Penguin Reference Books

THE PENGUIN DICTIONARY OF
DESIGN AND DESIGNERS

Born in 1943 in Suffolk, Simon Jervis read Classics and History of Art at Cambridge. After two years at Leicester Museum and Art Gallery he joined the Department of Furniture and Woodwork at the Victoria and Albert Museum in 1966. He has worked there ever since and is now the Department's Deputy Keeper. His interests extend beyond furniture to the history of interior decoration, architecture, design and ornament. His books include *Victorian Furniture* (1968), *Printed Furniture Designs before 1650* (1974), *Woodwork of Winchester Cathedral* (1976) and *High Victorian Design* (1983). He has published many articles in *Apollo*, the *Burlington Magazine*, *Connoisseur*, *Country Life*, *Furniture History* and other magazines. He translated Georg Himmelheber's *Biedermeier Furniture* (1974) and has been involved in many exhibitions on subjects ranging from Ludwig II of Bavaria to Eileen Gray. The most memorable was perhaps Victorian and Edwardian Decorative Art, The Handley-Read Collection, held at the Royal Academy in 1972, whose catalogue is still a work of reference.

Merry Christmas,

Richard —

From: Joy

'87

Simon Jervis

The Penguin Dictionary of
DESIGN AND DESIGNERS

Penguin Books

Penguin Books Ltd, Harmondsworth, Middlesex, England
Penguin Books, 40 West 23rd Street, New York, New York 10010, U.S.A.
Penguin Books Australia Ltd, Ringwood, Victoria, Australia
Penguin Books Canada Ltd, 2801 John Street, Markham, Ontario, Canada L3R 1B4
Penguin Books (N.Z.) Ltd, 182–190 Wairau Road, Auckland 10, New Zealand

First published 1984
Copyright © Simon Jervis, 1984
All rights reserved

Typeset, printed and bound in Great Britain by
Hazell Watson & Viney Limited,
Member of the BPCC Group,
Aylesbury, Bucks
Set in VIP Times Roman

For Thalia and John

Contents

Contents

This book is a historical dictionary of design and designers, not a handbook for contemporary designers. It attempts to provide brief biographies of leading designers, mainly from about 1450 to the present day, and briefer accounts of some minor and a few insignificant figures. The basis of selection is thus predominantly anthological but there is a degree of representativeness, though this is emphatically not proportional. The browser or dipper should, it is hoped, come across a wide cross-section of those involved in design. These have not been confined to designers: some patrons, impresarios, pundits and historians are also included. Exhibitions, which were so important in the diffusion of design in the nineteenth century, have been described under their locations, and accounts are provided of some design institutions.

Design is a field where modern literature is both scanty and patchy; no up-to-date bibliographies have therefore been given. But particular emphasis has been laid on published designs, ornament, pattern-books and periodicals. The question of the definition of design is begged, although the introductory essay tries to make some useful generalizations. Some entries cover styles, concepts and motifs but there is no attempt to provide a detailed glossary of design and ornament. Many design terms are taken from architecture or the crafts, and definitions for these are readily available in *The Penguin Dictionary of Architecture* or in *The Penguin Dictionary of Decorative Arts*.

The types of design covered here are not precisely delimited; ceramics, furniture, glass, interior decoration, metalwork, ornament and textiles get frequent mention, while graphic design, consumer durables and typography surface only on occasion. Heavy industrial design, theatre design and dress design are almost wholly excluded. Geographically this dictionary concentrates on Europe and North America, with a few outliers.

The lack of a solid tradition of research into the history of design means that this dictionary rests upon some foundations which are both narrow and insecure. But because the history of design is here regarded as closely linked to the history of art and architecture and because many artists and architects have been designers and are therefore included, it has been possible to use the literature and works of reference in those fields, pride of place going to Thieme and Becker's monumental *Künstlerlexikon*, as is usual with art-historical dictionaries.

The dictionary does not attempt to present the designer as the protean and heroic figure described by some modern promoters of design. It is precisely because many designers have been obscure figures that their resurrection in a dictionary is such a fascinating albeit difficult task. The variety in the status and role of designers makes the study of their contacts, sources, patrons, clients and interrelationships very complex, but it is hoped that the use of capitals for cross-references may shed a raking light on this world – or underworld.

Facts are the business of reference books and as many as possible are included. Opinions have inevitably crept in; but I hope that most of them are recognizable as such and that covert expressions of prejudice and unconscious displays of bias are not too frequent. There are not many jokes. Omissions are a more serious matter; some are calculated, but many more the result of ignorance or inadvertence. I would be grateful if any reader who finds a factual error, a mistaken judgement, or an inexplicable omission, would draw it to my attention; only through such corrections and suggestions can a second edition be an improvement on this first.

*

Personal acknowledgements must cover first those friends and colleagues in Europe, the United States of America and in England whose researches and ideas they will recognize as borrowed here. Since 1966 I have had the good fortune to work at the Victoria & Albert Museum, the greatest repository of the arts of design in the world; this dictionary, although a private project, is its product and, I hope, reflects, however dimly, the influence of its collections, its library and my colleagues, especially those in my own Department, and particularly my Keeper, Peter Thornton. Our secretary, Louisa Warburton-Lee, has worked early and late to transform inchoate manuscript into impeccable type. Finally I must thank my wife, Fionnuala, who has had to put up with preoccupied evenings and occupied weekends for too long.

In England at least design history has been a growth area from the 1970s. It is in many ways unfortunate that this growth has taken its main institutional form in polytechnics, where design history is on the syllabus of practical design students. Rightly or wrongly it has been felt that with few exceptions only the past hundred years or so of the history of design is relevant to these future designers. The stress has been on the emergence of the Modern style and on the effects of the Industrial Revolution. An unfortunate side-effect of this blinkered approach is that, now that the Modern style is being replaced or perhaps supplemented by various Post-Modern historicisms, the main non-Modern prototypes readily available to fledgling designers for imitation tend to be Art Nouveau, Arts & Crafts and Art Déco, with results that are all too familiar.

For similar reasons the English word 'design' has entered the vocabulary in France, Germany and Italy to mean 'industrial design'; in 1962, for example, a 'Design Center' was founded in Stuttgart. This usage is ironical in the case of Italy in that the word 'design', meaning a drawing to serve as a model and thence the making of such drawings, comes from the Italian '*disegno*'. A designer is one who makes designs. These meanings have been current in English since the 17th century. This etymology is simplified and there is no doubt that since the foundation of Schools of Design in 1836 restrictive definitions of 'design' and 'designer' have been increasingly current, particularly within the design establishment. None the less, this is no reason to abandon or outlaw their more broadly accepted significance.

If the term 'design' is thus embattled, the meaning of 'craftsman' has become opaque indeed. Thanks to Ruskin and Morris, and more so their followers, the 'craftsman' has become tainted with the 'artist-craftsman' and is now consciously or unconsciously accepted as a standard prototype, sharing many attributes with those other stock romantic images, the noble savage and the heroic proletariat. At the beginning of this century, especially in England, it was normal to believe that the craftsman was his own best designer, despite all evidence to the contrary, and this belief is still prevalent. The craftsman has also tended to dominate the academic study of the arts of design. This is partly due to the nature of the evidence; the artefacts themselves and the surviving documents tend to lead more directly to the craftsman than the designer. And it is partly due to Gottfried

Semper. When he proposed a division of the arts of design based on technical processes, and therefore in practice on different materials, he tended to encourage a fragmented study of design.

The South Kensington Museum and its followers, set up to improve public taste in design, have tended to divide into departments of ceramics, metalwork, textiles and so on, partly because of Semper's influence but also in response to the nature of their collections. Such museums collect and display artefacts, abetting the modern cult of the artefact as sacred relic and investment trophy. The massive interest and market in such artefacts has encouraged the growth of scholarly societies such as the Furniture History Society, the Glass Circle and the Jewellery History Society; their journals are an important vehicle for research, but this is naturally biased towards craftsmen or techniques within their specialized fields. And even when scholars discuss design it tends to be a range of ceramic designs, furniture designs or metalwork designs which are treated, not the whole range. The polymathic comprehensive approach is all too rare.

It is significant that the study of engraved ornament, surely a vital key to the general history of design, is neglected, and designers of ornament often receive summary treatment in books on the arts of design, just as in general histories of art the arts of design tend to be relegated to appendices. The neglect of ornament is of course not only the result of concentration on craft divisions, it is also a reflection of the Modern distaste for ornament. Ornament is such an important and perennial ingredient of art that it is to be hoped that the Post-Modern revival of complexity of texture, articulation and historical reference may bring with it a revival of interest in ornament.

There have recently been signs of such a revival among designers. But so far their ornament has too often consisted in defiant or ironic anti-Modern gestures, displaying all the crudity and inarticulateness which often succeeds a bout of iconoclasm. It may seem sanguine to suggest that the reintegration of ornament and design, until the early 20th century a continuum, is a task in which historians may play a creative role. But there are precedents. From about 1750 onwards archaeologists, antiquaries and historians supplied both material and inspiration for the classical and Gothic revivals. Their role is not and never was a mere historicist motif-mongering. They have reinterpreted and modulated earlier systems of ornament and design for new generations of designers.

It is sad that recent scholars have not so far established a solid bridgehead on this territory, especially as social and economic historians are showing increasing interest in the production of luxury goods. Their demographic approach and lack of art-historical knowledge reinforce the existing emphasis on the craftsman and neglect of the designer. A contributory factor, no doubt, is that design and ornament have in the past been rightly associated with luxury and wealth, and therefore carry unfashionable associations. The craftsman, by contrast, is sentimentally associated with the industrial worker and thus a respectable figure. There is a continuing reluctance to admit that design and ornament filter downwards, however vernacular or egalitarian their outward guise. Even to acknowledge that designers are employed to make objects of utility beautiful is a heresy against Modern utilitarianism.

But who was the designer? By about 1500 it seems that in Italy and Germany design and ornament were dominated by the goldsmith/ engraver/painter. Polliauolo, Dürer and Holbein are notable examples. As engraving developed it became a more specialized trade, and those engaged in producing engraved designs, although often trained in metal-work, were less likely to double as painters, at least not at a very elevated level, professionals like Solis and Passe being typical instances. The German engravers of Augsburg and Nuremberg who published endless series of designs for every type of object, as well as a mass of ornament, belonged to this tradition, which seems to have petered out in about 1780. Such engravings were occasionally designed by craftsmen, among the most notable being crude and vigorous designs for ironwork produced in Paris in the 17th century. Some engraver designers displayed originality and power. Wachsmuth and Göz are German 18th-century examples but the main products of their contemporaries were straight copies of Parisian ornament or variations on themes established by, say, Meissonier and Boucher in Paris, Cuvilliés in Munich and Hoppenhaupt in Berlin. Unoriginal though they often were, such designs were an immensely important channel for the dissemination of new styles. Their marketing, usage and relative popularity deserve investigation.

From about 1530 a new species of designer became dominant, the painter/sculptor/architect. Raphael, Giulio Romano, Michelangelo and Vasari are among the great 16th-century examples. They were influential not only as designers themselves but also because they created more or less structured hierarchies of designer specialists trained to meet the needs of the great courts, and thus providing models for the organization of designers and their education elsewhere. When Jacopo da Strada, having worked under Giulio Romano in Mantua, and Giovanni da Udine, having served Raphael in Rome and Michelangelo in Florence, travelled elsewhere, they were missionaries not only for a new style of design, whose vocabulary they disseminated by making drawings available for copying as well as by their own works, but also for this new system of organization and education.

With Le Brun the status of the artist as a dictator of design and co-ordinator of lesser designers reached its apogee. His commanding role is well known and with Gobelins tapestries it is possible to gain a fairly clear picture of the design process from the basic cartoon by Le Brun, to the working-up of details by painter designers who specialized in borders, or wild-life, or flowers, to the preparation of full-scale cartoons for weaving by a third tier of more mechanical craftsmen. But although the leading figures in many court design hierarchies are known – Sustris in Munich, Bernini in Rome, Knobelsdorff, Nahl and the Hoppenhaupts in Berlin, Cameron and Brenna in St Petersburg and so on – it is rarely possible to pin down their precise practical workings in this way. In the period after Le Brun, for example, the exact roles of Berain and Boulle with regard to practical furniture design have not been defined, although both published highly competent furniture designs. Even in the cases of the commode from Louis XV's bedchamber at Versailles, now in the Wallace Collection in London, and the elaborate *encoignure* by Dubois, now in the J. Paul Getty Museum in California, where there is unquestionable similarity to drawings by Slodtz and Pineau respectively, the pieces are so different from the drawings that the precise relationship or function of the latter is difficult to determine. Although there are exceptions it is surprising how many such unanswered questions remain even in fields where there is a wealth of documentation and no lack of scholarly delving. To what extent, for example, did such celebrated designers as Lalonde, Delafosse and Neufforge actually design objects?

Whereas in the 16th and 17th centuries sculptors and painters were among the dictators of design, in the 18th century the architect became a progressively more dominant figure, although it must be remembered that professional identities were by no means exclusive or enduring; Brenna, who described himself as '*architetto romano*' in 1767, was mainly active as a painter and draughtsman until in about 1790 he began to usurp Cameron's role as architect and designer, and Abildgaard, who began as a painter, was a prolific and influential designer and architect from the mid-1790s. But whoever may have been at the head of the great design establishments there is no doubt that their existence encouraged the development of a new type of professional designer, who may have been trained as a painter, architect or sculptor, who looked to official academies for education and to court hierarchies for preferment, and who often lacked the traditional craft training of the goldsmith/engraver/painter designer discussed above. The emergence of unofficial or semi-official schools of design such as the St Martin's Lane Academy or that founded by Bachelier reflects the spread of new methods of design education to centres which lacked official academies and to craftsmen who had become aware of the inadequacy of traditional craft training in design.

Many of the most interesting designers are difficult to fit neatly into the categories so far outlined. Vredeman de Vries and Dietterlin made their reputations by exploiting perspective and the orders. Sheraton, Brown and Nicholson were drawing-masters. Unteutsch, Chippendale and Danhauser were craftsman entrepreneurs. Designers were often autodidact and eccentric. Occasionally, as with Schübler, they designed for the sake of designing.

Since the Select Committee on Arts and Manufactures of 1835 to 1836 and the consequent establishment of the Schools of Design, there has been a continuing trend towards the professionalization of designers, reflected in specialized training, in the growth of professional associations, institutions and journals, and buttressed by an extensive literature of design, technical, theoretical and historical. In 1891 Richard Norman Shaw, Walter Crane, Philip Webb and many others protested against a parliamentary bill to make architecture a closed profession; their arguments were laid out in *Architecture, A Profession or an Art* (1892), in which the architect Gerald C. Horsley (1862–1917), a pupil of Shaw, quoted a saying of Alfred Stevens, 'I know but one art'. The fostering of technical expertise in design is a desirable goal. But the recent tendency of some promoters of the design profession to present the designer, and more particularly the industrial designer, as a modern equivalent of the Renaissance man, a romantic superhero of the consumer society, is misguided puffery. Design is so wide and various in its applications that the designer cannot become a wholly independent and distinct species. Design will probably continue to occupy a lower position in the hierarchy of the arts than painting and sculpture. According to Ruskin 'architecture must be the beginning of arts' and many of the best designers will continue to be architects. Indeed the pattern of industrial designer as functional technician may yet prove short-lived. The Modern style is under attack and, ironically, the new miniaturized technology is tending to liberate designers from the dominance of 'form follows function'. The sentimental ideas of Horsley and his generation about the unity of the arts and crafts may be outmoded, but perhaps Alfred Stevens's belief in 'one art' is due for revival among designers.

An important figure in the history of design is the middleman between client and craftsman or manufacturer. He may have organized a complex series of commissions; upholsterers seem often to have taken on the role. Or he may have been the equivalent of the modern retailer; the 18th-century Parisian *marchand-mercier* is the obvious example. Some of these hybrid figures were themselves designers; an instance is Jean Hauré, the sculptor who was *fournisseur de la Cour* to Louis XVI. Others were not designers themselves but were obviously in a position to influence design. How did the patron himself influence design? An elite of patrons could initiate or encourage stylistic revolutions. La Live de Jully, Marigny, Walpole, Beckford and Frederick the Great may all be placed in this class. Occasionally, as with Thomas Hope, patron and designer are one. More often patrons expressed advanced taste through the talents of designers in the painter/sculptor/architect tradition outlined above. This variety of patron has been much celebrated, and rightly so, but much more needs to be known about the detailed *minutiae* of how new ideas, or the appearance of new ideas, were translated into three dimensions via designers and craftsmen. The reactionary patron is much more difficult to pin down than his progressive contemporary. The 9th Earl of Exeter, who employed Ince & Mayhew at Burghley House in the late 1760s to execute work consistent with that abandoned at his grandfather's death in 1700, is an instance, although by no means a straightforward example as the 17th-century marquetry he had re-used is embellished with fashionable neo-classical mounts. Ultra-conservatism of an even more undiluted variety must have been common if not commonplace, but its influence on design has received little notice, perhaps because of the difficulty of documentation, perhaps because of a Whiggish tendency of historians to focus on the progressive.

Even less likely to attract attention, because it is inconspicuous, is the influence on design of the mass of patrons. In general it is probable that they accepted what was available and that their influence on design was a neutral confirmation of the *status quo*. Plain practical objects supplied to such clients and for functional use in more extravagant houses have appealed to Modern taste, and a prevalent belief has arisen that such objects are evidence for a proto-Modern simple style. A case can be made for a self-conscious taste for plainness at certain periods, but in general simplicity was surely the result of practicality and economy rather than taste. Indeed in 18th-century America, where a general puritanism and plainness is sometimes posited, furniture for the rich seems to have displayed all the showier characteristics of artisan mannerism in design.

To attempt an anatomy, however crude, of the mechanics of design, as experienced and influenced by designers, craftsmen and patrons, is evidently all too ambitious a task for an essay such as this. It has merely hatched the sketchiest outlines of the designer in history and indicated a few of the topics which should occupy historians of design. If it has concentrated on the past at the expense of the present this is intentional. Too much design history has progressed backwards from the present and viewed the past through Modern spectacles. In practice it has tended to become a functional fragment of a subject, analogous to Russia for scientists. There is for instance little or nothing substantial in English on designers as important as DuCerceau, Vredeman, Schor, Le Brun, Cuvilliés and Rastrelli, and many other fascinating figures are waiting to be rescued from oblivion. How much richer and more interesting a subject design history might be if it explored this wider territory. Thus developed it could illuminate perennial and vital aspects of the history of art. If this dictionary can encourage this process it will have performed its task.

A

Aalto, Hugo Henrik Alvar (1898–1976)
Born in Kuortane in Finland, the son of
a surveyor, Aalto fought against the
Bolsheviks in 1917. He then studied
architecture at the Helsinki Polytechnic
under the architect Armas Lindgren,
graduating in 1921. He became a practising architect in 1923. Aalto's early
architectural works were in a stripped-
down NEO-CLASSICAL style. At this
period he also designed some book-
jackets. In 1925, when he married Aino
Marsio, Aalto designed furniture for a
competition organized by the arts and
crafts journal *Käsiteollisuus*; the designs
are simple, mildly classical or cottagey,
including a Windsor-type chair. In 1927
Aalto moved his office from his home
town of Jyväskylä to Turku, and, influenced by the architect Erik Bryggman
(1891–1955), moved decisively towards
the MODERN style. From 1929 Aalto
attended CONGRÈS INTERNATIONAUX
D'ARCHITECTURE MODERNE conferences and was thus in contact with the
Modern establishment, among them P.
Morton Shand. Aalto's sanatorium at
Paimio (1929–33), strongly influenced
by Jan Duiker's Hilversum Sanatorium
(1926–8), was one of the great monuments of the Modern style. In 1927
Aalto designed his first Modern piece of
furniture, a wooden stacking chair for
Jyväskylä Civil Guard House; this was
followed by furniture for his own children (1927–8). From 1929 he was closely
involved with Otto Korhonen, a furniture manufacturer at Turku, and
designed for him a chest-of-drawers with
recessed handles, and a moulded ply-

wood chair on tubular metal legs, later
replaced by wood. Aalto exploited
moulded plywood shapes which had
been manufactured for cheap seating by
the Luther Company of Talinn since
1900. His Paimio chair (1930–33) also
uses similar shapes, as does a related tea
trolley. In 1930 Aalto designed simple
Modern rooms for the Helsinki Museum
Minimum Apartment exhibition; work
by Pauli and Märta Blomstedt, Erik
Bryggman and Werner West was also
shown. In the same year Aalto entered
a Viennese furniture design competition
with cantilevered bentwood chairs and
a stacking table. Aalto attended the
STOCKHOLM 1930 EXHIBITION, and
was in contact with the architects Gunnar ASPLUND (1885–1940) and Sven
MARKELIUS. In 1933 he moved his
office to Helsinki and his furniture was
shown at the London store, Fortnum &
Mason, the first time it had been seen
outside Finland. Also in 1933 Aalto
patented a method of bending wood for
stools, used on his most famous design,
a stool with three straight legs bending
over at the top to support a disk-like
seat. In 1935 Aalto developed a patent
sprung chair support of wood. About
this date he met Maire Gullichsen, the
wife of an industrialist who became an
architectural patron, and formed with
her and with his wife Aino a company
named Artek to produce his furniture,
as it still does. In 1937 Aalto designed
vases for the Savoy Restaurant in Turku
with flowing curvilinear free-form bases
and straight sides; they were produced
by the Iittala glass works and shown at

the PARIS 1937 EXHIBITION and the New York 1939 Exhibition. Aalto's pavilion at the latter exhibition was in a free expressive version of the Modern style and declared his freedom from its formulae. His later furniture developed and refined his earlier designs. Aalto also took great care over the design of such details as door furniture and lighting in his buildings, which display a high degree of originality.

Abbott, Edward Abbott was active as a heraldic painter and coach painter in Long Acre in London. He also executed landscapes, and issued competent designs for coaches captioned in both English and French, probably in the 1760s. He retired in 1782 to Hereford, where he died in 1791.

Abildgaard, Nicolai Abraham (1743–1809) Born in Copenhagen, the son of a draughtsman, Abildgaard trained as a decorative painter under J. E. Mandelberg, and also studied at the Copenhagen Academy, where he won several medals between 1764 and 1767. In 1772 he won a scholarship to Italy, where he remained until 1777, mainly in Rome, but also visiting Naples and Pompeii. In 1777 he returned to Copenhagen via Paris, and in 1778 became a member of the Academy. From 1780 to 1791 he painted allegorical decorations in Schloss Christiansborg, destroyed by fire in 1794. He was Director of the Academy from 1789 to 1791 and from 1801 to his death, and exercised a wide influence as the leading NEO-CLASSICAL artist in Denmark. From the mid-1790s, when he designed rooms and furniture for Christian VIII, Abildgaard was also active as designer and architect. Chairs of the purest klismos form, X-framed stools, desks, a cradle and commodes display refined and sometimes extreme neoclassicism, with some quirky detailing. The klismos chairs, for his own use,

incorporate legs of curved wood especially collected for this purpose. Abildgaard also designed medals.

Acanthus A plant with boldly indented and scrolled leaves, the acanthus was a common element in Greek and Roman architectural ornament. According to Vitruvius the marble sculptor Callimachus was inspired by a basket of offerings left on a young girl's grave, overgrown with acanthus and surmounted by a tile, to invent the Corinthian capital which is enriched with acanthus. The Ara Pacis, an altar dedicated by Augustus in 9 B.C., provided a model of Roman acanthus ornament at its richest: parts were probably in the collection of Cardinal Andrea delle Valle in the 1520s and further elements were discovered in 1568. The Ara Pacis was in the Medici collection in Rome from 1584. Acanthus was an ubiquitous RENAISSANCE motif, but enjoyed its widest popularity during the 17th century. SCHOR and FERRI were the greatest BAROQUE exponents of acanthus in Italy and prints by such designers as PASSARINI, CERINI and CRECCOLINI confirmed the development of an acanthus style. This exuberant manner was most pronounced in Germany and Austria, where it was propagated by ECHTER, INDAU, BICHEL and UNSELT, among others. A more feathery but equally powerful handling of acanthus is displayed by Stefano DELLA BELLA and STEINLE. Acanthus continued as a stock motif throughout the 18th century but enjoyed a final flowering in early 19th-century England, fostered by such designers as PIRANESI, TATHAM and Richard BROWN.

Ackermann, Rudolf (1764–1834) Born in Stolberg, Saxony, the son of a coachmaker, Ackermann followed his father's trade in Switzerland, France and Belgium before settling in London in about

1783. He was there active as a coach designer for some ten years, designing a state coach for the Lord Lieutenant of Ireland in 1790. In 1795 Ackermann opened his Repository of Arts, a shop for prints, books and fancy articles, modelled on J. Lackington's Temple of the Muses, and employing many French noblemen who had fled the revolution. Up to 1806 he also ran a drawing school and in that year he achieved some fame by designing the ornaments for Nelson's funeral car. Ackermann's *Repository of Arts* (1809–28), dedicated to the Prince of Wales, was a magazine of art, science and fashion, among other subjects. J. B. PAPWORTH was the leading architectural contributor, and also designed Ackermann's showroom (1812) and his later new premises (1826). Furniture designs were contributed to the *Repository* by George SMITH (from 1809), the inventor, Mr Gregson (1813), George BULLOCK (from 1816), textile designs by Mr Allen of Pall Mall, including chintzes for Carlton House (1811) and Endsleigh (1813), and designs for curtains by Mr STAFFORD of Bath (from 1819). The dominant style was Grecian, and HOPE, and PERCIER and FONTAINE, were recognized as its leaders. *Fashionable Furniture* (1823, reprinted later as *Modern Furniture*; forty-four plates) was an anthology of furniture designs mainly printed in the 1822 *Repository*. Although the GOTHIC conservatory at Carlton House was illustrated in 1811 there were few Gothic designs in the *Repository* until 1825, when A. C. PUGIN began regularly to publish Gothic designs reissued as his *Gothic Furniture* (1827). The *Repository* also contained some remarkable early 16th- and 17th-century designs (1813 and 1817). Ackermann was interested in scientific matters and published Frederick Accum's *A Practical Treatise on Gas-Light* (1815), Accum being a close friend. *A Selection of Ornaments* (1817,

1818 and 1819) presented designs of Grecian ornament and furniture on 120 lithographed plates; Ackermann was also friendly with Senefelder, the pioneer of lithography, and in 1819 presented a lithographic press to the Society of Arts. In 1807 Ackermann had suggested a scheme to scatter anti-Napoleonic propaganda from balloons, and after the 1813 battle of Leipzig he was much involved in raising funds for the relief of suffering, charitable work which later earned him public honours in Germany.

Adam, Robert (1728–92) Born at Kirkcaldy in Fife, the second surviving son of William Adam (1689–1748), the leading Scottish architect of his day, Adam was educated at Edinburgh High School and University and early made the acquaintance of the Scottish intelligentsia. On his father's death he and his brothers John (1721–92) and James (1732–94) continued the business until in 1754 Adam was prosperous enough to set out on an architectural grand tour with an aristocratic companion, the Hon. Charles Hope. In Florence, Adam was introduced by Joseph Wilton to Charles-Louis CLÉRISSEAU, who had previously met and quarrelled with CHAMBERS, and employed the French draughtsman as a tutor in NEO-CLASSICISM. In Rome, Adam devoted himself to the study of antiquity under Clérisseau's guidance, while not neglecting opportunities to cultivate noble and rich English tourists and potential patrons. In 1755 Clérisseau and he visited Naples and Herculaneum. Adam also established a close Roman friendship with PIRANESI, whose *Antichità Romane* (1756) incorporated a laudatory mock tomb to Adam, and whose *Campo Marzio* (1762), dedicated to Adam, included a portrait of himself and Adam on the plan of the site engraved in 1757. In 1755 Adam initiated a scheme to update Desgodetz's *Les Édifices Antiques de Rome* (1682) but, although he took on draughtsman assistants, including Laurent-Benoît Dewez and Agostino Brunias, and later confined the project to Hadrian's Villa and the Baths of Diocletian and Caracalla, nothing came of it. However, when Adam left Rome in 1757 he not only possessed a collection of antiquities and paintings, he had also turned himself into an accomplished draughtsman and virtuoso acquainted with the latest currents in architectural and decorative theory and practice and with many of the rich, influential and cultivated. In 1757 Adam broke his return journey from Rome to set out from Venice to Spalatro (now Split in Yugoslavia) to examine Diocletian's palace. The outcome was *Ruins of the Palace of the Emperor Diocletian at Spalatro in Dalmatia* (1764), a sumptuous scholarly survey dedicated to George III, whose engraving had been supervised by Clérisseau. On his arrival in London in early 1758 Adam set himself up as the new architect, but despite his election to the Society of Arts (see Royal SOCIETY OF ARTS) and such *douceurs* as the presentation of a design for a snuff-box to Lord Bute, success was not instant. In 1760, however, Adam was established as architect to Edwin Lascelles, later Lord Harewood (1760), at Harewood, to the 6th Earl of Coventry, at Croome Court, and to Sir Nathaniel Curzon, later Lord Scarsdale (1761), at Kedleston, where he ruthlessly supplanted STUART. In 1761, as well as starting work at Syon for the 1st Duke of Northumberland, he became a Fellow of the Royal Society and one of the first two Architects of the King's Works, with Chambers, who despised Adam's taste and ensured his exclusion from the Royal Academy. Adam's output rapidly burgeoned: to quote Sir John SOANE, writing in 1812, 'the light and elegant

ornaments, the varied compartments in the ceilings of Mr Adam, imitated from Ancient Works in the Baths and Villas of the Romans, were soon applied in designs for chairs, tables, carpets, and in every other species of furniture. To Mr Adam's taste in the ornament of his buildings and furniture we stand indebted, inasmuch as manufacturers of every kind felt, as it were, the electric power of this revolution in Art.' Not the least of his innovations were the introduction of elaborate colour schemes into interior decoration and the complete control he exercised over every detail of an interior. The Adam office depended upon a team of draughtsmen, including George RICHARDSON, Agostino Brunias and Jean Baptiste Lallemand (1716–1803). His works gave patronage to a wide range of craftsmen, from painters, for example Antonio Zucchi (1726–95) and Michelangelo PERGOLESI (active from 1762, died 1801), to plasterers, notably Joseph ROSE, senior (about 1723–80) and junior (1745–99). Adam designs were executed by cabinet-makers (for instance Thomas CHIPPENDALE), by carpet manufacturers (Thomas Moore of Moorfields), by silversmiths (Daniel Smith and Robert Sharp), by ormolu manufacturers (Matthew Boulton) and even by amateur embroiderers (Lady Mary Hog). Such uses of Adam's designs were often without sanction: in 1770 James Adam complained to Matthew Boulton that grates, doors and chimneypieces had been pirated. A canon of the Adam style was provided in 1773–8 by the publication of the *Works in Architecture of Robert and James Adam* (second volume, 1779, third, 1822). The first volume laid particular stress on his invention of a supposedly 'Etruscan' decorative style derived from Greek vases, unsanctioned by MONTFAUCON, Gori, CAYLUS or Passeri. Although the *Works* were exclusively classical, Adam occasionally designed fittings in the GOTHIC style – for instance at Strawberry Hill for Horace WALPOLE in about 1766, and Gothic interiors at Alnwick in the 1770s. Adam continued to be the dominant architect in England until about 1780 when James WYATT gained an ascendancy and Adam's practice became almost exclusively Scottish and often castellated. After his death the Adam firm survived until 1794, but Adam's library and collections were later dispersed, nearly 9,000 drawings being sold to Sir John Soane in 1833 for £200. The Adam style was by then held in general contempt. Based on knowledge of Greek and Roman antiquity and strongly influenced by the example of Piranesi, and – unacknowledged – of Stuart, it had in the 1760s retained a certain Palladian solidity. However, Adam's handling of ornament became increasingly mannered, delicate, linear and – to some extent – stereotyped towards the end of his career. In 1775 Horace Walpole condemned him as 'all gingerbread, filigraine, and fan-painting', and although *Designs for Vases and Foliage*, supposedly by Adam but derived perhaps from drawings by Brunias, was published in 1821 by Priestley & Weale, who in 1825 were to reissue *Spalatro* and the *Works*, this adverse view became the prevailing opinion in the early 19th century. At the LONDON 1862 EXHIBITION, however, the stand of the cabinet-makers Wright & Mansfield of Great Portland Street included furniture in which the details were 'gleaned from the works of the Messrs (Adelphi) Adam'. Thenceforward the Adam Revival, which still survives, flourished.

Adams, Maurice Bingham (1849–1933) Adams trained as an architect under H. M. Goulty of Brighton and was then assistant to Sir William Emerson. In 1872 he moved to London to become a member of the staff of 'BUILDING NEWS', of which he became editor before his retirement in 1923. He initiated the Building News Designing Club, organizing competitions and writing reports, and was reckoned the best architectural perspectivist of his day, showing at the Royal Academy from 1876 to 1919. In 1878 Adams drew the illustrations to R. Norman SHAW's *Sketches for Cottages*. He completed Shaw's church in Bedford Park, where he lived himself from 1880 and built several houses, some illustrated in *Artists' Homes* (1883); in 1880 he collaborated with E. W. GODWIN on *Artistic Conservatories*. In 1881 EDIS illustrated a mantelpiece in Burmantofts faience designed by Adams. In *Examples of Old English Houses and Furniture* (1888) Adams illustrated a 'SHERATON settle from Fonthill' and some early furniture borrowed from Henry SHAW's *Specimens*, as well as his own furniture designs for Hollands (an interior sent out to Australia), Robertson & Son of Alnwick, Shapland & Petter, William Watt, and Gillows (for example a bedroom suite shown at the Manchester 1886 Exhibition), and a cast-iron mantelpiece for the Coalbrookdale Company. Adams favoured a hybrid Queen Anne/CHIPPENDALE/ADAM style.

Adams, Maurice S. R. The son of Maurice B. ADAMS, Maurice S. R. Adams was trained as an architect, but in about 1905 resigned from the Royal Institute of British Architects to engage in furniture design and manufacture. In *My Book of Furniture* (1926), Adams boasted that he was 'originator and inventor of the "King George V" style of design'. The style, exemplified by the 'King George' and 'Queen Mary' dressing-tables shown at the Wembley 1924 and Olympia 1925 exhibitions respectively, was characterized by soapy Queen Anne forms covered in showy walnut veneers; Adams both designed and manufactured. In *My Connaught and Marlborough Furniture* (about 1928) Adams stressed that his own designs had been widely plagiarized. *Modern Decorative Art* (1930) included not only furniture but also light fittings, door handles, furnishing fabrics etc.; in it Adams, styled 'Designer and Craftsman' on the title-page, expatiates on his own skill and originality with the greatest complacency and describes the evolution of his style from 18th-century models. But in *Modern Furniture* (1931) Adams illustrated his own conversion to a flashy MODERN manner. He died in 1941.

Aglio, Agostino (1777–1857) Born in Cremona, Aglio studied painting in Milan. From 1797 he was active as a landscape painter in Rome. There he met the architect William Wilkins (1778–1839), whom he accompanied on part of his travels in Greece. Aglio settled in England in 1803 and was active as a decorative painter. His *Architectural Ornaments* (London, 1820; 100 lithographed plates) contained line drawings of capitals, friezes, ceiling roses, vases, lights and silver, all in a pure late-NEO-CLASSICAL style and mostly borrowed from NORMAND. It is similar to works by George SMITH (1812) and ACKERMANN (1817–19).

Aitchison, George (1825–1910) The son of an architect, Aitchison was trained by his father, whose partner he became in 1859. In 1853 to 1855 he travelled in France and Italy with William BURGES. Aitchison's best-known work was his house for Lord Leighton, begun in 1865, for which he designed Islamic windows in 1870 and to which he added the Arab Hall in 1879, with elements designed by Walter CRANE and William DE MORGAN. Aitchison was professor of architecture at the Royal Academy from 1887 and published a new edition of James Ward's *The Principles of Ornament* (1892). Aitchison was an expert at interior decoration, designing a sideboard with panels by Albert Moore (1874), and furniture shown in 'GEWERBEHALLE' and in the 'CABINET MAKER AND ART FURNISHER' (1884), the latter in the Empire Revival style.

Albers, Josef (1888–1976) Born in Bottrop, Westphalia, Albers trained as a school teacher, and then in 1913 went to art school in Berlin. In 1919 to 1920 he studied in Franz von STUCK's studio in Munich. From 1920 to 1923 Albers was a student at the BAUHAUS where, despite Walter GROPIUS's displeasure, he worked on stained glass after attending ITTEN's preliminary course. In 1923 Albers was appointed a craft teacher to run the practical preliminary course as a complement to MOHOLY-NAGY's visual education course, developing the use of folded paper as a teaching medium; he was the first Bauhaus student to become a teacher. He became a full master in 1925 and succeeded BREUER as head of the furniture course from 1928 to 1930. He moved with the Bauhaus to Berlin in 1932 as head of the preliminary course. From 1923 Albers designed furniture, for instance church seats and a showcase, glass, metalwork and typography in the Bauhaus style. In 1933 Albers started to teach at Black Mountain College, North Carolina, where he remained until 1949. He held many academic posts and honours, lecturing at the Harvard Graduate School of Design from 1936 to 1940 and acting as visiting professor at the ULM HOCHSCHULE FÜR GESTALTUNG in 1953 to 1954. His later works, pedagogical explorations of the perceptual effects of colour, pattern and geometry, were much admired during the Op Art craze of the 1960s.

Albert, Prince (1819–61) Born at

Rosenau, Coburg, as the second son of Ernst, Duke of Saxe-Coburg-Gotha, in 1840 Prince Albert married Queen Victoria, who had succeeded to the English throne in 1837. Albert dedicated himself to a gruelling programme of public works. In 1841 he was appointed by Sir Robert Peel to chair the Royal Commission to use the rebuilding of the Houses of Parliament to further the fine arts. It focused on fresco painting, which Albert used in a pavilion in Buckingham Palace Garden (1842–4), published in 1846 by Ludwig GRUNER. For Albert, Gruner designed carpets at Windsor Castle, candelabra by Barbedienne at Buckingham Palace, and a coal seat at Osborne House, built from 1845. In 1842 Albert designed a silver centrepiece by Garrard's decorated with the Queen's animals. He also designed naturalistic jewellery for the Queen and a billiard table at Osborne, where WHITAKER designed furniture. In 1843 Albert became President of the Royal SOCIETY OF ARTS and involved himself in the movement to improve design. From 1848 he and Henry COLE projected a scheme for a series of national design exhibitions. This evolved into the LONDON 1851 EXHIBITION of whose Royal Commission Albert was chairman. After the great success of the 1851 Exhibition, Albert watched over the development of the SCHOOL OF DESIGN and the South Kensington Museum, now the VICTORIA & ALBERT MUSEUM. The LONDON 1862 EXHIBITION, where great improvements in the standard of English design were apparent, was in a sense his memorial.

Albertolli, Giocondo (1742–1839) Born at Bedano in Ticino, the son of an architect, Albertolli moved in 1753 to Parma, where he was taught at the flourishing Accademia, founded in 1742, and influenced by the NEO-CLASSICAL French architect PETITOT, appointed

ducal architect in 1753. At the beginning of his career Albertolli was mainly active as a designer of stucco, working on ceilings in the villa at Poggio Imperiale in Tuscany in 1770. After a further stay in Parma in 1772 he moved to Rome and Naples to devote himself to the study of antiquity. In 1774 Albertolli went to Milan, where he designed an interior for the royal palace. From 1774 to 1775 he was in Florence, where he designed plaster ceilings in the Uffizi and the Pitti, and in 1775 he finally settled in Milan. He was closely linked with the newly founded Milan Accademia, and taught ornament there up to 1812. His decorative works in Milan were numerous, including many interiors in the royal palace and the royal villa at Monza (1777–80). Albertolli also published a series of books, *Ornamenti diversi* (1782), *Alcune Decorazioni* (1787) and *Miscellanea* (1796), which include powerful and refined neo-classical designs for furniture, for Monza and Milan Cathedral, and for silver, metalwork and wall and ceiling decorations; *Miscellanea* contains a striking series of decorative eagles of fierce NATURALISM. A second edition was published in 1843. Albertolli also published an elementary manual on ornament (1805). His pupils included MOGLIA.

Albini, D. M. Albini published *Libro I Divary Disegni Moderni di Gioiglieri* (1744), six plates of bows and brooches, encrusted with large stones. He was probably an Italian jeweller working in Spain.

Albini, Franco (1905–78) Born in Robbiate, Como, Albini trained as an architect, qualifying in Milan in 1929. During the 1930s he was influenced by Edoardo Persico and Giuseppe PAGANO, and the group associated with the architectural review 'CASABELLA', whose editor he was from 1945 to 1946, with Gian-carlo Palanti. Albini showed furniture at the MONZA 1930 Triennale, and later at MILAN TRIENNALES. In 1938 he designed a wireless whose works and loudspeaker were suspended between two sheets of glass and a stylish iron X-framed table with a glass top. An armchair of 1940, a version of a deck-chair with a heavy wooden frame, well upholstered, contrasts with the light Luisa armchair in production in various versions from 1937 to 1955. A 1941 bookcase of wood, glass and metal, a curious tensile structure supported by wires and diagonal struts, makes another contrast with a marble-topped table with massive steel pedestals of 1957, which harks back to Renaissance prototypes. Other Albini designs are uncomplicatedly MODERN. He also designed lighting and metalwork. His Museo di Palazzo Bianco, Genoa (1951), and Museo di San Lorenzo, Genoa (1952–6), introduced a new dramatic mode of museum display, in which early works of art are perched, spot-lit, on steel supports at once elegant and brutal. From 1952 Albini worked in collaboration with Franca Helg; from 1963 he was professor of architectural composition at Milan Polytechnic. The eclecticism and variety of Albini's designs reflects the Italian independence from Modern orthodoxies.

Aldegrever, Heinrich Born in 1502 in Paderborn, Aldegrever settled at Soest in about 1527 and died there between 1555 and 1561. A Protestant, Aldegrever worked as a painter but may have been trained as a goldsmith. He also painted glass and engraved seals and medals. From the late 1520s Aldegrever published some 300 prints, including about forty-two horizontal panels of early RENAISSANCE ornament, dated from 1527 to 1549, and about thirty-four similar vertical panels, dated from 1528 to 1553. The main elements are dolphins, scrolls, sirens, VASES, medallion heads and balusters, while fleshy leaves and foliate masks represent an element of GOTHIC survival. Some late prints of 1549 seem to show an awareness of the Flemish STRAPWORK GROTESQUE ornament pioneered by Cornelis FLORIS and BOS. However, the strongest influences on Aldegrever were the prints of DÜRER and the BEHAMS, probably known to him through BINCK's copies. Two panels depict the alphabet. Aldegrever also issued some sixteen designs for dagger sheaths, dated from 1528 to 1539, decorated with figures above foliate and Renaissance ornament. Other prints show the decorated end of a sheath (1537), three brooches (1536) and two richly decorated spoons and a whistle (1539). The latter served as an inspiration for a spoon made for William BECKFORD in 1812. Aldegrever's prints had earlier been applied to stoneware, stoves, arms and armour, and twelve English silver plates were engraved after his Labours of Hercules (1550) in 1567. OSTAUS published copies after Aldegrever.

Algardi, Alessandro (1595–1654) Born in Bologna, the son of a silk merchant of good family, Algardi studied at the academy of Lodovico Carracci and then under the sculptor G. C. Conventi. In 1622 he moved to Mantua and in 1625, after a stay in Venice, to Rome, where he started work as a restorer of antique sculpture. Algardi began to establish his own reputation as a sculptor in the late 1620s; his heyday was from 1644 under Pope Innocent X Pamphili. He was also active as a designer of metalwork, especially church metalwork, including reliquaries, frames and monstrances and in 1637 an urn in the Gesù to contain the bones of St Ignatius. He may also have designed furniture.

Alken, Samuel (1756–1815) Son of the celebrated wood-carver Sefferin Alken,

Samuel Alken studied at the Royal Academy Schools from 1769 and won a silver medal in 1773. He subsequently worked with his father at Somerset House and elsewhere. In 1779 he published *A New Book of Ornaments*, with ACANTHUS scrolls, putti and VASES in the ADAM style, handled in a spiky idiosyncratic manner. In 1780 he showed a design for monument at the Royal Academy, describing himself as 'Architect'.

Allard, Charles Born in Amsterdam in 1648, the son of a publisher, Allard followed his father's trade; he was still active in 1706. His *Ornemens d'Orfevrerie propres pour Flanquer & Emailler* comprise ACANTHUS friezes and shaped panels of floral scrolled ornament, in the manner of Paul Androuet DuCERCEAU, for the use of goldsmiths.

Allgemeine Bauzeitung The founder editor of this Viennese journal in 1836 was C. F. L. Förster (1797–1863). Ferstel and HANSEN were among its later editorial advisers. Although mainly architectural and often very technical, it contains much on ornament and design in plates of the highest quality.

Allori, Alessandro (1535–1607) Born in Florence, the son of a sword-cutler who died in 1540, Allori was subsequently brought up by BRONZINO, a friend of his father. In 1549 to 1553 Allori designed for Bronzino the borders of the tapestries for the Salone dei Dugento in the Palazzo Vecchio. He spent the years from 1554 to 1559 in Rome. Back in Florence, Allori assisted on the design of MICHELANGELO's funeral in 1564 and on the decorations for the marriage of Francesco I and Giovanna d'Austria in 1565. He became a member of the FLORENCE ACCADEMIA DEL DISEGNO in the same year. As official artist to the Medici court, Allori was enormously prolific, his works including GROTESQUE painted decorations executed in the Uffizi in about 1581. From 1576 he designed cartoons for tapestries on mythological and sacred themes in a MANNERIST style derived from VASARI and Bronzino. A suite of tapestries on the theme of aquatic birds designed by Allori in 1576 for the Villa Medici at Poggio a Cajano displays the direct influence of STRAET, also visible in Allori's four tapestry cartoons on bullfighting woven in 1583. From 1594 he was engaged on designing tapestries for the Salone dei Cinquecento in the Palazzo Vecchio. In 1613 to 1617, after his death, a set of pastoral scenes were woven to Allori's designs; with their grotesque borders and close-packed compositions they must have seemed old-fashioned in Roman terms.

Alma-Tadema, Sir Lawrence (1836–1912) Born in Dronryp, Friesland, the son of a notary, Alma-Tadema entered the Antwerp Academy in 1852 as a pupil of Baron Gustaf Wappers (1803–74). In 1860 he became an assistant to Baron Henri Leys (1815–69). In 1870 Alma-Tadema moved from Brussels to London, already celebrated as a painter of classical scenes, heavily promoted by the dealer Ernest Gambert (1814–1902). In about 1879, when he was elected to the Royal Academy, Alma-Tadema, assisted by George E. Fox, designed an elaborate Byzantine piano and seat for his own use. From 1884 to 1885 he recast his new house, 17 Grove End Road, designing couches with one side Pompeian, based on a model excavated in 1868, the other Egyptian; one couch was shown at the LONDON 1893 ARTS & CRAFTS EXHIBITION and illustrated in the 'STUDIO' (1894). He also designed a rich NEOCLASSICAL seat, similar to a piano and seat furniture designed for Henry G.

Marquand of New York. Made by Johnstone, Norman & Co., the suite was praised in the 'ART JOURNAL', 'BUILDING NEWS', and in Moyr SMITH's *Ornamental Interiors* (1887); its detailed designs were by W. C. Codman. Alma-Tadema owned glass by LA FARGE, and knew George AITCHISON. He was knighted in 1899.

Alphabet (1964) This short-lived but high-quality annual on alphabet design was edited from London by R. S. Hutchings.

Alphabet and Image (1946–8) Edited by Robert Harling and published by James Shand's Shenval Press, *Alphabet and Image* was a high-quality journal on typography and book design and illustration, comparable to the earlier 'TYPOGRAPHY' by the same team.

Altdorfer, Albrecht Altdorfer was probably born in Regensburg in about 1480, the son of the painter Ulrich Altdorfer, who left the city in 1491. Albrecht Altdorfer returned to Regensburg from Amberg in 1505 and remained there for the rest of his life, apart from a journey to Vienna in 1535. He died in 1538. In about 1515 Altdorfer designed elements for the great woodcut Triumphs and Triumphal Arch of the Emperor Maximilian, and drew brilliant marginal decorations in the Emperor's prayerbook, a mixture of late-GOTHIC and RENAISSANCE ornament, including putti, foliage, a candelabrum and a trophy borrowed from Mantegna. A woodcut of the Holy Family, executed at this period, includes a fountain strongly influenced by Zoan ANDREA's Fountain of Neptune. In about 1520 to 1525 Altdorfer published a suite of twenty-five etched plates of metalwork and ornament. The metalwork designs represent a synthesis of late-Gothic forms, such as the double cup, with Renaissance ornament, including shells, fluting, GROTESQUES, and ACANTHUS, but are simpler than comparable designs by HOLBEIN. Small copies of these designs were later published by Jerome Hopfer, and the Deutsches Ritter Orden in Vienna has a covered beaker of 1534 derived from an Altdorfer design. The suite also includes two bases and capitals derived from Giovanni Antonio da BRESCIA. At the same period Altdorfer also published two panels of late-Gothic foliate ornament, one with an oyster, one with pomegranates, a small design for a bell, and two vertical panels of early Renaissance ornament. A woodcut design for a door anticipates FLÖTNER, and the Masters H. S. and H. G.

Alte und Neue Glasmalerei, Zeitschrift für (1912–14) Published in Munich and Leipzig, this magazine covered stained-glass technique and design including articles on modern glass, for instance on Max Pechstein (1913) and Wilhelm Pütz of Cologne (1914).

American Architect and Building News (1876–1938) First published in Boston in the year of the PHILADELPHIA Centennial, this major American magazine revealed its models in a comment on the English exhibit there, 'The books of TALBERT and others are familiar to us, and we have watched with interest the illustrations of the "BUILDING NEWS" and "ARCHITECT".' It contains much information on design.

Amman, Jost (1539–91) Amman was born in Zürich, a member of a humanist and protestant household. By 1560 he had moved to Basel, where he probably designed stained glass, and in 1561 he moved to Nuremberg. There he concluded a contract with the great publisher Simon Feierabend to execute illustrations, a role previously filled by Virgil SOLIS, who died in 1562 and whom Amman probably met. Amman's first big series of 134 woodcuts was for the 1564 Frankfurt Bible; his second Bible (1571) contained a series of 198 woodcuts. He married in Nuremberg in 1574 but in 1575 he bought a house in Zürich. However, in 1577 Amman forswore his Zürich citizenship and was awarded honorary citizenship of Nuremberg as a painter and engraver of exceptional fame and talent. Amman later visited Augsburg (1578), Frankfurt (1578), Heidelberg (1583), Würzburg (1586–7) and Altdorf (1590). He was an enormously prolific designer of book illustrations and ornaments, and his designs were widely used for decoration by goldsmiths, gunstock-makers and other craftsmen. He was a friend of Wenzel JAMNITZER and engraved the plates to his *Perspectiva* (1568). Other works included portraits, coats-of-arms, almanacs, printers' marks, plates and cups. A new card game with fifty-two plates published by Amman in 1588 had suites of printers' bales, books, goblets and beakers; it was probably more for the amusement of connoisseurs than for use. Amman also issued a drawing manual with 108 plates, *Kunst und Lehrbüchlein* (Zürich, 1578). Another influential group of illustrations were the 220 blocks in Hans Weigel's *Trachtenbuch* (1577), a work on dress. Amman's inventions were propagated after his death by collections such as *Kunstliche Wohlgerissene Figuren* (1592) and, above all, the *Kunstbüchlein* (Frankfurt, 1599). A Bacchus from the latter is used on an enamelled flask of the 1720s by Ignaz Preissler. Amman also had a direct influence on other designers, especially SIBMACHER and FLINDT.

Andêl, Anton Born in 1844 in Mähren, Andêl studied painting in Vienna, and then became a teacher of design in Graz, where he taught ornament. He published

ambitious books on geometrical ornament (1877), polychrome ornament (1880), with fine chromolithographic plates in the NATURALISTIC, Pompeian, RENAISSANCE, Indian and Arabic styles, and plant ornament (1894). He also wrote on the history of ACANTHUS (1891), the spiral (1892) and colour (1900).

André, Émile (1871–1933) The son of the architect Charles André, who had promoted the Nancy 1894 Exhibition, Émile André followed his father's profession. In 1901 he collaborated with the cabinet-maker and designer Eugène Vallin (1856–1922) on the Magasins Vaxelaire & Pignot, Rue Raugraff, Nancy, and, with Henri Gutton, planned a model suburb at Nancy, the Parc de Saurupt; its entry has elaborate ART NOUVEAU iron gates. André later designed numerous houses in Nancy. He also designed furniture similar in style to that of MAJORELLE. He showed designs of all types at the Paris 1904 École de Nancy Exhibition.

Andrea, Zoan Andrea was a painter and engraver in Mantua, whose style was based on that of Mantegna. In 1475 he alleged that he had been attacked by armed men on Mantegna's orders. Andrea seems as a result to have moved to Milan. His engravings include copies after DÜRER. He also engraved twelve panels of ornament, tall thin candelabra-shaped compositions incorporating VASES, putti, ACANTHUS, merfolk, trophies, animals, masks, griffins and sphinxes. They were copied by the Italian potter Nicoluso in Spain, on the choir-stalls at Gaillon (1508) and Chartres (1529), and also in Germany. Although they represent a primitive stage of the GROTESQUE, they had a renewed period of influence in French ornament of the 1540s, together with the prints of Nicoletto da MODENA, Agostino VENEZIANO and Enea VICO.

Annales Archéologiques (1844–70) Founded by Adolphe-Napoléon Didron and continued after his death in 1864 by his son Édouard-Aimé, this learned journal combined archaeology with propaganda for the GOTHIC Revival in architecture and design.

Anthéaume, Baptiste Anthéaume published *Livre de meuble propre pour Mrs les brodeurs et tapissiers*, six plates of designs for bed valances for embroidering, decorated with BERAINESQUE STRAPWORK. They probably date from about 1700.

Antonini, Carlo From 1777 to 1790 Antonini published a *Manuale de Vari Ornamenti* in Rome. After title-pages in the style of PIRANESI its 213 plates include antique rosettes, candelabra and sundials, for the use of sculptors, architects, plasterers, stone-carvers and wood-carvers, silversmiths, jewellers, embroiderers, cabinet-makers, etc.; the candelabra were mainly from Roman collections such as the Museo Pio Clementino but also included six from English collections. In his preface Antonini alluded to his edition of Vignola. Antonini's *Manuale* was copied by the architect Thomas Hardwick (1752–1829). A sequel with antique VASES was published in Rome in 1821 (193 plates). An 1832 London reprint of the *Manuale* petered out after a mere four plates. Antonini also engraved after Pannini.

A.P. Some fifty printed designs for the decoration of silver in the dotted manner are attributed to a designer, A.P. or A.B., who signed some of them. One suite (twenty plates) is dated 1604, another (twelve plates) 1610. A.P.'s style is close to that of Paul FLINDT. The 1610 suite includes a dotted represen-tation of a goldsmith's workshop, while another design has a dotted architectural perspective, reminiscent of Hans VREDEMAN DE VRIES's designs for inlay, but enlivened by gondolas in the foreground.

Arabesque The term 'arabesque' was used in the 16th century in a sense identical or nearly identical to MORESQUE. TAGLIENTE (1527) called his designs '*moreschi et arabeschi*' and PELLEGRINO (1530) used the word '*arabicque*'. In 1611 Cotgrave's French–English dictionary included the definition 'Rebeske worke; a small, and curious flourishing'. In about the year 1760 STUART revived the RENAISSANCE GROTESQUE style, which was later used by CLÉRISSEAU. Grotesque was then called 'arabesque'. Arabesques, in this new sense, were designed by SALEMBIER, QUEVERDO, TIBESAR, FAY, PRIEUR and DUGOURC. They were gathered together in 1802 in a collection which also included prints after RAPHAEL's grotesques in the Vatican, under the title *Recueil d'arabesques*.

Architect, De (1890–1907) This luxury journal published by the Amsterdam association Architectura et Amicitia, which later published 'WENDINGEN', is a rich source of decorative designs by BERLAGE and other Dutch architects.

Architect Portfolio, The (1929–37) Published as a supplement to the *Architect and Building News*, the *Portfolio* contains a valuable range of detailed design drawings by Sir Giles Gilbert Scott, Oswald Milne, Oliver BERNARD, Joseph Emberton and others, thus covering the full spectrum of contemporary English styles.

Architect, The Subtitled *A Weekly Illustrated Journal of Art, Civil Engineering* *and Building*, this was one of the most important late-Victorian architectural papers, containing much information on design. Its first editor from 1869 was T. Roger Smith. In its latter years it has become a trade journal.

Architectural Annual (1900–1901) Published in Philadelphia under the auspices of the Architectural League of America, this magazine included a wide range of articles and illustrations, including surveys of Wilson EYRE (1900) and Louis H. SULLIVAN (1901).

Architectural Design Although it has usually played second fiddle to the 'ARCHITECTURAL REVIEW' and has undergone several changes of editorial policy, this London magazine founded in 1930 has useful information on design.

Architectural Digest Published from Los Angeles, this is now the most prominent American glossy magazine on interior decoration and design. It was founded in 1920.

Architectural Review The first editor of what is now the leading English architectural journal was Henry WILSON. The first volume of 1896 included an article on George Charles HAITÉ, and design has always formed an important part of the magazine's content.

Architecture d'Aujourd'hui, L' Under its founder editor, André Bloc (1896–1966), this Paris journal acted from 1930 as a mouthpiece for the promoters of the MODERN style; although mainly architectural it frequently contained information and illustrations on design. The magazine 'AUJOURD'HUI' was an off-shoot.

Architecture Illustrated (1930–57) Especially in its early years this magazine is a valuable source of illustration of designs by English architects over the full spectrum of styles. Its proprietors had published *Academy Architecture* since 1889.

Architecture Vivante, L' (1923–5) Edited by Jean Badovici, this de luxe Paris magazine promoted MODERN architecture and design. The first issue included windows designed by Maurice DENIS in Perret's Notre Dame de Raincy, a shop interior by SÜE & MARE, and a dining-room by RUHLMANN. Designers treated later included JOURDAIN, Mendelssohn and Eileen GRAY, whose house designed in collaboration with Badovici took up a whole issue.

Architettura e Arti Decorative (1921–40) This well-illustrated journal of architecture and design was published from Rome. In 1932 the title changed to *Architettura* and the magazine became the organ of the National Fascist Union of Architects.

Arfe y Villafañe, Juan de (1535–1603) Born in Leon, the son of a goldsmith, Arfe made famous tabernacles for the cathedrals of Avila, Seville, Valladolid and Burgos. He published a technical manual on goldsmiths' work (Valladolid, 1571) and a description of his tabernacles at Seville (1587). *De Varia Commensuracion para la Esculptura y Architectura* (Seville, 1585) covered geometry, proportion, anatomy and architecture, but also contained model designs for a chalice, ewers, candlesticks, crosses, a crozier, a censer, lamps, tabernacles and a monstrance. Arfe enjoyed great contemporary fame and always stressed his status as a sculptor rather than as a mere goldsmith; in 1597 he was involved in the completion of sixty-four reliquary busts of saints for the Escorial. In his *Commensuracion* Arfe argued for a pure classical style and against the

MANNERIST extravagances of Flemish and French pattern-books.

Arkady (1935–9) This well-illustrated Polish journal, published in Warsaw, covered most aspects of art and design.

Armstrong, John (1893–1973) Born in Hastings, Sussex, the son of a parson, Armstrong was trained as a painter at St John's Wood School of Art. He became a leading surrealist, joining UNIT ONE in 1933. His interior decorations included eight mural panels for the dining-room of Shell Mex, for whom he also designed posters from 1932 to 1952, commencing with 'Everywhere you go you can be sure of Shell'.

Arnoux, Joseph François Léon (1816–1902) Born in Toulouse, son of a successful potter, Léon Arnoux studied engineering in Paris, where he gained experience at the Sèvres factory under BRONGNIART. He later managed an unsuccessful new pottery for his father. Arnoux moved to England in the mid-1840s, met Herbert Minton (1793–1858), and in 1849 was appointed the Art Director of Mintons. He transformed the factory's techniques and its standards of design. His English maiolica was a great success at the LONDON 1851 EXHIBITION, and from 1858 he worked on the revival of Henri II ware. Arnoux was responsible for the employment of JEANNEST, Protat, and CARRIER-BELLEUSE as Minton designers. He was deeply involved in many international exhibitions, sitting on juries and writing reports. Arnoux retired in 1892 but continued to advise Mintons up to his death.

Arp, Hans (1886–1966) Born in Strasbourg, Arp studied in Weimar, and in 1910 helped to found Der Moderne Bund at Lucerne. In 1911 to 1912 he was in Munich and met Kandinsky and the Blaue Reiter group. Then he moved to Paris, which he had visited in 1904, and made contact with Picasso and Braque through the poet Apollinaire. In 1915 he met Sophie Taeuber in Zürich and from 1916 to 1920 they were both involved in the Dada movement. They married in 1921. Sophie Taeuber-Arp (1889–1943) was born at Davos and from 1908 to 1910 trained as a teacher of textile design at the school of applied art in St Gallen, and in 1912 studied in Hamburg. In 1915 she joined the Swiss Werkbund, and from 1916 to 1929 she taught textile design at the applied art school in Zürich. In 1927 she published *Dessin pour les métiers du textile*, a manual of textile design. From 1916 to 1920 Hans Arp and Sophie Taeuber collaborated on geometrical abstract embroideries and textiles. In 1919 Hans Arp was in Cologne, where he met Max Ernst and Kurt Schwitters. In 1925 he collaborated with El LISSITZKY on *Les Ismes de l'Art*. The Arps had established links with the DE STIJL group and in 1926 to 1928 they collaborated with Theo Van Doesburg on the resolutely abstract decorations of L'Aubette in Strasbourg, an entertainment centre with bars, ballroom and a cinema. Sophie Taeuber-Arp designed stained glass for L'Aubette and from 1928 to 1935 she designed furniture and other decorations for the Galerie Goemans in Paris. In 1939 she designed Aubusson tapestries. Hans Arp, although mainly active as a sculptor from 1930, designed Aubusson tapestries in the 1950s, and also designed silver for Christofle.

Arrowsmith, Henry, William and Arthur Described as 'Decorators to Her Majesty', the Arrowsmiths founded a London decorating firm in the late 1830s; they were based in New Bond Street from 1840. Their *The House Decorator and Painter's Guide* (1840) contains sixty-one mainly coloured plates of designs for wall decoration, incorporating some furniture, in the GOTHIC, Elizabethan, Louis XIV, Moorish and Pompeian styles, among others. (Tredgold's *New and Improved Practical Builder* (1848–50) contained a design by the Arrowsmiths for an Elizabethan bookcase.) James Arrowsmith, who published *An Analysis of Drapery* and *The Paperhanger's and Upholsterer's Guide* in about 1850, may be a relation.

Art Amateur, The (1879–90) Subtitled *A Monthly Journal Devoted to the Cultivation of Art in the Household*, this magazine was edited and published in New York by Montague Marks. It contains many full-scale decorative designs in Japanese and other fashionable styles. It was a direct competitor to the 'ART INTERCHANGE'.

Art and Decoration (1885–6) Subtitled *An Illustrated Monthly Devoted to Interior and Exterior Ornament*, this New York journal was edited by George R. Halm, who himself contributed many designs. It included a wide range of illustrations, representative of commercial taste in design.

Art Déco The style known as Art Déco takes its name from the PARIS 1925 Exposition Internationale des Arts Décoratifs et Industriels Modernes, which was its definitive showplace, but its sources go back to the years after 1905 when designers in France reacted against the curvilinearity and insubstantiality of much ART NOUVEAU design. A taste for more solid rectilinear shapes, a distaste for the 'macaroni' aspect of Art Nouveau ornament and a revival of interest in the 18th century were accompanied by influences from *avant-garde* painters. The Fauves, abetted by the Russian ballet, encouraged bold colours and strong patterns; the cubists intro-

duced African influences and a quasi-geometrical dissection of forms. Art Déco was a luxury style, sponsored by such *mondain* figures as DOUCET and POIRET, and rich materials, such as ebony, shagreen, lacquer, ivory and enamel, were ubiquitous. Art Déco protagonists such as RUHLMANN, LALIQUE and DUNAND might seem to have little in common with puritan advocates of an industrial aesthetic, but many designers, including Eileen GRAY and MALLET-STEVENS, spanned the distinction between Art Déco and MODERNISM, and even the most incorruptible Modernists, for instance LE CORBUSIER and Jean PROUVÉ, sometimes present an Art Déco aspect. Art Déco was an important source of popular design in the 1920s and 1930s and was particularly influential in America. From the late 1960s pastiches of a simplified and cheapened Art Déco have been a stock ingredient of Post-Modern design.

Art Décoratif, L' (1898–1914) After his resignation from 'PAN', Julius MEIER-GRAEFE founded *L'Art Décoratif* as a French companion magazine to 'DEKORATIVE KUNST'. The first volume included an article on MACKINTOSH and the Glasgow group. Later articles covered Vever's jewels (1901), SERRURIER's wallpapers (1902) and René BINET's drawings (1907).

Art Decorator (1890–1929) Subtitled *A Periodical Publication of Select Samples of Decorative Art, Old and New*, this was an English edition of 'DEKORATIVE VORBILDER'. From 1926 it was entitled the *Artworkers' Studio*.

Arte Italiana Decorativa ed Industriale (1890–1911) Edited by Ferdinando Ongania, this Italian magazine was mainly historical in bias, but its excellent plates, some in colour, also included modern design.

Art et Décoration Published by the Librairie Centrale des Beaux-Arts, this Paris magazine began in 1897 as a crusading organ of design reform, with GRASSET a vigorous member of its committee of direction. The first issue contained well-illustrated articles on HORTA, MUCHA, the London ARTS & CRAFTS EXHIBITION, and, by Gleeson White, on 'The Tree in English Ornamental Design'. Later articles included accounts of RUHLMANN, and SÜE & MARE, in 1920, at a time when Francis JOURDAIN was a regular contributor, and a survey of metal furniture in 1930. The magazine is now more middle-of-the-road.

Art et Industrie (1909–14) This luxurious and eclectic journal covered a wide field, including eastern decoration and theatre as well as the decorative arts. It was edited from Paris by G. Grouthière-Vernolle, but often acted as a mouthpiece for the Nancy School under the leadership of Victor PROUVÉ.

Art et les Artistes, L' (1905–39) Despite its title, this Paris journal contains much well-illustrated information on contemporary decorative arts, for example articles on LALIQUE in 1905 and 1921.

Art et l'Industrie, L' (1877–88) This journal published a wide variety of fine illustrations of designs for the decorative arts, some in colour, mainly by French- and German-speaking designers, with an emphasis on the RENAISSANCE Revival style. It was published in Paris.

Art in Industry (1946–60) Published by the Indian Institute of Art in Industry, this magazine combined a Council of Industrial Design approach with coverage of Indian art and crafts. The first

issue included articles by Gordon RUSSELL and Nikolaus PEVSNER.

Art Interchange, The (1878–1904) This magazine, subtitled *A Household Journal*, was published in New York, with Russell Sturgis as its architectural contributor. It took a strong interest in interiors and home decoration and incorporated many full-scale decorative designs. An English edition was briefly published from 1890 to 1891.

Artisan Mannerism In 1953 Sir John Summerson coined the term 'artisan mannerism' to describe the style of architecture practised in England from about 1615 to 1675 by craftsmen rather than architects. Its vocabulary was probably derived from pattern-books, MANNERIST and BAROQUE, but its syntax was the product of the instincts of craftsmen untrained in the classical language of architecture. The term artisan mannerism is also useful in a much more general sense to indicate the character of design by craftsmen without an academic background. Typical features are repetition, the overt display of technical tricks, over- or under-scaling of motifs, oddities of proportion, simplifications, exaggerations, and simple misunderstanding of sophisticated systems of design and ornament. Artisan mannerism often overlaps and coincides with provincialism in design, but is frequently evident in metropolitan products which mask academic ignorance in luxury of materials and virtuosity of technique.

Artist, The (1880–1902) With its supplementary title of *Journal of Home Culture*, this magazine seems to have been intended at first as an unillustrated and modest version of the 'ART JOURNAL'. From 1895 it adopted a new large format and a mass of illustrations as well as a new form of title, *The Artist, Photographer & Decorator, An Illus-*

trated *Monthly Journal of Applied Art*, further changed in 1896 to *The Artist, An Illustrated Monthly Record of Arts, Crafts & Industries*. An American edition was published from 1898 to 1902. The *Artist*'s post-1895 format was clearly a direct response to the success of the 'STUDIO', but although it failed as a competitor it is an important source for design history up to 1902.

Artistic Japan (1888–91) Subtitled *A Monthly Illustrated Journal of Arts and Industries*, this magazine was edited by Samuel BING, with Marcus S. Huish as English editor. There was a French edition, *Le Japon Artistique*, and a German, *Japanischer Formenschatz*. It comprised a brilliant variety of illustrations, many in colour, and included articles on Japanese jewellery by L. Falize (1888), on Japanese art by Justus Brinckmann (1890) and on the influence of Japanese art by Roger Marx (1891).

Art Journal (1839–1911) Founded by the journalist Samuel Carter Hall (1800–1889) as the *Art Union*, the magazine ran at a loss, despite a high reputation, until 1847, when Prince ALBERT gave his patronage. Virtue & Co. took over in 1848 and in 1849 the title was changed to the *Art Journal*. Its illustrated catalogues to the LONDON EXHIBITIONS of 1851, 1862 and others are an important source of information about design.

Art Nouveau The term Art Nouveau is derived from the gallery of that name opened by BING in Paris in 1895. Art Nouveau is used in a general sense to describe the great revival in the decorative arts which spread across Europe from about 1890, with roots in England and offshoots in Belgium, France, Germany, Italy and elsewhere. This broad definition encompasses MACKINTOSH and the Glasgow School, Josef HOFF-

MANN and the WIENER WERKSTÄTTE and even Elbert HUBBARD and his Roycrofters. Magazines such as the 'STUDIO', 'PAN', 'ART DÉCORATIF' and 'KUNST UND KUNSTHANDWERK' encouraged interest in design and local terms for Art Nouveau came into currency, such as Jugendstil in Germany, derived from the magazine 'JUGEND', and Stile Liberty in Italy, derived from the LIBERTY shop in London. Art Nouveau is also used in a narrow sense to denote a specific style of ornament, linear, sinuous and vegetal, with resemblances to the ROCOCO and AURICULAR styles. The great protagonists of this Art Nouveau style, which lasted from about 1895 to 1905, were HORTA and GUIMARD; it reached its apogee in the PARIS 1900 EXHIBITION. The origins of Art Nouveau in designs by MACKMURDO, SUMNER and Beardsley were first traced by PEVSNER (1936), but English designers such as CRANE and VOYSEY disowned their foreign offspring in a symposium published in the 'MAGAZINE OF ART' (1904). The style was often overladen with explicit symbolic overtones, usually evocative of Nature (see NATURALISM), through the use of flowers, leaves and insects, or of the Eternal Feminine or the Femme Fatale, through the use of female nudes. By 1905 the curvilinear Art Nouveau style was in full retreat. It was later forgotten, or even disowned, for instance by VAN DE VELDE, but from the publication of Brian Reade's *Art Nouveau and Alphonse Mucha* (1963), Art Nouveau enjoyed a sudden but brief period of revival, as the medium for the 'psychedelic' posters which appeared in the late 1960s.

Art pour Tous, L' (1861–1906) Subtitled *Encyclopédie de l'Art Industriel et Décoratif*, this magazine was founded by Émile REIBER, together with Théodore DECK; its principal editor was Charles

Sauvageot. It presented designers with a magnificent range of predominantly historic designs and illustrations, sometimes in colour, with captions in French, German and English.

Art Record, The (1901–2) Subtitled *A Weekly Illustrated Review of the Arts & Crafts*, this London magazine, edited by Arthur F. Phillips, seems to have been intended as a cheaper competitor to the 'STUDIO'

Arts and Crafts (1904–6) Subtitled *A Monthly Practical Magazine for the Studio, the Workshop and the Home*, this London magazine placed a strong emphasis on practical methods and on design by students, but also included work by professional designers such as Walter CRANE.

Arts and Crafts (1925–9) This London quarterly, edited by Claude Flight, was mainly craft-oriented, although it included articles on ornament and design by Maxwell Armfield and A. Romney Green respectively. It went monthly in 1927 under the editorship of Herbert Furst. He was succeeded in 1928 by W. L. Hanchant, who turned it progressively more MODERN and design-oriented until its demise in 1929.

Arts & Crafts Exhibition Society The idea of a society to organize exhibitions of the decorative arts in London was first mooted in about 1886. Walter CRANE and the painters George Clausen (1852–1944) and Holman Hunt (1827–1910) discussed the possibility of a national exhibition of the fine and decorative arts. Clausen and Hunt were considering the reform of the Royal Academy, but Crane found support for an independent exhibition among the members of the publicity-shy ART-WORKERS' GUILD. A committee was formed with W. A. S. BENSON as its

most energetic member to mount an exhibition called 'The Combined Arts', but the title 'Arts & Crafts', suggested by the bookbinder T. J. Cobden Sanderson, was adopted for the first exhibition, held at the New Gallery in Regent Street in 1888. The first president of the Arts & Crafts Exhibition Society was Crane, who designed the catalogue cover for the 1888 exhibition and held office until 1912, apart from a break from 1893 to 1896, when William MORRIS was President; Morris had been a sceptical member of the original committee. Apart from Benson and Crane the main activists were Heywood SUMNER, Emery Walker, Henry Longden, J. D. SEDDING and Lewis F. DAY. The 1888 exhibition was a great success, as was the second in 1889; however, that held in 1890 was a loss. *Arts and Crafts Essays by Members of the Arts and Crafts Exhibition Society* (1893), including essays by Ford Madox BROWN, John Hungerford POLLEN and Selwyn IMAGE as well as many of those already mentioned, provided a conspectus of Arts & Crafts attitudes. From about this date the Society and its members had an international influence and demonstrated the practical application of the ideas of RUSKIN and Morris. The fifth exhibition in 1896 included a selection of Ford Madox Brown's pioneer works. The Society was involved in the English contributions to the TURIN 1902 and ST LOUIS 1904 EXHIBITIONS and organized both the Ghent 1913 Exhibition and a larger version sent to Paris but cut short by the outbreak of war. After the war the Society published *Handicrafts and Reconstruction* (1919), with essays by Wilson, LETHABY, Benson and others, and briefly issued an *Arts & Crafts Quarterly* (1919–20) which, *mirabile dictu*, included a translation of the Futurist manifesto, sympathetically introduced by Wilson. By this date, however, the Arts & Crafts Exhibition

Society was rapidly declining in influence.'

Arts de la Maison, Les From its first issue in 1923, with a polemic foreword by Frantz (sic) Jourdain on the revival of decorative art, which looked forward to 'the triumph of truth' at the PARIS 1925 EXHIBITION, this luxury magazine edited by Christian Zervos was the showcase of what has come to be known as the ART DÉCO style. Designers illustrated included RUHLMANN, SÜE & MARE, GROULT, FOLLOT, CHAREAU, DUFY, Eileen GRAY, LURÇAT and LEGRAIN.

Arts et Métiers Graphiques (1927–39) This luxury Parisian journal covered all aspects of graphic design, including for instance DUFY as an illustrator (1928).

Artwork (1924–31) Subtitled *An Illustrated Quarterly of Arts & Crafts*, the first issue of this magazine, edited by Herbert Wauthier, contained an article on mosaic by R. Anning Bell and another on posters by E. McKnight KAUFFER. Under its later editors (D. S. MacColl from 1929, Randolph Schwabe from 1930) the stress moved towards the fine arts.

Art-Workers' Guild, The Early in 1883 some pupils of Richard Norman SHAW formed a society to discuss art and architecture, the St George's Art Society. The committee comprised Ernest Newton, E. S. Prior, Mervyn Macartney, Gerald C. Horsley, W. R. LETHABY and E. J. May (only May was not a Shaw pupil). After consultation with Shaw they decided to widen their aim to promote the unity of the arts. The Fifteen, founded in 1882 with Lewis F. DAY as secretary, were approached, and the two groups were transmuted into the Art-Workers' Guild, whose first formal meeting was held in May 1884.

BENSON suggested the Guild of Art Workers as a title; this was rejected and Prior proposed the exact formula adopted. Day became treasurer and the sculptor George Blackall Simonds, also a member of The Fifteen, became first master. Later masters included SEDDING (1886), Walter CRANE (1888 and 1889), William MORRIS (1892) and SUMNER (1894). Crane designed the badge and stationery and in 1888 the Guild bought turned chairs from Philip Clissett of Bosbury for its hall, chairs which were to inspire GIMSON. The Guild acted as a forum for discussion for craftsmen, architects and designers, including VOYSEY, MACKMURDO, Henry WILSON and ASHBEE. In its early years its masques, for instance *Beauty's Awakening* (1899), were fascinating expressions of Arts & Crafts sentiments. In 1915 its premises in Queen Square were used by the nascent DESIGN AND INDUSTRIES ASSOCIATION.

Art Workers' Quarterly (1902–6) Subtitled *A Portfolio of Practical Designs for Decorative and Applied Art* this journal, edited by W. G. Paulson Tounsend, had a strong Arts & Crafts flavour, with a stress on the practical applications of the designs it published, which included works by Stephen WEBB, W. J. NEATBY, Harold STABLER and Walter CRANE. These were issued on a large scale. A special number was published in 1908 and in 1914 a supplement called the *Annual of Art Work*.

Art-Workman, The (1873–83) Subtitled *A Monthly Journal of Design for the Artist, Artificer and Manufacturer*, this magazine was published in London by James Haggar. The first editor was Julius Schnorr, and the fine illustrations, some in colour, were predominantly by modern German or Austrian designers.

A.S. This German engraver, probably a goldsmith, published three fine panels of ornament in the ALDEGREVER style, two vertical with foliage and putti dated 1538 and 1539, and one circular, with an allegorical figure of Fortune, dated 1540.

Ashbee, Charles Robert (1863–1942) The son of a rich businessman and collector of pornography, Ashbee studied history at Cambridge, where he was influenced by the socialist simple-lifer, Edward Carpenter (1844–1929). From 1883 he was in the office of the architect G. F. BODLEY (1827–1907). He then lived and studied at Toynbee Hall, the philanthropic foundation in London's East End, and in 1886 founded a RUSKIN reading class in Whitechapel. The group executed a plasterwork panel for the dining-room at Toynbee Hall, and evolved into the Guild of Handicraft, which was inaugurated in June 1888 as a cooperative group of craftsmen. The formation of the Guild was welcomed by Walter CRANE, HERKOMER, MACKMURDO, Lewis F. DAY and others, but greeted with some scepticism by William MORRIS. The Guild practised woodwork, leatherwork, metalwork and jewellery. They showed at the 1889 and later ARTS & CRAFTS EXHIBITIONS. In 1891 they moved from premises in Commercial Street to Essex House, a Georgian house in the Mile End Road. In 1893 to 1894 Ashbee designed a house, The Magpie and Stump, Cheyne Row, for his mother, and the Guild did the interiors. He designed several houses in Cheyne Row in the 1890s, and was sporadically active as an architect up to the First World War. After William Morris's death in 1896 Ashbee acquired some of the Kelmscott Press equipment to start the Essex House Press; its first book, CELLINI's *Treatises on Goldsmithing and Sculpture* (1898), translated by Ashbee, was dedicated to the Guild. In 1900

Ashbee designed his own typeface, Endeavour, first used on *An Endeavour towards the Teaching of John Ruskin and William Morris* (1901). In 1897 Ashbee was elected to the ART-WORKERS' GUILD and in 1896 and in 1900 he visited America, meeting Frank Lloyd WRIGHT in Chicago on the latter trip; he later wrote a preface to the 1911 Wasmuth book on Wright. Ashbee also admired Charles Sumner GREENE and 'JUGEND'. In 1898 the Guild became a limited company and was employed to execute BAILLIE SCOTT's furniture for the Grand Duke of Hesse at Darmstadt. They opened a retail shop on a corner of Bond Street in 1899, showed at the Vienna 1900 Secession Exhibition, and in 1901 received a Royal Warrant as jewellers and silversmiths to Queen Alexandra. The lease of Essex House was nearing an end and in 1901 the Guild – some 150 people – moved to Chipping Campden in Gloucestershire. Greetings arrived from Elbert HUBBARD in 1902, and a steady stream of advanced and admiring visitors arrived to admire the Guild in their new rural quarters. In the 'STUDIO' winter number of 1901 to 1902 Aymer Vallance recognized Ashbee's pre-eminence as a designer of jewellery, and he was fêted in Budapest in 1905. A laudatory account of the Guild appeared in 'KUNST UND HANDWERK' (1907), but in the same year the Guild, which had been struggling since 1905, failed. Ashbee published an inquest, *Craftsmanship in Competitive Industry* (1909). His *Should We Stop Teaching Art?* (1911) advocated government endowed 'small artistic workshops'. From 1917 he was involved in town planning in Egypt and Jerusalem, but in 1924 returned to England and devoted himself to theorizing and his memoirs. Ashbee was the dominant designer of the Guild. Its furniture was usually plain, even dim, in form, and lent interest by iron hinges, and painted, gesso or stamped leather decoration; the overblown library at Madresfield for Lord Beauchamp (around 1905) was the most remarkable Guild interior. In silver Ashbee developed a personal style, in which rounded forms are relieved by elegant wire handles and mouldings, and by semi-precious cabochons or disks of enamel. *Modern English Silverwork* (1909; 100 plates drawn by Philippe Mairet, 1886–1975) summarized this style, which was much copied by LIBERTY's and others. Ashbee's jewellery designs, in which peacocks were prominent, were also widely imitated. Ashbee also designed wallpapers, pottery and carpets, and a Coalbrookdale cast-iron fireplace illustrated by MUTHESIUS, but his experience of dealing with manufacturers was not happy.

Aspertini, Amico Born in Bologna in about 1475, the son of a painter, Aspertini moved to Rome in about 1500, where he worked under Pinturicchio and devoted himself to the study of GROTESQUE ornament. Back in Bologna from 1503 Aspertini was mainly active as a painter but also in 1529 designed a triumphal arch for the entry of Pope Clement VII and the Emperor Charles V. A group of grotesque tapestries woven in Brussels in about 1550 are also attributed to Aspertini. He died in 1552.

Asplund, Erik Gunnar (1885–1940) Born in Stockholm, Asplund considered painting as a career but in 1909 began to study architecture at the Stockholm Academy of Art. In 1913 he travelled to Italy and Greece. On his return Asplund went into partnership with Sigurd Lewerentz (1885–1975). From 1917 to 1920 Asplund was editor of the magazine *Arkitektur*. He showed a celebrated kitchen and living room at the 1917 exhibition of Slöjdföreningen, the Swedish

Society of Arts & Crafts, founded in 1844, and from 1924 he served on the Society's council. In 1921 Asplund designed furniture and fittings for Stockholm City Hall, designed by Ragnar Ostberg (1866–1945), and from 1920 to 1928 every detail of Stockholm City Library, including sophisticated NEO-CLASSICAL furniture and door handles formed as Charles Atlas-like figures of Adam and Eve. Asplund was the chief architect of the STOCKHOLM 1930 EXHIBITION and thus presided over the breakthrough of the MODERN Functionalist style in Sweden, although he was never personally a whole-hearted adherent.

Asprucci, Antonio (1723–1808) Born in Rome, the son of an architect, Asprucci studied under the architect Niccola Salvi (1679–1751), whose assistant he became. Once independent, Asprucci worked for the Duca di Bracciano and Marcantonio Borghese. From 1782 to about 1800 Asprucci was employed by Prince Borghese on the re-arrangement, redecoration and refurnishing of the Villa Borghese in a delicate and suave NEO-CLASSICAL style. His son, Mario Asprucci (1764–1804), also worked on the Villa Borghese. He supplied designs for Ickworth in 1794 and was a friend of TATHAM.

Asti, Sergio Born in Milan in 1926, Asti qualified as an architect in 1953. He organized the Industrial Design Exhibition at the 1957 Milan Triennale. Asti designed for several Italian firms, including glass for Salviati of Venice.

Aubert, Félix Born in 1866 at Langrune-sur-Mer near Bayeux, Aubert was in 1892 one of the founder members of the decorative art group Les Cinq, with CHARPENTIER, DAMPT, SELMERS-HEIM and Moreau-Nélaton. In 1896 they were joined by Charles PLUMET to become Les Six. Aubert, working in a naturalistic ART NOUVEAU style, designed carpets, fabrics, pottery and glass. Around the turn of the century his designs were illustrated in the 'STUDIO', 'DEKORATIVE KUNST' and elsewhere. Aubert later helped to revive the lace industry in Calvados, supplying many designs.

Aubert Parent, Henri Joseph (1753–1835) Born in Cambrai, Aubert Parent worked as a wood-carver in Paris for the court. From 1784 to 1788 he made a subsidized visit to Italy. After the French revolution he lived in Berlin, St Petersburg and Switzerland before settling in Valenciennes in 1813. He taught architecture there until his death. In 1788 Aubert Parent published suites of designs for seat furniture, beds (1789), furniture, VASES, clocks, iron balconies and ARABESQUES, of four or six plates each. They are in an elaborate but slightly artisan NEO-CLASSICAL style.

Audran, Claude III (1658–1734) Born in Lyon, the son of an engraver who worked for CHARMETON, Audran was taught by his father and his uncles Claude II (1639–84) and Gérard (1640–1703), also engravers. Claude II had worked at Versailles as a decorative painter under LE BRUN, and Claude III Audran also worked in this capacity in the royal palaces. In 1693 his style was described as '*plus exquis et plus svelte*' than that of Jean I BERAIN. But Audran was not in opposition to Berain; indeed his *singeries* at Marly (1709) are directly inspired by Berain. He rather continued Berain's development of a spirited and elegant GROTESQUE style to a pitch of unstructured lightness which acted as a springboard for the early ROCOCO style, developed by Audran's pupil, WATTEAU, and by GILLOT. Audran painted at Anet (1698 and 1733), Versailles (from 1699) and Fon-

tainebleau (from 1703). In 1714 he painted the choir of Notre Dame with Dagly, in 1727 he painted a coach for the Princesse de Conti, and he also decorated many harpsichords. Audran designed stained glass for the chapel at Versailles (1705–10), Savonnerie carpets (1711), embroidery and church vestments. When the Gobelins tapestry factory reopened in 1699 Audran was employed as a designer. In the same year he was commissioned by Mansart to design the Portières des Dieux, a suite comprising grotesque ornament with figures by Louis de Boulogne, which was so popular that it was still being woven in the 1780s. In 1709 Audran designed the Douze Mois Grotesques par Bandes for the Grand Dauphin at Meudon, a series engraved by Jean Audran in 1726 and copied by ROGG in Augsburg. Audran also reworked Noel COYPEL's earlier Rabesques designs, and designed borders for Charles Antoine COYPEL's Don Quixote series in 1716. In 1704 he was appointed curator of the Luxembourg and he later set up his own tapestry factory there. In about 1693 and again in 1732 efforts were made to attract Audran to Sweden to work for the court. These failed, but after Audran died the Swedish architect Carl Johan Cronstedt acquired some 4,000 drawings from his estate.

Audsley, George Ashdown (1838–1925) Born in Elgin, Audsley trained there as an architect under A. & W. Reid. In 1856 he moved to Liverpool and worked as an architect in partnership, first with John Cunningham and then with his brother William James Audsley. Their first published works were *The Sermon on the Mount* (1861), *The Guide to the Art of Illuminating* (1861, twelfth edition 1868), *The Prisoner of Chillon* (1865) and *The Handbook of Christian Symbolism* (1865), one of the most important and attractive groups of chromolithographic books. In about 1868 they issued *Cottage, Lodge and Villa Architecture.* From 1870 to 1884 Audsley was a prolific publisher on Japanese art, including *Keramic Art of Japan* (Liverpool 1875, London 1881) and *The Ornamental Arts of Japan* (1882–4); in 1872 he lectured on Japanese art at the Architectural Association in London. Both brothers published *Outlines of Ornament* (1878), a manual of flat pattern ranging from Japanese to VIOLLET-LE-DUC's decorations in Notre Dame, Paris, and *Polychromatic Decoration as Applied to Buildings in the Mediaeval Styles* (Paris and London, 1882, Stuttgart, 1883), with splendid coloured plates by Firmin-Didot in a vigorous and sometimes grotesque GOTHIC style. Some designs in *Polychromatic Decoration* were borrowed from COLLING. The Audsleys' *Popular Dictionary of Architecture and the Applied Arts* (1878–83) petered out in the fourth volume; its dedicatees were Viollet-le-Duc, Charles Barry, Frederick Leighton and James Fergusson. In 1892, with Maurice Ashdown Audsley, presumably his son, G. A. Audsley published *The Practical Decorator and Ornamentist.* He then moved to New York. In 1911, with his son Berthold, Audsley published books on *Stencilling* and *Turning*, the latter with bold designs for furniture and inlay in an unregenerate Reformed Gothic style. In 1919 he published *The Organ of the Twentieth Century.*

Aujourd'hui (1955–67) Founded and edited by André Bloc (1896–1966), a friend and associate of LE CORBUSIER, *Aujourd'hui* presented a Parisian view of international modern art, architecture and design, the latter being most fully treated in its earlier years.

Auricular Auricular ornament is an early 17th-century style so named because of the similarity of its lan-guage to the curved and melting forms of the human ear. Its sources lie in MANNERIST design, in the flaccid spouts of vessels by POLIDORO DA CARAVAGGIO, in the labial fleshiness of a candlestick by Enea VICO, the scaly distorted denizens of Cornelis FLORIS's prints, the bulging monsters of Erasmus HORNICK and the melting mask forms used by BUONTALENTI. The stretched GROTESQUE manner of around 1600 as practised by Matthias BEYTLER and Johann ŠMIŠEK shades into auricularity. However, the cradle of advanced auricular seems to have been Haarlem in about 1600 and the style achieved its full expression in the hands of a series of Dutch goldsmith designers, Paul and Adam van VIANEN, Johannes LUTMA and Gerbrand van den EECKHOUT, the son of a goldsmith. In Germany, Christoph JAMNITZER, Gotfried MÜLLER and Lucas KILIAN pioneered the style, while Nikolaus ROSMAN was one of its extremists. Later practitioners include UNTEUTSCH and ERASMUS. Auricular ornament, although deriving from mannerist sources, shares a BAROQUE sensuality with Stefano DELLA BELLA's cartouches. As a system of quasi-abstract curvilinear and liquescent ornament the auricular style was at once a bridge from mannerism to ROCOCO and an anticipation of rococo forms.

Averbeke, Emil van (1866–1946) Born in Berchem, Averbeke studied architecture at the Antwerp Academy and then worked under the architect Emil Thielens (1854–1911) from 1892 to 1899. Averbeke then concentrated on interior decoration and the design of furniture, glass, posters, stained glass and book illustrations. From 1902 Averbeke's work was illustrated in Julius Hoffmann's *Moderne Bauformen.* In 1906 Averbeke was responsible for the Antwerp section at the Milan Exhibition.

Awashima, Masakichi Born in 1914, Awashima studied design in Japan and then from 1935 to 1946 with Kozo Kagami, a pupil of Wilhelm von Eiff (1890–1943), the glass designer who taught at the Stuttgart school of applied arts from 1922. From 1946 to 1950 Awashima worked at the Hoyar Chrijstal Glassworks. In 1950 he set up the Awashima Glass Design Institute; in 1956 it became the Awashima Glass Company.

B

Babel, Pierre Edmé Babel was active in Paris as a wood-carver from at least 1736, when the Swedish court tried to secure his services. In 1738 he designed *vignettes* for Jeaurat's *Traité de Perspective* (Paris, 1740). Babel later designed decorations for albums commemorating the royal stay in Strasbourg (1744) and the marriage of the Dauphin (1745) and for 'Jacques Barozzi', *Le Nouveau Vignole* (1755). In 1754 he was recommended by C.-N. COCHIN to the young Robert ADAM 'as a good man to do any ornaments for our books etc. as having a genteel taste in that way'. In 1755 Babel became Directeur Garde of the Académie de Saint-Luc. He executed plates of carved panelling for the architect Charles Étienne BRISEUX (1680–1754), and carved extensively for the crown from 1763 to 1775, the year of his death. Babel issued some fifteen suites of engraved ornament, including *Cartouches Nouveaux* (four plates), in the early ROCOCO style, very scrolly but mainly symmetrical. Later suites, such as *Differens Compartimens d'ornemens* (eight plates), and *Fontaines en forme de cartouches* (four plates), are heavily, indeed grossly asymmetric, elaborate and rococo. Babel also issued clumsy designs for *buffets*, for a clock and for ironwork. However, *Fragments d'Ornemens* (six plates) and *Recueil d'Ornemens et Fleurs* (six plates), the latter dedicated to the chaser Pierre Dumarais, seem to be directly from sketches by Babel and display a fluent rococo wit and delicacy often lacking in his works. It is conspicuously absent in *A New Book of Ornaments* (London, 1752; six plates), published by George BICKHAM, which includes a rococo chair of wild asymmetry. Other suites by Babel were issued in London by François Vivares, and he must have been connected with a Peter Babel 'Designer and Modeller' and papier-mâché manufacturer, in London in 1763. In 1765 Babel engraved the NEO-CLASSICAL jewellery designs in Nicolas Joseph MARIA, *Livre de desseins de Joaillerie et Bijouterie*. Many of Babel's prints were copied by HERTEL in Augsburg.

Babin A professional designer, Babin issued seven suites of simple ROCOCO designs for wrought-iron balconies, gates, staircases, signs, keys and keyhole escutcheons, amounting to sixty-eight plates, in Paris in about 1750. They were still offered for sale by Jean-Félix Watin in 1773. His *Nouveau Livre* comprised simple designs for floral brooches and pendants. A 'Babin' who supplied some of LA MÉSANGÈRE's earliest designs may have been a relation.

Bacchiacca, Francesco (1494–1557) Born Francesco d'Ubertini Verdi, at Mugello near Florence, the son of a goldsmith, Bacchiacca studied painting under Perugino, probably in Perugia. In 1514 he was in Florence and in 1515 assisted PONTORMO and Franciabigio on the decoration of the residence of the Medici Pope, Leo X (1475–1521) in Florence. Bacchiacca later collaborated with Pontormo and others on the decoration of the celebrated Borgherini bridal chamber. In 1525 he went to Rome, where he became friendly with Benvenuto CELLINI and Giulio ROMANO, but he returned to Florence before the Sack of Rome in 1527. From the end of the 1530s Bacchiacca worked mainly for Cosimo de' Medici. In 1545 he was commissioned by Cosimo to design a series of GROTESQUE tapestries to be made by the new Florentine tapestry factory and to hang in the Sala dell'Udienza of the Palazzo Vecchio, with its painted decoration executed by SALVIATI from 1543 to 1545. The tapestries, woven from 1546 to 1553, display fresh and delicate grotesques on a yellow ground. Bacchiacca also designed a suite of tapestries representing the months, with charming rustic scenes within grotesque borders. Before his death Bacchiacca was engaged on the decoration of a bed for Cosimo de' Medici, which incorporated scenes woven and embellished with pearls by his brother, Antonio, a weaver. The design was completed after his death by VASARI.

Bachelier, Jean-Jacques (1724–1805) Bachelier was active as a specialist flower and animal painter, exhibiting regularly at Paris Salons from 1751 to 1767. He did numerous paintings for the court, charging very high prices. In 1748 Bachelier was commissioned to provide designs for artists at the Vincennes porcelain factory to copy, and in 1751, thanks to the protection of Mme de Pompadour, he was appointed Directeur Artistique, a post he held after the move to Sèvres in 1756 until 1793, but which he shared with LAGRENÉE from 1785, by which time he was a spent force. In 1753 Bachelier opened a design school for apprentices at Vincennes. At this period he was also interested in encaustic painting and in 1755 he wrote a pamphlet disputing the views of the Comte de CAYLUS on this subject. Bachelier designed numerous brilliant

floral *culs-de-lampe* and *fleurons* engraved by CHOFFARD for the 1762 edition of La Fontaine. These were published separately in two series of six plates announced in the *Mercure* in 1760 and 1762. The 1760 announcement states that they had already been used to decorate a Sèvres service for the King and were also useful for engravers, jewellers and textile designers. In 1766 Bachelier set up an École Gratuite de Dessin, which received royal approval in 1767 and was the original predecessor of the present École Nationale des Arts Décoratifs; it soon had as many as 1,500 students. He also wrote widely on art education and, in 1781, a history of the Sèvres factory.

Bacon, Francis Born in Dublin in 1909 of English parents, Bacon set himself up as an interior decorator in London in 1929 after time in Berlin (1926–7) and Paris (1928–9). He held two exhibitions of design work in 1929 with moderate success, the first publicized in the 'STUDIO' (1930). His furniture of chromed-steel tubing, white plywood and plate glass, white rubber curtains, and cubist rugs displayed a modish but quirky version of the MODERN style. Since 1931 Bacon has devoted himself to painting.

Bacqueville, P. P. Bacqueville designed a *Livre d'Ornemens propres pour les meubles et pour les Peintres* (twelve plates), probably published in Paris in about 1710; it comprises elaborate BERAINESQUE designs for bedheads, bed canopies and valances, some with CHINOISERIE elements. The suite was later copied in Nuremberg by Weigel.

Baeck, Elias (1679–1747) Baeck studied painting in Rome, where he acquired the nickname Heldenmuth. He was in Venice in 1705, then spent some time in Laibach, and finally settled in Augsburg, where he was active as a painter and engraver. Baeck designed five suites of CHINOISERIES of six plates each, published by Leopold, and a further two similar suites, published by Wolff. Some are applied to porcelain shapes, and Baeck's designs were copied by the Meissen porcelain factory and by Augsburg painters of Meissen porcelain, as well as by decorators of Durlach faience in about 1760.

Baile, Jacques Joseph (1819–56) Baile studied from 1833 to 1839 at the Lyon École des Beaux-Arts, where his teachers included THIERRIAT and LE PAGE. He then worked as a textile designer for the Grange & Schulz manufactory, and, after moving to Paris, for the well-known firm of Ladevèze. After returning to Lyon in 1844 he concentrated on flower painting.

Baillie Scott, Mackay Hugh (1865–1945) Born near Ramsgate of wealthy parents, Baillie Scott was articled in 1886 to C. E. Davis, City Architect of Bath. In 1889, after marriage, he settled in Douglas, Isle of Man, where his teachers at the School of Art included Archibald KNOX, with whom he collaborated on the design of stained glass and ironwork. His architectural practice began with a number of villas which owe much to the Shingle School, to Ernest George and above all to VOYSEY. In 1894 Baillie Scott entered a 'STUDIO' competition to design a coal scuttle, without success, but from 1895 when his 'The Decoration of the Suburban House' appeared he was a regular contributor. In 1896 he designed mosaics for J. L. Pearson's St Matthew's, Douglas, and showed furniture, metalwork and wallpaper at the ARTS & CRAFTS EXHIBITION. In the same year his 'Manxman' design was hailed as a solution to the problem of the cottage piano. Scott's design relied heavily on MACKMURDO, Voysey and

inglenookery, buttressed by a RUSKINIAN distaste for the sham and luxurious, and he wore a modish simplicity very much on the sleeve. In 1897 he was commissioned by Ernest Ludwig, Grand Duke of Hesse, to decorate a drawing-room and a dining-room in his palace at Darmstadt. Baillie Scott publicized his own designs, which were executed by ASHBEE's Guild of Handicraft, in two articles in the *Studio* (1898 and 1899). His bold simplifications, glowing colours and fanciful symbolism had a great success in Europe, where MUTHESIUS's pioneering appraisal in 'DEKORATIVE KUNST' (1900) was followed by repeated notice in 'KUNST UND KUNSTHANDWERK' (1901 onwards) and 'DEUTSCHE KUNST UND DEKORATION' (1903 onwards), and in America (the 'HOUSE BEAUTIFUL', 1904). A signal accolade was Baillie Scott's gaining of the highest award in the 'Zeitschrift für INNEN-DEKOR-ATION's 1901 competition for a house for an art-lover. His designs were published as one of Alex Koch's *Meister der Innenkunst* series in 1902. Baillie Scott had moved to Bedford in 1901 and in that year J. P. White, for whom Scott had designed furniture since 1898, published *Furniture Made at the Pyghtle Works, Bedford . . . Designed by M. H. Baillie Scott*. This book comprised colour plates of Baillie Scott's interior designs, of great vigour and freshness; a particular interest was appliqué embroidery, further demonstrated by his 1903 *Studio* article, 'Some Experiments in Embroidery'. From about 1900 to 1914 Baillie Scott designed furniture, tapestries and interiors for the Deutsche Werkstätten, rooms for Karl Schmidt's Dresden Werkstätten and for Wertheimer in Berlin. His architectural practice, based on simple cottagey exteriors with flexibly planned interiors, extended even to Romania, where he designed a forest eyrie, Le Nid, for Queen Marie, together with its interior fittings. Baillie Scott subscribed to 'JUGEND' and recommended it to friends, his book, *Houses and Gardens* (1906), helped to promote his style, and Muthesius's *Das Englische Haus* (1904–5) further promoted his international influence. In 1909 he designed furniture for Dr Rolf Bühler in Switzerland, and there was a continuing trickle of foreign commissions. However, from about 1907 Baillie Scott's English architectural practice took off, much assisted by A. Edgar Beresford, who had joined him in 1905 and became his partner in 1919. Scott was the favoured architect of the *Studio Yearbook of Decorative Art* until the *Studio*'s switch to MODERN in 1929. He continued to encourage craftsmanship, for instance employing G. P. Bankart to execute plasterwork, but his style stagnated and became provincial; it is recorded in *Houses and Gardens* (1933), of which Beresford was co-author. Baillie Scott fulminated against building regulations and the Modern style, much like Voysey, whom he had celebrated in a 1907 *Studio* article. Baillie Scott retired in 1939, a spent force: those drawings which had escaped a 1911 fire were destroyed in the Blitz.

Baily, Edward Hodges (1788–1867) Born in Bristol, the son of a ship's carver, Baily showed precocious talent as a sculptor and became a pupil of FLAXMAN. In 1808 and 1809 he won medals at the Society of Arts (see Royal SOCIETY OF ARTS) and the Royal Academy respectively. From 1815 Baily worked as a designer for the goldsmiths Rundell, Bridge & Rundell. Until 1817 he worked under THEED, but after Flaxman's death in 1826 he was appointed chief modeller. For Rundells Baily not only supplied designs but also adapted designs by Theed, Flaxman and Thomas STOTHARD. In 1828 Baily executed reliefs for the throne room at Buckingham Palace after designs by Stothard. In 1833 he moved from Rundells to the rival firm of Storr & Mortimer, later Hunt & Roskell, for whom he worked until 1857.

Baldi, Lazzaro Born in Pistoia in about 1624, Baldi trained as a painter and worked in Rome under Pietro da CORTONA with Ciro FERRI. In 1663 Cardinal Francesco Barberini commissioned a series of twelve tapestries on the life of Urban VIII from Baldi and Ferri. As only wool from the Cardinal's own flocks was to be used the project took more than twenty years. Baldi died in Rome in 1703.

Baldovinetti, Alessio (1425–99) Born in Florence, Baldovinetti became a member of the guild of painters in 1448; he was influenced by Domenico Veneziano, Fra Angelico and Castagno. A notebook begun in 1449 records his close contacts with craftsmen of all types. In 1463 he designed intarsia in the sacristy of Florence Cathedral executed by Giuliano da Maiano, who had previously employed the goldsmith Tommaso Finiguerra as his designer. Baldovinetti was also active as a designer of mosaics, for instance in Pisa Cathedral (1461), San Miniato (1481) and the Baptistery (1482) in Florence, and is said to have written a manual on mosaic work. He designed stained glass for Santa Trinità in Florence (1466), San Martino in Lucca (1472) and Sant'Agostino in Arezzo (1481).

Baldung Grien, Hans Born in Schwäbisch Gmund in about 1484, Baldung was brought up in Strasbourg. In 1503 he moved to Nuremberg, where he worked in DÜRER's workshop. In 1507 he went to Halle to paint two altarpieces. He then moved back to Strasbourg, apart from a four-year spell in Freiburg from 1513 to 1517. Baldung executed decorations for the prayer-book of the Emperor Maximilian I in 1515. He was also a prolific designer of stained glass. Baldung's largest output was as a designer of book illustrations, and he executed at least 387 woodcuts, including some for a book on anatomy published in 1541. He died in Strasbourg in 1545.

Ballantine, James (1808–77) Born in Edinburgh, Ballantine started life as a house painter and then studied drawing under Sir William Allen at the EDINBURGH TRUSTEES' ACADEMY. He later became involved in the revival of stained glass; his firm won the 1843 competition to execute stained glass for the House of Lords. Ballantine's *Treatise on Painted Glass* (London, 1845) was dedicated to Lord Colborne, President of the Government School of Design. It includes plates of stained-glass styles, Norman to Elizabethan, and a tribute to HAY, who was a friend. His *Tradesman's Book of Ornamental Designs* (Edinburgh, 1847; forty plates) seems to have been produced in collaboration with Samuel Leith. It presents designs in the NATURALISTIC, GOTHIC, GROTESQUE and ROCOCO styles, and even an AURICULAR firescreen. The prefatory *Essay on Ornamental Art* suggested a link between Elizabethan and American art. Ballantine also published songs and verses and a life of the painter David Roberts.

Ballin, Claude I (1615–78) Born in Paris, the son of a goldsmith, Ballin was patronized by Richelieu in 1634 and later became principal goldsmith to Louis XIV, for whom he executed numerous works including silver tables and gueridons as well as table plate. Ballin often carried out designs by LE BRUN. He himself designed thirteen celebrated bronze VASES for the gardens at Versailles, engraved by Jean LE PAUTRE in 1673. In 1676 he was appointed master of the Paris Mint. Most of Ballin's works were melted down in 1689 to 1690 to pay for Louis XIV's wars. He was succeeded by his nephew Claude II Ballin (1661–1754), who executed the celebrated monstrance designed by De COTTE for Notre Dame in 1708.

Banderoles, Master of the The Master of the Banderoles was an engraver active from about 1450 to 1475, probably in the North Netherlands between Zwolle and Bocholt. His title, coined in 1834, is misleading; banderoles, or ribbons for inscription and ornament, were by no means exclusive to his works. The Master engraved a surviving total of some 100 prints, almost all derived from the Master of the PLAYING CARDS, E. S. and others. A suit of playing cards with cups probably copy an Italian original, while an alphabet formed of figures uses a woodcut prototype of 1464. Two panels of GOTHIC foliage with wildmen, copied from the Master of the Nuremberg Passion, were used on a carved box of about 1470, now in Vienna.

Bang, Hieronymus Born in Osnabrück in 1553, Bang settled in Nuremberg in 1587, becoming a master goldsmith there in 1588 and a citizen in 1589. He died between 1629 and 1633. Bang published some fifty plates of accomplished stretched GROTESQUE ornament, several on a black ground for enamelling. He also engraved a suite of the twelve months after SIBMACHER (1596).

Bang, Theodor Bang became a master goldsmith in Nuremberg in 1609. He was probably a relation of Hieronymus BANG. He published some forty plates of ornament, including a suite of friezes combining stretched STRAPWORK and scrolled floral decoration with parrots, cranes, peacocks, eagles and other birds. This suite is dated 1617.

Barbet, Jean Born in 1591 of a Norman family, Barbet was in Rouen in 1616. He moved thence to Paris, where in 1633 he worked as an architect for Cardinal de Richelieu, the dedicatee of his *Livre d'Architecture d'Autels et de Cheminées* (Paris, 1632, second edition, 1641; twenty plates engraved by Abraham Bosse). The first plate depicts the altarpiece of the chapel of the Hôtel des Ardelliers. It and the following altars and chimneypieces are in an elaborate late MANNERIST style, with complex broken pediments, cartouches, sculptural figures and allegorical paintings; one chimneypiece bears the royal arms. Inigo JONES was among those influenced by Barbet's chimneypieces, which were copied at Skokloster in Sweden and in part reprinted in Robert Pricke's *The Architects Store-house* (London, 1674). In 1642 Barbet was appointed Architecte du Roi in Touraine. He was dead before 1654.

Barcelona, Foment de les Arts Decoratives This association for the encouragement of the decorative arts published an annual (1919–25), and a journal, *Arts i Bells Oficis* (1927–30), both in Catalan. They are well-illustrated records of 1920s design in Catalonia.

Barley, William In 1596 Barley, an important early publisher of music, published *A booke of curious and strange inventions, called the first part of needleworkes*, one of the earliest English pattern-books in this field. It was a straight copy of Giovanni Battista CIOTTI's *Prima parte de' fiore* (Venice, 1591).

Baroque The term 'baroque' is derived from an Italian word meaning a tortuous device in logic and/or from a Portuguese and Spanish word meaning a misshapen pearl. Baroque was used by the NEOCLASSICAL architect and critic Francesco Milizia (1725–98) to condemn certain aspects of 17th-century architecture, especially the architecture of Francesco Borromini (1599–1667). From about 1855 onwards baroque has become the accepted neutral term to describe both 17th-century art in general and, more specifically, the style of art, architecture and design which developed in early 17th-century Rome, to a large extent as the language of a revived and newly militant Catholic church, and spread thence all over Europe. The CARRACCI family of painters from Bologna, who rejected the elongated and contorted forms of MANNERISM and returned to the grander and simpler style of RAPHAEL and, as they saw it, of classical antiquity, were the pioneers of baroque and its greatest early protagonists were RUBENS and BERNINI. Baroque retained the familiar RENAISSANCE repertoire of motifs, but, unlike mannerism, favoured the grand scale, theatrical naturalism and palatial display. Scrolls, ACANTHUS, masks and putti were ubiquitous, and bold and ostentatious craftsmanship tended to replace the miniaturist perfectionism of mannerism. Great impresarios of design such as Bernini and LE BRUN orchestrated a host of lesser designers and craftsmen, encouraging a unity of the arts which is a baroque hallmark. The AURICULAR style had mannerist roots but its palpitating transmogrification of natural forms was baroque, as was the floral style of ornament exemplified by Paul Androuet DuCERCEAU, and the acanthus style of INDAU and others. In about 1700, however, there were the first signs of a reaction to the grand gestures and massive architectural statements of baroque. In France a lighter and more delicate version of GROTESQUE began to evolve. Combined with increasing asymmetry and an insubstantial framework of scrolls, this was to lead to the ROCOCO style. None the less the baroque style continued to be dominant in Italy, Spain and many of the outlying parts of Europe up to about 1750. When, by another reaction, the heavier forms of neo-classicism replaced the rococo style, it was to baroque that many designers turned back for inspiration.

Barozzi, Serafino Lodovico An ornament and architecture painter in Bologna, Barozzi studied under his elder brother, Giuseppe Gioachino Barozzi, and accompanied him to Russia in about 1762. Barozzi executed ornamental painting in St Petersburg, in the Chinese palace at Oranienbaum and elsewhere. In 1770 he returned to Bologna and was active as a fresco painter. Barozzi belonged to the last generation of painters to work in the virtuoso PERSPECTIVE technique known as quadratura. He also contributed designs for NEO-CLASSICAL VASES to PANFILI's *Frammenti di Ornati* (1783). Barozzi died in Bologna in 1810.

Barraband, Jacques Born in Aubusson in about 1767, a member of a family of tapestry makers, Barraband worked as a flower painter at the Sèvres porcelain factory, and also as a designer at the Gobelins tapestry factory. From 1798 to 1806 he showed porcelain paintings at the Paris Salon, winning a gold medal in 1804. He also did book illustrations. Barraband worked under PERCIER, and in 1807 was appointed professor of floral design at the newly founded Lyon École des Beaux-Arts. He died in 1809.

Barre, Pierre de la Barre, a Parisian goldsmith, designed *Livre de Toutes sortes de feuilles Servant a l'orphevrerie* (six plates), probably in about 1640. It contains very large jewelled sprays in the COSSE-DE-POIS manner, with landscapes below. Barre's designs tend to the eccentric, one, for instance, being formed as a tree.

Basile, Ernesto (1857–1932) Born in Palermo, the son of a distinguished architect, Basile studied under his father and from 1877 was an assistant professor of architecture in Palermo. From 1880 to 1890 he taught architecture in Rome. He was successful in several national competitions and designed many buildings in Rome and Sicily, including those for the Palermo Exhibition (1891–92). Around 1900 Basile designed furniture in an elegant linear ART NOUVEAU style with carved foliate ornament for the Palermo furniture factory owned by the business tycoon Vittorio Golia Ducrot. Basile's furniture was praised at the TURIN 1902 EXHIBITION, at the Venice 1903 Biennale, and in the 'STUDIO' (1904), where he was called the centre and leader of the art movement in Sicily.

Basoli, Antonio (1774–1843) Born at Castel Guelfo, Bologna, son of a decorative painter, Basoli was trained as a painter at the Accademia Clementina in Bologna, where he became friendly with PALAGI. Basoli taught ornament at Bologna from 1803 and also travelled widely in Italy as a decorative painter. Some of his works are recorded in *Compartimenti di camere* (1827). Basoli lost an eye in 1837 and in the following year published *Vari ornamenti*, which includes furniture and other designs in the NEO-CLASSICAL style executed in various Bolognese palazzi. Basoli occasionally worked in a thin GOTHIC Revival style. He also published *Guernizioni dlversi di maniera antica* (1814) and *Alfabeto pittorico* (1839), the latter a bizarre series of architectural fantasies in the form of letters.

Batley, Henry W. A pupil of TALBERT, Batley designed furniture for Collinson & Lock, including an elaborate drawing-room illustrated in 'DECORATION' (1884), for Shoolbred & Co., notably their interiors for Doultons' terracotta house at the PARIS 1878 EXHIBITION, and a cabinet for Henry Ogden & Son of Manchester. He also designed wallpapers for Jeffrey & Co., and textiles. Batley's *Series of Studies for Domestic Furniture, Decoration &c.* (1883; ten plates) contains richly textured etchings begun as early as 1872; the earliest is for a dining-room with Egyptian details, but most are in a dense version of Talbert's style with the addition of Japanese details influenced by GODWIN and JECKYLL. In his preface Batley states: 'The Gothic revival some years back, although sound and good in its way, was soon found to be too heavy and severe for domestic use . . . We have naturally dropped into a more comfortable, easy, a more wooden and less stony style . . .' Batley described himself as 'Architect and etcher' and showed his etchings at the Royal Academy from 1873 to 1893, at Berlin in 1891, and at Munich in 1893. In 1908 Batley was the founder of the Guild of Decorators Syndicate Ltd, together with W. G. Paulson Townsend, Alfred Martin, Henry Poole and others.

Battini, Benedetto Battini, a Florentine painter, designed a suite of cartouches (1553; twenty-eight plates), published by Hieronymus Cock in Antwerp. Vigorous and early examples of STRAPWORK GROTESQUES, they enclose moral sentiments in Latin.

Baudin, Eugène Benoît (1843–1917) Born in Lyon, Baudin studied at the École des Beaux-Arts; REIGNIER was among his teachers. In 1865 he left to work in the textile design studio of Marc Bruyas (1821–96). In 1868 he went into business as a textile designer with his friend Mesonniat; they later designed and manufactured wallpapers. After the business had failed Baudin joined the firm of Bresson & Agnès and established himself as the foremost Lyon textile designer of his day.

Baudouin, Christopher Baudouin, a Huguenot refugee, was a celebrated silk designer in Spitalfields from at least 1709, when he was described as 'a patron drawer', to 1726, the latest date on his surviving designs. He was already in London in 1685.

Bauduin de Bailleul In 1448 Bauduin, who worked in Arras, was recorded as bringing cartoons of a tapestry of the Golden Fleece to the Duke of Burgundy in Bruges. His reputation as a tapestry designer lasted into the 16th century.

Bauhaus In 1919, under the direction of Walter GROPIUS, the two art schools in Weimar, the Grossherzogliche Sächsische Kunstgewerbeschule and the Grossherzogliche Sächsische Hochschule für Bildende Kunst, were merged under the new title of Staatliches Bauhaus Weimar. Its first manifesto, with a woodcut cover by Lyonel Feininger (1871–1956), proclaimed in somewhat mystical language the unity of the arts within building and the duty of artists to be craftsmen. The first teachers were Feininger, Johannes ITTEN and Gerhard Marcks. Later arrivals included Adolf Meyer (1881–1929) in 1919, Georg Muche in 1920, Paul Klee (1879–1940) in 1921, Wassily Kandinsky (1866–1944) in 1922 and MOHOLY-NAGY in 1923. The main elements of the Bauhaus curriculum were the six-month preliminary course (*Vorlehre*) under Itten, an exploration of form and materials, followed by simultaneous education in a craft (*Werklehre*) under a craftsman, and in formal problems (*Formlehre*) under an artist; the third stage was the study of architecture and building (*Bau*). In 1921 several disaffected teachers whom Gropius had inherited withdrew in protest against his innovatory and doctrinaire policies. However, Gropius demonstrated that the Bauhaus approach was the logical extension of ideas expressed by the DEUTSCHE WERKBUND, and by Bruno PAUL and Richard RIEMERSCHMID. Indeed at the beginning the Bauhaus, whose teachers were called Masters, owed much to the example of the medieval guild. Itten, artistic and mystical, acted as a focus for internal opposition to Gropius's more pragmatic and technological approach. Theo van Doesburg was in Weimar in 1922 and attracted support among Bauhaus students for the ideas propagated in 'DE STIJL'. In 1923 a Bauhaus exhibition held in Weimar, at the same time as a meeting of the Deutsche Werkbund, demonstrated the achievement of the fledgling institution. It included a model house, Am Horn, furnished by the Bauhaus workshops. These had proved an educational success but made no profits; Bauhaus publications also lost money and had to be sold off below cost when the Bauhaus moved to Dessau. This move followed the dissolution of the Weimar Bauhaus on 31 March 1925 in response to political and economic pressures. Dessau was suggested as a new location by the art-historian Ludwig Grote and the advent of the Bauhaus was welcomed by the liberal Mayor of Dessau, Fritz Hesse. At first the Bauhaus shared premises with the Dessau School of Arts & Crafts, but in 1926 it was granted an official identity as an Institute of Design. At Dessau Moholy-Nagy taught in the metal workshop, Muche textiles, BAYER typography and advertising, BREUER furniture and ALBERS the preliminary course. In 1927 Hannes Meyer (1889–1954) came in as head of the new department of architecture. Meyer harboured strongly collectivist views which were in direct opposition to Moholy-Nagy's concern with form. By the time of his arrival the Bauhaus had developed its own style, displayed in the STUTTGART 1927 EXHIBITION. A journal, *Bauhaus* (1926–31), and a series of Bauhaus

books propagated Bauhaus ideas. The latter included Walter Gropius's *Internationale Architektur* (1925) and *Neue Arbeiten der Bauhauswerkstätten* (1925), both designed by Moholy-Nagy, and Moholy-Nagy's own *Von Material zu Architektur* (1929). In 1928 Gropius, together with Breuer, Moholy-Nagy and Bayer, resigned and Meyer, whose socialist zeal and condemnation of formalism had driven the Bauhaus towards a divisively collectivist policy, was appointed director. He held the post until 1930. Under Meyer, Bauhaus products enjoyed some success and Bauhaus wallpapers and cheap furniture were developed. However, continuous reorganization led to discontent and in 1930 Mayor Hesse appointed MIES VAN DER ROHE director. Mies restored order but in 1932, after a period of harassment by the National Socialist local government, he was obliged to move the Bauhaus to Berlin, where from 1932 it survived in an abandoned telephone factory. The building was seized in April 1933 and in July the faculty decided to dissolve the Bauhaus. In 1937 Moholy-Nagy founded the New Bauhaus in Chicago and in 1938 an exhibition at the NEW YORK MUSEUM OF MODERN ART surveyed the work of the Bauhaus from 1919 to 1928. Such events and institutions and the writings of such scholars as Sigfried Giedion (1888–1968) and Sir Nikolaus PEVSNER established the reputation of the Bauhaus as the MODERN academy *par excellence*. The ULM HOCHSCHULE FÜR GESTALTUNG, founded in 1950 and opened in 1955, is the most celebrated German epigone of the Bauhaus. Works by Bauhaus designers such as BRANDT, WAGENFELD, Breuer and Mies van der Rohe are firmly established as 'Modern CLASSICS', and it is generally recognized that Modern industrial design takes much of its doctrinal basis from the Bauhaus. This posthumous reputation has tended to obscure the true character of the Bauhaus in its heyday, faddish, volatile, experimental and fissile.

Bauhütte, Die (1877–94) Published in Stuttgart and edited by the architect Professor H. Herdtle of the Museum for Art and Industry in Vienna, this magazine comprised a collection of 1,000 plates of historic architecture and design, including ornament, ironwork and furniture.

Baukunst und Werkform (1948–62) This straightforward German post-war architecture and design magazine was founded by Alfons Leitl.

Baumann, David Baumann published *Ein neues Buch von Allerhand Gold-Arbeit auff unterschiedliche Art und Manier . . .* (1695; seventeen plates), accomplished jewellery designs in the style of F. J. MORISSON, including also a sword-hilt. Baumann died before 1703.

Baumgartner, Johann Jakob Baumgartner was active in Augsburg as an engraver and publisher of ornament. His *Gantz Neu Inventiertes Laub und Bandwerck* (Augsburg, 1727; three parts on eighteen plates) comprises handles for knives and spoons, decoration for coffee and chocolate cups and other utensils in a BERAINESQUE strapwork GROTESQUE style full of CHINOISERIES and putti. Other suites of designs by Baumgartner depict snuff-boxes, swordhilts, borders and cartouches in the same style, sometimes interspersed with insects.

Baumgartner, Johann Wolfgang (1712–61) Born at Kufstein in the Tyrol, Baumgartner was taught to paint by Johann Georg BERGMÜLLER, director of the Augsburg Academy from 1730. Baumgartner was one of the first wave

of German ROCOCO ornamentists in the 1740s and designed a large number of suites of ornaments published in Augsburg by HERTEL and ENGELBRECHT. Some display pure and powerful rococo ornaments, others contain figures, which symbolize such themes as the continents, the elements and the arts, in rococo frameworks.

Baur, Johann Baur designed some fifteen suites of cartouches, shellwork, swords, goldsmiths' work and altars, published in Augsburg, mainly by Martin ENGELBRECHT. They are in the ROCOCO style and probably date from around 1740. A suite of VASES (four plates) uses unusually graceless shell forms twisting harshly in every direction.

Bawden, Edward Born in Essex in 1903, the son of an ironmonger, Bawden studied at the Cambridge School of Art from 1919 and then from 1922 to 1925 at the Design School of the Royal College of Art, where he was taught by Paul NASH and became friendly with Eric RAVILIOUS. Bawden was influenced by 'IMPRINT' and the 'FLEURON' and collected posters by KAUFFER. From 1925, when he illustrated *Pottery Making at Poole* for Harold STABLER, Bawden often worked for the Curwen Press, for whom he designed pattern papers and wallpapers around 1930. Bawden also did posters for the London Underground, for Shell, for Westminster Bank and others. He has been a prolific designer of book-jackets, illustrations and ephemera, all in a bold graphic style with much humour. In 1939 Bawden designed linocut wallpapers for Cole & Son, in 1950 a tapestry, Farming, for the Edinburgh Tapestry Co., and in 1955 a metal garden seat.

Bayer, Herbert Born at Haag, near Salzburg, in 1900, the son of a tax collector, Bayer studied arts and crafts in Linz after military service and in 1920 moved to Darmstadt to work in the office of the architect Emanuel Margold. In 1921 Bayer became a student at the BAUHAUS in Weimar under Kandinsky and MOHOLY-NAGY. In 1923 Bayer designed sans-serif banknotes for the State Bank of Thuringia and in 1925 he was put in charge of the typographic workshop at the Bauhaus in Dessau, for which he designed many posters, ephemera and the journal *Bauhaus* (1928). Building on foundations laid by Moholy-Nagy Bayer argued for a single-alphabet, sans-serif style of typography and designed a new typeface, Universal, composed of a small repertoire of curves and lines (conceived 1925, revised 1928). In 1928 Bayer left the Bauhaus and set up a design studio in Berlin, where he was active as commercial artist, display designer and typographer. In 1930 he worked with GROPIUS, Moholy-Nagy and BREUER at the Paris DEUTSCHE WERKBUND exhibition, and in 1931 with the former two on the Berlin building exhibition. In 1938 Bayer left Germany for the United States and was immediately involved in the NEW YORK MUSEUM OF MODERN ART Bauhaus exhibition, designing and selecting displays and editing the catalogue. In 1946 Bayer moved to Aspen, Colorado, where he has been active as a design consultant.

Bayeu, Francesco (1734–95) Born in Saragossa, Bayeu trained as a painter there until 1758, when he won a prize from the Real Academia di San Fernando and moved to Madrid to work under Antonio González Velasquez. Bayeu subsequently became a protégé of the painter Anton Raffael Mengs (1728–79), and worked from 1763 on the royal palaces of Carlos III. He then had a successful official career culminating in his appointment as Director of Painting at the Real Academia in 1788, and Director General shortly before his death. In the 1780s Bayeu designed tapestries for the Royal Manufactory of Santa Barbara, and also arranged for the dismissal of CASTILLO from the manufactory, thereby promoting the interests of his brother Ramon and his brother-in-law, GOYA.

Bazel, Karel Petrus Cornelis de (1869–1923) Born in Den Helder, Bazel was brought up from 1873 in The Hague, where he trained as a carpenter. After evening studies at the Hague Academy from 1882 to 1888, Bazel entered the office of the architect J. J. van Nieukerken in The Hague, and then in 1889 became an assistant to P. J. H. CUYPERS (1827–1921) in Amsterdam. Bazel's earliest projects, of about 1891, are in the GOTHIC style. In 1893 Bazel visited London with his friend J. L. M. Lauweriks (1864–1932) and drew the Egyptian and Assyrian objects in the British Museum. He was at the same time increasingly interested in anarchist and theosophic ideas. From 1894 to 1896 he supplied woodcut illustrations for the theosophical weekly *Licht en Waarheid*. In 1895 Bazel and Lauweriks left the office of the Catholic Cuypers and set up a design studio in Amsterdam for interior decoration, furniture and the graphic arts which lasted until 1900. Lauweriks later taught with BEHRENS at Düsseldorf from 1904 to 1909. From 1898 to 1899 Bazel and Lauweriks were editors of the periodical 'BOUW- EN SIERKUNST'. Bazel's earliest piece of furniture was a chair of 1893 of simple turned elements with an Egyptian-style back strut. Furniture designed by Bazel in 1898 for houses in The Hague and Amsterdam combines plain rectilinear frames with some Assyrian-style carved decoration. From 1899 to 1900 Bazel was president of the Amsterdam architectural group, Architectura et Amicitia. In 1904 he founded a cabinet-making workshop, De Ploeg, in Amsterdam with his brother-in-law C. A. Oosschot as manager. From 1909, when he designed a cradle for Princess Juliana, to 1913 Bazel was founder president of the Bond van Nederlandsche Architecten. In 1916 he was invited to design glass for the Leerdam factory and from 1917 to 1923 he produced a series of simple designs which represented a new approach to glass design.

Beaumont, Adalbert de In 1853 Beaumont published a book which traced the origin of heraldry to Middle Eastern sources; at the end he stressed the implications of his discovery for ornament in general. In 1859 Beaumont collaborated with the potter Eugène-Victor Collinot on *Recueil de dessins pour l'art et l'industrie* (217 plates), with designs and ornament in the Venetian, Islamic, Chinese and Japanese styles. In 1861 he urged the creation of a museum of eastern textiles, the creation of workshops for the production of textile samples, the abandonment of the *trompe-l'œil* style in tapestry, and simple colour harmonies in textiles. In 1862 Collinot founded a pottery in Boulogne-sur-Seine; Beaumont and Léon PARVILLÉ were his designers. Collinot's Persian wares were widely praised and in 1863 Beaumont was awarded a medal by the Union Centrale des Beaux-Arts Appliqués à l'Industrie for the promotion of the French ceramic industry and for publications which furnished industries with models of Persian ornament. Beaumont also designed the early Persian-style wares of Théodore DECK (1823–91). After Beaumont's death in 1869 Collinot was assisted on design by Adrien Dubouché, director of the Museum at Limoges. The *Recueil de dessins* formed the basis of *Ornements de la Perse* (1880; sixty coloured plates), and later volumes (1883) on Japanese, Arab, Turkish, Venetian, Hindu and Russian ornament. The polychrome interiors in the Turkish volume no doubt inspired many gaudy smoking-rooms.

Beaumont, Claudio (1694–1766) Born in Turin, Beaumont travelled in 1716 to Bologna and thence to Rome, where he studied under the painter Francesco Trevisani (1656–1746) until 1719, when he returned to Turin. From 1723 to 1731 he was again in Rome. Back in Turin, Beaumont was appointed court painter to the King of Sardinia. Already in 1734 he was in contact with the weaver Vittorio Demignot, who founded the royal tapestry factory officially recognized in 1736. Beaumont designed tapestries for the Turin factory on the histories of Alexander (seven pieces), Julius Caesar (six pieces), Hannibal and Cyrus. He also designed carpets. Beaumont's tapestries comprise lively historical scenes within rich fictive frames composed of late-BAROQUE scrolls supported and attended by putti.

Beauvais, Jacques Philippe de (1739–81) Born in Paris, the son of an engraver, Beauvais won the Prix de Rome in 1767, and eventually returned from Rome by way of Genoa where, in 1773, he was responsible for the sculptural decoration of the Salon of Palazzo Spinola. He is the probable author of three suites of 'VASES' (1760), of six plates each, in the most advanced and geometrical NEO-CLASSICAL style, complete with heavy swags. The second was dedicated to the architect Laurent Destouches, and the third to the painter Charles-Michel-Ange CHALLE, a leading neo-classical pioneer.

Beckford, William (1760–1844) Born in London, the son of a millionaire Lord Mayor of London, Beckford was taught to draw by Alexander Cozens and to design by CHAMBERS. In 1782 he wrote *Vathek*, a chilling oriental fantasy published in 1786. In 1784 the threat of a scandal arising from his liaison with William Courtenay drove Beckford to travel and seclusion from English society. In Madrid in 1787 he admired silver by Auguste designed by MOITTE, whom Beckford subsequently patronized. He also employed BOILEAU as both painter and designer. From 1796 Beckford began to plan a colossal romantic GOTHIC house, called Fonthill Abbey, near the site of his father's Palladian house, Fonthill Splendens; James WYATT was his architect, and William Hamilton designed stained glass for Fonthill. Beckford filled the Abbey with a prodigious collection of paintings, books and *objets d'art*, and some modern Gothic furniture probably designed by Beckford himself. From about 1815 to 1820 Beckford designed a large group of silver in an advanced RENAISSANCE Revival style, using MORESQUE, STRAPWORK and GROTESQUE ornament; Beckford seems to have dictated the outlines, details were designed by Gregorio FRANCHI (1770–1828), whom Beckford first met in a choral seminary in Lisbon in 1787; Franchi entered Beckford's service in 1788 and became his confidant and factotum. A silver ladle (1812) is derived from an ALDEGREVER print; Beckford also owned ornament by J. A. DU-CERCEAU, DIETTERLIN, VICO, the BEHAMS and others. In 1822 he had to sell Fonthill, whose great tower collapsed in 1825. He retired to Bath and from 1824 to 1827 built Lansdown Tower in a Grecian/Italianate style with a quasi-Romanesque gateway. His architect, H. E. Goodridge, designed synthetic Renaissance Revival furniture for the Tower, some made in 1841. Some was lithographed in 1844 by C. J. RICHARDSON, who illustrated Beckford silver in his *Studies* (1851).

Bedeschini, Francesco Born in Aquila, the son of a painter, Bedeschini was

active there as both painter and architect from the 1640s. He published some sixty plates of cartouches in several suites dated from 1672 to 1688, and variously dedicated to the Bishop of Aquila, to Prince Maffeo Barberini and to the Magistrates of Aquila. Bedeschini's cartouches are vigorous BAROQUE designs, boldly scrolled. A collected edition was published in Rome in 1770.

Beer, Jan de A pupil of Gillis van Everen, Beer became a master painter at Antwerp in 1504. He died there before 1536. Beer was a prominent artist in Antwerp and designed stained glass, often late GOTHIC in sentiment despite the inclusion of RENAISSANCE details.

Begbie, P. Begbie engraved a number of plates in Robert and James ADAM's *The Works in Architecture*, dating from 1776. In 1779, giving his address as Dukes Court, St Martin's Lane, London, Begbie issued three small suites of *Vases after the Manner of the Antique*. He also issued a suite of NEO-CLASSICAL friezes at the same date. His designs, which include a ewer and girandoles, are in an elegant and accomplished Adamesque style.

Beham, Barthel (1502–40) Born in Nuremberg, Barthel Beham was banished thence in 1525 for free-thinking, together with his elder brother, Hans Sebald BEHAM. He then worked as court painter to Duke Wilhelm IV of Bavaria in Munich. He died on a journey to Italy. Beham published some twenty delicate panels of early RENAISSANCE ornament, one dated 1525, including putti, VASES, sea-horses and dolphins and three designs for dagger sheaths. His manner is close to his brother's. VAVASSORE was among the many who borrowed ornament from Barthel Beham.

Beham, Hans Sebald (1500–1550) Born in Nuremberg, Beham was strongly influenced by DÜRER. In 1525 he was banished from the city for free-thinking in politics and religion, together with his young brother, Barthel BEHAM, and the painter Georg PENCZ. After that Beham led an unsettled existence, but contrived to spend much time in Nuremberg and even after a second trial in 1528 for the misuse of Dürer manuscripts returned there in 1529. In 1531 he was in the Frankfurt area where he settled, becoming a citizen of Frankfurt in 1540. Beham designed painted glass panels and book illustrations, including 265 woodcut blocks for Martin Luther's *New Testament* (1526). He also engraved many coats-of-arms and a set of playing-cards with clubs, leaves, roses and pomegranates as suits. From 1524 to 1544 Beham designed about twenty plates of exquisite early RENAISSANCE ornament, with some elements of GOTHIC survival in foliage. A panel of 1542 shows the alphabet on banderoles over which putti are striding, while a woodcut panel of 1548 shows Renaissance ornament in a manner close to FLÖTNER. Beham also engraved two plates in 1530 and 1531 with four designs for silver double cups embellished with Renaissance ornament. Beham exercised a widespread influence on other designers of ornament, including BINCK and ALDEGREVER.

Behrens, Peter (1869–1940) Born in Hamburg, the son of well-to-do parents, Behrens studied painting from 1886 to 1889 at the Karlsruhe School of Art, and then in 1889 in Düsseldorf under Ferdinand Brütt. In 1890 he visited Holland before settling in Munich. He was a member of the Munich Secession and in 1897, after a visit to Italy in 1896, he was one of the founders of the MUNICH VEREINIGTE WERKSTÄTTEN. Behrens formed a close friendship with Otto ECKMANN and designed for 'PAN'. Behrens designed covers for Otto Julius Bierbaum's advanced literary magazine, *Die Insel* (1899), his *Der Bunte Vogel* (1899) and for his *Pan im Busch* (1901). In 1899 he was invited to Darmstadt to join the artists' colony set up by Grand Duke Ernst Ludwig II von Hessen. The Haus Peter Behrens, which he designed for the DARMSTADT 1901 EXHIBITION, was the only building on the Mathildenhöhe not designed by OLBRICH. It received general praise, and was published in 'DEUTSCHE KUNST UND DEKORATION'. Behrens wrote the preface and designed the ornament for the record of the exhibition presented to Grand Duke Ernst Ludwig, *Ein Dokument Deutscher Kunst* (1901). In 1902 Behrens designed the German entrance hall at the TURIN EXHIBITION, with rectilinear furniture covered with leatherwork by Georg Hulbe. In 1904 he designed the decorations for the catalogue of the German section at the ST LOUIS EXHIBITION. From 1903 to 1907 Behrens was director of the Düsseldorf School of Applied Arts. In 1906 he was asked to design publicity material for A.E.G., the great electrical combine in Berlin, which had previously employed Adolf Messel and Otto Eckmann as designers. In 1907 Behrens was appointed architect of the A.E.G. by Emil Rathenau, its Director. He held the position until 1914 and designed not only buildings, such as the great turbine factory of 1908 to 1909, but also products – lamps, electric fans, ovens and kettles, and shop-fronts and advertising. Also in 1907 Behrens, who was closely associated with MUTHESIUS, became a founder member of the DEUTSCHER WERKBUND. In 1908 he designed four typefaces for Klingspor Brothers of Offenbach-am-Main, Behrensschrift, Behrens Antiqua, Behrens Cursiv and Behrens Mediäval. From about 1901 Behrens was a prolific designer of bookbindings, earthenware, glass, cutlery and fabrics; he was also responsible for the ship trademark of the publishers Insel Verlag. In 1910 GROPIUS, MIES VAN DER ROHE and LE CORBUSIER all worked in his office. In 1912 Behrens designed suites of cheap but sturdy furniture for the living-room, bedroom and kitchen of a worker's dwelling, in a style part BIEDERMEIER and part Arts & Crafts. It is in contrast to his earliest furniture, which was curvilinear in a style similar to that of VAN DE VELDE, and even more so to his contemporary furniture for rich patrons, brilliant exercises in a sophisticated NEO-CLASSICAL style influenced by SCHINKEL, for example for the Haus Schröder (1908) and the Haus Wiegand (1911–13). Around the First World War Behrens was a prolific pundit on design, deeply involved in the Deutscher Werkbund. This didactic importance has tended to overshadow his great all-round gifts as a designer, although his industrial work for A.E.G. has received more than its due from historians of the MODERN style and industrial design. From 1922 to 1936 Behrens taught architecture at the Vienna Academy, and in 1936 he conducted architectural masterclasses at the Berlin Academy.

Bélanger, François-Joseph (1744–1818) Born in Paris, Bélanger entered the Académie Royale d'Architecture in 1764 under the protection of the Comte de CAYLUS and studied there under Julien-David Le Roy (1724–1803). In 1766 Bélanger visited England and probably met CHAMBERS. In 1767 he was appointed Dessinateur des Menus Plaisirs, where he assisted Charles-Michel-Ange CHALLE, and in 1777 became Inspecteur des Menus Plaisirs. The actress Sophie Arnould was his mistress and later his friend; he designed a house for her in 1773. In 1777 Bélanger designed the Pavilion de Bagatelle for Charles Phi-

lippe, Comte d'Artois, brother of Louis XVI. Bélanger designed many royal ceremonies, including the funeral of Louis XV in 1774 and Louis XVI's coronation coach in 1775. In 1769 he designed a jewel cabinet made by Maurice-Bernard Évald which was presented by Louis XV to his daughter, the Dauphine Marie-Antoinette, in 1770, and which is the first major monument of the refined late-18th-century NEO-CLASSICAL style in furniture. Its gilt-bronze mounts were by Pierre Gouthière, who worked to Bélanger's designs on other occasions. In 1778 Bélanger designed a scheme for the gallery at Lansdowne House in London. Bélanger also designed silk for Camille Pernon. DUGOURC was his brother-in-law and pupil. Bélanger was a supporter of the revolution but was arrested for six months in 1794. He was active as an architect before and after the restoration of 1814, when he designed the new French official seal and further royal ceremonies.

Bel Geddes, Norman (1893–1958) Born in Adrian, Michigan, Bel Geddes studied briefly at the Art Institute of Chicago but, after meeting the Norwegian painter Hendrik Lund, struck out on his own, working at first as an advertising draughtsman. In 1927 he took up industrial design, and in his *Horizons* (1932), dashingly bound in blue and silver, described his own projects and the rosy future for design with a stress on the purity of grain elevators, power plants and suchlike. Bel Geddes's designs were often streamlined, prototype cars for the Graham Paige Company (from 1928), coaches, locomotives (from 1931) and air liners. He also designed interiors for J. Walter Thompson, the advertising agency (1932), S.G.E. gas stoves, scales for the Toledo Company (1929), Philco radios (1931), and slick abstract window displays for Franklin Simon (1928–30).

Eero SAARINEN was his pupil in the early 1930s. Bel Geddes was closely involved in theatre design, including a Soviet Mass Theatre for the Ukraine (1931), and later published *Magic Motorways* (1940), a paean to the motor car with many illustrations borrowed from General Motors' Futurama exhibit at the New York 1939 World's Fair.

Bell, John (1811–95) Born in Hopton, Suffolk, Bell trained as a sculptor at the Royal Academy Schools from 1829. In 1844 he enjoyed his first great success with 'The Archer'. In 1845 he designed the cast-iron Deerhound hall table for the Coalbrookdale Company. In about 1848 he was involved in Henry COLE's Summerly's Art-Manufactures designing ceramics, including the Sabrina urn and the Sugar Cane treacle pot, glass, and metalwork, including the Flying Fish scissors, and the thimble of Industry. The *Art Union* was 'unable to appreciate' his 1848 matchbox in the form of a crusader's altar-tomb. The 'JOURNAL OF DESIGN' illustrated many of Bell's designs including his cast-iron Cerberus hall-stand by Stuart & Smith (1849), a sideboard by Hollands (1849), and papier-mâché objects by Jennens & Bettridge of Birmingham (1850). The *Journal* stated that his ornamental breadplatter had created 'a trade in that article not only in Sheffield, but all over the country'. His electro-bronze clock case by Elkingtons, The Hours, was shown at the LONDON 1851 EXHIBITION. In 1852 and 1854 Bell published outline drawings as *Rudimentary Art-Instruction for Artizans and Others*. From 1854 he designed terracotta ornaments for Blashfield.

Bell, Robert Anning (1863–1933) Born in Soho in London, Bell started to study architecture but later studied painting at the Royal Academy Schools. His book illustrations of the 1890s, influenced by the 'HYPNEROTOMACHIA POLIFILI', made his reputation; they included *Keats* (1897), *The Tempest* (1901) and *Shelley* (1902). Bell also designed many book-plates at this period. Gesso reliefs by Bell were discussed in the 'STUDIO' (1893), and he later designed reliefs for the Della Robbia pottery. Bell designed mosaics for Townsend's Horniman Museum (1902) and J. F. BENTLEY's Westminster Cathedral, as well as stained glass. Bell was Master of the ART-WORKERS' GUILD in 1921. From 1918 to 1924 he was professor of design at the Royal College of Art in succession to LETHABY. In 1929 he listed conversation with VOYSEY among his recreations.

Bellin, Nicolas Born at Modena in the early 1490s, whence his alternative name, Nicolas de Modena, Bellin was in France by about 1515. He was trained as a plasterer and worked for the French crown from at least 1516 to 1522 and 1532 to 1534, including work on the King's chamber at Fontainebleau, where he was under PRIMATICCIO. By 1537 he was in England on Henry VIII's payroll. He executed chimneypieces at Whitehall Palace in the 'antique' style in 1540, and worked on Nonsuch Palace from 1541 to 1545. Bellin continued in royal employment until his death in 1569. A few drawings for decorations for English palaces have been attributed to him and it is probable that he helped to transmit the style of decoration evolved at Fontainebleau to England.

Bellini, Mario Born in 1935, Bellini was trained as an architect in Milan. He opened an office there in 1962. Bellini's main activity has been as consultant designer to Olivetti, whose electronic typewriter (1978) he designed. Other designs include a folding bed for Oggioni (1966), armchairs for Cassina (1967), stacking plastic table/chairs for C. & B. (1968), and the smart leather-covered Cab chair for Cassina (1977). Bellini has also designed lighting for Flos.

Benson, William Arthur Smith (1854–1924) Born in London, Benson was educated at Winchester and Oxford, where in 1874 he noted with amusement RUSKIN's abortive experiment in road-making at Hinksey. Benson was in the office of the architect Basil Champneys (1842–1935) up to 1880, and shared lodgings with Heywood SUMNER. In 1886 he was represented as Nicolo Pisano in Walter CRANE's watercolour, The Arts of Italy. Through his friendship with BURNE-JONES he met William MORRIS, whom he had long admired, and was inspired to set up a workshop for the manufacture of metalwork in 1880. He later opened a well-equipped factory in Hammersmith and in about 1887 a shop in Bond Street; the firm survived until his retirement in 1920. Benson was an active member of the ART-WORKERS' GUILD from 1884, a leader in the formation of the ARTS & CRAFTS EXHIBITION SOCIETY from 1886, and wrote an essay on metalwork in the catalogue of the first exhibition in 1888. On Morris's death in 1896 Benson became chairman of Morris & Co., for whom he designed furniture and wall-papers. He also designed furniture for J. S. Henry, and grates and fireplaces for the Coalbrookdale and Falkirk Iron Companies. In 1914 he was a founder of the DESIGN AND INDUSTRIES ASSOCIATION. Benson's firm produced some simple furniture, but his great output consisted in well-designed utilitarian metalwork, usually in copper and brass, including lamps, teapots, food-warmers etc. Benson metalwork was sold by BING and praised by 'DEKORATIVE KUNST' and MU-THESIUS, who liked Benson's electrical fittings. Their distinction derived from Benson's intimate knowledge of the mechanical processes involved. He had always been interested in engineering and, unlike so many of his Arts & Crafts contemporaries, had little squeamishness about the use of the machine. His *Elements of Handicraft & Design* (1893) deals with simple design in a commonsensical way. The posthumous *Drawing* (1925) is a short general treatise.

Bentley, John Francis (1839–1902) Born in Doncaster, Bentley was placed by his father with a firm of mechanical engineers in Manchester. In 1855 he moved to a firm of London builders and in 1857 entered the office of Henry Clutton (1819–93), who had broken with BURGES in 1856 and who became a Roman Catholic in 1857. In 1862 Bentley set up his own practice and himself became a Roman Catholic. At the LONDON 1862 EXHIBITION Hart & Son showed a great brass eagle lectern designed by Bentley. He continued to design ecclesiastical metalwork to the end of his career. Bentley also designed stained glass in the 1860s, and from 1863 to 1883 in collaboration with WEST-LAKE. At Carlton Towers (1875–7) Bentley designed inventive secular furniture, some in brass, using a refined but luxurious combination of late-GOTHIC and 17th-century forms, and also curtains and wallpaper. His greatest architectural work was Westminster Cathedral (1894–1903), which includes electric-light pendants executed after his death, probably to his design.

Bentley, Richard (1708–82) The son of the great classical scholar Dr Richard Bentley (1662–1742), Bentley studied at Trinity College, Cambridge, where his father was master. In 1751, with John Chute, he became a member of the 'Committee on Taste' which presided over Horace WALPOLE's transformation of his 'little plaything house' at Twickenham into Strawberry Hill, the most celebrated early GOTHIC Revival villa. Bentley designed brilliant *vignettes* and illustrations for poems by Thomas Gray published in 1753 under Walpole's auspices. Bentley's designs for Strawberry Hill itself included Gothic chairs (1754) made by William Hallett (1707–81) in 1755, the heraldic ceiling in the library painted by Andien de CLERMONT in 1754, and the screen and chimneypiece of the HOLBEIN chamber (1758), derived respectively from the choir-screen at Rouen and the tomb of Archbishop Warham at Canterbury. Walpole wrote that Bentley alone could 'unite the grace of Grecian architecture and the irregular lightness and solemnity of Gothic'. Bentley and Walpole quarrelled finally in 1761, and Bentley's later career, dogged by money troubles, was as an unsuccessful dramatist.

Berain, Claude A younger brother of Jean I BERAIN, Claude was active as an engraver. He published seventy-six plates of designs for book-plates, boxes and monograms, including a suite of *Diverses Inventions*, published by N. Langlois in the late 1660s, on which his brother collaborated. He died in 1729.

Berain, Jean I (1640–1711) Born at Saint-Mihil, Lorraine, the son of a gunsmith, Jean I Berain was brought up in Paris, where his family moved in about 1645. In 1659 he published a suite of designs for the decoration of guns, *Diverses Pièces très utiles pour les Arquebuzières* (second edition 1667) and in 1663 a suite of ironwork designed by a master smith, BRISVILLE, *Diverses pièces de serruriers*. In 1670 Berain was employed by Charles Perrault to engrave plates depicting the decorations of the Galerie d'Apollon at the Louvre, a task he completed in 1678 (reprinted 1710). These engravings were conscious

propaganda, intended to spread abroad the fame of Louis XIV's achievements and of the art they had inspired. Berain's appointment as engraver must have been approved by LE BRUN, who was godfather to Berain's daughter Catherine in 1675. But more direct influences were Jean Lemoyne, who had painted some of the Galerie d'Apollon decorations and who designed and engraved a book of ornaments published by Berain in 1676, and Henry de Gissey (1621–73), Louis XIV's official designer, Dessinateur de la Chambre et du Cabinet du Roi, from 1660, whom Berain succeeded in 1674. Further official success was marked by Berain's appointment as royal garden designer in 1677 and the grant to him of a lodging in the Louvre in 1679. The main task of the royal designer was to devise the decorations and costumes for all the royal ceremonies and entertainments, including ballet and opera; Berain seems to have been fond of music, working with the composer Lulli (1632–87) as designer to the Royal Academy of Music. But designs for decorations and furnishings for the royal palaces were also a major part of his work. Documentation is scarce, so it is difficult to establish the scale of Berain's decorative design work and the extent to which he delegated details to his team, following the pattern established by Le Brun. Certainly for tapestries he used Louis-Gui Vernansal the Elder (1648–1728), and Jean-Baptiste MONNOYER (1636–99), who painted the cartoons for Berain's highly successful set of GROTESQUES on a yellow ground, designed before 1689 and still in production at Beauvais in 1725. Berain's designs for textiles also included embroideries for the Dauphine (1680), chair covers for his wife (1695), the lining for a coach (1696), silks made at Lyon for Nicodemus TESSIN the Younger (1695) and even richer silks woven by Marcelin Charlier at Saint-

Maur to serve as portières at Versailles (1701). He is also known to have designed a clock for the Petite Galerie, as well as its floor (1685), a desk for the Cabinet de Médailles (1684), executed by Jean Oppenord, and a throne for the Salle d'Audience (1687) at Versailles, and an organ-case for the church of Saint-Quentin (1698). Some of his furniture designs were executed by André Charles BOULLE, notably the Dauphin's desk at Meudon (about 1699) and in 1701 Daniel Cronström dispatched three designs for tables by Berain to Sweden. His carriage designs included one for the King of Sweden (1696) and he also designed a sedan chair for the Princesse de Conti, which was painted by Jean Lemoyne (about 1692). From 1687 he designed the decoration of ships. His metalwork included a toilet service for the Dauphine (1680), pistols for the King of Sweden (1697) and silver girandoles for Versailles (1700). His decorative paintings for the Hôtel de Mailly-Nesles (1687) introduced a taste for wall and ceiling schemes completely composed of grotesque ornament. By 1689 Berain was rich enough to buy a country house at Bièvres, where he retired to work when under pressure. He also built up a large collection of paintings, prints and books. Evidence of entrepreneurial activity is the grant of an exclusive right to exploit an imitation rock-crystal he claimed to have invented (1699). Also in 1699 the Ambassador of Morocco visited Berain's lodging at the Louvre and saw designs for tapestries, mirrors and fabrics. These may have been drawings for specific jobs, but the main means by which Berain promulgated his style was through prints. He engraved only forty-seven prints himself, but about 300 were engraved after his designs, his engravers including Jean and Pierre LE PAUTRE and Daniel MAROT. Many prints were in commemoration of ceremonial events but the decorative designs included

chandeliers, VASES, furniture, ironwork, capitals, ceilings and, predominantly, panels of ornament. Four suites of designs for chimneypieces, dedicated to Jules Hardouin-Mansart, were issued from 1700 to 1711 but the dates of Berain's designs are otherwise difficult to establish. Copies were published by the Augsburg publisher Jeremias Wolff from as early as 1703, and after Berain's death further impressions were issued by his son-in-law, Jacques Thuret, clock-maker to Louis XIV. In 1849 another wave of reprints began. Berain's style in his early designs for gunsmiths is much the same as that of similar works by François MARCOU (1657) and by THURAINE and Le Hollandois (1660). However, by the late 1670s he had evolved a new manner of grotesque ornament which, although derived from the immediate example of Le Brun and Jean Le Pautre, introduced a new element of lightness and fantasy, a plethora of varied motifs – animals, trophies, terms, swags, scrolls, ACANTHUS, gods and so on – being symmetrically arranged in a thin geometrical structure of STRAPWORK. Although some of his prints had a specific functional destination, the majority were intended for general use. In the 1690s Berain became resentfully aware that his reputation as a designer was being overtaken by Claude III AUDRAN and others, and by his death he was looked upon as old-fashioned. None the less Berain had played a crucial role in the evolution from BAROQUE to ROCOCO and his designs had entered the international repertoire of ornament, applied to tapestries in Berlin, Erlangen and Schwabach, and to chintzes on the coast of Coromandel.

Berain, Jean II (1674–1726) Having worked with his father, Jean I BERAIN, Jean II was in 1704 guaranteed the succession as Dessinateur de la

Chambre et du Cabinet du Roi to Louis XIV, and duly succeeded on his father's death in 1711, when he took over his lodging in the Louvre. In 1695 he designed tapestry borders to be sent to Sweden by Daniel Cronström, and at the same period he copied his father's designs for Cronström. In 1718 he designed embroidery for the Duchesse de Lorraine. However, Jean II Berain lacked his father's genius, and seems to have relied heavily on Claude GILLOT as an assistant. On his death Berain was succeeded by MEISSONIER.

Béraud, Michel (1810–82) Béraud studied at the Lyon École des Beaux-Arts, where he was taught by THIERRIAT from 1827 to 1829. He then worked as a textile designer for the Schulz manufactory to 1875. He won many awards at exhibitions; Empress Eugénie's coronation cloak was his most celebrated design.

Berckhusen, Hieronymus Berckhusen, presumably a German goldsmith, published two suites of small black stretched GROTESQUE ornaments for enamelling on jewels, dated 1592 and 1597; the former includes an alphabet and rings.

Bergmüller, Johann Andreas Bergmüller, active as a sculptor and designer in Augsburg in about 1730, published five suites of designs for doors, columns, altars, and organ-cases (six plates each). His early altar designs are late BAROQUE in style and a little crude, but a later suite, *Unterschiedliche neue Altär*, is more ambitious and sophisticated, with some early ROCOCO elements.

Bergmüller, Johann Georg (1688–1762) Born at Türkheim in Bavaria, Bergmüller studied painting in Munich. In 1713 he became a master in Augsburg, where he was active as a fresco painter. Bergmüller was also a theorist, publish-

ing *Anthropometria* (1723) and a book on the ORDERS (1752). From at least 1728 to 1730 he published some six suites of ornament (four plates each) on allegorical themes in the light early ROCOCO manner influenced by GILLOT. In 1730 Bergmüller was appointed Director of the Academy in Augsburg. His pupils included J. W. BAUMGARTNER, WACHSMUTH and GÖZ, among the first Augsburg generation of full-blooded rococo designers.

Berjon, Antoine (1754–1843) Born in Lyon, the son of a baker, Berjon studied drawing under the sculptor Antoine Michel Perrache (1726–79). He then worked as a silk designer and painter. He was ruined by the Siege of Lyon in 1793, and then lived in poverty in Paris. After returning to Lyon, Berjon designed for an embroidery workshop and from 1810 to 1823 taught flower painting at the Lyon École des Beaux-Arts.

Berlage, Hendrik Petrus (1856–1934) Born in Amsterdam, Berlage studied from 1875 to 1878 at the Zürich Polytechnic, where he came under the influence of Gottfried SEMPER, who had taught there from 1855 to 1871. From 1880 to 1881 Berlage travelled in Italy, Austria and Germany. Back in Amsterdam, Berlage entered into an architectural partnership with the engineer Thomas Sanders, which lasted until 1889. Berlage's early works were in the RENAISSANCE Revival style, but in 1893 to 1894 he contributed ART NOUVEAU decorations to an elaborate edition of Joost van den Vondel's *Gysbreght van Aemstel*. Also in 1894 Berlage was commissioned by Carel Henny, director of the De Nederlanden van 1845 insurance company, to design new office buildings; in the event Berlage even designed the firm's office stationery. Berlage's Villa Henny of 1898 was his first major Art Nouveau work, with bare brick walls inside, and spare and angular ironwork, chairs and furniture of explicit honesty of purpose and construction. Berlage's furniture style, comparable to A. W. N. PUGIN's simple furniture, was already fully formed in his 1895 designs for the De Nederlanden company, and in his own drawings cabinet of the same year. From 1898 to 1903 Berlage's masterpiece, the Amsterdam Stock Exchange, was under construction; Berlage designed its furniture, ironwork and electric lighting. The publication of Haeckel's *Kunstformen der Natur* (1899) presented Berlage with a rich source for the geometrical adaptation of natural forms which he favoured in ornament. In 1900 Henny financed 't Binnenhuis, a combined workshop and saleroom run by Berlage, Jacob van den Bosch (1868–1948) and W. Hoeker; 't Binnenhuis sold furniture designed by K. van Leeuwen (1867–1935) and batiks by Chris Lebeau (1878–1945), and in 1904 showed furniture and glass designed by Berlage in Copenhagen. In 1904 Berlage published *Over stijl in bouw- in meubelkunst* (later editions 1908, 1917 and 1921), a simple history of furniture design with illustrations by Berlage, some adapted from Semper. In 1906 to 1907 Berlage gave a course on interior design at the Zürich Polytechnic. In 1909 his work was shown there at the Kunstgewerbemuseum alongside designs by RIEMERSCHMID. Berlage designed the bindings, end-papers, title-pages and ornament for his own books, including *Studies* (1910), essays on design illustrated by designs for a table, clock, chairs, a light and a stove. In about 1910 Berlage visited America; his *Amerikaansche reisherinneringen* (1913) recorded his enthusiastic reaction to H. H. RICHARDSON, SULLIVAN and WRIGHT. In an introduction to the development of the applied arts, published in 1923, adapted from lectures given in Rotterdam, Berlage illustrated silver designed by Lauweriks, carpets by Gidding, COLENBRANDER and LION CACHET, glass and furniture by BAZEL, and a poster by Toorop. In the 1920s Berlage himself designed glass for the Leerdam factory. In 1928 he was a delegate to the first CONGRÈS INTERNATIONAUX D'ARCHITECTURE MODERNE conference. Berlage's last major building was the Gemeentemuseum in Rotterdam, first designed in 1919, redesigned in 1927 to 1929 and built from 1931 to 1935.

Berlin Kunstgewerbemuseum The decorative arts and design museum of Berlin started in 1867 as a private foundation, the Deutsches Gewerbemuseum. In 1879 it became the Königliches Kunstgewerbemuseum and helped new museums of design and design schools all over newly united Germany by donations of objects from its collection. The museum devoted its own limited funds to the purchase of historic examples, but already in 1867 acted as a repository for 900 specimens purchased by the Prussian government at the PARIS EXHIBITION, including 404 examples of glass and mosaic by Salviati, enamels by Barbedienne and Christophle, and textiles from Vienna. These were at first loans, but were acquired by the museum in 1874. Other official purchases of contemporary art-manufactures to enter the museum included pottery by Doulton from the LONDON 1871 EXHIBITION, ceramics by Collinot and M. L. E. SOLON, and also Islamic and oriental specimens, from the VIENNA 1873 EXHIBITION, and TIFFANY glass from the PARIS 1878 EXHIBITION. Julius Lessing, Director from 1889, reacted against these large-scale intakes of contemporary specimens, and bought modern objects sparingly, with a stress on advanced designers and craftsmen such as GALLÉ and Delaherche. Lessing purchased from the CHICAGO 1893 WORLD COLUMBIAN EXPOSITION and the PARIS 1900 EXHIBITION, but when he was succeeded in 1908 by Otto von Falke contemporary acquisitions virtually ceased. After losses in the Second World War, when the furniture and textiles were entirely destroyed, the museum has made major efforts to rebuild its collections, including many 19th- and 20th-century purchases.

Berlin Passion, Master of the Although the Master of the Berlin Passion has retained the name coined for him in 1889, he has since 1907 been convincingly identified with Israhel van Meckenem, father of the goldsmith and engraver of the same name. In 1457 he was in Bocholt, and he was paid as municipal goldsmith there in 1458 to 1459. In 1464 he sold some property in Bonn, but in 1465 and 1470 he is again recorded as a goldsmith in Bocholt. The Master of the Berlin Passion's surviving *œuvre* comprises 117 engravings, mainly religious subjects, animals and birds. A suite of twelve panels of GOTHIC foliage with wrestlers, riders, hunters, etc., were probably intended for the use of goldsmiths and other craftsmen; their use is recorded on stoves and panelling. The Master also designed four panels of Gothic foliate ornament with the Madonna, a pair of chess players, a pelican and flowers.

Berliner Möbel-Journal (1860–61) This part-publication, issued in Berlin by Alexander Jonas, comprised thirty coloured lithographic designs for upholstery and thirty for cabinet-makers' work. Mainly in the ROCOCO revival style, they provide an excellent illustration of commercial German taste in about 1860. Jonas also issued *Berliner Compositionen*, a series of plates of ornament, and an *Album für Wagenbauer*, with designs for carriages.

Bernard, Oliver P. (1881–1939) Bernard worked as a scenery painter and later as a theatre designer in Manchester, London and Boston. He did decorations for the Wembley 1924 Empire Exhibition and was technical director for the British exhibit at the PARIS 1925 EXHIBITION. From 1929 to 1930 Bernard designed the chrome and glass entrance of the Strand Palace Hotel. He placed two Thonet tubular-steel chairs in the foyer, and as a consequence was in 1931 employed as designer by Practical Equipment Ltd, newly founded to produce tubular-steel furniture as a subsidiary of Accles & Pollock. Bernard designed PEL's London showrooms and, although he ceased to be their designer in 1932, maintained links with the firm through the 1930s. He also designed steel furniture for Cox & Co., interiors of Lyons Corner Houses and snack bars, and interiors for Bakelite Ltd.

Bernini, Gian Lorenzo (1598–1680) Born in Naples, the son of a sculptor who settled in Rome in about 1604, Bernini was himself a child prodigy as a sculptor. One of his earliest works, the St Lawrence of about 1618, rests on a table-like base formed as a burning tree-trunk. In 1621 Bernini was President of the Accademia di San Luca, and in the same year designed a catafalque for Pope Paul V. In 1623 he was appointed by Urban VIII master of the papal foundry. From 1624 to 1633 Bernini worked on the *baldacchino* above the high altar in St Peter's, whose architect he became on the death of Maderno in 1629. In 1631 he designed a frontispiece for Urban VIII's poems. He also designed silver, including a reliquary of Sant'Elena, made by Francesco Spagna as a gift to Queen Henrietta Maria of England (1636), silver torchères (1637), a shell-shaped silver basin (1643) and from 1673 candlesticks and the tabernacle for the Cappella del Sacramento in St Peter's, where from 1657 to 1666 he worked on the Cathedra Petri. In 1655 Bernini designed for Queen Christina of Sweden a coach, a seat for her to use at a banquet given by Pope Alexander VII, and, according to an inscription, a sculptural mirror formed as Time unveiling Truth. In 1644 John Evelyn wrote in his diary that 'Bernini . . . gave a public opera wherein he painted the scenes, cut the statues, invented the engines, composed the music, writ the comedy, and built the theatre'. Such universality involved the talents of many assistants; Bernini's specialist in ornamental works was SCHOR. Many of Bernini's cartouches were published by Francesco Aquila in 1719. Boldness, NATURALISM and the grand scale are the hallmarks of Bernini's works and of the BAROQUE style which he embodied. Bernini was also a fervent Catholic, and à close friend of Giovan Paolo Olivar, the General of the Jesuits, for whose published works he designed frontispieces.

Berthault, Louis Martin (1771–1823) Trained as an architect under PERCIER, Berthault was mainly active as a garden designer. In 1798 he designed a bed for Mme Récamier. He was a protégé of the Empress Joséphine (1763–1814) and redecorated her apartments at Compiègne before her divorce from Napoleon in 1809. In 1812 he designed a Sèvres porcelain service for Joséphine but her death prevented its execution. Berthault continued to work at Compiègne after the restoration.

Berthault, Pierre Gabriel (1737–1832) Born at Saint-Maur (Seine), Berthault travelled to Rome under the protection of Comte Tessé. His main activities were as an engraver, including plates by DELAFOSSE, J.-F. BOUCHER and RANSON, and as a designer of book ornaments, including *vignettes* and *culs-*

de-lampe for Saint-Non's *Voyage de Naples et de Sicile* (1781). He published three suites of such ornaments (eighteen plates in all), mainly floral but with some delicate NEO-CLASSICAL details. *Livre de Differents Trophées Representant L'Amour Des Arts* (four plates) combines doves and the attributes of the arts, a little surrealistically in the case of a female bust. Berthault also published suites of medallions and cartouches.

Berthélemy, Jean Simon (1743–1811) Born in Laon in Picardy, Berthélemy studied painting under Noel HALLÉ. Having won the Prix de Rome in 1767, he stayed in Rome from 1770 to 1774. He was then active in Paris as a decorative painter, and his 1777 painting on the Siege of Calais served as the cartoon for a Gobelins tapestry woven for Louis XVI. From 1791 to 1807 Berthélemy designed costumes for the Paris Opéra.

Berthon, Paul Émile (1872–1909) Born in Villefranche, where he studied as a painter, Berthon came to Paris in 1893 and entered the independent École Normale d'Enseignement du Dessin. There he became a disciple of Eugène GRASSET, the professor of decorative arts. Berthon showed bookbinding and furniture designs at the 1895 Salon, and designed ceramics for Villeroy & Boch in the late 1890s. However, his main output comprised posters and decorative panels, almost invariably depicting alluring ART NOUVEAU girls, some printed under the direction of Jules CHÉRET at the Imprimerie Chaix. He also did a few magazine covers, for example *L'Image* (July 1897) and the 'POSTER' (May 1899).

Bertoia, Harry Born in San Lorenzo in Udine in 1915, Bertoia went to America with his father in 1930. In 1936 he graduated from the Cass Technical High School in Detroit and in 1937 took up a scholarship to the Cranbrook Academy, where he taught metalwork from 1939 to 1943. At Cranbrook, Bertoia met Eliel and Eero SAARINEN, Charles EAMES, and Brigitta, daughter of the art-historian William Valentiner (1880–1958), whom he married in 1943. In that year Bertoia left Cranbrook for California, where he worked with Eames on chair design. Also in 1943 he showed jewellery in New York. In 1952 Bertoia's elegant wire shell chair, of welded steel wire and rod and foam rubber, was produced by Knoll International. It was an immediate success and is still in production. Since the 1950s Bertoia has mainly been active as a sculptor.

Bertolani, Gaetano Born in Mantua in about 1758, Bertolani ran away to Faenza, where he was employed as a specialist painter of ornament in the studio set up in about 1794 by the NEO-CLASSICAL painter Felice GIANI (1758–1823), who had rescued him from poverty and illness. He accompanied Giani to assist on the decorations of Montmorency in France (1812–13) and the Quirinale in Rome (1812). Bertolani was acquainted with Antonio BASOLI, who dedicated a plate in *Raccolta di Prospettive* (Bologna, 1810) to him. In 1819 he married and settled finally in Faenza, where he continued to work in the Giani style. He died in 1856. Bertolani designed furniture, textiles and bronzes, in a heavy neo-classical manner, with a few lighter details which recall late-18th-century models.

Beuth, Peter Christian Wilhelm (1781–1853) Trained as a lawyer, Beuth was an official in the Prussian treasury when in 1819 he was appointed director of the newly founded Königliche Technische Deputation für Gewerbe, a committee of eight, including SCHINKEL, intended to improve design standards in Prussia. In 1821 Beuth's Deputation

began to publish *Vorbilder für Fabrikanten und Handwerker*, a series of designs for ornament, furniture, ironwork, ceramics and textiles. The first series, mainly by Schinkel, were in the NEO-CLASSICAL style and included illustrations of classical models. A complete edition was published in 1830, with ninety-four plates, and another, with 150 plates, in 1837. Some of the later designs were after Islamic and RENAISSANCE models. Designers involved included Johann Matthäus Mauch (1792–1856), Carl Boetticher (1806–1899), Gustav STIER and Ludwig Lohde. The *Vorbilder* had great influence on design in Berlin, and a reprint was published in 1863. Also in 1821 Beuth established the Verein zur Beförderung des Gewerbefleisses in Preussen, a private association for the promotion of industry, and founded the first technical school in Berlin. This was renamed the Königlich-Preussisches Gewerbeinstitut in 1827, and by 1835 Beuth had set up twenty technical schools throughout Prussia. In the 1820s he travelled with Schinkel to London and commissioned the architect, who was a close friend, to design furniture for him, executed in 1828 to 1829. Until his retirement in 1845 Beuth was closely involved in Prussian design at the highest level; from 1842 to 1844, for instance, he directed the production of a remarkable giltbronze frame, designed by Gustav Stier, for a portrait of Friedrich Wilhelm IV. Beuth was also a distinguished collector of prints, paintings and decorative art, and after his death his collection joined that of Schinkel.

Bevan, Charles In 1865 the 'BUILDING NEWS' illustrated a davenport designed by Charles Bevan, which is one of the earliest commercial designs in the High Victorian Reformed GOTHIC style, its chunky form enlivened by geometric inlay, stump columns, chamfering and notching. Bevan's style seems to derive directly from that of J. P. SEDDON, who showed a similar desk at the LONDON 1862 EXHIBITION, and it seems likely that Bevan was his pupil. Also in 1865 Bevan advertised a 'New Registered Reclining Chair' made to his design by Marsh & Jones of Leeds, 'Mediaeval Cabinet Makers', who supplied the industrialist Titus Salt with a quantity of furniture designed by Bevan in 1865 and in 1867 with a grand piano and ottoman by Bevan. At the PARIS 1867 EXHIBITION James Lamb of Manchester showed a bookcase designed by Bevan and in 1868 in commenting on his design for a 'Plain Oak Cabinet' the *Building News* linked his name with those of BURGES, William BUTTERFIELD, STREET, TALBERT and Jefferson as a designer of 'Modern Gothic Furniture'. In May 1872 'Mr C. Bevan, Mediaeval Art Designer, having taken his son, Mr George Alfred Bevan, into partnership, they will carry on business as . . . C. Bevan & Son, Designers, Wood Carvers, and Manufacturers of Art Furniture'. Bevan designed furniture shown by Gillows at the LONDON 1872 EXHIBITION, including two ebonized cabinets incorporating Doulton stoneware. Bevan's factory produced patterns of ebonized clock-cases at this date and his studio was said to be prolific. Designs for furniture by Bevan and his son were published by the *House Furnisher and Decorator* in 1871 to 1872. But although evidently a gifted and vigorous designer, Bevan remains an obscure figure.

Beyer, Johann Christian Wilhelm (1725–1806) Born in Gotha, Beyer studied as a sculptor, painter and architect in Paris and Rome. From 1759 to 1767 he worked for Duke Carl Eugen of Württemberg, designing for the porcelain factory at Ludwigsburg founded in 1758. Beyer later moved to Vienna, where he executed garden statues at Schönbrunn. In *Österreichs Merkwürdigkeiten* (1779) and *Die neue Muse* (1784) Beyer published designs for garden figures, but stated that most had already served as patterns for porcelain figures made by Ludwigsburg. They are among the few published designs for ROCOCO porcelain figures.

Beytler, Matthias Beytler was probably a pupil of the Ansbach goldsmith and etcher Stefan HERMAN. His *Thier Buechlein* (1582; six plates) was published by Herman in Ansbach. It comprises rectangular designs for box lids, with oval reserves containing animals in landscapes. *Bosen Buechlein* (1582; six plates) follows the same formula. From 1612 to 1616 four suites of black ornament for enamelling by Beytler in the stretched GROTESQUE manner were published in Augsburg. They are among the finest accomplishments of this miniature genre, inhabited by sinister devils, hunters, butterflies, farmers and birds. One plate of 1614 was dedicated to the memory of the Emperor RUDOLF II, for whom Beytler may have worked. Jacob Beytler, who published six suites of designs for boxes, trophies and goldsmith's ornament in Ravensburg in about 1588, is likely to have been a relation of Matthias Beytler.

B.G. Master B.G. was active as an engraver, probably in the Middle Rhine area, from about 1470 to 1490. His forty-four surviving plates include four designs for GOTHIC foliate ornament enlivened with hares, a fox and birds; one, with a thistle and a wildman, dates from before 1485.

Bianco, Baccio del (1604–56) Born in Florence, Bianco studied painting under Giovanni Bilivert (1576–1644) and architecture with Giulio Parigi. In 1620 he went to Vienna, Regensburg and

Prague, working as an engineer for the Emperor Ferdinand II. In 1623 he returned to Florence, where he ran a school of architecture and painting. He acted as an engineer to the Medici but also collaborated with Alfonso Parigi on the decorations for the marriage of Grand Duke Ferdinand in 1637, and designed tapestries and goldsmith's works for the court workshops. In 1651, summoned by Philip IV of Spain, he went to Madrid to design ceremonial decorations and gardens.

Bianconi, Carlo (1732–1802) Born in Bologna, from an intellectual family, Bianconi was trained as painter, sculptor and architect. In 1755 Winckelmann stayed with him during his first visit to Italy. Bianconi was a close friend and collaborator of Mauro T E S I, and in 1768 supervised the execution of the tomb designed by Tesi for their mutual friend, Algarotti. In 1767 he had designed Tesi's own tomb. In 1770 Bianconi became a member of the Accademia Clementina in Bologna, but in 1777 he was in Rome and then in 1778 settled in Milan, having been appointed secretary of the newly founded Accademia della Brera. In this role he acted as an impresario of N E O - C L A S S I C I S M, with A L B E R T O L L I among his colleagues. Bianconi published *Esemplare di alcuni ornamenti per la gioventu amante del disegno* (1780; twenty-four plates of neo-classical ornament) and contributed one plate to the *Raccolta di disegni* (1787), which consisted otherwise of ornament designed by Mauro Tesi. Bianconi was active as archaeologist, topographer and architectural historian. He sold his enormous collection of drawings to finance the publication of his translation of Vitruvius, but Napoleon rejected the dedication and the project foundered.

Biard, Pierre (1592–1661) The son of an architect and sculptor, Biard worked as a sculptor for the French court, executing decorations in Marie de Médicis' grotto in the Jardin de Luxembourg. He designed a few decorative prints, including one with two sinister female terms flanking an elaborate trophy of Roman armour, and published a suite of allegories on the arts (1627).

Biarelle, Paul Amadeus Born in Liège, Biarelle was active as designer from the mid-1730s, when he worked with his brother, the painter Johann Adolphe Biarelle, at Schloss Falkenlust under the direction of C U V I L L I É S. From 1736 Biarelle was in Ansbach where, under the architect Leopold Retti (1705–51), he designed panelling, mirrors and furniture for the Ansbach Residenz, and administered a team of carvers there. He worked in a R O C O C O style much influenced by Cuvilliés but comparatively restrained in character. His brother also worked in Ansbach and died there in 1752.

Bichel, Aegidius An ornamental designer, Bichel published a suite of A C A N T H U S-style friezes and cartouches (twelve plates) in Augsburg in 1696, although one is dated 1698. *Allerhand inventiones von Frankolischem Laubwercth* (twelve plates) comprises cartouches, friezes and V A S E S in the same style, and a third suite of twelve plates (1704) also includes torchères, candelabra and a cup of traditional German R E N A I S S A N C E form, still in a late-B A R O Q U E acanthus style.

Bichweiler, Hermann Robert An architect, Bichweiler designed furniture and interiors in the G O T H I C and R E N A I S S A N C E styles for the furniture manufacturer H. C. Wolbrandt of Hamburg from 1872. In 1878, with Dr E. Berlien, he founded a highly successful art manufactory in Altona, whose products, designed by Bichweiler, included

German maiolica, terracotta, silver and copper wares, glass and leather. The business was wound up in 1893. Although his 'Venetian' glass was delicately archaeological, Bichweiler's designs usually employed mainly NATURALISTIC, Gothic and Renaissance elements, in a dense synthetic style highly influential in Hamburg in the late 19th century.

Bickham, George (1684–1758) A pupil of the engraver John Sturt (1658–1730), who had run a drawing school with Bernard LENS, Bickham was active as an engraver from 1705. His first book, *The British Penman* (1711), established his skill as an engraver of calligraphy, most remarkably displayed in *The Universal Penman*, published in fifty-two parts and 212 plates from 1733 to 1741. The 1743 fourth edition of the *Penman* had a frontispiece by GRAVELOT. Some of the ROCOCO decorations of the *Penman* were borrowed by CHIPPENDALE, and much later used as ornaments to Clough Williams-Ellis's *Architect Errant* (1971). The title of Bickham's *Drawing and Writing Tutor* stated 'Rooms, Ceilings, fitted up with Paper in the English and Chinese Tastes', as well as offering tutoring in drawing and calligraphy. Bickham engraved many book illustrations, some after GILLOT, and sold prints, including coach designs by FERRI. The *Museum of Arts, or the Curious Repository* (eighty-one plates) presented miscellaneous motifs; Bickham also published a guide-book, *The Beauties of Stow* (1750), and engraved tickets for the coronation of George III (1761). His son, also George, published *The Musical Entertainer* (1733–9) and *The Oeconomy of Arts* (1747), with accounts of drawing, japanning etc. The works of both Bickhams were widely copied on ceramics.

Biedermeier The term Biedermeier is a combination of the German adjective '*bieder*', meaning plain, unpretentious and inoffensive, with '*Meier*', one of the commonest German surnames. 'Biedermeier' was first used in 1853 as the surname of an imaginary poet invented by Adolph Kussmaul and Ludwig Eichrodt, and poems under his name were published regularly in the humorous journal *Fliegende Blätter* from 1855 onwards. Kussmaul was inspired by the unconscious humour in the poetry of Samuel Friedrich Sauter (1766–1846), a village schoolmaster from Baden. In the 1890s Biedermeier came to be used as a term for the style of the 1820s and 1830s, at first in a mocking and derogatory sense. However, from about 1900, designers, both advanced and commercial, began to draw inspiration from Biedermeier forms, and in the 1920s the simplicity of Biedermeier was seen to prefigure MODERN predilections. Biedermeier is used both to describe the lifestyle of German-speaking countries between 1815 and 1848, and in a more restricted art-historical sense to describe the NEO-CLASSICAL style prevalent in Germany and Austria and, to a large extent, neighbouring countries from 1815 to 1830. The style, most evident in furniture, was evolved by craftsmen for the middle class. Although its basic language was derived from the French Empire style, Biedermeier also used some late-18th-century neo-classical elements, and on occasion English models and GOTHIC motifs. The simple classicism of Biedermeier furniture has similarities to the more sophisticated abstract classicism practised on occasion by SCHINKEL. But the style is best considered as an expression of ARTISAN MANNERISM, a provincial, un-academic final manifestation of neo-classicism. Although Biedermeier objects were usually designed by craftsmen rather than designers, designs by DANHAUSER and

WÖLFER provide perfect illustrations of its character.

Bigaux, Louis An architect, Bigaux began to design furniture in the ART NOUVEAU style in the 1890s. His work was shown at the PARIS 1900 EX-HIBITION, and from that year Bigaux ran a furniture workshop. His designs were at first simple but from about 1910 he produced more luxurious furniture in precious woods or lacquer.

Bijou, Le (1874–1914) Subtitled *Revue Artistique & Industrielle de la Bijouterie, Joaillerie, Orfèvrerie,* this Parisian journal was edited by J. Rothschild. It contains a rich series of designs for fashionable jewellery, etc., many in colour.

Bijouterie, Revue de (1900–1905) First issued during the PARIS 1900 EXHIBITION this well-illustrated Parisian magazine gave a full coverage of ART NOUVEAU jewellery, under the editorship of the Vicomtesse de Reville. It contained not only information on contemporary jewellery, for instance that designed by COLONNA for BING (1900), but also important historical articles, notably those by Henri Vever on 19th-century jewellery in France (1903–5).

Biller, Albrecht (1663–1720) Biller was a member of an influential Augsburg family of silversmiths. In 1703 he published a suite of heavily scrolled BAROQUE cartouches containing busts (six plates). There followed a suite of designs for embossed silver (1716; seven plates), including BERAINESQUE STRAPWORK, frames, a table and a fire-screen. The ornament is similar to that on English gesso tables of this period. Biller also published a baroque VASE, *Ein Waasen,* and designed one of the

plates in DRENTWETT'S *Ein neües Lauber and Goldschmieds Buch.*

Biller, Johann Jacob A silversmith in Augsburg, Biller died there in 1723. His *Neues Zierathen Buch von Schlingen und Bändelwerk* (six plates) and *Neu inventirtes Formular Büchlein vor Gold und Silber Arbeiter* (seven plates) comprise BERAINESQUE STRAPWORK, panels, lights, boxes, tables, candlesticks, etc., all in an elaborate late-BAROQUE style, and intended for execution in silver.

Binck, Jacob Born in about 1500 in Cologne, Binck was a prolific engraver strongly influenced by DÜRER and the brothers BEHAM. He issued about fifty-one plates of ornament, mainly panels but including three dagger sheaths; many are copied from Hans Sebald Beham, and Binck's original designs use Beham's early RENAISSANCE vocabulary of ornament, including dolphins, putti and VASES. Binck worked as a court painter in Copenhagen in the 1530s, in 1541 to 1542 he was in Sweden, and in 1543 he designed medals and panelling for Duke Albrecht of Prussia in Königsberg. He died in Königsberg in 1569 after further travels, including two trips to Antwerp in 1549 and 1552, when he ordered tombs from Cornelis FLORIS for the Danish court.

Bindesbøll, Thorvald (1846–1908) Born in Copenhagen, the son of Michael Gottlieb Birkner Bindesbøll (1800–1856), architect of the Thorwalden Museum (1838–47), Thorvald Bindesbøll was himself trained as an architect and practised from 1876. From 1883 he designed earthenware for the Copenhagen Valby factory and others, and he later designed posters, bookbindings, embroidery, furniture, including a NEO-CLASSICAL cupboard (1900), and metalwork, including silver shown by the Danish court jewellers, A. Michelsen, at the PARIS 1900 EXHIBITION, ironwork, and electric chandeliers. Bindesbøll favoured undulating forms and vigorous cloud- or tadpole-like decorative motifs; he was the most prolific and influential of Danish ART NOUVEAU designers. The Carlsberg lager label is perhaps his most enduring work.

Bindoni, Giovanni Antonio di Bernardino Bindoni was responsible for two small two-part books of designs for lace; *Il monte* (Venice 1557 and 1559) and *Ricchezze* (also Venice 1557 and 1559). Some of his designs, elaborately redrawn, were reproduced by the VIENNA MUSEUM OF APPLIED ARTS in 1874.

Binelli Presumably a smith working in Paris, Binelli designed at least nineteen suites of designs of ironwork entitled *Cahiers de Serrureries Modernes*, including overdoors, balustrades, church screens, gates etc. They probably date from about 1780 and are in a neat thin NEO-CLASSICAL style. Some were engraved by QUEVERDO.

Binet, René (1866–1911) Born at Chaumont, Binet studied briefly at the École des Beaux-Arts in Paris, and then under the architect V. A. Laloux. In about 1895 he published *Esquisses Décoratives* (sixty plates), elaborate designs for interiors in a variety of styles. In 1897 he designed silver and jewels. Binet's most famous work was an entrance to the PARIS 1900 EXHIBITION, embellished with ceramics by Alexandre Bigot. He was later mainly active as a watercolourist, his drawings being praised in 'ART DÉCORATIF' (1907), but also designed tapestries for the Gobelins factory.

Bing, Samuel (1838–1905) Born in Hamburg, Bing worked in a ceramic factory there up to 1870. In 1871, after the Franco-Prussian war, he moved to Paris and opened a shop. In 1875 he travelled to China and Japan, and in 1877 set up a second shop, La Porte Chinoise, to sell Far Eastern objects; TIFFANY was among his customers and the shop soon became a meeting place for enthusiasts of Japanese art, including the Goncourts and Roger Marx. Bing showed his own collection at the PARIS 1878 EXHIBITION, and later published 'ARTISTIC JAPAN' (1888–91). In 1889 he became Tiffany's exclusive European distributor, and in 1892 travelled to America with a commission from the French government to survey American art and architecture. He attended the CHICAGO 1893 WORLD COLUMBIAN EXPOSITION, publishing his findings in *La Culture artistique en Amérique* (1895). In December 1895 Bing opened his new Paris gallery, inspired by the Brussels shop À la Toison d'Or, for which Combaz designed a poster. Bing's gallery was called L'Art Nouveau, and gave its name to ART NOUVEAU. The *Figaro* greeted its products as a *mélange* reflecting the influence of the vicious English, Jewish morphine addicts and Belgian spivs. On view were stained glass by Tiffany, designed by Vuillard, Toulouse-Lautrec, Sérusier and others, art glass by Tiffany, GALLÉ and Koepping, posters by BRADLEY and Beardsley, metalwork by W. A. S. BENSON, jewellery by LALIQUE and COLONNA, wallpapers and fabrics by CRANE, MORRIS and VOYSEY, and furniture by VAN DE VELDE and Gallé. Among the other designers employed by Bing at this period was BRANGWYN. At the PARIS 1900 EXHIBITION Bing had his own pavilion, with rooms designed by Georges DE FEURE, Edward Colonna and Eugène GAILLARD. Among its many admirers was Gabriel Mourey, writing in the 'STUDIO'. Bing was a propagandist for MODERN design, for example writing an article on the future of design in 'DEKORATIVE KUNST' (1897) and on Tiffany glass in 'KUNST UND KUNSTHANDWERK' (1898). Another means by which he exercised influence was the sale of objects to museums. Bing's son Marcel (1875–1920) designed some jewellery for his father and took over his shop in 1905; however, he soon turned to antique dealing. Samuel Bing's own collection of oriental art, amounting to 951 lots, was sold in 1906.

Birckenfeld, Johann Samuel (1732–69) The son of a celebrated smith, Johann Balthasar Birckenfeld (1690–1764), Johann Samuel Birckenfeld was responsible for a wide range of crude but vigorous designs for ROCOCO ironwork published in Augsburg around 1760 by HERTEL and ENGELBRECHT. His designs include locks, keys, cartouches, balconies, stairs, signs, gates, gutters and lights.

Birckenhultz, Paul (1561–1634) Born in Aachen, Birckenhultz worked as a goldsmith and engraver in Frankfurt from 1589 to his death. He travelled to Antwerp, France and Italy. Birckenhultz published four suites of delicate black designs in the stretched GROTESQUE style, intended for enamelling, with six plates each, all titled *Varii generis opera aurifabris necessaria*, and a further four similar suites, *Quatuor Mundi Elementa Elegantibus, Omnia Conando Docilis Solertia Vincit, Omnia Generis Instrumenta Bellica* and *Ars His Myronis Nobilis Effingitur Pagellulis*, a pretentious series of Latin titles, the last of which alludes to the Greek sculptor and bronze-caster Myron. They include very fine designs for jewelled pendants, several incorporating initials, as well as further enamel designs.

Black, Misha (1910–77) Black was trained as an architect. In 1933 he helped to found the Artists' International Association, a left-wing pressure group. In 1938 he was the coordinating architect to the MARS Group exhibition on the elements of modern architecture, and in the same year designed displays for the Glasgow Empire Exhibition. In 1939 he designed the corporate identity of the Kardomah chain of restaurants and interiors for London Transport buses. From 1940 to 1945 Black worked with Milner Gray as exhibition architect to the Ministry of Information. From 1945 Black ran a prolific partnership, the Design Research Unit. In 1946 he was chief designer to the Britain Can Make It Exhibition, and in 1951 an architect to the Festival of Britain (see LONDON EXHIBITIONS). In *Exhibition Design* (1950) and *Public Interiors* (1960) Black illustrated many of his own interior schemes, in an increasingly bland MODERN manner. Black was Professor of Industrial Design (Engineering) at the London Royal College of Art from 1959, and a prominent member of the industrial design establishment.

Blain de Fontenay, Jean Baptiste (1653–1715) Born in Caen as Jean Belin, Blain de Fontenay moved to Paris to become a pupil of the flower painter J.-B. MONNOYER (1636–99), whose daughter he married in 1687. Also in 1687 Blain became a member of the Academy; he was much patronized by Louis XIV and had a lodging in the Louvre. From 1699 Blain was a specialist flower painter for the Gobelins tapestry factory: he designed the first borders for C. A. COYPEL's Don Quixote suite. With Vernansal, Blain designed a series of delightful CHINOISERIE tapestries for the Beauvais factory, later copied at Berlin. He also designed for the Savonnerie carpet factory.

Blätter für Kunstgewerbe (1872–1898)

Edited from Vienna by Valentin Teirich, professor at the applied arts school attached to the VIENNA MUSEUM OF APPLIED ARTS, this distinguished magazine included not only articles, news and book reviews, but also designs, many in colour, by Teirich himself, Hasenauer, Ferstel, HANSEN and others, including STORCK, who was editor from 1877 to 1897. Historic examples were also illustrated. The style was predominantly RENAISSANCE Revival, and every sort of applied art object was represented.

Blondel, Jacques-François (1705–74) Born in Rouen, the nephew of the architect François Blondel (1683–1756) and the son of a hatter, Blondel was already established as an architect in Paris in 1729. He designed plates for Mariette's *Architecture Française* and for C. A. D'AVILER's *Cours d'Architecture* (fourth edition, 1737). Blondel's first book, *De la distribution des maisons de plaisance* (1737), was dedicated to the economist and statesman Turgot (1727–81), who became his protector. It included fine ROCOCO designs for interior decoration and ornament, and ironwork designs copied in the Palais de Justice at Liège (1739–43). In 1743 Blondel opened an École des Arts, where he taught drawing and architecture. It became the most important school in Paris and his pupils the elite of the NEO-CLASSICAL generation. *Architecture Française* (1752–6, four volumes) was intended as a sequel to Mariette, and in 1757 Blondel published an augmented edition of Vignola. He was elected to the Académie d'Architecture in 1755 and became a professor there in 1764. In 1759 Blondel subscribed to *Civil Architecture* by his former pupil, CHAMBERS. In 1767 he was given a lodging in the Louvre. In his 1762 article on Architecture in Diderot and D'Alembert's *Encyclopédie*, and in

his *Cours d'architecture* (six volumes, 1771–7), completed after Blondel's death by Pierre Patte, Blondel presented a rationalist middle-of-the-road view of architecture, anti-rococo and also against extreme forms of neo-classicism. The *Cours* included an excellent analysis of ornament and its uses with plates of VASES, ironwork, furniture, plasterwork, panelling and other architectural ornaments.

Blum, Hans Born at Lohr on the Main, Blum settled in Zürich in about 1549, and was active as architect, stonemason and wood engraver. His work on the ORDERS, *Quinque columnarum exacta descriptio atque delineatione* (Zürich, 1550), was the most popular work of this kind, going through fourteen editions by 1668, including a Dutch edition in 1612 and an English edition in 1660. Blum published similar works in 1558, 1560 and 1562. The Lyon publisher of ornament, Jean Le Maistre, and KASEMANN were among the many who borrowed or copied from Blum.

Bodley, George Frederick (1827–1907) Born in Hull, the son of a doctor, Bodley became in 1845 the first pupil of the GOTHIC architect Sir George Gilbert Scott (1811–78), with whom he stayed until 1850. Bodley then practised independently. His St Michael's, Brighton (1858–61), which Bodley later described as a 'boyish antagonistic effort', includes some of the William MORRIS firm's earliest stained glass and decorative work. In 1869 Bodley entered a partnership with Thomas Garner (1839–1906), another Scott pupil; it lasted until 1897. In about 1872 with Garner and George Gilbert Scott, junior (1839–97), Bodley founded a church furnishing firm, Watts & Co., which still survives. For Watts & Co., Bodley designed metalwork, much of it executed by Barkentin & Krall, including the Westminster Abbey memorial brass to G. E. STREET, as well as textiles and wallpapers. The designer H. H. Mott supervised Watts' textile and wallpaper designs. EDIS (1881) included a fender designed by Bodley. In 1894 Bodley redecorated Fishmongers' Hall, sweeping away Owen JONES's 1866 decorations; Bodley's work was superseded by that of H. S. Goodhart Rendel (1887–1959) in 1929. Bodley's mature architecture and designs were distinguished for their refinement. COMPER was Bodley's best-known pupil.

Boener, Johann Alexander (1647–1720) Born in Nuremberg, where he was active as an engraver and art dealer until his death, Boener was a pupil of the Dutch engraver Matthias von Somer. His *Neue Erfindungen für Gold- Silber- und Drahtarbeiter* (six plates) comprises BAROQUE ACANTHUS ornament incorporating animals; it was aimed at silversmiths.

Boeri, Cini After studying architecture at the Milan Polytechnic, Boeri worked with Studio Zanuso from 1953 to 1963. She showed at the Milan Triennale in 1963 and 1968. She has designed plastic lights for Arteluce (1968) and seating for Arflex, including the Bobolungo chair (1969) and the polyurethane Serpentone seat (1970–71). In 1979 her Strips seating system won the Compasso d'Oro of the Italian Institute for Industrial Design.

Bogaert HOPE, in his *Household Furniture* (1807), names Bogaert as a Flemish carver whom he had found to be sufficiently skilful to work at Duchess Street. Bogaert was still working for Hope in 1810, and in 1814 was listed as 'Bogairts & Co, Carvers & Gilders', 23 Air Street, Piccadilly. Bogaert, with the young Chantrey in his employ, also worked for Samuel Rogers (1763–1855) in 1803 to 1804. In 1824 George SMITH

stated that Bogaert, as well as being a carver, also designed for furniture and other branches of interior decoration.

Boileau, Jean Jacques Boileau came over from France in about 1787 to London, where he worked under Henry HOLLAND at Carlton House as a mural painter. He also worked as a painter at Fonthill for William BECKFORD, and was employed by Messrs George and Frederick Eckhardt to finish by hand their printed wallpapers. In 1799 he subscribed to TATHAM's *Etchings*. Boileau designed silver from at least 1799 to 1804 in a refined NEO-CLASSICAL style strongly influenced by MOITTE. He was well known as a designer of furniture, including Turkish tripods at Fonthill, and ormolu. In 1828 he designed a carpet for Windsor Castle. Designs by Boileau were in A. C. PUGIN's library sale in 1833, but Boileau seems to have survived until at least 1851.

Boler, James In 1634 Boler published *The Needle's Excellency*, described as a tenth edition. It was a fine copy of needlework patterns published by Johann SIBMACHER in 1597 and 1601, and of lace patterns published by Jacques FOILLET in 1598, with a lengthy preface by John Taylor, the Water Poet. Boler died in 1635.

Bölmann, Hieronymus Bölmann was active as an engraver and publisher in Nuremberg from about 1710 to 1730, engraving designs by DECKER, EYSLER, SCHÜBLER and others. His own designs include a suite of stolid early ROCOCO cartouches.

Bolten, Arent van Bolten was born in Zwolle in about 1573 and was active there as a goldsmith and designer. The publication of a portrait in 1607 suggests that he had by then achieved a substantial reputation. A number of silver reliefs of religious subjects by Bolten are known; they have a melted quality which recalls early 16th-century German landscape drawings and is stylistically close to AURICULAR ornament. Drawings in the British Museum show that Bolten was an imaginative designer of silver beakers, salts, VASES, frames and ornament in the auricular style. There are also a number of fantastic monsters related to those of Christoph JAMNITZER and Wendel DIETTERLIN THE YOUNGER. Bronzes of monsters similar to those in Bolten's drawings are known. He published a suite of monsters and another of auricular spoons. Bolten's place in the creation of the auricular style is not yet defined, but it seems likely that he was in contact with Adam and Paul van VIANEN in its earliest stages. Bolten died before 1633.

Bömmel, Wolfgang Hieronymus von Bömmel published in Nuremberg a suite of ornaments for goldsmiths, *Neu ersonnene Gold-Schmieds Grillen*, in two parts (nine plates in all). The title shows pendants composed of ACANTHUS scrolls, while the plates comprise lively animals – cats, dogs, horses, rams, lions and men, all made up out of tight black acanthus scrolls against a background of looser scrolls, droll inventions. They probably date from about 1690.

Bonasone, Giulio di Antonio Born in Bologna, Bonasone was a pupil of the painter Lorenzo Sabbatini. From 1531 to 1574 he published some 370 plates in Bologna and Rome, mainly copies after MICHELANGELO, RAPHAEL, Titian and other painters, in the tradition of Marcantonio Raimondi. His *Amori Sdegni et Gielosie di Giunone* (twenty-one plates) have extremely varied GROTESQUE frames which Bonasone claimed to have designed himself. Another print shows an antique frieze with ACANTHUS scrolls, a winged sphinx and an altar.

Bondol, Jean de Born in Bruges, whence his alternative name, Jean de Bruges, Bondol was from 1368 in the service of Charles V of France as a court painter. In 1376 he was commissioned by the King's brother, Duke Louis I of Anjou, to design the great suite of tapestries on the Apocalypse woven in Paris by Nicolas Bataille and now in Angers. He received a payment for '*pourtraictures et patrons*' in 1378 and seems to have completed the commission in 1379. He is last recorded in 1381. The Apocalypse designs were partly based on an illuminated manuscript borrowed from Charles V by Duke Louis for that purpose.

Bonito, Giuseppe (1707–89) Born in Castellmare di Stabia, Bonito entered the studio of the painter Francesco Solimena (1657–1747) at an early age. From Solimena's death onwards Bonito had a successful establishment career in Naples. In 1758 he was commissioned by Carlo III to design tapestries on the theme of Don Quixote for Caserta.

Bonnard, N. Bonnard issued in about 1730 *Nouveau Livre de Grille* (six plates), simple but competent early ROCOCO designs for iron screens for churches.

Bonnard, Pierre (1867–1947) Born at Fontenay-les-Roses, the son of an official in the War Ministry, Bonnard was intended for the law but in 1888 studied painting at the École des Beaux-Arts and at the Académie Julian in Paris. With Maurice DENIS, Vuillard and others he became a member of the Nabis group, which took a strong interest in the decorative arts. In 1889 Bonnard designed a poster for France-Champagne, directly influenced by Hokusai, and decided to become an artist. In 1894 he designed a poster for *La Revue Blanche*, for which he later did decorations and illustrations and, reportedly, a Nabique desk for the editor, Natanson. In 1895 Bonnard designed a stained-glass window, Maternité, for TIFFANY, which was shown by BING. A screen decorated with nursemaids and cats was designed in about 1894 and lithographed in 1897; it was influenced by Hiroshige and Kuniyoshi. For Vollard, Bonnard illustrated *Parallèlement* (1900) and *Daphnis et Chloé* (1902). In 1904 he designed a bronze table centrepiece. Bonnard painted decorative panels for Misia Godebska in 1909 and was active as a decorative painter until about 1920.

Bonomi, Joseph (1739–1808) Born in Rome, Bonomi studied architecture there under the Marchese Teodoli and CLÉRISSEAU. In 1767 he came to London to work for ADAM, and later for Thomas Leverton (1743–1824). He was active as an independent architect from at least 1782. In 1783 he went to Italy, probably with the Earl of Aylesford (1751–1812), a gifted amateur architect who etched his own book-plate in the manner of PIRANESI. For Aylesford, Bonomi designed the Pompeian Gallery (1785–8) at Packington, with wall decorations derived from Ponce's *Description des Bains de Titus* (Paris, 1786) and some of the earliest klismos chairs in Europe. The gallery is a remarkably early archaeological ensemble, and the church at Packington (1789–90) was an equally precocious, indeed ruthless example of advanced NEO-CLASSICISM.

Bonthomme, Gabriel Bonthomme, a Parisian smith, published seven suites of designs for ironwork in an ARTISAN NEO-CLASSICAL style with titles such as *Livre de differents Balcons* (1775); others are dated 1777.

Bony, Jean François (1754–1825) Born at Gisors, near Lyon, Bony studied flower painting under Gonichon at the Lyon school of design. He subsequently worked as a designer of textiles and embroidery for Lyon manufacturers. After the revolution, Bony continued to design textiles as a partner in the Bissardon, Cousin & Bony manufacture. In 1809 he succeeded BARRABAND as teacher of floral design at the Lyon École des Beaux-Arts. He taught there until 1810, and in 1811 moved to Paris, where he worked successively for Napoleon and Louis XVIII. After being ruined by a partner he committed suicide. Bony's designs for the Empress Marie-Louise are among the finest French NEO-CLASSICAL textile designs of the Napoleonic period.

Book Design and Production (1958–64) Published from London, a high-quality journal with fine illustrations, *Book Design* contained articles on typography and book design both national and international. It was succeeded by *Print Design and Production* (1965–7).

Booth, Lorenzo The 'ART JOURNAL' of October 1863 contained a lukewarm criticism of Booth's *The Exhibition Book of Original Designs for Furniture*, which had by then reached fifty plates. It was probably the same as his *Original Design Book for Decorative Furniture* (London, 1864), which contains 132 lithographed plates of competent designs for all types of furniture in a synthetic mixture of the GOTHIC, Elizabethan, RENAISSANCE and ROCOCO styles, one sometimes predominating. It is an interesting document of the change in taste since the decade before, best represented by Peter THOMSON's designs. Booth's lengthy text contains a long exegesis of the problems of style in furniture, illustrated by criticisms of objects shown at the LONDON

EXHIBITIONS of 1851 and 1862. Booth also published a *New Book of Ornamental Designs* (1861) and an *Original Design Book for Cornices and Draperies*.

Börgemann, Karl (1851–1938) Like Edwin OPPLER, Börgemann was a pupil of Conrad Wilhelm Hase, whose partner he became. As well as activity as an architect in Hanover, Börgemann designed some competent furniture in the late-GOTHIC style executed by Louis Günther in 1894.

Borra, Giovanni Battista Borra was employed as a draughtsman by Robert Woods and James Dawkins on their tour of Asia Minor and Syria from 1750 to 1751. Borra came to London in 1751 and worked on the drawings for the plates of *The Ruins of Palmyra* (1753) and *The Ruins of Balbec* (1757). He also designed interior decorations for the Duke of Norfolk at Norfolk House (1755), and from 1752 to about 1760 for Lord Temple at Stowe, the latter including the state bed. Borra used motifs from Palmyra in his designs, although his basic style was North Italian ROCOCO. It is probable that Borra is to be identified with G. B. Borra (1712–86) of Turin, an architect who trained under B. A. Vittone, and from 1756 to 1757 worked at Racconigi, where there is decoration similar to some at Norfolk House.

Borsato, Giuseppe (1770–1849) Born in Venice, son of an ornamental painter, Borsato studied at the Accademia there. He later worked in Rome in the Canova circle before returning to Venice to work as a decorative painter. He achieved fame designing for Napoleon and his regime, and in 1812 became professor of ornament at the Venice Accademia. In 1815 he designed a table presented to Austria as a token of Venice's loyalty. This was illustrated in Borsato's *Opera ornamentale* (Venice, 1822, reprinted

Milan, 1831; sixty plates), which also includes silver, furniture, lights, church decoration and mantelpieces. Borsato worked in a highly competent and sometimes elaborate late NEO-CLASSICAL style handled in a slightly mechanical manner. In 1844 Borsato issued an edition of PERCIER and FONTAINE's *Recueil*.

Bos, Cornelis Born at Hertogenbosch as Cornelis Wellem Claussone, Bos was admitted as a citizen of Antwerp in 1540, when he also became a member of the Guild of St Luke as a '*figuersnyder*'. His earliest known works were engravings of anatomy. He may have visited France in the 1530s and probably executed illustrations to COECK's books, many of which he bought from Coeck for resale in 1542, a transaction which left him with a debt which was still unpaid at Coeck's death in 1550. In 1544 Bos, a member of the fanatic sect of Loïsts, then being suppressed, had to flee Antwerp. He probably went to Haarlem and thence in about 1548 to Rome. In about 1550 he settled in Groningen, where he died in 1556. Before his exile in 1544 Bos issued a book of *Moresken* (forty plates), mainly copied from PELLEGRINO's *La Fleur de la Science de Pourtraicture*, which was probably in the enforced sale of Bos's property held in 1545. A Paris edition appeared in 1546. Bos's title to *Moresken* is one of the earliest developed examples of the Flemish STRAPWORK GROTESQUE ornament mainly created by Cornelis FLORIS. In 1546 Bos issued a plate of ornament in the same manner. While in Rome he issued three suites of grotesque ornament, totalling twenty plates, derived from RAPHAEL's Vatican Loggie, with details from Mantegna, and the Domus Aurea, in some cases enmeshed in Northern strapwork. A suite of vertical trophies of arms (seven plates) probably appeared about the same date.

On his return to Groningen in 1550 Bos issued a suite of eight fantastic cars, extreme variations on classical themes, with the most grotesque juxtapositions and distortions supported on a scaffolding of strapwork. The type derives from Cornelis Floris, who drew such a car in 1543. From 1550 to 1554 Bos issued nine engravings of strapwork grotesque ornament, one of which, incorporating a marine monster, later influenced Cornelis Floris's *Veranderinghe van Grottissen ende Compartimenten* (Antwerp, 1556). Bos's last series of ornamental prints are strapwork grotesque cartouches enclosing German proverbs (1554; five plates). Bos was also responsible for a suite of similar cartouches with French proverbs (twenty plates) copied from an anonymous suite, a suite of caryatids and terms (sixteen plates), some copied from Agostino VENEZIANO, and a total of ten plates of strapwork grotesque designs for the decoration of daggers or engraving on silver. Although Bos has at times been credited with a major role in inventing the Flemish style of strapwork grotesques in about 1540, it appears that he was in fact a designer of limited invention who followed prototypes invented by Floris and others.

Bossi, Benigno (1727–92) Born in Arcisate, Varese, Bossi was the son of a plasterer who worked in Germany. He was taught to engrave there, but in about 1759 settled in Parma. There he worked as a plasterer and also as an engraver, engraving PETITOT's *Suite des Vases* (1764) and *Mascarade à la Grecque* (1771). In 1766 Bossi was appointed court plasterer and became a member of the Parma Academy; he was also active as a painter. He published a suite of trophies (1770), one of which was copied in PANFILI's *Frammenti di Ornati* (1783). His *Opere Varie* (1789) included ten plates of panels of NEO-CLASSICAL ornament with a strong BAROQUE cast, some dated 1787. Bossi also designed book illustrations and ornament.

Botticelli, Sandro Born in Florence in about 1445, the son of a tanner, Botticelli was trained as a goldsmith, and was then from about 1461 an assistant to the painter Fra Filippo Lippi. He was an independent painter from about 1467, but also designed embroidery and appliqué work, as well as a number of mosaics for Florence Cathedral. From 1481 to 1482 Botticelli was in Rome. He died in Florence in 1510.

Bottomley, Joseph In 1793 to 1794 Bottomley published in London a two-part design book for blacksmiths, containing numerous neat NEO-CLASSICAL designs for ironwork, including door lights, balustrades, grilles etc.

Boucher, François (1703–70) Born in Paris, the son of an embroidery designer, Boucher was at first taught by his father and then, in 1720, entered an engraver's workshop. In 1721 to 1722 he illustrated Père Daniel's *Histoire de France*. In the next year he won the first prize of the Academy for painting. From 1722 to 1725 Boucher engraved drawings by WATTEAU. In 1727 he went to Italy with the painter Carle Van Loo, and stayed in Rome from 1728 to 1731. In 1731 he engraved *Diverses Figures Chinoises* (twelve plates), after Watteau. Boucher continued to design book ornaments and illustrations, including some for Regnier's *Satires et autres Œuvres* (1733) and Molière's *Œuvres* (1734). Also in 1734 Boucher became a member of the Academy as a history painter, and provided his first tapestry designs to the Beauvais factory, then being administered by OUDRY. In 1739 his painting of Psyche, a tapestry design for a series woven at Beauvais from 1741, was shown at the Salon. In 1740 he designed a device for the shop, À la Pagode, of the famous dealer, Gersaint; this was engraved by CAYLUS. From 1740 to 1742 Boucher designed illustrations for La Fontaine's *Fables*. In 1745 he began to design for the Vincennes porcelain factory: after the move of the factory to Sèvres in 1753 he increased his involvement at the request of Falconet, being paid 485 livres for designs in 1755. Chinese tapestries were first woven at Beauvais to Boucher's designs in 1743; eight such designs were shown at the 1748 Salon and in 1860 a suite of the tapestries was presented to the Emperor of China. In 1751 Boucher began to teach drawing and engraving to Mme de Pompadour (1721–64), who in 1755 engraved a suite of designs for gems (fifty-two plates), of which Boucher designed the frontispiece and thirty-six plates, the remainder being by VIEN and Guay. In 1753 Boucher showed the Rising and the Setting of the Sun, designs for Gobelins tapestries, at the Salon and in 1755, on the death of Oudry, was appointed Inspecteur des Gobelins; he was succeeded on his death by HALLÉ. In 1758 Boucher collaborated with Carle Van Loo, Jean Baptiste PIERRE and Vien on the Gobelins suite of Les Amours des Dieux. Boucher's assistants at the Gobelins included JACQUES and TESSIER. In 1765 Boucher succeeded Van Loo as Premier Peintre du Roi. However, in 1763 and 1765 he was attacked by Diderot, and a few late designs, for instance a tomb to Mlle Sandow, show him using the NEO-CLASSICAL vocabulary of ornament, of which his son, J.-F. BOUCHER, was to be an adept. Boucher himself had been one of the great masters of ROCOCO ornament. His early *Livres d'Écrans* (six plates), and *Nouveaux Morceaux pour des paravants* (1737; five plates), present panels for screens in a light early rococo manner comparable to GILLOT and Watteau, but the *Nouveaux Morceaux*

also include one design for a *rocaille* in the fully developed rococo style of MEISSONIER, who was a friend of Boucher and stood god-father to his son in 1736. Meissonier also influenced Boucher's *Recueil de Fontaines* (1736; seven plates) and his *Second Livre de Fontaines* (seven plates). In about 1740 Boucher issued the first of many suites of CHINOISERIES, *Diverses Figures Chinoises* (nine plates), Chinese figures supported by umbrellas, chairs, tables and other attributes in the Chinese style. As well as numerous suites of pastorals, putti, and female nudes, Boucher published a vigorous rococo *Livre de Cartouches* (twelve plates), a *Livre de Vases* (twelve plates), and his contributions to MacSwiny's *Tombeaux* included a splendid rococo tomb to 'Sir Clowdisley Shovell'. Prints after Boucher were widely copied, for instance on Sèvres, Chelsea, Frankenthal and Lowestoft porcelain, and on gold and enamel snuff-boxes. As late as 1784 his paintings were considered useful models at both the Sèvres and Gobelins factories.

Boucher, Juste-François (1736–82) Born in Paris, the son of François BOUCHER, Juste-François Boucher was a god-son of MEISSONIER. In 1761 and 1763 he won the second prize for architecture and in 1764 he went to Rome under the protection of the Marquis de MARIGNY; he returned to France in 1767. Before 1773 Boucher issued an edition of Vignola's ORDERS with a NEO-CLASSICAL frontispiece designed by GRAVELOT. From about 1774 onwards he was responsible for some 500 plates with highly professional designs for ornament, furniture, VASES, ironwork and every aspect of the decorative arts. They are '*à la moderne*', that is in the fashionable neo-classical style, of which they provide a conspectus. Copies were published in Augsburg. Boucher also designed wallpaper for the factory of

Jean Baptiste Réveillon. His designs rarely display originality and his competence often produces blandness.

Boucheron, Giovan Battista (1742–1815) Boucheron's father, Andrea Boucheron, was court goldsmith in his native Turin; he had been trained in Paris under Thomas Germain (1673–1748). In 1760 Boucheron went to Rome to study sculpture. In 1763 he returned to Turin to work in the court goldsmith's workshop, his father having died in 1761. A design for a ewer of 1768 shows Boucheron working in a rich ROCOCO style influenced by MEISSONIER. In 1775 he was appointed head of the court workshop and in 1776 director. From 1778 he taught at the Accademia, for whose printed *Regolamenti* (1778) he designed NEO-CLASSICAL ornaments. From 1776 Boucheron's silver designs were in a sophisticated and elaborate neo-classical style influenced by DELAFOSSE. A number of extant pieces are known as well as drawings. Boucheron also drew a portrait of Vittorio Amadeo III, King of Sardinia, with a fine neo-classical frame; it was engraved in Paris and shows him to have been an accomplished artist. His son, Michelangelo Boucheron, known as Angelo, was in 1796 appointed architect to the University of Turin and designed fine neo-classical maces and decorations for the inauguration of the university in the presence of Napoleon in 1805. However, his career later petered out into a series of professorships of drawing. He died in 1859.

Boucquet, Pierre Boucquet designed *Livre de Toutes Sortes de Feuilles pour Servir à l'Art D'Orfeburie* (Paris, 1634), published by MONCORNET on six plates. The book was dedicated to Christoffel Swager and comprises large sprays of fleshy leaves in the COSSE-DE-POIS style, intended for the use of goldsmiths; one has a panel of rabbits in its centre.

Boulle, André Charles (1642–1732) Born in Paris, the son of a cabinet-maker of Flemish origin, Boulle followed his father's trade from at least 1664. In 1672, at the recommendation of Jean-Baptiste Colbert (1619–83), Boulle was appointed Ébéniste du Roi and took over the lodgings of the cabinet-maker, Jean Macé, at the Louvre. He worked for the court, the government and the rich. Marquetry, both in woods and in tortoiseshell and brass, and bronze ornaments were his specialities. The sculptor François Girardon (1628–1715) designed some of his bronzes. Boulle was often in financial difficulties but was a passionate collector of prints and drawings. The large majority of his vast collection perished in a tragic fire in 1720. The remainder, listed after his death, included works by LE BRUN, COTELLE, LOIR, POLIDORO, Enea VICO, Agostino VENEZIANO, LE PAUTRE, BERAIN, DUCERCEAU and MITELLI. Boulle himself designed furniture and bronzes. Drawings survive and his *Nouveaux Deisseins de Meubles et Ouvrages de Bronze et de Marqueterie* (eight plates), published by Mariette, contains designs for clocks, bronzes, inkstands, commodes, desks, medal cabinets, torchères, tables, mirrors, firedogs and candelabra. It was reprinted by Bölmann in Nuremberg. Boulle's style is close to that of Jean I Berain. His eldest son, Jean-Philippe Boulle (1680–1744), published three designs for marquetry in a lively Berainesque manner. Two templates for marquetry in Boston may also be by Jean-Philippe; one includes a quotation from an engraving of 1550 by Cornelis BOS.

Bourdon, Pierre An accomplished engraver of ornament from Coulommiers in Brie, Bourdon published *Essais* *de Gravure* (Paris, 1703–7), three suites of seven plates each with fine ornaments for watches, box-lids, a cane handle, keys, flasks, etc., in either a black scrolled ACANTHUS or a BERAIN-ESQUE style. Each suite includes an amusing depiction of a man smoking by a table, probably a self-portrait, and some of the designs have captions, for instance 'À Étoilles et Fortifications', 'À piramides et troffées' and 'À festons Grotesque', a rare insight into trade nomenclature at this date. The book was partly intended for the education of young craftsmen, like BOURGUET's earlier work. Copies were later published in Nuremberg and an English engraved silver tobacco box of 1718 used one of Bourdon's smoking men.

Bourguet, Jean Bourguet, a Parisian goldsmith, published in 1702 a *Livre de taille d'épargne de goût ancient et moderne* (twelve plates). It contained designs for box-lids, pendants, an alphabet, a clock and similar small pieces of metalwork decorated with BERAINESQUE GROTESQUES, ACANTHUS and floral ornament. Already planned in 1716, Bourguet's *Second Livre de taille d'épargne* (1723; twelve plates) is a similar work on a larger format with designs for rings, jewels, box-lids, etc. Both Bourguet's works were specifically aimed at the instruction of apprentices, and contained some old-fashioned designs, some, Bourguet stated in 1723, of the fashion of forty years earlier. His designs are elaborate and finely engraved, but it is surprising to learn from POUGET that they were still being used by apprentices in 1762.

Boutemie, Daniel Born in Beauvais, Boutemie was active as a goldsmith in Paris from at least 1628 to 1636. Nicholas COCHIN engraved his portrait. Boutemie assisted Louis XIII in his cabinet of inventions. In 1636 he published the design of an extraordinary cup he had given the King at Chantilly, which could be used a different way each day for three months. It is in a wild and jagged AURICULAR style. Boutemie also published an *Ouvrage Rare et Nouveau* (1636; twenty plates), dedicated to Louis XIII. This has extreme auricular cartouches on title and dedication followed by plates in which a hat is tortured into an amazing variety of sinister dragon and bird-like forms. The designs were for the use of goldsmiths, engravers, chasers, sculptors, furniture-makers and others. Boutemie also published a suite of surrealistically auricular figures of the months, influenced by CALLOT.

Bouw- en Sierkunst (1897–1904) This expensive journal, published in Amsterdam and Haarlem, juxtaposed modern and historic art and design. The first issue included work by Toorop, LION CACHET, NIEUWENHUIS and CUYPERS.

Bowles, Carington (1724–93) From 1754 to 1764 Bowles was in partnership with his father, John Bowles, as a publisher. In 1756 to 1757 they published a *Drawing Book* with ROCOCO motifs which were used to decorate many English ceramics, including Liverpool tiles. Bowles's later publications include *Britannia Depicta* (1764), *Bowles' Young Lawyer's Tutor* (1764), a writing manual, and *Bowles's Art of Painting*, of which German translations were published in Leipzig in 1797 and Coblenz in 1800.

Boy, Peter de (1648–1727) Born in Lübeck, Boy settled in Frankfurt in 1675. He was active there as goldsmith and painter. He later moved to Düsseldorf as cabinet painter to Elector Johann Wilhelm von Pfalz, and died there. A surviving design for an embossed silver dish with a mythological scene within a floral BAROQUE border demonstrates that Boy designed metalwork.

Boyvin, René Born in Angers, Boyvin worked there as a coin engraver at the mint from 1542. From the late 1540s he was active as an engraver in Paris, succeeding FANTUZZI as the main popularizer of the Fontainebleau style. His engravings included a suite of MANNERIST metalwork designs derived from ROSSO FIORENTINO, nine plates of cups, salts, ewers, candlesticks etc. densely decorated with STRAPWORK and writhing nudes, a suite of twenty GROTESQUE masks after Rosso, and the *History of Jason* (1563; twenty-six plates), narrative scenes in strapwork grotesque borders after Rosso's pupil Léonard THIRY who worked with PRIMATICCIO at Fontainebleau. Boyvin also published jewellery designs (twenty plates), dedicated to the royal jeweller Aulbin du Carnoy, appointed in 1598. In 1566 he designed plates and a title for *Architecture* by the Huguenot architect Julien Mauclerc, only published in 1648. One of the plates, a panel of ACANTHUS after Marcantonio Raimondi, was issued by Boyvin in 1575. In 1569 Boyvin engraved plates for the edition of Besson's *Theatrum Machinarum* with J. A. DUCERCEAU.

Bracquemond, Joseph Auguste, called Félix (1833–1914) Bracquemond studied painting under Joseph Guichard. He was later distinguished as an etcher and showed at the first Impressionist exhibition in 1874. His discovery of some woodcuts by Katsushika Hokusai (1760–1849) in the print-seller Delâtre's shop in 1856 led to an interest in Japanese art. In the early 1860s Bracquemond designed plates for DECK. In 1866 he wrote to the Emperor Napoleon III asking for employment at the Sèvres porcelain factory. In 1866 to 1867 he designed an earthenware service for Lebœuf & Milliet decorated with animals and birds taken from Japanese *ukiyo-e* albums, mainly Hokusai's Mangwa; it was painted by the potter and glass-maker Eugène Rousseau (1827–91) and shown at the PARIS 1867 EXHIBITION and the VIENNA 1873 EXHIBITION. In 1867 Bracquemond became a member of the Société du Jing-Lar, which united French enthusiasts for Japan, including M. L. SOLON. In 1870 Bracquemond worked briefly at the Sèvres factory, but in 1872 he persuaded his American friend Charles Haviland to set up a design studio attached to the Limoges porcelain factory founded by his father. It started operations in Auteuil in 1873 with Bracquemond as artistic director; he brought in Albert and Édouard Dammouse, Eugène Delaplanche and in 1875 Ernest Chaplet. In 1875 Bracquemond designed Le Service Parisien, with Japanese-style landscapes, and in 1879 a service produced by Barluet & Co. of Creil-Montereau, painted with flowers and scrolling tendrils anticipating ART NOUVEAU ornament. In 1882 the Haviland studio closed. In 1885 Bracquemond published *Du Dessin et de la couleur*, a treatise on colour in design. In about 1900 he designed jewels, including an enamelled mirror with a figure by Rodin, and the decorations of a villa, La Sapinière, for the wealthy banker Baron Vitta (1860–1940). Alexandre CHARPENTIER and Jules CHERET were also involved in Vitta's billiard-room, exhibited in Paris in 1902.

Bradley, Will (1868–1962) Born in Boston, the son of a cartoonist, Bradley began work as a wood engraver in about 1879 and pursued that trade in Chicago. In 1893 he opened a studio there. Under the influence of GRASSET and Beardsley, Bradley designed covers (1894) for the Chicago trade magazine *The Inland*

Printer and posters which gave rise to much international acclaim, shown by BING in 1895, illustrated in *La Plume*, the 'POSTER' and 'Das PLAKAT'. From 1896 his Wayside Press in Springfield, Massachusetts, published *Bradley His Book* (1896–7), a short-lived magazine; Bradley also intended to produce wallpapers, tapestries and fabrics. In 1897 he showed furniture designs at the Boston Arts & Crafts Exhibition and designed six covers for *International Studio*. From 1901 to 1902 Bradley published designs for furniture and interiors in the *Ladies' Home Journal*, some later republished in *Documents d'Architecture Moderne*; their style is strongly influenced by MACKINTOSH, VOYSEY and, above all, BAILLIE SCOTT. Bradley was later mainly active as a typographer and illustrator, and from 1915 was art director of the Hearst publishing and film corporation. He retired in 1930.

Brandely, Jean Brandely worked as a designer of furniture in Paris in the 1850s and 1860s. His designs won a medal at the PARIS 1855 EXHIBITION, after which he published *Le Glaneur ornemaniste*, twenty-five lithographed plates of elaborate ornament in the GROTESQUE, ROCOCO and NEO-CLASSICAL styles, many with a strong ingredient of NATURALISM. At the PARIS 1867 EXHIBITION, Charles-Guillaume Diehl showed an extraordinary Merovingian medal cabinet and three pieces in the Greek style, all designed by Brandely.

Brandt, Marianne Born in Chemnitz in 1893, Brandt studied painting in Weimar, before travelling to Norway and France. In 1923 she became a teacher in the metalwork shop of the BAUHAUS, run by MOHOLY-NAGY. In 1924 she designed a nickel-silver ashtray and teapot composed of ruthlessly geometric forms. There followed an adjustable ceiling light (1926, with Hans Przyrembel), a glass and aluminium globe ceiling light (1926), a wall light with a folding arm (1927) and the Kandem bedside table lamp (1927). Several of Brandt's designs were industrially produced by Körting & Matthieson of Leipzig and other firms. They have been established as MODERN CLASSICS. From 1949 Brandt was professor of industrial design in Dresden. She later settled back in Chemnitz, now called Karl-Marx-Stadt.

Brangwyn, Sir Frank (1867–1956) Born in Bruges, the son of an émigré Anglo-Welsh architect who ran a church furnishing shop, Brangwyn moved to London in 1875. He was befriended by MACKMURDO and by Harold Rathbone. Brangwyn studied in the South Kensington Museum and from about 1882 to 1884 was employed in the William MORRIS shop in Oxford Street. From 1885 he exhibited paintings at the Royal Academy; he was elected to the Academy in 1919 and was knighted in 1941. In 1895 Brangwyn designed murals for BING. He also designed stained glass for Bing in 1897 and in 1899 a poster for the Bing Exhibition held at the Grafton Gallery in London. Brangwyn's bedroom for E. J. Davies was illustrated in the 'STUDIO' (1900) and in Walter Shaw Sparrow's *The British Home of Today* (1904). He designed interiors for the British pavilions at the Venice Biennales of 1905 and 1907, the former by J. S. Henry. In 1906 Brangwyn supplied unexecuted designs for a dining-room at Ca' Rezzonico, but his dining-room for Casa Cuseni, Taormina (1910), survives. It includes panelling, chairs, sideboard and table in an elegant rectilinear Arts & Crafts style. In 1910 Paul Turpin executed a large cabinet for Brangwyn's own use; he also made the Brangwyn furniture shown in the Ghent 1913 Exhibition. Around this date Brangwyn's reputation as a designer was considerable; his carpets were praised by MUTHESIUS. However, he designed little more until about 1930. At that period he designed marquetry panels for the Rowley Gallery, and in 1931 three dining-rooms for the Canadian Pacific S.S. *Empress of Britain*. In 1930 E. Pollard & Co. of London mounted an exhibition of furniture, ceramics, glass and electric lights by Brangwyn, together with rugs by Alexander Morton and carpets by Templetons of Glasgow. It was not a commercial success. In 1931 stained glass by Brangwyn was installed in St Patrick's Cathedral, Dublin.

Brenna, Vincenzo Born in Florence in about 1745, Brenna was in Rome in 1767, when he described himself as '*architetto romano*'. In the early 1770s Brenna investigated Roman wall-paintings for the antiquary Ludovico Mirri, and did drawings together with Franciszek Smuglewicz (1745–1807), published as *Vestigia delle Terme di Tito* (Rome, 1776–8; eighty plates). Brenna also drew the plates and designed decorative frames for a three-volume numismatic treatise (Rome, 1781, 1783 and 1788). In 1777 he was employed as a draughtsman by Count Potocki and moved to Poland, where he worked as a painter of NEO-CLASSICAL GRO-TESQUE wall decorations for Princess Lubomirska, the Potocki family and the King, Stanislas Augustus Poniatowski. In about 1784 Brenna moved to St Petersburg, where he worked as a decorative painter for Grand Duke Paul at Pavlovsk under CAMERON. He became involved in architectural works and when Paul succeeded as Tsar in 1796 supplanted Cameron as court architect. Brenna worked for the Tsar at Gatčina, where he designed many interiors, including furniture, and also designed many court ceremonies including the funeral of the Duke of Württemberg in 1797. In 1802 he moved to Dresden,

where he died, probably in 1814. Avid for honours and wealth, Brenna developed from an archaeological grotesque manner towards a more massive and imperial style similar to that of Cameron and suited to the taste of his Russian patrons.

Brentel, Friedrich The son of a painter and engraver from Lauingen, Brentel settled in Strasbourg in 1601 and died there in 1651. He was active as heraldic artist, calligrapher, engraver and painter, running a large and prolific workshop. In 1596 Brentel published some twelve plates of friezes, borders and ornament clearly intended for engraving on silver; they incorporate medallion heads and light scrolled foliate ornament. Brentel also published in 1617 a suite of STRAPWORK cartouches enclosing landscapes.

Brescia, Bartolomeo da Born in Brescia in 1506, Bartolomeo was active there as an engraver until his death in about 1577. He designed elaborate STRAP-WORK cartouches, probably influenced by BOS, for a book of EMBLEMS, *Carmina accademicorum occultorum* (Brescia, 1568; fifteen plates).

Brescia, Giovanni Antonio da Giovanni Antonio da Brescia, two of whose prints bear dates, 1507 and 1509, was responsible for some of the earliest Italian engravings of ornament, candelabra-shaped compositions with RENAIS-SANCE GROTESQUES. He was strongly influenced by Mantegna. In about 1515 he seems to have moved from Brescia to Rome, where he did prints of Roman antiquities, one of which, a base and capital, was copied by ALTDORFER. His prints of Roman metal vessels, a VASE with an embossed mask and a bowl supported by a tripod, were the earliest such patterns for Renaissance goldsmiths. Brescia's later works were much influenced by Marcantonio Raimondi. His ornaments were widely copied, for instance by Italian potters and by J. A. DuCerceau.

Bretschneider, Andreas the Younger Born in Dresden in 1578, Bretschneider moved to Leipzig in about 1611, becoming a citizen there in 1615. He was a painter, book illustrator and designer of title-pages. His *New Modelbuch* (1619) contains forty-eight plates of free scrolled floral grotesque designs for needlework, much more accomplished than most designs of this type. His title-page borrows from Lucas Kilian's *Newes Gradesca Büchlein* (1607).

Breu, Jörg Born in Augsburg in about 1475, the son of a weaver, Breu was a pupil of the painter Ulrich Apt from 1493. He went to Austria during his journeyman years, and in 1502 became a master in Augsburg. Breu was active as a designer of stained glass, and in 1515 designed decorations for the prayer-book of the Emperor Maximilian I. Breu travelled to Italy about that date and thenceforward worked in a Renaissance style, especially in designs for woodcuts, notably those for Alciati's *Emblematum Liber* (Augsburg, 1531). In about 1520 he designed a suite of the twelve months to be executed in stained glass for Georg Hoechstetter. Among the many designers influenced by Breu, Stimmer was perhaps the most important. Breu retired in 1534 and died in 1537.

Breuer, Marcel Lajos (1902–81) Born in Pécs, Hungary, the son of a doctor, Breuer spent a brief period in Vienna, working with the architect Bolek, before moving to the Bauhaus in Weimar in 1920. At the Bauhaus, Breuer specialized in furniture. Apart from his African chair, a rough-hewn throne, representing a brief excursus into the romantic

handcraft tradition, Breuer was from the beginning inclined towards purity of form. An early tea-table (1921), a round slab held towards the top of five square-section legs, and an armchair (1922) of ruthless rectilinearity reflect this orientation. In 1922 to 1923 Breuer executed furniture, some designed by Georg Muche, for the Bauhaus model house, Am Horn, erected at Weimar. From 1925 to 1928 Breuer taught at the Bauhaus in Dessau as head of the furniture workshop. In 1925 Breuer is said to have bought an Adler bicycle and to have had the idea of using the material and technology of its chromed-steel handlebars for a chair. The Wassily chair, named after Kandinsky, resulted. Fabric in tension as upholstery, structure of seat and frame clearly separated by space, the chair seems influenced by Constructivist ideas. Apart from a technical experiment shown by the mechanic Gerhard Stüttgen in Cologne in 1923, the Wassily chair was the first tubular-steel chair. In 1926 Breuer designed a stool with legs, side stretchers and top rails formed as one continuous length of tubular steel, an object of irreducible simplicity. In 1925 Breuer designed a modular system of storage furniture with rectangular units. He helped design interiors at the Bauhaus and in 1927 designed the interior of the Piscator house in Berlin. In 1928 Breuer set up in private practice in Berlin and around 1930 designed several interiors of spartan and clinical Modernity, overwhelmingly horizontal and rectilinear, for example Dr Paul Vogler's clinic and Dr Leopold Reidermeister's house. In 1928 Breuer designed the Cesca chair, his own enormously successful version of the cantilever chairs pioneered by Stam and Mies van der Rohe. It had a caned back and seat, and used a new heavy tubing. Writing in 1928 Breuer described metal furniture as style-less and stated that it was intended as nothing less than the necessary apparatus of modern life. At this period he also designed a glass table (1928), a tea trolley (1928) and other chairs. From 1931 Breuer travelled widely in Europe and North Africa. In 1932 his first building, the Haus Harnischmacher, was erected in Wiesbaden. In 1933 Breuer designed a group of aluminium furniture of curvilinear outline for an international competition in Paris, including chairs, a chaise longue and stacking tables. In 1935 Breuer came to England, where he practised as an architect in partnership with F. R. S. Yorke. In 1936 he designed nesting tables, a dining table, a square table, dining chairs and the Long chair for ISOKON. All used laminated wood. The Long chair, made in a short and a long version, was similar to Breuer's aluminium chaise longue. In 1937 Breuer succeeded GROPIUS as Controller of Design at Isokon and designed the Isobar at the Lawn Road flats, but then left England. In America, Breuer worked as an architect in partnership with Gropius from 1937 to 1941. He was a professor of architecture at Harvard from 1937 to 1947. In 1946 he designed a new group of laminated-wood furniture. At his death Breuer was a revered master of the Modern style, and his early furniture, accorded 'CLASSIC' status, was again in production.

Briceau In 1709 Briceau, a master goldsmith in Paris, published a suite (eight plates) of delicate and scrolly ACANTHUS ornament for enamelling or engraving on watch-cases etc., one plate including an alphabet. He was mentioned by POUGET in 1762.

Bridgens, Richard Bridgens was in contact with George BULLOCK in Liverpool from about 1810; he showed a view of Bullock's Egyptian Hall in Piccadilly at the Liverpool Academy in 1812. In 1813 'Richard Bridgens Architect' used Bullock's London address when showing at the Royal Academy. In 1817 ACKERMANN's *Repository* illustrated a chair in the late-17th-century style made by Bullock and designed by Bridgens for Battle Abbey. Bridgens also designed furniture for Abbotsford, Sir Walter Scott's house, where Bullock worked, and in 1818, the year of Bullock's death, Bridgens showed a view of the armoury at Abbotsford at the Royal Academy. He had a London address then. Also in 1818 Bridgens prepared the text and drawings for *Sefton Church* (1822, second edition 1835). He probably then travelled to Italy and prepared his *Costumes of Italy, Switzerland and France* (1821). In 1820 Bridgens showed at the Royal Academy a restoration of stained glass from Malines and in 1822 an 'Attempt to improve the Barberini candelabra'. From about 1819 to 1824 he was engaged on the design of Elizabethan furniture and interior decoration at Aston Hall, Birmingham, for James Watt, with whom Bridgens had been in contact in 1816 when he was involved with Bullock. In 1820 he was also working as an interior designer for the Boulton family. In 1824 he engraved plates for Samuel Rush Meyrick's *A Critical Inquiry into Antient Armour* (1824). In 1825 Cockerell reported that Bridgens had left Birmingham for lack of work. His last Royal Academy exhibit, of 1826, showed the east front of Aston Hall. He subsequently went to the West Indies for a period of seven years, recorded in his *West Indian Scenery* (1836). Bridgens was back in England by 1834, when he worked as a draughtsman on Henry SHAW's *Details of Elizabethan Architecture* (1839). In 1833 Augustus PUGIN's sale included 'Bridgens's (R.) Furniture with Candelabra and Interior Decoration'. This may represent drawings or a lost early edition of Bridgens's most ambitious work, *Furniture with Candelabra and Interior Decoration* (1838;

fifty-eight plates). The handsome coloured plates contain twenty-five 'Grecian' designs, twenty-seven 'Elizabethan' and seven 'GOTHIC'. Many show executed designs, mainly for Aston Hall, both from the 1820s and from Bridgens's second involvement there from about 1834 to 1837. Others are of existing objects, for instance the Gothic chair in St Mary's Hall, Coventry, also shown in Shaw's *Ancient Furniture* (1836). Bridgens's main importance is as the most significant pioneer of the Elizabethan revival.

Brin, Hertzig von Brin worked as an imperial goldsmith in Vienna. He published three suites of black designs for enamelling including GROTESQUES, animals, trophies, birds, butterflies etc., of four plates each; one suite is dated 1589, another 1592.

Briseux, Charles Étienne (1680–1754) Born in Baume-les-Dames, Franche-Comté, Briseux was active as an architect in Paris. He also published architectural textbooks. His *L'Art de bâtir des maisons de campagne* (1743) includes ROCOCO VASES, cartouches, panelling, chimneypieces, overdoors, bed niches, and iron balconies, stairs, gates and grilles. His text praises Vassé and PINEAU. Briseux practised a vigorous but slightly coarse rococo, and his panelling designs may have been supplied by his engraver, BABEL. Briseux's ironwork designs were re-used in a *Nouveau Livre de serrurerie* (1756) by a smith named Michel.

Brisville, Hugues Brisville, a Parisian smith, was responsible for a suite of competent designs for BAROQUE ironwork, *Diverses pièces de serrurerie* (1663; sixteen plates, engraved by Jean I BERAIN). A copy was owned by the English architect John James in the early 18th century.

Brongniart,   Alexandre-Théodore (1739–1813) Born in Paris, Brongniart studied architecture under Jacques-François BLONDEL and Étienne-Louis Boullée (1728–99). From 1765 he was a prolific designer of buildings in Paris and elsewhere, his final project being the Bourse in Paris, begun in 1807. In 1800 his son, Alexandre, was appointed administrator of the Sèvres porcelain factory, and from 1801 until his death Brongniart designed for the factory on a regular basis. His works include the Olympic service (1804–7), Napoleon's private service (1807–10), on which he collaborated closely with Vivant DENON, and the Seasons service, uncompleted at his death. Brongniart also, in 1808, designed carpets.

Bronzino, Angelo (1503–72) Born in Monticelli near Florence as Angelo di Cosimo di Mariano, Bronzino was taught by PONTORMO, whose assistant and collaborator he became. From 1530 to 1532 Bronzino was in Urbino, and in 1539 he entered the service of Duke Cosimo de' Medici in Florence and designed decorations for his marriage to Eleanora da Toledo. Bronzino was the principal decorator in Florence up to VASARI's arrival in 1554. From 1545 Bronzino was employed by Cosimo to design for his newly founded tapestry manufactory, manned by Flemish weavers. Three portières (1545 and 1546) were his first executed designs. Bronzino's main project, however, was a series of twenty tapestries on the Life of Joseph, for the Salone dei Dugento of the Palazzo Vecchio, of which SALVIATI designed one and Pontormo three, but the rest were by Bronzino, who from 1548 was assisted by Raffaelino dal Colle. In 1549 the young ALLORI assisted on some borders. Bronzino's tapestry designs are predominantly MANNERIST, elegant and sometimes contorted figure compositions, with strong echoes of RAPHAEL and Giulio ROMANO.

Brosamer, Hans Born in about 1500, probably in Fulda, Brosamer was active as painter, engraver and sculptor there and in Nuremberg, Erfurt and Frankfurt, where his death in 1552 probably took place. He was strongly influenced by BINCK and ALDEGREVER, and supplied fifty-seven illustrations to the Luther Bible of 1550. Brosamer's *New Kunstbüchlein* of about 1545 contained thirty-nine woodcut plates, a second edition quickly adding a further seven plates. They consist principally of silver cups of the traditional German type, together with four designs for pendants and another four for whistles. His ornamental vocabulary, handled with great directness and simplicity, is close to FLÖTNER'S, and includes putti, ACANTHUS, medallion heads and dolphins, applied to lobed and fluted forms influenced by Italian RENAISSANCE prints of candelabra. Brosamer's pendants are also Italianate. In 1570 the *Kunstbüchlein* was reissued on a smaller scale. Its designs were widely influential, even on cups made in England. Brosamer also published a very fine engraving of a mannered ewer with a shell spout and snake handle.

Brown, Ford Madox (1821–93) Born in Calais, the son of a ship's purser, Brown studied painting in Bruges and Ghent under pupils of DAVID and in Antwerp under Baron Gustave Wappers (1803–74). He later travelled to Paris (1840) and Rome (1845–6), where he became acquainted with the work of the German Nazarenes. In London in 1848 he met ROSSETTI, Holman Hunt and Millais and was closely associated with the Pre-Raphaelite Brotherhood, although he was never a member. In the early 1850s Brown was involved in worker education. In 1856 he met William MORRIS and in 1861 became a founder member of the Morris firm. In 1858 he joined the Hogarth Club but resigned in 1859, because they refused to allow him to exhibit his furniture designs, probably four designs for chairs executed in 1857. About this date Brown designed a massy X-framed dining table for Holman Hunt. In 1861 Brown helped to decorate SEDDON'S King René cabinet, shown at the LONDON 1862 EXHIBITION along with a turned sofa designed for Brown by Rossetti, and a bookcase by Brown himself, with painted decoration depicting the life of an English family from 1810 to 1860. Brown also designed furniture for Charles Seddon. Up to about 1874 he designed for the Morris firm not only furniture – he was the pioneer of Morris rush-seated furniture – but also wallpaper, embroidery, velvet, tiles and glass. In 1868 Brown illustrated *Lyra Germanica*. From 1878 to 1893 Brown was engaged on decorations for Manchester Town Hall. In 1887 he designed a dressing chest, 'something a clever workman could make for himself', for an artisan cottage shown at Manchester. The 'CABINET MAKER AND ART FURNISHER' noted cut-out holes for handles as a novel feature, but was generally slighting. Furniture by Brown was shown at the 1890 ARTS & CRAFTS EXHIBITION, and after his death his role as a pioneer design reformer was widely recognized.

Brown, Richard Probably of Devon origin, Brown had a small London practice as an architect, exhibiting designs at the Royal Academy from 1804 to 1828. His main activity was as a 'Professor of PERSPECTIVE' and M. A. NICHOLSON was among the pupils at his drawing school in 1812. Brown's *Principles of Practical Perspective* (1815, reprinted 1835) was dedicated to Sir John SOANE (1753–1837) and its plates reveal an acquaintance with Soane's virtuoso draughtsman, Joseph Gandy (1771–1843). *Principles* is technically an accomplished work, enlivened by many irrelevant but entertaining observations, as 'Whitewashed towers injurious to the picturesque'. *The Rudiments of Drawing Cabinet and Upholstery Furniture* (1822, reprinted 1835) was ostensibly another work on drawing but in fact one of the most interesting and handsome early 19th-century English furniture pattern-books. CHIPPENDALE and SHERATON are scorned in the preface, and HOPE, George SMITH, PERCIER, PIRANESI, HAMILTON, TATHAM and MOSES named as models. The twenty-five coloured plates of furniture are in a heavy Grecian style, with lavish use of associative ornament, for instance a mask of Clio, the muse of history, on a library table. Brown pays a tribute to the originality of the designs of George BULLOCK, who had been in partnership with Brown's friend Gandy in 1810; and it is possible that Brown himself may have been a designer in the Bullock stable, certain of the designs in the *Rudiments* being close to the Bullock style. *An Elucidation of the Principles of Drawing Ornaments* (1822; seven plates) is mainly devoted to the rich ACANTHUS ornament fashionable at this date. Brown seems later to have retired to Devon and published from there his *Domestic Architecture* (1842), an over-weeningly ambitious performance, with information and illustrations on furniture design from Greece to Burma: Henry SHAW's *Specimens of Ancient Furniture* (1836) was among Brown's source-books. *Domestic* was followed by *Sacred Architecture* (1845).

Brun, Franz Brun was probably active in Cologne. He published a number of very old-fashioned plates of ornament, including leafy MORESQUES around medallion heads, reminiscent of English plasterwork, friezes with scrolly leaves and buds in a manner looking back to the BEHAMS and ALDEGREVER, and some designs for moresque borders. One suite is dated 1596.

Brunetti, Gaetano An ornamental painter from Bologna, Brunetti published the first book of ornaments in the ROCOCO style to appear in England, *60 Different Sorts of Ornaments* (1736). The plates were said to be '. . . very usefull to Painters, Sculptors, Stone-Carvers, Wood-Carvers, Silversmiths, &c.' and included cartouches, mantelpieces, tombs, tables and chairs, all of them in a very vigorous and sometimes almost BAROQUE early rococo style. Brunetti worked with Amigoni at Chandos House and elsewhere in about 1736. By 1739 he was in Paris, where he was active as a decorative painter with his son Paolo Antonio Brunetti (1751–83). Brunetti's *Ornaments* was reprinted in Paris in about 1857.

Brunn, Isaac Brunn was active as an engraver in Strasbourg. In 1624 he published *Animalium Quadrupedum variorum typi varii* (ten plates), depictions of animals for the use of engravers on silver. He also engraved some of SYMONY's designs and copied from LE BLON.

Brustolon, Andrea (1662–1732) Born at Belluno, the son of a wood-carver, Brustolon trained first under his father and then from 1677 in Venice under Filippo Parodi (1630–1702). From 1679 to 1680 Brustolon was in Rome. Thereafter he stayed in Venice until 1695, when he settled in his native Belluno. Brustolon designed and executed furniture for Venetian patricians and altars, tabernacles and other furnishings for churches in Venice and elsewhere. He practised an elaborate BAROQUE style incorporating figures and scrolled ACANTHUS, directly influenced by BERNINI and

Ciro FERRI. Surviving designs by Brustolon include armchairs, frames, tables, VASES, crucifixes, tabernacles and a baldachin.

Bruyn, Abraham de Born in 1540 in Antwerp, Bruyn settled in Breda in 1570, but was by 1577 in Cologne. He was again in Antwerp in 1580 but probably died in Cologne in 1587. Bruyn issued about 240 finely engraved plates, many of costume. His *Equitum Descriptio* (1576; twelve plates) has a title with a rusticated gable at its summit, influenced by Hans VREDEMAN DE VRIES. His earliest designs for ornament, friezes with hunting scenes, were published in 1565 to 1566. Bruyn also published fine GROTESQUE ornaments for pendants, and a series of oval mythological figures in grotesque borders (1584). Two of the latter, Andromeda and Danae, were used as the basis of overmantels at Charlton House, Kent, about 1607, and Boston House, Brentford, about 1623.

Bruyn, Nicolas de Born in Antwerp, the son of Abraham de BRUYN, Nicolas de Bruyn became a member of the Antwerp Guild in 1610. In 1617 he was in Rotterdam, where he died at an advanced age in 1652. His earliest dated prints were published in 1594. They include bold medallion heads of the Caesars (twelve plates, some with STRAPWORK frames). A suite of medallion heads of kings, also 1594, have very rich and fine GROTESQUE borders with flowers, birds, animals and insects. Another 1594 suite, friezes with putti, hounds, vines and a skull, represents an evocation of the early RENAISSANCE style of Lucan van LEYDEN and ALDEGREVER. Bruyn also published oval allegories of the virtues and the elements in grotesque borders. All his engraved designs are of high quality and refinement.

Bry, Johann Theodor de (1561–1623)
Born in Liège, the son of Theodor de BRY, Johann Theodor de Bry was active as designer and engraver of ornament in Frankfurt, working in the style of his father, and sometimes collaborating with his brother Johann Israel de Bry. In 1604 Johann Theodor de Bry engraved a dish for the Archduke Maximilian of Tirol; he also issued a number of circular designs for engraving on such dishes, some with central scenes after other artists, including H. S. BEHAM and Abraham Bloemart. Other designs by Bry include scissor cases, thimbles, buttons, daggers, knives and châtelaines, the latter entitled *PENDANTS de cleffs pour les Femmes propre pour les Argentiers*. Bry also copied pendant designs by Daniel MIGNOT.

Bry, Theodor de (1528–98) Born in Liège, Bry left the Netherlands in 1570 to avoid religious persecution and settled in Frankfurt. There he was a prolific designer of engraved ornament. His works include four circular panels with medallions surrounded by dense GROTESQUE ornament (1578): they are virulently anti-Catholic, one depicting William of Orange as 'Capitaine prudent', another the Duke of Alba as 'Capitaine des Follie'. Another series of round panels has medallion heads of Roman emperors and Latin mottos linked by STRAPWORK grotesques. *Manches de Coutiaus* presents designs for knife handles, and other Bry designs show ornaments for swords, daggers and scabbards, and straps, buckles, bracelets, rings and other types of jewellery. *Spitze und Laubwerck fur Die Goldschmit: Grotis e point pour graver Bassin aeigir tass et sallir* (1589; four plates) comprises designs for scrolly grotesque borders inhabited by birds and insects for engraving on silver ewers, cups and salt-cellars. *Grotish fur alle Kunstler: Grotis pour Tous Artisien* (four plates) contains friezes, and Bry issued many others including a lively marine series. *Emblemata Nobilitati et Vulgo Scitu Digna* (1593; sixty plates) presents emblems and heraldic shields within elaborate grotesque frames; in the similar *Icones quinquaginta virorum illustrium* (1597; fifty plates) the borders contain portraits of famous men, including Erasmus and the Emperor RUDOLF II. *Nova Alphati Effictio* (1595, second edition Cologne, 1613, Johann Bussemacher; twenty-four plates) presents an alphabet in the manner of Cornelis FLORIS's initials of the 1540s, each letter carrying a portentous theological message; this surprising throwback to the style of Bry's youth was designed in collaboration with his sons, Johann Theodor and Johann Israel. In 1587 Bry engraved commemorative plates of Sir Philip Sidney's funeral in London, and the influence of his engraved ornament was equally wide. A panel of ornament by Bry was incorporated in the title of *Erotopaegnion Herus et Leandri* (Frankfurt, 1627).

Bücherfreunde, Zeitschrift für (1897–1921) Published from Bielefeld and Leipzig under the editorship of Fedor von Zobeltitz, this finely illustrated magazine combined excellent technical and historical articles with a wide coverage of contemporary book, poster and postcard design.

Buffágnotti, Carlo Antonio Born in Bologna in 1660, Buffagnotti was taught to draw by Domenico Santi (1621–94), a pupil of Agostino MITELLI. Buffagnotti engraved a number of ornaments after Santi's designs, one suite being dated 1683 and another 1694. From 1690 to 1698 he was a music publisher and issued richly decorated scores by Torelli and other composers. From 1703 he was an assistant to Ferdinando Bibiena and engraved many prints of architecture and theatre after his designs. Buffagnotti himself designed a suite of VASES (eight plates) and *Varii capricii di fughe* (twelve plates), a series of free and BAROQUE cartouches, consoles and ornament, reminiscent of Mitelli. Buffagnotti, who worked in Genoa, Turin and Ferrara as well as his native Bologna, was still active in 1715.

Bugatti, Carlo (1856–1940) Born in Milan, the son of a sculptor, Bugatti was educated at the Brera. An early interest in architecture gave way to a concentration on furniture. In 1880 he designed a bedroom suite for his sister Luigia, who married the painter Giovanni Segantini (1858–99) in that year. In 1888 he set up a workshop in Milan and showed furniture at the Italian exhibition in London; it enjoyed some success and by 1895 his designs seem to have been pirated by Ernst Kopp of Berlin. In 1900 his furniture was awarded a silver medal at the PARIS EXHIBITION. This was followed by a Diploma of Honour at the TURIN 1902 EXHIBITION. Bugatti moved from Milan to Paris in about 1904 and mainly devoted himself to painting, but his furniture designs continued to be produced by De Vechi of Milan. In 1907 the Galerie Hébrard in Paris showed silver designed by Bugatti: more was shown at the Salon des Artistes-Décorateurs in 1910 and 1911. Bugatti was very much the self-conscious autodidact, jealous of his originality and individuality. His furniture designs express an indeterminate exoticism in decoration, similar to but not precisely identifiable with the international Moorish craze of the 1880s: in 1888 the 'CABINET MAKER AND ART FURNISHER', which also pertinently compared Bugatti to DRESSER, suggested Rider Haggard as a parallel! But his furniture forms, when they were not wilfully eccentric, can display a radical originality which anticipates the possibilities of modern materials. His metalwork, using imaginary zoomorphic forms and decoration, is equally idiosyncratic. Bugatti's work at Turin attracted attention in 'DEUTSCHE KUNST UND DEKORATION' and 'KUNST UND KUNSTHANDWERK' and his silver was later praised by 'ART ET DÉCORATION'. His son Ettore (1881–1947) and grandson Jean (1909–39) achieved fame as automobile designers.

Builder, The (1843–present) Subtitled *An Illustrated Weekly Magazine for the Drawing-Room, the Studio, the Office, the Workshop and the Cottage* this was the most important mid-19th-century English architectural paper. From 1844 to 1883 its editor was George Godwin (1815–88). It contained much information on design. In 1966 its title changed to *Building* and it is now mainly a technical trade journal.

Building News (1855–1926) Subtitled *A Weekly Illustrated Record of the Progress of Architecture*, the *Building News* was one of the great late-19th-century architectural magazines. It contained much information on design. At the end it merged with the 'ARCHITECT'.

Bull, Hans de Bull issued about thirty plates of small black ornaments for enamelling on jewellery, some dated 1592 and others 1595. A suite engraved in Prague by Aegidius Sadeler in the year 1604 (six plates) includes black stretched GROTESQUES for rings, pendants and other jewels and a plate of monkeys.

Bullet, Pierre (1639–1716) The son of a mason, Bullet was trained as an architect under François Blondel (1617–86) and practised in Paris from 1672. He became a member of the French Academy in 1685. Bullet's *Livre nouveau de Cheminées* (six plates) was reprinted in Amsterdam, together with the similar designs by FRANCARD.

Bullock, George Born in Liverpool, Bullock exhibited as a sculptor at the Royal Academy and the Liverpool Academy from 1804 to 1816. He was President of the Liverpool Academy from 1810 to 1811. In 1805 Bullock, in partnership with a man named Stoakes, had a business as cabinet-makers, general furnishers and marble workers. From 1809 to 1811 Bullock's partner was the architect and draughtsman Joseph Gandy (1771–1843); they were 'Architects, Modellers, Sculptors, Marble Masons, Cabinet Makers & Upholsterers'. The *Stranger in Liverpool* (1812) stated that Bullock's showrooms contained '. . .tripods, candelabras, antique lamps, sphinxes, griffins, etc., in marble, bronze and artificial stone'. By 1813 Bullock had established himself in London, where he continued to work as a sculpture- and furniture-maker; he was also the proprietor of the Mona Marble Works, which exploited quarries on Anglesey. From 1816 to 1817 ACKERMANN'S *Repository* contained six plates of Bullock designs for furniture and for chimneypieces. A seventh plate appeared in 1824. From 1814 to 1819 furniture by Bullock was supplied to Blair Castle, and from 1816 to 1818 to Abbotsford, in collaboration with the architect William Atkinson. Sir Walter Scott, who was friendly with Bullock, described his stand for a bust of Shakespeare as 'positively the most elegant and appropriate piece of furniture I ever saw'. Bullock died in 1818. Daniel Terry, Scott's adviser, wrote: 'Poor Bullock's concern is entirely to cease and in another week or two is to be sold up. Mr BRIDGENS is gone to Italy, and all the rest gone to the Devil I believe . . .' In 1819 *The Times* announced that 'British Oak Furniture . . . to the late Mr Bullock's designs' was being made by the cabinet-maker E. T. Cox. The 1819 sale of Bullock's house amounted to 250 lots. Bullock worked mainly in a massive NEO-CLASSICAL style but he was also a pioneer in the use of native plants for ornament and in the revival of GOTHIC and Elizabethan forms. He also revived the brass inlay technique associated with BOULLE. Bullock was a designer himself, and his stable of designers included Bridgens and, probably, Richard BROWN, who praised his works, although describing them as 'massy and ponderous'.

Buoll, Hans Friedrich In 1679 the Zürich engraver Conrad Meyer (1618–89) published a plate of a triumphal car designed and made by Buoll, who worked in Kaiserstuhl. It is one of the jolliest of the genre, elaborated with scrolly ornament, including tamed AURICULAR elements.

Buontalenti, Bernardo (1531–1608) Born in Florence, Buontalenti was taken under Medici protection as an orphan in 1547. He acquired a knowledge of painting and architecture in the circle of SALVIATI, BRONZINO and VASARI. In 1556 he was active as a military engineer and probably visited Rome. From 1557 he was in Florence, although he visited Spain in 1563 with Francesco de' Medici, whose teacher he had been appointed by Grand Duke Cosimo and whose passion for scientific and mechanical studies Buontalenti shared and fostered. He was appointed to an official post as an engineer in 1568. From 1569 to 1580 he designed decorations at Francesco de' Medici's villa at Pratolino, including the extraordinary grotto. From 1574 to 1589 he created the Tribuna in the Uffizi, including its inlaid floor and a central table supporting an ebony temple, completed in 1587 and removed in about 1634. Buontalenti also designed many silver vessels in 1575 and 1576, and many

hardstone vessels, including in 1583 a lapis lazuli VASE which was mounted by the virtuoso goldsmith from Delft, Jacques Bilivert (1550–1603). Buontalenti collaborated with Grand Duke Francesco in his search for the secret of oriental porcelain, and almost certainly designed some of the pieces produced by his factory from 1575 to 1587. Buontalenti designed decorations for the marriage of Francesco I to Giovanna d'Austria in 1565 in collaboration with Vasari and for the funeral of Cosimo I in 1574 with Allori. He later became Francesco I's director of such events, including the marriages of Virginia de' Medici to Cesare d'Este in 1585, and Ferdinando I to Christina of Lorraine in 1589. In 1577 he designed a baptismal font for Prince Filippo de' Medici. Buontalenti worked in a refined but energetic MANNERIST style. His use of distorted and melting mask forms anticipates AURICULAR ornament.

Burges, William (1827–81) Born in London, the son of a successful engineer, Burges was given a copy of A. W. N. PUGIN's *Contrasts* on his fourteenth birthday and Pugin became a life-long inspiration. Burges started to study engineering at King's College, but after a year took up articles in 1844 in the office of the architect Edward Blore (1787–1879). In 1859 he moved to the office of Matthew Digby WYATT, whom he assisted on *Metal Work and its Artistic Design* (1852) and *The Industrial Arts of the Nineteenth Century* (1851–3), gaining a detailed knowledge of design and techniques in the applied arts; his first publication was an article on 'Damascening' in the 'JOURNAL OF DESIGN' (1850). In 1853 Burges designed candlesticks and vestments shown in Leighton's painting, *Cimabue's Madonna*. In 1851 Burges became assistant and later partner to the architect Henry Clutton (1819–93), another product of Blore's office, whose *Domestic Architecture of France* (1853) Burges helped to prepare. In 1856 the partners won the 1854 competition for Lille Cathedral, but they subsequently quarrelled. The Lille designs were in a massive French 13th-century style, with a painted organ-case, which anticipated Burges's later furniture. In 1857 Burges won the competition for a Crimea Memorial Church in Constantinople, with a richly polychrome design in a 13th-century style. Neither Lille nor the Crimean church were built. In 1858 Burges began to design furniture. His Yatman cabinet (1858) proclaimed a new style based on the only two surviving pieces of elaborate French 13th-century furniture, cupboards at Noyon and Bayeux; both were illustrated by VIOLLET-LE-DUC in 1858 and Burges himself had sketched that at Noyon in 1853. Burges's furniture style was characterized by massy slab-like forms, beefy finials and elaborate painted decoration expressing carefully worked out iconographic schemes. DRESSER was not an admirer. The furniture received its first public showing at the London 1859 Architectural Exhibition. It was later shown in the Mediaeval Court of the LONDON 1862 INTERNATIONAL EXHIBITION, including the Wines and Beers cabinet with painted decoration by E. J. Poynter (1836–1919) and Burges's own Great Bookcase, painted by ROSSETTI, BURNE-JONES and many others. Burges was very impressed by the Japanese Court at the London 1862 Exhibition which he called 'the real mediaeval court of the exhibition'. Burges was an accomplished antiquarian, with close French contacts. His style of drawings was modelled on VILLARD D' HONNECOURT, and his *Architectural Drawings* (1870) comprised details of French GOTHIC buildings. He much admired Viollet-le-Duc as an archaeologist – 'we all cribbed from Viollet-le-

Duc,' he stated. Burges was an active member of the Royal Archaeological Institute, showing many objects from his own collections at meetings, and published extensively on antiquarian subjects in the *Gentleman's Magazine* and elsewhere. In 1857 Burges, clubbable, Bohemian and jovial, was a founder of the Mediaeval Society and from 1858 to 1862 he was a member of the Hogarth Club; William MORRIS and RUSKIN were members of both. In 1863 he was elected a member of F.A.B.S., the Foreign Architectural Book Society, founded in 1859, an elite, expensive and convivial architectural club. In 1864 Burges delivered the Royal SOCIETY OF ARTS' Cantor Lectures on *Art Applied to Industry*, published as a book in 1865. He commemorated the book by having executed an 1858 design for a decanter, incorporating porphyry, lapis lazuli, Chinese jade, Persian seals and Greek coins. Its refinement of execution, vigour of form and extraordinary variety of material is characteristic of Burges's metalwork, which ranged from chalices to ink-pots and jewellery. In 1875 Burges's Dunedin crozier (1866–7) was published as a 13th-century French original in the French magazine 'ART POUR TOUS'. For his restoration of Waltham Abbey from 1860 Burges employed Burne-Jones as a stained-glass designer but he designed fine stained glass at Cork Cathedral (1869) and elsewhere, although sketches and cartoons were executed by H. W. Lonsdale, F. Weekes and others. Burges was not prolific. The interiors of his own flat at 15 Buckingham Street, London, decorated from 1858 to 1871, and of his own house in Melbury Road, built from 1875 to 1878, were among his most finished creations. In 1865, however, Burges met the Marquis of Bute, the richest man in Britain, for whom he restored Cardiff Castle from 1869 and Castell Coch from 1875, designing a series of elaborate interiors, mainly GOTHIC but culminating in the extraordinary vaulted Arab Room at Cardiff (1881). In about 1871 Burges designed some vigorous wallpapers for Jeffrey & Co. However, he neither worked for nor secured popular success as a designer. For all that Mrs Haweis included a chapter on Melbury Road in *Beautiful Houses* (1882), Burges's 13th-century Gothic was out of date by then. But Burges remained true to his early inspiration; in 1875 he had his own copy of Tennyson's *Poems*, acquired in 1853, illuminated by his assistant, T. M. Deane (1851–1933).

Burgkmair, Hans (1473–1531) Born in Augsburg, the son of a painter, Burgkmair trained in his father's workshop and then under Martin SCHONGAUER in Colmar from 1488 to 1490. Thenceforward Burgkmair stayed in Augsburg apart from a short visit to Italy in 1507. In 1515 he designed borders for the prayer-book of the Emperor Maximilian I. Burgkmair designed many woodcut book illustrations including those for Luther's New Testament translation (1523). He also designed woodcut medallion heads of Caesars for Konrad Peutinger. Burgkmair's woodcuts were influential in Augsburg and Germany for their use of early RENAISSANCE ornament.

Burne-Jones, Sir Edward (1833–98) Born in Birmingham, the son of a carver and gilder, Burne-Jones studied at King Edward School, Birmingham, which had furniture by A. W. N. PUGIN, and, from 1848, at evening classes at the Birmingham School of Design. In 1853 he went up to Exeter College, Oxford, planning to take orders. There he met William MORRIS and after they had travelled together to France in 1855 Morris decided to become an architect and Burne-Jones a painter. In 1856 they started the *Oxford and Cambridge*

Magazine, praised by Tennyson and RUSKIN, and in the same year Burne-Jones met ROSSETTI and became his pupil. Morris and Burne-Jones set up house in Red Lion Square in the same year. Burne-Jones painted some of Morris's early furniture and in 1857 painted the Chaucer wardrobe, designed by Philip WEBB and given as a wedding present to Morris in 1860. In 1857 Burne-Jones designed his first stained glass, a panel of the Good Shepherd for Powells of Whitefriars. In 1858 he became a member of the Hogarth Club, and showed stained-glass designs at their Dudley Gallery exhibition. In 1859 Burne-Jones designed the St Frideswide window in Christ Church Cathedral for Powells, from 1859 to 1860 glass in Waltham Abbey for BURGES, and in 1860 glass at Topcliffe church which was made by Lavers & Barraud for William BUTTERFIELD. At Morris's Red House, built from 1858, Burne-Jones designed glass and hangings, and in 1860 he painted a figure of Art on Burges's Great Bookcase. In 1861 Burne-Jones was involved in the foundation of the Morris company and participated in the firm's first stained-glass commission, for BODLEY's Selsey church. He also designed tiles for the firm from 1861 to 1863. Also in 1863 Burne-Jones designed embroideries with the Legend of Good Women for Ruskin; he later designed embroideries for the Royal School of Art Needlework, founded in 1872. In 1871 and 1873 Burne-Jones visited Italy. At this period his stained glass became less overtly GOTHIC and more RENAISSANCE in style. He designed figures on a plate by William DE MORGAN (about 1875), jewellery (from 1880), piano decorations (from 1880), some painted, some with gesso ornament by Kate FAULKNER, and mosaics for the American Church in Rome (1881). Burne-Jones designed all the figurative tapestries made by the Morris Company from 1881 to 1894. The most notable suite was the Holy Grail (five pieces; 1894). For Morris's Kelmscott Press, founded in 1891, Burne-Jones designed illustrations for the Kelmscott *Chaucer* (1895), fifty-seven in all, and illustrations for *Sigurd the Volsung* and *Love is Enough*. Burne-Jones's themes, derived from Malory, Tennyson and similar sources, remained constant from the 1850s. His style developed towards an abstracted, mannered and expressive late manner, most strikingly demonstrated in his stained-glass designs for Birmingham Cathedral (1897). In 1897 Burne-Jones was made an honorary member of the newly founded Vienna Secession.

Butterfield, Lindsay Philip (1869–1948) Butterfield was a prominent designer of textiles and wallpapers from about 1890. In 1892 he was working at the same address as Harrison Townsend. In the 1890s Butterfield designed tapestry fabrics for Morton & Co., including Squill (1899), illustrated in the 'ART JOURNAL' (1901). From 1902 he had an exclusive agreement to design tapestries for Mortons. Butterfield also designed tapestries and cretónnes for Liberty's, linen for G. & P. Baker and wallpapers for Essex & Co. and A. Sandersons. In *Floral Forms in Historic Design* (1922; eighteen plates) Butterfield illustrated examples taken from objects in the VICTORIA & ALBERT MUSEUM, as well as designs by William MORRIS and VOYSEY.

Butterfield, William (1814–1900) Born in London, the son of a Nonconformist chemist, Butterfield was apprenticed to a Pimlico builder in 1831. From 1833 to 1836 he studied architecture under E. L. Blackburne, an antiquarian. He then travelled and worked in Worcester before setting up office in London in 1840. In 1842 Butterfield wrote to the *Ecclesiolo-*
gist to suggest that the Cambridge Camden Society should sponsor and supervise the manufacture of chalices 'of the ancient form'. In 1843 Butterfield himself was retained as the Society's arbiter of ecclesiological taste in church fittings. His designs were published in *Instrumenta Ecclesiastica* (1844–7, seventy-two plates, mainly designed by Butterfield, and 1850–56, seventy-two plates, some designed by Butterfield). The church plate he designed was made under his supervision by John Keith & Son, who won a medal for their church plate designed by Butterfield at the LONDON 1851 EXHIBITION, and showed further examples at the LONDON 1862 EXHIBITION. His precious metalwork, based on archaeological examples, combines refinement with power. In church furnishings of wood and iron power and invention come to the fore. These attributes are most marked in a series of eighty fonts and font covers of great geometric pungency. Butterfield had strong views on the practicalities of church furniture, exemplified in his *Church Seats and Kneeling Boards* (1885). He also designed some simple secular furniture for Milton Ernest Hall (about 1858), as well as many embroideries, wallpapers and book covers. Although Butterfield was personally withdrawn and ascetic, his many buildings from All Saints, Margaret Street (1849), London, onwards breathe a passionate High Anglican Catholicism, inevitably expressed in the language of GOTHIC. But his approach to design was pragmatic and practical; he accepted modern timber sizes and his chimneys worked.

Byblis (1921–31) Subtitled *Miroir des Arts du Livre et de l'Estampe* this de luxe Parisian journal was devoted to book design, typography and illustration; its own illustrations are exceptionally distinguished.

C

Cabinet and Upholstery Advertiser, The (1877–8) Subtitled *A Journal of Modern Designs in Furniture & Upholstery*, this trade journal published many designs representative of commercial taste by A. JONQUET, among others. It was an almost direct precursor of the 'CABINET MAKER AND ART FURNISHER'.

Cabinet Maker and Art Furnisher, The (1880–present) Subtitled *A Monthly Budget of Designs and Information . . .* this trade magazine was at first edited by J. Williams Benn; it was a fierce rival of the 'FURNITURE GAZETTE'. The many designs illustrated in early issues included work by A. JONQUET, Henry SHAW, W. Timms and, posthumously, Bruce J. TALBERT. In 1902 the title changed to the *Cabinet Maker and Complete Home Furnisher*.

Caillart, Jacques A Parisian jeweller, Caillart published *Livre de Toutes Sorte de Feuilles pour Servir à l'Art d'Orfeburie* (Paris, 1627, reprinted in The Hague, 1638; six plates). These comprise fleshy leafed *aigrettes* for jewellers in the COSSE-DE-POIS style.

Caillouet Caillouet designed some twenty-four plates of NEO-CLASSICAL ironwork published in about 1780, including gates, balconies, balustrades and screens. Coarse copies were published in Augsburg by J. M. WILL in 1788. Caillouet also designed a *Premier Livre de Vases* (four plates of neo-classical VASES).

Calegari, Giovanni Born in Bologna in about 1753, Calegari died there in 1812. He studied architecture at the Accademia Clementina from 1772 to 1775, under Carlo BIANCONI and Mauro TESI. Calegari designed interiors for Bianconi at the Palazzo Zambeccari in Bologna in about 1780, some of which were executed by the plasterer A. Gambarini. He also designed altars and funerals. A censer designed by Calegari was included in PANFILI's *Frammenti di Ornati* (1783).

Callet, Antoine (1741–1823) Born in Paris, Callet trained as a painter under Antoine Boizot. In 1764 he won the Prix de Rome and in 1780 he became a member of the Academy. Callet designed a suite of four tapestries, the Seasons, for the Gobelins factory, whose cartoons were shown at the Salons from 1783 to 1791.

Callot, Jacques (1592–1635) Born in Nancy, the son of a herald, Callot was in 1607 apprenticed to a goldsmith. After training as an engraver he settled in 1612 in Florence, where he entered the studio of Giulio Parigi, the virtuoso designer of court fêtes. Callot's own prints incorporate many cartouches of a macabre and AURICULAR character. He also designed fountains, which may be VASES, and a title-page to a poem by G. D. Peri (1619). His *Varie Figure Gobbi* (1616; twenty-one plates of grotesque dwarfs) were reinterpreted by Wilhelm Kooning in *Il Calotto resuscitato* (Amsterdam, 1716) and used as a source by the goldsmith Johann Melchior Dinglinger (1664–1731) and the glass engraver Frans Greenwood (1680–1762) as well as by the porcelain factories of Meissen, Vienna and Chelsea. A series of twenty-five prints of beggars of about 1615 were used as designs for Naples porcelain figures of about 1790. However, Callot's greatest influence on design was through his follower, Stefano DELLA BELLA.

Cambiaso, Luca (1527–85) Born in Moneglia, Liguria, the son of a painter, with whom he later collaborated, Cambiaso's earliest and independent works as a painter date from 1547. In 1562 to 1563 he provided the design for the silver Corpus Christi shrine in the church of San Lorenzo in Genoa. In the later 1560s he frequently collaborated with CASTELLO on decorative painting in Genoa. Cambiaso designed two major suites of tapestries for weaving in Flanders, the Story of Moses and the Story of Ulysses, the latter for Battista Grimaldi. A design of about 1570 includes not only an altarpiece but also its frame and tabernacle. Cambiaso visited Rome and Florence in 1575, and in 1583 left Genoa for Spain, where he died at the Escorial.

Cameron, Charles Born in London in about 1743, the son of a Scottish carpenter and builder, Cameron was apprenticed to the Palladian architect and ROCOCO decorator Isaac Ware. On Ware's death in 1766 Cameron decided to execute Ware's project to re-edit Lord Burlington's edition of Palladio's drawings of the Roman baths (1730). He therefore went to Rome and in 1772 published *The Baths of the Romans* (reprinted 1774 and 1775), dedicated to Lord Bute (1713–92), a source-book of NEO-CLASSICAL ornament. Cameron seems to have returned to London in 1769 but by 1778 he was in Russia in

the service of Catherine the Great (1729–96). At Tsarskoe Selo he designed the Agate Pavilion (1782–5), the Cameron Gallery (1783–5) and the Empress's private apartments, including furniture and fittings in a rich and brilliant neo-classical style; some of his designs for painted decorations were based on CLÉRISSEAU and J. G. LEGRAND. From the year 1781 Cameron designed the palace of Pavlovsk for the Grand Duke Paul, but their relationship was strained and when Paul became Emperor in 1796 he was dismissed in favour of BRENNA. After the accession of Paul's son Alexander in 1801 Cameron was again employed as an official architect. He died in St Petersburg in 1812.

Cammermeir, Simon Cammermeir published a *Neues Zierrathen Buch* (Paulus Fürst, Nuremberg) which contained altars, tabernacles, monuments, panels and brackets in an AURICULAR style related to that of UNTEUTSCH. He also published a book of the ORDERS in 1678.

Cancio, Pedro Cancio worked as a designer in the Madrid tapestry manufactory from 1796, and also designed carpets. He was decorator to the Duke of Berwick and in 1816 travelled to Rome on his behalf. He died in Madrid in 1834.

Candid, Pieter The son of a Bruges tapestry maker, Pieter Candid was born there as Pieter de Witte in about 1548. In 1558 his father moved to Florence to work for the Medici. Pieter Candid was trained as a painter and worked under VASARI in the Vatican from 1569. In 1576 Candid became a member of the FLORENCE ACCADEMIA DEL DISEGNO, to which his elder brother, a sculptor, had earlier belonged, and about this date he was active as a tapestry designer under STRAET. In 1578 Candid was working as a painter in Volterra, but he was back in Florence by 1585, after paying a visit to Rome in 1581. In 1586, at the recommendation of the sculptor Giovanni Bologna (1529–1608), Candid was summoned by Duke Wilhelm V of Bavaria to Munich, where he found GERHARD and SUSTRIS, whom he had earlier known in Florence. Candid's first job in Munich was to work on the frescoes of the Grottenhalle in the Residenz, mainly designed by Sustris. However, from 1596, owing to the financial stringencies which led to Wilhelm V passing the regency to his son, Maximilian I, in 1598, Candid, who had received a salary, was discharged from regular court employment. His salary was restored in 1602 and in 1611, according to HAIN-HOFER, Candid was recognized as the leading painter at the Munich court. From 1604 he designed tapestries for the Munich workshops of Hans van der Biest. They comprised a series of GROTESQUES (twelve pieces; 1604–15), a series on the deeds of Otto von Wittelsbach (twelve pieces; 1604–14, rewoven in Paris, 1614–17), the Twelve Months, the Four Seasons, Day and Night (1612–14), and a series of Heroes for the Kaisersaal in the Residenz (twelve pieces; 1615–18), the latter woven by Biest and Hans van den Bosschen in Enghien. Candid's refined and colourful grotesque tapestries are related to Sustris's designs for the Grottenhalle, but his figurative compositions often seem to look back beyond his MANNERIST teachers to the heroic forms of Bernart van ORLEY. Candid was also responsible for several painted decorative schemes including the Altes Schloss at Schleissheim (1617) and the Goldener Saal of the Augsburg Rathaus (1619), as well as providing designs for goldsmiths' work. He died in 1628.

Cano, Alonso (1601–67) Born in Granada, Cano moved in 1614 to Seville, where he studied painting in the studio of Francisco Pacheco (1564–1654) and sculpture under Juan Martinez Montañes. He moved to Madrid in 1638, and finally to Granada, where he designed a new façade for the cathedral. Cano also designed massive silver altar lamps, a lectern (both about 1652 to 1656) and altars for the cathedral, as well as picture frames and illustrations for Quevedo Villegas's *El parnaso español* (Madrid, 1648).

Canonica, Luigi (1762–1844) Born at Tessereti near Lugano, Canonica was appointed royal architect by Napoleon and designed the throne for his coronation as King of Italy in Milan in 1805. Canonica, an efficient practitioner in the style of PERCIER and FONTAINE, designed many works for the Napoleonic regime in Milan. In 1821 he retired through disability.

Capronnier, Jean Baptiste (1814–91) The son of François Capronnier (1789–1833), a Sèvres porcelain painter who settled in Brussels in 1820 and in about 1830 established himself as a stained-glass painter and designer, Jean Baptiste Capronnier was trained by his father, and took over his factory. He designed and supplied a vast number of stained-glass windows in Belgium, Holland, England and Germany. Some 3,500 cartoons were included in his 1892 sale. In 1844 glass restored by Capronnier for Saint-Jacques in Liège was illustrated in John WEALE's *Quarterly Papers on Architecture*. Capronnier also employed other designers, including the painters Charles de Groux (1825–70), Constantin Meunier (1831–1905), Ernst Kathelin and François Joseph Navez (1787–1869).

Carabin, François Rupert (1862–1932)

Born in Saverne, the son of an Alsatian forester who opted for France in 1871, Carabin suffered hard times as a boy in Paris, working from 1873 as an engraver of cameos. He took evening drawing classes and later did architectural sculpture. In 1884 he was a founder of the Société des Artistes Indépendants, where he showed figures of Loie Fuller in 1896 to 1897. Carabin was a friend of Huysmans, Manet, Toulouse-Lautrec, GALLÉ and CHARPENTIER. In 1889 he was commissioned by the collector Henry Montandon to make a bookcase. He produced a massive structure embellished with vigorous female nudes. It was rejected by the Salon des Indépendants in 1890 and in 1891 was the first piece of applied art shown at the Société Nationale des Beaux-Arts. In all Carabin designed and made some twenty pieces of furniture, all incorporating female nudes, including a showcase for the Musée Galliéra. He also designed some jewellery and ceramics. In about 1899 Carabin was offered a position in Darmstadt by the Grand Duke of Hesse, but French patriotism led him to refuse. He disliked HORTA, 'who introduced the macaroni style which, when GUIMARD brought it to Paris, arrested the French movement launched by a few artists four or five years earlier'. In 1919 Carabin was appointed Director of the École des Arts Décoratifs in Strasbourg.

Carder, Frederick (1863–1963) Born in Staffordshire, Carder worked for various local potteries and glass factories before becoming a designer for Stevens & Williams of Brierley Hill. He left England in 1903 to found the Steuben Glass Works at Corning, New York. At Corning, Carder acted as designer and developed intarsia, iridescent, bubbled and metallic glasses which competed with TIFFANY's products. When the factory was taken over by Corning Glass in 1918

Carder continued in the post. From 1929 Steuben also produced architectural glass. Carder held the post of Art Director from 1932 and only retired in 1959, at the age of ninety-six.

Carême, Marie Antoine (1794–1833) Born in Paris, the son of a street cleaner, Carême was abandoned at the age of ten but subsequently rose to become one of the greatest cooks in France. Having studied architectural books at the Bibliothèque Royale, including SERLIO, Durand, PERCIER and FONTAINE, and NORMAND, Carême began to design architectural table decorations of icing sugar. His *Le Patissier Pittoresque* (Paris 1815) was often reprinted. The third edition of 1828 contains 125 witty designs for brightly coloured icing-sugar follies, in a whole gamut of styles, Polish, Turkish, Greek, Egyptian, Chinese, GOTHIC and so on. Carême also published twenty-eight plates of architectural projects for Paris and St Petersburg (1821–6).

Caron, Antoine (1521–99) Born in Beauvais, Caron was trained as a painter but also worked as a stained-glass designer. In the 1540s and before 1560 he worked as a decorator at Fontainebleau. In 1561 he was commissioned by the City of Paris to design decorations for the entry of Charles IX, but this did not take place until 1571. From 1562 Caron designed a large suite of tapestries on the History of Artemisia, commissioned by the scholar Nicolas Houel as an act of homage to Catherine de' Medici. Houel also ordered a large suite on the History of the Kings of France from Caron. Caron designed several court entertainments for Catherine de' Medici and succeeded Niccolo dell'Abbate as chief court designer. His designs for various events, including the entry of Henry III in 1573, served as the basis for tapestries designed by Lucas de

HEERE. Caron, who had a high reputation among his contemporaries, also designed illustrations for the *Livre de Philostrate*.

Carracci, Agostino (1557–1602) Born in Bologna, Carracci trained as a goldsmith and then as a painter. In 1582 he founded the Accademia degli Incamminati with his brother Annibale CARRACCI. Agostino was mainly active as an engraver and designed a number of book ornaments and illustrations, including an allegory in honour of Philip II of Spain as the title-page to *Cremona Fedelissima* (1585). In about 1590 he engraved a design for a fan. Carracci often worked in Venice, and also collaborated with Annibale in Rome in the 1590s.

Carracci, Annibale (1560–1609) Born in Bologna, Carracci studied painting under his cousin Lodovico Carracci (1555–1619). In 1582 he helped to found the Accademia degli Incamminati. From 1594 to his death Annibale was in Rome, where his painted decorations in the Galleria Farnese (1597–1600) and elsewhere displayed a grandeur which looked back to RAPHAEL and MICHELANGELO but which also acted as an important basis for the BAROQUE style of decoration. In about 1597 Cardinal Odoardo Farnese ordered engraved silver dishes from Annibale Carracci and his brother Agostino CARRACCI. Agostino's was to have represented Bacchus and Annibale's Silenus, but Agostino dropped out of the scheme. Annibale then designed a dish and a bread basket, which was executed by Francesco Villamena; both are engraved with bacchic subjects. They may have been made in connection with the marriage of Ranuccio Farnese and Margherita Aldobrandini in 1600.

Carriage Builders' and Harness Makers' Art Journal (1859–62) Published in London, this trade journal contained fine illustrations on all aspects of carriage design. In emulation of the 'ART JOURNAL' itself they issued an *Illustrated Catalogue of the 1862 London Exhibition*.

Carrier-Belleuse, Albert Ernest (1824–87) Born at Anizy-le-Château, the son of a public notary who deserted his family in 1834, Carrier-Belleuse was brought up in Paris by his Arago cousins, prominent republican intellectuals. In about 1837 he entered the studio of a chaser, Bauchery, whence he moved to the workshop of the goldsmith Fauconnier. Fauconnier died in 1839 and Carrier-Belleuse then worked for his nephews the Fannière brothers. He studied briefly at the École des Beaux-Arts and became friendly with Péquegnot and Jules Salmson. He later studied at the École Royale Gratuite de Dessin. Carrier-Belleuse soon left the Fannières to go freelance, designing metalwork for Barbedienne and for Michel Aaron's porcelain factory. He was in contact with leading designers such as Jules KLAGMANN (1810–67) and FEUCHÈRE. In 1850 Carrier-Belleuse followed VECHTE, ARNOUX and JEANNEST to England, where he designed for Mintons in Stoke-on-Trent and taught at the Schools of Design in Stoke and Hanley. He was recommended in Mintons by Jeannest and designed many Parian and maiolica wares for the factory. While in England Carrier-Belleuse also designed for Wedgwood and for William Brownfield & Sons, as well as continuing to send metalwork designs to Paris. Back in Paris in 1855 he became a successful sculptor prominent in the art establishment and friendly with leading artists and writers. He continued prolifically active as a designer, winning two medals at the PARIS 1855 EXHIBITION. At the LONDON 1862 EXHIBITION the ironfounders Durenne showed torchères by Carrier-Belleuse and the Compagnie des Marbres-Onyx d'Algérie a *tazza* to his design. In 1863 Carrier-Belleuse had his own stand at the first exhibition of the PARIS UNION CENTRALE DES ARTS DÉCORATIFS, which he had helped Klagmann to found. In the 1860s he began to teach design at the Académie Julian. At the PARIS 1867 EXHIBITIONS Mintons showed candelabras supported by negroes based on earlier bronze examples designed for Saïd Pasha, Viceroy of Egypt in 1862. For the great courtesan La Paiva, Carrier-Belleuse designed side-tables supported by kneeling male nudes (1866) and a massive silver centrepiece (1867). In 1869 he designed decorations for the Grande Galerie of the Louvre. In 1866 Carrier-Belleuse published *Études de figures appliquées à la décoration*, a selection of his own drawings. In 1884 he published his *Application de la figure humaine à la décoration et à l'ornementation industrielles*, a similar selection of drawings mainly dating from the mid-1870s or later. Carrier-Belleuse's style remained constant throughout his career, an assured neo-MANNERIST manner congruous with both RENAISSANCE and NEO-CLASSICAL ornament. He designed metalwork for Christofle, jewellery for Lucien Falize and Alphonse Fouquet, and furniture for Grohé, and was from 1876 artistic director at Sèvres. The Sèvres stand at the PARIS 1878 EXHIBITION showed a dramatic improvement in design attributable to Carrier-Belleuse's influence and in about 1880 he began to introduce simple new VASE forms. However, he was later in dispute with Charles Lauth, the director of the Sèvres factory, whose phrase '*trop de sculpture*' summarizes his verdict on Carrier-Belleuse, who began to go blind in 1886. Rodin entered Carrier-Belleuse's large studio in 1864 and in 1868 Gustave-Joseph

CHÉRET married his daughter Marie.

Carter, John (1748–1817) The son of a London mason and monumental sculptor, Carter was trained as an architect. In 1774 he began to design for the *Builder's Magazine* (1774–86, reprinted 1820), an encyclopaedic work projected by the publisher Newbery. His designs were mainly architectural but also included grates, ironwork, silver, doorcases, chimneypieces, friezes, ceilings, furniture designs, VASES and panels of ornament. They are in a hectic and spiky NEO-CLASSICAL manner in which ornaments form part of structure, regardless of congruity. However, Carter's interest in GOTHIC, already apparent in some of the *Magazine* designs, led to a career as a passionate and influential defender of Gothic antiquity, which was illustrated in his *Specimens of Ancient Sculpture and Painting* (1780–94) and his *Views of Ancient Buildings in England* (1786–93). John Carter also designed in the Gothic manner, notably the altar and organ of Peterborough Cathedral (about 1780).

Carteron, Stephanus Born at Châtillon-sur-Seine, Carteron published in 1615 a series of eight plates of very fine large black stretched GROTESQUE designs for enamelling on pendants, boxes, rings and jewellery.

Carwitham, John Carwitham was an engraver who worked for Batty LANGLEY. He also published in *Various Kinds of Floor Decorations* (1739; twenty-four plates) his own designs for stone or marble pavements, or floor cloths. The charming plates show the patterns flat and in PERSPECTIVE attended by harlequins, shepherdesses and huntsmen.

Casabella Casabella was founded in 1928

by the socialist art-educator Guido Marangoni (1872–1941), who also conceived
the MONZA BIENNALES, as *La Casa
Bella*. From 1930 to 1932 it was edited
by Arrigo Banfiglioli. In 1933 it was
taken over by 'DOMUS', and Giuseppe
PAGANO was appointed editor with Persico as assistant and later co-editor.
Casabella was closed in 1943, briefly
revived in 1945, and returned as *Casabella – Continuità* in 1953, under the
editorship of E. N. Rogers, who was succeeded by G. A. Bernasconi in 1965 and
A. Mendini in 1971. In 1975 *Casabella*
was taken over by Electá, who appointed
Tomás Maldonado as editor under a
managing committee.

**Cassandre, Adolphe Jean Marie Mou-
ron, called** (1901–68) Cassandre was
born of French parents in Kharkov in
the Ukraine. In 1915 he came to Paris
where he studied painting at the Académie Julian. From 1922 he worked as
a publicity artist. In 1923 Cassandre
designed his first poster for Boucheron
and thenceforward created a series of
striking posters in a vigorous MODERN
style. They include Étoile du Nord
(1927) for the Paris–Amsterdam train,
Dubonnet (1932) and Normandie
(1935). From 1927 Cassandre was in a
partnership, l'Alliance Graphique, with
Charles Loupot (1892–1962) and Maurice A. Moyrand. It disbanded in 1935,
Moyrand, the administrator, having
been killed in a car accident in 1934.
Afterwards Cassandre designed typography. He went to America in 1936 and
on his return designed for the theatre
and ballet. In 1929 he designed and
edited *Publicité* in the series *L'Art International d'Aujourd'hui*; it illustrated
work by Jan Tschichold, McKnight
KAUFFER, MOHOLY-NAGY, Jean
Carlu and Herbert BAYER, as well as
work by himself and Loupot. Cassandre
designed ninety-five posters in all,

although about a third were not published.

Castello, Giovanni Battista Born at
Gandino in Bergamo, whence his nickname Il Bergamasco, Castello probably
trained as a painter in Rome and Florence, but he is first documented in
Genoa in 1552. In Genoa, Castello
enjoyed the patronage of the great
banker Tobia Pallavicino, and from 1558
he acted as architect, decorative painter
and furniture designer for the Palazzo
Pallavicino. It was probably for the same
client that Castello designed a large suite
of tapestries with the Story of Cupid and
Psyche; their mannered figures and GRO-
TESQUE borders seem to be influenced
by the Florentine tapestries designed by
BRONZINO and others. In 1561 Castello
contracted to paint an altarpiece for
Taddeo Spinola, and to design its frame.
In the 1560s he often collaborated on
paintings with CAMBIASO, and in about
1565 designed the stucco framework for
Cambiaso's painted decorations at the
Palazzo Grimaldi. In 1567 Castello
moved to Spain as painter and court
architect to Philip II of Spain. He
worked on the decoration of the Madrid
Alcazar in the year of his death, 1569.

Castex-Dégrange, Adolphe Louis
(1840–1918) Born in Marseilles, Castex-
Dégrange studied at the Lyon École des
Beaux-Arts under REIGNIER, whom he
hated. From 1855 he worked as a textile
designer, moving to Paris in 1874. He
returned to Lyon in 1884 and succeeded
Reignier as professor of floral design at
the École des Beaux-Arts. His textile
designs were much praised at the PARIS
1889 EXHIBITION and up to 1914 Castex-Dégrange did much to revitalize the
Lyon tradition of floral textiles. He also
decorated ceramics and was successful
as a painter.

Castiglione, Achille Born in Milan in

1918, Achille Castiglione qualified as an architect in 1944. In 1938 his brothers Pier Giacomo (1913–68) and Livio, with the architect Luigi Caccia Dominioni, had designed the plastic-cased Phonola radio, which was in production from 1939 to 1945. Achille Castiglione set up his office in 1945 with Pier Giacomo, who remained a partner until his death, and Livio, who left in 1952. Castiglione was involved in all MILAN TRIENNALES from 1947. A founder of the Associazione Design Italiano in 1956 he has since 1969 taught industrial design at the Turin Polytechnic and is a prominent member of the Italian design establishment. The elegant tubular Tubino desk-light for Arredoluce (1950), the Mezzadro stool (1955) with its tractor-like seat, the REM vacuum cleaner (1956), the narrow Luminator light on spindly tripod legs (1956), and the Toio light (1962), its light hanging from a steel arch set in a block of marble, are a few of his better-known designs. Others have included glass, silver and electrical gadgets.

Castillo, José del (1737–93) Born in Madrid, Castillo was a pupil of the painter José Romeo (1701–72). In 1751 he was given a private scholarship to Rome, where he studied under Corrado Giaquinto, with whom he returned to Madrid in 1753. After winning prizes at the Real Academia di San Fernando in 1755 and 1756, Castillo won an official scholarship to Rome from 1758 to 1764, returning to Madrid in the latter year after visiting Herculaneum with the young architect Juan de Villanueva. He was recommended by Giaquinto for work in the royal tapestry factory, Santa Barbara, and executed over 100 cartoons. In about 1771 he completed the BAROQUE GROTESQUE tapestries designed for the bedroom of Carlos III by Guillermo Anglois. He followed these with a set of hunting tapestries and

some brilliant Pompeian grotesques for the cabinet of the Princess of Asturias at the Escorial. In 1770 Castillo designed illustrations to a celebrated edition of *Don Quixote*. As a tapestry designer, however, he was superseded by BAYEU and GOYA.

Cauvet, Gilles Paul (1731–88) Born at Aix-en-Provence, Cauvet was active as architect, sculptor and designer. He became a member of the Académie de Saint-Luc in 1762 and in 1774 was appointed sculptor to Monsieur, the King's brother. His architectural works were mainly decorative. Cauvet also designed clocks and furniture, including a pair of steel tables with silver inlay for Marie-Antoinette. In the Louvre are bronze candelabra by Cauvet dated 1783. Cauvet's designs were among those used in 1767 in the trade school of design founded by Jean-Jacques BACHELIER in 1766. *Recueil d'ornements à l'usage des jeunes artistes qui se destinent à la décoration des bâtiments* (1777; fifty-nine plates), dedicated to Monsieur, comprises large finely engraved plates of ornament, friezes, ACANTHUS and VASES in a very elaborate and refined NEO-CLASSICAL style, typical of their period. Borrowings from POLIDORO, DELLA BELLA and SALY are evident and, although brilliantly professional, Cauvet's designs display a certain chill sterility.

Cave, Walter Frederick (1863–1939) Cave, the son of a rich banker, was at school at Eton, studied art in Bristol and at the Royal Academy Schools, and then studied architecture under Sir Arthur Blomfield (1829–99). From 1889 Cave was a member of the ART-WORKERS' GUILD, of which he was secretary from 1898 to 1905. In 1893 Cave designed an oak case for a Bechstein piano for Maples. He also designed a showroom for Bechstein with plaster ornament by

Stephen WEBB. Cave designed metal-work, wallpaper and furniture. His work was praised in the 'STUDIO' and by MUTHESIUS, who compared him to VOYSEY.

Cavelier, Adrien-Louis-Marie (1785–1867) Born in Paris, Cavelier worked as an architect and designer in NEO-CLASSICAL style. He collaborated with PRUD'HON on the cradle of the King of Rome and the toilet service of the Empress Marie Louise.

Caylus, Anne-Claude-Philippe, Comte de (1692–1765) The son of a niece of Mme de Maintenon, Caylus had a brief but distinguished military career up to 1715, when he embarked on a life of travel and scholarship. In 1731 he was elected to the Académie de Peinture as an amateur. From 1729 Caylus built up a collection of antiquities which he published in his monumental seven-volume *Recueil d'antiquités égyptiennes, étrusques, et romaines* (1752–7), for which drawings were supplied by many prominent NEO-CLASSICAL designers. Caylus engraved the plates himself having been taught to engrave by WATTEAU. Before 1722 he engraved designs by GILLOT and in 1737 engraved a suite of drawings by his friend, the sculptor Edmé Bouchardon. From the mid-1740s Caylus began to take a more and more active role as lecturer and connoisseur, and in the 1750s he designed some neo-classical ornaments himself. In 1755 he attempted to revive the classical technique of encaustic painting, and in 1756 LE LORRAIN, a protégé, designed reconstructed shields of Achilles and Aeneas for him. Caylus's key role as a pundit in the 1750s, fully recognized by his contemporaries, was in supporting the '*goût grec*' of Le Lorrain, PETITOT, BÉLANGER and others. His *Recueil* was widely influential, being admired by Wedgwood and listed in the bibliography of Thomas HOPE's *Household Furniture* (1807).

Celle, Dominique de Born in Toulouse, Celle was a professional designer of embroidery who claimed to have lived in Spain, Italy and Germany. His first book, *Ce Livre est plaisant et utile* (Lyon, 1531; twenty-four plates), was reprinted with an Italian title at Lyon in 1532, and in Paris in 1583 and 1584 with six additional plates designed by Jehan Cousin the Younger (see Jehan COUSIN). Copies published under various titles at Venice from 1543 to 1584, the earliest issued by Matio PAGANO, reflect the popularity of Celle or Domenico de Sera, as he was known in Italy. Some Celle designs were borrowed by Bernhard JOBIN's 1579 Strasbourg pattern-book. They consisted mainly of geometric and interlace ornament.

Cellini, Benvenuto (1500–1571) Born in Florence, the son of an architect, Cellini trained as a goldsmith under Michelangelo Bandinelli and then under Martino di Sandro. In 1519, after a spell in Bologna, he moved to Rome, where he worked for the leading Roman goldsmiths Giovanni de Georgis and Lucagnolo di Jesu. With the latter he made a ewer and candlesticks designed by Giovanni Francesco Penni for the Bishop of Salamanca. Cellini also designed '*bizzarri vasetti*', presumably small MANNERIST VASES, and made two in silver; earthenware versions were later produced in Ferrara. In 1540 he was paid by Benedetto Accolti, Bishop of Ravenna, for 300 designs of various kinds. From 1540 to 1545 Cellini was in France. He then returned to Florence, where he designed vases for Duke Cosimo de' Medici and also a seal for the FLORENCE ACCADEMIA DEL DISEGNO. In 1564 he was noted as supplying designs for the banker Piero Salviati of Lyon. Although most famous for the skill in goldsmith's work and the picaresque adventures celebrated in his autobiography, Cellini seems to have been an important disseminator of the mannerist style through his designs as well as his works.

Cerini, Pietro Cerini designed at least three suites of about ten plates each, with bold BAROQUE ACANTHUS-style ornament and cartouches. A further small suite includes jewellery designs in the same manner. All were published in Rome in the 1680s and 1690s and one was dedicated to the goldsmith Samuelle Jacomini, who was active in Rome from before 1668 to at least 1690.

Chabal-Dussurgey, Pierre Adrien (1819–1902) Born at Charlieu near Roanne, Chabal-Dussurgey studied at the Lyon École des Beaux-Arts, where he was taught by THIERRIAT in 1836. He subsequently worked as a designer for Cinier, a manufacturer of church vestments. In 1844, at the suggestion of the architect Jacques-Félix Duban (1797–1870), he was employed by the Duc de Luynes to execute floral decorations at Dampierre. Chabal-Dussurgey also showed flower paintings in Paris winning a gold medal in 1847. At this period he was involved with the pioneer photographer Adolphe Braun (1812–77) in the publication of albums of flowers for the use of designers. In 1849 he became teacher of design at the Gobelins tapestry manufactory, and later designed many tapestries for that factory and for Beauvais, as well as Savonnerie carpets; a speciality was seat coverings, including some designed for Compiègne, and an 1874 Beauvais firescreen designed in collaboration with Godefroy; a firescreen by Chabal-Dussurgey was shown at the PARIS 1878 EXHIBITION. He also collaborated with DIÉTERLE. Chabal-Dussurgey's lithographed *Études et compositions de fleurs* (1867), a graphic course in floral design, was widely influential and often reprinted. In the mid-1870s he retired to independent practice, but in 1881 he was appointed first director of the Nice École de l'Art Décoratif, which he ran until 1892.

Challe, Charles-Michel-Ange (1718–78) Born in Paris, Challe trained as an architect and then as a painter, winning the Grand Prix in 1741. In 1742 he travelled to Rome, where he remained until 1749. In Rome he was in contact with LE LORRAIN and with the painter Joseph-Marie VIEN (1716–1809). His designs for the 1744 celebrations of Louis XV's recovery from illness were among the earliest demonstration of NEO-CLASSICISM, strongly influenced by PIRANESI. On his return to France, Challe was in 1753 elected to the Academy, and in 1758 appointed its professor of perspective. In 1764 he succeeded M.-A. SLODTZ as Dessinateur de la Chambre et du Cabinet du Roi, and designed neo-classical decorations for several ceremonies, including the funerals of the Duchess of Parma (1766) and Louis XV (1774). BÉLANGER was among his assistants. Challe spent his last years translating Piranesi. His brother, the sculptor Simon Challe (1719–65), published a suite of VASES (six plates), energetic and vigorous neo-classical designs strongly influenced by SALY.

Chambers, Sir William (1723–96) Born in Gothenburg in Sweden, the son of a Scottish merchant, Chambers was educated in Yorkshire before entering the Swedish East India Company in 1739. In 1749, after three voyages on which he gained direct knowledge of Chinese design, he left this service and moved to England, where he probably met FREDERICK LEWIS, PRINCE OF WALES. Late in 1749 he moved to Paris to study at the École des Arts run by Jacques-François BLONDEL, and gained contact with advanced Parisian taste; in later years he retained an affectionate memory for his fellow students. A sketch-book he began in Paris includes, surprisingly, sketches of OPPENORD'S ROCOCO work in the Palais Royal, together with designs copied from the advanced French architect LE GEAY. Chambers later owned a set of etchings (1770) by Le Geay, who drew Chambers's Casino near Dublin in about 1766, a drawing for which Chambers probably designed the NEO-CLASSICAL frame. Two trips to Rome, 1750 to 1751 and 1752 to 1755, finished his education; on the second he spent two years in the same house as PIRANESI. Back in London, Chambers published in 1757 his influential *Designs of Chinese Buildings, Furniture, Dresses, Machines and Utensils* (French edition also 1757). The book was dedicated to George, Prince of Wales, to whom he was appointed architectural tutor in 1757, the year he began to embellish Kew Gardens for the Prince's mother, Princess Augusta, and was proposed to the SOCIETY OF ARTS by Grignion, the engraver. In 1759 Chambers designed some proto-neo-classical furniture for the Society's Great Room, and in 1760 similar seat furniture for Sir Joshua Reynolds. The State Coach, designed by Chambers in 1760 and executed by Joseph Wilton and Giambattista Cipriani before 1762, is however predominantly rococo. In 1759 Chambers published his lessons to Prince George in the form of *A Treatise on Civil Architecture*, the first of many editions. His official career commenced as Architect of the Works in 1761 and culminated in his appointment as Surveyor General in 1782. He received many national and foreign honours, being made Treasurer of the new Royal Academy in 1768 and a Swedish Knight in 1770. In 1763 *Plans*

etc. of his work at Kew were published; these were widely plundered by designers, for instance on a 1766 printed cotton by John Collins of Woolmers, Hertfordshire. Like ADAM, Chambers supervised all aspects of his interiors. As well as furniture for the Society of Arts and Reynolds, he designed furniture at Blenheim, from 1765 to 1769, including pieces made by INCE & Mayhew, and a fine table made for him by the Swede Georg Haupt in 1769. In 1773, complaining that he had not been consulted over furniture to be supplied by CHIPPENDALE, Chambers asserted himself to be 'really a Very pretty Connoisseur in furniture'. Ornaments, particularly those using ormolu, seem to have been a special interest. In 1761 he showed a model for a candlestick at the Society of Arts, in 1767 he designed a medal cabinet with bronze mounts by Anderson for Lord Charlemont, and in 1768 a case for an astronomical clock for George III. In 1770 he showed at the Royal Academy various VASES to be executed in ormolu for the King by Matthew Boulton, who records that he received 'some valuable usefull and acceptable models' from Chambers in that year. In 1771 Chambers designed the Boulton case for an eight-day clock for George III. Some of Chambers's ormolu designs also seem to have been used by Wedgwood. Chambers's gravity may be broadly contrasted with Adam's elegance, but his part in naturalizing the neo-classical style in design, if less conspicuous, was no less important than the latter's.

Chareau, Pierre (1883–1950) Born in Bordeaux of a shipbuilding family, Chareau worked before 1914 as a draughtsman for the furniture manufacturers Waring & Gillow in London. From 1919 he showed sophisticatedly austere furniture in rich materials – macassar ebony and amboyna – at the

Salon d'Automne and the Salon des Artistes-Décorateurs. At the PARIS 1925 EXHIBITION he designed the study in the Ambassade Française. From 1928 to 1931 Chareau collaborated with the Dutch architect Bernard Bijvoet on the celebrated Maison de Verre for Dr Dalsace with glass brick walls, exposed metal structure and studded white-rubber floors supporting metal furniture. In 1929 he edited *Meubles* in the series *L'Art International d'Aujourd'hui*, illustrating furniture by LE CORBUSIER, Pierre Jeanneret and Charlotte PERRIAND, Marcel BREUER, MALLET-STEVENS, Oud, Eileen GRAY, DJO-BOURGEOIS, Mondrian and HERBST. In 1930 Chareau was one of the founders of the Union des Artistes Modernes with Francis JOURDAIN and others, and his furniture, rectilinear and metallic with an imaginative use of pivoting members, his lights, abstract arrangements of opaque glass, and his textiles, were stylishly MODERN. In 1930 he produced tubular-steel chairs designed by Jean Burkhalter and in 1938 he designed interiors at the Collège de France. After the fall of France in 1940 Chareau moved to America.

Charles, Richard Born in Caernavon in 1823, Charles worked as a cabinet-maker in Warrington. He came to public notice as the designer and maker of the Warrington State Bedstead, a gigantic affair in an incoherent mixed RENAISSANCE style, which attempted to emulate the furniture by Leistler shown in the Austrian section of the LONDON 1851 EXHIBITION and which was shown at the 1857 Manchester Art Treasures Exhibition. The bedstead, which was put to a lottery, brought Charles to bankruptcy in 1859. However, he later moved to London and became a successful interior designer. The first of Charles's published works, the *Cabinet Maker's*

Monthly Journal of Designs (1860), a short-lived periodical edited from Wigan and printed in Manchester, was intended to raise the quality of British furniture design. It contained forty designs by Charles, of dashing fluency, by turns conventional and eccentric, composed of NATURALISTIC, Renaissance Revival and Puginian GOTHIC elements. His *Cabinet Makers' Sketch Book*, published in London in 1866, presented sixty lithographed plates of sideboards in a competent eclectic manner spanning Reformed Gothic and Renaissance Revival. A second abortive attempt to found a periodical, the *Cabinet Maker: A Journal of Designs* (1868), consisted of ninety-six plates mainly by Charles in the Reformed Gothic, Renaissance Revival and 'Néo-Grec' styles. A few designs by Owen W. DAVIS and 'E.' LORMIER were also included. In 1873 Charles published *Designs for Window-Draperies, Fringes and Mantelboard Decorations* (reprinted 1874), whose frontispiece incorporates a portrait of the author, and also an improved version of his 1857 bed, and whose 100 plates are in variegated ADAM, Néo-Grec, Italian, Elizabethan and other styles. The escutcheons for the page numbers are highly eccentric; one overmantel is a tribute to the ALBERT Memorial. *Designs in Various Styles* (1877; fifty-one plates of fringes, valances and pelmets) was succeeded by *The Compiler* (1879), whose 240 designs are mainly reprinted from SHERATON, Adam, PERGOLESI and others. Charles's last work, *Decorative Designs by Robert Adams* (sic) (1883), comprises six plates traced from Adam drawings in the SOANE Museum.

Charmeton, Georges (1623–74) Born in Lyon, the son of a painter, Charmeton moved to Paris, where he became a pupil of Jacques STELLA. In 1663, under the direction of Sebastien Bourdon

(1616–71), Charmeton painted the decorative and landscape elements of the gallery of the Hôtel Bretonvilliers (J.-B. MONNOYER (1636–99) painted the flowers). This work made his reputation as a painter of ornament and in 1665 he became a member of the Academy. After his death some fourteen suites of ornament were published after his drawings, many dated 1676,and with six plates each. They are characteristic representations of the French BAROQUE style of ornament, with masks, ACANTHUS scrolls, putti and sphinxes playing prominent roles. Particularly interesting are designs for embroidery to be used on beds, for carved ornament on coaches, and *Plusieurs Vaze*, a bold and sculptural series of six designs for VASES. A large suite of *Corniches* (thirty plates) contains elaborate baroque mouldings; dedicated to the architect Claude Perrault (1613–88), it was later reprinted in Augsburg.

Charpentier, Alexandre (1856–1909) Charpentier started work as an apprentice jewel engraver, but later studied at the École des Beaux-Arts under the medallist Hubert Ponscarmé (1827–1903). From 1879 he showed as a sculptor at the Salon. He was a friend of CARABIN and in 1893 followed him in showing furniture at the Société Nationale. In 1892 he was a founder member of Les Cinq with DAMPT, AUBERT, SELMERSHEIM and Moreau-Nélaton (it became Les Six when Charles PLUMET joined in 1896). Charpentier was friendly with Octave Maus and showed in Brussels with Les Vingt in 1895 and the Salon de la Libre Esthétique in 1899. He designed posters, furniture, metalwork, ceramics and interiors. His work was widely published for instance in the 'REVUE DES ARTS DÉCORATIFS' (1895), for which he designed a luxury binding in 1899, the 'STUDIO' (1897) and the 'ARTIST'

(1901). At the PARIS 1900 EXHIBITION Charpentier designed a dining-room for the Magasins de Louvre. He worked with BRACQUEMOND, Besnard and Jules CHÉRET for Baron Vitta, and also designed a dining-room for Adrien Benard (1846–1912), who had commissioned GUIMARD'S Métro entrances. Charpentier's decorative style is elegant and curvilinear and makes generous use of female nudes, in each respect typical of French ART NOUVEAU.

Charvet, Jean Gabriel (1750–1829) Born at Serrières, Ardèche, Charvet was a pupil at the École de Dessin at Lyon and of the painter Donat Nonotte (1708–85). In 1785 Charvet founded a drawing school in Annonay. He was active as a painter and ornamental designer. In about 1805 Charvet designed a scenic wallpaper, Les Sauvages de la Mer Pacifique, recording Captain Cook's discovery of the Sandwich Islands in 1778, printed from 1806 by Joseph Dufour & Cie at Mâcon.

Chateauneuf, Alexis de (1799–1853) Son of a French diplomat who opened a bookshop in Hamburg after the French revolution, Chateauneuf was trained as an architect by Lectère in Paris (1817) and by Weinbrenner in Karlsruhe. After travels, Chateauneuf settled in Hamburg in 1823. His furniture (1835) for the house he designed for Dr Abendroth in 1831 to 1834 displays a tense mixture of massy NEO-CLASSICAL detailing with curved forms which owe more to the early phase of the German ROCOCO Revival. Chateauneuf's *Architectura Domestica* (London, Paris and Hamburg, 1839) includes a Romanesque/GOTHIC interior with two Glastonbury chairs, as well as classical designs for Dr Abendroth.

Chedel, Pierre Quentin (1705–63) Born

at Châlons-sur-Marne, Chedel was a prolific engraver in Paris, his works including prints after MEISSONIER, and the engraving of OUDRY's illustrations to La Fontaine's *Fables* (1755–9). Chedel's own *Fantaisies Nouvelles* (1738; six plates) were intended to be useful for textile design and similar purposes; they are stiff but imaginative compositions of shells, water, sea creatures and ROCOCO scrolls. He also designed two *Livres de Fantaisies* (twelve plates in all), with cartouches, ornaments, fountains, etc.

Chenavard, Aimé (1798–1838) An architect, in 1830 Chenavard was appointed as an adviser to the Sèvres porcelain factory by Alexandre Brongniart. His *Recueil de Dessins* (Paris, 1828; thirty plates) was also distributed by 'Akerman 96 strand LONDON' (sic). It included designs for furniture, stained glass, tapestry and carpets in the Chinese, Egyptian, Turkish, RENAISSANCE and GOTHIC styles, but is predominantly in a rich and refined late-Grecian style. His *Nouveau Recueil de décorations intérieures* (1833–5; forty-two plates) and its sequel, *Album de l'ornemaniste* (1836; seventy-two plates), contained designs of furniture, textiles, glass, metalwork and porcelain. In these the predominant style is Renaissance, although many designs are in the Persian, Chinese and Gothic styles and a few in the late Grecian style. Designs include a silver-gilt ewer for the Duc d'Orléans made by M. Durand and shown at the PARIS 1834 EXHIBITION, VASES in 16th-century stoneware style, shown at the Sèvres 1833 Exhibition, the title-page of the magazine *L'Artiste*, for 1828, and furniture made in the Chenavard factory. Many of these designs were printed, with some by LECONTE, in Louis Zoellner's *Der Ornamentist* (Leipzig, 1843). The posthumous *Le Mosaïque* (1851; twenty-four plates)

contains many official commissions and a similar mix of styles, with some particularly elaborate designs for cutlery and Sèvres vases in a late-16th-century style, and a complete redecoration of the chapel at Eu in the Gothic style, on which Chenavard collaborated with Achille Mascret.

Chéret, Gustave-Joseph (1838–94) The younger brother of Jules CHÉRET, Gustave-Joseph Chéret worked successively for an ornamental sculptor Gallois, for a porcelain factory at Boulogne and then for the sculptor and designer LIÉNARD. Chéret showed as a sculptor at the Salon from 1863. He then became a pupil of CARRIER-BELLEUSE and married his daughter Marie in 1868. Chéret designed metalwork for Christofle, glass for the Baccarat factory (from 1877), as well as designs for many other manufacturers, including in about 1870 the Cologne furniture manufacturer Pallenberg. At the end of Carrier-Belleuse's life Chéret succeeded him for a brief period as Directeur des Travaux d'Art at Sèvres. A Sèvres VASE to Chèret's design, with masks, putti and jolly nudes, was shown at the PARIS 1900 EXHIBITION and some designs are still in production. At the PARIS 1889 EXHIBITION Chéret won a gold medal for his designs for the furniture manufacturer Fourdinois.

Chéret, Jules (1836–1932) Born in Paris, the son of a typographer, Chéret trained from 1849 as a lithographer, also attending evening classes at the École Nationale de Dessin. In 1854 he went to London, where he designed a furniture catalogue. Back in Paris his first major commission was a poster of 1858 for Offenbach's *Orpheus in the Underworld*. From 1859 to 1866 he was again in England and perfected his technique as a lithographer, designing book covers for the publisher Cramer and posters for the circus, theatre and music halls.

Chéret travelled to Italy and North Africa with the perfume manufacturer Rimmel, for whom he designed labels and packaging. On their return to Paris in 1866, Rimmel financed Chéret to set up a lithographic press with modern English machines. Chéret was then able to produce the first French coloured posters. In 1881 he sold the press to the Imprimerie Chaix but he kept artistic control, publishing not only his own posters but also those of other designers, including BERTHON. In all Chéret designed some 1,200 posters. His formula of attractive women in active poses, visible for example in his poster for Loie Fuller at the Folies Bergère (1893), was enormously successful and widely imitated. His poster for Zola's *La Terre* (1889) is atypically bleak. In 1895 to 1896 Chéret did murals for Baron Vitta's villa, La Sapinière, and in his later years he executed a number of decorative schemes, and designed VASES for Vitta, fabrics for the collector Fenaille and tapestries for the Gobelins factory.

Chermayeff, Serge Born in 1900 in the Caucasus of an oil-rich family, Chermayeff was educated at Harrow. From 1918 to 1922 he was a journalist in London with Amalgamated Press and then from 1922 to 1924 he worked in Argentina. From 1924 to 1927 he worked as chief designer for the decorating firm E. Williams Ltd. In 1928 he was appointed director of the Modern Art Studio set up by the London furniture manufacturers Waring & Gillow, who also employed FOLLOT. Chermayeff's designs for furniture, carpets and decoration were strongly influenced by the PARIS 1925 EXHIBITION, sometimes ART DÉCO in character, sometimes more MODERN. He used black glass, silver cellulose, macassar ebony and abstract patterns. His designs were a revelation to English commercial manufacturers. In the 'CABINET MAKER' (1930) Chermayeff envisaged the elimination of ornament and the evolution of 'as pure a style as was finally achieved by the Greeks in the age of Pericles'. From 1931 to 1933 he was in private practice as an architect and designed Modern interiors for the B.B.C., including stacking tubular-steel chairs made by P.E.L. (1931–2). His plastic AC74 radio case for Ekco was one of the best early designs in this field. From 1933 to 1936 Chermayeff was in partnership with Eric Mendelsohn (1887–1953); their best-known joint work is the De La Warr pavilion at Bexhill. In 1936 Chermayeff designed Unit furniture for Plan Ltd. In 1939 he emigrated to America and taught design and architecture at Chicago (1946–51), Harvard (1953–6) and Yale (1962–71).

Chevreul, Michel Eugène (1786–1889) Born in Angers, Chevreul studied chemistry at the Collège de France in Paris and subsequently taught at the Lycée Charlemagne. In 1826 he entered the Academy of Sciences, and in 1830 became professor of organic chemistry at the Natural History Museum in Paris. His discoveries as a chemist included margarine. From 1824 Chevreul was director of dyeing at the Gobelins tapestry manufactory, a post which led in 1825 to profound research into colour theory and to his *The Principles of Harmony and Contrast of Colours* (1839, English edition 1854), which developed lectures given in 1828, 1836 and 1838. Chevreul applied his insights to tapestries, carpets, mosaics, stained glass, calico-printing, wallpapers and so on. In 1872 he was accused of having reduced tapestry to a detestable rivalry with oil painting, but was able to defend himself with considerable vigour, citing his own teachings. Owen JONES was among the many designers who relied heavily on Chevreul for colour theory.

Chicago 1893 World Columbian Exposition Chicago was in 1890 chosen as the site of an exhibition to celebrate the four-hundredth anniversary of the discovery of America by Columbus in 1493. Daniel H. Burnham (1846–1912) was chief architect and the appointed style was 'Roman classic' chosen as 'capable of variation according to the best Italian and RENAISSANCE models'. Exuberant wedding-cake architecture resulted and attracted over twenty-seven million visitors, significantly fewer than the PARIS 1889 EXHIBITION, but nearly three times as many as the PHILADELPHIA 1876 EXHIBITION. Frank Lloyd WRIGHT was a disparaging visitor, finding the Japanese pavilion alone worthy of praise.

Chinoiserie Chinoiserie is the term for the European use of Chinese or pseudo-Chinese motifs in ornament and design. Although trading links with China can be traced back to antiquity and Marco Polo's memoirs of his supposed travels in China in the late 13th century enjoyed some currency, direct imitations of Chinese art are rare until the 17th century. The soft-paste porcelain produced by the Medici factory in Florence between 1575 and 1587 included pieces with decoration based on Chinese prototypes, although others are decorated with GROTESQUES probably designed by BUONTALENTI. A new source of inspiration were lacquers and other wares imported from China and Japan, particularly by the Dutch East India Company, founded in 1602; one English ship, the *Clove*, brought back a cargo of Japanese lacquer in 1614. However, a new impulse towards the imitation of Chinese art was given by the Dutch embassy to Peking in 1656, or more particularly by the account of it by Jan Nieuhof, 'steward to the ambassadors', first published in Dutch in 1665, translated into French in the same year and into English in 1669. Nieuhof's book was followed by accounts of China by Athanasius Kircher (1667), Arnoldus Montanus (1671, following a book on Japan of 1669) and Jean Baptiste Du Halde (1735). A new fashion for things Chinese was reflected in the Trianon de Porcelaine at Versailles, designed by Louis Le Vau (1612–70) in 1670 as a present from Louis XIV to his mistress, Madame de Montespan (1641–1707); demolished in 1687, it seems to have been BAROQUE in form but Chinese in detail, covered in blue-and-white tiles and with blue-and-white interiors. STALKER and Parker's *Treatise of Japanning* (1688) presented models, many derived from Nieuhof, for the lacquered decoration of furniture etc.; a later pattern-book of the same kind is FRAISSE's *Livre de Desseins Chinois* (1735). Influences from India, China and Japan were often confounded by contemporary designers, and even Indian chintzes were decorated with chinoiserie ornament for the English market. BERAIN incorporated Chinese figures in his grotesques, and Chinese figures and Chinese attributes were combined to form a new ornamental genre by WATTEAU in paintings of 1709, later engraved by BOUCHER. Boucher himself designed numerous chinoiseries, including in 1740 a trade card for Gersaint's shop, À La Pagode. In England chinoiserie elements were used by such designers as DE LA COUR, DARLY, CHIPPENDALE, HALFPENNY and LINNELL. *Designs of Chinese Buildings* (1757) by CHAMBERS provided designs for furniture and other utensils based on his observations in China, but a more fantastical chinoiserie manner survived in designs by PILLEMENT. SHERATON and RANSON later executed chinoiserie designs, but the swansong of chinoiserie was in the interiors of Brighton Pavilion designed by Frederick Crace.

Chippendale, Thomas (1718–79) Born in Otley, Yorkshire, the son of a joiner, Chippendale retained his links with his birthplace until his death. He probably received his training as a cabinet-maker under Richard Wood of York. However, from at least 1748, when he married at St George's Chapel, Mayfair, and probably from before 1747, when he was paid a small sum by Lord Burlington, he was in London. There is no firm evidence as to who taught Chippendale how to design, but the best candidates are Matthias LOCK and Matthias DARLY. The latter not only engraved most of the plates, all dated 1753, for Chippendale's *The Gentleman and Cabinet-Maker's Director* (1754) but also shared his house in Northumberland Court in 1753. In the same year Chippendale moved to grander premises in St Martin's Lane, probably financed by his Scottish partner, James Rannie. The street was then a centre of artistic life in London, and Slaughter's Coffee House, opposite Chippendale's shop, was a meeting place for artists, craftsmen and patrons. The *Director*, first announced in March 1753, appeared in April 1754. It was dedicated to the Earl of Northumberland and attracted several subscribers among wealthy and noble patrons of the arts as well as a large following from tradesmen, ranging from cabinet-makers to enamellers and jewellers. It was also supported by booksellers, including Robert SAYER, who took six copies. The second edition of the *Director*, which appeared in 1755, was in fact marketed by Sayer; it was an almost unaltered reprint of the first edition. The *Director* had 161 plates which depicted first the orders of architecture borrowed from James GIBBS's *Rules for Drawing the Several Parts of Architecture* (1732), and then a whole range of 'household furniture in the GOTHIC, Chinese and modern taste'. 'Modern' here means ROCOCO. In July 1759 INCE & Mayhew

announced their *Universal System of Household Furniture*, modelled on and intended as a rival to the *Director*. Chippendale was quick to respond, announcing in October 1759 the publication of a third edition of the *Director* to appear in parts. The full volume appeared in 1762, dedicated to His Royal Highness Prince William Henry (1743–1805), and at the same time a French edition was issued; examples of the latter were in the libraries of Catherine the Great of Russia and Louis XVI of France. The third edition dropped nearly half the plates of the first and added 106 new plates, bringing the total up to 200. Among the new engravers was Isaac Taylor (1730–1807), founder of a dynasty of architectural publishers. In his preface Chippendale indignantly refuted critics who had queried the practicality of the designs in the first edition, and in several of his notes to the plates vaunted the effect of his designs when executed. The new edition illustrated a wider range of furniture and tended to elaboration rather than simplicity. Two years earlier in 1760 Chippendale contributed at least six plates to Robert Sayer's unpretentious publication *Household Furniture in Genteel Taste* (further editions 1762, 1763 and about 1764). Also in 1760 he had been elected to the SOCIETY OF ARTS, being proposed by the accomplished amateur architect Sir Thomas Robinson of Rokeby (about 1702–77). Firm evidence exists that Chippendale designed not only for publication and for his own firm, but also for other craftsmen, including furniture, carpets and wallpaper; his *Director* designs were even borrowed on other cabinet-makers' trade cards. Chippendale seems only rarely to have executed the designs of architects, a solitary exception being a suite of chairs designed by Robert ADAM for Sir Lawrence Dundas in 1764. Adam may have brought Chippendale his first major known commission, the furnishing of Dumfries House from 1759 onwards: the design for a bed made for Dumfries House, dated 1759, is included in the third edition of *Director* (1762). The first signs of a response to the new NEO-CLASSICAL ideas then being introduced to London by STUART, CHAMBERS and Adam are apparent in the 1762 *Director*, which integrates ram's heads, husks, caryatids and lion masks into designs which are otherwise little different from those of 1754. The effect is of an *ad hoc* response to the new style rather than any real understanding of it. During the 1760s however Chippendale worked in a number of houses which were decorated by Adam, who seems to have been his principal avenue of patronage, including Croome Court, Nostell Priory and Harewood House, and developed an accomplished range of neo-classical designs. In 1766 Chippendale's partner James Rannie died, leaving Chippendale a legacy of financial insecurity. In 1771 he took Thomas Haig, Rannie's book-keeper, into partnership, and the firm remained Chippendale Haig & Co. until Chippendale's death, although a third partner, Henry Ferguson, probably had a financial interest in the firm, which was one of the top cabinet-making businesses in London. Towards the end of his career his son Thomas CHIPPENDALE THE YOUNGER probably played a major role in designing for the firm. But Chippendale's own gifts as a designer, although often questioned in recent years, were evidently considerable; rarely innovative or brilliant, he was always competent. He borrowed little (some putti from BICKHAM'S *Universal Penman* (1734) in the 1762 *Director* are an exception), and his subscription to Thomas MALTON'S *A Compleat Treatise on Perspective* (1775) demonstrates his professionalism. His versatility is demonstrated by his move from rococo to neo-classicism. After his death SHERATON and George SMITH praised him, and in the 1830s John WEALE paid him a curious compliment by attaching his name to reprints of designs by JOHNSON and others to satisfy rococo revival designers. Modern reprints of the *Director* go back to 1900; what is still needed is an edition of his drawings, which are mainly divided between the Metropolitan Museum in New York and the VICTORIA & ALBERT MUSEUM in London.

Chippendale, Thomas, the Younger (1749–1822) Thomas Chippendale the Younger entered his father's firm and signed business letters from 1767. He seems to have taken over the effective running of the firm at about the date of his father's apparent retirement to Kensington in about 1777, and after his father's death he continued as a partner in the firm until its bankruptcy in 1804. He then restarted it and was in business until at least 1820. In 1772 Chippendale designed a cartouche for a map of Hull and its river, and in 1779 he published *Sketches of Ornament*, five panels of NEO-CLASSICAL ornament with VASES, sphinxes, griffins and scrolling ACANTHUS in a rich version of the ADAM manner. Chippendale subscribed to several of George RICHARDSON'S works and had pretensions as a painter, exhibiting five genre works at the Royal Academy from 1784 to 1801. From 1797 to 1820 Chippendale supplied handsome and often inventive neo-classical furniture to Stourhead in Wiltshire. In about 1820 he designed a chair made from the elm which was Wellington's command post at Waterloo (1815). In 1826 George SMITH coupled him with Thomas HOPE as one of the two English 'artists who have excelled in their designs for furniture' and stated that 'Mr Thomas Chippendale (lately deceased), and known only amongst a few, possessed a very great degree of taste, with great ability as a draughtsman and designer'. All too little is known about his activities.

Chodowiecki, Daniel (1726–1801) Born in Danzig of mixed Polish and Huguenot ancestry, Chodowiecki settled in Berlin in 1743 and established himself first as a painter of enamel boxes. He taught himself to engrave and became a prolific and brilliant book illustrator. In 1787 he engraved two designs for commemorative fans. His illustrations were widely used to decorate porcelain, for example by the Höchst and Volkstedt factories. He became a member of the Berlin Academy in 1764 and was its Director from 1797 until his death, when he was succeeded by his friend MEIL. The NEO-CLASSICAL realism which Chodowiecki practised in miniature was tempered by a delicacy and intimacy derived from French ROCOCO models.

Choffard, Pierre Philippe (1730–1809) Taught by P. E. BABEL, Choffard became the leading French designer and engraver of book ornaments in the late 18th century. He engraved some 855 plates, many after other designers, including BACHELIER's ornaments for the 1762 edition of La Fontaine and the drawings by the architect Pierre-Adrien Paris (1747–1819) illustrated in Saint-Non's *Voyage pittoresque de Naples et de Sicile* (1781–86), but the majority designed by Choffard himself and including a wide range of titles, *culs-de-lampe*, addresses, *vignettes*, etc., as well as suites of nervous and varied cartouches part NEO-CLASSICAL and part ROCOCO in style. *Diversi Trofei e Ornamenti* (six plates) comprises highly sophisticated neo-classical trophies depicted as classical stone reliefs, designed by Choffard and by Benigno BOSSI.

Chopard, Jean François In about 1750 Chopard published a suite of designs for carriages (twelve plates) in a restrained but accomplished ROCOCO style; the plates included many technical details. On the title Chopard is called '*menuisier du Roi*'. Chopard was also probably responsible for five designs for carriages published with harness designs by Baudouin. In 1767 Chopard designed a NEO-CLASSICAL carriage for the Marquis de MARIGNY, and in 1773 to 1774 he executed carriages designed by BÉLANGER for the Comte d'Artois and the Duc de Bourbon-Condé. Chopard was still in the royal service in 1780.

Ciampoli, Carlo Ciampoli, born in Ancona, published *Adornamenti di gioie* (Rome, 1711; twenty-eight plates), with drawings of rings, earrings, watches, box-lids etc.

Ciotti, Giovanni Battista Ciotti was the publisher of a basic but competent twenty-plate book of lace designs, *Prima parte · de' fiore* (Venice, 1591), which was copied by William BARLEY in 1596, and by Tomaso Pasini (1591), Florimi (1591 and 1594) and Gargano (1601).

C.L. In 1757 Giovanni Carlo Mallia published in Rome a *Racolta di Disegni d'Ornati*, dedicated to Prince Rospigliosi (seven plates designed by C.L.). The *Racolta* presents elaborate jewels, miniature frames, brooches, etc., mainly set with gemstones; they incorporate foliate, floral and ROCOCO ornament with some architectural elements.

Clarke, Harry (1889–1931) Born in Dublin, the son of a church decorator and stained-glass manufacturer from Leeds, Clarke was trained in his father's business, and in the Dublin and South Kensington Schools of Art, winning many scholarships and prizes. His master in Dublin was A. E. Child, who had arrived there in 1903 after working in

Christopher WHALL's London studios. From 1909 Clarke was active as a graphic artist and from 1910 he showed glass with the Arts & Crafts Society of Ireland. In 1914 he met E. A. TAYLOR and Jessie KING in Paris, and his work was noticed in the 'STUDIO', where Oswald Reeves praised his hieratic windows for the Honan Chapel, Cork, in 1918 and Thomas Bodkin published an appreciation of his art in 1919. In the latter year Clarke was commissioned to design handkerchiefs and textiles by Walter Sefton of Belfast. After his father's death in 1921 Clarke took over the business with his brother and his activity as a stained-glass designer further intensified. Among the many exhibitions at which he showed was one in London in 1925 with John Austen, Alan Odle and Austen O. Spare, and at the end of his life Clarke spent much time in London. His book illustrations were very popular: the principal are Hans Andersen's *Fairy Tales* (1916), Poe's *Tales of Mystery and Imagination* (1919), *The Year's at the Spring* (1920), Perrault's *Fairy Tales* (1922), Goethe's *Faust* (1925) and Swinburne's *Poems* (1928). The dominant influence on Clarke, as on his friend John Austen, was Beardsley, whose work he would have seen together with that of BURNE-JONES, ROSSETTI, Walter CRANE and others at the Dublin 1907 Irish International Exhibition. The decadent symbolism of Clarke's work was out of fashion at his death and his religious windows can be mawkish and formulaic. But at his best he displays a febrile intensity and luminosity of vision, for instance in his jewel-like *Eve of St Agnes* window (1923–4).

Classic Two London exhibitions, Classics of Modern Design (1977) and Classics (1981), the latter organized by Heal's, the furniture shop, reflect the MODERN hankering after a canon of approved models, formally and historically irreproachable. The NEW YORK MUSEUM OF MODERN ART has been most influential in establishing what is 'Classic' and what, by implication, is not. BREUER, BRANDT, MIES VAN DER ROHE, LE CORBUSIER and AALTO are typical of the designers given the 'Classic' accolade. In the late 1970s Cassina and other manufacturers reissued many 'Classic' designs which had not survived in production, with great commercial success. But although the authority of the Classic remained intact, detailing proved all too mutable, and such later versions are often coarse or prettified. One of the more curious aspects of the cult of the Classic is a tendency to fix on an object from an earlier century and to give it Modern Classic status. Le Corbusier's canonization of the THONET bentwood chair was an early example of this process, obscuring the chair's origins in the ROCOCO revival.

Clein, Francis (1582–1658) Born in Rostock, the son of a goldsmith, Francis Clein was by 1611 in the service of Christian IV of Denmark. He then went to Italy for four years, which included a stay in Venice, where Clein met Sir Henry Wotton. Back in Denmark by 1617, Clein was employed from 1618 to 1623 on the decoration of the royal castle of Rosenborg, where he painted Italianate GROTESQUES in the King's writing closet. In 1623 Sir Arthur Anstruther, English Ambassador in Copenhagen, recommended Clein to the Prince of Wales as 'a very eminent artist working in tapestry'. Prince Charles was in Spain when Clein arrived but he was well received by James I and appointed designer to the Mortlake tapestry factory founded in 1620 by Sir Francis Crane. James I then sent Clein back to Denmark but requested his brother-in-law Christian IV to release him permanently from his service. Clein completed his work in Denmark and returned to

London in 1625. Charles I granted him a pension and he was soon employed to design a triumphal arch to celebrate Queen Henrietta Maria's arrival in London, under Inigo JONES's supervision. He also decorated the Queen's cabinet at Old Somerset House, the façade of Wimbledon House, and after 1625 designed interiors, including shell-backed Italianate chairs, for Holland House. As tapestry designer at Mortlake, Clein executed working cartoons from RAPHAEL's Acts of the Apostles and designed borders for them, as well as suites of Hero and Leander (completed 1636), Horses, and the Five Senses. The death in 1636 of Sir Francis Crane, whose house, Stoke Bruerne, Clein had decorated, led to the sale of the Mortlake works to Charles I and to Clein's continued employment there at a higher salary. Under the Commonwealth the ageing Clein continued at Mortlake until at least 1657. He also executed decorative paintings at Ham House, partly based on POLIDORO DA CARAVAGGIO and probably designed other decorations at Ham. He published several suites of ornament in London, *Septum Liberales Artes* (1645; eight plates), *Quinque Sensuum descriptio* (1646; six plates), *Varii Zophori figuris animalium* (1645; twelve plates) and *Several Borders of Grotesk Works useful of Painters . . .* (1654; fourteen plates). Clein's ornament comprises highly competent BAROQUE grotesque and ACANTHUS friezes and panels, incorporating many animals and birds. He was also a prolific illustrator of books, including Ovid's *Metamorphoses* (Oxford, 1632, Paris, 1637), Virgil (London, 1654) and Homer (1660). His Homer and Virgil plates served later as the basis for wall-paintings at Adlington in Cheshire.

Clerget, Charles Ernest Born in Paris in 1812, Clerget was active as a designer of ornament, title-pages, porcelain, for the Sèvres factory, and tapestry, for the Gobelins factory. He was responsible for a number of books of ornament, working first for LECONTE but later issuing *Nouveaux Ornements* (1840; eighteen plates), *Ornements Teintés* (1841; eighteen plates) and the *Encyclopédie Universelle d'Ornements* (eighty-four plates). These ranged from Virgil SOLIS to India for inspiration, but most designs shared a fascination with interlaced ornament, including a remarkable Saxon carpet in the *Encylopédie*, which was designed by Ovide Regnard, not Clerget himself. Clerget also published designs for wallpapers and goldsmiths' work and several anthologies of mainly 16th-century ornament, on one of which, of 1841, he collaborated with Riester, among others. His *Collection Portative d'Ornaments de la Renaissance* (1851; thirty-six plates) reprinted plates from 16th-century embroidery and lace pattern-books. In 1859 Clerget wrote on typographic ornament. He was later a librarian to the Union Centrale des Beaux-Arts Appliqués à l'Industrie.

Clérisseau, Charles-Louis (1721–1820) Born in Paris, the son of a seller of scented gloves, Clérisseau was trained as an architect by Jacques-François BLONDEL. In 1746 he won the Grand Prix d'Architecture and in 1749 set off for Italy to study at the French Academy in Rome until 1754. He was taught perspective by the painter Gian Paolo Pannini and himself taught a number of English tourists, including CHAMBERS, with whom he fell out. While staying at the house of the connoisseur and art dealer Ignazio Hugford (1703–78) in Florence on his way back to France, Clérisseau met Robert ADAM, who engaged him as his tutor in drawing and antiquities. In 1755 they went to Rome together and until their departure in 1757 Clérisseau lived in Adam's lodgings. He assisted Adam's survey of Diocletian's palace at Split and back in Venice supervised the engraving of the plates for Adam's resultant *Spalatro* (1764), until James Adam's arrival in 1760, after which he returned with James Adam to Rome, accompanied by George RICHARDSON. After James Adam's return to England in 1763 Clérisseau stayed in Rome until 1767. He was friendly with Mengs and PIRANESI and in about 1766 designed a remarkable ruin room at Trinità dei Monti, which contained a bed formed as an antique basin, a desk as a damaged sarcophagus, and tables and chairs as a fragment of cornice and inverted capitals. It was much admired by Winckelmann. On his return to France Clérisseau became a member of the Académie Royale de Peinture in 1769. He visited England in 1771. In about 1774 he designed for the Hôtel Grimod de la Reynière wall-paintings '*dans le style arabesque*' and, probably, a carpet, furniture and candelabra. Clérisseau also worked for the Empress Catherine of Russia and advised JEFFERSON on the Virginia State Capitol. Only the first volume of his *Antiquités de France* (1778) was published: it is in the bibliography to HOPE's *Household Furniture* (1807). At the end of his life Clérisseau lived in Auteuil, where Hubert ROBERT was a neighbour. He left a large collection of designs, and of notes for his *Antiquités*.

Clermont, Andien de Probably a pupil of the flower painter Antoine Monnoyer (1670–1747), Clermont may have come to England with his master in 1717. In England, Clermont worked not only as a flower painter but also as a painter of delightfully light and colourful *singeries* and GROTESQUES in a BERAINESQUE or early ROCOCO manner, at Kirtlington Park, Oxfordshire, Langley Park, Norfolk, and elsewhere. In 1754 he painted the heraldic ceiling of the Library at Strawberry Hill designed by Richard BENTLEY for Horace WALPOLE. His sale in 1740 included 'Designs for Screens and Chairs in Needlework or Tapestry' and Clermont is believed to have designed grotesque tapestries woven by Joshua Morris at Frith Street, Soho, in the 1720s. In about 1756 Clermont returned to France, where he may have worked at Chantilly. He died in 1783.

Cliff, Clarice (1899–1972) Born in Tunstall in Staffordshire, Cliff became in 1912 an apprentice enameller at a local pottery. She went to evening classes and in 1918 joined A. J. Wilkinson Ltd, Royal Staffordshire Pottery, Burslem. In about 1925 the managing director of Wilkinsons, Colley Shorter, whom she married in 1941, allowed Cliff to experiment in the Newport Pottery, which Wilkinsons had taken over. She produced patterns called Bizarre, decorated with Modernistic geometric patterns, and from 1928 Cliff designed a vast variety of 'Hand Painted Bizarre' wares in a popular jazzy idiom; they were a great success. In 1932 she employed contemporary artists to design wares for the pottery – Duncan GRANT, Vanessa Bell, Paul NASH, Graham Sutherland and Laura Knight; these were not such a success and the experiment ended. Clarice Cliff remained Art Director of the Newport Pottery until 1963.

Coates, Wells (1895–1958) Born in Japan, the son of a Canadian missionary, Coates studied engineering in Vancouver from 1913. After the war, when he trained as a pilot, he gained a London doctorate in 1924 for research on the diesel engine. He then worked as a journalist, with a special interest in advanced technology, and became acquainted with the MODERN style of LE CORBUSIER and others. After marrying in 1927 Coates began to work as a designer. In 1928 he designed a shop for Crysede silks, and in 1929 a factory and the first of many shops for the breakaway Cresta Silks, in which he exploited plywood and made the first use of a bow- or D-handle, an innovation still in use. Jack Pritchard of the Venesta plywood company recognized his talent and in 1931 Wells Coates won a competition to design a stand for Venesta for the Manchester British Empire Trade Exhibition. Also in 1931 he and Pritchard formed the ISOKON Company for 'the application of modern functional design to houses, flats, furniture and fittings'. Its major project from 1932 was the Lawn Road Flats; a specimen minimum flat with built-in furniture was shown at the Dorland Hall British Industrial Art Exhibition (1933). The flats were opened in 1934; among the early tenants were GROPIUS, BREUER and MOHOLY-NAGY. Wells Coates also designed bookcase units for Isokon. In 1931 he designed sound studios for the British Broadcasting Corporation in Portland Place, and recast the interiors of 1 Palace Green, a Victorian mansion, in the Modern style, with murals by John ARMSTRONG; it was published in the 'ARCHITECTURAL REVIEW' (1932), with 'before and after' views. In 1933 Wells Coates helped to form the MARS Group as an English CONGRÈS INTERNATIONAUX D'ARCHITECTURE MODERNE chapter, and became a member of Paul NASH's UNIT ONE. He was at this period leading the vanguard of the Modern movement in England. In 1932 he won a competition to design a wireless case for Ekco; his circular plastic design, the AD65, was produced from 1934. In 1935 he designed tubular-steel furniture for PEL, and in 1936 wood furniture for Ganes of Bristol. He was an advocate of built-in furniture and his own one-room flat in Yeoman's Row, Hampstead, incorporated a low room divider doub-

ling as a back rest, a tubular-steel bed ladder and a movable desk fitted into a wall unit. His later designs included the Thermovent Ekco fire (1937), and Ekco television with a lift-up top (1946), the Radio Time combined wireless and alarm clock (1946), aircraft interiors for De Havilland and BOAC (1946–7), and the portable Princess Handbag wireless (1948). But, although appointed a Royal Designer for Industry in 1944, Wells Coates's post-war career was a sad series of false starts and he produced little more.

Cochin, Charles-Nicolas (1715–90) The son of an engraver under whom he studied, Cochin was appointed Dessinateur et Graveur des Menus Plaisirs in 1739. From 1749 to 1751 he travelled in Italy as a companion to Mme de Pompadour's brother Abel Poisson, later Marquis de MARIGNY, together with the architect Soufflot and the Abbé Le Blanc. After returning to Paris he was appointed curator of the King's drawings in 1752. In 1754 he published *Observations sur les antiquités de la ville d'Herculaneum*, with illustrations by the architect J.-C. Bellicard (1726–86), and in the same year recommended the designer Pierre-Edmé BABEL to Robert ADAM. Also in 1754 he published an article in the *Mercure de France*, a heavily witty attack on the ROCOCO style, repeated in 1755. Cochin was a prolific engraver, after Vassé, OUDRY, François BOUCHER, LA JOUE and others. His posthumous memoirs, published in 1880, were critical of the more extreme productions of the NEO-CLASSICISM '*à la grecque*', of which he had been an early advocate.

Cochin, Nicolas (1610–86) Born in Troyes, the son of a glass painter, Cochin was active as an engraver in Paris from about 1640. His prolific output included a portrait of the goldsmith and engraver

Daniel BOUTEMIE, and *Livre Nouveau de Fleurs Tres Util pour l'Art d'Orfevrerie, et Autres* (Paris, 1645). This depicts naturalistic flowers for engraving on silver above small and delicate landscapes and battles.

Codman, Ogden (1863–1951) Codman was born in Boston of a well-connected family; his uncle was the architect John Hubbard Sturgis (1834–88). He spent much of his youth in France but returned to America in 1882 and spent an unhappy year at the Massachusetts Institute of Technology. In 1893 the novelist Edith Wharton (1862–1937) employed Codman to redecorate her Rhode Island house. From 1894 he designed Empire Revival interiors at the Harold Brown House, Newport, Rhode Island, and from 1895 decorated the top floors of Cornelius Vanderbilt's nearby The Breakers in a neat Louis XVI NEO-CLASSICAL style. In 1897 with Edith Wharton Codman published *The Decoration of Houses* advocating 18th-century good taste for the rich. In 1903 he designed Louis XV ROCOCO interiors at Château-sur-Mer, Newport. Codman accumulated a distinguished library of architectural books; his designs for furniture and interiors are distinguished by blandness and expertise.

Coeck, Pieter, van Alost (1502–50) Born in Alost, Coeck probably travelled to Italy and spent some time in the Brussels studio of the painter Bernart van ORLEY, where he may have met DÜRER and would have made the close acquaintance of RAPHAEL's style, before becoming a master painter in Antwerp in 1527. He was dean of the Guild of St Luke there in 1537. A woodcut of the triumph of Jacopus Castricus, about 1530, incorporating a triumphal arch and chariot, and the equally RE-NAISSANCE mark of the printer Jan Graphaeus, first used in 1527, have been

convincingly attributed to Coeck. During the 1530s he was active as a designer of tapestries, including the Story of David (five pieces, after 1531), the Histories of St Paul and Joshua (nine and eight pieces, both about 1535) and the Seven Deadly Sins (1537). In 1533 Coeck travelled to Constantinople probably in order to gain commissions for tapestries, a project which was commemorated in a series of woodcuts of Turkish scenes, apparently conceived as tapestry designs, published by his widow, the painter Maeyken Verhulst, in 1553. In about 1541 Coeck set up a workshop to draw tapestry cartoons in Antwerp. In 1534 he is said to have designed a great figure of the giant of Antwerp, Druon Antigon, for the entry to the town of the Emperor Charles V, to whom Coeck is said to have been painter in ordinary. He was also a designer of stained glass, including a documented window of 1537 in Antwerp Cathedral, for which the design survives; at St Catherine, Hoog-straten, are windows dated 1535 attributed to Coeck. In 1539 he published in Antwerp *Die Inventie der Colomnen*, a brief treatise on the ORDERS of which only one copy is known, and in the same year issued his Flemish translation of Book IV of SERLIO's *Architectura*, devoted to the orders, which thus appeared only two years later than the publication of the original in Venice. A German translation of Serlio's Book IV was issued by Coeck in 1542, dedicated to Ferdinand, King of the Romans (1503–64), brother of Charles V. The idea of the German edition was suggested to Coeck by Jacob Seisenegger, painter to Ferdinand. Its preface explains that Coeck's aim was to follow Dürer's theoretical work on fortification with equivalent treatises on architecture and decorative art. In 1545 Coeck published a French translation of Serlio's Book IV, dedicated to the Governor of the Netherlands, Marie of Hungary, thus ignoring Serlio's complaints about pirated editions of his books in the 1545 Paris edition of his Books I and II. In 1546 and 1550 Coeck produced Flemish and French translations of Serlio's Book III, devoted to the monuments of Rome, thus pirating, as it were, the foreign rights to both Book III and IV, the two parts of the *Architectura* with most practical use to designers. In his edition of Book IV Coeck underlined this practicality by substituting for a plate of shields an alphabet based on Luca Pacioli's *De Divina Proportione* (Venice, 1509), because shields were not manufactured in the Netherlands. In 1553 Coeck's widow completed his Flemish translation of Serlio by publishing Books I, II and V, on geometry, perspective and temples respectively. Coeck seems to have entrusted part of the marketing of his books to Cornelis Bos, who may also have been employed to re-engrave Serlio's illustrations. Coeck's 1542 German edition of Serlio's Book IV has a GROTESQUE frontispiece, an indication that Coeck was abreast of the advanced grotesque and STRAPWORK ornament associated with Cornelis FLORIS and Cornelis Bos. Coeck's title-page for Cornille Graphaeus's *Le Triomphe d'Anvers* (1550), a luxury album commemorating the triumphal entry of the future Philip II of Spain to Antwerp in 1549, is an even more developed example of the strapwork style. The programme of the entry was worked out by Graphaeus, secretary of the town of Antwerp, a humanist who had known Erasmus and Thomas More. Graphaeus had written a Latin poem in Coeck's praise in Coeck's German edition of Serlio's Book IV (1542), and it is highly probable that he employed Coeck as an adviser on the design of the entry, if not as director. The triumphal arches set up for the entry by Antwerp organizations made a lavish use of strapwork, in contrast to the more subdued classicism of the foreign arches, and this was probably due to Floris. Hans VREDEMAN DE VRIES, who had first been inspired by Coeck's Serlio translation, worked on the entry and was doubtless influenced by its early use of strapwork. However Coeck's most lasting influence was through his Serlio edition, which was reissued in Holland after the fall of Antwerp in 1567, and formed the basis for Robert Peake's 1611 London edition, dedicated to Henry, Prince of Wales.

Cole, Sir Henry (1808–82) The son of an officer in the dragoons, Cole was at Christ's Hospital School, and then from 1823 in the government service under Sir Francis Palgrave. In 1833 he was appointed a sub-commissioner of records. He studied watercolour under David Cox (1783–1859) and showed at the Royal Academy. Cole led a campaign for better conservation of records and in 1838 was appointed a senior assistant keeper in the reformed Public Record Office. He was also involved in postal reform, and, thanks to a friendship with Francis Douce (1757–1834), took an interest in antiquarian matters. From 1841 he published *Felix Summerly's Home Treasury*, a series of children's books illustrated by Mulready and others, followed by a series of guidebooks. In 1843, as Felix Summerly, Cole published the first Christmas card, designed by J. C. Horsley. In 1846 Cole won a silver medal from the SOCIETY OF ARTS for a tea service; it was produced by Herbert Minton, to whom Cole was introduced by WILLEMENT, and admired by Prince ALBERT. Cole joined the Society of Arts in the same year, becoming its chairman in 1851 and 1852. In 1847 Cole launched Summerly's Art-Manufactures, a series of model designs commissioned from artists of his acquaintance, including John BELL, Richard REDGRAVE and Daniel

MACLISE. In 1848 Cole announced the end of his connection with the venture which had 'established the compound work "art-manufactures" in our language'. From 1847 to 1849 Cole organized annual exhibitions of art-manufactures through the Society of Arts and in 1850 an exhibition of Ancient and Mediaeval Decorative Art. These were forerunners of the LONDON 1851 EXHIBITION, which was largely organized by Cole, working closely with Prince Albert. Cole was on the executive committee from 1849 and from 1850 served under Prince Albert with Digby WYATT and others on the Royal Commission for the exhibition. From 1851 to 1852 Cole served with Redgrave, A. W. N. PUGIN and Owen JONES on a committee to buy objects from the exhibition. He was later general adviser to the LONDON 1862 EXHIBITION, and manager of the unsuccessful LONDON EXHIBITIONS of 1871 to 1874, as well as secretary of the British commissions at the PARIS EXHIBITIONS of 1855 and 1867. From 1847 onwards Cole mounted an assault on the organization and methods of the SCHOOL OF DESIGN. Cole's 'JOURNAL OF DESIGN' was the mouthpiece of the campaign but the appointment in 1849 of a Select Committee on Schools of Design provided the engine of reform. In 1851 Cole was offered the job of Secretary to the School of Design, but he held out for more power and in early 1852 was appointed Secretary to a new government department formed at his suggestion, the Department of Practical Art, which administered the Schools of Design (there were thirty-six subordinate schools in 1852 and ninety-one in 1864) and created a museum; in 1853 it became the Department of Science and Art. The first major test of the reformed School of Design was the rapid production in 1852 of a massive car for the funeral of the Duke of Wellington. The Department's museum was first shown in a display at Marlborough House designed by Cole and Owen Jones; it included not only the objects bought from the London 1851 Exhibition but also 'Examples of False Principles in Decoration', attacked as 'A House full of Horrors', in Dickens's *Household Words*. Cole was also satirized in the ruthless utilitarian, Gradgrind, in *Hard Times* (1854), but Dickens and he were personally friendly. Cole's Museum moved to South Kensington in 1857 and rapidly expanded; it is now the VICTORIA & ALBERT MUSEUM. Cole retired from the Department in 1873, but continued to lead an active life.

Cole, Thomas (1801–48) Born at Bolton in Lancashire, Thomas Cole emigrated to America in 1819. He later became one of the founders of the Hudson River school of landscape painters, working in a romantic style strongly influenced by Claude, Turner and Martin. From 1821 to 1823, however, he worked as a wallpaper designer in his father's factory at Steubenville, Ohio.

Coleman, William Stephen (1829–1904) Born in Horsham in Sussex, the son of a doctor, Coleman studied medicine before turning to art. He trained at the Stoke-on-Trent School of Design. In the 1860s he worked as a book illustrator and for the Copeland factory. From 1869 he worked for Mintons and was from 1871 to 1873 director of Minton's Art Pottery in Kensington Gore. Coleman also designed Christmas and other cards for De La Rue.

Colenbrander, Theodor Christiaan Adriaen (1841–1930) Born in Doesburg, Colenbrander first worked for the Arnhem architect L. H. Eberson. In 1869 to 1870 they visited Paris. From 1884 to 1889 Colenbrander was director of the Rozenburg pottery in The Hague and designed ornament in a bold floral style with angular abstract elements influenced by Javanese batik. From 1895 he was director of a carpet factory at Amersfoort and from 1901 of that at Deventer. Colenbrander designed from 1912 to 1913 for a pottery in Gouda, and from 1913 lived in Arnhem, where he designed for the Ram pottery.

Collaert, Adriaen Born in Antwerp in about 1560, Collaert died there in 1618. In 1586 he married the daughter of the engraver and publisher Philippe Galle. Collaert was a prolific engraver working mainly after designs by contemporary artists, including Goltzius. A suite by Collaert on the theme of the Judgement of Paris has narrative roundels set in panels of elaborate scrolled STRAPWORK GROTESQUE ornament, comparable to that of Nicolas and Abraham de BRUYN. Collaert also designed suites of flowers (thirty-six plates in all), a suite of fishes (twenty-five plates), and two suites of ornament for engraving on dishes (four plates each), one round, one oval, both with fishes and sea monsters round their borders, and sea gods in the centre. As late as about 1735 a Collaert garden view was used to decorate a Castelli maiolica dish.

Collaert, Hans Collaert was active as an engraver in Antwerp from at least 1555 to his death in about 1581. In 1562 he supplied the design for the surviving pectoral cross of the Abbot of Averbode, elaborately decorated with enamelled and jewelled STRAPWORK. Designs of the planets by Collaert were used to decorate an astronomical clock made for the Elector August of Saxony in about 1567. Before 1573 he designed two suites of pendants (ten plates each), published by Hans Liefrinck. All are decorated with delicate black scrolled flowers and foliage, and nine have elaborate MANNERIST architectural niches that

have figures superimposed on this background. Other pendant designs engraved by Collaert about this date consist entirely of niches of architecture. Liefrinck published delicate friezes of birds by Collaert, some perched on scrolling tendrils; these were later copied by Henri Le Roy and Hans JANSSEN. Philippe Galle published two posthumous suites of designs for pendants by Collaert, *Monilium Bullarum Inaurumque Artificiocissimae Icones* (1581; ten plates) and *Bullarum inaurum &c. archetypi artificiosi* (1582, second edition, 1604; ten plates); the 1581 suite is decorated with figures, GROTESQUES and stones, while the 1582 suite is entirely composed of figures riding massive sea monsters. Designs by Collaert are known to have been available in England before 1618.

Collan, Jacques An engraver in Rotterdam, Collan published *Nouveau Livre d'Ornemens*, with rich dense ACANTHUS ornament for boxes, watch-cases, seals and buckles, some with monograms or allegorical scenes. One plate is dated 1702. In 1728 Collan engraved a title-page.

Collcutt, Thomas Edward (1840–1924) Born in Oxford, Collcutt was articled to the architect R. E. Armstrong. After working for Miles & Murgatroyd he became an assistant to G. E. STREET, in whose office he met Philip WEBB and Richard Norman SHAW. Collcutt reacted against GOTHIC to become one of the leading protagonists of the Queen Anne style. In 1870 he designed new premises in Fleet Street for the luxury cabinet-makers Collinson & Lock, for whom he also designed furniture, including pieces shown in their 1871 catalogue *Sketches of Artistic Furniture*, to which J. Moyr SMITH also contributed, and an influential ebonized cabinet with painted decoration shown in London in 1871, Vienna in 1873 and Philadelphia in 1876. Colcutt's first offices, in Essex Street, Strand, were below those of GODWIN. For the PARIS 1878 EXHIBITION Collcutt designed a house in the Street of Nations for Collinson & Lock, together with much of its furniture. Collcutt also designed furniture for Jackson & Graham, Gillows and Maples. A Collcutt cabinet of 1884 with a scrolled broken pediment and RENAISSANCE-style inlaid decoration is comparable to contemporary designs by Maurice B. ADAMS, who was a close friend. Collcutt was enormously successful as an architect, his best-known building being the Imperial Institute (1887–93). He also designed a hanging lamp illustrated by EDIS (1881), a Della Robbia pottery fountain for the courtyard of the Savoy Hotel (about 1898), and interiors for many P. & O. steamships. Collcutt's work was praised by MUTHESIUS.

Colling, James Kellaway (1816–1905) In 1832 Colling entered the office of the architect Matthew Habershon (1789–1852). From 1836 to 1840 Colling practised in Norfolk, assiduously drawing GOTHIC antiquities. In 1841 to 1842 he was in Scott & Moffatt's office, and in the latter year was, with his brother William, one of the founders of the Association of Architectural Draughtsmen. He was also a founder member of the Architectural Association in 1846. In 1843 a design for an inlaid marble table by Colling was illustrated in the 'BUILDER'. His Norfolk studies led to *Gothic Ornaments* (1848–50). This was followed by *Details of Gothic Architecture* (1852–6). *Art Foliage for Sculpture and Decoration* (1865), based on a series of articles in the 'BUILDING NEWS', was a *tour-de-force* of Reformed Gothic formalized foliage; a second edition appeared in 1878. His last book, *Examples of English Mediaeval Foliage and*

Coloured Decoration (1874), was Batsford's first book. In 1880 Colling supplied the 'Descriptive and Historical Letterpress' to John LEIGHTON's *Suggestions in Design*.

Collot, Pierre In 1631 Collot published *Pièces d'architecture* (Paris, second edition 1633), twelve plates of chimneypieces, triumphal arches, a tabernacle and doors. He also published a suite of twelve chimneypieces, one with a bust of Richelieu, another with Louis XIII. Collot's designs are in an elaborate late-MANNERIST style comparable to that of BARBET.

Cologne 1914 Deutsche Werkbund Exhibition The Cologne 1914 Exhibition which was organized by the DEUTSCHE WERKBUND represented the first major showing of architecture and design by Werkbund members. The poster was by the typographer Fritz Helmuth Ehmcke (1878–1965), there were buildings by GROPIUS, VAN DE VELDE and Bruno Taut (1880–1938), and the designs included railway interiors by Gropius and by ENDELL, and a tea service by RIEMERSCHMID. During an important debate held at the exhibition MUTHESIUS pronounced that the Werkbund was not a confederation of artists but an association of artists, manufacturers and salesmen, attacked the pretentious use of the word 'art' for every aspect of domestic design, and affirmed the necessity of developing from an individualistic conception of design towards standardization of types, stressing the importance of such a development for German exports. The opposing case for the individual artist as free creator was put by Van de Velde, supported by Endell, Gropius, OBRIST and Taut.

Colombo, Joe Cesare (1930–71) Trained as an architect at the Milan Polytechnic,

Colombo was associated from about 1951 with the painters Enrico Baj and Sergio Dangelo in the Movimento Nucleare. He gave up painting and sculpture to set up his own design office in 1961. A curved perspex light for O-Luce (1965) was followed by the Spyder light, with a fitment sliding up a narrow upright, also for O-Luce (1966). Furniture by Colombo included the 4801 armchair for Kartell (1963) formed ingeniously from three interlocking curved plywood shapes, the 4860 armchair for Kartell (1967), the first all-plastic chair to be made by injection moulding and Sormani seating (1968), a flexible arrangement of narrow polyurethane units. In 1966 Colombo designed the Smoke range of glasses. He also designed garden lights, kitchen units and complete furniture ranges.

Colonna, Edouard (1862–1948) Born near Cologne, Colonna studied architecture in Brussels. In 1882 he moved to New York, where he worked briefly for TIFFANY's Associated Artists before moving to Dayton, Ohio, where he designed railroad cars for the Barney & Smith Company and published his *Essay on Broom-Corn* (1887). This remarkable work had a photograph of broom-corn followed by ten ornamental variations on its theme and a photograph of an executed mirror decorated with broom corn, a formula which anticipated WRIGHT's *The House Beautiful* (1897). The *Essay* seems to have influenced Edward C. MOORE and John T. Curran's design for a Tiffany punch-bowl shown at the PARIS 1900 EXHIBITION; Curran had already in 1890 designed Broomcorn cutlery for Tiffany. In 1898 Colonna arrived in Paris via Canada and designed jewellery, furniture, fabrics and porcelain for BING. Colonna designed the drawing-room in Bing's L'Art Nouveau pavilion at the Paris 1900 Exhibition, on which Georges DE FEURE and Eugène GAILLARD also worked. Colonna designed not only for Bing but also jewellery for Henri Vever (1854–1942) and ceramics for Gérard, Dufraissex & Abbot. His work, in a smooth, flowing and elegant ART NOUVEAU style, was widely illustrated, for instance in 'ART ET DÉCORATION' (1899) and 'KUNST UND KUNSTHANDWERK' (1900). In 1905, after Bing's death, Colonna went to New York, where he worked as an antique dealer and interior decorator. In 1923 he retired to the French Riviera.

Columbani, Placido A Milanese architect, Columbani lived for most of his life in England, working in the ADAM style. He is first noticed as contributing to *The Chimney-piece Maker's Daily Assistant ... from the original drawings of Thomas Milton, John Crunden and Placido Columbani* (1766). This was followed by his *Vases and Tripods* (I. Taylor, 1770), *A New Book of Ornaments* (1775) 'pour embellir des chambres à l'Angloise', and *A Variety of Capitals, Friezes and Corniches* (1776). Columbani was active as designer and architect until at least 1801.

Commercial Art (1922–59) This copiously illustrated London monthly was devoted to posters, packaging, display and advertising design in general. It was taken over by the 'STUDIO' in 1926. The title changed in 1932 to *Commercial Art and Industry*, in 1937 to *Art and Industry*, and in 1959 to *Design for Industry*, the changing titles reflecting an increasing interest in industrial design. 'MODERN PUBLICITY' was an off-shoot which outlived its parent.

Comper, Sir John Ninian (1864–1960) Born in Aberdeen, the son of an Episcopalian clergyman and the god-son of John Mason Neale (1818–66), one of the founders of the Cambridge Camden

Society in 1839, Comper studied at the RUSKIN School in Oxford, the South Kensington School in London, and under C. E. KEMPE, before entering the architectural office of BODLEY and Garner in 1882. He remained there until 1887, setting up independently in the next year. Up to 1904 Comper was in partnership with Arthur Bucknall. Until his death Comper was a prolific designer for every aspect of church decoration and furnishing, stained glass, embroideries, metalwork, etc. He worked mainly in a refined and elaborate late-GOTHIC style, sometimes incorporating classical elements.

Congrès Internationaux d'Architecture Moderne In 1928 Mme Hélène de Mandrot, a wealthy amateur of architecture who knew MALLET-STEVENS and LE CORBUSIER, asked the historian and critic Sigfried Giedion (1888–1968) to organize a meeting of leading MODERN architects at her house near Geneva, Château La Sarraz. A one-day conference during the STUTTGART 1927 EXHIBITION provided a partial precedent. Architects including Le Corbusier, STAM, RIETVELD, El LISSITZKY and BERLAGE duly met at La Sarraz, elected the Zürich architect Karl Moser (1860–1936) as their first president, and initiated the Congrès Internationaux d'Architecture Moderne, known as C.I.A.M. The programme of the first C.I.A.M. congress in 1928 was rigorously Modern, including standardization of furniture; '*Le mobilier (sauf les sièges et les tables) peut se réduire à des casiers.*' Later conferences at Frankfurt (1929), Brussels (1930), Athens (1933), and Paris (1937) explored Modern themes such as the minimum dwelling and the planning of cities. The increasingly grandiloquent proclamations and statements issued by C.I.A.M. acted as rallying calls to the Modern movement and the congresses themselves promoted

contacts and solidarity between Modern architects all over the world. After the Second World War C.I.A.M. was progressively less effective and it finally dissolved in disarray after the 1956 Dubrovnik congress.

Cooper, G. Describing himself as 'Draftsman & Decorator', Cooper published *Designs for the Decoration of Rooms* (1807), twenty etched plates in the Egyptian, Hindoo, Chinese, GOTHIC, ARABESQUE, Etruscan and Roman styles. Elaborate but unrefined, they may have been among the coarse imitations of his style censured by HOPE's *Household Furniture* (1807).

Cooper, Susan Vera Born in 1902 Susie Cooper studied at the Burslem School of Art under Gordon M. Forsyth (1879–1953). From 1922 to 1929 she worked for the pottery decorating firm of A. E. Gray & Co., Stoke-on-Trent, starting as a painter but later designing. A ginger jar decorated by Cooper in 1924 was shown at the PARIS 1925 EXHIBITION. In 1929 she started her own firm, and began to design shapes ordered from other firms which she decorated, at first by hand, from 1933 by lithography. In about 1933 she designed her Curlew shapes and in about 1935 the Kestrel shapes, which remained in production into the 1960s. Her decorative patterns for tableware included Polka Dot (1932), Exclamation Mark (1933) and Wedding Ring (1934), all simple but effective. Cooper showed at the PARIS 1937 EXHIBITION and in 1937 to 1938 she designed tableware for Imperial Airways. The factory closed in 1942 but Cooper restarted successfully in about 1950. In 1961 her factory merged with the Tuscan works and in 1966 became a semi-autonomous unit within Wedgwoods.

Copier, Andries Dirk Born in 1901 in

Leerdam, Copier entered the glass factory there in 1914. From 1917 to 1919 he studied typography in Utrecht and then from 1920 to 1925 went to evening classes at the Rotterdam Academy, where he was taught by the painter and designer Jacob Jongert (1883–1942), who introduced him to Ernst Haeckel's *Kunstformen der Natur* (1899). Copier was appointed designer to the Leerdam glass factory by the director P. M. Cochius and in 1923 designed both his first mass-produced glass and his first Unica glass, individual unique pieces. In 1924 he showed at The Hague Arti et Industriae Exhibition and in 1925 won a silver medal for mass-produced glass at the PARIS EXHIBITION. His early work was influenced by the glass designs of BERLAGE and BAZEL, and was based on natural forms. An exhibition of Copier's work, organized by Professor Gustav Pazaurek, was shown in Stuttgart in 1927. Copier was much influenced by the Weissenhof exhibition of MODERN housing and design, which was taking place in Stuttgart at the same time, and from about 1930 his glass designs became more pure, geometric and Modern. Copier has designed porcelain and textiles but glass has dominated his life. In 1940 he became director of the newly founded Glass School at Leerdam, and he has continued to act as a publicist for modern glass design as well as designing glass himself.

Copland, H. An engraver, Copland's first recorded work was a trade card (1738) for Benjamin Rackstrow, 'Cabinet & Picture-frame Maker', in a heavy early ROCOCO style. This was followed by *A New Book of Ornaments* (1746), ten plates of vigorous rococo cartouches and details, *A New Book of Ornaments* (with Matthias LOCK, 1752), eleven plates of tables, mirror-frames, etc., *A New Book of Ornaments*, six plates, a manual for drawing rococo ornament comparable to but livelier than Lock's *The Principles of Ornaments*, and six plates of chairs with rococo STRAP-WORK backs forming part of Robert MANWARING'S *The Chair-Maker's Guide* (1766), but probably originally published in about 1750 at the same time as two suites of similar chairs by DARLY. Copland died in 1761. In view of his role as one of the earliest English disseminators of the rococo style and his contacts with Lock and Darly tantalizingly little is known about him.

Cortona, Pietro da (1596–1669) Born Pietro Berrettini in Cortona, of a family of stonemasons, Pietro da Cortona entered the studio of the Florentine painter Andrea Commodi at an early age. In 1612 he followed his master to Rome and in 1614 moved to the studio of Baccio Carpi. In 1618 he executed some illustrations of anatomy eventually published in 1741 as *Tabulae Anatomicae*. From about 1620 Cortona was associated with virtuosi and scholars such as Cassiano del Pozzo and Marcello Sacchetti, who bought his paintings. In the late 1620s he built the Palazzetto del Pigneto for the Sacchetti and began to gain a reputation as an architect. In 1630 he was commissioned by Cardinal Francesco Barberini to complete the seven pieces of the RUBENS History of Constantine tapestries presented to Barberini by Louis XIII in 1625, with five extra subjects plus portières, overdoors, etc. Weaving was completed in 1641. Cortona had already in 1627 designed minor elements for a suite of Castles, the first woven at the Barberini factory. In 1637 Cortona briefly visited Florence and was commissioned by Grand Duke Ferdinand II to decorate the Palazzo Pitti; it was probably on this visit that he designed intarsia panels in the Casa Buonarroti. The completion in 1639 of the great BAROQUE fresco in the Saloon of the Palazzo Barberini represented the summit of Cortona's career. From 1640 to 1647 he worked mainly at the Palazzo Pitti, designing elaborate baroque plasterwork decorations; the later elements of the scheme were mainly by Ciro FERRI. Cortona was involved in 1643 in the Life of Christ tapestry suite commissioned by Francesco Barberini and from 1663 in Barberini's final tapestry commission, the Life of Urban VIII, completed after 1683. In 1651 Cortona designed mosaics for St Peter's. He also designed VASES and cartouches engraved by Francesco Aquila.

Cosse-de-pois The term 'cosse-de-pois' (pea-pod) has been used since the late 19th century for a scrolled foliate style of ornament, embellished with seed-like and sometimes fleshy sprays, closely related to the stretched GROTESQUE. Jean TOUTIN, Peter SYMONY and Jacques CAILLART were notable exponents of this manner.

Costantini, Giovanni Battista Costantini published three suites of sophisticated black stretched GROTESQUE STRAPWORK ornament for enamelling on pendants, earrings and jewellery, of six plates each, dated 1615, 1622, and 1625. The first is entitled *Invenzioni di ornementi*, while the title of the second hovers over a view of Rome. Costantini also engraved a design for a dish with bacchic decorations after Guido Reni.

Cotelle, Jean (1607–76) Born at Meaux, the son of a mason, Cotelle was a pupil of Laurent GUYOT and Simon VOUET. At first he assisted with tapestry design at the Gobelins factory, but he was independent from 1633, when he executed decorative paintings at the Hôtel Rohan. He later worked at the Tuileries and in about 1650 at Fontainebleau. He became a member of the French Academy in 1651. In about 1640 Cotelle published *Livre De divers Ornemens*

Pour plafonds, Cintres surbaissez Galleries & autres (twenty-two plates), dedicated to his patron at the Hôtel Rohan, the Princesse de Guémené. It comprises designs for boldly compartmented ceilings decorated with sculptured figures, ACANTHUS, swags etc., early examples of the French BAROQUE style. The *Livre* was reprinted by JOMBERT in 1765. Cotelle probably influenced Inigo JONES, who may have owned the Cotelle drawings now in the Ashmolean Museum in Oxford. Nicolas LOIR was Cotelle's son-in-law.

Cotelle, Jean (1642–1708) The son of the painter Jean COTELLE, Cotelle followed his father's profession. In 1662 he travelled to Italy at the expense of his father's patron, Princesse de Guémené: he remained in Rome until 1670. He became a member of the French Academy in 1671. Cotelle decorated manuscripts, designed ceremonial decorations and in 1688 executed decorative paintings at the Trianon. His *Nouveaux livre de Chenest et autre ouvrage dorfeverie* (six plates), probably published in about 1675, comprises andirons and other metalwork designs in a bold BAROQUE style with swags, putti and scrolls, derived from LE BRUN. One andiron has Atlas supporting the globe with Louis XIV's sun-King emblem above.

Cottart, Pierre Cottart was active as an architect in Paris from 1655 to 1686. In 1660 he published a book of recent Parisian church façades, including his own design for the 'Peres de la Mercy'. Cottart published a suite of designs for panelling (six plates copied in Augsburg in about 1690 and reissued by JOMBERT in 1765), a suite of designs for doors (six plates, including a door designed by Mansart) and *Recueil de plusieurs morceaux d'ornements* (1685; eight plates).

The English architect John James owned a copy of Cottart's panelling designs.

Cotte, Robert de (1656–1735) Born in Paris, the son and grandson of architects, Cotte began as a building contractor with a partner, Rocher. From about 1676 he worked for the architect Jules Hardouin-Mansart (1646–1708); in 1682 he married Mme Mansart's sister. In 1684 Cotte abandoned building for architecture and helped to complete the Château de Marly. In 1687 he became a member of the Académie d'Architecture and in 1689 he travelled to Italy. In 1699 Cotte was appointed director of the refounded Gobelins factory, a post in which he was succeeded by OUDRY. In 1708 Cotte followed Mansart as Premier Architecte du Roi and from 1708 to 1714 reordered the choir and sanctuary of Notre Dame, an elaborate scheme swept away by VIOLLET-LE-DUC; Cotte's work for Notre Dame included a celebrated monstrance executed by Claude II Ballin (1661–1754) and a wrought-iron screen executed by Louis FORDRIN. Cotte presided over the transition between the BAROQUE and ROCOCO styles, for which the impetus was given by such designers as Pierre LE PAUTRE and Vassé. Cotte's influence was felt in Germany, where his work included palaces at Bonn and Poppelsdorf for the Archbishop Elector Joseph Clemens of Cologne (1712 onwards), with Guillaume d'Auberat as executant architect, and in Spain, where he advised Philip V.

Cottier, Daniel (1838–91) Born in Glasgow, Cottier studied there under the local glass painter David Kier (1802–64). By 1862 he had moved to Edinburgh, where he designed stained glass for Field & Allan. By 1866 he was back in Glasgow. Cottier's early stained glass was strongly influenced by William MORRIS & Co. In 1870 he left Glasgow for London, where he formed a brief partnership with TALBERT. In 1873 he opened branches of his business in New York and Sydney. In New York, Cottier sold Anglo-Japanese furniture influenced by GODWIN. Cottier's later stained glass is in a personal and advanced Artistic style. Mrs Haweis's *The Art of Decoration* (1878) praised his schemes of interior decoration.

Cottingham, Lewis Nockalls (1787–1847) Born at Laxfield in Suffolk, Cottingham, after training as a builder, began to work as an architect in London in 1814. He built up a large practice as a church restorer, evincing a knowledge of and regard for GOTHIC architecture well ahead of his time. John CARTER was among his friends. For Snelston Hall, Derbyshire, a Gothic mansion designed in 1828, Cottingham designed a wide range of Gothic furniture in the early 1840s. Some of this furniture incorporated genuine fragments of Gothic carving collected in the 1830s, and Cottingham himself was an avid collector of such fragments and also of casts and drawings. His London house incorporated a museum of which a *Descriptive Memoir* was published in 1850, and which formed a basis for the Architectural Museum established in Westminster in 1852. In 1834 Cottingham designed a 'Louis XIV drawing room' for Combe Abbey. His *Ornamental Metal Worker's Director* (1823), lithographed by Hullmandel, was enlarged and reissued as *The Smith and Founder's Director, Containing a Series of Designs and Patterns for Ornamental Iron and Brass Work* (1824) and a later edition published in 1845 as *The Smith's, Founder's and Ornamental Metal Worker's Director*. It is a record of 1820s design in iron, for instance the gates to John Nash's house in Waterloo Place, but also includes numerous designs by Cottingham himself in both the Roman and Gothic styles, many from drawings &

casts in the author's possession'. Cottingham also published works on *Westminster Hall* (1822) and *Henry VII's Chapel* (1822–9). His *Working Drawings of Gothic Ornaments, etc., with a Design for a Gothic Mansion* (1824) incorporates magnificent large-scale lithographs of Gothic mouldings, finials, etc., among the most powerful images of all Gothic Revival ornament. Cottingham also designed encaustic tiles for St John, Barr & Co. of Worcester in the 1840s. His son Nockalls Johnson Cottingham (1823–54), who continued his father's architectural practice after his death, designed stained glass at Hereford Cathedral and elsewhere. Cottingham's own private museum was sold up in 1851.

Couder, Jean-Baptiste-Amédée (1797–1864) A brother of the painter Louis-Charles-Auguste Couder (1790–1873), Jean-Baptiste-Amédée Couder worked in Paris as a designer and architect. His design for a shawl in the Persian style won a medal at the PARIS 1839 EXHIBITION, and with Alaux he designed a suite of tapestries for the Salon Louis XIV at the Tuileries, ordered by Louis Philippe. His *L'Architecture et l'industrie comme moyen de perfection sociale* (Paris, 1842, new edition, 1844) suggested a gigantic palace of art and industry; Couder's text is full of the rhetoric of progress with references to Fourier, Chateaubriand and Lamartine. Couder published several other pamphlets on design and exhibitions.

Courtois A silk designer in Lyon, Courtois was credited by JOUBERT DE L'HIBERDERIE (1764) and DUTILLIEU with the invention in 1730 of a subtle method of shading by juxtaposing carefully gradated colours, further developed by REVEL. Courtois was said to have died in 1750.

Cousin, Jehan Probably born in about 1490 in the Sens area, Cousin was active in Sens in 1526 as a surveyor. In 1530 he repaired a clock in Sens Cathedral and was also recorded as a painter. He is reported to have designed stained glass in Sens and in the late 1530s executed sculpture at the Château de Pagny. In 1540 Cousin moved to Paris, becoming a citizen and '*maître peintre*' in 1541, in which year he designed three tapestries for the confraternity of Sainte-Geneviève-du-Mont. In 1543 he designed eight tapestries for Langres Cathedral with the History of St Mammès, with gesticulating figures and hectic perspectives of architecture. In 1549 Cousin designed an arch for the entry of Henri II to Paris and in 1557 he contracted to design stained glass for the goldsmiths' hospital; Cousin may also have worked as a goldsmith, having signed a protest by the Paris goldsmiths against a royal decree of 1540. In 1560 Cousin published his *Livre de Perspective*, a primer of PERSPECTIVE, whose title-page, a combination of geometric solids, contorted nudes, scrollwork influenced by Fontainebleau and vertiginous perspective, is a quintessential example of MANNERIST design. Cousin also prepared a posthumous *Livre de pourtraicture* (1571), a manual for drawing figures which was repeatedly reprinted, sometimes under the title *L'Art de Dessiner*, including a revised edition by P. T. LE CLERC. Vasari mentioned Cousin for his engravings and books. He seems to have been a prolific book illustrator, although none of his designs can be securely identified for lack of evidence. He died in about 1560 and was succeeded by his son and pupil, also Jehan Cousin, who designed decorations for the entry of Charles IX to Paris in 1563, glass for Saint-Gervais in about 1586, and in 1583 extra embroidery designs for an edition of Dominique de CELLE's pattern-book, retitled *Le Livre de lin-*

gerie. Jehan Cousin the Younger died in about 1594.

Couven, Johann Joseph (1701–63) Born in Aachen, the son of an architect, Couven established himself as the leading architect in the town, building churches and houses in a late BAROQUE style. In 1739 he was supplying designs to local cabinet-makers for chairs, cabinets, commodes, chimneypieces, windows and mirrors. A surviving design for panelling is in an elaborate early ROCOCO manner. Couven also designed decorative VASES.

Coxcie, Michiel (1499–1592) According to VASARI, who met him in Rome in 1532, Coxcie spent a number of years there studying painting. In 1531 he executed murals in the Santa Barbara chapel in Santa Maria dell'Anima in Rome, and in 1534 he joined the Accademia di San Luca. In 1539 Coxcie became a master in Mechlin. In 1542 he was summoned to Brussels to complete and continue Bernart van ORLEY's work as a tapestry and stained-glass designer, including the windows for Sainte-Gudule in Brussels, and in 1543 he was made a citizen of Brussels and awarded 50 florins a year. Coxcie became painter to the court of Philip II and Marie of Hungary, Governor of the Netherlands. Among his official commissions was a copy of the Van Eyck polyptych in Ghent, painted in 1557. Coxcie's tapestry designs for the Brussels factory were extremely successful – often woven and often imitated. His Raphaelesque style was based on that of Bernart van Orley, by whom he was probably taught, but also reflects his first-hand experience of art in Rome around 1530. Among the suites designed by Coxcie were the Story of Adam and Eve (six pieces, before 1553), the Story of Noah (eight pieces, before 1553), the Story of Moses (five pieces, before 1553) and the Story of the Tower of Babel (four pieces, probably after 1553). The first sets of these stories were woven after 1548 and before 1567 for Sigismund II Augustus of Poland (1520–72) for his Castle of Wawel, at Cracow; their GROTESQUE borders are assigned to Cornelis FLORIS. Other tapestries attributed to Coxcie include the Seven Virtues, a Cyrus cycle and the Victories of Saxony. A baldaquin tapestry in Vienna designed by Hans VREDEMAN DE VRIES has figures designed by Coxcie. He remained in Brussels until 1563, when he was succeeded by Pieter de Kempeneer, and retired to Mechlin, where he retained the favour of the Spanish authorities. Coxcie's death was caused by a fall from his scaffold while he was restoring his 1582 Judgement of Solomon mural in Antwerp Town Hall.

Coypel, Antoine (1661–1722) Born in Paris, the son of Noel COYPEL, Antoine Coypel accompanied his father to Rome in 1672. Back in Paris in 1676 he had a rapid rise to success as a painter, and was also active in intellectual circles, a friend of Racine, Boileau and La Fontaine. He was successively Premier Peintre to Philippe Duc d'Orléans, Louis XIV's brother, and from 1716 to the King himself. He was ennobled in 1717. In 1691 Coypel began to design 200 medals on the King's achievements for the Académie des Inscriptions, a project carried to completion and publication in 1702. In 1710 he began to design a suite of tapestries on the Old Testament for the Gobelins factory, followed by the Iliad. A painting by Coypel of Alceste, executed for the Dauphin at Meudon in 1700 and engraved in 1715, served as a model for a Frankenthal porcelain group in about 1775.

Coypel, Charles Antoine (1694–1752) Born in Paris, the son of Antoine COYPEL, Charles Antoine Coypel was taught by his father. Thanks to this connection he had a precocious success as a painter, and an energetic involvement in artistic matters culminated in his appointment in 1746 as Premier Peintre du Roi; he had a lodging at the Louvre from 1722. He was possessed of literary talent and ambition, writing many plays, and moved in intellectual circles, his friends including Mariette and CAYLUS. Coypel was also a collector, and his sale in 1753 was a major event. His many book illustrations included those to the 1734 edition of Molière, but his forte was as a tapestry designer for the Gobelins manufactory. He completed the Old Testament and Iliad series commenced by his father, and from 1714 designed twenty-eight pieces for a Don Quixote series, which was enormously successful, being rewoven up to 1794, and, engraved by Picart, turned into illustrations for the 1746 Hague edition of the book. Coypel also designed two Gobelins suites of theatrical scenes, 1733 to 1741 and 1744 to 1752, the latter for the Queen of Poland.

Coypel, Noel (1628–1707) Born in Paris, the son of a merchant, Coypel studied under the painter Pierre Poncet (1574–1640) at Orleans, and then under Noel Quillerier (1594–1669) in Paris. From about 1646 he was active as a decorative painter, and worked for a while under Charles ERRARD. In about 1661 he decorated the Palais de Justice at Rennes with GROTESQUES of great lightness and elegance. From 1672 to 1676 he was director of the Académie at Rome, succeeding Errard. Official success continued on his return to Paris, where Coypel designed a number of tapestries for the Gobelins factory, including an eighth for the series known as the Rabesques of RAPHAEL but more probably by Giulio ROMANO, rewoven at the Gobelins in 1686 to 1687. From 1695 he received a salary of 3,000 livres a year from the Gobelins.

Crabeth, Dirck Pietersz Born in Gouda, the son of a glass painter, Crabeth was, with his brother Wouter, who died before 1590, the leading Dutch stained-glass designer from about 1545 until his death in Gouda in 1577. His works included windows in the Oude Kerk in Amsterdam and in the St Jans Kerk in Gouda (1562). A number of designs survive, including one for a window to Charles V dated 1549, and another for a Last Judgement derived from Lucas van LEYDEN's 1526 painting in the Lakenhal in Leiden. Crabeth's style was influenced by COECK and COXCIE's work in Antwerp, Brussels and elsewhere.

Crace, John Gregory (1809–89) In about 1750 Edward Crace founded a decorating firm in London; in 1780 he was appointed curator of royal pictures. He died in 1799. His son John Crace (1754–1819) worked under Henry HOLLAND at Carlton House and Althorp. Frederick Crace (1779–1859) worked under his father and was then responsible for the decoration of the Royal Pavilion in Brighton from 1815 to 1822, designing elaborate schemes in a gaudy Chinese style; while working on the Pavilion he had over thirty assistants, of whom the chief was Robert Jones. Frederick's son John Gregory Crace entered the family firm in 1826. He was closely associated with A. W. N. PUGIN from 1843, when he began to execute decorations in the New Palace of Westminster. Crace was one of those persuaded by Henry COLE to join the Royal SOCIETY OF ARTS in 1846 to 1847 and was a special commissioner on decoration, furniture and paper hangings at the LONDON 1851 EXHIBITION, where he supervised the decoration of Pugin's Mediaeval Court. Crace was a critic of

Owen JONES's 1851 decorative scheme and himself suggested a scheme of maroon and bronze green with gilt details. Crace himself designed decorations for the Manchester 1857 Art Treasures Exhibition and for the LONDON 1862 EXHIBITION. Crace designed furniture, wallpaper and stained glass, as well as decorative schemes. He travelled widely and was prominent in his profession's establishment. His son, John Diblee Crace (1838–1917), entered the Crace firm in 1854 and rose to an equal prominence. He was a specialist in Italian RENAISSANCE decoration, described in his *The Art of Colour Decoration* (1912). Among his better-known schemes were Longleat in Wiltshire and Fishmongers' Hall in London.

Craftsman, The (1901–16) Published from Eastwood, New York, by Gustav STICKLEY, who started to write for it in 1903, this magazine started with the motto 'The lyf so short the craft so long to lerne' and its first three issues were devoted to William MORRIS, RUSKIN and the medieval guilds. It was well illustrated, and, although there was a stress on work produced by Stickley or under his influence, ranged from John LA FARGE to German designers, and even to Maxim Gorky (1868–1936).

Crane, Thomas Born in 1843, the elder brother of Walter CRANE, Thomas Crane started as a designer of greetings cards, calendars and children's books for Marcus Ward & Co. in the 1870s. By 1885 he was Art Director of the firm. He designed the nineteen colour plates in M. S. Lockwood and E. Glaister's *Art Embroidery* (1878).

Crane, Walter (1845–1915) Born in Liverpool the son of an artist, Crane was apprenticed in 1859 to William Linton, a radical London wood engraver, and trained as a draughtsman on wood. Having served his time, in 1862 Crane graduated from hack work to a minor place among the 1860s black-and-white illustrators, influenced by the work of ROSSETTI and Millais in the Moxon *Tennyson* (1857) and by Leighton's illustrations for *Romola* (1862–3). His first major work, *The New Forest* (1863), displayed refined naturalism, but by 1870 he had developed a more vigorous manner. From that time this was devoted to eye-catching covers for novels and above all to children's books, mainly for the firm of Routledge. Under the aegis of the printer Edmund Evans (1826–1906), Crane revealed a growing mastery of colour printing, and from about 1870 the influence of Japan and the Art style of GODWIN, for example *One, Two, Buckle my Shoe* (1868). From 1873 Crane's name was used by Routledge to advertise a new series of sixpenny books, which ended in 1876 after thirteen had been published. In these and his later books for children Crane displayed a virtuoso range of antiquarian knowledge, stylistic wit and formal device. The wide circulation of the books in England and abroad helped to popularize the decorative language of the Pre-Raphaelites and Queen Anneites, of Bedford Park and BURNE-JONES. In about 1871 Crane came to know DE MORGAN, Philip WEBB, Hungerford POLLEN, William MORRIS and Burne-Jones, whose Cupid and Psyche series he helped to complete from 1876. In the late 1870s Randolph Caldecott and Kate GREENAWAY also entered the children's book market, but Crane continued to develop the genre and his reputation as a general illustrator. To the influence of Burne-Jones and BOTTICELLI was added that of William Blake. In 1883 Crane designed the cover for the new *English Illustrated Magazine* and in 1889 delivered the Cantor Lectures on *The Decorative Illustration of*

Books to the SOCIETY OF ARTS: in 1896 these were recast in a book with the same title. Crane's earliest decorative designs were ceramics for Wedgwoods from 1867 to 1871. From about 1874 he designed tiles for Maws and in 1889 a group of VASES for that firm. (Tiles to designs pirated from Crane's children's books were widely produced by amateurs and commercial makers in both England and America.) In 1880 Crane became Art Superintendent of the London Decorating Company, which made encaustic tiles, and from 1900 he designed for Pilkington's Tile and Pottery Company. In the 1870s Crane moved from mural painting to the design of wallpapers; introduced by TALBERT to Metford Warner, the proprietor of Jeffrey & Co., he designed fifty papers for this firm from 1874. In 1888 Crane wrote an essay 'Of Wallpapers' for the ARTS & CRAFTS EXHIBITION catalogue. From about 1874 he designed embroideries for the Royal School of Art Needlework and others, and from the 1880s woven and printed textiles, including ultimately carpets for Templetons of Glasgow. At Combe Bank in 1874 Crane pioneered the revival of gesso decoration, on which he wrote in the 'STUDIO' of 1893. Crane also designed mosaics for Leighton's Arab Hall (1877–9), and stained glass for Vinland, Rhode Island, U.S.A. (1883) and elsewhere. From 1882 Crane attended meetings of The Fifteen (secretary Lewis F. DAY), and in 1884 was a founder member of the ART-WORKERS' GUILD, becoming third Master in 1888–9. In 1888 Crane also led the splinter-group which constituted the Arts & Crafts Exhibition Society, and served as President until 1912, with a break for William Morris from 1893 to 1896; in 1894 he illustrated *The Story of the Glittering Plain* for Morris's Kelmscott Press. The 1899 Art-Workers' Guild masque *Beauty's Awakening* was coordinated by Crane: it represented a summary of the ideals of the movement, and was published as the *Studio Summer Number*. From about 1885, thanks to the influence of Morris, Crane was a committed and active socialist, supporting the movement with cartoons, reprinted in *Cartoons for the Cause* (1896), and designs for union banners. His book *The Claims of Decorative Art* (1892) echoed the Morris line, politically and artistically. In 1893 Crane was appointed Director of Design at the Manchester School of Art: his lectures there were printed as *The Bases of Design* (1898) and *Line and Form* (1900). In 1897 he moved briefly to the Art Department at Reading, and in 1898 became Principal of the newly constituted Royal College of Art, London, for a year. Crane supported a freer and less dominantly historic approach to design than had been South Kensington usage, but had not the time or application to press his ideas, expressed in *Ideals in Art* (1905), into practice. In 1891 a Crane retrospective was held at the Fine Art Society, London; the exhibition later toured America and Europe, ending in Sweden in 1896. Crane himself visited America in 1891–2. Despite an early eulogy of his and Caldecott's children's books by J.-K. Huysmans in 1881, Crane's European reputation only took off in about 1890: in 1891 and 1893 articles praising his books and decorative work were published in *Art Moderne*, those of 1893 by VAN DE VELDE, and in 1895 Crane was among the designers whose work was shown at BING's L'Art Nouveau. Dutch and German editions of *The Claims of Decorative Art* appeared in 1893 and 1896, and in 1898 Crane did a cover for 'JUGEND'; he had been made an honorary member of the Vienna Secession in 1897. In 1900 Crane attended a successful exhibition of his work in Budapest; a Hungarian edition of *Line and Form* appeared in 1910. The exhibition moved to Vienna in 1901, and in 1902 to Turin, where Crane provided the lion's share of the English section. His later books were *Ideals in Art* (1905), *An Artist's Reminiscences* (1907) and *William Morris to Whistler* (1911). His last major scheme was the planning of the PARIS 1914 EXHIBITION, based on that held in 1913 in Ghent, and the decorations he designed for this war-stricken project were used for the PARIS 1925 EXHIBITION.

Creccolini, Giovanni Antonio Born in .1675 Creccolini was trained as a painter under G.-B. Lenardi (1656–1704) and Benedetto Luti (1666–1724); in 1702 he won a prize from the Accademia di San Luca. He designed a splendid BAROQUE coach for the Prince of Liechtenstein's entry to Rome in 1691, published in 1694. A suite of six elaborate coaches are also recorded in prints after Creccolini, in an ACANTHUS style which owes much to Ciro FERRI, who was, like Creccolini's master Lenardi, a pupil of CORTONA.

Crivelari, Gasparo Crivelari almost certainly designed an eighteen-plate pattern-book of lace designs, *Nova scielta di varii fiori di mostre da ago* (Padua, 1612), similar to other Paduan books by TOZZI and RIZZARDI.

Crüger, Dietrich Born in Hamburg in about 1575, Crüger worked as an engraver in Nuremberg, Bologna, Florence and, from 1618, Rome, where he died in 1624. In 1614 he published in Nuremberg a suite of twelve plates of fruit ornament.

Crunden, John Born in Sussex in about 1745, Crunden worked as architect and surveyor in London. Boodle's Club (1775–6) is his best-known work. He died in 1835. His *The Joyner and Cabinet-Maker's Darling* (1765; twenty-six plates) and *The Carpenter's Companion for Chinese Railings and Gates* (1765; sixteen plates), the latter in collaboration with J. H. Morris, 'carpenter', both contain GOTHIC and Chinese frets to be used on furniture, doors and garden buildings. *Designs for Ceilings* (1765; twelve plates), comprised forty-eight designs for ceiling corners in the ROCOCO and Gothic styles. Crunden also contributed two extra plates of Gothic gates to Robert MANWARING's *The Carpenter's Compleat Guide to the Whole System of Gothic Railing* (1765). Crunden was responsible for designs in the rococo, Chinese and Gothic styles in *The Chimney-piece Maker's Daily Assistant* (1766) to which Thomas Milton, Placido COLUMBANI and Thomas Collins Overton also contributed. Crunden's *Convenient and Ornamental Architecture* was mainly concerned with exterior architecture but did include rococo doors and wall elevations with plasterwork and mirror-frames.

Cuvilliés, Jean François Vinzent Joseph (1695–1768) Born at Soignies, François de Cuvilliés entered the service of the Elector Max Emanuel of Bavaria in Brussels as a court dwarf in 1706. In 1715 he travelled with the court to Munich and in 1716 began to train there as an architectural draughtsman. Cuvilliés was destined to serve as a fortification engineer, and was in 1717 appointed an ensign in the life-guards, but, although he passed his exams, he was not allowed on the Hungarian campaign because of his small size. In 1720 Cuvilliés was sent by the Elector to Paris to complete his architectural training under François Blondel (1683–1756). Back in Munich in 1725 Cuvilliés was appointed court architect alongside Josef Effner (1687–1745). In 1728 he travelled to Bonn to work for the Elector Clemens August at Schloss Brühl and his nearby hunting-box, Schloss Falkenlust, and was by him given the title of gentleman in 1730. In 1754 to 1755 he revisited Paris. Although Cuvilliés worked at Mergentheim (1734), Kassel (1749) and elsewhere, and his advice was sought by princely patrons all over Germany, the majority of his works were in Munich where he was in 1763 appointed director of architecture to the Elector Maximilian III Joseph. Cuvilliés was the central figure in the great flowering of the ROCOCO style which took place in Munich from the 1720s. His greatest achievements were the interior decoration of the *Reichen Zimmer*, the parade rooms of the Munich Residenz (1730–37), the Amalienburg (1734–9), a hunting-box in the park of Schloss Nymphenburg and the theatre of the Munich Residenz (1750–53). Cuvilliés disseminated his designs by publishing from Munich engravings executed from his drawings there and also in Augsburg and Paris. The first series, which appeared from 1738, comprised thirty suites of six plates each, and included cartouches, frames, ceilings and wall elevations with panelling and furniture. From about 1745 a second series was published, twenty suites of four to six plates each, including cartouches, panels of ornament, tables, commodes, beds, ironwork, ormolu, girandoles, gueridons, VASES, mirrors, chandeliers, snuff-boxes, watch-cases, cane handles, picture-frames, etc. The third series, twenty-four suites of four to six plates each, published from 1756, consisted almost entirely of architecture. Many of Cuvilliés's later designs were produced in collaboration with his son, François Joseph Ludwig Cuvilliés (1731–77), also an architect. Cuvilliés's handling of the rococo style is brilliant, his ornament vertiginously distorting architecture, PERSPECTIVE, symbol and reality, sometimes flowing, sometimes spiky and sprightly. Asymmetry is ubiquitous and waterfalls sparkle over ceilings and tables alike. Cuvilliés's

inventory included ornament by Jean I BERAIN and D'AVILER'S *Cours d'architecture*, but it is clear from his works that he was well acquainted with the works of François BOUCHER, LA JOUE, MEISSONIER and other French rococo designers. His prints were often copied, and some were reissued by his son in *École de l'Architecture Bavaroise* (Munich, 1770 onwards), an ambitious project to survey every aspect of Bavarian architecture. Cuvilliés junior tended to trade on his father's name but produced some remarkable designs for fountains (1769) and stoves (1770), which combine NEO-CLASSICAL motifs and rococo forms; he also published in 1770 a rococo VASE design copied from François Boucher and a neo-classical vase copied from DELAFOSSE.

Cuypers, Pierre Joseph Hubert (1827–1921) Born in Roemond, Cuypers trained as an architect from 1847 at the Antwerp Academy and then from 1850 practised in his home town. In 1852 he founded a workshop for Christian art which survived into this century, producing stained glass and other ecclesiastical artefacts designed by Cuypers. In 1863 Cuypers won second prize in a competition to design a museum of art in Amsterdam; he was by this date well known as a designer of GOTHIC churches, strongly influenced by VIOLLET-LE-DUC. In 1865 he moved to Amsterdam and in 1867 became a member of the Amsterdam Arti et Amicitiae association. The Rijksmuseum (1877–85) in Amsterdam was his most celebrated building. Cuypers' pupils included BAZEL and Lanooy and his designs were illustrated alongside those of the younger generation in 'BOUW- EN SIERKUNST'.

Czeschka, Carl Otto (1878–1960) Born in Vienna, Czeschka studied at the Academy there under the painter Christian Griepenkerl (1839–1916). From 1901 to 1907 he taught at the school of applied art in Vienna; Kokoschka was among his pupils. In 1904 he joined with Josef HOFFMANN, Koloman MOSER and others in designing for the WIENER WERKSTÄTTE. Czeschka designed postcards, book illustrations, jewellery, embroidery and stained glass, including some for the Palais Stoclet (1911). He also designed ceramics for

the great patron Karl Ernst Osthaus, for whom Lauweriks and VAN DE VELDE worked. Czeschka was in 1907 invited by Justus Brinckmann to teach at the school of applied arts in Hamburg, became a professor there in 1909 and only retired in 1943. Czeschka continued to be an active and versatile designer in Hamburg, his work including cigar posters and in 1947 a title for the newspaper *Die Zeit*.

D

Dali, Salvador Born in Figueras in 1904, Dali studied painting from 1921 at the Academy of San Fernando in Madrid; he was expelled in 1926. In 1928 he met the surrealists on a visit to Paris, where he moved in 1929, and joined André Breton's surrealist group, whence he was expelled in 1934. In that year Dali designed book illustrations for *Les Chants de Maldoror*. In 1936 he gave a lecture in a diving suit in London, and designed a sofa in the shape of Mae West's lips (reissued in 1980) for Edward James, for whom he also designed a telephone with a lobster receiver and a chair with hands as its back. Dali has also designed Steuben glass (1938 and 1940), scarves for Simpsons of New York (1946) and a whole series of surrealist kitsch jewels, mainly for American clients.

Dampt, Jean (1854–1946) Born at Vénarey on the Côte d'Or, Dampt studied at the École des Beaux-Arts in Dijon under the sculptor François Dameron (1835–1900). In 1874 he moved to the Atelier Jouffroy in Paris, where he was active as a sculptor from the mid-1870s. In the 1880s he travelled to Italy, Spain and North Africa and developed a rich chryselephantine style. In 1892 Dampt was a founder of Les Cinq, a group of designers and craftsmen which also included CHARPENTIER, AUBERT, SELMERSHEIM and Moreau-Nélaton. Dampt designed ART NOUVEAU furniture, interiors, goldsmiths' work, clockcases, electric lights and jewellery, showing at the Salon du Champ de Mars. His work was illustrated in the 'STUDIO' and praised there by Gabriel Mourey (1897). Dampt was an admirer of RUSKIN and the Arts & Crafts movement; his pupils included Jean DUNAND. In his later years Dampt was mainly active as a religious sculptor.

Dandridge, Joseph (1667–1746) As a naturalist Dandridge was a distinguished follower of John Ray (1627–1705), with a specialist interest in insects and birds. However, he earned his living as a competent silk designer working in Moorfields for the weavers in Spitalfields. He was active as such from at least 1706 to 1737, and John Vansommer (1705–74) was among his pupils.

Danhauser, Josef Ulrich (1780–1829) Born in Vienna, the son of a sculptor, Danhauser entered the Vienna Academy of Fine Arts in 1793 to study sculpture. His factory, founded in 1804, was in 1807 granted an official permit to make gilt, silvered and bronze ornaments. In 1808 an imperial licence was awarded and in 1814 a permit to manufacture all types of furniture. Already in 1808 he was employing 130 workers and the scale of his operations seemed prodigious to his contemporaries. In 1825 he bought the former Karoly Palace as showrooms, but after his death in 1829 the firm went into a decline, finally disappearing in 1842. Little of Danhauser's furniture has been identified apart from some of that supplied to Archduke Carl for the Albertina in Vienna and Schloss Weilburg near Baden in 1822 to

1823. But in the Museum for Applied Arts in Vienna is a collection of some 2,500 designs representing the whole output of the Danhauser firm. These designs are the finest surviving record of the BIEDERMEIER style in furniture. They cover all types from spittoons to beds, from pipe-racks to sofas, and display both the pure classical side of Biedermeier and the more idiosyncratic Viennese variant. Some of the later designs, reflecting the onset of the ROCOCO revival, are attributed to Danhauser's son, Josef Franz Danhauser (1805–45), who achieved fame as a painter of genre scenes and executed furniture designs engraved in a newspaper, the *Wiener Zeitschrift*, in about 1835.

Danieli, Bartolomeo A professional lace designer, Danieli was the final representative of the RENAISSANCE tradition of VINCIOLO, VECELLIO and PARASOLE. His books included *Fiore pretioso d'ogni virtu* (Siena, 1610; fourteen plates), *Libro di diversi disegni* (Bologna, about 1630; twenty-six plates) and *Vari disegni di merletti* (Bologna, 1639; probably fourteen plates).

Darling, William An engraver, Darling designed book-plates and trade cards. He also published a trophy of music after PEYROTTE, a suite of ornaments for carving or plasterwork (1771), of at least six plates, in the NEO-CLASSICAL ADAM manner, and another, *Ornaments* (1775; five plates). Darling also engraved the otherwise unknown T. Laws's *A New Book of Vases* (1773; six plates), competent designs in the Adam style.

Darly, Matthias Darly was active as a caricaturist in London from 1741. His trade cards describe him as engraver and drawing master, and he engraved patterns for textiles and wallpapers, as well

as book illustrations, trade cards and coats-of-arms on silver. In 1748 his premises faced Old Slaughter's Coffee House in St Martin's Lane, a seed-bed of English ROCOCO. His first known pattern-book, *A New Book of Chinese Gothic and Modern Chairs* (1750–51; eight plates), comprises dumpy designs for chairs, incorporating rococo STRAPWORK and scrolls, Chinese frets and the odd GOTHIC quatrefoil. They were reprinted in MANWARING's *The Chair-Maker's Guide* (1766), which also included five plates of Parlour Chairs and a Settee probably designed by Darly in about 1751. They have much in common with designs by LOCK reprinted at the same time. In 1753 Darly, who was then living at the same address as CHIPPENDALE, engraved the majority of the plates of his *Director* (1754). It is possible that Darly may have taught Chippendale to design, although Lock is perhaps a better candidate. In *A New Book of Chinese Designs* (1754; 120 plates) Darly collaborated with George Edwards (1694–1773), ornithologist, book illustrator and caricaturist. The illustrations comprise CHINOISERIE landscapes and ornaments useful to painters, japanners and embroiderers. They were used on cotton and on Bow porcelain and some were reprinted in Robert SAYER's *The Ladies Amusement* (1762) and again in DECKER's *Chinese Architecture* (1769). The *New Book* includes designs for furniture, chimney furniture, VASES and stands in the Chinese and rustic tastes. In 1759 to 1760 Darly engraved the plates for INCE and Mayhew's *Universal System* (1762) and he later engraved for *Household Furniture in the Genteel Taste*, published by SAYER from 1760. Darly later published *A New Book of Ceilings* (1760), and *Sixty Vases of English, French and Italian Masters* (1768) of forty-nine plates, including one after POLIDORO DA CARAVAGGIO and copies from NEO-CLASSICAL designers, including SALY; these vases were used on English tiles. *The Ornamental Architect or young Artist's Instructor* (1770, reprinted 1773) included competent neo-classical ornament tripods, vases and frames. Darly's last work in this field was *A New Book of Ornaments in the Present (Antique) Taste* (1772). From 1765 to 1771 as 'architect' Darly showed architectural designs, vases and antique ornaments at the Society of Artists, and in 1771 as 'Professor and Teacher of Ornament' designs of vases 'for the different manufactures of Great Britain' at the Free Society. In a 1771 self-portrait he called himself 'The Political Designer of Pots, Pans and Pipkins', and on another 'P.O.A.G.B.' (Painter of Ornaments to the Academy of Great Britain).

Darmstadt 1901 Mathildenhöhe Exhibition At the Darmstadt 1898 Exhibition the applied arts section, organized by the influential publisher Alexander Koch (1860–1939), included works by the painter and designer Hans Christiansen (1866–1945). In December 1898 Christiansen was invited by Grand Duke Ernst Ludwig von Hessen to come to Darmstadt as a founder member of an artists' colony. The colony was publicly initiated in 1899 and situated on the Mathildenhöhe. Designers involved at the outset were Christiansen, Paul Bürck (1878–1947) and Patriz Huber (1878–1902). OLBRICH and BEHRENS soon followed, and in late 1899 the artists of the Mathildenhöhe colony proposed to Grand Duke Ernst Ludwig a great exhibition of art and design to be held in 1901 under the portentous title Ein Dokument Deutscher Kunst. Olbrich took the leading part in organizing the exhibition and designed most of its buildings. On show in 1901 were not only the artistic centre of the colony, the Ernst-Ludwig-Haus and various

temporary structures, but also the houses of the artists themselves. The exhibition was a financial failure and met a mixed critical response but was none the less perceived as a milestone in the development of design in Germany. SEDER saw it as a turn for the worse and blamed the influence of the 'STUDIO'. A less ambitious exhibition was held in 1904, and in 1906 an exhibition of art from Hesse was shown in the Mathildenhöhe buildings. The colony was represented at the PARIS 1900, TURIN 1902 and ST LOUIS 1904 EXHIBITIONS. However, Christiansen, Bürck and Huber left in 1902 and Behrens in 1903. The painter and designer Johann Vincenz Cissarz (1873–1942) arrived in the same year and left in 1906. Other artists and designers continued to settle in the colony, and a Grand-Ducal ceramic factory opened in 1906, and a glass factory in 1908. The First World War put an end to the whole venture.

Daubigny, Philippe Cordier Daubigny, who came from a family of gunsmiths, issued sixteen plates of designs for the decoration of guns from 1634 to 1644. They were republished as a suite in 1665 in Paris and Antwerp. Daubigny's designs are crude but vigorous, with scrolly ACANTHUS ornament accompanied by putti, masks, etc.

Daudet, Étienne Joseph An engraver and goldsmith in Lyon, Daudet published *Nouveaux Livre d'Ornemens Propre pour Peintre, Graveur, Orphevres et autres* (1689; twelve plates). It has the French royal arms on its title and presents friezes, panels and ornamental motifs of scrolling ACANTHUS for the use of goldsmiths, engravers and others.

Davesne, Robert A Parisian smith, Davesne published *Livre de Serrurerie nouvellement inventé* (Paris, 1676; fourteen plates), dedicated to the architect

Bruant. It comprises able designs for BAROQUE ironwork, with an element of coarseness common in designs by practising smiths. Similar designs occur in *Rampes d'Escailler et Balcons* (1687), which has a title with smartly dressed but naïvely drawn figures looking over a balcony and ends with a doggerel quatrain by Claude Prieurs praising Davesne's works.

David, Jacques Louis (1748–1825) David, a distant relation of François BOUCHER, studied painting under Joseph-Marie VIEN, the pioneer of NEO-CLASSICISM in painting, whose *La Vertueuse Athénienne* (1763), praised by Diderot, depicted an antique tripod, manufactured as a novelty in furniture by the banker J. H. Eberts in about 1773. David won the Prix de Rome at his fourth attempt in 1774, and spent from 1775 to 1780 in Rome, returning again in 1784 to paint the *Oath of the Horatii*, commissioned by d'Angiviller for Louis XVI. By 1788 David, assisted in the designs by his pupil Charles MOREAU, had furniture similar to that shown in the *Oath* executed for his studio by Georges Jacob (1739–1814). By 1814 the *Oath* was a standard subject for clocks. As virtual dictator of art under the revolution (he designed the president's chair of the Convention) and as Premier Peintre to Napoleon, David had a wide influence on the arts. He helped Vivant DENON (1745–1825) at a crucial moment and his archaeologically accurate depictions of antique furniture and utensils were a major source of inspiration to designers. Despite qualms as to its suitability for this purpose, David's painting of the *Coronation of Napoleon* (1805–8) was woven as a Gobelins tapestry. He was also involved with PERCIER on the design of Napoleon's imperial throne, made by Jacob-Desmalter (1770–1841) in 1804. David designed ebony furniture and a Gobelins

screen with figures of the Gods for Napoleon's cabinet at the Tuileries (1812). After Waterloo he retired to Brussels, where he died.

D'Aviler, Charles Augustin (1653–1700) Born in Paris, D'Aviler studied architecture in Rome from 1676 to 1681 after capture by pirates and two years as a prisoner in Tunis. He then spent eight years working discontentedly under Jules Hardouin-Mansart (1646–1708) before finally settling in Montpelier, where he was extremely active as writer and architect. D'Aviler's translation of Book VI of Scamozzi (1685) was followed by his *Cours complet d'architecture* (1691; 2 volumes), conceived as a commentary to Vignola. It contained some highly accomplished designs for BAROQUE ironwork, including balcony patterns used by Jean Tilman for the stair of the Hôtel de Ville at Liège (1719–20). The second volume of the *Cours* was published separately as the *Dictionnaire d'architecture* (1693, new editions 1720 and 1755), and the *Cours* was also the basis for the popular *Vignole des ouvriers* (1825–6).

Davis, Alexander Jackson (1803–92) Born in New York City, Davis was active as an architectural draughtsman from 1826. In 1829 he entered an architectural partnership in New York with Ithiel Town of New Haven, which lasted until 1844, after which Davis practised on his own until 1884. Davis worked prolifically in a wide range of styles from Tuscan to GOTHIC and Swiss. From 1839 to 1852 he designed illustrations for the books of Andrew DOWNING, borrowing from English sources such as LOUDON and Robinson's *Rural Architecture* (1823); in 1838 he had started his own short-lived publication of *Rural Residences*. For houses such as Lyndhurst (1838, extended 1864) Davis designed competent albeit often quirky

GOTHIC furniture. Some furniture by Davis was directly based on A. W. N. PUGIN's 1835 book.

Davis, Owen William Davis described himself as an architect and worked for many years as an assistant to Sir Matthew Digby WYATT at the India Office and elsewhere. In 1868 he contributed some designs for furniture to Richard CHARLES's *The Cabinet Maker*. Davis subsequently designed furniture for James Shoolbred & Co. in the Japanese, 'Adams', Stuart, Medieval, Louis Seize, Old English and Jacobean styles, published in their *Designs of Furniture* (1876). Shoolbred furniture designed by Davis was shown at the PHILADELPHIA 1876 EXHIBITION. In about 1870 Davis published a number of designs and archaeological drawings in 'BUILDING NEWS'. He showed designs for interiors at the Royal Academy from 1874 to 1884. His *Art and Work* (1885; eighty-five plates) is partly archaeological and partly devoted to Davis's own designs, including decoration for ceramics made by Copeland of Stoke-on-Trent, a metal bed for Gillows, an ADAM-style room for Messrs Nosotti (1882), an Adam-style piano for James Plucknett of Warwick, wallpapers for Messrs Jeffrey, William Woollams & Co. and Mr James Toleman, ecclesiastical and secular metalwork for Benham & Froud, and carpets in the Indian style. Davis also illustrated works by earlier designers from SERLIO to Adam, and birds by Hokusai. His work was praised by J. Moyr SMITH.

Dawson, Nelson Ethelred (1859–1942) Born in Stamford, Dawson studied architecture there under his uncle. From about 1885 to 1887 he studied painting at the South Kensington Schools. After a spell in Scarborough he came to London in 1891 and took up metalwork, studying under the enameller Alexander Fisher (1864–1936). In 1893 he married Edith Robinson, whom he taught to enamel. Dawson designed and made a wide range of metalwork, including lights, bath taps, church metalwork and the trowel used by Queen Victoria in laying the foundation stone of the VICTORIA & ALBERT MUSEUM in 1899. In 1900 the Dawsons showed 125 pieces of jewellery at the London Fine Art Society. In 1901 Dawson became Art Director of the new-founded Artificers' Guild, but retired when in 1903 Montague Fordham, former director of the Birmingham Guild of Handicraft, took over the venture. In 1907 Dawson published *Goldsmiths' and Silversmiths' Work*. In 1912 he was involved in a school of colour printing and from 1914 he was active as a painter.

Day, Lewis Foreman (1845–1910) Born in Peckham Rye, the son of a Quaker wine-merchant, Day entered the office of Lavers & Barraud, the stained-glass manufacturers, in 1864. He subsequently spent two years as keeper of cartoons for glass with Clayton & Bell, and in 1870 worked with Heaton, Butler & Bayne on the decoration of Eaton Hall. Also in 1870 Day started his own designing business. Day's stained-glass designs were mainly for domestic uses, although he collaborated with Walter CRANE on glass at Christ Church, Streatham Hill (1891). Day designed wallpapers for W. B. Simpson & Co. and Jeffrey & Co., tiles for Maws, Craven Dunnill, and Pilkington, and textiles for many manufacturers, including Turnbull & Stockdale, whose Art Director he became in 1881. He also designed furniture, silver and jewellery. Day was Secretary of The Fifteen, founded in 1882, a founder (1884) and later Master of the ART-WORKERS' GUILD, a founder activist in the ARTS & CRAFTS EXHIBITION SOCIETY (1888), and from 1890 examined at the South Kensington SCHOOL

OF DESIGN. Day was a prolific journalist, contributing to the 'MAGAZINE OF ART', the 'ART JOURNAL' and the 'JOURNAL OF DECORATIVE ART'. He also published many books on aspects of ornament and design, most of which went through several editions. They include *Instances of Accessory Ornament* (1880), *Every-Day Art* (1882; this book, translated and reworked by C. Vosmaer in 1884, had wide influence in Holland), *The Anatomy of Pattern* (1887), *The Planning of Ornament* (1887), *The Application of Ornament* (1888), *Nature in Ornament* (1892), *Alphabets Old and New* (1898), *Art in Needlework* (1900, with Mary Buckle), *Lettering in Ornament* (1902), *Pattern Design* (1903), *Enamelling* (1907), *Windows, a Book about Stained and Painted Glass* (1909) and *Nature and Ornament* (1908–9). Day also published the first monograph on his friend William MORRIS, in an 1899 *Art Journal* extra number. Day was an important and influential educator in design but his own designs, based on a profound knowledge of historic ornament, together with nature and Japan, tend to lack spirit and breadth for all their professionalism.

Day, Robin Born in High Wycombe in 1915 Day studied at the local art school from 1931. He then worked for a local furniture manufacturer for a year before moving in 1935 to the Royal College of Art (see SCHOOL OF DESIGN). He opened his London office in 1948 with his wife Lucienne Day and practised as a designer of posters, exhibitions, graphics and typography, as well as teaching design. In 1948 Day, with Clive Latimer, won the first prize for storage furniture in the NEW YORK MUSEUM OF MODERN ART's Low Cost Furniture Competition. He was then commissioned by Hille Ltd to design a dining-room for the 1949 British Industry Fair.

From 1950 Day was consultant designer to Hille. He designed their trade-mark, their letterheads and other graphics. Day's furniture for Hille included the plywood Hillestack chair (1950), Q-Stack chair (1953) with plywood one-piece seat and back and metal legs, and his elegant Gatwick seating (1958). In 1951 he designed the auditorium seating for the London Festival Hall. Day has also designed storage units and office furniture for Hille, but his greatest success is the injection-moulded flexible shell Polyprop chair. The material, polypropylene, had been discovered in 1954. Day's Mark I chair was produced in 1962 and his revised Mark II of 1963 has been produced in millions. Lucienne Day has her own reputation as a textile designer, winning a gold medal at the Milan 1951 Triennale for her design Calyx. More recently she has designed Thai silk appliqué wall hangings.

Déchazelle,   Pierre   Toussaint (1752–1833) Déchazelle studied under Nonotte at the Lyon School of Design and then under Dodet. He subsequently worked as a textile designer for the Guyot manufactory. After spending the revolution in Paris he returned to Lyon in 1798, and helped to modernize the silk industry by supplying Dutch-inspired floral designs. In 1801 he showed a flower painting at the Paris Salon. Déchazelle was a strong influence on the newly founded Lyon École des Beaux-Arts, and a vigorous advocate of links between art and industry.

Deck, Joseph-Théodore (1823–91) Born in Guebwiller in Alsace, the son of a silk-dyer, Deck at first followed his father's trade and then became an apprentice potter in a Strasbourg stove factory, also studying design with a sculptor named Friedrich. From 1844 he travelled widely in Germany and Austria but in 1847 he settled in Paris. After the

1848 revolution he returned to Gueb-willer, but back in Paris from 1851 he worked for the stove factory of Dumas before setting up his own pottery in 1856. From 1859 Deck produced earthenware pots influenced by Persian models, influenced by Adalbert de BEAUMONT. In 1861 he showed earthenwares in the Henri II style in Paris and at the LONDON 1862 EXHIBITION lustre with Hispano-Moresque and RENAISSANCE-style decoration. He worked with BRACQUEMOND among others. At the PARIS 1878 EXHIBITION Deck was awarded the Grand Prix for ceramics for Renaissance-style wares with a gilt ground. In 1887 he was appointed director of the Sèvres porcelain factory and published *La Faïence*. In technique and design Deck's works helped to pave the way for ART NOUVEAU innovations in ceramics.

Decker, Paul (1677–1713) Born in Nuremberg, in 1699 Decker went to Berlin and was strongly influenced by the BAROQUE architect and sculptor Andreas Schlüter. In 1705 he returned to Nuremberg. Decker was from 1708 court architect to Pfalzgraf Theodor zu Sulzbach and from 1710 served Markgraf Georg Wilhelm of Brandenburg Bayreuth. He died in Bayreuth. Decker's first published designs were titles and decorations for J. C. Volckamer's *Nürnbergische Hesperides* (Nuremberg, 1708, 1714), one of the finest of gardening books. Decker's *Civilbau-Kunst*, dedicated to Volckamer, included, as well as the ORDERS and architecture, designs for doors, tombs and wall and floor decoration. *Fürstlicher Baumeister oder Architectura Civilis* (Augsburg, 1711, 1716) is a magnificent evocation of an ideal baroque palace complete with interiors, wall decoration, state beds and other furniture. Decker also published a number of suites of ornament includ-ing *Groteschgen-Werk* (ten plates in two parts), *Neues Groteschgen-Werk* (four plates), *Neues Goldschmiedsbüchlein* (four plates) and *Neu inventirtes Wercklein vor underschiedliche Künstler*. They include panels of ornament, designs for metalwork — chalices, VASES, dishes, cups, snuff-boxes, watches and ironwork, cartouches, details of plasterwork, and furniture, including one extraordinary contorted commode. Decker's style, derived from Jean I BERAIN and Daniel MAROT, with occasional CHINOISERIE elements, looks forward to that of SCHÜBLER, with richly elaborate GROTESQUE ornament applied to every object, sometimes sprightly, sometimes overpowering. Decker's ornament was emulated and used by glass enamellers, among others.

Decoration (1881–9) Further titled *in Painting, Sculpture, Architecture and Art Manufactures* this magazine was published in London with J. Moyr SMITH as its art editor. He contributed many illustrations especially in the early issues. The magazine was strongly oriented towards the decorating trades and in 1888 it started to incorporate an *Art Trades Review*.

Decoration (1930–39) Subtitled successively *Beauty and the Home* (1930–31), *of the House Beautiful* (1932–4), and *of the English Home* (1934–9), this London magazine reflected the MODERN attitude to interior decoration in the 1930s. Its editor and assistant editor from 1938 were John Betjeman and Hugh Casson.

Decorator, The (1864) Subtitled *An Illustrated Practical Magazine and Advertiser for the Furnishing Trades*, this London magazine, though short-lived and modest, contained a large design or illustration in each issue, interesting as representations of unreformed commercial taste.

Decorator (1902–36) This London trade journal for 'house painting, decorating and kindred trades' was edited by Arthur Seymour Jennings. It contains much information on the design of wallpaper and decorations.

Decorator and Furnisher (1882–94) Edited from New York by A. Curtis Bond, the first issue of this magazine contained an article on the decoration and furniture of modern houses by R. W. EDIS, and another on the sunflower. Its excellent illustrations, a few in colour, cover all aspects of decorative design with a stress on 'Art' styles.

Decorators' and Painters' Magazine, The (1902–7) Edited by Arthur Seymour Jennings, this superior trade journal was a successor to the *Plumber and Decorator* (1879–1901): it contains useful information and illustrations on the design of stencilling, wallpapers, etc.

De Feure, Georges (1868–1928) Born in Paris as Georges Joseph van Sluijters, the son of a Dutch architect, De Feure started work as a craftsman in Holland. In 1891, after a spell in a bookbindery in The Hague, he moved to Paris, where he designed illustrations for the newspapers *Le Courrier Français* and *Le Boulevard*, and changed his name successively to Van Feuren and De Feure. In 1894 an exhibition of his drawings was admired by the painter Puvis de Chavannes (1824–98). De Feure designed many posters, at first influenced by Jules CHÉRET, with whom he studied; they included a dashing virtuoso performance for Loie Fuller (1895). De Feure also designed elegant and delicate ART NOUVEAU interiors, furniture, porcelain and glass. Like GAILLARD and COLONNA he was much patronized by BING and designed two rooms in his L'Art Nouveau pavilion at the PARIS 1900 EXHIBITION. De Feure also

founded the Atelier De Feure to produce furniture, with the Aachen architect Theodor Cossmann as his partner. In 1903 Bing mounted a De Feure exhibition. De Feure later designed for the theatre, working in London. In the 1920s he designed interiors for the modiste Madeleine Vionnet. At the PARIS 1925 EXHIBITION he designed the pavilions of the towns of Roubaix and Tourcoing. De Feure was also active as a book illustrator, being encouraged by Octave Uzanne.

Dekorative Kunst (1897–1929) This Munich magazine edited by H. Bruckmann and J. MEIER-GRAEFE who contributed under several pseudonyms, opened with an article by Samuel BING on the future direction of design; a major article on VOYSEY followed, and among the designers treated later were ENDELL, William MORRIS, Henry WILSON, BENSON, ECKMANN, VAN DE VELDE and ASHBEE.

Dekorative Vorbilder (1889–1929) Published by Julius Hoffmann in Stuttgart, this magazine provided a copious representation of modern designs for all aspects of allied art, mostly in colour. An English edition, the 'ART DECORATOR', was also published.

Dekorativnce Iskusstvo (1957–present) This magazine on decorative art in Russia combines articles on historic and folk design with coverage of the gradual assimilation by Russia of the MODERN Western style of design, heavily illustrated and with strong nationalist and propaganda overtones.

De La Cour, William Presumed to be of French origin, De La Cour painted scenery for the opera *Busiri* in London in 1740. His *First Book of Ornament*, dedicated to Lord Middlesex, and engraved by Vivares, appeared in 1741; eight books were published, the last in 1747. De La Cour's designs for ornament, metalwork and furniture were among the earliest to introduce the ROCOCO style to England. After activity as a decorative and portrait painter De La Cour settled in Edinburgh in 1757, and in 1760 became first master of the EDINBURGH TRUSTEES' ACADEMY. He died in 1767.

Delafosse, Jean Charles (1734–89) Born in Paris, the son of a wine merchant, in 1747 Delafosse was apprenticed to the carver Jean-Baptiste Poulet of the Académie de Saint-Luc. He later worked as an architect and designer in Corsica. In 1771 Delafosse became professor of drawing at the Académie de Saint-Luc, and in 1777 assistant professor of geometry and PERSPECTIVE. He became a member of the Académie of Bordeaux in 1781. Delafosse was the architect of several houses in Paris from 1776 and also published a *Mémoire pour une boucherie et tuerie générale*, proposing a general abattoir on an island in the Seine. In 1768 Delafosse published *Nouvelle Iconologie Historique* (111 plates); it included designs prepared over several years. A second edition (1771) contained 126 plates. A Dutch edition was published in Amsterdam with 103 plates. The *Nouvelle Iconologie* comprises designs for trophies, chimneypieces, friezes, bases, medallions, cartouches, clocks, pedestals, VASES, tripods, tables and doors, in the most strenuous early NEO-CLASSICAL style with tough geometric forms, chopped-off columns and heavy swags; there are frequent echoes of BAROQUE design and occasional disconcerting displays of ROCOCO lightness. The work is tied together by complex and comprehensive iconography, interpreted in lengthy introductions; it covers such themes as the four elements, the four parts of the world, the four seasons and so on. Delafosse's remaining designs were conceived as supplements to the *Nouvelle Iconologie*. They include magnificent suites of neo-classical architectural compositions influenced by PIRANESI for their titles. There are also suites of designs for every aspect of metalwork and church furniture, and for every type of domestic furniture. A few of the latter are rococo, '*dans le goût Pictoresque*'. Delafosse's designs amount to some 500 plates, and thus rival NEUFFORGE's *Recueil*. However, his designs were far more imaginative than those of Neufforge, and were often executed, especially in marquetry. Copies were published in Augsburg. In 1773 the gilder and print-dealer Jean-Félix Watin, while praising Delafosse's genius, criticized his designs as too elaborate, even for the very rich, and offered to simplify them or supply substitutes. BLONDEL described Delafosse as '*homme de génie, mais peu conséquent*'. In 1785 the Sèvres factory owned prints by Delafosse. GÜNTHER copied some of his vases for the Nymphenburg garden in Munich in about 1770.

Delaunay, Sonia (1885–1979) Born in Gradizhsk in the Ukraine, the daughter of a factory worker, Delaunay was in 1890 adopted by a wealthy Jewish lawyer in St Petersburg, Henri Terk. In 1903 she went to Karlsruhe, where she studied drawing under Schmidt Reutter, and in 1905 she moved to Paris and the Académie de la Palette. In 1908 in order to avoid returning to Russia she married Wilhelm Uhde, a German gallery-owner in Paris. She was at this period painting in a manner strongly influenced by the Fauves and by Douanier Rousseau. In about 1909 she turned to embroidery under the influence of Robert Delaunay (1885–1941), whom she married in 1910, having divorced Uhde. In 1911 she designed and made a completely abstract appliqué quilt for her son, Thomas. This and her later paintings used bright contrasted colours, influenced by CHEVREUL. In 1913 Delaunay designed coloured paper collage bookbindings, lampshades, curtains and posters shown in Berlin. She also designed brightly coloured abstract ornaments for Blaise Centrars's *La Prose du Transsibérien* (1913), published in a two-metre-long folded format. During the First World War the Delaunays were in Portugal and Spain; in 1918 Sonia Delaunay opened a shop in Madrid, the Casa Sonia, to sell her designs. Back in Paris in the 1920s she was closely associated with Dada and surrealism. She designed bookbindings for Tzara, the interior of a bookshop in Neuilly (1922) and decoration for a Citroën B12 (1925). Delaunay began to design textiles for a Lyon manufacturer in 1923; thenceforward cheerful and colourful abstract textiles were the main part of her design output. However, her Boutique Simultanée at the PARIS 1925 EXHIBITION included furniture with geometrical marquetry as well as textiles. In 1930 she published *Compositions Couleurs Idées* (forty plates of abstract designs). At the PARIS 1937 EXHIBITION she designed decorations for the Air Pavilion. She later designed playing-cards, mosaics, stained glass, ceramics and Aubusson and Gobelins tapestries. In 1977 many of her early textile designs were reissued.

Delaune, Étienne Born in Orleans in about 1518, Delaune was in 1552 appointed engraver to the Paris mint of Henri II of France (1519–59), who succeeded in 1547. Delaune's first dated engraving was made in 1561; he published a grand total of some 450. A protestant, Delaune fled Paris after the St Bartholomew's Day massacre in 1572, was in Strasbourg in 1572 and in Augsburg from 1575. While there he published two informative views of a goldsmith's workshop (1576). After returning to Strasbourg in 1580 Delaune

died in Paris in 1583. Many of Delaune's prints are small oval panels with figures allegorical of such themes as the senses, the months, hunting (1573), the Gods, the Labours of Hercules, the virtues and the Bible. His figures are almost invariably elongated MANNERIST nudes. Delaune also published numerous small panels of elaborate and dense GROTESQUE ornament, some oval, others rectangular, and many of his allegorical figures have borders of brilliant STRAPWORK grotesque. Other prints depict friezes of battles, trophies and triumphs, particularly suitable for the decoration of arms and armour. Indeed in the 1550s Delaune designed some elaborate armours for Henri II and others associated with his court. Delaune's first suite of prints (1561; twenty-six plates) included hand-mirrors, whistles, handles and decoration for cups. They use a refined and delicate version of the type of strapwork used at Fontainebleau in the 1530s, combined with grotesques and elegantly posed figures. Many drawings for jewels, rings, pendants, medals, necklaces, belts and whistles in this manner survive and probably date from the 1550s and 1560s. During his Strasbourg and Augsburg period Delaune published numerous dense grotesques for engraving or enamelling on pendants, crosses, miniature cases, etc., some dated 1573, 1578 or 1579. Some were engraved by his son, Jean Delaune. These grotesques were widely influential and often used by engravers, enamellers and inlayers, not only by Delaune's contemporaries but also in the 19th century, when, for instance, C. H. Ahrens of Hamburg followed a Delaune print of 1573 on an ebony panel inlaid with engraved ivory (1866–7).

Della Bella, Stefano (1610–64) Born in Florence, the son and nephew of sculptors who worked in the studio of Giovanni Bologna (1529–1608), Della Bella was trained as a goldsmith. He copied the etchings of CALLOT and in 1627 issued a plate of a banquet, which was dedicated to Gian Carlo de' Medici. He was thereafter patronized by the Medici, many of whose entertainments he commemorated in prints, and designed, for instance, the funeral of Emperor Ferdinand II (1637). In 1633 Lorenzo de' Medici financed a journey to Rome, where Della Bella remained until 1639. In that year he left for Paris in the train of Alessandro del Nero, Florentine Ambassador Extraordinary to France. Through his career Della Bella executed over 1,000 prints, many issued by the Parisian publishers François Langlois (Ciartres), Israël Henriet and Pierre I Mariette. In 1649, as a result of the Fronde disturbances, Della Bella left Paris for Florence, where he remained until his death, still working for Parisian publishers and serving for a while as drawing-master to Cosimo III. Della Bella's etchings of ornament comprise *Frises, feuillages et grotesques* (eight plates), staccato friezes of ACANTHUS enlivened with masks, rams' heads and other lively devices, probably influenced by MITELLI, *Ornamenti di fregi e fogliami* (sixteen plates), again friezes but in this case flowing and brilliant acanthus incorporating hounds, panthers, grapes, mermen and putti, *Ornamenti o Grottesche* (twenty plates), upright panels in the same manner, with sphinxes, goats, bats and symbols of hunting and mortality, *Raccolta di vasi diversi* (six plates), vigorous VASES both mannered and BAROQUE, *Raccolta di varii cappriccii et nove inventioni di cartelle et ornamenti* (Paris, 1646; eighteen plates) and *Nouvelles inventions de cartouches* (Paris, 1647; twelve plates), two sets of incomparable cartouches containing centaurs, swans, skeletons and dragons. Della Bella also designed fans and, in 1644, a series of educational card games which helped to teach the young Louis

XIV mythology, geography and history. He was responsible for several title-pages, for instance that for the works of Scarron (1649), and made etchings of antiquities, notably a plate of the Medici vase (1656). Many drawings for ornament and metalwork by Della Bella survive, together with the odd furniture design. His designs look back to the MANNERIST inventions of LIGOZZI and Callot; his ornament, on the other hand, although synthetic rather than innovatory, with many echoes of the AURICULAR style, looks forward to the ROCOCO of MEISSONIER. The seduction of his manner was such that as late as 1824 Edward Farrell used a cartouche by Della Bella to emboss a sideboard dish and borrowings from his works by other designers, for instance SCHOR, CAUVET and TESI, are frequent. Many of his drawings were lost in the 1720 BOULLE fire.

De Marteau, Gilles (1722–76) Born in Liège, the son of an armourer, De Marteau was a pupil of La Collombe, whose *Nouveaux Desseins d'Arquebuseries* (Paris, 1730) presented accomplished BERAINESQUE designs for engraving on fire-arms, influenced by SIMONIN, one engraved as early as 1702. After La Collombe's death De Marteau reissued his *Nouveaux Desseins* with some extra plates in the ROCOCO taste, engraved from 1743 to 1749. He also issued *Nouveaux Ornemens D'Arquebuseries* (twenty plates), rococo designs for gunsmiths, and *Plusieurs Trophées* (six plates), rococo trophies. He engraved TESSIER's Livre de Fleurs, as well as many paintings by François BOUCHER, HUET and others. In 1769 De Marteau became a member of the Academy in Paris.

De Morgan, William Frend (1839–1917) Born in London, the son of a professor of mathematics, from 1859 De Morgan studied painting at the Royal Academy Schools, where he met Henry HOLIDAY. In 1861 De Morgan was involved in stained-glass design and from 1863 he designed tiles and glass for the William MORRIS firm. His novel *Alice for Short* (1907) describes a stained-glass workshop. In 1869 De Morgan began to decorate pottery, and was by 1873 running a successful pottery. He revived lustre techniques and from about 1875 used 'Persian' colours. De Morgan lustre wares were shown in the drawing-room by the cabinet-makers Collinson & Lock at the PARIS 1878 EXHIBITION. De Morgan tiles were sold by the Morris firm from 1872 and he later designed mosaics for Morris & Co. De Morgan tiles were used to decorate the Arab Hall (1879) in Lord Leighton's house designed by George AITCHISON and Richard Norman SHAW's Tabard Inn in Bedford Park, London (1880). Also in 1880 De Morgan published a pattern-book of tiles made at his Chelsea pottery. About this date De Morgan established a close friendship with William Morris and moved his pottery to a site close to Morris's Merton Abbey works; he was also friendly with BURNE-JONES. In 1888 De Morgan became involved in the first ARTS & CRAFTS EXHIBITION and set up a new factory in Fulham with the architect Halsey RICARDO (1854–1928), who designed relief tiles. From the mid-1890s De Morgan spent much of his time in Italy; in about 1900 he designed ornament influenced by Italian maiolica for pottery fired at the Cantagalli factory in Florence. The Fulham factory closed in 1907, although the Passenger brothers and Frank Iles carried on until 1911. De Morgan himself turned to novel-writing with *Joseph Vance* (1906). 1,248 designs for ceramics by William De Morgan are in the possession of the VICTORIA & ALBERT MUSEUM.

Denis, Maurice (1870–1943) Born in Granville, Denis was brought up in Paris, where he met Roussel and Vuillard while studying classics at the Lycée Condorcet. In 1888 he entered the Académie Julian and then moved to the École des Beaux-Arts, where his master was Gustave Moreau (1826–98). In 1888 Denis was one of those who formed the Nabis group; their leader was Paul Sérusier (1864–1927), while Denis himself was active as propagandist and theoretician. In 1892 Denis designed a poster for the newspaper *La Dépêche de Toulouse*, and in 1893 illustrations for André Gide's *Le Voyage d'Urien*. From 1899 Denis, a fervent Catholic, designed stained glass; in 1912 he was a founder member of the Société des Amis des Cathédrales and in 1919 founded the Atelier d'Art Sacré in Paris: windows by Maurice Denis were illustrated in 'L'ARCHITECTURE VIVANTE' (1923). Denis also designed mosaics, wallpapers and ceramics, and in 1930 a tapestry, Rinaldo and Armida, for the Gobelins factory.

Denon, Dominique Vivant (1747–1825) Born at Givry, near Chalon-sur-Saône, of minor nobility, Denon was sent to Paris to study law but turned to the arts and literature. He studied drawing under Noel HALLÉ, and having charmed himself into court circles was appointed by Louis XV curator of Mme de Pompadour's collection of medals. In 1772 he went as a diplomat to St Petersburg and then from 1776 to Naples. He was involved in the Abbé de Saint-Non's *Voyage pittoresque de Naples et de Sicile* (1781–6) but they quarrelled and Denon later published his own *Voyage en Sicile* (1788). He was recalled to Paris in 1785, but in 1788 sold his collection of VASES to Louis XVI and set off for Italy on the proceeds. Returning to France at the Terror he was protected by DAVID, and published an *Œuvre priapique* (twenty-four plates), derived from Pompeii. He then frequented Joséphine de Beauharnais' salon, where he met Napoleon and as a result accompanied him to Egypt. His *Voyage dans la Basse et la Haute Égypte* (1802) immediately became a standard NEO-CLASSICAL textbook, cited in the bibliography to HOPE's *Household Furniture* (1807); it was followed by a monumental *Description de l'Égypte* (1809–22). In 1802 Denon was appointed by Napoleon director of his museum, and in 1803 head of the Monnaie des Médailles, most of whose medals were based on his sketches. Denon conceived and supervised the design of the Sèvres porcelain Egyptian service (1804–8), and was ubiquitous as Napoleon's art adviser. After 1815 he resisted the break-up of the Musée Napoléon, resigned his office and devoted the rest of his life to forming a great collection of drawings.

Depero, Fortunato (1892–1960) Born in Fondo in Trentino, Depero was rejected by the Vienna Academy of Fine Arts in 1909. In 1913 he moved to Rome, where he became involved in Futurist circles, producing his first Futurist paintings in 1914. In 1915, with Giacomo Balla (1871–1958), he issued a manifesto, *Ricostruzione futurista dell'universo*. From 1916, when he designed for Diaghilev and Stravinsky, Depero was closely involved with the theatre. In 1919 he established the Casa d'Arte Depero in Revereto, and began to design tapestries, interiors and, in 1921, inlaid boxes and panels. In 1923 Depero designed a Futurist room for the first MONZA BIENNALE, including felt wall-hangings. He also showed at the PARIS 1925 EXHIBITION and the Monza 1927 Biennale. In 1926 he designed a Campari poster and in 1927 a cover for *Emporium*. From 1928 to 1930 Depero was in New York, where he designed covers for *Vanity Fair* (1930), the *New Auto Atlas* (1930) and *Sparks* (1930). Returning to Italy he continued to advocate and practise Futurism with great perseverance. His house in Revereto is now a museum.

Design (1949–present) Published by the Council of Industrial Design, this magazine is the official mouthpiece of British design. Its first article, 'What is Good Design?', was by Gordon RUSSELL. The first editor, Alex Davis, was succeeded by Michael Farr in 1952.

Design and Art Direction (1964–present) This annual of the Designers' and Art Directors' Association comprises an anthology of British poster, packaging and advertising design.

Design and Industries Association (1915–present) After the 1912 ARTS & CRAFTS EXHIBITION a group of young designers, of whom the most active member was Harold STABLER (1872–1945), attempted to set up a permanent showroom for their works. This initiative failed, but in 1914 Stabler, Ambrose HEAL, his cousin Cecil Brewer, and Harry Peach (1874–1936) of the Dryad Works in Leicester all visited the COLOGNE DEUTSCHE WERKBUND EXHIBITION, and determined to set up an English equivalent. The original committee also included Hamilton Smith, Ernest Jackson and J. H. Mason. In 1914 a memorandum was sent to the Board of Trade, with Frank PICK and H. G. Wells among its signatories, to suggest an exhibition of high-quality German and Austrian goods, in order to arouse emulation among British manufacturers. The exhibition, held in 1915 in Goldsmiths' Hall, was followed by the launch of the Design and Industries Association, with Cecil Brewer as its founding secretary, operating from 6 Queen Square, also the premises of the ART-WORKERS' GUILD. W. R. LETHABY, then professor of design at the Royal College of Art (see SCHOOL OF DESIGN), was an inspiration and father-figure to the young enthusiasts of the D.I.A., as it came to be known, and his 'Art & Workmanship', first published in 'IMPRINT' (1913), was reissued as a D.I.A. pamphlet in 1915. The *Imprint* group were closely involved in the D.I.A.'s first exhibition, held in 1915 at the Whitechapel Art Gallery on the theme of Design and Industry in Printing. In 1916 the Arts & Crafts Exhibition at Burlington House incorporated a D.I.A. room of the Products of Industry. Although GIMSON declined Lethaby's suggestion to design for industry under D.I.A. auspices, the close links between the Arts & Crafts establishment and the D.I.A. were reflected in the D.I.A.'s membership, which included W. A. S. BENSON, Graily Hewett and Selwyn IMAGE, and the D.I.A. was slow to display any positive response to the European MODERN style, its *Yearbook* (1922–30) being dominated by objects which toed the 'fitness for purpose' line but were distinctly products of the Arts & Crafts tradition. Others were clearly Neo-Georgian. In 1927, under the auspices of the D.I.A., Harry Peach organized the English design exhibition at the Leipzig Fair: its miscellaneity and lack of purpose was evident by the side of the foreign displays, a point forcefully made by the textile designer Minni McLeish, who had been partly responsible: 'We do not understand this modern movement in design, and we do not like it.' None the less CHERMAYEFF'S 1928 furniture for Waring & Gillow attracted praise from John C. Rogers in the D.I.A. *Journal* and, with Gordon RUSSELL'S switch to Modern, Jack Pritchard's commission of a stand for Venesta from LE CORBUSIER in 1930, and the B.B.C.'s series of talks on Modern design from 1932, the D.I.A. became intimately involved in the promotion of the Modern style. The first issue of its

short-lived magazine *Design in Industry* (1933), edited by Maxwell Fry, was devoted to 'The Office, its Planning and Equipment'. Its successors, *Design for Today* (1933–5) and *Trend* (1936), supplied a comprehensive representation of MCGRATH, O'RORKE, Wells COATES, BREUER and other leading Modern designers. The 1933 Dorland Hall exhibition of British Industrial Art, although not officially sponsored by the D.I.A., was organized by D.I.A. activists, as a response to the 1931 Swedish design exhibition at Dorland Hall. Its success and a rise in membership up towards a thousand in the mid-1930s (from 1917 the figure had stuck around the 600 mark) represented the high-water mark of the D.I.A.'s influence. The foundation of the Society of Industrial Artists in 1930 and of the Council for Art and Industry, in 1933, with Frank Pick as Chairman, succeeded in 1944 by the Council of Industrial Design, created new institutions which supported D.I.A. principles. The D.I.A. was thus to a large extent replaced by its progeny. As a forum for discussion and an educational pressure group, producing exhibitions and publications, it had prepared the way for the Modern style in design. It continues to educate and discuss. However, in contrast to the Werkbund, its model, the D.I.A. never provided forceful leadership; PEVSNER'S phrase 'patient progress' summarizes its approach.

Design Quarterly (1946–present) Founded as the *Everyday Art Quarterly* this journal changed its title to the current one in 1954. Published by the Walker Art Center, Minneapolis, it provides useful if variable academic coverage of most aspects of mainly American design.

Deskey, Donald Born in 1894 Deskey began to work as a designer in the late

1920s. He came to prominence as the designer of furniture in the Radio City Music Hall which formed part of the Rockefeller Center in New York. Deskey's furniture, executed in about 1932, used aluminium and bakelite among more conventional materials and was in a dashing MODERN style. Other furniture by Deskey used glass, chrome and lacquer. In 1933 Deskey wrote in the 'STUDIO' on 'The Rise of American Architecture and Design', illustrating work by Paul T. Frankl and Walter Dorwin TEAGUE as well as a Radio City interior. Deskey designed not only furniture but also interiors, exhibitions, products and packaging. An advertisement in the 1940 *Architectural Record* refers to 'the designing genius of Donald Deskey' and illustrates a pierced metal chair for the Royal Metal Company. In the 1950s Donald Deskey Associates was one of the leading American firms of industrial designers. Deskey himself not only designed but also invented a high-pressure laminate called Weldtex.

Desportes, François-Alexandre (1661–1743) Born at Champigneul-Champagne, Marne, the son of a labourer, Desportes went to Paris in 1673 and was taught to paint animals by an old Flemish painter, Nicasius, a pupil of Frans Snyders (1579–1657). From 1678 Desportes worked as a painter of details for others, including Claude AUDRAN. In 1695 he visited Poland and on his return to Paris in 1696 devoted himself to animal and still-life painting; he became a member of the Academy in 1699, and was given a lodging in the Louvre. Desportes painted decorations for Louis XIV at Marly and for the Dauphin at Meudon. He designed carpets and screens for the Savonnerie factory and in 1735 was asked to revise the cartoons of tapestries woven from 1687 to 1730 at the Gobelins factory after paintings of exotic subjects by Albert Eckhout, given by Prince Maurice of Nassau to Louis XIV. The Desportes cartoons were shown at the Salon from 1737 to 1741 and the tapestries, the Nouvelles Indes (eight pieces) were very successful.

Desprès, Jean Born in 1889 at Souvigny in Allier, from a family of glass manufacturers, Desprès trained as a goldsmith in Avallon and Paris, then studied design. In the years around the First World War, during which he worked on aircraft construction, Desprès was friendly with painters such as Georges Braque and Joan Miró. After the war he devoted himself to jewellery design and construction, showing at the PARIS 1925 EXHIBITION, and at the 1926 Salon des Indépendants. His earliest jewellery designs, executed in 1912, are in a massive geometric cubist style. Jacques DOUCET, to whom Desprès was introduced by Rose Adler, was one of his earliest patrons. From about 1927 Desprès collaborated with the glass painter Étienne Cournault on the creation of '*bijoux surréalistes*', and in 1930 he showed jewellery in a style inspired by the aeroplane. Desprès later became a doyen of French jewellery design, showing at the PARIS 1937 EXHIBITION and many others.

Destailleur, Hippolyte Alexandre Gabriel Walter (1822–93) Born in Paris, the son of an architect, Destailleur studied architecture at the École des Beaux-Arts from 1842. He designed many houses in France and also the Palais Albert von Rothschild in Vienna (from 1879), Waddesdon Manor for Baron Ferdinand von Rothschild (from 1874) and the mausoleum at Farnborough for the Empress Eugénie (1887). Destailleur was an expert designer of furniture and interiors in a wide range of historic styles. He was a great collector of drawings and prints of ornament: his first collection was bought by the BERLIN KUNSTGEWERBEMUSEUM in 1879 and part of the second later entered the Bibliothèque Nationale in Paris. His books include *Recueil d'estampes relatives à l'ornementation des appartements* (1863 and 1871) and an edition of J. A. DUCERCEAU'S *Les Plus Excellents Bastiments* (1868–70).

De Stijl (1917–32) The magazine *De Stijl* was founded and edited by Theo van Doesburg (1883–1931) a Utrecht-born painter, art critic and architect. It propagated the views of a group led by him which included the painter Piet Mondrian (1872–1944), the architects Vilmos Huszar and J. J. P. Oud (1890–1963) and the poet Antony Kok. Mondrian wrote an article in the first issue of *De Stijl* proposing abstraction as the representation of pure spirit; the De Stijl group believed in the unity of the arts and was strongly influenced by the mystical teaching of Dr Schoenmakers. The straight line was supreme. The group soon gained the architects Jan Wils, Robert van t'Hoff and RIETVELD as members. In 1918 the architects Bart Van der Leck and P. J. C. Klaarhamer showed an interior designed in De Stijl principles in Utrecht. In 1919 Huszar designed stained glass and in 1921 a set of chessmen. Also in 1921 van Doesburg visited the BAUHAUS, where he exercised considerable, albeit disputed, influence and in the same year he met El LISSITZKY, who was the subject of two issues of *De Stijl*. In 1923 a De Stijl exhibition was held at the Léonce Rosenberg gallery in Paris. It was repeated in 1924, in which year van Doesburg settled in Paris. In 1925 Mondrian left the group. At the PARIS 1925 EXHIBITION the Austrian architect Frederick Kiesler (1890–1965), a De Stijl member who had worked with LOOS, showed his City in Space project; he moved to New York in 1926 and after a spell with Saks on Fifth Avenue wrote *Contemporary Art Applied to the Store and its Display*. From 1926 to 1928, in collaboration with the ARPS, Theo van Doesburg designed abstract decorations for L'Aubette in Strasbourg. The last issue of *De Stijl* was an obituary tribute to his memory.

Deutsch, Niklaus Manuel Born in Bern in about 1484, the son of an apothecary of German descent from Piedmont, Deutsch was trained as a glass painter. He was also active as a designer of stained glass. His earliest windows at Kirchberg, of about 1508, are accompanied by others designed by Hans Baldung Grien, by whom Deutsch was influenced. He continued to design stained glass up to at least 1537. In 1522 Deutsch designed new choir-stalls for Bern Cathedral executed from 1523 to 1525 by Jacob Rüsch and Heini Seewagen, in the RENAISSANCE style. In his last years Deutsch, who died in 1530, was active as a politician, a satirical poet and an impassioned supporter of the Reformation. Two pattern-books of about 1520 by Deutsch survive. Possibly intended for publication they include figures, and GOTHIC and Renaissance ornament, panels with putti, foliage, candelabra and battle friezes, a formula which anticipates VOGTHERR.

Deutsche Kunst und Dekoration (1897–1933) Issued by the Darmstadt architect and editor Alexander Koch, publisher of 'INNEN-DEKORATION', this well-illustrated journal was a leading propagandist for improved standards of design in Germany. Its first year included articles on ECKMANN, ENDELL, OBRIST, the Munich 1897 Exhibition and Melchior LECHTER's stained glass.

Deutsche Werkbund The Dresden 1906 Exhibition of applied art seemed to many German designers and manufacturers to open a new era in German design. Before it was over twelve manufacturers and twelve designers, including BEHRENS, Josef HOFFMANN, OLBRICH, PAUL and RIEMERSCHMID, suggested a new organization to promote German design. In 1907 MUTHESIUS published a report which stressed the commercial penalties of backwardness in design. His views attracted much opposition but were defended at a debate in Berlin in June 1907 by the writer Wolf Dohrn (1874–1914), Secretary of the Dresdener Werkstätte, the writer Josef August Lux (1871–1947) and the industrialist Peter Bruckmann (1865–1937). In October 1907 the Deutsche Werkbund was founded in Munich with the architect Theodor Fischer (1862–1938) as first chairman. Apart from Muthesius the main activists included the architect Fritz Schumacher (1869–1947) and the theologian and writer Friedrich Naumann (1860–1919). Karl Schmidt-Hellerau (1873–1948), director of the Dresdener Werkstätte, joined in 1908. The purpose of the Deutsche Werkbund was 'die Veredelung der gewerblichen Arbeit im Zusammenwirken von Kunst, Industrie und Handwerk' ('the improvement of industrial products through the combined efforts of artists, industrialists and craftsmen'). As Muthesius stressed in 1914 the Werkbund was not an artists' club but an alliance of artists, manufacturers and commercial interests. The Werkbund yearbook (1912–20) illustrated approved designs by, among others, Behrens and VAN DE VELDE; the Deutsches Warenbuch (1916) illustrated utilitarian objects of irreproachable simplicity. In 1914 the Deutsche Werkbund organized an exhibition in Cologne with buildings by Van de Velde, Walter GROPIUS and Taut. The Cologne exhibition was the occasion of a debate between Muthesius and Van de

Velde, in which Muthesius advanced the case for industrial design while Van de Velde stressed the contribution of the individual creative artist. From 1925 to 1934 the Werkbund published a magazine, Die Form, and in 1924 circulated an exhibition entitled 'Die Form ohne Ornament' ('Form without Ornament'). In 1927 the Werkbund organized a major exhibition on housing at Stuttgart, building a model suburb, Die Weissenhof Siedlung; the architectural director was MIES VAN DER ROHE. Werkbund exhibitions were also held in Paris in 1930 and as part of the German building exhibition in Berlin in 1931. By 1930 the Werkbund, which had begun with about 500 members, had about 3,000. Its chairmen had included Bruckmann from 1909 to 1919 and 1926 to 1931, the architect Hans Poelzig (1869–1939) from 1919 to 1921 and Riemerschmid from 1921 to 1926. In 1933 after a long debate only Gropius, WAGENFELD and the architect Martin Wagner (1885–1957) stood out against an accommodation with the Hitler regime. But despite the efforts of the president Ernst Jäckl the Werkbund was faded out of effective existence in 1934. It was revived in 1947 and has since 1952 published a magazine, Werk und Zeit. The Werkbund was greatly admired in other countries as an efficient promoter of good industrial design. It formed the model for the British DESIGN AND INDUSTRIES ASSOCIATION and in 1921 the French writer Sedeyn asked, 'Quel homme d'action, quel esprit vraiment moderne fondera un Werkbund français?'

Devarenne, Jean (1743–1806) A Lyon textile designer who worked for the manufactory of Devarenne & La March, Devarenne worked as professor of floral design at the Lyon school of design from 1799 to 1806, when the Lyon École des Beaux-Arts superseded it.

Diéterle, Jules-Pierre-Michel (1811–89)
Born in Paris Diéterle began as a decorative painter at the Opéra, working on
Robert le Diable in 1831. With three
other students he formed Séchan,
Feuchères & Cie, later Séchan, Diéterle
& Despléchin (1841–8), a firm of theatrical designers. In 1848 Diéterle was
appointed to the newly created post of
Artiste en Chef at the Sèvres porcelain
factory and in the same year was chosen
to serve on the official Conseil Supérieur
de Perfectionnement des Manufactures
Nationales. At Sèvres, Diéterle designed
VASES in the ROCOCO, Indian and
RENAISSANCE styles, with refined
NATURALISTIC and geometric ornament. Promoted in 1852 to Chef des
Travaux d'Art he left Sèvres in 1855,
when he designed a room in the rococo
style for the cabinet-maker E. S. Rou-
dillon, which won a silver medal at the
PARIS EXHIBITION. In the 1850s Diéterle was involved with Séchan, now his
father-in-law, and the decorator Hau-
mont on designs for the Sultan in Istanbul, including a Louis XIV-style
bedroom (1851) and a Louis XIII-style
dining-room (1853). They also decorated the Conversationshaus at Baden-
Baden in a variety of styles. The association ended in 1862. Diéterle designed
silver for Christofle and, from 1861,
tapestries for the Gobelins factory,
including the Cinq Sens (1864–7), compositions strongly influenced by AU-
DRAN's Portières des Dieux (1699),
which were intended for the Élysée
Palace. Diéterle also designed Savonnerie carpets for the Empress Eugénie
at the Tuileries, and, in 1878 and 1882,
carpets in the 17th-century style for the
Pope's apartments at Fontainebleau. In
1867 Diéterle was responsible with M.
Digby WYATT for the international
jury's report on decoration at the PARIS
EXHIBITION. In 1877 he became director of the Beauvais tapestry factory.

Dietterlin, Wendel (1551–99) Born in
Pullendorf, the son of a protestant pastor, Dietterlin's original name was
Wendling Gapp. His mother became a
citizen of Strasbourg in 1562. In 1571
Dietterlin himself became a citizen also,
buying a house in Strasbourg. His main
activity was the execution of mural
paintings. In 1590 he moved to Stuttgart
to execute paintings for Duke Ludwig
of Württemberg, returning to Strasbourg in 1593. In 1593 Dietterlin published the first part of his *Architectura
und Ausztheilung der V Seülen* (forty
plates) in both Stuttgart and Strasbourg.
A second Strasbourg instalment with
fifty plates followed in 1594, and the
definitive Nuremberg edition of 1598
contained 194 plates. Dietterlin's designs
comprise windows, chimneypieces,
doors, fountains and monuments,
ordered thematically by the five ORDERS
of architecture. They are in a brilliantly
extreme three-dimensional version of
the STRAPWORK GROTESQUE style,
with an inventive and expressive use of
crestings and contorted figures, both
human and animal. Dietterlin inspired
many imitators, who included Eck,
GUCKEISEN, EBELMANN, KRAMMER
and KASEMANN, but his intensity is
turned to incoherence by their lesser
talents. *Architectura* was reprinted in
Nuremberg in 1655, and some of its
plates were copied in Daniel MEYER's
Architectura, and in Amsterdam editions of BLUM from 1617. Charlton
House in Kent, built in about 1610,
displays the influence of Dietterlin in
the ornament of its frontispiece.

Dietterlin, Wendel the Younger The son
of the painter and designer Wendel
DIETTERLIN, Wendel Dietterlin the
Younger was active as a goldsmith and
engraver in Strasbourg and Lyon in the
early 17th century. He published a suite
of six plates of ornament (Lyon, 1614)
in a combination of the stretched GRO-

TESQUE style and the scrolled foliate manner known as COSSE-DE-POIS. In 1615 he published in Nuremberg fourteen plates of sinister monsters, insects, birds and snails, together with panels of extreme stretched grotesque ornament interlaced with monsters; they are close to Christoph JAMNITZER'S 1610 suite and FLINDT'S 1611 suite and thus on the margin of the AURICULAR style.

Dilettanti, Society of Founded in 1732 as a dining club by a group of wealthy young Englishmen who had travelled in Italy – Horace WALPOLE said '. . . the nominal qualification is having been in Italy, and the real one, having been drunk' – the Society of Dilettanti helped to encourage classical studies. The painter George Knapton (1698–1778), a founder member, painted portraits of many members and also in 1736 to 1737 designed for the Society a box known as Bacchus's Tomb, embellished by Nicholas Revett (1720–1804) in 1766, a balloting box and a chair. From 1742 until 1756 the Society seriously planned a building. When this scheme was abandoned Spencer House became the focus of the Society's attentions and its decoration of about 1760 by James STUART was the earliest important NEO-CLASSICAL scheme in London. In 1751 Stuart and Revett had been elected members of the Society, while in Venice, and the first volume of their *Antiquities of Athens* (1762) was the direct result of the Society's patronage. The Society later published several handsome works on classical archaeology, including *Ionian Antiquities* (1769), the result of an expedition led by Richard Chandler (1738–1810) in 1764, financed by the Society. Sir William HAMILTON became a member in 1777. From 1806 the Society lost some of its authority in matters of taste and scholarship by acting as a centre of opposition to the Elgin marbles, led by the collector and pundit Richard Payne Knight (1750–1824), who dismissed them in 1806 as 'Roman of the time of Hadrian'. The Society later published Francis Cranmer Penrose's *Athenian Architecture* (1851, revised edition 1888), which included an account of Greek polychromy.

Djo-Bourgeois, Édouard-Joseph (1898–1937) Born at Bezons, Djo-Bourgeois was a pupil of MALLET-STEVENS and a disciple of Francis JOURDAIN. He became a member of the Société du Salon d'Automne and showed at their Salons from 1922, and was also a member of the Société des Artistes-Décorateurs. He worked with Kohlmann and Mattet at Studium, the design studio of the Grands Magasins de Louvre, designing an office in their pavilion at the PARIS 1925 EXHIBITION, for which his wife Élise designed textiles. From 1925 Djo-Bourgeois was involved in the decoration of the Villa of the Vicomte de Noailles at Hyères. He designed many villas in the South of France, and many shop interiors in Paris. His work was often illustrated in 'ART ET DÉCORATION', *L'Art Vivant* and the 'STUDIO'. The *Répertoire du goût moderne* (1929) included a rectilinear pastel-coloured nursery suite designed by Djo-Bourgeois, including a carpet with a puffer-train. He was a strong supporter of MODERN materials and took a typically Modern anti-ornament line.

Documents d'Architecture Moderne (1902–7) German in origin this French-text collection of mainly coloured illustrations of houses and interiors showed the work not only of German designers but also that of ASHBEE, Edgar WOOD, VOYSEY, G. M. ELLWOOD, Eliel SAARINEN, George LOGAN and Will BRADLEY.

Domus (1928–present) The founder-editor of this Milan-based magazine was

Gio Ponti (1892–1979). Always well illustrated, it commenced as a vehicle for educated middle-class interior design, but became increasingly stylish and MODERN in the 1930s. In recent years it has combined the promotion of Italian design with de luxe avant-gardism of a mainly conceptual variety.

Dorn, Marion (1899–1964) Born in San Francisco, Dorn studied graphic art at Stamford University. In the early 1920s she came to England and designed resist printed fabrics and soft furnishings. In 1929 she illustrated William BECKFORD's *Vathek* with bold coloured lithographs for the Nonesuch Press. In the same year she shared an exhibition of hand-knotted rugs by the Wilton Royal Carpet Factory with McKnight KAUFFER, with whom she had lived since 1923 and whom she married in 1950; the exhibition was reported in the 'STUDIO'. Thenceforward Dorn was a prolific designer of MODERN and often abstract textiles and carpets for interiors in private and public buildings, including the Savoy and Claridges, and for liners including the *Orion* and *Queen Mary*. She established her own firm Marion Dorn Ltd in 1934. Dorn's clients included Warners, Edinburgh Weavers, the Old Bleach Linen Co., Syrie MAUGHAM, Gordon RUSSELL and Donald Brothers. Her work was illustrated in magazines such as 'DECORATION' and shown in exhibitions. In 1940 she and Kauffer left England for America but failed to repeat their London success. Dorn died in Tangier.

Dosio, Giovanni Antonio (1533–1609) Born in Florence, Dosio moved to Rome in 1548 to study as a goldsmith. From 1549 to 1551 he was in the studio of the architect and sculptor Raffaelo da Montelupo. He subsequently worked in Rome as a sculptor, restorer of antiqui-

ties and art dealer. He did the illustrations for Bernard Gamucci's *Antichità di Roma* (Venice 1565) and in 1569 published a suite of engravings of Roman antiquities dedicated to Cosimo I de' Medici. In about 1575 he gave up sculpture for architecture and was at this period planning a treatise on architecture to supersede that of SERLIO; it was to include chimneypiece designs. He was often in Florence and from 1590 in Naples, where he became royal engineer, and died. Dosio designed altars, tabernacles, monuments, and furniture, including an elaborate architectural cabinet.

Dossi, Dosso Born Giovanni de Lutero and also known as de Constantino, Dossi probably trained as a painter in Venice. In 1512 he was working for Federigo Gonzaga in Mantua, but by 1514 he was in Ferrara, where his father served Ercole d'Este as a steward. In 1517 he was in Florence and in 1518 in Venice, where he became friendly with Titian, with whom he visited Mantua in 1519. Back in Ferrara, Dossi designed tapestries (1536), maiolica (1529), horse armour (1526), coins (1528) and decorations for court entertainments. He died in 1542. Many of his designs had been done in collaboration with his younger brother, Battista Dossi, who probably worked in RAPHAEL's workshop in Rome in about 1520. Battista designed coins (1526), brocades (1540), armour (1541), a triumphal arch for the visit of Pope Paul III to Ferrara in 1543, and tapestries, including suites on the History of Hercules (1545) and Ovid's *Metamorphoses* (1543–5), woven by the Flemish weaver Hans Karcher in Ferrara. Battista Dossi died in 1548.

Doucet, Jacques (1853–1929) Born in Paris, Doucet became a great couturier there, mentioned as such by Proust; Paul POIRET was a protégé and Madeleine

Vionnet worked under him. From 1907 to 1912 he built up a great collection of 18th-century art in his house in the Rue Spontini, a collection which he sold in 1912. He then rapidly created an important art library which he gave to the University of Paris in 1918. Reserved, imperious and exclusive, Doucet became a great patron of advanced artists and decorators; he owned Picasso's *Les Demoiselles d'Avignon*. In 1912 he bought furniture by Paul Iribe, in 1914 lacquer by Eileen GRAY, and in about 1920 furniture by Marcel Coard. From 1917 to 1919 he employed LEGRAIN as a bookbinder; he later employed Rose Adler in the same role. In 1926 the architect Paul Ruau designed for Doucet a villa at Neuilly for which MIKLOS designed sculpture, carpets and door handles, Czaki a black glass staircase, Lipchitz a chimneypiece and LALIQUE glass doors. In 1928 Doucet had mounted by '*mon décorateur Legrain*' some decorated mirrors by Étienne Cornault. Legrain predeceased Doucet by three months.

Downing, Andrew Jackson (1815–52) Born in Newburgh, New York, Downing became an American equivalent of LOUDON, a pundit on landscape gardening who was also an authority on houses and their furnishing. His *A Treatise on the Theory and Practice of Landscape Gardening* (1841), *Cottage Residences* (1842) and *The Architecture of Country Houses* (1850) borrow heavily from Loudon and other English works. The illustrations, mainly drawn or designed by A. J. DAVIS, include furniture and interiors.

Drentwett, Abraham Born in about 1647, Drentwett was a member of a celebrated Augsburg family of goldsmiths. He was also active as a wax modeller. He died in 1727. Drentwett was responsible for three undated suites of designs for silver in the Augsburg manner of about 1700, *Neue Inventiones von underschidlich nutzlicher Silber-Arbeit* (eight plates), *Unterschiedlich Augspurgischer Goldschmidts Arbeit* (twelve plates in two parts) and *Ein neües Lauber und Goldschmieds Buch* (twelve plates in two parts). Drentwett's designs are in an elaborate late-BAROQUE style, incorporating figures into richly scrolled supports and frames. They comprise friezes, cartouches, VASES, ewers, tables, stands, wine-coolers, chairs, stools and andirons. His designs for the embossing of silver tables are closely related to the ornament of English gilt gesso tables of about 1720.

Dresser, Christopher (1834–1904) Born in Glasgow, the son of an excise officer of Yorkshire origin, Dresser entered the government SCHOOL OF DESIGN at Somerset House in 1847. He was a star pupil and in about 1854 began to lecture at the School on botany, his main interest. In 1856 he supplied the plate in Owen JONES's *Grammar of Ornament* depicting the geometrical arrangement of flowers, and in 1857–8 published on *Botany as Adapted to the Arts and Art Manufactures* in the *Art Journal*. In 1860 he was given a doctorate at the University of Jena in recognition of his botanical researches, and accumulated several botanical professorships, notably that of Botany applied to the Fine Arts in the Department of Science and Art, South Kensington. His first book on design, *The Art Decorative Design* (1862), expanded an 1857 article. Dresser designed a number of objects shown at the London 1862 Exhibition, where the display of Sir Rutherford Alcock's collection provided the first full introduction to Japanese work; Dresser made drawings and purchases from this collection. In the 1860s Dresser established himself as a leading commercial designer, and in 1869 moved into a large house, Tower Cressy, in Kensington. The only known Dresser sketch-book (Ipswich Museum) dates from the mid-1860s and displays his mature style, which did not change. *The Principles of Decorative Design* (1873), based on a series of articles in Cassell's *Technical Educator*, reflects Dresser's continued indebtedness to Owen Jones, on whom he lectured at Jones's Memorial Exhibition in 1874. In 1875 he began to design silver and plate for Elkington & Co., from 1878 for Messrs Hukin & Heath, and from 1879 for James Dixon & Sons. In 1876 he saw the PHILADELPHIA EXHIBITION en route for a semi-official visit to Japan, whence he returned in 1877 with a large collection of art objects partly assembled for TIFFANY & Co. of New York and partly for the London oriental dealers, Londros & Co. In 1878 he was a wallpaper juror at the PARIS EXHIBITION, and in 1879 with Charles Holme of Bradford set up the firm of Dresser & Holme to trade in Japanese and other oriental imports. Also in 1879 Dresser became Art Director of the newly formed Linthorpe pottery, for which he designed prolifically until 1882: at the same period he was designing porcelain for Mintons. His appointment in 1880 as Art Editor of the 'FURNITURE GAZETTE' initiated a vigorous but hopeless one-year campaign to improve design on Jones/Dresser principles. At the same time he became Art Manager of the Art Furnishers' Alliance, and attempted to put these principles into commercial practice. The Alliance, whose backers included Arthur Lasenby LIBERTY, went into liquidation in May 1883. In 1882, after illness, Dresser published his magnum opus, *Japan, its Architecture, Art and Art Manufactures*. Illness and business troubles probably led to a move to Sutton in 1883, but in 1886 Dresser's *Modern Ornamentation* appeared and in 1889 he moved to Barnes, where he ran

a studio with ten assistants during the 1890s. In that decade he designed glass for James Couper & Sons of Glasgow's Clutha range. In November 1904, still actively engaged in design, he died while on a business trip to Alsace. As well as the silver, plate, ceramics, furniture and glass already mentioned, Dresser was a prolific designer of textiles, carpets and wallpapers for leading firms such as Warner & Sons, Crossley & Co. and Jeffrey & Co., among many others. He also designed cast-iron for the Coalbrookdale Company. Christopher Dresser always acknowledged his debt to the teachings and example of Owen Jones. His admiration for Egyptian, Greek, GOTHIC, Persian, Indian, Chinese and Japanese ornament reflected Jones's taste, as did his dislike of Roman, RENAISSANCE and ROCOCO decoration. Dresser's grounding in botany further encouraged his adoption of an analytical, systematic and quasi-scientific approach to such topics as colour and proportions. His moral objection to 'dishonesty' in design, veneering for instance being taboo, is a strain common to most Victorian theorists of design, including A. W. N. PUGIN, whose work Dresser admired. However he also advocated refinement of finish, criticizing Charles EASTLAKE's *Household Taste* for its shortcomings in this respect, and was fully attuned to the needs of machine production. Some of Dresser's metalwork exhibits strikingly rigorous and stark forms, in astonishing prefigurement of the BAUHAUS manner, but his style is better understood as an extreme version of the High Victorian geometric style, which also provided a disciplined framework for his abstract explorations of polychromatic ornament, and his usage of an extraordinarily wide range of historic and exotic prototypes, even including Peruvian pottery.

Drews, Marie Sister of the Berlin potter Otto Drews, Marie Drews produced painted pottery in the 1870s and 1880s, which she called 'Majolika'. In 1879 and 1880 her firm showed at exhibitions in Berlin; it foundered in 1894. Marie Drews published an introduction to maiolica painting in 1883 and before that, in collaboration with Minna Laudien, *Vorlagen für Majolikamalerei*, a series of models mainly based on Islamic prototypes.

Dreyfuss, Henry (1903–72) Born in New York, Henry Dreyfuss was active as a stage designer on Broadway from 1921. In 1929 he opened a design office after an unhappy period as a design consultant for a department store. Dreyfuss established a versatile and prolific practice although he never allowed the firm to become impersonally large. Among objects designed by Dreyfuss were aircraft interiors, hearing-aids, clocks, farm equipment, Bell telephones (from 1930), Hoover products (from 1934), television sets for R.C.A. (from 1946) and passenger cars for the New York Central Railroad (1941). Dreyfuss worked hard to establish a system of anthropometrics to provide a basis for ergonomic design. This preoccupation is reflected in books such as *Designing for People* (1955) and *The Measure of Man* (1959). By the mid-1950s Henry Dreyfuss Associates had offices in both California and New York. In 1965 he became the first president of the Industrial Designers Society of America. In 1972 Dreyfuss and his wife killed themselves; she had been his business manager.

Drusse, Nikolaus (1584–1629) Drusse worked in Augsburg, where he lodged for many years with the goldsmith David Flicker. From 1607 to 1625 he published seven suites of six plates each with very fine black designs for enamelling in the stretched GROTESQUE style, with a scatter of silhouetted birds, flowers and landscapes, similar to BEYTLER's later designs.

Dubost, Michel (1879–1952) Born at Lyon, Dubost studied at the École des Beaux-Arts there. His teachers included CASTEX-DÉGRANGE, whom he succeeded as professor of floral design at the École in 1914, after working as a textile designer. From 1923 to 1933 Dubost designed textiles for François Ducharne, among them some shown at the PARIS 1925 EXHIBITION. Ducharne published a suite of Dubost's designs with a preface by Colette.

DuCerceau, Jacques Androuet Nothing definite is known of the origin and education of DuCerceau, whose name may derive from his trade sign, a circle or hoop. He has been stated to have been born in Paris in 1515 and to have travelled to Rome in 1533, and again after 1544, then as a protégé of Georges Cardinal d'Armagnac, a relation of Georges d'Amboise, the builder of Château Gaillon. The facts start in Orleans in 1549, when DuCerceau published a suite of *Arches* there. This was followed by *Temples* (1550), in whose preface DuCerceau makes it clear that he was running a publishing house, an '*officina*', with an ambitious programme of publications on architecture and ornament, a programme which DuCerceau was largely to fulfil. *Fragmenta structurae veteris* (1550) presented imaginary views of Roman ruins after Léonard THIRY, named as their author and probably known to DuCerceau. DuCerceau's most interesting early publication was a suite of *Grotesque* (1550, second edition Paris, 1562; fifty plates), which included close copies from Enea VICO's 1541 GROTESQUES, as well as adaptations and borrowings from other Italian engravers including Peregrino da Cesena, Agostino VENEZIANO, Giovanni

Antonio da BRESCIA and Nicoletto da MODENA (a plate adapted from the latter was used on an armour of Henri II), and, probably, from Italian book ornament. DuCerceau also used Flemish sources, such as the Master of the HORSE HEADS, Cornelis BOS and Cornelis MATSYS. In 1551 DuCerceau published *Vues d'Optiques* and *Compositions d'architecture*. Of the same period are the *Grands cartouches de Fontainebleau* (ten plates) and the *Petits cartouches de Fontainebleau* (thirty-two plates), which include copies after FANTUZZI and thus promulgated the vigorous scrolled STRAPWORK initiated by ROSSO at Fontainebleau in the 1530s, which is otherwise uncommon in DuCerceau's works. In the mid-1550s DuCerceau moved to Paris where he published his *Livre d'architecture* (1559), dedicated with a French nationalist stress to Henri II (1519–59). *Arcs et monuments antiques d'Italie et de France* (1560) was followed by the *Second Livre d'architecture* (1561), dedicated to the new king, Charles IX (1550–74); the Château de Lourmarin, Provence, has chimneypieces of the early 1560s based on the *Second Livre*. In 1562 a second edition of his *Grotesque* appeared with ten additional plates in the grotesque manner derived from RAPHAEL'S Vatican Loggie, which was practised by PRIMATICCIO. In the mid-1560s DuCerceau, a protestant, had to leave Paris and retire to Montargis, where he came under the protection of Renée de France, sister of François I and consort of Ercole II d'Este. To her he dedicated his second book of *Grotesques* (1566; thirty-six plates). DuCerceau claimed that his grotesques would be useful to goldsmiths, painters, stonemasons, cabinet-makers etc., and stated that the plates were in part his own invention and in part copied from Monceaux-en-Brie, built by Catherine de' Medici (1519–89) from 1547, and

from Fontainebleau. Certain plates are direct but distorted copies from Primaticcio's Galerie d'Ulysse at Fontainebleau and most plates reflect the Roman and Mantuan prototypes used by Primaticcio. *Grotesques* (1566) is thus essentially a record of the Henri II style of ornament, rather than an original contribution by DuCerceau himself. In 1569 DuCerceau and BOYVIN engraved plates for Jacques Besson's *Theatrum Instrumentorum et Machinarum*, a book of mechanical devices in whose preface Besson refers to DuCerceau as 'architecte du Roy et Madame la Duchesse de Ferrara'. In 1572 he published his third *Livre d'Architecture* and in 1576 *Leçons de perspective pratique* (a copy belonged to Turner!), dedicated to Catherine de' Medici, who was also the dedicatee of DuCerceau's *Plus Excellens Bastimens de France* (first volume 1577, second volume 1579): in the *Plus Excellens Bastimens* DuCerceau illustrated many of the great RENAISSANCE palaces built in France during his lifetime. There followed his *Petit traité des cinq ordres de colonnes* (1583), on the ORDERS, and DuCerceau's last work, *Le livre des édifices antiques romains* (1584), dedicated to the Duc de Nemours, son-in-law of his patron Renée de France. DuCerceau also published many prints of ornaments, including MORESQUE niello designs, cartouches, trophies, friezes, terms and caryatids, and designs for VASES, ewers and *tazze*, some derived from Vico, Veneziano and POLIDORO DA CARAVAGGIO, locks and keys. Apart from one table dated 1550, DuCerceau's fifty furniture designs all seem to date from about 1560 and are the earliest large group of such designs, all in a frenetic MANNERIST style. One design was used for a surviving table 'standing uppon sea doges' listed in the 1601 inventory of Hardwick Hall. DuCerceau's role as an architect is ill-defined but it seems probable that he did work as a designer at Verneuil from 1568 and Charleval from 1570. He certainly founded a dynasty of architects with which GENTILHÂTRE was probably associated. As a designer Du-Cerceau was not a great innovator but he played a role comparable to that of VREDEMAN DE VRIES in disseminating mannerist and grotesque ornament in France and Northern Europe.

DuCerceau, Paul Androuet The son of Jacques Androuet DuCerceau of Ver-neuil-sur-Oise and a kinsman of the famous 16th-century designer, Paul Androuet DuCerceau was probably in contact with the royal decorator, Charles ERRARD, whose ornaments in the Vieux Louvre he engraved in about 1650. DuCerceau later published over twenty suites of ornament, usually with six plates each. Typical titles are *Nouveau Livre de Montans, Livre de diverse Frises*, and *Livre d'Ornemens de feuil-lage*, panels, friezes and ornaments with an admixture of masks and STRAPWORK but predominantly composed of ACAN-THUS and/or flowers; some suites incorporate mythological scenes such as the Labours of Hercules. DuCerceau clearly had direct experience of designing for textiles and embroidery, as is evident from plate titles such as 'Fleurs à la Persienne pour la Broderie et les Étoffes de soye' and 'Dessein Nouveau pour Étoffes de Brocart a Fond Dor ou d'Argent', as well as from suites specifically aimed at embroiderers. Other designs were intended for engraving or embossing on silver, for marquetry, and for carving, while *Ornements d'orfevrerie pour Flenquer et Émailler Cinq Desseins de Boëstes de Miroirs faits pour les Ambassadeurs de Siam* records executed enamel designs. However, the greater part of his designs were for decorative painting and many bear indications that sections are to be marbled; a few incorporate royal emblems.

DuCerceau also engraved one suite after designs by CHARMETON and in 1654 a view of the door of Rheims Cathedral, where Louis XIV was crowned.

Duflos, Augustin Duflos was trained as a jeweller in Paris under Jean Denis L'Empereur, jeweller to the crown, who died in 1735. In 1722 Duflos assisted the goldsmith Claude Ballin II in the making of Louis XIV's throne. His *Recueil de Desseins de Joallerie* (1767; thirty-three plates) alludes to this early triumph in the preface, which also stresses the importance of practical experience and simplicity to designers; many designs, Duflos states, are only beautiful on paper. His own are NATUR-ALISTIC. Duflos bewails the fact that coloured stones are out of fashion and only diamonds are *à la mode*.

Dufrène, Maurice (1876–1955) Born in Paris, Dufrène studied at the École des Arts Décoratifs. In 1899 he started to work as a designer for MEIER-GRAEFE'S La Maison Moderne, while still a student, and in 1901 he was a founder member of the Société des Art-istes-Décorateurs. In about 1906 Duf-rène reacted against the curvilinear extravagance of the ART NOUVEAU style. He taught at the École Boulle from 1912 to 1923. From 1921 Dufrène established a second reputation as founding director of La Maîtrise, the design studio of the Galeries Lafayette department store. Dufrène edited three volumes of *Ensembles mobiliers* (thirty-two plates each), devoted to interior design shown at the PARIS 1925 EXHIBITION; his own designs comprised five rooms for La Maîtrise, including a dashingly curvaceous woman's bedroom with a polar-bear rug. Dufrène also published an album of plates of interiors at the 1926 Salon des Artistes-Décorateurs, including work by JALLOT, SELMERSHEIM, CHAREAU,

FOLLOT and others, and a similar album for the PARIS 1937 EXHIBITION; in 1937 Dufrène was still working for La Maîtrise. He was a versatile and prolific designer who advocated mass production but whose MODERNISM was usually applied to comfortably traditional forms.

Dufy, Raoul (1877–1953) Born in Le Havre, Dufy was trained as a painter; from 1905, under the influence of Matisse, he was associated with the Fauve group. In 1910 Dufy executed his first book illustrations, for Fleuret's *Friperies* and Apollinaire's *Bestiaire*. In 1909 he designed letter headings for Paul POIRET, who in 1911 commissioned Dufy to design textiles. The venture, which was associated with Poiret's Atelier Martine, progressed on an *ad hoc* basis but none the less produced designs of remarkable vigour and colour. In 1912 Bianchini, of the Lyon silk manufacturers Atuyer, Bianchini & Férier, offered Dufy such good terms that he left the association with Poiret to design for them, which he continued to do until 1928. In the latter year Aldous Huxley had sofas and cushions covered in material designed by Dufy. Up to about 1919 his designs were still in the same vigorous manner as those for Poiret, often using imagery and techniques borrowed from popular woodcuts. Later however Dufy's designs tended to become freer and more spontaneous. Flowers were his basic theme but butterflies, marine subjects, the races and other subjects familiar from his paintings were also used. In 1931 to 1934 the firm of Onondaga of New York commissioned some designs for printed textiles from Dufy. In 1953 several of his early designs were reissued by the Parisian firm of Corot. In 1924 Dufy was commissioned by the Beauvais tapestry factory to design a tapestry screen and seat coverings; they were completed in 1930, and were based on the theme of the City of Paris. Dufy also designed Aubusson tapestries in 1940 and later. Although he was at this stage in contact with LURÇAT, Dufy's own style, painterly and sketchy, seems to have been ill suited to the medium of tapestry. More successful are hangings he designed for Paul Poiret's show at the PARIS 1925 EXHIBITION. Dufy also decorated vases and architectural *jardinières* made by the Catalan potter Joseph Lhorens i Artigas from 1922 to 1930 and 1937 to 1940. A brief flirtation with the Sèvres porcelain factory proved abortive; its disciplines did not suit Dufy.

Dugourc, Jean Démosthène (1749–1825) Born in Versailles the son of a controller in the household of the Duc d'Orléans, Dugourc went to Rome in 1764 and there met Winckelmann. In 1776 he married one of the elder sisters of the architect and designer BÉLANGER whose pupil he became. Dugourc was appointed designer to the Duc d'Orléans in 1780 and in 1783 designer to the Paris Opéra. In 1782 he published a suite of *Arabesques* (six plates) which were reprinted in *Recueil d'arabesques* (1802) together with others by PRIEUR, SALEMBIER, QUEVERDO and J.-F. BOUCHER. In 1784 Dugourc was appointed Dessinateur du Garde-Meuble de la Couronne and designed furniture for the King, for his brothers the Comtes de Provence and d'Artois, and for his sisters Mmes Adelaide and Elisabeth, working at Maisons and Bagatelle in 1777–8, and at Fontainebleau in 1785. Dugourc designed silks and embroidery for the Lyon firm of Pernon between 1774 and 1790. He claimed to be the pioneer of the Etruscan taste, and the leading arbiter of design in the decade before the revolution. In about 1790, having been appointed a general inspector of French manufactures Dugourc founded a wallpaper factory with the printing pioneer Jean Louis Duplat (1757–1833). Dugourc later ran a play-ing-card factory and a glass factory. At the end of 1799 Dugourc went to Spain, where from 1800 to 1814 he was Premier Architecte du Roy d'Espagne, for whom he designed highly refined NEO-CLASSICAL furniture, bronzes and silks. In 1814 Dugourc returned to France, where Bélanger secured him the appointment as designer to the Menus Plaisirs in succession to J. M. MOREAU (1741–1814), an influential post he held until his death.

Duguers de Montrosier, Pierre-Louis-Arnulphe (1758–1806) Born at Landau, the son of a soldier, he served in the Anhalt infantry regiment until 1779. During the French revolution he estab-lished himself at Neuilly on the western outskirts of Paris as a promoter of enter-tainments in the Parc des Sablons. In about 1800 he set up an ambitious fur-niture business with borrowed money in association with a cabinet-maker named Hutin. At the 1806 Paris Exhibition of products of industry he showed an ambitious but unwieldy group of furni-ture designed by himself in a highly allegorical version of the Empire style of PERCIER and FONTAINE, including a clock in the form of a memorial to Frederick the Great and a trophy of arms dedicated to Napoleon; their exe-cution was subsidized by a large govern-ment loan. Duguers commemorated these products in a nicely engraved *Recueil de Dessins de Meubles, Pendules & Candelabres* (1806). After Duguers' death Napoleon refused to buy his fur-niture, understandably objecting to its excessive elaboration, but in 1812 it was accepted from Duguers' widow by the state in satisfaction of his debt to the government.

Duhn, Rudolf von A furniture designer and publisher, Duhn, issued the *Mobi-lien-Magazin* (Altona, 1860), containing 218 designs for every type of furniture in the ROCOCO revival style. In 1842 Duhn had issued views of Hamburg after the fire.

Dumée, Guillaume Dumée was active as a decorative painter in Paris from 1601 to 1626. From 1605 he was curator of the royal paintings at Saint-Germain. He worked for the King in the Tuileries, and decorated the Grand Cabinet of the Queen in the Louvre. In 1610 he won the competition to succeed LERAMBERT as royal tapestry designer, together with GUYOT, who married his sister in 1613. The two artists collaborated on a suite of twenty-six tapestries on the theme of *Il Pastor Fido*, which had formed the subject of the competition. Dumée received payment for tapestry designs in 1618.

Dumons, Jean Joseph (1687–1779) Born at Tulle, Limousin, Dumons was trained as a painter, became a member of the Academy in Paris in 1735, and showed at Salons there from 1737 to 1753. From 1731 to 1754 he was painter and designer at the Aubusson carpet factory, where he spent three months every two years. In 1756, after the death of OUDRY, he was appointed artistic director of the Beauvais tapestry factory.

Dunand, Jean (1877–1942) Born at Lancy near Geneva, Dunand trained in Geneva as a sculptor and designer. In 1897 he came to Paris on a scholarship and worked in the studio of the sculptor and furniture designer Jean DAMPT. In 1903 Dunand began to work in beaten metal, with richly varied surface treat-ments, and from about 1905 was pro-ducing vases in an ART NOUVEAU style from which he turned in 1913 to more geometric forms. Dunand continued to produce such vases to the end of the 1930s, with an increasingly powerful use of geometry. During the 1914 to 1918 war he designed a new helmet for the French army, but only a few thousand were produced. From 1912 Dunand learnt the technique of Japanese lacquer from Sugawara, who had taught Eileen GRAY, and from 1919 he built up a lacquer manufactory which eventually employed as many as 100 workers; the use of crushed eggshell in lacquer was his hallmark. Dunand became a French citizen in 1922 and from 1921 to 1932 showed vases and lacquer at the Galerie Georges Petit together with GOULDEN, Jouve and Schmied. Dunand was well publicized by Émile Sedeyn and others in magazines such as 'ART DÉCORATIF' and 'ART ET DÉCORATION'. At the PARIS 1925 EXHIBITION he executed a black lacquer smoking-room in the French Embassy. He also made lacquer panels for Pierre LEGRAIN, Printz and RUHLMANN, and in about 1929 a particularly dashing geometric MODERN card-table for the couturière Madeleine Vionnet. Among his largest commissions were lacquer panels for the liners *Île de France* (1928), *L'Atlantique* (1931) and *Normandie* (1935), and for the 1931 Colonial Exhibition. Primarily a craftsman, Jean Dunand was an eclectic designer, sometimes NATURALISTIC, sometimes cubist, and with a frequent use of African motifs. As well as vases and furniture he designed some geometric jewellery. From 1908 to his death Dunand exhibited regularly at the Société des Artistes-Décorateurs, of which he became Vice-President in 1927.

Dunstan, Saint (924–88) Educated at Glastonbury, where he was taught to write and paint, Dunstan provided designs for embroideries on a stole for a noble matron called Aethelwynn in about 940. He later became a great reformer of the Anglo-Saxon church.

Duplessis, Jean-Claude Born Jean-Claude Chambellan in Turin, Duplessis worked there as a silversmith until at least 1739, when Amadeo, Duke of Savoy, owed him money. In about 1740 he moved to Paris, where he died in 1774. From about 1745 Duplessis worked as a designer to the Vincennes porcelain factory, which moved to Sèvres in 1756. He also supplied and designed gilt-bronze mounts for both porcelain and furniture. Duplessis owned engraved ornament by BABEL, BEAUVAIS, SALY, DELAFOSSE, PETITOT and J.-F. BOUCHER. But despite the predominance of NEO-CLASSICAL designers in this list, it is probable that most of the neo-classical designs associated with Duplessis, such as the Sèvres Vase Duplessy and the mounts to the Bureau du Roi (1760–69), were due to his son and collaborator Jean-Claude-Thomas Duplessis, who published two handsome suites of VASES in the neo-classical style, both of four plates, and was described in 1777 as 'an accomplished designer who can work from his own drawings'. In about 1776 he made and probably designed a set of gilt-bronze candelabra for the Hôtel Grimod de la Reynière, decorated by CLÉRISSEAU. He died in 1783.

Dupré, Augustin (1748–1833) Born at Saint-Étienne of a poor family, Dupré first entered a gunsmith's workshop and then studied at the Saint-Étienne school run by the medallist Jacques Olanier (1742–98). In 1768 he decided to try his fortune in Paris and rapidly built up a prolific activity designing jewellery, metalwork and ornament. Dupré began to produce medals in 1776 and soon became dominant in this field. In 1791 he was appointed Graveur Général des Monnaies Français and designed silver coins for Louis XVI, the first of many coin designs. Deprived of office in 1803 he subsequently worked privately, designing ornament for guns, silver and the inkstand of the Empress Marie-Louise. The goldsmith Biennais and the gun-maker Boutet were among those who probably used Dupré's designs.

Durant, Jean Louis (1654–1718) Born in Geneva and recorded in Rome in 1673 and 1698, Durant was active as an engraver of ornament and as an enameller; enamelled watches signed by Durant survive. He engraved MUS-SARD's *Livre de Divers Ornements d'or-fèvrerie* (Geneva, 1673) and himself designed and engraved *Livre de diverses pièces d'orfèvrerie* (six plates) and *Livre de feuilles orfèvriques* (six plates), both published in Geneva in 1682. The latter was republished in London as *A New Book of Ornaments, Leaves, Frize-Work, Moresk-Work, Masks, Cyphers &c*; Durant's brother Jacques worked as an engraver in London and may have arranged this edition. Durant's designs are similar to those of Mussard and comprise ornament, watch-cases, monograms, etc., in a rich late-BAROQUE ACANTHUS style.

Dürer, Albrecht (1471–1528) Born in Nuremberg, the son of a goldsmith from Hungary, Dürer was first apprenticed to his father but then in 1486 entered the workshop of the painter and woodcut designer Michael Wolgemut, where he remained until 1490. In 1492 Dürer was in Colmar and then in Basel, where he executed woodcuts. After a spell in Strasbourg in 1493 Dürer returned to Nuremberg in 1494 and married. In the same year he travelled to Venice, but he was back in Nuremberg in 1495. In 1498 he produced his first woodcut masterpiece, the *Apocalypse* (1498). At this period Dürer also designed stained glass, including windows in St Lorenz, Nuremberg (1502). Dürer made a second Italian journey in 1505 and stayed in Venice until 1507. It was probably at this period

that he executed six woodcut copies of elaborate knots designed under the influence of Leonardo da Vinci. From 1512 to 1519 Dürer worked for the Emperor Maximilian I, designing decorations for his prayer-book (1515), for his great woodcut Triumphal Arch (1515–17) and Triumphal Procession (unfinished in 1519), and for the Emperor's silvered armour made by Koloman Helmschmied (1517). In 1520 Dürer travelled to the Netherlands to meet Charles V; on this journey he was lionized by local artists and met Lucas van LEYDEN and Dierick VELLERT, to whom he presented a copy of the Six Knots. Dürer's interest in PERSPECTIVE and proportion was probably first stimulated by the Venetian Jacopo de' Barbari, whom he met on his first Venetian trip or in Germany in about 1500. It culminated in his *Underweysung der Messung* (Nuremberg, 1525), a brilliant illustrated treatise on perspective, which included an ambiguous and possibly ironic monument to commemorate victory over the peasants in the war of 1525. It was followed by a book on fortification (1527) and a book on human proportion (1528). Throughout his career Dürer was a prolific designer of metalwork, for example cups, lights, whistles, etc. His designs, even the latest, used lobed GOTHIC forms and contorted Gothic foliage, sometimes combined with RENAISSANCE motifs. Dürer, a Protestant, was in contact with humanist scholars and designed many title-pages, book-plates and book illustrations which helped to disseminate the language of Renaissance ornament in the North. His works were widely used as decorations, for example on Limoges enamels and on Italian maiolica. Wenzel JAMNITZER and the Emperor RUDOLF II were both collectors of Dürer drawings. As late as 1671 a paten for Southwell Cathedral was engraved with a Virgin and Child after a Dürer print of 1512, and in 1826 to 1827 a silver cup after a Dürer design was made in London for George IV. Dürer's brother Hans was also trained as a goldsmith, and designed a silver altar frontal made for the King of Poland in 1531 to 1538 by Melchior Baier, a Nuremberg goldsmith; Peter FLÖTNER collaborated on this project.

Dutillieu, Jacques Charles (1718–82) The son of a Parisian painter and decorator, Charles Gille Dutillieu (1697–1738), who worked at Chantilly, Dutillieu was trained by his father. In 1736 to 1738 he visited Lyon and studied silk design. In 1739 he worked at Versailles on decorations for the marriage of Louis X V's eldest daughter. In 1742 Dutillieu settled in Lyon and became a successful silk designer; he may have been responsible for the introduction of a new ROCOCO lightness of design. In 1747 he was allowed to open his own factory, a singular honour for an outsider. Dutillieu's *Livre de Raison*, a genealogical and autobiographical work, gives a fascinating insight into commerce and sentiments in mid-18th-century Lyon.

Duvet, Jean Born in Dijon in 1485, the son of a prominent goldsmith, Duvet followed his father's trade, becoming a master in 1509. In 1521 Duvet was involved in the decorations for the entry of François I to Langres and in 1529 he made a bowl with MORESQUE inlaid decoration for the King. Duvet was prominent in civic affairs in Langres and in 1533 designed decorations for the entry of François I and Eleanora of Toledo. From at least 1539, Duvet, a Protestant, was in exile in Geneva, where he worked for the mint, designing coins in 1554, and was made a citizen in 1541. In this year he worked on Geneva's fortifications and did a mural painting in the Hôtel de Ville. Duvet was elected to the Conseil des Deux-Cents in 1546.

His *Apocalypse figurée* (Lyon, 1561) comprised elaborate Apocalypse illustrations, for which Henri II gave Duvet a *privilège du Roi* at Fontainebleau in 1556. Duvet visited Langres on many occasions from 1544 to 1562. He died before 1570. Duvet published in all some seventy engravings. The History of the Unicorn (six plates) is closely related to tapestry designs such as those by COUSIN on the History of St Mammès (1543) in Langres Cathedral, to which Duvet himself had supplied a reliquary of the head of St Mammès in 1524. It is possible that there were two Jean Duvets, one in Langres and one in Geneva, and that they have been wrongly identified.

Dyce, William (1806–64) Born in Aberdeen, Dyce studied at Marischal College there from 1819 to 1823. In 1824 he studied painting briefly at the Royal Academy Schools in London and in 1825 he travelled to Rome. In 1826 Dyce decorated a room in his father's house in Aberdeen with ARABESQUE designs. In 1827 and 1832 Dyce was again in Italy and became friendly with the Nazarenes; in 1829 he won a prize from Marischal College for an essay on electricity and magnetism. He etched illustrations for *The Morayshire Floods* (1830) and *The Highland Rambler* (1837) by Sir Thomas Dick Lauder (1784–1848), an encourager of art schools. In 1837 with the art teacher C. H. Wilson (1809–82) Dyce wrote to Lord Meadowbank of the EDINBURGH TRUSTEES' ACADEMY on *The Best Means of Ameliorating the Arts and Manufactories of Scotland in Point of Taste*. Dyce was in the same year appointed Master of Colour at the Trustees' Academy and visited schools of design in Prussia, Bavaria, Saxony and France on behalf of the Council of the London SCHOOL OF DESIGN. Dyce then presented a report on the application of design to manufactures advocating a practical involvement with industry. In 1838 Dyce was appointed Superintendent of the London School of Design at Somerset House and restored the study of the human figure. In 1842 he published a modest elementary *Drawing Book* for use in Schools of Design, stressing the geometrical basis of ornament. In 1843 Dyce resigned and became Inspector of the Spitalfields and provincial schools. In 1847 he returned to the head school to take charge of the School of Ornament, but in 1848 he finally severed his connection with Schools of Design. His ideas on design education were widely admired and copied but he had found dealing with the Council of the School an impossible task. Dyce was heavily involved in the fresco revival of the 1840s, working on the New Palace of Westminster, Osborne House (Prince ALBERT was an admirer) and William BUTTERFIELD'S All Saints, Margaret Street, London, commissioned in 1849. Dyce was a juror at the LONDON 1851 and 1862 EXHIBITIONS for ironmongery and stained glass respectively. He designed stained glass for Ely Cathedral, Alnwick church (1856) and elsewhere. Dyce was also an authority on church music and a prominent High Church controversialist.

E

Eames, Charles (1907–78) Born in St Louis, Eames was trained as an architect, opening his own office in 1930. From 1936 he was at the Cranbrook Academy of Art, Michigan, where his colleagues included Harry BERTOIA, Eero SAARINEN and Ray Kaiser. From 1939 to 1940 he worked in Eliel SAARINEN's office. In 1940 Eero Saarinen and he jointly entered the competition 'Organic Design in Home Furnishings', organized by the Industrial Design Department of the NEW YORK MUSEUM OF MODERN ART. Their entry, which won, was exhibited at the Museum in 1941 and comprised seating using plywood moulded in complex three-dimensional curves, some with sprung upholstery, others with cloth on foam rubber, and rectilinear modular storage cabinets set on benches. In 1941 Eames married Ray Kaiser, who had executed the competition drawings, and henceforward they worked as a design team. They moved to Southern California and formed the Plyformed Products Company (taken over by the Evans Products Company in 1944) to exploit their ideas. From 1942 to 1945 these were concentrated on moulded plywood splints and litters for the U.S. Navy, and from about 1943 on aircraft parts, using technology developed in Britain for Mosquito aircraft. At this time Eames also worked on plyformed chairs, welding their backs and seats to rubber shock mounts bolted to their simple steel-rod frames; other designs used plywood for legs, seats and backs. In 1946 these designs were shown at a small one-man

furniture show at the Museum of Modern Art, and some began to be marketed by the Herman Miller Furniture Company of Zeeland, Michigan, who took over production by 1948. Among Eames's plywood designs was an elegantly undulating screen with canvas hinges (1946). In 1948 the Museum of Modern Art ran an 'International Competition for Low-cost Furniture Design', directed by Edgar Kaufmann, junior. Working with a University of California team Eames submitted designs for stamped metal chairs, which won second prize and were eventually produced as moulded glass-fibre-reinforced polyester shells with metal-rod legs by Herman Miller and Zenith Plastics. The latter firm also supplied some components for Eames's own house, built in 1949 as one of a series of Case Study Houses commissioned by John Entenza of the magazine *California Arts and Architecture*, and a key MODERN building using ready-made industrial parts in a cheerfully *ad hoc* manner. Also in 1949 Eames's Contract Storage System – versatile and modular – was first shown at the 'For Modern Living' exhibition at the Detroit Institute of Arts. In 1951 Herman Miller began to manufacture woven wire versions of the polyester shell chairs, and in 1954 a stacking version was introduced. Also in 1954 Eames designed a sofa with a square-section steel frame and legs. In 1956 came the famous lounge chair and ottoman, derived from a project for a TV chair for the film director Billy Wilder. The chair is formed as three rosewood shells, upholstered in leather, joined by aluminium connectors, standing on a five-pronged aluminium base; it was promoted in a film with music by Bernstein. In the vinyl-seated Aluminium Group of chairs, introduced in 1958, Eames refined the steel sofa of 1954, and with leather cushions the Aluminium Group became in 1969 the Soft Pad Group. Another development in metal-framed furniture was The Tandem multiple seating, first designed for O'Hare Airport, Chicago, in 1962. In the 1960s Eames used foam with naugahyde or vinyl to make his earlier shell designs more comfortable. As well as the seat furniture for which he is most famous Eames's designs included plywood animals for children (about 1944), the Toy, the Little Toy, the House of Cards, and Giant House of Cards (1951–3) and the Hangitall (1953). Having become seriously interested in photography in 1942 he later produced many films for I.B.M. and the U.S. government, as well as designing a wide range of exhibitions, including the American display at the 1959 Moscow World Fair, with multi-screen projection under a Buckminster Fuller geodesic dome, and I.B.M.'s Mathematica in 1961. These display a polymathic variety of subject and a zestfully undoctrinaire approach to graphic design. Eames's formulation of the three most important things about design, 'the connections, the connections, and the connections', is misleadingly lapidary for one whose work, although rigorously tested, never relied on fixed formulae. In his latter years Eames became the recipient of many honours both in America and elsewhere, including for instance the 1978 gold medal of the American Institute of Graphic Arts.

Eastlake, Charles Locke (1836–1906) Born at Plymouth, as a nephew of the painter Sir Charles Lock Eastlake (1793–1865), Eastlake was virtually adopted by his uncle. He studied architecture under Philip Hardwick and then at the Royal Academy Schools, winning a silver medal for drawing in 1854. He showed a few architectural projects at the Royal Academy in 1855 and 1856, but turned to journalism as a career. In 1866 he became Assistant Secretary to the Institute of British Architects and in 1871 Secretary. In 1878 he resigned to become Keeper of the National Gallery, whence he retired in 1898, thwarted of the Directorship by intrigue. In 1868 Eastlake recast articles he had written for the *Cornhill Magazine* (1864) and *The Queen* (1864–6) to form *Hints on Household Taste in Furniture, Upholstery and Other Details*. *Hints* was a popular manual on that style of decoration and design derived from architect-designers such as STREET, Norman SHAW and SEDDON which began to be commercialized in the late 1860s. Honesty of construction and materials, rectilinear forms, and tough geometric patterns and ornament were its hallmarks. *Hints* included designs by Eastlake himself for furniture and for wallpapers made by Woollams, as well as a fender designed by A. W. Blomfield, picture frames designed by E. J. TARVER, a frieze by Clement HEATON and jewellery designed by Sir Matthew Digby WYATT. Eastlake also showed metalwork by Benham & Froud, geometric tiles by Maw, parquetry by Arrowsmith, glass by Salviati and ceramics by Copeland. The book went to a fourth edition in England in 1878 but its real success was in America, where six editions appeared in Boston from 1872 to 1879 and *The House Beautiful* (New York, 1877) by C. C. Cook (1828–1900), and *Art Decoration Applied to Furniture* (New York, 1878) by H. P. Spofford (1835–1921) recognized Eastlake's influence. The American 'Eastlake' style often bears little relation to Eastlake's designs or precepts. Indeed in 1878 he stated that 'I find American tradesmen continually advertising what they are pleased to call "Eastlake" furniture, with the production of which I have had nothing whatever to do, and for the taste of which I should be very sorry to be considered responsible.' Eastlake also published *Lectures on Decorative Art and Art-Workmanship* (1876) and *The Present Condition of Industrial Art* (1877) and designed wallpapers for Jeffrey & Co. in 1871. His magnum opus, however, was *A History of the Gothic Revival* (1872).

Eastlake, E. Eastlake published in Brussels in 1866 *Recueil de Meubles et d'Ornements Intérieurs* (fifty plates), competent and fluent designs for furniture and curtains in the GOTHIC, RENAISSANCE, Louis XIII, XIV, XV, XVI, Néo-Grec, and '*fantaisie*' styles. A second part with a further fifty plates, including some in the '*Élizabethienne*' style, ends with Gothic overmantels and a door executed for M. J. H. Johnson at St Osyth's Priory in Essex.

Ebelmann, Johann Jakob Born in Speir, Ebelmann was a citizen of Strasbourg, where he probably worked as a cabinetmaker. In 1598 he published a suite of cabinets (six plates) in an intense and incoherent MANNERIST architectural style derived from Wendel DIETTERLIN, and in 1609 a suite of twenty-four architectural inventions, including altarpieces and ceilings with some borrowing from Wenzel JAMNITZER's *Perspectiva*. He also collaborated with Jakob GUCKEISEN on three further books. All his works seem to have been published by Johann Bussemacher of Cologne.

Ecclesiological Society, The In 1839 John Mason Neale (1818–66) and Benjamin Webb (1819–85), then undergraduates at Trinity College, Cambridge, founded the Cambridge Camden Society to promote the study of Ecclesiastical Architecture and the restoration of mutilated architectural remains'. But although named after the Elizabethan antiquary William Camden (1551–1623) the Society adopted a crusading attitude in such works as *A Few Words to Church Builders* (1841), *A Few Words to Churchwardens on Churches and Church Ornaments* (1841) and *Twenty-three Reasons for Getting Rid of Church Pues*, attempting to propagate fixed solutions to problems of ecclesiology. Its language was GOTHIC and Neale and Webb's translation of Durandus's *Rationale Divinorum Officiorum* as *The Symbolism of Churches and Church Ornament* (1843) included a lengthy foreword proposing the symbolism and arrangement of the Catholic Gothic church of the 14th century as an ideal model. From 1841 to 1868 the Society disseminated its views in a journal, the *Ecclesiologist*. By 1843 there were 700 members and the Society was attracting accusations of Popery. In 1846 it changed its name to the Ecclesiological Society and transferred to London. The Society promoted a design guide to church metalwork and furniture, *Instrumenta Ecclesiastica* (first series 1844 to 1847, second series 1850 to 1856); this was edited by William BUTTERFIELD, who provided the majority of designs, although STREET and R. C. Carpenter (1812–55) also contributed. Street was the Society's official metalwork designer from 1857 to 1864, when he was succeeded by BURGES.

Échantillon, J. B. Échantillon, whose name sounds suspiciously like a *nom-de-plume*, called himself 'Brodeur Royal à Lion' on his *Desseins des Fleurs Platitudes et Guirlandes pour le Tambour et pour la Broderie* (Lyon, 1784–5; at least seventeen plates), a collection of accomplished NEO-CLASSICAL designs for embroidery.

Echter, Matthias Born in Weiz, Steiermark, before 1642, Echter was later active in Graz as painter, draughtsman and engraver. His *Raccoltà Di Varij Cappricij et Noue Inventionij di fogliami Romane* (Graz, 1679; six plates) contains frames, friezes, VASES and coach decorations in a vigorous ACANTHUS style peopled by eagles and lions. Its title, borrowed almost exactly from Stefano DELLA BELLA's 1646 *Raccolta*, denotes one source of Echter's inspiration, while the mention of Rome in the title suggests that he may have spent time there, perhaps with SCHOR. INDAU was directly influenced by Echter, who also published cartouches and friezes in his *Neues Romanisches Laubwerkbüchlein* (six plates).

Eckmann, Otto (1865–1902) Born in Hamburg, Eckmann was educated at the applied arts schools there and in Nuremberg. After studying at the Munich Academy he was active there as a painter from about 1890. In 1894 however he auctioned his paintings in Frankfurt, and transferred his attention to decorative art and design. Strongly influenced by Japanese art, and particularly by the collection assembled at Hamburg by Justus Brinckmann, Eckmann supplied illustrations to both 'PAN' (from 1895) and 'JUGEND' (from 1896). In 1897 he was appointed to teach decorative painting at the Berlin school of applied art, and in the same year designed a study for the Grand Duke Ernst Ludwig's Neues Palais at Darmstadt. Furniture to Eckmann's design was also commissioned in about 1898 by Wilhelm Hirschwald, proprietor of the Hohenzollern-Kaufhaus in Berlin. Eckmann also designed light fittings, ceramics, for H. A. Kähler, tiles, for Villeroy & Boch, wall hangings, for the Scherrebeck

school of weaving (1896 and 1897), furnishing fabrics and every variety of graphic design, including wallpapers for H. Engelhard of Mannheim (1900), publicity material (1900–1902) for the electricity company A.E.G., for which Peter BEHRENS later worked, and a poster for the publisher, E. A. Seeman of Leipzig. In 1897 he published *Dekorative Entwürfe*. His style made a bold use of asymmetry, strong outlines and colours and energetically scrolled ornament derived from natural forms. In about 1901 Eckmann designed a new type for the Klingsor printing works at Offenbach, and issued a *Schriftmusterbuch* (1901); the Eckmann script became a classic ART NOUVEAU typeface. Eckmann's works were illustrated in such magazines as 'DEUTSCHE KUNST UND DEKORATION', 'DEKORATIVE KUNST' and 'TEXTILE KUNST UND INDUSTRIE', and despite his early death he was recognized as a principal pioneer of German Art Nouveau. Among his pupils was Gustav GOERKE.

Écrin, L' (1863–5) This Paris magazine was subtitled *Moniteur de la Bijouterie-Joaillerie*. Under its editor Antonio Violli it presented fine coloured designs for jewels, mainly in a part-geometric part-RENAISSANCE Revival style. Designers included N. Magnan, C. Foucher, F. Fernoux, H. Gandon and C. Beauregard.

Edinburgh Trustees' Academy In 1754 the painter Allan Ramsay (1713–84), a NEO-CLASSICAL intellectual, founded the Edinburgh Select Society for 'the encouragement of arts, sciences, manufactures and agriculture'. The Society offered prizes for drawings of flowers, fruit and foliage and the classical ORDERS, but standards were so low that an appeal was made to the Board of Trustees for Improving Fisheries and Manufactures in Scotland. As a result the Trustees' Academy was founded in 1760. The stress was on practical applications of design and students included cabinet-makers, calico printers, goldsmiths etc. The first master was William DE LA COUR, and from 1765 John Baptist Jackson received an annual grant for drawing patterns and training apprentices of designers. David Allan, a later master who served from 1786 until his death in 1796, continued the emphasis on ornament, providing designs for carpets, damasks and printed calicos. After 1800, when John Graham became master, the Academy was principally devoted to the fine arts. In 1798 a sister institution, a drawing school, was founded, and in 1837 William DYCE was invited to draw up a scheme for reorganization. His resulting pamphlet had an important influence on the nascent SCHOOL OF DESIGN-in London, where Dyce became Superintendent in 1838.

Edis, Robert William (1839–1927) Born in Huntingdon, Edis began to work as an architect in London in 1861. He had a wide practice, and was one of the protagonists of the red-brick Queen Anne style in the 1870s. He was knighted in 1919. Edis published articles on decoration and furniture in *The Week* and *The Queen*. In the latter he was probably responsible, under the pseudonym 'Scorpio', for a series of articles entitled 'Modern Mansions' (1877), which included a long description of Owen JONES's Carlton House Terrace interiors for Alfred Morrison. In 1880 Edis delivered the Cantor Lectures to the SOCIETY OF ARTS on 'Decoration Applied to Modern Houses'. These he turned into a book, *Decoration and Furniture of Town Houses* (1881), which advocated a middle-brow Queen Anne style. It included interiors and Minton tiles designed by Edis himself, together with wallpapers by Walter CRANE and

TALBERT, furniture by William MORRIS & Co., Holland & Son, and Gillows, and metalwork by BODLEY, COLLCUTT, JECKYLL and Somers Clarke. Edis paid tribute to the pioneers in the improvement of furniture and decoration, whom he lists as STREET, Norman SHAW, WATERHOUSE, GODWIN, BURGES and Philip WEBB. His admiration extended to FLAXMAN, William Morris and Doulton's 'Lambeth' ware. Maurice B. ADAMS was responsible for the illustrations. Edis later contributed to the New York 'DECORATOR AND FURNISHER' (1882) and wrote a handbook, *Healthy Furniture and Decoration*, for the London 1884 International Health Exhibition. In 1893 Edis was honorary architect for the Royal Commission for the CHICAGO WORLD COLUMBIAN EXPOSITION.

Ednie, John After studying at the Edinburgh and Glasgow Schools of Art in the 1890s, Ednie worked as a furniture designer for the Glasgow cabinet-making firm of Wylie & Lochhead, together with George LOGAN and E. A. TAYLOR. He designed a dining-room shown by Wylie & Lochhead at the 1901 Glasgow International Exhibition. His style was similar to Logan's and Taylor's.

Eeckhout, Gerbrand van den (1621–74) Born in Amsterdam, the son of a goldsmith, Eeckhout became in the late 1630s Rembrandt's favourite pupil. It was probably as a result of Rembrandt's friendship with LUTMA that Eeckhout produced some designs for ornament and cartouches in an extreme AURICULAR style similar to Lutma's. They comprise *Veelderhande Niewe Compartimente* (twenty-four plates), *Verscheyde Aerdige Compartimenten* (1655; twelve plates) and contributions to *Verscheyde Constige Vindingen on in Gout, Silver Hout en steen te Wercken*, which also included designs by Lutma, Adam and Paul van VIANEN and others.

Egell, Paul (1691–1752) A ROCOCO sculptor in Mannheim, Egell designed altars, plasterwork and church fittings, as well as a competition design for the great barrel of Heidelberg (1751) and many illustrations for *Scriptores Historiae Romanae* (Heidelberg, 1743 and 1748).

Ehrensvärd, Carl August (1745–1800) Born in Örebro, Sweden, the son of a field-marshal, Ehrensvärd himself rose to the rank of admiral. He began to study art on a visit to Holland and France in 1766, and from 1780 to 1782 travelled to Italy as a connoisseur. Ehrensvärd became an honorary member of the Stockholm Academy in 1783. In 1786 he published his views on art in Italy. He was active as a NEO-CLASSI-CAL theorist in contact with L. A. MASRELIEZ, and also as a caricaturist, working in a strongly neo-classical style influenced by Sergel. Ehrensvärd, who owned D'Hancarville's volumes on the HAMILTON vases, designed neo-classical silver for his own use, including a tea urn (Ystad, 1795) by Hans Jakob Hagman and a dish (Stockholm, 1798), by Simson Ryberg.

Eichel, Emanuel (1717–82) Born in Augsburg, the son of a designer and silversmith from Danzig who specialized in silver furniture, Eichel was trained by the engraver Daniel Herz. He taught at the protestant drawing school in Augsburg and directed it from 1770. Eichel was responsible for many book illustrations and also for some nine suites of ROCOCO ornament (four plates each) published by HERTEL. They include rococo altars, not inspired, VASES, and furniture, very scrolly and deft rococo ironwork for balconies, stairs, gates and signs, and a set of grand rococo cartouches symbolizing such titles as *Il Generalissimo*, treated with macabre humour.

Eichler, Gottfried (1715–70) Born in Augsburg, the son of a painter, Eichler worked in Vienna and Nuremberg. In 1743 he was appointed drawing-master at Erlangen University. Eichler later returned to Augsburg where he designed 200 allegorical ROCOCO compositions for HERTEL's 1760 edition of Ripa's *Iconologia*.

Eisen, Charles (1720–78) Born in Valenciennes, the son of a painter and engraver, Eisen worked in Paris from 1742 to 1777, and then moved to Brussels to escape his debtors; there he died. Eisen was extremely prolific as a book illustrator, his masterpiece being the 1762 edition of La Fontaine, for which BACHELIER designed the ornaments. Voltaire much admired his illustrations to *La Henriade* (1767). Eisen was drawing-master to Mme de Pompadour and Dessinateur du Roi. His *Premier Livre d'une Œuvre Suivie contenans différens sujets de décoration et d'ornemens* (1753; six plates) was the first of six suites of six plates each, containing spirited but derivative ROCOCO designs for VASES, fountains, cartouches and ornament. A *vignette* designed in 1756 for a book on the Dresden Gallery (Dresden, 1757) shows Eisen tentatively adopting the NEO-CLASSICAL style, the vehicle for his later works. Subjects by Eisen were sometimes copied on Sèvres porcelain.

Eisler, Caspar Gottlieb An engraver and medallist active in Nuremberg around 1750, Eisler designed about seven suites of ROCOCO ornament published by Martin ENGELBRECHT and others. They include designs for silversmiths' work, for cartouches, for lights, and *Essai de dessins servant à l'embellissement des*

Carrosses de cérémonie et autres (eight plates), rococo designs for the decoration of coaches.

Eitelberger-Edelburg, Rudolf von (1817–85) Born in Olmütz, Eitelberger studied classics in Vienna University and then from 1847 taught art history there, becoming a professor in 1864. In 1848 he published a work urging the reform of art education and in 1862 a similar work, in response to his observations at the LONDON 1862 EXHIBITION. These initiatives led to the foundation in 1864 ·of the Austrian Museum for Art and Industry, the first museum in Europe to follow the South Kensington model, and, in 1868, of the attached School of Applied Art. As first director of the Museum, Eitelberger was in close and influential contact with such manufacturers as Lobmeyr. He continued to press for reform in Austrian art education, and helped to establish the Viennese tradition of art history. In 1873 to 1874 Eitelberger published a reprint of 16th-century needlework designs.

Ellis, Harvey (1852–1904) Born in Rochester, New York, the son of a hardware merchant, Ellis attended the military academy at West Point in 1881, but was dismissed and travelled to Venice. He subsequently studied art in Albany under Edwin White and, after a brief return to Rochester, worked under the architect Arthur Gilman in New York. Back in Albany, Ellis met the architect H. H. RICHARDSON, who was a life-long influence. In 1879 Ellis set up as an architect with his younger brother Charles, with rapid success. In 1885 he moved to Utica and thence in 1886 to St Paul, Minnesota, where he worked as a designer for other architects, notably Leroy S. Buffington. Back in Rochester from 1893 Ellis was mainly active as a painter but also designed posters for the *Rochester Herald* (1895) and *Harper's*

Magazine (1898). In 1902 he moved to Syracuse to work for STICKLEY's the 'CRAFTSMAN', for which he designed interiors, furniture and textiles, including a child's bedroom with a Puss-in-Boots frieze. This late work was strongly influenced by VOYSEY and BAILLIE SCOTT.

Ellwood, George Montague Born in London in 1875, the son of a civil servant, Ellwood studied at the Camden School of Art and then at South Kensington, where he was a conspicuously successful student. In about 1897, when a chair to his design was shown in Brussels, Ellwood began to establish a reputation as a furniture designer, working for J. S. Henry, for Trapnell & Gane of Bristol and for the Guild of Art Craftsmen. Ellwood showed designs of interiors at the Royal Academy from 1899 to 1906. Designs by Ellwood were illustrated in 'DOCUMENTS D'ARCHITECTURE MODERNE'. In 1909 he published *English Furniture and Decoration 1680–1800* (fourth edition, 1933, German edition, Stuttgart, 1913). From 1916 to 1924 he was editor of *Drawing and Design*. He was also active as a designer of advertising. Ellwood published several works on drawing in the 1920s including *The Art of Pen Drawing* (1927). From 1942 he taught at the Camden School of Art. A member of the ART-WORKERS' GUILD from 1925, Ellwood died in about 1960.

Elmslie, George Grant (1871–1952) Born in Aberdeenshire, Elmslie moved to America in 1885 and was in 1887 in the office of the architect J. L. Silsbee at the same time as Frank Lloyd WRIGHT. In 1889 he joined the partnership of Adler & SULLIVAN as a draughtsman, becoming chief designer in 1895. Elmslie executed the detailed designs of much of Sullivan's ornament. He remained with Sullivan until 1909 and always stayed faithful to his master. From 1909 to 1913 Elmslie was in partnership with William Gray Purcell and George Feick, and from 1913 to 1922 with Purcell alone. Elmslie designed furniture, stained glass, embroidery, carpets and metalwork in a style derived from that of Sullivan.

Emblems In about 1419 a manuscript of the *Hieroglyphica* of Horapollo was introduced to Florence. The work aroused great interest in humanist circles. Leone Battista Alberti (1404–72) advocated the use of hieroglyphics in design and interior decoration and hieroglyphics were a major theme of the 'HYPNEROTOMACHIA POLIFILI' (1499). Aldus Manutius (1450–1515), the publisher of the *Hypnerotomachia*, also published the first edition of Horapollo's *Hieroglyphica* (1505). In the Latin translation of 1517 Filippo Fasanini wrote of the use of hieroglyphics to decorate swords, rings, bells, beds, doors and ceilings. By about 1521 the humanist Andrea Alciati (1492–1550) had prepared for publication his *Emblematum Liber*. It was published in Augsburg in 1531, dedicated to the archivist Conrad Peutinger (1465–1547), and comprised epigrams, mainly derived from the anthology of Greek poems re-edited in 1301 by the monk Planudes, matched to hieroglyphic illustrations. Alciati's book of emblems went through over 150 editions and translations and served as the foundation for a new literary and artistic genre. Later such works include Corrozet's *Hecatomgraphia* (1540), Georgette de Montenay's *Emblemes ou devises chrestiennes* (1571), the first book of Christian emblems, *Iconologia* (1603) by Cesare Ripa (1560–1625), Geoffrey Whitney's *A Choice of Emblems* (1586) and Henry Peacham's *Minerva Brittana* (1612). Emblems, sayings and/or images, at once moralistic and hermetic, were

ubiquitous as decorative motifs from the 16th to the 18th century, and even the BIEDERMEIER glass of Anton Kothgasser (1769–1851) used the 1798 Vienna edition of Ripa as a source of motifs. Emblems anticipated the use of images for teaching in *Orbis Sensualium Pictus* (1658) by J. A. Comenius (1592–1670) and prefigure the methods of modern advertising. Lyle's Golden Syrup tin, with its lion and bees combined with the text 'Out of the strong came forth sweetness', represents a survival of the emblem tradition, at once oblique and pregnant.

Endell, Ernst Moritz August (1871–1925) Born in Berlin, the son of an architect, Endell studied philosophy in Tübingen, before moving in 1892 to Munich. In Munich he was active as a self-taught architect and designer, strongly influenced by OBRIST. Endell's Photoatelier Elvira (1897–8) had on its façade an extraordinary plaster composition of frothing and lashing wavelike forms. In 1898 Endell was involved with the MUNICH VEREINIGTE WERKSTÄTTEN. He designed textiles, jewellery and graphic ornament, including *vignettes* for 'PAN' (1897). In 1901 Endell moved to Berlin. In 1903 he designed furniture made by Theophil Müller of Dresden. From 1904 to 1914 he ran a school of design in Berlin and wrote on the theory of design and architecture. In 1918 Endell was appointed director of the Breslau Academy.

Engelbrecht, Martin (1684–1756) Johann Georg HERTEL and Martin Engelbrecht were the main publishers of ornament in Augsburg in the mid 18th century. Engelbrecht trained as an engraver, executing the illustrations to Paul DECKER's *Fürstlicher Baumeister* (1711), and then worked as a partner in the press of his brother, Christian (1672–1735). He founded his own press in 1719 and when Christian died in 1735 Martin took over his plates. Among those whose works he printed were HABERMANN, BAUR, EISLER, PIER, RUMPP, WACHSMUTH, Hildt, Craaz, BIRCKENFELD, Leuchte, BAUMANN and GRENDEL. Engelbrecht also engraved and published his own ROCOCO designs for metalwork and CHINOISERIES. He was succeeded by his son-in-law Christian Wilhelm, who did not however change the name of the firm.

Erasmus, Georg Caspar Born in Bopfingen, Erasmus worked as a cabinet-maker in Nuremberg in the late 17th century, gaining civic commissions. His *Seülen-Buch* (Nuremberg, 1666, reprinted 1667 and 1672; fifty-five plates) displays the ORDERS and also doors, windows, tables, and beds in the AURICULAR style. An appendix has seven plates of friezes, brackets and cartouches. *Neues Zierahten Büchlein von allerhand Schreinwerck* (Nuremberg, 1695; sixteen plates) contains brackets, aprons, doors, cupboards and chair-backs in a subdued ACANTHUS style. Erasmus died in 1695. His son, Johann Georg Erasmus (1659–1710), a mathematician and architectural theorist, published *Fünff Seulen* (twelve plates), a book of the orders which includes a cupboard with auricular ornament, and, on the title, the designer's initials leaning together in a manner anachronistically reminiscent of LENCKER.

Erdmannsdorff, Friedrich Wilhelm (1736–1800) Born in Dresden, the son of a court official, Erdmannsdorff became friendly with Duke Friedrich-Franz of Anhalt-Dessau in 1757. In 1761 he travelled to Italy, where he studied painting in Florence and Venice. In 1763 he went to England with Duke Franz and turned to architecture, influenced by ADAM and CHAMBERS. In 1765 he returned to Italy where he met Winck-

elmann and studied architecture under CLÉRISSEAU, who became a close friend. Back in Dessau, Erdmannsdorff was employed by Duke Franz to rebuild Schloss Dessau (1767–8) and, from 1769, to build Schloss Worlitz, his masterpiece. He designed chairs influenced by CHIPPENDALE in about 1766 and by Chambers's *Chinese Buildings* (1757) in 1771, but his main distinction was to have acted as the pioneer of NEO-CLASSICISM in Germany, naturalizing a decorative vocabulary derived from Adam, Clérisseau and PIRANESI. In 1771 he designed furniture made for Worlitz by David Roentgen; it is inlaid with neo-classical VASES, swags and altars. As late as 1787 he was still designing tables in a massy early neo-classical style. In 1771 he proposed the foundation of a school of design for craftsmen, and he opened his own house and library to students. Erdmannsdorff revisited England and Italy, meeting Angelica KAUFFMANN and Canova in Rome in 1789 to 1790, and in 1787 to 1789 he worked in Potsdam and Berlin, where he taught GILLY. However, he preferred the seclusion of Dessau and for all his talents and distinguished connections Erdmannsdorff's influence was limited.

Errard, Charles Born at Nantes in about 1606, Errard went to Rome in 1627 to train as a painter. In about 1637 he returned to Nantes and thence to Paris. After another period in Rome he was in 1643 appointed Peintre Ordinaire du Roi in Paris and granted a pension and lodgings in the Louvre. In 1647 he became a founder member of the Académie Royale, at a time when he was directing decorations in the Louvre, the Tuileries, Fontainebleau, and later at Versailles (1661). In 1651 he published three suites of BAROQUE ornament dedicated to the Queen of Sweden, *Divers Ornements* (eight plates), *Divers*

Trophées (six plates, after POLIDORO DA CARAVAGGIO), and *Divers vases antiques* (twelve plates). A little later he issued *Ornements des appartements de la Reine au Vieux Louvre* (six plates). Errard also designed graphic ornaments and illustrations for the *Breviarum Romanum* (Paris, 1647) and Chambray's *Parallele de l'architecture antique avec la moderne* (1650). After 1661 he was increasingly eclipsed by his rival Charles LE BRUN, and in 1666 he returned to Rome to head the Académie de France, where he was able to pursue his scholarly interests and to design the ornaments for Bellori's *Vite* (1672). In 1683 he returned to France, where he died in 1689. Errard represented a continuation of the classical tradition established by Poussin and his important influence on mid-17th-century French decoration needs further investigation.

E.S. The Master E.S. was active as an engraver from about 1450 to 1467. He was a goldsmith, probably of North Swiss origin. In 1466 he designed three prints to commemorate the 500th anniversary of the Benedictine Abbey of Einsiedeln, and he was probably in Constance about this date. E.S. was influenced by Flemish sculpture and painting. His surviving *œuvre* amounts to 317 engravings, mainly of religious subjects. He also engraved ten coats-of-arms and two packs of playing-cards; of the first, probably before 1463, fifteen plates survive with animals, helmets, shields and flowers as suits, and of the second, of about 1463, forty-two plates with men, dogs, birds and shields as suits. The latter were soon used to decorate bookbindings as had been the cards designed by the Master of the PLAYING CARDS. An alphabet (twenty-three plates) of GOTHIC letters formed of men and animals probably dates from about 1464 to 1467. A large engraving of an elaborate Gothic monstrance by E.S. is the earliest known design of this type. He also published two panels of Gothic foliate ornament, one with a Joust between the Sexes, the other with Women struggling over Men's Hose, and five separate Gothic leaves. Many of E.S.'s prints were copied by Israhel van MECKENEM.

Esprit Nouveau, L' (1920–26) The magazine *L'Esprit Nouveau* derived its title from an essay of 1918 by the poet Guillaume Apollinaire (1880–1918) entitled 'L'esprit nouveau et les poètes'. At first the editor was Paul Dermée, but the real powers behind the magazine were Amedée Ozenfant (1886–1966) and LE CORBUSIER, who used it to propagate their MODERN views. In 1920 a famous essay by LOOS was published, translated as 'Ornement et Crime', and in 1921 Le Corbusier, in an essay on steamships, announced that '*Le paquebot est la première étage dans la réalisation d'un monde organisé selon l'esprit nouveau.*' The Esprit Nouveau pavilion at the PARIS 1925 EXHIBITION, designed by Le Corbusier, was a concrete manifesto of the Modernism he had so often preached in its pages.

Estampe et l'Affiche, L' (1897–9) Published in Paris this poster design magazine included copious illustrations of the main ART NOUVEAU designers. Its cover listed Jules CHÉRET, Willette, GRASSET, Steinlen and, inevitably and incongruously, William MORRIS.

Ewald, Ernst (1836–1904) After working as a fresco painter in Berlin from 1865 in a manner strongly influenced by Italian RENAISSANCE prototypes, Ewald was appointed in 1868 to teach design at the BERLIN KUNST-GEWERBEMUSEUM, where he exercised widespread influence. His wish to supplement the theoretical study of design with practical work led him in the mid-

1870s to found a workshop for decorating earthenware, with two partners, Hermann Ende (1829–1907), later a prominent architect, and Louis Ravené, a connoisseur who probably supplied the capital. The workshop, which dissolved in 1877, produced maiolica wares in the Italian Renaissance manner, based on examples in the Kunstgewerbemuseum. Ewald also designed stained glass and mosaics. His *Farbige Dekorationen alter und neuer Zeit* (Berlin, 1889) is a monumental two-volume chromolithographed work, which covers painted wall decorations from antiquity to the 18th century.

Eyre, Wilson (1858–1944) Born in Florence of American parents, Eyre was brought up in Newport, Rhode Island, and elsewhere. In 1876 he turned to architecture, studied for two years at the Massachusetts Institute of Technology and then worked as a draughtsman in the office of the Philadelphia architect James P. Sims (1849–82). Eyre succeeded to Sims's practice and built many buildings public and private in the Philadelphia area. In 1883 he was a founder of the Philadelphia T-Square Club. Eyre was much influenced by English Queen Anne and Arts & Crafts architects and designed furniture and interiors influenced by VOYSEY and BAILLIE SCOTT. From 1901 to 1906 Eyre was editor of the Philadelphia magazine *House and Garden*.

Eysler, Johann Leonhard Eysler became a master goldsmith in Nuremberg in 1697. He died there in 1733. His *Neu inventirtes Laub und Bandlwerck* (twelve parts of six plates each), published by J. C. Weigel, comprises borders of BERAINESQUE interlaced STRAPWORK for engraving on silver, for inlay, for gesso and for similar purposes. Eysler also issued a manual on designing such borders (six plates), a suite of putti in BAROQUE cartouches representing the zodiac (twelve plates) and two suites of swags of fruit and flowers (six plates each).

F

Falize, Alexis (1811–98) Born in Liège, the son of a bootmaker, Falize was in 1833 employed as a clerk by the Parisian jewellers Mellerio Frères. He then began to design jewellery for them, and from 1835 for the firm of Janisset. From 1838 to 1871 he ran his own jewellery business, subcontracting for Janisset up to 1848 and later for other jewellers, including Boucheron. In 1864 he became president of the Syndicat de la Bijouterie, a trade association. Falize retirèd in 1876. He was particularly associated with the Greek and Egyptian styles. He was succeeded by his son, Lucien Falize (1842–97), who was also active as designer and writer, publishing an essay on Japanese jewellery in 'ARTISTIC JAPAN' (1888).

Fantastici, Agostino A Sienese architect, Fantastici designed furniture in a handsome late NEO-CLASSICAL style for Mario Bianchi-Bandinelli (1799–1854) and others from the 1820s. A volume of drawings by Fantastici is in Siena public library.

Fantuzzi, Antonio Born in Bologna, Fantuzzi is recorded as working at Fontainebleau as a painter and stucco worker from 1537 to 1540 at a low wage. After ROSSO's death in 1540 Fantuzzi seems to have been promoted by his fellow Bolognese, PRIMATICCIO, and worked at Fontainebleau from 1541 to 1550 at a much higher salary designing 'grottesques' for painters. Fantuzzi executed some 100 engravings, some of which bear dates from 1542 to 1545, after Giulio ROMANO, Rosso, Primaticcio and others. Two plates of VASES, a ewer and a cup all probably record Rosso metalwork designs. Fantuzzi also published a number of STRAPWORK frames incorporating MANNERIST nudes, and helped to disseminate the Fontainebleau style of ornament.

Faulkner, Kate The sister of Charles Faulkner, one of the founding partners of MORRIS, Marshall, Faulkner & Co. in 1861, Kate Faulkner painted tiles for the firm in its early days. She later executed gesso decorations to Philip WEBB's design, notably on a Broadwood grand piano (1883) shown at the first ARTS & CRAFTS EXHIBITION in 1888. Kate Faulkner also designed a number of wallpapers for Morris & Co. and for Jeffrey & Co. in 1883. She died in 1898. Her sister Lucy, as Mrs Orrinsmith, wrote *The Drawing Room, its Decoration and Furniture* (1878).

Fay, Jean Baptiste As an engraver, Fay engraved designs by PRIEUR and LALONDE. As a designer he issued several suites of *Arabesques*, competent panels of ornament in the French NEO-CLASSICAL style of the 1780s. He also published a *Cahier de Bijouteries dans le Goût Moderne* (six plates), designs for neat gold boxes and other trinkets, a *Cahier de dessins pour étoffes, indiennes et papiers* (four plates), designs for fabrics and wallpapers, at least two suites *De Serrurerie Moderne*, with coarse but effective designs for iron balconies, doors and gates, and also some suites of

Vases. More unusual are neo-classical designs for the decoration of plates and cups, and a suite of awkward but elaborate frames which include ROCOCO elements alongside the familiar neo-classical vocabulary. In 1785 Fay designed an ARABESQUE wallpaper, Coq et Perroquet, for the wallpaper factory of Jean Baptiste Réveillon. He was clearly the type of the versatile professional, but his designs show little vigour, refinement or originality.

Feldscharek, Rudolf Born in Vienna in 1845, Feldscharek was principally active as an architect, but also designed for the applied arts, including bronzes for Dziedzinsky & Hanusch of Vienna and a cabinet by Heinrich Irmler of Vienna (1894). He was partly responsible for the Austrian sections in the Brussels Exhibitions of 1888 and 1897.

Ferri, Ciro (1634–89) Born in Rome, Ferri trained as a painter under Pietro da CORTONA (1596–1669), with whom he worked on the decoration of the Pitti Palace, Florence, in the 1660s. In 1673 he was appointed drawing-master at Cosimo III de' Medici's new Florentine Academy in Rome, a post he occupied until the Academy closed in 1686. Also in 1673 Ferri designed the tabernacle of Santa Maria in Vallicella in Rome; it had already been planned by Pietro da Cortona in 1653, and was completed in 1684. In 1675 Ferri was commissioned to decorate the choir chapel of Santa Maria Maddalena de' Pazzi in Florence, whose bronze altar frontal, executed in Rome in 1683, uses rich ACANTHUS ornament, finer even than SCHOR's work on the Cathedra Petri. Ferri was mainly responsible for the transmission of the Roman BAROQUE style of ornament to Florence. Ferri designed many frontispieces, including that for Pallavicini's *Difesa della Divina Providenza* (1679), dedicated to Queen Christina of Sweden, for

whom Ferri designed a coach. Later coaches designed by Ferri included the great state coach for the 1687 Earl of Castlemaine's embassy to Pope Innocent XI (published Rome 1687, London 1688, and reprinted Augsburg, 1700); the remaining coaches were designed in the same style by the carver Andrea Cornely, active from 1678. Ferri also designed coaches for the entry of Cardinal Rinaldo d'Este to Rome in 1688 (published Rome 1691). Ferri's coach decorations exploit baroque sculptural figures and exuberant acanthus ornament, anticipating the designs of CRECCOLINI and PASSARINI. VASES by Ferri were later published by Aquila (1719). Ferri also designed reliquaries, tombs, lights, tables and ciboria.

Feuchère, Jean-Jacques (1807–52) Born in Paris, Feuchère was trained as a sculptor by Cortot and Ramey. He was one of those instrumental in pioneering the RENAISSANCE Revival style in France, designing for the goldsmith FROMENT-MEURICE and for the Sèvres porcelain factory. VECHTE was among his pupils. Feuchère designed the title-page of *L'Artiste* (1837) and in the same year published *Ornements dédiés à S.A.R. La Princesse Marie*. In 1851 he issued *Figures applicables à l'ornementation*, including a remarkable GROTESQUE cup with lobster feet. His *Coupe de Travail*, shown at the PARIS 1855 EXHIBITION, was completed by DIÉTERLE.

Feuchère, Léon (1804–57) Born in Paris, Feuchère studied architecture at the École des Beaux-Arts. His first experience was as a theatre designer, with DIÉTERLE, among others. He later established himself as a leading decorative arts designer, describing himself as 'Architecte Décorateur'. His *L'Art Industriel* (1842; seventy-two plates) is a comprehensive display of his expertise in design. Centred on an imaginary palace it includes extraordinarily elaborate designs for furniture, silver, enamel, porcelain, gasoliers, etc., in the NATURALISTIC, Louis XIV, Louis XV, Byzantine, GOTHIC, RENAISSANCE, Moorish and Chinese styles. A Moorish smoking-room is one of the earliest of that genre. In 1844 Feuchère was referred to in the *Art Union*, the predecessor of the 'ART JOURNAL', as 'the most celebrated of the designers in France', a claim which received some confirmation in his appointment in 1848 to the Conseil Supérieur for the French national manufactories.

Fiéret, Pierre Born in Bruges, Fiéret studied painting there under Jan Fabiaen. He was from 1480 in Tournai where he became a master in 1483. In 1498 Fiéret designed two tapestries illustrating the History of Hercules for an Oudenarde weaver.

Fietta Fietta and Company at Kriegshaber near Augsburg published prints of VASES in a tough NEO-CLASSICAL style, chairs in the latest fashion, that is a quirky provincial German neo-classicism, designs for ironwork, and pilasters filled with gauche neo-classical GROTESQUES. All presumably date from about 1785.

Fiore, Nicola A member of a Neapolitan family of craftsmen, Fiore was probably the son of Gennaro Di Fiore, who designed and executed decorations for the royal palaces of Naples from at least 1759 to 1781. In 1775 Nicola Fiore designed a brilliant ROCOCO interior for the palace of Caserta, incorporating delicate CHINOISERIE panels. With his brother Pietro, Fiore later executed carved ornaments for the Crown Prince from 1796 to 1797.

Fiosconi, Cesar *Espingarla Perfeyta* (Lisbon, 1718) is a treatise on gunmaking dedicated to King John V of Portugal (1706–50) by its authors, Cesar Fiosconi and Jordam Guserio. It includes a few crude BAROQUE ACANTHUS designs for gun decoration.

Fjerdingstad, Carl Christian Born in Christianso, Denmark, in 1891 Fjerdingstad was trained as a goldsmith. He designed silver for the Parisian firm of Christofle from 1925 to 1938. His designs were much praised at the PARIS 1925 EXHIBITION.

Flach, Thomas *A book of Jewellers Work designed by Thomas Flach in London* (1736; six plates) comprises designs for pendants, châtelaines, étuis, a swordhilt, boxes and a fan handle. They are decorated with floral motifs, and curious nervous scroll ornaments derived from 17th-century jewellery designs, but not dissimilar to tentative early ROCOCO.

Flamen, Albert Flamen was prolifically active as an engraver and draughtsman in Paris from 1648 to 1669. His *Livre de Plusieurs Cartouches* (1664; twelve plates) comprises competent but timid BAROQUE cartouches decorated with fruit, flowers, masks and scroll ornament.

Flaxman, John (1755–1826) Born in York, the son of a successful plaster-cast maker and sculptor, Flaxman was brought up in London, where he entered the Royal Academy Schools in 1770. From 1775 he designed ceramics for Wedgwood and Bentley, to whom his father had supplied plaster casts. At first he modelled low-relief portrait busts, but later he supplied delicate reliefs of figures for plaques and VASES. His *Dancing Hours* and *Apotheosis of Homer*, both 1778, marked Flaxman's establishment as a major designer of NEO-CLASSICAL ornament. The

Apotheosis was admired by Sir William HAMILTON; its subject came from a vase in the d'Hancarville volumes on his collection (1766–7), which was the prime source of Flaxman's early designs. Flaxman also designed a GOTHIC chess set for Wedgwood (1783) as well as basic shapes (about 1786). He also began at this period to supply designs for silver. Flaxman's wish to further his education as a sculptor led to a journey via Paris to Rome, where he remained until 1794, partly financed by Wedgwood. While in Rome his patrons included Thomas HOPE. In 1794 his outline compositions from the *Odyssey*, the *Iliad* and Dante were published, 213 drawings in all, having been engraved by Thomas Piroli; William BECKFORD was his patron for the Dante drawings. Many later editions were published in London, Paris and Germany. In 1807 Thomas Hope named them as 'the finest modern imitations I know of the elegance and beauty of the ancient Greek attire and furniture, armour and utensils'. In 1794 Flaxman returned to England. He was elected A.R.A. in 1797, R.A. in 1800, and in 1810 was appointed Professor of Sculpture at the Royal Academy, beginning to lecture in 1811. His works as a sculptor included Josiah Wedgwood's tomb in Stoke-on-Trent (1803). From 1805, when he designed the Trafalgar vase, Flaxman worked regularly for the royal goldsmiths, Rundell, Bridge & Rundell, including a sideboard design probably for their showrooms. The Theocritus cup (1811) was his finest variation of the Greek vase theme, while the National cup (1819) was a Gothic equivalent. However Flaxman's masterpiece was the Shield of Achilles, on which he worked from 1810 to 1818. He also designed medals, including the prize medal of the SOCIETY OF ARTS (1805). Flaxman's sources were eclectic, including Greek vases, Roman sarcophagi and Gothic sculpture, but his ideal was a Christian-ized Grecian antiquity. His reputation was international and his designs continued to be used for ornament long after his death, for instance to decorate tiles made by Richard Davis on Tyneside in the 1830s, or on an Etruscan tea kettle supplied by the silversmiths Barnard to Widdowson & Veale in 1848. An electrotype version of the Shield of Achilles was shown at the LONDON 1851 EXHIBITION.

Fleuron, The (1923–30) The *Fleuron* was concerned with all aspects of typography, historic and modern. From 1923 to 1925 it was edited by Oliver Simon of the Curwen Press, by whom it was printed, and from 1926 to 1930 it was edited by Stanley MORISON and printed by the Cambridge University Press. Its own typography is of great distinction.

Flindt, Paul Born in Nuremberg in 1567, the son of a goldsmith, Flindt published two suites of VASES and metalwork (eight plates and thirty-six plates) in Vienna in 1592 and 1593. His next suite (forty plates) was published in Nuremberg in 1594 and he seems thenceforward to have settled there, becoming a master goldsmith in 1601. Flindt died after 1631, in which year he was entrusted with the embossed work on a cup to serve as a pattern for prospective Nuremberg master goldsmiths. Flindt published in all some 200 plates of goldsmith's work and ornament in the dotted manner, stylistically similar to the designs of ZAN and SILBER. His *Zwölf Schtucklein etliche Schnaulwaidt* (1611; twelve plates) comprises monsters similar to those of Wendel DIETTERLIN THE YOUNGER and Christoph JAMNITZER.

Florence Accademia del Disegno In 1562, after the death of PONTORMO, VASARI called a meeting of leading Florentine artists to discuss the founding of an academy. A set of regulations were drawn up, presented to Cosimo de' Medici (1519–74) in early 1563, and approved. The Accademia del Disegno had Cosimo and MICHELANGELO as its leaders and the connoisseur and writer Vincenzo Borghini as its first chairman. There were thirty-six artists in the original foundation and the funeral of Michelangelo in 1564, organized by Vasari, gave the Accademia an opportunity to display its talent. It pretended from the beginning to an educational as well as a representative role. By 1567 the Accademia had enough authority to be consulted by Philip II of Spain about the plans for the Escorial. It tended to lapse into an artists' guild and between 1575 and 1578 Federigo Zuccaro urged the revival of the Accademia's teaching role. Foreign members included Peter CANDID (1576). In 1675 Cosimo III de' Medici set up a branch of the Accademia in Rome, where Ciro FERRI taught until its closure in 1686.

Floris, Cornelis (1514–75) Born in Antwerp, the son of Cornelis de Vriendt, Floris travelled to Rome in the late 1530s, returning to Antwerp in 1538 on the death of his father. He became a master in the Guild of St Luke in 1539, as a sculptor like his uncle, Claudius, who had been dean of the Guild in 1538. From 1541 to 1560 Floris decorated the ledgers of the Guild of St Luke with a series of thirty-two decorated initials, which include the earliest documented instances of the Flemish STRAPWORK GROTESQUE, a style of ornament of which Floris appears to have been the main pioneer. Surviving drawings of 1542 and 1543 in the same manner seem to confirm his status; it is probable that Floris was also the designer responsible for the elaborate strapwork decorations set up for the entry of the future Philip II of Spain to Antwerp in 1549, recorded by COECK. In 1548 Floris issued a suite of twenty-one designs for cups and ewers, which include copies after designs by VICO, and employ an extraordinary variety of scaly, bulgy forms, often with watery associations, including snails and fish, interfused with MANNERIST nudes. In 1556 the goldsmith Gomes Alonso of Barcelona used a Floris design of a cup for his masterpiece. *Masques*, a suite of eighteen plates, is probably contemporary; the vigorous and extremely grotesque masks use lobsters as noses, wings as ears and snakes as eyes. In 1552 followed a suite of four fantastic cars, similar to those issued by BOS in 1550, variations on a motif already used by Floris in 1543. A suite of six panels with cartouches enclosing sayings of philosophers (1554) uses a lighter and more delicate touch. In *Veelderley Veranderinghe van Grottissen ende Compartimenten* (1556; twelve plates), Floris designed spectacular and often sinister panels of grotesque ornament, drawing on the same watery vocabulary as his 1548 metalwork designs, which had already been used in a 1554 panel of ornament by Bos. A second suite in the same manner, *Veelderley niewe inventien . . .* (1557; sixteen plates), included eight elaborate designs for tombs. From the late 1540s Floris's main activity was as sculptor of tombs and other church decorations. In 1560 however he won the competition to design the new Antwerp Town Hall, completed in 1565, burnt in 1576, but restored by 1582. He also designed the house of the Hanseatic merchants in Antwerp (1564–8) and other buildings. Floris's decorative style was disseminated through Europe by his own prints and also through those of followers, notably Hans VREDEMAN DE VRIES.

Floris, Jakob (1524–81) Born in Antwerp, the younger brother of Cornelis FLORIS, Jakob Floris, a member of the Guild of St Luke from 1551, was a glass painter, executing a Last Judgement window for Sainte-Gudule, Brussels, and an Adoration of the Shepherds window in Antwerp Cathedral. He also produced three suites of engraved GROTESQUE cartouches, highly competent works in the manner of his brother, Cornelis. They are *Veelderhande cierlycke Compertementen* ... (Antwerp, 1564; thirteen plates), *Compertimentorum quod vocant multiplex* ... (Antwerp, 1566; seventeen plates) and *Compertimenta pictoriis flosculis manubiisq bellicis variegata* (Antwerp, 1567; twelve plates).

Flötner, Peter Born in about 1490 in Thurgau, Flötner may have worked in Augsburg as a sculptor from about 1512. He was later in Ansbach, but in 1522 the council of Nuremberg decided to grant him citizenship. He may have travelled to Italy around this date. Flötner died in 1546 in Nuremberg. Strongly influenced by DÜRER, he was active in many fields. His earliest published works were Bible illustrations, and there followed furniture designs, some dated 1533, designs for goldsmith's work, church furniture, daggers, playing-cards and an alphabet with figures. Flötner's best-known works are a long series of some 130 small bronze reliefs which were frequently copied in metalwork long after his death. In 1530 he designed a silver cup for the Holzschuher family incorporating reliefs he had carved, and in 1538 he designed a silver altar for Cracow Cathedral for King Sigismund I of Poland. Three years after Flötner's death, his *Kunstbuch* (forty plates) was published in Zürich; it comprised extremely fine and elaborate MORESQUE designs for ornament, which were often used to decorate books. The single GROTESQUE panel in the book, dated 1546, was re-used as late as 1596 in *Architectura antiqua* (Zürich). Flötner was comparable to HOLBEIN for his mastery of early RENAISSANCE ornament, and had an extremely wide influence in Germany.

Foggini, Giovanni Battista (1652–1725) Born in Florence, the nephew of a sculptor, Foggini was trained in Rome from 1673 to 1676 by Ciro FERRI and Ercole Ferrata, as one of the first students of the Accademia Fiorentina. On his return to Florence he worked mainly for Grand Duke Cosimo III de' Medici (1642–1723), succeeding Ferdinando Tacca as court sculptor in 1687 and being appointed court architect in about 1695. Part of his duties in the latter post was to direct the Galleria dei Lavori, workshops which executed works in marble, ebony and metal for the Medici Chapel in San Lorenzo and for princely gifts. Foggini seems to have been responsible for a large increase in the output of the Galleria, but even before he took it over he had been involved in ecclesiastical design, for instance a prodigiously elaborate ciborium for the Chapel of the Blessed Sacrament in Pisa Cathedral. Among his finest designs executed by the Galleria were a frame (1697) for a Madonna by Carlo Dolci (1616–89), a lavabo (1704), a prie-dieu (1706) and a cabinet (1709) for Anna Maria Luisa de' Medici; the latter is one of the great *tours-de-force* of BAROQUE furniture design. A journal of Foggini's work from 1713 to 1718 survives with designs for interior decoration, lights, cups, boxes for cosmetics and medicines, tables, cupboards, candelabra, monstrances, tabernacles, etc. His objects are richly embellished with ACANTHUS, birds, fruits, flowers, swags and VASES, and make bold use of the strongly coloured materials at his command. The baroque vocabulary Foggini had learnt in Rome thus takes on a mannered intensity which foreshadows the less frivolous aspects of the ROCOCO. Long after Foggini's death, in about 1750, the Doccia porcelain factory produced groups based on his bronzes.

Foillet, Jacques (1554–1619) Born at Tavare near Lyon, Foillet was a prolific publisher, operating from Montbéliard, a Huguenot refuge. His *Nouveaux pourtraicts de point coupé* (1598; eighty-seven plates) contained an almost indefinite variety of geometric designs for lace. Some copies are found in Wilhelm Hoffmann's 1604 *Modelbuch* and in James BOLER's 1634 book. In 1599 Foillet published a book of designs by VINCIOLO.

Folkema, Johannes Jacob A goldsmith and engraver in Dokkum and Amsterdam, Folkema published *Alderhande Voorbeelden van Doorgebroken Zilversmids werk* (Amsterdam; twelve plates) in about 1680. It comprises delicate scrolled floral and ACANTHUS ornament formed into borders, friezes, cartouches, and brooch or locket shapes. Folkema also engraved some of Théodore LE JUGE's designs.

Follot, Paul (1877–1941) Son of a successful wallpaper manufacturer, Follot studied design under Eugène GRASSET, whom he later succeeded as a teacher. Early designs by Follot published in 'ART ET DÉCORATION' were in the GOTHIC style, but after a period of interest in sculpture he began in 1901 to design bronzes, jewellery and textiles for MEIER-GRAEFE's La Maison Moderne. These were in the ART NOUVEAU style as were combs designed by Follot illustrated by Gabriel Mourey in the 'STUDIO' special number (1902), and a study shown at the first Salon (1904) of the Société des Artistes-Décorateurs, of which Follot was a founder member. A later interior for the same Salon in 1909 demonstrated a change towards calm and simplicity, which derived from Follot's studies of 18th-century NEO-CLASSICAL design. Some of the furniture shown in 1909 was acquired by the Musée des Arts Décoratifs, and in the following years Follot was a prolific and highly regarded de luxe designer, showing at the Turin 1911 and Munich 1913 Exhibitions, and designing furniture, ceramics, carpets, for Marcel Coupé and Savonnerie, textiles, for Cornille & Cie, and tapestries for Aubusson, as well as collaborating with SELMERSHEIM on the design of his own Paris house (1912–14). In 1911 he was commissioned by Cecil Wedgwood to design ceramics, and designed three services, one called Pomone, for Wedgwoods. In 1923 Follot was appointed head of the design studio at the Paris department store Le Bon Marché, called the Atelier Pomone; Follot there presided over a group of designers including Germaine Labaye, Mme Schilf and Dumouchet. At the PARIS 1925 EXHIBITION Follot designed not only the Pavilion Pomone, but also textiles, pianos, silver and a room in the Ambassade Française. As a result he participated with Dubocq, Brandt and LALIQUE in an interior commissioned by the New York textile manufacturer Schumacher. When in 1928 Waring & Gillow of London established a MODERN department under the direction of Serge CHERMAYEFF, Follot was employed to design furniture and interiors. He rarely visited England, but designed many of the interiors shown in London in 1928, and a sumptuous dining-room shown by Waring & Gillow at the Salon des Artistes-Décorateurs in 1929. Follot's style remained consistent throughout, opposed to Germanic systems and to the austere mechanism of the Modern style, and employing rounded Louis XVI forms, carved fruit, garlands and cornucopiae, gilding and light woods. He was replaced at the Atelier Pomone by René Prou, a Modernist, but continued to practise in the 1930s, designing an *appartement de luxe* on the *Normandie* (1935).

Foltz, Ludwig (1809–67) Born in Bingen, the son of a miniaturist, Foltz was first educated as a builder and stonemason. However he eventually worked as a favourite pupil under the sculptor Ludwig von Schwanthaler (1802–48) in Munich and at the end of the 1830s started a career as a decorative sculptor in the area of Regensburg, where he taught at the school of applied arts. In 1845 Foltz designed a stoneware beaker in the GOTHIC style, made by Villeroy & Boch, sold to raise funds for the completion of Cologne Cathedral: Foltz later designed similar beakers for the Berlin firm of Ernst March. In 1852 he was appointed to teach at the Munich Polytechnic, but continued to execute schemes of sculptural ornament, notably the re-gothicizing of the Munich Frauenkirche from 1863. Foltz also designed furniture, ceramics, a chess-set and statuettes, in the Gothic and RENAISSANCE styles.

Fontaine, Jacques Valentin Fontaine worked as Serrurier du Roy at the Gobelins factory, to which he seems to have been strongly attached. His *Livre de Differens Couronnemens* (six plates) was dedicated to the architect Jules Robert de Cotte, titular director of the Gobelins from 1735 to 1737. It comprises designs for ironwork crestings with heraldic supporters and cartouches, in a rich, lively and asymmetric ROCOCO style, sometimes vigorous to excess. *Nouveau Livre d'Études* (twelve plates) was dedicated to colleagues and apprentices at the Gobelins factory; it is a manual in drawing scrolled leaf ornaments for ironwork, including a 'Nouveau feuille de Rocaille'. A third book, *Nouveau Livre de Serrurerie*, was dedicated to Jean-Charles Garnier, the controller general

of the royal manufactories.

Fontaine, Pierre François Léonard (1762–1853) Born in Pontoise, the son of an architect and hydraulic engineer, Fontaine studied at the École des Beaux-Arts in Paris under PEYRE, in whose studio he met PERCIER in 1779. He completed his studies under Jean François Heurtier (1739–1822). In 1785 he was beaten to the Grand Prix by Charles MOREAU, but in 1786 he set off to Rome, where he earned a living by doing topographical watercolours. In 1786 he was joined in Rome by Percier and their friendship blossomed. Back in Paris in 1791 Fontaine designed silks and wallpapers and ran a drawing school. In 1792 he sought employment in England, where he worked briefly as a designer. Returning again to Paris, Fontaine assisted Percier on decorations for the Opéra, and their partnership began. In 1793 they designed furniture for execution by Jacob for the Convention. Their first book, *Palais, maisons, et autres édifices modernes dessinés à Rome* (1798), illustrated RENAISSANCE buildings in Rome. Fontaine then designed illustrations and ornaments for the Didot *Horace* (1799) and *La Fontaine* (1802). In 1799 Fontaine designed interior decorations for M. de Chauvelin, a neighbour of Joséphine de Beauharnais, and thus met Napoleon. As a result he and Percier began work on the decoration of Malmaison in the same year. In 1800 they designed a memorial service for Washington, and in 1801 published the first edition of their *Recueil de décorations intérieures* (forty-three plates; second edition 1812, seventy-two plates), which presented their fully developed NEO-CLASSICAL style, the official style of the Napoleonic regime. The style used not only Roman and Greek objects and motifs, but also Renaissance ornament, embellished where appropriate with Napoleonic emblems. Percier and Fontaine designed Napoleon's coronation by Pius VII at Notre Dame in 1804 and his marriage to Marie-Louise in 1810, both recorded in albums (1807 and 1810). They designed furniture and interiors for Napoleon's palaces, including Saint-Cloud (from 1804) and the Tuileries (from 1804). Fontaine appears to have been the entrepreneur in the partnership, with the larger ideas, while Percier executed the detailed designs. After the fall of Napoleon, Fontaine became architect to Louis XVIII, and he continued in royal service until the fall of Louis Philippe in 1848. His later books included *Le Palais-Royal* (1829) and *Résidences de souverains* (1833). An edition of the *Recueil* was published in Venice in 1843, with a commentary by BORSATO. Fontaine was buried in the same grave as Percier.

Fontana, Carlo (1638–1714) Born in Rancate near Como, Fontana came to Rome in 1650. By 1658 he was working as a draughtsman in the studio of Pietro da CORTONA. In 1659 he worked under BERNINI, his principal master, on the colonnades of St Peter's. His first independent work as an architect dates from about 1664. Fontana became architect of St Peter's in 1697 and was by then the leading architect in Rome, working in a highly professional late-BAROQUE style. He designed ecclesiastical fittings such as candlesticks, lamps, altars, tombs and so on, and secular furniture such as chairs, cabinets, frames and pedestals, as well as ironwork, including a door knocker and a papal galley. His pupils included Nicodemus TESSIN, Fischer von Erlach, and James GIBBS.

Fontanieu, Pierre Élisabeth de The son of the Intendant et Contrôleur Général des Meubles de la Couronne, Fontanieu succeeded his father in that post on his death in 1767, and held it himself until he sold it in 1783. He died in 1784. Fontanieu was thus in charge of the furnishing of the French royal palaces at the period when the ROCOCO style gave way to the NEO-CLASSICAL, and exercised the closest control over designs and craftsmen, in particular the cabinet-maker J. H. Riesener (1734–1806). Fontanieu was a highly expert amateur of turning and his *Collection de Vases* (1770; forty-seven plates) comprises imposing designs for VASES which are shown both in their basic turned form and as embellished with ornament. A few are simple virtuoso turnery, but most use the full neo-classical repertoire of fluting, ACANTHUS, swags, husks and so on. Their outline is rich and lively, and the character of some very BAROQUE. Most elaborate is a columnar musical clock topped by an urn with the signs of the zodiac. One of the vase designs was produced by the Sèvres porcelain factory from 1772. Fontanieu also published *The Art of Making Coloured Crystals to Imitate Precious Stones* (Paris, 1778, London, 1787).

Fordrin, Louis Fordrin was a member of a family of smiths. He executed ironwork at Versailles from 1703 and in 1714 made parts of the choir-screen in Notre Dame, Paris, to the design of the architect Robert de COTTE (1656–1735). In 1723 Fordrin reissued TIJOU's *A New Book of Drawings* (1693), without acknowledgement, as *Nouveau Livre de serrurerie de composition anglaise*, and in the same year published his own *Nouveau Livre de Serrurerie* (thirty plates), dedicated to the Duc d'Épernon, Surintendant des Bâtiments du Roy. It comprises gates, balconies, staircases, signs and choir-screens in a rich scrolly late BAROQUE style with a generous use of ACANTHUS and royal emblems. Some of Fordrin's designs were later copied by LUCOTTE in plates to Diderot and D'Alembert's encyclopaedia.

Foresto, Iseppo Trained as a manuscript illuminator, Foresto designed a successful series of lace and embroidery pattern-books, similar but superior to the works of PAGANO. They comprise *Splendore delle virtuose giovani* (Venice, 1557; sixteen plates), *Lucidario di recami* (Venice, 1557; eighteen plates) and *Bellezze de racami* (Venice, 1558; twenty plates). He was also probably responsible for the very fine lace designs in *Corona de le mostre* (Venice, about 1566; sixteen plates) edited by Armenio Corte and published by VAVASSORE.

Form (1905–present) Published in Stockholm by the Swedish Society of Industrial Design, this generously illustrated magazine is an invaluable source on Swedish design. Until 1932 its title was *Svenska Slöjdföreningens Tidskrift*.

Form (1957–present) Wilhelm WAGENFELD was one of the original editors of this semi-official West German design periodical.

Form, Die Published in Berlin from 1925 and subtitled *Zeitschrift für Gestaltende Arbeit*, *Form* was first edited for the Deutsche Werkbund by Walter Curt Berendt; he was succeeded in 1927 by Walter Riezler. The magazine had a serious MODERN approach to design in the widest sense; its very title was attacked on ideological grounds by MIES VAN DER ROHE in 1927. Professor Adolf SCHNECK wrote on furniture (1926, 1927) and the STUTTGART 1927 EXHIBITION was fully covered.

Formenschatz, Der (1877–1911) Published from Munich by Georg Hirth, whose foreword stresses the strong impulse towards the RENAISSANCE style in evidence at the MUNICH 1876

EXHIBITION, this magazine was an enormous collection of prints, drawings and objects illustrated to inspire contemporary craftsmen and designers. After Dr E. Bassermann-Jordan became editor in 1902 the slant was almost exclusively art-historical.

Forseth, Einar Born in 1892 in Linköping, Sweden, the son of a Norwegian draughtsman and lithographer, Forseth studied from 1908 to 1911 at Gothenburg Art School and then from 1912 to 1915 at Stockholm Academy. He worked under the church decorator Professor Olle Hjortzberg, and became interested in stained glass and mosaics. His first stained glass (1917) was for Frövi church; from 1918 Forseth's stained glass was made by his partner Gustaf Ringström. After 1918 Forseth travelled widely. From 1919 he designed many Swedish postage stamps. From 1921 to 1923 he designed splendid mosaics for the Golden Room of Stockholm City Hall, by the architect Ragnar Östberg (1866–1945), and in 1924 tapestries, mosaics and plasterwork for Stockholm Concert Hall. His later stained glass included work at the English church in Stockholm (1940) and Coventry Cathedral (1951–62), where he also designed a floor mosaic at the Chapel of Unity. Forseth's style ranges from expressionist to abstract to naïve.

Förster, Heinrich Gottfried Förster was trained as a smith in Leipzig. He was established as court smith in Nikolsburg before 1727, but in 1728 became a citizen of Brünn, where he died in 1760. Förster issued two suites of designs for ironwork, published by HERTEL in Augsburg. They comprise gates, balconies, brackets, shop signs, grilles, locks, keys, etc., mainly in a crude but vigorous ACANTHUS or BERAINESQUE style, with some exercises in a coarse ARTISAN ROCOCO.

Fortuny y Madrazo, Mariano (1871–1949) Born in Granada, the son of a painter and collector who died in Rome in 1874, Fortuny was brought up in Paris, where he studied under his uncle the painter Raymondo de Madrazo. In 1889 Fortuny moved with his mother to Venice, where he studied painting at the Accademia. In 1904 he published a new system of electrical lighting for the theatre. He also designed kite-like electric-light shades and textiles. Fortuny's textiles – silks, velvets and cottons – were based on historic models, many in his own collection, from Japan, China, Spain, the Near East, Italy and Byzantium. He designed furniture for his own house, the Palazzo degli Orfei. From about 1906 Fortuny became famous as a dress designer, praised by Proust among many others.

Forty, Jean François Almost no biographical details are known about Forty, although he was among the most accomplished and sophisticated professional designers to have worked in the NEO-CLASSICAL style. His *Œuvres d'orfèvrerie* (three suites of six plates each), covering chalices, ciboria and candlesticks, and his similar *Œuvres de serrureries*, with designs for ironwork, appeared before 1768. Both were advertised in 1773 by the gilder and print-dealer Jean-Félix Watin. In the 1760s Forty was lodging with the chair-maker, Louis Delanois (1731–92), one of the first craftsmen to embrace the neo-classical style, who may have executed designs by Forty. His *Œuvres de sculptures en bronze* comprises forty-eight plates of girandoles, firedogs, clocks, barometers, chandeliers, etc., intended for execution in gilt bronze, and represents the summit of refined and highly finished neo-classical French bronze design of the late 18th century. Not advertised by Watin in his 1776 edition but present in 1785, they probably fall between those dates. In the early 1790s Forty published a *Projet de deux Toilettes* (twelve plates).

Fouquet, Georges (1862–1957) In about 1895 Fouquet took over the jewellery business of his father, Alphonse Fouquet. In 1900 he enjoyed an enormous success at the PARIS EXHIBITION with jewellery designed by Alphonse MUCHA, who also designed the shop in the Rue Royale which Fouquet occupied until 1936. In the 1900s Fouquet designed jewellery in the ART NOUVEAU style himself, but in 1922 he changed to a rich ART DÉCO style using a wide variety of materials, platinum, diamonds, onyx, coral, jade and enamel. He presided over the jewellery sections of the PARIS EXHIBITIONS of 1925 and 1937. Among the designers who worked for Fouquet were his son, the architect Eric Bagge, the poster designer CASSANDRE, the sculptor and painter Jean Lambert-Rucki, the painter André Léveillé, and his own *chef d'atelier*, Louis Fertey.

Fouquet, Jean Born in Paris in 1899, the son of Georges FOUQUET, Jean Fouquet entered the family jewellery business as a designer and was active as such until 1964. He exhibited at the PARIS 1925 EXHIBITION, and from 1926 at the Salon d'Automne. His late-1920s jewellery designs are in a severe and geometric ART DÉCO style. Fouquet continued to exhibit both in Paris in 1937 and Brussels in 1958. In 1930 he was a founder member of the Union des Artistes Modernes. In 1928 he published *Bijoux et Orfèvrerie*. On his retirement he passed his clientele to Raymond TEMPLIER.

Fowler, John (1906–77) Fowler was educated at Felsted School and then worked in a bank and a printing works before in the mid-1920s starting to paint Chinese wallpaper in Thornton Smith's studio in Soho. He then became head of the Peter Jones studio in Sloane Square. In 1935 Fowler joined the decorating firm founded by Lady Sybil Colefax and Countess Munster, who had by then left, and in 1938 became a partner. Fowler was a prolific interior decorator working both in private houses and in many houses owned by the National Trust. He designed many adaptations of 18th-century and early 19th-century wallpapers and textiles.

Fraisse, Jean-Antoine From 1733 to 1740 Fraisse was employed as a painter by Louis-Henri, Duc de Bourbon, at Chantilly. In 1735 he issued an enchanting *Livre de Desseins Chinois*, engraved by himself, with fifty-three plates. These represent a considerable advance in sophistication on STALKER & Parker but are still in a wholly pre-ROCOCO manner, in contrast to Christophe HUET's contemporary painted *singeries* at Chantilly. On his title-page Fraisse claims that his designs were copied from originals from Persia, India, China and Japan. These, it is implied by the fulsome dedication, had been collected by the Duc de Bourbon, whose porcelain factory at Chantilly, founded in 1725, was another expression of his enthusiasm for oriental art.

Francard, Laurent Born in Paris, the son of a painter, Francard worked as a designer for the great military engineer Sébastien de Vauban (1633–1707), and was in 1686 Ingénieur du Roy. He is last recorded in 1690. Francard published a book of handsome French BAROQUE designs for doors (six plates), engraved by Jean MAROT. They were reprinted by Danckerts in Amsterdam, and were owned by the English architect John James. Francard also issued a suite of chimneypieces (six plates); he described himself 'Architecte du Roy' on the title.

Franchi, Gregorio (1770–1828) Franchi met William BECKFORD in 1787 when he was a pupil at the Patriarchal Seminary of Music in Lisbon. In 1788 he entered Beckford's service and became his confidant and general factotum. Franchi had a facility for ornamental design, especially MORESQUES, and designed some remarkably advanced and sophisticated silver in a synthetic 16th-century style made in London from 1815 to 1820 for Beckford, who supplied the basic ideas. Franchi assembled an important collection of early metalwork which he was forced to sell in 1827. He died in poverty.

Franck, Kaj Born in Viipuri, Finland, in 1911 Franck studied furniture design at the Institute of Industrial Art in Helsinki from 1929 to 1932. From 1946 to 1961 Franck was head of the design department at the Arabia pottery and porcelain factory and from 1950 to 1973 he was Art Director of the Nuutajärvi glass factory. Franck also designed lighting for Taito Oy, Helsinki, textiles for Associated Woollen Mills in Hyvinkää, and furniture for Te Ma Oy, Helsinki. Franck worked in a MODERN manner both elegant and cheerful, many of his designs being well suited for industrial production, and helped to establish the Finnish reputation for Modern good taste in design.

Franco, Battista Born in Venice in about 1510, Franco went to Rome in about 1530 to study painting. He executed decorations for the entries of Emperor Charles V to Rome and Florence in 1536. Franco remained in Florence until 1539 and then returned to Rome. Summoned to Urbino by Duke Guidobaldo to decorate the choir of the Cathedral, Franco proved unequal to the task. He then designed at least two maiolica services for the Duke, one presented to the Emperor Charles V, the other to the

Duke's brother-in-law, Cardinal Alessandro Farnese (1500–1558). One had as its theme the War of Troy, other maiolica designs by Franco depicted the Labours of Hercules and subjects from Greek mythology, Roman history and the Old Testament. He was paid for forty designs in 1551. Surviving drawings have central narrative scenes with borders composed of figures. His designs seem to have remained in use until as late as 1600. In 1548 Franco decorated triumphal arches for the marriage of Duke Guidobaldo to Vittoria Farnese. By 1554 Franco was in Venice, where he died in 1561.

Franco, Giacomo (1550–1620) An illegitimate son of the painter Battista F R A N C O, Franco was responsible for many book illustrations and title-pages. In 1596 Franco published the last Venetian pattern-book to contain designs for needle lace, *Nuova inventione de diverse mostre* (twenty-six plates): he claimed responsibility for the designs, but a number were copied after T O Z Z I's slightly earlier book. Franco also published a writing book, *Il franco modo di scrivere cancellaresco moderno*, and two books on dress, *Habite delle donne venetiane* (1610) and *Habiti d'huomini e donne venetiane* (1610).

Fraser, Claude Lovat (1890–1921) Born in London, the son of a solicitor, Fraser was educated at Charterhouse and read law from 1907. In 1911 he turned to art and studied at the Westminster School of Art under Walter Sickert and Sylvia Gosse. From 1913 Fraser issued a series of hand-coloured broadsides and chapbooks under the Flying Fame imprint. He also designed painted wooden toys. Fraser served in the First World War but was gassed in 1916. From 1916 he designed book-jackets, covers and illustrations for the Poetry Bookshop. He also designed a mass of advertisements and other graphics for the Curwen Press, for Heal & Son, for Eno's Fruit Salt, for the London Underground and others. In about 1920 he designed a number of cheerful textiles for William Foxton & Co. of London. Fraser's most famous poster was that for a production of *The Beggar's Opera* at the Lyric Hammersmith in 1920, for which Fraser designed bold 18th-century-style sets and costumes.

Frederick Lewis, Prince of Wales (1707–51) Born in 1707 in Hanover, the son of the future George II of England, Frederick was made Duke of Gloucester in 1717 and Duke of Edinburgh in 1727. In 1728 he came to England and in 1729 was created Prince of Wales. In 1736 he married Princess Augusta of Saxe-Gotha. Frederick was continually at odds with his parents and from about 1737 his house became a centre of the opposition. He was the ground landlord of Vauxhall Gardens, where Jonathan Tyers developed a pleasure ground with R O C O C O decorations by G R A V E L O T, G. M. M O S E R, Roubiliac and others. From 1738 to 1742 the Prince's Pavilion was erected at Vauxhall for Frederick and his friends. In 1749 he had a Chinese barge with Chinese boatmen and erected an Indian temple at Kew. Despite such evidence of involvement in and patronage of the English rococo, Frederick's barge (1732) was designed by William K E N T, who also designed a masquerade for the Prince in 1731 as well as a silver centrepiece made by George Wickes in 1745, and in 1749 the Prince asked Horace W A L P O L E for a copy of *Aedes Walpolianae*.

Froment-Meurice, François Désiré (1802–55) Born in Paris, the son of a jeweller who had founded a firm in 1794, Froment-Meurice was taught to draw by the painter Girodet (1767–1824). He took over the firm in 1825 and built up a towering reputation as a virtuoso, working in the GOTHIC, RENAISSANCE and NATURALISTIC styles. He was admired by Victor Hugo and Balzac and won medals at the PARIS EXHIBITIONS of 1839, 1844, 1849 and 1855 and at the LONDON 1851 EXHIBITION; he was nearly ruined by the 1848 revolution. Froment-Meurice designed himself to a limited extent, but also employed FEUCHÈRE, KLAGMANN, LIÉNARD and Pradier as designers; VECHTE was an employee of his for a while. The firm was taken over in 1859 by Froment-Meurice's son, P. H. Émile Froment-Meurice (1837–1913), who maintained its high reputation. Prestige commissions which involved him included the cradle presented to the Prince Imperial by the City of Paris in 1856 and a centrepiece for Napoleon III shown at the PARIS 1867 EXHIBITION. He developed a luxurious chryselephantine style and at the PARIS 1889 EXHIBITION showed GALLÉ glass mounted in silver-gilt.

Fry, Roger Eliot (1866–1934) Born in Highgate, the son of a judge, Fry studied natural sciences at Cambridge from 1885 to 1888. After Cambridge Fry devoted himself to the history of art, although he also painted, studying briefly at the Académie Julian in Paris in 1892. He travelled widely, helped to found the *Burlington Magazine* and from 1905 to 1910 was director of the Metropolitan Museum in New York. Back in London in 1910 Fry organized an exhibition of post-impressionist paintings at the Grafton Gallery. In late 1912 Fry planned with the Vorticist painter Wyndham Lewis (1884–1957) the Omega Workshops, announced in the *Art Chronicle* (1913) as 'a new movement in decorative art'. The Workshops, in Fitzroy Square, produced furniture, textiles, mosaic, stained glass and pottery from July 1913.

Design was anonymous but designers involved included Fry himself, Duncan GRANT, Vanessa Bell and Dora Carrington (1893–1932). Lewis also designed but in October 1913 quarrelled with Fry and left the Workshops, taking with him Frederick Etchells (1886–1973), Cuthbert Hamilton (1884–1959) and Edward Wadsworth (1889–1949). William Roberts and Henri Gaudier-Brzeska (1891–1915) also designed briefly for Omega, but left in 1914, when Brzeska described the lounge shown by Omega at the Allied Artists Salon as 'too much prettiness'. The Omega Workshops petered out in 1919 to 1920, but survived in name until 1921. Though the idea of the Workshops looked back to William MORRIS, the Omega style of decoration was influenced by Fauvism and cubism. Some products were handmade and amateurish, others, such as Wilton carpets, were executed by professional firms to Omega designs.

Fumiani, Giovanni Antonio (1643–1710) Fumiani, a Venetian-born painter, made his reputation by his decoration of the church of San Pantaleone in Venice from 1684 to 1704. He also designed mosaics for St Mark's in 1690 and 1691. In about 1702 he painted for Ferdinando de' Medici an extraordinary series of designs for torchères, and a VASE. The former are contorted and teetering allegorical erections, while the latter is comparable to vases by SOLDANI BENZI.

Functionalism In 1757 the NEOCLASSICAL theorist Marc-Antoine Laugier (1713–69) in his *Essai sur l'architecture* emphasized the logic of construction as the basis of architectural design and looked back to the primitive hut, described by Vitruvius, as the archetype of classical architecture. Laugier owed much to J. L. de Cordemoy's *Nouveau Traité de toute l'architecture* (1706), which advocated the fusion of the Greek and GOTHIC systems. An even more radical Functionalism was propounded by Carlo Lodoli (1690–1761), who did not fear to reject classicism. Lodoli's views were propagated by Andrea Memmo (1729–93) in his *Elementi d'architettura lodoliana* (1786), and, in a muted form, by Francesco Algarotti (1717–64) in his *Saggio sopra l'architettura* (1753). The American sculptor Horatio Greenhough (1805–52) was an extreme mid-19th-century Functionalist; in his *American Architecture* (1843) he stated: 'In nakedness I behold the majesty of the essential instead of the trappings of pretension.' For A. W. N. PUGIN from the 1830s the logic of construction was one of the factors pointing inevitably to Gothic as the only honest Christian style, a doctrine preached with even greater eloquence by RUSKIN. VIOLLET-LE-DUC's rationalist dissection of architectural structure and acceptance of new materials – at least in theory – was also widely influential. On the other side of the stylistic divide Owen JONES's fifth proposition, 'Construction should be decorated. Decoration should never be purposely constructed,' implied a structural honesty of which Pugin would have approved. Although SULLIVAN's oft-quoted formulation of Functionalism, 'Form follows function' (1895), belies Sullivan's own achievement as a creator of ornament, there is no doubt that ornament was increasingly under attack from around 1900, notably at the hands of Adolf LOOS. The NEO-CLASSICAL tendencies evident in the work of such early 20th-century designers as Loos himself and BEHRENS encouraged the use of pure, simple forms. Add to these factors the cult of the machine-made object common to MUTHESIUS, Futurists, Constructivists and LE COR-BUSIER, and the conditions were ripe for the emergence in the 1920s of a Functionalist style, which pretended to base itself on Sullivan's 'Form follows function' dictum but was in fact determined to be MODERN. Functionalism, at once slogan and style, spread from France and Germany in the 1930s, and Le Corbusier's admiration of grain silos, aeroplanes and ships became an international commonplace.

Furness, Frank (1839–1912) Born in Philadelphia, the son of a distinguished clergyman, Furness entered the office of the Philadelphia architect John Fraser in 1857 and then worked under the New York architect Richard Morris Hunt (1827–95) from 1859 to 1861, when he joined the Union cavalry. From 1866 Furness practised as an architect in Philadelphia in partnership with John Fraser and George W. Hewitt (1841–1916) and from 1871 with the latter alone. SULLIVAN was a pupil in 1873. Furness made his reputation with the Pennsylvania Academy of Fine Arts (1871–6). At the PHILADELPHIA 1876 EXHIBITION Furness designed the Brazilian Pavilion in the Moorish style. He worked mainly in a violent GOTHIC style, influenced by both English and French prototypes and using polychromy and geometric ornament. He designed furniture, light fittings, ironwork and stained glass. A desk and chair of 1875 for his brother, probably made by the cabinet-maker and furniture designer Daniel Pabst (1827–1910), are unusually vigorous examples of American Reformed Gothic. From 1875 to 1881 Furness practised alone and from 1881 in partnership with his former draughtsman Allen Evans (1845–1925).

Furnisher, The (1899–1901) A trade journal, which seems to have attempted to capture the 'FURNITURE AND DECORATION' market when the latter changed its title, its illustrations are a useful index of commercial design standards in England during its brief existence: it also contained a few useful historical articles, notably one on Ford Madox Brown's furniture (1900).

Furniture and Decoration (1890–98) This trade magazine, published by Timms & Webb, incorporated the 'Furniture Gazette' in 1894. Publishing a wide range of designs by J. Moyr Smith and others, it is representative of English commercial design. It was succeeded by the 'Furniture Record'.

Furniture Gazette, The (1872–93) This London based trade journal contains many useful illustrations of designs, highly representative of commercial taste. It was superseded by 'Furniture and Decoration'.

Furniture Record, The (1899–1928) This trade journal, at first edited by Timms and Webb, was merely a new title for 'Furniture and Decoration'.

Towards the end it contained little on design.

Fürst, Rosina Helena A daughter of the great Nuremberg publisher Paul Fürst, Rosina Fürst was responsible for the needlework designs in his *Model Buch*, which appeared in four large parts from about 1660 to 1676, and was the first new pattern-book of this type to appear after the Thirty Years War. A few designs were borrowed from Georg Herman and from Sibmacher. The *Model Buch* was last re-issued in 1728.

F.V.B. The Master F.V.B. engraved fifty-nine surviving plates, dating from about 1480 to 1500. The majority are religious subjects, but F.V.B. also engraved seven panels of Gothic ornament. Four are copies after Schongauer, the remaining three designed by F.V.B. himself comprise Gothic foliage and flowers. F.V.B., the most gifted 15th-century Flemish engraver, may have been a goldsmith in Bruges.

G

Gabriel, René (1890–1950) From 1916, when he had left the École des Arts Décoratifs in Paris, Gabriel was active as a producer of hand-blocked wallpapers, which he designed himself. They comprise landscape, floral and abstract designs in an ART DÉCO manner. Gabriel, an admirer of Francis JOURDAIN, showed a walnut room for a young girl at the 1920 Salon des Artistes-Décorateurs, and later designed simple rectilinear oak unit furniture which was illustrated in 'ART ET DÉCORATION' (1934).

Gaddi, Agnolo Born in Florence before 1351, the son of a painter and the grandson of a mosaicist, Gaddi is recorded as working at the Vatican in 1369. By 1381 he was a member of the painters' guild in Florence, where he designed sculpture for the Loggia dei Lanzi in 1383 to 1386, and, in 1394 to 1396, stained-glass windows for the cathedral, mainly executed by Leonardo di Simone. Gaddi died in 1396. Among his assistants was Cennino Cennini, whose *Libro dell'arte* records techniques and procedures he had learned in Gaddi's workshop.

Gaillard, Eugène (1862–1933) With Georges DE FEURE and Édouard COLONNA, Gaillard designed fabrics, furniture and interiors for BING's pavilion at the PARIS 1900 EXHIBITION. In *À Propos du Mobilier* (Paris, 1906) Gaillard advocated decoration inspired by nature but not the literal imitation of natural forms. Sedeyn's *Le Mobilier*

(1921) illustrates a table and chair of 1913 by Gaillard, which are still in an elegant ART NOUVEAU manner.

Gajani, Egisto Born in 1832, Gajani was a virtuoso carver and designer of carved ornament in the Italian RENAISSANCE manner, taught by Barbetti, who had in 1830 moved his workshop from Siena to Florence and who showed at the LONDON 1851 EXHIBITION. At the PARIS 1867 EXHIBITION and later exhibitions Gajani showed spectacular demonstrations of his skill. In about 1880, together with another Florentine virtuoso carver, Luigi Frullini (1839–97), Gajani published in Paris twenty-eight plates of *Panneaux et ornements en bois sculptés*.

Gallé, Émile (1846–1904) Born in Nancy, the son of the proprietor of a shop selling glass and ceramics who had revived a pottery at Saint-Clément, Gallé designed floral decoration for his father's wares from about 1860, when he was studying botany under Dominique Alexandre Godron, a professor at the university of Nancy. From 1865 to 1866 Gallé studied design, botany and mineralogy in Weimar. From 1866 to 1867 he studied glass-making at the factory of Burgun & Schwerer at Meisenthal in the Saar. He then returned to Nancy and continued to experiment with glass. After service in the Franco-Prussian war Gallé travelled in 1871 to London with Édouard Du Sommerard to help organize the Art de France Exhibition. Back in Nancy again, he set up his own glass workshop and in 1874 took over direction of the Saint-Clément pottery, which had moved to Nancy. Gallé showed earthenware at the PARIS 1878 EXHIBITION. At the 1884 PARIS UNION CENTRALE DES ARTS DÉCORATIFS Exhibition he showed 300 pieces of pottery and glass in the Islamic, GOTHIC and NATURALISTIC styles. His glass was influenced by the example of the Brandt collection of Chinese glass which he saw at the BERLIN KUNSTGEWERBE-MUSEUM in 1884. Also in 1884 Gallé set up a furniture workshop. At the PARIS 1889 EXHIBITION his glass and his furniture employed natural forms redolent with symbolism. In the 1880s and 1890s Gallé's factory was enormously prolific; he had by 1900 some 300 workers. The admirers and patrons of his glass included Proust and Count Robert de Montesquiou. He was given public commissions, for instance glass vases given in 1896 by the City of Paris to Nicolas II of Russia. In 1900 Gallé won prizes for both glass and furniture at the PARIS EXHIBITION. In 1901 with the support of his friends Victor PROUVÉ and Louis MAJORELLE he founded the Alliance Provinciale des Artistes, known as the École de Nancy and heavily backed by Eugène Corbin (1867–1932) in the Nancy journal 'ART ET INDUSTRIE'. There was a successful exhibition of the École de Nancy in Paris in 1903. In 1904 Gallé opened a shop in London. In the same year he died of leukaemia, from which he had suffered since 1898. Gallé was a passionate botanist; the posthumous anthology of his writings, *Écrits pour l'Art* (Paris, 1908), includes many articles on botanical and horticultural subjects. An admirer of Maeterlinck – and Loie Fuller – Gallé thought of himself as a symbolist working in glass, and his glass, and even more so his furniture, is overlaid with high-falutin' symbolism; on the design of the latter he was assisted by Victor Prouvé and Louis Hestaux. In an article in the 'REVUE DES ARTS DÉCORATIFS' (1900), advocating natural ornament in furniture, he attacked the vermicelli style of contemporary ART NOUVEAU, echoing CARABIN. The Gallé factory finally closed in 1935.

Garthwaite, Anna Maria (1690–1763) The daughter of a Lincolnshire parson, Garthwaite worked as a silk designer in Spitalfields, where she lived with a widowed sister, from the 1720s to 1756. She worked freelance for the leading weavers, producing about eighty highly competent designs a year, many influenced by Jean REVEL and other French designers. She may have been the author of an essay on 'designing and drawing Patterns for the Flower'd-silk Manufactory' in G. Smith's *Laboratory, or School of Arts* (1756). Her reputation long outlived her.

Gate, Simon (1883–1945) Born in S. Fågelås, Skaraborg, in Sweden, the son of a farmer, Gate studied at the applied arts school of the Stockholm Academy from 1905 to 1909. From 1909 to 1916 he travelled widely and was mainly active as a portrait painter, although in 1912 he designed book illustrations for the publisher B. Wahlström. From 1916 Gate designed glass at the Orrefors factory, where he collaborated with Edward HALD and the glass-blower Knut Bergqvist (1873–1953). Gate designed simple geometric forms, NEOCLASSICAL figures and abstract patterns for engraving, and free-form glass. He won a Grand Prix at the PARIS 1925 EXHIBITION. Among the many designers influenced by Gate was G. M. B. STELLA.

Gaudernack, Georg (1865–1914) Born in Bohemia and trained at the Vienna school of applied arts, Gaudernack designed glass for Lobmeyrs of Vienna up to 1891, when he moved to Oslo, where he designed glass for the Christiania Glasmagazin. In 1892 he was attached as a designer to the silversmiths David Anderson. From 1910 Gaudernack was an independent silversmith.

Gaudí i Cornet, Antoni (1852–1926) Born in or near Reus in Tarragona, the son of a copper-smith, Gaudí studied architecture at Barcelona University from 1873 to 1878 under the GOTHIC Revival architect Juan Martorell. He was much influenced by VIOLLET-LE-DUC. Gaudí designed Gothic church furniture and metalwork for Martorell's chapel at Comillas in 1878 and in the same year designed a showcase for the PARIS EXHIBITION. In 1879 he designed cast-iron street lamps for Barcelona. In the Vicens House (1883–5), the house El Capricho (1883–5) and the Güell pavilions (1884–8), Gaudí used a highly personal Moorish style incorporating tiles, plasterwork, and ironwork. Ferocious Chinese dragons in the iron gate to the Güell pavilions and iron whiplash scrolls above the entrance to the later Güell palace (1885–90) display an extraordinary vigour, also reflected in Gaudí's development of an idiosyncratic organic style analagous to ART NOUVEAU to express his fervent Christianity and Catalan patriotism. The Güell palace also contained furniture designed by Gaudí, including a perversely contorted and asymmetric dressing-table. The Calvet House (1898–1904) had an elaborate iron lift and furniture designed by Gaudí in a knobbly osteomorphic manner, also displayed in the irregularly lobed and twisted woodwork and furniture of the Batlló House (1904–5). The crypt at Santa Coloma (1908–14) incorporates holy water stoups of shells clasped by ironwork and curvilinear pews of wood and iron.

Gautier, Pierre Gautier, a smith, executed works in Toulon Cathedral in 1648 and 1658 in collaboration with P. Augier. In 1657 they made a gate for Toulon Town Hall to the design of Pierre Puget. Gautier was later employed in the arsenal at Marseille and there published *Divers ouvrages de balustrades cloisons paneaux et autres ornemens* (1685; fourteen plates), to which his son, Jean Gautier, later added a further six plates (1688). All the plates are in an accomplished BAROQUE style with a generous use of ACANTHUS, scrolls, fleurs-de-lys and crowns.

Gebrauchsgraphik (1925–present) Founded and first edited by H. K. Frenzel, this German magazine was published from Berlin. It covers all aspects of graphic and advertising design, including posters, books and so on. In 1972 it adopted the additional title *Novum*.

Gedde, Walter Gedde was author of *A Booke of Sundry Draughtes, principaly serving for Glasiers: and not Impertinent for Plasterers, and Gardiners: be sides sundry other Professions . . .*, London (Walter Dight, 1615). The book contains 103 plates of patterns for leaded windows, followed by a brief treatise on glass painting. It was reprinted in 1848 by Henry SHAW. Nothing is known of Gedde, although he is assumed to have been a glazier. In the National Museum in Copenhagen is a glazier's book of 1670 with leaves of thin beech wood on which similar leading patterns are incised. But, as its title makes clear, Gedde's book was intended to have a wider application. It is important as one of the earliest English design manuals.

Geeraerts, Marcus Geeraerts was born in Bruges in about 1520, the son of a painter. He became a member of the guild of painters in Bruges in 1558, but in 1568 he moved to London. In 1577 he moved to Antwerp, where he remained until 1586. He seems to have died in London before 1604. In Bruges, Geeraerts supplied designs for stained glass and designed illustrations for the influential 1567 edition of Aesop. During his Antwerp period Geeraerts published oval STRAPWORK GROTESQUES containing the Labours of Hercules (twelve plates), a series of variously shaped panels of grotesque ornament (eight plates), a suite of oval scenes of the Passion with grotesque borders (fourteen plates) and further similar suites representing the continents and the elements. These prints of ornament are all of the highest quality and comparable to works by DELAUNE. Geeraerts also published prints of birds, butterflies and animals, and designed illustrations for Holinshed's *Chronicles* (1577).

Gelys, Meinert Gelys published *Grateske*, aimed at goldsmiths, cabinetmakers and other craftsmen. It comprises sinister mask-like GROTESQUE motifs formed of elongated black scrolls, some with landscapes below, others with birds and insects about them. They are presumed to have been published in the Netherlands in about 1620, and are closely related to contemporary AURICULAR grotesques.

Geminus, Thomas Probably born in Lys-le-Lannoy near Lille, Geminus was in England from about 1540. His *Compendiosa totius Anatomie delineatio* (London, 1545, reprinted 1552, 1557 and 1559) had a title-page which employed the new STRAPWORK GROTESQUE style associated with Cornelis FLORIS. It was dedicated to Henry VIII. There followed *Morysse and Damashin renewed and encreased Very profitable for Goldsmythes and Embroderars* (London, 1548; thirty plates of delicate scrolled MORESQUES), the earliest pattern-book of designs produced in England. The

only known full copy of this work was discovered early in this century in the possession of working goldsmiths in Westphalia. In 1556 Geminus published *Tectonicon*, a work on mensuration. Before 1570 he was in contact with the geographer Ortelius.

Gensler, Johann Martin (1811–81) One of a family of Hamburg painters, Gensler was also active as a designer, with a passionate interest in GOTHIC. He designed Gothic furniture and stained glass, the Gothic silver-gilt Lukas-Pokal of the Hamburg Society of Artists (1851–7), a glass cup (1868) and an elaborate casket to contain Bismarck's honorary citizenship of Hamburg (1871) made by the horn furniture manufacturer Heinrich Rampendahl (1822–91).

Gentile, Antonio (1519–1609) Born in Faenza, the son of a goldsmith, Gentile was himself active as a goldsmith in Rome from 1550. He was appointed warden of the papal mint in 1584 and frequently worked for the papal court. In 1581 he designed and made a torchère for the Chapel of the Sacrament in St Peter's, commissioned by Pope Gregory XIII, and an altar cross and candlesticks for St Peter's, commissioned by Cardinal Alessandro Farnese. In 1582 Gentile published a full-size engraving of the design of the silver and crystal cross. Parts of this were illustrated by CHAMBERS in his *Treatise on Civil Architecture* (1759), and used on a clock by Matthew Boulton of 1771 to 1772, and on a Wedgwood VASE of about 1780.

Gentilhâtre, Jacques Born in 1578 at Sainte-Menchauld in north-east France, Gentilhâtre, a master mason, probably spent a period in the DUCERCEAU family workshop, based at Verneuil-sur-Oise, near Senlis. He may also have worked for Henri IV's architect, Rémy Collin, at Fontainebleau from about

1601 to 1609. A sketch-book by Gentil-hâtre bearing dates up to 1623, in the London R.I.B.A. Drawings Collection, is a remarkable document of provincial French late-MANNERIST design, including organ-cases, cartouches, and chimneypieces.

Gentzsch, Andreas In 1567 Gentzsch published in Augsburg his *Spitzen büchle* (twelve plates), consisting of charming panels of light STRAPWORK GROTESQUE ornament incorporating fruit, flowers, etc. Gentzsch later engraved plates designed by Matthias BEYTLER.

Gerhard, Hubert Probably born in Amsterdam in about 1550, Gerhard trained as a sculptor in Italy, possibly in Florence and Venice. In 1581 he moved to Augsburg to work for the Fugger banking family. In about 1584 he was appointed sculptor to Duke Wilhelm V of Bavaria. From 1590 he lived in Munich and from 1602 to 1613 in Innsbruck, although he also executed works in Prague (1604) and Brussels (1607). Gerhard designed some fine church metalwork, including candelabra for the St Michaelskirche in Munich. Hans KRUMPER was probably his pupil. Gerhard died in about 1622.

Germain, Pierre Perhaps a relation of the great ROCOCO goldsmith Thomas Germain (1673–1748), Pierre Germain was in Rome in 1730. In Paris in 1736 he entered the Louvre workshop of the goldsmith Nicolas Besnier and on Besnier's retirement in 1737 served under his son-in-law, J.-J. Roettiers, until in 1744 Germain had his own workshop in the Louvre. He died in Paris in 1783. In *Elements d'orfèvrerie* (1748; 100 plates) Germain presented fine designs for all aspects of ecclesiastical and secular silverware in a subdued but accomplished rococo style derived from MEISSONIER. *Elements* also included

seven designs by Roettiers for elaborate pieces under execution for the Dauphin; these incorporate figures but are otherwise close in style to Germain. Germain also published a *Livre d'Ornemens* (1751; ten plates), with rococo friezes, cartouches and lights.

Gewerbehalle (1863–97) Published from Stuttgart, this well-illustrated design magazine was subtitled *Organ für den Fortschritt in allen Zweigen der Kunst-Industrie*; its editors were Wilhelm Bäumer, professor of architecture at the Stuttgart Polytechnic, and the designer Julius Schnorr. Its first issue included the cabinet designed for the PARIS 1855 EXHIBITION by SEMPER, and a GOTHIC clock designed by Peter HERWEGEN. Later designs included glass by HANSEN for Lobmeyr (1868), Alfred Normand's Pompeian house for Prince Napoleon (1869), a sideboard by E. J. TARVER (1871) and another by TALBERT for Gillows (1872). From 1877 a larger format was accompanied by some colour. Towards the end, historic examples dominated the illustrations. An English edition, *The Workshop*, was issued from 1868 to 1872.

Gherardi, Antonio (1638–1702) Born in Rieti, Gherardi was trained as a painter in Rome by P. F. Mola and on his death in 1666 by P. Berettini. He was later active in Rome as engraver, painter and architect. He designed two large silver VASES to be made by Tomasso Spagna for the Marchese Francesco Ruspoli. The vigorous design with two dryad supporters shows him a master of the late-BAROQUE style; it is dated 1684. In 1682 Gherardi had designed illustrations for Elpidio Benedetti's encomium of Louis XIV, published in Lyon, *Le Glorie della Virtù*.

Ghiberti, Lorenzo Born in Florence in about 1380, Ghiberti became a goldsmith there in 1406 and also a member of the painters' guild in 1423. In 1402 he had won the competition to design and make a bronze door (1403–24) for the Baptistery, and in 1404 had designed stained glass for the cathedral. Ghiberti designed more glass for the cathedral from 1434 to 1443, although in 1434 he lost one commission to the sculptor Donatello. He also designed mitres and morses for the popes Martin V (1368–1431) and Eugenius IV (1383–1447), and a frame for Fra Angelico's Linaiuoli Madonna (1433). Ghiberti died in 1455.

Giancarli, Polifilo Giancarli, a Venetian, designed two suites of bold scrolling ACANTHUS ornament of a BAROQUE character, peopled by birds, beasts, satyrs, putti, etc., which were engraved by the Venetian painter and engraver Odoardo Fialetti (1573–1638). *Disegni Varii* (ten plates) consists of upright panels; it was later reprinted in Paris. The second suite comprises of thirteen friezes. It was reprinted in Rome, in 1628, and then dedicated to the antiquary and connoisseur Cassiano del Pozzo. The friezes were also reissued in Paris in 1646, and, in a reduced format, in Amsterdam in 1636, and in London in 1672, by John OVERTON.

Giani, Felice (1758–1823) Born near Genoa, Giani was a pupil of Carlo Antonio Bianchi and Antonio Galli Bibiena in Pavia, then from 1778 of Domenico Pedrini (1728–1800) and Ubaldo Gandolfi (1728–81) in Bologna. In 1780 he went to Rome where he worked under the painters Pompeo Batoni (1708–87) and Christoph Unterberger (1732–98) and the architect Giovanni Antolini (1754–1842). In 1788 Giani executed wax paintings for a mirror room for Catherine II of Russia, working for Unterberger. In 1792 he designed illustrations for Conte Veri's *Notti Romane al Sepolcro dei Scipioni.* From 1793 Giani worked in Faenza, where he executed decorations in many houses, including the Palazzo Laderchi. Giani also worked in Forlì, Ravenna and Bologna, and from about 1800 to 1809 in Paris for Napoleon, in the Tuileries and elsewhere. Later he worked in Venice, Bologna and Rome, where he died. Giani enjoyed a wide contemporary reputation as a painter but also was possessed of brilliant facility as a draughtsman and designed accomplished and elegant NEO-CLASSICAL furniture and interiors.

Giannini, Orlando (1861–1928) Born in Cincinnati, Ohio, Giannini was active as a sculptor from 1878. He was manager of the Cincinnati Art Pottery Company from 1883 to 1885 when he moved to New York. From 1890 he was active as a designer in Chicago where in 1899 he formed the firm of Giannini & Hilgart, glass stainers, his partner Fritz Hilgart (1869–1942) providing technical expertise. Giannini designed glass mosaics, stained glass, book covers and posters. His firm supplied stained glass to Frank Lloyd WRIGHT.

Giardini, Giovanni (1646–1721) Born at Forlì in 1646 Giardini moved as a child to Rome, where he was apprenticed to the silversmith Marco Gamberucci from 1665 to 1668. In 1675 he became a master and set up a company with Gamberucci and Marco Ciucci to run the former's workshop. In 1680 Giardini and his brother Alessandro took over the enterprise. He repeatedly held office in the Congregazione (guild) of goldsmiths and silversmiths in Rome and in 1698 was appointed bronze-founder to the papal court, for which he did much work from 1700. In 1712 Giardini engaged the engraver Massimiliano Limpach of Prague to engrave 100 of his designs. These were published in Rome in 1714 as *Disegni Diversi*, dedicated to Pope Clement XI; the original drawings by Giardini are in Berlin. The inventory of his effects made after his death in 1721 reveals that Giardini's possessions included prints by Stefano DELLA BELLA and DÜRER as well as a relief by FOGGINI. A second edition of his *Disegni* was published in Rome in 1750 under the title *Promptuarium artis argentariae*. The *Disegni* display powerful and accomplished BAROQUE designs for ecclesiastical metalwork, VASES, candelabra and ornaments. Three designs for massive console tables must have had a direct influence on William KENT, who was in Rome in 1714 when the *Disegni* were first published. Although the influence of Jean LE PAUTRE is apparent Giardini's decorative language is basically that of BERNINI and Borromini (1599–1667) and he may thus be seen as one of the final and most accomplished practitioners of the Roman baroque tradition. Most of his works as a silversmith have disappeared, but those that survive show the same combination of richness and strength as revealed by his designs.

Gibbs, James (1682–1754) The son of an Aberdeen merchant, Gibbs was a Catholic and entered the novitiate in Rome in 1703. But he soon turned to architecture, becoming a pupil of Carlo FONTANA. Gibbs returned to England in 1709, and thenceforward had a prolific architectural career, presenting himself as an Italian, known as 'Signor Gibbi' (Kent was also known as 'Signior'). In 1712 he designed a pedimented frontispiece to Flamsteed's *Historia Caelestis*. His *A Book of Architecture* (1728, second edition 1739) included designs for ceilings, doorways, buffet-niches, tables, pedestals, fireplaces, garden seats, cartouches and urns in an accomplished Roman BAROQUE manner. One of the urns had been executed by

Andries Carpentière for the garden at Wimpole Hall. *Thirty Three Shields & Compartments . . . from the Designs of that Curious Architect Mr James Gibbs* (1731; eleven plates) contains baroque scrolled cartouches decorated with masks and foliage. Gibbs designed chandeliers, pulpits etc. for his churches, and also domestic furniture, including a cabinet and bookcases for Wimpole Hall (1719), mirrors for Fairlawne, Kent (1721–2), and for the Duchess of Norfolk's house in Arlington Street, London (about 1736), console tables, clock-cases and sconces. Gibbs owned designs by Jean I BERAIN, Daniel MAROT and PINEAU. He was probably in contact with BRUNETTI.

Gibbs, John A sculptor and architect, Gibbs published a number of pattern-books mainly in the GOTHIC style. The first, *A Series of Designs for Gothic Monuments* (London, 1852), was written while Gibbs was in Wigan and dedicated to Hon. Colin Lindsay. The subscribers included Skidmores and Mintons. It was followed by *Designs for Gothic Ornaments and Furniture* (London, 1854), written in Manchester and dedicated to Lord Lindsay. The designs include furniture and metalwork, all in a competent but uninspired Gothic. His preface, originally a lecture given in Liverpool in 1854, is passionately pro-Gothic but anti-gargoyles and GROTESQUES. He later moved to Oxford, designing Banbury cross (1859) and a number of houses in North Oxford. His later books, *Domestic Architecture and Ornament in Detail* (Oxford, 1868) and *Studies for Art Designers and Manufacturers* (Oxford, 1869), the latter dedicated to George Godwin, editor of the 'BUILDER', are fine large-scale designs for architectural details, ironwork, formalized foliage and polychrome tiles. The style is a coarse Reformed Gothic.

Gill, Arthur Eric Rowton (1882–1940) Born in Brighton, the son of a dissenting minister, Eric Gill studied at Chichester Art School. Then from 1899 to 1903 he was in the London office of the architect W. D. Caröe (1857–1938). While there he studied lettering on stone at the Central School of Arts & Crafts, where the example of Edward Johnston changed his life. From 1902 he shared Johnston's rooms in Lincoln's Inn. From 1904 Gill supported himself as a letter-cutter and in the same year he was commissioned by Count Kessler to design title-pages for the Cranach Press. Gill was subsequently a prolific illustrator not only for Kessler but also for Robert Gibbings's Golden Cockerel Press, for which he designed *Troilus and Criseyde* (1927), *The Canterbury Tales* (1928–31) and *The Four Gospels* (1931). In 1918 he did illustrations for *Woodwork* by A. Romney Green (1872–1945). From 1925 Gill discussed with Stanley MORISON (1889–1967) the possible designing of typefaces for the Monotype Corporation. The results were Gill's Perpetua and Felicity, Roman and Italic types (1925–9) and Gill Sans (1928), a sans-serif type adopted by the L.N.E.R. railway as its typeface in 1929. Gill, a fervent Catholic from 1913, felt passionately about the sacredness of craftsmanship. He was also active as a sculptor and designed book-plates, silver and emblems for postage stamps (1937).

Gillot, Claude (1673–1722) Born in Langres, the son of a painter and embroiderer, Gillot was taught painting and engraving in Paris by the history painter Jean-Baptiste Corneille (1649–95). After the death of Corneille Gillot set up his own studio, where WATTEAU was his pupil from about 1705 to 1708, followed by Lancret. Gillot was admitted to the Académie in 1710 and became Peintre du Roi in 1716. In 1712 Cronström predicted a brilliant career for him as the exponent of a new taste in ornament. Gillot was active as a book illustrator and illustrations account for many of the 225 designs he engraved himself and the 275 engraved by others. The first category also includes six *Nouveaux Desseins d'Arquebuseries*, published by François Chereau in about 1720, ornament for guns in a brilliant light scrolled and foliate manner. Gillot also partly engraved a set of six *Portières*, which were completed after his death by C.-N. CoCHIN and published by Jacques-Gabriel HUQUIER in 1737; one, Neptune, was adapted in reverse by George BICKHAM as a frontispiece. Among the 275 prints after Gillot are two designs for harpsichord lids engraved before 1722 by the amateur Comte de CAYLUS (1692–1765), which were finished by Crepy and published in about 1731, probably at the same time as a similar design by Watteau. Huquier owned over 300 designs for ornament by Gillot and engraved a twelve-plate *Livre d'ornaments, de trophées, culs de lampe, et devises* (1732), which were copied in Augsburg by Johann Georg MERZ, a ten-plate *Deuxième Livre* and, after 1759, a twelve-plate *Nouveau livre de principes d'ornements*. Gillot also designed metalwork, fabrics and tapestries, including a suite of Italian comedy subjects in light GROTESQUE frameworks with the arms of Joseph Bonnier de la Mosson, woven at Beauvais in about 1719. Gillot's style, strongly influenced by AUDRAN, and closely related to that of OPPENORD, represents the initiation of the ROCOCO spirit in ornament.

Gilly, Friedrich (1772–1800) Son of the architect, David Gilly (1748–1808), Friedrich Gilly studied architecture under his father, and from 1788 at the Berlin Academy. His intensely NEOCLASSICAL project for a monument to

Frederick the Great of 1796 was a revelation to the young SCHINKEL, who was also deeply impressed by Gilly's studies of the GOTHIC Schloss Marienburg, of which Gilly published a print in 1797. From 1798 Gilly taught at the Academy. Schinkel was his pupil and took over his uncompleted projects on Gilly's death in 1800. Gilly's advanced neo-classical designs for furniture and interiors were the direct inspiration for Schinkel's early designs.

Gimignani, Giacinto (1611–1681) Gimignani, a pupil of Pietro da CORTONA, was active as a painter and engraver in Rome. In 1653 he designed a tapestry for the Florentine factory depicting the entry of the Grand Duchess Joanna d'Austria to Florence. His son Lodovico Gimignani (1643–97) designed some of the silver plates presented by the heirs of Cardinal Lazzaro Pallavicini to the Grand Duke of Tuscany, others of which were designed by Carlo MARATTI.

Gimson, Ernest (1864–1919) Born in Leicester, the son of a self-made industrialist, Gimson was in 1881 articled to the local architect Isaac Barradale. He also attended the Leicester School of Art, and in 1885 won a national prize with furniture designs. In 1884 he met William MORRIS and in 1886, on Morris's recommendation, entered the office of J. P. SEDDING, situated next to Morris & Co.'s showrooms. There he met Ernest Barnsley (1863–1926) and through him came to know his brother Sidney Barnsley (1865–1926), LETHABY, and Robert Weir SCHULTZ, all of whom were in Richard Norman SHAW's office. In 1888 Gimson left Sedding's office, and travelled and studied. In 1890 he learned chair-turning under Philip Clissett, a chair bodger of Herefordshire who had supplied rush-seated ladder-back chairs to the ART-WORK-ERS' GUILD in 1888, and about the same date studied plasterwork with the London firm of Whitcombe & Priestley. He published an essay on plasterwork in *Plain Handicrafts* (1892), edited by A. H. MACKMURDO. In 1890 he showed plasterwork and furniture at the ARTS & CRAFTS EXHIBITION and the same year, with Lethaby, Mervyn Macartney, Reginald Blomfield and Sidney Barnsley, founded Kenton & Co., to supply 'furniture of good design and good workmanship'. The designs were made up by professional cabinet-makers. Gimson's designs used plain, mainly 17th-century forms, decorated with chamfering and geometrical or floral inlay influenced by George JACK. The firm was disbanded in 1892. In 1893, with the Barnsley brothers, Gimson moved to the Cotswolds, renting Pinbury Park from Lord Bathurst. From 1894 they produced furniture, mainly designed and made by Sidney Barnsley. Gimson was principally interested in plasterwork; the plaster expert G. P. Bankart was a friend. From 1901 Gimson returned to furniture design, and in that year a Dutch cabinet-maker, Peter van der Waals (1870–1937), was hired from London by Gimson and Ernest Barnsley, who in 1902 moved their enterprise to Sapperton, setting up workshops in Daneway House. In 1903 'MODERNE STIL' illustrated their work. The partnership broke down in about 1905 and Gimson continued the business on his own. It was successful, attracting a wealthy clientele; some 800 furniture designs by Gimson survive. From about 1902 Gimson also designed iron sconces, firedogs, hinges, etc., in a 17th-century style. His furniture designs range from cottagey adaptations of 17th-century forms to some stark and original inventions. Inlay, chamfering and dovetails were his standard ornaments; his style seems to have been mainly formed in the 1880s. In 1907 Gimson mounted a large exhibition of his furniture at the London store Debenham & Freebody's, and in 1916 he designed two room settings for the Arts & Crafts Exhibition. Gimson was aware that the DEUTSCHE WERKBUND was partly based on his 'Craft Eden', but in 1916 he rejected Lethaby's invitation to join the DESIGN AND INDUSTRIES ASSOCIATION on the basis that he did not wish to design for machinery. After Gimson's death Waals continued his business in Chalford; the workshops finally ended activity in 1938.

Godwin, Edward William (1833–86) Born in Bristol, the son of a currier, Godwin was trained by the local architect William Armstrong and set up as an architect in Bristol in 1854. In 1857 he built a church in Donegal, but his first conspicuous success was in winning the 1861 Northampton Town Hall competition, with a Reformed GOTHIC design influenced by John RUSKIN. Godwin designed Gothic furniture for Northampton. In 1862 he moved to a new house in Bristol which he furnished with Japanese prints, Persian rugs and antique furniture. In 1864 Godwin won the competition for Congleton Town Hall and in the same year entered a partnership with Henry Crisp which lasted until 1871. Godwin opened a London office in 1865. In 1866 he assisted BURGES on his designs for the Law Court competition; the two had been firm friends since Godwin introduced himself to Burges in 1858. In 1867 they visited Ireland together and Godwin began to design Dromore Castle for the Earl of Limerick. Also in 1867 Godwin designed for his own use furniture of ebonized deal decorated with gilt lines, but with 'no mouldings, no ornamental work and no carving', its effect dependent on the 'grouping of solid and void'. Godwin set up his own Art Furniture Company, but it failed and he subsequently designed furniture for Gillows, Green & King, and W. A. Smee. In the 'FURNITURE GAZETTE' (1877) he was listed as a designer. He was for a while under contract to the cabinetmakers Collinson & Lock at £450 a year; he designed their shop-front in 1873. In about 1868 Godwin designed a small square coffee-table for William Watt, a light ebonized piece based on Egyptian prototypes; it was widely plagiarized. William Watt later issued a catalogue, *Art Furniture Designed by Edward W. Godwin F.S.A.* (1877; twenty plates), with a letter from Godwin as its introduction, in which he lays stress on the importance of refined proportions. The majority of designs in *Art Furniture* are in the Anglo-Japanese style of which Godwin was the main pioneer and protagonist, using details of wood construction borrowed from Hokusai prints such as he had illustrated in 'BUILDING NEWS' (1875). Other pieces are in the Old English and Jacobean styles but are much lighter and more elegant than TALBERT's designs in this manner. *Art Furniture* also contains Gothic church furniture, stained glass, and wallpapers printed by Jeffrey & Co. of Islington, for whom Godwin had worked since 1866 when Metford Warner joined the firm. *Art Furniture* seems to have been highly successful; EDIS (1881) included a chair borrowed from Godwin on his frontispiece. Godwin was a close friend of Whistler. In 1874 he designed decor for Whistler's exhibition and in 1877 Whistler's White House in Tite Street. Whistler decorated some of Godwin's furniture shown by William Watt at the PARIS 1878 EXHIBITION. Many of Godwin's furniture designs borrowed from Greek prototypes, for instance an armchair illustrated in *Building News* (1885). However Godwin's later furniture, including 'The Shakspere Dining-Room Set' (*Building News*, 1881), seems to have been mainly Jacobethan in style.

Godwin was an extremely prolific theatre designer, a dress reformer, and had an extensive journalistic output. In 1880 he published *Artistic Conservatories* with Maurice ADAMS. Godwin's importance as a design reformer was recognized by MUTHESIUS among many others. It has probably been exaggerated in recent years.

Goerke, Gustav Born in Hanover in 1881, Goerke studied at the Kunstgewerbeschule there and subsequently in that of Berlin, where he was a pupil of Otto ECKMANN. He designed interiors, furniture and fittings in a style strongly influenced by Vienna, and Josef HOFFMANN in particular, and also by MACKINTOSH. He worked mainly in middle-class apartment blocks in Berlin and Breslau, but also decorated a number of villas in that area. His work was noticed in magazines such as 'Die KUNST' (1904), 'DEUTSCHE KUNST UND DEKORATION' (1910, 1913) and 'INNEN-DEKORATION' (1917).

Goldfinger, Ernö Born in Budapest in 1902, the son of a doctor, Goldfinger moved to Paris in 1920 and from 1923 studied architecture at the École des Beaux-Arts. In 1924 with twelve others he set up the Atelier Perret to work under the architect Auguste Perret (1874–1954). Goldfinger practised as an architect with Andre Sive from 1924 to 1929. In 1926 he designed MODERN furniture for M. Coutrot in Paris and the Helena Rubinstein Shop in Grafton Street, London, including tubular-steel furniture. Goldfinger used bakelized paper and pressed plywood for chair seats and backs; his furniture was described in 'ART ET DÉCORATION' (1930). Goldfinger was a French delegate to CONGRÈS INTERNATIONAUX D'ARCHITECTURE MODERNE but in 1934 he moved to London, where he lived from 1935 in High Point and then

from 1939 in a Modern house of his own design in Willow Road, Hampstead. In 1936 he designed a toyshop and toys for Paul and Marjorie Abbatt, and in 1938 unit furniture for Easiwork. His *British Furniture of To-day* (1951) illustrates his own designs alongside those of BREUER, R. D. Russell, RACE, Robin DAY and others.

Gold und Silber (1948–present) This glossy German trade magazine for goldsmiths, silversmiths and jewellers is full of information and illustrations on design in this field.

Gomm, William Born in about 1698, the son of a yeoman farmer of Chinnor in Oxfordshire, Gomm completed his apprenticeship as a cabinet-maker in London in 1720. In 1736 he had premises in Clerkenwell near those of the well-known cabinet-maker Giles Grendey (1693–1780); his journeymen included the great German cabinet-maker Abraham Roentgen (1711–93). In 1764 Gomm supplied furniture to Lord Leigh for Stoneleigh Abbey. From the 1750s he was in partnership with his son Richard, who was a subscriber to CHIPPENDALE's *Director* (1754), and in 1776 went bankrupt. William Gomm was a competent designer of furniture in the Chippendale style. At the Winterthur Museum are designs for the furnishing of a drawing-room, chairs, tables, cabinets, beds, bookcases and commodes, dated 1761. Two designs for pier glasses are copied from LOCK and COPLAND (1752). Gomm died in 1780.

Gondoin, Jacques (1737–1818) Born at Saint-Ouen-sur-Seine, the son of a gardener, Gondoin studied architecture under J.-F. BLONDEL. He was from 1759 to 1763 in Rome, where he knew PIRANESI. Before returning to Paris in 1766 he also visited England and Holland. His major architectural work, the

École de Chirurgie (1769–75), was one of the great Parisian monuments of advanced NEO-CLASSICISM. In 1769, on the death of PEYROTTE, Gondoin was appointed Dessinateur du Mobilier de la Couronne, a post he held until 1784. He was elected to the Academy in 1774 and visited Italy in 1775. After the revolution Gondoin posed as a gardener at his own country house, but from 1795 he was again active as an architect. As royal furniture designer Gondoin specialized in carved furniture, particularly in beds and chairs. He was highly paid and provided not only detailed drawings but also models in wood and wax. Gondoin designed chair covers, and in 1769 spent a month in Lyon designing silks. In 1769 he designed gueridons made for the Galerie des Glaces at Versailles by the carver Toussaint Foliot. In view of his evidently key role in the development of French neo-classical furniture tantalizingly little is known about the detail of Gondoin's designing activity.

Gooden, Robert Yorke Born in Over Compton, Dorset, in 1909, Gooden graduated as an architect from the Architectural Association School in London in 1932. He then worked briefly as a furniture designer for Gordon RUSSELL in Broadway, and then started practice as a designer and architect in Oxford. In 1934 he designed pressed glass for Chance Bros. of Birmingham. In 1948 Gooden was appointed professor of jewellery, silversmithing and industrial glass at the Royal College of Art (see SCHOOL OF DESIGN); he retired in 1974. Gooden designed much presentation silver such as a box made by Aspreys given by the Royal SOCIETY OF ARTS to Princess Elizabeth in 1948, a tea service with marine subjects made by Leslie Durbin for the royal pavilion at the London 1951 Festival of Britain (see LONDON EXHIBITIONS), and in 1953 the Queen's Cup made by Wakely & Wheeler for the Goldsmiths' Company. In 1960 Gooden designed glasses made by Thomas Webb of Stourbridge for use in British embassies.

Good Furniture (1913–32) Published in Grand Rapids, Michigan, the centre of the American furniture industry, this magazine placed a revealing emphasis on antique and reproduction furniture, but also gave good coverage to recent developments in America, England and France. The title changed in 1929 to *Good Furniture and Decoration*, and finally, in 1932, to *Interior Architecture and Decoration*.

Goodridge, Henry Edmund (1797–1864) The son of a successful Bath builder, Goodridge was taught architecture by John Lowder and practised in Bath from the 1820s. He built Lansdown Tower for William BECKFORD from 1824 to 1827, employing a picturesque NEO-CLASSICAL style, and later designed for it furniture in a remarkable early eclectic RENAISSANCE revival style. In 1847 he designed a library at Hamilton Palace for Beckford's son-in-law, the Duke of Hamilton, with coloured decorations executed by Sang.

Gossaert, Jan, called Mabuse Born in about 1480 at Mauberge in Hainault, Gossaert worked as a painter in Antwerp from 1503 to 1507. In 1508 he went to Rome by way of Verona and Florence in the entourage of Philip of Burgundy (1465–1524), who was both humanist and dilettante, having dabbled in painting and goldsmith's work. In Rome Gossaert drew antique statues for Philip and imbibed the RENAISSANCE language of ornament. After his return from Rome in 1509 he was mainly resident at Middelburg, but also lived at

Mechlin, Brussels, Bruges and Utrecht, in the service of great lords. In 1516 he designed a triumphal chariot for the obsequies of Ferdinand of Spain in Brussels. Gossaert's paintings, influenced by DÜRER and Jacopo de' Barbari, used both flamboyant GOTHIC ornament and Renaissance GROTESQUES, and sometimes a combination of both. Designs for a monstrance in the late-Gothic style and for a purse cover and a mirror employing a mannered fusion of late-Gothic and Renaissance forms suggest that Gossaert may have specialized as a designer of goldsmiths' work. As a designer he was also responsible for stained glass and in 1526 for the magnificent Renaissance tomb of Queen Isabella of Denmark. In 1527 Gossaert travelled with Lucas van LEYDEN. He died in 1532.

Gothic The Gothic style of architecture, which first came to fruition at the Abbey of Saint-Denis in about 1140, affected all aspects of design and ornament. Its characteristic forms, the pointed arch, geometric tracery and columnar and ribbed construction, were all used on the decoration of small artefacts from metalwork to floor tiles. The other most prominent ingredients of Gothic ornament were natural forms, especially foliage. In the 19th century, thanks to the writings of RUSKIN and his followers, the still potent idea became current that advances in Gothic design were the product of craftsmen. Certainly some Gothic craftsmen possessed skill as designers but architects seem to have played the leading role; the sketch-book of VILLARD D'HONNECOURT is a unique document of this activity. Painters were also active as designers, particularly of tapestry and stained glass; instances are BONDOL, VULCOP and SPICRE. Gothic printed designs and ornament of the late 15th century attest the growing importance of designers

trained as goldsmiths and engravers, such as Master WꝮ, SCHONGAUER and OLMÜTZ. From the 15th century, RENAISSANCE critics saw the Gothic style as an ugly creation of the German and Gothic barbarians who had destroyed the Roman Empire. The term Gothic became current from the early 17th century. Already in about 1600 there was a minor MANNERIST Gothic Revival in Northern Europe: examples include the adaptation of a Master WꝮ monstrance design by Jacob MÜLLER in 1591 and a Gothic interior of 1606 by Hans and Paul VREDEMAN DE VRIES. In England, in particular, antiquarian interest in Gothic had a long tradition, founded on such works as the *Monasticon Anglicanum* (1655–73) by Sir William Dugdale (1605–86) with illustrations by Wenceslas Hollar (1607–77). From the early 18th century many Gothic Revival buildings were erected in England, the style being particularly popular in gardens. William KENT designed Gothic furniture for York Cathedral and Batty LANGLEY codified Gothic into an equivalent of the Roman ORDERS. The use of Gothic by such ROCOCO designers as CHIPPENDALE and HALFPENNY and WALPOLE's description of Strawberry Hill as a 'small capricious house' has encouraged a view of mid-18th-century Gothic as a frivolous diversion. However, even at Strawberry Hill, particularly in the work of James Essex (1722–84), an increasingly archaeological approach is evident. The cult of the sublime and the picturesque often took Gothic form, most spectacularly in the case of BECKFORD's Fonthill. The novels of Sir Walter Scott (1771–1832) encouraged the romantic taste for Gothic and RICKMAN provided a scholarly analysis of the style. Gothic designers such as PORDEN, A. C. PUGIN, COTTINGHAM and BRIDGENS established Gothic as a stock manner handled with fluency, and, in the case of Cottingham, force. In the mid-1830s A. W. N. PUGIN developed a faith in Gothic as the only Christian style, preaching this belief with great vehemence. Pugin's stress on honesty was to be echoed by Ruskin and by the ECCLESIOLOGICAL SOCIETY, the leading mid-19th-century advocates of Gothic in England. The structural toughness of some of Pugin's furniture and the vivid polychromy of his flat patterns anticipate the uncompromising severity of form and inventive ornament of much High Victorian Gothic. The term 'Reformed Gothic' has been coined to describe the style of STREET, William BUTTERFIELD, BURGES, SEDDON and their contemporaries, 'Reformed' in the sense that they purged Gothic of the superficiality and dishonesty of early 19th-century work and 'Re-formed' in that, often basing themselves on French 13th-century models, they invented new forms appropriate to the needs of the 19th century. Reformed Gothic was rejected by most young architects and designers in about 1870; it had never been popular with the public. Thenceforward English Gothic design tended towards refinement rather than vigour, enjoying a prolonged afterlife in the work of COMPER and his followers. However the vision of Gothic propagated by Ruskin and William MORRIS had a pervasive influence on Arts & Crafts designers, even though they tended to abandon the recognizable details of the style. On the continent the Gothic Revival tended at first to follow developments in England. By about 1850, however, architects and designers such as VIOLLET-LE-DUC and UNGEWITTER possessed an archaeological expertise fully equal to their English contemporaries. With exceptions, continental Gothic of the 19th century tends to lack the force and originality of English work, although the influence of Pugin and Reformed Gothic seems to be reflected in the work of BERLAGE and MOHRMANN in the 1890s.

Goulden, Jean (1878–1947) Born at Charpentry, Meuse, of a wealthy Alsatian landed family, Goulden trained and practised as a doctor. After the First World War he was active as a patron, and designed and made very tough ART DÉCO geometric boxes of silver and enamel. He also designed lacquer commodes made by Jean DUNAND, which were shown at the Galerie Georges Petit in 1925. Goulden in that year married the daughter of SCHMIED, another of the group who exhibited at the Galerie Georges Petit. In 1928 Goulden moved his workshop from Paris to Reims.

Goya y Lucientes, Francesco de (1746–1828) Born in Saragossa, the painter Goya visited Madrid in 1763 and 1766 and Italy from 1770 to 1771. He then returned to Madrid to work under Francesco BAYEU, whose sister Josefa he married in 1773. Thanks to Bayeu's influence Goya was subsequently commissioned by Mengs to design tapestries for the royal manufactory of Santa Barbara. His cartoons, thirty from 1776 to 1780, eleven from 1786 to 1788, and five in 1791, depict scenes of popular life, hunting, games etc. whose surface cheerfulness is pervaded by sinister and tragic overtones.

Göz, Gottfried Bernhard (1708–1774) Born at Wehlerad in Moravia, Göz was a pupil of Johann Georg BERGMÜLLER (1688–1762), director of the Augsburg Academy from 1730. Göz was active as engraver, miniaturist, and painter, executing frescoes on numerous houses and churches in Augsburg and South Germany in a ROCOCO version of the Italian BAROQUE style of virtuoso PERSPECTIVE illusionism called quadratura. Göz was responsible for a number of book illustrations, and for at least twenty suites of rococo ornament (from four to twenty plates each); they include many with allegorical figures, such as the seasons, or the virtues and vices, in rococo frameworks, and designs for altars, doors and fountains. Göz's rococo is on occasion conspicuously wild and flamelike, and always charged with energy. A suite of the senses comprises sparkling rococo compositions set around an ear, a hand, a nose, a mouth and an eye! Some of his prints were published in Augsburg by HERTEL or by Göz himself; others were published by Wagner in Venice.

Graf, Urs Born in Solothurn, the son of a goldsmith, Graf worked at first with his father and then completed his training in Basel, which remained his base although he spent periods in Strasbourg and accompanied various German campaigns into Italy as a mercenary. He designed stained glass and also published nine designs for ornament for dagger and sword sheaths, one, dated 1512, with RENAISSANCE candelabra decoration, others incorporating nude women, scrolling GOTHIC foliage, and depictions of mercenaries. Graf also designed book illustrations, title-pages, and borders, working in a late Gothic style up to about 1510 and thenceforward using the Renaissance vocabulary of ornament. He died in Basel in about 1527, a popular but stormy character.

Graff, Karl Ludwig Theodor (1844–1906) Born in Grabow in Mecklenburg-Schwerin, Graff studied architecture in Hanover and Berlin. At first he was mainly active as a GOTHIC church architect and restorer, but later, in Vienna, he went over to the RENAISSANCE style, working under SEMPER at the Opera and museums. Graff supplied designs for objects shown at the VIENNA 1873 EXHIBITION, including bronzes by Dziedzinsky & Hanusch of Vienna, and in 1874 was appointed Director of the new school of applied arts at Dresden, where he died.

Graffico, Camillo Graffico was active as an engraver and publisher in Rome from about 1589 to 1595. He was born in Friuli. In 1591 he published a series (eight plates) of medallion heads of Sultans of Turkey in crude and heavy STRAPWORK cartouches. He also issued a suite of Christian kings, similarly framed.

Grant, Duncan (1885–1978) A Scot, Grant studied painting in London (1902–5) and Paris (1907–9), undergoing direct influence from Matisse and the Fauves. In 1910 he met Roger FRY, for whom he designed the poster of the Second Post-Impressionist Exhibition (1912), and began to paint murals for the Bloomsbury set. In 1912 he began to design and paint furniture, textiles and ceramics for the Omega Workshops, of which he was a codirector, before the opening in 1913. In 1916 he began to live at Charleston in Sussex with Vanessa Bell. After the demise of the Omega Workshops Grant continued to work with Vanessa Bell as decorative designer and painter; in 1930 they won third prize in the 'ARCHITECTURAL REVIEW'S Lord Benbow competition for an interior, in 1925 an exhibition included his needlework designs, from 1931 to about 1938 he designed textiles for Alan Walton, and also in 1931 he designed a poster for Shell. A music room shown at the Lefevre Galleries in 1933 was a *succès d'estime*, and in 1934 he designed dinner and tea services for Foley China and Clarice CLIFF's Bizarre range. In 1935 he designed decorations for the *Queen Mary*, which were rejected by the chairman of Cunards. Grant's graphic designs included Christmas cards, book-plates, book-jackets and illustrations. His style remained consistent: occasional cubist elements, decorative abstraction and flowers, swags, gods, goddesses and putti, usually with no very precise meaning, handled with strong colours, dash and invention. His room decorations, in a provincial BAROQUE manner, were among the most original of the 1930s, swimming very much against the MODERN stream.

Graphis (1944–present) Edited from Zürich by Walter Herdeg this glossy international magazine covers all aspects of graphic design. Offshoots are *Graphis Annual* (1952–present) and *Graphis Posters* (1973–present).

Grasset, Eugène (1841–1917) Born in Lausanne, Grasset studied architecture at the Zurich Polytechnic. After a visit to Egypt in 1869 he went to Paris in 1871, and worked at first as a textile designer. His early studies were much influenced by VIOLLET-LE-DUC. In 1878 he began to design ornamental letters and 1880 decorated *Les Fêtes Chrétiennes* by Abbé Drioux, his ornaments for which were reprinted in 1896. Also in 1880 he designed a studio for his friend, the printer Charles Gillot, who in 1881 commissioned illustrations for the *Histoire des Quatre Fils Aymon*. These appeared in 1883 and the book, a *tour-de-force* of antiquarian expertise reflecting strong Japanese influence, represented a major innovation in book design. In the 1880s Grasset established himself as a protagonist of ART NOUVEAU poster design, and in 1899 was bracketed with MUCHA and Jules CHÉRET as a leader in this field in the 'MAGAZINE OF ART'. Other graphic works included a folio of allegorical drawings, *Iconographie Décorative* (1887), a calendar reflecting the influ-

ence of Kate GREENAWAY, *La Belle Jardinière* (1896), and magazine covers for *Harper's Bazaar* (1889, 1891 and 1892). Grasset also designed stained glass, mostly executed by Félix Gaudin, but including a panel by TIFFANY shown at the opening of BING's Maison de l'Art Nouveau in 1895. Other works were Limoges ceramics, stoneware decorative panels for Emile Müller & Co., wallpapers, bookbindings, tapestries and stamps. At the PARIS 1900 EXHIBITION the celebrated firm of Vever exhibited a large group of highly symbolic jewellery designed by Grasset, and in about 1900 Grasset designed a successful and restrained Art Nouveau typeface for Peignot Frères. He was also a successful teacher, acting as professor of decorative arts at the independent École Normale d'Enseignement du Dessein founded by M. A. Guerin in 1881. His most celebrated pupil was Paul FOLLOT. In 1897 Grasset published *La Plante et ses Applications Ornementales* (seventy-two coloured plates incorporating usages of plant ornament in furniture, wallpapers, stained glass, silver, glass, iron and textiles). A second volume appeared in 1900. Grasset also wrote the introduction to *L'Animal dans la Décoration* by his pupil M. P. Verneuil, which transferred the method of the 1897 book to animals. Grasset's last didactic books were *Méthode de Composition Ornementale* (1905) and *Ouvrages de Ferronerie Moderne* (1906), but as a member of the editorial board for 'ART ET DÉCORATION' (founded 1897) he also published many articles on design topics. In 1901 he was among the founders of the Société des Artistes-Décorateurs, and he was one of the first honorary members of the Vienna Secession, founded in 1897, who also included Walter CRANE. Crane and Grasset have much in common as highly professional pioneers in the improvement of design who emerge as influ· · ' ıl teachers. The first exhibition of Grasset's work was held at the Salon des Cent in 1894. A retrospective exhibition took place in 1906 at the Salon des Artistes-Décorateurs. In 1909 Grasset was a founder member of the Société d'Art Décoratif Français.

Gravelot, Hubert François (1699–1773) Born in Paris, the son of a tailor, Gravelot was trained as a draughtsman and painter under Jean Restout and François BOUCHER. In 1732 he came to London to work for the French publisher Claude Du Bosc. According to Vertue (1741) Gravelot designed for 'Gold & Silver works', and Pye (1745) stated that he designed for joiners and cabinet-makers. He was friendly with the painter Francis Hayman (1708–76), and the elegant ROCOCO furniture seen in some of Hayman's paintings of the 1740s may have been designed by Gravelot. Certainly his decorations for *Heads and Monuments of the Kings* (1736) and his cartouches, begun in 1738, for Birch's *The Heads of Illustrious Persons of Great Britain* (1745–52), are the most exuberant specimens of rococo decoration published in England. Gravelot often worked with George BICKHAM and Bickham borrowed from Gravelot. Thus putti designed by Gravelot for the title-page of *Ceremonies and Religious Customs* (1734) crop up in Bickham's *The Universal Penman* (1743) and later on a state bed and a dressing table in CHIPPENDALE's *Director* (1762). Gravelot compositions were repeatedly used on English porcelain made at Chelsea, Worcester and elsewhere. Gravelot designed some extremely elaborate rococo cartouches for John Pine's *Tapestry Hangings in the House of Lords* (1739). Gravelot ran a drawing-school of his own, and was by 1745 involved in the ST MARTIN'S LANE ACADEMY, which was the seed-bed of rococo in England. He left for France in 1745.

He continued to design book illustrations for publication in London, notably Boccaccio's *Decameron* (1757–61), and was prolific in Paris up to his death. Before 1773 Gravelot designed a NEOCLASSICAL frontispiece for J.-F. BOUCHER.

Gray, Eileen (1878–1976) Born at Enniscorthy, Wexford, Ireland, Eileen Gray came from a wealthy, aristocratic and artistic background. In 1898 she went to study at the Slade School of Art in London, and soon developed an interest in Japanese lacquer. In 1902 she moved to Paris and studied at the Académies Colarossi and Julian, and, later, lacquer with a Japanese craftsman, Sugawara. In 1907 she bought an apartment in Rue Bonaparte, Paris, where she lived until her death. Before the First World War the great couturier and patron Jacques DOUCET bought some of her lacquer furniture, notably a part-abstract part-symbolist screen, Le Destin, dated 1914. After a spell driving ambulances in Paris she spent the war in London with Sugawara. On her return to Paris in 1918 she extended her sphere to interior decoration, in 1919 to 1922 designing a spectacular apartment in the Rue de Lota for Suzanne Talbot, a well-known modiste, and in 1922 opening her Galerie Jean Désert in the Rue du Faubourg Saint-Honoré. This gallery was a shop-window for her lacquer and the many abstract carpets she designed and had made in collaboration with Evelyn Wyld, and also advertised her talent as a decorator. Evelyn Wyld left Jean Désert in 1927 and it was wound up in 1930. In 1923 Eileen Gray exhibited a room at the Salon des Artistes-Décorateurs: its highly abstract design attracted contumely except from J. J. P. Oud, the leading DE STIJL architect, who wrote admiringly. Contact with the De Stijl group had been initiated in 1922 and led to the June 1924 issue of

'WENDINGEN', the Dutch magazine, being devoted to her work. At the same time she developed contacts with the Parisian *avant-garde* and was encouraged by Jean Badovici, a Romanian architect/journalist to try architecture. The first result was a house at Roquebrune in the South of France, nicknamed E-1027, built in collaboration with Badovici from 1926 to 1929, when an issue of his magazine, 'ARCHITECTURE VIVANTE', described the house. She later converted a Paris apartment for Badovici (1930–31) and built a house for her own use at Castellar (1932–4). Each building contained furniture in advanced materials such as chromed steel, aluminium and mirror glass. Later Eileen Gray designed a number of architectural projects, most notably a cultural centre shown in the Pavillon des Temps Nouveaux at the PARIS 1937 EXHIBITION by LE CORBUSIER, who had admired her work since the 1920s. In the late 1960s she was rediscovered and in her nineties witnessed her own revival, furniture to her early designs being reproduced in Italy, France and England, and carpets in Ireland and Spain. Eileen Gray's stylistic development from late ART NOUVEAU to abstraction in lacquer, and thence to a mastery of the International MODERN repertoire both as architect and designer was characterized by fastidiousness and wit – wit which was most evident in her predilection for hinged, pivoting, transparent, convertible and adjustable forms.

Greef, Jan de (1784–1834) Born in Dordrecht, Greef studied at first to be a painter. He then studied architecture in Paris, where he was a pupil of Hippolyte Le Bas in 1809, and visited Italy. From 1816 he was active as an architect in The Hague, where he was engaged up to 1825 on interiors for Willem I of Holland at the palace of Noordeinde. His furniture is in an accomplished late NEOCLASSICAL manner, including very inventive mahogany pier commodes carved with winged lions (1825). Greef later worked as an architect in Amsterdam.

Greenaway, Kate (1846–1901) Born in London, the daughter of a draughtsman and engraver, Kate Greenaway was trained from 1857 to 1867 at the National Art Training School at South Kensington. She began to exhibit drawings in 1868 and was thenceforward busy as an illustrator, designing cards and calendars for Messrs Marcus Ward & Co. from 1870 to 1876, as well as work on books and magazines. In 1878 the printer Edmund Evans (1826–1906) published her *Under the Window*. Kate Greenaway enjoyed great international success with this and a whole series of books for children, in most of which slightly melancholy small children pose in elaborately simple clothes against Artistic Queen Anne backgrounds. The style is a delicate version of Walter CRANE's. Kate Greenaway was much admired and criticized by H. Stacy Marks, whom she first met in 1871, and by RUSKIN, whom she first met in 1882. Her drawings were widely used to decorate plates, tiles, vases and even wallpaper. Kate Greenaway also designed book-plates and a wide range of ephemera. At the height of her success, in 1885, she moved into a house in Hampstead designed by R. Norman SHAW.

Greene, Charles Sumner (1868–1957) Born near Cincinnati, Ohio, the son of a doctor, Greene was brought up from 1874 in St Louis, Missouri, together with his younger brother, Henry Mather Greene (1870–1954). The Greenes attended Calvin Milton Woodward's Manual Training School at the University of Washington, St Louis, a school strongly influenced by RUSKIN and

William MORRIS. From 1889 C. S. Greene studied architecture at the Massachusetts Institute of Technology in Boston. In 1891 he worked with the architect H. Lawford Warren, and then with Winslow & Wetherall. H. M. Greene followed his brother to the Massachusetts Institute in 1892 and then worked with the architects Shepley, Rutan & Coolidge, and Chamberlin & Austin. In 1893 the brothers left Boston to join their parents in Pasadena, California; on the way they saw the Japanese section at the CHICAGO 1893 WORLD COLUMBIAN EXPOSITION. Edward Morse's *Japanese Homes and Their Surroundings* (1885) was another probable influence. By late 1894 the Greenes had begun to establish an architectural reputation in Pasadena. Their furniture was influenced by BRADLEY's designs in the *Ladies' Home Journal* (1901) and in 1902 they used STICKLEY furniture in a house. In 1903 the Greenes opened an office in Los Angeles and from 1905 worked in a refined style which reflected the influence of Chinese and Japanese prototypes, although the underlying influence was the English Arts & Crafts movement with which C. S. Greene had become acquainted on his honeymoon trip to England in 1901. The work of the Greenes was often praised in the 'CRAFTSMAN' from 1907 to 1915 and in 1909 Ashbee was an enthusiastic visitor to their furniture workshop. In 1912 C. S. Greene applied to register a trademark to be branded on his furniture; this had been made since 1905 by John and Peter Hall. C. S. Greene moved to Cartmel in 1916 and the partnership petered out being finally dissolved in 1922. C. S. Greene, the more creative partner, designed some furniture thereafter, but became increasingly taken up with Buddhism. H. M. Greene continued for a while to practise as an architect in Pasadena.

Grendel, Gerrit de Grendel was active as a sculptor and designer in Middelburg in Holland from 1719 to 1741. He designed two suites entitled *Nouveau Livre de Cheminées Hollandaises* (four plates each), published by MERZ in Augsburg in about 1735. They depict chimneypieces in a jolly early ROCOCO style. A third similar suite was published by ENGELBRECHT in Augsburg; its six plates include doors and a fountain. A Grendel design for a high-backed garden bench in the Dutch manner, decorated with putti, also survives. Such documents of 18th-century Dutch design are very rare.

Gribelin, Simon (1661–1733) Born in Blois, Gribelin came to London in about 1680. He became a member of the Clockmakers' Company in 1686, but worked as an engraver. He executed *A Book of severall ornaments* (1682), *A Book of Ornaments usefull to jewellers watchmakers and all other Artists* (1697), *A Book of Ornaments useful to all Artists* (1700), *A new book of ornaments useful to all artists* (1704), engravings of the Raphael Cartoons (1712) and Rubens's Banqueting House ceiling (1722), and many illustrations in anatomical, botanical and topographical books. In the British Museum is an album entitled *Livre d'Estampes de Sim. Gribelin*, assembled in 1722, which belonged to Horace WALPOLE. It includes pulls from many of his engravings on silver; among his works in this medium is an altar dish at Dunham Massey engraved in about 1706 with a Deposition after Annibale CARRACCI. Gribelin's decorative style comprises well-disciplined putti, scrolls, VASES and foliage in the French manner of about 1700.

Grimaldi, Giovanni Francesco (1606–80) Born in Bologna, where he trained as a painter, Grimaldi moved to Rome in about 1628. In 1648 he arrived in

Paris at the summons of Cardinal Mazarin, who also employed the painters ROMANELLI and Pietro da CORTONA. Before his return to Rome in 1651 Grimaldi designed *buffets*, cabinets, mirrors, silver and tapestry borders, and thus helped to transmit the Roman BAROQUE style to France.

Grognard, Alexis (1752–1840) Born in Lyon, Grognard studied painting at the École de Dessin there under Donat Nonotte (1708–85) and then in Rome under J.-M. VIEN (1716–1809). He himself taught at the École de Dessin in Lyon from 1780 and at the École des Beaux-Arts there from 1807. Grognard designed accomplished NEO-CLASSICAL decorations, including a room scheme for a royal patron dated 1790.

Grondoni, Giovanni Battista An Italian goldsmith and jeweller active in Brussels, Grondoni published there two suites of designs (seven plates and ten plates) for ornament and jewellery in an elaborate ACANTHUS style; they are dated 1709 and 1715 and the later suite is dedicated to the Elector Max Emanuel of Bavaria.

Gropius, Martin (1824–80) Born in Berlin, the son of a silk manufacturer, Gropius was brought up in the circle of SCHINKEL, Schadow, Boetticher and BEUTH, whose Preussisches Gewerbeinstitut he attended, as well as the Bauakadamie, where, in 1856, he taught ornamental drawing. He practised as an architect from 1864, founding in 1866 a partnership with the builder Heino Schmieden, which was the most prolific and successful in late-19th-century Berlin. From its foundation in 1867 to 1874 he taught at the BERLIN KUNST-GEWERBEMUSEUM, whose building, begun in 1877, he designed, and from 1869 he was head of the applied arts school in Berlin, and consequently of

all the other similar schools in Prussia, exercising great influence on the teaching of design in the kingdom. Gropius was a committed NEO-CLASSICIST in the tradition of Schinkel and Boetticher. His buildings fully exploited the effects of coloured bricks, and of terracotta ornament, which was manufactured by Ernest March. His *Archiv für Ornementale Kunst* (1871–9) contains seventy-two plates, almost exclusively of antique models for ceramics, furniture and ornament, while his *Dekorationen Innerer Räume* (1877–83) consists of nineteen magnificent chromolithographed plates of Gropius's own wall decorations. Gropius also designed for almost every aspect of the decorative arts, including furniture, textiles, ceramics, tiles and wallpaper.

Gropius, Walter (1883–1969) Born in Berlin, the son of an official architect, Gropius studied architecture in Munich and Berlin from 1903 to 1907. From 1908 to 1910 he worked in the office of Peter BEHRENS in Berlin, and then started an independent architectural practice. In 1913 Gropius designed furniture for Dr Karl Hertzfeld in a stripped NEO-CLASSICAL style similar to that of Behrens, and a diesel locomotive for the Königsberg locomotive factory. He showed interiors at the Ghent 1913 Exhibition and in the same year published an article in the DEUTSCHE WERKBUND yearbook praising the unadorned majesty of American grain silos. At the COLOGNE 1914 DEUTSCHE WERKBUND EXHIBITION Gropius designed the model factory and also showed a railway compartment designed for the Deutsche Reichsbahn. Before the dissolution of the Weimar school of applied arts in 1915 Gropius was approached by the then director, VAN DE VELDE, as a potential successor. Gropius served in the war from 1914 to 1918 but was in 1919 appointed director of both the applied and fine arts schools in Weimar. He merged them into the Staatliches BAUHAUS, whose manifesto, with a woodcut cover by Lyonel Feininger (1871–1956), proposed the unity of the arts. Gropius's designs for the director's office at the Bauhaus (1923) included a tubular lamp derived from that by RIETVELD (1920). Gropius directed the Bauhaus during the move to Dessau in 1925 but resigned in 1928 to set up office in Berlin. In that year he designed unit furniture for the Feder department store in Berlin. In 1929 he became vice-president of CONGRÈS INTERNATIONAUX D'ARCHITECTURE MODERNE. In 1930 he designed coachwork for the Adler Cabriolet, and the Paris 1930 Deutsche Werkbund Exhibition, on which he was assisted by BREUER, BAYER and MOHOLY-NAGY. In 1934 Gropius emigrated to England, where he worked with E. Maxwell Fry from 1934, in partnership from 1936 to 1937. In London Gropius published *The New Architecture and the Bauhaus* (1935). He lived in the Lawn Road flats in Hampstead and designed furniture for ISOKON, including a perforated aluminium wastepaper basket (1935) and a plywood chair and table (1936). Gropius became Controller of Design to the new Isokon Furniture Company in 1936. In 1937 he went to America and became a professor in the Graduate School of Design at Harvard, where he taught architecture until 1952. From 1938 to 1941 he was in partnership with Marcel Breuer, and in 1945 he founded The Architects Collaborative (T.A.C.) for which he designed a tea and coffee service in 1968 with Louis McMillen. In 1979 a chair designed by Gropius in 1910 for the Fagus works was manufactured by Tecta.

Grossmann, Carl August Born in Königsbruck in 1741, Grossmann studied

engraving in Dresden but was settled in Augsburg in 1765. His brother Christian Gotthelf Grossmann worked as a porcelain painter at Meissen and Ludwigsburg, specializing in flowers and fruit. Grossmann himself published numerous designs for VASES, pedestals, candlesticks, watch-stands, ironwork, furniture and trophies, many dated 1776. They are in a mannered and typically German NEO-CLASSICAL manner, by turns refined and comic. Grossmann stressed his French stylistic orientation by signing some works 'Grand'home'. He died in about 1798.

Grotesque Roman wall and ceiling paintings in the Domus Aurea, the Golden House of the Emperor Nero (37–68), were submerged in the foundations of baths erected by the Emperor Trajan. From about 1480 the Domus Aurea was explored by artists and archaeologists. A manuscript in the Escorial, the Codex Escurialensis (about 1493 to 1494), contains drawings attributed to a pupil of Domenico Ghirlandaio (1449–94) after paintings in the Golden House. Because such paintings were found underground in grottoes they were known as grotesques. Typical grotesques were composed of circular or rectangular panels containing figures, connected into an overall composition by an elaborate framework or by an insubstantial scaffolding of chimerical monsters, attenuated architecture, VASES, trophies, ACANTHUS, putti, scrolls and so on; a variety of such motifs were often formed together into upright candelabra-like components, well adapted to decorate panels or pilasters. From the mid-1480s Bernardino Pintoricchio revived grotesque decoration in Rome and in the Piccolomini Library of the Cathedral of Siena (1503–8); the contract for the Library (1502) speaks of '*disegni che hoggi chiamano grottesche*' ('designs which are now called grotesques'). Among other painters who made an early use of grotesque ornament were Filippino Lippi, from about 1488, Luca Signorelli, from about 1500, and Perugino, from about 1494, and the genre rapidly spread all over Italy, its diffusion assisted by engraved designs by Zoan ANDREA, Nicoletto Rosex da MODENA, Agostino VENEZIANO and Giovanni Antonio da BRESCIA, and, later, by Enea VICO. From 1517 to 1519 RAPHAEL, a pupil of Perugino, directed the decoration of the Loggie of the Vatican with virtuoso grotesques, assisted by Giovanni da UDINE and other pupils. Raphael also projected grotesque decorations for the Villa Madama, executed by Udine and PERUZZI, a former associate of Pintoricchio. Raphael's adoption of the grotesque assured its lasting popularity: SERLIO specifically recommended the imitation of the Vatican grotesques. Already in 1532 a French inventory mentioned 'ces gentilles crotesques nouvellement inventées' and the next major development took place at Fontainebleau, where ROSSO combined grotesque elements with heavy scrolled STRAPWORK probably derived from Venetian models. At Antwerp the strapwork grotesque was developed by Cornelis FLORIS and Cornelis BOS into a versatile and independent style, which Hans VREDEMAN DE VRIES did much to disseminate. In 1550 J. A. DUCERCEAU copied grotesques by Enea Vico and others and in 1566 grotesques by PRIMATICCIO. VASARI discerned elements of the grotesque in the work of MICHELANGELO and thus identified the grotesque as a key MANNERIST ingredient. Although the 1561 inventory of Mary Queen of Scots mentioned 'twa paintit broddis (boards) in crotesque or conceptis', the usual English term was 'anticke' or 'antique' – hence the modern 'antic'. Around 1600 designers such as MIGNOT, BEYTLER, KILIAN and ŠMIŠEK introduced curves

and asymmetry into the strapwork grotesque, and created a new stretched grotesque manner, which was a direct antecedent of the AURICULAR style of ornament. In Italy BAROQUE designers favoured a massive, naturalistic and sculptural version of the RENAISSANCE grotesque. This bolder manner was transmitted to France by VOUET. From the late 1670s however Jean I BERAIN developed a light and sprightly system of surface ornament which combined grotesques with delicate strapwork, but Berain's designs had none of the muscular and sinister quality of 16th-century strapwork grotesques. The Berainesque grotesque was widely influential and formed the basis for an even lighter manner developed by AUDRAN, GILLOT and TORO. This was the final stage before the emergence of the ROCOCO proper, of which grotesque was an ingredient. The grotesque surfaced again as an independent style in the hands of NEO-CLASSICAL designers such as STUART, ADAM and CLÉRISSEAU. The manner was at this date usually called ARABESQUE and a celebrated *Recueil d'Arabesques* (1802) paired modern designs by SALEMBIER, DUGOURC and others with prints after Raphael's grotesques, which had by then the authority of antique ornament. The most recent episode in the grotesque's long history was its popularity among Renaissance Revival designers of the 19th-century such as SYKES and M. L. E. SOLON. Recently the grotesque has been described by Gombrich (1979) as 'a guidebook to chaos': its revival seems overdue.

Groult, André (1884–1967) Groult was active in Paris as a designer of furniture and interior decoration. His work was shown at the Salon d'Automne and the Salon des Artistes-Décorateurs from 1910, when it was illustrated in 'ART ET DÉCORATION'. Groult worked in a plump and luxurious modified Louis XVI style comparable to that of SüE & MARE and opposed to the FRANCIS JOURDAIN MODERN line, although his designs were illustrated alongside GRAY, CHAREAU and other Modern designers in 'ARTS DE LA MAISON'. Groult was prominent at the PARIS 1925 EXHIBITION, where he designed the lady's bedroom, sponsored by the Société des Artistes-Décorateurs, in the Ambassade Française. He also designed textiles and wallpapers.

Gruber, Jacques (1870–1936) Born in Sundhouse in Alsace, Gruber was employed as a designer by the glass manufacturers Auguste Daum (1853–1909) and his brother Antonin (1864–1931) at Nancy from 1891. He then had a scholarship from the city of Nancy to the École des Beaux-Arts in Paris, where he studied painting under Gustave Moreau (1826–98). From 1894 to 1897 Gruber continued to design for the Daums. He also taught design at the Nancy École des Beaux-Arts, where his pupils included Jean LURÇAT and the poster designer Paul Colin. Gruber designed furniture for MAJORELLE, ceramics for the Mougin brothers and bookbindings for Wiener. From 1900 he both designed and manufactured furniture and stained glass. He showed at the 1908 Salon d'Automne. After the First World War Gruber moved to Paris and was mainly active as a designer of stained glass.

Grundler, Marcus Born in 1560, Grundler was a member of an Augsburg family of goldsmiths. He died in about 1613. He was responsible for three posthumously published suites of stretched GROTESQUE designs for enamelling of six plates each, two dated 1617, the third 1618. They include jewels, crosses, miniature cases and military trophies.

Gruner, Ludwig (1801–82) Born in Dresden, Gruner at first worked as a decorative painter there. After studying at the Dresden Academy, he spent the years from 1836 to 1843 in Rome. Gruner then travelled to London, where he became an art adviser to Prince ALBERT. From 1845 to 1849 he was again in Rome. Designs by Gruner in the LONDON 1851 EXHIBITION included a cabinet by Messrs Dowbiggin, a Wilton carpet for Windsor Castle and a Derbyshire marble table by Woodruffe of Bakewell. His books, including *Fresco Decorations . . . in Italy* (1846) and his *Specimens of Ornamental Art* (1850; eighty plates), encouraged a taste for RENAISSANCE polychromy and GROTESQUES which was to be influential at South Kensington. The *Specimens* derived from a suggestion by C. H. Wilson of the SCHOOL OF DESIGN for a replacement to DYCE'S 1842 *Drawing Book*. In 1856 Gruner was appointed director of the Dresden print room. He was responsible for the German report on metalwork in the LONDON 1862 EXHIBITION. His last major work was *The Terra-Cotta Architecture of North Italy* (1867).

Gruntler, Michel A goldsmith from Steier, Gruntler published in 1592 a suite of eight plates of small black enamel motifs for jewellery.

Guckeisen, Jakob Born in Cologne, Guckeisen is said to have been a pupil of the architect Hans Schoch. In 1596 he was described as citizen and cabinetmaker of Strasbourg. In 1596 in collaboration with Veit Eck he published *Kunstbüchlein Darin etliche Architectischer Portalen Epitaphen Caminen Schweiffen* with designs for altars, doors, monuments etc., in a style strongly indebted to Wendel DIETTERLIN whom Guckeisen probably knew. In 1599 he published a suite of chests in the same incoherent manner. Other works were in collaboration with Johann Jakob EBELMANN: *Schweyfbuch* (1599), consisting of ornament for woodwork, *Architectura Lehr und Kunstbuch* (1599), and *Seilenbuch* (1600, second edition 1611), a book of the ORDERS. Apart from his *Kunstbüchlein*, whose first edition appeared in Strasbourg, all Guckeisen's works were issued by Johann Bussemacher of Cologne. Several were dedicated to the Strasbourg cabinet-maker Jacob Riebel.

Guérard, Nicolas (1648–1719) Born in Brie, Guérard was taught to engrave in Paris by François Chareau (1613–76) and later worked with Jean LE PAUTRE. Guérard was active as both engraver and publisher, and was responsible for numerous maps and book illustrations. His *Diverses pièces d'arquebuserie* (ten plates) contains fine BERAINESQUE designs for the decoration of fire-arms; they were copied in both Augsburg and Nuremberg. *Livre nouveau de principes d'ornemens* (eight plates) was a teaching manual for designers, demonstrating the construction of lively scrolled and STRAPWORK ornament on the verge of ROCOCO. Other published designs by Guérard include box-lids, chimney-pieces, embroidery and ironwork, although some of his plates of ironwork are records of executed works including gates designed by Robert de COTTE in Notre Dame.

Guilmard, Desiré From about 1840 to about 1880 Guilmard was the most prolific Parisian publisher of high-quality designs for furniture and upholstery. From 1844 to 1882 he edited the illustrated journal *Le Garde Meuble* (1844–1903) whose excellent plates were widely imitated for instance by the English firm of Gillows and the Dutch firm of Horrix. Guilmard described himself as '*dessinateur et éditeur du Garde Meuble*' but its plates were mainly supplied by Parisian firms or by other designers. Guilmard's numerous publications include *Albums* of the 1844, 1849 and 1855 PARIS EXHIBITIONS, *Album du Menuisier Parisien* (1855–61), *Le Menuisier Moderne* (1860), *Album du Sculpteur Parisien* (1869), *Le Carnet de l'Ébéniste Parisien*, a collection of designs for simple furniture from examples by leading cabinet-makers of the Faubourg Saint-Antoine, *La Tenture Parisienne*, *Le Portefeuille Pratique de l'Ébéniste Parisien*, *Album Gothique*, *Album du Fabricant de Billards*, and *Album du Tourneur Parisien*. Among designers published by Guilmard were PRIGNOT, SANGUINETI and Beaucé. In *Les Maîtres Ornemanistes* (1880) Guilmard provided an invaluable international survey of historic ornament. According to Baron Davillier's preface, 'The superiority of France in matters of taste has been recognized and accepted by the whole world for two centuries; its artists and craftsmen will only retain their supremacy by the constant study of the great works of the old masters.'

Guimard, Hector (1867–1942) Born in Lyon, Guimard studied at the École des Arts Décoratifs in Paris from 1882 to 1885, and subsequently at the École des Beaux-Arts, where his teacher, Gustave Raulin, was a follower of VIOLLET-LE-DUC, whose writings strongly influenced Guimard. In the early 1890s Guimard began to evolve a new architectural style, characterized by asymmetry, variation in texture, rationality in construction and planning, and originality in ornament. These characteristics are apparent in his Hôtel Jassedé (1893), whose façade incorporated ceramic panels executed by Emile Müller of Ivry, for whom Grasset also designed, and in the contrastingly simple École du Sacre-Cœur (1895), with splayed iron columns directly based on Viollet-le-Duc. From 1894 to 1898 Guimard worked on the Castel Béranger, a block of flats built for Mme Fournier, who allowed him carte-blanche to experiment. While it was building Guimard visited England and Belgium, where he met Paul HANKAR and Victor HORTA, whose Hôtel Tassel was a revelation and inspired Guimard to develop a system of ornament based on Horta's. Guimard treated the Castel Béranger as a personal manifesto. He published an album, *Le Castel Béranger L'Art dans l'Habitation Moderne* (1898), which illustrated every aspect of the building, architecture, ironwork, carpets, furniture, stained glass, wallpaper and so on, all unified by Guimard's flowing scrolls, whirls and waves of abstracted vegetal or aqueous ornament. In 1899 he held an exhibition on the Castel Béranger at the Salon du Figaro, and in the same year designed the first cover of the *Revue de l'Art*, which contained a laudatory article on his work by Frantz Jourdain. At this period Guimard was for the only time in his life a busy architect. He designed Sèvres porcelain shown at the PARIS 1900 EXHIBITION, and from 1903 to 1904, and also, in about 1902, tiles for Alexandre Bigot. From 1900 he designed his celebrated entrances for the Paris Métro, commissioned by Adrien Bénard. In 1903, when he designed a pavilion in the Paris Exposition de l'Habitation, Guimard issued a series of postcards of his own work, entitled 'Le Style Guimard'. In 1907 he promoted this style in his *Fontes Artistiques pour Constructions, Fumisterie, Articles de Jardins, et Sepultures*, which illustrated over 200 models of ironwork from gates to door furniture to fenders made by the Fonderies de Bayard et Saint-Didier. Also in 1907 he showed furniture, jewellery, textiles and wallpapers at the Salon des Artistes-Décorateurs, where he also showed in 1910 to 1913. By this date, however, his influence was waning, and his own style tending to ossify, although his own house (1909–12) is handled with refinement and ingenuity. Guimard died in New York, where he moved in 1938 after a period of inactivity.

Günther, Franz Ignaz (1725–75) Born at Altmannstein in Bavaria, Günther was trained as a sculptor by his father and later by the Munich court sculptor Johann Baptist Straub (1704–84). After travelling he became in 1754 a court sculptor in Munich. His designs included altars, church metalwork, a calendar case, a frontispiece (1763) and pulpits. The latter display exceptional invention and freedom, couched in Günther's ethereal ROCOCO style. His 1771 designs for the doors of the Frauenkirche in Munich, rococo in spirit although NEOCLASSICAL in detail, seem to have been influenced by DELAFOSSE's *Premier Livre de Trophées* (1768), and in 1770 a suite of VASES designed by Günther after Delafosse were engraved by Joseph Kattner. In about 1758 Günther designed and executed rococo tables for Schloss Sünching.

Guyot, Laurent On the death of LERAMBERT, Guyot won the competition to succeed him as '*peintre ordonnée pour faire les patrons des tapisseries que S.M. fait faire*' being appointed royal tapestry designer in 1610, together with DUMÉE whose sister he married in 1613. For the competition Guyot had to prepare a design taken from Guarini's *Pastor Fido*, and subsequently he and Dumée designed a twenty-six-piece suite of tapestries on this theme. Other tapestry suites designed by Guyot include the History of Constantine, the Kings of France (nine pieces), the Hunts of François I (with the arms of Louis XIII) (eight pieces), Astrée (nine pieces) and the Marriage of Gombaut and Macée (eight pieces). Payments to Guyot are recorded in 1618, 1625 and 1636, the last at the Gobelins. In 1642 to 1644 he collaborated with Noel Quillerier (1594–1669) on decorative paintings in the Hôtel de la Vrillière.

Gwatkin, Arthur Gwatkin, a partner in a firm of decorators, was a leading designer of wallpapers in the 1890s, working in a flowing floral style. He designed for Wylie & Lochhead of Glasgow, among others, and showed designs for friezes at the Royal Academy from 1890 to 1899.

H

Haase, Hermann Haase was a Hamburg decorative painter taught by Hans Speckter (1848–88). In the late 1880s he supplied designs for ceramic decoration for the firm of Villeroy & Boch, and for the Hamburg 1889 Exhibition he designed an interior decorated with coloured chip-carving. Haase was closely associated with the revival of folk art led by SCHWINDRAZHEIM, and contributed designs of furniture and drawings of plants to his *Beiträge zu einer Volkskunst* (1891–3). The two also collaborated on a *Neues Stickmusterbuch* with designs for embroidery.

Habermann, Franz Xaver (1721–96) Born in Habelschwerdt in Glatz, now under Polish rule, Habermann was trained as a sculptor and travelled to Italy before settling in Augsburg in 1746, when he married the widow of Peter Georg Wörle, a miniature painter. In 1747 he purchased the right to practise as a sculptor and in 1755 to 1757 carved the organ case of the Barfüsserkirche in Augsburg. However, because of a lack of work he turned to a career as a designer, especially of silver, and ornamentist. From 1781 to his death he taught architectural and PERSPECTIVE drawing. He published over 500 prints, usually in suites of four, which were mostly issued by Johann Georg HERTEL or by Martin ENGELBRECHT. None is dated but stylistic analysis suggests a development from a vigorous and massy ROCOCO before 1750, towards a free and lively mastery until about 1765, followed by a mannered late ROCOCO phase up to about 1770, which was succeeded by a relatively small and unoriginal sequence of twenty-four NEO-CLASSICAL designs for silver engraved and published by Habermann himself. Drawings for neo-classical chalices dated 1787 and 1792 also survive. Habermann's designs cover church furniture, from altars to organs, doors, secular furniture, wall panelling, frames, coaches and sedan chairs, ironwork, church metalwork, VASES, and purely ornamental compositions, cartouches and *vignettes*. His prints were widely disseminated and uses have been noted on a desk by Abraham Roentgen, on pottery from Ansbach and Spain, and on Fürstenburg porcelain. Many of his designs were reprinted in Leipzig and Berlin from 1887 to 1893. The main influences on Habermann were MEISSONIER, BABEL and J. M. HOPPENHAUPT.

Hailler, Daniel Hailler was active as a goldsmith in Augsburg where in 1604 he published a *Libellus Aurifabris* (six plates), fine stretched GROTESQUE black ornaments for enamelling. In 1616 Hailler moved to Kremnitz in Hungary, where he died before 1630.

Hainhofer, Philipp (1578–1647) Born in Augsburg, the son of a merchant, Hainhofer was brought up in Ulm from 1584 and in 1594 went to Padua to study law. He travelled widely, learning Italian, French and Flemish, and visiting monuments and art collections all over Europe. From 1601, when he married, Hainhofer was active as a merchant in

Augsburg. He soon established a reputation as a collector, as an artistic middleman and impresario, and as a diplomat. Hainhofer was agent and correspondent to Duke Wilhelm V of Bavaria, to Henri IV of France, to the Margrave of Baden, and above all to Duke Philipp II of Pommern and his brother-in-law Duke August of Brunswick. Hainhofer had made a series of extraordinary and elaborate cabinets, for which he devised complex iconographic programmes. One, constructed from 1610 to 1617, he sold to Duke Philipp of Pommern, another, begun as a speculation in about 1624, was finally bought in 1628 by Leopold, Grand Duke of Austria, as a gift for Ferdinand II, Grand Duke of Tuscany, and a third was presented to King Gustavus Adolphus of Sweden in 1632 by the City of Augsburg. Hainhofer suffered grave financial difficulties after the withdrawal of Swedish troops and in 1647 was obliged to sell his collections and his last cabinet (1631–4) to Duke August of Brunswick. Hainhofer was in contact with all the leading Augsburg artists, craftsmen and designers, including ROTTENHAMMER.

Haité, George Charles (1855–1924) Born in Bexley, Kent, the son of George Haité, a textile designer, Haité was among the most prolific of late-19th-century pattern designers. He designed wall decorations, for example the Sunflower decoration shown at the European Galleries in 1881, wallpapers, for Essex & Co. and for Sandersons, fabrics for G. P. & J. Baker, stained glass, copper grills, electric-light brackets and the cover of the *Strand Magazine*. Nature and Japanese art were his main springs of inspiration; he wrote on both, his *Plant Studies* (1883–5), a large-scale work with fifty plates of accomplished plant ornament after a solid botanical text, being his most important book, dedicated to Princess Louise. He also wrote on wallpaper design in Gleeson White's *Practical Designing* (1893) and on design in the 19th century in the 'ARCHITECTURAL REVIEW' (1897), where an article by White on Haité's work had appeared in 1896. After an abortive attempt to found a Decorative Arts Association, Haité was instrumental in founding a Society of Designers in 1896, and became its first President, a role he also undertook when the London Sketch Club was founded in 1908. He had shown both oils and watercolours at the Royal Academy. From 1887 Haité lived in the 'aesthetical' suburb of Bedford Park, where his evident self-satisfaction with his talents caused some amusement.

Hald, Edward Born in Stockholm in 1883, the son of an engineer, Hald studied under the painter Johan Rohde in Copenhagen, and then from 1908 to 1909 in Paris under Henri Matisse. In 1912 he travelled to Italy. From 1917 to 1924 he designed for the Rörstrand porcelain factory and then from 1924 to 1933 for the Karlskrona porcelain factory. From 1917 onwards Hald designed at the Orrefors glass factory, where he worked with Simon GATE. He became artistic director at Orrefors from 1924 to 1933.

Halfpenny, William Halfpenny, who occasionally called himself Michael Hoare, was active, from 1722 as the author of over twenty manuals and pattern-books on architecture, PERSPECTIVE, geometry, building and allied subjects. He described himself as 'architect and carpenter', but his known buildings are few and scattered. He was based in Bristol from about 1730 and the altarpiece for the Redland Chapel, Bristol (1742), was made by William Brooks, a London joiner, to Halfpenny's design. His *New Designs for Chinese Temples, Triumphal Arches, Garden Seats, Pal-*

ings &c (1750–52; sixty plates) was the earliest work of this kind and includes entertaining designs for railings, terms, doors, windows, seats, chairs, chimney-pieces and ceilings in the Chinese taste. *Rural Architecture in the Chinese Taste* (1752) and *Rural Architecture in the Gothick Taste* (1752) also included garden ornaments. Halfpenny's later works were done in collaboration with his son, John Halfpenny. William Halfpenny himself died in debt in 1755.

Hall, John Hall was active in 1840, when his *The Cabinet-Makers Assistant* was published in Baltimore. He is described on the title page as 'Architect and Draftsman'. The book contains 198 figures on forty-three plates, depicting a wide range of furniture in the provincial scrolled Grecian style then current in America. The text includes a short treatise on linear PERSPECTIVE.

Hallé, Noel (1711–81) Born in Paris, the son of the painter Claude Guy Hallé (1652–1732), one of a large family of artists originating in Rouen, Hallé was taught to paint by his father and by his brother-in-law Jean Restout (1692–1768). He also studied architecture. Hallé won the Prix de Rome for painting in 1736 and stayed in Rome from 1737 to 1744. Back in Paris he had a successful and prolific career as a painter and also designed book ornaments, for example for Félibien's *Histoire de La Ville de Paris* (1755). In 1771 he succeeded François BOUCHER as artistic director of the Gobelins factory for which he designed, as did his pupil Jean Simon BERTHÉLEMY (1743–1811).

Hamburg Museum für Kunst und Gewerbe The Hamburg Museum of Applied Arts began in 1869 as a private foundation but was in 1877 taken over by the state. Justus Brinckmann (1843–1915) was then appointed director. Born in

Hamburg, Brinckmann had studied science, law and economy in Leipzig and Vienna, where, under the influence of Rudolf EITELBERGER, he developed an interest in the history of art. Back in Hamburg, Brinckmann was active as lawyer and journalist but was also instrumental for making purchases from the VIENNA 1873 EXHIBITION for the Hamburg Museum. He was early a collector of hymenoptera and later collected prints of ornament. In developing the Museum Brinckmann was influenced by SEMPER and by his friend Alfred Lichtwark, who founded the Hamburg Kunsthalle in 1886. Brinckmann's published works included treatises on Japanese art (1883 and 1889) and a celebrated guide to his Museum (1894). Brinckmann energetically collected Japanese art for Hamburg and in 1900 made extensive purchases of ART NOUVEAU at the PARIS EXHIBITION which included objects designed by COLONNA, GAILLARD, GUIMARD and LALIQUE. Through Brinckmann's purchases of Japanese and Art Nouveau design the Hamburg Museum exercised a wide influence in Germany around 1900.

Hameel, Alart du Probably born in Hertogenbosch, Hameel was assistant architect to the St Janskerk there in 1478, and was involved in the church until the consecration in 1494 of a chapel he had designed. In 1484 Hameel designed a monstrance for the St Janskerk, which was made by the Cologne goldsmith, H. de Borchgrave. In 1494 or 1495 he was appointed the municipal architect of Louvain, where he worked on the church of St Pieter. In 1496 he was held hostage in Mecheln, and in 1500 he was in Antwerp. Hameel resigned his post in Louvain in 1502 and died in Hertogenbosch before 1509. An engraving by Hameel of a GOTHIC monstrance, possibly the one he designed in 1484, is the largest known 15th-century print, 110 centimetres high on three plates. Hameel also engraved a Gothic canopy, and a panel of seaweed ornament.

Hamilton, Sir William (1730–1803) Born near Henley, the son of Lord Archibald Hamilton whose wife was mistress of FREDERICK LEWIS, PRINCE OF WALES, Hamilton was educated at Westminster School. From 1747 to 1758 he was a soldier. In 1764 Hamilton was appointed Envoy Extraordinary to the Court of Naples, where he remained until 1800. In Naples Hamilton took a close interest in the excavations at Herculaneum and Pompeii, directed since 1755 by the Royal Herculanean Academy, and reported on them to the Society of Antiquaries in London. In 1777 he was elected a member of the DILETTANTI SOCIETY. In Naples, Hamilton was visited by many distinguished travellers, including BECKFORD and Goethe, and built up a distinguished collection of antiquities. Hamilton published his collection in a splendid four-volume *Catalogue of Etruscan, Greek and Roman Antiquities* (1766–7) with coloured plates and a text by the French art-historian D'Hancarville; it was dedicated to George III and cost Hamilton £6,000. Hamilton's explicit aim was to provide model designs for modern artists and craftsmen. Josiah Wedgwood was shown proof plates by Lord Cathcart, Hamilton's brother-in-law, before the publication of the *Catalogue*, and in 1769 Wedgwood and his partner Thomas Bentley celebrated the opening of their factory at Etruria by making six black basalt VASES decorated with figures from the *Catalogue*. FLAXMAN and other Wedgwood designers later made frequent use of the *Catalogue*. The collection was in 1772 bought by the British Museum for £8,400 and put on display. In 1791 to 1795 Wilhelm Tischbein published four volumes of line engravings, *Collection of Engravings from Ancient Vases*, after Hamilton's second collection of vases. Most of the collection was sunk with the ship *Colossus* in 1799, but some vases were bought from Hamilton by Thomas HOPE. The beneficent influence of Hamilton's vase catalogues on English industry was attested by Charles MOREAU.

Hancock, Robert Possibly born in Burslem in Staffordshire in about 1731 and trained as an engraver by George Anderton of Birmingham or, more probably, in London, Hancock worked from 1753 to 1756 at the York House enamel factory in Battersea under John Brooks, the pioneer of transfer printing, and his associates the French engravers Simon-François Ravenet (1706–74) and Louis P. Boitard. After the failure of York House, Hancock moved to the Worcester porcelain factory where he became a partner in 1772. Hancock was responsible for many designs at Worcester; his pupils included the engravers Valentine Green (1739–1813) and James Ross (1745–1821). After leaving Worcester in 1774 Hancock became a partner in the Caughley porcelain factory but seems to have left by 1780. He engraved many designs for *The Ladies' Amusement, or the Whole Art of Japanning Made Easy* (1762), a compendium of fashionable motifs borrowed from François BOUCHER, WATTEAU, Lancret, GRAVELOT, PILLEMENT among others; first published by SAYER, it was claimed to be 'extremely useful to the Porcelaine and other Manufactures depending on design'. Hancock also contributed to such similar works as *The Artist's Vade Mecum* (1762), *The Compleat Drawing Book* (1762) and *The Compleat Drawing Master* (1763). He also engraved book-plates and probably engraved plates for calico printers. In his later years he was mainly active as an engraver of book illustrations and portraits. He showed at the

Royal Academy in 1802. Hancock died in 1817.

Hankar, Paul (1859–1901) Born at Frameries, the son of a stonemason, Hankar worked under a decorative sculptor named Houtstont, and then from 1879 under the Brussels architect Henri Beyaert, with whom he remained until Beyaert's death in 1894. He studied briefly at the Brussels Academy from 1882 to 1883, and was strongly influenced by the writings of VIOLLET-LE-DUC. In 1893 Hankar was a founder member of the Le Sillon group. He much admired the Glasgow contribution to the Liège 1895 Exhibition. At this period Hankar was designing furniture and interiors similar in style to VAN DE VELDE, and was regarded as the peer of HORTA as a pioneer of ART NOUVEAU. He designed every detail of the exterior and interior of his buildings in a crisp calligraphic manner. Hankar was particularly adept at the design of ironwork, working for several Brussels manufacturers, notably P. Desmedt. He was friendly with the poster designer Adolphe Crespin (1859–1944), who showed a poster of 'Paul Hankar Architecte' at the 1896 Cercle Artistique et Littéraire Exhibition, and designed sgraffito mural decorations for Hankar's ethnographic room at the Tervueren 1897 Colonial Exhibition. Hankar showed ironwork at the PARIS 1900 EXHIBITION, praised in 'ART ET DÉCORATIONS' (1901). His pupils included Leon Sneyers (1877–1949).

Hansen, Theophilus Edvard von (1813–91) Born in Copenhagen, Hansen studied architecture under his brother Christian (1803–83), and then at the Copenhagen Academy of Architecture from 1824 to 1837 under HETSCH (1788–1864). In 1838 he travelled on a scholarship to Germany, Italy and Athens, where he remained until 1846

teaching and practising as an architect. In 1846 he settled in Vienna at the invitation of the architect Ludwig Förster (1797–1863), whose partner he became and whose daughter he married in 1851. Hansen built a series of great public and private buildings in Vienna, notably the Parliament (1873–83). His work employed a synthesis of Greek and RENAISSANCE forms. He frequently designed schemes of polychromatic painted decoration for interiors, for example in the Greek Catholic Church am Fleischmarkt, Vienna (1858–61). From 1864 Hansen supplied many glass designs to Ludwig Lobmeyr; glass designed by Hansen was shown at the PARIS 1867 and VIENNA 1873 EXHIBITIONS and glass designs by Hansen were illustrated in 'GEWERBEHALLE' and 'BLÄTTER FÜR KUNSTGEWERBE'. In about 1866 Hansen designed furniture for Ludwig Lobmeyr.

Hårleman, Carl (1700–1753) The son of the garden designer Johann Horlemann and a pupil of the architect Adelcrantz (1668–1739), Hårleman travelled in Italy with Carl Gustav Tessin (1695–1770) and Carl Johan Cronstedt (1709–79) from 1731 to 1737. He became architectural adviser to Tessin and in 1741 succeeded him as superintendent of the royal buildings. Hårleman's most notable works, designed in the 1740s in collaboration with REHN, were elegant ROCOCO interiors in Stockholm Palace. Hårleman's collection of drawings included one of a fashionable French rococo commode and clock by Jean-Pierre Latz. Hårleman had earlier designed in the French BAROQUE style, for instance a candelabrum for Riddarholm church, Stockholm, made by Gustaf Stafhell in 1735.

Hartmann, Gottfried A smith from Breslau, Hartmann published several suites of designs for ironwork, one of which is dated 1736. They include grilles, brackets, keyhole escutcheons, locks etc., and are in an old-fashioned style composed of scrolled ACANTHUS and STRAPWORK.

Has, Georg Born in 1521 Has was described on the title of his portrait, engraved in 1581 by Nicolaus Andrea, as a citizen of Vienna and court cabinet-maker to the Emperor RUDOLF II. In 1571–2 he executed an elaborately inlaid ceiling in the Landhaus in Vienna. His *Künstlicher und Zierlicher Newer Funfftzig Perspectifischer Stück*, published in Vienna in 1583, contains fifty designs for ceilings which incorporate elaborate PERSPECTIVE effects, mythological scenes and GROTESQUE ornament.

Haste, Michel A smith in Paris, Haste worked at Versailles and other royal palaces from 1676 to 1688. He published a suite of handsome BAROQUE designs for ironwork dedicated to Nicolas L'Espine, Architecte des Bastimens du Roy, and is also likely to have designed the *Livre Nouveau de Serrurerie*, published by Antoine PIERRETZ, and other ironwork designs published by François de POILLY: the crossed Ls on a key in one of the latter presumably refer to the patronage of Louis XIV.

Hauer, Johann Paul Born in Nuremberg in 1629, Hauer issued in 1650 a suite of six plates of fine black floral enamel designs for crosses, flasks, miniature cases, étuis, etc.

Havinden, Ashley Eldred (1903–73) Havinden studied drawing and design at the Central School of Arts & Crafts in London. From 1922 he worked for the W. S. Crawford advertising agency of which he was appointed Director of Art and Design in 1929. The clients for his many posters, signed 'Ashley', included Eno's Fruit Salt, the Milk Marketing Board and Simpson's of Piccadilly. From 1933 he designed rugs and textiles for J. Duncan Miller, who organized an exhibition of Havinden's work in 1937. Havinden also designed rugs and textiles for Edinburgh Weavers, Campbell Fabrics and the Wilton Carpet Factory. He designed the British book section of the PARIS 1937 EXHIBITION. In 1956 Havinden published *Advertising and the Artist*.

Hay, David Ramsay (1798–1866) Born in Edinburgh, Hay was apprenticed in 1812 to Gavin Beugo, a heraldic and decorative painter. Hay's early ambition was to be an artist, but he was advised to become a house painter by Sir Walter Scott, who employed him as such at Abbotsford from about 1820. In 1828 Hay set up his own business as a decorator, which thrived and was highly regarded: in 1843 he described himself as 'Decorative Painter to the Queen'. Hay moved in the learned society of Edinburgh and published numerous works on art theory. His *The Laws of Harmonious Colouring adapted to interior decorations, manufactures, and other useful purposes* (1828, sixth edition 1847, German translation Weimar, 1848) was one of the most important 19th-century manuals on colour, although Hay was despised by Owen JONES as a poor copyist of George Field. *Proportion, or the Geometrical Principle of Beauty, Analysed* (1843) used music as an analogy for the analysis of ornament, and also pointed towards a geometrical basis for ornament, which was developed in his *Original Geometrical Diaper Designs* (1844), and applied to art manufactures in his *First Principles of Symmetrical Beauty* (1846). Hay also applied geometry to anatomy and architecture, and his emphasis on this theme may be regarded as prophetic of the High Victorian Geometric style.

Among Hay's own decorative works was the hall of the London SOCIETY OF ARTS, executed in about 1846.

Heal, Sir Ambrose (1872–1959) The son of Ambrose Heal, of the bedding and furniture manufacturers and retailers, Ambrose Heal, junior, was educated at Marlborough and the Slade School. Then, after serving an apprenticeship as a cabinet-maker with Messrs Plucknett of Warwick from 1890 to 1893, he entered the family firm. He designed furniture for Heal's from 1896, became a partner in 1898, managing director in 1907 and chairman in 1913. He was knighted in 1933. His first catalogue, *Plain Oak Furniture* (1898), comprised designs in a simple cottagey Arts & Crafts manner, also adopted in *Simple Bedroom Furniture* (1899) for which Gleeson White (1851–98) wrote an introductory essay on 'Simplicity of Design'. Heal's designs were also praised by MUTHESIUS. A member of the ART-WORKERS' GUILD, Heal was in 1915 an active founder member of the DESIGN AND INDUSTRIES ASSOCI-ATION, together with his cousin Cecil Brewer and Hamilton Smith, another director of Heal's. He remained faithful to his early Arts & Crafts style until the 1930s when, influenced by other Heal's designers, including J. F. Johnson, Leonard Thoday and Arthur Greenwood, he began to design for modern laminated woods and steel tube. The success of a range of cheap furniture designed by Greenwood and E. W. Shepherd of Greenings of Oxford enabled Heal to pilot Heal's through the depression. He retired in 1953. Heal was also a distinguished scholar. His works include *London Tradesmen's Cards of the Eighteenth Century* (1926), *The English Writing Masters and their Copy Books 1670–1800* (1935) and *London Furniture Makers from 1660 to 1840* (1953).

Heartfield, John (1891–1968) The son of a socialist poet, Heartfield was born Helmut Herzfeld in Berlin. From 1909 to 1912 he studied at the Munich School of Applied Arts. In 1912 he designed his first book-jacket, for an edition of his father's poems. Also in 1912 he moved to Berlin and in 1914 he won a prize for a mural design shown at the Cologne DEUTSCHE WERKBUND exhibition. After meeting Georg Grosz (1893–1959) in 1915 he destroyed his earlier work and in 1916 changed his name to John Heartfield in protest against anti-British propaganda. Heartfield produced adventurous typography for the magazine *Neue Jugend* (1917), published by the left-wing Malik Press, run by his brother Wieland, for which Heartfield was to design many books and bookjackets. In 1918 he joined the Communist Party, for which he designed many posters up to 1933. He and Grosz had begun to play with photomontage in 1916, and had produced some specimens of a Dada character in about 1919. From about 1924, however, when he designed a photomontage display for the Malik bookshop, Heartfield converted this device into a powerful propaganda medium. Among his most celebrated inventions were the dove speared on a bayonet (1932) and Goering with a bloodstained axe (1933). He was a close disciple of Bertholt Brecht (1898–1956). He was the subject of an article in 'GEBRAUCHSGRAPHIK' (1927) and an exhibition in Moscow in 1931. In 1933 he fled to Prague and in 1938 to London. There he designed book-jackets for Penguin Books and others and published photomontages in *Lilliput* and *Picture Post*. In 1950 Heartfield settled in Leipzig, where he was revered as a great communist typographical pioneer.

Heaton, Clement John (1861–1940) Born in London, the son of Clement Heaton (1824–82), the founder of Heaton, Butler & Bayne, stained-glass manufacturers and decorators, Heaton succeeded his father in the firm in 1882 but left in 1885 after a dispute. Heaton developed a speciality in cloisonné enamel and set up his own firm Heaton's Cloisonné Mosaics Ltd. In the early 1880s Heaton was closely associated with MACKMURDO and the Century Guild, for which he designed metalwork and lights. In the early 1890s Heaton settled in Neuchâtel in Switzerland, where he designed and made stained glass and enamels and patented a method of making embossed wallpapers. In 1912 Heaton moved to the United States, where he was active as a stained-glass designer.

Heckell, Augustin Born in Augsburg in about 1690, the son of a goldsmith, Heckell spent some time in Paris but was established as a leading London chaser by 1732. He was still active as such in 1749, but later, having made a fortune, he retired to Richmond and painted flowers and landscapes as a hobby until his death in 1770. Drawings by Heckell for watch-cases and snuff-boxes decorated with allegorical scenes, some within ROCOCO cartouches, survive. He also designed *A NEW BOOK of Sheilds usefull for all sorts of Artificers* (six plates of very asymmetric and bold early rococo cartouches) and *A Select Collection of the most beautiful Flowers . . . disposed in their proper Order in Baskets: Intended either for Ornament, or the Improvement of Ladies in Drawing or Needlework* (six plates).

Hecken, Abraham van den A goldsmith and engraver active in Amsterdam, Hecken published *Konstbuechlein den Goldschmieden dienstlich* (1608; twelve plates), mythological scenes for engraving on boxes, and the similar *Konst Boexken dienstlich den Goudsmeden* (1634; six plates).

Heckenauer, Leonhardt Heckenauer, a member of an Augsburg family of gold-smiths and engravers, published a wide range of engravings there from 1678 to 1704. He issued two suites of *Romanisches Laubwerck*, of twelve plates each, containing ACANTHUS-style cartouches, friezes and ornaments: Heckenauer claimed that he had personally designed the plates in Rome. His *Neues sehr dienliches Goldschmidts Buch* (twelve plates) contains designs for screens, firedogs, candelabra and lights in a late-BAROQUE acanthus style enlivened by figures. Heckenauer's son, Jacob-Wilhelm, issued a third suite of *Romanisches Laubwerck* (twelve plates) and also engraved copies after MAROT as well as illustrations to Goldman's *Civilbaukunst* (1708); he died in 1738.

Hedouyns, Anthoine Hedouyns, a Parisian goldsmith, published in 1633 a suite of six designs for jewelled sprays, one with crossed and smoking tobacco pipes at the top; they were engraved by Michel van Lochom (1601–43) and are in the COSSE-DE-POIS style.

Heel, Johann Wilhelm (1637–1709) Born in Augsburg, Heel was a pupil of Matthäus Schaffhauser. In 1668 he moved to Nuremberg, where he died. He was active as goldsmith, enameller and glass engraver as well as designer of ornament. Five small suites of engravings after Heel are known, the *Schneid-Büchlein* and *Goldschmidts-Büchlein*, both published by David Funck, the *Neues Blum- und Lauber-Büchlein*, first issued in 1664, and six panels of ornament, first issued in 1665, both reissued later by Paulus Fürst, and six plates of ornament which he engraved himself, partly copied from Jean MUSSARD. Heel was a competent practitioner of the late-17th-century BAROQUE repertoire of ornament in which floral and

ACANTHUS motifs surround putti and VASES.

Heere, Lucas de (1534–84) Born in Ghent, Heere worked under Frans Floris, brother of Cornelis FLORIS, in Antwerp and was subsequently active as a designer of glass and tapestries. He worked in the latter capacity for Catherine de' Medici in about 1560 and may have met CARON at this period. From about 1567 to 1576 Heere was in exile in England. He then returned to Ghent, where he designed the decorations for the entries of William of Orange in 1577 and of the Duc d'Anjou in 1582. Heere designed the Valois tapestries, now in Florence, adding figures to basic schemes by Antoine Caron (woven in Brussels in about 1582). They were an elaborate expression of protestant aspirations.

Heiberg, Jean (1884–1976) Heiberg studied painting in Munich under Knirr and then from 1908 to 1910 in Paris under Matisse. He returned from Paris to Norway in 1929. In 1930, while teaching at the National Academy of Fine Art, Heiberg was commissioned to design a telephone for the L. M. Ericsson Company's Oslo branch. The telephone, at once sturdy and smoothly sculptural in black bakelite, was produced in Stockholm in 1931 and thenceforward enjoyed international and prolonged success, being made in the United States, England, France and elsewhere, and eventually celebrated as a CLASSIC.

Heidel, Hermann Rudolf (1810–65) Born in Bonn, Heidel was a pupil of the sculptor Ludwig von Schwanthaler (1802–48). In 1843 he settled in Berlin, and was active as a ceramic designer as well as sculptor. His designs for the Berlin Royal Porcelain Factory were particularly successful.

Heideloff, Carl Alexander von (1789–1865) Born in Stuttgart, the son of a decorative painter, Heideloff was at first active in this field. In architecture he was a pupil of Nicolaus Thouret, whose GOTHIC chapel in the park at Hohenheim (1797) may have prompted Heideloff's early love of Gothic. Heideloff collected Gothic objects from as early as 1808 and came to regard Gothic as the German national style. In 1817 he designed the Gothic Schloss Rosenau for Duke Ernst of Saxe-Coburg, where Prince ALBERT was born in 1819. Heideloff also designed a tournament held at Rosenau. In 1821 he moved to Nuremberg, at whose polytechnic he taught until 1856 and where he was in charge of the conservation of ancient monuments, which involved the design of much church furniture and stained glass. His many restorations included the Veste, Coburg (1838–40), and Burg Lichtenstein (1837) for Graf Wilhelm von Württemberg (1810–69), where he designed a large amount of Gothic furniture. Heideloff's handling of Gothic was partly archaeological, partly fanciful, as appears in the designs of his furniture pattern-book, *Der Bau- und Möbelschreiner oder Ebenist* (Nuremberg, 1832–7), which also included designs in a rich late-Empire style. His many books also included works on the ORDERS (1827), on plasterwork (1835), designs for turners, potters, silversmiths and jewellers (1851–2), and *Arabesken im griechischen, byzantinischen, altdeutschen und Renaissance-Styl* (1851). However his most important works treated of German Gothic architecture, *Die Bauhütte des Mittelalters in Deutschland* (1844), and German Gothic ornament, *Die Ornamentik des Mittelalters* (1843–52). An Italian edition of the latter was published in Venice in 1859. From 1845 Heideloff was a contributor to the *Art Union*, the predecessor of the 'ART JOURNAL', on Gothic furniture and allied subjects. In 1856 he retired to Hassfurt, where he died.

Heiglen, Johann Erhard (1683–1757) Heiglen became a master goldsmith in Augsburg in 1717 and died there in 1757. In 1721 he published three suites of ten plates each, with artisan designs for engraved borders on silver and for tureens, dressing-table articles, ewers, funnels, casters, candlesticks etc., with BERAINESQUE ornament. Heiglen also published some designs for keys.

Heller, B. Karl A sculptor, Heller spent some years in Greece in the 1830s and published a book of lithographic illustrations of the excavations of the Acropolis in Athens carried out from 1835 to 1837. He later taught at the Nuremberg Polytechnic. His *Darstellungen sämtlicher Haus- und Luxusartikel im deutschen Style* (Nuremberg, 1849) contains sixty plates of designs for furniture, jewellery, teapots, beer-mugs and much besides in an accomplished, unarchaeological and sometimes fantastic GOTHIC style, much in contrast to UNGEWITTER'S designs of the same period.

Henequin, Jean A Metz gun-maker who made a wheel-lock gun for Louis XIII, a great gun collector, in 1621, engraved with figures in scrolly foliage, Henequin published seven crude plates of designs for the decoration of wheel-lock weapons. They incorporate masks, putti, GROTESQUE animals, dolphins and foliate scrolls.

Hepplewhite In 1788 I. & J. Taylor published *The Cabinet-Maker and Upholsterer's Guide*, containing 126 plates of furniture 'from drawings by A. Hepplewhite and Co. Cabinet-makers'. All its plates were dated 1787. A. Hepplewhite (Alice) was the widow of George Hepplewhite, who had died at Redcross Street, Cripplegate, in 1786. He is an obscure figure. It has often been stated that he was apprenticed to Gillows of Lancaster but there is no firm evidence of this: in 1801 Gillows wrote: 'We have not Hebblethwaite's Publication.' A second edition of the *Guide* appeared in 1789 with slight alterations. In 1791 in the preface to his *Cabinet-Maker and Upholsterer's Drawing Book* SHERATON commented unfavourably on the standard of design in the *Guide*, stating it had 'already caught the decline'. He was more favourable to *The Cabinet-Makers' London Book of Prices* (1788), mainly designed by SHEARER, whose second edition (1793) contained six plates signed by 'Hepplewhite'. The third edition of the Hepplewhite *Guide* (1794) contained a number of new designs for chairs and sofas in the square-backed Sheraton manner, clearly a response to his earlier criticism. Who in the Hepplewhite firm was responsible for all or any of the designs in the succeeding editions of the *Guide* or in the *Book of Prices* has never been established. The *Guide* was the first major furniture pattern-book to appear after the third edition of CHIPPENDALE'S *Director* (1762), and the first to exhibit the NEO-CLASSICAL style. The gap from 1762 to 1788 was filled by the first two volumes (1773–9) of the *Works* of Robert and James ADAM, whose influence on the *Guide* was immense, many of its designs being elegant ARTISAN variations of Adam themes. But the *Guide* also laid a strong stress on practicality and much of the furniture it contains is in a solid sub-Palladian manner going back to Chippendale and beyond. The influence of the *Guide* went far beyond England, for example to America and to Denmark, where J. C. Lillie used it in 1793 when designing chairs for Liselund. In 1897 the *Guide* was reprinted by Batsford, a token of the widespread revival of Hepplewhite designs from the late 19th century onwards.

Herbst, Johann Bartholomaus A goldsmith and engraver from an Augsburg family of goldsmiths, Herbst published *A Book of Severall Ornaments fitt for Jeweler* (London, 1708), black scrolled ACANTHUS ornament for enamelling on boxes etc., and *A Book of Several Juwelers work* (London, 1710), with floral and acanthus designs for étuis, seals, flasks and ornament.

Herbst, René Born in Paris in 1891, Herbst trained as an architect from 1908, spending time in London and Frankfurt. He practised as an architect in Paris from 1919. Herbst designed stands at the PARIS 1925 EXHIBITION and was in 1930 on the original committee of the Union des Artistes Modernes with Francis JOURDAIN, Robert MALLET-STEVENS, Raymond TEMPLIER and Hélène Henry. He designed interiors and furniture in the MODERN style, including, from 1927, tubular-steel chairs manufactured for his own firm, which published a catalogue in 1933. In 1949 to 1950 Herbst, by then president of the Union, helped to organize their exhibition of design, Les Formes Utiles, at the Musée des Arts Décoratifs. In 1954 he published a book on Pierre CHAREAU.

Heritage, Robert Born in Birmingham in 1927, Heritage studied furniture design at the Royal College of Art under R. D. Russell (1904–81). Heritage has been an independent designer from 1953. In 1974 he was appointed professor in the School of Furniture Design at the Royal College of Art (see SCHOOL OF DESIGN). Heritage has designed furniture for Archie Shine, for Race Furniture, including the Q.E. II chair (1969) and Molecula seating (1978), and for Gordon RUSSELL Ltd.

Herkomer, Sir Hubert van (1849–1914) Born in Munich in 1849, the son of a carver, Herkomer was taken as an infant to the United States in 1851, but the family settled in Southampton in England in 1857. By 1873 Herkomer was established as a successful painter at Bushey outside London, and there he erected Lululaund, an ambitious romanesque house destroyed in 1938, to designs by H. H. RICHARDSON, whom he met in America in 1886, the year of Richardson's death. Herkomer's decorations for Lululaund, partly executed by his father, his uncle John, another carver, and his uncle Anton, a weaver, comprised furniture, woodwork, metalwork, including pewter cutlery, in a remarkable style which combined late German GOTHIC with proto-ART NOUVEAU motifs, including draperied nudes à la Loie Fuller. In the 1890s Herkomer experimented with enamels. In 1895 he designed the insignia for the Welsh Eisteddfod, and in 1897 the presidential badge of the Royal Society of Painters in Watercolour.

Herman, Georg Born in Ansbach in 1579, Herman followed his father, Stefan HERMAN, as both goldsmith and engraver. He published suites of beasts (1594), birds and insects (1596) for goldsmiths, a suite of cartouches with landscapes (1595) and a suite of arms (1596). His *Ein new Kunstlich Modelbuch* (Nuremberg, 1625; fifty-four plates) was published by Balthasar Caymox, SIBMACHER's publisher. It contains some borders in Sibmacher's manner and many very geometric designs for lace.

Herman, Stefan Herman worked in Ansbach as a goldsmith, engraver and publisher from 1568 to 1596. He also lived in Kulmbach at some stage. Herman published designs by his pupil, Matthias BEYTLER, and by ZAN,

PLEGINCK and AMMAN, who may have been his master. Herman's own designs for GROTESQUE borders for goldsmiths' work (1586; twelve plates) are in the dotted manner and resemble designs by Zan. Herman was succeeded by his son, Georg HERMAN.

Herold, Johann Gregor (1696–1775) Born in Jena, Herold was in 1718 working as a painter in Strasbourg. In 1719 he moved to Vienna, where he painted paper hangings, and joined the staff of the Vienna porcelain factory. In 1720 he accompanied Samuel Stöltzel, a runaway chemist from the Meissen porcelain factory, back to Meissen, where Herold was appointed artistic director. He instituted formal training for the Meissen painters in 1722. In 1726 he issued a suite, six plates of fanciful CHINOISERIES, printed for the instruction of his pupils and to assist the transfer of his designs to porcelain. Herold also knew SCHENCK's chinoiseries and Martin ENGELBRECHT's *Habitus et mores Sinensium* (Augsburg, about 1719). By 1731 he had twenty-five painters and ten students under his direction. Despite an attack on his methods by Johann Joachim Kändler (1706–75) in 1734, Herold continued in the post and in 1751 had 190 painters under him. He received extra payment for new designs. During the Seven Years War, from 1756 to 1763, Herold fled to Frankfurt. He then returned to Meissen, where he taught in the school of art under Christian Wilhelm Ernst Dietrich (1712–74), and continued his researches on the chemistry of paints for porcelain. Herold retired in 1765.

Herrera, Francisco de (1622–85) Born in Seville, Herrera was taught to paint by his father. He subsequently went to Rome, where he published a suite of cartouches (1649; twelve plates) dependent on MITELLI. After his father's death in 1656 Herrera returned to Seville and was notably successful as both painter and architect.

Hertel, Johann Georg the Elder (1700–75) Martin ENGELBRECHT and Hertel were the two main publishers of design and ornament in Augsburg in the mid 18th century. Hertel was trained as a plasterer in his youth but in 1748 bought a share in the former press of Jeremias Wolff from the latter's son-in-law Johann Balthasar Probst (1686–1750). Hertel published at least 404 suites of prints, the work of at least thirty-five designers, including his son, Georg Leopold Hertel, STOCKMANN, HABERMANN, EICHEL, WACHSMUTH and Thelot. He also copied prints of others, including designs by BABEL, F. BOUCHER, DELAFOSSE, RANSON and J. M. HOPPENHAUPT.

Herwegen, Peter (1814–93) Born in Cologne, Herwegen trained there as a painter from 1826 to 1830 under E. Mengelberg (1770–1849). From 1837 Herwegen lived in Munich, where he was regarded as a follower of Eugen NEUREUTHER (1806–82). He designed many objects in the GOTHIC style, notably, in 1869, preliminary designs for LUDWIG II's bedroom at Neuschwanstein. In 1863 a Gothic clock design by Herwegen was illustrated in 'GEWERBEHALLE'.

Hess, Gotlieb Hess published a series of designs for ironwork grilles incorporating heavy swags, wreaths etc. in an advanced NEO-CLASSICAL style derived from NEUFFORGE and DELAFOSSE. Bold but provincial, they are probably German of the 1780s.

Hetsch, Gustav Friedrich (1788–1864) After studying architecture in his native Stuttgart under Eberhard von Etzel, Hetsch moved in 1808 to Paris, where in

1809 he began to study at the École des Beaux-Arts, working under Charles PERCIER and H. LE BAS. In 1812 he went to Italy where, in Rome, he became friendly with the Danish architect P. Malling and other Danes. In 1815 he came to Denmark with Malling, and taught in the newly founded school of ornament for architects. Hetsch became a naturalized Dane in 1822. He was an intimate friend of C. F. Hansen and designed the redecoration of Hansen's rebuilding of Schloss Christianborg from 1826. From 1828 to 1857 he designed for the Copenhagen porcelain factory. He was also involved in Ipsen's terracotta factory and L. Rasmussen's zinc factory, and taught at the Copenhagen Polytechnic from 1829, becoming director in 1844. Hetsch worked exclusively in the NEO-CLASSICAL style, with an emphasis on ACANTHUS and anthemion ornament. He designed furniture, silver and, in 1839, an unexecuted proposal for the decoration of the Thorvaldsen Museum. Hetsch was an important pioneer of design education in Denmark and published a number of books on drawing and design, including *Models for Artisans* (1839–43).

Hettwig, Carl A furniture designer in Berlin, Hettwig was a prolific publisher of charming coloured lithographs of his varied and typical designs for the bourgeois interior, many in a RENAISSANCE Revival style. They include *Album moderner Verzierungen für alle Zweige der Möbel-Industrie* (1867), *Journal für Tapezierer und Decorateure* (1871), *Kunstgewerbliche Ornamentik* (1871) and *Deutsches Musterbuch für Bildhauer und Dreehsler*. The title of his later *Sammlung moderner Sitzmöbel* (Dresden, 1882–94), with designs for every variety of seat furniture, describes Hettwig as 'furniture manufacturer in Berlin'.

Heumann, Georg Heumann published in Nuremberg in about 1720 *Neu inventirte Degengefass*, six plates of ornament for hunting knives incorporating ACANTHUS, BERAINESQUE STRAPWORK and hunting imagery such as hounds. He was probably related to the engraver Georg Daniel Heumann (1691–1759).

Heyden, Adolf (1838–1902) Born in Krefeld, Heyden began his architectural career as a restorer. In 1868, however, he formed the partnership of Kyllmann & Heyden, which was one of the most successful in Berlin in the late 19th century. Heyden's specialities were interior design, for instance the Emperor's BAROQUE revival study in the Berlin Schloss, and design for the applied arts, including the design of the magnificent state wedding present to Crown Prince Wilhelm (1881–3), consisting of 809 pieces of silver and glass in a synthetic baroque revival style.

H.G., Master Possibly a pupil of Master H.S., Master H.G. was a cabinet-maker whose known works are dated 1563 and 1565. He probably worked in the Oberpfalz. Seven crude woodcut designs for furniture by Master H.G. are known. They are in the early Renaissance manner of Peter FLÖTNER; one is dated 1551.

Hieronimo da Cividad di Frioli A Franciscan monk, Hieronimo was responsible for the only early book of lace designs not published in Venice, *Triompho di lavori a fogliami* (Padua, 1555; sixteen plates). His designs resemble those of Matio PAGANO.

Hill, Oliver F. (1887–1968) After working in a builder's yard for eighteen months at LUTYENS's suggestion, Hill spent three years with the architect William Flockhart (1907–10), also attending classes at the Architectural

Association. From 1910 Hill had his own practice, building a great number of town and country houses in styles which ranged from Lutyensesque to Provençal Basque to International MODERN. His conspicuously smart clientele included Kenneth Clark, Lord Mount Temple and Syrie MAUGHAM, for whose house he designed additions in 1933. In 1924 Hill designed the pottery section of the Wembley British Empire Exhibition. He was also supervising architect for the British Industrial Art Exhibition at Dorland Hall in 1933 (see LONDON EXHIBITIONS), and designed the British Pavilion at the PARIS 1937 EXHIBITION. Oliver Hill was a prolific and inventive designer of interior furniture and fittings, down to 'maids' dresses, summer and winter'. As did his architecture his designs ran the gamut of styles, and he used a wide variety of materials, including engraved glass, silver foil, chromed steel, vitrolite, fluted marble and onyx. His furniture, sometimes in dashing materials such as sycamore and maple inlaid with marble and ivory, was highly successful, whether neo-Georgian, neo-Regency or Modern. Hill had wide contacts in the world of design; for example his Midland Hotel, Morecambe (1931–2), incorporated reliefs by Eric GILL (1933). Throughout his career he had a close relationship with the magazine *Country Life*, which publicized his work, and later published his books and articles on the history of architecture. Hill spent his last years at Sapperton in a house, Daneway, which had been Ernest GIMSON's.

Hirschvogel, Augustin (1503–53) Born in Nuremberg, the son of a glass painter, Hirschvogel worked in his father's workshop until he died in 1525. He executed many designs for stained glass at this period. After financial difficulties Hirschvogel entered into an association with two Hafner potters, Hanns Nickel and Osswald Reichardt, in 1531. Probably about this date he studied glass and pottery techniques in Venice. In 1536 he moved to Laibach, in Austrian territory, where he seems to have been involved in a maiolica workshop and also started activity as an engraver of maps, including a map of Austria for the Emperor Ferdinand I. In 1543 Hirschvogel was back in Nuremberg to arrange the publication of his *Geometria*, dedicated to the Emperor. The frontispiece of *Geometria* incorporates a virtuoso PERSPECTIVE of geometric solids which looks forward to the designs of LENCKER, Wenzel JAMNITZER and STÖER. In 1543 Hirschvogel published eight designs for ewers (one 1544), three cups and covers (one 1544), one VASE, two daggers with sheaths, two hilts, nine panels of ornament of various shapes, two designs for pendants and one tripod candelabrum. The metalwork designs are in the GROTESQUE style and display bizarre and inventive combinations of natural forms. In 1543 Hirschvogel moved to Vienna where he was active as cartographer, musician, glass painter, heraldic and portrait engraver, die cutter and maker of mathematical instruments. In 1549 he painted a plan for the fortifications of Vienna. Hirschvogel was a famous artist in Vienna, with the honorary title 'Mathematicus'. His works are remarkable for their variety and invention.

Hittorff, Jacques Ignace (1792–1867) Born in Cologne, the son of a tinsmith, Hittorff was there a pupil of the architects C. Löwenstein and Leidel, and of the painter Caspar Arnold Grein (1764–1835). In 1810 he went to the École des Beaux-Arts and studied architecture under PERCIER and BÉLANGER and drawing under Jean Baptiste Isabey (1767–1855). In 1814 he assisted Bélanger on decorations for the return of the Bourbons. In 1818, on Bélanger's death, he was appointed joint architect '*pour* *les Fêtes et Cérémonies'* with Joseph Lecointe (1783–1858). In this capacity Hittorff designed the funeral of the Duc de Berry (1820), the baptism of the Duc de Bordeaux (1821) and the coronation of Charles X (1825), for whom Hittorff designed a carpet in 1827. In 1820 he visited England and sketched buildings by SOANE, Cockerell and STUART and George IV's throne for the opening of Parliament. In 1821 he went to Germany and was in contact with SCHINKEL. From 1822 to 1824 he travelled in Italy and Sicily with Karl Ludwig von Zanth (1796–1857) and Gustav STIER. His *Architecture Antique de la Sicile* (1827) was the first full account of Greek polychromy, also the theme of his *Architecture polychrome chez les Grecs* (1830); Owen JONES was among the many influenced by Hittorff's discoveries. Hittorff designed stained glass and metalwork for his church of Saint-Vincent-de-Paul (from 1824), lights for the Place de la Concorde (1836 to 1840, and 1853) and the frame for a portrait of Prince Napoleon by INGRES (1855). He became a French citizen in 1842.

H.N.D.C. These initials refer to the publisher and possibly the designer of *Winter- und Sommer-Gärtlein* (Linz, 1691; thirty-six plates), a book of simple, mainly geometric, designs for embroidery.

Hoeder, Friedrich Wilhelm Born in Kottbus in about 1715, Hoeder studied painting in Berlin, probably under Antoine Pesne (1683–1757), and from 1736 in Paris under the architect and painter G. N. Servandoni (1695–1766). He also travelled to Italy. Back in Berlin from 1745 Hoeder worked as a decorative painter for Frederick the Great there and in Potsdam. He also designed textiles, embroidery and goldsmiths' work. In 1761, about the time of Hoeder's death, sixteen plates of ROCOCO

VASES, cartouches and fountains after his designs were published in Potsdam.

Hoffmann, Friedrich Gottlob A cabinet-maker in Leipzig, in 1789 Hoffmann issued an illustrated catalogue of his furniture as an explicit reaction to French and English competition, *Abbildungen der vornehmsten Tischlerarbeiten, welche verfertiget werden und zu haben sind bey Friedrich Gottlob Hoffmann, wohnhaft auf dem alten Neumarkt in Leipzig*; this catalogue contains designs in both French and English styles. In 1795 he issued a second catalogue, *Neues Verzeichnis und Muster-Charte des Meublen-Magazins von F. G. Hoffmann in Leipzig*, completely in the English style, many of its designs being copied directly from HEPPLEWHITE's 1788 *Cabinet-Maker and Upholsterer's Guide*. On at least one occasion a design was in turn copied by F. J. Bertuch, and, although intended as catalogues, Hoffmann's books must also have provided models for craftsmen, helping to disseminate French and, even more, English NEO-CLASSICISM in Germany.

Hoffmann, Hans Hoffmann was both designer and engraver of a pattern-book for embroidery, *New Modelbuch* (Strasbourg, 1556; twenty-eight plates). His style resembles that of Narcissus RENNER.

Hoffmann, Josef (1870–1956) Born in Pirnitz in Moravia, Hoffmann studied architecture in Munich and Vienna. In Vienna he was briefly a pupil of Otto Wagner (1841–1918) and, after travelling in Italy in 1895, worked in Wagner's studio until 1899. In 1892 Hoffmann founded the Siebener Club, whose members included OLBRICH and Koloman MOSER, and in 1897, one day after the actual event, he joined the Vienna Secession, led by Gustav Klimt (1862–1918). The 'VER SACRUM' room at the first Secession Exhibition (1898) was designed by Hoffmann and his work was praised by Loos in 'Dekorative Kunst' (1898). In 1899 Wagner recommended Hoffmann to be his successor as professor of architecture at the Academy, but in the event Hoffmann was appointed professor of architecture at the School of Applied Arts, a post for which Wagner had recommended Olbrich but which Hoffmann held until 1941. Until about 1900, for instance in a house near Hohenburg (1899), Wagner's interior designs were in a simple but curvilinear Art Nouveau style. Shortly afterwards Hoffmann turned to an almost total rectilinearity, most remarkably demonstrated in abstract reliefs for the Vienna 1902 Secession Exhibition. The elongated abstraction of Hoffmann's designs owed much to Mackintosh. Hoffmann visited England with Koloman Moser and in 1903, backed by Fritz Wärndorfer, they founded the Wiener Werkstätte, inspired by the example of Ashbee's Guild of Handicraft; Koloman Moser left in 1905 but Hoffmann designed for the Werkstätte until 1931. For the Puckersdorf Sanatorium (1903–6) Hoffmann designed bentwood chairs; he also designed jewellery, leatherwork, textiles, metalwork, often pierced with a lattice of small squares, and also glass for the Lobmeyr firm, at the invitation of Stephan Rath (1876–1960). The Palais Stoclet, Brussels (1905–11), for the Belgian industrialist Adolphe Stoclet, was Hoffmann's greatest achievement as architect and designer; his collaborators there included Klimt and Czeschka. In 1905 Hoffmann joined Klimt in seceding from the Secession to form the Kunstschau, whose building he designed in 1908. Hoffmann designed many Austrian pavilions at exhibitions, for example the Cologne 1914 Deutsche Werkbund Exhibition and the Paris 1925 and Stockholm 1930 Exhibitions. In the 1920s Hoffmann turned to a curvilinear style in metalwork, much in contrast with his earlier manner. In 1978 Hoffmann's Kubus armchair (1910) and other models were reproduced by Franz Wittmann in Austria. The designer and architect Oswald Haerdtl (1899–1959) was Hoffmann's most direct successor.

Hohlwein, Ludwig (1874–1949) Born in Wiesbaden, Hohlwein studied at the Munich Polytechnic under Thiersch and was then an assistant to Wallot at the Dresden Academy. After visiting London and Paris he settled in Munich, where he designed interiors, books and ceramics. From 1906 Hohlwein designed a masterly series of posters for the Munich tailors Hermann Scherrer (1907 and 1908) and others. Their stylish use of asymmetry, bold lettering and large blank areas, derived from Japan, France and England, made them, according to 'Art et Décoration' (1911), much collected by French and English designers; among those who were probably influenced by Hohlwein was McKnight Kauffer. After the First World War, Hohlwein was less original but still prolific.

Holbein, Hans Born in Augsburg, the son of the painter Hans Holbein, in the winter of 1497 to 1498, Hans Holbein the Younger was trained in his father's workshop. In about 1515 he was in Basel, where he painted a table-top for the standard bearer Hans Baer. In 1517 he moved to Lucerne, where he designed stained glass and painted the façade of the Hertenstein house. In 1519 Holbein became a member of the Basel guild and in 1521 to 1522 decorated the Great Council Chamber of Basel Town Hall with paintings in fictive architectural frames. In about 1523 he visited France, and around this date designed his woodcut *Dance of Death*, first published in

Lyon in 1538, as well as many other book decorations, title-pages and initials. In 1526 Holbein travelled to England for the first time and worked on the temporary banqueting hall erected at Greenwich for the French Ambassadors in 1527. Back in Basel in 1528 he designed ninety-four woodcut biblical illustrations published at Lyon in 1538, and continued to design stained glass. In 1532, after a month in Antwerp, Holbein returned to England. In 1533 Holbein was commissioned by the merchants of the Steel Yard to design an arch and decorations for the coronation of Anne Boleyn. In 1535 he designed a cover for the Coverdale Bible. However, Holbein's main activity in London was as a designer of silver and jewellery; he was a friend of the goldsmith Hans of Antwerp. Holbein designed a silver cradle for the Princess Elizabeth (1533) and a table fountain (1534) given by Anne Boleyn to Henry VIII. From 1536 Holbein worked for the King, decorating for him the Privy Chamber in Whitehall Palace (1537) and, after a return visit to Basel in 1538, the ceiling of the Chapel in St James's Palace, modelled on a plate in SERLIO's Book IV (1537). A large design for a mantelpiece by Holbein was probably intended for Bridewell Palace; it once belonged to William BECKFORD. Thirteen Holbein designs for silver and arms, including ewers, salts, cups, swords and daggers, were engraved by Wenceslas Hollar from 1642 to 1646. Designs for jewels also survive, and a combined sand-glass, compass and sundial for presentation by Sir Anthony Denny to Henry VIII in 1545, Holbein having died in 1543. Holbein worked in an accomplished Italianate early RENAISSANCE style, comparable to that of Peter FLÖTNER; he was moreover a master of MORESQUE ornament. However, his 1535 portrait of Erasmus is framed in an arch which shows a precocious awareness of STRAPWORK

looking forward to Cornelis FLORIS and BOS. Holbein's designs were frequently imitated in the 19th century, for instance a cup and cover by Garrards of London (1861 to 1862) presented by Edward VII to the Town of Hamburg in 1904.

Holiday, Henry George Alexander (1839–1927) Holiday studied painting at Leigh's Life School and at the Royal Academy Schools, where his fellow students included William DE MORGAN and he fell under the influence of the Pre-Raphaelites. Holiday helped to decorate BURGES's Great Bookcase (1859–62) and painted the Sleeping Beauty panel (1866) on his bed. In December 1862, at the recommendation of the painter Albert Moore, he succeeded BURNE-JONES, whom he had met in 1861, as designer to the stained-glass firm of James Powell & Sons of Whitefriars. Holiday's early style was strongly influenced by ROSSETTI and Burne-Jones. His first big success was a window for Burges at Worcester College Chapel, Oxford (1864), where he took over the commission from Millais, who had provided an unsatisfactory design. Holiday worked not only for Powell's but also for Lavers & Barraud, and for Heaton, Butler & Bayne. In 1867 he travelled to Italy via Chartres and the PARIS EXHIBITION with Burges's pupil W. Gualbert Saunders; they had a brief partnership. About this time Holiday broke with Burges, refusing to match his own stained glass to Burges's architecture. By this date he was working in a pictorial style characterized by rich draperies. In 1882 Holiday became a member of The Fifteen, the designers' club, which had Lewis F. DAY as its secretary. In 1891, dissatisfied with Powell's work, Holiday set up his own stained-glass studio. His *Stained Glass as an Art* (1896) includes chapters on Burne-Jones and Richmond.

Holland, Henry (1745–1806) The son of a prominent London builder, Holland trained under his father until 1771, when he became the partner of the landscape gardener Lancelot 'Capability' Brown (1716–83), whose daughter he married in 1773. From 1776, when he was employed on Brooks's Club, Holland enjoyed the patronage of the Whig aristocracy, and thence that of the Prince of Wales, for whom he designed Carlton House (1783–96). Holland's style was strongly influenced by his French contemporaries and he procured French furniture and decorations for the houses of his clients, through the Parisian *marchand-mercier* Dominique Daguerre. An assistant, Jean-Pierre Théodore Trécourt, was French, as were his painters, BOILEAU, Delabrière and Pernotin. In 1785 Horace WALPOLE wrote of Carlton House: 'Every ornament is at a proper distance, and not one too large, but all delicate and new, with more freedom and variety than Greek ornaments; and though probably borrowed from the Hôtel de Condé and other new palaces, not one that is not rather classic than French.' In some objects Holland articulates chaste outlines and plain surfaces with passages of reeding or fluting, favourite motifs; in others, sometimes directly based on classical prototypes, he used a stronger palette of ornament, chimaerae, gryphons, ACANTHUS and anthemions, all handled with exquisite refinement. The materials for this more archaeological aspect of Holland's designs were doubtless supplied by TATHAM, who was his assistant. SOANE was a pupil of Holland and SHERATON was strongly influenced by his furniture designs.

Holly, Henry Hudson (1843–92) Holly was active as an architect in New York, from 1887 in partnership with his pupil Horatio F. Jelliff (1844–92). His *Holly's Country Seats* (New York, 1866) contains designs in the Tudor and Swiss manners, which look back to the age of LOUDON. *Church Architecture* (Hartford, Connecticut, 1871) is a total contrast: dedicated to G. E. STREET it has a long ecclesiological introduction and plates in an English Reformed GOTHIC manner, notably some tough gas fixtures by the Archer & Pancoast Company of New York. Its title, in the style of TALBERT, is by Edward Neville Stent, whom Holly described as 'an artist whose designs for interior color decoration are unrivalled in this country'. Holly was one of the pioneers of the Queen Anne style in America. In *Harper's Monthly* (1876) he echoed C. L. EASTLAKE's doctrines on furniture design and illustrated a bedroom in the Eastlake manner. Holly's *Modern Dwellings in Town and Country* (New York, 1878) acknowledges his debt to Eastlake.

Hone, Evie (1894–1955) Born in Dublin, the daughter of a prosperous maltster, Hone studied painting in London at the Westminster and Central Schools of Art under Walter Sickert (1860–1942), Bernard Meninsky (1891–1950) and Glen Byam Shaw. In 1920, with her life-long friend Mainie Jellett (1897–1944), she entered the studio of André Lhôte (1885–1962) in Paris; in 1921 the two became pupils of Albert Gleizes (1881–1962). Hone painted abstracts and was elected to the Abstraction-Création group. In 1933 she designed abstract stained glass, made by Wilhelmina Geddes; thenceforward she was a regular stained-glass designer, strongly influenced by the painter Georges Rouault (1871–1958). From 1933 to 1943 her glass was made by Sarah Purser at An Túr Gloine; Michael Healy was her mentor in stained-glass techniques. Hone admired GRUBER and Louis Barillet in France and THORN PRIKKER, R. N. R. Hulst and Joseph

Nicholas in Holland. Her most celebrated commission was a window for Eton College Chapel (1949–52).

Honervogt, Jacob In 1608 Honervogt moved from his native Cologne to Paris, where he was active as a publisher. He became a naturalized Frenchman in 1620. In about 1619 he published two suites, each of twelve plates, for richly jewelled embroidery: his designs may have derived from those published by Daniel MEYER in 1618. Honervogt also issued a number of designs for STRAPWORK cartouches, and for jewellery in the COSSE-DE-POIS manner; he further reprinted Balthasar SYLVIUS, *Variarum protactionum quas vulgo maurusias vocant.*

Hope, Thomas (1769–1831) Born in Amsterdam, Hope was a member of a wealthy and cultivated Scots-Dutch banking dynasty. His father, John Hope, had been a patron of PIRANESI. From 1787 to 1795 Hope embarked on a prolonged and exceptionally extensive Grand Tour, travelling to Turkey, Egypt, Syria, Greece, Sicily, Spain, Portugal, France, Germany and England. In Rome in 1792 he ordered from the young sculptor FLAXMAN a group, Aurora and Cephalus, and a series of illustrations to Dante; while there he also collected antique statues, including Egyptian pieces. Later voyages included Egypt (1797), Athens (1799), Naples (1802), Rome (1803) and Italy (1815). However, from 1795, when the French installed a revolutionary republican regime in Holland, Hope's permanent place of residence was England. In 1799 he bought a house in Duchess Street, London, designed by Robert ADAM, and immediately proceeded to convert and redecorate it in an advanced NEOCLASSICAL style. In 1801 he purchased Sir William HAMILTON's second collection of vases, as a foundation for his own

collection, and in 1803 he purchased from the sculptor Thorwaldsen his unfinished Jason (only delivered in 1828). Hope's activity as a collector was accompanied by an active participation in the politics of art. He had been elected a Fellow of the Society of Antiquaries in 1794. In 1800 he became a member of the Society of DILETTANTI. In 1804 he published *Observations on the Plans and Elevations designed by James Wyatt, Architect, for Downing College, Cambridge . . .*, a highly polemical pamphlet which attacked WYATT, then President of the Royal Academy, and promoted Greek Revival principles. Also in 1804 Hope opened Duchess Street to the public as a lesson in taste (Horace WALPOLE's opening of Strawberry Hill provides a partial precedent). He was at this stage closely involved in design. The silversmiths Paul Storr (1798 and 1801) and Rundell, Bridge & Rundell (1805) both executed his designs and in 1805 Matthew Boulton sent his protégé John Philip (1780–1820) to make drawings at Duchess Street. In 1807 Hope published 'A Letter on Instruction in Design' in the *Artist*, in which he initiated the English 19th-century effort to improve standards of design by education. His *Household Furniture and Interior Decoration Executed from Designs by Thomas Hope* (1807), a book with sixty plates, was intended to further this cause by illustrating the objects that Hope had designed for Duchess Street as models for designers and craftsmen. The plates were engraved by George Dawe (1781–1829) and Edmund Aikin (1780–1820). In 1809 *Household Furniture* was followed by *Costume of the Ancients* and in 1812 by *Designs of Modern Costume*, which illustrated many of Hope's furniture designs in use. An edition of the latter with nine extra plates was issued by its engraver, Henry MOSES, in 1823. Hope's next book was a novel, *Anastasius* (1819), a great success, which recorded the picaresque adventures of a Greek Christian in the Eastern Mediterranean. After his death his *Historical Essay on Architecture* (1835) was issued; like *Costume of the Ancients* it went through many editions. In 1807 Hope bought a country house, The Deepdene, in Surrey; he was engaged until his death in its remodelling and improvement, in a picturesque variety of styles. It was described in a manuscript *History* by John Britton, who had dedicated Volume II of his *Architectural Antiquities* (1809) to Hope. In his later years Hope continued to collect, ordering a Venus from Canova in 1819. However, Duchess Street (demolished in 1851) and *Household Furniture* were the main avenue by which his gifts as designer and propagandist influenced contemporary taste, despite an attack by Sydney Smith in the *Edinburgh Review* (1807). George SMITH's *Designs for Household Furniture*, published in 1808 but announced as ready in 1806, probably reflects the direct influence of visits to Duchess Street. Richard BROWN and John STAFFORD are among those later indebted to the book, which crops up in most bibliographies of the period, including that in LOUDON's *Encyclopaedia* (1833). Hope listed his own sources: they include Flaxman's drawings to Aeschylus and Homer (1793), DENON's *Voyage dans la Basse et la Haute Égypte* (1802), STUART's *Antiquities of Athens* (1762, 1789 and 1795), Piranesi's works, and the illustrations of Hamilton's vases by d'Harcanville (1766–7) and Tischbein (1791–5). Charles PERCIER was a personal friend of Hope, who specifically mentions his illustrations to the Didot edition of *Horace* (1799) as a source of inspiration, but Percier and FONTAINE's *Recueil* (1801 and 1812) represents a parallel experiment in design rather than an influence. Even Hope's use of outline engravings was derived from Tischbein and Flaxman rather than the *Recueil*. Hope does not acknowledge TATHAM's *Ancient Ornamental Architecture* (1799), but he owned it and is likely to have used it. Hope's designs for Duchess Street incorporated Greek, Roman and Egyptian elements, with an admixture of Indian or Turkish. It was a highly personal mixture, and Hope ultimately influenced taste more by the general example of his seriousness of attitude and method than by the provision of specific models for imitation. After the sale of The Deepdene in 1917 his collection and designs enjoyed a new lease of life as a major influence on the Regency Revival.

Hopfer, Daniel Born in about 1470 in Kaufbeuren, the son of a painter, Hopfer became a citizen of Augsburg in 1493 and a master in the painters' guild in the same year. In 1497 Hopfer, a militant protestant, married Justina, sister of the humanist and publisher Sigismund Grimm, for whom he designed initial letters in 1522 to 1523. Hopfer designed borders for title-pages from 1514. His main activity was as an etcher of decoration on armour, and he remained active as such until the year of his death, 1536, the date of a signed shield in Madrid. Hopfer invented the technique of taking prints on paper from etched plates, and was already famous for this achievement in 1593. Hopfer issued some fifty etched plates of ornament, which included GOTHIC foliage, RENAISSANCE GROTESQUES from Zoan ANDREA and Nicoletto da MODENA, medallion heads, and designs for ceilings, lavabos, towel-rails, daggers, alphabets, monstrances, tabernacles and altars. In some instances Hopfer combines Gothic foliage with early Renaissance motifs. In the 17th century his designs were reprinted from the original plates by the Nuremberg publisher David Funck. Two of Hopfer's sons, Jerome and Lambert, produced prints in their father's manner. A print by Lambert was used to illustrate an English cup of 1540. Jerome moved in 1529 to Nuremberg, where he died in 1550; his prints include copies after Andrea, ALTDORFER and Giovanni da BRESCIA.

Hoppenhaupt, Johann Christian Born in 1719 in Merseburg, the son of a carver, Hoppenhaupt came to Berlin in 1740 with his elder brother, Johann Michael HOPPENHAUPT, and thenceforward they worked together on Frederick the Great's palaces in Berlin and Potsdam under KNOBELSDORFF and NAHL; when Nahl left Berlin in 1746 Hoppenhaupt succeeded him as Directeur des Ornements. His style is difficult to distinguish from this brother's, whose engravings he used as inspiration when he worked on the Neues Palais in Potsdam from 1763 to 1769, but seems to have been at once lighter and stiffer. They shared a predilection for NATURALISTIC ornament. In the 1760s Hoppenhaupt probably supplied the Berlin porcelain factory with ROCOCO models; he is known to have executed NEOCLASSICAL models in 1772. He also designed for goldsmiths. He died in Berlin between 1778 and 1786.

Hoppenhaupt, Johann Michael Born in Merseburg in 1709, the son of a carver, Hoppenhaupt was at first trained by his father but later worked in Dresden and Vienna before coming to Berlin in 1740. Hereafter Hoppenhaupt collaborated with his younger brother, Johann Christian HOPPENHAUPT, on the carving and design of interior decoration in Frederick the Great's palaces in Berlin and Potsdam under the direction of KNOBELSDORFF and NAHL, the creators of the Berlin ROCOCO style. In 1746 Hoppenhaupt designed and carved a coach and a throne for Empress Elisa-

beth of Russia and about the same date published a suite of designs for clockcases later copied by HERTEL in Augsburg. From 1746 to 1748 he designed and executed decorations for Schloss Zerbst. Hoppenhaupt also issued seventy designs for decorations engraved by MEIL from 1752 to 1755. They include panelling, chimneypieces, console tables, commodes, chairs, clocks, chandeliers, coaches and sedan chairs, and are in an extreme rococo style influenced by CUVILLIÉS, full of asymmetry, vigour and invention (sometimes to the extent of gawkiness) and with a generous use of naturalistic ornament, not to mention Chinamen, dragons and putti and some surprisingly oldfashioned masks and trophies. Certain motifs seem to have acted as a direct inspiration for Thomas JOHNSON. In 1755 Hoppenhaupt designed a pair of commodes in the Residenz at Ansbach for the Prussian Queen Mother Sophie Dorothea made by the cabinet-maker Schilansky; furniture to his designs was exported to Sweden about this date. Afterwards he left Berlin and may have returned to Merseburg, but nothing definite is known of his later life and death.

Horn, Donath Born at Pirna in Meissen, Horn became a cabinet-maker in Frankfurt in 1673. Earlier, in Nuremberg, he had issued a *Neues un Wohl Inventiertes Buch* (thirty-nine plates), which contained extremely vigorous AURICULAR brackets and other ornaments for the use of carvers and cabinet-makers.

Horne, Herbert Percy (1864–1916) Born in Chelsea in 1864, the son of an architect and collector, Horne trained as a surveyor from 1880. In 1883 he entered MACKMURDO's office to learn architecture, and became a declared member of the Century Guild. Horne was in partnership from 1885 to 1890. He was coeditor with Mackmurdo of the Century

Guild journal the *Hobby Horse* (1884) and designed many of its decorations. From 1886 to 1892 he was co-editor with Selwyn IMAGE, and he himself became editor in 1893 when the *Hobby Horse* was taken over by The Bodley Head and became mainly art-historical. As a member of the Century Guild, Horne designed the swirling fabric, The Angel with the Trumpet, in about 1884; it was produced both as a cretonne and a velveteen. He also designed a number of Century Guild wallpapers, powerful patterns using leaves, flowers and birds; they were printed by Jeffrey & Co. of Islington. In 1896 Horne helped to decorate Arnold Dolmetsch's first harpsichord shown at the ARTS & CRAFTS EXHIBITION in that year. In 1900 Horne moved to Florence, where he was active as both collector and art-historian and designed typefaces, including the Florence (1909). He produced a major life of BOTTICELLI and left his house and collection to the City of Florence.

Hornick, Erasmus A goldsmith from Antwerp, Hornick became a citizen of Augsburg in 1555. In 1559 he moved to Nuremberg, where he was made an honorary citizen and, in 1563, a master goldsmith. In Nuremberg, Hornick published two suites of designs for jewels (1562 and 1565; nineteen and twenty plates) and a suite of designs for VASES (1565; eighteen plates). His ornamental vocabulary is comparable to that of ZÜNDT. In 1566 Hornick left Nuremberg and by 1568 had moved back to Augsburg, where in 1578 he was working on the design of military equipment. In 1582 he was appointed imperial goldsmith to the Emperor RUDOLF II in Prague, where he died in 1583. In the VICTORIA & ALBERT MUSEUM are 275 designs by Hornick, probably dating from around 1560. They include titlepages, braziers, bowls, buckets, candelabra, cups, chalices, knives, forks, egg-

cups, ewers, salvers, hunting horns, lamps, pilgrim bottles, plates, pomanders, salts, snuffers, tankards, toothpicks, swords, vases, etc. Some designs are influenced by Giulio ROMANO and similar to those of URSONI, others are embellished with STRAPWORK, but the most extreme, many of them ewers, are contorted and bulging encounters of monstrous imaginary creatures. Hornick's designs seem to have been for a wide range of rich and exotic materials. A group of designs by Hornick in Munich was already attributed to Jacopo da STRADA in 1582, and said to be after the antique. Hornick would have seen designs by Strada in Nuremberg, and was clearly indebted in Strada's transmission of Giulio Romano's style to Germany.

Horse Heads, Master of the The Master of the Horse Heads was a Flemish engraver active in the first third of the 16th century. He was strongly influenced by ALDEGREVER, one of whose friezes of ornaments he copied. The Master also engraved some ten plates of RENAISSANCE ornament, incorporating dolphins, ACANTHUS, sea-horses, horse heads, etc., and five plates of dagger scabbards. Ornament by the Master was used to decorate the staircase of the Town Hall at Görlitz in 1537.

Horta, Victor (1861–1947) Born in Ghent, the son of a cobbler, Horta at first studied music, and then from 1874 to 1877 drawing and architecture at the Ghent Academy. In 1878 he worked with the Paris architect and decorator Jean Dubuysson at Montmartre. In 1881 he entered the Brussels Academy. From 1884 he was a pupil of Alphonse Balat (1818–95), architect to Leopold I. Horta was also influenced by VIOLLET-LE-DUC. His first buildings date from 1885. In 1891 he designed a silver centrepiece for the City of Brussels in collaboration with the sculptor Van der Stappen. In 1892 to 1893 Horta designed a house in Brussels for the engineer Emile Tassel which was the first monument of the fully developed ART NOUVEAU style, especially in its staircase where ironwork, glass, woodwork and wall decorations alike are animated by scrolling stems and whiplash tendrils. English wallpapers were used elsewhere in the house, and LIBERTY silks bought by Horta from VAN DE VELDE. His house for the industrialist Armand Solvay (1894–5) and the Maison de Peuple in Brussels (1895), a socialist meeting place, reinforced his reputation. In 1895 he was invited by SERRURIER-BOVY to participate in the Liège exhibition and met BING at Tassel's house. He subsequently went to Paris to visit him, and designed a façade for Bing's shop, completely altering Bonnier and BRANGWYN's original scheme. Horta's designs were not executed. In 1896 he was in contact with GUIMARD, who wrote him admiring letters, and in 1897 the first issue of 'ART ET DÉCORATION' included an article on Horta's work. In 1896 Horta designed a pavilion for the Val Saint Lambert glass factory at the Brussels Exhibition. In 1897 he showed a dining-room for Baron Van Eetvelde at the Libre Esthétique Exhibition. Horta designed decorations and furniture for the Belgian pavilion at the TURIN 1902 EXHIBITION. His last main work was the Palais des Beaux-Arts in Brussels (1920). Towards the end of his life, despite academic honours, Horta became increasingly inactive, melancholy and embittered. He particularly resented Van de Velde's self-promotion. Horta designed only for his own buildings, but for these he executed every detail, lighting, carpets, stained glass, furniture etc., all in that energetic vegetal Art Nouveau which CARABIN referred to as the 'macaroni style'.

House Beautiful, The Founded in 1896, the *House Beautiful* was a Chicago based version of the 'STUDIO'. Frank Lloyd WRIGHT designed for the magazine and it described the work of ASHBEE, VOYSEY, BAILLIE SCOTT and others.

Houte, Adrian van den Born in Malines in about 1459, the son of a stained-glass painter, Herman van den Houte, Adrian van den Houte worked as a stained-glass designer and painter in Malines, supplying windows to the Town Hall in 1513 and to Margaret of Austria's palace in 1519. Around 1510 Houte designed stained glass for Arnold Ortkens van Nijmegen, later the great rival of VELLERT. Houte also designed tapestries in the late-GOTHIC style, although using classical motifs; they include two on the Romaunt of the Rose in the Hermitage, Leningrad. Houte seems to have been an important influence on Bernart van ORLEY. He died in 1521.

Høye, Emil (1875–1958) Born in Denmark, where he was influenced by Georg JENSEN, Høye settled in Bergen in 1905. He was artistic director for Marius Hammer's goldsmiths' firm from 1910. He set up independently in 1916 but continued to design for Hammer on occasion.

H.S., Master An obscure figure, H.S. seems to have worked as a cabinetmaker in the Thurgau but to have received his artistic education in Augsburg. His importance lies in his authorship of a group of eight crude woodcut designs for furniture and panelling in an early Renaissance manner derived from the designs of Peter FLÖTNER. They probably date from about 1530 to 1540 and are among the earliest furniture designs to have been produced at ARTISAN level. He influenced Master H.G.

Hubbard, Elbert (1856–1915) Born in

Bloomington, Illinois, Hubbard was a successful soap salesman until 1893, when he settled in East Aurora, near Buffalo, New York. In 1894 he travelled to England and was much influenced by William MORRIS and the Kelmscott Press. On his return to America, Hubbard bought a press, which he named the Roycroft Press, and began to publish a magazine, *The Philistine*. *The Song of Songs* (1895) was the first of many books published by Hubbard, their designers including Will Denslow, Samuel Warner and Dard HUNTER. Many had soft chamois bindings. The press became the centre of a thriving artistic community over which Hubbard, 'the Sage of East Aurora' or 'Fra Elbertus', presided. A Roycroft leather shop was soon opened; from 1901 furniture was made and in 1903 the Roycroft Inn opened. Janet Ashbee visited the Roycrofters in 1900, by which date 175 people were employed. Roycroft furniture was usually of oak in a massive Arts & Crafts style; in 1905 it was called 'Aurora Colonial Furniture'. Roycroft lines included hand-carved mottoes such as 'Build strong' on half logs. Metalwork was produced at the Roycroft Copper Shop under Karl Kipp. In 1915 Elbert Hubbard and his wife Alice went down on the *Lusitania*; the Roycroft Shops survived until 1938 under Bert Hubbard. Of Elbert Hubbard, Kornwolf has written 'he popularized RUSKIN'S and Morris's ideas to the point of boredom, the Arts and Crafts to the point of vulgarity'. Gustav STICKLEY much resented Hubbard's success.

Huet, Christophe (1700–1759) Born in Pontoise, Huet was active as a decorative painter at Versailles from 1723. In 1733 he worked with Claude III AUDRAN at the Château d'Anet, and in 1735 and 1740 painted the Grande et Petite Singeries at Chantilly. In 1755 he painted the Salon Chinois at the Châ-

teau de Champs in Brie. Huet published *Singeries* (twelve plates), in which ROCOCO monkeys are seen hunting, painting, playing musical instruments, and in much less dignified anthropomorphic poses. A *Nouveau Livre de Singeries* followed. *Trofées de Chasse* (six plates) presents lively and naturalistic rococo hunting trophies; they were copied in reverse in London and said to be 'Properly adapted to the New Method of Ornamenting Rooms and Screens with Prints'.

Huet, Jean-Baptiste (1745–1811) The nephew of Christophe HUET, and the son of Nicolas Huet '*peintre du Garde-Meuble du Roi*', Jean-Baptiste Huet studied under the animal painter Dagomer, and afterwards under François BOUCHER'S pupil, LE PRINCE. In 1769 he showed an animal painting at the Salon, and his later works were mainly animal or pastoral paintings. Huet also designed book illustrations, tapestries for Aubusson and Beauvais, including a set of *Pastorales*, wallpapers for Réveillon, and porcelain for the manufactory at Sèvres where he had a country house. In 1783, the year in which the venture became a Manufacture Royale, he began to design printed cottons for the manufactory at Jouy founded by Christophe Philippe Oberkampf (1738–1815) in 1759. Huet's first design for Jouy's *Travaux de la Manufacture* (1783) illustrated the making of the cottons. It and his other early designs, including *Les Plaisirs de la Ferme* (about 1785), are free compositions of scattered scenes. Next came scenes in a structure of ARABESQUES, including the unlikely *Louis XVI restaurateur de la Liberté* (about 1789). From 1796 Huet used a more rigid geometrical framework, for instance *Psyché et l'Amour* (1810). Huet published a wide range of prints after his designs in eighteen suites of *Fragments* (1778) and twelve suites of *Œuvre* *de Différens Genres* (one dated 1783). Some are painterly pastoral scenes, animals, hunting subjects and putti. Others present designs for tapestry, textiles and embroidery for chair covers, wall hangings and other purposes, designs for gilt-bronze clocks and chimney furniture, designs for ornamental trophies, panels and friezes, and a few *singeries* in the manner of his uncle. One plate, entitled 'Model d'un Écran executé pour la Reine', shows Huet as a royal furniture designer. Like the majority of his works, it is in a graceful late NEO-CLASSICAL style in which doves and putti play a prominent part. Some of Huet's plates were copied at Augsburg by the engraver and publisher J. M. WILL (1727–1805).

Hulme, Frederick Edward (1841–1909) Born in Hanley, Staffordshire, the son of a landscape painter, Hulme studied at the SCHOOL OF DESIGN in London from 1858, and was then art master at Marlborough College. From 1870 he taught geometrical drawing at King's College, London. Hulme was a passionate botanist and an influential advocate of formalized natural ornament; he admired the works of Matthew Digby WYATT, of Owen JONES and of VIOLLET-LE-DUC. Hulme's many books include *A Series of Sketches from Nature of Plant Form* (1868), *A Series of 60 Outline Examples of Freehand Ornament* (1870), *Plants, Their Natural Growth and Ornamental Treatment* (1874), *Principles of Ornamental Art* (1875, based on articles in the 1875 'BUILDING NEWS'), *Examples for Fret-Cutting and Woodcarving* (1877) and *The Birth and Development of Ornament* (1893).

Hulsen, Esaias van The son of a mathematician from Ghent, who moved in about 1590 to Nuremberg, settled in Frankfurt in 1602, and died there in 1606, Hulsen was born in Middelburg,

probably in about 1570. In 1612 in Frankfurt he married the daughter of a tapestry worker of Flemish origin working in Frankenthal, and in the same year moved to Stuttgart, where he was active as a goldsmith and where he died shortly before 1626. Hulsen published five suites of black ornament for enamelling in 1606, 1609, 1616 (two) and 1617. The 1616 and 1617 designs, published in Stuttgart, were fine exercises in the stretched GROTESQUE manner, compilations including animals, reptiles, birds, flowers and architecture, some incorporated into landscapes, hunting scenes, or spiders' webs of scrolls. Hulsen was an engineer and assisted Gerhard Philippi on the waterworks of a famous grotto built in Stuttgart from 1613 to 1621.

Hunter, Dard (1886–1966) While at Ohio State University in 1903 Hunter was inspired by a copy of Elbert HUBBARD's magazine, *The Philistine*, to seek work with the Roycrofters in East Aurora, New York. There he designed furniture, metalwork and books in the Arts & Crafts style. Hunter travelled to Vienna in 1908 and again in 1910, after which he founded the short-lived Dard Hunter School of Handicraft, where he taught stained glass and jewellery making. In 1915 Hunter made the paper, cut the type and printed W. A. Bradley's *The Etching of Figures*. He became an expert on paper and from 1928 to 1931 revived hand paper-making at Lime Rock, Connecticut. Hunter's books include *Papermaking through Eighteen Centuries* (New York, 1930).

Huquier, Gabriel (1695–1772) Born in Orleans, Huquier was from 1732 a member of the Académie de Saint-Luc in Paris. He was active there as an engraver and publisher of ornament by such leading designers as GILLOT, Bouchardon, LA JOUE, MEISSONIER, OPPENORD, PEYROTTE, WATTEAU and François

BOUCHER, being responsible for about 1,000 plates. Huquier was also a designer himself. His works include ten suites under the title *Nouveau Livre de Ser-rurerie*, sixty plates in all of fluent ROCOCO designs for ironwork of all types, and *Nouveau Livre de Trophées de Fleurs et Fruits Étrangers*, twelve plates, rococo floral compositions with a delightful Chinaman at the top of the title-page cartouche. A very large rococo floral cartouche published in about 1749 may have been a template for an embroidered chair-back. Huquier had a fine collection of drawings, which young students were able to visit on certain days in every week. It included many drawings by Meissonier, Oppenord and Gillot, as well as a large group of Chinese paintings.

Hurtu, Jacques Hurtu published three suites of black stretched GROTESQUE designs for enamelling, about thirty plates in all, some with COSSE-DE-POIS elements. One suite was dated 1614, another 1619, and two were engraved by the Parisian publisher Pierre Firens.

Hvidt, Peter Born in 1916, Hvidt was trained as an architect and at the School of Applied Art for Cabinet-Makers in Copenhagen (1942 to 1945), where he also taught. In 1944 he formed a design partnership with the similarly qualified Orla Mølgard-Nielsen, born in 1907. In 1950 they designed a series of chairs, the A X range, made by Fritz Hansen of Copenhagen, which represented a breakthrough in knock-down, mass-produced laminated-wood construction.

Hypnerotomachia Polifili A Dominican monk, Fra Francesco Colonna (1433–1527) was born in Venice but worked in Treviso from at least 1465 to 1477,

when he returned to Venice. Colonna's *Hypnerotomachia Polifili*, conceived in 1467 and published by Aldus Manutius (1450–1515) in Venice in 1499, was a strange allegorical romance, full of obscure symbolism and detailed descriptions of hieroglyphics and of classical buildings. This interest in architecture, strongly influenced by Vitruvius and Leone Battista Alberti (1404–72), has led to the description of the *Hypnerotomachia* as the first Italian architectural treatise. DÜRER and François I owned copies and Peter FLÖTNER's furniture designs seem to have been directly influenced by the superb line woodcut illustrations of the *Hypnerotomachia*; their author has not so far been identified. They were also used on Venetian glass. A second Venetian edition was published in 1545. The edition published in Paris in 1546 by Jean Martin (reprinted 1553 and 1561) had new illustrations, elaborate MANNERIST versions of those in the 1499 edition. These plates were reissued in 1600 with a new translation by Béroalde de Verville, who laid stress on the alchemical content of the *Hypnerotomachia*, which was also an encouragement to the cult of EMBLEMS. An English part translation appeared in 1592. The *Hypnerotomachia* was still popular in the 17th century. Tapestry cartoons illustrating the *Hypnerotomachia* were commissioned from VOUET and executed by his pupil Eustache Le Sueur. In 1685 François Blondel (1617–86) mentioned it as a useful book for the study of architecture. In 1802 Didot published an unillustrated translation by J. G. Legrand (1743–1808), pupil and son-in-law of CLÉRISSEAU. The *Hypnerotomachia* illustrations were later an important influence on RICKETTS and his generation.

I

Illustrated Carpenter and Builder (1877–present) Subtitled originally *A weekly journal for joiners, decorators, painters, plumbers, gas-fitters, architects &c.*, the 19th-century volumes of this trade magazine are a useful guide to design at the ARTISAN level.

Image, Selwyn (1849–1930) Born in Bodiam in Sussex, the son of a clergyman, Image met RUSKIN at Oxford and was taught drawing by him; he later stated: 'Whatever small power of design I may possess, I date the dawn of it from that lesson.' After graduation Image became a curate but he continued to design and showed stained glass at the PARIS 1878 EXHIBITION. In 1881 he shared a studio with Ruskin's assistant Arthur Burgess and in 1882 he resigned Holy Orders in favour of Art. From its beginning Image was very closely associated with MACKMURDO'S Century Guild. He designed the cover for the first number of its journal, the *Hobby Horse* (1884). He was an active stained-glass designer up to at least 1913. The 'STUDIO' devoted an article to his stained glass in 1898 and MUTHESIUS illustrated his work, which was in a vigorous manner derived from William MORRIS. Image also designed embroideries for the Royal School of Needlework and others, as well as bindings for Michael Field's *The Tragic Mary* (1890) and *Stefania* (1893), the latter shown at the ARTS & CRAFTS EXHIBITION, the title of *The Pageant* (1896), and pictures for the Fitzroy Picture Society (1893). In 1896 he helped to decorate the first

harpsichord made by Arnold Dolmetsch (1858–1940), and in 1904 he designed mosaic for Mortehoe church, North Devon. Image contributed to *Arts and Crafts Essays* (1893). He was Master of the ART-WORKERS' GUILD in 1900 and Slade Professor of Fine Arts at Oxford in 1910 and 1913. Image also was a member of the DESIGN AND INDUSTRIES ASSOCIATION. His *Letters* were edited by Mackmurdo in 1932.

Imprint (1913) This high-quality but short-lived London journal was devoted to the improvement of design in printing. The first issue opened with an essay on 'Art and Workmanship' by LETHABY.

Ince, William Born in London, the son of a glass grinder, Ince was in 1752 apprenticed to John West, a cabinet-maker of Covent Garden. After West's death in 1758 Ince entered into a partnership with the upholsterer John Mayhew, which they announced publicly in January 1759. The firm prospered and from 1766 to about 1776 the Duchess of Northumberland listed Ince & Mayhew among the leading London furniture makers. The partnership was formally dissolved in 1800 but continued in business until Ince's death in 1804. Ince was the partner concerned with 'designing and drawing', while Mayhew contributed capital and managerial skills. Ince subscribed to CHIPPENDALE'S *Director* (1754), and in 1759 Ince & Mayhew announced the publication of an 160-plate work intended as a competitor to the *Director* and as an advertisement of the capacities of its authors. In the event *The Universal System of Household Furniture* reached eighty-nine plates, and was topped up in 1760 with small designs for grates, firedogs, etc., two to a page on six pages, to reach a total of 101 plates when the book was published in 1762, with a dedication to the Duke of Marlborough. Mayhew contributed eleven plates but the vast majority of the designs were by Ince. Their style is close to that of Chippendale, who seems to have effectively replied to Ince & Mayhew's competition by issuing the third edition of the *Director* in 1762. SHERATON, while conceding that the *Universal System* was 'a work of merit in its day', thought it 'much inferior to Chippendale's'. *Household Furniture in Genteel Taste* (1760), a collaborative pattern-book produced by a 'Society of Upholsterers, Cabinet-Makers etc.', contains about twenty plates attributed to Ince & Mayhew, several of which are simplified from designs in the *Universal System*. Ince owned a copy of Isaac Ware's *Designs of Inigo Jones* and subscribed to George RICHARDSON's *The Five Orders of Architecture* (1787). The partnership owned ADAM's *Spalatro* and Mayhew owned Batty LANGLEY's *Treasury of Designs* (1740) with designs by Matthias LOCK bound in. Ince & Mayhew worked for Robert Adam at Croome Court, and seem to have evolved their own distinct NEO-CLASSICAL manner, presumably designed by Ince, in which blockish forms are decorated with bold neo-classical marquetry and neo-classical gilt-bronze mounts. In 1771 Ince was asked to recommend a draughtsman to Boulton and Fothergill, and they subsequently asked for the loan of Gori's *Museum Florentinum*.

Indau, Johann (1651–90) An architect and cabinet-maker active in Vienna, where he is first noted in 1682, Indau was in 1686 cabinet-maker to the Dowager Empress Eleonora. His *Neue Romanische Zierathen* (eleven plates) was published before 1685. It contains crestings, frames, brackets, stools, tables, chairs and altars in a rich ACANTHUS style, similar to that practised by FERRI and PASSARINI in Rome. *Nova Invenzione di Rabeschi, e Fogliami Romani* (Vienna, 1686, later reissued by Jeremias Wolff, Augsburg; six plates) contains scrolled acanthus friezes inhabited by putti and eagles. From the stress on Rome in the title of these two works and the character of their ornament it seems likely that Indau had been in Rome, perhaps with SCHOR. In 1686 he also published an architectural pattern-book.

Industrial Art (1877–8) Subtitled *A Monthly Review of Technical and Scientific Education* this London magazine, edited by J. H. Lamprey, adopted a format similar to the 'ART JOURNAL'. Although short-lived it was full of illustrations and information.

Industrial Design (1954–present) Published in New York, this is the leading American journal of design, founded in the same year as the Italian 'STILE INDUSTRIA'. George NELSON is among its regular contributors.

Ingres, Jean Auguste Dominique (1780–1867) Born in Montauban, the son of an ornamental sculptor, Ingres studied painting in Toulouse and then from 1797 under DAVID in Paris. He was in Rome from 1806 to 1820, when he moved to Florence. In 1824 he returned to France. Ingres was in Rome again from 1834 to 1841. In 1842 he designed hieratic stained glass made by Sèvres for the Chapel of Saint-Ferdinand at Neuilly and in 1844 another series of windows for the Chapelle Royale at Dreux, where Delacroix (1798–1863) played a minor role. From

1848 to 1850 five tapestries were woven at Gobelins after the Dreux cartoons. As a member of the Conseil Supérieur de Perfectionnement des Manufactures from 1848 Ingres advocated the role of tapestry as the sister art to painting. He showed twenty-five stained-glass cartoons at the PARIS 1855 EXHIBITION. In 1861 Ingres designed a great NEO-CLASSICAL cameo that depicted the Apotheosis of Napoleon I, based on a ceiling painting of 1853, and in 1864 he designed decorations for the Paris house of his friend HITTORFF.

Innenarchitektur (1953–60) Merged in 1961 into *Moebel + Decoration*, *Innen-architektur* was published from Essen. While it lasted it provided a broad and serious coverage of 1950s interior design with a stress on Germany.

Innen-Dekoration, Zeitschrift für (1889–1939) Published in Darmstadt by Alexander Koch, the publisher of 'DEUTSCHE KUNST UND DEKOR-ATION', this periodical is a rich source of information and illustration relating to design. In 1901 it sponsored the interior design competition in which BAILLIE SCOTT and MACKINTOSH were successful.

Interieur, Das (1900–4) This well-illus-trated Viennese decorative arts monthly was first edited by Dr Ludwig Abels; he was succeeded in 1903 by Josef August Lux. Josef HOFFMANN appears as the dominant figure, but major designers such as Koloman MOSER and minor designers such as Hartwig Fischel are also well represented. Its publisher, Anton Schroll, also issued *Der Architekt* (1895–1922).

Interiors (1888–present) This New York magazine is concerned with all aspects of interior design. It is now a well-illustrated glossy.

Isäus, Magnus (1841–90) Isäus became one of the leading Swedish practitioners of the RENAISSANCE Revival in architecture during the 1880s. In the early 1870s he was active as a designer for the Gustavsberg porcelain factory in Stockholm, working in a modified 'Louis XVI' style.

Isokon In 1929 the architect and designer Wells COATES met Jack Pritchard of the Venesta Plywood Company, who had come into contact with the ideas of LE CORBUSIER and the BAUHAUS while working in Paris. Coates and Pritchard then planned to build model MODERN houses, which they called Isotype dwellings, in Lawn Road, Hampstead. In 1931 a company was formed with the name 'Isokon', derived by Pritchard from 'Isometric Unit Construction', to exploit their ideas, which attached great importance to built-in furniture. In 1932 they began to plan a block of flats at Lawn Road and in 1933 a specimen 'minimum' flat designed by Wells Coates was shown at the Dorland Hall British Industrial Art Exhibition (see LONDON EXHI-BITIONS). The flats were built in 1934 and the tenants included Walter GRO-PIUS, Marcel BREUER and MOHOLY-NAGY. In 1937 an 'Isobar', designed by Breuer, opened on the ground floor. Pritchard had designed a sideboard using Plymax, a metal-faced plywood, as early as 1928, and he and Wells Coates later designed furniture made by Isokon from 1932. From 1934 Isokon marketed a plywood trolley designed by Gerald Summers for Makers of Simple Furniture in about 1933. In 1935 Pritchard decided to develop the furniture side of Isokon and enlisted Gropius as Controller of Design of the new Isokon Furniture Company, launched in early 1936, with plywood as its basic material and graphics designed by Moholy-Nagy. Isokon subsequently manufactured a wide range of plywood tables and chairs designed by Breuer, notably the Long Chair. Illustrated in *Circle* (1937) and shown by the MARS Group in 1938, such pieces became totems of Modernism in England. Gropius designed a few pieces, including a perforated aluminium waste-paper basket (1935) and in 1939 Egon Riss and Jack Pritchard designed the Penguin Donkey, to hold Penguin paperbacks, the Gull, a small bookshelf, and the Pocket Battleship. The war brought Isokon to an end but it was revived by Jack Pritchard in 1963.

Isselburg, Peter Born in about 1580 in Cologne, Isselburg was active there as an engraver from 1607. In about 1610 he moved to Nuremberg and in 1622 to Bamberg. There he published *Schönes Grottessken Bücklein* (1625; twelve plates), jolly GROTESQUE panels with ornaments which include symbols of the Passion and bacchic subjects; it was aimed at painters, goldsmiths, embroiderers, cabinet-makers and other craftsmen. In 1626 Isselburg moved to Coburg, but in 1630 he was back in Nuremberg, where he probably died in that year. He published over 440 plates in all.

Itten, Johannes (1888–1967) Born in the Bernese Oberland, the son of a teacher, Itten himself became an elementary school teacher in 1908. In 1910 he decided to study art in Geneva but, disillusioned by academic methods, he started to train as a high-school teacher at the University of Berne. Then, after a journey to Holland and Cologne, he decided in 1912 to become a painter. He studied the geometric basis of form under Professor Gilliard in Geneva, then from 1913 to 1916 he studied under Adolf Hölzel in Stuttgart, his fellow students including Oskar Schlemmer (1888–1943) and Willy Baumeister (1889–1955). In 1916 Itten moved to Vienna, where he painted and taught. In 1919 he showed abstract paintings at the Freie Bewegung exhibition, organized by Adolf LOOS. In the same year he was introduced by Alma Mahler to her then husband, Walter GROPIUS, and was engaged to teach at the newly founded BAUHAUS in Weimar. Itten taught the basic course, concentrating on such fundamentals as tone, texture, colour, movement and so on. His own designs were influenced by folk art. Itten's idiosyncratic and mystical approach led to conflict with the pragmatic Gropius and in 1923 he left the Bauhaus to study oriental philosophy at Herrliberg near Zürich, where he designed and made abstract carpets. At the Bauhaus, Itten was succeeded by MOHOLY-NAGY. In 1926 he opened his own design school in Berlin, and then from 1931 to 1938 he directed the school of textile design in Krefeld. In 1938 Itten fled the Nazis to Holland and thence to Zürich, where he ran the Museum and school of applied arts from 1938 to 1953, and the Zürich school of textile design from 1943 to 1960.

Ivanov, Ivan Alexeivich (1779–1848) Born in Moscow, Ivanov attended the St Petersburg Academy from 1789. He was mainly active as draughtsman and painter, but from 1806 spent a period designing for the Imperial Glass Factory, and in the 1830s designed for the Imperial Porcelain Factory.

J

Jack, George Washington Henry (1855–1932) Born in New York, the son of an engraver, Jack was brought to Glasgow while a boy, and was then articled to the architect Horatio K. Bromhead. In about 1875 he came to London and before 1880 entered the office of Philip WEBB, whose practice he took over on Webb's retirement in 1900. Jack designed furniture for William MORRIS & Co. from about 1880 until Morris's death in 1896. He was also active as a wood-carver, and his skill was admired by LETHABY, for whose Artistic Arts & Crafts Series he wrote *Woodcarving, Design and Workmanship* (1903). Jack also designed embroidery, stained glass, mosaics and cast-iron chimneypieces. He was a member of the ART-WORKERS' GUILD and showed regularly at ARTS & CRAFTS EXHIBITIONS. In 1913 he designed a balustrade for 8 Addison Road, London. Jack was steeped in the teaching of RUSKIN, Morris and Webb. His own designs, full of sincerity, tend to a sentimental NATURALISM most effective in marquetry. His furniture tended to employ simplified 18th-century forms.

Jacobsen, Arne (1902–71) Born in Copenhagen, the son of a merchant, Jacobsen was trained as a mason and then, from 1924 to 1927, trained as an architect at the Copenhagen Academy. He showed a book cover and a chair at the PARIS 1925 EXHIBITION. At the Academy Jacobsen formed a friendship with Gunnar ASPLUND (1885–1940) which lasted until the latter's death.

Jacobsen's earliest buildings were in a late NEO-CLASSICAL manner, but from about 1930, when he began to practise independently, he worked in the International MODERN style, becoming one of its most accomplished and celebrated practitioners. While in exile in Sweden from 1943 to 1945 Jacobsen designed some charmingly NATURALISTIC patterns for textiles and wallpapers. In 1952 he designed a neat stacking chair with moulded plywood back and seat on three tubular-steel legs. It was made by Fritz Hansen, as was all Jacobsen's later furniture, including the Egg and Swan chairs (1959) with curvaceous upholstered glass-fibre shells supported on aluminium bases, and his elegant and mannered tall-back chairs for St Catherine's College, Oxford (1963). Jacobsen designed lights for Louis Poulsen & Co. from 1955 and steel cutlery for A. Michelsen from 1957. In 1957 his elegant loudspeaker for Poul Lehmbeck won a silver medal at the Milan Triennale. For the Royal Hotel in Copenhagen (1958–60) Jacobsen designed not only furniture, door handles, lighting, etc., but also abstract patterned textiles and porcelain ashtrays. In 1967 he designed the Cylinda-line range of stainless-steel hollow-ware and its packaging.

Jacquard, Antoine Jacquard was active as an engraver in Poitiers from 1615 to 1624. He may be the same as an Antoine Jacquard who died there in 1652. He published a number of title-pages and a total of fifty-four plates of ornamental designs, including *Différents Portraitz*

Pour les Serruriers (1615; six plates) and a suite of the Senses (1624; five plates). His designs are intended for the decoration of boxes, swords, daggers and watch-cases, and are in a concentrated GROTESQUE style reminiscent of Étienne DELAUNE.

Jacques, Maurice Born in Paris in about 1712, Jacques was trained as a painter and elected to the Académie de Saint-Luc in 1755; he showed three flower-pieces at the 1756 Salon. He died in 1784. From 1756 Jacques was employed as '*peintre et dessinateur*' at the Gobelins tapestry factory where, under the close supervision of the factory's director, the architect Jacques Germain Soufflot (1713–80), he specialized in designs for borders, chair seats, etc., often collaborating with François BOUCHER and with the Gobelins flower painter Louis TESSIER. In 1772 Jacques designed a new border for the Histoire d'Esther tapestries designed by François de TROY in 1737. Jacques published designs of ROCOCO fantasy architecture for the decoration of panels and coaches in his *Suittes de Décorations* (1756; six plates). His *Vases nouveaux* (about 1765; six plates), although containing rococo survival elements, are predominantly NEO-CLASSICAL. They depict VASES garlanded with flowers, and were widely used on snuff-boxes and to decorate marquetry, both in France and England.

Jallot, Léon Albert Born in Nantes in 1874, Jallot trained as a wood-carver in Paris, where he worked with GAILLARD, DE FEURE and COLONNA, BING's designers. From 1904 Jallot was an independent designer of interiors, textiles and furniture, his work being frequently illustrated in 'ART ET DÉCORATION' and other magazines from 1905. In the 1920s he worked in a rich ART DÉCO style, from 1921 in partnership with his son Maurice Jallot, born in

1900. They designed interiors for the Ambassade Française at the PARIS 1925 EXHIBITION.

Jamnitzer, Christoph (1563–1618) A grandson of Wenzel JAMNITZER, Christoph Jamnitzer was a goldsmith in Nuremberg. He was employed by the Emperor RUDOLF II, also designed sculpture, and very probably travelled in Italy. His *Neuw Grotszken Buch* (Nuremberg, 1610; sixty-three plates in three parts) is an extraordinary compilation of ornamental fantasies, including GROTESQUE monsters, often fighting, putti engaged in violent or absurd activities, and purely decorative compositions which could be models for jewels or furniture escutcheons. Its second part, *Der Schnacken Markt*, has on its title a stall tiled with grotesque masks, at which grotesque monsters are being sold; in another plate is a prototype for Edward Lear's Dong with a Luminous Nose. '*Schnacken*' in the title was a term for the AURICULAR style which dominates Jamnitzer's ornament, similar to that of Lucas KILIAN.

Jamnitzer, Wenzel Born in Vienna in about 1507, the son of a goldsmith, Jamnitzer became a citizen of Nuremberg in 1534 and in the same year a master goldsmith. In 1543 he was appointed engraver to the city mint, and he was later given many important civic appointments. In his early years in Nuremberg, Jamnitzer worked in collaboration with his brother Albrecht, and was expert not only as a goldsmith but also as a glass enameller, engraver and perspectivist. A speciality was the casting of small reptiles or insects in silver. Jamnitzer was soon acknowledged as the leading Nuremberg goldsmith of his day, his patrons including the city of Nuremberg and four Emperors. Already in 1544 he designed a sword of state for the Emperor Charles V. A sketch-book of about this date in Berlin shows him designing jewellery in the manner of HOLBEIN. In 1556 Jacopo da STRADA was his assistant, and Jamnitzer is also likely to have been influenced by Erasmus HORNICK of Antwerp, the leading MANNERIST designer of goldsmith's work, who became a citizen of Augsburg in 1555. Most remarkable of Jamnitzer's works was a three-metre-high ornamental fountain presented to the Emperor RUDOLF II in 1578 and intended not only as an allegory to the house of Habsburg, but also as a compendium of physical, metaphysical, political, philosophical and poetical knowledge. Jamnitzer also designed an allegorical print on the Habsburg Empire engraved in 1571 by Jost AMMAN, whose ornament was strongly influenced by Jamnitzer, as was that of Virgil SOLIS and Mathias ZÜNDT. In 1568 Jamnitzer published *Perspectiva Corporum Regularium* (fifty plates), engraved by Jost Amman and dedicated to the Emperor Maximilian II. In its foreword Jamnitzer alludes to a forty-year experience as a perspectivist; the plates consist of complicated geometric solids comparable to those published by LENCKER in 1567, and related to STÖER's designs. The decorations to the text are influenced by the ornament of Cornelis FLORIS and BOS. Jamnitzer died in Nuremberg in 1585, the date of a two-volume manuscript in the VICTORIA & ALBERT MUSEUM, which describes the contents of a cabinet, including flasks, cups and mathematical instruments and their uses, with a strong emphasis on surveying. His collection included a large number of drawings by DÜRER.

Janel Janel designed five suites of coaches (six plates in each suite), engraved in Paris by CHOFFARD in about 1780.

Jansen, Michel Jansen was active as a furniture manufacturer for seven years in the early 1830s. From 1835 he was active as a designer, describing himself as 'Professeur de Dessin' and 'Compositeur de Meubles'. He designed furniture shown at the PARIS EXHIBITIONS of 1839, 1844 and 1849. He published numerous books of furniture designs, with such titles as *Le Guide du Fabricant de Meubles*, usually coloured lithographs with constructional details; his furniture is mainly in a crude sub-ROCOCO style, but 17th-century models and GOTHIC elements also crop up. The 1841 edition of SANTI incorporates twelve plates by Jansen.

Janssen, Hans Born in Amsterdam in 1605, the son of an engraver, Janssen followed his father's trade. In 1631 he published *Verscheyden Randen en Spitzen*, twelve plates of borders for engraving on silver; they are composed of GROTESQUES with fine AURICULAR STRAPWORK containing fruit and flowers. A suite of small vertical panels (four plates) depicts fashionably dressed figures before dense black scrolled tendril ornament peopled with birds and monkeys. Dense spiralling and scrolling tendrils cover four small oval designs for the decoration of miniature cases etc.; their effect is surrealistically three-dimensional. Similar ornament is used by Janssen on four large oval designs symbolic of the elements, and as the border to an oval depiction of the Marriage at Cana. Theodor de BRY or DELAUNE are the sources of four designs by Janssen for knife handles, but the auricular ornament which surrounds his figures is a new ingredient. He also copied Hans COLLAERT's friezes of birds.

Jaquet In about 1430 Jaquet *'le peintre'* was given the commission to produce a small design, *'petit patron'*, for tapestries for the church of La Madeleine in

Troyes, and later to draw and paint the designs full size on cloth.

Jeannest, Émile (1813–57) Born in Paris, the son of a sculptor and bronze chaser, Jeannest was a pupil of the painter Paul Delaroche (1795–1856). In about 1845 he emigrated to England, where he worked for Mintons in Stoke-on-Trent, and from about 1850 for Elkingtons. He also designed furniture and taught in the Stoke-on-Trent School of Design. Jeannest designed the Minton maiolica shown at the PARIS 1855 EXHIBITION.

Jeckyll, Thomas (1827–81) Jeckell, as his name was originally spelt, was active as an architect and designer in both London and Norfolk. At the LONDON 1862 EXHIBITION Barnard, Bishop & Barnard of Norwich showed a prodigious set of cast-iron gates in the GOTHIC style with lavish foliate decoration, designed by Jeckyll; they were bought by the gentry of Norfolk as a wedding present for the Prince of Wales and set up at Sandringham. In the late 1860s Jeckyll was in contact with WHISTLER and GODWIN. It was probably the painter Thomas Armstrong (1832–1911) who introduced him to Edward Green of Heath Old Hall, for which in the late 1860s Jeckyll designed furniture in a sometimes cumbersome mixed Japanese and Jacobean style. In 1870 Jeckyll designed a new wing to 1 Holland Park, London, for the advanced collector Alexander Ionides; it incorporated bracketed overmantels for the display of blue-and-white porcelain. In 1875 Jeckyll designed furniture for Ionides with elaborate mouldings, subtle asymmetry and Chinese-style brackets. In 1876 Jeckyll designed a room for F. R. Leyland with a Tudor-style ceiling, elaborate bracketed shelves and walls covered in Spanish leather; in 1877 Whistler painted it blue and gold with

peacocks. From 1873 Jeckyll designed a number of Anglo-Japanese brass and cast-iron grates for Barnard, Bishop & Barnard. They were very popular, being used for instance in Waterhouse's Blackmoor and Devey's Betteshanger: EDIS (1881) praised them. Jeckyll's culminating achievement was a great cast-iron Japanese pavilion, railed with iron sunflowers, shown at the PHILADELPHIA 1876 and PARIS 1878 EXHIBITIONS. From 1877 Jeckyll was mad.

Jefferson, Thomas (1743–1826) Born in Shadwell, Virginia, the eldest son of a landowner and surveyor, Jefferson studied at the College of William and Mary, Williamsburg, from 1760. In 1767 he became a barrister. From 1769 to his death Jefferson was occupied in the building and embellishment of his own house, Monticello, acting as his own architect and designer (Shadwell was burned in 1770). Jefferson's deep involvement in politics led to his drafting the Declaration of Independence (1776). From 1784 to 1789 he was in Paris, from 1785 as American Minister; in 1786 he travelled in England and in 1787 in Southern France and Italy. He took a close interest in art and design and was advised by CLÉRISSEAU and J. G. LEGRAND on the State Capitol at Virginia (1787). In 1789 he designed a NEO-CLASSICAL silver coffee urn and goblets made by Odiot. A Roman wine jug excavated at Nîmes was later used by Jefferson as a model for a silver version by Simmons & Alexander of Philadelphia. In 1803 Jefferson designed a parquetry floor for Monticello, where he also designed an ingenious revolving door/shelf unit and several pieces of furniture. After two terms as President (1801 to 1809) Jefferson retired to Monticello. The University of Virginia (1817 to 1824) was his last major project.

Jensen, Georg Arthur (1866–1935) Born at Raadvad near Copenhagen, the son of a cooper, Jensen served his apprenticeship as a goldsmith, becoming a journeyman in 1884. From 1887 to 1892 he studied sculpture at the Copenhagen Academy, where he was influenced by C. C. Peters (1822–99), who had designed NEO-CLASSICAL metalwork and ceramics. From about 1895 Jensen designed and made sculptural ceramics with Joachim Petersen (1870–1943); some of these were shown at the PARIS 1900 EXHIBITION. In 1900 Jensen travelled to France and Italy and after this became increasingly involved in the design and manufacture of jewellery and silver, opening a small shop in Copenhagen in 1904. Except around 1926, when he briefly moved to Paris, Jensen's business was extremely successful; by the year 1930 he was employing about 250. After a brief ART NOUVEAU period Jensen's own designs for silver and jewellery employed simple stumpy forms embellished with concentrated passages of ornament, usually composed of fruit or flowers. From 1907 the painter Johan Rohde (1856–1935) was a close collaborator and was responsible for many simple and striking designs. Among the many other designers who have been used by the Jensen firm have been his two sons Jørgen and Soren Georg Jensen, Henning Keppel, Arno Malinowski and Sigvard Bernadotte.

Jobin, Bernhard A very active publisher, Jobin issued a forty-plate embroidery pattern-book, *Neu Künstlichs Modelbuch*, at Strasbourg in 1579. It borrowed from CELLE, PAGANO, VAVASSORE and SCHÖNSPERGER, but also contained a number of lively and original designs incorporating animals and figures. The *Modelbuch* was reprinted seven times by 1600, and again in 1607 by Jobin's successor, Johann Carolus. Jobin was a close friend of Tobias STIMMER, who supplied him with many illustrations. He died in Strasbourg in 1597.

Joel, Betty Born in 1896, the daughter of Sir James Stewart Lockhart, Joel started a furniture workshop on Hayling Island in 1921 with her husband, David Joel, an ex-naval officer. A factory was soon opened in Portsmouth and a shop in Sloane Street, London. Joel's early furniture, mainly in oak and teak, uses a stripped-down Arts & Crafts style with Neo-Georgian overtones. In the 1930s she developed a more dashing Modernistic manner. At the Royal Academy 1935 British Art in Industry exhibition (see LONDON EXHIBITIONS) she showed a revolving bed. In the 'ARCHITECTURAL REVIEW' (1935) she was criticized by Geoffrey Boumphrey for not toeing the MODERN FUNCTIONALIST line. She designed not only furniture but also carpets, made in China, and fabrics, woven in France, with abstract patterns. In 1937 she showed chairs with Aubusson tapestry covers designed by Anna Zinkeisen. Her Knightsbridge showrooms were in this year given a new façade by H. S. Goodhart Rendel (1887–1959), who had also designed the Joel works on the Kingston by-pass. Betty Joel retired in 1937. After the war her works were revived by David Joel, whose *The Adventure of British Furniture* (1953) includes an account of Betty Joel furniture.

John, William Goscombe (1860–1952) Born in Cardiff, the son of Thomas John (1834–93), wood-carver to the 3rd Marquess of Bute (1847–1900), who worked for BURGES at Cardiff Castle, from 1881 Goscombe John carved architectural decorations for Thomas Nicholls, Burges's sculptor, but from 1884, when he entered the Royal Academy Schools, John established a career as the leading

Welsh sculptor. As a designer he was responsible for the Hirlas Horn of the Gorsedd of Bards (1898), the investiture regalia of the Prince of Wales (1911), and the ceremonial tools and seal of the National Museum of Wales (1912, 1927). He also designed medals including that of the National Eisteddfod Association (1899) and one for George V's jubilee (1935).

Johnson, Thomas (1) In 1630 Johnson published *A Booke of Beasts, Birds, Flowers, Fruits, Flies and Wormes, exactly drawne with their lively colours truly Described*, a successor to Jacques LE MOYNE's *La Clef des Champs* (1586). Johnson's sources included Crispin van de PASSE's *Hortus Floridus* (1614) and Jacob Hoefnagel's *Archetypa Studiaque Patris Georgii Hoefnagelii* (1592). In 1706 Grisell and Rachel Baillie used Johnson's *Booke* when embroidering a panel at Mellerstain under the direction of their governess May Menzies. Johnson was a predecessor of Peter STENT, but no link is known.

Johnson, Thomas (2) Born in London in 1714, Thomas Johnson was active as a carver from at least 1755; in 1763 he was described as 'Carver, Teacher of Drawing and Modelling the author of a Book of Designs for Chimney-pieces and other ornaments and of several other pieces'. After moving address several times he ended in Tottenham Court Road. Although the size of his premises, especially in the early 1760s, denotes a successful career, Johnson seems to have worked exclusively as a specialist subcontractor to cabinet-makers and upholsterers, including George Cole, who supplied Johnsonesque carved pieces to Corsham Court (1761), Dunkeld House (1761) and Blair Castle (1763). Johnson is last recorded in 1778. His first published designs, *Twelve Gerandoles* on

four plates, appeared in 1755 when he announced a larger part-work, *A New Book of Ornaments*, of which the plates appeared in 1756 and 1757. The book, without a title, was published in 1758: it was dedicated to Lord Blakeney, the aged Grand President of the Anti-Gallican Association, which had been founded in 1745 against French influence and which encouraged English trade. Johnson was a member. In the dedication plate he specifically attacks 'French paper Machée', a response perhaps to the threat posed to his trade as a carver by Dufour, a close neighbour and maker of 'papie machie'. The book contained fifty-three plates and a second edition with the misleading title *One Hundred and Fifty New Designs* was issued by Robert SAYER in 1761. In 1760 Johnson had contributed six plates to *Household Furniture in the Genteel Taste*, a compilation by 'a Society of Upholsterers, Cabinet-makers, etc.', and also in 1760 he issued *A New Book of Ornaments* of unknown size; seven plates survive. A different book with the same title containing six plates of ornaments 'Design'd for Tablets & Frizes for Chimney-Pieces' appeared in 1762. Johnson's designs were in a vigorous, imaginative and intense ROCOCO manner. He borrowed ornaments directly from Daniel MAROT, from DE LA COUR and, above all, from TORO. J. M. HOPPENHAUPT also seems to have been used. *Aesop's Fables* illustrated by Francis Barlow (1687) was a favourite source of quotation. All his designs, with the exception of a handful for ceilings, grates and silver, are for carver's work – tables, mirror-frames, stands, etc. Although many appear fantastic Johnson asserted that they 'may all be performed by a Master of his Art'. Later, it appears, Johnson converted to NEO-CLASSICISM: a single plate of three workmanlike neo-classical mirror-frames, published in 1775, survives from a set of at least five. In the 1830s his rococo designs were much reprinted by WEALE, who pretended they were by CHIPPENDALE.

Jombert, Charles Antoine (1712–84) Born in Paris, Jombert was active there as a publisher and author. In 1755 he published *Méthode pour apprendre le dessin* (later edition, 1784), a drawing manual with model ROCOCO ornaments by BABEL. He published architectural books including those of BLONDEL, the ORDERS after Vignola (1760) and *Bibliothèque portative d'Architecture élémentaire* (1764), and catalogues of the prints of C. N. COCHIN (1770), Stefano DELLA BELLA (1772) and Sebastien Le Clerc (1774). Jombert's greatest work was his *Répertoire des Artistes* (two volumes, 1765), which contained a total of no less than 688 plates of design and ornament after J. A. DUCERCEAU, the MAROTS, P. LE PAUTRE, the LOIRS and others, and thus made the French BAROQUE language of ornament easily accessible to the NEO-CLASSICAL generation of designers.

Jones, Inigo (1573–1652) Born in London, the son of a clothmaker, Jones was in 1603 described as a 'picture maker'. He may have travelled in Italy from 1598 to 1601 in the train of Lord Roos. In 1605 he designed sets and costumes for Ben Jonson's *Masque of Blacknesse*, given at Whitehall for Anne of Denmark, and until 1640 such stage designs were his main activity. From around 1608, when he produced designs for the New Exchange, Jones developed into an architect. In 1609 he visited France. In 1610 he was appointed Surveyor to Henry, Prince of Wales, but Henry's death in 1612 cut short the promise of this post. From 1613 to 1614 Jones travelled throughout Italy with the virtuoso 2nd Earl of Arundel (1586–1646) and acquired drawings by Palladio and

Scamozzi, a purchase which was to change the course of English architecture and design. In 1615, on his return, Jones was appointed Surveyor of Works to James I and in 1616 he began to design the Palladian Queen's House at Greenwich for Anne of Denmark, whose hearse he designed in 1619. Jones's Banqueting House in Whitehall (1619–22) is the great monument of his early Palladianism. In 1625 Jones designed a catafalque for James I; in the same year he designed a triumphal arch for Queen Henrietta Maria. Jones later designed interiors for her at Somerset House (1626), St James's (1629–31), the Queen's House (1630–38), Oatlands (1636) and Whitehall (1637). In interior decoration Jones's sources included both Italy and Palladio and contemporary French designers. His designs for Ben Jonson's *Love's Triumph* (1631) include a splendidly BAROQUE throne for Venus. The King's Bedroom at the Queen's House, designed by Jones's pupil John Webb (1611–72) in 1665, was decorated with palm trees derived from Prado and Villalpando's *In Ezechielem explicationes* (II, 1604), a reconstruction of Solomon's Temple. This scheme may go back to Inigo Jones; it was certainly considered to be his by VARDY in *Designs of Mr Inigo Jones and Mr William Kent* (1744). William KENT's *Designs of Inigo Jones* (1727) and Isaac Ware's *Designs of Inigo Jones and Others* are earlier instances of the English 18th-century cult of Jones and Palladio, promoted by Lord Burlington (1694–1753), who in about 1720 bought Jones's Palladio drawings.

Jones, Owen (1809–74) The son of a prosperous London furrier who was also a prominent Welsh antiquary, Jones was in 1825 articled to the architect Lewis Vulliamy (1791–1871). After a spell in the Royal Academy Schools from 1829 and a short tour of the continent, he embarked on a grand tour to Egypt (1832–3), Istanbul (1833) and Spain (1833–4). He was accompanied by a French architect, Goury, whom he met in Athens, where Goury had been working with SEMPER on the polychrome decoration of Greek temples. In Egypt they met Robert Hay (1799–1863), a rich Egyptologist and his party, including Joseph Bonomi (1796–1876), a lifelong friend of Jones. *Views on the Nile* ... (1843) was one product of Jones's and Goury's studies, the second being Jones's *Plans, Details and Sections of the Alhambra* (1836–45). Goury had died in 1834 after six months' work on the Alhambra. The book was a massive chromolithographic production printed by Jones himself; its preparation involved not only a second visit to Spain in 1837, but also the sale of inherited land in Wales. In the *Alhambra*, reprinted by Quaritch in 1877, Jones displayed his strong views on colour by depicting columns gilt in the face of the evidence because gilding seemed to him necessary. In the 1830s he was active in architectural politics, joining the Architectural Society in 1833 and the future R.I.B.A. in 1836. In a lecture of 1835 'On the Influence of Religion in Art' he advocated the use of cast-iron and a new architecture for the age. Jones was in touch with advanced and radical French and German theorists but he designed few buildings himself. In the 1840s his reputation was as a designer of tiles and mosaics, partly through contacts with Herbert Minton, but mainly through his involvement with John Marriott Blashfield, a terracotta manufacturer and entrepreneur who had subscribed to the *Alhambra*. Jones produced two books for Blashfield, *Designs for Mosaic and Tessellated Pavements* (1842), with plates of Jones's highly geometric designs, and *Encaustic Tiles* (1843), after drawings of ancient examples. In 1844 he showed designs for the floors of the

New Palace of Westminster, but these were considered too Moorish for execution. Jones later designed tiles for Maw and the cover of their catalogue of about 1871. Through an ill-fated Blashfield property speculation Jones became the architect and decorator of 8 and 25 Kensington Palace Gardens, London (1843 and 1845). Although basically Italianate their detailing was Moorish and it was with this style that Jones was identified, although at 22 Arlington Street, London, he had worked in the French RENAISSANCE manner. In about 1850 he decorated the apse of Lewis Vulliamy's All Saints, Ennismore Gardens, London, in the 'Byzantine' style, although the *Ecclesiologist* (1850) said it looked Elizabethan, and by 1851 he had decorated Christ Church, Streatham (1841), in the same style. Its architect was James Wild (1814–92), an expert in Egyptian and Islamic architecture, who married Jones's sister in 1842 and in 1878 succeeded Bonomi as Curator of the SOANE Museum. Having printed his own *Alhambra* Jones maintained a vigorous activity as printer and graphic designer, designing titles to Robert Hay's *Views in Cairo* (1840) and to *Views of Ancient Monuments in Central America* ... (1844) by his friend Frederick Catherwood, which he also printed. E. Adams's *The Polychromatic Ornament of Italy* (1846) and plates for John WEALE's *Quarterly Papers on Architecture* (1844) are other works which reflect Jones's specialized interests. However, in the early 1840s he began to produce books for commercial publishers which used the chromolithographic technique for a wider range of subjects than the architectural polychromy it was developed to illustrate. Jones's edition of J. G. Lockhart's *Ancient Spanish Ballads* (1841) for John Murray was the first illuminated gift book: it went through five editions, and was succeeded by the *Book of Common*

Prayer (1845) and *Works of Horace* (1849). Jones began to work for Longmans in 1842: his *Sermon on the Mount* (1844) was a marked success, going through three editions, but the most interesting product of the Longmans association was due to Jones's polymathic friend Henry Noel Humphreys, who suggested the *Home Illuminated Diary and Calendar for 1845*, with illustrations from medieval manuscripts, whence *Illuminated Books of the Middle Ages* (1850). Jones and Humphreys collaborated on a series of small books, including *A Record of the Black Prince* (1849) with black papier-mâché bindings made by G. Jackson, whose fibrous plaster Jones used in interior decoration. For *Gray's Elegy* (1846) Jones used a binding of 'patent relievo leather', while his *Preacher* (1848) had a stamped wood binding whose model had been carved to Jones's design by W. G. Rogers. Jones's collaborator on *The Good Shunamite* (1847) was Ludwig GRUNER, who had also worked on the *Book of Common Prayer*. Gruner was a member of the set round Henry COLE, which Jones joined in the mid-1840s. In 1847 Jones joined the SOCIETY OF ARTS at Cole's suggestion and in 1850, doubtless through Cole's influence, was appointed as joint architect of the LONDON 1851 EXHIBITION. In 1850 his scheme for the interior decoration of Paxton's new exhibition building was accepted. Jones's interest in colour had first been roused by his experience of colour on Egyptian buildings in 1832. That experience and the writings of CHEVREUL and Field led Jones to use the primary colours separated by white in the ratio, blue 8: red 5: yellow 3, which he calculated would merge into bright neutrality over long distances. The scheme attracted strong criticism from decorators, including Frederick Sang, J. G. CRACE and L. W. Collmann, but when executed it was a triumphant success.

Jones designed many details of the building and worked with Cole and M. D. WYATT on the arrangement of the exhibits. In 1851 Cole's 'JOURNAL OF DESIGN' included a textile designed by Jones, praised his shop front for Chappells, the music publishers, in New Bond Street, and contained four articles by Jones entitled 'Gleanings from the Great Exhibition of 1851' which singled out Indian design for praise. Jones sat from 1851 to 1852 with Cole, REDGRAVE and the dying A. W. N. PUGIN on a committee to spend £5,000 on exhibition objects and a large proportion went on Indian and Near Eastern examples. Jones helped Cole to display these and other objects at Marlborough House, including a selection 'illustrating false or wrong principles'. In his *Journal of Design* articles Jones had begun to formulate correct principles, setting out six of which the first was 'The construction is decorated; decoration is never purposely constructed'. An extra nineteen were added in a lecture on colour at the Society of Arts in 1852 and ten more in Jones's Marlborough House lectures in the same year, when a pamphlet with the full thirty-four was published. Cole had helped to evolve the principles and by 1852 the Department of Practical Arts' plans included the idea of the *Grammar of Ornament* which Jones issued in 1856 with Day & Sons as publishers. Three extra principles were added in the *Grammar*, including 'All ornament should be based upon a geometrical construction'. Jones's collaborators on the text included J. B. WARING on Byzantine and Elizabethan ornament, M. D. Wyatt on Renaissance and Italian ornament, and John Westwood on Celtic ornament. He was assisted on the plates by Joseph Bonomi and James Wild on Egyptian ornament, T. T. Bury on stained glass, C. J. RICHARDSON on Elizabethan ornament and Christopher DRESSER on leaves and flowers. But

Jones himself did the bulk of the work and the *Grammar*, with its 100 elaborate chromolithographed plates, immediately established itself as an ornamental repertoire of international importance: a scaled-down edition appeared in 1865. The *Grammar* was more expensive than the book originally envisaged by Cole, whom Jones had offended in 1852 by accepting a post as Director of Decorations for the Crystal Palace in Sydenham, opened in 1854. With Joseph Paxton and M. D. Wyatt, Jones created courts representing various cultures, travelling to Europe with Wyatt in 1852 to arrange plaster casts. His colour decoration of the reconstructed building attracted high praise. In the late 1850s Jones was responsible for a group of iron and glass buildings and their decoration, St James Hall (1858), a concert hall complex, the Crystal Palace Bazaar (1858) and a showroom for Messrs Oslers, the glass manufacturers (1859), for whom he also designed a showcase for the LONDON 1862 EXHIBITION. Several other grandiose iron and glass schemes came to nothing. Although Jones gave up his own printing business in 1853 he continued to produce elaborately chromolithographed books for Day & Son, of whom he became a director in 1865: they included *Paradise and the Peri* (1860), in the Persian style, the *Victoria Psalter* (1861), dedicated to the Queen, in the GOTHIC style, and the *History of Joseph and his Brethren* (1862), in the Egyptian style. Jones also did a mass of graphic design for De La Rue, for whom he first worked in 1844 – playing-cards, stamps, menus, calendars, paper currency and so on. He had begun to design wallpaper in the early 1840s for Townsend & Parker and in the 1850s and 1860s he worked for John Trumble & Sons and Jeffrey & Co. Linens for Erskine Beveridge & Co. in 1851, biscuit labels for Huntley & Palmer of Reading, silks for Warners of

Braintree (1870–74) and even silver designs for Hancocks (1867 and 1868), in collaboration with Raphaelle Monti, are further evidence of Jones's success as a commercial designer. However, his most elaborate works were interiors. His clients tended to be public, commercial or rich, including the Indian, Chinese and Japanese Courts at South Kensington (1863–4), Fishmongers' Hall (1865–6) and work at Fonthill and 16 Carlton House Terrace, London, for Alfred Morrison (from 1863). *Examples of Chinese Ornament* (1867) reflected a new interest; previously Jones had criticized Chinese work. For interiors Jones designed carpets, kamptulicon, silks, wallpaper and furniture. From the early 1850s he had a link with the luxury cabinet-makers Jackson & Graham, who showed pieces designed by Jones for Morrison at the PARIS 1867, LONDON 1871 and VIENNA 1873 EXHIBITIONS, winning gold medals at the former and latter. These were elaborate inlaid pieces of a Grecian character, but Jones also designed simple furniture for Eynsham Hall in 1872. As a designer Jones lacked the natural gifts of Pugin, whom he admired, but his energy, allied to a passionate interest in colour, geometry, new materials and new techniques, allowed him to create ornament which epitomizes High Victorian taste, and in particular the geometric style. As a friend of Henry Cole and of George Henry Lewes and George Eliot (he decorated their house in 1863 and advised on the wrapper of *Middlemarch* in 1871), Jones, cultivated and musical, represented a new breed of professional designer. But, although Dresser was a direct follower, Jones's greatest influence was through his *Alhambra* and *Grammar* which demonstrated to an international readership (including Frank Lloyd WRIGHT!) the potential of non-European, and in particular Islamic, decoration and of the systematic study of the principles of design, colour and ornament.

Jones, William Jones contributed designs for six tables and fourteen mirrors, as well as doors and overmantels to James Smith's *Specimen of Antient Carpentry* (1736), which Jones republished as *The Gentleman's or Builder's Companion* (1739; sixty plates). The 'Slab Tables' and 'Pier Glasses', the earliest published group of furniture designs by an English designer, are mainly in the style of William KENT, although some tables are lighter in character, inspired by Nicolas PINEAU. James's later career was as a minor architect, although his Rotunda at Ranelagh Gardens, Chelsea (1742), achieved some notoriety.

Jonquet, Adolf In his *Thirty Original Designs for Window Draperies* (thirty coloured plates) Jonquet described himself as 'Designer of all branches of art industry'. His *Original Sketches for Art Furniture* (1877; forty plates) contains a few designs in the TALBERT manner followed by a great many in a vapid 'Adams' style. *Original Sketches for Art Furniture, in the Jacobean, Queen Anne, Adams and other styles* (1879; sixty plates) is very similar, and Jonquet contributed many designs of the same kind to the 'CABINET AND UPHOLSTERER ADVERTISER' and 'CABINET MAKER AND ART FURNISHER'. His *Present Day Furniture* (1890; nine plates) contains designs in a heavy RENAISSANCE style called 'Free Classic'.

Jordaens, Jacob (1593–1678) The son of an Antwerp linen-draper, Jordaens was a pupil of the painter Adam van Noort (1562–1641). He began to work as an assistant to RUBENS in about 1620. Rubens was the principal influence on Jordaens's painting. In 1634 Jordaens worked on the decorations for the state entry of the Cardinal-Infant Ferdinand,

under the direction of Rubens. Before 1628 Jordaens designed a suite of eight tapestries on the History of Alexander the Great and a similar series of Scenes of Country Life. A suite of the story of Ulysses followed in the 1630s. In 1644 Jordaens signed a contract with certain Brussels tapestry weavers to provide designs for a suite of tapestries of Proverbs, which he had been planning since at least 1638; a set was woven by 1647. A more drawn-out project was a suite on Horses, probably begun in about 1640 but only completed after 1652. He designed vigorous architectural and floral BAROQUE borders for his tapestries. A similar vigour informs a frame for a print, the Fool and the Cat, and the few surviving drawings for frames and ornament by Jordaens.

Jores, J. Jores was the author of *A New Book of Iron Work* (London, 1759; twenty plates), published by Robert SAYER, which comprised gates, pedestals, signs, brackets and staircases in wrought iron of a lively scrolled variety derived from French models.

Joubert de l'Hiberderie A silk designer in Lyon, Joubert published a manual on his trade, *Le Dessinateur pour les Fabriques d'étoffes d'or, d'argent et de soie* (1764). It includes mention of Deschamps, MONLONG, RINGUET, COURTOIS and REVEL as important designers.

Jourdain, Francis (1876–1958) Born in Paris, the son of Frantz Jourdain (1847–1937), architect of La Samaritaine (1905) and a supporter of advanced designers such as Hector GUIMARD, Francis Jourdain was trained as a painter and also, like his friend Jacques Villon, practised engraving. In about 1909 Jourdain gave up painting and applied himself to interior design, winning a Grand Prix at the Turin 1911 Exhibition as an *ensemblier*. In 1912 Jourdain founded Les Ateliers Modernes to execute furniture to his own design and at the 1913 Salon d'Automne he showed a MODERN living-room of integrated informality, studiously rectilinear and unornamented (also in 1913 Jourdain had read LOOS). Jourdain was interested in low-price adaptable furniture for the mass-market; at the Paris 1916 'La Cité Reconstituée' Exhibition he showed a prefabricated dining-room and bedroom. Les Ateliers Modernes were a notable success, with 130 workers in 1919, when Jourdain opened a shop, Chez Francis Jourdain, to sell its products. Its clients however were the rich, not the workers. In the 1920s Jourdain was widely influential, his work being illustrated in such magazines as 'ARCHITECTURE VIVANTE' and 'ARTS DE LA MAISON'; DJO-BOURGEOIS and René GABRIEL were among his disciples. He designed not only furniture but also lights and cheerful textiles and wallpapers; on occasion he used tubular steel. At the PARIS 1925 EXHIBITION Jourdain showed a Salle de Sport and a smoking-room which led into Pierre CHAREAU's library. In 1929 he published *Intérieurs*, with illustrations of designs by Chareau, MALLET-STEVENS, LE CORBUSIER, RIETVELD and himself; he stated '*On peut aménager luxueusement une pièce en la démeublant plutôt qu'en la meublant*', in others words 'Less is more'. Jourdain joined Mallet-Stevens, Chareau and HERBST in the schism from the Société des Artistes-Décorateurs which led to the formation of the Union des Artistes Modernes, whose first Salon Jourdain organized in 1930. At the PARIS 1937 EXHIBITION he showed a student's room and in 1939 he decorated interiors at the Collège de France. Jourdain ceased to be active designer in that year and from 1945 was a prolific art-historian, who continued to preach against ornament and for that MODERN simplicity and logic of which he was the pioneer in French interior design.

Journal des Luxus und der Moden (1786–1827) Friedrich Justin Bertuch (1747–1822) was born in Weimar, the son of a doctor, and studied theology and law before becoming a private tutor. Back in Wiemar, Bertuch went into Grand-Ducal service from 1775 to 1796 when he retired to devote himself to his flourishing publishing and bookselling business. In 1786 he founded the *Journal der Moden*, which became the *Journal des Luxus und der Moden* in 1787, and survived under various permutations of title until 1827. Bertuch was a keen gardener and freemason, and both writer and translator. His position at the head of the German book trade was recognized by his being chosen to represent its interests at the Congress of Vienna in 1814; in the event his son and partner Karl Bertuch (1777–1815), a close friend of Goethe, attended. The *Journal des Luxus und der Moden* provided news of the latest fashions in dress, interior decoration, design, gardening, music and the theatre, thus anticipating the formula of ACKERMANN'S *Repository of Arts*. It published reports from London, Paris and various German cities. Almost every issue included at least one design for furniture, silver, lighting or some novelty. Up to about 1803 English fashions were dominant. An 'Englische Commode' (1786), in fact French in appearance, was offered at various prices depending on quality from 'our capable English cabinet-maker Herr Holzhauer junior'. Later English illustrations included a globe-shaped tea machine (1797), similar to English desks and anticipating a shape common for BIEDERMEIER desks, a cucumber cutter (1800), a FLAXMAN Iliad outline (1802) and a typical English convex circular mirror surmounted by an eagle

(1803). In 1786 Bertuch described a crimson damask room decorated with ARABESQUES, a term he carefully explained, and in 1797 he illustrated an Athénienne, distantly related to the French model invented by J.-H. Eberts in 1773, inspired by VIEN. A semicircular Parisian 'Divan' (1808) seems to anticipate SCHINKEL. French NEO-CLASSICAL influence is reflected in ornaments by Joseph Beaunat of Sarrebourg and Paris and by Spoerlin & Rahn, wallpaper manufacturers of Vienna, both illustrated in 1813. After Waterloo, English influence was once more dominant. In 1816 a table given by the Prince Regent to the Royal Palace in Stuttgart was illustrated, and a remark in the same year makes it evident that Bertuch was familiar with Ackermann's *Repository*. Bertuch provided news of a wide variety of German designs, inventions and manufactures in addition to his coverage of foreign design.

Journal of Decorative Art, The (1881–1937) Subtitled *An Illustrated Technical Journal for the House Painter, Decorator and all Art Workmen* this London magazine contains a wide range of information together with illustrations of designs. From 1887 an American edition was published in New York as *Beck's Journal of Decorative Art*.

Journal of Design and Manufactures (1849–52) Published by Chapman & Hall as the mouthpiece of Henry COLE's campaign for improvement in design and design education, the *Journal* was edited by his friend Richard REDGRAVE; 'our aim is to foster ornamental art in all ways ... which would be the appropriate business of a Board of Design ... if such a useful department of the Government actually existed'. The *Journal* included real samples of textiles. Its criticism was directed against literal NATURALISM and excessive and inap-

propriate ornament. Redgrave, William DYCE, Matthew Digby WYATT and Owen JONES all reinforced this message in articles, and a general air of purposeful optimism prevailed, although this was disappointed by the standard of design in the LONDON 1851 EXHIBITION, a main focus of the *Journal*'s interest.

Jousse, Mathurin Born in La Flèche in 1607, Jousse started his life as a locksmith in the service of the local Jesuits. They encouraged his interest in architectural and mechanical theory, which resulted in four books, an edition (1635) of Jean Pélerin's *De Artificiali Perspectiva* (1505) 'augmentée et illustrée par maistre Étienne Martel Ange' the Jesuit architect, *La Fidelle Ouverture de l'Art du Serrurier* (1627) with provincial BAROQUE designs for locks, keys, handles, escutcheons and for two wheelchairs, *Théâtre de l'Art de Charpentier et des cinq Ordre des Colonnes* (1627), a work on structural carpentry, and *Secret de l'Architecture* (1642). All were published at La Flèche, where Jousse was active as architect and craftsman. He died before 1692.

Judson, William Lees (1842–1928) Born in Manchester, England, Judson moved to Brooklyn, New York, whence having established himself as a portrait painter he moved in 1893 to Chicago and California. In 1897 he founded the Judson Studios, in Los Angeles, which supplied stained glass to Frank Lloyd WRIGHT. Judson was mainly active as a landscape painter but also designed stained glass and mosaics.

Jugend (1896–1914) Founded by Georg Hirth as a lighter Bavarian riposte to 'PAN', *Jugend* was published in Munich and was decorated by Julie Wolfthorn (1897), Otto ECKMANN, Julius Diez (1899) and Ludwig von Zumbusch

(1897). It gave its name to ART NOUVEAU in Germany, 'Jugendstil', and, although it was not specifically devoted to design, acted as a show-window for the new style.

Juhl, Finn Born in 1912, Juhl was trained as an architect at the Copenhagen Academy. In 1939 he designed an upholstered sofa for Niels Vodder, whose sculptural curves, reminiscent of Arp, represented a new ingredient in Danish furniture design. In 1942 Juhl designed a prize-winning house for his own use, and from 1944 to 1955 he lectured on Interior Design at Fredericksberg Technical School, where he exercised wide influence. A sculptural easy chair of 1945 was succeeded in 1949 by the almost expressionist Chieftain chair. In 1951 Juhl designed a whole range of furniture for Baker Furniture Inc. of Grand Rapids, including chairs, tables, storage units, sideboards and desks. In the same year he designed the Trusteeship Council Room at the United Nations Headquarters, and was given the ultimate Nordic seal of approval by being invited to design a room in the Trondheim Kunstindustrimuseum, executed in 1952. Juhl has also designed glassware for Georg Jensen, refrigerators for General Electric, and ceramics for Bing & Grøndahl among many other commissions.

Julienne, Eugène In the 1830s Julienne was a painter in the Paris pottery of Pichenot & Loebnitz. He later worked at Sèvres, probably mainly on special commissions such as two vases given by Napoleon III to the King of Portugal in 1856. In about 1840, with another Sèvres painter, Ferdinand Regnier, Julienne published *L'Industrie Artistique*, a collection of ornament in the GOTH-IC, RENAISSANCE, ROCOCO and BA-ROQUE styles, including a seal for Queen Victoria. It was reprinted at

Offenbach in Germany in 1842, in Paris in 1845 and in Venice in 1853. In about 1865 Julienne designed jewellery for the *Journal du Bijoutier* and in 1862 to 1868 published *L'Orfèvrerie Française, les Bronzes et la Céramique*, highly accomplished designs for silver, etc. in all the current styles, similar to objects executed by Barbedienne and others. They have captions in German and English, including 'Price-Cups for Agricultural and Hyppic Concurrences'.

Junck, Ignaz Carl Born in Neuss in Silesia, Junck was active as a painter in Augsburg, where he married in 1750. He issued four suites of four plates each, published by HERTEL, showing designs for pulpits, altars and confessionals in a flaky, jagged and aggressive ROCOCO style.

Juvarra, Filippo (1676–1736) Born in Messina, the son of a goldsmith, Juvarra entered the priesthood but also studied architecture. In 1701 he designed decorations in Messina for Philip V of Spain. He then went to Rome, where he studied under Carlo FONTANA and in 1706 became a member of the Academy. In Rome, Juvarra began to produce designs for the theatre some of which incorporate vigorous BAROQUE furniture. His *Raccolta di Targhe* (Rome, 1722; seventy-two plates) is a collection of mainly baroque cartouches, designed by BERNINI, Borromini, Pietro da CORTONA, ALGARDI, Carlo Fontana and Juvarra himself. In 1714 he met Victor Amadeus II of Savoy and was appointed Primo Architetto Civile del Re. His many buildings for the King include the Palazzo Madama in Turin (1718–21) and the hunting palace at Stupinighi (from 1729). However, he revisited Rome on many occasions and in 1719 to 1720 travelled to Portugal, and on his return to London and Versailles (he is recorded as having worked for English 'Milordi' in Rome in 1716). In 1723 Juvarra designed an urn to contain the corpse of Amadeus IX of Savoy in the Cathedral of Vercelli, and in 1728 silver chandeliers sent from Turin as presents to Pope Benedict XIII. Juvarra's brilliant drawings include many baroque designs for altars, tabernacles, VASES, lights, table centres, tables and plasterwork, and a series of enjoyable imaginary tombs to famous contemporaries, including Carlo Fontana and Sebastiano Ricci. He also illustrated Scarlatti's *Il Ciro* and Amadei's *Teodosio il giovane*. In 1735 Juvarra went to Spain to design the Royal Palace in Madrid; he died there suddenly the next year.

Käckenhoff, H. Käckenhoff designed furniture in the peasant style for W. Schmidt & Son of Hamburg in the 1890s. He was also a contributor to SCHWINDRAZHEIM'S *Beiträge zu einer Volkskunst* (1891–3), which was also concerned with the revival of folk art.

Kåge, Wilhelm (1889–1960) Kåge was trained as a painter at Valand art school in Gothenburg, and then from 1908 to 1909 under Carl Wilhelmsson in Stockholm, and from 1911 to 1912 under Johan Rohde in Copenhagen. In 1914 he was at the Plakatschule in Munich and he afterwards made a reputation as a poster designer. In 1917 Kåge was employed by the Gustavsberg porcelain factory as a designer. He subsequently became their Art Director, only retiring in 1949 to devote himself to painting. Kåge was a prolific designer at Gustavsberg and his designs were shown with success at all the major exhibitions from the Stockholm 1917 Exhibition onwards: he was awarded a Grand Prix at the PARIS 1925 EXHIBITION. Kåge's designs include the cheerfully folksy workers' service (1920), the graceful fluted Pyro service (1930), the MODERN and modular Praktika service (1933; a softer version, Praktika II, was produced in 1945), the K. S. Service (1934), based on English creamware, and the subtly curvilinear Soft Forms service (1940). Kåge also designed a wide variety of forms for his Farsta stoneware, first produced in 1930. He was succeeded at Gustavsberg by Stig Lindberg.

Kager, Johann Matthias (1575–1634) Born in Munich, Kager trained as a painter under Jacob Zeller, Jörg Karl and Friedrich SUSTRIS. He worked for the Bavarian court under Wilhelm V and Maximilian I of Bavaria on the Munich Residenz and elsewhere. In 1595 to 1596 he travelled to Italy and in 1597 became a master in Munich. In 1603 Kager moved to Augsburg where he became a citizen in 1604 and a civic painter in 1615. In Augsburg, Kager was extremely successful as a painter of both easel pictures and frescoes. He was a friend of Philipp HAINHOFER, for whom he painted miniatures and designed many elements of the great cabinet delivered to Philipp II of Pommern in 1617. Kager also did drawings of the Antiquarium at Munich for Philipp II. He designed the interior decoration of Augsburg Town Hall from 1619 to 1622 under the architect Elias Holl, including panelling, stoves and furniture. Kager also did numerous book illustrations and designed ornamental frames in the second edition of *Fuggerorum et Fuggerarum ... Imagines* (Augsburg, 1618). These are in the Augsburg version of the AURICULAR style of which Kager was a leader together with KILIAN. He also published a suite of thirteen plates of ornament in this manner engraved by Raphael Custos. In 1631 Kager was one of the six burgomasters of Augsburg.

Kahr, Andreas In 1626 Kahr published a fifty-two-plate pattern-book for embroidery, *New Modelbuch*; some designs are taken from SIBMACHER, others are original, consisting of crude but vigorous figures on a net ground.

Kamien, Erasmus Born in Posen, Kamien was the son of a goldsmith and himself became a master there in 1553. In 1568 after an exodus from Posen caused by the plague Kamien became Mayor. In 1552 he published a suite of thirteen plates of GROTESQUE ornament for goldsmiths, reprinted in 1592 and sometimes attributed to Kamien's cousin, Erasmus Kosler, a goldsmith from Wilna who worked in Nuremberg. In 1582 Kamien published a further suite of twelve plates.

Kasemann, Rutger Described as Vitruvian architect, sculptor and cabinetmaker, Kasemann designed a series of architectural pattern-books, *Architectura Lehr Seiulen Bochg* (Cologne, 1615; twenty-four plates) and *Architecture*, after Hans BLUM, both published by Johann Bussemacher, the latter republished by Abraham Hogenberg in 1644, *Seilen Bochg* (Cologne, 1616; twenty-seven plates) and *Architectur* (Cologne, 1630; sixty-one plates), both published by Hermann Esser, the latter reprinted by Gerhard Altzenbach in 1653. Kasemann's designs include not only architecture but also columns, doors, gables, cornices, brackets and furniture in a wild and incoherent STRAPWORK style influenced by Wendel DIETTERLIN and comparable to designs by Veit Eck, Jakob GUCKEISEN and Johann Jakob EBELMANN, also published by Bussemacher. *Architectura Lehr Seiulen Bochg* was dedicated to the cabinetmakers of Cologne. Surprisingly Batty LANGLEY was acquainted with Kasemann's works.

Kauffer, Edward McKnight (1890–1954) Born in Great Falls, Montana, the son of a popular musician, Kauffer was working in a bookshop in San Francisco when, in 1912, he met Professor McKnight of Utah University, who paid for him to travel to Paris to study painting and whose name Kauffer adopted in gratitude. Passing through Chicago, where he saw the Armory Show (1913), and Munich, Kauffer reached Paris in 1913, but left for England in 1914. In 1915 he was given his first commission for a poster by Frank PICK of the London Underground Railway. He was soon influenced by Vorticism, and his *Flight* (1916), a geometric flock of birds derived from a Japanese print, reflected the Vorticist advocacy of tough and striking images; it was published in *Colour* (1917) and used as a *Daily Herald* poster in 1919. In 1917 Kauffer became secretary of the London Group and Roger FRY sold his drawings at the Omega workshops. After the war Kauffer's career as a poster designer blossomed and in 1920 he gave up painting. In 1924 he published *The Art of the Poster*, dedicated to Frank Pick, and in 1927 his posters were cited in *The Times* as representative of good British design. In 1925 an exhibition of his posters was held in Bloomsbury. From 1921, when he designed a book-jacket for *Eminent Victorians*, Kauffer was involved in book design and in 1925 he illustrated *The Anatomy of Melancholy* for Francis Meynell's Nonesuch Press. In 1929 rugs by Kauffer were shown alongside those by Marion DORN, with whom he had lived since 1923 and whom he married in 1950. From the late 1920s Kauffer adopted a more MODERN manner in his posters, using photographic images and the airbrush; in 1929 his work was featured in 'GEBRAUCHSGRAPHIK'. He worked for most of the great design patrons of the 1930s, for Crawfords, for Shell, for Cresta Silks, for the Orient Line (on the *Orion*, 1935) and for the Great Western Railway. He became a member of the Modern design establishment and was in

1936 made the first Honorary Designer for Industry, chosen by the Royal SOCIETY OF ARTS. He was in contact with Wells COATES, with Stephen Tallents and with T. S. Eliot. In 1940 he left England for New York with Marion Dorn. For the NEW YORK MUSEUM OF MODERN ART Kauffer designed a poster for the organic furniture competition of 1940 won by EAMES and Eero SAARINEN, and in 1941 a cover for the Britain at War exhibition catalogue. But he never recovered his English success, and turned to drink, a forlorn and withdrawn figure by his death. He had designed some 250 posters and 150 book-jackets, apart from innumerable smaller jobs.

Kauffmann, Angelica Catherina Maria Anna (1741–1807) Born at Coire in the Grisons, the daughter of a painter, Kauffmann worked with her father in Northern Italy before moving in 1763 to Rome, where she met Winckelmann (1717–68). After a journey to Naples she returned to Rome in 1764 and thence, after visiting Venice in 1765, travelled in 1766 to England, where she became in 1768 a founder member of the Royal Academy. Her works were widely disseminated in prints by Francesco Bartolozzi and others, and were used to decorate porcelain and enamels in England and Europe. In 1772 Christopher Fürlohg executed a marquetry panel of the Muse Erato after Kauffmann's design and in 1780 she showed a design for a fan at the Royal Academy. She did decorative paintings for STUART, CHAMBERS and ADAM. In 1781 she married Adam's chief decorative painter, Antonio Zucchi (1726–95), and retired to Italy where, after a brief stay in Venice, she settled in Rome and was part of an artistic circle which included Goethe, Tischbein and Canova.

Keller, Johann Heinrich (1627–1708) A Basel cabinet-maker, Keller published a book of the ORDERS and ornament (Strasbourg, 1680; sixteen plates). It includes brackets and panels in a crude but vigorous AURICULAR style.

Keller-Leuzinger, Franz (1835–90) Born in Mannheim, Keller-Leuzinger studied painting at the Karlsruhe Polytechnic. After returning in 1870 from a voyage of exploration to Brazil, he applied himself to design, becoming Director of the Karlsruhe school of applied arts and designing for the Grand Duchess Luise's embroidery school. In 1874 to 1876 he revived the Heimberg pottery in Switzerland, preserving old techniques but introducing new designs based on oriental and RENAISSANCE modes with great success; he also revived potteries in Villingen in the Black Forest. From 1877 to 1879 Keller-Leuzinger was in Hamburg, where he designed glass in the Venetian style for C. H. F. Müller's factory, and earthenware decoration for the girls' school of applied art. He later worked in Stuttgart and Munich.

Kellerthaler, Hans The son of a goldsmith, Kellerthaler became a master in Dresden in 1585. He specialized in the embellishment of luxury cabinets, and was still active in 1637. In 1589 Kellerthaler issued four highly MANNERIST plates of the elements within oval GROTESQUE cartouches in the dotted manner.

Kempe, Charles Eamer (1837–1907) Born in Ovingdean, near Brighton, Kempe was a member of an old Sussex family. He was intended for the priesthood, but a stammer prevented his ordination. In 1862 he worked for BODLEY, whom he assisted on the design of embroidery and furniture. Kempe was acquainted with the William MORRIS circle and attempted to go into partnership with the painter Arthur Hughes. In 1865 he designed a stained-glass window at Gloucester Cathedral for Clayton & Bell. In 1866 he set up as an independent architect, designing stained glass made by the London firm of Thomas Baillie. In 1869 he set up his own prolific stained-glass firm, which often worked for Bodley. Kempe's style was based on late-15th-century models, with pale stains, elaborate details and canopy work; his later works can be overblown and stereotyped. His nephew Walter Ernest Tower (1873–1955) entered the firm in the 1890s and carried it on until 1934.

Kendrick, George Prentiss Kendrick was a director of the Grueby Faience Company of Boston, founded in 1894 by William Henry Grueby (1867–1925). Kendrick designed Grueby's early vases, massy forms decorated with curving leaves and flowers, influenced by French prototypes by Delaherche and Chaplet; few were made after 1911.

Kent, William Born in Bridlington in Yorkshire in 1685 or 1686, Kent is said to have been apprenticed to a coach-painter in Hull. His talent attracted attention and in 1709 he was sent to Italy by a group of wealthy patrons; he travelled with John TALMAN. In Rome, Kent bought works of art for his backers, while studying painting under Benedetto Luti. He 'became acquainted with many English Noblemen', including Thomas Coke, later Earl of Leicester, with whom he toured northern Italy in 1714. In 1713 Kent won a prize for painting at the Accademia di San Luca and in 1717 he did a fresco ceiling in San Giuliano dei Fiamminghi. In 1719 the Earl of Burlington, who had met Kent in the winter of 1714 to 1715, brought him back to England and employed him as a painter. In the Presence Chamber of Kensington Palace, Kent executed a ceiling in a

revived GROTESQUE style (about 1724), but most of his decorative paintings were unremarkable. In 1724 Burlington employed Kent to edit *Designs of Inigo Jones, with some Additional Designs* (1727), the latter by Burlington himself, and at this period Kent turned from painting to the design of architectural decorations, such as frames and chimneypieces and a triumphal arch in Westminster Hall for the Coronation of George II (1727). From 1726, thanks to Burlington's influence, Kent was on the Board of Works, first as Master Carpenter and then, from 1735, as Master Mason and Deputy Surveyor. In 1732 he designed the Royal State Barge for FREDERICK LEWIS, PRINCE OF WALES. *Some Designs of Mr Inigo Jones and Mr William Kent* (1744), published by his disciple, John VARDY, includes designs by Kent for furniture and silver. Kent designed furniture for Lord Burlington's villa at Chiswick, for Houghton Hall, for Sir Robert Walpole, both in about 1730, and at Sherborne House, Gloucestershire, for Sir John Dutton in 1728. A gold cup designed by Kent for Colonel Pelham in about 1736 was repeated in silver mugs for Sir Charles Hanbury Williams in 1745. In 1736 he designed two silver chandeliers for Herrenhausen, George II's German palace, and in 1745 a silver centrepiece for Frederick, Prince of Wales. In 1725 Kent did some easel paintings of GOTHIC subjects, and he sometimes designed in the Gothic style, including a pulpit and choir furniture for York Minster in 1741; he also designed a pavement for York in 1731 to 1735. Kent's Merlin's Cave at Richmond (1735) included rustic tree-trunk book-cases. He also illustrated several books, including Gay's *Poems* (1720), Thomson's *Seasons* (1730) and Spenser's *Faerie Queene* (1751). However, Kent's main achievement was the creation of a system of interior decoration congruous with the Palladian architecture of his patron, Lord Burlington. It was a sober version of Roman BAROQUE with a stress on architectonic elements. Kent anticipated Robert ADAM's later role as a complete interior architect, able to design every detail of a room, and Adam recognized Kent's role as a pioneer in the revival of grotesque ornament. Kent's designs had a wide and prolonged influence; John LINNELL, for instance, copied a Kent design for a settee. Kent seems to have possessed great personal charm; he was an intimate friend of Burlington, whom he left 'two yellow Marble VASES with Vine Leaves' and in whose house he died in 1748.

Keramic Studio (1899–1923) Subtitled *A Monthly Magazine for the Designer Potter Decorator Firer*, this New York journal contained high-quality illustrations of ceramic designs, some in colour.

Kilburn, William (1745–1818) Born in Dublin, the son of an architect, Kilburn was apprenticed to a cotton and linen printer at Lucan. He subsequently moved to London, where he sold designs to calico printers, and in 1777 was responsible for plates in William Curtis's *Flora Londiniensis*. He later managed and owned a calico printing factory at Wallington in Surrey. In 1787 Kilburn, whose designs were widely pirated, petitioned Parliament to protect his copyright. His designs of about 1790 are of great delicacy, with flowers in compartments and seaweed patterns.

Kilian, Lucas (1579–1637) Born in Augsburg, the son of a goldsmith, Kilian became a draughtsman and engraver under his stepfather, Domenicus Custos. From 1601 to 1604 he was in Italy, including a long stay in Venice. He engraved for the Custos press until the death of Domenicus in 1617, after which he worked for his brother, Wolfgang

Kilian. Lucas Kilian was a militant protestant. He was a prolific engraver of portraits and landscapes as well as ornament. In 1606 he published a book of goldsmith's designs. His *Newes Gradesca Buchlin* (1607; ten plates) comprises delicate and witty panels of GROTESQUE ornament, with certain stretched and scrolled elements which look forward towards the AURICULAR style. A later *Newe Gradisco Buech* (1624; twelve plates) is more vigorous and auricular than its predecessor. The *Newes ABC Buechlein* (1627; twenty-five plates), dedicated to the goldsmith Melchior Gelb, shows the alphabet enmeshed in auricular ornament with industrious putti, a strange prefigurement of Godfrey SYKES's 1864 alphabet. *Ein Newes Schildt Buech* (1630), engraved by Raphael Custos, has gobbets of pious doggerel in bold auricular cartouches. Kilian himself engraved silver ornament on a table made for Maximilian I of Bavaria in 1626 by Hans Georg Hertel, probably to Kilian's design. Hertel also made an architectural model to Kilian's design. Kilian was among the most important pioneers of the auricular style in Germany, imitated by BRETSCHNEIDER among others.

Kimball, J. Wayland Kimball's *Book of Designs: Furniture and Drapery* (Boston and New York, 1876) presents designs in the fashionable Néo-Grec and EASTLAKE styles made by such manufacturers as George Hunzinger and Kilian Brothers of New York.

Kimbel, Martin (1835–1921) The third son of Wilhelm KIMBEL, Martin Kimbel worked as a cabinet-maker in New York, before finally settling in Breslau in 1866. He published a pattern-book for woodwork (Mainz, 1864) and another for decorative painters (Breslau, 1872).

Kimbel, Wilhelm (1786–1875) Born in Mainz, Kimbel commenced a highly successful cabinet-making business there in 1815. He showed at the Darmstadt 1839, Mainz 1842 and Berlin 1844 Exhibitions. From 1835 to 1853 he issued a *Journal für Möbelschreiner und Tapezierer*, with slight variations of title. This contains numerous highly competent designs for furniture, starting with pieces in the late BIEDERMEIER style and then including a whole range of styles, GOTHIC, RENAISSANCE, and, above all, ROCOCO revival. It is the most valuable source for German furniture design of its period. One plate in 1842 shows chairs directly borrowed from Henry SHAW's *Specimens of Ancient Furniture* (1836).

King, Jessie Marion (1876–1949) Born in Glasgow, Jessie M. King was educated at the Glasgow School of Art, whose history she illuminated on vellum to be laid under its foundation stone in 1898. She won a travelling scholarship to Germany and Italy and later claimed that BOTTICELLI drawings in the Uffizi in Florence were a chief inspiration. Her style, a gossamer version of Charles Rennie MACKINTOSH's, strongly influenced by Aubrey Beardsley, was fully formed by about 1900. In 1902 book covers, book-plates and book illustrations of Jessie M. King were illustrated in the 'STUDIO', and in the same year she won a gold medal for watercolours shown in the Scottish Section at the TURIN EXHIBITION, organized by Mackintosh, with whom she was friendly. At this period she was also designing tiles, fabrics, wallpaper and jewellery, some made by LIBERTY'S. From 1902 until about 1915 she was a fertile designer of bindings, title-pages, ornaments and illustrations, her masterpieces being William MORRIS's *The Defence of Guenevere and Other Poems* (1904) and Oscar Wilde's *A House of*

Pomegranates (1915). She also published a book of plant drawings, *Budding Life* (1906). From about 1920 her main interest was batik, explained in her *How Cinderella Was Able to Go to the Ball* (1924), although a number of later book designs are known. In 1908 she married the Glasgow painter and furniture designer Ernest A. TAYLOR, with whom she shared a studio in Paris.

King, Thomas In about 1835 King described himself as an upholsterer of forty-five years' experience with leading London firms. He was responsible for some fifteen pattern-books for furniture from 1829 to 1839. *The Modern Style of Cabinet Work Exemplified* (1829; seventy-two plates, some coloured) contains neat Grecian and GOTHIC designs; King claimed that it represented 'English style blended with Parisian taste' and issued twenty-eight *Supplementary Plates*, some of almost BIEDERMEIER simplicity. In *Designs for Carving and Gilding* (about 1830; forty-one plates, some coloured) King alternated between Grecian and a rich ROCOCO revival style; his *Modern Designs for Household Furniture* (thirty-five coloured plates) is similar but simpler. King's *Working Ornaments and Forms* (1833; thirty plates) contained details of furniture in the Grecian and Gothic styles; it was praised in LOUDON's *Architectural Magazine*. *A Compilation of Splendid Ornamental Designs* (twenty-four plates) was presumably similar. *Shop Fronts and Exterior Doors* contained designs in the Egyptian, Greek and Roman styles. *The Upholsterer's Accelerator* (about 1835), reprinted as *The Upholsterer's Guide* (1848) includes a long technical text on upholstery, and thirty-seven plates. *Valences and Draperies, Original Designs for Chairs and Sofas* (thirty-two coloured plates) and *Original Designs for Cabinet Furniture* (forty-six plates, mainly coloured) are all of about 1835. *The Cabinet Maker's Sketch Book* appeared in two parts of twenty-four and thirty-six plates in 1835 and 1836; it was treated at length in Loudon's *Architectural Magazine*. *Fashionable Bedsteads* (about 1839; sixteen coloured plates) contains basic designs, but *The Upholsterer's Sketch Book* (1839; sixteen plates) had elaborate designs in the rococo and Elizabethan styles which, with Gothic, dominate King's posthumous *Specimens of Furniture*, whose title was presumably intended to recall Henry SHAW's *Specimens of Ancient Furniture* (1836). King's works provide the most comprehensive document of commercial taste in furniture design in the 1830s, reflecting the move from simple Grecian forms to the richer ornamental vocabulary of rococo and Elizabethan. He was long in use among the trade and his *Modern Style of Cabinet Work Exemplified* was reprinted as late as 1862.

King, Thomas Harper A Catholic architect working in Bruges, King published in 1850 a revised and expanded edition of A. W. N. PUGIN's *True Principles*, incorporating plates from Pugin's *Contrasts*. King hoped that the book would encourage the revival of the GOTHIC style in Belgium and praised Pugin and Hansom, the English Catholic architect. At the end is an advertisement for Louis Grossé, an ecclesiastical supplier in Bruges, illustrating vestments and metalwork probably designed by King. His next book, *Orfèvrerie et Ouvrages en Metal du Moyen Âge* (Brussels and Ghent, 1852–4; 200 plates), contains excellent full-scale drawings of Gothic metalwork. King also published *Études pratiques tirées de l'Architecture du Moyen Âge* with a text by the Catholic writer George James Hill; it appeared in an English edition, *The Study Book of Mediaeval Architecture and Art* (1858–68; 400 plates).

Kinsman, Rodney Born in 1943, Kinsman trained at the Central School of Art in London and in 1966 set up O.M.K. Design Limited with Jerzy Olejnik and Bryan Morrison. O.M.K.'s chairs of chrome-plated tubular steel, tractor stools, T10 table, Petal table, Omkstack chair and Sanpan light use MODERN materials with zest and Modern forms with wit; they have been among the most successful English designs in recent years.

Kips, Alexander (1858–1910) Born in Berlin, Kips studied at the BERLIN KUNSTGEWERBEMUSEUM and subsequently with the history painter Schaller. From 1886 to his retirement in 1908 Kips was artistic director of the Berlin porcelain factory, where he was responsible for the revival of 18th-century ROCOCO models, which led to an upturn in the fortunes of the factory. In 1893 he travelled to Italy to gather inspiration for porcelain decoration. Kips developed painted decoration on porcelain tiles and showed large symbolic compositions in this technique at several exhibitions, for instance 'The German Applied Arts' at the CHICAGO 1893 EXHIBITION.

Kjaerholm, Poul Born in 1929, Kjaerholm was trained at the School of Arts & Crafts in Copenhagen, where he lectured from 1952 to 1956. He has designed furniture for E. Kold Christiansen of Copenhagen from 1956 and also for Ejnar Pedersen of P.P. Furniture. Kjaerholm's designs reflect the Danish tradition of elegant detail and careful craftsmanship, but he has combined wood with other materials – chromium-plated steel, marble and fibre glass, or used these on their own, and his stylistic language is MODERN. His hammock chair 24 (1965), an elegant curved-steel frame covered in canework, resting on a slender steel stand, is a refined version of LE CORBUSIER's 1928 chaise longue.

Klagmann, Jean-Baptiste Jules (1810–67) Born in Paris, the son of a shoemaker, Klagmann first worked in a copper foundry. He later studied sculpture under J.-J. FEUCHÈRE and E. J. Ramey (1796–1852), and had an active career as a monumental and decorative sculptor. From the 1840s he was prolific as a designer of goldsmiths' work, in an accomplished RENAISSANCE manner, including the Goodwood Race cup of 1844 and a sword made by FROMENT-MEURICE presented by the City of Paris to the Comte de Paris in the same year. He also designed Sèvres maiolica executed for Fontainebleau. Klagmann was appointed in 1848 to the Conseil Supérieur de Perfectionnement des Manufactures Nationales, and was later among the more active founders of the Union Centrale des Beaux-Arts Appliqués à l'Industrie.

Klauber, Joseph Sebastian (1700–1776) Klauber and his brother, Johann Baptist Klauber (1712–87), were pupils of Johann Georg BERGMÜLLER at the Augsburg Academy. They were active as engravers and publishers, issuing many suites of lively ROCOCO ornament, including *rocailles* on such themes as the seasons, the elements, the times of the day and the quarters of the compass. Some suites were later republished by HERTEL. The Klauber brothers also published the works of other designers, including J. W. BAUMGARTNER and GÖZ.

Kleiber, Anton Born in about 1580 probably in Strasbourg, Kleiber was active as a glass painter and designer there from 1609. In about 1614 to 1616 he was paid for work in Stuttgart.

Klenze, Leo von (1784–1864) Born at Bockenem near Hildesheim, the son of a wealthy lawyer, Klenze studied architecture in Berlin under GILLY from 1800, in Paris under Durand, PERCIER and FONTAINE, and then in Italy. From 1808 to 1813 Klenze was architect to Jérôme Bonaparte, King of Westphalia. He then studied architecture in Paris, where he met Crown Prince Ludwig of Bavaria in 1814. In 1816 he moved to Munich to work for Ludwig and became the leading architect and town planner in Munich. In 1853, having quarrelled with Maximilian II, he resigned his offices. Klenze travelled to Italy in 1818 and 1823 to 1824 and to Greece in 1834. Klenze designed furniture and lighting for many of his buildings, including the Max-Palais (1822–6), the Königsbau (1826–35) and Festsaalbau (1837–42) of the Residenz, and the Alte Pinakothek (1825–36), all in Munich, and the Hermitage Museum in St Petersburg (1842–51). His designs were in a rich and massive NEO-CLASSICAL style.

Klint, Kaare (1888–1954) The son of the leading Danish architect P. V. Jensen Klint (1853–1930), Klint studied painting under Johan Rohde and architecture under his father and under the Professor of architecture at the Copenhagen Academy, Carl Petersen (1874–1923). In 1914 Klint collaborated on the design of NEO-CLASSICAL furniture for the art gallery at Faalborg with Petersen, who also designed for Bing & Grøndahl's porcelain factory. In 1917 Klint did studies on human proportions in relation to furniture and worked out ideal dimensions for storage furniture based on the objects to be stored: he then designed sectional units for storage to be factory made, but these were not produced. In 1924 Klint was appointed lecturer in furniture design at the Copenhagen Academy, where he exercised a wide influence, his pupils including MOGENSON and KOCH. He became professor of architecture at the Academy in 1944. Most of Klint's later designs were made by the cabinet-maker

Rudolf Rasmussen. He was given many official commissions, including in 1922 to 1925 furniture for the Thorwaldsen Museum, and his designs were shown at many exhibitions, including the Barcelona 1929 Exhibition and the PARIS 1937 EXHIBITION. Klint's own style was much influenced by English 18th-century furniture and, unlike many MODERN teachers, stressed the value of traditional design, although he did not advocate the imitation of earlier styles. A deck-chair (1933) and an X-framed folding stool exemplify Klint's calculated mastery of construction and detail.

Knight, Frederick Knight published a range of pattern-books for silversmiths, engravers, jewellers, carvers and founders. They include *Knight's Modern and Antique Gems* (1828; eighty-six plates), *Knight's Scroll Ornaments* (about 1830; fifty plates), including designs derived from LE BRUN, Le Potre (sic), GRIBELIN, MEISSONIER and so on, as well as the designs for the cast-iron gates by Bramah at Hyde Park Corner, *Knight's New Book of Cyphers* (1832), *Knight's Ornamental Alphabets* (five plates), *Knight's Unique Fancy Ornaments* (1834) and *Knight's Vases and Ornaments* (122 plates), the latter published in Edinburgh, the rest in London. Although repetitive and derivative, using mainly 17th- and 18th-century sources with a stress on ACANTHUS ornament, Knight's books present a neglected conspectus of English taste in about 1830.

Knobelsdorff, Georg Wenzeslaus von (1699–1753) Born near Crossen, of noble descent, Knobelsdorff joined the infantry at Küstrin in 1712, but had to retire owing to ill health in 1729 with the rank of captain. He then studied painting and drawing under Antoine Pesne (1683–1757) and subsequently architecture under Wangenheim and

Kemmeter. From before 1732 Knobelsdorff was friendly with Crown Prince Frederick of Prussia, who financed a visit to Rome from 1736 to 1737, after which Knobelsdorff worked for him at Schloss Rheinsburg. When Frederick became King in 1740 he appointed Knobelsdorff Surintendant des Bâtiments et Jardins, and in the same year Knobelsdorff briefly visited Paris. On his return to Berlin he immediately began a new wing to Schloss Charlottenburg which, after continuous pressure from Frederick, was inaugurated in 1746 and completed in 1747. In 1744 Knobelsdorff began to rebuild the Schloss in Potsdam, and to build Frederick's summer residence, Schloss Sanssouci, but after a quarrel with the King he ceased to be involved at Potsdam in 1746. Knobelsdorff, influenced by MEISSONIER and LA JOUE, introduced to Berlin a light, brilliant and confident ROCOCO style of interior decoration. He himself designed furniture and other details, but usually worked in collaboration with NAHL and the HOPPENHAUPT brothers. After Knobelsdorff died, worn out by Frederick's ruthless demands, the King paid him the unusual tribute of a personal obituary.

Knox, Archibald (1864–1933) Born in Cronkborne, Isle of Man, son of a marine engineer, Knox studied from 1878 to 1884 at Douglas School of Art, where he subsequently taught. From 1892 to 1896 Knox was probably attached to BAILLIE SCOTT's office in the Isle of Man. In 1897 he moved to London and in 1898 was attached to the SILVER studio, who marketed some of his textile designs. In about 1898 Knox began to design for LIBERTY'S, to whom he was probably introduced by Baillie Scott, who had designed Liberty textiles in 1893. Liberty's had been importing pewter by Kayser of Krefeld designed by Hugo LEVEN. Knox designed metalwork to compete with Kayser, the Cymric range of silver from 1899 and the Tudric range of pewter, probably from 1900. Knox's designs used interlaced ornament of a Celtic character; as well as metalwork he designed carpets, textiles and jewellery. From 1900 to 1904 Knox went back to the Isle of Man. He then returned to London teaching at various art schools, including that at Kingston, whence he resigned when in 1911 his methods were criticized by the South Kensington examiners. A group of Kingston students then seceded and set up the Knox Guild of Craft and Design, which survived until 1939. Knox's style seems to have gone out of fashion in about 1909, when Liberty's sold a number of his metalwork designs to James Connell & Co. He ceased work for Liberty's in 1912 and went to America, where he designed carpets for Bromley & Co. of Philadelphia. He returned to the Isle of Man in 1913. Knox designed Arthur Lasenby Liberty's tomb (1917). After the First World War he painted and taught.

Koch, Mogens Born in 1898, the son of an engineer, Koch studied architecture at the Copenhagen Academy, and worked under Carl Petersen (1874–1923) and Kaare KLINT. In 1950 Koch became professor of architecture at the Copenhagen Academy. Koch designed furniture very much in the Klint tradition, much of it made by N. C. Jensen Kjaer or Rudolf Rasmussen, both of whom also worked for Klint. One of Koch's most celebrated designs, the Safari chair, was designed in 1933 but only produced in 1958.

König, Ignaz-Carl König was responsible for two suites of designs for cabinets (five plates each), published by HERTEL in Augsburg in about 1750. They are of conservative late BAROQUE form with ROCOCO crestings. König also issued a suite of rococo altars, and another of doors.

Kontur (1950–64) Published by the Swedish Society of Industrial Design, this well-illustrated magazine contains much useful information including, for instance, articles on Bruno MATHSSON (1963) and Sigurd PERSSON (1964).

Krammer, Gabriel Krammer was born in Zürich. From 1599 he was active in Prague as a cabinet-maker and as a bandsman in the Emperor RUDOLF II's life guards. He seems to have died before 1606. His *Architectura* (Prague, 1600; twenty-eight plates) was dedicated to Rudolf II: it comprises plates of geometry and the ORDERS, followed by brackets, gables, windows, terms, doors, panelling and cresting in an exuberant STRAPWORK GROTESQUE style, with the stress on strapwork, apart from one plate of scrolling ACANTHUS brackets. Later editions were published in Prague (1606), Nuremberg (1608, and, in part, 1649) and Cologne (1610), the latter issued by Johann Bussemacher and dedicated to cabinet-makers. Krammer's second book was *Schweiff Buchlein* (Prague, 1602; twenty-three plates). It includes designs for brackets, chairbacks, stools, panels, an alphabet, and cartouches, mainly in a vigorous strapwork grotesque manner, and based on the theme of the orders. A second edition was published by Bussemacher in Cologne in 1611. A crude broadsheet on the orders by Krammer is bound in with ERASMUS's 1666 book on the subject, and it seems that Krammer had a prolonged influence on design at the ARTISAN level. Andreas Krammer, who in 1659 published a suite (six plates) of black designs for enamelling of mediocre quality, with putti, birds and squirrels, may have been a relation.

Krug, Ludwig Krug was the son of a

prominent Nuremberg goldsmith and die-cutter, who had worked after designs by Cranach. Krug was an important member of the DÜRER circle, and was active not only as a goldsmith – he became a master in 1522 – but also as sculptor, medallist, engraver and painter. A ciborium of about 1520, designed and made by Krug, combines a NATURALISTIC foot formed as a tree-trunk, complete with woodcutter, and embossed scenes of the Passion on the bowl; in both respects its design was influenced by DÜRER. His later works abandon late-GOTHIC naturalism in favour of a wholly RENAISSANCE vocabulary of ornament.

Krumper, Hans Born in Weilheim, the son of a sculptor, Krumper followed his father's trade. He seems to have been active at the Munich court from 1584 and was in 1587 said to be a pupil of Hubert GERHARD. In 1590 he travelled to Italy at the expense of Duke Wilhelm V of Bavaria, probably visiting Venice and Florence. After his return to Munich in 1592 Krumper married the daughter of Friedrich SUSTRIS, whom in 1599 he succeeded as private architect and Kunstintendant to Wilhelm V, although without achieving Sustris's complete dominance of court art in Munich. In 1609 Maximilian I appointed Krumper as court painter, but his main job was to supervise the rebuilding and redecoration of the Residenz in Munich. He also advised on the decoration of the Goldener Saal at Augsburg. Krumper was an important designer of goldsmiths' work, including reliquaries, lamps, altars, etc. One of the few securely identified designs is a reliquary of about 1612 for the parish church of St Wolfgang bei Dorfen made by the Augsburg goldsmith Hans Lencker. Krumper's style was strongly influenced by Gerhard, Sustris and CANDID. His metalwork makes use of elongated scrolls in the stretched GROTESQUE manner which looks towards the AURICULAR style. Krumper died in 1634, still in the service of Maximilian I.

Kübler, Werner Born in Schaffhausen in 1555, Kübler was active there as a stained-glass designer in a manner influenced by Tobias STIMMER and similar to that of Christoph MURER. His frames make a lavish use of STRAPWORK GROTESQUE ornament. Kübler died in about 1586. His widow married Daniel LINDTMAYER in 1588, and his son, another Werner Kübler (1582–1621), was also active as a stained-glass designer in Schaffhausen.

Kulmbach, Hans Süss von Kulmbach was probably born at Kulmbach in the late 1470s. In about 1500 he became a pupil of DÜRER in Nuremberg, and later assisted Jacopo de' Barbari. From 1508 Kulmbach was a prolific designer of stained glass, probably for the workshop of Veit Hirschvogel, father of Augustin. His major designs include windows presented by the Markgrave of Brandenburg and by the Emperor Maximilian to the church of St Sebald in Nuremberg in 1514 to 1515. A design for an elaborate late-GOTHIC monstrance is also attributed to Kulmbach. He died in Nuremberg in 1522.

Kunst (1899–1905) Published in Copenhagen, this well-illustrated Danish magazine covered most aspects of art and design.

Kunstgewerbe, Das (1890–94) Published from Dresden, this magazine was founded by Ferdinand Avenarius, who also created a fine arts magazine, *Der Kunstwart*, in 1887. *Das Kunstgewerbe*, part edited by Paul Schumann, contained illustrations and information on ancient and modern design and ornament.

Kunstgewerbeblatt (1889–1916) Published from Leipzig by E. A. Seemann, this well-illustrated journal of design was edited by Professor Karl Hoffacker, Director of the Karlsruhe school of applied arts. Among the many excellent articles was one by J. A. Lux, the editor of 'Das INTERIEUR', on J. M. OLBRICH (1909).

Kunstgewerbe in Elsass-Lothringen, Das (1900–1906) Published in Strasbourg, this well-illustrated magazine of the applied arts was edited by Dr Friedrich Leitschuh of Strasbourg University and Professor Anton SEDER, Director of the Strasbourg school of applied arts. Seder is notable for his virulent attack of 1901 on the Mathildenhöhe exhibition in DARMSTADT, in which he blamed the influence of the 'STUDIO'.

Kunst im Dritten Reich, Die (1937–44) Published in Munich with Albert Speer as one of three editors this magazine contains useful coverage of design under the Hitler regime.

Kunst und Handwerk (1898–1932) As the *Zeitschrift des Bayerischen Kunstgewerbeverein zu München* this journal had started in 1850, and was thus the oldest German art magazine. Its fine illustrations covered most aspects of ART NOUVEAU design. In 1928 it became the official organ of several other South German applied arts associations, and before its disappearance issued an English edition, *Creative Hands* (1931).

Kunst und Kunsthandwerk (1898–1921)

Published by the VIENNA MUSEUM OF APPLIED ARTS and edited by its director, A. von Scala, until 1908, this monthly magazine contained a series of richly illustrated articles on modern design, for example BING on TIFFANY glass (1898), E. H. Berlepsch on Eugène GRASSET (1898), and B. Kendell on the Glasgow School and on ASHBEE at Essex House (1902), and on historic subjects, for instance August Schestag on BIEDERMEIER (1906).

Kurtz, Georg In about 1695 Kurtz designed a book for the use of jewellers (eight plates), published in Rome and dedicated to Vincenzo Rota, jeweller to Pope Innocent XII. Reprinted in Augsburg as *Neu Inventiertes Zierathen Buch*, probably in about 1710, the book comprises large plates of scrolled ACANTHUS ornament and designs for jewellery incorporating stars, ribbons, eagles, etc., as well as acanthus.

Küsel, Maria Philippina Born in Augsburg in 1676, Maria Philippina Küsel was a member of a family of goldsmiths and engravers. She published two suites of BERAINESQUE ornaments for goldsmiths (six plates each) and a suite of flowers in VASES (six plates), as well as copies after Sebastien Le Clerc. She probably died in Vienna.

Küsthardt, Friedrich (1830–1900) Born in Göttingen, Küsthardt was active in Hildesheim as a sculptor, mainly of funerary monuments, from 1859. In the early 1880s he designed for Robert BICHWEILER's 'German Majolika' factory in Hamburg.

L

Ladenspelder, Johann Ladenspelder was probably born in Essen in about 1512. Working in Cologne up to at least 1561 he was influenced by the early RENAISSANCE ornament of DÜRER and the BEHAMS. He copied the so-called Tarocchi cards of Mantegna. Ladenspelder's own prints of ornament range from a self-portrait as a medallion head flanked by scrolling foliage (1540), and a knife design (1540) to two panels of ornament (1550 and 1552) incorporating heavy STRAPWORK.

La Farge, John (1835–1910) Born in New York of wealthy French parents, La Farge spent a brief period in the Paris studio of Thomas Couture (1815–74) in 1856. After travels in Europe, including England, he returned to New York in 1858 and then studied with William, brother of the architect Richard Morris Hunt (1828–1895), in Newport. From about 1860, when he married a grandniece of Commodore Perry, he was influenced by Japanese prints, the Pre-Raphaelites and Blake. An early interest in stained glass and the colour theories of CHEVREUL was revived by a trip to Europe in 1873, and in the late 1870s La Farge began to add a thriving career as a designer of stained glass to his established practice as a painter of murals. From 1878 he designed glass in Holy Trinity, Boston, for H. H. RICHARDSON, who had noticed La Farge's paintings at the 1867 National Academy of Design. His many distinguished clients also included Henry Marquand (about 1878), ALMA-TADEMA (1882) and Cornelius Vanderbilt (1882). After 1882 when an agreement with Herter Brothers failed he set up the short-lived La Farge Decorative Art Company (1883–5) to produce his glass, but from 1885 it was made by John Calvin and Thomas Wright. His interest in technique was demonstrated by his 1879 patent for a method for opalescent glass, which anticipated Tiffany. His window, The Sealing of the Twelve Tribes, earned him a medal at the PARIS 1889 EXHIBITION, and in 1894 he was in close contact with BING. At this period his glass combined a strong Japanese influence with brilliant technical effects. But an increasing eclecticism, drawing on RENAISSANCE and BAROQUE elements, led to a more and more pictorial style. His writings included *An Artist's Letters from Japan* (1897), and by his death La Farge had achieved great status as a pundit.

Lafitte, Louis (1770–1828) Born in Paris, Lafitte was trained as a painter under G. Demarteau and J.-B. Regnault, winning the Grand Prix de Rome in 1791. In 1799 he designed the decorations of the dining-room at Malmaison. At the restoration in 1815 he was appointed Dessinateur du Cabinet du Roi. Lafitte designed the wallpaper suite Les Amours de Psyche for Dufour in 1816, and designs for the royal goldsmith, Cahier, shown in the PARIS 1819 EXHIBITION, were illustrated in NORMAND'S *Modèles d'Orfevrerie* (1822). Lafitte was also responsible for medals, book illustrations and porcelain designs for the Sèvres factory.

Lagrenée, Jean Jacques (1739–1821) Born in Paris, Lagrenée was taught to paint by his brother Louis-Jean-François Lagrenée (1725–1805), whom he accompanied to St Petersburg in 1760 and by whose style he was much influenced. From 1763 to 1768 Lagrenée was in Rome, where he published *Recueil de Desseins à la Plume de Composition et d'après l'antique* (Rome, 1765, reissued Paris, 1784; twelve plates, including VASES, tripods etc. after the antique). From 1785 to 1800 Lagrenée was Directeur Artistique at the Sèvres porcelain factory, at first with BACHELIER as co-director. Lagrenée was already working at Sèvres before his appointment; his designs were completely NEO-CLASSICAL in style, some using the Greek vases from the collection of Vivant DENON deposited at the Sèvres factory in 1786 by the Comte d'Angivillier to serve as an inspiration to designers. In 1787 d'Angivillier encouraged Lagrenée to design gilt-bronze mounts for Sèvres porcelain to be manufactured by J. J. Thomire. Also in 1787 Lagrenée bought prints of ARABESQUES after RAPHAEL to serve as models at Sèvres. His own *Recueil de Différentes Compositions Frises et Ornements* included vases and ACANTHUS friezes.

Laîné, Thomas (1682–1739) Born in Paris, Laîné worked as a sculptor on the chapel at Versailles in 1708 to 1709, in 1710 at Fontainebleau, and in 1711 on the choir-stalls of Notre Dame in Paris. In 1716 he moved to Avignon and was active there and in Aix-en-Provence as an architect and interior designer. His *Livre de divers desseins d'ornements* (Aix-en-Provence, 1740; thirty plates) comprises ornaments, mouldings, frames, doors, chimneypieces, tables, sideboards and church plate in a very rich scrolly late-BAROQUE style on the verge of ROCOCO, influenced by TORO. An edition appeared later in Paris.

La Joue, Jacques de (1686–1761) Born in Paris, the son of an architect, La Joue was active as a painter, working with WATTEAU, Lancret and François BOUCHER, and exhibiting landscapes, seascapes, hunting scenes, interiors, architectural fantasies and garden scenes at the Salon from 1738 to 1753. He was patronized by Madame de Pompadour, was a Peintre Ordinaire du Roi, and seems to have had excellent connections. La Joue was named in 1774 by BLONDEL as one of the three first inventors of the '*genre pittoresque*', together with MEISSONIER and PINEAU. He issued some seventeen suites of designs for ornament in the ROCOCO style. Occasionally, as in his *Livre de Cartouches de Guerre* (seven plates), dedicated to the Duc de Mortmart, there is an echo of MITELLI in his cartouches, but usually these, and La Joue's other inventions, are of an exhilarating vigour, freedom and originality. His *Livre nouveau de douze morceaux de Fantaisie* (twelve plates) and his *Troisième Livre de Cartouches* (twelve plates) are both dedicated to the Duc d'Antin, Directeur Général des Bâtiments du Roi, and must precede his death in 1736. In 1739 La Joue designed the title for a book of pieces for the organ by the royal organist, Dandrieu. Among his most enjoyable inventions is the *Livre de Buffets* (1735; seven plates), dedicated to M. Bonier de la Mosson, the royal huntsman. It comprises details of fantastic rococo sideboards-cum-fountains to be set up in the open air for hunting picnics. In his *Recueil Nouveau De differens Cartouches* (twelve plates) La Joue turns a cartouche into the sail of a boat with a dragon figurehead, a typical caprice. CHINOISERIES, *singeries*, rocks, shells, waterfalls and architecture are but part of the material La Joue dissolved into the quintessence of rococo ornament. His prints were extensively copied in Augsburg by Johann Georg MERZ (1694–1762), but to C. N. COCHIN and other NEO-CLASSICISTS they became a symbol of the worst excesses of the rococo style.

Lalique, René (1860–1945) Born in Ay, Marne, the son of a Parisian businessman, Lalique studied drawing in Paris under J. M. L. Père (1796–1881) and then from 1876 studied goldsmith's work under the jeweller Louis Auroc (1850–1932). From 1878 to 1880 Lalique was in London. On returning to Paris he worked as a jewellery designer, at first for Auguste Petit and later as a freelance. He also designed fans and textiles. In about 1883 Lalique contributed designs to the magazine 'Le BIJOU'. In 1884 he formed a partnership to market his jewellery designs with a friend, M. Varenne. Some were shown in the same year at the Louvre and attracted the attention of the jeweller Alphonse Fouquet. In 1885 Lalique took over the workshop of the jeweller Jules Destape, and began to manufacture jewellery as a sub-contractor to well-known firms such as Boucheron, Vever and Cartier. By 1890 he had thirty employees. In 1891 Lalique began to design stage jewellery for Sarah Bernhardt, and at the same time began to interest himself in glass. In 1894 he showed an ivory bookbinding and an iron vase at the Salon de la Société des Artistes Français, where he regularly showed jewels from 1895 to 1909, becoming '*hors concours*' as early as 1897, the year in which he was given the Légion d'Honneur for his display at the Brussels Exhibition. Lalique's jewellery was also shown by BING in 1895. His greatest triumph as a jeweller was at the PARIS 1900 EXHIBITION, and the influence of his rich and rare materials and artificial NATURALISM was patent in the work of such followers and imitators as Lucien Gaillard, Vever Frères, Georges FOUQUET and Philippe WOLFERS. Lalique also showed jewellery at the TURIN 1902 EXHIBITION, the ST LOUIS 1904 EXHIBITION, the Liège 1905 and Turin 1910 Exhibitions, and at the Grafton Gallery and Agnews in London in 1903 and 1905 respectively. At this period Lalique began to produce mirrors, textiles, paper-knives etc., and, from 1905, to use engraved glass in jewellery. In 1906 he was commissioned to produce pressed-glass scent bottles for François Coty and glass became his main interest. In 1908 Lalique rented a glass factory at Combs-le-Village near Paris, taking it over in the next year. In 1918 he founded a new glass factory in Alsace; a Dane, Christian Christensen, acted as his manager until 1930 when his son Marc Lalique succeeded. At the PARIS 1925 EXHIBITION, Lalique not only had his own pavilion but also designed and manufactured a glass table, wine-glasses and candlesticks for the Sèvres porcelain pavilion. In 1932 he supplied glass panels and chandeliers to the dining-room of the liner *Normandie* and in 1933 he was accorded a retrospective exhibition at the Musée des Arts Décoratifs. He continued to design glass up to the war. Lalique's early jewellery designs were in a simple NATURALISTIC manner up to 1890 and after that followed RENAISSANCE prototypes. From about 1895 he developed an independent ART NOUVEAU manner, with sinuous combinations of natural and symbolic motifs in rich and rare materials. His later glass still used natural ornament but handled it in a more geometric manner, typical of the ART DÉCO style.

Lalonde, Richard No biographical details are known about Lalonde, although he was one of the most prolific and professional French designers in the NEO-CLASSICAL style of the 1780s and 1790s, publishing a total of some 500 plates. The gilder and print-dealer Jean Félix Watin was among those who sold prints by Lalonde. Already in 1787 a design school in Gyöv in Hungary possessed 102 plates by Lalonde from the series of 156 plates known as the *Œuvres diverses*, which included borders, frames, legs for furniture, tables, lights, VASES, chimneypieces, goldsmiths' work, secular and ecclesiastical, jewellery, locks and ironwork. Copies of Lalonde's designs were published in Augsburg. He also designed clocks, coaches, curtains, lights, trophies and so on. Although Lalonde shows little originality he seems to have evolved from a sophisticated neo-classical style based on the work of NEUFFORGE, DELAFOSSE, J.-F. BOUCHER and others, to a relatively crude but vigorous interpretation of the more archaeological treatment of neo-classicism in the 1790s. His designs are particularly valuable for constructional details.

Lamb, Edward Buckton (1806–69) The son of an amateur artist and government official Lamb was articled to the architect L. N. COTTINGHAM. He exhibited at the Royal Academy from 1824, and in 1830 published *Etchings of Gothic Ornament*, twenty dryly etched plates of GOTHIC capitals, foliage and details in the Cottingham tradition. In the 1830s Lamb supplied designs for three of LOUDON's works, the *Encyclopaedia* (1833), the *Architectural Magazine* (1834–8) and the *Suburban Gardener and Villa Companion*. His fortes were the Gothic, Tudor and Elizabethan styles, but he could also design in the Grecian and Italian manners. The 1834 *Architectural Magazine* contained designs by Lamb for an interior with furniture based on carved ivory chessmen in the British Museum, a classic

document of the Norman revival. Lamb had an extremely fertile later career as an architect, principally of churches, and mainly in a quirky Gothic manner, which was not approved by the ECCLESIOLOGICAL SOCIETY. His furniture and fittings were richly inventive but formally heterodox. In 1846 Lamb published *Studies of Ancient Domestic Architecture*.

Lambert, Théodore Born in Besançon in 1857, Lambert was a pupil of the Parisian architect L. J. André (1819–90). He was mainly active as a designer of interiors and furniture. His furniture of about 1910 is in a subdued late ART NOUVEAU manner. Lambert's book of Japanese motifs, *Motifs Décoratifs Tirés des Pochoirs Japonais*, was used by FORTUNY. Lambert may have been a relative of Henri Lucien Lambert, a Sèvres porcelain painter, who in about 1880 published *La Flore Décorative*, thirty charming hand-coloured plates of floral ornament displaying Japanese-influenced asymmetry.

La Mésangère, Pierre Antoine Leboux de (1761–1831) Born at Baugé in Anjou, La Mésangère later taught literature and philosophy in La Flèche. Dismissed as a consequence of the revolution, in 1799 he took over the *Journal des Dames et des Modes*, founded in 1797 by Sellèque; although the role of a fashion journalist was a curious one for a priest, La Mésangère performed it with great success. An eccentric and a philanthropist, his collection took six days to sell after his death. From 1802 to 1835 the *Journal* contained as a supplement a *Collection de Meubles et Objets de Goût*, 678 handsome coloured plates for furniture, upholstery and other decorative objects, including a stove for Joubert & Bance's print shop. The *Collection* provides a superb conspectus of the Empire style, illustrating several versions of designs by

PERCIER and FONTAINE. La Mésangère also published works on topography (1796–8), costume (1827) and French women (1827).

Lamour, Jean (1698–1771) Lamour was born in Nancy, the son of a smith from Charleville. He worked as a smith in Metz in 1712, and after two trips to Paris settled in Nancy, succeeding his father as Serrurier de la Ville in 1720. Lamour's great opportunity came when in 1737 King Stanislas Leszczynski (1677–1766) took possession of the Duchy of Lorraine and from 1738 employed him on a wide range of commissions. These culminated in Lamour's works from 1751 to 1759 in the Place Stanislas in Nancy, the greatest *tour de force* of French ROCOCO ironwork, both in design and execution. Lamour recorded his best works in *Recueil des Ouvrages* (Nancy, 1767; twenty plates), one of the finest collections of designs for ironwork. Its dedication page includes a scene of Stanislas visiting Lamour's atelier. An earlier version was published at Lunéville in 1762. Lamour was something of a connoisseur and collected paintings and curiosities.

Landi, Gaetano A native of Bologna, Landi styled himself, with no known justification, 'Professor in the University of Bologna, and Member of the Clementine Academy'. His *Architectural Decorations* (London, 1810; twenty-seven coloured plates) lists in its title designs for interiors, metalwork, etc., in the 'Egyptian, The Greek, The Roman, The Etruscan, The Attic, The Gothic &c.' styles; the work was dedicated to the Marquess of Douglas. The executed plates, Chinese, Egyptian, GOTHIC and Roman, are of a theatrical indeed almost barbarous richness and vigour, a stark contrast to the chaste presentation of Thomas HOPE's *Household Furniture* (1807). Landi was in

financial difficulties in 1810 and probably left for Russia soon after.

Landry, Abel Born in Limoges, where he studied design, Landry also studied at the École des Arts Décoratifs in Paris before spending some time in London, where he came under the influence of William MORRIS. Having returned to Paris he designed porcelain and metalwork for MEIER-GRAEFE's La Maison Moderne. Landry also designed interiors and was associated with Victor PROUVÉ and Jules-Paul Brateau (1844–1923) in the group La Poignée. In 1912 he was associated with the Société des Artistes-Décorateurs. Landry was praised by Sedeyn (1921) as a precursor of the ART DÉCO style.

Lang, Hans Caspar (1571–1645) Born in Schaffhausen, the son of Daniel Lang and the grandson of Hieronymus Lang, both stained-glass designers, Lang followed the family trade. In his journeyman years he travelled to Freiburg and Strasbourg, settling in Schaffhausen in 1595. Lang, whose designs employed much scrolled STRAPWORK, was also active as a painter of mural decorations. He was the last major stained-glass designer to work in Schaffhausen.

Lang, Hieronymus Born in Hüfingen, Lang came to Schaffhausen in 1541. He died there in 1582. Lang was a prolific designer of stained glass who founded a dynasty of stained-glass designers.

Langley, Batty (1696–1751) Born in Twickenham, the son of a gardener whose trade he at first followed, Langley manufactured artificial stone in about 1731 and in about 1740 established a drawing school in Soho, in partnership with his brother Thomas, an engraver born in 1702; this academy became a seed-bed for artisan ROCOCO. Batty Langley had little success as a practising architect, although he submitted plans to the Mansion House competition in 1735 and for Westminster Bridge in 1736. His claim to fame was through a large number of works on gardening, estate management, architecture, geometry and allied subjects, published from 1724 to 1750, most of which went through several editions. Langley was an active freemason, as is reflected in the title of his *Ancient Masonry* (1734–6), whose 494 plates included copies after Hans VREDEMAN DE VRIES, who had already influenced the frontispiece of his *Young Builder's Rudiments* (1730), and KASEMANN, as well as more familiar models such as Vitruvius, Palladio and SERLIO; the Langley architectural library appears to have been extensive. In his *Antient Architecture Restored and Improved* (1741–2, reissued as *Gothic Architecture* in 1747) he devised GOTHIC orders on the classical model, and Langley's Gothic was widely influential, although later derided by writers as diverse as WALPOLE (1754) and EDIS (1881). *The City and Country Builder's and Workman's Companion* (1740), engraved by Thomas Langley, includes among designs for urns, fireplaces and floors about twenty-five designs for furniture, mainly dated 1739, in a neat, basically Palladian, style with BAROQUE and rococo exceptions borrowed from SCHÜBLER, LAUCH and PINEAU. For all the basic Palladianism of many of his designs Langley came to share the anti-Palladianism of Hogarth. But his influence was more provincial than metropolitan. For example the American architect William Buckland (1734–74) owned books by Langley, and at Tissington Hall, Derbyshire, is a Gothic fireplace based on his designs.

Lapp, Henry L. (1862–1904) Born in an Amish family in rural Pennsylvania, Lapp was trained as a carpenter. Although deaf and partially mute he set up a prospering business as carpenter and cabinet-maker in 1898. His death was due to lead poisoning. In the Philadelphia Museum of Art is a forty-seven-page manuscript pattern-book drawn by Lapp: it presents a repertoire of cheerfully painted furniture and utensils from flour chests to mouse traps which, when not purely functional, are in a simple early Victorian style. The book is a remarkable and endearing document of design at the most basic level in about 1904.

Larsson, Carl Olof (1853–1919) Born in Stockholm, Larsson studied painting at the Stockholm Academy under Georg von Rosen from 1866. At that time he was earning his living by retouching photographs. From about 1871 he illustrated books and the satirical journal *Kasper*. Larsson visited Paris in 1876 and 1880, and lived there from 1882 to 1884. From about 1885 he was extremely successful as a painter, executing several monumental frescoes on grandiose historic themes. Larsson lived in Göteborg from 1886, in Stockholm from 1891, and in Sundborn near Falun from 1901. His country house there, Lylla Hyttnäs, had been given to him in 1888. In 1897 Larsson showed watercolours of his home at the Stockholm Exhibition with the conscious aim of improving Swedish taste and the tenor of Swedish family life. They were published as *Ett Hem* ('A Home') in 1889, followed by *Spadarfvet* ('At Home in the Country') in 1906, and *At Solsidan* (1910). All celebrated the joys of an idyllic domesticity. Larsson's illustrations, influenced by Japanese prints and French posters, depicted his interiors, which he himself had designed, as seductively fresh, light and informal, mixing simple NEO-CLASSICAL or peasant furniture with brightly coloured textiles, flowers and the practical paraphernalia of living. They had a wide influence on domestic design in both Scandinavia and Germany.

La Rue, Louis Félix (1731–64) Born in Paris, La Rue was a pupil of Lambert Sigisbert Adam (1700–1759); he won the Grand Prix de Sculpture in 1750 and spent 1754 to 1755 in Rome. La Rue taught at the Paris Académie de Saint-Luc from 1762, sculpted in the style of Clodion (1738–1814), and designed for the Sèvres porcelain factory and for bronze manufacturers. Many suites of ornament were delicately and posthumously engraved after his designs by Philippe Louis Parizeau (1740–1801) and published in 1771 to 1772. They included VASES, tripods, altars, tables, chairs, chandeliers, clocks, incense burners and figures, all in an advanced NEO-CLASSICAL style. La Rue had contacts with the Marquis de MARIGNY and with Lalive de Jully. Had he lived longer, he might have developed his role as a pioneer of neo-classical design.

Lasalle, Philippe de (1723–1805) Born at Seyssel near Aix-les-Bains, Lasalle moved as a child to Lyon, where he studied under the painter and textile designer Daniel Sarrabat (1676–1748), who also taught PILLEMENT. He then moved to Paris, where he attended BACHELIER's design school and later worked under François BOUCHER and DUTILLIEU. By 1760 Lasalle was back in Lyon, where he married the daughter of Charryé, a textile designer and manufacturer, and established a fruitful connection with the firm of Pernon. In 1773 Lasalle was given the order of Saint-Michel, in 1780 a royal pension and in 1783 a gold medal. He was responsible for a number of mechanical improvements to silk weaving and his silk designs were woven for the courts in Paris, Madrid and St Petersburg. They were mainly rich but refined floral patterns incorporating trophies and other NEO-

CLASSICAL motifs. Lasalle also designed embroideries. He was ruined by the French revolution and died in poverty, leaving his collection of designs and samples to the Lyon Conservatoire; it was later dispersed. Lasalle's funeral oration was delivered by the designer Picard: a memorial plaque erected in the Conservatoire in 1805 stated that Lasalle had brought to maturity what Jean REVEL began.

Lassus, Jean-Baptiste-Antoine (1807–57) Born in Paris, Lassus studied as an architect under Louis Hippolyte Lebas (1782–1867) and from 1830 under Henri Labrouste (1801–75). In 1835 he won a medal for a project for restoring the Sainte Chapelle and in 1837 helped to restore Saint-Séverin. In 1844, with VIOLLET-LE-DUC, Lassus won the competition to restore Notre Dame in Paris, a scheme on which he was engaged until his death. In 1848 he designed a GOTHIC house in Paris for Prince Alexis Soltykoff. Lassus became architect to the Paris diocese in 1849 and in 1852 to Le Mans and Chartres. In 1856 he came third after BURGES and STREET in the Lille Cathedral competition. Lassus designed illustrations for *De Imitatione Christi* (1855) and Gothic furniture and fittings, including the elaborate reliquary of St Radegunda (1852). His great edition of VILLARD D'HONNECOURT was published posthumously in 1858.

Latrobe, Benjamin Henry (1764–1820) Born at Fulneck, near Leeds, the son of a Moravian minister, Latrobe attended the Moravian college at Niesky in Saxony from 1776. In 1784 he was briefly in the Stamp Office and then became a pupil of the architect Samuel Pepys Cockerell (1753–1827). Practising on his own from 1790, Latrobe worked in an advanced NEO-CLASSICAL style. In 1796 he emigrated to America, where he designed such Greek Revival master-pieces as the Bank of Pennsylvania in Philadelphia (1798–1801). In about 1809 he designed neo-classical furniture, lights, carpets etc. for the Capitol and the White House in Washington, includ-ing bold painted klismos chairs made for the latter by the Finlays of Baltimore.

Lauch, Johann Fridrich A member of a Leipzig family of goldsmiths, Lauch was active from 1724 to 1757. His *Neue Uhr Gehause* (six plates) comprises var-ied and inventive designs for clock-cases and brackets in a manner derived from Jean I BERAIN and BOULLE. One was later copied by Batty LANGLEY. It was published in Nuremberg, as was a suite of jolly Berainesque designs for box-lids by Lauch (six plates).

Laurenziani, Giacomo Laurenziani was a member of a family of founders from Reggio Emilia, who was active in Rome as a founder, sculptor and engraver. He became a member of the Accademia di San Luca in 1607 and in 1649 of the Congregazione Virtuosi. He died in 1650. Laurenziani executed a brass grille in St John Lateran in 1607 and many other important works in metal. His *Opere per Argentieri et Altri* (Rome, 1632; eleven plates) contains BAROQUE designs for reliquaries, monstrances, chalices etc. They are highly accom-plished documents of early baroque goldsmiths' design.

Lautensack, Heinrich (1522–68) Born in Bamberg, the son of a painter and theologian, Lautensack moved in 1527 to Nuremberg, where he worked for the goldsmith Melchior Bayer from 1532 to 1538. He was then taught PERSPECTIVE by the Zürich goldsmith Jacob Stampfer (1505–79). From 1548 Lautensack lived in Frankfurt. His *Des Circkels unnd Richtscheyts auch der Perspectiva* (Frankfurt, 1564, second edition 1618) is a treatise on perspective comparable to that by RODLER. It includes plates of complicated geometrical figures related to those of STÖER and Wenzel JAM-NITZER, and anatomical diagrams de-rived from DÜRER.

Lavallée-Poussin, Étienne (1722–1805) Born in Rouen, Étienne Lavallée stud-ied painting under J. B. Descamps and J. B. PIERRE. He won the Premier Prix de Peinture in 1759 and lived from 1762 in Rome, where his close study of Pous-sin led him to add the name of that painter to his own. In 1764 he designed the illustrations of a book commemorat-ing the visit to Rome of the financier Watelet and his mistress and tutor; the book was decorated by Weirotter, Dura-meau and Radel. In Rome, Lavallée-Poussin designed five parts of the twelve-part *Nouvelle Collection d'Arabesques*, engraved by Guyot in about 1785 and later reissued with a preface by Alex-andre Lenoir in 1810. The *Collection* includes enchanting ARABESQUES by Lavallée-Poussin alongside others by VOISIN, LE CLERC, Berthelot, de Claire and L. Janneret; its plates were sometimes coloured. Lavallée-Poussin also designed two suites of tapestries for the Beauvais factory, the Conquest of India (1785) and the History of Alex-ander (1798), as well as designing wall-papers for Réveillon.

Lawford, Henry Described as an 'Archi-tectural Designer and Lithographer', Lawford issued three furniture pattern-books. *The Chair and Sofa Manufac-turers' Book of Designs* (101 plates) was probably published after the visit of Queen Victoria to the PARIS 1855 EXHIBITION – witness the inclusion of the 'Napoleon Settee' and the 'Eugene (sic) Lounge'. The designs are in the basic mid-Victorian ROCOCO revival style. Equally lumpen-bourgeois but more comprehensive is *The Cabinet of*

Practical, Useful and Decorative Furniture (1856; 126 plates): its furniture designs are enlivened by a few interiors. Lawford's last book, *Designs in Buhl & Marquetry* (1867; twenty coloured plates), contains coarse designs for gaudy cabinets influenced by French 18th-century prototypes and decorated with marquetry, boulle work and porcelain plaques.

LCZ The Master LCZ is probably to be identified with the Bamberg painter Lorenz Katzheimer. He was active from about 1480 to 1505, and may have studied in about 1490 in the Nuremberg studio of Michael Wolgemut (1434–1519), DÜRER's teacher. Only twelve prints by LCZ are known but they include the finest early jewellery design, a superb pendant of 1492 with a lady and unicorn within a border of GOTHIC foliage.

Le Bas, Hippolyte (1782–1867) Born in Paris, Le Bas was taught architecture by his uncle the architect Laurent Vaudoyer (1756–1844) and by PERCIER. He travelled to Rome in 1804 and from 1819 to his death taught at the École des Beaux-Arts. Gustav Friedrich HETSCH was among his pupils. From 1815 Le Bas designed a number of printed cottons for the Jouy manufacture, including Monuments de Paris (1816), Marchande d'Amours (1817) and Monuments du Midi (1818). In 1828 he designed for the Sèvres porcelain factory.

Le Blon, Michel (1587–1656) Born in Frankfurt, Le Blon was trained as a goldsmith but was already active as an engraver in 1605. He probably settled in Amsterdam in about 1610. In 1627 he travelled to Venice and thence to Rome. Le Blon spent many years in England as agent of the Swedish court, and was also a frequent visitor to Stockholm in this capacity. Van Dyck painted his portrait.

His earliest prints (1605) were small black stretched GROTESQUE ornaments for enamelling on jewels. Two suites of knife handles (six plates each) combine fine black scrolled tendrils with figures and animals, in a manner similar to Hans JANSSEN's designs. Le Blon also published several suites of friezes and borders for engraving on silver, incorporating STRAPWORK of an almost AURICULAR character: one suite is for engraving on an octagonal dish. *Versheyden Wapen-Schilden* comprises heraldic shields and mantling, for engraving on silver. In 1611 Le Blon published *Eenvoldige Vruchten en Spitsen* (fourteen plates of borders, alphabets, etc.), later copied by Isaac BRUNN. Le Blon also engraved heraldic shields, emblems and small scenes in cartouches for box-lids and watches; he issued a collected edition of such works in 1627. The prints of Le Blon, known as Blondus, were always prized for their delicacy and invention.

Le Blond, Jean Born in Paris in about 1635, Le Blond was active there as engraver and publisher. He died in 1709. His *Plan et élévation des plus beaux confessionaux de Paris très fidellement mesuré* (1688; six plates) depicts handsome French BAROQUE confessionals. In 1703 Le Blond published a collection of designs for woodwork, including doors by FRANCARD, panelling by Feuillet and choir-stalls.

Le Bouteiller Le Bouteiller was editor of a short-lived magazine, *L'Exposition* (Paris, 1839), whose coloured lithographs cover a wide range of Parisian manufactures, giving an excellent picture of French middle-class taste in the late 1830s. The plates include curtains, furniture and ironwork. A GOTHIC shop-front and chair by M. Ramée are particularly charming.

Le Brun, Charles (1619–90) Born in Paris, the son of a sculptor, Le Brun studied painting under François Perrier from 1632, and from about 1634 under Simon VOUET. He also studied the decorations of Fontainebleau. Under the protection of the Chancellor Séguier, in 1638 Le Brun became a painter to the King. His close links with writers began at this stage and he designed a number of frontispieces, for example for the 1639 edition of Guarini's *Il Pastor Fido*. In 1641 he was working for Richelieu and in 1642 he travelled with Poussin to Rome, where he was strongly influenced by antiquity and RAPHAEL on the one hand, and by the BAROQUE decorations of painters such as Pietro da CORTONA (1596–1669) on the other. After the death of Pope Urban VIII (1568–1644) Le Brun suffered from the eclipse of French influence at Rome and in 1645 left for France. Back in Paris he married Suzanne, daughter of the painter Robert Butay in 1647, when he also designed a frontispiece for Corneille's *Rodogune*. In 1648 he became a founder member of the Académie. By the deaths of Simon Vouet in 1649 and Eustache Le Sueur in 1655 two potential rivals to Le Brun's future artistic supremacy were removed (ERRARD was eclipsed a little later). His activity as a decorative painter in the Hôtel Louis La Rivière (1652–3) and elsewhere led to a commission in 1658 from Nicolas Fouquet (1615–80) to decorate the chapel at his splendid new château, Vaux. While at Vaux, Le Brun directed the tapestry workshop set up by Fouquet at Maincy, supplying designs for a suite of portières and a series of the History of Constantine, partly after RUBENS, among others, and beginning to gather about him a group of assistant painters which was to include the Yvarts, Van de Meulen, MONNOYER, Boels and several others. He also designed a suite of six tapestries of the story of Meleager for Jean Valdor, an engraver with great

influence at court. While at Vaux, Le Brun also designed furniture. In 1660 he designed a triumphal arch for the entry of Louis XIV and Marie-Thérèse to Paris, was appointed Premier Peintre du Roi and summoned by the King from Vaux to Fontainebleau. After the death of Mazarin and the arrest of Fouquet in 1661 Le Brun joined the artistic team being assembled by Jean-Baptiste Colbert (1619–83) and started to decorate the Galerie d'Apollon at the Louvre. Ennobled in 1662, he established his dominance over the Académie in 1663, and in the same year was appointed director of the Gobelins tapestry manufactory, which took over many of the designs done for Fouquet at Maincy – with suitable adjustments to their heraldry. The confirmation in 1664 of Le Brun's status as Premier Peintre du Roi established his complete dominance of the arts under Louis XIV. In 1665 he designed a coach to be sent to the Great Mogul, and began to design silver, including tables, gueridons and mirrors; already in 1654 he had designed an elaborate baroque silver tabernacle for a Carmelite church in Paris. His tapestries on the themes of the four elements (1666) and the four seasons (1667) were the subject of printed eulogies by André Félibien. In 1667 the Gobelins royal furniture manufactory was founded under Le Brun's direction and his close relations with Louis XIV, expressed in his decorations of the Tuileries (1666) and for the celebrations of the baptism of the Grand Dauphin, and of the Flanders campaign (1668), were reflected in the King's ceremonial visit to the Gobelins factory (1667). This was commemorated in a tapestry designed by Le Brun as part of the Histoire du Roi series conceived in 1662 and woven from 1665 to 1678. His other tapestries included the History of Alexander suite (1664–84) and the Months or Royal Houses, woven seven times from 1668 to

1694. In the 1670s Le Brun's star was still in the ascendant, the design of the Escalier des Ambassadeurs (1675) and the Grande Galerie (1678) at Versailles, and his façade for Marly (1679), all confirming his paramount status, as did the gift of land from the Great Condé (1621–86) near Le Brun's country estate, Montmorency. But in 1683 the death of Colbert brought the Marquis de Louvois (1641–91) to power. Louvois and his protégé, the painter Mignard, were sworn enemies to Le Brun, who kept his titles but lost most of his power. In 1683 he designed two extra tapestries to complete a set of the History of Moses after Poussin, first suggested by Chantelou in 1665. In 1686 he completed the decorations of the Salons de la Guerre and de la Paix at Versailles. But in 1689 the formation of the Grand Alliance against Louis XIV led to the meltingdown of the royal silver, destroying a whole section of Le Brun's work as a designer. In 1690 he died and the contents of his studio were secured for the royal collection. Le Brun introduced a new style of decoration to France, an accomplished Roman baroque style in which a massive architectural vigour was relieved by scrolls, putti, swags, dolphins, lions, sphinxes and so on, all handled in a highly sculptural manner. This style became identified with Versailles, whose interior decoration, furniture and silver became the model of princely splendour, and its influence spread throughout Europe, from TESSIN in Sweden to Verrio in England, especially as transmitted by the engravings of Jean LE PAUTRE. As a tapestry designer Le Brun helped to perfect a tradition of tapestries conceived as woven paintings. In this field, as in his whole activity, Le Brun was a masterly impresario, able to divide and delegate the execution of the largest schemes, while preserving the unity of his original conception.

Lechter, Melchior (1865–1937) Born in Münster, Lechter was apprenticed to a glass painter in 1879 and studied art in Berlin from 1884. He was much influenced by a visit to Bayreuth in 1886 when he attended performances of *Parsifal* and *Tristan und Isolde*. From 1892 Lechter was active as a painter. In 1895 he met the poet Stefan George (1868–1933) and from 1897 designed his books, including the binding of *Das Jahr der Seele* (1897) and every detail of *Der Teppich des Lebens* (1899). He also designed an edition of Joris Karl Huysmans's *À Rebours* (1897) and Maurice Maeterlinck's *Der Schatz der Armen* (1898). Lechter also designed tapestries (1895), posters, stained glass and GOTHIC furniture (from 1896), the latter described in 'DEUTSCHE KUNST UND DEKORATION' (1897). His 1896 windows for the Romanisches Haus in Berlin and an exhibition in the same year established his reputation. He designed every detail of his own house, with stained glass on themes from Nietzsche and Wagner, and a chandelier inscribed with the names of Nietzsche, Wagner and Böcklin. At home Lechter wore a velvet monastic habit. From 1898 to 1900 he designed and decorated a reception room donated to the Museum of Applied Arts in Cologne by the industrialist Jakob Pallenberg; it won a Grand Prix at the PARIS 1900 EXHIBITION. From about 1905 Lechter retired from the world, devoting himself to Indian philosophy, theosophy and mysticism. He emerged in 1934 to deliver a memorial lecture on Stefan George.

Le Clerc, Pierre Thomas Le Clerc was a pupil of the painter L.-J.-F. Lagrenée (1725–1805) at the Académie Royale. He designed many book ornaments, including *vignettes* for La Fontaine's *Fables* (new edition, 1765–75) and illustrations including those to Desmarais's *Jérémie* (1771). Le Clerc published a new edition of Jehan COUSIN's *L'Art de Dessiner*, its plates curiously and unhappily transmogrified by re-engraving. His *Principes de dessins* (1773) is one of a series of prints of ornament which Le Clerc seems to have issued over a long period. He also contributed six plates to the *Cahiers d'Arabesques* engraved by Guyot in about 1785, of which LAVALLÉE-POUSSIN designed the lion's share. Le Clerc showed paintings at the 1795 and 1796 Paris Salons, and was still active in 1799.

Leconte, Émile In the 1830s Leconte was a major Parisian dealer in old and new books as well as publishing and editing books of design and ornament. They included the works of Aimé CHENAVARD, *Ornemens Gothiques* (1839; fifty plates), designed by H. Roux and others, which in fact ranges from GOTHIC to ROCOCO and includes stained glass, manuscript illustrations and furniture designs borrowed from A. W. N. PUGIN's *Gothic Furniture* (1835), *Mélanges d'Ornamens divers* (1837; seventy-two plates) by CLERGET, and *Variété ou choix d'ornemens* (1838; seventy-two plates). Leconte also published flowers after Redouté and *Choix de nouveaux Modèles de Serrurerie* (1838; seventy-three plates), designs for iron doors, railings, lights and balconies, both Gothic and classical, as well as structural ironwork, including some designed by Duban.

Le Corbusier (1887–1965) Born Charles Édouard Jeanneret in Le Chaux de Fonds in the Swiss Jura, the son of an engraver of watch-cases, Le Corbusier studied his father's trade at the civic art school and showed a watch-case which combined NATURALISTIC and geometrical ornament at the TURIN 1902 EXHIBITION. He was encouraged by his teacher Charles L'Eplattenier (1874–1946) to study architecture, and fell

under the influence of John RUSKIN, Owen JONES and GRASSET. Clement HEATON, who designed decorations for Neufchatel Museum in around 1900 and was a friend of L'Eplattenier, may have influenced the young Le Corbusier. In 1907 Le Corbusier travelled to Italy and Vienna, where he later claimed that Josef HOFFMANN had offered him employment, and thence in 1908 to Paris where, having approached Frantz Jourdain, Charles PLUMET and Henri Sauvage, he was recommended by Grasset to approach the architect Auguste Perret (1874–1954). Le Corbusier then worked for a spell in Perret's office; while there he bought VIOLLET-LE-DUC's *Dictionnaire*. At the end of 1909 Le Corbusier returned to Le Chaux de Fonds and then in 1910 went to Germany to study the teaching of the decorative arts there. He travelled to Munich, to Hagen, to Dresden, where he met Wolf Dohrn (1874–1914), Director of the Dresdener Werkstätte, and to Berlin, where he met MUTHESIUS and BEHRENS, in whose office he worked for a while. In 1911 Le Corbusier travelled to Eastern Europe, and then from 1912 to its collapse in 1914 he taught in L'Eplattenier's Nouvelle Section in the art school at Le Chaux de Fonds. In 1912 he published an approbatory report on design teaching in the decorative arts in Germany. From 1914 to 1916 he occupied himself in architectural theory, in antique dealing and, briefly, in planning to set up a lighting factory. In 1917 Le Corbusier moved to Paris and through Perret met the painter Amedée Ozenfant (1886–1966). In 1911 Ozenfant had designed coachwork for a car and both he and Le Corbusier were influenced by cubism and futurism. Together they invented Purism, promulgated in a manifesto, *Après le cubisme* (1918). In 1920, when Le Corbusier adopted the name by which he is now known, they began to promote their ideas in the periodical 'ESPRIT NOUVEAU'. *Vers une architecture* (1923, translated into English in 1931 as *Towards a New Architecture*) presented Le Corbusier's architectural theories in book form. His ideas on the decorative arts were set out in *L'Art décoratif d'aujourd'hui* (1925), partly based on articles published in *L'Esprit Nouveau* (1924). He illustrated machines, office furniture and cheap commercial products. '*L'art décoratif est de l'outillage, du bel outillage*' and '*L'art décoratif moderne n'a pas de décor*' are among his pronouncements. For the uncompromisingly MODERN L'Esprit Nouveau pavilion at the PARIS 1925 EXHIBITION Le Corbusier selected THONET bentwood chairs as furniture. In 1928 together with his brother Pierre Jeanneret (1896–1967) and Charlotte PERRIAND, Le Corbusier began to design a range of Modern furniture shown at the 1929 Salon d'Automne. It included the Siège à Dossier Basculant (a wooden version was designed by Perriand in 1935), the Fauteuil Grand Confort, in a large and a small version, the Siège Tournant, and the corresponding stool, a bathroom stool, the Table en Tube d'Avion, and a series of modular steel storage units, further developed in 1935. These pieces, all using tubular steel and almost all first manufactured by Thonet, are now in production again, firmly established as Modern CLASSICS. Le Corbusier designed little furniture from then onwards, although a marble-topped table on two columnar steel legs (1934) is noteworthy. His participation in the CONGRÈS INTERNATIONAUX D'ARCHITECTURE MODERNE from its start in 1927 and his burgeoning architectural reputation ensured a wide-ranging influence on designers as well as architects, especially through his Modulor system of harmonic proportions based on human dimensions. His Venesta stand for the London 1930 Building Trades Exhibition, commissioned by Jack Pritchard of ISOKON, marks the beginning of his influence in England; in 1938 he was an approving visitor to the London MARS exhibition. In 1935 Le Corbusier was commissioned by Marie Cuttoli to design a tapestry for her Aubusson studio. In 1955 to 1956 he designed tapestries executed in Kashmir for the Law Courts at Chandigarh, and in 1956 a tapestry for the Unesco Building in Paris made in the Ateliers Pinton at Felletin.

Le Febure, François A goldsmith in Paris, Le Febure published in 1635 a *Livre de fleurs et de feuilles*, six plates engraved, like all Le Febure's works, by Balthasar MONCORNET. In it floral cartouches, sprays and oval designs for miniature cases hover above pungently comic figures derived from CALLOT; Salomon Savery published a copy in 1639 omitting the Callot elements. *Livre de Feuilles et de Fleurs* (Paris, 1657 and 1661; six plates) has on the title a floral cartouche above a view of Paris, followed by floral sprays and cartouches over landscapes. *Livre Nouveau* (Paris, 1665; twelve plates), with its title in German as well as French, has a title-page with a cartouche of flowers, jewels, tools and musical instruments, followed by magnificent jewelled brooches in floral cartouches above views of Rouen and Paris. The final plate incorporates a miniature of the young Louis XIV. *Livre de fleurs et de feuilles* (Amsterdam, 1679) is derived from Le Febure's earlier works.

Lefèvre-Chauveaux, Alphonse Born at Corbeny in Aisne in 1789, Lefèvre-Chauveaux worked as a drawing-master and teacher of mechanics, etc. His *Le Parfait Menuisier Ébeniste* (forty-one plates) was intended to vie with Roubo's *L'Art du Menuisier* (1769). It included a design for a confessional executed at

Lyon and a plate of beds executed in 1841. There are also shop-fronts, doors, staircases and furniture. The styles are a crude late-Empire manner, a naïve ROCOCO revival, which may even be survival, and, in the case of some chairs, a 17th-century manner. The book is thus an excellent illustration of provincial French taste in design in about 1841.

Lefuel, Hector-Martin (1810–80) Born at Versailles, Lefuel was a pupil of his father, the architect Alexandre Lefuel (1782–1850) and of Jean Nicolas Huyot (1780–1840). He won the Prix de Rome in 1839 and was then from 1848 architect to Château Meudon, from 1852 to the Sèvres porcelain manufactory, from 1853 to Fontainebleau, and from 1854 to the Louvre in succession to Visconti (1791–1853). Lefuel designed the fine arts building at the PARIS 1855 EXHIBITION. In 1867 he published his designs for the Empress Eugénie's apartment at the Tuileries; their style, described in the introduction as '*le style Napoléon III*', was a refined synthesis of BAROQUE, ROCOCO and NEO-CLASSICAL elements. The bronzes were made by Christofle.

L'Égaré, Gédéon (1615–76) L'Égaré worked in Paris as a goldsmith and from 1671 shared a lodging in the Louvre with his brother-in-law, the enamel painter Pierre Bain. His *Livre de Feuilles d'Orfèvrerie* (seven plates) comprises sprays or cartouches for jewellers, in the foliate style known as COSSE-DE-POIS, above landscapes. He also published a suite of six small plates of black enamel designs in the same manner.

L'Égaré, Gilles Born in Chaumont en Bassigny, L'Égaré was active as a goldsmith in Paris from at least 1663 to 1685, when he emigrated as a result of the Revocation of the Edict of Nantes. He worked in the Louvre under LE BRUN

and described himself as royal goldsmith on the title of his *Livre des Ouvrages d'Orfèvrerie* (1663; eight plates). This has a rich jewelled clock on the title-page, followed by rings, seals, pendants, crosses and brooches, all in a rich BAROQUE floral style. L'Égaré also published a *Nouveau Livre d'Ornements* (1692), of which only the title is known.

Le Geay, Jean Laurent Born in about 1710, Le Geay won the Grand Prix d'Architecture in 1732 and stayed at the French Academy in Rome from 1738 to 1742, whence he returned to Paris. François de Troy, the painter Director of the Academy, then announced that Le Geay's designs exhibited fire and genius ('*feu et génie*') and C.-N. COCHIN later dated the rise of NEO-CLASSICISM from his return. Le Geay worked successively and unsuccessfully as architect to the Duke of Mecklenburg from 1748, and from 1756 as Premier Architecte to the King of Prussia, until they fell out in 1763. He was in England in 1766 and 1767, and died, probably in France, after 1786. He published four small suites of etchings – *Fontane* (1767), *Rovine* (1768), *Tombeaux* (1768) and *Vasi* (n.d.). In 1770 they were assembled as *Collection de Divers Sujets de Vases, Tombeaux, Ruines, et Fontaines Utiles aux artistes Inventée et Gravée par G. L. Le Geay architecte*. These extreme examples of neo-classical design, some with a strong PIRANESIAN flavour, were probably composed long before their publication; Sir William CHAMBERS copied Le Geay designs before 1755. Through him and through his pupils, E. L. Boullée, P. I.. Moreau-Desproux, M. J. Peyre and Charles de WAILLY, Le Geay exercised a profound influence on the beginnings of neo-classical design.

Legrain, Pierre Émile (1889–1929) Born in Levaillois-Perret, the son of a wealthy distiller, Legrain broke with formal education in 1901 and studied drawing. In 1904 he attended the École des Arts Appliqués Germain Pilon. After his father's ruin and death Legrain worked from 1908 for the cartoonist and decorator Paul Iribe (1883–1935), who in 1912 supplied furniture to Jacques DOUCET. In 1917 Legrain was commissioned by Doucet to design bookbindings; they fell out in 1919 and Legrain thenceforward executed bindings for many other clients. His bindings, mainly abstract or cubist in style, were shown at the 1920 Salon des Décorateurs and at the PARIS 1925 EXHIBITION, on which occasion he protested publicly about the plagiarization of his designs. Doucet recalled Legrain in 1922 to decorate his flat in Rue Saint-Jacques and in about 1925 his villa at Neuilly. For Doucet, Legrain designed furniture, picture frames, plinths and the coachwork of a car. The display of his furniture for Doucet at the 1924 Salon des Artistes-Décorateurs was designed by Pierre CHAREAU. Other commissions included two flats in Paris and a villa at Celle for Mme Tachard, a friend of Doucet. Legrain's furniture was strongly influenced by Egyptian and African prototypes and used a rich variety of materials, including ebony, vellum, shagreen, chromed metal, zebra skin and lacquer, some of the latter executed by Jean DUNAND. A celebrated piano by Pleyel had a glass case which revealed its mechanism. At the time of his death Legrain was planning to devote himself exclusively to bookbinding.

Legrand, Augustin Born in Paris in 1765, Legrand was a prolific engraver after painters. His *Galeries des Antiques* (1803) comprised basic lithographs of classical sculpture in the Musée Napoléon. As well as a drawing book he published the *Petit Nécessaire des jeunes Demoiselles* (1819; thirty-two plates),

which includes charming coloured designs for purses, chair covers etc.

Legrand, Jacques Guillaume (1743–1808) Born in Paris, Legrand was a pupil of CLÉRISSEAU, whose daughter he married. As an architect Legrand had a small output although he assisted ADAM at Split, JEFFERSON on the Virginia State Capitol designs, and, involuntarily, CAMERON on Tsarskoe Selo. He continued the publication of his father-in-law's works, and published a life of PIRANESI and a work on Greek architecture. Legrand formed a collection of plaster casts of plants for the inspiration of designers, and with his partner, Jacques Molinos (1743–1831), designed a NEO-CLASSICAL candelabrum for the Hôtel de Marbœuf, which was illustrated in NORMAND's *Nouveau Recueil* (1803).

Leighton, John (1822–1912) Leighton often worked as a designer and illustrator under the pseudonym Luke Limner. In 1848 he published *The Comic Art Manufactures*, a spoof on Henry COLE's Summerly venture. In 1852 to 1853 he published a number of decorative motifs later incorporated into *Suggestions in Design* (1880; 100 plates), with a text by James K. COLLING. *Suggestions* comprised ornamental motifs in all styles for execution in most materials; its introduction stated that Leighton's designs had been included in many great international exhibitions and that he had served on the jury of the PARIS 1878 EXHIBITION. Leighton designed the title of the *Art Journal Catalogue of the 1851 Exhibition*, which included his bindings for Bunyan's *Pilgrim's Progress* and for the Bible. He showed stained glass at the Royal Academy in 1854, designed a memorial *tazza* to Prince ALBERT in 1862, made by Copelands for the Art Union of London, and in 1863 delivered a pioneering lecture on Japanese art at the Royal Institution. In

1879 he was a co-founder of the *Graphic* and designed its annual title. Leighton was an enthusiast for book-plates and also designed Christmas cards and valentines.

Le Juge, Théodore Le Juge was a member of a mid-17th-century Parisian family of engravers. His *Livre de Feuillages et d'Ouvrages d'Orfevrerie* (seven plates) comprises delicate ACANTHUS and floral scrolls both as large friezes and panels and in the form of small lockets and brooches, sometimes juxtaposed to disconcerting effect. An adapted copy was later published by Peter SCHENCK in Amsterdam. Le Juge published two further suites (twenty plates in all), with similar titles and contents; one suite was engraved by FOLKEMA.

Le Lorrain, Louis-Joseph (1715–59) Trained as a painter under Dumont le Romain, Le Lorrain won the Grand Prix de Peinture in 1739, and on the recommendation of the architect Ange-Jacques Gabriel (1699–1782) was sent to the French Academy in Rome in 1740. In Rome he designed advanced architectural decorations for the annual festival of the Chinea, and came under the influence of PIRANESI, for whose *Opere Varie* he supplied a title-page in 1750, after his return to Paris in 1749. In 1751 he designed a title for the play *Cénie*, and in 1752 he joined the Académie as a *peintre d'histoire*, and in the same year designed a suite of eleven VASES, which were engraved by the amateur and patron of art Claude-Henri Watelet (1718–86) and dedicated to Madame Geoffrin (1699–1777). Le Lorrain was taken up by the Comte de CAYLUS, and thanks to him received a commission from the Swedish Count Tessin to design advanced NEO-CLASSICAL wall decorations for his country house, Åkerö, in 1754. In 1753 he was commissioned by Lalive de Jully to paint a St Elizabeth (1754) for the church of Saint-Roch in memory of Lalive's wife, who had died in 1753. In 1756 Le Lorrain, who had executed painted decorations in Parisian hotels, designed a 'cabinet à la grecque' for Lalive, which comprised the first furniture in an advanced neo-classical manner. According to C. N. COCHIN, whose *Mémoires* described the furniture as heavy, its success was due to praise from Caylus. For Caylus, Le Lorrain designed reconstructed shields of Achilles and Aeneas (1756) and improved the drawings by Julien-David Le Roy, *Les Ruines des plus beaux monuments de la Grèce* (1758), engraved by NEUFFORGE, Patte and Le Bas. In 1758 Le Lorrain accepted an appointment to teach at the new Academy in St Petersburg. He had hoped to specialize in furniture design, but his own furniture was lost in the voyage, and he died in Russia, where he had been followed by his pupil, J. M. MOREAU, before he had had time to accomplish much.

Leman, James (1688–1745) The son of a Spitalfields silk weaver of Huguenot origin, Leman followed his father's trade. From at least 1706 to 1722 he was active as a silk designer, strongly influenced in certain designs by French bizarre patterns. Leman also commissioned designs from other designers, and became an important figure in the London silk trade.

Le Mersier, Balthasar Le Mersier designed a suite of jewellery designs (Paris, 1626; six plates) engraved by Balthasar MONCORNET; it was reissued by Michel Van Lochem in 1647. The plates show sprays of jewelled flowers above landscapes, one spray spewed out by a dragon. Le Mersier also published a single similar design in 1625.

Lemmen, Georges (1865–1916) Born in

Brussels, the son of an architect, Lemmen was trained as a painter. From 1884 to 1889 he was associated with Les Vingt and from 1894 to 1914 with La Libre Esthétique. Lemmen was encouraged to take an interest in the decorative arts by VAN DE VELDE for whose edition of Nietzsche's *Also Sprach Zarathustra* (1908) he designed the typeface. In 1891 Lemmen wrote an article in Octave Maus's *L'Art Moderne* (1889–1914) on Walter CRANE. Lemmen himself designed rugs, tapestries, ceramics, jewellery for Philippe WOLFERS, mosaics, book illustrations and posters.

Le Moyne, Jacques Born in about 1533 probably near Dieppe, Le Moyne was employed in 1564 as a recording artist on Laudonnière's Huguenot expedition to Florida, of which Le Moyne's map was published posthumously by Theodor de BRY (1528–98) in 1591. In 1581 Le Moyne settled in England 'for religion'. In 1586 his *La Clef des Champs* was published, ninety-six woodcuts of animals, birds and plants intended as models for painters, engravers and embroiderers. Two albums of drawings by Le Moyne are also known, one in the VICTORIA & ALBERT MUSEUM of about 1565, the other in the British Museum of 1585. In 1588 he died in London.

Lencker, Hans Lencker, a goldsmith, became a citizen of Nuremberg in 1551. His *Perspectiva Literaria* (Nuremberg, 1567; twenty-one plates) displays imaginative virtuoso variations on PERSPECTIVE and geometry, anticipating and excelling Wenzel JAMNITZER'S slightly later *Perspectiva*. The plates were engraved by ZÜNDT. *Perspectiva Corporum* (1571), a textbook, followed, and from 1572 to 1576 Lencker worked at the court of Saxony, teaching perspective to the Elector Christian I. He also executed goldsmith's work for the

courts of Bavaria and Hessen in about 1574. He died in 1585 at Nuremberg.

Lens, Bernard (1659–1725) Born in London, the son of a painter, Lens was a prolific engraver and also ran a drawing school with the engraver John Sturt (1658–1730) in St Paul's Churchyard. In about 1707 he published *A Sett of Indian Figures for the Use of Japanning*, ten plates with Chinese figures accompanied by CHINOISERIE furniture, utensils and rockwork. They are important as the earliest known successors to STALKER and Parker's 1688 *Treatise*.

Le Page, François (1796–1871) The son of a Lyon hairdresser, Le Page studied at the Lyon École des Beaux-Arts and subsequently worked as a designer for a Saint-Étienne ribbon factory. Returning to Lyon, he taught design from 1825 to 1827 at the École des Beaux-Arts. He was also active as a flower painter.

Le Pautre, Jean (1618–82) Born in Paris, Le Pautre was a pupil of the cabinet-maker PHILIPPON, who was probably a relation and whose *Curieuses Recherches* (1645) Le Pautre engraved. In his career as a designer and engraver Le Pautre produced some 1,100 plates of ornament out of a total *œuvre* of some 2,200 plates, which also included illustrations for Desgodetz's *Les Édifices Antiques de Rome* (1682). Some of Le Pautre's suites of ornament bear dates from 1657 to 1678, and the majority of his output probably lies around the 1660s. He was employed by the Crown from 1670 and in 1677 was elected to the Academy as 'Dessignateur et Graveur'. Le Pautre's designs include friezes, mouldings and panels of ornament, for example *Frises ou montans à la moderne* (1657), *Rinceaux de diferents feuillages*, *Frisses Feuillages et Ornements*, *Livre de Frises et Ornemens*, *Rinceaux de Frises et Feuillages*, *Bordures de Tableau* *à la Romaine* and *Nouveau Livre de Cartouches*. He also designed panelling and ceilings, for example *Desseins de Lambris à l'Italienne pour orner et embellir les Chambres, Sales, Galeries et autres lieux magnifiques* (1659), *Lambris à la Françoise, Plafons à la Romaine* (1665), *Plafonds Modernes, Quarts de Plafons* and *Nouveaux Desseins de Plafons*. Chimneypieces, bed alcoves and doors were a speciality of his, for example *Cheminées à l'Italienne* (1665), *Nouveaux Desseins de Cheminées à l'Italienne, Cheminées à la Romaine, Cheminées à la Moderne, Nouveaux dessins de Cheminées à peu de Frais, Cheminées et Lambris, Grand Alcoves à la Romaine* (1667), *Alcoves à la Romaine, Differens Desseins d'alcauve*, dedicated by the editor Jean Le Blond (1635–1709) to his best friend, the doctor Charles Patin, *Alcoves à la Françoise* (1678), and *Nouveau Livre d'Porte d'La Chambre*. Le Pautre also designed trophies and VASES, for example *Montans de trophées d'armes à l'antique* (1659), *Trophez à l'antique, Vases d'Ornemens* and *Vases à l'Antique* (1661). Le Pautre's vases were widely copied, for instance in a Still Life by Berentz (1680). Ecclesiastical designs form a large group including *Chaires de Predicateur* (1659), *Chaires des Predicateurs et Œuvres de Marguilliers, Retables d'autels à l'italienne, Nouveaux Dessins d'Autels à la Romaine, Tabernacles* and *Clostures de Chapelles tant de Menuiserie que Serrurerie*. The latter designs, for wood or iron church screens, are among many by Le Pautre for metalwork, such as *Vases ou Burettes à la Romaine, Fontaines et Cuvetes*, and *Inventions pour faire des placques ou des Aubenetiers servans aux Orfevres* (1659), and designs for keys, keyhole escutcheons and andirons. Le Pautre also designed furniture in *Les Cabinets, Livre de Lit à la Romaine, Livre de Miroirs Tables et Gueridons*, and in a series of designs for torchères supported by carved figures. Designs by Le Pautre were reissued in London by John OVERTON, in 1676, and Samuel Sympson, in Amsterdam by Danckerts and SCHENCK, by Stapff in Augsburg and by Sandrart in Nuremberg. The English architect John James, who died in 1746, owned engravings by Le Pautre, and 765 were reissued in Paris by JOMBERT in 1751. In 1850 engravings by Le Pautre were in a cabinet-makers' library in the Tottenham Court Road, London. Although Le Pautre described his designs variously as in the antique, Roman, Italian, French and modern manners, he was in fact faithful to one style, the Roman BAROQUE, which he had first tasted under Philippon, and which, under LE BRUN, became the official style of Louis XIV. Le Pautre's designs were dense, bold, rich, varied and professional. They formed the main channel by which the style of Le Brun spread throughout Europe. But Le Pautre developed little and at the end of his life his designs were made to look heavy by those of Jean I BERAIN, some of which Le Pautre engraved, and which were in turn to be superseded by the designs of Le Pautre's son Pierre, among others.

Le Pautre, Pierre The eldest son of Jean LE PAUTRE, Pierre Le Pautre was born in about 1648, and trained as an engraver by his father. He engraved ornaments by Jean I BERAIN and numerous plates of architecture by D'AVILER, Jules Hardouin-Mansart (1646–1708) and others. While his *Cheminées et Lambris à la Mode* (six plates) shows relatively old-fashioned chimneypieces, *Cheminées à la Royalle à grand Miroir et Tablette avec Lambris de Menuizerie* (six plates), published in about 1698, comprises tall mirrors some with delicate borders above rectangular chimneypieces; a copy belonged to the English architect John James. Le Pautre's evident talent for fashionable interior design attracted the attention of Mansart, and when in 1699 Mansart became Surintendant et Directeur des Bâtiments du Roi, he appointed Le Pautre Dessinateur et Graveur des Bâtiments du Roi, a post he held until his death in 1716. Already in 1699 Le Pautre was employed to design furniture and chimneypieces for Louis XIV at Marly; the chimneypieces were published and show a new integration of ornament and panelling far in advance of the designs of his predecessor Lassurance and surpassing Le Pautre's own *Cheminées à la Royalle*. In 1701 Le Pautre revised the decoration of the Chambre du Roi at Versailles, and in 1703 he designed the King's apartment at the Trianon. His designs integrated panelling into an overall scheme of novel lightness which abandoned the BAROQUE architectonic structure framing Berain's ornament. The most notable surviving monument by Le Pautre is the organ-case in the chapel at Versailles of about 1709. Because of his position in the royal design hierarchy Le Pautre received little credit for his innovations, which marked an important stage in the creation of the ROCOCO style. Le Pautre also taught drawing and planned to publish a parallel of ancient and modern architecture.

Le Prince, Jean Baptiste (1734–81) Born at Metz, the son of a carver and gilder, Le Prince studied painting under François BOUCHER and VIEN. In 1754 he travelled to Italy and in 1757 to St Petersburg, where he did much decorative painting in the Winter Palace. Back in Paris in 1763 he was active as a book illustrator and also designed in 1769 a suite of Beauvais tapestries, Les Jeux Russes, first woven in 1769 and often thereafter. They were used as models by J. J. Spängler, a Swiss modeller who worked at the Derby porcelain factory in the early 1790s.

Lerambert, Henri Lerambert worked as a painter at Fontainebleau in 1568 to 1570. He later worked as royal tapestry designer to the factory set up in 1607 in the Faubourg Saint-Michel under the protection of Henri IV. Suites on the stories of Coriolanus and Artemisia are attributed to Lerambert, who died in 1609 and was succeeded by GUYOT and DUMÉE.

Lethaby, William Richard (1857–1931) Born in Barnstaple, Devon, the son of a Bible Christian carver and gilder, Lethaby entered the office of Alexander Lauder, a local architect. In 1879 he won the Soane Medallion and joined the office of Richard Norman SHAW as chief clerk in succession to Ernest Newton (1856–1922). In 1884 he helped to found the ART-WORKERS' GUILD, of which he was master in 1911. Lethaby was also active in starting the ARTS & CRAFTS EXHIBITION SOCIETY in 1887. He set up in independent practice in 1889 but continued to work part-time for Shaw; in 1889 he designed some of the decorations for Stanmore Hall executed by William MORRIS & Co. In 1890 Lethaby and GIMSON were the leading forces in the creation of Kenton & Co., set up to supply 'furniture of good design and good workmanship'. At the 1889 Arts & Crafts Exhibition, Lethaby had shown designs for chairs, for embroidery and for wrought iron and leadwork executed by Wentham & Waters. In 1890 he showed cast-iron designs for the Coalbrookdale Company and furniture designed for Marsh, Jones & Cribb, described by Gimson as 'wonderful furniture of a commonplace kind'. In 1891 Lethaby amicably severed his connection with Shaw and became active in the Society for the Protection of Ancient Buildings, which led to a close friendship with Philip WEBB. Lethaby's Kenton & Co. furniture shown in 1891 ranged from plain inlaid oak chests to a more elaborate hexagonal workbox. Kenton & Co. was disbanded in 1892. In that year Lethaby published *Architecture, Mysticism and Myth* and contributed an essay on cabinet-making to *Plain Handicrafts*, edited by MACKMURDO. Lethaby had a relatively small output as an architect, including Avon Tyrrell (1891), a house for Lord Manners, and Melsetter House, Isle of Hoy, Orkney (1898), for which he designed furniture. In 1894 Lethaby and the sculptor George Frampton were appointed the first art inspectors to the Technical Education Board of the London County Council and in 1896 they became joint directors of the new Central School of Arts & Crafts. Lethaby was sole Principal from 1900 to 1912; his protégés at the Central School included Edward Johnston. From 1900 to 1918 Lethaby was first professor of ornament and design at the Royal College of Art (see SCHOOL OF DESIGN). In 1915 he was active in the creation of the DESIGN AND INDUSTRIES ASSOCIATION; he tried but failed to persuade Gimson to join. Lethaby remained an active propagandist in the field of design until his death, regarded as a father figure by many of his juniors. He was also a distinguished medievalist.

Levati, Giuseppe (1739–1828) Born in Concorrezzo near Milan, the son of a carpenter, Levati moved to Milan to study under a painter, who introduced him to the works of Vignola, SERLIO, Palladio and Scamozzi. Levati then became an assistant to the decorative painter Comaschino. The architect, designer and inventor Agostino Gerli, who returned from Paris in 1769, introduced Levati to the NEO-CLASSICAL style; he later referred to Levati as the 'Giovanni da UDINE de' nostri tempi'. From 1765 Levati designed marquetry in both the Chinese and the neo-classical styles for the cabinet-maker Giuseppe Maggiolini (1738–1814), including the parquetry floors of the Archducal Palace in Milan (1771). From 1802 to 1806 Levati taught PERSPECTIVE at the Milan Academy.

Leven, Hugo (1874–1956) Born in Benrath near Düsseldorf, Leven was active as a designer of pewter for the Kayser factory at Krefeld. ART NOUVEAU pewter designed by Leven was imported to England by LIBERTY'S and inspired Alexander KNOX's pewter designs. From 1910 Leven was professor and director of the academy in Hanau.

Leyden, Lucas van Born in Leiden in 1489 to 1494 Lucas was the son of a painter. After being taught painting by his father he worked under Cornelis Engebrechtsen (1468–1533). Lucas is said to have begun to engrave as early as 1503. In 1521 he met DÜRER, who was a life-long influence and rival, in Antwerp, and in 1527 he travelled with Jan GOSSAERT in Flanders. Lucas died in 1533. He had engraved twelve plates of ornament of admirable delicacy and vigour. Six, dating from 1517 or earlier, display putti, arms and foliate ornament in a basically late GOTHIC manner. The remainder, dated 1527 or 1528, are RENAISSANCE GROTESQUES, with a full complement of sphinxes, dolphins and sirens, derived from the engravings of Agostino VENEZIANO and others. They probably reflect the influence on Lucas of Gossaert and Jan van Scorel, who had returned from Rome in 1509 and 1524 respectively. Lucas's Passion series of 1509 has circular frames decorated with ACANTHUS and putti, and many of his later prints include Renaissance ornament in details or frames. He was also active as a book illustrator and as a designer of stained glass. Lucas's prints were a widely used source of images for decoration from Limoges enamels and Vellert's windows at King's College, Cambridge, to a church screen in Norfolk. The Lucas Months, whose design was wrongly attributed to Lucas, were a popular tapestry subject, being rewoven at the Gobelins factory in 1688.

Liart, Matthew (1736–82) Born in London, the son of a Huguenot sausage-maker, Liart was active as an engraver after old masters and after West. He was taught by Ravenet and in 1764 won a premium from the SOCIETY OF ARTS. He has been identified with a 'Mattieu Liard' who published a *Recueil de differents Meubles garnies* (Paris, 1762; four plates), very competent late-ROCOCO designs for various sofas with elaborate embroidered upholstery, and similar suites in the NEO-CLASSICAL style, including his *Cahier de petits meubles* (Paris, 1774).

Liberty, Sir Arthur Lasenby (1843–1917) Born in Chesham, the son of a draper, Liberty was in 1859 apprenticed to a London draper, and then in 1862 moved to Farmer & Rogers' Great Shawl and Cloak Emporium in Regent Street. He was soon made one of the managers of their Oriental Warehouse, an annex which sold Japanese and other exotic goods, some of them originally purchased from the Japanese section at the LONDON 1862 EXHIBITION. In 1875 Liberty opened his own shop in Regent Street selling silks, Japanese porcelain, fans, screens and so on. His first published catalogue was entitled *Eastern Art Manufactures and Decorative Objects* (1881). Another shop, Chesham House, was opened in 1883, incorporating an Eastern Bazaar and a furnishing and decorating studio. This was run by Leonard F. Wyburd, who designed woodwork in the Moorish style, the well-known Thebes stools (1884), based on Egyptian models, and other furniture. In 1884 SERRURIER-BOVY was supplied with stock by Liberty's. Among the designers who worked for Liberty's

were: furniture – George WALTON, and E. G. Punnett, who worked for William Birch of High Wycombe in 1909; textiles – VOYSEY, Frank Miles, Lindsay P. BUTTERFIELD, Arthur Wilcock, J. Scarratt-Rigby, Sidney Mawson and Arthur SILVER; carpets – Mrs G. F. Watts, who also designed garden pottery; and metalwork – KNOX, Oliver Baker, Bernard Cuzner and Jessie M. KING. As well as papers on Japanese art and furniture Liberty published *Japan, A Pictorial Record* (1910), based on photographs of his trip to Japan in 1888 to 1889. Thanks to the international popularity of its products Liberty's was closely identified in Europe with progressive design, and in Italy ART NOUVEAU was sometimes called Stile Liberty.

Liebart, Philip Born in Liège, Liebart fled to England to escape the French occupation and was active as chief jewellery designer to Rundell & Bridge during the 1820s and 1830s. He designed jewels for George IV, among others.

Liénard, Michel Joseph Napoléon Born near Rouen in 1810, Liénard was trained as a sculptor. He was active as a designer by the 1840s, for Salomon de Rothschild, among others, and at his death in about 1875 had risen to a position of celebrity among French '*artistes industriels*'. At the LONDON 1851 EXHIBITION Gauvain showed guns in the NATURALISTIC and ROCOCO styles after his designs. He also designed ironwork, furniture and ornament in all the fashionable styles. His *Spécimens de la Décoration et de l'Ornementation* (Liège, 1866; 126 plates) even includes an overmantel in the Elizabethan style for a London house, as well as a portrait of the designer. The posthumous *Portefeuille de Liénard* (Liège, 1876; 125 plates) was similarly comprehensive, from Byzantine to Louis XIV; the selection was made by his pupil and son-in-law, A. Doussamy.

Lightoler, Timothy A carver, Lightoler was responsible for numerous designs for ceilings, chimneypieces and wall decorations, the latter incorporating mirrors and lights, mainly in the ROCOCO style, but some GOTHIC and some Palladian, in *The Modern Builder's Assistant* (1757) to which W. and J. Halfpenny and Robert Morris also contributed. In about 1760 Lightoler designed a Gothic altarpiece for the Beauchamp Chapel, Warwick, executed by the sculptor William Collins (1721–93). From 1763 to 1768 Lightoler worked at Burton Constable in Yorkshire, where he designed furniture and interiors in the rococo, Gothic and NEO-CLASSICAL styles. He was active as an architect up to 1775, mainly in the Midlands, and in 1774 published *The Gentleman and Farmer's Architect*.

Ligozzi, Jacopo (1547–1627) Born in Verona, the son of a painter, Ligozzi seems to have worked for the Medici court in Florence from at least 1577. In addition to being active as a painter Ligozzi did illustrations of natural history for the scientist Ulisse Aldrovandi (1522–1605), supplied embroidery designs to Bianca Capello in 1584 and designed for the Grand-Ducal manufactory of inlaid marbles. His most celebrated work in the latter field was the design of a famous octagonal *pietrè dure* table with elaborate natural and grotesque decoration, which was made from 1634 to 1649 and then, until the 19th century, stood in the centre of BUONTALENTI's Tribuna in the Uffizi. Ligozzi also designed glass vessels made in Florence, similar to examples shown in MAGGI's *Bicchierografia*, and also seems, in 1617, to have worked up Ferdinando I de' Medici's own ideas for joke vessels of this kind. Some of

Ligozzi's designs for glass are exceedingly ingenious and fantastic, incorporating water-wheels, frogs and gloves. Stefano DELLA BELLA and Baccio di BIANCO designed in a similar vein. Ligozzi also did designs for the decoration and costumes of court ceremonies. Some of his drawings of dress and animals were used to decorate Doccia porcelain in about 1750.

Lindstrand, Vicke Viktor Emanuel Lindstrand was born in 1904 in Göteborg, where he studied at the school of the Swedish Society of Arts & Crafts from 1924 to 1927. From 1928 he worked as a designer at the Orrefors glass factory under HALD and GATE; his work was shown at the PARIS 1937 EXHIBITION. In 1940 Lindstrand left Orrefors to design for the Uppsala-Ekeby ceramics factory and from 1950 he was Director of Design for the Kosta glass factory. Lindstrand's glass designs include engraved work, simple industrial forms and a wide range of free-form art glass.

Lindtmayer, Daniel Lindtmayer was born in Schaffhausen in 1554, of a family of glass painters which had moved there from Zürich in about 1514. The Lindtmayer glass workshop finally came to an end in 1586. From the late 1560s to at least 1603 Lindtmayer was active as a designer of stained glass: about 350 drawings survive, in an accomplished MANNERIST manner, spanning religious, secular and heraldic subjects. Lindtmayer was trained in Basel in 1574 to 1575 but thenceforward was active in Schaffhausen. Family troubles and mental illness drove him to desert his family in 1595 and to move to Schwyz in 1597 and in about 1598 to Luzern; at this time Lindtmayer also converted to Catholicism. The main influence on him was Tobias STIMMER, his main contemporary rival was Christoph MURER. With Murer he provided extra illustrations to the 1588 edition of Melchior Sebizius's book on agriculture, published in Strasbourg by Bernhard JOBIN, whose first 1580 edition had been illustrated by Tobias Stimmer. In 1597 Lindtmayer designed vigorous GROTESQUE frames influenced by Wendel DIETTERLIN. He also designed wall decorations. He is presumed to have died about 1607. Lindtmayer's only follower in Schaffhausen was Hans Caspar LANG (1571–1645).

Lingg, Bartholomäus Born in Zug in about 1555, Lingg was active as a glass painter and designer in Strasbourg from about 1580. He became a citizen of Strasbourg in 1581 and died there after 1629. Lingg was strongly influenced by Tobias STIMMER.

Linnell, John (1729–96) Born in London, the son of the successful carver and furniture manufacturer William Linnell, John Linnell was taught to design at the St Martin's Lane Academy. In 1753 he designed an imaginative CHINOISERIE bedroom for Badminton House. In 1760 he published a BAROQUE design, dedicated to Lord Scarsdale, for a new state coach for George III, designed in association with his uncle Samuel Butler, a coach builder. *A New Book of Ornaments Useful for Silversmiths &c.* (1760; four plates) was Linnell's only published suite of designs. It contains coffee-pots, jugs, sugar castors and VASES which are among the liveliest examples of English ROCOCO. Linnell was clearly established as the designer to his father's firm and when the latter died in 1763 the inventory of his premises included 'Mr John Linnell's Drawing-Room'. Linnell took over the business and kept it going until his retirement in about 1793. In 1770 he lost on a speculative venture to sell prints in India. His private life was picaresque; known as the 'Noble Squire', he had a mistress, Polly Perfect, a clergyman's daughter, and their attempt to fleece Lord Conyngham led to a prolonged fraud case. His friends included the French sculptor Pierre Étienne Falconet. Linnell had pretensions to be a painter and a country gentleman, moved in theatrical circles, and was a Colonel of Volunteers in 1790. From 1793 he spent time in Bath. Linnell was a fluent and versatile draughtsman. He owned a copy of MONTFAUCON's *Antiquité Expliquée*, borrowed from KENT and from DELAFOSSE, and subscribed to MALTON's *Perspective* (1775) and to George RICHARDSON's *Orders* (1787). The designer C. H. TATHAM, a cousin of Linnell, was also his pupil and always remained grateful to his mentor. Linnell's own style, revealed in a volume of over 350 drawings in the VICTORIA & ALBERT MUSEUM put together by Tatham in 1800, spanned rococo and NEO-CLASSICISM. In about 1765 Linnell delivered a pair of massive sofas to Kedleston, Lord Scarsdale's neo-classical house; they were supported by merfolk in a baroque style probably influenced by VARDY. Linnell worked for ADAM on several occasions. His later designs are close in style to HOLLAND, for whom his cousin Tatham worked.

Lion Cachet, Carel Adolph (1864–1945) Born in Amsterdam, Lion Cachet studied design there under B. W. Wierink and others. His work was illustrated in 'BOUW- EN-SIERKUNST' (1897) and from 1898, with NIEUWENHUIS and Gerrit Willem Dijsselhof (1866–1924) he designed furniture for the Amsterdam firm of Wisselingh. In 1901 Lion Cachet opened his own Atelier voor Vercierungskunst, a design workshop, in Vreeland. He designed furniture, carpets, bookbindings, posters and bank notes and showed at many exhibitions, including the TURIN 1902 EXHIBITION. Lion Cachet's interiors included saloons on the steamships *Gro-*

tius (1907), *Princess Juliana* (1910) and *J. P. Coen* (1915).

Lissitzky, El (1890–1941) Born in Polschinok near Smolensk, the son of an estate steward, Lazar Markovich Lissitzky was brought up in Vitebsk. From 1909 to 1914 he studied engineering and architecture at the Darmstadt Technische Hochschule where his teachers included OLBRICH. In 1911 he visited Paris, where he met the sculptor Ossip Zadkine (1890–1967), also from Vitebsk; in the same year he met VAN DE VELDE. In 1914 he returned to Russia, where he was active as an architect from 1915. Lissitzky was a fervent supporter of the Russian revolution and in 1918 designed a Soviet flag carried in procession across the Red Square. From 1917 to 1919 he designed a number of experimental Yiddish picture books. In 1919 Lissitzky was invited by the painter Chagall to teach architecture and graphic art at Vitebsk, where he was strongly influenced by the painter Kasimir Malevich (1878–1935), who had been in Vitebsk since 1912. In 1919 Lissitzky helped to organize the publication of Malevich's *New System of Art*, a manifesto of Suprematism, designed a celebrated abstract Soviet propaganda poster, Beat the Whites with the Red Wedge, and produced his first PROUN. The PROUN, a dynamic rectilinear abstract intended to effect a union between painting and architecture, took its acronymic name from the Russian for Project for the Affirmation of the New; in 1923 Lissitzky designed a PROUN room in Berlin and in 1927 another in Hanover. From 1920 to 1924 Lissitzky worked on the design of the Lenin podium, a prow-like steel structure symbolic of Soviet optimism. In 1921 Lissitzky taught architecture in Moscow at the Vhkutemas, the Russian BAUHAUS, where his colleagues included Vladimir Tatlin (1885–1953), and in 1922 he participated in the Constructivist International. At the end of 1921 Lissitzky was in Berlin and designed a cover for 'WENDINGEN'. In 1922 he edited *Veschch*, a pro-Soviet periodical to which LE CORBUSIER and Theo van Doesburg contributed, and published his abstract children's book, *Of Two Squares*, designed in 1920; it was reprinted in 'DE STIJL'. Also in 1922 Lissitzky designed a cover for the American Matthew Josephson's magazine *Broom*, met Kurt Schwitters (1887–1948) and became friendly with MOHOLY-NAGY, whom he later on regarded as a plagiarist. In 1923 he designed typography for a book of poems by Mayakovsky. In 1924 he had to go to Switzerland for his health, but before moving to a sanatorium near Locarno he met Hans ARP and Mart STAM in Zürich. While ill Lissitzky helped to edit and design the 1924 issue of Schwitters's *Merz*, contributed to the Merz journal *Nasci* and to Stam's periodical, *ABC*, and, to earn money, designed vigorous abstract posters and publicity material for Pelikan ink. In *The Isms of Art* (1925), in collaboration with Hans Arp, Lissitzky gave a summary of the aims of cubism, futurism, expressionism, constructivism and other MODERN isms. In 1925 he moved back to Moscow where he became professor of interior decoration and furniture at the Vhkutemas. Lissitzky appears to have designed little furniture himself, apart from some for the Narkomfin apartment building, by the constructivist architect M. Y. Ginzburg (1892–1946), and some bent-plywood chairs for the Soviet section at the Leipzig 1930 International Fur Trade Exhibition. He designed several important exhibitions, notably the Soviet pavilion at the Cologne 1928 International Press Exhibition. Also in 1928 Lissitzky published a children's arithmetic book in which typographic pin-men express improving

Soviet slogans, and his contribution to Modern typography was recognized by Jan TSCHICHOLD (1902–74) in *Die neue Typographie*. During the 1930s Lissitzky devoted himself mainly to teaching. His last posters, against Hitler, were in a weak realistic manner.

Liverpool 1886 Exhibition The Liverpool 1886 International Exhibition of Navigation, Travelling, Commerce and Manufacture included a stand for furniture, stuffs, papers and decoration by the Century Guild of Artists, whose members were MACKMURDO and HORNE, who also designed a stand for Cope Brothers, tobacco importers. The *Art Designer* showed needlework designs by Walter CRANE and Mawe & Co. 'an Old Damascus Room'.

Lobmeyr, Ludwig (1829–1917) Second son of Josef Lobmeyr (1792–1855) who, in 1822, had founded the celebrated Viennese glass factory, Ludwig Lobmeyr became a partner with his elder brother, Josef (1828–64), in 1860. Ludwig designed for the factory himself, creating in 1856 a service which dispensed with ornament altogether, and always tending away from the heavy opaque effects of BIEDERMEIER glass. His prolific designs also covered the Moorish, RENAISSANCE and NEO-CLASSICAL styles, and on taking over the direction of the firm when his brother died in 1864, Lobmeyr established a close relationship with the Österreichisches Museum für Kunst and Industrie, its director, EITELBERGER, and with the architect Theophil von HANSEN, who supplied designs. Other designers employed by Lobmeyr were STORCK, Frederick von SCHMIDT, Teirich and Eisernmenger. His nephew Richard Kralik, whose father had pioneered iridescent glass in 1875, designed a Parsifal service in 1888 and in the same year Moritz Knab designed

a much-praised Alhambra service. In 1902 Lobmeyr's nephew Stephan Rath took over the factory and began to introduce the ART NOUVEAU style.

Lock, Matthias In 1724 Lock was apprenticed to a London carver, Richard Goldsaddle. Lock's recorded activity as a carver began in the 1740s, when he designed and carved some elaborate furniture for the Earl of Poulett, including a mirror, stands and table in the late-BAROQUE style, a table in the style of William KENT, and another in the manner of PINEAU. He was still active as a carver in 1752, probably as a sub-contractor, and about that date probably carved a gilt 'French chair' later used by Richard Cosway as a studio prop. Lock died in 1765. His main fame had been as a designer of carved furniture, 'having been reputed the best draughtsman in that way that had ever been in England'. Lock published eight suites of ornament, one in collaboration with COPLAND. Most were reprinted after Lock's death by Robert SAYER from about 1767, and again by WEALE and Taylor from about 1830 to 1860. In the latter reprints the authorship of the designs was credited to CHIPPENDALE. Lock also engraved a few trade cards. Lock's printed designs are as follows: *Six Sconces* (1744), *Six Tables* (1746), *A Book of Shields* (eight plates), *A New Drawing Book of Ornaments, Shields, Compartments, Masks &c.* (two suites of six plates), *A New Book of Ornaments* (with Copland, 1752; twelve plates), *A New Book of Ornaments . . . in The Chinese Taste* (six plates), and *The Principles of Ornament* (twelve plates). The designs include mirror-frames, tables, stands, clock-cases, cartouches, a chandelier, a bowl and a watch-case. The latter two designs for metalwork and the existence of a drawing for a salt-cellar with spoons, one identical to an executed spoon (1742) by Nicholas SPRIMONT, suggest that Lock may have been active as a designer in this field. Lock's ornamental vocabulary is ROCOCO, but his scrolls, dragons, flowers, masks, birds and Chinamen are all handled with a zest and freedom rare in the English product, with a strong dash of asymmetry. His *Principles of Ornament* are an interesting rococo anticipation of PETHER's similar manual of draughtsmanship. This evidence of an ability to teach design, combined with Lock's activity as a rococo designer from the early 1740s, makes him a better candidate than DARLY as Chippendale's mentor in the rococo style. In 1769 two books by 'M. Lock' were published, *A New Book of Foliage* (eight plates) and *A New Book of Pier-Frame's, Oval's, Gerandole's, Table's &c.* (seven plates). The first is a NEO-CLASSICAL version of the *Principles of Ornament*, the second an artisan but competent neo-classical pattern-book. 'M. Lock' may be a son of Matthias Lock, and may be identified with a carver of that name recorded at Clerkenwell Green between 1788 and 1797.

Loewy, Raymond Born in Paris in 1893, Loewy designed, built and sold a successful model aeroplane in 1909, inspired by Santos-Dumont's first flight. He then studied electrical engineering before serving with distinction in the First World War. In 1919 Loewy moved to New York, where he was hired as a window dresser at Macy's department store but rapidly resigned. Thenceforth Loewy worked as a fashion illustrator, mainly for *Harper's Bazaar*, and as a commercial artist; in 1923 he designed the Nieman Marcus trademark. In 1929 Loewy redesigned a duplicating machine for Sigmund Gestetner, using modelling clay to give it a sleek new shape; it was marketed from 1933 to 1949. A 1930 design for a car, patented in 1931, represented the beginning of Loewy's interest in car design, whose first fruit was the

1934 Hupmobile for the Hupp Motor Company. Later car designs included the 1945 design for the Studebaker Champion, produced in 1947, and the 1961 design for the Studebaker Avanti, produced in 1962. The Sears, Roebuck & Company Coldspot refrigerator, designed in 1934, was successfully marketed on its looks in 1935. In 1934 a mock-up of Loewy's office, a dashing combination of black and white linoleum, gun-metal furniture and fittings and built-in lighting, was shown at the Metropolitan Museum in New York, and marked his early apotheosis as a leader of American industrial design; his appearance on the cover of *Time* magazine (1947) sealed his public reputation. Celebrated designs by Loewy include the Lucky Strike cigarette packet (1940), the Pepsodent toothpaste packet (1945) and the Dole Coca-Cola dispenser (about 1948). The streamlined S-I locomotive for the Pennsylvania Railroad, designed in 1937, was shown at the New York World Fair in that year, and from 1935 Loewy was consultant designer to the Greyhound Coach Corporation. Loewy was particularly proud of his work from 1967 to 1972 for NASA, including the interior of Skylab. Other designs have included electric shavers, radios, postage-stamps, trademarks, porcelain, textiles and furniture. An ardent self-publicist, Loewy built up an international practice with offices in California, New York, London and Paris.

Logan, George A minor member of the Glasgow School, Logan showed projects for interior decoration in the Scottish Section of the TURIN 1902 EXHIBITION. In 1904 Logan's furniture designs for Messrs Wylie & Lochhead of Glasgow were illustrated in the 'STUDIO'. They display a highly professional, but muted, cosy and prettified version of the style of Charles Rennie MACKINTOSH.

Loh, F. Loh published four accomplished plates of designs for pendants, brooches, sword-hilts, cane handles etc., in a floral ROCOCO style. They probably date from about 1760.

Loir, Alexis (1640–1713) Born in Paris, the son of a goldsmith and younger brother of Nicolas LOIR, Alexis Loir was active as engraver and goldsmith, becoming a master in 1669, and executing many commissions for the court. He engraved his brother's designs and also published several suites of ornament to his own design. *Nouveaux Dessins de Guéridons dont les pieds sont propres pour des Croix, Chandeliers, Chenets et autres Ouvrages d'Orfevrerie et de Sculpture* (six plates) presents varied BAROQUE designs for candle-stands, whose sculptural feet were, as the title suggests, also applicable to crucifixes and other uses. *Desseins de Brasiers* (six plates) shows similarly versatile designs for braziers, applicable to tables and other uses. *Panaux D'Ornements* (six plates), *Nouveaux desseins d'ornemens de paneaux, lambris, carosse &c.* (six plates), *Frises et Ornemans de Paneaux* (twelve plates) and *Plafons à la Moderne* (twelve plates) include designs for panelling, friezes, coach ornaments and ceilings. Frieze designs by Loir were copied by John OVERTON in London in 1675, and the architect John James owned a copy of his *Nouveaux Dessins de Guéridons*. Loir's style was close to that of his brother, a rich baroque derived from Roman prototypes and similar to the designs of LE BRUN and Jean LE PAUTRE.

Loir, Nicolas Pierre (1624–79) Born in Paris, the son of a goldsmith, Loir trained. as a painter under VOUET and Bourdon. From 1647 to 1649 he was in Rome, where he was influenced by Poussin. Loir

designed for the Gobelins tapestry factory, specializing in GROTESQUES and also designed a number of prints of ornament, which were engraved by his younger brother, Alexis. They include *Desseins pour embellir les Chaises Roulantes* (twelve plates), *Nouveaux Dessins pour l'embellissement des Carosses, Panneaux, Lambris* (twelve plates) and *Desseins d'Éventails et Écrans* (six plates) with designs for the decoration of coaches, panelling, fans and screens. Loir's style, similar to that of LE BRUN and Jean LE PAUTRE, transmitted the BAROQUE forms of Rome to France.

Londerseel, Assuerus van Born in Antwerp in about 1572, Londerseel was settled in Amsterdam in 1595 and was there active as an engraver. He died in Rotterdam in 1635. Londerseel published copies of Hans COLLAERT'S sea-monster pendants and of FLINDT'S *Visirung Buch* (1593), some elaborate frames (eight plates) in the Flemish GROTESQUE STRAPWORK manner of Hans VREDEMAN DE VRIES, and some crude COSSE-DE-POIS sprays for jewellers (ten plates) with fleshy leaves and birds, insects, soldiers etc., in the foreground. Londerseel also published the works of his brother-in-law, Nicolas de BRUYN.

London Exhibitions Although various bazaars had been held for the sale of local products, for example in Dublin in 1827, Great Britain had no tradition of exhibitions of design and industry to compare with France or Germany. In the 1840s, however, the success of Paris exhibitions encouraged emulation. In 1845 a Free Trade Bazaar was held in Covent Garden, London, and in 1849 an exhibition of manufactures was held in Birmingham on the occasion of the visit of the British Association. Prince ALBERT, President of the SOCIETY OF ARTS, was one of those instrumental in

1845 in setting up a committee to consider the need for British exhibitions. The Society itself organized three exhibitions in London in 1847, 1848 and 1849. Prince Albert himself was eager in 1848 to promote a full-scale British industrial exhibition. Nothing came of this, but in June 1849, influenced by an abortive scheme of M. Buffet, the French Minister of Agriculture, and by Matthew Digby WYATT's report on the PARIS 1849 EXHIBITION, Prince Albert announced to a meeting at Buckingham Palace his plan for a Great Exhibition of the Industry of All Nations to be held in 1851. A Royal Commission met in January 1850 and, despite much public scepticism, the project forged ahead with Henry COLE as its most active promoter. A competition for the building failed, a Building Committee produced its own cumbrous plan, and then at the last minute Sir Joseph Paxton (1801–65) produced a scheme for a gigantic greenhouse; Owen JONES designed its polychrome decorations. The Crystal Palace, as it was soon known, was opened on 1 May 1851. The London 1851 Exhibition was a prodigious success, and actually made a profit of £173,896. Design in the exhibition, amply illustrated in the *Art Journal Illustrated Catalogue*, was dominated by NATURALISM. Typical examples are the carpets designed by E. T. Parris for Messrs Turberville Smith of London, the Lotus table and Victoria Regia cot by John BELL for Jennens & Bettridge of Birmingham, and J. N. Paton's tablecloth for Birrell of Dumfermline, incorporating thistles and Queen Victoria. Naturalism blended with RENAISSANCE was also popular, as in T. R. MACQUOID's bookcase for Holland & Sons of London, and in W. Harry ROGERS' many designs, which included the Prince of Wales's Bridle by Mr Penny. Design reformers, however, found little to encourage their hopes

except in A. W. N. PUGIN's Mediaeval Court, which contained GOTHIC metalwork, carving and furniture to his design by Hardman, Myers and CRACE. The London 1862 Exhibition has been overshadowed by that of 1851. But, although the expense of the 1862 buildings, designed by Captain Fowke (1823–65) and decorated by J. G. Crace, caused an overall loss, the exhibition was popular and seemed to contemporaries to mark a great advance in English design. In retrospect 1862 rather than 1851 is the great exhibition of High Victorian design. The Reformed Gothic style was represented in the Mediaeval Court, organized by the ECCLESIOLOGICAL SOCIETY, where designs by BURGES, Philip WEBB and others were condemned by the antiquary Charles Boutell (1812–77), 'the very best things in this Mediaeval Court are parodies of something which refuses to be parodied successfully': none the less even Boutell praised designs by SEDDON and R. N. SHAW. H. H. Armstead, Matthew Digby Wyatt and Owen Jones were instances of a new professionalism among English designers, although immigrant designers such as JEANNEST, WILLMS, Monti, MOREL-LADEUIL and CARRIER-BELLEUSE were also well represented. The Japanese stand, admired by Burges, was to have a far-reaching influence on design, and the first signs of a revival of late-18th-century NEO-CLASSICISM were visible in furniture by Wright & Mansfield with 'details . . . gleaned from the works of the Messrs (Adelphi) ADAM' and in Jackson & Sons' Louis XVI style mirrors and stands. Four London exhibitions of diminishing importance were held from 1871 to 1874, when the idea of an annual exhibition was abandoned: the French caused bad feeling by converting their section into a bazaar in 1871 and the 'ART JOURNAL' dismissed the London 1874 Exhibition as 'Odds

and Ends'. None the less the series gave
a new generation of designers, including
TALBERT, COLLCUTT, TARVER and
Owen W. DAVIS, their London exhibition debut. From 1888 onwards the
exhibitions held by the ARTS & CRAFTS
EXHIBITION SOCIETY acted as an
unofficial focus for advanced designers.
The next large official exhibition was the
London 1924 British Empire Exhibition
at Wembley. The British exhibits were
displayed by Sir Lawrence Weaver, who
used his experience as the basis for
Exhibitions and the Arts of Display
(1925). Decorations included polychrome tiles by Oliver P. BERNARD,
stained glass with animals of the Empire
by Reginald Bell, and ceramic roundels
by Phoebe Stabler. In the afterglow of
STOCKHOLM 1930 EXHIBITION the
magazine *Country Life* sponsored in
1933 an exhibition, British Industrial
Art in Relation to the Home, at the
Dorland Hall in London. The leading
spirit was Oliver HILL, and with a
minimum flat by Wells COATES, a study
by R. D. Russell (1904–81) and a bedroom by Raymond MCGRATH, the
exhibition was the first major display of
MODERNISM in England. The London
1935 Royal Academy exhibition, British
Art in Industry, sponsored by the Royal
Society of Arts, was less stylistically
unequivocal, but none the less marked
a further step in the naturalization of
Modernism. After the war the Council of Industrial Design, encouraged by
Sir Stafford Cripps, President of the
Board of Trade, organized the London
1946 Britain Can Make It Exhibition,
held at the VICTORIA & ALBERT
MUSEUM. In 1945 Gerald Barry, editor
of the *News Chronicle*, had written to
Cripps suggesting an exhibition to commemorate the London 1851 Exhibition
and to celebrate post-war recovery. In
1947 Herbert Morrison took over the
scheme and made Barry Director General. The London 1951 Festival of Brit-

ain was a great popular success. Under
the aegis of a mutedly patriotic Britannia head symbol, designed by Abram
Games, design at the Festival ranged
from etiolated Modernism to cheerful
whimsy. Acting on a suggestion of Kathleen Lonsdale (1903–71) that crystal
structure diagrams be applied to textiles,
the Festival Pattern Group used crystal
forms on wallpapers, pottery and textiles, some used in Misha BLACK's
Regatta Restaurant. Spindliness was in
vogue, for instance in Ernest RACE's
Antelope chair and Robin DAY's direction signs. The Lion and Unicorn pavilion by R. D. Russell and Robert
GOODEN, with a mural by Edward
BAWDEN, summed up the mood of
quirky self-congratulation. It was generally agreed that the Festival's influence on design was ephemeral.

Loos, Adolf (1870–1933) Born in Brno,
the son of a stonemason, Loos studied
building at Liberec from 1887 to 1888
and then after military service studied
at the Dresden Institute of Technology.
From 1893 to 1896 Loos was in America,
where he did a variety of jobs and
visited the CHICAGO 1893 WORLD
COLUMBIAN EXPOSITION. Back in
Vienna Loos devoted himself to architecture, working until 1897 under Carl
Mayreder. From 1897 Loos wrote numerous articles on architecture and design;
those of 1897 to 1900 were collected as
Ins Leere Gesprochen (1921) and those
of 1900 to 1930 in *Trotzdem* (1931).
Loos's 'Die Potemkinischer Stadt' in
'VER SACRUM' (1898) attacked extravagance and dishonesty in architecture.
Loos disliked the transitory modishness
of Secession designers, although he
admired Otto Wagner. In 1898 he
designed a shop interior for Goldman
& Salatsch and in 1899 the Café
Museum, the Stössler apartment and the
Turnowsky apartment. His furniture for
these was mainly rectilinear, solid,

simple and unornamented. For the Café Museum, which was nicknamed the Café Nihilismus, Loos designed THONET chairs with an oval bentwood section. His first building, the Villa Karma, near Montreux in Switzerland (1904–6), included Egyptian-style stools similar to the LIBERTY three-legged Thebes pattern, which were made by Loos's favourite cabinet-maker, Josef Veillich, and crop up in many of his houses. In 1908 Loos published a celebrated article, 'Ornament und Verbrechen', in which he linked cultural evolution to the removal of ornament from articles in daily use, attacked the built-in obsolescence of ornament by such designers as ECKMANN and VAN DE VELDE, and claimed that lack of ornament is a sign of spiritual strength. Such tenets and the purity of some of Loos's own designs led to his canonization as a pioneer of the MODERN style. However the designs executed in the architectural school which he opened in 1912 are unequivocally NEO-CLASSICAL and he had a life-long admiration for the Greeks and for SCHINKEL. His 1922 competition design for the Chicago Tribune building was a skyscraper in the form of a colossal Doric column. Recently the Lanvin shop in Zürich (1978) by the Swiss designers Robert and Trix Haussmann has revived the mannered classical aspect of Loos's Kärntner bar (1908). Loos admired English and American practicality, simplicity and engineering, and many of the houses he designed contained plain English 18th-century furniture. He regarded the artist-designer as a largely superfluous figure and believed in the inevitable rightness of simple forms evolved by the craftsman, an idea which owes much to SEMPER. From 1920 to 1922 Loos was chief housing architect in Vienna. The next five years he spent mainly in Paris and on the French Riviera, and he continued to travel widely to the end. In 1931 Loos designed a series of simple glasses for the firm of Lobmeyr; they are still in production.

Loose, Hermann (1848–99) A son of the leading Hamburg marquetry specialist of the late 19th century, Julius Rudolf Loose (1823-1901), Hermann Loose supplied NATURALISTIC marquetry designs to his father's firm. He also contributed to SCHWINDRAZHEIM'S *Beiträge zu einer Volkskunst* (1891–3).

Loreck, Johann Anton Loreck was probably trained as a goldsmith in Vienna. In about 1720 he published there a book of designs for jewellery (eight plates) dedicated to the Archduchesses Maria Josepha and Maria Amalia, whom he likened to two diamonds. It is one of the finest records of late-BAROQUE court jewellery design, displaying grand jewels heavily set with stones above CHINOISERIES, garden views and PERSPECTIVES with VASES and architecture. As well as jewels the plates incorporate many passages of fine scrolling ornament for the chaser. After the marriage in 1722 of Maria Amalia to the future Elector Karl Albrecht of Bavaria, Loreck probably moved to Munich, where he became keeper of the crown jewels and, though not a member of the Munich goldsmiths' guild, supplied jewellery to the court of Karl Albrecht from at least 1731. He died between 1741 and 1745.

Lorimer, Sir Robert Stodart (1864–1929) Born in Edinburgh, the son of a professor of law, Lorimer left his studies at Edinburgh University in 1884 to take articles with the architect Hew Wardrop (1856–87) and remained after Wardrop's death with his partner Rowand Anderson (1834–1921). In 1889 he spent some time in BODLEY's office in London. In 1893 Lorimer returned to Edinburgh to set up his own office. By

1900 he had established himself as a leading Scottish architect. Lorimer showed furniture at the London ARTS & CRAFTS EXHIBITION in 1893 and 1896, when he was elected to the ART-WORKERS' GUILD. He had a deep admiration for William MORRIS, on whom he lectured in 1897, and became friendly with MUTHESIUS, who praised his work. For his houses, Lorimer designed some furniture in the GOTHIC style, some based on English, Dutch and French 18th-century prototypes, and some in a more timeless Arts & Crafts manner. Much of it was made by Whytock & Reid of Edinburgh, and some was illustrated by W. Shaw Sparrow's *Hints on House Furnishing* (1909). Lorimer also designed stained glass, plasterwork, ironwork and embroidery, including bedspreads for Kellie Castle shown at the 1899 Arts & Crafts Exhibition. In about 1915 he designed the Remirol (Lorimer backwards) water closet for Messrs Shanks. Lorimer was an activist in the DESIGN AND INDUSTRIES ASSOCIATION, to which he was probably introduced by his friend William Scott Morton.

Lorm, Cornelis de (1875–1942) Lorm studied law and then worked for the Dutch Post Office in The Hague: he remained there until 1929, and subsequently moved to the Dutch Home Office. While at the Post Office, Lorm was a designer and patron of design. In 1913 he commissioned jubilee stamps from BAZEL and in 1917 he set up a shop, De Zonnebloem, to sell modern design of which he approved; it was closed in about 1927. Lorm's own designs included furniture, pottery, silver and embroidery, mainly dating from after 1916. In 1917 he was commissioned by Cochius of the Leerdam glass factory to design glass, and up to 1921 Lorm produced bold and competent designs in

this medium, influenced by BERLAGE and Bazel.

Lormier, Alfred Lormier was a French furniture designer employed by the English firm of luxury cabinet-makers, Jackson & Graham, who also employed Eugène PRIGNOT and Owen JONES. He designed cabinets shown by them at the LONDON 1862, PARIS 1867 and LONDON 1871 EXHIBITIONS. J. Hungerford POLLEN said that Lormier was the first to design the ebony and marquetry cabinets for which Jackson & Graham were celebrated. He is probably the 'E. Lormier' who contributed a number of designs to Richard CHARLES's *The Cabinet Maker* (1868).

Loudon, John Claudius (1783–1843) Born at Cambuslang, Lanarkshire, in Scotland, the son of a farmer, Loudon was apprenticed to a series of landscape gardeners from 1798. In 1803 he moved to London and began a distinguished career as a 'Designer of Rural Improvements', strongly influenced by Repton and the theorists of the picturesque. A first article in the *Literary Journal* (1803), 'Observations on Laying Out the Public Squares of London', was followed by a series of works on landscape gardening and estate management. After travels in Northern Europe he began in 1817 to experiment with the construction of conservatories and in 1822 published *An Encyclopaedia of Gardening*. In 1831 Loudon married Jane Webb (1807–58), who actively supported and supplemented his prodigiously intensive work as a writer. His most important contribution to the literature of design was his *Encyclopaedia of Cottage, Farm and Villa Architecture and Furniture* (1833), which is the crucial document of 1830s middle-class taste. A *First Additional Supplement* was published in 1842 and a second in 1843; a new edition edited by Mrs Loudon was issued in

1846. Among the architectural contributors were Charles Barry (1795–1860), W. H. Leeds (1786–1868), W. F. Smallwood, Charles Fowler (1791–1867) and Edward Buckton LAMB (1806–69). Their styles ranged from Grecian to GOTHIC and also included Indian and Swiss. The furniture was revealingly divided into four styles, Grecian or modern, Gothic or perpendicular, Elizabethan, and style of Louis XIV or florid Italian. Designs were supplied by E. B. Lamb, by George Fildes, a professional designer who worked for the London cabinet-maker W. F. Dalziel, and, for cast-iron, by Robert MALLET. Among the source-books praised by Loudon were Thomas HOPE's *Household Furniture* (1807), Thomas Hunt's *Exemplars of Tudor Architecture* (1830) and, in later editions, Henry SHAW's *Specimens of Ancient Furniture* (1836). Loudon's *Architectural Magazine* (1834–8), to which the young RUSKIN contributed from 1837 on 'The Poetry of Architecture', also contained much information on design, and his *Suburban Gardener and Villa Companion* (1838) included many illustrations of his own model London house, built in 1824, and replete with much ingenuity. Loudon was an active member of many societies and associations and a paradigm of industry. His influence was strong in America, particularly through A. J. DOWNING.

Louis, Victor (1731–1800) Born in Paris, Louis studied architecture under Louis-Adam Loriot. He won the Grand Prix and spent from 1756 to 1759 in Rome. In 1764 he went to Warsaw as architect to the King of Poland, but he was back in Paris by 1766 leaving his scheme for the royal palace and its furniture, designed in collaboration with PRIEUR, to be completed under the supervision of his pupil Anatole Amoudru (1739–1812). The palace is among the earliest elaborate NEO-CLASSICAL decorative ensembles and its design was approved by the Marquis de MARIGNY. In 1767 Louis designed a choir-screen for Chartres Cathedral, executed by the smith Joseph Pérez. His greatest architectural work was the Bordeaux Theatre (1775–80). In 1780 Louis became architect to Louis Philippe, Duc d'Orléans.

Loy, Erasmus Loy was active in Regensburg in about 1550 to 1560. He was granted an imperial privilege for the production of 'Kunst- und Flattenpapier', which seems to have implied bold two-coloured woodcuts for decoration for furniture and walls. In 1557 to 1561 he complained to the Regensburg council that his imperial privilege was being breached by Utz Meyer, a cabinet-maker who was copying his papers. Eighteen prints by Loy are known; they are mainly bold RENAISSANCE architectural PERSPECTIVES, but also include a frieze with medallion heads, vertical STRAPWORK GROTESQUES and candelabra, and the arms of the City of Regensburg. One of Loy's architectural prints is copied on the arcaded front of an early 17th-century Bavarian chest, and a bed in Nuremberg uses his frieze of medallion heads.

Luce, Jean (1895–1964) Born in Paris, Luce worked in the ceramic shop his father had founded in 1888 and then from 1923 had his own shop. Luce was active as a designer of both ceramics and glass, exhibiting from 1911. His early glass used clear enamel decoration; from about 1924 he used sandblasting. Luce favoured simple forms, ART DÉCO abstract patterns and stylized flowers. He designed porcelain and glass for the *Normandie* and served on the juries at the PARIS EXHIBITIONS of 1925 and 1937.

Lucotte, J. R. Lucotte designed many

of the plates in Diderot and D'Alembert's *Encyclopédie*, from 1763. These include designs for goldsmith's work, jewellery, ironwork, saddles and coaches; many of Lucotte's designs are derivative and some copies, for instance after jewellery designs by MARIA. He also published *Le Vignole Moderne* (1772–84), three suites of thirty-six plates each with the ORDERS, doors, windows, cornices etc.

Ludwig II of Bavaria (1845–86) In 1864 Ludwig succeeded his father Maximilian II as King of Bavaria. In the first few years of his reign Ludwig took some part in affairs of state but from about 1870 he retreated into seclusion. His extravagance and eccentricity led to his being officially pronounced insane in 1886 and a few days later he drowned in mysterious circumstances. Brought up in the Bavarian Alps in the BIEDERMEIER GOTHIC castle of Hohenschwangau, designed by Domenico Quaglio from 1833 to 1838, Ludwig was from the late 1850s a passionate admirer of Wagner. This relationship, his identification with the Bourbon Kings of France, especially Louis XIV and Louis XV, and his belief in absolute monarchy were the inspiration for Ludwig's patronage of architecture and design. Ludwig used the Louis XIV style for his apartments in the Munich Residenz (from 1865 to 1869), by the theatrical designer Franz Seitz, and at Herrenchiemsee (from 1878 to 1886), an extraordinary reconstruction of Versailles designed by Georg Dollmann and Julius Hoffmann. Herrenchiemsee also includes some Louis XV interiors and this style is dominant in Linderhof (1870 to 1884), a luxurious royal villa designed by Sietz and Christian Jank, another theatrical designer, Dollmann, Adolph Seder, Eugen Drollinger, Franz Stulberger, Franz Brochier and Franz Widnmann. In the Alps near Linderhof, Ludwig had built a Moorish

house whose interior, designed by Dollmann, borrowed from Thomas Allom's *Constantinople* . . . (London, 1840) and from Owen JONES's *Alhambra*. At Neuschwanstein (1869–86), a romantic mountain-top castle, the interiors evolved from Gothic to Romanesque; the designers involved included Jank, Peter HERWEGEN, Michael WELTER and Hoffmann. Ludwig, whom Verlaine apostrophized as '*seul vrai roi de ce siècle*', did not encourage originality in the designers of the sets in which he played out his solipsist fantasies; it is thus a vindication of their professionalism that the interiors of Neuschwanstein, Linderhof and Herrenchiemsee are full of texture, variety and conviction.

Luining, Andreas Luining was active in Vienna in about 1589. He published some sixty plates of ornament for engraving on silver. They include delicate GROTESQUES, foliage, fruit, flowers, medallion heads and STRAPWORK. Luining also engraved portraits of DÜRER and the Emperor RUDOLF II.

Lurçat, André (1894–1970) Born at Bruyères in the Vosges, the younger brother of Jean LURÇAT, Lurçat became a leading MODERN architect in Paris in the 1920s after studying at the École des Beaux-Arts. *Répertoire du goût moderne* (1929) included three offices by Lurçat with simple blockish furniture, lighting and an amusing chromed-steel plant-stand supporting a cactus. Lurçat also designed tubular-steel furniture for THONET. His book *Architecture* (1929) encapsulated the Modern line; he later published a five-volume work of architectural theory, *Formes, composition et lois d'harmonie* (1953–7).

Lurçat, Jean (1892–1966) Born at Bruyères in the Vosges, the son of a postmaster, Lurçat gave up medicine in 1911 to study under Victor PROUVÉ and Jacques GRUBER. In 1912 he moved to Paris, and in 1914 determined to devote himself to mural painting, a project interrupted by the war. From 1917 he designed needlework pictures for his mother and others. During the 1920s Lurçat was mainly active as a painter, but in 1933 he designed his first Aubusson tapestry and in 1936 his first tapestry for the Gobelins factory. In 1938 he designed chair covers to accompany his tapestry suite, Les Illusions d'Icare, and in the same year saw for the first time the GOTHIC Apocalypse tapestries in Angers, which exercised a major influence on his later designs. He was in 1939 appointed permanent designer to the Aubusson factory and in 1940 collaborated on design with André Derain (1880–1954) and with Raoul DUFY, sharing an exhibition with the latter in New York in 1942. In 1945 at the end of the war, during which he had been active in the Resistance, Lurçat became founder president of the association of tapestry designers, and thenceforward until his death he was involved in an endless series of exhibitions, conferences and other activities as the protagonist of the tapestry revival, which his *Tapisserie Française* (1947), translated as *Designing Tapestry* (London, 1950), helped to promote. In 1961 he became founder president of the Lausanne Centre International de la Tapisserie. Lurçat's tapestry designs rejoice in natural forms – birds, fish, animals and trees, with a particular predilection for stars, suns and flames – and in a small palette of strong colours; his themes tend to be grandiloquent celebrations of life, nature and suchlike, inspired by his own poems, or those of Apollinaire and others. Lurçat also designed book illustrations, mosaics, ceramics executed from about 1950 by the Poterie Saint Vicens at Perpignan, and in about 1960

jewels for François Hugo of Paris and Patek Philippe of Geneva.

Luthmer, Ferdinand (1842–1921) Born in Cologne, Luthmer was from 1879 to 1912 director of the Kunstgewerbemuseum in Frankfurt, where he also directed the school of applied art. His designs included glass, for Fritz Heckert of Petersdorf (1873), interiors, goldsmiths' work, for example the civic plate of Frankfurt, and books. He was a prolific writer on the history of the decorative arts, and furniture in particular, but also published a number of books on the design of ornament, including *Flachornamente auf der Grundlage von Naturformen* (Karlsruhe, 1895), which contained eighteen highly competent chromolithographed plates of natural ornament.

Lutma, Johannnes (1587–1669) Born in Emden, East Friesland, Lutma was apprenticed to a goldsmith there. He seems to have been in Paris in 1615 but from 1620 was active as a goldsmith in Amsterdam. He executed many civic commissions, including an AURICULAR silver trowel for the laying of the foundation stone of the new Amsterdam Town Hall (1648) and the extraordinary auricular brass choir screen for the Nieuwe Kerk in about 1649. Lutma must have had some direct contact with Adam van VIANEN, whom he succeeded as the great master of the auricular style, developing Vianen's fleshy inventions to a further extreme of palpitating abstraction. His designs were recorded in two suites of prints, *Veelderhande Nieuwe Compartemente* (1653; six plates) and *Versheide Snakeryen* (1654; ten plates). The title 'Snakeryen' may be compared with that of Christoph JAMNITZER'S 'Schnacken'. Lutma was a friend of Rembrandt, who etched his portrait. A fine posthumous portrait was engraved by his son, Johannes Lutma (1624–89), a silversmith who also published *Einige nieuwe compartimente* (eleven plates), auricular cartouches in his father's style.

Lutyens, Sir Edwin Landseer (1869–1944) Born in London, the son of an animal painter, Lutyens entered the South Kensington School of Art in 1885. In 1887 he moved to the office of the architects Ernest George (1839–1922) and Harold Peto (1828–97). In 1889 Lutyens set up on his own as an architect. By 1900 he had built up a successful practice, designing country houses in a sophisticated Arts & Crafts style praised by MUTHESIUS. He did not however respond to Arts & Crafts idealists, describing ASHBEE as 'artist and furniture freakist . . . most to me distasteful'. Heathcote (1906) marked a return to classicism, and henceforth Lutyens revealed himself as a great MANNERIST architect, notably in Castle Drogo (1910–30), the Thiepval Arch (1926), The Viceroy's House at New Delhi (1912–31) and his scheme for Liverpool Cathedral (1929–41). In 1901 he designed a successful grand-piano case for Broadwoods. Lutyens also designed furniture for many of his buildings, ranging from RENAISSANCE-style oak in his own house, 29 Bloomsbury Square, London (1897), to Arts & Crafts oak for Deanery Garden, Sonning (1899–1902), to 'CHIPPENDALE' chairs for the Midland Bank (1929) and to BAROQUE stateroom furniture and jokey painted nursery lights for New Delhi (1930). Queen Mary's Dolls' House (1920–24) is a miniature compendium of Lutyens interior design.

Lux, Wolff Lux was the publisher of the only 16th-century Austrian lace pattern-book, *Mödel Büchel* (Vienna, 1596), a modest production with simple geometric designs, probably by a woman. It is also the first book published in a German-speaking country to show designs for the sort of lace which had spread from Italy, and Venice in particular, all over Europe.

M

Maandblad voor Beeldende Kunsten (1924–48) This general art magazine, published in Amsterdam, contains useful information on design, for instance articles on NIEUWENHUIS (1924) and on the DEUTSCHE WERKBUND'S STUTTGART 1927 EXHIBITION (1928).

Macdonald, Frances (1874–1921) Born in Newcastle-under-Lyme, Frances Macdonald moved to Glasgow in about 1890 with her sister, Margaret. From about 1891 they studied at the Glasgow School of Art, where in about 1893 they met Herbert J. MACNAIR and Charles Rennie MACKINTOSH. The style of the sisters, heavily influenced by Toorop and Beardsley, is hard to distinguish. In about 1894 they opened a studio in Glasgow where they entertained other artists and designers, and practised embroidery, metalwork, gesso, book illustration and illumination, and stained glass. Their work was shown at the 1896 ARTS & CRAFTS EXHIBITION and, with that of Mackintosh, was the subject of an article in the 'STUDIO' (1897). In 1899 Frances married Herbert J. MacNair, and moved to Liverpool, where he taught at the university. Both sisters participated in the Vienna 1900 and TURIN 1902 EXHIBITIONS. In 1903 Frances designed the cover of a book on dress by Anna, wife of Hermann MUTHESIUS. From 1907 she taught enamelling, gold- and silversmithing and metalwork at the Glasgow School of Art.

Macdonald, Margaret (1865–1933) Born in Newcastle-under-Lyme, Margaret Macdonald's career was almost identical to that of her younger sister, Frances, until she married Charles Rennie MACKINTOSH in 1900. Her forte was painting and two-dimensional design. In 1897 an 1893 watercolour, *Ill Omen*, was illustrated in the 'YELLOW BOOK', and in May 1902 she designed a cover for 'DEUTSCHE KUNST UND DEKORATION'. From her marriage she closely collaborated in Mackintosh's work, particularly in textiles and painted or gesso wall decoration. Like him she designed textiles for Foxton's & Sefton's in London from about 1916 to 1923. Margaret Macdonald has been accused of encouraging the decorative and therefore less serious aspects of her husband's work, but there is limited evidence for this view, which reflects Mackintosh's canonization by historians of the MODERN movement.

McGrath, Raymond (1903–77) McGrath studied architecture at the Sydney School of Architecture from 1921. In 1926 he travelled to England on a scholarship and became a research student of architecture in Cambridge, where in 1929 to 1930 he remodelled a house, Finella, for Mansfield Forbes using glass and the metal-faced plywood made by Jack Pritchard of Venesta. Also in 1930 McGrath won the 'ARCHITECTURAL REVIEW' interior design competition. At this period he met Charlotte PERRIAND, Wells COATES and Serge CHERMAYEFF. From 1930 to 1932 McGrath was engaged on the designing of strikingly MODERN interiors for Broadcasting House. He also designed wallpapers for Sandersons, radio cabinets for Ekco, unit furniture for Easiwork, interiors for Atalanta aircraft and a sales trophy for Austin Reed Ltd. His *Twentieth Century Houses* (1934) and *Glass in Architecture and Decoration* (1937) helped to promote the Modern style.

Mackintosh,   Charles   Rennie (1868–1928) Born in Glasgow, the son of a police superintendent, Mackintosh was apprenticed in 1884 to a local architect, John Hutchison. In 1889 he joined the architectural firm of Honeyman & Keppie, where he became friendly with a fellow draughtsman, H. J. MACNAIR. Reacting against the Glasgow classical tradition, Mackintosh displayed an early interest in GOTHIC and Scottish architecture. He was a successful student, winning prizes, notably the Alexander Thomson Travelling Scholarship (1890) which took him to Italy, France and Belgium in 1901. By 1892 Mackintosh had developed a fully ART NOUVEAU decorative style, using elongation, abstraction and rhythmic polychromy, a style much influenced by the appearance of the 'STUDIO' in 1893, with its illustrations of the work of VOYSEY, Beardsley and, especially, the Java-born symbolist painter Jan Toorop (1859–1928). At this time Mackintosh was also much affected by LETHABY's *Architecture, Mysticism and Myth* (1892), and in 1893 he praised the work of R. Norman SHAW, J. F. BENTLEY, BODLEY and SEDDING among others. From 1894 he made several English tours sketching Gothic and vernacular buildings. The energetic head of the Glasgow School of Art, Francis H. Newbery, and his wife, Jessie NEWBERY, encouraged Mackintosh and his friend, MacNair, to join forces with the Macdonald sisters, Margaret and Frances. 'The Four', as they became

known, executed posters, metalwork and other decorative work, developing a common style. Posters such as Mackintosh's for the *Scottish Musical Review* (1896) publicized its work, which attracted much criticism for its affectation and abstraction when shown at the 1896 ARTS & CRAFTS EXHIBITION. By this date Mackintosh had begun to design furniture for Messrs Guthrie & Wells of Glasgow. In 1897 he won the competition for the new Glasgow School of Art building, whose first stage was erected from 1897 to 1899, and the second, designed in 1906, from 1907 to 1909. Also in 1897 Gleeson White, editor of the *Studio*, who had admired the work of The Four at the 1896 Arts & Crafts Exhibition, published two articles on their work and that of Talwin MORRIS. Again in 1897 Mackintosh was commissioned by Miss Cranston to decorate her tea-rooms, first doing the wall decorations for the Buchanan Street rooms, while George WALTON designed the furniture, and next designing furniture for the Argyle Street rooms, where Walton did the walls. In 1898 an article about the group appeared in Alexander Koch's magazine, 'DEKORATIVE KUNST', and henceforward Mackintosh was better known abroad than in England. His foreign fame was confirmed at the 1900 Vienna Secession Exhibition, where he designed for the Scottish Section a setting and furniture, illustrated in 'Die KUNST', whose refinement and invention caused a sensation. In Vienna, Mackintosh met and was fêted by Josef HOFFMANN and his fellow Secessionists. Also in 1900 Mackintosh married Margaret Macdonald, for whose parents he had designed a drawing-room at Dunglass Castle in 1899, and for his Glasgow flat and for Windyhill, his first major house, built in 1900, Mackintosh designed interior ensembles, including furniture. In 1901 'VER SACRUM', the Secession magazine, was devoted to

Glasgow and Mackintosh entered the competition organized by Alexander Koch's magazine, 'Zeitschrift für INNEN-DEKORATION', to design a house for an art-lover: he did not keep to the rules and was therefore awarded only a special prize, BAILLIE SCOTT winning the second prize, a first not being given. Mackintosh's project was published by Koch with an introduction by MUTHESIUS, and the illustrations were shown at the TURIN 1902 EXHIBITION, where Mackintosh was responsible for the very successful Scottish section, which was illustrated both in *Decorative Kunst* and in 'ARTE ITALIANA DECORATIVA ED INDUSTRIALE'. Also in 1902 Mackintosh was commissioned to design a music room in Vienna for Fritz Wärndorfer, who would be the future financial backer of the WIENER WERKSTÄTTE (1903), and, recommended by Talwin Morris, designed a house and furniture, Hill House, Helensburgh, for W. W. Blackie, the publisher. In 1903 work by Mackintosh was shown in Moscow, and illustrated in 'MIR ISKUSSTVA'. From 1901 he had worked on Miss Cranston's Ingram Street tea-rooms, and in 1904 he designed her Willow Street rooms, and this project, the climax of his decorative style, was illustrated in *Decorative Kunst* (1905); also in 1905 'DEUTSCHE KUNST UND DEKORATION' published thirty-five illustrations of Hill House. In the same year Hermann Muthesius, a personal friend of Mackintosh's, devoted a chapter to his work in *Das Englische Haus*. But Mackintosh's last Glasgow masterpiece, the School of Art Library, completed in 1909, received no publicity, and in 1914 Mackintosh, difficult, drinking and neglected, left Glasgow for ever. He settled in Chelsea in 1916. From 1916 to 1917 he designed graphic display matter for W. J. Bassett-Lowke, for whom he also transformed a dull terrace house, 78 Derngate, Northampton, with highly rectilinear furniture and decorations reflecting Viennese influence. Parts of this scheme were later transported to New-ways, the house designed for Bassett-Lowke by Peter BEHRENS in 1925. While in London Mackintosh also executed textile designs, some produced by Foxton's & Sefton's. In 1923 he left for France, where he painted until his death from cancer in London in 1928. Although much promoted from the 1930s onwards as a precursor of the MODERN movement, it was Mackintosh's skill as a designer of elegantly ornamental ensembles – from lettering, furniture, cutlery, jewellery, stained glass, carpets and wrought iron to gravestones – which received most contemporary attention. He does not seem to have shared the Arts & Crafts concern with honesty or sturdiness of construction (he habitually stained or painted wood and his furniture is sometimes structurally unsound), but rather concentrated on formal effects, usually the product of a contrast between attenuated forms, either rectilinear or gently curved or tapered, and squat rounded decorative motifs. The rose was a favourite device, and a mystic delicacy pervaded many of his rooms. Since 1975 Mackintosh's furniture has been reproduced in Italy, and his lettering and decorations were among the main ingredients of the Art Nouveau revival of the 1970s.

Mackmurdo, Arthur Heygate (1851–1942) Born in London, the son of a wealthy chemical manufacturer, Mackmurdo began to study architecture in 1869. In 1873 he entered the office of the great Gothic architect James Brooks (1825–1901) and began to attend RUSKIN's drawing classes in Oxford. In 1874 Mackmurdo went to Italy as companion and assistant to Ruskin. On his return Mackmurdo set up practice in London, but soon returned to Italy to study classical and RENAISSANCE architecture. In 1877 he was active in the foundation of the Society for the Protection of Ancient Buildings and thus came in contact with William MORRIS, whom he later advised on the establishment of the Kelmscott Press. In about 1880 Mackmurdo met Whistler. Mackmurdo offered in 1882 to teach at Ruskin's St George's Guild in Sheffield, but instead founded his own Century Guild. Its only formal members were himself and the young Herbert HORNE, who had joined his practice in 1883; Selwyn IMAGE and Clement HEATON were among those closely involved. The purpose of the Guild was 'to render all branches of art the sphere no longer of the tradesman but the artist'. In 1883 Mackmurdo's *Wren's City Churches*, a topographical work, was published by G. Allen, Ruskin's publisher; its extraordinary title-page was composed of undulating flowers and leaves probably influenced by William Blake (1757–1827). Mackmurdo used a similar design for the back of a chair made by Collinson & Lock; its plagiarization in a design by Fred Miller published in 'Der MODERNE STIL' (1899) is a graphic demonstration of its anticipation of ART NOUVEAU ornament. Also in 1883 Mackmurdo set up a workshop in Enfield. In 1884 the Century Guild published the first volume of its journal, the *Hobby Horse*, and showed a Music Room at the London International Health Exhibition. Mackmurdo was involved in the 1885 Home Art and Industries Exhibition and showed at the LIVERPOOL 1886 EXHIBITION (Music Room and a stand for Cope Brothers, tobacco importers) and the Manchester 1887 Jubilee Exhibition (an Entrance Hall based on the Guild's extensive work at Pownall Hall from 1886). Mackmurdo's furniture used flowing natural forms in its carved and inlaid decoration and in upholstery fabrics, but its struc-

ture tended to be rectilinear, with mannered mouldings and cornices. Mackmurdo also designed wallpapers, embroidery, light fittings, metalwork and book-plates. VOYSEY was strongly influenced by his designs. In 1888 Mackmurdo dissolved the Century Guild and his partnership with Herbert Horne came to an end in 1890. In 1888 he was involved with Walter CRANE in the foundation of the National Association for the Advancement of Art. He also knew ASHBEE, and his house at 20 Fitzroy Street, London, the erstwhile headquarters of the Century Guild, continued to be a centre of art and music; Arnold Dolmetsch (1858–1940) gave concerts there from 1892 and Mackmurdo lent the young BRANGWYN a studio in the house. Mackmurdo continued active as an architect up to about 1906, but thenceforward his main energies were devoted to theories of social reform, which he published in *The Human Hive* (1926) and *A People's Charter* (1933). In 1904 Reginald Blomfield rightly attributed the first beginnings of Art Nouveau ornament to Mackmurdo and Horne in the 'MAGAZINE OF ART'.

Maclise, Daniel (1806–70) A painter, born in Cork, Maclise was involved in 1843 in the fresco decorations of the garden pavilion at Buckingham Palace, planned by Ludwig GRUNER; he also executed frescoes at the New Palace of Westminster from 1845 to 1865. In 1848 Maclise designed a bracelet for Summerly's Art-Manufactures, in 1859 the Turner Prize Medal of the Royal Academy, and in 1862 the Prize Medal for the London International Exhibition. He helped to illustrate the Moxon *Tennyson* (1857), and his *Story of the Norman Conquest*, engraved by Gruner, was issued by the Art Union of London in 1866.

MacNair, Herbert J. (1868–1953) Born near Glasgow from a military family, MacNair, although intended for an engineer, studied painting at Rouen, before being apprenticed in about 1888 to the architect John Honeyman. He was a draughtsman with Honeyman & Keppie when Charles Rennie MAC-KINTOSH joined them in 1889, and the two young men struck up a close friendship. They both studied at the Glasgow School of Art and were introduced by its head, Francis H. Newbery, to the two Macdonald sisters, Margaret and Frances, in about 1893. 'The Four' soon formed a close-knit group. Mac-Nair may have been the first to experiment with the highly symbolic and tortuously decorative ART NOUVEAU style practised by The Four, given its earliest public showing at the 1896 ARTS & CRAFTS EXHIBITION. Already in 1895 MacNair, an independent spirit, had resigned from Honeyman & Keppie, and established himself as an 'architect and designer' in Glasgow. He specialized in designs for furniture and the applied arts, although two drawings were published in the 'YELLOW BOOK' (1896) and a book-plate in the 'STUDIO' (1897). In 1897 MacNair was, with Talwin MORRIS, the subject of one of Gleeson White's two articles on Glasgow designers in the *Studio*. In 1898 this was followed up in an article in Alexander Koch's 'DEKORATIVE KUNST'. Also in 1898 MacNair was appointed Instructor in Decorative Design at the School of Architecture and Applied Art at Liverpool University, and in 1899 he married Frances MACDONALD. In 1900 they participated in the Vienna Secession Exhibition, and in 1902 in the TURIN EXHIBITION, on both occasions under the aegis of Mackintosh. MacNair remained at Liverpool until about 1906, and continued his activity as a designer of furniture and interiors. After his wife's death in 1921, however, he gave up his artistic career. MacNair's style was a subdued and on occasion quirky version of Mackintosh's, but he was a gifted and versatile designer, not a mere follower of his more famous friend.

MacQuoid, Thomas Robert (1820–1912) Born in London, MacQuoid showed watercolours at the Royal Academy from 1838 to 1894. He was trained as an architect under H. E. Kendall (1805–85) with WARING. MacQuoid designed an elaborate bookcase shown by Holland & Sons at the LONDON 1851 EXHIBITION. He also illustrated *Robinson Crusoe* (1864), designed initial letters for *Rhymes and Roundelayes* (1875) and worked on the *Graphic* and the *Illustrated London News*. His son, Percy MacQuoid, became a painter and a celebrated pundit on antique furniture and silver.

Maes, Godfried (1649–1700) Born in Antwerp, Maes was active there as a painter and book illustrator. He also designed a suite of tapestries, on the four continents, accomplished BAROQUE GROTESQUES woven by Jan van der Beurcht of Antwerp.

Magasin de Meubles, Le (1865–75) Subtitled *Journal d'Ameublement*, this Paris magazine published forty-eight plates annually of furniture designs in all styles executed by its editor/designer, Victor Quetin. It provides an excellent index of prosperous French taste and was a dominant competitor for the 'MONITEUR DE L'AMEUBLEMENT'.

Magazine of Art, The (1878–1904) Prompted by the PARIS 1878 EXHIBITION and published by Cassell & Co. this periodical included Lewis F. DAY and Henry HOLIDAY among its early contributors. Its editors included M. H. Spielmann and W. E. Henley

(1849–1903). HERKOMER supplied a poster and later writers included Aymer Vallance. The *Magazine* was a precursor of the 'STUDIO' and, although overtaken by it, a very valuable source on design matters, especially from 1895.

Maggi, Giovanni (1566–1618) Born in Rome, Maggi was there active as a painter and engraver. He specialized in views of Rome, publishing two series in 1600 and 1618. In 1604 Maggi presented to Cardinal Francesco Maria Del Monte a four-volume collection of some 2,000 designs for glass vessels. Del Monte was an important patron of the arts who acted as an agent for Grand Duke Ferdinando I de' Medici and Maggi's designs were probably intended for manufacture in Florence. Some are inspired by BUONTALENTI and LIGOZZI's designs, others are Maggi's own invention. Simple and practical designs are outnumbered by others which run the gamut of MANNERIST invention using every combination of distorted, NATURAL, GROTESQUE and perverse forms. The work was entitled *Bicchierografia*.

Magistretti, Vico Born in Milan in 1920, Magistretti graduated as an architect there in 1945 and thenceforward worked as an architect, town planner and designer. A beech and leather armchair for Cassina (1964), a plastic light for Artemide (1968), the Selene moulded glass-fibre chair for Artemide (1968) and the Broomstick range of furniture (1978) are among the better-known designs in a prolific output much publicized in 'OTTAGONO' and elsewhere.

Magyar Iparművészet (1897–1909) This Hungarian applied arts and design magazine, published in Budapest, supplies not only an excellent coverage of the rapid growth of ART NOUVEAU in Hungary, but also good articles on for-

eign topics, for instance the PARIS 1900 EXHIBITION and Walter CRANE (1900).

Mair, Wolf Mair became a master goldsmith in Nuremberg in 1552 and died there in 1592. He published a suite of six plates of small black ornaments for enamel in 1586. They are in a basic stretched GROTESQUE manner typical of this Nuremberg genre.

Maîtres de l'Affiche, Les (1896–1900) This monthly magazine, edited from Paris by Roger Marx, published splendid colour illustrations of posters designed by Jules CHÉRET, GRASSET, Lautrec and others, including American, English and Belgian designers.

Majorelle, Louis (1859–1926) Born in Toul, Majorelle was trained as a painter, spending two years at the École des Beaux-Arts in Paris from 1877. In 1879 his father died and Majorelle returned to Nancy to take over his cabinet-making and ceramic business, founded in 1860. Majorelle concentrated on producing furniture, at first mainly in the ROCOCO style. However, in the 1890s he came increasingly under the influence of GALLÉ and began to design in NATURALISTIC ART NOUVEAU style. At the PARIS 1900 EXHIBITION Majorelle showed a room whose theme was the waterlily. Although he sometimes used Gallé's literally naturalistic carved details and marquetry, Majorelle's designs were usually more elegant and abstract than those of his mentor, while his use of gilt-bronze mounts on furniture echoed rococo prototypes. In 1901 he was a Vice-President of the newly founded École de Nancy and at the Paris 1903 École de Nancy Exhibition he showed furniture and gilt-bronze lights alongside Victor PROUVÉ, Émile ANDRÉ, Gallé and others. By 1914 his forms were more subdued and rectilinear. His factory was burned in 1916 but he started production again in Nancy in 1918 and by the time of the PARIS 1925 EXHIBITION, where he served on the jury, he was working in a subdued ART DÉCO style.

Malaine, Joseph Laurent (1745–1809) The son of a Tournai painter, Malaine succeeded JACQUES as '*peintre de fleurs*' at the Gobelins tapestry factory in 1786. He also worked as a wallpaper designer for Arthur & Robert in Paris. After the French revolution he retreated to Alsace, where he designed floral wallpapers for the firm of Jean Zuber in Rixheim. In 1798 he returned to Paris.

Mallet, Robert (1810–81) Born in Dublin, the son of an ironfounder from Devonshire, Mallet became a partner in his father's works in 1831 and built it up to a great concern. He was an important innovative engineer, publishing numerous papers; in 1865 to 1869 he edited the *Practical Mechanics Journal*. Mallet designed a number of cast-iron chairs, brackets and X-supports for tables published in LOUDON's *Encyclopaedia*. The majority had GOTHIC detailing but the structure of many was brutally radical.

Mallet-Stevens, Robert (1886–1945) Born in Paris, the son of an art-historian, Mallet-Stevens studied between 1905 and 1910 at the École Spéciale d'Architecture. He was an admirer of MACKINTOSH and also of Josef HOFFMANN, whose Palais Stoclet belonged to his uncle. His earliest interior designs, published in the Belgian journal *Le Home*, display Hoffmann's influence. Among his early friends were Frantz and Francis JOURDAIN. From 1912 Mallet-Stevens showed interiors and furniture at the Salon d'Automne. From 1923 he was involved in the journal *L'Architecture Moderne*, and in the same year his first building, a villa for the Vicomte de Noailles at Hyères, included stained glass by Joël and Jan Martel, and furniture designed by DJO-BOURGEOIS and Pierre CHAREAU. In 1924 Mallet-Stevens designed a villa for Jacques DOUCET, which was not executed, met the painter Fernand Léger (1881–1955) and also established links with the Dutch DE STIJL group. In 1925 he wrote on Frank Lloyd WRIGHT in 'WENDINGEN' and designed several pavilions at the PARIS EXHIBITION. In 1929 he became founder President of the Union des Artistes Modernes. Two books on his work published in 1930 and 1931 confirmed Mallet-Stevens's status as a member of the MODERN establishment. At the PARIS 1937 EXHIBITION he designed several pavilions, and in the same year he published a book on modern stained glass. In his own furniture designs Mallet-Stevens used modern materials such as aluminium and steel; he also encouraged the work of other Modern designers. He was, as might be expected, strongly opposed to ornament.

Malton, Thomas (1726–1801) Born in London, Malton was active as a cabinetmaker in the Strand up to at least 1761. In 1761 he showed at the Free Society of Artists two drawings of St Martin-in-the-Fields, and thenceforth he showed at the Incorporated Society of Artists and, from 1772 to 1785, at the Royal Academy. His *The Royal Road to Geometry* (1774) was a mathematics textbook; its second edition (1793) included a criticism of SHERATON's *Drawing Book*. From 1772 to 1780 Malton gave lectures on PERSPECTIVE at his house in Poland Street; J. B. PAPWORTH was a pupil. His *Compleat Treatise on Perspective* (1775, second edition 1779, *An Appendix or Second Part*, 1783) was dedicated to the President and Members of the Royal Academy; the architects ADAM, STUART and

James WYATT subscribed. The *Treatise* included a section specifically aimed at 'the Cabinet-maker and Upholder', illustrated with fine plates showing a bookcase, an organ, a table and two chairs (1775), and a pedestal and vase, a pier table, a dressing-table, a lady's secretary, a bed and a chair (1779). Malton died in Dublin, where he had retreated to escape financial difficulties.

Mannerism The term 'mannerism' has been current since the 1920s to describe certain aspects of 16th-century art and design (mainly Italian), by extension to cover all or almost all 16th-century art and design, and by analogy to categorize other periods or aspects of art and design similar in detail or general character to 16th-century mannerism. The word mannerism, or rather *manierismo*, first used in Italy in 1792, derives from the Italian *maniera* (style). *Maniera* was a quality much prized in the 16th century by, among others, RAPHAEL and VASARI. It connoted grace, learning, virtuosity, refinement and sophistication. The artistic perils of such qualities were soon recognized and 17th-century critics such as Bellori used *maniera* to denote self-indulgent, self-conscious and empty artificiality, which sundered art from its proper inspiration in nature. Ornament and design were ideal vehicles for the display of *maniera* and in this field at least it is over-restrictive to confine the term to Italy. The development of the GROTESQUE from about 1500 made available to mannerist designers a language of ornament which was divorced from reality but sanctioned by antiquity. MORESQUE and STRAPWORK ornament, the latter a mannerist invention, lent themselves to virtuoso adaptation and PERSPECTIVE was also suited to ornamental exploitation. Mannerist craftsmen such as Benvenuto CELLINI were encouraged to combine rich and rare materials with ever-increasing virtuosity. Mannerist scholars such as the STRADAS devised iconographic schemes of bewildering complexity, often using the new language of EMBLEMS to salt designs with extra layers of meaning. Courtly patronage was essential to the development of such a hot-house style. The Gonzagas employed Giulio ROMANO at Mantua from 1524, François I of France employed ROSSO at Fontainebleau from 1530. BRONZINO, Vasari, Strada and BUONTALENTI were among the many who served the Medici in Florence, and Cosimo de' Medici was a patron of the FLORENCE ACCADEMIA DEL DISEGNO, which was dominated by mannerist ideas. The greatest individual patron of mannerist design was the Emperor RUDOLF II, who attracted designers from all over Europe to his court at Prague in about 1600. By that date mannerist design was the style of mercantile centres such as Antwerp, Nuremberg and Augsburg and the prints of designers such as Jacques Androuet DUCERCEAU, Hans VREDEMAN DE VRIES, Virgil SOLIS and many others had made mannerist ornament available to craftsmen everywhere. Apart from the ornamental ingredients already mentioned mannerist designers revelled in attenuated classical architecture, in elegantly elongated nudes, in perversely distorted monsters, and in scaly crustaceans and slimy amphibians. The latter taste lay directly behind the development of the AURICULAR style, but the wider influence of mannerist ornament was such that there are few later developments in ornament, apart from the GOTHIC, Chinese and Japanese manners, which were not derived from or anticipated by mannerist designers. Certainly the vocabulary of BAROQUE ornament was essentially mannerist, even if the language was different. In the mid to late 19th century, designers such as MOREL-LADEUIL and M. L. E.

SOLON worked in a highly sophisticated mannerist revival style. More recently much Post-MODERN design has been mannerist in the widest sense. The detailed vocabulary of 16th-century mannerism awaits revival.

Manwaring, Robert A cabinet-maker, Manwaring published *The Carpenter's Compleat Guide to the Whole System of Gothic Railing* (1765), fourteen plates of GOTHIC gates and railing, five signed by Manwaring and two by MÜNTZ, with two extra plates by CRUNDEN. Manwaring stated in the preface that Müntz had given him his designs before leaving England, and these stand out by their crispness and confidence above the engaging but amateurish inventions of Manwaring. *The Cabinet and Chair-Maker's Real Friend and Companion* (1765; forty plates) comprised about 100 designs for chairs in the ROCOCO, Chinese, Gothic and rustic styles. Manwaring stated that the latter, which imitated natural tree branches, were 'the only ones of the kind that ever were published'. His lengthy technical introduction included quotations from CHIPPENDALE and Müntz. *The Chair-Maker's Guide* (1766; seventy-five plates), by Manwaring 'and others', incorporates as its first twenty-eight plates chair designs earlier issued as the first part of *Genteel Household Furniture in the Present Taste* (1760), issued by a Society of Upholsterers, Cabinet-Makers &c. Two of these are by INCE & Mayhew, and the later plates in the *Guide* include designs by Chippendale, DARLY and COPLAND. Manwaring's own designs make up for their lack of elegance in variety and invention. SHERATON, not surprisingly, considered them worthless.

Maratti, Carlo (1625–1713) Born in Camerano, Maratti trained as a painter in Rome under Andrea Sacchi (1599–1661) and later became the leading representative of the classical tradition there. In the 1680s Maratti designed the silver plates presented by the heirs of Cardinal Lazzaro Pallavicini to Cosimo III, Grand Duke of Tuscany. His designs were influenced by RAPHAEL and POLIDORO DA CARAVAGGIO, drawings by whom Maratti is known to have owned.

Marchant, Pierre Marchant was active as an engraver in Paris where, in 1601, he published a suite of small black ornaments for jewellers (six plates). In 1623 he designed a suite of not very accomplished COSSE-DE-POIS sprays for jewellery (seven plates).

Marcou, François Born in Paris in 1595, Marcou was active there as a gunsmith. His *Plusieurs Pièces d'Arquebuzeries* (fifteen plates) contains designs for the decoration of guns in a lively but incoherent scrolly floral style derived from earlier enamel designs, with an admixture of GROTESQUE masks and monsters. It appeared in or after 1657 and was engraved by C. Jacquinet, who also engraved the contemporary pattern-book of THURAINE and Le Hollandois, and was probably part designer. Marcou's designs were later copied by Alexandre de Rochetaille, 'Armurier Ordinaire du Roy', in a six-plate suite, *Divers Ornemens* (1687).

Mare, André (1887–1932) Born in Argentan, Mare was trained as a painter at the Académie Julian. From about 1910 he was active as a designer, producing bookbindings and furniture, and at the 1912 Salon d'Automne he showed the controversial Maison Cubiste, for which he designed the furniture and wallpapers and coordinated the work of Roger de la Fresnaye, Marie Laurencin, Maurice Marinot and others. In 1919 Mare entered a partnership with the architect Louis SÜE to found the Compagnie des Arts Français, in which he was active until 1928. After this Mare returned to painting.

Maria, Nicolas Joseph A wood-carver in Paris, Maria became a member of the Académie de Saint-Luc there in 1751 and a director in 1763. He died in 1802. His *Premier Livre de desseins de Jouaillerie et Bijouterie* (1765; thirty-six plates) was engraved by BABEL. It comprised designs for jewellery of all types, and for snuff-boxes, fans, buckles and handles. They are either NATURALISTIC or NEO-CLASSICAL, or a combination, with the exception of a few ROCOCO handles. Their competence was paid the compliment of copies by J. R. LUCOTTE in the plates on jewellery (1771) in Diderot and D'Alembert's *Encyclopédie*.

Marigny, Abel-François Poisson, Marquis de (1727–81) The brother of Madame de Pompadour (1721–64), Marigny early showed an interest in architecture and geometry. In 1745 it was decided that he should succeed Le Normant de Tournehem as Directeur Général des Bâtiments and in 1749 he was sent on an educational trip to Italy with the architect Jacques Germain Soufflot, C.-N. COCHIN, and the Abbé Le Blanc (1706–81), all early champions of NEO-CLASSICISM. On his return to Paris in 1751 Marigny was appointed Directeur Général, Le Normant having died; he held the post until 1774. In 1755 Marigny had Soufflot appointed director of the Gobelins tapestry factory and of the Savonnerie carpet factory. The Gobelins suite of Les Amours des Dieux was first woven for Marigny after paintings in his possession by François BOUCHER, Van LOO, PIERRE and VIEN. Soufflot designed neo-classical interiors for Marigny's house in the Rue Saint-Thomas-du-Louvre in the mid-

1760s and for his villa at Roule from 1768 to 1771; the upholsterer Antoine Godefroy supplied neo-classical seat furniture to both houses. In 1764 Marigny inherited his sister's notable collections. Although himself not an extreme Grecian, Marigny played a key role in the advance of neo-classicism.

Marillier, Clément Pierre (1740–1808) Born in Dijon, Marillier was there a pupil of a painter named Morlot, to whom he dedicated a suite of twelve NEO-CLASSICAL trophies published in Paris by Mondhare. In Paris, Marillier studied under the painter Noel HALLÉ. In 1763 Mondhare published Marillier's *Recueil de Nouveau Ornements* (twelve plates), designs for secular and ecclesiastical metalwork dedicated to '*Messieurs les Orfevres, Fondeurs et Ciseleurs*'; they apply neo-classical ornament to mainly BAROQUE forms and are among the earliest designs in this manner. Marillier later became one of the leading French neo-classical book illustrators and decorators, active from 1772 to 1804. In 1782 he designed decorations to Abbé de Lille's *Les Jardins*.

Marmi, Giacinto Maria A member of a Florentine family of decorators, Marmi worked for the Medici from at least 1658, and was still active in Florence in 1697. His designs included tables, cabinets, caskets, beds, VASES and schemes of interior decoration in a rich BAROQUE style. He was sometimes assisted by his son, Giovan Battista Marmi (1656–86), a pupil of FOGGINI and Ciro FERRI, who in 1685 designed an altar for Santa Lucia delle Rovinate.

Marot, Daniel Born in Paris in about 1663, the son of Jean MAROT and the nephew of the royal cabinet-maker, Pierre Golle, Daniel Marot was a pupil of his father. He was responsible for prints commemorating the funeral of

Maria Teresa in 1683, and others after Jean I BERAIN, Louis XIV's official designer, and it thus seems probable that he was involved in the royal design establishment. Upon the revocation of the Edict of Nantes in 1685 Marot, a Huguenot, entered the service of Prince William of Orange, Williàm III of England (1650–1702), who in 1698 granted him a pension, confirmed by a States General after the death of the Prince. Marot lived in both The Hague and in Amsterdam until 1713, when he settled in the former. He died in 1752. From as early as 1689 to 1706 he spent periods in England, working at Hampton Court, Petworth and Montagu House. Although titled 'Architecte de Guillaume III roi de la grand Bretagne', Marot was mainly active as an interior designer, his greatest achievement being his decoration of Prince William's palace Het Loo, where he worked with the architect Jacob Roman (1640–1716) from 1685 to 1702. His later works included the Huis Schuylenburch in The Hague (1715) and involvement at Kasteel Duivenvoorde (1717) and Huis ten Bosch (1734). Marot published numerous designs in suites of six plates, the earliest dated suite being *Dessins de Carrosses* (1698); his *Œuvres* were collected at The Hague in 1703 in 108 plates, in Amsterdam in 1713 in 126 plates, and in a further Dutch edition in two volumes with a total of 237 plates. Marot's designs include VASES, doors, chimneypieces, clocks, panelling, ironwork, goldsmiths' work, upholstery, beds, embroidery and so on. His style is basically the French court style of the late 17th century, as developed by LE BRUN, Berain and Jean LE PAUTRE, but Marot enlivened his prototypes with a plethora of porcelain, CHINOISERIES, fringes, tassels, flowers, swags and scrolls. His most characteristic designs are exaggeratedly tall and elaborate state beds, which are the culmination of BAROQUE upholstery. However, Marot's originality consisted more in his ability to coordinate and control every element of a palatial baroque interior, even designing Delft pots, rather than in specific inventions. His influence was widespread, especially in the Low Countries, England and Germany, but he never fully adapted to the ROCOCO style and was in his later years outmoded.

Marot, Jean (1619–79) Marot, the son of a *menuisier*, was active in Paris as an architect but is best known as an engraver of architectural subjects. His ornamental prints include some fifty plates of ironwork, some forty-five plates of VASES, large and small, and several suites of chimneypieces, doors, ceilings, alcoves and mouldings. Marot also designed iron railings and gates for Notre Dame in Paris and for the Château de Maisons. *Tombeaux ou Mosolées* (eleven plates, one dated 1640) comprises tombs formed as elaborate architectural structures peopled by elongated figures, a throw-back to J. A. DU-CERCEAU, but Marot's designs are usually bold and vigorous – even heavy – with a generous use of swags, gadrooning, masks, etc. Many were reissued by Mariette in the 18th century. Marot also acted as an engraver for other designers, for example FRANCARD's *Portes Cochères de Menuiserie*.

Mason, Henry W. A book of drawings in the VICTORIA & ALBERT MUSEUM is entitled *Selection of Ornamental Work Designed & modelled by Henry Mason 1857*. It includes designs for cast-iron furniture and stoves in the NATURALISTIC style shown at the LONDON 1862 EXHIBITION. Later, Mason seems to have been active as a draughtsman rather than as a designer, working for Cox & Son, among others.

Masreliez, Jacques Adrien (1717–1806)

Born in Grenoble, Masreliez was trained as a decorative carver. In 1748 he was summoned to Stockholm, where he taught at the Academy and from 1750 to 1775 worked as a sculptor and designer of interior decorations and furniture in the Swedish royal palaces, including the Stockholm Palace, and Drottningholm. He sometimes worked to the designs of HÅRLEMAN and REHN, and spanned the transition from a heavy ROCOCO style to full-blown NEO-CLASSICISM.

Masreliez, Louis Adrien (1748–1810) Born in Paris, the son of J. A. MASRELIEZ, Louis Adrien Masreliez joined his father in Stockholm in 1753. He was a child prodigy, winning his first medal at the Stockholm Academy in 1759. He travelled in 1769 to Paris, thence in 1770 to Bologna, and then stayed from 1774 to 1782 in Rome, where he became friendly with the painter Anton Raphael Mengs (1728–79). In 1783 Masreliez returned to Stockholm via Venice, Verona, Mantua, Augsburg and Berlin accompanied by EHRENSVÄRD, with whom he corresponded from 1781 to 1794. In Stockholm, Masreliez became a member of the Royal Academy, where he taught from 1784 to 1797, and whose director he became in 1805. From 1784 he was Gustav III's leading decorator, designing furniture and interiors in the royal palaces, including the Pavilion at Haga, and also designed for many private clients. He worked in a highly sophisticated and advanced NEO-CLASSICAL style, although in some chairs he followed English CHIPPENDALE prototypes. Masreliez also designed medals. His younger brother, Jean Baptiste Édouard Masreliez (1753–1801), studied in Paris and then worked as a sculptor in Stockholm under Adelcrantz and REHN, and from 1785 collaborated with his brother. He taught ornament at the Academy from 1775 and designed furniture and decorations in the Swedish royal palaces and elsewhere.

Masson 'Le Sieur Masson' designed and engraved *Nouveaux Desseins pour graver sur l'orfevrerie* (six plates), published by Mariette. It comprises BERAINESQUE designs for engraved ornament on silver boxes, lockets, bowls, teapots, coffee-cups, sugar-castors and so on; it shows not only ornament but also the form of many pieces and is thus an invaluable document of the style of French silver in about 1700. *Nouveaux Desseins* was reissued by JOMBERT, *Répertoire des Artistes* (1765).

Mathsson, Bruno Born in 1907, the son of a fourth-generation cabinet-maker, Mathsson was trained in his father's workshop in Värnamo, Sweden, where he worked from 1923 to 1931. In the latter year he designed furniture for Värnamo general hospital. His Eva chair (1934) had a light curvilinear laminated-wood frame and webbing in the place of upholstery; it was produced from 1935 and exhibited in Gothenburg in 1936. Furniture by Mathsson was also shown at the PARIS 1937 EXHIBITION. An armed version of the Eva chair, the Pernilla chair (1941), was brought back into production by Dux in 1966. From 1945 to 1957 Mathsson was mainly active as an architect. He then returned to furniture design in collaboration with Piet Hein. Mathsson's Jetson chair (1966) stands on an elegant circular base of thin steel members, while his Karin chair (1968) has a solid tubular-steel frame on massy castors.

Matsys, Cornelis Born before 1508 in Antwerp, the son of a painter, Matsys became a master there in 1531. His main activity was as a painter of landscapes, but he also engraved several panels of GROTESQUE ornament, some derived from VENEZIANO and dated around

1540, others in the Flemish STRAPWORK grotesque style of Bos and Cornelis FLORIS, dated about 1560.

Maugham, Syrie (1879–1955) The daughter of Doctor Barnardo (1845–1905), Syrie Maugham married the novelist and playwright Somerset Maugham (1874–1965) in 1917; they were divorced in 1929. In 1922 she opened a shop, Syrie, as an interior decorator and furniture dealer, probably influenced by the example of Elsie de Wolfe. Syrie Maugham's heyday as a decorator lasted from about 1927 to 1937 and spanned the Atlantic, with shops in London, Chicago and New York. She was an original of Mrs Beaver in Evelyn Waugh's *A Handful of Dust* (1934) and helped to introduce a widespread taste for whites and beiges, mirror glass and pickled wood and muted BAROQUE and Regency forms. Her interiors often included rugs by Marion DORN.

Mazell, Peter Probably of Irish origin, Mazell designed a series of floral swags and pendants published in London in 1755 and 1756. He later worked as an engraver and flower painter, last exhibiting in 1797. In 1775 Mazell showed at the Royal Academy his engraved frontispiece for Thomas MALTON's *Perspective*.

Meckenem, Israhel van Meckenem was probably the son of the goldsmith and engraver of the same name, known as the Master of the BERLIN PASSION. He was probably born before 1450 in Bonn or Bocholt and seems to have spent some time in the late 1460s in the workshop of Master E.S. In 1470 he was in Bamberg but from before 1480 to his death in 1503 he was settled in Bocholt. He was active as a goldsmith and works by him survive, including a reliquary case of 1470 in Munich. In Nurem-

berg is a drawing for a silver double cup attributed to Meckenem. He also issued over 620 engravings of which some three-quarters are copies after other engravers, who include E.S., SCHONGAUER and the young DÜRER. Meckenem designed two alphabets with GOTHIC foliage and flowers, in about 1465 and about 1485, a highly elaborate Gothic design for a crozier, about 1500, and a number of elaborate panels of Gothic foliage with the infant Christ and John the Baptist, with the Tree of Jesse, with Hares Cooking a Hunter (later adapted by Virgil SOLIS), with Morris dancers (later used on an English stained-glass window of about 1620), with a Pair of Lovers, and with Meckenem's own name. Meckenem also engraved a series of twelve scenes of daily life, about 1500, which are valuable records of interior design. Many of his prints were copied by later designers, for example by VELLERT at Cambridge.

Meier-Graefe, Julius (1867–1935) Born at Pesitza in Banat, Hungary, the son of an innovative German industrialist, Meier-Graefe studied engineering in Munich and Zürich. From 1890, in which year he moved to Berlin, Meier-Graefe devoted himself to writing and frequented Bohemian circles. In 1893 he travelled to England, where he met William MORRIS, BURNE-JONES, Beardsley and others. In 1894 he helped to found the Pan association, but he was dismissed as editor of 'PAN' in 1895, despite his having done much to raise money and influential patronage for the magazine. Like many *Pan* contributors Meier-Graefe worked for the magazine *Die Insel* from 1899. In 1895 Meier-Graefe moved to Paris and met BING, to whom he may have suggested the foundation of L'Art Nouveau; also in 1895 they travelled together to Brussels to meet VAN DE VELDE. In 1897 Meier-Graefe founded 'DEKORATIVE

KUNST'; he wrote almost all its first issue under a *nom-de-plume* and up to 1900 he was responsible for over half the magazine. The subjects of his articles included VOYSEY, Van de Velde, BEHRENS, GALLÉ and MACKINTOSH. In 1899 Meier-Graefe founded La Maison Moderne, a shop on the Rue de la Paix which was to serve as a showplace for the best MODERN design; its façade and interior were designed by Van de Velde, who had also designed the offices of *Dekorative Kunst*, and other designers involved were Behrens, Karl Koepping (1848–1914), DUFRÈNE, FOLLOT, Orazi and LANDRY. La Maison Moderne showed at the TURIN 1902 EXHIBITION but closed down in 1903. In 1902 Meier-Graefe refuted Van de Velde's egocentric account of the recent revival in the decorative arts. His own last article in this field was on Behrens (1905), and thenceforward Meier-Graefe became increasingly disillusioned with the movement of the 1890s, which he came to regard as an outbreak of misguided idealism. For the rest of his life he was a prominent art critic and historian and travelled widely. MUTHESIUS designed his house in Berlin in 1921 but in 1934, having fled Hitler, Meier-Graefe applied for French citizenship.

Meil, Johann Wilhelm (1733–1805) Born in Altenburg in Thuringia, the younger son of a sculptor, Meil was educated in Bayreuth and Leipzig. In 1752 he moved to Berlin and there worked as a self-taught engraver for the brothers Johann Michael and Johann Christian HOPPENHAUPT, then mainly engaged on the decoration of Frederick the Great's palaces in Potsdam. Meil soon began to design furniture, goldsmith's work and ornament, including a series of twelve VASES for the picture gallery at Sanssouci in Potsdam. He published suites of trophies, mirrors and

tables, and later designed for the Royal Porcelain Factory in Berlin. In about 1755 he commenced a fertile career as a book illustrator and designer of graphic ornaments. In 1766 he became a member of the Berlin Academy, where he taught design from 1787. His proposals for design education may be summarized: (1) Geometry, the ORDERS, technical drawing, (2) Free drawing, (3) Modelling, using prints of vases, plants, etc. In 1801 Meil succeeded his friend and mentor CHODOWIECKI as Director of the Academy. He had been closely linked with the set of Berlin intellectuals associated with Frederick the Great, illustrating for instance the *Memoirs* and *Works* of Count Algarotti (1712–64). But although he survived into the NEO-CLASSICAL epoch his works always retained the grace and delicacy which had distinguished his handling of the ROCOCO, the style of which he was a natural master.

Meissonier, Juste Aurèle (1695–1750) Born in Turin, the son of a Provençal goldsmith and sculptor who had settled there, Meissonier had moved to Paris by 1718. In 1724 he was appointed royal goldsmith to Louis XIV, a signal favour, and a month later became a master in the goldsmiths' guild, bypassing all the usual requirements; he registered his mark in 1725. In 1726 Meissonier was named 'Dessinateur de la Chambre et du Cabinet du Roi' in succession to Jean II BERAIN, a further mark of royal favour. Most of the information on Meissonier derives from his published *Œuvre* (118 engravings on seventy-four plates, of which about fifty plates were extant in 1734); the final edition, published by Gabriel HUQUIER (1695–1772), appeared in about 1750. The earliest dated design in the *Œuvre* is a wine cooler (1723) for the Duc de Mortemar, for whom Meissonier also designed a wind indicator (1724). Other designs include sword hilts (1725), a decorated ceiling (1730) and chronological chart (1733) for Louis XV, a garden sleigh for the Dowager Queen of Spain (1735), a cabinet (1734) and a sofa (1735) for Count Bielinski, and a salon for Princess Sartorinski (1748). He designed the decorations for royal events in 1725, 1729 and 1739, and in the 1730s designed a house at Bayonne for Léon de Bréthous, a rich provincial bourgeois. The *Œuvre* also included designs for vegetable ornaments, porcelain, picture frames, church metalwork, cartouches and tombs. Of Meissonier's works as a goldsmith only three survivals have been identified, a snuff-box for Charles II of Spain (1728), a silver candlestick (1734–5) and a pair of tureens (1734–6) for the Duke of Kingston. He was recognized by contemporaries as the only rival to the supremacy of the goldsmith Thomas Germain (1673–1748), who owned a copy of Meissonier's *Œuvre*. However, although his forte was as a goldsmith, Meissonier was ambitious to be recognized as an architect, and on two plates depicting masterpieces of world architecture from Egyptian to modern times, and with GOTHIC and Chinese examples, included four ambitious projects by himself for monumental buildings in Paris. In his day, C.-N. COCHIN states, Meissonier was regarded as a divinity, and NEO-CLASSICAL pundits such as J.-F. BLONDEL (1705–74) stressed his role in the creation of what they considered the bizarre irregularity of the ROCOCO style. Cochin linked Meissonier with the Italian architect Francesco Borromini (1599–1667) and in 1727 the *Mercure de France* noted that a monstrance by Meissonier was in the taste of the painter Pietro da CORTONA (1596–1669) and the sculptor Pierre Puget (1620–94). The *Mercure* also stated in 1734 that his engravings were in the taste of Stefano DELLA BELLA. The BAROQUE ornament of Italy, where

Meissonier was brought up, was evidently an important influence on his treatment of the rococo style. For Meissonier's rococo was strongly sculptural in character, handling the shell-like, watery or vegetal matter of rococo ornament with great vigour, and excelling in three-dimensional objects such as candlesticks. His asymmetry was often attacked by neo-classical critics, but in many cases this is more apparent than real; asymmetry in details was balanced in his larger compositions, whether by means of the complementary treatment of pairs or of the different sides of the same object. Although he did not discover the rococo style, it is just that Meissonier should have been named by J.-F. Blondel in 1774 as one of the three first inventors of the '*gen. e pittoresque*', with LA JOUE and PINEAU.

Mellor, David Born in 1930, Mellor studied design at Sheffield School of Art and at the Royal College of Art in London. He was then retained as a design consultant by Walker & Hall of Sheffield and designed for them the Pride range of cutlery (1954), the Campden range (1957), in collaboration with Robert WELCH, the Symbol range (1961) and several other cutlery ranges. Mellor has also designed silver, including many presentation pieces and the official pattern for British embassies (1963), as well as many products from calculating machines to traffic signals. In 1974 he set up his own factory in Sheffield.

Memorie di un Architetto (1887–1906) Published from Turin, this informally conducted 'album' of architecture includes interesting illustrations of Italian design around 1900.

Menuiserie, Journal de Edited by the architect Adolphe Mangeant, this Paris periodical presented from 1863 fine drawings of furniture and woodwork, both ancient and modern, in all styles, sometimes in colour and usually with long and informative captions. They are mainly French but outsiders crop up, including Reformed GOTHIC by Cox & Sons (1877) and TALBERT influence in Sweden (1878).

Menuiserie Pratique, Recueil de (1876–92) Edited by the architect N. Gateuil, who issued a similar work on *Serrurerie Pratique*, this Paris magazine contains plates of modern furniture in all styles, including for instance a piece shown by Gillows at the PARIS 1878 EXHIBITION.

Mercker, Friedrich Wilhelm Mercker was active as a designer in Leipzig from at least 1829. He published a number of part-works on the design of VASES (1829), metalwork (1832), house-carpentry (1832) and upholstery (1832). His *Practische Zeichnungen von Meubles im neuesten und geläutertsten Geschmack* (1830–43) survived for twenty-nine parts, with designs for furniture mainly in a conventional BIEDERMEIER style, with some GOTHIC and Egyptian pieces and few grotesque oddities described as Moorish or Chinese.

Merian, Matthäus (1593–1651) Born in Basel, Merian trained as engraver in Zürich from 1609. After spells in Strasbourg (1610), Nancy and Paris (1614), Basel (1615), Augsburg and Stuttgart (1616) he joined the firm of Johann Theodor de BRY, whose daughter he married in 1617. After a further spell in Basel in 1619, Merian took over his father-in-law's press in Frankfurt in 1625, becoming a Frankfurt citizen in 1626. Merian was a prolific designer of book illustrations, and his Bible subjects are found on 18th-century Nuremberg enamel and Liverpool tiles. Merian also designed a suite of seventeen panels of dense GROTESQUE ornament (Augs-

burg, 1616, reprinted Bamberg, 1625, as *Schönes Grottesken Büchlein*). A suite of putti playing at goldsmiths in scrolled STRAPWORK frames (eight plates), probably also 1616, were republished by MONCORNET in Paris in 1666 as *Livre Nouveau De toutes sortes d'Ouvrages d'Orfevries recueillies des meilleurs Ouvriers de ce temps*, a misleading title.

Merz, Johann George (1694–1762) Merz engraved RUDOLPH'S suite of table designs, as well as copies after GILLOT and LA JOUE. He also published *Neue Inventiones auf Tobac Dosen* (four plates), lively but not very accomplished designs for ROCOCO snuffboxes, four to a plate.

Métaux Ouvrés, Les (1882–1906) J. Bréasson was the first editor of this Paris magazine which comprised fine designs for metalwork, principally ironwork, mainly designed by contemporary architects but also including some historic models.

Metzmacher, Pierre Guillaume Born in Paris in 1815, Metzmacher drew and engraved the designs, adapted from Virgil SOLIS, ALDEGREVER, Mantegna and others, in *Portefeuille Historique de l'Ornement* (1841; thirty-two plates), a work in the manner of CLERGET which was recommended in the bibliography of J. C. ROBINSON's *Coloured Ornament* (1853).

Meyandi, Giovanni Sebastiano Meyandi, a jeweller, worked in Siena from 1762 to 1794. Many designs by Meyandi for jewellery survive, some in a ROCOCO style influenced by C. L.

Meyer, Daniel (1576–1630) Born in Frankfurt, the son of a glass painter, Meyer published *Architectura oder Verzeichnis allerhand Einfassungen* (Frankfurt, 1609; fifty plates), a book of architectural ornaments including lavabos, VASES, cartouches and masks covered with wild STRAPWORK in the Wendel DIETTERLIN tradition, which was reprinted with a French title in Heidelberg in 1609 and 1664. He also issued a book of the ORDERS and architectural ornaments such as brackets, likewise called *Architectura* (Frankfurt, 1612; eighty-eight plates), copied from Dietterlin and Hans VREDEMAN DE VRIES, and a lost book of embroidery or jewellery designs, *Zierat Buch von allerhandt Hutschur* (Frankfurt, 1618), which may have been copied by Jacob HONERVOGT.

Meyer, Eduard Lorenz (1856–1926) Born in Singapore, where he drew native plants, Meyer settled in Hamburg in 1888 and became a well-known amateur heraldic artist and scholar. He designed some remarkable plain silver in the GOTHIC style (1886–90), Gothic jewellery (1891) and book-plates. Chairs after his design were shown at the Hamburg 1889 Exhibition.

Meyer, Theodor (1572–1658) Born in Eglisan, Meyer was active as an engraver in Zürich, where he died. He issued a number of suites of friezes with dancing couples (1599), hunting scenes (1599), the months (1599), birds (1603), gods, the planets and so on, as well as a suite of twelve lively designs for pendants in the GROTESQUE style, mainly pear-shaped and surrounded by animals and figures.

Michel Michel designed the *Cahier d'Arabesques* (six plates), competent panels of NEO-CLASSICAL ornament for wall decoration incorporating sphinxes, scrolls, tripods, lyres, putti etc., in a series published in Paris by Mondhare in about 1780 which included similar designs by TIBESAR, FAY and PRIEUR.

Michelangelo Buonarroti (1475–1564) Born at Caprese, the son of the local magistrate, Michelangelo became in 1488 an apprentice in the Florentine workshop of the painters Domenico (1449–94) and Davide Ghirlandaio (1452–1525). In 1489 he entered the school for sculptors run by Bertoldo, curator of the sculpture garden of Lorenzo de' Medici (1449–92). From 1490 to 1491 Michelangelo was a guest in Lorenzo's palace, and he remained there until 1494 under the protection of Piero de' Medici (1471–1503). After periods in Bologna, Venice and Florence, Michelangelo spent the years from 1496 to 1501 in Rome. He was then in Florence from 1501 to 1505, when he was summoned back to Rome by Pope Julius II (1443–1513). For the tomb of Julius, which occupied him from 1505 to 1545, Michelangelo designed some superb panels of GROTESQUE ornament which were carved by Antonio del Pontasieve in 1513. From 1506 to 1534 Michelangelo was mainly in Florence but also visited Rome many times as well as Bologna, Ferrara and Venice. In 1524 he designed the Biblioteca Laurenziana in Florence, including its carved ceiling, executed in 1534; its pavement, executed in 1553, followed the same design. The reading desks in the library, carved by Battista del Cinque and Ciappino in 1534, incorporate grotesque panels probably designed by Michelangelo. From 1534 until his death he was in Rome. In 1537 he designed an inkwell for the Duke of Urbino; he also designed ciboria, including one for Santa Maria degli Angeli, and crystal plaques executed by Giovanni Desiderio Bernardi (1496–1553). From about 1540 there was a cult of Michelangelo, promoted by VASARI's *Life* (1550, second edition 1568). His funeral in Florence on 14 July 1564 was attended by over a hundred artists, including the members of the FLORENCE ACCADEMIA DEL DISEGNO, of which he had been an acknowledged inspiration. As architect, painter and sculptor, Michelangelo was a major influence on MANNERIST designers. Although his own *œuvre* as a designer was relatively small, ornament by Michelangelo was always of the highest quality. Examples are the panels of grotesque ornament of the Julius tomb and in the Biblioteca Laurenziana, and the sinister melting masks which occur in the Medici Chapel (1520–34), which also included a marble candelabrum by Michelangelo, and on the Porte Pia (1562). In 1789 Carlo Lasinio (1759–1838) published a number of grotesques by Michelangelo.

Mickle, Samuel Born in 1746 in Haddonfield, New Jersey, Mickle was in 1760 apprenticed to the Philadelphia cabinetmaker Jonathan Shoemaker (1726–93). He returned to New Jersey to marry in 1776 and was active until about 1800. Mickle left the only surviving design book of a Philadelphia cabinet-maker, containing crude ARTISAN designs for furniture.

Mies van der Rohe, Ludwig (1886–1969) Born in Aachen, the son of a stonemason, Mies was trained at a building trade school. He then worked as a draughtsman of stucco ornaments for a local architect before moving in 1905 to Berlin, where he studied under Bruno PAUL until 1907. His first house, designed in 1907, was in an 18th-century style. In 1908 Mies moved to the office of Peter BEHRENS, where he stayed until 1911 and came to share Behrens's deep admiration for SCHINKEL'S NEO-CLASSICISM. After the war Mies was involved from 1919 in the revolutionary Novembergruppe and became a vociferous proponent of MODERN ideas, for instance through his projects for glass skyscrapers. In 1926 he became Vice-President of the DEUTSCHE WERK-

BUND, and in 1927 organized the STUTT-GART EXHIBITION. At Stuttgart, Mies showed his cantilevered steeltube chairs, a development of Mart STAM's earlier designs, in which Mies exploited the resilience of steel tube. He took out a patent for the MR chair on 24 August 1927. Mies also designed a steel-tube stool with a sling seat and a glass-topped table with a simple tubular-steel frame. For the Barcelona 1929 Exhibition, Mies designed the ceremonial German pavilion, furnished with two X-framed chairs for the use of the King and Queen, two unstable X-framed and glass-topped tables, one for the signing of a Golden Book, the other for champagne, and X-framed ottomans; all the furniture frames were of chrome-plated steel strip. The Barcelona chairs represented a brilliantly detailed synthesis of neo-classicism and Modernity, and have since been canonized as 'CLASSICS'. For the Tugendhat house in Brno (1928–30) Mies designed a steel chair with an S-shaped support, and another, the Brno chair, in which the front legs rise in a curve to form arms, and the Tugendhat coffee-table, a glass top supported on an elegant rectilinear X-frame with vertical legs, as well as simple rosewood-veneered chairs and tables. Many of these designs were shown at the Berlin 1931 Building Exhibition together with an ungainly steel-tube chaise longue derived from the MR chair. The latter was already an icon of Modernism and was shown en masse together with the BREUER chair at the Paris 1930 Werkbund Exhibition. From 1927 to 1931 Mies's chairs were produced by a small firm, Berliner Metallgewerbe Joseph Müller, and then from 1931 by Bamberger Metalwerkstätten, set up by Joseph Müller's business manager. In 1931 Mies signed a contract with Thonet-Mundus for the marketing of his chairs; it brought him a substantial income. Fifteen designs were involved, mainly by Mies, the others by Lilly Reich (1885–1947), a wealthy pupil of Josef HOFFMANN who was a Werkbund activist from 1913, and collaborated with Mies at the Berlin 1927 fashion exhibition, and the Barcelona 1929 and Berlin 1931 Exhibitions, designing furniture in a style indistinguishable from his. They also worked together on furniture designed for Philip Johnson's New York apartment in 1930. In 1930 Mies became the last director of the BAUHAUS, which he moved from Dessau to Berlin but closed in 1933. Around this time he became interested in laminated-wood chairs, influenced by AALTO's work, shown in Zürich in 1933, and he later sketched designs for plastic chairs, but little came of these projects. In 1938 Mies left for America to teach at the Illinois Institute of Technology, Chicago, leaving his affairs in Lilly Reich's hands. He became a United States citizen in 1944, and was by his death universally recognized as a great master of Modern architecture. From 1947 Knoll Associates produced his Barcelona chair (Florence Knoll had been his pupil in Chicago), and most of Mies's furniture is in production in 1981.

Mignerak, Matthias In 1605 Jean Le Clerc, the Paris publisher of VINCIOLO's books, published *La pratique de l'aiguille industrieuse* (seventy-six plates) by Mignerak, described as an English 'Milour' and as a professional embroiderer. The book contains a wide range of lively and competent designs for embroidery influenced by Vinciolo and a few for bobbin lace in the PARASOLE manner.

Mignot, Daniel A goldsmith, Mignot was active as a designer in Augsburg from 1593 to 1596, publishing some 100 plates of designs for jewellery in eleven suites. Many of his designs were reprinted in 1616. Mignot's designs consist mainly of brilliant pendants decorated with black stretched GROTESQUE STRAPWORK for enamelling; some are jewelled. He also designed small black motifs for jewellery, and grotesques with scattered snails, monsters, birds, etc. Johann Theodor de BRY copied pendants by Mignot.

Miklos, Gustave (1888–1967) Born in Budapest, Miklos studied painting there. In 1909 he came to Paris and continued to paint. After spending the 1914–18 war in the Foreign Legion he returned to Paris in 1919, becoming a French citizen in 1923. A friendship with the couturier and art-collector Jacques DOUCET led to a commission to design carpets and silver, and a move towards decorative sculpture in an ART DÉCO cubist style. Miklos showed at the PARIS EXHIBITIONS of 1925 and 1937 and designed jewellery for Raymond TEMPLIER. In 1940 he retired to the country to teach.

Milan Triennales After the last Monza exhibition in 1930, which was a Triennale as opposed to the earlier MONZA BIENNALES, the event moved to Milan, where the first Milan Triennale was held in 1933 at the Palazzo d'Arte, planned by Giovanni Muzio. It included a memorial exhibition to the Futurist architect Antonio Sant'Elia (1888–1916), and the work of MODERN architects including LE CORBUSIER, LOOS, MIES VAN DER ROHE and Walter GROPIUS. The 1936 Milan Triennale had Giuseppe PAGANO as one of the directing triumvirate: Persico, NIZZOLI and others were involved with him in the design of the Salone della Vittoria, a ceremonial hall in which rationalism and classicism combined in queasy grandeur. Foreign designers, limited for political reasons, included AALTO from Finland and Max Bill from Switzerland. The 1940 Milan Triennale was closed prematurely because of Italy's entry into the war and the proposal for a 1943 Milan Triennale failed. In 1947, however, the sequence was renewed and thenceforward Milan Triennales, at more or less regular three-year intervals (1951, 1954, 1957, 1960, 1964 and so on), have served as the major international showplace for Italian design.

Milde, Carl Julius (1803–75) Educated as a painter in Dresden (1824), Munich (1825) and Rome, Milde settled in Lübeck in 1838. He was a designer of stained glass, goldsmiths' work and furniture, working in the NEO-CLASSI-CAL, GOTHIC and NATURALISTIC styles. He also published the *Lübecker ABC*.

Minozzi, Flaminio Innocenzo (1735–1817) Born in Bologna, Minozzi was active there as a painter of architecture and ornament; he was a pupil of C. G. Bibiena. He designed a cartouche and church plate published in PANFILI'S *Frammenti di Ornati* (1783), and surviving drawings combine NEO-CLASSICAL details with BAROQUE form.

Mintalopek (1895–1905) This official Hungarian publication, edited from Budapest by Jozsef Szterényi, presented a superb series of designs for the decorative arts, including many full-scale details, which constitute a basic record of Hungarian ART NOUVEAU.

Mir Iskusstva (1899–1904) Subtitled in French *Le Monde Artiste*, this Russian art periodical included work by MACKINTOSH and OLBRICH, as well as work by native designers, such as J. Fomine, A. Braïlowsky, N. Davidoff, C. Orloff and C. Korovine. Its editor was Serge Diaghilev, assisted by Alexandre Benois.

Mitelli, Agostino (1609–60) Born near

Bologna, Mitelli studied architecture and fortification and afterwards trained as a painter under Girolamo Curti (1583–1632). He became a virtuoso in the illusionist PERSPECTIVE painted decoration known as quadratura, working with his partner, Angelo Michele Colonna (1604–87), in Tuscany and Emilia and later in Spain, where he died. Mitelli issued a number of engravings of cartouches, a suite of twenty-four (Bologna, 1636), a suite of twelve (one dated 1640, reissued by Rossi, Rome, 1642, and again by Wijngaerde, 1664) and a suite of eleven (also reissued by Rossi, Rome). After Mitelli's death his son Giuseppe Maria (1634–1718) published *Disegni et Abbozi di Agostino Mitelli* (Bologna; twenty-four plates), which include capitals, VASES and panels of ornament as well as cartouches. The cartouches are often composed of conventional ingredients such as masks and ACANTHUS but they are always invested with great energy, and sometimes, when they employ asymmetric and almost AURICULAR leathery scrolls, great power. They probably influenced DELLA BELLA, whose prints Mitelli owned, together with those of CAL-LOT and Jean LE PAUTRE. *Freggi dell'architettura* (Bologna, 1645; twenty-four plates) contained depictions of the RENAISSANCE GROTESQUE ornament on pilasters in the church of San Barto-lomeo in Bologna, begun in 1516 and designed by Andrea Marchesi; its plates are thus an early and significant example of a Renaissance revival.

Mobilia (1955–present) This predominantly Danish design monthly, published in Copenhagen, contains excellent illustrations, although the text tends to sparseness.

Modena, Nicoletto Rosex da Presumably born in Modena, Nicoletto published engravings from 1500 to 1512. He was influenced by Mantegna, SCHONGAUER and DÜRER. In 1507 he scratched his name in the Domus Aurea of Nero in Rome, the main source of RENAISSANCE GROTESQUE ornament, as 'Nicholetto da Modena Ferara 1507', presumably implying that he had been in Ferrara before coming to Rome. Nicoletto published many panels of grotesque ornament, incorporating trophies, masks, monsters, satyrs, sphinxes, VASES, baskets, etc.; on occasion he quotes directly from the Domus Aurea. Some of his compositions are based on a central candelabrum, others comprise small scenes connected by narrow interlacing borders, the source of STRAPWORK ornament. Nicoletto's designs were widely copied and influential; as early as 1518, for instance, relief decoration in the Fugger chapel in the Annakirche in Augsburg was based on one of his designs, and J. A. DuCERCEAU leant heavily on his example.

Moderne Stil, Der (1899–1905) Published from Stuttgart by Julius Hoffmann, junior. *Moderne Stil* consisted of thousands of illustrations of designs of all types, giving an invaluable broad international coverage.

Modernism At the beginning of the 20th century the search for a totally new style of architecture and design – a constant preoccupation of Victorian theorists – took a radical turn. LOOS associated the disappearance of ornament with the evolution of culture. Wagner, Josef HOFFMANN and Koloman MOSER practised an abstract rectilinearity. MUTHESIUS and the DEUTSCHE WERKBUND identified industrial projects as the proper province of the designer. The DE STIJL group enforced abstract purity. Futurists and Constructivists praised the machine and modern materials. LE CORBUSIER and Walter GROPIUS extolled the beauty of grain silos, ocean liners and motor cars. After the First World War the architects and designers who shared such ideas saw as their task the development of a fundamentally new aesthetic. The new approach to design found its ideological base in FUNCTIONALISM. The German term '*Sachlichkeit*' (objectivity) made clear that the goal was not a new style to add to the museum of historical styles, but an inevitable and rational response to Modern needs using Modern materials. Idealism, iconoclasm, puritanism, socialism and, for some, revolution were all involved in this pursuit. The vision of a brave new world of justice, light, health, equality and order, stripped of the clutter of the past, seemed a real and enticing prospect. By the time of the STUTTGART 1927 EXHIBITION a consensus as to what Modern architecture and design should look like had emerged: rectilinear white buildings of glass and concrete contained minimal dwellings furnished with metal and bentwood chairs, while built-in storage units housed industrially made products. Le Corbusier's celebrated dictum that 'a house is a machine for living in' might have served as a motto for the whole event. Modernism, which disowned academies and institutions, invented its own; the BAUHAUS was the first. In Paris the Union des Artistes Modernes, founded in 1928, was a focus for Modern designers. In the same year the CONGRÈS INTERNATIONAUX D'ARCHITECTURE MODERNE (C.I.A.M.) began to formulate and to propagate the tenets of Modernism, whose products were to be collected by the NEW YORK MUSEUM OF MODERN ART, founded in the following year. Historians such as Giedion and PEVSNER traced the origins of Modernism in industrial buildings or in the work of 'pioneering' 19th-century designers. Emigrants to England and America such as Gropius and MIES VAN DER ROHE acted as Modern missionaries and after the Second World War Modernism, called 'Modernismus' by Sir Reginald Blomfield (1856–1942) in 1934, was recognized as the doctrine of the coming establishment. In 1932 the New York Museum of Modern Art mounted an exhibition, The International Style, with a book by Henry-Russell Hitchcock and Philip Johnson. In 1958 Hitchcock was to use 'modern architecture of the second generation' as a more neutral term, avoiding the pejorative overtones which had by then attached themselves to International Style. By the 1960s it was generally recognized that whatever else Modernism represented it was also a style. The dominant characteristic of Modern design was simplicity; ornament was eliminated, clean sleek forms were achieved at whatever cost to functional efficiency or 'honesty', repetition took precedence over articulation, materials were allowed direct expression, sometimes fictive, and historical references were outlawed. Modernism so dominated the teaching of architecture and design from the 1940s onwards that when the inevitable reaction came, generally known as Post-Modernism, it was at first a rebellion of scattered underground resistants rather than a unified revolution. Expressionists, who had always refused to toe the Modern line, unregenerate historicists and old-fashioned Arts & Crafts men were thrown into the limelight. A crude NEO-CLASSICISM with strong ART DÉCO overtones, a 'vernacular' Arts & Crafts revival and a refined and mannered revival of Modernism itself were among the styles favoured by a new generation in the 1970s. The reign of Modernism as a fundamentally new – and completely dominant – aesthetic was over.

Modern Publicity (1927–present) Commenced as *Posters and Publicity*, the 1927 Annual of 'COMMERCIAL ART'. The title changed to *Modern Publicity* in 1930. This London-based annual provides an international survey of posters, advertising and packaging design.

Moeglich, Andreas Leonhard (1742–1810) A citizen of Nuremberg, Moeglich was taught to engrave by Johann Justin PREISLER (1698–1771) and Johann Eberhard Ihle (1727–1814). His prolific output included engraved frames, *culs-de-lampe* and commemorative portraits with refined NEO-CLASSICAL ornament. He was called 'Stadtdekorateur', civic decorator.

Moelder, C. de Moelder published *Proper Ornaments to be Engrav'd on Plate* (London, 1694; twelve plates), with a dedication to the Earl of Ranelagh. It comprises friezes, mouldings, frames, masks, keyhole escutcheons, boxes, *écuelles* and lights in a rich scrolled ACANTHUS style or in an imitation of French BAROQUE ornament. One plate shows a silver pin-cushion, and another a tea-caddy with CHINOISERIES. A silver toilet service of 1728 to 1729 by Isaac Liger has engraved decoration copied from this pattern-book.

Mogenson, Børge Born at Aalborg in Denmark in 1914, Mogenson was in 1934 a cabinet-maker. He studied furniture design at the College of Arts and Crafts (1936–8) and the Royal Academy (1938–41), in Copenhagen. From 1938 to 1942 Mogenson worked under various architects including Mogens KOCH and Kaare KLINT, with whom he collaborated on research into ideal dimensions. He was in 1942 appointed head furniture designer to the Danish Co-operative Wholesale Society, through the influence of the director, Frederik Nielsen, and the designer, Steen Eiler Rasmussen. In 1946 Mogenson showed a flat at the annual Copenhagen Cabinet-Makers' Guild Exhibition with furniture designed by himself and by Hans WEGNER. In 1953 he set up as an independent designer. He has collaborated on textile design with the weaver Lis Ahlmann. Mogenson designed two elaborate systems for storage, Boligens Byggeskabe, from about 1952, and Øresund, from about 1955, both in collaboration with the designer Grethe Meyer. Although opposed to stylistic revivals, Mogenson shares Kaare Klint's respect for traditional forms, and has made direct use of English Windsor chairs, Shaker furniture and Spanish leather-backed chairs, the latter adjustable through straps (from about 1951). On Klint's death in 1954 Mogenson took over his role as designer to the Museum of Decorative Arts in Copenhagen. His plain, eclectic, well-detailed style has brought Mogenson many honours.

Moglia, Domenico (1780–1862) Born in Cremona, Moglia was trained by ALBERTOLLI in Milan, where he later worked. His *Collezione di oggetti ornamentali ed architettonici* (Milan, 1837–8; fifty-six plates) includes designs for furniture, silverwork, bronzes, mantelpieces and an episcopal mitre, all in an elaborate and highly competent late-NEO-CLASSICAL manner. Particularly remarkable is a table with a micromosaic top made as a present from Pope Leo XII to the Austrian Ambassador in 1825. Moglia also published an elementary manual on architectural ornament (1837).

Moholy-Nagy, Laszlo (1895–1946) Born in Bacsborsod, Hungary, Moholy-Nagy began to study law before the First World War, in which he served as an artillery officer. In 1917, recovering from wounds, Moholy-Nagy began to draw and paint and when in 1918 he resumed his law studies in Budapest, he became increasingly interested in art. From 1919 he devoted all his time to painting and art, helping to found the *avant-garde* MA group. In late 1919 he moved to Vienna and thence to Berlin. His writings in the journal *MA* included proposals for glass architecture (1921) and a discussion of Constructivism and the proletariat (1922). In 1921 Moholy-Nagy attended the congress of progressive artists in Düsseldorf, where he met Theo van Doesburg of the DE STIJL group and El LISSITZKY. In Berlin in 1921 Moholy-Nagy met Schwitters, Gabo and ARP. He had an exhibition there in 1922 and met Walter GROPIUS who in 1923 summoned him to teach at the BAUHAUS. Moholy-Nagy was put in charge of the metal workshop, where his pupils included WAGENFELD, and took over the preliminary course from ITTEN. Moholy-Nagy designed covers for *Der Sturm* from 1923 to 1924, typography for the 1923 Bauhaus catalogue and the Bauhaus books published from 1925, including his own *Malerci, Photographie, Film* (1925) and *Von Material zu Architektur* (1929). In 1924 he wrote an essay on modern typography which was published in 1926. In 1928 Moholy-Nagy left the Bauhaus and settled in Berlin, where he was active as a typographer. In 1930 his Licht-Raum-Modulator, a Constructivist sculpture using light and movement, was exhibited. Moholy-Nagy had been working on this theme since 1922, from which year he also explored the possibilities of photography. He attended the meeting of the CONGRÈS INTERNATIONAUX D'ARCHITECTURE MODERNE in Greece, was in Amsterdam in 1934, and in 1935 moved to London, where he designed for the 'ARCHITECTURAL REVIEW', produced publicity for Empire Airways, and in 1936 had an exhibition devoted to his work. In 1937, on Gropius's recommendation, Moholy-Nagy was appointed Director of the New Bauhaus in Chicago. After it failed in 1938 Moholy-Nagy opened his own school in 1939; it was in

1944 recognized as the Institute of Design. On his death Moholy-Nagy was succeeded as Director by Serge CHERMAYEFF. In Chicago, Moholy-Nagy had also been active as an industrial designer, designing a plastic pill-box for Foley & Co. in 1940 and the Parker 51 pen in 1941.

Mohrmann, Karl (1857–1927) Mohrmann studied architecture at the Hamburg Polytechnic and under Conrad Wilhelm Hase. After a period as professor at Riga from 1887 to 1892, Mohrmann took over Hase's practice. In 1890 to 1891 he designed for his own use some GOTHIC furniture which is remarkable for its display of English Reformed Gothic influence, with massive forms, stump columns, chamfering and notching. A cupboard of 1899 is more German Gothic with flat-relief carved foliage ornament.

Moithey l'Aîné Moithey published *Atribues de Vases* (six plates), *Nouveau Vases Antiques* (six plates), *Nouveau Livre de Vases* (1767; six plates) and *2me Suitte de Vases* (1768; six plates), all coarse designs for VASES in an advanced NEO-CLASSICAL style. He also published some ten plates of trophies and in 1773 a very ARTISAN suite of frames, in a ROCOCO survival style.

Moitte, Jean-Guillaume (1746–1810) Born in Paris, the son of an engraver, Moitte trained as a sculptor under J. B. Pigalle (1714–85) and J. B. Lemoyne (1704–78). Having won the Prix de Rome in 1768 he stayed in Rome from 1771 to 1773. After his return to Paris he was a prolific designer for the great goldsmith Robert-Joseph Auguste, working in a pure and advanced NEO-CLASSICAL style which ensured Auguste's ascendancy over his competitors, and influenced J. J. BOILEAU. Moitte also designed illustrations for

Fénelon's *Télémaque* (Didot, 1785) and for the Didot edition of Racine (1801). His portrait was painted by DAVID.

Moncornet, Balthasar Moncornet was active as an engraver and publisher in Paris, where he died in 1688. Among the designers he published were MOSBACH, LE MERSIER, HEDOUYNS, LE FEBURE and BOUCQUET. Moncornet himself designed a suite of coarse COSSE-DE-POIS sprays for jewellers.

Mondon, Jean By training an engraver of jewels, Mondon was also active as a designer and in 1736, when a young man, began to issue a long series of plates of advanced ROCOCO ornament with his *Premier Livre de Forme Rocquaille et Cartel* (seven plates), dedicated to the Prince of Carignano. Also in 1736 he published five further suites with similar titles, as well as a *Livre de Trophée*, trophies on themes such as the arts. Typical of Mondon are plates from his *Cinquième Livre* showing a very unwarlike 'Trophée d'Armes d'un Grand de la Chine', and 'Le Sultan de Lachine (sic) avec une Esclave', the latter with the sultan carrying an outsize pipe alongside his slave, both perched with perilous insouciance upon a lofty plinth of rococo scrollwork. Mondon also published a book of designs for panelling, with a bed alcove on its title (1749), and two suites of jewellery designs, fourteen plates in all. In 1738 the *Mercure* announced his four-plate suite *Les Heures du Jour*. Mondon also designed some highly accomplished rococo snuff-boxes. Many of his printed designs for ornament were reissued by MERZ in Augsburg.

Mongin, Antoine Pierre Born in Paris in about 1761, Mongin was trained as a painter at the Academy from 1782 to 1785 and exhibited at the Salon from 1791 to 1824. He died in 1827. Mongin succeeded MALAINE as chief designer for the Zuber wallpaper factory. His first scenic wallpaper, Les Vues de Suisse (1804), which won a silver medal at the Paris 1806 Exhibition, was followed by L'Indoustan (1807), L'Arcadie (1811), L'Helvétie (1813–14), Vues d'Italie (1818), Jardins Français (1821) and Les Lointains (1825).

Moniteur de l'Ameublement, Le (1863–8) This monthly Parisian journal published furniture designs in all fashionable styles by A. SANGUINETI, who advertised his services as a designer in the text, which is full of interesting information on French furniture styles in the 1860s.

Monlong, Jean Monlong was a silk weaver in Lyons from at least 1714 to 1751. He was also active as a silk designer from 1715 to 1731, and his reputation for design was still alive in 1764 when he was praised by JOUBERT DE L'HIBERDERIE.

Monnoyer, Jean-Baptiste (1636–99) Born in Lille, Monnoyer studied painting in Antwerp and then moved to Paris where he became a member of the Academy in 1665. Monnoyer, a specialist flower painter, worked at the Trianon, Marly, Meudon and other palaces of Louis XIV. He designed flowers and fruits in LE BRUN's Months or Royal Houses tapestries and assisted on Jean I BERAIN's GROTESQUES. In about 1685 Monnoyer travelled with the Duke of Montagu to London, where he died. Many prints of flowers were engraved by Monnoyer himself; others were engraved after his designs by VAUQUER, and like Vauquer's engravings were widely copied in Strasbourg faience.

Montano, Giovanni Battista (1534–1621) Born in Milan, Montano came to Rome in about 1572 and was there active as carver, architect, designer

and goldsmith. In 1590 he designed the church of San Giuseppe dei Falegnami for the guild of joiners. Montano also carved the organ-case of St John Lateran. After his death Montano's pupil, the architect and wood-carver G. B. Soria (1581–1651), who worked on occasion for BERNINI, sponsored a series of publications of his master's designs, adding a few of his own. *Scielta di varii Tempietti antichi* (Rome, 1624; sixty-six plates) comprises naïve architectural reconstructions of antique temples; it was dedicated to Cardinal Borghese. *Diversi Ornamenti capricciosi per depositi e altari* (1625; forty plates), dedicated to Cardinal Aldobrandino, and *Tabernacoli diversi* (1628; twenty-eight plates), dedicated to Tadeo Barberini, contain designs for monuments, altars and tabernacles, in a sophisticated ARTISAN MANNERIST style. *Architettura* (1636) contains the ORDERS and architectural details after the antique, neatly handled, with two lively plates of terms.

Monteforte, Alexander Wielemans von (1848–1911) Born in Vienna, Monteforte was trained as an architect at the academy there, subsequently working with Friedrich von SCHMIDT, one of his teachers. Monteforte designed interiors and furniture in his Justizpalast (1874–81) and other buildings in an eclectic RENAISSANCE manner.

Montfaucon, Dom Bernard de (1655–1741) Born into a noble family at the Château de Soulages in Languedoc, Montfaucon was brought up and largely self-educated at the Château de Roquetaillade. He became a military cadet in 1672, but after briefly serving in the army of Turenne he became in 1675 a Benedictine monk and rapidly became conspicuous for learning, specializing in the Early Fathers of the Church. In 1687 he moved to Paris. Montfaucon travelled to Rome and Italy from 1698 to 1701 and in 1702 published an illustrated account of his travels. He became a member of the Académie des Inscriptions in 1719. Montfaucon's *Antiquité Expliquée* (1719–24; fifteen volumes) included copious plates of Roman antiquities; an English edition appeared from 1721 to 1725 and a German abridgement at Nuremberg in 1757. Montfaucon was used by KENT, CHAMBERS, ADAM and Wedgwood and included by HOPE in his *Household Furniture* bibliography (1807). Montfaucon's *Monumens de la Monarchie Français* (1729–33; five volumes) used the topographical collection of François-Roger de Gaignières (1642–1715) to give an illustrated account of medieval France.

Monza Biennales In December 1917 the art teacher and socialist politician Guido Marangoni (1872–1941) wrote an open letter to Milan Council suggesting a major biennial exhibition of decorative art. The idea was influenced by the TURIN 1902 and Milan 1906 Exhibitions and encouraged by the Milan 1919 Exhibition of Decorative Arts in Lombardy. In 1923 the Prima Mostra Internazionale delle Arti Decorative was held at Monza in the palace designed for Archduke Ferdinand of Austria by Giuseppe Piermarini (1734–1808) and built from 1777 to 1780. Among the exhibits were glass, pottery and furniture designed by G. B. STELLA, a massy classical chest by Duilio Cambellotti (1876–1960), ceramics by PONTI, furniture by Vittorio Zecchio and Giuseppe Berti, and a Futurist room by DEPERO. The French showed furniture by RUHLMANN and SUE & MARE. The second Monza Biennale followed in 1925 (including furniture by Cambellotti and shawls by NIZZOLI), and the third in 1927 (with a poster by Nizzoli, furniture by Ponti, Orrefors glass by GATE and

HALD, and another Futurist room by Depero). In 1930 the last Monza exhibition was held, the precursor of the MILAN TRIENNALES. Gio Ponti was on the committee and also showed vases made by Richard Ginori. The English section included furniture by Gordon RUSSELL and Betty JOEL, and the Belgian a family bar with chrome-steel furniture by Alphonse Barrez.

Moore, Edward Chandler (1827–91) Moore worked in his father's New York silver firm, which made silver exclusively for Tiffany & Co. from 1851, and in 1868, when Tiffany & Co. took over the Moore firm, became TIFFANY'S chief silver designer. His works used Indian, Persian and NATURALISTIC ornament and from 1871 incorporated Japanese motifs. His work for Tiffany won a gold medal at the PARIS 1878 EXHIBITION and he was a strong influence on the young Louis Comfort Tiffany. In 1881, with the cabinet-maker Christian Herter (1840–83), Moore was a judge on the Warren, Fuller and Co.'s wallpaper competition which was won by Candace WHEELER. He was a distinguished collector of Persian glass and metalwork, leaving nearly 900 pieces to the Metropolitan Museum, New York.

Moreau, Charles (1762–1810) Born at Rimancour-près-Neufchâteau, Haute Marne, Moreau trained as an architect, winning the Prix de Rome in 1785. He then spent four years in Rome. On his return Moreau became pupil of the painter Jacques Louis DAVID and won the second prize for painting in 1792. Moreau assisted David in designing the furniture made by Jacob by 1788 after that shown in his *Oath of the Horatii* (1784). Moreau's *Fragments et Ornemens d'Architecture dessinés à Rome, d'après l'antique* (Paris, 1800, second edition, 1827) was intended as an ornamental supplement to Desgodetz's *Les*

Édifices antiques de Rome (Paris, 1682); it contained details of architectural ornament, objects in the Vatican Museum, the Medici VASE etc. In his preface Moreau paid tribute to the encouragement given to English industry by HAMILTON's *Vases*, to the detriment of French industry, but was confident that the French would surpass their rivals. Moreau showed at the Salon from 1791 to 1827. He had a reputation as a calm calculating professional in design.

Moreau, Jean Michel (1741–1814) Known as Moreau Le Jeune, Moreau was born in Paris. He was trained as an engraver and draughtsman. He worked on CAYLUS's *Recueil*, and in 1758 followed his teacher, LE LORRAIN, to St Petersburg, where he taught drawing at the Academy. On Le Lorrain's death in 1759 Moreau returned to Paris, where he was appointed Dessinateur des Menus Plaisirs as successor to C.-N. COCHIN. He illustrated works by Rousseau, Voltaire and Restif de la Bretonne, his illustrations including excellent representations of modern interior design. As Dessinateur et Graveur du Cabinet du Roi, Moreau recorded royal ceremonies. Moreau also contributed a design of ARABESQUE ornament to LAVALLÉE-POUSSIN's *Premier Cahier d'Arabesques*.

Morel-Ladeuil, Léonard (1820–88) Born in Clermont-Ferrand, Morel-Ladeuil became a pupil and collaborator of Antoine VECHTE, whom in 1859 he followed to England to work for Elkingtons of Birmingham as a designer of electroplate. His designs, all in a sophisticated RENAISSANCE revival style, included the Milton Shield, shown at the PARIS 1867 EXHIBITION; designs by Morel-Ladeuil were also shown at the VIENNA 1873 and PARIS 1878 EXHIBITIONS. In 1878 he was referred

to in the 'ART JOURNAL' as 'a master hand, an artist who has obtained the highest renown'.

Mores, Jacob Probably born in Hamburg in about 1550, Mores was working as a jeweller for Frederick II of Denmark in the 1570s, becoming a master in 1576. His clients included the town of Hamburg and local ruling families. He died before 1612. Designs by Mores for MANNERIST cups and ewers have survived, eighty-seven in all, including one in the form of an elephant and two, even more bizarrely, in the shape of the Holy Roman Emperor and Empress. He also designed jewels, similar in general form to those of MIGNOT, but encrusted with table-cut stones, mainly pendants but also including crowns, sword-hilts and a jewel casket. The surviving album of jewellery designs dates from between 1593 to 1607. The sketchier drawings must be designs, but Mores's finished representations may either be presentation designs or records of executed pieces.

Moresque The inventories of Piero de' Medici in 1463 and Lorenzo de' Medici in 1492 included many pieces of Islamic metalwork. In about 1500 Moslem craftsmen working in Venice were producing brass vessels with damascened ornament in a Turkish style composed of interlacing bands or stems, embellished with subsidiary tendrils and leaves and forming a dense carpet of polygonal and ogival compartments. DÜRER was in Venice before 1507 and about this date published woodcut copies of elaborate knots probably designed under the aegis of Leonardo da Vinci, themselves influenced by Islamic ornament. TAGLIENTE's collection of embroidery designs *Essempio di ricammi*, published in Venice in 1527, is the first pattern-book to include unequivocally moresque ornament, although it had been used earlier to decorate the title-page of Baptista da Crema's *Via de aperta verita* (Venice, 1523), and on many Venetian bookbindings. Tagliente also included knots similar to those copied by Dürer, which he called '*groppi moreschi et arabeschi*' (moresque and arabesque knots). The terms moresque and ARABESQUE were interchangeable at this period but, as in the 18th century arabesque came to mean GROTESQUE, moresque is a less confusing term. The most influential early moresque pattern-book was Francesco PELLEGRINO'S *La fleur de la Science de Pourtraicture* (Paris, 1530). Pellegrino worked at Fontainebleau under ROSSO, the pioneer of STRAPWORK. Pellegrino's designs were copied by BOS and later by Gourmont. It is probable that the band-work aspect of moresque encouraged Cornelis FLORIS and Bos in the development of a lighter more versatile form of strapwork. The first English pattern-book, Thomas GEMINUS'S *Morysse and Damashin* (London, 1548), was in the moresque style, while the best-known work was Balthasar SYLVIUS's *Maurusias* (1554). By about 1600, however, the moresque had been subsumed into the grotesque and had lost its own stylistic identity.

Morghen, Filippo Morghen was born in Florence in 1730, the son of a businessman from Montpelier. He was trained as an engraver and worked first in Rome and later in Naples, where he became engraver to the King. He was responsible for most of the plates in *Antichità di Ercolano* (Naples, 1757–62) and forty plates in *Antichità di Pozzuoli* (1769). Morghen's *Raccolta delle Cose più notabile vedute dal Cavaliere Wild Skull, e dal Sigr. de la Hire nel lor famoso viaggio della Terra alla Luna* (nine plates) is one of the most enchanting *jeux-d'esprit* in the history of ornament. It comprises lunar CHINOISERIES of sparkling invention, wholly ROCOCO in style and

spirit; the work was dedicated to Sir William HAMILTON ('Guglielmo Amilton'), appointed British Ambassador in Naples in 1764. Morghen's son Raphael Morghen (1758–1833) married Volpato's daughter and became a celebrated engraver.

Morien, Jean Morien published in 1612 a suite of six black designs for enamelling on jewels.

Morison, Stanley Arthur (1889–1967) Born in Wanstead, Essex, the son of an unsuccessful commercial traveller, Morison was successively office boy and clerk before in 1912 joining the printing journal, the 'IMPRINT' (1913), through an advertisement in *The Times*. After its demise he designed books for the Catholic publishers Burns & Oates. In 1919 he joined Francis Meynell's Pelican Press as 'designer of printed matter'. He left in 1921 to work for the Cloister Press but when this failed in 1922 helped to launch the 'FLEURON' with Oliver Simon. Also in 1922 he was appointed typographical adviser to the Monotype Corporation. For Monotype, Morison revived Garamond (1922), Baskerville (1923) and Fournier (1924) among other old typefaces. New typefaces introduced by Morison included Gill Sans (1928) by Eric GILL and Albertus (1935–40) by WOLPE. His most famous personal achievement was Times New Roman (1932). His *First Principles of Typography* (1936, but earlier published in *Encyclopaedia Britannica*, 1929) reflects the authority which Morison established in this field; it has repeatedly been republished and translated. Morison exercised influence not only through Monotype – he was also typographical adviser to the Cambridge University Press from 1925, designed book-jackets for Victor Gollancz in 1929, wrote widely and learnedly on the history of calligraphy, typography, printing and allied subjects, and was friendly with many distinguished typographers at home and abroad, including, for example, Bruce Rogers (1870–1957) and Giovanni Mardersteig (1892–1977). Converted to Catholicism in 1908, Morison was a conscientious objector in the First World War, a railway enthusiast, a socialist and a republican.

Morisson, Friedrich Jacob Morisson published two suites of designs for jewellery and enamelling (1693 and 1697) in Vienna, ten plates in all. A third suite, *Unterschidliche neue Feston, von Blumen und Früchten* (twelve plates), comprises NATURALISTIC swags of fruit and flowers, combined with small black scrolled motifs for enamel. It seems to have been published first in Vienna in 1697 and then in Augsburg in 1699 by Jeremias Wolff, presumably after Morisson's death. Wolff later issued *Unterschiedliche neüe Inventionen* (two parts, fourteen plates in all), engraved posthumously after Morisson's designs; it shows brooches, aigrettes, pendants, etc., many with large stones, and also boxes, flasks, handles, sword-hilts, fan handles, and a prayer-book cover, in a rich combination of scrolled, floral and BERAINESQUE ornament.

Morris, Talwin (1865–1911) Born in Winchester, Talwin Morris was trained as an architect under his uncle, Joseph Morris of Reading. He then was on the staff of the periodical *Black and White*, and subsequently, in 1893, became Art Director of Blackie & Sons of Glasgow. In this capacity he was a gifted and prolific designer of ART NOUVEAU bookbindings. He also designed some stained glass, furniture and metalwork. Morris was associated with the Glasgow School, his work being discussed with that of Herbert J. MACNAIR in an article by Gleeson White in the 'STUDIO' (1897). In 1902 he introduced

Charles Rennie MACKINTOSH to Mr W. W. Blackie, an introduction which resulted in Hill House, one of Mackintosh's masterpieces.

Morris, William (1834–96) Born in Walthamstow on the outskirts of London, the son of a wealthy stockbroker, Morris was educated at Marlborough, one of the new Victorian public schools. In 1853 he went to Exeter College, Oxford, intending to become a clergyman, and rapidly struck up a friendship with BURNE-JONES. Architecture and design became his main interests and RUSKIN and the 'BUILDER' prominent in his reading. In 1854 he visited Amiens, Beauvais and Chartres. He returned there in 1855 with Burne-Jones, the two friends committing themselves at the end of their holiday to art, Morris to architecture and Burne-Jones to painting. In 1856 Morris entered the office of G. E. STREET, where Philip WEBB was senior clerk, and began to study architecture. However, he soon fell under the influence of ROSSETTI and started to paint. In 1856 Burne-Jones and Morris moved into a house in Red Lion Square for which Morris designed some massive GOTHIC furniture. In 1857 they were involved with Hungerford POLLEN and others painting murals in the Oxford Union, designed by the architect Benjamin Woodward. In 1858 Morris travelled to France once more, this time with Philip Webb, who then built the Red House at Bexley Heath near London for Morris from 1859 to 1860. It is a handsome red-brick house in the style of William BUTTERFIELD and Street, which Morris decorated in the Gothic style, with furniture designed by Webb. Morris's experience in commissioning appropriate decorations and furniture for the Red House led him, at Ford Madox BROWN's suggestion, to form a cooperative firm to produce well-designed and executed decorative work. Morris, Marshall, Faulkner & Co. began business in 1861 with Burne-Jones, Webb, Rossetti and Madox Brown as partners, as well as those names in the title. At the LONDON 1862 EXHIBITION the firm filled two stalls with its products, including the St George cabinet (1861), designed by Webb and painted by Morris. Morris himself, the main financial prop of the firm, gradually took over complete control in the mid-1860s, but with his private income declining and the firm's accounts ill disciplined the future of the venture was doubtful until Warington Taylor started as accountant in 1865. In 1875 Morris took over complete control of the firm himself. In 1865 he had given up the Red House and moved to London. The main early product of Morris & Co. was stained glass, in whose design Burne-Jones, Webb and Rossetti played the main roles. Morris himself designed some figure subjects, but was mainly active as a designer of lay-outs and backgrounds, especially around 1870. Morris & Co. also executed many decorative schemes, ecclesiastical and secular, including Queen's College Hall (1875) and Jesus College Chapel (1867–74) in Cambridge, the Green Dining Room (1866) in the VICTORIA & ALBERT MUSEUM, and two rooms in St James's Palace (1866–7). Morris's own designing work included a group of three wallpaper patterns issued from 1864 to 1866; one of them, Trellis, incorporated birds and insects by Philip Webb. They repeated simple naturalistic motifs, but were not successful until the 1870s. In 1871 Morris designed three more geometric patterns. From 1872 to 1876 he designed seventeen wallpaper patterns, including Jasmine, Vine and Apple, in which natural forms are arranged in rich and vigorous scrolled patterns. After 1876 Morris's wallpaper designs tended to a more formal treatment of flowers and foliage,

although a final group designed in the 1890s combines naturalism and formalism. Having designed an experimental chintz, Tulip and Willow, in 1873, Morris began in 1874 to work seriously on the design and technique of textiles, investigating the latter at Thomas Wardle's factory in Leek in Staffordshire from 1875. In 1875 his scrolling Honeysuckle chintz was produced and Wardle printed five other designs, including Tulip, up to 1877. From 1881 to 1885 Morris designed over twenty patterns for chintzes printed at Merton Abbey, where he set up print works in 1881, including Bird and Anenome, and Strawberry Thief. Later chintz designs include Daffodil (1891). Morris & Co. supplied embroidery kits including designs by Morris, who also designed embroidery for the Royal School of Needlework (founded 1872). In 1878 Morris started to make hand-tufted carpets in the stables of his house in Hammersmith. However, his finest carpets were woven at Merton Abbey from about 1881, including the great carpet of 1887 for Clouds, the house designed by Philip Webb for Percy Wyndham from 1877. Morris also designed several machine-made carpets for the Wilton, Axminster, Kidderminster and other factories. He also designed silk and woollen fabrics for Morris & Co., many influenced by the textile collection at South Kensington which he studied assiduously; they include the woollen tapestry Bird of 1878, which he used in the drawing-room at Kelmscott House, the Oxfordshire country house he had occupied since 1871, and the silk Oak designed in 1880 to 1881 for the Throne Room at St James's Palace. In 1878 Morris began to experiment with weaving tapestry; he completed his first piece, Cabbage and Vine, in 1879. For other tapestries woven by Morris & Co. at Merton from 1881 Morris designed only foliate backgrounds, figures being by Burne-Jones, except for the Woodpecker (1885). From 1870 to 1876 Morris was active as an illuminator of manuscripts. In around 1870 he planned editions of his poems *The Earthly Paradise* and *Love is Enough* with illustrations by Burne-Jones, but it was only in 1888 that Morris, influenced by a lecture in printing by his Hammersmith neighbour Emery Walker (1851–1933) at the ARTS & CRAFTS EXHIBITION, designed his first book, *The House of the Wolfings*, printed by the Chiswick Press. In 1889 Morris decided to set up his own press and in 1891 the Kelmscott Press began printing. It closed in 1898, having produced fifty-three books. Morris designed three typefaces, Golden (1889), Troy (1891) and Chaucer (1892), the former Roman, based on Jenson, the latter two Gothic. For the Kelmscott Chaucer (1896) Burne-Jones designed eighty-seven illustrations. Morris himself produced in all some 664 designs for initials, borders, title-pages etc. for the Kelmscott Press. Kelmscott books were mainly expensive de luxe products for the collector. One of the earliest was Ruskin's *The Nature of Gothic* (1892). Ruskin was a life-long influence on Morris, and Morris was always at his happiest with the Gothic style. Born a High Victorian, Morris was not an innovator in design; his foundation in 1877 of the Society for the Protection of Ancient Buildings reflected conservation as well as an enlightened attitude towards conservation under Ruskin's influence. But Morris's designs, especially his flat patterns, display a marvellous fusion of richness and power. Morris's greatest influence was as a teacher and as a leader. His gifts as a poet, his inherited wealth and status, his power as an orator and propagandist, his generosity and his apparently inexhaustible energy, a happy combination of advantages and talents, all fitted him for this role. Loved and admired as Morris was, it is not surprising that his followers should have exaggerated his role as a pioneer reformer of design, especially given his involvement in the proposed reform of society through Socialism, which he took up seriously from 1883. There were tensions and inconsistencies in this socialist who spent many of his best years 'ministering to the swinish luxury of the rich', this artist-craftsman who designed for the machine, this Victorian businessman who was buried from a hay-cart in Kelmscott churchyard, with a gravestone designed by Philip Webb. But of Morris's greatness as a designer and his international influence from the 1880s there can be no question.

Mosbach, Hans Georg Mosbach designed a suite (six plates) of jewellery in the COSSE-DE-POIS manner, with frames and brooches suspended above figures, engraved by Balthasar MONCORNET in 1626.

Moser, George Michael (1704–83) Born in Schaffhausen, the son of an engineer and metalworker, Moser was trained as a chaser in Geneva. He then moved to London in about 1721 and was at first employed by the cabinet-maker John Trotter, who later subscribed to CHIPPENDALE's *Director* (1754), as a chaser of furniture mounts. Moser later became the leading gold chaser in London and was also an enamellist, responsible for many watches and snuff-boxes. Moser was manager and treasurer of the ST MARTIN'S LANE ACADEMY, founded in 1735. He was also a drawing-master to the young George III, and engraved his great seal on his accession in 1760. Moser was a founder member of the Society of Artists, and became founder Keeper of the Royal Academy in 1768. Moser illustrated a book of *Fables* (1746), and also provided designs for silver. One of these, a candlestick influenced by MEISSONIER, probably dating from about 1740, provided a model for more than one silversmith, and represents one of the rare fully ROCOCO silver designs to have been executed in England. Moser also designed decorations for the Rotunda at Vauxhall in the 1740s.

Moser, Koloman (1868–1918) Born in Vienna, where his father was a school porter, Moser entered the Academy to study painting in 1888. He earned money by doing illustrations to *Wiener Mode* and other journals. In 1892 he moved to the school of applied arts to study design and in 1894 he was a member of the Siebener Club with OLBRICH and Josef HOFFMANN. In 1895 Moser designed a set of leafy and bosomy ART NOUVEAU allegories for the publisher Martin Gerlach. Through Gerlach Moser met Klimt and in 1897 he was a founder member of the Vienna Secession. He designed postcards and *vignettes* for the first Secession Exhibition (1898) and decorations and a stained-glass window for Olbrich's Secession building (1898). Also in 1898 Moser designed the cover for *Die Kunst für Alle* and began to design for 'VER SACRUM'. In 1899 he began to teach at the School of Applied Arts, refusing an invitation from Olbrich to move to Darmstadt; Moser was a professor at the School from 1900 to his death. In 1899 he designed glass for Bakalovits, furniture for Portois & Fix, and textiles for Johann Backhausen & Sons. Furniture by Moser was shown at the 1900 Secession Exhibition and he organized the Secession section in the Austrian pavilion at the PARIS 1900 EXHIBITION. Moser's title-page for Arno Holz's *Die Blechschmiede* (1901) had a border of small black squares, and his poster for the 1902 Secession Exhibition employed schematic geometric patterns, also used in his publication of surface ornament as the third volume of *Die Quelle* (1901). In 1903 Moser founded the WIENER

WERKSTÄTTE together with Hoffmann and Fritz Wärndorfer, the financial backer for whom Moser designed a Beardsleyesque book-plate (1903). Until 1907, when he quarrelled with Wärndorfer and left the venture, Moser was a prolific designer for the Werkstätte. His designs include furniture, jewellery, metalwork, leather, toys and bookbindings, usually in a decorative rectilinear style. In 1904 he designed vigorous stained glass for Wagner's Kirche am Steinhof. In 1908 he designed postage stamps for the Emperor Franz Josef's jubilee and in 1909 he won a competition to decorate the Heilige-geistkirche in Düsseldorf, a scheme which remained unexecuted. From about 1908, however, Moser was mainly active as a painter working in a style similar to that of Ferdinand Hodler (1853–1918).

Moses, Henry Moses, who was born in about 1782 and died in 1870, was a specialist in the use of line engraving in the manner of FLAXMAN. He engraved the plates to Thomas HOPE's *Costume of the Ancients* (1809) and in 1812 published *Designs of Modern Costume* (second expanded edition, 1823), whose twenty plates incorporate many objects designed by Hope. Moses's *A Collection of Antique Vases, Altars, Paterae, Tripods, Candelabra, Sarcophagi, etc.* (1814; 150 plates) was dedicated to Hope and listed by J. C. ROBINSON in his 1853 bibliography. Moses also published *Vases from the Collection of Sir Henry Englefield* (1819), among other works.

Motif (1958–67) Subtitled *A Journal of the Visual Arts* this luxury magazine was edited by Ruari McLean and published by the Shenval Press, founded by James Shand (1905–67) in 1930. Its emphasis was on book illustration and typography, and a dashing variety of lay-out and style matched its subjects.

Mourei, Homer Presumably French, Mourei published in 1636 a series of designs for keyhole escutcheons, lockplates and their ornament, coarse but vigorous exercises in an early BAROQUE manner.

M.T. The Master M.T., long identified for no good reason as Martin Treu, was probably active in North Germany. He published some fifty-five plates dated from 1540 to 1543: he was strongly influenced by ALDEGREVER. M.T.'s designs include a dagger and sheath, a cutlery case, hunting whistles and panels of early RENAISSANCE ornament. His vocabulary of masks and fleshy leaves was old-fashioned by 1540, but M.T. handled his style with a crude energy.

Mucha, Alphonse (1860–1939) Born at Ivancice in Moravia, Mucha worked as a theatrical painter in Vienna from 1879, coming under the influence of Hans Makart (1840–84). In 1883 he was employed on a scheme of decoration by Count Khuen-Belassi, who encouraged him and financed his studies of painting in Munich from 1884 to 1887, and in Paris from 1888. There Mucha soon commenced his prolific career as a book illustrator, a decorative artist and a graphic designer; his first stamp designs were made in 1889, his first poster in 1892. Mucha's breakthrough to success came with his poster for Sarah Bernhardt as *Gismonda* (1894), which led her to secure his services under contract for six years and to later posters including *Lorenzaccio* (1896) and *Médée* (1898). In 1897 an exhibition of 107 works by Mucha was held in Paris, and a special number of the magazine *La Plume* devoted to his work; part of the exhibition later travelled to Prague, Munich, Brussels, London and New York. His posters for the Salon des Cent (1896), Job cigarette papers (1898), Waverley Cycles (1898) and Moët & Chandon

(1899) consolidated his reputation; in all he designed at least eighty-three posters, as well as numerous calendars, menus and other publicity material, including biscuit tins, and the packaging of a soap which bore his name (1907). Mucha also issued a series of decorative panels, posters without a title, such as Les Quatre Saisons (1896), Les Fleurs (1897), and Les Quatre Arts (1898), and these, together with postcards issued in 1900, and pressed metal and ceramic wall ornaments, helped to publicize his work. Of his book illustrations the most successful are those for *Ilsée* (1897) and *Cloches de Noël et de Pâques* (1900); each page is fully integrated, with interlace borders and richly varied formats. *Le Pater* (1899) is overpoweringly symbolical. Mucha also designed covers for many magazines, including *L'Image* and *Cocorico*. In about 1897 Mucha opened his own school of design; he taught up to 1904. Also around 1897 he designed floral prints for textiles; they seem to have been commissioned by Karl Gustave Forrer, a Swiss designer working in Paris for whom Georges DE FEURE also designed. Mucha textiles were later illustrated in 'TEXTILE KUNST UND INDUSTRIE'. In 1899 Mucha was asked to design the Bosnia-Herzegovina pavilion at the PARIS 1900 EXHIBITION, which was awarded a medal. The Paris 1900 Exhibition also included jewellery, scent bottles and a carpet designed by Mucha. The jewellery was for Georges FOUQUET (1862–1957), whose shop Mucha subsequently designed (1900–1901) in every detail, stained glass, furniture, door handles, lights and, on the outside, an alluring female seminude in bronze relief. Jewellery designed by Mucha for Fouquet was later shown at the Liège 1905 and Milan 1906 exhibitions. Mucha's *Documents Décoratifs* (1902; seventy-two plates) comprised designs for posters, book covers, plant studies, letters, wall decorations, furniture, carpets, lights, ceramics, cutlery and jewels, many in colour, using a wide range of printing techniques. It was followed by *Figures Décoratives* (1905; forty plates), which presented a repertoire of female figures for decorative purposes. From this period Mucha began to spend an increasing proportion of his time in his native Czechoslovakia. He settled there in 1910, although he continued to work for spells in Paris up to 1913, and from 1904 to 1909 spent periods in America. It was at a Smetana concert in Boston in 1908 that he determined to devote his life and art to the Slav cause, of which the most notable result was his suite of twenty paintings on the Slav epic (1909–28). However, he continued to be active as a designer, producing the first Czechoslovakian stamps in 1918 and designing a window for Prague Cathedral in 1931. Mucha had a lifetime devotion to the theatre, his memoirs (1936) being divided into acts and scenes like a play. The most important influences on his work were CHÉRET and GRASSET. In the mid-1890s he developed a basic formula of attractive girls with swirling hair and draperies entangled in flowers, part formalized and part representational, in subtle combinations of often pale colours. These provided and, since the 1963 VICTORIA & ALBERT MUSEUM Exhibition and the accompanying booklet by Brian Reade, have continued to provide archetypally ART NOUVEAU pin-ups. As a designer Mucha was highly professional – for example he made extensive use of photography. However, his vocabulary varied little according to material, and his style, once fixed, underwent no significant development.

Müller, Gotfried In 1620 Müller moved from Hamburg to Brunswick and was there active as a publisher. His *News Compertament Buchlein* (1621; about eighteen plates) displays aprons, brackets and cartouches in a scrolly AURICULAR style, and is one of the earliest pattern-books in this manner.

Müller, Jacob Müller wrote *Ornatus Ecclesiasticus* (Munich, 1591), published simultaneously in German as *Kirchen Geschmuck*. He was a vicar of the Bishop of Regensburg and his book is a liturgical manual illustrated by model designs for fonts, altars, candlesticks, censers, chalices, ewers, etc., some in the RENAISSANCE style, others in a GOTHIC survival manner. A monstrance is indebted to the Master W⸶. *Ornatus* was published by Adam Berg, court printer in Munich, and the leading South German publisher of the counter-reformation.

Munari, Bruno Born in Milan in 1907, Munari was active as a second-wave futurist painter around 1930. In 1933 he showed *Macchine inutili*, machines with no function. After 1945 Munari was an abstract painter and in 1948 a founder of the Movimento Arte Concreta, with which Dorfles and COLOMBO were also associated. He designed more *Macchine inutili* and in his *Macchinismo* manifesto (1952) announced '*Noi scopriremo l'arte delle macchine!*' ('We shall discover the art of machines!'). Munari published much portentous *avant-garde* theorizing on communication and design but was also active as a designer himself. His cube ashtray for Danese was much admired, as were many lights and toys. Munari's Blocco Abitabile (1968) and Abitacolo (1970) were minimum flexible dwelling units, the one composed of blocks, the other a flexible scaffold.

Munich 1876 Exhibition The Munich 1876 Exhibition was organized by the Bayerischer Kunstgewerbe-Verein under its president, the sculptor Ferdinand von Miller (1813-87), to celebrate its twenty-fifth anniversary. The exhibition, exclusively devoted to German art, had a strongly nationalistic character. A German RENAISSANCE room designed by Gabriel von SEIDL attracted much attention and imitation. The exhibition was later seen as the beginning of a revival in German design. A repeat was planned for 1886 but clashed with the Berlin Exhibition of that year and was postponed to 1888. The Munich 1888 Exhibition was again exclusively German, an aspect stressed in the poster by Rudolf von SEITZ (1842–1910). The main styles were GOTHIC, Renaissance, as in a cabinet by Himmelheber of Karlsruhe, and ROCOCO, exemplified in a large group of objects designed for LUDWIG II.

Munich Vereinigte Werkstätten In 1897 the Munich Glaspalast Exhibition included a small applied arts section with works designed by PAUL, PANKOK and OBRIST. Its success led to the foundation in 1898 of the Vereinigte Werkstätten für Kunst im Handwerk (United Workshops for Art in Handwork). The Vereinigte Werkstätten, directed by the painter Franz August Otto Krüger, had workshops and a showroom, and was the first German venture of this kind. Designers associated with the Vereinigte Werkstätten included BEHRENS, Obrist, Pankok, Paul and RIEMERSCHMID. The Vereinigte Werkstätten showed first at the Munich 1898 Glaspalast Exhibition; three rooms by Pankok, Paul and Riemerschmid were shown at the PARIS 1900 EXHIBITION, and a room by Paul at the ST LOUIS 1904 EXHIBITION. In 1902 VAN DE VELDE praised the achievement of the Werkstätten in 'INNEN-DEKORATION' but they had little commercial success and most of their designers soon left Munich. However, the Brussels 1910 Exhibitions contained several rooms by the Vereinigte

Werkstätten designed by Paul, Troost and Schröder.

Muntinck, Adrian A goldsmith and engraver from Groningen, Muntinck seems to have worked there as well as in Amsterdam. In 1597, 1610, 1611 and 1614 he published suites of designs for engraving on silver, a total of some thirty-six plates. They include birds and insects, and STRAPWORK GROTESQUES for the borders of vessels. Muntinck was probably brother to Hinrich Muntinck, whose suite of terms (ten plates) he engraved in 1604. These are handsome designs in the manner of Hans VREDEMAN DE VRIES, based on the five ORDERS of architecture.

Müntz, Johann Heinrich (1727–98) Born in Mülhausen in Alsace, Müntz was recorded drawing Moorish architecture in Spain in 1748. From 1749 to 1753 he was in Rome,, where from 1751 he did many drawings of Egyptian and Roman urns and VASES; gathered together for publication in 1772, they included examples from the Villa Borghese and the Villa Medici in Rome, from the Palazzo Reale in Parma and from the HAMILTON collection. In 1753 he was an officer in the French army in Nantes, but his regiment disbanded and in 1755 he came to England with an introduction from Richard BENTLEY, whom he had met in Jersey, to John Chute (1701–76) and Horace WALPOLE, for both of whom he worked. Müntz was mainly active as a draughtsman and landscape painter but also designed the GOTHIC Cathedral at Kew (1759), where he worked with CHAMBERS, a Gothic room (1761–2) for Dicky Bateman, and a Gothic 'Egyptian Room' (1762) at Lord Charlemont's house at Marino near Dublin, for which he did more designs in 1768; he was probably in contact with LE GEAY at this period. In 1759 Müntz did drawings of St Albans Cathedral and in 1760 proposed *A Course of Gothic Architecture*, which came to nothing. In 1760 he published *Encaustic*, observations on the book by CAYLUS. Müntz moved to Holland in 1763 and showed paintings there until 1776. In 1765 MANWARING published two Gothic designs by Müntz, whom he described as 'one of the most ingenious Gentlemen that ever was in England'. Müntz was in Poland and Ukraine from 1780 to 1783, travelling with Count Stanislaw Poniatowski, in Florence in 1785 and from 1792 in Kassel.

Murer, Christoph (1558–1614) Born in Zürich, the son of the glass painter and designer Jos Murer (1530–80), Christoph Murer travelled as a journeyman to Basel from about 1580, and to Strasbourg from about 1583 to 1586. Back in Zürich from 1586 he worked as a prolific designer of stained glass and woodcuts. His main contemporary rival was LINDTMAYER. From 1611 Murer lived in Winterthur, where he died.

Murray, Keith (1892–1981) Born in Auckland, New Zealand, Murray trained as an architect at the Architectural Association school after the First World War, in which he served in the air force. He was interested in old glass, and after the PARIS 1925 EXHIBITION, impressed by the design of Swedish, Viennese, Czech and Finnish glass shown there, determined to improve the low standard of English glass design by reviving the plainness he liked in old English glass and by using flat rather than deep cutting. He began to experiment at the Whitefriars glassworks. Then from 1932 he was employed as designer by Hubert S. Williams-Thomas of Stevens & Williams of Brierley Hill, Staffordshire, whose blown method of production better suited his approach to design. Before putting Murray's designs

into production Williams-Thomas consulted Gordon RUSSELL and Ambrose HEAL. As a result of their advice Stevens & Williams produced Murray's entire design output of simple and brilliant geometric forms decorated with simple repeated cut motifs. The range was widely publicized and attracted much praise. In 1933 Murray published an article 'The Design of Table Glass' in *Design for Today* in which he set forth a typical FUNCTIONALIST credo. Also in 1933 Murray was engaged by Wedgwoods as a designer, and his bold geometric forms for their earthenware and basalt were as successful as had been his glass designs. They employed fluted and ridged ornament, sometimes hand-thrown, sometimes engine-turned, and the Moonstone (1933), Matt Green (1935) and Matt Straw (1935) glazes developed by the Wedgwood chemists. Murray was also used as a designer from 1934 by the silversmiths, Mappin & Webb. In 1935 an exhibition, Glass, Pottery and Silver Designed by Mr Keith Murray, was held at the Medici Galleries. Murray's work was also shown in the exhibitions British Industrial Art in Relation to the Home (Dorland Hall, London, 1933), the MILAN 1933 TRIENNALE, English Pottery Old and New (VICTORIA & ALBERT MUSEUM, 1935), British Art in Industry (Royal Academy, 1935) and at the PARIS 1937 INTERNATIONAL EXHIBITION. In his chosen fields he was unassailably the leading MODERN British designer. After 1939 however he exchanged his role as a designer for that of architect, the new Wedgwood factory (1938–40) being the first work in this new career.

Mussard, Jean (1644–1703) A member of a celebrated Geneva family of goldsmiths and enamellers, Mussard published *Livre de Divers Ornements d'orfèvrerie* (Geneva, 1673; six plates engraved by J. L. Durant). It was copied in London as *A Book of Divers Ornaments proper for most sorts of Artificers, but particularly for such who Engrave on Plate, &c.*, and comprises scrolly ACANTHUS and floral ornaments and brooches, including fierce masks formed of leafy scrolls. REUTIMANN later borrowed from Mussard.

Muthesius, Hermann (1861–1927) Born in Gross-Neuhausen in Thuringia, the son of a mason, Muthesius worked under his father and then from 1881 to 1883 studied philosophy in Berlin. From 1883 to 1886 he studied architecture at the Technische Hochschule in Berlin; he then worked for a while under the architect Paul Wallot (1841–1912). From 1887 to 1891 Muthesius worked as an architect in Tokyo. Then, in 1893, he became a Prussian government architect; from 1894 to 1895 he edited the official architectural journal. In 1896 Muthesius was appointed to the German Embassy in London and began to study English progress in architecture and design. He published numerous articles in 'DEKORATIVE KUNST' and elsewhere, for example on William MORRIS and the 5th ARTS & CRAFTS EXHIBITION (1897), on ASHBEE's Guild and School of Handicraft (1898), on BENSON's lights (1902), on MACKINTOSH (1902) and on WALTON's Kodak shops (1903). In England Muthesius was friendly with Walter CRANE, the M*/*· NAIRS and MACKINTOSH, and wrote books on the Arts & Crafts movement (1900) and English architecture (1900). After returning to Berlin he published the three-volume *Das Englische Haus* (1904–5, second revised edition 1908–11), a comprehensive account of the history, architecture and interior of the English house in which he illustrated and praised the work of Norman SHAW, VOYSEY, BAILLIE SCOTT, Edgar WOOD, Walton, Benson, LUTYENS, LORIMER and many others. From 1904 to 1926 Muthesius was an official in the Prussian trade ministry and helped to reform Prussian schools of design. He also built a large number of houses influenced by English prototypes, many, including his own (1906), including furniture and fittings designed by Muthesius. A prolific journalist, Muthesius tirelessly agitated and propagandized for improvement in German design, goading manufacturers with his attacks on historicism to such an extent that a debate was held in Berlin in 1907 to respond to his strictures. Muthesius was the moving spirit behind the foundation of the DEUTSCHE WERKBUND in 1907, delivered the keynote address at the 1911 Werkbund congress and at the COLOGNE 1914 EXHIBITION was involved in a public debate with VAN DE VELDE, in which he asserted that the designer must be concerned with standardization and, by implication, with industrial products. In 1922 Muthesius edited *Die Schöne Wohnung* (1922, second edition, 1926), in which he published modern houses by himself, RIEMERSCHMID and others.

N

Nahl, Johann August (1710–85) Born in Berlin, the son of a sculptor who worked under Schlüter, Nahl trained in Paris and, from 1736, in Strasbourg, where he worked on the Palais Rohan. In 1741 he returned to Berlin, where as Directeur des Ornements under KNOBELSDORFF he developed a graceful and brilliant ROCOCO style of decoration as carver and designer. Nahl worked in Schloss Charlottenburg, and in the Stadtschloss and Schloss Sanssouci in Potsdam. In 1746 however, tired of being overworked by the insatiable Frederick the Great, he fled first to Strasbourg and thence to Bern. From 1755 he was in Kassel, where he executed the decoration of Schloss Wilhelmsthal (1755–73), and in 1777 became director of the academy.

Nash, Paul (1889–1946) Trained from 1906 as a painter, Nash enrolled at the Slade School in 1910, paying his fees from the proceeds of book-plates designed in a style derived from William MORRIS, the Century Guild and Beardsley. In 1914 he was briefly involved with the Omega Workshop. His textile designs, encouraged at first by Claud Lovat FRASER, were produced from 1925 to 1929 by the Footprints Workshop for Miss Little's Modern Textiles shop, from 1929 by Cresta Silks Ltd, and from 1936 by the Old Beach Linen Company. In the early 1930s he designed rugs for R. W. Symonds and upholstery for London Transport. He also did posters for the latter, and from 1932 to 1937 for Shell-Mex and B.P. Ltd. In 1931 Nash provided designs for Chance Brothers' rolled glass, and in about 1934 for E. Brain & Co.'s Foley China, for Clarice CLIFF's Bizarre range and for Stuart & Sons' crystal table glass. His most spectacular commission was in 1932, a bathroom for Tilly Losch, the dancer wife of Edward James, in which he used an abstract combination of mirrors, coloured and textured glass, chrome tubing, black glazed earthenware, a pink rubber floor and tube lighting. In 1936 a large abstract wood mural was exhibited by the Timber Development Association. Throughout his career Nash did book illustrations and ephemera, mainly for private presses. He was also an accomplished photographer. Nash's · Presidency of the Society of Industrial Artists from 1932 to 1934, his own exhibition Room and Book, and his participation in the Royal Academy British Art in Industry Exhibition, 1935 (see LONDON EXHIBITIONS), were further evidence of a serious interest in design on the part of one who, as an official War Artist in the First and Second World Wars, as a founder of UNIT ONE in 1933 and as an exhibitor at the 1936 Surrealist Exhibition, was one of the pillars of the MODERN art establishment. His designs often incorporate naturalistic elements and romantic and surrealist motifs, yet are far more abstract than his paintings. But despite this, and Nash's advocacy in writing of abstraction and of natural and artificial materials in the raw, much of his *œuvre* as a designer represents a Modern version of the de luxe one-off aspect of the Arts & Crafts movement.

His involvement in design petered out from the mid-1930s, but Nash remains the pattern of the English Modern artist-designer of that decade.

Nasoni, Nicolau (1691–1773) Trained in Siena, Nasoni worked for a while in Malta before emigrating in 1725 to Oporto, where he was active as painter and architect. He also designed silver and woodwork in a rich BAROQUE style into which he later incorporated vigorous ROCOCO ornament, a mixture which had a wide influence in Portugal.

Naturalism The use of natural forms for ornament has been continuous throughout history. GOTHIC ornament represents a high-water mark of naturalism; even late-Gothic foliage such as that designed by MECKENEM and SCHONGAUER can exhibit great vigour. Renaissance designers, drawing their inspiration from Roman architecture and artefacts, tended to use nature at second-hand, the floral swags and ACANTHUS of the Ara Pacis being particularly popular models. However, Giovanni da UDINE made direct use of natural forms in his GROTESQUE decorations and Wenzel JAMNITZER made direct casts of small reptiles in silver, reflecting not only technical virtuosity but also the MANNERIST fascination with the miniature and the extreme in nature. The potter Bernard Palissy is a similar case. The early 17th-century COSSE-DE-POIS style, practised by French jewellery designers such as TOUTIN, SYMONY, CAILLART and MONCORNET, represents an artificial naturalism. A simpler taste for flowers and leaves is apparent in the early 17th-century embroidery designs of Thomas TREVELYON. In the later 17th century, at the same time as an acanthus style, an international floral style developed; MONNOYER, VAUQUER, REUTIMANN and Paul Androuet DUCERCEAU were among its practitioners. The latter designed textiles, and floral ornament was from REVEL to LASALLE and onwards the stock-in-trade of most textile designers. In the late 18th century the elegant realism of Louis TESSIER's designs contrasts with Jean PILLEMENT's fantastic flowers. The use of native plants for ornament by George BULLOCK and Richard BROWN marks the beginning of the 19th-century fascination with botanical ornament. At the LONDON 1851 EXHIBITION the use of realistically treated natural forms for decoration was widely condemned. In reaction the conventional treatment of nature, advocated by A. W. N. PUGIN and Owen JONES, RUPRICH-ROBERT and Christopher DRESSER, became an important element in design education, and textbooks on the subjects were produced by G. C. HAITÉ, F. E. HULME and many others. RUSKIN and William MORRIS were both ardent advocates of nature as the source of ornament and the Arts & Crafts generation of designers followed their teaching. ART NOUVEAU designers were equally committed to nature as the source of their designs. COLONNA, GRASSET and MAJORELLE are instances and GALLÉ published extensively on botany and horticulture. A cheerful and colourful naturalism dominated the vocabulary of some ART DÉCO designers, notably DUFY and the working girls who designed for POIRET's Atelier Martine. Although textile designers have continued to use natural forms, innovatory naturalism has been uncommon in the 20th century. The project to use crystal structure diagrams as a basis for ornament, suggested by Kathleen Lonsdale (1903–71) and taken up by many manufacturers at the London 1951 Festival of Britain (see LONDON EXHIBITIONS), represents a short-lived exception.

Neatby, William James (1860–1910)

Born in Barnsley, Yorkshire, Neatby was articled to a local architect in 1875 and from 1881 practised as an architect in Whitby and elsewhere. In 1883 he became a tile designer for Burmantofts Potteries in Leeds. In 1889 he joined Doulton's of Lambeth. Neatby was in charge of Doulton's architectural department from 1890 to 1907; he was succeeded by Barry Pittar but continued to act as a consultant. His many ceramic schemes included polychrome ART NOUVEAU tile cladding for the Winter Gardens, Blackpool (1896), the Royal Arcade, Norwich (1899), Harrod's Meat Hall (1901) and the Everard Building, Bristol (1901). Neatby also designed stained glass, metalwork, furniture and jewellery, and published designs in the 'ART-WORKERS' QUARTERLY'. His work as a designer of interiors and furniture was praised by MUTHESIUS.

Nelson, George Born in Hartford, Connecticut, in 1907, Nelson studied architecture at Yale University, graduating in 1931. From 1935 to 1944 he was an editor of *Architectural Forum*: in 1935 he published articles on LE CORBUSIER and other MODERN architects in the magazine *Pencil Points*. Nelson opened his own architectural office in New York in 1936. In 1944, with Henry Wright, he designed the Storagewall concept. It was published in *Life* (1945) and led to his being appointed design director to the Herman Miller Furniture Company, replacing Gilbert ROHDE. In 1947 Nelson established his own industrial design firm. Nelson was responsible for Herman Miller employing the designers Charles EAMES (from 1946) and Alexander Girard (from 1952). His own designs included Basic Storage Components, a development of the storage wall and a slat bench (1946), the Steelframe group (1954), the Sling sofa and Action Office (1964), the latter based on an idea of Robert PROPST. Nelson has also

designed many exhibitions and has been a prolific lecturer and writer, often contributing to 'INDUSTRIAL DESIGN'. Among his books are *Tomorrow's House* (1945), *Living Spaces* (1952), *Chairs* (1953) and *Problems of Design* (1957).

Neo-Classicism The ROCOCO style was already under attack in Paris in the late 1730s as frivolous, bizarre and irrational. The reaction against rococo seems to have found its first expression in ephemeral and ornamental designs by students at the French Academy in Rome in the 1740s, including PIERRE, LE GEAY, SALY, CHALLE, VIEN and PETITOT. These were aggressively classical, using massy geometric forms and boldly emphasized classical ornament – swags, fluting, paterae, frets and scrolls. PIRANESI'S example encouraged an infusion of drama and texture. Despite MARIGNY'S visit to Rome in 1750 and continuing anti-rococo pronouncements by C.-N. COCHIN and others radical neo-classical designs seem to have remained unexecuted until about 1756 to 1757, when a group of furniture designed by LE LORRAIN for Lalive de Jully acted as a manifesto for the new style. By this date the *Essai sur l'architecture* (1753) of the Abbé Laugier (1713–69), tracing all architecture back to the primitive hut described by Vitruvius, and anticipating an architecture of simple geometric forms, and *Gedanken über die Nachahmung der Griechischen Werke . . . (Reflections on the Imitation of Greek Art)* (1755) by Johann Joachim Winckelmann (1717-68), stressing the noble simplicity and calm grandeur of Greek art, had provided an ideological basis for the new style. Julien David Le Roy's *Les Ruines des plus beaux monuments de la Grèce* (1758) provided a hasty canon of Greek monuments suitable for imitation. Le Lorrain was involved in its production, as was

NEUFFORGE, whose *Recueil* (1757–80) was the greatest compendium of advanced neo-classical designs. New archaeological models were produced by the excavations at Herculaneum (1738–40 and 1745–65), Pompeii (1748 onwards) and elsewhere. Another ingredient in early neo-classical design was the use of BAROQUE and earlier prints; this taste was catered for by JOMBERT's reprinting of designs by the LOIRS, the MAROTS and others. French patrons of the 1760s seem to have avoided extremes and favoured a compromise in which rococo is reduced to symmetrical and measured curves and neo-classicism to a rectilinear framework and a veneer of refined classical ornament. Nevertheless briefly, in 1763 to 1764, there seems to have been a general fashion for designs '*à la grecque*' ('in the Greek manner'). In England rococo never established an impregnable bridgehead and the Palladian tradition of Inigo JONES and William KENT provided a solid foundation for neo-classical developments. CHAMBERS, who had studied in Paris and knew Le Geay and Piranesi, practised a sophisticated neo-classical style strongly influenced by French design. However, the work of James 'Athenian' STUART at Spencer House from 1758 and the first volume of his *Antiquities of Athens* (1762) represented the first conspicuous display of the new style and its sources in England. Stuart rapidly lost his leading role to ADAM, whose style developed from an early vigorous manner towards, in the 1770s, an increasing delicacy and elegance. French neo-classical design of the 1770s also tended to elegance and refinement and as in England ARABESQUE ornament enjoyed great popularity. A gradual reaction in the direction of massive forms and of grandly scaled ornament took place in the 1790s. In 1800 the artist and poet William Blake (1757–1827) referred to 'the immense flood of Grecian light & glory which is coming on Europe' and the Grecian style, later regarded by A. W. N. PUGIN as alien and mechanical, was often at this stage associated with the romantic cult of nature and the picturesque. In France this phase of neo-classicism took a particularly opulent and grandiloquent form, with PERCIER as its leading designer. As the official style of Napoleon's empire it spread over his dominions; PALAGI, who designed a monument to Napoleon in 1800 and furniture shown at the LONDON 1851 EXHIBITION, exemplifies the style's longevity in Italy. In Germany there was a late flowering of neo-classicism under the influence of SCHINKEL but from the mid 19th century neo-classicism was in general decline. In France the Néo-Grec style, typified by Prince Napoleon's Maison Pompéienne, designed in 1856 to 1860 by Alfred-Nicolas Normand (1822–1909), was characterized by polychromy, abstraction and eclecticism, a far remove from most earlier neo-classicism. From the 1860s a revival of late-18th-century neo-classicism, sometimes known in England as the 'Adams' style, was popular among commercial designers. Shortly after 1900 a more profound classical revival is apparent in the work of designers as various as LUTYENS, BEHRENS and Walter GROPIUS, and the BIEDERMEIER style was widely admired and imitated in Germany. This neo-classicism was a vital ingredient of MODERNISM, most clearly in the work of MIES VAN DER ROHE. More recently a crude neo-classical revival has surfaced in the work of Post-Modern designers.

Neroni, Bartolomeo Born in Siena in about 1500, Neroni, called Il Riccio, was a pupil of Peruzzi, and in 1543 married the daughter of the painter Il Sodoma (1477–1549). He was in 1552 appointed Siena's military engineer. Neroni designed the organ in Siena Cathedral in 1547, and from 1567 to 1570 the stalls, benches and bishop's throne; his design for the latter was in VASARI's collection, and is richly decorated with putti, sphinxes and masks. Neroni was also active as a painter and miniaturist. He died in 1571.

Nesfield, William Eden (1835–88) Son of the landscape gardener W. A. Nesfield, he studied architecture under William Burn (1789–1870) from about 1850 and again, after a spell in J. K. COLLING's office, from 1851 to 1853. He then entered the office of his uncle Anthony Salvin (1799–1881), where his friend, Richard Norman SHAW, was also working. From 1856 to 1858 Nesfield travelled in Europe, spending a short stint in VIOLLET-LE-DUC's office in 1856. Later trips to France led to his book *Specimens of Mediaeval Architecture* (1862), whose title-page had figures by the painter Albert Moore (1841–93), who had travelled with Nesfield to France in 1859 and who did decorative painting for Nesfield at Combe Abbey (1863) and elsewhere. Nesfield's independent architectural practice began in about 1859; he shared his offices with Shaw from 1863 to 1876, but although they were partners from 1866 to 1869 they never directly collaborated. Nesfield started as a Goth, helped to pioneer the Old English style, and anticipated Shaw's later move towards classicism. Nesfield was convivial and Bohemian, a sparring-partner of Whistler and a friend of BURGES, and during the 1860s he was more exuberantly inventive than Shaw. By 1880, when he retired, however, Nesfield had lost his impetus. Nesfield had a reputation as a furniture designer but little has come to light. His GOTHIC organ at Radwinter (1871), where he designed all the church fittings, is a handsome Reformed Gothic job, while his interiors at Kinmel Park

(1868–74) represent, as it were, Queen Anne and Jacobean details on Gothic foundations.

Neufforge, Jean François (1714–91) Born at Comblain-au-Pont near Liège, Neufforge is said to have studied under the architect J.-F. BLONDEL (1705–74). His first work, *Nouveau livre de plusieurs projets d'autels et de baldaquins* (1747; six plates), was engraved by BABEL and comprised altars and canopies in the ROCOCO style. In 1756 Neufforge advertised his *Recueil élémentaire d'Architecture* (1757–80; 906 plates divided into suites of six, and forming eight volumes and a supplement). The *Recueil* is the greatest compendium of designs in the advanced NEO-CLASSICAL style of the 1750s and remained consistent to its finish. It was widely praised and received the official approval of the Académie. Neufforge stated his aim to imitate 'the masculine, simple, and majestic manner of the ancient architects of Greece, and of the best modern architects'. His style is sometimes tough and geometric, and sometimes has strong echoes of the sculptural BAROQUE style of the mid 17th century. Few of his designs seem to have been executed, many are pedestrian, awkward or doctrinaire, but Neufforge had widespread influence as a propagandist for the new style. He also engraved plates after Le Roy and LE LORRAIN for *Les Ruines des plus beaux monuments de la Grèce* (1758), and Neufforge's designs must have been strongly influenced by Le Lorrain. The *Recueil* includes in Volume I (1757) wall decorations, alcoves, beds, tables and VASES, in Volume IV (1761) chimneypieces, a range of guilloches and Greek frets, and some schemes for rooms, in Volume V (1763) iron gates, balconies and stoves, marquetry, furniture and frames, vases and plinths, in Volume VI (1765) church furniture (altars, pulpits, organs, choir-stalls etc.), in Volume VII (1767) more altars and interior schemes, and in Volume VIII (1768) interiors with a wide range of furniture, frames, mouldings, doors and floors. The *Supplement* (1772–80) included further church fittings and ironwork.

Neureuther, Eugen Napoleon (1806–82) Born in Munich, the son of a painter, Neureuther acted as an assistant to Peter von Cornelius (1783–1867). From 1847 to 1856 he was artistic director of the Nymphenburg porcelain factory. In 1846 he designed a silver table for presentation to the Crown Prince of Bavaria. In 1868 to 1876 he was professor at the Munich applied arts school. Neureuther was also a prolific book illustrator.

Newbery, Jessie Rowat Born in Paisley in 1864, the daughter of a shawl manufacturer, William Rowat, Jessie Rowat married in 1889 Francis H. Newbery, the energetic head of the Glasgow School of Art. She taught embroidery at the school from 1894 to 1908, and was closely associated with 'The Four', MACKINTOSH, MACNAIR and the MACDONALD sisters. Her embroidery designs are in their style, and were shown in the Scottish Section of the TURIN 1902 EXHIBITION, organized by Mackintosh. In her introduction to the 1933 Mackintosh Memorial Exhibition in Glasgow she gave one of the first retrospective accounts of the Glasgow School.

New York Museum of Modern Art Founded in 1929 with Alfred H. Barr as its first director, the Museum of Modern Art mounted in 1932 an exhibition of MODERN architecture. Among the architects represented were WRIGHT, Walter GROPIUS, LE CORBUSIER, MIES VAN DER ROHE, and Oud, and the catalogue, mainly by Philip Johnson and Henry-Russell Hitchcock, sup-

ported the Modern line. The Museum opened a department of Industrial Design in 1933 and its 1934 Machine Art exhibition included chairs by Le Corbusier and BREUER, Steuben glass by Walter Dorwin TEAGUE and Frederick CARDER, and a Hermann Miller clock by Gilbert ROHDE. In 1938 there was an influential BAUHAUS exhibition and in 1940 the Museum's Organic Design competition was won by EAMES and Eero SAARINEN. Its design collection has continued to serve as a shop window of the Modern style, inclusion often being cited in advertisements as a seal of excellence. In recent years, however, there have been signs of a failure of the Modern nerve in some of the Museum's architectural exhibitions.

Nicholson, Michael Angelo (1796–1842) The son of Peter NICHOLSON, Michael Angelo studied drawing under Richard BROWN, and was subsequently a pupil of the architect John Foulston (1772–1842). He was closely involved with and shared the interests of his father. They collaborated on *The Practical Cabinet Maker, Upholsterer and Complete Decorator* (1826; eighty-one plates), for which Michael Angelo supplied the designs, some dated 1827. These are mainly accomplished and vigorous variations on late Grecian themes, with a few competent GOTHIC examples. The work was dedicated to George IV and had bound in a recommendation from leading cabinet-makers such as Wilkinson & Sons, Thomas & George Seddon and Edward Bailey, whose chair for the late Duke of York (1763–1827) was illustrated. Nicholson also published *The Carpenter and Joiner's Companion* (1826) and two similar works, practised a little as an architect, but was mainly active as an architectural drawing master.

Nicholson, Peter (1765–1844) Born at

Prestonkirk, East Lothian, the son of a stonemason, Nicholson was trained as a cabinet-maker. In 1788 he came to London, and taught in the evenings at a school for mechanics, earning enough by 1792 to finance the publication of his *The New Carpenter's Guide*. His many later works included *The Principles of Architecture* (1795–8), *The Student's Instructor in . . . the Five Orders of Architecture* (1795), *The Carpenter's and Joiner's Assistant* (1797) and *A Treatise on Practical Perspective* (1815), which described his invention of the centrolinead, a drawing instrument which had been awarded £20 by the SOCIETY OF ARTS in 1814. Nicholson's works covered mathematics, PERSPECTIVE, architecture, carpentry and building: they went through numerous editions and had an immense influence on the technical education of craftsmen and mechanics. From 1800 to 1810 Nicholson was active as architect and engineer in Scotland and Cumberland. He then returned to London and published his *Architectural Dictionary* (1812–19), the plan of which was suggested by SHERATON's *Cabinet Dictionary* (1803) and *Encyclopaedia* (1805). From 1810 Nicholson was friendly with LOUDON, a kindred spirit. In 1826 with his son, Michael Angelo, Nicholson published *The Practical Cabinet Maker, Upholsterer and Complete Decorator* (eighty-one plates), containing designs for furniture by Michael Angelo; it seems probable that Nicholson himself was responsible for the planning of the work and for its lengthy text on geometry and perspective, subjects of which he was a master. Impoverished in 1829 by the failure of a publishing venture, Nicholson retired to Morpeth. From 1834, when Sir Jeffry Wyatville subscribed £10 to his annuity, Nicholson ran a school in Newcastle-upon-Tyne, where he was recognized as a pundit.

Nicolai, Johann Ernst Nicolai published in 1695 *Vorstellung Allerhand Lauber, Bandel, Carmosirter und anderer . . . Erfindungen* (eight plates). Aimed at craftsmen working in gold and silver, it comprises very scrolly ACANTHUS ornament, including jewelled pendants, buckles, brooches, and watch-cases, and sinister and energetic putti, birds and dogs entirely composed of tightly scrolled black leaves.

Niedecken, George M. (1878–1945) Born in Milwaukee, Wisconsin, Niedecken showed designs for friezes at the 1897 Chicago Arts & Crafts Society Exhibition. In 1899 he travelled to Germany and Austria and in 1900 to Paris, where he studied at the École des Beaux-Arts. By 1904 he was regularly working for Frank Lloyd WRIGHT: in that year he executed the painted frieze in the Dana House. In 1907 Niedecken, with John Walbridge, founded the Niedecken-Walbridge Company, interior designers, who were responsible for the execution of the decorations of several Wright houses. In 1913 the firm advertised itself in the *Western Architect* as 'Specialist in the design and execution of interior decorations and mural paintings'. Niedecken's own designs were sometimes in the Wright manner but as an accomplished professional designer he could work in a number of fashionable styles.

Nielsen, Harald Christian Born in Baarse in 1892, Nielsen studied silversmithing under Georg JENSEN and drawing under Carl Vilhelm Meyer (1870–1938). He briefly intended to paint, but in the event became a designer of silver for the Jensen firm, collaborating with Jensen himself and with Johan Rohde (1856–1935). Nielsen worked in a muted ART DÉCO manner and showed at the PARIS 1925, Barcelona 1929 and PARIS 1937 EXHIBITIONS.

Nieuwenhuis, Theodoor Willem (1866–1951) Born in Noord-Schar-woude, Nieuwenhuis studied art in Amsterdam. In 1886 he met Gerrit Willem Dijsselhof (1866–1924), with whom he travelled to Berlin, Dresden, Prague, Vienna and Paris from 1889 to 1890. Back in Amsterdam, Nieuwenhuis was mainly active as a graphic designer and illustrator; in 1898 he illustrated the poems of Perk. Also in 1898 Nieuwenhuis, together with Dijsselhof and LION CACHET, began to design ART NOUVEAU furniture for the Wisselingh furniture firm. In 1911 they published a handsome portfolio of elaborate interiors, furniture, stained glass and metalwork designed by Nieuwenhuis; it also illustrated his textiles for Ramaer & Co. of Helmond and the Hengelosche Trijpweverij of Hengelo. Nieuwenhuis's work was also illustrated in 'BOUW- EN SIERKUNST' and 'MAANDBLAT VOOR BEELDENDE KUNSTEN'.

Nilson, Johann Esaias (1721–88) Born in Augsburg, Nilson came from a family of miniaturists of Swedish origin. He was taught by Johann Georg BERGMÜLLER (1688–1762) at the Augsburg Academy, of which he himself became director in 1769. Nilson married the daughter of a pastor and thus entered the merchant class. From 1750 he ran his own publishing house. Nilson was a vastly prolific designer of sparkling ROCOCO ornament, and in his later years made a successful transition to NEO-CLASSICISM. His plates total some 400 in all, some forty of which were published by HERTEL. His output consisted mainly of allegorical figures in rococo frameworks or cartouches – the seasons, the elements, the months and so on. Nilson also designed garden decorations, VASES, particularly in his neo-classical phase, snuff-boxes, and in 1756 a mirror frame decorated with putti representing the four times of life, and with a pair

seated on rococo chairs in the foreground. Nilson was also responsible for many decorations for almanacks, *vignettes* and book illustrations, for instance those to Schiller's *Die Räuber* (1781). His designs were used on Liverpool tiles and Frankenthal porcelain in the 1750s, on Ottweiler and Brunswick earthenware in the 1760s and on Kiel and Stockelsdorf earthenware in the 1770s.

Nizzoli, Marcello (1887–1969) Born in Boretto, Reggio Emilia, Nizzoli studied ornament, figure drawing and architecture at the School of Fine Arts in Parma to 1913. In 1914 he showed embroideries worked by his sister Matilde with the group Nuove Tendenze in Milan. In 1923 he won a competition at the Monza Biennale with silk shawls embroidered in a lively ART DÉCO style; they were later shown at the PARIS 1925 EXHIBITION. Nizzoli designed many posters at this period, for instance for OM (1924) and for Campari (1931). In the 1930s Nizzoli was associated with Razionalismo and showed at the 1932 Rivoluzione Fascista Exhibition and the PARIS 1937 EXHIBITION. He often collaborated with Edoardo Persico (1900–1936). From the late 1930s Nizzoli designed for Olivetti. His works include the Summa 40 adding machine (1940) and the Lettera 22 and Diaspron 82 typewriters (1954 and 1959). Nizzoli also designed exhibitions and many other products, such as the Necchi Supernova Bu Kitchen mixer (1955), the Necchi sewing machine (1956) and Ronson lighters. Nizzoli's industrial designs are characterized by calculated purity of outline and epicene elegance of form.

Noguchi, Isamu Born in Los Angeles in 1904, the son of a Japanese poet father and an American writer mother, Noguchi was brought up in Japan. In 1917 he started to train as a cabinet-maker in

Chigasaki. In 1918 he was sent to America and from 1919, while doing a variety of jobs, became increasingly committed to sculpture. In 1927 he went to Paris, where he was for a period in Brancusi's studio. From 1932 he lived mainly in New York. In 1937 Noguchi designed a helmet-like bakelite wireless for the Zenith Radio Company of Chicago and in 1940 he designed decorations for Steuben glass. A glass-topped coffee-table with sculptural wood supports made for A. Conger Goodyear in 1939 was pirated by ROBSJOHN-GIBBINGS but in a later version of 1944 was produced from 1945 by the Herman Miller Company. Noguchi also designed lights (1944), stools and a table (1955) for Knoll, and from 1951 to 1966 designed many variations on the theme of lights with sculptural paper shades on bamboo and metal supports. Noguchi also studied ceramics in Japan and designed ceramics made there.

Nolin, Pierre Nolin engraved part of SYMONY's suite of jewellery designs published in Strasbourg in 1621. He himself issued two suites of black ornament of six plates each, with pendants and small motifs, enlivened by devils, insects and jewels, in the stretched GROTESQUE manner, and another similar suite (1619) of ten plates, with backs for miniatures, watches and boxes and more small motifs, mainly in the scrolled foliate style known as COSSE-DE-POIS. Nolin later engraved a collection of coats-of-arms, published in Paris in 1654.

Nonnenmacher, Marcus (1653–1720) Born in Constance, the son of a cabinet-maker, Nonnenmacher became in 1677 a citizen of Prague, where he became court cabinet-maker and ran a successful and prolific workshop. His *Der Architectonische Tischler* (Nuremberg, 1710; thirty-two plates) is a furniture pattern-book which began with an account of the ORDERS, but also included altars, cartouches, chairs, tables, beds, cradles, overmantels, and cupboards, all in a rich ACANTHUS style, similar to that of INDAU and ECHTER. A second edition appeared in 1751, only three years before CHIPPENDALE's *Director*, a book similar in format, however different in style.

Normand, Charles Pierre Joseph (1765–1840) Born at Goyencourt, Somme, Normand was taught architecture by J. E. Thierry (1750–1832) and G. Gisors (1762–1835). A suite of six NEO-CLASSICAL VASE designs may date from this period. In 1792 Norman won the Grand Prix and travelled to Rome. From about 1800 to 1815 he is said to have engraved at least 7,000 plates, including those for PERCIER and FONTAINE's *Recueil de décorations intérieures* (1801). He also designed the new French republican banknotes. His *Nouveau Recueil en Divers Genres d'Ornemens* (1803; thirty-six plates) comprised candelabra, vases, tripods, furniture and ornament. It included a candelabrum in the antique style by J. G. LEGRAND and Jacques Molinos (1743–1831) for the Hôtel de Marbœuf. The preface refers to Legrand's collection of plaster casts of plants to serve as an inspiration to designers. Normand was closely associated with Pierre Nicolas Beauvallet (1749–1828), a sculptor born in Le Havre and taught by Augustin Pajou (1730–1809), whose revolutionary principles he followed, executing a bust of Marat in 1793. The first edition of Beauvallet's *Fragmens d'Ornemens* (1804; 144 plates dated from 1804 to 1807) was dedicated to J. L. DAVID (1748–1825), whose *Oath of the Horatii* was incorporated in the dedication plate: Normand signed one engraving. Some of the textiles were designed by A. R. de Montferrand

(1786–1858), a pupil of Percier who moved to St Petersburg in 1816. The second edition of *Fragmens* (1820) has Normand's name on the title with that of Beauvallet and was dedicated to the genius of the French school of painting. The plates include the widest possible range of ornament and design in the neo-classical style; some plates were contributed by Alexandre Lenoir (1761–1839), for whose *Musée des Monuments Français* Normand engraved plates. Normand and Beauvallet collaborated on *Decorations intérieures et extérieures* (1803), forty-eight plates of furniture, tripods, vases and ornament in a rich and refined neo-classical style; it later included designs after RAPHAEL and PRUD'HON, the latter executed in part by Thomire and Odiot. A second edition (1828) had eleven plates of friezes in a style reminiscent of Jean I BERAIN. In 1813 Normand designed architectural ornaments for the manufacturer Joseph Beunat of Sarresbourg and Paris, and his *Recueil Varié des Plans et de Façades* (1815), although mainly architectural, included seven fine plates of ornament and furniture. It was followed by *Modèles d'Orfévrerie* (1822; seventy-two plates), which included examples of goldsmith's work from the PARIS 1819 EXHIBITION. Apart from the odd GOTHIC design the plates are in a rich Grecian style. Normand designed many of the pieces; others were by Bury, LAFITTE and Cavallier. *Le Guide de l'Ornemaniste* (Paris, 1826, second edition Liège, 1847; thirty-six plates) comprised ornament and vases in the same rich Grecian style. In 1841 Normand's son, Louis, who was also active as designer and engraver, published the second edition of his father's *Cours de Dessin Industriel* (thirty-four plates), with instructions on the design of ornament, ironwork and carpenter's work. Normand's most famous book was his *Nouveau Parallèle des Ordres* (Paris, 1819), repeatedly reprinted and translated into German (1830), and into English (1819) by Augustus PUGIN. It became the standard work on the ORDERS, recommended in a design bibliography by J. C. ROBINSON in 1853.

Nüscheler, Hans Jakob (1583–1654) The son and father of glass painters and designers in Zürich, Nüscheler was himself the most important designer of stained glass there after MURER.

O

Obrist, Hermann (1863–1927) Born at Kilchberg near Zürich, the son of a doctor, Obrist studied at the applied arts school in Karlsruhe in 1888 and then in Weimar and Paris. In 1892 he founded an embroidery workshop in Florence with Bertha Ruchet, which he transferred to Munich in 1894. In 1895 'PAN' devoted an article to his work, which illustrated his Cyclamen embroidery (1895), whose whiplash form was to enter the ART NOUVEAU vocabulary. Obrist's work had a direct influence on ENDELL. At the Munich 1897 Glaspalast Exhibition, Obrist showed textiles and an oak chest. He was then involved in the foundation of the MUNICH VEREINIGTE WERKSTÄTTEN, for which he designed embroideries, tapestries, ceramics and ironwork. Chairs designed by Obrist were included in RIEMERSCHMID's Room for an Art Lover at the PARIS 1900 EXHIBITION. In 1901 he bewailed public indifference to the Werkstätten. From 1902 to 1904 he ran an applied arts school in Munich with Wilhelm von Debschitz (1871–1948). He was subsequently active as a propagandist for improvement in design and in 1919 was shortlisted for the directorship of the BAUHAUS.

Olbrich, Joseph Maria (1867–1908) Born in Troppau in Silesia, the son of a baker, Olbrich studied building in Vienna from 1882 and then, from 1890, architecture under Carl von Hasenauer at the Academy of Fine Arts. Olbrich was a star pupil, winning the Rome Prize in 1893; JOSEF HOFFMANN was one of his contemporaries. In 1893 he worked as an assistant to Otto Wagner for a few months before travelling to Rome and North Africa. Back in Vienna in 1894 Olbrich went back to Wagner's office to work on Vienna's railway, and was joined there by Hoffmann. From 1895 Olbrich, Hoffmann and Wagner were involved with Koloman MOSER and others in discussions which led to the foundation of the Vienna Secession which broke away from the conservative Künstlerhaus in May 1897. Olbrich supplied illustrations to the Secession magazine 'VER SACRUM' from 1898 and designed the lay-out of the first Secession Exhibition early in the same year. By November 1898 he had designed and completed the building erected for the second Secession Exhibition. He designed its poster, and wallpapers shown in the exhibition. Also in 1898 Olbrich designed elaborate interiors for the Villa Friedmann in a curvilinear ART NOUVEAU style. His 1899 interiors for the Villa Stift and the David Beil apartment integrate furniture into brilliantly coloured decorative schemes. In August 1899 Olbrich moved to the Darmstadt Artists' Colony established by Grand Duke Ernst Ludwig of Hesse (1868–1937) in July 1899. At Darmstadt, Olbrich was soon joined by Peter BEHRENS. Olbrich designed the room which was the Darmstadt exhibit at the PARIS 1900 EXHIBITION, a cooperative venture markedly more restrained than Olbrich's earlier Viennese room shown in the Austrian section. The

Darmstadt room won a gold medal. Olbrich had the largest salary of the artists in the Darmstadt colony and was its *de facto* leader. As the only architect he was able to design the public buildings and artists' houses on the Mathildenhöhe, which were to be presented as the DARMSTADT 1901 MATHILDENHÖHE EXHIBITION. In the event Olbrich designed the central studio building, the Ernst Ludwig House, seven houses, including his own, and many temporary buildings for the 1901 Exhibition. Olbrich designed furniture, lighting and other decorations for most of the buildings. The exhibition was a financial failure and relatively few buildings were added after 1901, the most celebrated exception being the Wedding Tower (1905–6) for the Grand Duke's second marriage, and the adjacent exhibition buildings (1905–6). The Opel Worker's House (1908) included simple furniture designed by Olbrich and made by Schöndorff Brothers of Düsseldorf. Olbrich's contributions to the TURIN 1902 EXHIBITION were regarded by critics as simpler and less extravagant than his earlier designs. At this period the 'STUDIO' considered him superior to Behrens. Olbrich also showed rooms at the ST LOUIS 1904 EXHIBITION, winning lavish praise from MUTHESIUS for their lightness and delicacy, and the Grand Prix and a gold medal. Throughout his career Olbrich was designing embroideries, posters, cutlery, lighting, etc. His last work was the redecoration in 1908 of parts of his Gluckert House (1901). For the original dark and sometimes spindly furniture and woodwork, and light walls, he substituted richly coloured walls and light painted woodwork of a massive NEO-CLASSICAL character, comparable to contemporary designs by Behrens.

Olmütz, Wenzel von From Olmütz, east of Prague, Wenzel engraved ninety-one surviving plates from about 1475 to 1500, most of which are copies after SCHONGAUER, the young DÜRER and others. Wenzel also published an elaborate GOTHIC design for a covered cup, another for a monstrance, and seven plates of elaborate Gothic canopies, mainly with ground plans.

Olsen, Thorwald (1870–1941) Son of a well-known Norwegian goldsmith, Olsen studied design in Paris, and was also active as a painter. He designed and made goldsmiths' work, including an elaborate punch service which won a medal at the PARIS 1889 EXHIBITION. This was in an involved Nordic style; Olsen later moved to a more plain functional manner.

Omega Workshops The Omega Workshops were officially opened at 33 Fitzroy Square, London, in July 1913, under the direction of Roger FRY. His aim was to harness the talents of artists to the design of furniture, interiors, carpets, textiles, pottery, stained glass, etc. The designers included Fry himself, his two fellow directors, Duncan GRANT and Vanessa Bell, and Wyndham Lewis, Edward Wadsworth, William Roberts, Frederick Etchells, Nina Hammett, Edward Wolfe and Gaudier-Brzeska. The Omega style, remarkably advanced for England at this date, ranged from Fauvism to Cubism, but the technical quality of the brightly coloured Omega products was sometimes amateurish. The Workshops, after struggling through the First World War and internal disagreements inflamed by Wyndham Lewis, were finally liquidated in 1921.

Oppenord, Gilles Marie (1672–1742) Oppenord was born in Paris. His Flemish father, who died in 1715, was cabinetmaker to Louis XIV and had an *atelier* in the Louvre from 1684. Oppenord studied under his father and then under the architect Jules Hardouin-Mansart (1646–1708). From 1692 to 1699 he was in Italy, mainly in Rome, but in 1698 in Venice and Lombardy. On his return to France, Oppenord had a period of relative inactivity during which he developed his talent as a designer. In 1704 Oppenord designed the high altar of Saint-Germain-des-Prés, and this and other early designs for churches display the influence of BERNINI and Borromini, whom he had studied in Italy. His early publication, *Desseins de Couronements* (four plates), contains dense BAROQUE ornament in the manner of Jean LE PAUTRE. The English architect John James owned a copy. However, a set of drawings for fountains, which in 1715 belonged to Oppenord's friend WATTEAU, display a brilliance of touch which belies their debt to Bernini. Also in 1715 Oppenord became an architect in the service of Philippe Duc d'Orléans (1674–1723), who appointed him director of the royal manufactures. In 1722 he designed the fête given by the Duc d'Orléans to celebrate Louis XV's coronation. But Oppenord's main activity was as a designer of interiors. His patrons included the Duchesse d'Orléans at the Palais Royal and, under the architect Robert de COTTE (1656–1735), the Elector Clement-Augustus of Cologne at Bonn, Brühl and Falkenlust. In the Salon d'Angle at the Palais Royal (1719–20), in the Salon of the Hôtel d'Assy (1719) and the Salon of the Château de la Grange-du-Milieu (about 1720) Oppenord developed a lighter system of ornament and a more curvilinear treatment of planes, which is the final stage before the full emergence of ROCOCO. Oppenord was to be closely involved in the development of the new style, but his later designs, wholly rococo in spirit and by turns delicate and lively, are always temperate in the use of such rococo mannerisms as asymmetry and C-scrolls. His designs were propagated after his death by HUQUIER, who owned over 2,000 drawings by Oppenord. They appeared in three collections, *Livre de Fragments d'Architecture* (1744; fourteen suites of twelve plates, 168 plates in all), known as 'Le Petit Oppenord', *Livre de différents morceaux* (1744–8), twelve suites of six plates, seventy-two plates in all), known as 'Le Moyen Oppenord', and *Œuvres* (from 1748; nineteen suites mainly of six plates, 120 plates in all), known as 'Le Grand Oppenord'; the *Œuvres* were dedicated by Huquier to De Tournehem, Directeur des Manufactures Royales. Oppenord's designs include lanterns, lights, brackets, crestings, trophies, cartouches, doors, altars, torchères, clocks, lecterns, chimneypieces, monuments, fountains, panelling, ceilings and obelisks. Oppenord also designed ironwork, including, in the 1720s, the choir-screen for Meaux Cathedral, the title-page to Jacques Dumont's *Livre de nouveaux trophez*, and illustrations to the 1734 edition of Molière. In the introduction to the *Œuvres* Oppenord is called 'le Le Brun *de l'Architecture*' and said to have worked in '*un goût contenant de l'antique mais plus riche*'. By contrast C.-N. COCHIN, writing from the NEOCLASSICAL viewpoint, in 1755 grouped Oppenord with Borromini as one of those who had debauched the classical language of architecture.

Oppler, Edwin (1831–80) A pupil of Conrad Wilhelm Hase, VIOLLET-LE-DUC and A. Oudinot, he was active as an architect in Hanover. From 1864 he worked with Hase on the decoration of Schloss Marienburg, designing vigorous and sometimes highly elaborate GOTHIC pieces influenced by Viollet-le-Duc. In 1872 he published his furniture designs in the Gothic style in *Die Kunst im Gewerbe*, the Hanover architects' magazine which he edited

(1872–8), including chairs whose construction was derived from UNGE-WITTER. Oppler also designed in the RENAISSANCE style.

Orders The Roman architectural writer, Marcus Vitruvius Pollio, whose works were rediscovered in the library of St Gall by the humanist Poggio Bracciolini (1380–1459), described in detail the orders of ancient architecture, comprising columns with their bases, capitals and entablatures. He also specified the character of each order. Thus Doric was expressive of power and appropriate for temples of Minerva, Mars and Hercules, Corinthian connoted feminine grace and was therefore suitable for Venus, Flora and Proserpina, while Ionic, between the other two, fitted Juno, Diana and Bacchus. The text of Vitruvius was printed in about 1486, and in 1511 the first illustrated edition appeared in Venice. SERLIO's *Regole Generali di Architettura* (1537), Book IV of his treatise on architecture, systematized the five orders, Tuscan, Doric, Ionic, Corinthian and Composite, and stressed the appropriate modern uses for each; thus Tuscan was for castles, prisons and arsenals. The Composite, not described by Vitruvius, was a vehicle for the exercise of free imagination. *Vitruvius Teutsch*, the first German edition of Vitruvius, published by Walter Ryff in Nuremberg in 1548, was widely influential, while Hans BLUM's *Quinque columnarum . . .* (Zürich, 1550) provided a brief summary of the orders, repeatedly reprinted; the 1635 London edition was designed for 'the benefit of Free-Masons, Carpenters, Goldsmiths, Painters, Carvers, Inlayers, Anticke-cutters, and all others that delight to practise with the Compasse and square'. The first English architectural pattern-book, John Shute's *The First and Chief Groundes of Architecture* (1563), was a work of the same kind. Up to the early 16th century

the Corinthian and Composite orders were by far the most popular, as shown for instance by VOGTHERR's *Kunst-büchlein* (1537). From the middle of the 16th century Northern MANNERIST designers played elaborate ornamental variations on the theme of the orders: Hans VREDEMAN DE VRIES, SAMBIN and Wendel DIETTERLIN were among the more powerful exponents of this genre, while certain designers such as KRAMMER and KASEMANN carried it to an incoherent extreme. BERNINI in 1665 expressed the profound significance of the orders for BAROQUE designers: 'The beauty of all things, including architecture, lies in proportion. One might say it is a divine attribute, since it takes as its origin the body of Adam, which was not only made by God's own hand, but was also formed in his semblance and image. The variety of the orders or architecture stems from the difference between the bodies of man and woman and their different proportions.' From 1758, when James 'Athenian' STUART designed a Greek Doric Temple of Theseus at Hagley, the orders, often now Greek, gained a renewed significance for NEO-CLASSICAL designers. That many furniture pattern-books, for example those of Crispin de PASSE II (1621), NONNENMACHER (1710) and CHIPPENDALE (1754), prefaced designs with an account of the orders argues their prolonged relevance, both practical and symbolic.

Orlandi, Stefano (1681–1760) Born in Bologna, the son of a painter and sculptor, Orlandi was a pupil of the painter Pompeo Aldrovandini, with whom he worked in Rome from about 1713 to 1715. He later worked as a theatre decorator with Giuseppe Orsoni (1691–1755). Orlandi collaborated with the painter Vittorio Maria Bigari (1692–1776) on the decoration of the Palazzo Aldrovandi, the Palazzo Manfredi in Faenza (1727) and elsewhere. He designed altarpieces, votive altars, metalwork and furniture, in a late-BAROQUE style reminiscent of GIAR-DINI but sometimes overladen with ROCOCO frills.

Orley, Bernart van (1488–1541) Born in Brussels, the son of a painter, Bernart was taught by his father. In 1515 he began to execute portraits for the Spanish royal family and in 1518 became painter to Margaret, the Regent. He was strongly influenced by RAPHAEL, above all through the medium of Raphael's tapestry cartoons, which were in Brussels from 1514 to 1519. He was also aware of Italian engravings of ornament, using one by Zoan ANDREA on his Job altarpiece (1521). Other cardinal influences were GOSSAERT and DÜRER, whom he met in Brussels in 1521. From about 1515 Bernart became increasingly involved in the design of tapestries. His main series included Scenes of the Passion (about 1520), the Founding of Rome (eight pieces, about 1524), the Battle of Pavia (seven pieces, from 1525), given by the Estates General to Charles V in 1531, the Hunts of Maximilian (twelve pieces, from about 1525), depicting scenes in the vicinity of Brussels, the Story of Abraham (ten pieces), the Genealogical Portraits of the House of Nassau, for Henri III of Nassau (1483–1538), the Story of Jacob (ten pieces, about 1528) and the Story of Tobias (eight pieces). Bernart also designed stained glass, including windows in Sainte-Gudule, Brussels (1537–40), which were painted by Jan Hack of Antwerp. As a designer Bernart was succeeded by disciples who became rivals, Pieter COECK and Michiel COXCIE, but his fame endured; in 1685 the Gobelins factory began to re-weave the Hunts of Maximilian. Bernart indeed consolidated the revolution in tapestry brought about by Raphael's Acts of the Apostles cartoon, and thus helped to determine the nature of tapestry design up to the late 19th century.

O'Rorke, Brian (1901–74) Born in New Zealand, O'Rorke moved to England, where he studied architecture at Cambridge University and at the Architectural Association School. He designed MODERN interiors for the passenger liner *Orion* (1934–5), published in the 'ARCHITECTURAL REVIEW' (1935), as well as domestic, train and aircraft interiors and the Mayor Gallery (1933), the leading Modern picture gallery in London during the 1930s.

Orsi, Lelio (1511–87) Born in Novellara, Orsi trained as a painter under the influence of Correggio, MICHEL-ANGELO and Giulio ROMANO. In 1536 he painted triumphal arches for the visit of Ercole II d'Este to Reggio d'Emilia. From 1546 to 1552 Orsi was in exile from Reggio in his native Novellara under the protection of Count Francesco II Gonzaga. In 1553 he travelled to Venice and in 1554 to 1555 to Rome. Thereafter Orsi worked in Novellara and Reggio. In 1567 to 1568 he designed accomplished MANNERIST GROTESQUE decorations for the Rocca di Novellara. In 1567 he designed a silver VASE for presentation to Duke Alfonso d'Este. Orsi also designed furniture, including an elaborate cradle, jewellery and, in 1576, a tabernacle for the cathedral at Reggio.

Osmont From about 1815 to 1839 seven series of about fifty plates of drapery designs, were published in Paris. The first *Recueil de draperies* was by Halla-vant, its successor, in a gaudy Empire style with a hint of GOTHIC in one plate, was credited to Osmont and Dezon, and Osmont was succeeded by Pinsonnière. The last series, called *Nouveau recueil de draperies* (1839), included designs in the Louis XIV and Louis XV styles. Osmont seems to have been the leading promoter of the designs, and two pattern books of furniture and drapery entitled *Die elegante Welt*, published in Augsburg in 1840 and 1847, use his name, while he seems to have influenced a Swedish book of drawings of curtains of about 1835.

Ostaus, Giovanni In 1557 Ostaus, a professional designer, published *La vera perfettione del disegno* (Venice; forty plates). The book contains a very wide range of designs for both embroidery and lace, some of them copied from SCHÖNSPERGER and RENNER, and for ornament, some copied from ALDEGREVER and Virgil SOLIS. Its popularity is shown by copies by Franceschi (1564), Le Maistre (1565) and Latomus (1606).

Ottagono (1966–present) This glossy magazine is issued from Milan by eight leading Italian design manufacturers, Arflex, Artemide, Bernini, Boffi, Cassina, Flos, ICF De Padova, and Tecno. It gives generous coverage to the work of designers such as Mario ZANUSO, Vico MAGISTRETTI and Gio PONTI, who have worked for them.

Oudry, Jean Baptiste (1686–1755) Born in Paris, the son of a painter, Oudry studied in 1704 under Michel Serre, painter of the royal galleys in Marseille. From 1706 Oudry studied painting at the Académie de Saint-Luc, becoming a master in 1708. From 1707 to 1712 he was in the studio of Nicolas de Largillierre (1656–1746), and from 1713 he worked independently. He became an academician in 1719. In 1724 he decorated a coach presented to Louis XV by the Marquis de Beringhen; he also executed decorative paintings in the style of his friend Claude III AUDRAN in 1725, and painted at least one harpsi-

chord lid. In 1726 Oudry was appointed designer to the Beauvais tapestry works. His first suite, the Chasses Nouvelles (1726–7), was followed by the Amusements Champêtres (1728), Molière subjects (1730), the Metamorphoses d'Ovide (1732), the Verdures Fines (1735) and the Fables de La Fontaine (1736). In 1734 Oudry became a director of the Beauvais factory, a post he held until 1754, when he was made Directeur Artistique. Although Oudry ceased to design for the Beauvais factory in 1736 and was involved in disagreements with his weavers, he presided over a period of success at Beauvais and professional jealousy rather than artistic principles seem to have been behind his troubles. In 1733 Oudry was commissioned to design three tapestries for Compiègne. The suite which resulted, the Chasses Royales, eventually included nine tapestries, and was completed in 1746; one of the Chasses includes a self-portrait of Oudry. In 1738 he was appointed to oversee the weaving of De Troy's Esther suite at the Gobelins factory, completed in 1745, and in 1748 he was appointed chief inspector of the Gobelins, a post in which he was succeeded by François BOUCHER. In 1751 Oudry proposed and prepared a suite of Combats d'Animaux to succeed his Chasses, but they were not woven. Oudry, although a versatile painter, specialized in hunting and animal subjects, which he also treated in illustrations to La Fontaine published in 1755 to 1759 in an edition which was purchased by the Sèvres porcelain factory in 1785.

Overton, John Overton was active from about 1667 as a publisher at the White Horse without Newgate, London, in succession to Peter STENT and in rivalry with Robert Walton. Overton was succeeded by a son of the same name. The Overtons published many prints of flowers, fruits, beasts and birds, some after Wenceslas Hollar and John Dunstall, similar to examples issued earlier by Thomas JOHNSON. They were intended as models 'for all sorts of Gentlewomen and School-Mistresses Works'. Other Overton books were second editions of ROUSSEEL's *De Grotesco* (1623), and of PIERCE's 1640 book of friezes, and Edward Cocker's *England's Penman* (1703).

P

Paganino, Alessandro Active as a printer at Toscolano near Salo from 1516, Paganino published a number of pattern-books for needlework in about 1532, including *Raccolta de tutti i ritratti & disegni di ricchami* (twenty plates) and *Libro de Rechami* (eighty plates), among which are copies after Quentel (1529) and VAVASSORE (about 1530), as well as some original designs for vigorous scrolled borders. A third book by Paganino, *Burato*, consisted merely of blank representations of canvas upon which the purchaser could draw designs.

Pagano, Giuseppe (1896–1945) Born Giuseppe Pogatschnig at Parenzo, Istria, the son of an archaeologist, Pagano changed his name on entering the army in 1915. After the war he returned to Parenzo, where he helped to found the local Fascist party. In 1924 he graduated as an architect in Turin, where in 1927 he was appointed technical director of the Turin 1928 Exhibition. In 1931 Pagano moved to Milan. In 1933 he became editor of 'CASABELLA', where he was assisted by Persico. With PONTI, Pagano designed a streamlined train shown at the MILAN 1933 TRIENNALE and in about 1939 he designed handsome simple laminated-wood chairs for the Università Commerciale Bocconi. In 1943, reacting against Fascism, Pagano joined the Resistance. He died in 1945 in Mauthausen concentration camp after capture, escape, recapture and torture.

Pagano, Matio From Treviso, Pagano was active as an engraver in Venice from 1515. He was almost certainly the principal designer of two needlework books published by Nicolo Zoppino, *Convivio delle belle donne* (Venice, 1531; twenty-four plates) and *Gli universali di tutti e bei dissegni, raccami, e moderni lavori* (Venice, 1532). His designs include interlace and foliate borders, and in the second book a sophisticated panel of GROTESQUE ornament in the manner of Nicoletto da MODENA. Later Pagano was the designer and publisher of the first pattern-book for cutwork, *Giardinetto nuovo di punti tagliati* (Venice, 1542; twenty-four plates); its designs were mainly geometric. The *Giardinetto* was extremely successful, an eighth edition appearing in 1558, as were his later books in the same manner, *Ornamento de le belle virtudiose dòne* (Venice, 1543; twenty-four plates), with some copies from VAVASSORE (1530) and ZOPPINO (1531), and *Il spechio di pensieri delle belle et virtudiose donne* (Venice, 1544; sixteen plates). His next book, *Lhonesto essempio* (Venice, 1550; sixteen plates), displayed a much richer vocabulary of ornament, with figures and flowers. *Specchio di virtu* (Venice, 1554; twenty-four plates) consisted of copies from TAGLIENTE (1527) and Pagano's earlier books. *La gloria e l'honore de ponte tagliati et ponti in aere* (Venice, 1554; sixteen plates) continued the manner of *Lhonesto essempio*: its title-page is the earliest representation of lace-makers. Pagano's last publication, *Trionfo di virtu* (Venice, 1559; sixteen plates), was in the same style. In 1543 he also published an edition of Dominique de

CELLE's 1531 book, which has much in common with some of his own early work for Zoppino. Pagano was also probably the designer of the first pattern-book for bobbin lace, *Le Pompe* (Venice, 1557; fourteen plates), published by the brothers Sessa. The designs are geometrical. Similar but more elaborate designs are found in the second part of *Le Pompe* (Venice, 1562; sixteen plates). Pagano may also have designed *I frutti* (Venice, 1564; sixteen plates), another Sessa publication, mainly for embroidery. Pagano's books of 1554 and 1559 were in 1579 copied by Bernhard JOBIN.

Page, James Describing himself as an 'Ornamental Draftsman and Designer', Page taught ornament and design at the Society for Promoting Practical Design's school in Savile House, Leicester Square, in 1839, and later set up a school of his own. His *Guide for Drawing the Acanthus and Every Description of Ornamental Foliage* (1839–40, reprinted 1886) is a vigorously illustrated compendium of most styles of ornament from Elizabethan to ROCOCO.

Pageant, The (1896–7) Edited by Charles Shannon and J. Gleeson White, this short-lived periodical in the 'YELLOW BOOK' manner had covers by Charles RICKETTS, a title by Selwyn IMAGE and end-papers by Lucien Pissarro.

Paiva, José Francisco de (1744–1824) Paiva was active in Oporto from at least 1780 to 1808. He started as a cabinet-maker, but from 1795 devoted himself exclusively to architecture. A book containing over 130 designs by Paiva is in the Museu de Arte Antiga, Lisbon. These include drawings for buildings, architectural details, church furnishings, chimneypieces and secular furniture. Paiva's style is basically Portuguese late BAROQUE, but the presence of an English mercantile community at Oporto encouraged him to imitate English models. Thus his works include direct or indirect borrowings from CHIPPENDALE, HEPPLEWHITE and SHERATON. He also seems to have known Roubo's *L'Art du Menuisier Ébeniste* (Paris, 1771), and owned a print by Johann Georg HERTEL of cabinets designed by I.-C. KÖNIG in Augsburg in about 1740. Paiva's designs perfectly illustrate late-18th-century Portuguese ARTISAN MANNERISM.

Palagi, Pelagio Filippo (1775–1860) Born in Bologna, Palagi was active there as a decorative painter from about 1795, and studied at the Accademia Clementina in 1798 to 1799. At this period he probably designed VASES for the ceramic factory set up in Bologna in 1798 by his principal patron, Count Aldrovandi. A monument to the glory of Napoleon (1800), a medal to commemorate the first electoral college of the new Italian Republic (1801), funerary monuments and decorative paintings, some in collaboration with Antonio BASOLI and recorded in the latter's *Compartimenti di camere* (Bologna, 1827), established Palagi's reputation as an artist. His early style was vigorously NEO-CLASSICAL, influenced by PIRANESI and Felice GIANI. In 1803 he was elected to the Bologna Academy and in 1806 he left for Rome to further his career. Success as a painter led to Palagi's involvement in the decoration of the Quirinale for Napoleon (1812), appointment as inspector of the Accademia Italiana (1813) and election to the Accademia di San Luca (1813). In 1815 he returned to Bologna and then settled in Milan, where he ran a painting school and continued his activity as a decorative painter. In the 1820s he became a serious collector. In 1832 Palagi moved to Turin, where he was entrusted by the King of

Sardinia, Carlo Alberto, with the total direction of the decoration of the palace of Racconigi. In 1834 he designed a GOTHIC Revival garden chapel for the Villa Traversi at Desio, and the Gothic Margheria in the park at Racconigi. In the same year he designed the Etruscan Cabinet at Racconigi, was appointed director of ornament at the Royal Academy in Turin, where he also designed the decorations of the royal palace, and was knighted. In the following years he was elected a member of almost every Italian academy. Palagi's designs extended to vases, carpets, silver, furniture, both in the classical and Gothic styles, fireplaces, and every element of interior decoration. Stendhal's *Chartreuse de Parme* (1838) alludes to silks woven at Lyon after the designs of '*le célèbre Palagi, peintre de Bologne*'. His ornamental language included winged victories, sphinxes, cornucopiae, caryatids and the whole vocabulary of PERCIER and FONTAINE, handled with almost BAROQUE exuberance and boldness. ALBERTOLLI and BORSATO were more immediate influences. At the LONDON 1851 EXHIBITION furniture designed in 1834 for the Etruscan Cabinet at Racconigi attracted favourable comment; it had been excuted in Turin by Guido Capello, called Monsalvo, while other inlaid pieces for Racconigi were made in Paris by Claude Chiavasso. Some of Palagi's grandest pieces of furniture were of gilt bronze, cast by the Viscari foundry in Milan. Palagi left his collection, including some 40,000 coins, Egyptian, Greek and Roman sculpture, Greek and Etruscan vases, and even some pre-Columbian pottery, to his birthplace, Bologna. In some respects Palagi was an Italian equivalent to SCHINKEL, having been active as decorative designer, architect, painter, sculptor and designer of sculpture.

Palmqvist, Sven Born in Lenhovda, the son of a soldier, in 1906, Palmqvist was trained from 1927 to 1930 at the Orrefors glass-engraving school and from 1930 to 1934 at Stockholm technical school. After studying sculpture at the Stockholm Academy from 1934 to 1936, he was in Paris from 1936 to 1939. Palmqvist has been a prolific designer of glass for the Orrefors factory, introducing many technical innovations and working mainly in an abstract style.

Pan (1895–1900) A magazine of the highest quality published in Berlin, *Pan* was founded by an association with royal patrons. The title *vignette*, a head of the god Pan, was by Franz von STUCK. *Pan* included poems, philosophy and painting, among which writings by Nietzsche and paintings by Böcklin were conspicuous. The final article was by Henri VAN DE VELDE. *Pan* suffered from internal strife, its first editors, the poet Otto Julius Bierbaum and the art critic Julius MEIER-GRAEFE, resigning after the third issue in 1895. After *Pan*'s end in 1900 Justus Brinckmann bought its graphic collection for the HAMBURG MUSEUM.

Panfili, Pio (1723–1812) Born in Fermo, Panfili studied painting at the Bologna Academy. He was active as both painter and engraver. His *Frammenti di Ornati per Li Giovani Principianti nel Disegno* (Bologna, 1783; twenty-four plates) is a fascinating anthology of early NEO-CLASSICAL design in Bologna, with strong BAROQUE elements. It includes copies after POLIDORO, DELLA BELLA and Jean LE PAUTRE. There are also designs by Mauro TESI, Flaminio MINOZZI, Benigno BOSSI, Giovanni CALEGARI and Panfili himself. He contributed several plates of rosettes, trophies and ACANTHUS ornament.

Pankok, Bernhard (1872–1943) Born in

Münster, the son of a cabinet-maker, Pankok studied painting at the academies in Düsseldorf (1889–91) and Berlin (1891–2). He then moved to Munich, where he designed decorations for 'JUGEND' and 'PAN' from 1896. The Munich 1897 Glaspalast Exhibition included an armchair and a mirror frame designed by Pankok; the former was praised by Wilhelm Bode in 'PAN'. In 1898 Krüger commissioned Pankok, PAUL and RIEMERSCHMID to design for the MUNICH VEREINIGTE WERKSTÄTTEN, whose first exhibition was held in that year. In about 1899 Pankok designed furniture for OBRIST's villa in Munich. He worked in a quirky and knobbly ART NOUVEAU style decorated with naturalistic carving and marquetry, with some similarities to the work of GAUDÍ and of ROHLFS. Furniture designed by Pankok was also shown in 1899 at the Munich Secession and Dresden Exhibitions. For the PARIS 1900 EXHIBITION Pankok designed the decorations of the German catalogue. Riemerschmid's Room for an Art Lover incorporated a cupboard, table and lights by Pankok. Pankok's own Alcove Room, with heavy built-in furniture animated by complex curves and decorated with carving and inlay, with appliqué wall embroideries incorporating birds, flowers and fierce C-curves, and with an elaborate arrangement of pendant electric lights, was described by Obrist as a mixture of ROCOCO curlicues and the style of Viking ships, at once fantastic and gloomy. The room was shown again at the Munich 1901 and TURIN 1902 EXHIBITIONS. In 1902 Pankok moved to Stuttgart, where in 1903 he became director of the royal workshops. He showed a Music Room at the ST LOUIS 1904 EXHIBITION and another at the 1917 Werkbund exhibitions in Basel and Bern; he had become a member of the DEUTSCHE WERKBUND in 1908. From 1913 to 1937 he was director of the applied arts school in Stuttgart.

Panton, Verner Born in Odensee in 1926, Panton qualified as an architect in Copenhagen and then worked for Arne JACOBSEN from 1950 to 1952; in the latter year he designed some experimental inflatable furniture. Panton set up his own office in Switzerland in 1955. In that year Thonet produced Panton's zig-zag laminated-wood chair, an advanced echo of RIETVELD. Among his later designs are a dashingly sculptural glass-fibre shell chair (1960), produced from 1967 by Herman Miller, a curvilinear easy chair for Stortz & Palmer (1962) and a circular television for Wega (1963). Panton has also designed interiors, carpets and lights, and has eagerly experimented with new materials.

Papworth, John Buonarotti (1775–1847) The second son of John Papworth (1750–99), who was a leading London stuccoist, Papworth was directed towards architecture by Sir William CHAMBERS, who frequently employed his father. He was taught PERSPECTIVE by Thomas MALTON, and then, after two years with the architect John Plaw and three (1789–92) with the builder Thomas Wapshott, spent a year (1793) with Sheringhams, the decorators. In the late 1790s Papworth began a prolific architectural career designing all sorts of buildings in every available style. In 1820 he was given the title of Architect to the King of Württemberg. Papworth was also active as a draughtsman, acting as secretary to the Associated Artists in Watercolours from 1808 to 1810. His versatility led him in 1815 to adopt the middle name Buonarotti, at the suggestion of friends. His contributions to ACKERMANN'S *Repository of Arts* (1809–28) were reprinted as *Select Views in London* (1816), *Rural Resi-*

dences (1818) and *Hints on Ornamental Gardening* (1823), the latter two important contributions to the picturesque, including many designs for rustic decorations and garden furniture. Later, in 1826, Papworth designed Ackermann's new premises; it is probable that he employed another Ackermann protégé, A. C. PUGIN, to design a GOTHIC summer house at Claremont (1817). In 1814 Papworth drew some illustrations for Peter Coxe's poem *The Social Day*, published in 1823. These included furniture in a neat but modest Grecian style. The design of furniture was one of Papworth's major activities. At Sheringhams he had met the cabinet-maker George Morant, for whom he designed a Bond Street shop-front in 1817, and in 1824 he designed a Piccadilly shop-front for Robert Hughes, later cabinet-maker to the Duke of Cambridge. In the 1830s he designed furniture for the cabinet-makers Edward & William Snell of Albermarle Street and for George and Thomas Seddon; among other furniture makers he also employed Johnstone & Jeanes, Taprell & Holland, Mr Dowbiggin and the carver William Gibbs Rogers (1792–1875). In 1824 Papworth complained that his designs had been widely plagiarized in Paris, and his son, Wyatt Papworth, later stated that many of the designs in LOUDON's *Encyclopaedia* (1833) were borrowed from his father. His stylistic inclination was NEO-CLASSICAL; giving evidence to the Select Committee on Arts & Manufactures in 1835 he praised PERCIER and FONTAINE and condemned the ROCOCO Revival. In a speech on Papworth's retirement in 1847 C. R. Cockerell singled out his furniture designs as a major achievement, but his designing activities ranged much wider. They comprehended silver for Rundell & Bridge, stained glass, church furniture, light fittings and chandeliers, including a Gothic example probably for Eaton Hall, a glass

throne for the Shah of Persia, made by the glass manufacturer, James Blades, for whom in 1823 Papworth designed a new showroom which was published by Ackermann. He also designed textiles, including a handkerchief (1815) for James Morrison (1790–1857), who became a leading client, fireplaces, book covers for the *Forget-me-not Annual* (1825–30), Grecian blinds for New York (1827) and the decorations and flags for the steamship *London Engineer*. He designed new shop-fronts for Sewell & Cross, silk mercers (about 1830), Collard & Co., piano manufacturers (1834), and Duppa & Collins, paper-hangers (1843). But Papworth not only practised but also preached the virtues of design. In 1835 he delivered a paper on the '. . . cultivation of architecture, and of the art of ornamental Design' to the new Institute of British Architects, which he had helped to found in 1834. As a result, in 1836 Papworth was appointed part-time Director of the new government SCHOOL OF DESIGN, which opened in 1837 with teachers selected and furniture designed by Papworth. He had to resign as a result of economies and reorganization in 1838. At Papworth's death the rational Grecian style which he had helped to form was in decline, but his role in forging the vocabulary of middle-class furniture and ornament in the period from 1820 to 1840 has received too little recognition. His elder brother, Thomas (1773–1814), mainly active as a sculptor, also designed silver from at least 1802 to his death, including a candelabrum for S. P. Cockerell (1802).

Parasole, Isabetta Catanea In 1595 Parasole published the first known pattern-book for lace by an Italian woman, *Specchio delle virtuòse donne* (forty plates), which was also the first lace book published in Rome. The designs are competent but unoriginal, a pattern followed in Parasole's second book, *Studio delle virtuose dame* (Rome, 1597; thirty-six plates). The *Specchio* was reprinted by the publisher Lucchino Gargano in 1598 and 1600 and by Guglielmo Facciotti in 1615 to 1621. *Fiori d'ogni virtu* (Rome, 1610; forty plates), later issued in several editions as *Teatro delle nobili et virtuose donne* (1616–36), was her last work and her finest, with a wide range of lace designs comparable to those of VINCIOLO and VECELLIO.

Paris Exhibitions In 1797 the Marquis d'Avèze, encouraged by the Minister of the Interior M. de Neufchâteau, projected an exhibition and lottery of products of the neglected French national manufactories (Sèvres, Gobelins and Savonnerie). The scheme foundered, but in 1798 he held a selling exhibition of French art-manufactures at the Maison d'Orsay in Paris. The idea was taken up by the French government and later in 1798 the first French Exposition de l'Industrie was held in a temporary pavilion on the Champ de Mars in Paris with 110 exhibitors. The second exhibition was in the courtyard of the Louvre in 1801 with 229 exhibitors, the third also in the Louvre in 1802 with 540 exhibitors, and the fourth on the Esplanade des Invalides in 1806, with 1,662 exhibitors, including DUGUERS DE MONTROSIER. After the Restoration the series of Paris exhibitions was revived with the fifth exhibition in the Louvre in 1819 with 1,662 exhibitors, including silver designed by NORMAND, a sixth in 1823 with 1,648 exhibitors, and a seventh in 1827 with 1,795 exhibitors. In 1834 the eighth was held in a new building on the Place de la Concorde with 2,447 exhibitors; the ninth, in the same location, had 3,281 exhibitors, including a shawl designed by COUDER. The tenth exhibition in 1844 and the eleventh exhibition in 1849, both on a site near the Champs Élysées, attracted

3,960 and 4,494 exhibitors respectively. These eleven Paris exhibitions were widely influential and imitated, leading to the first German exhibition of art and industry, held in Stuttgart in 1812 under the patronage of King Friedrich I of Württemberg, and to subsequent exhibitions held in Munich from 1815, Düsseldorf and Leipzig from 1816, Nuremberg and Augsburg from 1818, and Dresden from 1824. In England the Paris 1844 Exhibition led to the Birmingham 1849 Exhibition and to the various initiatives taken by the SOCIETY OF ARTS, with Prince ALBERT as its president, to improve standards of English design by means of exhibitions. In 1849 Matthew Digby WYATT reported on the Paris exhibition and his recommendations helped to prepare the way for the first great international exhibition, that held in London in 1851. In 1853 Napoleon III appointed commissioners for his response, the Paris 1855 International Exhibition, a massive event with 20,839 exhibitors but a financial disaster which attracted fewer visitors than 1851. Among the designers were PRIGNOT, SEMPER, STEVENS, COLLING and John BELL, working for English manufacturers, and Reister, CLERGET, DIÉTERLE and LIÉNARD for French. The Paris 1867 Exhibition, with 42,217 exhibitors and nearly 7 million visitors, was the last great High Victorian exhibition. Monti, Matthew Digby WYATT, MOREL-LADEUIL, WILLMS, VECHTE and TALBERT designed English exhibits, HANSEN, F. von SCHMIDT and STORCK Austrian; Prignot was back in Paris and Brangwyn of Bruges, father of Frank, showed ecclesiastical embroidery. At the Paris 1878 Exhibition COLLCUTT, Talbert, BATLEY, Lewis F. DAY and Walter CRANE represented the English Art style, TIFFANY showed silver by MOORE, and an elaborate vase designed by Gustave Doré (1832–83) attracted much attention. GALLÉ was prominent at the Paris 1889 Exhibition, famous for the Eiffel Tower. The Paris 1900 Exhibition represented the climax of the sinuous vegetal stage of ART NOUVEAU; Gallé, MAJORELLE, GRASSET and MUCHA were prominent and BING showed designs by COLONNA, DE FEURE and GAILLARD. In 1901 GUIMARD, Gaillard, Grasset, FOLLOT, DUFRÈNE and others founded the Société des Artistes-Décorateurs in an attempt to improve standards of French design. In 1907 the Société planned an exhibition of the decorative arts for 1915. The war put a stop to the project but it came to fruition in the Paris 1925 Exposition des Arts Décoratifs et Industriels, which marked the high-water mark of the ART DÉCO style, with RUHLMANN, DUNAND, CHAREAU and LALIQUE prominent as designers. LE CORBUSIER's Pavillon de l'Esprit Nouveau presented an uncompromisingly MODERN line. By the time of the Paris 1937 Exposition Internationale des Arts et Techniques Appliqués à la Vie Moderne, Modernism was established but Le Corbusier's canvas and metal Pavillon des Temps Nouveaux still appeared *avant-garde*. The German Pavilion was surmounted by an eagle and a swastika, the Russian by heroic workers. Oliver HILL designed the British pavilion.

Paris, Union Centrale des Arts Décoratifs In 1863 an association called the Union Centrale des Beaux-Arts Appliqués à l'Industrie was founded in Paris. Its president was Guichard, its founder members included the designers KLAGMANN, DIÉTERLE, DECK and CARRIER-BELLEUSE and the antiquary Edmond du Sommerard, and its purpose was to counter the threat posed to French trade and manufactures by improving English standards of design. The Union organized a museum, a

library, lectures and many important exhibitions, and published the 'REVUE DES ARTS DÉCORATIFS' from 1880. In 1877 an association was formed to found a decorative arts museum in Paris: in 1881 this merged with the Union under the new title Union Centrale des Arts Décoratifs, and the new body sponsored a lottery to raise funds for the museum. As a result the Musée des Arts Décoratifs was installed in the Palais de l'Industrie in 1882. The Union had a pavilion at the PARIS 1900 EXHIBITION, designed by Georges Hoentschel (1855–1915). This was partly reconstructed at the Pavillon de Marsan of the Louvre, which became the home of the Musée des Arts Décoratifs from 1905.

Particino, Antonio A Florentine woodcarver and architect, Particino executed works for VASARI for the decorations for the entry of Charles V in 1636 and for Francesco I de' Medici in 1567. Vasari owned elaborate MANNERIST designs for tabernacles and altars by Particino. He also designed door frames at Empole.

Parvillé, Léon Parvillé was employed by the Turkish regime to restore buildings in Istanbul from 1863. In 1867 he erected a mosque as the Turkish pavilion at the PARIS EXHIBITION. He subsequently worked as a ceramicist, attracting praise for his wares in the Turkish manner at the VIENNA 1873 EXHIBITION. His *Architecture et Décorations Turques* (1874) contains fifty fine plates of Turkish ornament, many in colour; it has a long preface by VIOLLET-LE-DUC. Parvillé died in Paris in 1885.

Pasquier, Théodore One of the leading decorators in Paris in about 1830, Pasquier published *Dessins d'ameublement* and *Recueil de fauteuils, lits de repos et chaises* (1837), the latter with at least seventeen coloured lithographs of sofas and chairs, all in a more or less elaborate heavy NEO-CLASSICAL style. Most were executed for the chair manufactory founded by the brothers Jeanselme in Paris in 1824, which continued as 'Jeanselme Frères' until 1840.

Passarini, Filippo Born in Rome in about 1638, Passarini designed a coach for the entry of the Ambassador Extraordinary of Parma to Pope Innocent XI in 1691. It employed rich ACANTHUS ornament and sculptural figures, which also occur in his *Nuove Inventioni d'ornamenti d'architectura e d'intagli diversi utile Ad Argentieri, Intagliatori, Ricamatori* . . . (Rome, 1698; thirty-two plates). This vigorous and theatrical book of designs includes clocks, mirrors, tables, brackets, pulpits, an organ, state beds and cradles, directly dependent on the style of SCHOR and FERRI, and employing the same vocabulary of scrolls, acanthus, trophies, etc.

Passarotti, Aurelio A son of the Bolognese painter Bartolomeo Passarotti, Aurelio Passarotti was a miniature painter who worked as an engineer of fortifications for the Emperor RUDOLF II, by whom he was imprisoned. Freed, he returned to Bologna, where he published a book of lace designs, *Libro di lavorieri* (1591; forty-six plates), which were old-fashioned and mainly uncomplicated, though with heraldic references to aristocratic Bolognese ladies, and with some eccentricities, including an elephant.

Passe, Crispin de I Born in Arnemuyden in Zeeland probably in about 1570, Passe may have been trained as an engraver by Dirk Volckkertsz Coornhert. In 1585 he became a member of the guild in Antwerp. From about 1595 to 1612 Passe was very successful as an engraver in Cologne. He then moved to

Utrecht, where he was made a citizen in 1613 and died in 1637. From 1603 Passe had English contacts: he also had a large trade with France. He was responsible for a large number of book illustrations, for instance a series for a 1602 edition of Ovid. He also produced plates of emblems, for example *Emblemata Amatoria* (designed in 1612, published in Leiden 1618) and the illustrations to Rollenhagen's *Nucleus Emblematum* (Utrecht, 1613), re-used in London in 1634 to 1635. Around 1601 Passe published series of EMBLEMS, of heroes, saints, biblical and classical heroines, etc., in superb STRAPWORK GROTESQUE cartouches. Passe engraved after many other artists, including the Four Ages of Man by Martin de Vos, copied on the Grand Staircase at Knole in about 1605.

Passe, Crispin de II Born in Cologne in about 1593 or 1594, the son of the engraver of the same name, Passe was trained by his father with whom he collaborated. Passe's first major work comprised the vast majority of the plates of *Hortus Floridus* (1614), illustrations of plants some of which were copied by Thomas JOHNSON in 1630. From about 1617 to 1630 Passe was in Paris, where he went to teach drawing on the recommendation of Prince Maurice of Orange. Among the books he illustrated were Pluvinel's *Manège Royal* (1623), dedicated to Louis XIII, and Sidney's *L'Arcadie* (1624). In 1621 Passe published in Utrecht *Oficina Arcularia*, an accomplished furniture pattern-book whose format, furniture designs following the ORDERS, anticipated that of CHIPPENDALE'S *Director*. Passe was clearly influenced by Hans VREDEMAN DE VRIES and *Oficina* (1621) contains two plates copied from Vredeman's *Differents pourtraicts de menuiserie*. However, Passe's own designs are not MANNERIST but BAROQUE in the manner of RUBENS, with whom Passe claimed friendship, and some incorporate AURICULAR elements. In around 1639 Passe seems to have moved from Utrecht via Rotterdam to Amsterdam, where he published a second edition of *Oficina* in 1642; a third appeared in Paris in 1651. The 1642 edition of *Oficina* is often bound with Passe's 1642 Amsterdam edition of Vignola, which contains an English text. Passe also published a drawing-book, *La lumière de la peinture* (1643). He was in a lunatic asylum in Delft in about 1645 and seems to have died after 1670. His brothers Willem and Simon were both active as engravers in England.

Paul, Bruno (1874–1968) Born in Seiffennersdorf in Lausitz, the son of a building contractor, Paul studied at the Dresden school of applied arts from 1886 to 1894 and then worked up to 1907 at the Munich Academy. In Munich, Paul executed brilliant illustrations for *Simplicissimus* from 1894 and in the same year designed furniture for its editor, Thomas Theodor Heine. In 1897 he illustrated Ludwig Thoma's *Agricola*. Paul designed furniture for the Munich 1897 Glaspalast Exhibition, and was in 1898 commissioned by Krüger to design for the MUNICH VEREINIGTE WERKSTÄTTEN, along with PANKOK and RIEMERSCHMID. At the PARIS 1900 EXHIBITION Paul showed a Hunting Room, with simple furniture and plain panelling relieved by an inlaid frieze. It was much praised and shown again at the Munich 1901 Exhibition and the TURIN 1902 EXHIBITION; Paul also designed a poster for the Munich 1901 Exhibition. At the ST LOUIS 1904 EXHIBITION, Paul won a Grand Prix for his Office for the government building in Bayreuth; its simplicity was in contrast to Pankok's Music Room. From 1907 Paul taught at the BERLIN KUNSTGEWERBEMUSEUM. His contributions to the Brussels 1910 Exhibition used an elegant late-18th-century manner; at the same time he was experimenting with unit furniture. Paul played a major part in the COLOGNE 1914 DEUTSCHE WERKBUND EXHIBITION, designing the beer hall, the restaurant and other public rooms. In 1929 he was associated with MIES VAN DER ROHE. In 1932 Paul handed over his influential post as director of state art schools in Berlin to Hans Poelzig (1869–1948).

Pauwels, Noe Pauwels, a goldsmith in Brussels, published there *Livre Dorfeferie* (1710), twelve plates of dense black scrolled ACANTHUS designs for boxes, buckles, brooches, crosses, some jewelled. The ornament is repetitive and ARTISAN in quality.

P.C. *Livre de Feuilles d'Orfeuvrerie et de taille dépargne* (Paris, 1672; seven plates) by P.C. comprises fine ACANTHUS ornament for goldsmiths and designs for miniature cases and box-lids. In his address to the public, P.C. proclaims his indifference to praise or blame. The designs, similar to some by ROUPERT, were reprinted in 1676.

Peche, Dagobert (1887–1923) Born at St Michael, near Salzburg, the son of a lawyer's clerk, Peche studied architecture at the Vienna Polytechnic from 1906 to 1908 and then until 1911 at the Vienna Academy, where he was taught by Friedrich Ohmann. Peche visited England in 1910 and Paris in 1912. In Paris he was much influenced by French ROCOCO furniture and GOTHIC tapestry; on his return journey he met the Darmstadt publisher Alexander Koch. Back in Vienna, Peche designed wallpapers and a room shown at the 1913 Secession exhibition; another room designed by Peche was shown in the Austrian pavilion at the COLOGNE 1914

DEUTSCHE WERKBUND EXHIBITION. In 1915 he began to design for the WIENER WERKSTÄTTE, whose branch in Zürich he ran from 1917 to 1919, designing silver, jewellery and embroidery. Returning to Vienna, Peche continued to design prolifically; in 1922 he visited Cologne to supervise the printing of his wallpapers. In all Peche made some 3,000 designs for the Wiener Werkstätte. As well as the fields already mentioned they covered graphic ornament, decorative papers, bookbindings, leather, textiles, ceramics, glass and ivory carvings. His ornament made generous use of gaily coloured fruit, flowers, birds and animals and his forms, often curved and fluted, were capricious, playful and varied. Rococo, provincial late-18th-century NEO-CLASSICAL ornament and BIEDERMEIER were among Peche's sources of inspiration. His style was in strong contrast to the early geometric Wiener Werkstätte manner of Josef HOFFMANN and Koloman MOSER; as might be expected, LOOS did not approve. However, Peche was a dominant influence on the design of Wiener Werkstätte products through the 1920s.

Pellegrino, Francesco A Florentine, Pellegrino travelled in 1528 to France to work for the court, with his friend the sculptor G. F. Rustici (1474–1554). He later worked under ROSSO from 1534 to 1536 on stucco work in the Galerie François I at Fontainebleau, and died in France in about 1552. His *La fleur de la Science de Pourtraicture. Patrons de Broderie. Façon arabique et ytalique* (Paris, 1530; forty-nine plates) was the most influential early pattern-book of MORESQUE ornament, only anticipated by TAGLIENTE in 1527. A copy of *Le fleur* probably belonged to BOS, who copied it in ninety of the 106 designs in his moresque book of about 1540,

reprinted in Paris by Hierosme Gourmont in 1546.

Pelliciolo Pelliciolo was probably the designer of two early Venetian pattern-books for cut-work of about 1545, *Fontana de gli essempli* (sixteen plates) and *Fior de gli essempi* (sixteen plates). Both comprise geometrical designs comparable to those of PAGANO.

Pencz, Georg Pencz became a citizen of Nuremberg in 1523. He was a pupil of DÜRER. In 1525, with his fellow pupils the BEHAM brothers, he was exiled for religious unorthodoxy, but was soon allowed to return. Pencz seems to have visited Italy in about 1529 and 1539 and was influenced by Giulio ROMANO and POLIDORO DA CARAVAGGIO. He was a successful painter in Nuremberg and died in 1550 in Leipzig on his way to take up a position as court painter to Duke Albrecht of Prussia at Königsberg. Pencz's many prints include two fine panels of early RENAISSANCE candelabrum ornament, with addorsed satyrs and mermen, and a frieze with the triumph of Bacchus.

Penrose Annual, The (1895–present) First entitled *The Process Work Year-Book*, the *Annual* is now subtitled *An international review of the graphic arts.* It covers all aspects of design in printing. It is published in London.

Percier, Charles (1764–1838) Born in Paris, Percier studied at the École Gratuite de Dessin founded by BACHELIER, where he was a star pupil. He then learned architecture under Antoine François Peyre (1739–1823) in whose office he met Pierre FONTAINE in 1779. Percier won the second prize for architecture in 1783 and the Grand Prix in 1786. He then travelled to Rome, where he became intimate with Fontaine, and stayed until 1792. Back in

Paris he worked as a designer and in 1793 collaborated with Lenoir on arranging the Museum of French Monuments. From 1794 he was in a close partnership with Fontaine. Their *Recueil de décorations intérieures* (1801) was the manifesto of a new archaeological classicism, which became the official Napoleonic style, with Percier and Fontaine as Napoleon's chosen architects. Percier, who suffered from ill health, seems to have handled the details of design, while Fontaine formed their projects and managed their execution. Percier designed furniture, carpets, porcelain, bronzes, silver and every other article of decoration. He specified the minutiae of every object with great care down to tassels and braids. Percier had known Thomas HOPE since 1791 and was called his '*carissimo amico*' in 1802. In the same year Percier became friendly with FLAXMAN, when he visited Paris, and he helped to disseminate Flaxman's engravings in France. Percier worked almost exclusively in the NEO-CLASSI-CAL style, although his designs often incorporate RENAISSANCE elements. However, his decorations for the coronation of Napoleon in 1804 were GOTHIC, and those for the coronation of Louis XVIII were part Gothic and part Renaissance. Percier's pupils included HETSCH. ACKERMANN'S *Repository* contained many designs in the style of 'Mr Persée'. He died fifteen years before Fontaine, but they share the same grave.

Pergolesi, Michelangelo Although probably brought to England from Italy through Robert ADAM, Pergolesi's only recorded work for Adam is the decoration of sixty-two pilasters in the Long Gallery at Syon House, executed in 1768: Adam's designs for the room were commenced in 1761. In 1765 Pergolesi was paid for 'Designs for the Carpet and Tapestry' at Syon. He also seems to have designed plasterwork for CHAMBERS at Gower House, London (1765–74). Sixty-six drawings by Pergolesi of GROTESQUE ornament and antiquities, dated 1776 and 1777, are in the Cooper-Hewitt Museum, New York. He published a long series of ornamental engravings as *Designs for Various Ornaments* (1777–1801): the final four plates (1801) were issued by Dulauchamp, 'successor to the late Signor Pergolesi'. In his proposals for this publication which eventually totalled sixty-six sheets Pergolesi stated that he had 'long applied his Attention to the Ornaments of the Ancients' and that he 'had the Honour of designing and painting Rooms, Ceilings, Staircases and Ornaments for many of the Nobility and Gentry in England and other Countries'. Some prints incorporate subjects drawn by the painter Giovanni Battista Cipriani, R.A. (1727–85), who had also worked at Syon and was presumably an associate of Pergolesi. Parts of the *Designs* were dedicated to Lord Scarsdale, Adam's patron at Kedleston, and to the Duchess of Northumberland, his patron at Syon. A drawing for a table by Pergolesi inscribed 'for the Duke of Northumberland' is in the VICTORIA & ALBERT MUSEUM. The *Designs* include panels, trophies, friezes, doors, ceilings, metalwork and furniture. A 1782 design for a silver tureen was borrowed by Matthew Boulton, and Pergolesi probably played a major part in disseminating Adamesque ornament. Pergolesi's *Original Designs . . . in the Etruscan and Grotesque Style* were published posthumously in 1814.

Perriand, Charlotte Born in 1903, Perriand studied interior design at the École de l'Union Centrale des Arts Décoratifs. She was strongly influenced by the writings of LE CORBUSIER and attracted his attention through a roof-top bar, shown at the Salon d'Automne of 1927.

Perriand then worked with Le Corbusier until 1937. *Répertoire du goût moderne* (1929) illustrated her aggressively healthy apartment entitled Travail et Sport, with a bar and open-plan terrace, as well as a Meuble-Phonograph and a typewriter table, couch and stools with tubular-steel supports. Perriand was closely associated with Le Corbusier's furniture designs and promulgated a ruthlessly MODERN line exemplified by her statements in the 'STUDIO' (1929): 'Metal plays the same part in furniture as cement has done in architecture. It is a revolution ... *Brightness loyalty liberty* in thinking and acting. *We must keep morally and physically fit.* Bad luck for those who do not.' Perriand showed at the PARIS 1937 EXHIBITION, and then went to Japan in 1938 to advise on industrial design. She stayed there until 1945, organizing an exhibition in Tokyo in 1941.

Perspective Perspective, a method of representing the recession of three dimensions on two-dimensional surfaces, was developed into a reliable system in Italy in the early 15th century. Architects such as Leone Battista Alberti (1404–72), Francesco di Giorgio Martini (1439–1502) and Bramante (1444–1514) and painters such as Paolo Uccello and Piero della Francesca helped to develop the techniques of perspective by example and by precept. *Prospectiva* by John Peckham (1240–92), published in Milan in about 1480, was an early printed treatise. The first illustrated work on perspective was *De Artificiali Perspectiva* (Toul, 1505) by Jean Pélerin, a cleric and civil servant; JOUSSE published a reprint of this work in 1635. The second edition (Toul, 1509) included on its title a couplet drawing attention to the usefulness of the book to craftsmen while a plate of a properly furnished room is early evidence of the especial importance of perspective to furniture

designers. DÜRER's *Underweysung der Messung* (1525) was an influential treatise; RODLER's 1531 book was intended to popularize Dürer's work. COUSIN (1560) and J. A. DUCERCEAU (1576) also wrote perspective manuals. In the mid 16th century a number of designers, including STÖER (1567), LENCKER (1567) and Wenzel JAMNITZER (1568), displayed pure or ornamental virtuosity in the use of geometry and perspective. However, the great MANNERIST master of perspective was Hans VREDEMAN DE VRIES. The standard 17th-century work was the *Perspective Pratique* (1642–9) by a Jesuit expert, Jean Du Breuil (1602–70). Other writers, including Salomon de Caus (1567–1626) in 1612 and Jean François Niceron (1613–46) in 1631, gave instruction in curious tricks of perspective. BAROQUE grandeur found its expression in books by Andrea Pozzo (1693–1700) and SCHÜBLER (1719–20). SHERATON was among the many furniture designers who gave instruction in perspective. MALTON's general work was aimed at the furniture trade, as was Richard BROWN's *Rudiments* (1822).

Persson, Sigurd Born in Helsingborg in 1914, the son of a silversmith by whom he was trained, Persson studied art in Munich and Stockholm, where he settled in 1942. From the late 1940s he was active as an industrial designer, producing many ranges of cutlery; in the late 1960s Persson designed for the Kosta glassworks. Persson has also worked as a silversmith, designing his own works in a massy, sculptural late-MODERN manner.

Peruzzi, Baldassare (1481–1536) Born in Siena, the son of a weaver, Peruzzi may have had the architect and engineer Francesco di Giorgio Martini (1439–1502) as his first teacher. In about 1503 he moved to Rome, where he joined the circle of Pinturicchio and was mainly active as an architect, with Sebastiano SERLIO (1475–1554) as his leading pupil. In 1520, on the death of RAPHAEL, he was appointed architect of St Peter's with Antonio da Sangallo the Younger (1485–1546). From 1525 he worked on Siena Cathedral, returning there in 1527 after the Sack of Rome. He was back in Rome in 1535. In 1525 Peruzzi designed a medal for the Holy War. For Siena Cathedral he designed bronze doors, stalls, the high altar and other altars, and for the Carmine in Siena an organ case. Peruzzi also designed metalwork, including a dish with the Story of Joseph. He was active as a painter of GROTESQUE ornament, influenced at first by Pinturicchio and later by Giovanni da UDINE, with whom he worked on the Villa Madama in the early 1520s.

Pesce, Gaetano Born in 1939 and trained as an architect at Venice University, in 1969 Pesce designed the doughnut-like polyurethane-foam Up 1 armchair. In 1972 he showed a cave-like commune for twelve people, and in 1975 designed for Cassina the Sit Down range of splodgy upholstered armchairs. In 1980 Cassina showed in Milan Pesce's grey amorphous resin Dalila chairs, jagged polychrome Samson tables and skyscraper sofa, Tramonto a New York. Like SOTTSASS, Pesce has been a prolific and portentous prophet of a new language of architecture and design.

Pether, Thomas Pether was described as 'Thos. Pether CARVER' on the title of his six-plate *A Book of Ornaments Suitable for Beginners* (1773), 'Sold at his Print Shop in Berwick Street, Soho. LONDON'. This *Book* was later available from I. & J. Taylor's Architectural Library and was probably reprinted by John WEALE in about 1834. It depicts husks, ribbons and ACANTHUS in the NEO-CLASSICAL manner, and is unusual as a book of designs evidently aimed directly at the craftsman and none other. Nothing more is known of Pether.

Petit, Jacob Born Jacob Mardochié in Paris in 1796, Petit later adopted his wife's surname. After studying painting under Baron Antoine Gros (1771–1835), he travelled widely, especially in England, where he published a *Series of Ornamental Books* (1824) with designs for floral jewellery, rings and seals, as well as luxuriant NEO-CLASSICAL designs for ornament (1823), ewers (1824), tureens and candelabra (1825). In the late 1820s he issued in parts of five plates his *Collection de Dessins d'Ornement*, comprising 100 handsome plates of designs for every aspect of interior decoration from furniture, goldsmiths' work, and bronzes to ceilings and pure ornament. His style varies between a rich dense late-Empire manner of startling luxuriance, ACANTHUS playing a leading role and motifs being crammed together with more vigour than congruity, and a GOTHIC equivalent, totally unarchaeological but rich in texture. Petit reissued his *Collection* under more than one title in 1831. Later he set up a pottery and produced wares somewhat in the Staffordshire style up to 1848. It seems probable that Petit's taste for acanthus and for a rich heavy variety of classical ornament may have been stimulated by the works of Richard BROWN and other English designers of the 1820s, which he would have come across during his period in England.

Petitot, Ennemond-Alexandre (1727–1801) The son of an architect, after studying under Soufflot in Lyon and at the Paris Academy, Petitot won the Grand Prix d'Architecture in 1745 and spent 1746 to 1750 with the French Academy in Rome, where he was associated with the pioneers of NEO-CLAS-

SICISM, and in 1749 designed a neo-classical backdrop for the Chinea festival. In 1753, through CAYLUS's influence Petitot was appointed architect to the Duke of Parma, whose wife, Marie Louise, was Louis XV's daughter. In Parma he published a *Suite de Vases* (1764, reissued in Milan in the same year; thirty-two plates), dedicated to Guillaume-Léon du Tillot, Marquis de Felino (1711–74), the prime minister of Parma. The VASES, incorporating grass-hoppers, chickens and elephants, are among the most *outré* neo-classical inventions. Later Petitot issued an amusing *Mascarade à la Grecque* (1771; ten plates), also dedicated to Felino, in which stock figures of theatre such as the shepherd, the bride and the priestess are clothed in neo-classical ornament. Both suites were engraved by Benigno BOSSI. Petitot executed many decorative schemes in Parma, and had a direct influence on ALBERTOLLI.

Pevsner, Sir Nikolaus (1902–83) Pevsner studied at the universities of Leipzig, Munich, Berlin and Frankfurt. From 1924 to 1928 he was an assistant keeper in the Dresden Gallery and from 1929 to 1933 a lecturer in the history of art and architecture at Göttingen, where he published an article on LE CORBUSIER in 1931. In 1933 he moved to England. In 1936 Pevsner's *Pioneers of the Modern Movement from William Morris to Walter Gropius*, praised in a review by Morton Shand, presented a fresh and persuasive chronicle of progress from the slough of Victorian historicism, via the Arts & Crafts and ART NOUVEAU, to the enlightened rationalism of the BAUHAUS. Many later editions have spread the message from Portugal to Japan. In articles in the 'ARCHITECTURAL REVIEW' (1936) and in *An Enquiry into Industrial Art in England* (1937) Pevsner used research done at Birmingham University in 1934

to 1935 to underpin a clear account of English progress in design; the *Enquiry* was revised by Michael Farr as *Design in British Industry* (1954). From 1935 to 1939 Pevsner was a buyer for his friend Gordon RUSSELL. He was a consistent advocate of the MODERN style in the *Architectural Review*, of which he became editor in the early 1940s. His pamphlet *Visual Pleasures from Everyday Things* (1946), with a bibliography including Herbert Read, John Gloag and Noel Carrington and praise for Gordon Russell's furniture, typifies Pevsner's sympathy for the commonsensical 'patient progress' of Modern design in England. Although his later fame has been as an architectural historian Pevsner continued to advocate the Modern style in design, although he chose to regard Modernism as a rational response to functional needs, rather than a style.

Peyrotte, Alexis (1699–1769) Born at Mazan, in Vaucluse, Peyrotte was in 1749 appointed Peintre du Roi et Dessinateur pour les Meubles de la Couronne. In this capacity he designed textiles and furniture for Versailles and other royal palaces. A silk woven to his design by Jean Charton in Lyon in 1757 may have been one of the earliest to incorporate NEO-CLASSICAL elements. The chair-maker Nicolas-Quinibert Foliot (1706–76) supplied furniture to Peyrotte's designs. Peyrotte issued some fifteen suites of engraved ornament. They are mainly cartouches in the ROCOCO style, one suite being dedicated to Gaspard de Fontanieu, administrator of the royal wardrobe from 1757 to 1767. Another, of rosettes for the decoration of furniture, is dated 1743. Peyrotte seems to have specialized in CHINOI-SERIES, but among his most interesting productions was *Divers ornements* (two suites of six plates), dedicated to the architect Michel Tannevot, which comprised full-scale rococo scrolls, ornaments and cartouches, presumably for the use of carvers. One of a set of trophies by Peyrotte was copied by William DARLING.

Philadelphia 1876 Exhibition In 1864 John L. Campbell, a professor from Indiana, suggested an international exhibition to celebrate the centenary of American independence. The idea was approved by Congress in 1871 and announced internationally in 1873. The Philadelphia buildings ranged from a competent free RENAISSANCE in the Memorial Hall to barbarous GOTHIC in the Agricultural Hall and hectic timber-work in many state buildings, notably those of Michigan and New Jersey. The Japanese dwelling and the half-timbered English building, designed by Thomas Harris (1830–1900), seemed relatively sophisticated, as did the iron pavilion of Barnard, Bishop & Barnard, designed by Thomas JECKYLL, with its sunflower railing. Wright & Mansfield showed elegant adaptations of SHERATON furniture designs, while Collinson & Lock exhibited furniture designed by COLLCUTT. Elkington's stand included cloisonné enamels designed by WILLMS. Of the American exhibits the Gorham Company's Century Vase, designed by George Wilkinson and Thomas J. Pairpoint, was perhaps the most spectacular.

Philippon, Adam Born in Paris in 1606, Philippon was a cabinet-maker and worked as an engineer for Louis XIII. In 1640 he was sent by the King to Rome to seek out talent. Philippon was probably accompanied on this journey by Jean LE PAUTRE, who may have been a relation; Philippon's wife was a Marie Le Pautre. Le Pautre engraved many of the plates for Philippon's *Curieuses Recherches de Plusieurs Beaus Morceaus D'ornemens Antiques, et Modernes*

(1645; thirty-eight plates), a compilation of brackets, friezes, bases, masks, ornaments, VASES, a tripod, trophies, ceilings and reliefs. Some are after the antique, others are in an up-to-date and vigorously BAROQUE style. In 1645 Philippon published a panel of rich ACANTHUS ornament from the Palazzo Medici in Rome.

Piat, Frédéric-Eugène (1827–1903) Born in Montfey in Aube, the son of a carpenter who settled in Paris in 1833, Piat worked under a number of designers, including Protat, before setting up on his own in 1845. He specialized in designing metalwork of all kinds, especially bronzes, for most of the main Parisian manufacturers, including Léon Marchand, who secured his exclusive services at the LONDON 1862 EXHIBITION. Piat worked in a wide range of styles, including Něo-Grec, Louis XVI and Chinese, frequently with great originality and refinement. He was friendly with his peers in design, SÉVIN and CARRIER-BELLEUSE. Piat received medals at the PARIS EXHIBITIONS of 1855 and 1867 and was still active at the PARIS 1900 EXHIBITION. He also established a decorative arts museum in Troyes, which opened in 1894.

Picart Le Doux, Jean (1902–82) Born in Paris, Picart Le Doux was at first interested in bookbinding and publishing, but in 1931 he turned to graphic art. In the 1930s he designed numerous posters and book-jackets. In 1939 he met Jean LURÇAT and from 1943 he was involved in tapestry design, becoming in 1945 a founder member and the vice-president of the Association des Peintre-Cartonniers de Tapisserie. Picart Le Doux designed some 300 tapestries in a style similar to that of Lurçat, abounding in universal themes, quotations from poetry and flame-like natural forms. He also designed mosaics, ceramics and, in 1957, a pack of cards for De La Rue.

Piccolpasso, Cipriano Michele di Born a gentleman in about 1523 in Castel Durante in the Duchy of Urbino, Piccolpasso received a humanist education. From 1558 he served as storemaster at the citadel of Perugia and gained a reputation as military engineer and topographer. In 1575 after a brawl he was exiled to Castel Durante where he died in 1579. In 1557, at the request of Cardinal François de Tournon (1489–1562), he prepared for publication the *Arte del Vasaio*, a technical treatise on the potter's art. At its end Piccolpasso records eighteen current designs for maiolica with trophies, MORESQUE, foliate, floral, GROTESQUE and landscape designs, as practised at Venice, Urbino, Genoa and elsewhere.

Pick, Frank (1878–1941) Born at Spalding, Lincolnshire, Pick was trained as a solicitor, but worked from 1902 as a railway administrator. In 1909 he became Traffic Development Officer of the London Underground and in 1912 its Commercial Manager. He subsequently rose to Chief Executive of the London Passenger Transport Board in 1933. Pick was an enthusiast for design, and was deeply involved in the creation of the DESIGN AND INDUSTRIES ASSOCIATION; he became its president in 1931. In 1920 he was the dedicatee of Hardie and Sabin's *War Posters* 'in honour of his brave and successful effort to link art and commerce'. For the London Underground, Pick commissioned buildings from Charles Holden (1875–1960), tiles from Harold STABLER, fabrics from Paul NASH and Marion DORN, and posters from KAUFFER, BAWDEN and many others. Most permanent was the Sans Serif typeface designed by Edward Johnston for the Underground in 1916. Pick was himself a life-long

admirer of William MORRIS; in 1928 he commissioned an Arts & Crafts cabinet from GIMSON's successor, Peter Waals (1870–1937). In 1933 Pick was deputy chairman of the London Dorland Hall British Industrial Art in Relation to the Home Exhibition, and in 1934 chairman of the Council for Art and Industry. Christian Barman, whom Pick had in 1935 appointed Publicity Officer to London Transport, described him in his 'ARCHITECTURAL REVIEW' obituary as 'a modern counterpart of Lorenzo the Magnificent', a judgement accepted, with qualifications, by PEVSNER.

Picquot, Thomas Born at Lisieux, Picquot described himself as a painter on the title of his *Livre de diverses Ordonnances de Feuillages, Moresques, Crotesques, Rabesques et autres inventions* (Paris, 1638; twenty plates). This was dedicated to Louis XIII, a great gun collector, and contains decorations for guns mainly in an energetic stretched GROTESQUE manner on a black ground, similar to earlier enamel designs. In 1634 Picquot succeeded Marin Le Bourgeois as keeper of the King's globes and mechanical devices. Le Bourgeois, also from Lisieux, probably invented the flintlock. When Picquot was granted a lodging in the Louvre in 1636 he shared it with François Duclos, another gunsmith. Picquot is thus likely to have been closely involved in this trade.

Pier, Carl Pier designed eleven suites of ROCOCO ornament of four plates each, published in Augsburg in about 1750 by ENGELBRECHT. They include designs for the corners of plaster ceilings in a free and spiky rococo manner influenced by CUVILLIÉS, as well as VASES, confessionals, pulpits and ornament.

Pierce, Edward Pierce was first recorded in 1630, as an apprentice to the London painter-stainer Rowland Buckett. In

1631 to 1632 he decorated Inigo Jones's St Paul's Covent Garden with 'perspective, groteske and other ornaments'; he also assisted on Jones's royal masques and worked in various royal palaces from 1634 to 1639, gilding and graining picture frames and painting GROTESQUE ornaments. He is said to have also been an assistant to Van Dyck. In 1640 Pierce published a book of twelve friezes which was later reissued by John OVERTON; they are among the very few English BAROQUE prints of ornament. In about 1652 Pierce was described as 'the only man that doeth understand perspective of all the painters in London'. Before 1654 he decorated the cove of the Double Cube Room at Wilton House and the Hunting Room there, the latter with subjects borrowed from TEMPESTA. Pierce later worked at Belvoir Castle, where he died in 1658.

Pierre, Jean Baptiste Marie (1713–89) Born in Paris, Pierre studied painting at the Académie Royale and in 1734 won the Grand Prix. He spent 1735 to 1740 in Rome. In 1749 he published *Sei vasi disegn dal sienor Pierre intagliati dal suo amico Watelet*, a suite of six VASES engraved by Claude-Henri Watelet (1718–86), a wealthy patron of the arts, for whose *L'Art du Peindre* (1759) Pierre designed NEO-CLASSICAL decorations. Pierre's vases, reprinted later, combine bold neo-classical forms with BAROQUE figures and GROTESQUE masks, treated in a manner influenced by PIRANESI. Pierre was a favourite of Mme de Pompadour and in 1770 succeeded François BOUCHER as Premier Peintre du Roi. Pierre worked with Carle Van Loo and VIEN on the Gobelins tapestry Les Amours des Dieux in 1757 to 1758, and from 1780 to 1789 was director of the Gobelins factory.

Pierretz, Antoine Probably a younger relation of D. Antoine PIERRETZ,

Antoine Pierretz was active as an engraver and publisher. He issued in 1666 suites of chimneypieces, ceilings and trophies, of six plates each. *Livre de Vases et Ornements* (twelve plates) comprises BAROQUE VASES and handsome mirror-frames decorated with ACANTHUS, swags, eagles etc.; it was twice reissued under different titles. *Livre de Divers Panneaux enrichis de plusieurs Ornemens & Grotesques* (eleven plates) presents handsome panels of baroque GROTESQUE ornament. A book of ironwork designs published by Pierretz was probably the work of HASTE.

Pierretz, D. Antoine Pierretz was active as an engraver in Paris. His *Livre d'architecture de Portes et cheminées* (1647; sixteen plates) comprises doors and chimneypieces in a subdued French BAROQUE style reminiscent of Jean MAROT. *Recherche de plusieurs beaux morceaux d'ornemens antiques et modernes, comme trophées, frises, masques, feuillages et autres* (1648; twenty-five plates) presents accomplished baroque cornices, swags, friezes, masks and mouldings; the work was reprinted by JOMBERT in 1765. *Livre d'Autels et d'Épitaphes* (thirteen plates) and *Desseins de cheminées à La Royalle* (thirteen plates) present designs for altars, monuments and chimneypieces. Pierretz also published *Feuillages Modernes*, six plates of panels of GROTESQUE ornament designed by PRIMATICCIO at Fontainebleau with the salamander of François I and the lilies of France.

Pillement, Jean (1728–1808) Born in Lyon, the son of a designer of ornament, Pillement was a pupil of the painter Daniel Sarrabat (1666–1748). He then worked in Paris as a designer at the Gobelins tapestry factory. In about 1745 Pillement set off for Spain, where he spent three years in Madrid, and subsequently a short period in Lisbon. In 1750 he settled in London, where he was active as both painter and designer. His *A New Book of Chinese Ornaments* (London, 1755; six plates), published by Robert SAYER, comprises enchanting light ROCOCO CHINOISERIE cartouches laden with birds, monkeys, bells, shells, and Chinamen. While in London Pillement also contributed to Robert Sayer's *The Ladies' Amusement* (2nd edition, 1762), and published *Recueil de differentes Fleurs de Fantaisie dans le Goût Chinois, Propres aux Manufactures d'etoffes de Soie et d'Indienne* (Paris and London, 1760; eight plates), designs for exotic flowers suitable for silk and cottons, as well as other designs for Chinese figures and flowers. Pillement exhibited landscapes and drawings at the London Society of Artists in 1760 and 1761; his drawings enjoyed a considerable vogue in England. Then, after a short stay in Paris, he moved to Italy, where he was in Turin, Rome and Milan. In 1763 he was working in the Kaiserhof in Vienna, and soon after made a bid for royal patronage in France, claiming in a memoir of 1764 to have invented a new method of printing flowers on silk. C.-N. COCHIN, asked by MARIGNY to comment on Pillement's abilities, was condescending and dismissive: Pillement's success in England was not surprising; such mediocre talents could shine in London, but in Paris, GRAVELOT and PEYROTTE were much superior. In 1766 Pillement was summoned by King Stanislas August of Poland to Warsaw, where he decorated the King's study in the Chinese style; he was in 1767 entitled *'pictor regius'* (royal painter). In the same year he moved to Bonn and in 1768 to Avignon. In 1770 he was travelling again, and throughout the 1770s he exhibited in both London and Paris; in 1772 he presented some of his works to David Garrick. In 1778 Pillement supplied three paintings to the Petit Trianon and was appointed painter to Marie-

Antoinette. Pillement also provided designs for the Parisian textile printing factory founded in 1779 by Jean-Baptiste André Gautier Dagoty (1740–86). In 1780 he was again in Portugal, and designed a rococo pavilion at Cintra which was admired by BECKFORD. In 1796 he settled in Pézenac, and in his last years moved back to his native Lyon, where he taught drawing and died in poverty. Up to 1774 Pillement continued to produce prints of ornament in large numbers, always in the rococo style and almost all chinoiseries. Some, such as *Recueil de Nouvelles Fleurs de Goût; pour la Manufacture des Etoffes de Perse* and his *Recoeil de fleurs de caprice*, representing strange imaginary exotic flowers, were specifically directed at textile manufacturers; the *Recoeil* was sold by *'Mr Menissier marchand detoffes'*. But Pillement designs were also copied in marquetry, by Januarius ZICK, who designed for the great cabinet-maker David Roentgen (1743–1807), on Liverpool tiles by Guy Green, on a plate made at Bovey Tracey, on a Worcester vase decorated by James Giles as well as on Staffordshire enamels.

Pineau, Nicolas (1684–1754) Born in Paris, the son of a sculptor who had worked at Versailles, Pineau studied under the architects Jules Hardouin-Mansart (1646–1708) and Germain Boffrand (1667–1754), and under the sculptor Antoine Coyzevox (1640–1720) and the goldsmith Thomas Germain (1673–1748). In 1716 with the architect Alexandre Le Blond (1679–1719) Pineau went to Russia, where in 1725 he designed the funeral of Peter the Great (1672–1725), for whose study he had earlier carved panels with trophies. Back in Paris from about 1730 Pineau was mainly active as a decorative carver. He became a member of the Académie de Saint-Luc in 1739 and its director in

1749. Mariette's *L'Architecture Française* (1727–38) includes beds, fireplaces, buffets, wall decorations,
mirrors, commodes, altars, chimneypieces and a fine privy after designs by
Pineau. Suites of tables, VASES and
consoles (six plates), and of beds (six
plates), were incorporated in Mariette's
Architecture à la Mode and some designs by Pineau were included in the Mariette edition of D'AVILER'S *Cours
d'Architecture* (1738), among them mirror heads copied from RASTRELLI, the
Italian architect whom Pineau had
known in Russia. Many of Pineau's
designs were later reissued by MERZ in
Augsburg. In 1774 J.-F. BLONDEL
named Pineau as one of the three first
inventors of the '*genre pittoresque*', with
LA JOUE and MEISSONIER. Pineau's
early silver designs, executed in Russia,
are in a BERAINESQUE style, and light
STRAPWORK in the manner of Berain
later reoccurs in his designs for beds.
His suite of tables, which were copied
by Batty LANGLEY in 1739, are ROCOCO
in spirit rather than in their detailed
vocabulary, which is similar to that of
GILLOT. But from the early 1730s in his
ceilings, panelling and furniture, much
of it designed for the architect Jean
Baptiste Le Roux, Pineau used fully
developed rococo scrolls, shellwork and
asymmetry with great delicacy and spirit,
deserving Blondel's tribute. His first
major interior in this style was the Hôtel
de Villars (1732–3); his last recorded
work was the Maison Claustrier (1752).
One of the few pieces of French rococo
furniture linked with a specific design is
a magnificent corner-cupboard with a
scrolled superstructure by Jacques
Dubois derived from a Pineau design.
An equally important document is a
carriage, one of five, designed by Pineau
for Prince Liechtenstein in 1738. His
son, Dominique Pineau (1718–86), was
also a designer, and published a suite of
tables in 1756.

Piper, John Born in 1903 in Epsom, the
son of a solicitor, Piper followed his
father's profession until the latter's
death in 1926. He then studied painting
in Richmond from 1926 to 1927 and until
1929 at the Royal College of Art (see
SCHOOL OF DESIGN) in London. In
1935 Piper designed the cover of the
'abstract' journal *Axis* (1935–7), edited
by Myfanwy Evans, whom he married
in 1937. In 1936 he designed a booklet
for Imperial Airways and in 1938
designed and wrote the *Shell Guide to
Oxfordshire*, under the editorship of
John Betjeman, who had admired articles by Piper in the 'ARCHITECTURAL
REVIEW' and whose *First and Last
Loves* (1952) Piper illustrated. In 1954
Piper began to design stained glass made
by Patrick Reyntiens: his first window
was for Oundle College Chapel, his most
celebrated for the Baptistery of Coventry Cathedral (1959–62). Piper has also
designed tapestries, including some for
Chichester Cathedral (1962), woven by
Pinton Frères of Aubusson, mosaics and
ceramics.

Piranesi, Giovanni Battista (1720–78)
Born at Mogliano near Venice, the son
of a builder, Piranesi was taught architecture by his uncle, Matteo Lucchesi,
an architect and hydraulic engineer. He
was early influenced by the Venetian
tradition of townscape painting as represented by Antonio Canaletto (1697–
1768), by theatre designers, particularly Giuseppe Galli Bibiena (1696–
1757), and by the free draughtsmanship
of Giovanni Battista Tiepolo (1696–
1770) and Francesco Guardi (1712–
93). Piranesi's early designs are in a
fantastic ROCOCO manner and include
frontispieces, a pulpit, wall panels,
a table and a ceremonial gondola. This
manner culminates in a suite of four
etchings on fantastic part archaeological part architectural themes, entitled
Grotteschi, published at Rome in

1750. Piranesi had arrived in Rome in 1740 and entered the studio of Giuseppe Vasi (1710–82), a Sicilian who was the leading producer of printed views of Rome. Piranesi was also influenced by the view-painter Giovanni Paolo Pannini (about 1692–1765/8), who taught PERSPECTIVE at the French Academy in Rome. Small views by Piranesi were published as early as 1741 and twenty-seven were included in *Varie Vedute di Roma* (1745). His exquisite *Archi Trionfali* (1748) also used a small format. Piranesi's most celebrated topographical works however were his sublime and monumental *Vedute di Roma*, which began publishing in about 1748 and only ended with his death 135 plates later. They were issued singly or in sets at various dates. Piranesi's first independent work was his *Prima Parte di Architettura e Prospettive* (1743), a series of architectural fantasies much influenced by the historical reconstructions included by the Austrian architect Johann Bernhard Fischer von Erlach (1656–1723) in his world history of architecture (1721). Piranesi's fantasies were a vital influence upon the whole first generation of NEO-CLASSICAL designers, both the group of students at the French Academy in Rome, among whom were LE GEAY and LE LORRAIN, and travelling English architects including Sir William CHAMBERS, Robert Mylne (1733–1811), George Dance (1741–1825) and Robert ADAM. Piranesi's close friendship with Adam is reflected in his dedication of his *Campo Marzio* (1762) to Adam. *Campo Marzio* was one of a series of archaeological works, commenced in 1750, in which Piranesi attempted the description, interpretation and reconstruction of Ancient Rome. These were also intended as a quarry for modern designers: in 1761 for instance Robert Adam used reliefs depicted in Piranesi's *Trofei di Ottaviano Augusto* (1753) to

decorate the Ante-room at Syon House. *Antichità Romane* (1756), a work with 250 plates, was the culmination of Piranesi's archaeological activity; it brought him international acclaim and election as an Honorary Fellow of the Society of Antiquaries of London in 1757. The new view of Greece as the source of architectural excellence which was expressed in Laugier's *Essai sur l'architecture* (1753), in Winckelmann's *Reflections on the Imitation of Greek Art* (1755) and in Le Roy's illustrations of Greek monuments (1758) was perceived by Piranesi as a direct threat to his own belief in the superiority of the Etruscans and in the richness and variety of the Roman civilization they had founded. Even the second edition of his etchings of fantastic prisons, the *Carceri*, issued after 1760, was intended to express Roman virtue, and his *Della Magnificenza ed Architettura de' Romani* (1761) represented a full-blooded riposte to the Hellenists. It was dedicated to Piranesi's patron Pope Clement XIII, for whose nephew Cardinal G. B. Rezzonico Piranesi projected an unexecuted remodelling of the interior of St John Lateran (1763–7) and the executed reconstruction of Santa Maria del Priorato (1764–6). In his *Parere su l'Architettura* (1765) Piranesi replied to criticisms of his *Della Magnificenza* voiced by the French critic Pierre-Jean Mariette by advocating the virtues of creative licence and imagination as opposed to the sterility of Greek simplicity. *Diverse Maniere d'Adornare i Cammini* (1769) was a record, focused on chimneypieces, of Piranesi's activity as a designer. Antique motifs are combined with intense, almost febrile originality; the results are often as much MANNERIST or rococo as neo-classical. The plates include tables and clocks designed for the Rezzonico family, and chimneypieces for Lord Exeter and John Hope, father of Thomas HOPE. There are also coaches, sedan chairs, mirrors,

VASES, commodes and much besides. The plates were widely circulated before publication; in 1767 Sir William HAMILTON praised their probable usefulness to English designers. Piranesi particularly stressed the novelty of his Egyptian designs, which were based both on his archaeological expertise and on his Egyptian decorations of the English Coffee House in Rome, executed in the early 1760s. Piranesi's activities as a designer and print-seller (he set up independently in 1761 and issued a revised *Catalogo* at intervals) closely interlock with his profitable business as a dealer in and restorer of antiquities, recorded in the 118 plates of his *Vasi, Candelabri, Cippi, Sarcofagi* (1778). Objects created by Piranesi out of antique fragments were exported to England, France, Sweden and Russia, and through his prints became a valuable source of inspiration to designers. The English silversmith Paul Storr (1771–1844) and the French bronze-founder Philippe Caffieri (1714–74) both owned Piranesi engravings, and silver more or less directly derived from his engraved vases is not uncommon. After Piranesi's death the rump of his collection was bought by TATHAM, and most of these pieces were finally purchased by SOANE, in 1821.

Pittoni, Giovanni Battista (1520–83) Born in Vicenza, Pittoni published in 1561 in Venice a suite of sixteen plates of ACANTHUS friezes enlivened with putti, sea-horses etc.; they are remarkable anticipations of BAROQUE ornament. His *Imprese di diversi principi* (Venice, 1566; fifty plates) makes lavish use of STRAPWORK, some reminiscent of Fontainebleau, some apparently influenced by Cornelis BOS. Pittoni also supplied illustrations to Scamozzi's *Discorsi sopra l'Antichità di Roma* (Venice, 1583).

Plakat, Das (1910–21) This Berlin magazine covered posters, advertising and graphic design. It was very well illustrated and included articles on such designers as William H. BRADLEY (1913) and C. O. CZESCHKA (1921).

Platzer, Ignác Michael (1757–1826) Born in Prague, son of Ignác František Platzer, a leading BAROQUE church sculptor and carver born in Pilsen, Platzer took over his father's workshop in 1787, his two elder brothers, a sculptor and a painter, having emigrated to Vienna. He designed clock-cases, frames for mirrors and pictures, candelabra, VASES, furniture and, at least once, cast-iron stoves. Platzer's ornamental repertoire was typical of provincial NEO-CLASSICISM of the late 18th century – the standard vases, swags, rams' heads etc. handled with the intensity associated with ARTISAN MANNERISM. But he may also have been influenced by the mannerist pattern-book of Ottavio Strada (see Jacopo da STRADA), still preserved in the Premonstratensian Abbey of Strahov in Prague, where Platzer executed decorations. His designs are notable for wit and elegance. Platzer's drawings, and those of his father and later generations of the Platzer dynasty, which ended in 1907, are in the Prague Museum of Applied Arts.

Playing Cards, Master of the The Master of the Playing Cards seems to have been active as an engraver from the mid-1430s to the mid-1450s. He probably worked at Mainz in about 1450, but based his activity somewhere in the Rhine Valley between Strasbourg and Constance. He is the earliest recognizable personality in the history of engraving. He published forty engravings on religious themes and a pack of sixty playing-cards with flowers, wildmen, birds, deer and beasts of prey as suits. They probably date from about 1440 and were soon widely used for ornament on manuscripts, bookbindings and glass.

Pleginck, Martin Pleginck designed a suite of box-lids with birds and animals published in Ansbach in 1594 by the goldsmith Stefan HERMAN (seven plates), and a suite of birds and fish (seven plates), engraved by Herman. Pleginck's designs are similar to those of Georg HERMAN and MUNTINCK.

Plepp, Hans Jakob Born in Biel, probably in about 1560, the son of a pastor, Plepp was active as the leading stained-glass designer in Basel from 1579, becoming a citizen there in 1581. In 1595 he moved to Bern, where he died in about 1597. The great painter Joseph Heintz (1564–1609), who worked for the Emperor RUDOLF II, was Plepp's brother-in-law.

Plumet, Charles (1861–1928) Born at Cirey-sur-Vezouze, Plumet was trained as an architect under Eugène Bruneau and Anatole Baudot (1834–1915). He built his first house in 1890. In about 1895 he turned his attention to furniture design, and in 1896, by joining the Les Cinq group founded in 1892 by CHARPENTIER, DAMPT, AUBERT, SELMERSHEIM and Moreau-Nélaton, changed it into Les Six. The Les Six exhibition of 1897 included Art Nouveau furniture by Plumet in collaboration with Selmersheim; it was described in the 'STUDIO' and the 'REVUE DES ARTS DÉCORATIFS'. Plumet was the author of Les Six manifesto, *Le Foyer Moderne*, which proposed a modern, simple, healthy, comfortable type of dwelling. He and Selmersheim showed a dining room at the PARIS 1900 EXHIBITION; by this date Plumet's ART NOUVEAU was shorn of any excesses. *Maisons de Rapport* (1923), introduced by Jean Badovici, is mainly concerned with blocks of flats by Plumet but also

shows simple furniture and ironwork and lighting in an ART DÉCO manner with floral and fluted ornament.

Poilly, François de (1622–93) Born in Abbeville, son of a goldsmith, Poilly was taught to engrave by Pierre Daret in Paris from 1639. He was in Rome from 1649 to 1656, and in 1669 became Graveur Ordinaire du Roi to Louis XIV. Poilly designed a suite of tight black scrolled ACANTHUS ornament for watches, boxes, flasks and miniature cases, some incorporating mythological figures and scenes. His main activity was as a publisher, his output including, at the end of his life, suites of modern designs for chimneypieces, doors and panelling.

Poilly, Nicolas de (1626–96) Born in Abbeville, the son of a goldsmith and brother of the engraver and publisher François de POILLY, Poilly published a suite of six plates of bold ARTISAN designs for ironwork – handles, locks, bolts, keyhole escutcheons, andirons, firebacks, hinges and street signs. They probably date from about 1660, and are close to the designs of HASTE.

Poilly, Nicolas Jean Baptiste de Born in Paris in 1712, the son and grandson of engravers, Poilly published a *Nouveau Livre de Rampes d'Escaliers et Balcons*, light graceful ROCOCO designs for ironwork, and a suite of lively details of rococo ornament (six plates).

Poiret, Paul (1879–1944) Born in Paris, the son of a shopkeeper, Poiret was apprenticed to an umbrella maker. In 1896 he met Jacques DOUCET and became a dress designer. He later worked for Worth and in 1904 went independent with great success. In 1910 he visited Vienna, where he met Josef HOFFMANN, and in 1911 he founded the Atelier Martine, a school which taught design to working girls. The Maison Martine on the Faubourg Saint-Honoré sold Martine products, notably textiles, rugs, carpets and wallpapers with bright floral patterns. Guy Pierre Fauconnet designed furniture, lights and vases for Martine, and the Atelier designed the packaging for Poiret's Rosine scents. Poiret was a patron of DUFY, employing him to engrave letter headings in 1909 and setting him up as a textile designer in 1911. For the PARIS 1925 EXHIBITION Poiret decorated three boats, 'Amours, Délices et Orgues', with hangings by Dufy. Poiret also produced de luxe brochures distinguished for their design and illustration, *Les Robes de Paul Poiret* (1908) by Paul Iribe and *Les Choses de Paul Poiret* (1911) by Georges Lepage. Poiret was closely associated with SÜE & MARE, and GROULT, his brother-in-law, and had a large collection of paintings by Picasso, Matisse, Derain and others. His period of fame and success ended at the Depression.

Polidoro da Caravaggio Born as Polidoro Caldara at Caravaggio in Bergamo in 1490, Polidoro worked in Rome from 1517, assisting Giovanni da UDINE on the Loggie of the Vatican from 1518 to 1520; he was also influenced by Giulio ROMANO. Polidoro was in Naples in 1524. He achieved fame by painting the façades of several Roman buildings with frieze compositions of battles, triumphs, ornaments etc., including the Palazzo Ricci, the Palazzo Milesi and the Casino del Bufalo. In 1527 Polidoro fled the Sack of Rome to Naples and thence to Messina, where he probably died soon after 1535, having designed decorations for the entry of the Emperor Charles V in that year. Charles I of England bought nine paintings of playing putti by Polidoro. These were used by Francis CLEIN as models for decorative paintings at Ham House and for tapestries made at Hatton Garden. But, although Polidoro seems himself to have designed VASES and jewellery, his greatest influence on design was through the fictive vases and trophies he painted on the façade of Palazzo Milesi. 'Golden vases invented with such bizarre imagination that mortal eye could not conceive others more beautiful or novel', stated VASARI, who said that 'these works have been imitated time without number'. Many artists, who included RUBENS and Stefano DELLA BELLA, owned drawings of the Palazzo Milesi designs. Their complexity, boldness and antique learning attracted MANNERIST, BAROQUE and NEO-CLASSICAL taste, and through prints their survival and influence were assured. The earliest, which were probably made in about 1540, were copied by J. A. DUCERCEAU and later reprinted by C. I. Visscher. The most important set of prints, produced by Cherubino Alberti in 1582, were reprinted in 1628, copied by Aegidius Sadeler and reissued by Vandergucht in London in 1752. A suite of prints by Galestruzzi, published in 1657, reprinted in 1660, formed the basis of reprints by Arnold von Westerhout in about 1690 and, remarkably, of *Designs for Vases and Foliage . . . By Robert Adam Esq.* (London, Priestley & WEALE, 1821). A version of the vases with landscape backgrounds was engraved by Francesco Aquila in 1713 and reissued in 1719. Fialetti, ERRARD and Bartoli were other engravers inspired by Polidoro. His vases were widely imitated in metal, stone and ceramics, for instance at William Duesbury's Chelsea-Derby porcelain factory in the 1770s. Hawksmoor owned vase prints after Polidoro.

Pollaiuolo, Antonio Born in Florence in about 1431 as Antonio Benci, the son of a poulterer, Pollaiuolo was trained as a goldsmith, possibly by Vittorio Ghiberti.

He was himself active as a goldsmith from at least 1457 and soon became prominent in Florence, designing and making tabernacles, reliquaries, incense boats and jewellery in an advanced early RENAISSANCE style. In 1477 he designed a silver altar frontal for the Baptistery, completed in 1483, for which he designed embroidery from 1466 to 1480. In 1469 and 1472 Pollaiuolo is recorded as decorating armour. In 1484 he moved to Rome and worked on the tombs of Sixtus IV and Innocent VII in St Peter's. He also designed a purse clasp and a bread-knife sheath for Cardinal Francesco Gonzaga. Pollaiuolo died in Rome in 1498. He signed one engraving, a battle of ten nude men, which may have been intended as a pattern for craftsmen.

Pollen, John Hungerford (1820–1902) From a well-connected family, Pollen, educated at Eton and Christ Church, Oxford, spent a period as a Puseyite clergyman in Oxford and Leeds before being received into the Church of Rome in 1852. In 1844 to 1845 he painted the ceiling of St Peter-le-Bailey in Oxford and in 1850 the ceiling of Merton College Chapel. At Newman's suggestion Pollen served from 1855 to 1857 as professor of fine arts at the Catholic University of Dublin, where he designed and decorated the remarkable Byzantine University Church in 1855 to 1856. In Dublin Pollen met the architect Benjamin Woodward (1815–61), who introduced him to ROSSETTI, a meeting which led to Pollen's involvement in the Oxford Union frescoes of 1857 to 1858. Pollen also designed the decoration for Woodward's 1857 Foreign Office competition entry and for his Oxford Museum (1858). Pollen settled in London in 1858 and from 1863 was employed as an editor by the South Kensington Museum; among the publications for which he was responsible were the *Universal Cata-logue of Books on Art* (1870–77) and his own *Ancient and Modern Furniture* (1874). In 1876 Pollen left South Kensington to become secretary to the Marquess of Ripon; in 1884 he visited India. Among many design commissions Pollen designed in 1861 the furniture and decorations for the library at Blickling Hall, interiors at Deane & Woodward's Clontra (1860–62) and Kilkenny (1862), painted tapestry hangings for Alton Towers in the 1870s and a carpet for Wilton in 1877. In 1881 Pollen showed a tapestry design at the European Galleries, and in 1887 participated in the founding of the ARTS & CRAFTS EXHIBITION SOCIETY, where he exhibited a design for a panel and a chimneypiece executed after his designs by the School of Art Woodcarving in 1889, and in whose 1890 catalogue he wrote an article on Decorated Furniture.

Ponti, Gio (1892–1979) Born in Milan, Ponti studied architecture there after serving in the First World War, graduating in 1921. He was then mainly active as a painter, but from 1923 to 1930 he designed ceramics for the Richard-Ginori Factory at Doccia, decorated with sinister MANNERIST nudes and architecture. In 1926 Ponti designed a house for Tony Bouilhet, president of the French firm of goldsmiths, Christofle, for whom he designed elegant cutlery and silver in 1956. In 1928 Ponti became founder editor of 'DOMUS', which he edited until his death, writing prolifically on art, architecture and design. He also was influential as a director of the second (1925) and later MONZA BIENNALES, and moved the event to Milan in 1933. From 1936 Ponti taught at the Milan Polytechnic. His Lotus armchair for Cassina (1937), a rounded sculptural form on spiky legs, anticipates the style of the 1950s. Spindly, spiky or polygonal elegance is also present in a desk for Altamira (1953), a coffee table for Giordano Chiesa (1953) and, above all, in the Superleggera chair for Cassina (1957). Also in 1957 Ponti published *Amate l'Architettura* (1957), an aphoristic and rambling manifesto. The rounded sculptural aspect of Ponti's approach to design is apparent in the dashing and celebrated chrome coffee machine for La Pavone (1949) and in an egg-like garden lamp for Arredoluce (1957), while his Ideal Standard bathroom ceramics (1954) display a 'CLASSIC' purity of form.

Pontormo, Jacopo (1494–1556) Born at Pontormo near Empoli as Jacopo Carucci, Pontormo came to Florence in about 1503 and was trained as a painter there from about 1508, being influenced by Leonardo, Piero di Cosimo and Mariotto Albertinelli, and entering Andrea del Sarto's studio in 1512. Neurotic and solitary, Pontormo was none the less the central creative figure in the development of MANNERISM, and from 1530 recognized as the leading painter in Florence. His disciples included BRONZINO, VASARI and SALVIATI. In 1545 Pontormo was commissioned to design tapestries on the Story of Joseph for the new Florentine tapestry factory, but no more than two were woven after his designs, which were found eccentric, and he was soon dropped from the project.

Popp, Alexander Popp was responsible for a furniture pattern-book with 180 plates, probably published in Vienna in about 1835. It contains a rich and varied assortment of late NEO-CLASSICAL designs, some copied from PERCIER and FONTAINE, others close to DANHAUSER, some sensible, others silly. The book also included a few crude GOTHIC and ROCOCO Revival designs. This Alexander Popp is not to be confused with a homonym born in 1891 who

was also a furniture designer, and was a pupil of Peter BEHRENS.

Porden, William Born in Hull in about 1755, the son of a labourer, Porden became a pupil of the architect James WYATT in 1774. After a spell as Paymaster to the 22nd Dragoons, Porden was appointed Surveyor to Lord Grosvenor in about 1785. He retired in 1821 and died in 1822. Porden was a specialist in the GOTHIC style. His Gothic Eaton Hall (1804–12) for Lord Grosvenor included inventive and elaborate Gothic furniture in a vigorous but wholly unarchaeological style.

Porta, Guglielmo della (1485–1577) Born at Porlezza near the Lake of Lugano, Porta was active from 1531 as a sculptor in Genoa, where he worked under Perino del VAGA in the Palazzo Doria. From 1537 he was in Rome, where he was strongly influenced by MICHELANGELO. Porta was there active as a restorer of antique statues, and also designed metalwork, including twelve reliquaries ordered by Pope Pius V from the goldsmith Antonio Gentile (1519–1609) in 1570. He was succeeded by Giovanni da UDINE in the sinecure post of Keeper of the Apostolic Seal.

Poster, The (1898–1901) This London magazine focused on poster design, English and foreign, illustrating works by such designers as MUCHA, Louis F. Rhead, John Hassall and Will H. BRADLEY.

Pottery and Glass (1918–1964) This well-illustrated London trade journal was founded in 1918 as the *Pottery and Glass Record*. Its title changed to *Tableware* in 1963 and in 1964 it merged with the *Pottery Gazette*. It contains much information on commercial design.

Pottery Gazette (1878–present) Published in London, this trade journal contains much information and illustrations on the design of ceramics and glass. For its first year it was the *Pottery and Glass Trades Journal*; in 1970 the title changed to *Tableware International*.

Pouget Pouget was a pupil of the jeweller Jean Denis II Lempereur. He was himself patronized by the Marquis de MARIGNY and died in 1769. His *Traité des pierres précieuses et de la manière de les employer en parure* (1762) includes a lengthy history of jewellery and seventy-nine charmingly coloured plates of designs for aigrettes, buckles, bracelets, watches, snuff-boxes, combs, fans, orders, a sword-hilt, etc. Pouget admired MEISSONIER but cautioned apprentices that the designs of BOURGUET were no longer fashionable. Pouget's own designs, composed of flowers and ribbons, have no decided stylistic orientation. A *Nouveau recueil de parures de joyaillerie* (forty-eight plates) appeared in 1764. Pouget's *Dictionnaire de Chiffres et de Lettres ornées* (1767), dedicated to the Marquise de Marigny, combines a history of calligraphy with a manual of cyphers, with a NEO-CLASSICAL frontispiece depicting the Graces.

Powell, John Hardman (1827–95) A nephew of John Hardman junior (1811–67) who in 1838 founded John Hardman & Co., 'Medieval Metalworkers', to produce ecclesiastical metalwork to A. W. N. PUGIN's design, Powell was first trained by Elkingtons. From 1844 however he entered Pugin's office as Pugin's only permanent pupil. Pugin educated him in true GOTHIC principles and from the mid-1840s Powell worked on Pugin's designs for stained glass. In 1850 he married Pugin's eldest daughter, Anne, and on Pugin's death in 1852 succeeded him as chief designer to John Hardman & Co., settling in Birmingham. As well as stained glass, Powell designed church plate and jewellery, including some notable plate shown at the LONDON 1862 EXHIBITION. He remained faithful to Pugin's style, although tending to favour a more mechanical and elaborate manner. Powell was succeeded by his son, Dunstan John Powell (1861–1932), who worked in the same style as his father.

Poyntz, Adrian In 1591 Poyntz issued *New and singular patternes and workes of linen*, a copy of VINCIOLO's 1587 book of lace designs. It was one of the earliest works of this type to be published in London.

Preisler, Johann Daniel (1666–1737) Born in Nuremberg, the son of a painter from Prague, Preisler studied painting in Venice and Rome from 1688 to 1696. From 1704 to 1737 Preisler was Director of the Nuremberg Academy, running its drawing school from 1716. He designed several suites of ornament, including decorated letters, terms and plates symbolizing the continents, the seasons, the elements, etc. Preisler also issued three practical handbooks on drawing ornament, *Anleitung zu Laub-und Blumen Rissen*, eighteen plates with floral friezes and BERAINESQUE STRAPWORK, *Anleitung zu Croteschen Schild und andern Verzierungen*, fourteen plates with BAROQUE cartouches, panels and friezes, and *Grundliche Anweisung*, on floral ornaments.

Preisler, Johann Justin (1698–1771) Born in Nuremberg, the son of Johann Daniel PREISLER, Preisler was a pupil of his father and then, from 1724 to 1731, worked in Italy, where he drew antique statues and gems for the antiquary Baron Philipp von Stosch. From 1742 Preisler was Director of the Nuremberg Academy, and from 1754 he ran its drawing school. His *Nüzliche Anleitung Rocailles* consists of four suites of four plates each demonstrating the construction of ROCOCO ornament and its application to metalwork. This manual of ornament is a direct successor to those designed by Preisler's father. *Allerhand neu erfundene Comperts* (Nuremberg, 1743; six plates) comprises bold and varied rococo cartouches on a wide variety of themes, including 'sea-battles' and 'flower-gardens'.

Prenzell, Robert (1866–1941) Born in Elling, Prussia, Prenzell came to Australia in 1888 for the Melbourne Centennial International Exhibition. There he established himself as a designer of terracotta architectural ornaments and furniture, which he produced himself, until 1896 in partnership with a German cabinet-maker, J. Treede. His work was illustrated in the Melbourne magazine *Arts and Crafts* in 1895. Later he underwent the influence of MAJORELLE and other exhibitors at the PARIS 1900 EXHIBITION, and developed the 'Gumnut Nouveau' style, a remarkably sophisticated Australian version of ART NOUVEAU, using Australian plants as ornament.

Prieur, Jean Louis Prieur became a member of the Paris Académie de Saint-Luc in 1765 as a sculptor; he was also from 1769 a founder and is later described as a chaser. In 1766 Prieur designed furniture, clocks, VASES, lights and other decorations for the Royal Palace in Warsaw, as a collaborator to Victor LOUIS. Prieur's drawings for this commission, still in Warsaw, are the finest record of an advanced French NEO-CLASSICAL scheme of the 1760s. In 1767 Prieur again worked under Victor Louis on the choir-screen for Chartres Cathedral made by the smith Joseph Pérez. In 1775 Prieur supplied the bronze ornaments for Louis XVI's coronation coach designed by BÉLANGER and recorded in a plate by

Prieur in 1783. Prieur published a number of suites of panels of ARABESQUES, incorporating scrolls, griffins and putti, several suites of vases, furniture, tripods, chimneypieces etc., and *Principes de dessin* (1783), six plates of scrolling foliate friezes. Prieur's designs are highly accomplished, sometimes delicate and elegant, sometimes, especially in vases, tough and geometric. Prieur also designed for the wallpaper factory of Jean Baptiste Réveillon.

Prignot, Alexandre Eugène Born in Paris in 1822, Prignot was a pupil of Cicéri. He was active as a designer in London from 1848 to 1855 and 1870 to 1875, as well as working in his native Paris, in the U.S.A., Belgium; Russia and Spain. The anthology *Les Ornemanistes du XIXme Siècle* (1851) included designs for a RENAISSANCE-style mantelpiece and panels of ARABESQUE ornament by Prignot. For the PARIS 1855 EXHIBITION Prignot designed a cabinet in a rich and elaborated Louis XVI style for Jackson & Graham. He later designed a cabinet of ebony inlaid with ivory for the same luxury cabinet-makers for the LONDON 1872 EXHIBITION. In 1870 Prignot began to issue a sixty-plate photographic anthology of his designs for furniture and decorations. *La Marbrerie Moderne* (Liège, 1879; twenty-five plates) contains highly competent designs for mantelpieces in the main fashionable styles, notably Renaissance and Louis XVI. This was followed by *La Tenture Moderne* (Liège, 1882; seventy-five plates), a series of designs for upholstery, which also included furniture and room settings.

Primaticcio, Francesco (1504–70) Born in Bologna, Primaticcio worked under Giulio ROMANO in Mantua from about 1525 and assisted him on the Palazzo del Tè. He was also influenced by Mantegna and Correggio. In 1532 Primaticcio was summoned by François I to work at Fontainebleau and brought with him designs by Giulio Romano for tapestries to be woven in Brussels. At Fontainebleau, Primaticcio collaborated with ROSSO on the Galerie François I, and himself decorated the Chambre de Roi, completed in 1539. In that year Primaticcio worked with Rosso on decorations for the visit to Fontainebleau of the Emperor Charles V. In 1540 he travelled to Rome to buy works of art for François I, especially antiques or plaster casts of antiques which could be cast in bronze. Back in Fontainebleau in 1542, after the death of Rosso, Primaticcio took over the direction of its decoration, above all the Galerie d'Ulysse, begun in 1542 and still incomplete at his death in 1570; it was destroyed in 1738. At Bolsover Castle in Derbyshire the Elysium room has a ceiling derived from a print of the Galerie d'Ulysse. Primaticcio did not continue the dynamic use of STRAPWORK visible in the Galerie François I, but instead produced GROTESQUE ornament composed of a multiplicity of small details. This approach may reflect Primaticcio's taste as opposed to that of Rosso, but is probably also due to the influence of SERLIO, who had been summoned to France in 1541 and whose Book IV, published in French in 1542, recommended grotesque ornament in the style of the Vatican Loggie, and recognized the role of Giovanni da UDINE in their creation. In 1545 Primaticcio made a second art-collecting journey to Rome, where he ordered plaster casts after sculptures by MICHELANGELO. Having returned to Fontainebleau after the death of François I in 1547 Primaticcio continued to be active there, and also from 1552 designed decorations for the Grotte de Meudon for Cardinal de Lorraine, in collaboration with Domenico del Barbiere. In 1559 on the death of Henri II,

Catherine de' Medici appointed Primaticcio *Surintendant* in succession to Philibert Delorme. In 1563 he revisited Bologna, where he met VASARI.

Printing Review (1931–59) Subtitled *The Magazine of the British Printing Industry*, this was a luxury production with good articles on design and developments in typography, lay-out and so on.

P.R.K. P.R.K. published a suite of seven plates of pendant designs (1609) probably influenced by MIGNOT. They have elaborate STRAPWORK GROTESQUE frames with pendant pearls and insects, containing black stretched grotesque panels, an alphabet, an I.H.S. badge etc. Below are small figures engaged in hunting and fishing. P.R.K.'s second work, *Spits-Boeck* (Amsterdam, 1617; six plates), has on its title scenes of goldsmiths and engravers at work, and a beaker and *tazza* with engraved decoration. The five following plates present borders for this purpose, virtuoso exercises in scrolled grotesque strapwork ornament incorporating birds, monkeys, etc.

Proger, Gilich Kilian Born in Dresden, Proger became a master goldsmith in Nuremberg in 1531 and was active there until 1540. Proger published a number of small prints of ornament influenced by ALDEGREVER, mainly candelabra or VASES with putti and female figures, surrounded by fleshy leaves. Some are dated 1533 or 1535.

Projekt (1956–present) Published from Warsaw, this well-illustrated magazine presents a full coverage of Polish art and design.

Propst, Bob Born at Marino, Colorado, in 1921, Propst studied at Denver University. In 1950 to 1953 he established the Propst Company in Denver, designing interiors, aircraft, playground equipment and much besides. From the mid-1950s Propst was heavily engaged in design research for the Herman Miller furniture company. Propst's company became part of Herman Miller as a research corporation in 1960. In 1964 the Action Office he had conceived was put into production, its design being detailed by George NELSON. A development of the idea, Action Office 2, was produced in 1968.

Prouvé, Jean Born in 1901, the son of Victor PROUVÉ, Jean Prouvé was trained as a blacksmith in Paris from 1917 to 1920 by Émile Robert, a friend of his father. He then studied at the École Supérieure de Nancy. In 1918 Prouvé executed his first commissions, for a lamp and a grille, and in 1923 he opened a metal workshop in Nancy. By 1924 he was designing and manufacturing steel chairs in the MODERN style, using sheet steel, and in 1925 he received a commission to execute metalwork from MALLET-STEVENS. He also worked for LE CORBUSIER during the late 1920s and was a founder member of the Union des Artistes Modernes. In 1929 he edited the volume on metal in the series *L'Art International d'Aujourd'hui*, including works by himself as well as by Adnet, CHAREAU, René HERBST, Le Corbusier, LEGRAIN, Mallet-Stevens and Theo van Doesburg. In 1931 Prouvé founded a limited company, Les Ateliers Jean Prouvé, which investigated industrial building in metal. In 1933 Prouvé designed wood and metal chairs, in 1935 sheet-steel desks for the Compagnie Parisienne d'Électricité and in 1937 steel school furniture. In 1949 he published *Le Décor d'Aujourd'hui*. Prouvé ceased designing and producing furniture in 1950. After this he was a prolific public architect in the Modern style, admired for his exploitation of engineering techniques. In 1958 Charlotte PERRIAND, a friend, designed interiors for Prouvé's Saharan house.

Prouvé, Victor (1858–1943) Born in Nancy, the son of an embroidery designer and ceramic modeller who worked for Émile GALLÉ's father, Prouvé struck up a close friendship with Émile Gallé and when barely in his teens began to assist him on ceramic design. From 1873 to 1877 he studied at the École de Dessin at Nancy, where he was much influenced by the painter Devilly and from 1877 to 1882 he was at the École des Beaux-Arts in Paris. From 1882 he showed paintings at the Paris Salon; in 1893 he showed a portrait of Gallé. Prouvé was also a prolific decorative painter. Ceramics to his design were shown at the Paris 1884 Exhibition organized by the Union Centrale des Arts Décoratifs and at the PARIS 1889 EXHIBITION. His designs were conspicuous at the Nancy 1894 Exhibition of decorative art, although he was then living in Paris. He supplied marquetry designs to both Gallé and MAJORELLE and also designed glass, posters, bookbindings, jewellery, lace and embroidery, working in an ART NOUVEAU style close to that of Gallé. When the École de Nancy was founded in 1901 Prouvé moved back to Nancy: he became president after Gallé's death. In a lecture given in 1903 Prouvé praised RUSKIN and William MORRIS: his views were often propagated by the magazine 'ART ET INDUSTRIE'. From 1919 to 1940 he served as director of the École des Beaux-Arts in Nancy. Prouvé's pupils had earlier included Jean LURÇAT.

Prud'hon, Pierre-Paule (1758–1823) Born at Cluny, the son of a stonemason, Prud'hon studied at Dijon from 1774 under the painter Antoine Desvosge. In 1779 he moved to Paris, and from 1783 to 1788 he was in Rome, where he met DAVID. When he returned to Paris,

Prud'hon was an enthusiastic supporter of the revolution, but in 1794 he fled to the Franche-Comté, where he remained until 1796. Back in Paris from 1797 he enjoyed the protection of Frochot, future prefect of the Seine under the Empire. At this period Prud'hon did many book illustrations including some for Rousseau's *Nouvelle Héloïse* (1804). Despite his friendship with the Empress Joséphine, Prud'hon was appointed artistic director of the celebrations organized in 1810 by the City of Paris to mark the marriage of Napoleon to the Empress Marie-Louise, whose drawing master he became. For her Prud'hon designed in collaboration with the architect Adrien-Louis-Marie CAVELIER the furnishings of a dressing room, as a wedding present from the City of Paris. It included a wash-stand, an armchair, a dressing-table, a cheval-glass, and a jewel casket, brilliantly refined and elegant NEO-CLASSICAL compositions, executed by Odiot and Thomire. In 1811 Prud'hon designed the magnificent cradle given by the City of Paris to the infant King of Rome. The whole group of designs were later published by NORMAND.

Prytz, Jacob Tostrup (1886–1962) Son of Thorolf PRYTZ, Jakob Prytz succeeded his father as chief designer of the Oslo firm of goldsmiths, Jacob Tostrup. His early work, for example that shown at the Oslo 1914 Centenary Exhibition, was in the ART NOUVEAU style. In 1918 he was one of the founder members of Foreningen Brukskunst, the organization which argued the case for MODERN design in Norway. Tostrup himself was the leading pioneer of Modern design in Norwegian goldsmiths' work. From 1914 to 1950 he taught at the Oslo school of art. In his later years he designed some elaborate enamelled pieces, reacting against the austerity of the Modern style.

Prytz, Thorolf (1858–1938) Born in Alstadhaugh, Thorolf studied architecture in Oslo and Hanover. From 1884 he worked as a designer for the Oslo firm of goldsmiths founded by Jacob Tostrup (1806–90), which he took over in 1890. His designs were mainly Nordic or NATURALISTIC. He was succeeded by his son, Jacob Tostrup PRYTZ.

Pugin, Augustus Charles (1769–1832) Born in France, Pugin entered the Royal Academy Schools in London in 1792. He was soon employed as draughtsman by the architect John Nash, then in Wales. In 1796 he accompanied Nash back to London and there established a career as a minor architect and a leading topographical artist with a specialized knowledge of the GOTHIC style. His *Specimens of Gothic Architecture* (1821 and 1823), published by John Britton with a glossary by E. J. Willson (1787–1854), was partly the product of the many pupils of his drawing school. It was a vital source book for designers and architects as were Pugin's later *Gothic Ornaments* (1828–31), *Ornamental Timber Gables* (1831) and *Examples of Gothic Architecture* (1831 and 1836), whose second volume was completed by his son, A. W. N. PUGIN. From 1825 to 1827 Pugin contributed competent designs of furniture in the Gothic style to ACKERMANN'S *Repository*; these were reprinted as a book, *Gothic Furniture*. Some gothic designs by Pugin were also included in Ackermann's *Fashionable Furniture* (1823). Pugin acted as an unsung Gothic designer for other architects, including probably J. B. PAPWORTH. Pugin's extensive architectural library was sold in 1833.

Pugin, Augustus Welby Northmore (1812–52) The son of A. C. PUGIN, A. W. N. Pugin began to draw seriously in 1819, while visiting French relatives in

Paris. He was subsequently trained as a draughtsman and designer by his father, and in 1827 was commissioned to design GOTHIC furniture for Windsor Castle made by Morel & Seddon. Although he later disclaimed these early works as a 'complete burlesque' of Gothic, Pugin's Windsor furniture is, within the conventions of 1820s Gothic, highly competent. Also in 1827 Pugin was spotted at the British Museum copying DÜRER prints by a member of the firm of silversmiths, Rundell & Bridge; a commission to design silver resulted, and among the pieces whose design is attributed to Pugin are the Coronation Cup (1826–7) and the plate in St George's Chapel in Windsor (1827) for George IV. From 1829 to 1832 Pugin worked successfully as a theatrical designer at Covent Garden, and his sense of the dramatic must have been encouraged by this experience; his designs for Kenilworth (1831) displayed his command of the Elizabethan style. Also in 1829 Pugin established his own decorating firm in Hart Street in Covent Garden. There he produced furniture and metalwork in the Gothic, Elizabethan and Jacobean styles. Despite an initial success the business failed in 1831. At this stage Pugin experimented with imaginary designs for furniture, brass, ironwork and silver; they were in an elaborate and increasingly archaeological Gothic style. Also in about 1830 Pugin, who was a keen sailor, began to import antiquities from the Low Countries, a trade which involved close contacts with antique dealers such as John Swaby, John Webb and Edward Hull. In 1834 he designed furniture for Hull, and it was through Hull that he met his greatest patron, Lord Shrewsbury. From about 1832 Pugin applied himself to the study of architecture, accumulating a major library of architectural books. A scheme of furniture for the architect Charles Barry (1795–1860) led to Pugin's design-

ing furniture and fittings in 1835 for Barry's Birmingham Grammar School, and thence to the preparation in late 1835 of Barry's winning competition design for the New Palace of Westminster, and of the estimate drawings (1836–7). In 1835 Pugin saw his first book, *Gothic Furniture in the Style of the 15th Century*, published by ACKERMANN; the original drawings had been made in 1834. *Gothic Furniture* has much in common with the imaginary designs of the early 1830s, some pieces being extremely fanciful; however other designs, notably a massive X-framed chair and a stool with a through tenon secured by a revealed peg, establish the mode of solid honesty which Pugin was to practise and advocate henceforth. In 1836 Pugin published *Designs for Gold and Silversmiths*, *Designs for Iron and Brass Work*, and *Details of Antient Timber Houses*, a group of works which, with *Gothic Furniture*, initiated the vocabulary of Pugin's Gothic style. In 1835 Pugin had converted to Catholicism, and his *Contrasts; or a Parallel between the Architecture of the 15th and 19th Centuries* (1836, second revised edition, 1841) presented his personal creed: Protestant religion and architecture were bad, Catholic religion and architecture, by which Pugin meant Gothic, and exclusively Gothic, were good: Gothic was good on theological, economic, structural, moral and practical grounds: it was the only Christian architecture. The illustrations brilliantly contrasted an idealized Middle Ages with the gimcrack regularity of modern Grecian and Gothic architecture and design. Pugin's message was repeated in his later polemical works, *The True Principles of Pointed or Christian Architecture* (1841), *An Apology for the Revival of Christian Architecture in England* (1843) and *The Present State of Ecclesiastical Architecture in England* (1843), and the important doctrines formulated that 'There should be no features about a building which are not necessary for convenience, construction or propriety' and that 'All ornament should consist of enrichment of the essential construction of the building'. Pugin's militant Catholicism was a brake on his popularity, even among some Catholics, but his ideas had immediate and widespread influence. In 1836 Pugin received his first major architectural commission, for Scarisbrick Hall, for a wealthy Catholic, Charles Scarisbrick (1801–60): the interiors incorporated old carvings in elaborate Gothic settings and the furniture developed the designs in *Gothic Furniture*, for Birmingham Grammar School and, for his own house, St Marie's Grange (1835). From the late 1830s, as his architectural activity expanded, Pugin developed Gothic design in the applied arts. In 1838 John Hardman & Co. of Birmingham began to execute Pugin's metalwork, in about 1840 Herbert Minton began to manufacture his tiles. In the 1840s Hardman executed monumental brasses and jewellery to Pugin's design. In 1844 Pugin was employed by Barry to work out the decorative details of the New Palace of Westminster, including furniture made by John Webb, Hollands, and Gillows, metalwork by Hardmans, tiles by Minton, and from 1846 stained glass, on which he was assisted by J. H. POWELL and Francis Oliphant. *The Glossary of Ecclesiastical Ornament and Costume* (1844, second revised edition, 1846), one of the finest early chromolithographed books, demonstrated Pugin's mastery of Gothic ornament; it was welcomed with a call for imitation by the *Ecclesiologist*. Pugin's work on the Palace of Westminster was a gruelling task, as he delegated almost nothing, and was kept on a tight rein by Barry, who often restrained his more exuberant inventions. However, it brought a close relationship with John Gregory CRACE

(1809–89), who was the decorator of the New Palace, for whom Pugin designed Gothic wallpapers and textiles in 1847, and Gothic carpets in 1848. *Floriated ornament* (1849) displayed in thirty-one chromolithographed plates Pugin's approach to flat pattern, with a stress on geometry, the formalization of nature and bold colours. In 1851 the *Builder* published a Crace advertisement for 'Ancient House Furniture . . . executed under the immediate supervision of Mr A. W. Pugin Architect'; it was Pugin's wish to create 'a sensible style of furniture of good oak'. However, he had to design for Crace some elaborate veneered furniture of which he himself disapproved, and had continually to recall Crace to the true principles of design. Around 1850 Pugin was busier than ever; Chirk Castle (from 1846), Eastnor Castle (from 1849) and Lismore Castle (from 1850), and the continuing demands of the New Palace of Westminster, finally drove him to breaking point and to an early death. In 1851, however, his ideas received a measure of public vindication. He organized the Mediaeval Court at the LONDON 1851 EXHIBITION, assembling objects made to his design by Hardman, Minton, Crace, Myers and his other favoured manufacturers; it was generally recognized to be the only section of the exhibition to display English design in a favourable light, being praised by, among others, Dr Waagen. Already in 1849 the 'JOURNAL OF DESIGN' had praised metalwork by Pugin and Hardman shown at the Birmingham Exhibition. Pugin was appointed member of a committee, with Owen JONES and others, to acquire objects from the 1851 Exhibition for the nation. He encouraged the purchase of Indian objects. However, when Pugin found that a neo-Renaissance shield designed by VECHTE had been purchased in his absence his opposition was uncompromising. Pugin's mastery of Gothic was based on study: he was a compulsive draughtsman and travelled in England, France, Italy, Germany and the Low Countries, sketching not only buildings but also objects in public and private collections, including those of Sauvageot (1837) and Soltikoff (1847). Pugin not only dealt in antiquities but also collected them himself and as teaching tools at Oscott College in the late 1830s and the New Palace of Westminster from 1844. He had a close acquaintance with printed sources such as Willemin and scholars such as Montalembert. His designs were often based on direct archaeological borrowing, for instance taking patterns for textiles from stained glass. The facility produced by the constant practice of design together with Pugin's creative energy prevented any hint of dry copyism. His Gothic breathes life. However, Pugin became disillusioned; in 1850 he said that he had 'passed his life in thinking of fine things, studying fine things, designing fine things, and realizing very poor ones'. St Giles, Cheadle (1846), was among the few churches where he saw his ideas realized in every detail, down to the brass mounts of the missal. His son, E. W. Pugin (1834–75), took over the practice on his death, but in the 1850s the modern style of Gothic moved back from Pugin's 14th century. But if his style soon appeared outmoded, Pugin's methods and his message were dominant influences on his successors, and writers as diverse as DRESSER and MUTHESIUS paid tribute to his achievement.

Puiforcat, Jean (1897–1945) Born in Paris, the son of a goldsmith, Puiforcat was self-taught as a designer, although he studied sculpture under Louis Lejeune. He was active as an independent goldsmith from 1922, designing his own works, mainly in a geometric ART DÉCO style; Puiforcat was addicted to geometry and the golden section. A friend of RAYMOND TEMPLIER, Puiforcat showed at the PARIS EXHIBITIONS of 1925 and 1937: at the former his silver was shown in RUHLMANN's Hôtel du Collectionneur. Renê HERBST published a life of Puiforcat in 1949.

Push Pin Studio Founded in 1954 by Milton Glaser (born New York 1930) and Seymour Chwast (born New York 1931) as a partnership to undertake illustration and graphic design work, the Push Pin studio established itself in the 1960s as the best-known American graphic design group. Its floating complement of twenty or more distinguished graphic designers and illustrators have produced an endless stream of striking albeit anaesthetized images for posters, book covers, record sleeves and so on. Its manner is various, inventive and slick, adapting modern and historic styles and conventions to commercial ends with wit and precision.

P.W. Master P.W. was active as an engraver, probably in Cologne, from about 1490 to 1510. He engraved six surviving plates of GOTHIC foliage and floral ornament, one dated 1484, and in about 1500 seventy-two small round playing-cards, with roses, columbines, carnations, parrots and rabbits as suits.

Q

Quarenghi, Giacomo (1744–1817) Born in Bergamo, Quarenghi was sent to Rome in 1763 to study painting under Mengs, but having become friendly with the youthful B R E N N A, was influenced to take up architecture, in which his masters were Antoine Derizet (1697–1768), Paolo Posi (1708–76) of Siena and Nicola Gian Simoni. He was strongly influenced by the writings of Palladio. Apart from a spell in Venice and a journey to Bergamo to marry in 1772 Quarenghi remained in Rome until 1779. In about 1774 he designed a chapel and altar for Lord Arundell of Wardour, for whom James Byres (1734–1817), another pupil of Mengs settled in Rome, also designed an altar and V A L A D I E R sanctuary lamps. Quarenghi designed for other English clients but in 1779, through the agency of Reiffenstein, Russian minister in Rome and a friend of Winckelmann, he was summoned to St Petersburg to work for Catherine the Great (1729–96). From 1780 until Catherine's death Quarenghi was extremely prolific working on the grand scale in a massive N E O - C L A S S I C A L style. His output thereafter was reduced. He went back to Bergamo in 1810 but returned to die in St Petersburg. In Russia, Quarenghi designed rich neoclassical furniture and interiors, usually as massive as his architecture. He also commissioned designs from A L B E R - T O L L I.

Quarti, Eugenio (1867–1831) Born at Villa d'Almé, Bergamo, the son of a carpenter, Quarti trained as a cabinet-

maker in Paris in the early 1880s. Returning to Turin at the end of the decade he worked briefly for Carlo B U G A T T I, and then set up his own small workshop in Milan. Quarti was taken up by the painter Vittore Grubicy de Dragon (1851–1920) and became friendly with the painter Luigi Conconi (1852–1917). Quarti showed at the P A R I S 1900 and at the T U R I N 1902 E X H I B I T I O N S. The magazine *Emporium* praised his work in 1900 and Quarti's business became fashionable and prosperous about this date. Quarti designed furniture and interiors in an elegant, refined and often understated A R T N O U V E A U style until about 1905, when he adopted a plainer manner. In the 1920s he designed in the A R T D É C O style.

Quellien, Artus (1609–88) Born in Antwerp, Quellien trained as a sculptor. He came early under the influence of R U B E N S. In about 1634 Quellien travelled to Rome, returning to Antwerp by 1639. In 1650 he began to work on the sculptural decoration of the new Town Hall in Amsterdam, designed by the architect Jacob van Campem (1595–1657), whose foundation stone was laid in 1648. Quellien worked on the Town Hall until 1664, and engravings after a whole range of swags, pendants and trophies by Quellien were published by his brother Hubertus from 1665 to 1669. Quellien's ornament is distinguished by freedom and naturalism. He was influenced by Roman A C A N T H U S ornament, for example the Ara Pacis, and was an influence on Grinling Gibbons (1648–1721), who worked on occasion with Quellien's son, Arnold (1653–86).

Quest, The (1894–6) The periodical of the Birmingham Guild of Handicraft, the *Quest* published texts by William MORRIS, W. R. LETHABY and other Arts & Crafts pundits. Its illustrators included Sydney Meteyard, Charles Gere, E. H. New and Arthur Gaskin. The latter three were admired by Morris who asked them to design for the Kelmscott Press.

Queverdo, François Marie Isidore (1748–97) Born in Josselin in Morbihan, Queverdo studied under J. B. M. PIERRE, and subsequently became an engraver. He was a prolific designer of almanacks, *vignettes*, trophies and allegories. His *Premier Cayer de Panneaux Frises et sujets Arabesques* (1788; six plates) was followed by a *Deuxième Cayer*. They comprise friezes, panels, overdoors and chimney-boards, predominantly in a refined NEO-CLASSI-CAL style, but including some panels of fine BERAINESQUE ornament.

Quewellerie, Guillaume de la Born in Oudenarde, Quewellerie became a master goldsmith in Leiden in 1612. In 1624 he was banished for dishonest jewel dealing and moved to Hanau and Frankfurt. In 1633 he petitioned for reinstatement in his Leiden guild from Amsterdam and returned to Leiden, where he died in 1661. Quewellerie published three suites of accomplished stretched GROTESQUE ornament on a black ground for enamelling on jewels, miniature cases, dagger ornaments and so on; one of six plates was published in Amsterdam in 1611, and two of seven plates each appeared in 1635.

Quien, Jean Quien worked as a jeweller in London; he was presumably of French origin. In 1712 he published in London *Livre d'Ouvrages de Jouaillerie* (*A Book of Ornaments for Jewellers &c.*), (reprinted Vivares, London, 1762; six plates). It comprises cartouches, watchcases, jewels, boxes etc. in a competent scrolly ACANTHUS style.

R

Raab, Heinrich Raab designed a suite of fine floral ornament for enamelling on pendants, boxes and crosses (six plates), published in Nuremberg in about 1650.

Rabel, Daniel Born in Paris in about 1578, Rabel was active as a designer and engraver from at least 1619. He died in 1637. He was responsible for ballet scenes, fashion plates, illustrations of flowers and butterflies, and those to the pastoral romance *Astrée* (1633) by Honoré d'Urfé (1568–1625). His *Cartouches de differentes inventions* (thirteen plates) and a second suite of cartouches (thirteen plates) are boldly scrolly and BAROQUE, with a frequent use of AURICULAR masks. They look forward towards cartouches by MITELLI and DELLA BELLA.

Race, Ernest (1913–64) Born in Newcastle-upon-Tyne, Race studied interior design at the Bartlett School of Architecture in London from 1932 to 1935. After this he worked for the forward-looking lighting firm, Troughton & Young, as a draughtsman. In 1937 he visited his missionary aunt, Blanche Tweddle, in India. She ran a weaving village near Madras and on his return to London Race opened a shop to sell these textiles woven to his own simple geometric designs. The shop closed in 1939, but, while serving in the Auxiliary Fire Service, Race worked on the design of unit furniture. In 1945, after a spell in an architects' office, he formed Ernest Race Ltd with the engineer J. W. Noel Jordan (1907–74). Their first great suc-cess was the neat cast-aluminium B.A.3 chair. Designed in 1945 it won a gold medal at the MILAN 1954 TRIENNALE and was produced until 1969. For the 1951 Festival of Britain (see LONDON EXHIBITIONS) Race designed the cheerful and popular bent-steel-rod chairs called Antelope and Springbok. He also designed successful upholstered furniture from about the same date, including the Woodpecker chair (1952) and the Flamingo armchair (1957). Through the 1950s the firm became increasingly successful, producing a wide range of contract furniture. Race was made a Royal Designer for Industry in 1953. In 1962 he resigned from the board of Ernest Race Ltd to follow a brief final career as consultant designer.

Racinet, Albert Charles Auguste (1825–93) Born in Paris, Racinet was active there as a draughtsman. From 1847 to 1851 he worked on the plates for Paul Lacroix's *Le Moyen Âge et la Renaissance*. Racinet's *L'Ornement Polychrome* (1869; 100 plates) presented fine chromolithographic illustrations of ornament in the manner of Owen JONES. A second series (120 plates) appeared in 1885 to 1887. Racinet also produced plates for *La Céramique Japonaise* (1880) by AUDSLEY and Bowes.

Racknitz, Joseph Friedrich (1744–1818) Born in Dresden, where he entered the service of the Elector in 1761, Racknitz later became court chamberlain of Saxony. He was also a composer of lieder, a dilettante and littérateur. His *Darstel-*

lung und Geschichte des Geschmacks (Leipzig, 1796; forty-eight coloured plates) is the earliest comprehensive history of furniture decoration and furniture. The text volume, with an allegorical frontispiece and charming *vignettes*, is supported by references to such works as CHAMBERS'S *Chinese Buildings*, DIETTERLIN'S *Architecture* and HAMILTON'S *Vases*: Racknitz supplies useful information on such subjects as woods and colours as well as interesting historical matter. There are two plates to each style, one of interiors and architecture, the second of furniture. The styles covered are Egyptian, Etruscan, RENAISSANCE Arabesque, Pompeian, Roman, Chinese, Greek, Old German, Persian, English, French GROTESQUE (ROCOCO), Tahitian, Late Greek, Moorish, Turkish, Old French (BAROQUE), Kamtschadalian (this amused Goethe and Schiller), Mexican, Old Persian, Indian, Siberian, GOTHIC, DELAFOSSE style and Jewish. The enchanting illustrations, although in some cases archaeological in intent, are a perfect conspectus of the range of 1790s German taste in design. Their wide influence is reflected by a copy of the plate of Old German furniture in ACKERMANN'S *Repository* (1819).

Radi, Bernardino (1581–1643) Born in Cortona, the son of an architect, Radi worked as an architect in Florence, Cortona and Rome, where he died. From 1618 to 1625 he published in Rome suites of designs for wall-monuments, altars and doors, all in an elaborate late MANNERIST style. His last collection of monuments (1625) was reprinted in Amsterdam in 1642. Radi's *Scudiero di varii disegni darme e targhe* (Florence, 1636), dedicated to Giovanni Carlo di Toscana, comprises large and imposing cartouches composed of drooping scrolls of STRAPWORK incorporating sinister masks; their style has much in common

with that of MITELLI. Radi later published another suite of cartouches *Disegni varii de Cartelle* (1649).

Raidel, Hans Friedrich An embroiderer from Ulm, Raidel published two embroidery pattern-books of lively floral scrolls, one of twelve plates published in Augsburg in 1613, and *Newes seidensstickherisches Groteschgen- vnnd Bluemen Bücchlen* (Memmingen, 1626; twelve plates).

Rams, Dieter Born in Wiesbaden in 1932, Rams was apprenticed as a joiner and later studied architecture and design. He then worked for the architect Otto Apel before in 1955 joining the Braun company of Frankfurt as a designer, as a result of his involvement with the Hochschule für Gestaltung in Ulm. He soon became head of design at Braun and has designed a series of Braun electrical consumer products – shavers, food-mixers, fans, wirelesses and so on, austere in colour and, to a mannered degree, elegant, pure and MODERN in their detailing. Rams, who describes himself as a *Gestalt* engineer, has an unflinching faith in the probity of his approach to design.

Ranson, Pierre (1736–86) Born in Paris, the son of a worker at the Gobelins factory, under whom he studied, Ranson was the great-nephew of the Gobelins flower-painter Louis TESSIER. In 1780 he succeeded Jacques Nicolas Julliard as painter designer at the Aubusson factory. On the death of Tessier, Ranson applied for his job, was refused in favour of JACQUES, applied again on the death of Jacques in 1784, but was again rejected and died two years later. From 1778 Ranson issued plates of ornament which amounted in total to 471. Although they incorporate ROCOCO survival elements, Ranson's designs are predominantly floral and NEO-CLASSI-

CAL. His main themes are flowers, trophies and VASES, but he also designed specifically for panelling, for embroidery on waistcoats, and for seat furniture and beds etc., including surprisingly fanciful designs in the Chinese manner, and imposing creations such as a '*Grand lit à la Duchesse dans le goût le plus nouveau*'.

Raphael (1483–1520) Born Raffaele Sanzio at Urbino, the son of a painter, Raphael studied painting under Perugino in Perugia from about 1494. By the end of 1504 he had settled in Florence, where he was influenced by Leonardo and MICHELANGELO. In 1508 he went to Rome to work for Pope Julius II. From 1510 Raphael was active as architect as well as painter, and in the same year he designed two bronze salvers made for Agostino Chigi by the goldsmith Cesarino of Padua. From 1515 to 1516 Raphael designed ten tapestries on the Acts of the Apostles for Pope Leo X. They were to hang in the Sistine Chapel. The cartoons were taken to Brussels, where the tapestries woven by Pieter van Aelst were completed by 1521. The cartoons then passed to Jan van Tiegen and his associates and further sets were woven. Seven of the cartoons were later taken to Genoa, where in 1623 they were bought by Charles I, then Prince of Wales. In London Francis CLEIN made copies of the cartoons, from which tapestries were woven at Mortlake. Cardinal Mazarin had an additional tapestry woven in Paris in about 1653 to complete his Mortlake set. A further set of the Acts was woven at the Gobelins tapestry factory in 1667. The cartoons, then at Hampton Court Palace, were engraved in 1719 by Nicolas Dorigny (1658–1746) as *Pinacotheca Hamptoniae*. In the 1830s they were copied in stained glass in the chapel at Bowood. Since 1865 the cartoons have hung on loan from the Royal Collection at the VICTORIA & ALBERT MUSEUM. From 1517 to 1518 Raphael directed the decoration of the Loggie and Loggetta in the Vatican with GROTESQUES, executed by Giovanni da UDINE and other pupils. Raphael also designed grotesques for Cardinal Giulio de' Medici's Villa Madama, also executed by his pupils. The influence of Raphael's grotesques was enormous, and they were widely copied, for example by Domenico da Barbiere. In 1811 twenty plates of ornaments in the choir of San Pietro in Perugia '*d'invenzione de Raffaele*' were published in Rome, and in 1850 a copy of 'Raphael's Pilaster Ornaments of the Vatican' was in the cabinet-makers' library of Tottenham Court Road, London. Before his death Raphael designed a bronze perfume burner for François I of France which later served as a basis for Germain Pilon's 1560 monument to the heart of Henri II. Prints after Raphael's works, many by Marcantonio Raimondi, were extensively copied on Italian maiolica and on Limoges enamels.

Rastrelli, Francesco Born in Paris in about 1700, the son of an Italian sculptor who moved to St Petersburg in 1716 to work for Peter the Great, Rastrelli began as an assistant to his father, but after travelling abroad in 1719 and 1725 became chief architect at the Russian court in 1736. He was ruined by the fall of Biron, the favourite of the Empress Anna Ivanovna, in 1740, but was reinstated by the Empress Elisabeth Petrovna (1709–62) in 1741 and thenceforward enjoyed twenty years of prolific activity, his great works including Tsarskoe Selo (1749–56) and the Winter Palace (1754–62). Rastrelli designed interiors, furniture, plasterwork and ironwork in a rich, gaudy and sculptural Russian variant of ROCOCO. He visited Italy in about 1763 and in 1768, but died in St Petersburg in 1771.

Rateau, Armand-Albert (1882–1938) Born in Paris, Rateau was trained as a designer and wood-carver at the École Boulle, and subsequently worked as an assistant to the architect, interior decorator and designer Georges Hoentschel (1855–1915). From 1905 to 1914 he was director of the Alavoine interior decoration firm. After the First World War, Rateau practised as an independent designer and interior decorator, working mainly for private clients in a stylish ART DÉCO manner, for instance his quasi-NEO-CLASSICAL bathroom (1920–22) for the actress Jeanne Lanvin, with a day-bed on deer feet and a table supported by pheasants.

Ravenna, Marco da Born Marco Dente in Ravenna, Marco da Ravenna was active as an engraver in Rome where he died in 1527. Like Agostino VENEZIANO he was a pupil of Marcantonio Raimondi. He issued many engravings after RAPHAEL and the antique, the latter including a plate of bas relief with cupids and a throne (1519). As well as some plates of RENAISSANCE ornament he produced one of the earliest designs for metalwork, three graces supporting a covered cup with lizards round its body.

Ravilious, Eric (1903–42) Born in Acton, the son of a shopkeeper, Ravilious was brought up in Eastbourne, where he attended the art school. In 1922 he won a scholarship to the Royal College of Art (see SCHOOL OF DESIGN), where he became friendly with Edward BAWDEN and was influenced by Paul NASH. From 1923 Ravilious developed a mastery of wood engraving. He designed illustrations and ornaments for the Golden Cockerel, Nonesuch and Curwen Presses, advertisements for Austin Reed and decorations for London Transport publications. Ravilious also designed many book-jackets, for instance for Edith Sitwell's *The Pleasures of Poetry* (1930) and for Osbert Sitwell's *Winters of Content* (1932). From 1935 he designed Wedgwood porcelain, including a coronation mug for Edward VIII (1937). In 1935 he also designed a range of glass for Stuart Crystal. In 1937 Ravilious designed chairs and a table based on neat early 19th-century prototypes for Dunbar Hay Ltd, for whom he also executed a trade card and a symbol. Ravilious also designed some textiles and, in 1937, a wall decoration for the British pavilion at the PARIS EXHIBITION.

Redgrave, Richard (1804–88) Born in London, the son of a clerk who turned to the manufacture of wire fencing, Redgrave began work as a clerk and draughtsman for his father. In 1826 he began to study at the Royal Academy and from 1830 he supported himself by teaching drawing, while developing his own reputation as a painter. In 1847 he was appointed botanical lecturer at the government SCHOOL OF DESIGN, where he had been on a temporary basis in 1846 and had agitated for improvement. Redgrave became one of Henry COLE's most important lieutenants at South Kensington. He became Headmaster in 1848, Art Superintendent in 1852, Inspector-General for Art in 1857, and finally in 1874 Director of the Art Division of the Department of Education; he resigned in 1875. For Henry Cole as Felix Summerly, Redgrave designed a glass jug, water bottles and glasses decorated with water-lilies, and paper hangings made by W. B. Simpson, illustrated in 1849 in the 'JOURNAL OF DESIGN', which Redgrave edited. He wrote a supplementary report on design at the LONDON 1851 EXHIBITION, which was published in 1852. In it he castigated excessive and ill-applied ornament, and attacked not only the taste of manufacturers but also the organization of schools of design. He praised the work of A. W. N. PUGIN, and advocated formalized and conventionalized ornament, which he himself had taught from 1848. In 1853 Redgrave published *An Elementary Manual of Colour* and in 1855 he was a member of the executive committee of the British Section at the PARIS 1855 EXHIBITION. He also designed many book illustrations, for example for Goldsmith's *Poetical Works* (1846) and Milton's *L'Allegro* (1859).

Regnière, Jean Hyacinthe (1803–70) Born in Paris, Regnière studied at the École des Beaux-Arts, where he met J.-J. FEUCHÈRE, a life-long friend. In 1827 Regnière entered the Sèvres factory, where he was active as a designer until his retirement in 1863, working in the Néo-Grec, RENAISSANCE and Chinese styles. His brother Joseph Ferdinand Regnière (1802–70) also worked at Sèvres, from 1826 to 1830 and 1836 to 1870.

Rehn, Jean Eric (1717–93) Born in Stockholm, Rehn began in 1730 to train as a military engineer. From 1740 to 1745 he was given a scholarship to study design in Paris under the engraver Jacques Philippe Lebas (1707–83). Back in Sweden in 1745 he was appointed designer and artistic director of the Stockholm silk manufactory of Barthelemi Peyron. In 1751 Rehn copied for the Royal Palace in Stockholm the throne designed for Louis XV by SLODTZ in 1743. He also designed medals and taught drawing, his pupils including Crown Prince Gustav. From 1755 to 1756 Rehn travelled in Germany, Italy, France and the Netherlands. He later taught at the Stockholm Academy. Rehn converted to the NEO-CLASSICAL style and designed the remarkable mineral cabinet by Georg Haupt, given to the

Prince of Condé in 1774 by Gustav III of Sweden. He also designed silver, ceramics and tapestries, and was active as an architect. Rehn visited Paris once more in 1778 to buy textiles, and from 1783 designed neo-classical furniture for St John's church in Stockholm.

Reiber, Émile Auguste (1826–93) Born in Schlettstadt in Alsace, Reiber studied architecture in Paris from 1847 but was mainly active as a designer, founding the influential periodical pattern-book 'L'ART POUR TOUS' in 1861. He was associated with Théodore DECK at the beginning of his career and supplied him with RENAISSANCE revival designs, and, for the LONDON 1862 EXHIBITION, designs in the arabic style. From the 1860s onwards Reiber also designed metalwork for Christofle, becoming the artistic director of the firm in about 1870. At the PARIS 1867 EXHIBITION Christofle showed imitations of Chinese cloisonné enamel designed by Reiber. In the early 1870s he entered on a study of Japanese art and began to design in this manner; in 1878 he was called the high priest of 'Japonisme'. In 1877 he began to issue *Les Album Reiber*, which reproduced his own sketches from objects in other collections, such as the Cernuschi collection of oriental art, and from his own private museum, and attempted to issue a basic course in design.

Reiff, Johann Conrad Reiff was an engraver in Augsburg, who engraved the designs of Paul DECKER; he was also active as a mechanic. He died in Nuremberg in 1726. Reiff's *Zierathen Büchel vor Glasschneider und Künstler* (six plates) and *Zierathen Büchlein 2ter Theil* (six plates) comprised friezes with scrolls, putti, STRAPWORK and figures, many derived directly from ŠMIŠEK. Intended for glass engravers and others, Reiff's designs were used in marquetry. Reiff also published a book of designs for locks, keys, gates, handles, signs and other ironwork (ten plates), in a scrolly ACANTHUS style embellished with dragons, putti, etc., and a *Neu inventirtes Laub Bandl und Groteschgen Werk*. In 1710 he issued a book on the ORDERS, reprinted in 1751.

Reignier, Jean-Marie (1815–86) The son of a Lyon concierge, Reignier studied at the Lyon École des Beaux-Arts, where THIERRIAT was among his teachers. He regarded himself as a disciple of BERJON, to whom he exhibited a memorial at the 1845 Paris Salon. He was in 1845 active as a textile designer and a teacher of floral design; in 1853 he succeeded Thierriat as professor of floral design at the Lyon École des Beaux-Arts. In 1864 he delivered an address, *De l'intime relation des Beaux-Arts et de l'Art industriel*. On retirement in 1885 he was appointed curator of the Lyon museum.

Renaissance In 1568 VASARI used the term '*rinascita*' (renaissance) to describe the gradual revival of art which had taken place in Italy from Cimabue onwards to culminate in the work of MICHELANGELO. The term Renaissance is now used to describe the revival of classical arts and letters which became a distinct new movement in Florence in about 1420; it is usually divided into Early Renaissance, up to about 1500, and High Renaissance, from about 1500 to the Sack of Rome in 1527. For design the most important aspect of the Renaissance was the systematic revival of the classical language of architecture. The works of the Roman architectural writer Vitruvius attained an almost scriptural authority and Leone Battista Alberti (1404–72) in his *De Re Aedificatoria* (1485) and other writings helped to establish the concept of Greek and Roman architecture as a classical canon

of excellence. The classical ORDERS became prominent in ornament, as did VASES, candelabra, roundels, cornucopiae, shells, masks, wreaths, swags, ACANTHUS, putti and enriched mouldings borrowed from sarcophagi, triumphal arches and other remnants of antiquity. PERSPECTIVE, as developed by the architect Filippo Brunelleschi (1377–1446) and others, was considered an essential part of the training of architects and designers. The Early Renaissance vocabulary of ornament was transmitted to Northern Europe by artists such as DÜRER and HOLBEIN, and in prints by the BEHAMS, PENCZ, ALDEGREVER, FLÖTNER and others. The development from the late 15th century of the GROTESQUE, used by both RAPHAEL and Michelangelo, introduced a new and flexible system of ornament, supplementing the Early Renaissance repertoire. However, the idea of the High Renaissance as a perfect moment of balance, valid though it may be for painting, is difficult to apply to design and ornament of the early 16th century. MANNERIST, BAROQUE and even NEO-CLASSICAL designers continued to employ a system of architecture and ornament founded on the Renaissance. Around 1800 neo-classical designers favoured the direct imitation of antique models. But at the very moment when this consciously archaeological approach was becoming most widespread the first seeds of the Renaissance Revival were sown. In 1798 PERCIER and FONTAINE published a book on Renaissance buildings in Rome and in about 1802 the architect John Nash (1752–1835) designed Cronkhill in Shropshire, the first picturesque Italianate villa. A more academic Renaissance Revival style was initiated at the Travellers' Club, designed by Sir Charles Barry (1795–1860) in 1829 to 1832, with Raphaelesque painted decorations by Frederick Sang. Henry WHITAKER designed furniture in a Renaissance manner for Osborne House, Prince ALBERT's favourite home, and under the influence of Ludwig GRUNER, Alfred STEVENS and Gottfried SEMPER, Renaissance Revival became the official style of the SCHOOL OF DESIGN in London. The sophisticated mastery of Renaissance Revival design displayed by imported French designers, for example ARNOUX, CARRIER-BELLEUSE and MOREL-LADEUIL, was widely influential on English commercial manufacturers, and, thanks to Semper, the style was dominant in German-speaking countries in the late 19th century. It was promoted by many magazines such as 'L'ART ET L'INDUSTRIE' (1877–88). RUSKIN hated the Renaissance Revival and in general it was abjured by designers in the William MORRIS and Arts & Crafts tradition. However, Early Renaissance 'Pre-Raphaelite' prototypes were used by Walter CRANE, Stephen WEBB and Charles RICKETTS, among others. Since about 1900, however, Renaissance design and ornament have been little imitated.

Renbage, Heinrich Working in Cologne in about 1590, Renbage published a suite of the five senses, in which allegorical figures are surrounded by black stretched GROTESQUE frames inhabited by birds, and a suite of six plates of small black enamel ornaments for jewellery, similar to those of Wolf MAIR.

Renner, Narcissus Born in 1503, Renner was active in Augsburg as a manuscript illuminator. He was responsible for the designs in one of the earliest pattern-books for embroiderers, *Modelbuch aller Art Nehewercks vnd Stickens* (Frankfurt, 1533), published by Christian Egenolff. The book contains about 180 borders, both GOTHIC and RENAISSANCE; they are mainly origi-nal, but details are borrowed from a panel of grotesque ornament by Master G. J. and some ARABESQUE interlace from Zoppino's 1529 book, a very early appearance of this style of ornament in Germany. Renner was also responsible for the designs in most of Egenolff's later books, continuing to borrow from PAGANO and Zoppino. They include *Modelbuch aller Art Nehens uñ Stickens* (Frankfurt, 1535; thirty-two plates). Renner also probably designed Johan Schwartzenberger's *Ain new Formbüchlein* (Augsburg, 1534; twenty plates), which presented symmetrical borders, predominantly Renaissance, white on black, a new departure for Germany, following TAGLIENTE's lead in 1527. Schwartzenberger's later books, the two versions of *Ain schöns nutzlich newes Formbüchlin* (Augsburg, 1534 and 1535), also included designs by Renner, together with copies from Pagano, VAVASSORE and Tagliente. Renner's style was later followed by Hans HOFFMANN.

Reutimann, Johann Konrad Probably a silversmith, Reutimann executed at least ten suites of ornament published in Augsburg from 1676 to 1691. They consist of friezes and panels of flowers, fruit or scrolling ACANTHUS. A typical title is *Ein Neüwes Büchlein mit Früchten für die Silber Arbeiter* (1691; six plates). Stefano DELLA BELLA and Johann HEEL were influences, and Reutimann also worked directly from MUSSARD's 1673 suite.

Revel, Jean (1684–1751) The son of a painter, Gabriel Revel, who had worked under LE BRUN at Versailles, Jean Revel was himself trained as a painter. In about 1710 he moved from Paris to Lyon, where he became active as a designer for the silk manufacturers. Revel is credited with having introduced in about 1733 a new painterly NATU-

RALISM into the treatment of flowers in silk design, by means of a subtle method of shading known as *points rentrés*, in contrast to the more stiff treatment practised by his predecessors COURTOIS and RINGUET. Revel seems later to have introduced ROCOCO scrolls and CHINOISERIES into his silks. In 1757 he was described as the RAPHAEL of silk designers. Among the many who underwent his influence was the Spitalfields designer Anna Maria GARTHWAITE.

Reverdy, Georges Born in Lyon, Reverdy was active as an engraver from about 1531 to 1564. He probably travelled to Italy early in his career, coming under the influence of Marcantonio Raimondi. Reverdy's fifty surviving engravings include an alphabet and other subjects within bold STRAPWORK frames.

Revue des Arts Décoratifs (1880–1902) Edited throughout its existence by Victor Champier the *Revue* succeeded the *Bulletin* of the Musée des Arts Décoratifs in Paris, and was also the magazine of the Union Centrale des ArtsAppliqués à l'Industrie. From its first issue which contained an article on VIOLLET-LE-DUC the *Revue* was filled with well-illustrated articles on most aspects of historic and modern design. When it closed, the *Revue*'s readers were advised to turn to 'ART DÉCORATIF'.

Revue Générale de l'Architecture (1840–88) This magazine edited by César Daly (1809–93) presented technical articles and illustrations of the highest quality, covering both historical and modern design, sometimes in colour. Daly's policy was eclectic, and his title-page was designed by Henri Labrouste.

Reybaud, Joseph Marie Jules (1807–68) Born in 1807, Reybaud studied at the Lyon École des Beaux-Arts, where he was taught by THIERRIAT in 1827. He subsequently worked as a textile designer for the Champagne & Rougier company. With Eugène Oyex (1816–86), a pupil of Thierriat in 1834, and a textile and wallpaper designer, Reybaud published *Album du dessinateur* (1840), *Groupes de fleurs* (1840) and *Choix d'ornements*.

Rhodes, Benjamin Born in Houghton, Northamptonshire, Rhodes was apprenticed in 1670 to David Venables, a goldsmith; he received his freedom in 1678, and thenceforward worked as an engraver on silver. At the end of his career, in 1723, he issued *A New Book of Ciphers . . . usefull for all sorts of Artists, as Painters, Carvers, Engravers, Chacers, Watchmakers, Imbroderars . . .* It contains ciphers in the manner of about 1700.

Ricardo, Halsey Ralph (1854–1928) Born in Bath, Ricardo was at school at Rugby while William BUTTERFIELD'S chapel was being built from 1870 to 1872. He was then articled to the architect John Middleton of Cheltenham, spent two years under Basil Champneys (1842–1935) and, after travelling in Italy, set up in independent practice in 1878. From 1888 to 1898 Ricardo was in partnership with DE MORGAN, for whom he designed relief tiles and vases. In 1888 Ricardo showed a chimneypiece at the ARTS & CRAFTS EXHIBITION and in 1901 he designed cast-iron fireplaces for Longden & Co. Ricardo's Debenham House (1906–7), colourfully tiled, was an advertisement of his belief in polychromy; it incorporated a plaster ceiling designed by GIMSON and a balustrade designed by JACK. Ricardo became Master of the ART-WORKERS' GUILD and taught architecture at the Central School of Arts & Crafts.

Richardson, Charles James (1806–71)

Trained as an architect under Sir John SOANE (1753–1837), Richardson practised independently from about 1832. In 1846 he was appointed to teach 'ornamental and geometrical drawing' at the SCHOOL OF DESIGN, Somerset House, where he taught until 1852, vigorously involved in its internal disputes. His *Observations on the Architecture of England during the Reigns of Queen Elizabeth and James I* (1837; fifty-seven plates) included copies after DIETTERLIN as well as ornament and architectural details. With his *Architectural Remains of the Reigns of Elizabeth and James I* (1840) and *Studies from Old English Mansions* (1841–8), the latter recommended by J. C. ROBINSON in 1853, Richardson won himself a position as leading expert on Elizabethan design, recognized in his execution of the plate on Elizabethan ornament in Owen JONES's *Grammar of Ornament* (1856). *The Workman's Guide to the Study of Old English Architecture* (1845; thirty-eight plates) was later incorporated into the last volume of *Studies from Old English Mansions*; it was dedicated to James Watt of Aston Hall, patron of BRIDGENS. The dedicatee of the first part of *Studies of Ornamental Design* (1851; twenty-six plates) was Prince ALBERT. It included silver in the collection of William BECKFORD, and designs for silver and ornament by Thomas STOTHARD, as well as GOTHIC, RENAISSANCE and Persian ornament. At the LONDON 1851 EXHIBITION Richardson showed Elizabethan furniture to his own design, and his *Picturesque Designs for Mansions ...* (1870, reprinted in 1870 as *The Englishman's House*) includes design for railings, stoves and tiles.

Richardson, George First noticed as 'apprentice' when witnessing the will of John Adam (1721–92) in Edinburgh in 1759, Richardson accompanied his brother James Adam (1732–94) on his grand tour to Italy from 1760 to 1763, employed as a draughtsman. Although treated meanly by James Adam, Richardson learned much from this contact with antiquity and was employed by the ADAM firm as draughtsman and designer for 'upwards of eighteen years' according to the preface (1774) to his *A Book of Ceilings in the Stile of The Antique Grotesque* (1776). This work was dedicated to Lord Scarsdale, for whom Richardson had designed the Great Hall ceiling at Kedleston, executed by the plasterer Joseph ROSE, who was among the subscribers to his book, which was reissued in 1793. The Kedleston design was shown at the Royal Academy in 1776, and a number of drawings for ceilings by Richardson survive; like his *Book of Ceilings* they are very much in the Adam manner. Richardson's work as a designer was accompanied by activity as a drawing-master and as engraver and author, his works including *A New Collection of Chimney Pieces* (1781), *A Treatise on the Five Orders of Architecture* (1787), *New Designs for Vases and Tripods decorated in the antique taste* (1793), *Capitals of Columns and Friezes measured from the Antique* (1793) and, posthumously, *A Collection of Ornaments in the Antique Style* (1816) by G. Richardson & Son (Richardson had died in about 1813). Among the subscribers to his *Iconology* (1779–80), an English version of Cesare Ripa's *Iconologia* (1593), were Robert Adam, Matthew Boulton, Sir William CHAMBERS, Thomas CHIPPENDALE and the japanner Henry Clay of Birmingham. It was dedicated to George III. Richardson's son William was also active as a designer, showing decorative designs at the Royal Academy in 1783, 1784, 1793 and 1794. In his old age George Richardson fell on hard times and was helped by, among others, the sculptor Joseph Nollekens

(1737-1823), who had collaborated with him before 1776 on two ceilings for Drapers' Hall.

Richardson, Henry Hobson (1838-86) Born of Louisiana plantation aristocracy, Richardson was brought up in New Orleans and then, during the Civil War, studied architecture at the École des Beaux-Arts in Paris before working in 1862 in the office of Henri Labrouste (1801-75). In 1865 Richardson returned to New York, where he practised as an architect. His drawings were probably influenced by BURGES, whose *Architectural Drawings* (1870) he owned. In 1874 he moved to Brookline near Boston to supervise the building of Trinity Church, for which he had won the competition in 1872. This great church, in the Romanesque style, had glass by LA FARGE, BURNE-JONES and Henry HOLIDAY. Richardson ran a prolific and congenial office, which produced many designs for lighting, ironwork and furniture in a manner which ranged from Reformed GOTHIC to a sturdy version of Queen Anne, often embellished with rich Romanesque ornament, as for instance in the New York State Capitol (1881 to 1882).

Richter, Ludwig (1803-84) Born in Dresden, the son of the painter and illustrator Carl August Richter (1770-1848), under whom he studied, Richter settled in Meissen in 1828 after extensive travels and taught drawing at the Meissen porcelain factory until 1835, also supplying designs for porcelain. Richter was a prodigiously prolific book illustrator and designed many titlepages. He was later professor at the academy in Dresden.

Ricketts, Charles de Sousy (1866-1931) Born in Geneva, the son of an English naval officer and his French wife, Ricketts was brought up in England, France and Italy. In 1882 he began to study wood engraving at the City and Guilds Technical Art School in London and there met Charles Hazlewood Shannon (1863-1937), who became his life-long friend. From 1889 to 1897 they issued an occasional magazine, the *Dial*, from their Chelsea house, The Vale. The *Dial* was strongly influenced by the 'HYPNEROTOMACHIA POLIFILI' and by the Century Guild *Hobby Horse*. Ricketts designed bindings much indebted to ROSSETTI for Oscar Wilde's *Dorian Gray* (1890), *Intentions* (1891), *The House of Pomegranates* (1891) and *Poems* (1892), and for Thomas Hardy's *Tess of the D'Urbervilles* (1891), Lord de Tabley's *Poems Lyrical and Dramatic* (1893), John Gray's *Silverpoints* (1893) and J. A. Symonds's *In the Key of Blue* (1893). Ricketts designed binding, frontispiece, illustrations and initials for Wilde's *The Sphinx* (1894). *Daphnis and Chloe* (1893) and *Hero and Leander* (1894), mainly designed by Ricketts with a format similar to the *Hypnerotomachia Polifili*, anticipated the style of the Vale Press, which was founded by Ricketts and Shannon in 1896; for it Ricketts designed three types, the Vale, Avon and King's Fount. *The Marriage of Cupide and Psyche* (1897) was the most notable Vale book. After a fire in 1899 the Vale Press petered to a close in 1903; Ricketts issued a bibliography in 1904. For Gleeson White, co-editor with Shannon of the 'PAGEANT', Ricketts designed a book-plate. From 1899 he designed jewellery for friends and also some embroidery executed by his friend May Morris. After the First World War, Ricketts designed a few more bindings and illustrations in an almost ART DÉCO manner.

Rickman, Thomas (1776-1841) Born in Maidenhead, the son of an apothecary, Rickman took an interest in medieval architecture from about 1807 as a distraction from financial and personal sorrows. By 1811 he had developed the typological analysis of English medieval architecture which formed the basis of *An Attempt to Discriminate the Styles of English Architecture from the Conquest to the Reformation* (1817, based on an earlier article and repeatedly reprinted); *An Attempt* established the Norman–Early English–Decorated–Perpendicular terminology which is still in existence. Rickman was active as an architect from about the year 1813 and developed a prolific career, specializing in churches and the GOTHIC style. In about 1816 he designed competent Gothic furniture for Scarisbrick Hall and he later designed Gothic stained glass, monuments, lighting, grates and so on.

Riedel, Gottlieb Friedrich (1724–84) Born in Dresden, Riedel worked as a painter at the Meissen porcelain factory from 1743 to 1756. After a visit to Paris and a short spell at the newly founded Höchst porcelain factory, Riedel moved to the Frankenthal porcelain factory, where he spent the years 1757 to 1759 as, successively, specialist bird and animal painter and director of painting. He then moved to the Ludwigsburg factory, where he remained until 1779, when he settled in Augsburg. In 1784 Riedel's services to design education in Augsburg were commemorated by a gold medal. Riedel was responsible for a large number of delicate printed designs, often NATURALISTIC and NEO-CLASSICAL in detail, but ROCOCO in spirit. Many, such as his *Samlung von Feder-Vieh besonders Haus-Geflügel* (Augsburg, 1776; fourteen plates), depict birds, fruit or flowers, his specialities in porcelain painting. His suites of VASES (1779) have basically BAROQUE forms embellished with flowers, and with a delicate veneer of neo-classical ornament. Riedel

also published designs for clock-cases (1779), trophies, some of them after DELAFOSSE (1779), and chair designs, four plates showing chairs, with their plans, derived from French neo-classical models.

Riemerschmid, Richard (1868–1957) Born in Munich, the son of a textile manufacturer, Riemerschmid studied painting at the Munich Academy. In 1895 he designed his own house and furniture and in 1896 designed a poster for the Nuremberg Bavarian Exhibition. At the Munich 1897 Glaspalast Exhibition Riemerschmid showed a wall hanging, stained glass and a yew-wood *buffet*, with iron mounts; the latter was praised by Wilhelm Bode in 'PAN' and shown again in Krefeld in 1898. In that year Riemerschmid designed furniture for the MUNICH VEREINIGTE WERKSTÄTTEN, together with PAUL and PANKOK. In about 1899 he designed furniture for OBRIST. At the PARIS 1900 EXHIBITION Riemerschmid's Room for an Art Lover was decorated with a frieze and door surrounds of elaborate interlacing plasterwork and with skeletal pendant electric lights probably influenced by BENSON. The wallpaper and carpet, with small leaf patterns, were comparatively subdued and Riemerschmid's furniture was simple, particularly a striking chair with a diagonal side strut connecting front feet to top back rail. Riemerschmid's room also contained works by other Munich Vereinigte Werkstätten designers. From 1902 to 1905 Riemerschmid taught at the Nuremberg school of art; in 1904 his room for the Rector of the school was shown at the ST LOUIS EXHIBITION. In the same year MUTHESIUS detected a certain coldness in his designs. At this period Riemerschmid collaborated with his brother-in-law, the cabinet-maker Karl Schmidt (1873–1948), on the design of furniture for industrial production; their earliest models were shown at the Dresden 1905 Deutsche Werkstätten Exhibition. In 1907 Riemerschmid was a founder member of the DEUTSCHE WERKBUND and taught at the BERLIN KUNST-GEWERBEMUSEUM. In 1908 he became Director of the applied arts section of the Munich exhibition. Also in 1908 Riemerschmid showed porcelain, glass and cutlery at the Wertheimer gallery in Berlin. In 1910 he showed at the Brussels Exhibition and at the Paris Salon d'Automne. From 1912 to 1924 he directed the school of applied arts in Munich, where in 1913 an exhibition was held of his architectural works. Riemerschmid was heavily involved in Werkbund activities and showed a living-room at the COLOGNE 1914 WERK-BUND EXHIBITION. In 1920 Walter GROPIUS stated that Riemerschmid's project for an art school was close to the programme of the BAUHAUS. From 1926 to 1931 Riemerschmid was head of the industrial school in Cologne.

Rietveld, Gerrit Thomas (1888–1964) Born in Utrecht the son of a cabinet-maker, Rietveld began to work in his father's workshop at the age of eleven. In 1911 he started his own cabinet-making business in Utrecht, and began to study architectural drawing at evening classes conducted by the architect P. J. Klaarhamer, a follower of BERLAGE. At this period Rietveld executed Klaarhamer's simple rectilinear furniture designs, and began himself to experiment with design, producing in about 1918 his famous red-blue chair, in which cheap wood cut into square sections and planks is screwed together with overlapping joints; all is transparent and rectilinear, only the seat and back being at an angle. Simple colours were used to emphasize its Mondrian-like abstract spatial presence, which owes much to

the example of Frank Lloyd WRIGHT. Through Klaarhamer, Rietveld met the stained-glass designer Bart van der Leck, then working closely with Berlage, and the architect Robert van 't Hoff, both of whom were founder members of DE STIJL; as a result Rietveld became a member himself in 1919, when the red-blue chair was illustrated in the magazine *De Stijl*, and remained one until 1931. His early furniture is all doctrinally and stylistically close to the red-blue chair, and several pieces have a CLASSIC authority, most notably his 1919 side-board of bleached wood, his 1920 hanging lamp in which three or four tubular lamps hang independently in a tense confrontation of different directions, and his 1925 radio cabinet, displaying its innards in a glass case. Rietveld's sparse early decorative and architectural commissions included a surgery for Dr Hartog (1920), a famous house for Mrs Schröder (1924) and interiors for her brother-in-law, Dr Harrestein (1925). During the 1920s Rietveld was in contact with many of the international *avant-garde*, for instance the German artist Kurt Schwitters (1887–1948) and the Russian Constructivist El LISSITZKY (1890–1941), who published an article on Rietveld's work on his return to Moscow in 1926. In 1927 Rietveld began to experiment with chairs of moulded fibre and, later, bent plywood on metal-tube frames. From about 1930 these were manufactured and sold by Metz & Co., of Amsterdam. In 1934, in response to slump conditions, Rietveld designed a basic range of furniture made from packing-crate wood for sale by Metz & Co., who marketed it in self-assembly packs, attracting strong criticism from the furniture trade. Also in 1934 Rietveld designed his celebrated zig-zag chair. His experimental models were in fibre on a metal frame, but this failed and wood and screws were used by Metz & Co. on the production model. Rietveld's 1935 upholstered armchair for Metz & Co. deserves to be better known; its seat and back are formed as a large L held at an angle by two smaller inverted Ls which form the arms. In 1942 Rietveld began to experiment with chairs to be stamped out of one piece of material. His aluminium armchair with stamped holes is an early ancestor of Rodney KINSMAN's Omkstack chair. After the war Rietveld's architectural career gradually took off: he had been a founder member of CONGRÈS IN-TERNATIONAUX D'ARCHITECTURE MODERNE in 1928 and was now one of the MODERN establishment. However, he continued to interest himself in design and his bent-metal chairs of 1957, later produced in polyester, are among the neater of the early mass-produced portable chairs. In contrast his chair for a jeweller's shop in Amsterdam (1963), based on a simple swastika-like radiation of arms and legs, represents a de luxe reversion to his early De Stijl manner. After Rietveld's death his 'classic' furniture designs were produced by Van der Groenekan, who had worked in his workshop. In 1971, however, the rights were bought by Cassina of Milan, and although Riet-veld's later work was strongly tinged with FUNCTIONALISM, it is for his early and striking formalist inventions that he continues to be remembered and reproduced.

Righetti, Luigi Born in Rome in 1780, Righetti was active there as a bronze caster. In 1815 and 1817 he designed elaborate NEO-CLASSICAL table centres, incorporating the rostral column among other motifs.

Ringuet, Jean Ringuet was a silk designer in Lyon from at least the 1720s. He is said to have been the first to introduce NATURALISTIC flowers into silk design, but a surviving design of 1728 shows that his was a formal naturalism compared to that of REVEL. Ringuet was still alive in 1764, when he was described as an 'ancien et fameux Dessinateur'. In 1748 the Swedish designer Anders Odel studied under Ringuet, or perhaps under his son, Jean-Pierre Ringuet, born in 1728, who was also a well-known silk designer.

Ripanda, Jacopo Born in Bologna, Ripanda was active as a painter from about 1490; he was strongly influenced by Mantegna. He was in Rome from at least 1507, and in 1516 was in Sulmona. A sketch-book at Lille by Ripanda includes a scene copied on several Faenza maiolica plates, one dated 1524. As no print is known it seems likely that Ripanda himself supplied this design.

Rizzardi, Giovanni Domenico Rizzardi published *Giardino nel quale si dimostra varij disegni per far ricami* (Padua, 1607; thirty-two plates), containing embroidery and reticella lace designs very similar to those published earlier by TOZZI and later by CRIVELARI.

R.M. In about 1561 Christoph Froschauer of Zürich published *Nüw Modelbuch, allerley Gattungen Däntelschnur... Zubereit* (twenty-four plates), designed by R.M., a woman lace-worker of twelve years' experience. The designs are practical but rudimentary.

Roberday, E. Roberday published two suites of BERAINESQUE ornament, *Livre nouveau D'ornements a divers usages* (Paris, 1697) and *Livre des principes de l'ornement* (1713). He is probably the same as the G. Roberday who published *Essais de Tabatères A l'usages des Graveurs et Sizeleurs* (1710), small panels of Berainesque ornament with monkeys, CHINOISERIES, putti and so on, for engraving on snuff-boxes.

Robert, Hubert (1733–1808) Born in Paris, Robert was at first destined for the priesthood but he turned to painting, spending the years from 1754 to 1765 at the French Academy in Rome under the protection of the Marquis de MARIGNY and the Duc de Choiseul. Back in Paris he became a prolific and successful painter of ruins, landscapes and architecture in a manner influenced by Pannini and PIRANESI. Robert provided the basic design for Marie-Antoinette's dairy at Rambouillet (1785), for which he also designed some handsome but unarchaeological mahogany chairs 'de forme nouvelle genre étrusque' made by Georges Jacob in 1787, but replaced in 1804. They are X-framed with partly trellised backs decorated with anthemia, paterae and laurels. From 1784 Robert was curator of the nascent gallery of paintings in the Louvre.

Robinson, George Thomas Born in about 1828, Robinson began as an architect in Wolverhampton, where in 1850 he designed the interior of the public baths. His *Military Architecture of the Middle Ages* (1859) illustrated Warwickshire castles. Robinson later worked as an art critic for the *Manchester Guardian* and for the 'ART JOURNAL'. From about 1875 Robinson designed interior decorations as Art Director of Messrs Trollope: he was also a well-known wallpaper designer and in 1882 was a founder member of the designers' club, The Fifteen, whose secretary was Lewis F. DAY. He was a pioneer in the revival of plasterwork and sgraffito decoration, on which he lectured to the SOCIETY OF ARTS in 1891. He contributed a historical introduction to William Millar's *Plastering Plain and Decorative* (1897). Robinson died in 1897.

Robinson, Sir John Charles (1824–1913) Born in Nottingham, Robin-

son studied painting in Paris under M. M. Drölling (1786–1851). In 1847 he was appointed headmaster of the Government School of Art in Hanley. In 1852 Robinson moved to London, where he was Superintendent of the Art Collection at South Kensington until 1869 and organized the circulation of works of art from the museum to provincial institutions. Distinguished for the range and quality of his museum acquisitions, Robinson was a prolific writer on many aspects of art. He published *A Manual of Elementary Outline Drawing* (1853) and *A Collection of Examples of Coloured Ornament* (1853), the latter with twelve chromolithographic plates adapted from HAMILTON'S *Vases*, Zahn's *Ornamente*, Henry SHAW's *Illuminated Ornaments* and Owen JONES's *Alhambra* and a useful bibliography on ornament. *An Introductory Lecture on the Museum of Ornamental Art* (1854) gave an account of the future VICTORIA & ALBERT MUSEUM when housed at Marlborough House, and objects from the museum were illustrated in *The Treasury of Ornamental Art* (1857; seventy-one chromolithographic plates), including works designed by Thomas Battam, A. W. N. PUGIN, VECHTE and CARRIER-BELLEUSE, and many Indian wares.

Robsjohn-Gibbings, Terence Harold (1905–76) Born in London, Robsjohn-Gibbings intended to become an architect but after working as an antique dealer moved to New York in about 1930 and became a successful designer and interior decorator. In about 1937 he designed for the Casa Encantada, Bel Air, California, a large houseful of smooth and sophisticated furniture in a NEO-CLASSICAL manner influenced both by French early 19th-century and Greek prototypes: he claimed to have been converted to Greek furniture by a visit to the British Museum in 1933. In

1944 Robsjohn-Gibbings published *Goodbye Mr Chippendale*, a journalistic attack on the cult of antiques which directed plausible brickbats at most other contemporary styles of interior design. *Homes of the Brave* (1954) was in the same vein. From 1946 to 1956 he designed for the Grand Rapids furniture industry. His 1948 range of furniture for the Widdicomb furniture company struck a Californian note, in 1950 he turned to New England, and in 1951 to the West, including a massive 'Mesa' table. Robsjohn-Gibbings later returned to private practice and in 1963 published a book on his reconstructions of ancient Greek furniture.

Rocchegiani, Lorenzo A number of designs for NEO-CLASSICAL table ornaments by Rocchegiani, dated 1803, are in the Museo Napoleonico in Rome. In 1804 he published a book an antique dress. This was followed by his *Invenzione diverse di mobili, utensili sacri e profani* (Milan, 1811. later editions 1814 and 1817), 100 plates engraved by Pietro Ruga incorporating a very wide range of coarse but varied and inventive neoclassical designs for furniture, metalwork, lighting etc., with griffins, Egyptian motifs and other fashionable ornaments.

Rococo From about 1734 the word 'rocaille', meaning rockwork and shell work for the decoration of grottoes, was used in France to describe a new fashion for such motifs in ornament. By 1772 'rocaille' was a general, albeit derogatory, term for the French style of ornament of the 1730s. In about 1796 the slang diminutive 'rococo' was in use, again derogatorily, among NEO-CLASSICAL painters and their pupils to describe the works of François BOUCHER and his contemporaries. Rococo has now become a neutral term for the French style of design and orna-

ment of the second quarter of the 18th century, which spread from France all over Europe. Martinets confine its usage to designs incorporating C or S scrolls; it is usually allowed a slightly wider application. French BAROQUE designers such as VOUET, LE BRUN and Jean LE PAUTRE had tended to favour massive forms and dense rich ornament. In the 1670s Jean I BERAIN began to develop a light and delicate form of GROTESQUE, supported on scrolled and interlaced STRAPWORK ultimately derived from 16th-century models. The Berainesque grotesque was carried to a further pitch of lightness by AUDRAN, GILLOT and WATTEAU. From about 1700 Pierre LE PAUTRE began the development of a delicate curvilinear system of wall decoration which abandoned the massive architectonic framework of baroque panelling. The process was carried further by OPPENORD and in designs for objects by TORO. Oppenord had early been influenced by BERNINI and by Francesco Borromini (1599–1667), the most complex and original of the great Roman baroque architects, while Toro, from the South of France, was particularly open to Italian influence. Toro's designs are characterized by great vigour. The same quality is apparent in the works of the goldsmith and designer Juste Aurèle MEISSONIER, who was brought up in Turin and must have been familiar with the architecture of Borromini's follower Guarino Guarini (1624–83), characterized by virtuoso spatial complexity. From the late 1720s Meissonier developed a new and bold form of ornament which combined asymmetry with vigorous three-dimensional C and S scrolls, rockwork, shellwork, fountains, waterfalls and boldly distorted cartouches and VASES. DELLA BELLA's influence was apparent to contemporaries; that of MITELLI is also probable. In 1774 Meissonier was named as one of the three founders of '*le genre pittoresque*', the purest form of what is now called rococo, along with PINEAU and LA JOUE. La Joue's rococo was an extreme and brilliant form of Meissonier's; Meissonier also influenced his friend Boucher. Pineau, back from Russia in about 1730, used scrolls and asymmetry but handled them with a linear delicacy in the Berain tradition which contrasts with the more sculptural or pictorial approach of Meissonier, La Joue and Boucher. From the beginning French rococo was attacked for illogicality and frivolity and for breaking classical rules; J.-F. BLONDEL wrote in 1737 of the '*amas ridicule de coquilles, de dragons, de roseaux, de palmiers et de plants*' ('ridiculous jumble of shells, dragons, reeds, palm-trees, and plants'). Despite such early criticisms, and later ones by such neo-classical pundits as CAYLUS in 1749, the Abbé Le Blanc (1706–81) in 1753, and C.-N. COCHIN in 1754, rococo continued to be an important ingredient of French design into the late 1760s, albeit in an increasingly symmetrical and subdued form. In Germany rococo was founded on French models, but REIFF's copies of about 1710 after ŠMIŠEK's designs on the cusp between the stretched grotesque and AURICULAR styles, indicate a predisposition towards rococo. In Munich, CUVILLIÉS, who was trained in Paris, practised a rococo almost as advanced and fully as brilliant as the latest French models, and from about 1740 KNOBELSDORFF and others brought a light and elegant rococo to Berlin. However, court designers apart, the great German centre of rococo was Augsburg, where HERTEL and ENGELBRECHT issued a mass of designs for rococo ornament by both French and German designers, some of the latter, such as WACHSMUTH and GÖZ, exhilarating extremists. English rococo was a less flourishing transplant despite the presence of capable designers, both immi-

grant, such as G. M. MOSER and SPRIMONT, and native, such as LOCK and LINNELL. JOHNSON's eccentric vigour is unusual. In America the influence of English pattern-books such as those of SWAN long survived English rococo. CHINOISERIES by Watteau, Boucher and others were an important source of rococo ornament all over Europe. In England, Chinese and Gothic ornaments had especial importance, both as independent manners, as in the work of HALFPENNY, or combined with rococo proper, as in many of CHIPPENDALE's designs. Although PILLEMENT survived as a designer into the 1780s, rococo was an all but dead style by 1780, except in provincial or remote centres. Its revival began in England in the 1820s when, as a Bourbon style, rococo had strong political overtones. The leading rococo revival architect was Benjamin Dean WYATT, whose clients included the Duke of Wellington. Early English rococo revival designs were characterized by a vegetal vigour in total contrast to the tentative linearity of much 18th-century English rococo design. In England the rococo revival rapidly descended the social scale, promoted by Thomas KING, J. C. LOUDON, and John WEALE in the mid-1830s. Thereafter the rococo revival became an international style. It still survives as such, although at a level usually scorned or ignored by designers and historians of design alike.

Rodler, Hieronymus Born in Bamberg, Rodler was from 1530 in charge of the press established at Simmern by the humanist Prince Johann II von Pfalz-Simmern (1486–1557). In 1531 he published *Eyn schön nützlich büchlin und underweisung der Kunst des Messens* (2nd edition, Frankfurt, 1546), a treatise on PERSPECTIVE intended to popularize DÜRER's 1525 work on the subject. The *Büchlin* was aimed at painters, sculptors, goldsmiths, embroiderers, masons, cabinet-makers and other craftsmen, and contained interesting delineations of interiors and furniture. Rodler died in 1539.

Rodríguez Tizón, Ventura (1717–85) Born in Ciempozuelas near Madrid, Rodríguez was trained as an architect by working on the royal palace at Aranjuez. In 1735 he became an assistant to the royal architect Filippo Juvarra (1676–1736) and subsequently to his successor Giovanni Battista Sacchetti. Rodríguez became chief royal architect in 1749. In 1752 he was appointed director of architecture at the newly founded Academy of S. Fernando. In 1760 Rodríguez was dismissed from the royal service after the accession of Charles III and replaced by Francesco Sabatini. In 1764 he was appointed municipal architect in Madrid, and pursued a prolific career until his death. Rodríguez worked at first in the Italian BAROQUE style, but later switched to NEO-CLASSICISM, before developing a spare and austere late style. In 1761 he designed florid baroque chairs and tables for the Madrid College of Surgery. His later furniture designs sometimes retain a baroque flavour, but are more often in a strongly French-influenced neo-classical style.

Rogers, William Harry (1825–73) A son of the celebrated wood-carver William Gibbs Rogers (1792–1875), William Harry Rogers designed for his father and others in an eclectic RENAISSANCE manner from at least 1847. He designed ornaments for the *Art Journal Illustrated Catalogue of the 1851 Exhibition* and a boxwood cradle for the Queen shown in the exhibition. Rogers also illustrated Shakespeare's *The Merchant of Venice* (1860).

Rogg, Gottfried (1669–1742) Rogg was active in Augsburg as designer, engraver

and publisher. He designed a suite of four coarse ROCOCO CHINOISERIE scenes in cartouches, and published a *Neues Unterschidliches Bilder Laub und Grodetschgenwerk* (six plates), including copies after Claude III AUDRAN's GROTESQUE months. Rogg's *Encyclopaedia oder Schaubühne curieuser Vorstellungen* (Augsburg, 1726; three suites of twelve plates) included friezes of ACANTHUS, scroll and STRAPWORK. It was aimed at painters, engravers, chasers, seal-cutters, goldsmiths, glass-cutters, enamellers and steel-workers.

Rohde, Gilbert (1894–1944) The son of a New York cabinet-maker, Rohde left high school in 1913 and then followed various trades, including a spell as reporter and political cartoonist on the *Bronx News*. From 1923 he was a full-time furniture illustrator with the Abraham & Straus department store. In 1927 he travelled to Paris and on his return began to produce his own furniture designs in a fashionable MODERN manner using bakelite and chrome. Many were marketed by Lord & Taylor. In 1927 to 1928 he redecorated the Avedon fashion stores (his wife was their advertising manager). His Norman Lee apartment, New York, 1928 to 1929, was widely praised and illustrated, and in 1930 Rohde began to design furniture for the Heywood-Wakefield Company of Gardner, Massachusetts, including a successful bentwood chair, neat but unadventurous, of which 250,000 had been sold by 1939 (variations were produced by the Kroehler Company and Herman Miller in about 1933). In 1930 Rohde visited Grand Rapids, centre of the American furniture trade, to sell his design skills. Only the John Widdicomb Company and Herman Miller responded. From 1931 Rohde designed prolifically for Herman Miller, having sold their chairman, D. J. De Pree, the idea of an ethical Modernism. De

Pree, however, hedged his bets by employing Frieda Diamond to design furniture in traditional styles. Rohde designed chrome chairs for the Troy Sunshade Co. in 1933 and tub chairs for Thonet Bros. in 1932. Rohde was involved in many exhibitions, including Design for the Machine (Philadelphia, 1932), Machine Art (NEW YORK MUSEUM OF MODERN ART, 1934), Art and Industry (New York, R.C.A. Building, 1934) and the New York World's Fair (1939). In 1935 he was appointed to direct the free Design Laboratory in New York, but pressure of commercial work forced his resignation in 1938. From 1939 to 1943 Rohde was head of industrial design at the New York University School of Architecture.

Rohlfs, Charles (1853–1936) Born in New York, Rohlfs studied at the Cooper Union for the Advancement of Science and Art, founded by Peter Cooper in 1859. By 1872 he was working as a designer of cast-iron stoves. From 1877 to the early 1890s Rohlfs was an actor. By 1890, however, he had begun to make plain oak furniture in Buffalo and his workshop there grew to employ eight craftsmen. Rohlfs evolved a personal Arts & Crafts manner, with quirky details, revealed construction and curvilinear carved decoration, perhaps influenced by COLONNA and SULLIVAN. Rohlfs was a friend of Elbert HUBBARD and in 1901 wrote an article for 'HOUSE BEAUTIFUL' on 'The Grain of Wood'. He retired in the mid-1920s.

Romanelli, Giovanni Francesco Born in Viterbo probably in 1610, Romanelli studied painting under Domenichino and Pietro da CORTONA. In 1627 Cardinal Francesco Barberini founded a new tapestry factory in Rome, and put Romanelli in charge of design. In 1638 he was appointed Principal of the Accademia di San Luca at the behest of Barberini. Romanelli's designs included a suite of putti in the manner of Giovanni da UDINE, and a suite of Dido and Aeneas, woven at least six times by Michel Wauters in Antwerp. In 1647 he followed Cardinal Francesco Barberini into exile to Paris, and commenced the decoration of Cardinal Mazarin's gallery, a scheme completed by GRIMALDI. Romanelli returned to Rome in 1648 but revisited Paris from 1655 to 1657 to work for the Queen Mother, Anne d'Autriche, in the Louvre. He died in Viterbo in 1662.

Romano, Giulio (1499–1546) Born Giulio Pippi in Rome, Romano entered RAPHAEL'S workshop as a boy, and became one of his chief assistants. After Raphael's death in 1520 Romano was regarded as one of his successors. In 1524 he moved to Mantua, where he worked for Federico II Gonzaga and, after Federico's death in 1540, for the Regent, Cardinal Ercole Gonzaga. Romano's great achievement in Mantua was the Palazzo del Tè (1527–35), where he was both architect and painter. But he was also prolific as a designer of goldsmith's work, jewellery and tapestries. His designs for silver include ewers, cups, salts and caskets; their ornament incorporates bacchic emblems, snakes, shells, dolphins, putti, ACANTHUS, masks and basket work. Their vigorous contortions were a major source of inspiration to MANNERIST designers, and although many appear impractical it is clear from inscriptions that most if not all were intended for execution, and that many were made, mainly for members of the Gonzaga family. Jewellery, belts and fan-holders designed by Romano for such patrons as Ferrante Gonzaga and Isabella d'Este made a bold and sculptural use of snakes, swans, peacocks and lions. Giulio Romano was designing jewellery until at least 1531. In 1562 Romano's drawings were sold by his son Raffaele to Jacopo de STRADA, and were widely copied. A group in Lord Arundel's collection were engraved by Hendrik van der Borcht (1583–1660), Arundel's curator of drawings. Romano's designs for tapestries included the lion's share of a suite of no less than twenty-two pieces on the History of Scipio, woven in Brussels for François I of France from before 1532 to 1535. Some of the designs were taken to Brussels by PRIMATICCIO in 1532. The History of Scipio was rewoven in 1686 to 1690 at the Gobelins tapestry factory as a ten-piece suite. Other tapestry suites designed by Romano included Playing Putti, the Fruits of War, and Mythological Subjects, the former rewoven at Mortlake in the 1620s, the latter two at the Gobelins factory in the 1680s. Many of Giulio Romano's tapestries include ornament and depict metalwork, and thus helped to transmit his early mannerist style to Northern Europe.

Rösch, Georg Sigmund Rösch, the son of an Augsburg painter, was active there as painter, designer and engraver. He also worked in Munich as court engraver to Duke Clemens Franz of Bavaria. While there in 1745 he engraved one of CUVILLIÉS's suites of ornament. Rösch died in 1766. His own designs comprise eight suites of four plates each published in Augsburg by HERTEL, and one suite published by ENGELBRECHT. They include ROCOCO clocks, mirror-frames and ornament, but Rösch's speciality was scrolly rococo structures containing figures emblematic of the senses, the seasons and suchlike.

Roscher, Georg Michael Roscher was responsible for about ten suites of four plates each published by J. G. HERTEL in Augsburg in about 1750. They comprise ornament, altars, cartouches, furniture, frames, organ-cases, altars and

so on. Roscher's ROCOCO in details for plasterwork is very extreme, and some of his furniture, notably a bed, almost wild. His altars are curvilinear in plan even by rococo standards.

Rose, Joseph (1745–99) One of the leading dynasty of plasterers in 18th-century England, Rose prepared for publication *Sketches of Ornamental Frizes* (1782), containing 331 designs not only by ADAM, James WYATT, STUART, CHAMBERS, Keene and, probably, YENN, but also by Rose himself and by his uncle, also Joseph Rose (about 1723–80).

Rosenbergh, Hendrik Rosenbergh decorated the Mayor's parlour at Franeker in 1762. In 1777, by which time he was well known as a wallpaper designer, Rosenbergh came from Leeuwarden to run the newly founded wallpaper factory at Hoorn. His assistant Jean Théodore da la Campaigne was also engaged.

Rosman, Nikolaus In 1627 Rosman published the first and only known part of his *Neuw Zirat Büchlein*, comprising eight plates of the most extreme and grisly AURICULAR ornament. He is described on the title-page as a painter in Halle.

Rossetti, Dante Gabriel (1828–82) Born in London, the son of a refugee professor of Italian, Rossetti studied painting at the Royal Academy from 1845 to 1847, and then in 1848 under Ford Madox BROWN. In that year Rossetti shared a studio with Holman Hunt, and with Millais and Hunt founded the Pre-Raphaelite Brotherhood. In early 1856 Rossetti met William MORRIS and BURNE-JONES. In 1857 he designed illustrations for the Moxon *Tennyson*. Rossetti became a member of the Hogarth Club in 1859 and helped to decorate BURGES's Great Bookcase

(1859–62). In 1861 he was involved in the foundation of Morris, Marshall, Faulkner & Co., and from 1861 to 1864 designed some stained glass for the firm. In 1861 he helped to decorate SEDDON's 'King René' cabinet, and about the same date painted decorations on a bookcase designed by C. F. Hayward (1830–1905). A sofa designed by Rossetti was shown by the Morris firm at the LONDON 1862 EXHIBITION, and his name was associated with one of the light turned chairs based on early 19th-century models, which were produced by Morris & Co. from about 1865. From 1861 to 1871 Rossetti designed eleven bindings, including those for Christina Rossetti's *Goblin Market* (1862) and Swinburne's *Atalanta in Corydon* (1865). He finally severed his connection with the Morris firm in 1875.

Rossi, Angelo (1670–1742) Rossi was born in Florence, studied painting in Bologna and worked as a decorative painter in Venice. *A New Book of Ornaments* (London, 1753) presents designs for ceilings, chimneypieces, doors and windows in a bold sculptural style, engraved after Rossi by Antonio Visentini (1688–1782).

Rosso Fiorentino (1495–1540) Born in Florence as Giovan Battista di Iacopo di Gasparre, Rosso was already active as a painter in 1513, under the influence of Fra Bartolommeo and Andrea del Sarto. In about 1514 he became friendly with Baccio Bandinelli. In 1517 Rosso became a master in Florence. After a prolific early career he travelled in 1524 to Rome, where in 1526 he was in contact with MICHELANGELO. Also in 1524 he designed a series of figures in niches which were engraved by Jacopo Caraglio and were subsequently copied by Jacob BINCK (1530), J. A. DU-CERCEAU (1550) and Virgil SOLIS, and used on Limoges enamels. After the

sack of Rome in 1527 Rosso lived alternately in Arezzo and Borgo San Sepolcro, but in 1530, after staying with Pietro Aretino (1492–1557) in Venice, he travelled to Fontainebleau to work for François I. At Fontainebleau Rosso's great work, in which he was assisted by PRIMATICCIO, was the Galerie François I (begun in 1535, plasterwork 1535 to 1537, paintings 1537 to 1539, and panelling, by Scibec de Carpi, 1535 to 1539). The distinguishing feature of the decorations at Fontainebleau was the combination of painted scenes with an elaborate plasterwork scheme incorporating figures and heavy and aggressive scrolled STRAPWORK frames. Rosso had already used a combination of plaster and painting in Rome in 1524, but the Fontainebleau style of decoration is probably more indebted to Venetian prototypes. However, the style came to be regarded in Italy as specifically French. The Galerie François I was reproduced in tapestries, now in Vienna, woven in Fontainebleau after Rosso's death to cartoons prepared by Claude Baudouin from 1540. Rosso is known to have designed a wide range of silverwork for François I including salts, VASES and mounted shells which displayed, according to VASARI, '*strane e bizzarre fantasie*' and were among the most influential early MANNERIST silver designs. Antonio FANTUZZI, a painter from Bologna who worked under Rosso from 1537 to 1540, subsequently issued prints of Rosso silver designs, as did René BOYVIN later. A Rosso design for a tabernacle was engraved as late as 1575 by Cherubino Alberti. Rosso also designed for court ceremonies including a triumphal arch for the visit of Charles V to Fontainebleau in 1540.

Roth, Christoph-Melchior Born in Nuremberg, Roth was active there as an engraver from 1744. In 1761 he moved to St Petersburg with his brother collaborator, Matthias, and worked until 1770 as an engraver for the Academy. After a spell in private practice he returned to Nuremberg in 1777. He died there in 1798. Roth engraved some of EISLER's designs, and also issued a suite of ROCOCO VASES and cartouches. His *Verschiedene Fenster nach der neuesten Facon* (six plates) applied absurdly incoherent rococo shellwork to BAROQUE pediments.

Roth, J. L. (1727–77) A Würzburg bronze-caster, Roth published *Unterschiedliche Zeichnungen von neuer Invention vor Goldarbeiter* (1763; seven plates), basic designs for floral jewellery.

Rottenhammer, Hans (1564–1625) Born in Munich, the son of the court riding-master, Rottenhammer studied painting under Hans Donauer up to 1588. In 1589 he travelled to Rome via Venice, and remained there until about 1595, becoming friendly with Paul Bril and Jan Bruegel. From 1596 to 1606 he was in Venice, where his patrons included the Emperor RUDOLF II. From 1606 Rottenhammer was in Augsburg, where he became a citizen in 1607. He executed many decorative paintings, including some in the Goldener Saal of the new Town Hall. He also designed a crucifix made by the goldsmith Christoph Lencker, and, in 1610, embossed work for another goldsmith, Bayr, who was one of his drinking companions. HAINHOFER employed Rottenhammer as a designer on his Pommersche Kunstschrank.

Rouillart, Noel Rouillart published a suite of black stretched GROTESQUE designs for enamelling on pendant backs and other types of jewellery, in about 1610. They are attended by lively devils.

Roumier, François Born at Corbigny, Roumier is recorded as working as a wood-carver from 1701. He worked for the crown at Versailles, Marly and Fontainebleau, and called himself 'Sculpteur de Roi'. His *Livre de plusieurs coins de Bordures* (1724; seven plates) contains light and lively borders and corners formed of scrolls and STRAPWORK, but looking forward to ROCOCO. His next published work, dedicated to the architect Robert de COTTE (1656–1735), recorded in eight plates trophies which Roumier had carved in the choir of the Jacobins' church. They are in the early rococo style and display a vigorous use of asymmetry. *Livre de plusieurs Pieds de tables ou de cabarets* (1750; six plates) shows console tables. It was issued posthumously; Roumier had died in 1748.

Roupert, Louis Born in Metz, Roupert was active there as a goldsmith. His *Dessins de feuillage et d'ornements pour l'orfèvrerie et la niellure* (1668) comprises scrolled foliate and ACANTHUS ornaments, black on white for engraving on silver, or white on black for niello. Putti drag great branches of ornament, or they grow out of a bellows or a pipe; on other plates ornaments are suspended above panoramic landscapes. A portrait after P. Rabon accompanies the suite; Roupert is shown holding a sheet of scrolling ornament, with another scroll growing out of a vase by his side. The work is dedicated to '*Monsieur Clavier mon amy*', and Roupert, in response to critics, allows that he has borrowed figures from Sadeler, MECKENEM and CALLOT, but states that he is not ashamed of being a student. He is writing from Paris, where he admits that there are better designers than he. *Dessins* appeared in more than one version.

Rousseel, Nicasius Born in Bruges, Rousseel arrived in London in about 1567 and was active there as a goldsmith. He was still alive in 1640. Rousseel seems to have acquired excellent contacts in artistic circles; one son became a painter and another was probably connected with the Mortlake tapestry works, while Cornelius Johnson and Isaac Oliver stood godfathers to other children. *De Grotesco* (London, 1623; twelve plates) was dedicated by Rousseel to George Heriot, goldsmith to James I. It comprises designs by Rousseel for engraving on silver, stretched early AURICULAR GROTESQUE ornament inhabited by elongated monsters and insects. Copies in reverse were published by J. C. Visscher in 1644, and *De Grotesco* was later reissued by John OVERTON.

Rubens, Peter Paul (1577–1640) Born at Siegen in Westphalia, the son of a lawyer from Antwerp, Rubens returned there by 1589. From 1591 he studied painting under, successively, Tobias Verhaecht (1561–1631), Adam van Noort (1562–1641) and Otto van Veen (1556–1629). In 1600 he travelled to Italy, where he became a court painter to Vincenzo Gonzaga, Duke of Mantua. In 1603 he travelled to Madrid and from 1604 to 1608 he was in Mantua, Rome, Genoa and Milan. He then returned to Antwerp, where he settled after being in 1609 appointed court painter to Archduke Albert and Archduchess Isabella, the Governors of the Netherlands. Rubens acquired a great reputation as scholar, collector and diplomat as well as painter. He visited Paris in 1622 and 1625, Madrid in 1628, London in 1629 and was repeatedly in Holland. Rubens designed many book illustrations and title-pages, mainly for Balthasar Moretus of the Plantin press, a school friend with whom he collaborated closely, first on Philip Rubens's *Electorum Libri II* (1608); their principal engraver was Cornelis Galle. From 1637 Rubens was assisted on the details by Erasmus Quellien. In 1634 Rubens designed a series of decorations to celebrate the entry of Ferdinand of Austria to Antwerp in 1635. In 1642 a great book, the *Pompa Introitus Ferdinandi*, was published to record the event; it also illustrated a magnificent triumphal car designed by Rubens in 1638 to commemorate Ferdinand's victory at Calloo. In 1622 Rubens published *I Palazzi di Genova* (later editions 1663, 1652, 1708 and 1755) illustrating great houses in Genoa; it had a wide influence on Northern architecture. In 1618 Rubens stated in a letter to Sir Dudley Carleton that he had extensive contacts with Brussels tapestry weavers, and in the same year offered Carleton tapestry cartoons on the History of Decius Mus, ordered by some Genoese nobles. In 1622 he was commissioned by Louis XIII of France to design tapestries on the History of Constantine and in about 1625 by Archduchess Isabella to design no less than twenty tapestries on the Triumph of the Eucharist for the Convent of the Descalzas Reales in Madrid. He also designed tapestries on the History of Aeneas. Rubens's last suite of tapestries, on the History of Achilles, was probably designed for his father-in-law, the tapestry merchant Daniel Fourment, in the early 1630s, although tapestries after his paintings on the History of Maria de' Medici were woven at the Gobelins factory from 1828 to 1840. In about 1630 Rubens designed a ewer and basin with the birth of Venus and a border of merfolk and tritons, said to have been executed for Charles I by Theodor Rogiers. In 1637 Sir Balthasar Gerbier obtained from Rubens 'certaine drawings for carving of cups', probably for execution in ivory by Lucas Faidherbe (1617–97), a sculptor from Mecheln who lived in Rubens's house from 1637 to 1640. In design as in painting Rubens was one of the great protagonists of the BAROQUE style.

Rudolf II (1552–1612) Born in Vienna,

Rudolf was in 1564 sent for his education to Spain, where he remained at the court of Philip II until 1571. He became King of Hungary in 1572, King of Bohemia, with the title of King of the Romans, in 1575 and Emperor on the death of his father, Maximilian II, in 1576. He continued to employ MANNERIST artists patronized by his father, including Bartholomaus Spranger (1546–1611) and Giuseppe Arcimboldi (1527–93). The latter designed costumes and equipment for many court festivals, assisted by Giovanni Battista Fonteo. In 1577 Rudolf made a series of formal entries to his domains; in Olmütz the Jesuits erected a triumphal arch designed by the English Jesuit Thomas Williams. Rudolf took a deep interest in the elaborate iconography of such celebrations of his imperial status, assisted by his court antiquary Ottavio Strada (1550–1612) among others. In his castle in Prague, Rudolf assembled a prodigious collection of works of art and nature, including paintings by DÜRER, Bruegel, Leonardo, RAPHAEL and Correggio: his contemporary the Flemish painter and biographer Karel van Mander (1548–1606) called Rudolf 'the greatest art lover in the world' and HAINHOFER admired his example. In 1585 Rudolf set up a hardstone cutting mill at Bubeneč, he sponsored Caspar Lehmann's development of wheel engraving on glass, and in 1588 he issued an edict urging his subjects to search for precious stones; his personal physician Anselm Boeth de Boot wrote a treatise on the subject, *Gemmarum et Lapidum Historia* (1609). Rudolf attracted craftsmen and designers from all over Europe to work in his imperial court workshops in Prague, including Ottavio Miseroni, Alessandro Abondio, Paul van VIANEN, Erasmus HORNICK, Adriaen de VRIES, Hans and Paul VREDEMAN DE VRIES. Rudolf also commissioned works from craftsmen, designers and artists living elsewhere, for example ROTTENHAMMER and the JAMNITZERS. The works they produced ministered to Rudolf's mannerist taste for the rich, the curious and the rare, but also reinforced the general purpose of his collection of Kunstkammer to represent and reinforce in microcosm Hapsburg domination of the universe.

Rudolph, Christian Friedrich (1692–1754) Rudolph was active in Augsburg as a designer from 1713, when he published a suite of elaborate BAROQUE pulpits (six plates). A suite of trophies, ecclesiastical and secular, intended for carving on panels, are probably a little later. *Livre de Tables françoises* (six plates) comprises tables in the early ROCOCO style of PINEAU, incorporating coarsely handled horses', dragons' and hairy satyrs' legs. *Einige Vases mit modernen Einfassungen* (six plates) shows VASES in frames in a fully developed rococo manner, very scrolly and incorporating several prehensile snails. Rudolph also published designs for altars, cartouches, capitals and locks, mainly in the rococo style. His brother, the cabinet-maker Johann Friedrich Rudolph, published a suite of pulpits (four plates).

Ruhlmann, Jacques Émile (1879–1933) Born in Paris, the son of a prosperous Protestant house-painter from Alsace, Ruhlmann showed luxury furniture at Salons d'Automne from 1913 onwards. After the First World War he built up a large furniture workshop, Établissements Ruhlmann et Laurent, and also designed silks, carpets, textiles, lighting and so on. He was the subject of an article in 'ART ET DÉCORATION' (1920), the *Gazette du Bon Ton* (1920) included a Ruhlmann bathroom and *Croquis de Ruhlmann* (1924; fifty-four plates) reproduced his design sketches. At the

PARIS 1925 EXHIBITION Ruhlmann's
Hôtel du Collectionneur, designed by
the architect Pierre Patout, was a centre
of attention, incorporating work by
PUIFORCAT, Brandt, LEGRAIN,
DUNAND and many others, alongside
Ruhlmann's own designs. He also
designed the study in the Ambassade
Française at the 1925 Exhibition. For
his furniture, exquisitely executed in
rich materials, particularly ebony,
amboyna and ivory, Ruhlmann often
used an elegantly pared-down 1760s
NEO-CLASSICAL idiom, although in the
late 1920s he sometimes switched to a
more MODERNISTIC manner, using
chromium-plated steel and black lacquer, for instance in a desk for the
Maharajah of Indore. *Répertoire du goût
moderne* (1929) included designs by
Ruhlmann, some in an unregenerately
luxurious ART DÉCO manner, alongside
Modern designs by G. Guévrekian and
MALLET-STEVENS.

Rumpp, Johann (1702–55) Born in
Kirchheim unter Teck, a centre of cabinet-making, Rumpp worked as a cabinet-maker specializing in silver furniture
in Augsburg, becoming a master there
in 1739. His *Tischler oder Schreiner
Risse* (forty-eight plates) comprises
cabinets, desks, chairs, cradles, clock-
cases, chests, tables etc. in an elaborate
late BAROQUE style. Like most of
Rumpp's designs, these were published
by ENGELBRECHT. Other designs for
cabinet-makers include crestings, win-
dow-frames, boxes and patterns for
inlaying in pewter and brass, the latter
panels with WATTEAUESQUE figures in
scrolling frames. Rumpp also issued
ROCOCO designs for VASES and stoves,
for cartouches, and for doors, some of
the latter published by HERTEL.

Ruprich-Robert, Victor-Marie-Charles
(1820–87) Born in Paris, Ruprich-Robert studied architecture under Constant-

Defeux. From 1843 he taught alongside
VIOLLET-LE-DUC at the École
Speciale de Dessin, where he influenced
a whole generation of architects and
designers. In 1856 Ruprich-Robert was
appointed Architecte-Dessinateur to
the Mobilier de la Couronne, and
thenceforward designed furniture and
decorations for many of the imperial
palaces, using styles appropriate to each
building, for instance a massive
RENAISSANCE style for furniture at
Fontainebleau (1860). He was a pioneering historian of French architecture and
was also interested in the theory of
ornament. His *Flore ornementale* (1866,
reprinted 1876; 151 plates) urged a
return to the study of nature as the basis
of ornament. The designs, which include
metalwork, ceramics and an ambitious
Monument to Agriculture as well as
ornament, are based on the geometrical
arrangement of natural forms. Ruprich-
Robert claimed to have first published
his ideas in 1850, and thus to have
anticipated Owen JONES's *Grammar of
Ornament* (1856) and Viollet-le-Duc's
*Dictionnaire raisonné de l'architecture
française*, V (1861).

Ruskin, John (1819–1900) Born in London, the son of a prosperous wine merchant, Ruskin received a sheltered and
intense Christian education which,
reflecting the Scottish background of his
admiring parents, incorporated the arts
and sciences as well as the more conventional subjects. Ruskin was a precocious
enthusiast for geology and drawing. He
published a poem in *Spiritual Times* as
early as 1830 and his first article
appeared in LOUDON's *Architectural
Magazine* (1837). Ruskin studied at
Oxford from 1837 and in 1843 published
the first volume of his *Modern Painters*,
a monumental vindication of the genius
of Turner, whom he had admired since
seeing Turner's illustrations to Rogers's
Italy in 1832. Ruskin's *Seven Lamps of*

Architecture (1849) and *Stones of Venice* (1851–3) used a similarly eloquent prose to establish the absolute and inevitable validity of GOTHIC. The proper subject of ornament, he stated, was nature: 'all noble ornamentation is the expression of man's delight in God's work'. Ruskin's catholic definition of nature, which included abstract lines and crystals as well as foliage, encouraged geometric ornament and the conventionalization of natural forms. Like A. W. N. PUGIN, Ruskin was a stickler for honesty in architecture and ornament. He detested the RENAISSANCE and machine-made ornament. In 1854 F. J. Furnivall of the Working Men's College distributed copies of the chapter on the Nature of Gothic from *Stones of Venice* at the opening lecture of the college, at which ROSSETTI and BURNE-JONES taught. In 1892 William MORRIS reprinted the same lecture at the Kelmscott Press. Ruskin's views on art had a social dimension; he strongly attacked 'the degradation of the operative into a machine' and stated: 'I believe the right question to ask, respecting all ornament, is simply this: Was it done with enjoyment – was the carver happy while he was about it?' In 1867 Ruskin began to plan the St George's Company which finally emerged in 1878 as the Guild of St George, a doomed attempt to put into practice his dream of a regeneration of society along medieval lines. In 1874, while Slade Professor at Oxford, Ruskin led an experiment in road-mending at Hinksey in which Oscar Wilde participated; W. A. S. BENSON was amused. But although his concrete attempts at reform foundered Ruskin had an immense general influence on designers and his works became sacred texts to devotees of the Arts & Crafts movement. MACKMURDO was a direct disciple, ASHBEE's *An Endeavour towards the Teaching of John Ruskin and William Morris* (1901) reflects his debt, and

LETHABY, JACK, Ernest Barnsley and MUTHESIUS were among Ruskin's many admirers. Ruskin was no designer himself; his windows for Scott's St Giles, Camberwell (1844), and for the Oxford Museum (1855) were unsuccessful and his personal taste in furniture was conventional. He did, however, have a limited direct influence on design, notably at the Oxford Museum, where carving by the O'Shea brothers reflected his doctrines. Ruskin also took a close interest in the typography of his own published works. Under his aegis his friend Burne-Jones designed embroideries for Winnington School for girls in about 1864 and in 1883 a gold cross to be given by Ruskin to the Whitelands May Queen. Ruskin and Morris met in 1857 but only became friendly after 1877, when Ruskin joined Morris's Society for the Protection of Ancient Buildings. Together they became the international patron saints of the revival of interest in the decorative arts which blossomed in the 1890s.

Russell, Sir Gordon (1892–1980) Sydney Gordon Russell was born in Cricklewood, the son of a bank clerk of an independent outlook, who in 1904 took over the Lygon Arms, Broadway, Worcestershire. He was educated in Chipping Campden shortly after the move of ASHBEE's Guild of Handicraft there in 1901. An early friend was F. L. Griggs (1876–1938), the Arts & Crafts book illustrator and etcher. After helping in his father's antiques business he was put in charge of the repair workshop, and in about 1910 began to design furniture made there for the Lygon Arms and other clients. After service in the First World War Russell began to produce hand-made furniture much in the manner of Ernest GIMSON. He was advised and encouraged by Percy Wells (1867–1956) of the Shoreditch Technical Institute, co-author with J. Hooper of

Modern Cabinet Furniture & Fitments (1909), and by John Gloag, then assistant editor of *The Cabinet Maker*. Russell quickly established contact with the DESIGN AND INDUSTRIES ASSOCIATION and began to propagandize in favour of honesty in the crafts. Among the many who lectured to his craftsmen was the elderly VOYSEY. Russell furniture was shown at the 1924 Wembley British Empire Exhibition (see LONDON EXHIBITIONS) and at the PARIS 1925 EXHIBITION, where he was awarded a gold and two silver medals. In 1926 he became a member of the ART-WORKERS' GUILD, and in the same year his company, Gordon Russell Ltd, was formed. From about 1925, however, he gradually introduced machinery in the workshops, and after a number of temporary London exhibitions a permanent shop was established at 24 Wigmore Street. At this period Russell also designed some glass for Whitefriars and Stevens and Williams of Brierley Hill, Staffordshire. In about 1930 Russell turned to a plain, unpretentious MODERN manner, also practised by other designers working for his firm, including W. H. Russell (no relation), Eden Minns and his brother, R. D. Russell. In 1931 Gordon Russell was approached by Frank Murphy of Murphy radios, and as a result produced a whole series of Modern radio cabinets designed by R. D. Russell. In 1935 larger London showrooms were opened at 50 Wigmore Street, designed by Geoffrey

Jellicoe, and Nikolaus PEVSNER was appointed as a buyer of textiles and glass for the firm, in succession to Marian Pepler, a post he held until 1939. Gordon Russell Ltd showed furniture at the LONDON 1934 EXHIBITION at the Royal Academy and the PARIS 1937 EXHIBITION. In 1938 Russell initiated a scheme for the mass-production of furniture by the firm for sale by a group of enlightened retailers called the Good Furnishing Group; the project was cut short by the war. From 1942 Russell was a member of the Board of Trade committee which initiated the production of Utility furniture in 1943, and from 1943 to 1947 Russell was Chairman of the Board of Trade Design Panel. In 1947 he became director of the Council of Industrial Design, of which he had been a member since its foundation in 1944. He served as director until 1959, opening the Design Centre in 1956. A knighthood was one of many honours, national and international, which reflected his leading role in the design establishment. The Mastership of the Art-Workers' Guild in 1962 was particularly appropriate, for although Russell had pioneered the industrial production of well-designed furniture and helped to propagandize Modern standards in design in Britain, his personal taste, especially in furniture designed for his own use, was for hand-made pieces in natural woods, in the Cotswold Arts & Crafts tradition with which he had been brought up.

S

Saarinen, Eero (1910–61) Born near Helsinki, Saarinen moved to New York in 1923 with his father, Eliel SAARINEN, and thence in 1925 to Cranbrook, north of Detroit. Saarinen at first intended to become a sculptor, studying in Paris in 1930 to 1931, but later trained as an architect at Yale, graduating in 1934. Already in 1929 he had designed furniture for his father's Kingswood School, Cranbrook. After Yale, Saarinen worked on furniture design with Norman BEL GEDDES. He returned to Cranbrook in 1936 and from 1937 worked together with Charles EAMES on furniture design. In 1941 they won the two first prizes in the 1940 organic furniture design competition organized by the NEW YORK MUSEUM OF MODERN ART. Saarinen later designed for Knoll Associates a bent plywood chair (1946), the Womb chair (1948), latex foam on a moulded plastic frame with chromed tubular-steel legs, and his winsomely elegant Pedestal furniture (1958), including tables and the Tulip chair (1957), with a fibre-glass shell on a cast-aluminium base. Saarinen saw himself as a pioneer of sculptural furniture, as opposed to the rectilinear forms of the 1920s. Until 1950 Saarinen was in his father's architectural practice. Some of his later architecture uses dramatically curved forms, notably his TWA Terminal at Kennedy Airport in New York (1956–62); the mobile lounges at Kennedy were an ingenious amalgam of architecture, design and engineering.

Saarinen, Gottlieb Eliel (1873–1950) Born in Rantasalmi, Finland, the son of a pastor, Saarinen was brought up in Russia. He was at first inclined towards painting but then in the 1890s decided to become an architect, studying at the Helsingfors Polytechnic. In 1896 he formed a partnership with his fellow students Herman Gesellius and Armas Lindgren; Lindgren left in 1905 and the remaining partnership was dissolved in 1907. In 1900 Saarinen and his partners designed the Finnish pavilion at the PARIS EXHIBITION, described in 'DEKORATIVE KUNST' (1900). In 1902 he designed a studio house, Hvitträsk, for the partnership; it became a centre of the arts and many distinguished friends stayed there including, in 1910, Julius MEIER-GRAEFE. Saarinen's early furniture at Hvitträsk and Suur-Merijoki (1902) displays the influence of MACKINTOSH and BAILLIE SCOTT. That at the Molchow Haus (1905) shows a move towards greater lightness and simplicity. Saarinen had wide international contacts and an equally wide reputation. In 1907 he met OLBRICH in Darmstadt and BEHRENS at Düsseldorf, and showed furniture at the Salon d'Automne in Paris. In 1913 he was made a corresponding member of the DEUTSCHE WERKBUND; he showed at the COLOGNE 1914 DEUTSCHE WERKBUND EXHIBITION. In 1923, Saarinen, having won second prize in the 1922 Chicago Tribune Tower competition, moved with his family to America. In 1924 he was appointed visiting professor of architecture at the University of Michigan and in 1925 was asked by George G. Booth, the wealthy proprietor of the *Detroit News*, to develop his Cranbrook educational centre at Bloomfield Hills, Michigan. The Cranbrook Foundation was set up in 1927 and in 1932 Saarinen was made President of the Cranbrook Academy of Art. Saarinen's own house at Cranbrook included furniture, glass, silver, brass and other furnishings to his own design. His wife Loja, whom he had married in 1904, the sister of his partner Gesellius, designed and executed rugs and textiles at Cranbrook, including curtains and carpets for the Kingswood School (1929–31) there, for which Eliel Saarinen's son Eero designed furniture. An exhibition of designs by the whole family was held at the Detroit Institute of Arts in 1932. In 1929 Saarinen designed a dining-room for the Architect and Industrial Art Exhibition, at the Metropolitan Museum of Art, New York, and in 1934 he and Loja showed a Room for a Lady at the same event. Silver by Saarinen was shown at the PARIS 1937 EXHIBITION. The teachers he assembled at Cranbrook included his son Eero, Charles EAMES and Harry BERTOIA.

Sagrestani, Giovanni Camillo (1660–1731) Born in Florence, Sagrestani was a pupil of Antonio Giusti and Romolo Panfi. He was strongly influenced by Luca Giordano and painted in Bologna and in Venice as well as in Florence. From 1715 he designed for the Medici tapestry factory in Florence a suite of the Four Continents, dashing late BAROQUE allegories whose weaving was completed in 1730.

Saint, Gideon (1729–99) A Huguenot, Saint was apprenticed to the London carver Jacob Touzey in 1743 and himself set up as a carver and gilder near Leicester Square in 1763. He moved to Hoxton in 1779 and was styled a gentleman on his death at his son's house in Groom-

bridge, Kent. A scrap-book assembled by Saint, probably in about 1763, is in the Metropolitan Museum in New York. It includes prints by Pierre LE PAUTRE, BOULLE, Jean I BERAIN, ROUMIER, PINEAU, Mariette, LOCK, COPLAND and Thomas JOHNSON (2). Saint also contributed his own designs in the ROCOCO style, some hesitant and others fluent, and many indebted to Lock and Johnson.

Saint-Ange-Desmaisons, Louis Born in Paris in 1780, Saint-Ange was a pupil of PERCIER, BRONGNIART and Vaudoyer. From 1806 he was a designer at the SÈVRES porcelain factory. In 1809 he designed a Gobelins tapestry of the arms of France for the Grand Cabinet of Napoleon at the Tuileries, and in 1810 he was appointed designer of the Mobilier Impérial. Saint-Ange, in this capacity, designed Savonnerie upholstery and carpets in a rich and colourful NEO-CLASSICAL style. In 1816 he was appointed designer to the Mobilier de la Couronne under Louis XVIII and continued to work in the same style up to 1825. DUGOURC was a colleague. In 1819, as a recognition for his design for the carpet of the Salle du Conseil du Roi at Versailles, Saint-Ange was appointed designer to the Comte d'Artois. In 1825 he designed a gaudy GOTHIC carpet presented to the choir of Notre Dame, Paris, by the King. Saint-Ange died after 1831. He had also been active as an engraver.

Saint-Aubin, Charles Germain (1721–86) Grandson of an embroiderer, son of the royal embroiderer, Saint-Aubin followed his father's profession, but as a designer rather than as a craftsman. He was taught to design ornament by Dutrou and in 1745 left his father's workshop to set up on his own. Saint-Aubin published two suites of cyphers (thirteen plates) and an *Essay de Papil-*

loneries humaines (1748; twelve plates), a ROCOCO fantasy in which butterflies mimic human behaviour. He also executed a large number of watercolour suites of flowers, as an inspiration to design, and is estimated to have executed no less than 40,000 designs for the textile industry. Saint-Aubin's pre-eminence in this field led a lace manufacturer to pay 1,200 livres for his exclusive services in 1761. In his *Art de Brodeur* (1770), part of the French Academy's *Description des Arts et Metiers*, Saint-Aubin stresses the fundamental importance of design for embroidery, as well as illustrating works by earlier but forgotten embroidery designers such as Bagueville, who worked for Louis XIV, and Seré, who was active in 1717. He also illustrated his own designs for the Dauphin in 1747, 1768 and 1770, as well as a caparison for the King of Portugal. One of his brothers, Louis-Michel, was a painter at the Sèvres porcelain factory.

Saint-Aubin, Gabriel Jacques (1724–80) A younger brother of Charles Germain SAINT-AUBIN, Gabriel Jacques Saint-Aubin was educated as a painter but after repeated set-backs devoted himself almost entirely to drawing. From 1747 to 1776 he taught architecture in BLONDEL's academy. In 1754 he engraved a design for four VASES of BAROQUE character in the advanced NEO-CLASSICAL style, with a tiny extra scene showing Lalive de Jully's cabinet in the same year. As well as many illustrations, vignettes and ephemera Saint-Aubin also designed snuff-boxes, watches and other trinkets. His drawings of interiors and entertainments and his sketches in the margins of sale catalogues are valuable documents of the progress of design during his lifetime.

Saint-Jean, Simon (1808–60) The son of a Lyon cooper, Saint-Jean studied at the Lyon École des Beaux-Arts, where he was taught floral design by THIERRIAT. He then worked as a textile designer for the Didier Petit company. Saint-Jean was later successful as a flower painter but also sat on the silk jury for the LONDON 1851 EXHIBITION.

St Louis 1904 Exhibition In 1901 the United States Congress approved an exhibition at St Louis to commemorate the centenary of the purchase of the Louisiana territory from France in 1803. In the event the exhibition was postponed to 1904. The French designer Georges Hoentschel (1855–1915), reporting on furniture, saw Germany as the most successful nation and as the chief rival to France, a position held twenty years earlier by England. Although the German pavilion was a version of Schloss Charlottenburg in Berlin, German designers represented included OLBRICH, PANKOK and RIERMERSCHMID and the German catalogue, similar to that by Pankok for the PARIS 1900 EXHIBITION, was a highly accomplished ART NOUVEAU design by BEHRENS. MUTHESIUS thought the British pavilion, a reproduction of the Kensington Palace Orangery furnished in period styles by George Trollope & Sons, appalling. However the small English Arts & Crafts section included objects designed by VOYSEY, ASHBEE and Walter CRANE. Crane thought that the LALIQUE jewellery was the only noteworthy French exhibit; Muthesius felt similarly about TIFFANY in the American section.

St Martin's Lane Academy, London Founded by William Hogarth (1697–1764) in 1735, the St Martin's Lane Academy was a nursery for English ROCOCO design. From 1738 the architect Isaac Ware helped to run the Academy. Its teachers also frequented Old Slaughter's Coffee House in St Martin's Lane, where anti-Palladian artists and designers gathered in the 1730s and 1740s. Its principal members in 1745 included GRAVELOT and G. M. MOSER, and many were involved in the rococo decorations of Vauxhall Gardens in the 1740s. James Paine, the architect whose design for Doncaster Mansion House, commissioned in 1744 and published in 1751, included rococo plasterwork, was a pupil as was the furniture designer John LINNELL.

Saint Sebastian, Master of An engraver who probably worked in the Rhine region in about 1480 and was possibly a goldsmith in Cologne, the Master of Saint Sebastian published a design for a pax with the Madonna and Child and, on the same plate, a beaker supported by a lion and an eagle.

Salembier, Henri Born in Paris in about 1753, Salembier issued a large range of printed designs in 1777 and 1778. They consist mainly of ornament and friezes in the NEO-CLASSICAL style. A suite of *Tables, Feux et Ornements* (1778; six plates) shows tables, candlesticks, firedogs and frames, all mingled but to different scales, with an uneasy effect heightened by Salembier's idiosyncratic handling of form and ornament. A second wave of printed designs of 1807 and 1809 culminated in *Modèles de Dessins d'Orfèvrerie* (thirty-six plates), published by Bance, which comprises a wide variety of silversmiths' work. The style is neo-classical in the 1780s mode, but treated in a quirky light GROTESQUE manner which sets butterflies, snails and snakes alongside Napoleonic bees. A reprint (1828), by a jeweller, S. Vallardi, also includes jewellery designs by Salembier. Bance published his *Principes d'Ornements* (forty plates), a typical design manual of foliate ornaments. Salembier died in 1820.

Salviati, Francesco (1510–63) Born in Florence as Francesco de' Rossi, Salviati received his earliest training, as a goldsmith, from his cousin Diacceto, who also taught him design. He later studied design under Baccio Bandinelli (1493–1560) and painting under Andrea del Sarto (1486–1530). He was in Rome from about 1530 in the service of Cardinal Salviati, whose name he adopted, and at this stage established his life-long friendship with VASARI. In Rome, Salviati collaborated on the design of a triumphal arch for Charles V in 1535 and designed tapestries on the History of Alexander commissioned by Pier Luigi Farnese in 1537. In 1539 he moved via Florence and Bologna to Venice, where he collaborated with Giovanni da UDINE on decorations in the Palazzo Grimani. After visiting Verona and Mantua Salviati came back to Rome in 1541. His murals in the Sala dell'Udienza in the Palazzo Vecchio in Florence (1543–5) reflect the influence of ornament at Fontainebleau as transmitted by FANTUZZI and Mignon. In 1545 Salviati designed a Dream of Pharaoh tapestry for the Florentine factory, as part of BRONZINO's Joseph suite. Salviati also designed tapestries with the History of Tarquin for Christofano Rinieri. Salviati was a close friend of Manno di Sebastiano Sbarri (1520–86), the goldsmith who made the Farnese casket (1547–61), which was probably designed by Salviati, although Perino del VAGA was also involved. In 1554 Salviati travelled to France, where he worked at Dampierre. Two plates of serving knives engraved by Cherubino Alberti after Salviati's designs in 1583 (copied 1605) demonstrate his mastery of MANNERIST metalwork design, their handles being composed of elaborate entanglements of figures. Many other elegant and complex designs by Salviati for goldsmiths' work survive and seem to have been widely copied. He may also have designed the mannerist title-page to Labacco's *Architettura* (1558).

Saly, Jacques François Joseph (1717–76) Born in Valenciennes, Saly was trained as a sculptor and won the Grand Prix in 1738. He spent the years 1740 to 1748 in Rome, where he published a suite of VASES (1746). These marvellously sensitive and inventive designs combine precociously pure NEO-CLASSICAL forms with ornament of BA-ROQUE character compounded of mer-folk, satyrs and fishy GROTESQUES. They reflect the influence of DELLA BELLA and, more immediately, PIRA-NESI and were very popular and influential, reprinted in Paris, owned by DU-PLESSIS, and copied in DARLY's *Sixty Vases* (1768). Saly's neo-classicism is further demonstrated by the fact that his drawing of a Roman tripod was engraved in CAYLUS's *Recueil* (1756). Saly lived from 1753 to 1774 in Copenhagen, where his friend, the architect Nicolas-Henri Jardin (1720–99), used vases by Saly to decorate Count Moltke's house in 1757.

Sambin, Hugues Born in Gray in about 1520, Sambin in 1548 married a daughter of Jean Boudrillet of Dijon, a carver from Troyes, who in 1527 had signed a contract to supply choir stalls to the church of Saint-Benignon in Dijon '*le tout à l'antique*'. Also in 1548 Sambin worked on decorations for the entry of Henri II to Dijon. In 1549 he became a master in the guild of *menuisiers* there. Sambin was active in Dijon as carver, engineer, designer and architect. In 1564 he designed decorations for the entry of Charles IX. On the title of his *Œuvre de la Diversité des Termes* (Lyon, 1572; thirty-six plates) Sambin described himself as '*Architecteur en la ville de Dijon*'; in his text Sambin claimed that he had dedicated himself to architecture since his early years and that he had studied '*les despouilles des vieilles et antiques Architectures*'. The *Œuvre* was dedicated to Léonor Chabot, Comte de Charny, for whom Sambin worked at the Château de Pagny, and prefaced by a sonnet by the local poet Étienne Taboureau which hailed Sambin as '*la perle de notre âge*'. The *Œuvre* consisted of MANNERIST designs of terms arranged in groups of six according to the character of the ORDERS – Tuscan, Doric, Ionic, Corinthian, Composite and a synthetic invention of Sambin's own. They are exuberantly rich and vigorous assemblages of masks, fruits, flowers, putti, satyrs, centaurs, breasts and so on, and seem to have been a potent influence on local carvers. In 1583 Sambin executed carved work in the Palais de Justice in Dijon, and in 1592 he provided a model for a rood-loft for a church in Dôle. He died in 1601 or 1602.

Sandoz, Gérard Born in Paris in 1902, from a family of clock-makers and jewellers from the Jura, who had shops in Paris from about 1865, Sandoz entered the family firm as a designer after studying art. Much influenced by Paul FOLLOT, his uncle, Sandoz designed very geometric and abstract ART DÉCO jewellery which was shown at the PARIS 1925 EXHIBITION, and at the Salons d'Automne, and des Artistes-Décorateurs up to 1931, when he gave up jewellery design for painting and films. In 1930 Sandoz was a founder member of the Union des Artistes Modernes.

Sandrart, Joachim von (1630–1708) Born in Frankfurt, Sandrart lived in Hamburg from 1635 and was subsequently taught to draw by his uncle Joachim Sandrart in Amsterdam in about 1640. He later moved to Danzig, Breslau, Vienna and Regensburg, settling in Nuremberg in about 1656. He was a prolific engraver and publisher, publishing ECHTER and copies after

Jean LE PAUTRE, as well as *Neues Romanisches Laubwerckbuchlein* (five plates), frames of vigorous scrolled ACANTHUS.

Sanguineti, A. Sanguineti, editor of the 'MONITEUR DE L'AMEUBLEMENT', advertised his services as a furniture designer. His *La Serrurerie Moderne* includes iron railings, balconies, screens etc., and structural ironwork. Some designs are after existing examples, including works by VIOLLET-LE-DUC and the architect A. N. L. Bailly (1810–92), and some are apparently by Sanguineti himself. Sanguineti also published *La Décoration en bois découpé* (1864).

Santi Santi designed the plates of *Modèles de Meubles* (Paris, 1828), seventy-two vividly coloured plates of furniture and curtains, mainly NEO-CLASSICAL but some GOTHIC. It was reprinted in 1841 with the addition of designs by PRUD'HON and JANSEN. Santi's name is sometimes spelt Centi.

Sarpaneva, Timo Born in 1926, Sarpaneva was trained as a graphic designer, graduating in 1948. From 1950 he has designed for the Karhula-Iittala glass works, working alongside Tapio WIRKKALA on a freelance basis. Sarpaneva has shown a penchant for moulded and textured effects. He has also designed cast iron, textiles and packaging.

Sauermann, Heinrich (1842–1904) Born in Flensburg, Sauermann founded a furniture factory there in 1869. In 1876 he presented his collection of North German decorative art objects to the town of Flensburg as the basis for a museum, and in 1877 founded an influential school of furniture design. Sauermann's earliest designs were in the Italian RENAISSANCE style, but he later adopted Dutch 17th-century models and finally used local prototypes. At the Munich 1888 Exhibition his North Frisian room was a great success, leading to official commissions to design and make rooms for the CHICAGO 1893 EXHIBITION and the PARIS 1900 EXHIBITION; their style was eclectic but distinctively German. Designs by Sauermann were illustrated in the 'GEWERBEHALLE' and 'KUNST-GEWERBEBLATT'.

Saur, Corvinianus Saur, probably Bavarian, entered the goldsmiths' guild in Copenhagen in 1606 and in 1613 became court goldsmith to Christian IV of Denmark. From 1591 to 1597 he published eight suites of miniature designs for jewellery, rings, pendants etc. in a white on black manner. His delicate STRAPWORK GROTESQUES sometimes incorporate insects, flowers and heraldic motifs. A single plate is dated 1606. Saur died in 1635.

Savoy, The (1896) Published by Leonard Smithers (1861–1907) and edited by Arthur Symons, the *Savoy* published Beardsley's post-'YELLOW BOOK' designs as well as illustrations by Shannon and others.

Sayer, Robert Sayer was active as a publisher and print-seller in London from 1751 to 1794 at the Golden Buck, opposite Fetter Lane in Fleet Street. He took six copies of CHIPPENDALE'S *Director* (1754), marketed the second edition (1755) and included designs by Chippendale in his *Household Furniture in Genteel Taste* (1760) by 'a Society of Upholsterers, Cabinet-Makers, etc.'. Sayer also published books by W. and J. HALFPENNY such as *Rural Architecture in the Gothick Taste* (1752), INCE & Mayhew's *Universal System* (1762), WILLSON's *The Antique and Modern Embellisher* (1766), MANWARING'S

The Chair-Maker's Guide (1766) and
SWAN's *Chimney Pieces* (1768). Sayer's
The Compleat Drawing Book (1757),
with plates borrowed from LE BRUN,
Barlow and others, was a useful source
for designers of ornament. Even more
popular was *The Ladies' Amusement*
(1762), a rich compendium of ROCOCO
designs by PILLEMENT and others.

Scalzi, Lodovico Born in Orvieto, Scalzi
worked there and in Perugia as a sculptor, painter and designer. In 1548 to 1551
he worked in Orvieto Cathedral. He
executed plasterwork designed by Galeazzo Alessi (1512–72). Scalzi published
fourteen plates of vigorous ACANTHUS
ornament dated 1599, 1607, 1610 and
1611.

Scarpa, Carol (1906–78) Scarpa was
born in Venice, where he studied architecture at the Accademia delle Belle
Arti, and practised from 1931, when he
designed the interior of a bar. From 1933
to 1947 Scarpa designed glass for Venini
of Murano; in 1977 he designed silver
for Rossi and Arcandi of Vicenza. He
was also involved in exhibition, interior
and museum design (notably the Cas-
telvecchio museum at Verona), and
designed furniture in an austere, mainly
rectilinear style, with elegant and
expressive effects; Scarpa was a great
admirer of Frank Lloyd WRIGHT.
Despite a small *œuvre* Scarpa was widely
influential through teaching and the
publicity attendant on his work for Olivetti. He died in Tokyo.

Schenck, Peter Born in Elberfeld in
1660, Schenck came early to Amsterdam, where he was a pupil of the painter
and engraver Gerard Valck. He then
established himself as an engraver and
publisher on a large scale, reprinting the
works of many French designers, including Jean LE PAUTRE and SIMONIN,
and regularly visiting Germany on busi-

ness. He died in Amsterdam in about
1718 to 1719. His *Topiarii operis orna-
menta varia* (Amsterdam, 1704; eight
plates) comprises accomplished
BAROQUE cartouches, scrolls, ACAN-
THUS ornament, etc. Schenck and his
son and successor, another Peter
Schenck, published a large number of
CHINOISERIES, including a suite
(twelve plates) adapted from Dapper's
1670 book on China, *Picturae Sinicae*
(1702), including representations of
Chinese porcelain, and *Chineese en
Vremden Nasie* (twenty plates). Many
were used on Meissen porcelain.

Schiavone, Andrea Born at Zadar in
Dalmatia, probably in 1503, as Andrea
Meldolla, Schiavone moved to Italy in
about 1530, and probably worked with
Parmigianino (1503–40). He was in Venice by about 1541, when VASARI commissioned a picture from him. He died
there in 1563. Schiavone's *Raccolta de'
Disegni Et Compartimenti Diversi*
(twenty plates) comprises frames in a
scrolled or MANNERIST architectural
manner; they are decorated with elongated figures, and some enclose medallion heads.

Schinkel, Karl Friedrich (1781–1841)
Born in Neurippen, Mark, the son of an
archdeacon and school inspector, Schinkel moved to Berlin in 1794. In 1797 he
was deeply impressed by Friedrich
GILLY's project for a monument to
Frederick the Great, and by Gilly's
drawings of the GOTHIC Schloss Marienburg. In 1798 Schinkel began to study
architecture with David Gilly
(1748–1808), Friedrich's father, while
Friedrich was away in England. When
he returned in 1798 Schinkel worked
closely with him, inheriting his unfinished projects on Gilly's premature
death in 1800. In about 1802 Schinkel
designed a number of interior schemes
with furniture directly based on Gilly's

earlier designs in a massy NEO-CLASSI-CAL manner, comparable to contemporary designs by HOPE. In the decade from 1805 Schinkel was mainly active as a painter and theatrical designer, but in 1809 to 1810 he designed interior decoration and furniture for King Friedrich Wilhelm III (1770–1840) of Prussia's Berlin palace, including a neo-classical bed and coach of wood with carved details, which displayed supreme elegance and understatement, especially by contrast to the designs of PERCIER and FONTAINE. Other early design commissions included a room (1813–14) for a silk manufacturer, Jean Paul Humbert, and a shop and fittings (1815) for the marzipan shop of Feige & Kessler in Königsberg. In 1815 he became an official architect and there followed a series of houses and interiors designed by Schinkel for members of the Prussian royal family: a house (1816) for Prince August (1779–1843); a house (1817) for Prince Friedrich (1794–1863), including Schinkel's first Gothic room; the casino in Schlosspark Klein Glienicke (1824–6) for Prince Karl (1801–83), including a mosaic table on a base both derived and simplified from a Percier and Fontaine design; the Neuer Pavilion in the park of Schloss Charlottenburg in Berlin (1824–6) for Friedrich Wilhelm III, which includes corner sofas, and a great half round sofa, a motif repeated in the contemporary rooms in the royal palace for Crown Prince Friedrich Wilhelm (1795–1861), which also included a Gothic study, gilt-bronze tables, and gilt armchairs with sphinx arm supports; the interior of Schloss Charlottenhof near Potsdam (1826–9), including a desk for the Crown Princess of silvered wood; the palace (1827–8) of Prince Karl; interiors (1829) for Prince Wilhelm (1797–1888), the future King and Emperor, including a sofa with a wooden frame but with scrolled ends of gilt iron, hall chairs based on basically 16th-century peasant models, and detailed plans of furniture placement; and, from 1830 to 1832, the palace of Prince Albrecht. Schinkel also designed interiors and furniture (1821–4) for Schloss Tegel, the home of Wilhelm von Humboldt (1767–1835), and furniture for his friend BEUTH. He was closely involved in Beuth's efforts to improve standards of manufacture and design. He was a founder member of the Technische Deputation in 1819 and was the leading contributor to *Vorbilder für Fabrikanten und Handwerker* (1821–37), model designs issued under the auspices of the Deputation. In 1830 Beuth's Berlin Gewerbeinstitut manufactured an elaborate plinth designed by Schinkel. His refined neo-classical designs were much influenced by visits to Italy in 1803 to 1805, 1824, when he was accompanied by Gustav Friedrich Waagen, and 1830, but a visit to France and England in 1826 also made an impact; some of Schinkel's chairs and tables reflect English prototypes. Schinkel had an abiding and romantic enthusiasm for Gothic, saw the Gothic and classical styles as complementary, and advocated their synthesis. The restoration of Schloss Stolzenfels on the Rhine for Friedrich Wilhelm IV occupied him from 1825 until his death. However Schinkel's own Gothic furniture designs, although competent, lack the invention of his neo-classical designs. In the 1820s he began to design cast-iron garden seats: he also designed textiles, draperies, light fittings for candles, oil and gas, picture frames, including Gothic, RENAISSANCE and BAROQUE examples, and silver. His favourite executants included the cabinet-maker Karl Wanschaff (1775–1848), the bronze-casters Werner & Neffen, the ceramicist Feilner (1773–1839) and the silk manufacturer George Gabain. In his final years Schinkel was mainly occupied with official duties and ambitious but unexecuted architectural schemes, including a romantic reconstruction of the Akropolis in Athens incorporating a palace for Prince Otto of Bavaria, the new King of Greece. He witnessed his own furniture being displaced by pieces in the newly fashionable ROCOCO and Renaissance Revival styles. None the less, the combination of monumentality with elegant refinement of ornament in his designs, as in his architecture, lent Schinkel's works an almost institutional authority-in Berlin. A coloured edition of his furniture designs edited by L. Lohde was published in Potsdam in 1852 (sixteen plates). Not for nothing did the Crown Prince keep Schinkel's drawings in a portfolio labelled 'Museo Pio Schinkelianum', by reference to the Museo Pio Clementino in the Vatican.

Schlick, Benjamin (1796–1872) Born in Copenhagen, Schlick studied architecture there from 1815 to 1818 and then, supported by a royal scholarship, travelled to Rome and Paris. He also copied paintings at Pompeii. In 1823 Schlick exhibited interiors after PERCIER and FONTAINE and in 1828 his scheme for a new interior for the Odeon theatre in Paris. Schlick was mainly active as a theatre designer. He lived most of the time in Paris and Italy but also in Berlin, Hamburg and London. From about 1844 Schlick was employed by Elkington, Mason & Co. of Birmingham to design electrotypes. Schlick's designs ranged from variations on classical originals to elaborate RENAISSANCE-style inventions. On some of the latter, shown at the LONDON 1851 EXHIBITION, Schlick was assisted by George Clark Stanton (1832–1894), a product of the Birmingham School of Design.

Schmidt, Christoph Born in Nuremberg in 1632, Schmidt was active as an engraver and publisher in Augsburg, where he married in 1654. His *Newes*

blumenbüchlein (1663; eight plates) comprises floral ornament with putti and birds; one plate, a scatter of NATURALISTIC flowers over small grey sprigs, appears to be a textile design. Schmidt also published copies after Jean LE PAUTRE and Stefano DELLA BELLA. In 1674 he published a suite of illustrations to Aesop's *Fables*.

Schmidt, Friedrich von (1825–91) Born in Frickenhofen in Württemberg, Schmidt studied architecture in Stuttgart and then, from 1843, worked as a mason on the completion of Cologne Cathedral. In 1855 he won third prize in the competition for the Votivkirche in Vienna, where he moved in 1859 after a period teaching in Milan. In 1863 Schmidt was appointed architect to St Stephan Cathedral, and soon became recognized as the main protagonist of GOTHIC in Vienna, his masterpiece being the Town Hall (1872–83), for which he designed Gothic furniture. Schmidt also designed Gothic-style glass for LOBMEYR, shown at the PARIS 1867 EXHIBITION. He was ennobled in 1889.

Schmidt, Hermann (1833–99) Born in Hamburg, where he was active as a decorative painter from 1857, Schmidt became the leading Hamburg church decorator, designing stained glass and furniture as well as murals. He showed at the Hamburg 1876 and 1889 Exhibitions. In 1889 his designs for embroidery were singled out for special mention, including some elaborate hangings in the late-GOTHIC style for the villa 'Haus Hauhopen', for which BICHWEILER had designed furniture.

Schmied, François Louis (1873–1941) Born in Geneva, Schmied studied at the École des Arts Industriels there, and became friendly with Jean DUNAND, a fellow student. In 1905 he moved to Paris, where he specialized in woodcuts.

A woodcut booklet published by Schmied in 1911 attracted the interest of Paul Jouve, who then commissioned Schmied to interpret his illustrations to Kipling's *The Jungle Book* as colour woodcuts. Schmied volunteered for the Foreign Legion during the First World War but was invalided out, having lost an eye, and resumed work on *The Jungle Book*, which he completed in 1919. After this success Schmied became a notable de luxe publisher, designing his own bindings, illustrations, typography and ornament, and also collaborating with other artists and craftsmen; he showed at the PARIS 1925 EXHIBITION. Notable books included *Les Chansons de Bilitis* (1922), Comtesse de Noailles's *Les Climats* (1924), Oscar Wilde's *Two Tales* (1926) and J. C. Nardrus's *Le Paradis Musulman* (1930). He employed Dunand on many of his bindings. In about 1939 he retired to Tahanaout in the Sahara, where he died.

Schmittmeyer, Paul A court goldsmith in Vienna, Schmittmeyer designed a suite of large and elaborate late-BAROQUE designs for jewellery, published by Jeremias Wolff of Augsburg in about 1715, and dedicated to Herr Paul Paulleti of Augsburg. It includes buckles, brooches, sword-hilts, etc., all heavily jewelled.

Schmittner, Franz Leopold (1703–61) Schmittner published in Vienna in about 1730 *Neu inventirtes Schlosser Reiss-Buch* (eight plates), with designs for iron keys, keyhole escutcheons, a crucifix, gates, screens, signs, etc., to be executed in an elaborate scrolled ACANTHUS and STRAPWORK style.

Schmoranz, Franz (1845–92) The son of an architect, Schmoranz was born in Slatinan. At the VIENNA 1873 EXHIBITION he designed the Khedive's pavilion. After having been inspector of textile instruction in Prague he was in 1885 appointed director of the applied arts school there. In 1889 he published a book on antique oriental glass. He designed glass in this manner for Lobmeyr, as did his brother Gustav, who also taught at the applied arts school from 1887 and whose glass designs were shown at the PARIS 1900 EXHIBITION.

Schmuz-Baudiss, Theodor Hermann (1859–1942) Born in Herrnhut, Schmuz-Baudiss studied at the Munich school of applied arts from 1879 to 1882 and then from 1882 to 1884 at the Munich Academy under Herterich, and from 1884 to 1890 under the painter Wilhelm von Lindenschmit (1829–95). Schmuz-Baudiss provided illustrations for 'JUGEND' and in 1896 trained as a potter at Diessen on the Ammersee. In 1897 he became a member of the MUNICH VEREINIGTE WERKSTÄTTE; from 1900 to 1901 he designed for the Werkstätte porcelain in a bold floral or foliate ART NOUVEAU style made by the Swaine & Co. factory at Hüttensteinach. Porcelain designed by Schmuz-Baudiss was shown at the PARIS 1900 EXHIBITION and the Dresden 1901 Exhibition. In 1902 he became a designer for the Berlin porcelain factory, where he became professor in 1904 and was from 1908 to 1926 artistic director, in succession to Alexander Kips (1856–1910). Schmuz-Baudiss's designs for Berlin used geometricized flowers and plants, and stylized landscapes.

Schneck, Adolf G. (1883–1971) Born in Esslingen, Schneck studied at Stuttgart school of applied arts, where he was a pupil of PANKOK and himself taught from 1923 to 1949. In 1924 Schneck designed for the Stuttgart Exhibition Die Form, in 1925 he joined the DEUTSCHE WERKBUND, from 1926 he contributed articles to 'Die FORM' and in 1927 he was involved in the

STUTTGART EXHIBITION. Schneck's *Der Stuhl* (1928) showed more or less MODERN chairs by Pankok, RIETVELD, BREUER, Dieckmann, CHAREAU, PERRIAND, DJO-BOURGEOIS, STAM, MIES VAN DER ROHE as well as many others: it also included designs by Schneck himself for the Deutsche Werkstätte and Thonet, English Windsor chairs and examples of Peach's Dryad cane chairs. In *Der Möbel als Gebrauchsgestand* (1928), which was dedicated to Pankok, Schneck presented his own decent, FUNCTIONAL, Modern designs for all types of furniture. PEVSNER, when he married, bought Schneck chairs. After the Second World War, Schneck continued to urge his commonsensical, Functionalist and Modern approach to design in teaching and writing.

Schongauer, Martin Born in Colmar in about 1450, Schongauer is recorded in 1456 at Leipzig University. He probably received some training from his father, a goldsmith, but later turned to painting. In 1469 he bought a house in Colmar and his earliest dated drawings are of this year. In 1489 he became a citizen of Breisach, where he was engaged on a large painting, but in 1491 he died in Colmar. Schongauer executed two superb engravings, one depicting an elaborate late-GOTHIC crozier, the other an equally splendid censer; whether these are designs or displays of virtuosity in draughtsmanship is difficult to determine. Schongauer also published four plates of single scrolled leaves for ornament, and five plates filled with scrolly Gothic foliage, one incorporating an owl being mobbed by birds. As one of the greatest late-Gothic artists in Germany, Schongauer had a strong influence on the young DÜRER, whose personal background was similar. His prints were widely copied, for example on Limoges enamels and on Italian maiolica.

Schönsperger, Johann the Younger Son of a celebrated publisher, Schönsperger experimented with printing designs on textiles. This was probably the inspiration for his creation of the first pattern-book for embroidery, *Furm- oder Modelbuchlein* (Augsburg, about 1523; twenty-four plates), consisting of geometric ornament or late-GOTHIC foliage, with some blanks to be filled out with designs by the purchaser. His *Ein new Modelbuch* (Zwickau, 1524; twenty-four plates) was very similar: the foliate border designs which it includes are attributed to Lucas Cranach the Elder. The last embroidery pattern-book published by Schönsperger, *Ein ney Fürmbüchlein* (Augsburg, about 1529; nineteen plates), displays Italian RENAISSANCE motifs, in the manner of Daniel HOPFER, who was then active in Augsburg. Schönsperger's pioneering pattern-books were copied in Italy, France and Germany, and his Gothic foliate borders were still retained in the repertoire of published embroidery designs in the early 17th century.

School of Design (Royal College of Art), London In 1835 the radical Member of Parliament William Ewart (1798–1839), prompted by the painter Benjamin Robert Haydon (1786–1846), moved the appointment of a Select Committee on Arts and Manufactures; it sat from 1835 to 1836. The Committee, impressed by design education in France and Bavaria and, particularly, by BEUTH's Gewerbeinstitut in Berlin, recommended the creation of a central school to train teachers and assist local schools. Even before the Committee reported the Board of Trade moved to set up a School of Design. Neither Ewart nor Haydon was involved. A Council was appointed including the pottery manufacturer William Copeland, the glass manufacturer Apsley Pellatt, and James Thomson of Clitheroe, a calico printer. They appointed J. B. PAPWORTH as first Director and the School opened at Somerset House in June 1837. Much to Haydon's disgust the study of the human figure was excluded from its curriculum, which comprised 'Elementary Outline Drawing' and 'Instruction for Design in Special Branches of Industry'. In June 1838 Papworth's post was abolished and DYCE, who had in 1837 published an influential pamphlet on the reorganization of the EDINBURGH TRUSTEES' ACADEMY and been sent by the Board of Trade to France and Germany to report on design education, was appointed Superintendent. The study of the human figure was admitted but a new stress was laid on knowledge of industrial techniques. By 1843 six branch schools had been founded, at Manchester, Spitalfields, York, Birmingham, Sheffield and Newcastle-upon-Tyne, and the Somerset House School was training teachers, as proposed in 1836. Dyce resigned and was appointed an Inspector to report on provincial schools in 1843 and succeeded by Charles Heath Wilson. In 1845 Haydon sent letters to *The Times* exposing a deep division between Wilson and J. R. Herbert (1810–90), who had successfully taught the figure since 1842 and was supported by a large faction of students. Herbert was dismissed but attacks continued; in 1845 A. W. N. PUGIN, a friend of Herbert, dismissed the School as 'a mere drawing school' in a letter in the 'BUILDER'. In 1845 Alfred STEVENS was employed as a teacher in the morning school; the evening teachers were H. J. Townsend (1810–90), drawing, ornament and modelling, J. C. Horsley (1807–1903), the figure class, replaced in 1846 by Richard REDGRAVE, and C. J. RICHARDSON, ornament and geometry. In 1846 Redgrave, Townsend

and Richardson protested about the shortcomings of the School; a Special Committee of the Council broadly endorsed their complaints and recommended reorganization. Three divisions resulted, a Class of Form, taught by Townsend, assisted by Richardson, a Class of Colour, taught by Horsley, and a Class of Ornament, with Dyce as master; Redgrave taught botanical drawing and WORNUM lectured. After criticism Dyce resigned and in 1849 the administration was once more changed. At this point Henry COLE's 'JOURNAL OF DESIGN AND MANUFACTURES' began to campaign for improvement in design education. A Select Committee was almost instantly appointed: it produced an equivocal report. However, Cole pressed his case for reform and at the beginning of 1852 was put in charge of the newly formed Department of Practical Art to administer the Schools, with Richard Redgrave as Art Superintendent. By 1860 the number of Schools had risen from twenty to eighty and pupils from 3,200 to 85,000. But despite an international *succès d'estime*, and the teaching of SEMPER and Owen JONES, whose *Principles of Decorative Art* (1853) provided the Thirty-Nine Articles of the reformed system, no great revival in design took place. The London School acted as the National Training School and taught teachers for the provincial schools. In 1857 the painter Sir Edward Poynter (1836–1919) became Principal and the bias towards the fine arts increased to such an extent that in 1888 more than three-quarters of the 426 students were fine artists. In 1896 Queen Victoria granted the School the title Royal College of Art. In 1898 Walter CRANE became Principal and in 1901 a complete reorganization divided the College into four schools, Architecture, Painting, Sculpture and Design; W. R. LETHABY was appointed professor of design. In 1936 the Hambledon

Committee recommended a fresh shake-up but this was delayed by the Second World War. In 1946 the Training Committee of the Council, under its secretary Professor Robert Darwen, proposed a new emphasis on design and a change of title to the Royal College of Design. Darwen was appointed Principal in 1948 and the Royal College of Art, title unchanged, became an independent national college. In 1967, on the recommendation of the 1963 Robbins Committee, the Royal College of Art became a university institution.

Schor, Giovanni Paolo (1615–74) Born in Innsbruck, the son of a painter, Schor worked in Rome from 1640, being elected a member of the Accademia di San Luca in 1654. In the late 1650s he worked under Pietro da CORTONA (1596–1669) on the painted decorations of the Palazzo Quirinale, together with his brother Egid (1627–1707), and in the 1660s he was a specialist in decoration in BERNINI's workshop, designing the floral ornament of Bernini's Cathedra Petri in 1665. The title-page for Kircher's *Musurgia Universalis* (1649), a coach and sugar table decorations for the entry of Queen Christina of Sweden (1655), a state bed for Pope Alexander VII (1660), the bed for the new-born son of Contestabile Colonna (1663), a shell drawn by sea-horses with flying putti holding a curtain above, and a golden rose (1680) are examples of Schor's work as a decorative designer, often on the papal pay-roll; he also designed candelabra, VASES, mitres, tapestry and embroidery. His reputation as a designer stood high, and his ornamental vocabulary, rich in ACANTHUS and sculptural figures, was, like that of Ciro FERRI, typical of the Roman BAROQUE.

Schorer, Hans Friedrich Born in about 1585 in Augsburg, the son of a painter, Schorer was a pupil of his father. He became a prolific designer of metalwork, working in an elaborate and accomplished BAROQUE style. His designs included cups, reliquaries, and statuettes. Schorer died in Augsburg after 1646.

Schreiber, Emma A needlewoman, Schreiber designed embroideries for the Hamburg embroidery workshop of Dr Marie Meyer (1878–90), some in a late-16th-century German style. Her work was praised by Justus Brinckmann of the HAMBURG MUSEUM FÜR KUNST UND GEWERBE.

Schübler, Johann Jakob Schübler was active as a mathematician and architectural theorist in Nuremberg from at least 1716. In 1738 he stated that he was also a painter and sculptor and a member of the Royal Prussian Academy of Science. He died in 1741. His many works covered the ORDERS, architecture, PERSPECTIVE, ornament and gardening. *Perspectiva, Pes Picturae* (Nuremberg, 1719, 1720) is one of the most spectacular treatises on perspective, with a text which refers to Sirigatti, SERLIO, Wenzel JAMNITZER and Hans VREDEMAN DE VRIES among many others, and fine plates which include designs for doors, urns and monuments. *Civil Bankunst* (Nuremberg, 1728) extends from the orders and architecture into ironwork and furniture. *Stüben-Oefen* (Nuremberg, 1728) displays elaborate and ingenious stoves and *Medaillen Schränke* (Nuremberg, 1730) equally prodigious bookcases and coin cabinets, several on the revolving principle. The culmination of Schübler's *œuvre* was the publication by Jeremias Wolff in Augsburg of a collection of 138 plates (1738), which includes beds, desks, one 'in the English manner', tables, clocks, church furniture, room settings, funerary decorations, etc. Although his works were based on a foundation of mathematics and perspective Schübler's style of ornament used an uninhibitedly elaborate BAROQUE GROTESQUE vocabulary which looked back to Jean I BERAIN, MAROT and DECKER. His works were widely disseminated; a desk was even copied by Batty LANGLEY.

Schulte, Rodolff Schulte was active as a jewellery designer in Paris in about 1620. His designs (six plates) were influenced by SYMONY and Wendel DIETTERLIN THE YOUNGER. They were reissued by Jacob HONERVOGT.

Schultz, Robert Weir (1860–1951) Born in Port Glasgow, Schultz was apprenticed in 1878 to the Edinburgh architect R. Rowand Anderson (1834–1921). In 1884 he moved to London to Norman SHAW's office, where LETHABY became his mentor (in 1899 Lethaby designed his book-plate). In 1885 Schultz became friendly with F. W. Troup (1859–1941), Ernest GIMSON, and Ernest and Sidney Barnsley. In 1889 he visited Greece with the latter, and their resulting *The Monastery of St Luke of Stiris in Phocis* (1901) is a major document of the Byzantine Revival. When Schultz set up practice in 1891 his first commissions were from the 3rd Marquess of Bute (1847–1900), BURGES's patron, for whom he designed furniture at St John's Lodge, Regent's Park, and the House of Falkland (1891–1909). From 1903 to 1908 he collaborated with Gimson on the furnishing of Old Place, Mochrum, for the 4th Marquess (1881–1947). In 1910 Schultz designed St Andrew's Chapel, Westminster Cathedral, including choir-stalls which were executed by Gimson, as were those designed by Schultz for Khartoum Cathedral. In 1920 Schultz was Master of the ART-WORKERS' GUILD.

Schuster, Franz (1892–1972) Born in Vienna, the son of a railway executive, Schuster studied at the school of applied arts in Berlin from 1912 to 1916, mainly under the architect Heinrich Tessenow (1876–1950). He worked in Tessenow's office up to 1922, moving with him to Hellerau in 1919 and working in Tessenow's community of craftsmen. In 1923 Schuster moved back to Vienna. From 1927 to 1936 he was in Frankfurt and from 1937 again in Vienna. Schuster was mainly active as a town planner and architect, but in Frankfurt he worked on the furnishing of modest houses and flats. His *Ein Möbelbuch* (1929) illustrated a series of 100 different types of simple furniture for machine production, based on four basic units. Schuster's unit furniture was widely produced in Germany and also in Sweden. It was used by Walter GROPIUS, MIES VAN DER ROHE and CHERMAYEFF.

Schwabe, Carlos (1866–1926) Born in Altona, Schwabe was brought up in Switzerland and was a pupil of the painter Joseph Mittey at the École des Arts Industriels in Geneva. In 1884 he moved to Paris, where he worked as a decorative painter, book illustrator and wallpaper designer. In 1892 he designed a poster for the Rose & Croix exhibition at the Galerie Durand-Ruel. Schwabe's book illustrations for Zola's *Le Rêve* (1892), d'Haraucourt's *L'Effort* (1894) and Baudelaire's *Les Fleurs du Mal* (1900) include superb examples of ART NOUVEAU floral ornament.

Schwartz, Stefan (1851–1924) Born at Neutra in Hungary, Schwartz was educated at the Vienna school of applied art, where he taught from 1876, becoming a professor in 1884. Schwartz was active as a sculptor, medallist and chaser, but also designed objects in silver, bronze and iron for all the leading Viennese manufacturers, such as Hanusch and Dziedzinsky and Politzer. His designs, often illustrated in 'BLÄTTER FÜR KUNSTGEWERBE', were usually in an elaborate and refined RENAISSANCE, MANNERIST, or BAROQUE style.

Schwertfeger, Johann Georg Schwertfeger was active in Nuremberg as an engraver of seals, armorials and stamps. His *Nutzliches Stempffelbüch* (Nuremberg, 1697; thirteen plates) is a manual of design for bookbinders. Schwertfeger favoured scrolly floral ornament, crudely executed but decoratively arranged.

Schwindrazheim, Oskar (1865–1952) Born in Hamburg, Schwindrazheim attended the applied arts schools there and in Munich. In 1889 he designed a poster for the Hamburg Exhibition. His main interest was German peasant art, and he helped to found an association, Volkskunst, which promoted its study, and a periodical, *Beiträge zu einer Volkskunst* (1891–3), which contained designs for ornament and furniture in peasant styles combined with formalized plant ornament by HAASE, KÄCKENHOFF and LOOSE, as well as Schwindrazheim himself. He specialized in designs for embroidery, wrought iron, ceramics and bookbindings, many of the latter being executed by Wilhelm Rauch (1868–1952). The peasant revival was encouraged by Justus Brinckmann. Schwindrazheim later published several historical works on peasant art, which included *Deutsche Bauernkunst* (1904).

Scoppa, Orazio Scoppa was active as a goldsmith in Naples from at least 1607 to 1668, when he executed the entrance screen to the chapel of the treasury in the cathedral of San Gennaro to the design of the architect Cosimo Fanzago (1591–1678). In 1642 and 1643 Scoppa published a series of large prints of chandeliers, sanctuary lamps, crozier heads, monstrances, VASES, etc. (eight-

een plates in all). They are in a massive and elaborate BAROQUE style, with a generous use of figures and scrolls. Considering their early date they are a remarkable anticipation of GIARDINI. Fanzago was doubtless the key influence on Scoppa.

Scott, Isaac Elwood (1845–1920) Born in Manayunk, Pennsylvania, Scott fought in the Civil War and then from 1867 worked as a carver in Philadelphia. By 1873 he was working as a designer in Chicago, and in 1875 he was designing furniture in the American 'EASTLAKE' style, strongly influenced by TALBERT. In 1874 to 1875 he went into partnership with Frederick W. Copeland as 'Designers, Carvers and Art Wood WORKERS'. In 1879 he designed vigorous earthenware vases made by the Chelsea Keramic Art Works of Massachusetts. In 1881 he exhibited frames at the Chicago Decorative Art Society, for which he designed an embroidered portière in 1885. In 1882 Scott described himself as a designer of interiors and architect, and·in 1883 he was in partnership with the architect Henry S. Jaffray. Scott later moved to New York and Boston (from 1889). He travelled to Europe in 1884 and 1900. Scott's most important patrons were the Glessner family of Chicago, for whom H. H. RICHARDSON designed a house in 1886.

Scott, William Bell (1811–90) Born in Edinburgh, the son of an engraver, Scott was educated at Edinburgh High School and afterwards at the EDINBURGH TRUSTEES' ACADEMY. After this he earned his living as an engraver, but also wrote poetry. In 1843 Scott sent a cartoon to the competition for decorations for the Houses of Parliament; it was unsuccessful but led to his appointment in 1844 as master of the School of Design at Newcastle, a post he held until 1864.

In 1845 Scott published *The Ornamentalist* (eighty-two plates), prefaced by an 'Essay on Ornamental Art': it included a wide variety of designs for ornament, etc., derived from prints by Wendel DIETTERLIN, Jean I BERAIN, BLONDEL, Zahn, Boetticher and others. In about 1847 Scott republished this material in selections of designs 'for Furniture and House Decoration', 'for Brass, Iron & Glass Work' and 'for Silver and Gold Work'. His *Antiquarian Gleanings in the North of England* (1851) is a compilation similar to Henry SHAW's *Specimens of Ancient Furniture* (1836). Scott was a prolific writer and book illustrator and also executed wall-paintings at Wallington (1856–68) and Penkill Castle (1868). In 1866 he designed a sideboard, 'all flowers and quatrefoils', for Calverley Lodge, a house designed for the Trevelyans of Wallington by Benjamin Woodward.

Sedding, John Dando (1838–91) Born in Eton, Sedding joined his elder brother, Edmund, in G. E. STREET's office in 1858. On leaving in 1863 he joined his brother's practice in Penzance. Edmund died in 1868 and Sedding moved to Bristol. In 1874 he moved to London and established himself as an architect and as a designer of embroidery, wallpapers and church metalwork. He was a great admirer of A. W. N. PUGIN and in 1876 met RUSKIN, by whom he was strongly influenced. Sedding's ecclesiastical designs are in a refined late-GOTHIC manner. In 1880 he contributed ten coloured plates of designs for interiors 'from the Tudor to the so-called Queen Anne' to T. Knight & Son's *Suggestion for House Decoration*. Sedding was a member of The Fifteen, founded in 1882 with Lewis F. DAY as its secretary. He was a member of the ART-WORKERS' GUILD, serving as its master in 1886 and 1887, and of the ARTS & CRAFTS EXHIBITION SOCIETY, showing the Westminster and Jacobean wallpapers at its first exhibition in 1888. Sedding's pupils included Ernest GIMSON, Alfred Powell and Henry WILSON, who took over his practice. His *Garden-Craft Old and New* (1891) was followed by the posthumous *Art and Handicraft* (1893). He was long revered by Arts & Crafts designers. In 1892 MACKINTOSH chose a Sedding statement as a motto for Glasgow designers: 'There is hope in honest error: none in the icy perfections of the mere stylist.'

Seddon, John Pollard (1827–1906) Born in London, the son of the cabinet-maker Thomas Seddon, Seddon was from 1848 to 1851 a pupil of the architect T. L. Donaldson (1795–1885). He then visited the continent and from 1852 to 1862 was in partnership with John Prichard (1818–86) in Llandaff. In 1852 he published *Progress in Art and Architecture, with Precedents for Ornament* (twelve plates), advocating GOTHIC ornament of a RUSKINIAN character. In 1857 he became a member of the Mediaeval Society and in 1860 he defended the Pre-Raphaelites at a meeting of the ECCLESIOLOGICAL SOCIETY. In 1862 Seddon moved to London. The LONDON 1862 EXHIBITION included on the William MORRIS firm's stand a roll-top desk designed by Seddon, made by Thomas Seddon, which employed geometrical inlay, notching, chamfering and stump columns, the whole vocabulary of Reformed Gothic furniture. His 'King René's Honeymoon Cabinet', shown on the same stand, uses the same style with the addition of painted panels by Morris, BURNE-JONES, ROSSETTI and Ford Madox BROWN; BURGES helped Seddon on the design of its inlay. Seddon published an account of the cabinet in 1898. Also in 1862 Seddon was appointed secretary of the Institute of British Architects with his friend,

Charles Forster Hayward (1831–1905), who designed some advanced and quirky Gothic furniture for the collector John Jones (1799–1882), including a bookcase with paintings by Rossetti. Seddon was a prolific designer of furniture from the late 1850s onwards, but little has been identified. He also designed vigorous stoneware for C. J. C. Bailey's Fulham Pottery from about 1875, including *jardinières* formed as Gothic capitals, and tiles for Maw & Co. Seddon designed stained glass for S. Belham & Co., church metalwork for Hart & Son, and church embroideries. At Abermad, a country house, he incorporated a rose window with Ruskin's Seven Lamps of Architecture in stained glass. From 1887 he was art editor of the *Building World*. A prolific architect and a steadfast Goth, Seddon was in partnership with J. C. Carter of Cardiff from 1893. His pupils included VOYSEY.

Seder, Anton (1850–1916) Born in Munich, Seder published in 1886 *Die Pflanze in Kunst und Gewerbe* (189 plates, many in colour); it comprised a wide range of plant illustrations by various artists, including ornamental treatments by Seder himself. In 1890 Seder was appointed director for the newly founded school of applied arts in Strasbourg. His *Naturalistische Decorationsmalereien* (1897–1903; sixty coloured plates) offered NATURALISTIC designs for decoration, mainly ART NOUVEAU in character. A book of controlled and professional designs for metalwork and glass (1899; fifty plates) was predominantly floral Art Nouveau in style. Seder was an editor of 'KUNSTGEWERBE IN ELSASS-LOTHRINGEN' and in 1901 published a 128-plate book of work done in the Strasbourg school. His elder brother, Adolph Seder, who died in 1881, designed furniture at Linderhof for LUDWIG II of Bavaria.

Seidl, Emanuel von (1856–1919) The younger brother of Gabriel von Seidl, with whom he worked at first, Emanuel von Seidl was an independent architect from 1888. He followed a more eclectic course than his brother, showing a Pompeian room at the Munich 1898 Exhibition but reverting to his brother's speciality, German RENAISSANCE, at Schloss Sigmaringen (1903). A prolific practice as an architect of town and country houses gave him an immense influence on interior design in Southern Germany, but he was not unsympathetic to newer trends, and Peter BEHRENS worked under his general direction on the German section of the Brussels 1910 Exhibition.

Seidl, Gabriel von (1848–1913) Born in Munich, Seidl worked in a locomotive factory until 1871, when he began to study architecture under Gottfried Neureuther (1811–87). In 1876 Seidl showed a Deutsche Wohnstube at the MUNICH EXHIBITION, a pioneering German RENAISSANCE Revival room, which successfully created a romantic ambience, complete in every detail. It was an enormous success and as a result Seidl, with the painter Rudolf von SEITZ, founded a decorating business in 1878, for which he designed furniture. Seidl and Seitz later collaborated in the decoration of the Bayerisches Nationalmuseum in Munich (1896–1900). There and in his many houses Seidl followed German Renaissance models.

Seitz, Rudolf von (1842–1910) Born in Munich, Seitz studied under his father, the painter Franz von Seitz (1817–83), and at the Munich Academy. In 1878 together with the architect Gabriel von SEIDL he founded an interior decorating business. Later, with Seidl, he decorated the Bayerisches Nationalmuseum in Munich, of which he was a curator from 1883. Seitz designed much ceremonial silver, posters, including one for the Munich 1888 Exhibition, and many diplomas and addresses.

Sellers, James Henry (1861–1954) Born in Oldham, the son of a cotton mill worker, Sellers started as office boy to a local architect. After working in various practices and having been from 1893 assistant county architect for Cumberland, Sellers set up practice in Oldham in 1899. In 1904 he went into partnership with Edgar WOOD and thenceforward designed refined furniture which combined some Arts & Crafts attitudes with rectilinear late 18th- and early 19th-century NEO-CLASSICAL forms. After Wood's retirement to Italy, Sellers continued to practise. He was active in the DESIGN AND INDUSTRIES ASSOCIATION and his designs were praised by John Gloag.

Selmersheim, Pierre The sons of an architect, Pierre Selmersheim and his brother Tony were collaborators of Charles PLUMET; Tony had been a founder member of Les Cinq. Pierre Selmersheim showed ART NOUVEAU furniture at the PARIS 1900 EXHIBITION and in 1925 edited a book of illustrations of architecture at the PARIS EXHIBITION, including his own folksy Lorraine restaurant.

Semper, Gottfried (1803–79) Born in Hamburg, where he received a good classical education before studying law and mathematics at Göttingen University from 1823 to 1825, Semper studied architecture in Munich in 1825 under Friedrich von Gärtner, and was then an assistant to Gau in Paris, where he met HITTORFF. From 1830 onwards Semper travelled widely in the South of France, Italy, Sicily and Greece. In 1833 he visited SCHINKEL in Berlin. Semper's travels gave him a lasting interest in antique polychromy, on which he published a paper in 1834, and an equally enduring taste for the ornament and architecture of the Italian RENAISSANCE. After briefly practising as an architect in Hamburg in 1834 Semper moved to Dresden, where he was professor at the school of building and established his fame with the design of the Dresden opera house (1838–41). In Dresden, Semper designed porcelain for the Meissen factory from 1835 to 1849, and metalwork such as lights for the Dresden Synagogue (1838–40). Having taken part in the revolution of 1849 Semper had to flee to Paris, where he became friendly with Jules DIÉTERLE and designed Sèvres porcelain. In 1850 Diéterle recommended Semper's services as a designer to Mr Graham of the London cabinet-makers Jackson & Graham. In September 1850 Semper moved to London, where in December he met Henry COLE. He subsequently designed the Egyptian, Swedish, Danish and Canadian sections at the LONDON 1851 EXHIBITION, the latter noted with approval in the 'JOURNAL OF DESIGN' (1851). In 1851 Semper was in contact with Herbert Minton and ARNOUX. His book *Wissenschaft, Industrie und Kunst* (1852) attracted the interest of Prince ALBERT. Semper was employed by Cole in 1852 at the SCHOOL OF DESIGN at Marlborough House, where he taught metalwork and furniture design. Semper designed furniture for Snell in 1852 and in 1854, assisted by his students, designed for Holland & Sons a cabinet in an eclectic Renaissance style shown at the PARIS 1855 EXHIBITION. However, Semper's most noted achievement at the School was the design in 1852 of the ornamental details of the rapidly produced funeral car of the Duke of Wellington, the main outline being by REDGRAVE. In 1854 Semper designed the Mixed Fabrics Court at the Crystal Palace in Sydenham; this project must have brought him into contact with

Owen JONES, but they do not seem to have been friendly. While in London, Semper elaborated the ideas on the origin of style in art expressed in his *magnum opus*, *Der Stil* (1861–3). According to Semper there were three basic methods of making, related to the structure of the primitive dwelling: weaving, derived from woven walls, ceramics, derived from the moulded earth, and joinery, derived from the wooden roof. Masonry, an extra which partly replaced the earlier methods of building, provided a fourth 'radical', and from these roots Semper derived the whole structure of style. His ideal museum, which united the arts and manufactures, was arranged according to the four radicals, although metalwork proved difficult to fit into the format. Semper's materialistic explanations of stylistic development and his respect for function and technique as the proper determinants of design had a profound influence, for instance on Meurer, GRAFF, Berlepsch, BERLAGE and LOOS. In 1906 Justus Brinckmann had executed for the Hamburg Senate an elaborate Semper design for a silver punch bowl, dated 1851. Semper moved in 1855 to Zürich, where he was professor at the polytechnic until 1871, exercising a dominant influence on Swiss architecture and design. From 1871 to 1876 he was in Vienna and then until his death mainly in Italy.

Sequeira, Domingos António (1768–1837) The son of a poor seaman of Belem, Sequeira was trained as a painter at the Royal School of Design and Sculpture in Lisbon from 1781. From 1788 to 1795 he studied in Rome, paid from the privy purse of Maria I. Back in Lisbon he was in 1802 appointed joint first painter to the court with Francisco Vieira (1765–1805). In 1811 he was commissioned by the Regent John VI to design a monumental silver service for presentation to the Duke of Wellington. Completed in 1816, when it was described in *Jornal de Bellas Artes ou Mnemosine Lusitana*, the service, executed under Sequeira's direct supervision, was a refined NEO-CLASSICAL exercise, comparable to contemporary designs by PRUD'HON and FLAXMAN.

Serlio, Sebastiano (1475–1554) Born in Bologna, Serlio worked as a painter of PERSPECTIVE in Pesaro from 1511 to 1514. He was thenceforward an assistant to Baldassare PERUZZI in Rome, inheriting many of his drawings and manuscripts. On the Sack of Rome in 1527 Serlio moved to Venice, where in 1528 he applied for a copyright to publish illustrations of the ORDERS, engraved by VENEZIANO, and in 1537 published Book IV of his treatise on architecture, dedicated to Ercole II of Ferrara. This work attracted a grant of 300 ducats from François I of France, to whom Serlio dedicated his Book III (Venice, 1540). In 1541 Serlio moved to France with the title of Peintre et Architecteur Ordinaire at Fontainebleau; it turned out to be an empty sinecure, as Serlio's French rivals ensured that he was excluded from practical design work. None the less, the French edition (1542) of his Book IV, which recommended the grotesque decoration of RAPHAEL, Giovanni da UDINE and, by implication, Serlio's fellow Bolognese, PRIMATICCIO, was probably influential. In Serlio's Books I and II (1545) he complained of COECK's unauthorized translations. On François I's death in 1547 Serlio ceded his title to Philibert de l'Orme and moved to Lyon with Cardinal Ippolito d'Este. His Book V was published in this year, and in 1551 his *Extraordinario Libro* on rustication. Books VI and VII were published posthumously by Jacopo da STRADA, who had bought their manuscripts from Serlio. Eclectic and autodidact though Serlio's works were, they had a profound influence in Northern Europe, above all through Coeck's editions, and especially by disseminating knowledge of the orders; Hans VREDEMAN DE VRIES was among those thus affected. A Spanish edition appeared in Toledo in 1563, and Robert Peake's 1611 London edition, dedicated to Henry, Prince of Wales, and also to 'Artificers of all sorts' noted that Serlio's ceiling designs could be applied to furniture.

Serrurerie, Journal de (1874–84) This Paris magazine contained fine designs for both structural and decorative ironwork, ancient and modern.

Serrurerie Pratique, Recueil de (1876–94) Edited by the architect N. Gateuil, who issued a similar work on 'MENUISERIE PRATIQUE', this Paris magazine contains designs for ironwork, mainly decorative and mainly modern.

Serrurier-Bovy, Gustave (1858–1910) Born in Liège, the son of a cabinet-maker, Serrurier studied architecture at the Académie des Beaux-Arts there from 1874, and was practising as an architect in 1883. He was early influenced by VIOLLET-LE-DUC. He seems to have visited England in 1884, when he married Maria Bovy, whose name he adopted, and opened a large shop in Liège to sell English and American furniture, wallpaper and fabrics, and Japanese goods, some supplied by LIBERTY's of London. His first catalogue (about 1890) borrowed designs from the 'CABINET MAKER' (1887) and the 'BRITISH ARCHITECT' (1887). In 1894, at VAN DE VELDE's suggestion, Octave Maus invited Serrurier to participate in the first La Libre Esthétique Salon in Brussels. He showed a Cabinet de Travail with furniture in a style described by a newspaper as '*rustico-gothico-britannique*', with a floral frieze

of English wallpaper. In 1895 Serrurier showed a Chambre d'Artisan, whose plain wood furniture with iron mounts incorporates strong curved elements, a departure from Serrurier's earlier English Arts & Crafts prototypes. Also in 1895 Serrurier helped to organize the Liège L'Œuvre Artistique exhibition, and showed a room. GUIMARD was also involved, and Francis Newbery brought a group of works from Glasgow. In 1896 he opened a shop in Brussels and showed at the London ARTS & CRAFTS EXHIBITION. In 1898 his Salon for the Hôtel Chatham in Paris was praised in 'ART ET DÉCORATION' and in 1899 he opened a branch of his shop, L'Art dans l'Habitation, in Paris, with the architect René Dulong as his partner. By this date he was running a large factory in Liège. Serrurier designed the interior for Dulong's Le Pavillon Bleu at the PARIS 1900 EXHIBITION and in 1901 they visited the DARMSTADT EXHIBITION together: Serrurier found OLBRICH's designs impressive but theatrical. His own career reached a prolific apogee in about 1902. In that year Van de Velde praised his achievement in 'INNEN-DEKORATION', he became president of the Avant-Garde group, and began to build his own villa near Liège. His style was by now a strong curvilinear ART NOUVEAU. He opened branches of his business in The Hague in 1904 and in Nice in 1907; his designs were ubiquitous at the Liège 1905 Exhibition. In 1907 Serrurier's business suffered a financial crisis, but he recovered to show at the Brussels 1910 Exhibition before his death. His style at this last moment changed towards reticence and rectilinearity. Apart from furniture Serrurier designed stained glass, wallpaper and ironwork. However his importance was more as a crucial link between English design and the continent than as a great innovative designer.

Sévin, Louis Constant (1821–88) Born in Versailles, the son of an actor, Sévin was apprenticed in 1834 to the Parisian sculptor Marneuf. In 1839 he went into partnership with two sculptors, Phénix and Joyau, to produce metalwork for leading manufacturers such as FROMENT-MEURICE, Sévin acting as designer. During the 1848 revolution Sévin went to London to work for Jean Valentin Morel (1794–1860), designing his contributions to the LONDON 1851 EXHIBITION, including rich cups in the Islamic, RENAISSANCE and ROCOCO styles. In 1851 Sévin returned to France, where he designed for the Limoges porcelain manufacturer, Jouhanneaud & Dubois, who showed ceramics based on 17th-century Italian and German prototypes to Sévin's design at the PARIS 1855 EXHIBITION. In 1855 Sévin went back to Paris, accepting a post as *sculpteur-ornemaniste* with Ferdinand Barbedienne (1810–92), where he remained until his death. Sévin designed bronzes for the Hôtel de Paiva (1855–66) and for the Royal Mausoleum at Frogmore (1861–2). He was awarded medals at the LONDON 1862 EXHIBITION and PARIS 1867 EXHIBITION. The main styles he used were Néo-Grec and Renaissance revival, with oriental and NATURALISTIC elements. But although his knowledge of historic styles was immense, Sévin was never a copyist; his was a synthetic eclectic style of great refinement and richness. His masterpiece was a cup with a jasper bowl, mounted in enamel with St George and the Dragon, in the style of about 1600, made for Henry Thomas Hope (1808–62), son of Thomas HOPE, shown at the Paris 1855 Exhibition.

Sezenius, Valentin Sezenius published three suites of black stretched GROTESQUE ornament for enamelling in 1619 to 1620, 1622, and 1622 to 1624, a total of some fifteen plates. Among them is a febrile and elongated representation of the Adoration of the Shepherds for execution in enamel. Sezenius's style is similar to the later manner of Matthias BEYTLER.

Shaw, Henry (1800–1873) Born in London, Shaw was employed by John Britton (1771–1857) as a draughtsman in his *Cathedral Antiquities of England*. Shaw's first book, *A Series of Details of Gothic Architecture* (1823; twenty-one plates), reflects this apprenticeship. *Examples of Ornamental Metalwork* (1836; fifty plates) contains designs dated 1825 and 1826 by Shaw himself for iron railings in the Grecian style, as well as designs by Lewis Vulliamy (1791–1871) and BRIDGENS; there are GOTHIC designs and an Elizabethan lantern in WILLEMENT's collection. *Illuminated Ornaments Selected from Manuscripts of the Middle Ages* (1833; forty plates dated from 1830), with a text by Sir Frederick Madden (1801–73), was the first of a series of works in which Shaw explored the antiquarian and practical sides of illumination and lettering. They include *Alphabets, Numerals and Devices of the Middle Ages* (1845; forty-eight plates), *Handbook of Mediaeval Alphabets and Devices* (1853; thirty-six plates), and *Hand Book of the Art of Illumination as practised during the Middle Ages* (1866) to promote which Shaw held an exhibition of his own copies of medieval illumination. Shaw copied manuscripts in the British Museum for BURGES, and designed numerous addresses and testimonials as well as decorations for the New Testament (Longmans, 1864) and G. W. Thornbury's *Two Centuries of Song* (1867). *Specimens of Ancient Furniture* (1836; seventy-four plates dated from 1832), with a text by Sir Samuel Rush Meyrick (1783–1848), contained illustrations of mainly Gothic and Elizabethan furniture and metalwork, including pieces belonging to prominent dealers, such as John Webb, or collectors, such as T. L. Parker (1779–1858), to whom *Specimens* was dedicated. *Specimens* was recommended by LOUDON, and by the 'BUILDER' (1844), which advised young cabinet-makers to buy sheets. Some of the plates were copied in Asselineau's *Objets du Moyen Âge et de la Renaissance* (Paris, 1844) and *Specimens* was listed with other works by Shaw in an 1853 bibliography by J. C. ROBINSON. *Details of Elizabethan Architecture* (1839; sixty plates, many dated 1834), with a text by Thomas Moule (1784–1851), contained mainly architectural ornament; *The Encyclopedia of Ornament* (1842; sixty plates) was more wide-ranging. In 1848 Shaw published a reprint of GEDDE's *A Booke of Sundry Draughtes*, with a few extra designs by Willement. *Dresses and Decorations of the Middle Ages* (1843; ninety-four plates) and *The Decorative Arts, Ecclesiastical and Civil, of the Middle Ages* (1851; forty plates) both include enamels, furniture and metal-work, among which an iron gate in COTTINGHAM's collection, which Shaw catalogued in 1851. *Specimens of Tile Pavements* (1858; forty-seven plates) depicted Gothic encaustic tiles; Herbert Minton, Anthony Salvin, Willement and Burges were subscribers. Shaw's works, although partly antiquarian in purpose, were also intended for the inspiration of designers, and exercised a wide influence.

Shaw, Richard Norman (1831–1912) Born in Edinburgh, the son of a struggling lace merchant, Shaw was articled to the architect William Burn (1789–1870) in about 1849, after a move to London. Early influenced by A. W. N. PUGIN, Shaw was soon converted to GOTHIC, which he studied in Europe from 1854 to 1856, making drawings published as *Architectural Sketches from*

the Continent (1858). In 1856 he entered the office of Anthony Salvin (1799–1881), whose nephew, W. E. NESFIELD, had become a close friend. In 1859 Shaw was made G. E. STREET's principal assistant in succession to Philip WEBB, and in the same year showed two extrovert designs of 1858 for Gothic organs, more influenced by BURGES than Street, at the Architectural Exhibition. In 1861 Shaw showed a desk made to his own design for his own use by James Forsyth at the same exhibition; it was shown again at the LONDON 1862 EXHIBITION. Architectural, with revealed construction, geometric inlay and stump columns, it is a classic of the Reformed Gothic style. Shaw began to practise on his own as an architect in 1862, sharing an office with Nesfield from 1863 until 1876, and a partnership from 1866 to 1869. In the 1860s Nesfield and Shaw evolved the Old English style, and from about 1870 Shaw used the Queen Anne style in towns. After 1880 he turned to classicism. Gothic remained his church style, as in the fittings for Bingley (1867 onwards), his altar frontal for Meerbrook (1870), and even secular furniture such as his cradle for Alfred WATERHOUSE's son Julian (1867) and his owl beds at Cragside (about 1876) often retain a massive Gothic character. But as early as 1865 at Willesley, Shaw had incised Japanese patterns on plaster and designed rush-seated corner chairs based on models of about 1730. Shaw was a collector of blue-and-white porcelain, and in 1875 designed a shop-front for Murray Marks, the leading dealer. From the mid-1870s Shaw designed furniture made by W. H. Lascelles and decorated by J. Aldam Heaton, Shaw's favoured decorator whose 1887 *Catalogue* shows a whole range of furnishings designed by or for Shaw. A group by Lascelles was shown at the PARIS 1878 EXHIBITION. Shaw also designed cast-iron fireplaces for Coalbrookdale and

Elsleys. However, he came to rely for fittings on the work of other designers, for example BURNE-JONES, WHALL and HOLIDAY for stained glass, and DE MORGAN for tiles, and on the assistants in his office, most notably LETHABY, for decorative details. His pupils provided the nucleus of the ART-WORKERS' GUILD, but Shaw stood apart, although he showed at the 1890 ARTS & CRAFTS EXHIBITION a silver box made to his design for presentation to the Royal Academy. Shaw was an avid clock collector, and a clock case in a highly personal English BAROQUE manner of about 1885 survives. But towards the end of his life most of Shaw's attention was occupied by his great works as an architect.

Shearer, Thomas Shearer signed seventeen of the twenty plates in *The Cabinet-Makers' London Book of Prices* (1788), a tabulated schedule of the cost of cabinet work. The designs are predominantly conservative with NEO-CLASSICAL details; some have changed little since CHIPPENDALE'S *Director* (1754). A dressing-table was anticipated by Thomas MALTON in 1779. The second edition of the *Book of Prices* (1793) contains extra plates by HEPPLEWHITE and by W. Casement. SHERATON, surprisingly, praised the designs in the *Book of Prices* by contrast to those of Hepplewhite.

Sheraton, Thomas (1751–1806) Born in Stockton-on-Tees, Sheraton is said to have worked for many years as a journeyman cabinet-maker. A long-case clock whose case is labelled by Sheraton is said to exist in Durham, but two engravings of Stockton High Street signed 'T. Sheraton' and dated 1785 are more prophetic of his future interests, as indeed is a Baptist tract on the Doctrine of Regeneration (1782). Having moved to London, Sheraton estab-

lished himself as a drawing-master specializing in furniture design. His first work, mainly published in parts from 1791 to 1793, was *The Cabinet-Maker and Upholsterer's Drawing Book* (1793–4). A second edition appeared in 1794, when a German version, translated by G. T. Wenzel, was published in Leipzig; a third English edition was issued in 1802. In the *Drawing Book*, dedicated 'To Cabinet-Makers and Upholsterers in General', Sheraton mentions the works of CHIPPENDALE, INCE and Mayhew, HEPPLEWHITE and others, but while his tone is charitable he finds them all deficient as teachers of PERSPECTIVE, the subject which, combined with geometry and the ORDERS, occupied the first two parts of the *Drawing Book*. MALTON in his *New Road to Geometry* (second edition, 1793) combined faint praise of Sheraton with some technical strictures on his perspective, and Sheraton, who had acknowledged Malton's earlier works on the subject, was stung to a riposte in his second edition. Sheraton's perspective is explicitly calculated to be of use to the furniture trade, although he cannot resist lengthy historical asides and references to such authorities as Vitruvius, CHAMBERS, Dr Brook Taylor and Mr Kirby. Part III of the *Drawing Book*, however, was intended to 'exhibit the present taste in furniture' and comprises mainly NEO-CLASSICAL designs, strongly influenced by the Frenchified style of HOLLAND, whose work Sheraton had seen at York House and Carlton House; the Chinese drawing-room at Carlton House was illustrated in the *Drawing Book*. Sheraton's designs, accompanied by lengthy and interesting technical commentaries, are competent and elegant, but display that tendency to over-ornament so common in the ARTISAN designer. The *Drawing Book* attracted over 600 subscribers, almost without exception connected with the furniture trade and including all the best firms; most were in London, but Sheraton's reputation in his native North-East is attested by a large group of subscribers in that area. Sheraton's trade card, issued from his Wardour Street address between 1795 and 1799, stated that he 'Teaches Perspective, Architecture and Ornaments, makes Designs for Cabinet-makers and sells all kinds of Drawing Books &c.'. In 1799 Sheraton moved back to Stockton-on-Tees and was ordained a Baptist minister. In 1802 however he returned to London and in 1803 published his *The Cabinet Diction-ary*, the first trade pattern-book to respond to the new archaeological approach to furniture design implicit in TATHAM's *Ancient Ornamental Archi-tecture* (1799). Sheraton's plates dem-onstrate that his was a distinctly *ad hoc* response to the change in fashion: the new motifs, particularly the animal ele-ments of Roman furniture, are applied to old forms. The entries in the text of the *Dictionary* are full of useful technical information but sometimes stray far from furniture. Sheraton's final work, *The Cabinet-Maker, Upholsterer, and General Artist's Encyclopaedia*, was uncompleted at his death in 1806. Its plates range in date from 1804 to 1807, some thus being engraved after his death: thirty accompanied the only full volume issued (1805), covering A to C, which sold nearly a thousand copies, some subscribers being canvassed by Sheraton during a trip to Ireland for that purpose. Also in 1805 he published a final religious pamphlet, *The Character of God as Love*. The plates of the *Encyclopaedia* resemble in character those in the *Dictionary*, at times inco-herent, but mainly competent and of a fashionable character; Sheraton would doubtless have been aware of the early plates of George SMITH's *Household Furniture*, which began to appear in 1804. The text of the *Encyclopaedia* is decidedly eccentric, the entries ranging from Baptism to Balls of Fire, but its indiscipline and ambition is surely char-acteristic of the artisan autodidact, not of the mental collapse discerned by some in Sheraton's later works. All the evi-dence agrees to his ability and energy. However Sheraton's death left his family in poverty. In 1812 a posthumous collec-tion of eighty-four *Designs for House-hold Furniture* taken from Sheraton's earlier works was published by J. TAYLOR. The influence of his designs on the furniture trade was immense. The firm of Gillows adapted his designs; in America the cabinet-maker John Sey-mour owned a copy of the *Drawing Book* and two others, William Camp in Baltimore and Joseph Barry in Phila-delphia, both used Sheraton designs on their trade cards. The *Drawing Book* was first republished in 1895 and Shera-ton has since become the popular adjective to describe the English furni-ture style from about 1790 to 1800.

Shorleyker, Richard A publisher, Shor-leyker succeeded Walter Dight, who had published GEDDE's book for glaziers (1615). Shorleyker issued *A schole-house, for the needle* (London, 1624; sixty-four plates), a pattern-book which included a wide range of original designs for leaves, flowers and animals, as well as some copies after SIBMACHER, VINCIOLO, MIGNERAK and others. *A schole-house* was reprinted at least three times up to 1632.

Sibmacher, Johann From about 1590, Sibmacher was a highly productive engraver and designer of ornament, working in Nuremberg in a manner often very close to Jost AMMAN. His works include copies after J. A. DuCER-CEAU's 1550 GROTESQUE book, a suite of twelve plates of grotesque panels and friezes for goldsmiths (1592), sixteen plates of beakers (1596), and another suite of designs for goldsmiths, *Fysirvn-gen Zum Verzeichnen Für Die Goldt-schmidt* (1599). It is probable that Hans Melchior Sibmacher, a court gold-smith in Vienna in about 1625, was a relation. However, Sibmacher was more eminent as a designer of needlework than of goldsmiths' work. His first work in this field, *Schön neues Modelbuch* (Nuremberg, 1597; forty-eight plates), was the earliest German embroidery pattern-book to be engraved rather than woodcut. It contains highly competent geometric designs for embroidery, remi-niscent of SCHÖNSPERGER, some incor-porating figures, and designs for cutwork in the PAGANO manner. Sibmacher's second embroidery pattern-book, *Newes Modelbuch in Kupffer gemacht* (Nuremberg, 1601; sixty-eight plates), was no less professional than his first, but even larger and richer, both in the range of techniques it represented and in its repertoire of ornament, including many figures in contemporary dress. Both Sibmacher's pattern-books were often reprinted and copied by KAHR, BOLER and others, the second being reissued in Leipzig as late as 1736. After 1601 Sibmacher devoted himself almost exclusively to heraldry, following his small *Wappenbuch* (Nuremberg, 1596) with his large *Wappenbuch* (Nuremberg, 1605 and 1609). The latter became a standard work on German heraldry, often reprinted up to 1806, and recast in a massive new edition from 1855. Sib-macher died in 1611.

Silber, Jonas Silber was first trained as a goldsmith by Samuel Spillmann in Bern and subsequently by Wenzel JAM-NITZER in Nuremberg, where he be-came a master in 1572. From 1578 Sil-ber spent two years as court goldsmith in Heidelberg and from 1587 worked for two years at the Danzig mint. In 1589 he was again in Nuremberg. Silber issued numerous prints in the dotted manner for the decoration of metalwork, with STRAPWORK and allegories, very much in the manner of ZAN. Many are dated 1582 or 1590.

Silver, Arthur (1853–96) Born in Read-ing, the son of a cabinet-maker, Silver attended Reading School of Art from 1869. After leaving in 1872 he was apprenticed to H. W. BATLEY and became a versatile professional designer. In 1880 he opened his own studio, which prospered. He designed some interior schemes, and many wallpapers for Jef-frey & Co., W. Woollams, including The Fig, shown at the 1888 ARTS & CRAFTS EXHIBITION, and Charles Knowles & Co., and many textiles, including silks for Warners & Sons such as Princesss May of Teck's wedding dress (1893). In 1888 Silver subscribed to BING's *Artistic Japan*. Japan, J. Moyr SMITH, Albert Moore, William MORRIS, Walter CRANE and VOYSEY were among the many influences he underwent. In 1889 Silver paid tribute to another source of inspiration by publishing the Silvern Series of photographs, representing tex-tiles in the South Kensington Museum (now the VICTORIA & ALBERT MUSEUM). In 1894 Silver's friend Glee-son White, to whose *Practical Design* (1894) Silver contributed textiles and floorcloths, wrote in the 'STUDIO' on the Silver Studio, and in 1895 Silver launched Rottmann-Silver Stencil dec-orations collaborating with Alexander Rottmann, an importer of Japanese papers. Silver was widely recognized as one of the leading commercial designers of the 1890s; MUTHESIUS for example praised his wallpapers and Walter Crane described him as 'an able and graceful designer'. His assistants included John Illingworth Kay (1870–1950) and Harry Napper.

Silver, Rex (1879–1965) The elder son of the designer Arthur SILVER, Rex

Silver became a member of the Junior Art-Workers' Guild in 1896. In 1901 he took over the management of the Silver Studio together with his brother Harry (1882–1972), a gifted designer in the ART NOUVEAU style, influenced by Archibald KNOX, who seems to have worked for the Studio in 1898. Since Arthur Silver's death in 1896 the Studio had been managed successively by the designers Harry Napper (to 1898) and J. R. Houghton. Under Rex Silver's management the Studio survived until 1963, responding to every change in style and particularly expert at neo-18th-century and floral patterns. In the 1900s many textile patterns, often influenced by VOYSEY, were exported to France and Belgium, and from about 1910 America became an important market. Designers employed by the Studio included Frank Price, Winifred Mold, Madeleine Lawrence and Lewis Jones.

Simonin, Claude (1635–1721) In 1685 *Plusieurs Pieces et Ornements D'arque-buzerie* (twelve plates) was published in Paris. It contains a wide range of French BAROQUE designs for ornamental engraving on fire arms. The title calls Simonin the designer, and states that the designs had been used by the royal gunsmith, Laurent de Languedoc, for whom Simonin presumably worked. A second edition was published in Paris in 1705, and pirated editions appeared in Amsterdam in 1691 and 1692, and in Nuremberg. Through dissemination Simonin's designs were widely influential.

Slodtz, Michel-Ange (1705–64) René Michel Slodtz, called Michel-Ange, was born in Paris a younger son of the sculptor and designer Sébastien Slodtz. He studied sculpture at the Academy, won the second prize, travelled to Rome in 1728 and remained there until 1746. In Rome Slodtz was probably respon-

sible for the design of a Chinese masquerade for the 1735 carnival, but also became friendly with the architect Jacques Germain Soufflot (1709–80), who arrived there in 1734. When Slodtz returned to Paris in 1746 he brought with him works by PIRANESI and, unlike his brothers Sébastien Antoine SLODTZ and Paul Ambroise, who worked in the ROCOCO style, was an early pioneer of NEO-CLASSICISM. He had an influential enemy in CAYLUS, but C.-N. COCHIN was a friend and engineered the protection of the Marquis de MARIGNY and, in 1755, a pension. In 1758 Slodtz succeeded his brother Paul Ambroise as Dessinateur de la Chambre et du Cabinet du Roi, and in 1760 designed a catafalque in Notre Dame, Paris, for the King and Queen of Spain, which was seen as a manifesto of neo-classicism. Slodtz also designed church furniture, including a heavily classical altar for Vienne Cathedral in 1744 to 1747, and neo-classical iron choir-screens for the cathedrals of Amiens (1758) and Bourges (1760), the latter by the smith Joseph Pérez. His pulpit at Saint-Merry of 1760 combines rich palm decoration, reminiscent of VARDY, with neo-classical details. Among the possessions listed in Slodtz's inventory were paintings by JACQUES and a drawing by DELLA BELLA.

Slodtz, Sébastien Antoine (1695–1754) A son of the sculptor and designer Sébastien Slodtz, who died in 1726, and a grandson of the royal cabinet-maker, Dómenico Cucci, Slodtz was mainly active as a designer. In 1750 he was appointed Dessinateur du Cabinet du Roi in succession to MEISSONIER. He collaborated closely with his younger brother, Paul Ambroise Slodtz (1702–58), a sculptor who became a member of the Academy in 1743. Paul Ambroise succeeded his brother as Dessinateur du Roi, and left a considerable fortune, his estate including the works of OPPENORD. Among the most celebrated designs by the Slodtz brothers were a clock for the King of Portugal in 1728, a medal cabinet made for Louis XV by Gaudreaux in about 1738, and a commode of 1739 for the King's bedroom made by Gaudreaux with bronzes by Caffieri. They also designed ROCOCO console tables for the Château de Compiègne in 1739, twenty-eight gueridons for Versailles in 1743, and a large bookcase for the King's cabinet there in 1744. A throne designed for Louis XV in 1743 carries asymmetry to the point of ungainliness; it was copied in 1751 by the Swedish designer and architect Jean REHN. The Slodtz brothers also designed picture frames, bronzes and church furniture.

Small, John W. An Edinburgh architect, probably a pupil of Rowand Anderson (1834–1921), Small published *Scottish Woodwork of the 16th and 17th centuries* (1878) and *Leaves from my Sketch Books* (1880, reprinted 1901), both with drawings of mainly Scottish furniture etc.; the latter included 'Robert P. Clark, Furniture Designer, of Edinburgh' among its subscribers. Small's next book, *Ancient and Modern Furniture* (1833, reprinted 1903), included twenty-five plates of competent designs for modern furniture in the Italian, Queen Anne, CHIPPENDALE and SHERATON, and ADAM's (sic) styles. Most of the leading English and Scottish cabinet-makers subscribed; among those who made the designs were Chapman & Son of Newcastle, John Pollock of Beith, and Robertson & Son of Alnwick.

Šmišek, Johann Born in Prague before 1585, Šmišek seems to have been in Innsbruck in 1603, and from 1604 to 1640 to have worked in Munich and Prague. His *Neues Groteschgen-Büchlein* (Munich, 1618; eighteen plates) is a perfect demonstration of how the Flemish STRAPWORK GROTESQUE of Cornelis FLORIS and others was stretched and curved into a degree of AURICULARITY. It consists of panels of lively ornament in this transitional style inhabited by vigorous huntsmen and peasants. This arrangement anticipates ROCOCO ornament and designs by Šmišek are used on lock designs (1736) by J. G. Tauber, on Vienna porcelain decorated in Augsburg and on Meissen porcelain, both dating from about 1730. Šmišek's designs were copied in J. C. REIFF's *Zierathen Büchel vor Glasschneider und Künstler*, in about 1710.

Smith, Bernard E. Smith's *Designs and Sketches for Furniture in the Neo-Jacobean and Other Styles* (1875; fifty-six plates) contains highly competent designs for furniture and interiors in the late TALBERT manner followed by three fascinating interiors, serving as advertisements for Henry Capel's Art Furniture, in part designed by Brightwen Binyon. Smith showed a design for a dining-room at the Royal Academy in 1875 and in 1876 travelled abroad as a Royal Academy student. He was later Assistant Colonial Engineer in Gibraltar, and published two books of sketches (1880 and 1883).

Smith, George In 1806 Smith, who described himself as 'Upholder Extraordinary to His Royal Highness the Prince of Wales', advertised in *The Times* the second part of his *Designs for Household Furniture* and announced that he was able to manufacture furniture from his designs. The complete work, *A Collection of Designs for Household Furniture and Interior Decoration* (1808), contained 158 coloured plates, predominantly of Grecian furniture but with some designs in the

GOTHIC, Egyptian and Chinese styles; two copies were in Thomas HOPE's library. Already at this date Smith described himself as 'Draughtsman in Architecture, Perspective and Ornament'. From 1801 he contributed designs to ACKERMANN's *Repository*. His *A Collection of Ornamental Designs* (1812; forty-three plates) contains neat outline lithographs of ornament, furniture, metalwork etc. in the Grecian style, influenced by TATHAM's *Examples*, and anticipating Ackermann's later *Selection*. Smith's last book, his *Cabinet-Maker's and Upholsterer's Guide, Drawing Book and Repository* (1826; 145 plates), described him as 'Upholsterer and Furniture Draughtsman to his Majesty, Principal of the Drawing Academy, Brewer Street, Golden Square', an address occupied about this date by an upholsterer called William Smith, who was presumably a relation; Smith himself claimed in his *Guide* that he had had forty years' experience in his trade. The plates are dated from 1826 to 1828, and cover geometry, PERSPEC-TIVE, as well as the design of ornament and furniture. The styles were Egyptian, Greek, Etruscan, Roman, Gothic and Louis XIV. Smith clearly disapproved of the latter, ascribing its introduction to Philip and Benjamin WYATT's work at Crockford's gaming-rooms 'in direct opposition to the chaste Grecian taste of the late Mr James Wyatt'. James WYATT, Hope, Thomas CHIPPENDALE THE YOUNGER, BOILEAU and BOG-AERT were designers admired by Smith. He also recommended DENON's *Égypte*, Gell's *Pompeii* and HAMILTON's *Vases* as source-books. Smith himself was one of the most gifted professional designers of the early 19th century and his admiration for Hope was probably, as he claimed, reciprocated. Hope's scorn was probably reserved for minor figures such as G. COOPER.

Smith, J. Moyr Smith commenced work in London as a designer in the studio of Christopher DRESSER, to whom he dedicated his first book, *Studies for Pictures* (Moxon, 1868; twenty-five plates); this sets a pattern of mawkish sentimentality, facetiousness and allegory, which was to remain constant throughout Smith's later work. In 1871 he lithographed all the plates and contributed designs to *Sketches of Artistic Furniture* by Collinson & Lock, the cabinet-makers, which also contained designs by COLLCUTT. A second book of illustrations, *Theseus, A Greek Fairy Legend* (1872; six plates), was followed by chromolithographed illustrations to *The Childhood of Christ*, published by F. Warne & Co., and by the magazine 'DECORATION', edited by J. Moyr Smith from 1881. His *Album of Decorative Figures* (1882; fifty plates) contained illustrations drawn from *Decoration*, which showed Minton tiles designed by Smith and shown at the PARIS 1878 EXHIBITION; other Smith designs included pottery plaques for W. B. Simpson & Sons, a bookcase for COX & Son, and decorations for J. G. CRACE and the Holloway Sanatorium at Virginia Water. Also in 1882 Smith published *Ancient Greek Female Costume*, an expanded version of HOPE's *Costume of the Ancients* (1809). Smith's last book, *Ornamental Interiors* (1887), was a history of interior decoration from Egypt to modern times, in which he traced recent improvement in design to TALBERT's *Gothic Forms* (1868). In it Smith alludes to his own designs for Marcus Ward's Christmas cards and fairy-tale books, and to thousands of designs for wallpaper, carpets, tapestries, metalwork, and pottery, many done in Dresser's studio. BATLEY, Lewis F. DAY, Owen DAVIS and Margetson were among the commercial designers praised by Smith, who also recognized the influence of STREET,

WATERHOUSE, Norman SHAW, GODWIN and SEDDON. From 1888 to 1894 Smith showed designs for decoration at the Royal Academy; he then described himself as 'Decorative Artist'.

Soane, Sir John (1753–1837) Born in Goring-on-Thames, the son of a bricklayer, Soane entered the office of the architect George Dance junior (1741–1825) in 1768 and in 1771 began to attend the Royal Academy Schools. His youthful *Designs in Architecture* (1778) included two very quirky NEO-CLASSICAL garden benches: Soane later tried to suppress this youthful work. He travelled to Italy from 1778 to 1780 and in the late 1780s began to establish a highly successful architectural career working in an increasingly abstract version of the neo-classical style. In 1788 he was appointed architect to the Bank of England and in 1832 he was knighted. In 1805 Soane designed dashing ivory and ebonized furniture for his GOTHIC Library at Stowe, also furnished with Goanese ebony chairs. Soane may also have designed neat neo-classical furniture made for his own house and elsewhere by the cabinet-maker John Robins, for whom he designed a house in Park Lane in 1812 and premises in Regent Street in 1820 to 1821. Soane's own house and collections in Lincoln's Inn Fields, of which he published a *Description* in 1833, was left to the nation, a remarkable and personal affirmation of the 'unity of the arts'; among its treasures are nearly 9,000 ADAM drawings, purchased by Soane in 1833.

Society of Arts, Royal In 1753 William Shipley (1715–1803), a painter, drawing-master and philanthropist, issued proposals for a fund to finance premiums to promote improvements in the 'Liberal Arts and Sciences, Manufactures, &c.' and seven months later a scheme for executing these proposals through 'a Society for the Encouragement of Arts, Sciences, and Manufactures'. The Dublin Society, founded in 1731, had from 1740 awarded premiums which acted as a precedent for Shipley's scheme. The Society was founded in 1754 and Shipley acted as its secretary until 1760. Shipley, who knew G. M. MOSER and probably had other contacts with the St Martin's Lane Academy, also ran his own drawing school, Shipley's School, which endured until 1761. In an advertisement of 1757 he offered 'to introduce Boys and Girls of Genius to Masters and Mistresses in such Manufactures as require Fancy and Ornament'. Many pupils won premiums for textile designs from the Society of Arts. In 1758 the Society recognized Shipley's personal services by the award of a gold medal designed by James 'Athenian' STUART. CHIPPENDALE was elected a member in 1760. Although in 1778 the Society claimed to have encouraged 'elegance of pattern' among weavers and calico printers, it seems to have been inactive in design improvement until 1843, when Prince ALBERT became its President. In 1845 the Society's annual competition was expanded to include 'industrial products embodying artistic design'. In 1846 a tea service designed by Henry COLE, as Felix Summerly, and made by Herbert Minton, was awarded a silver medal and ten guineas. Cole subsequently persuaded many of his friends to join the Society, including MACLISE, Owen JONES, John BELL and J. G. CRACE. In 1847, 1848 and 1849 the Society organized a series of exhibitions which were the direct forerunners of the LONDON 1851 EXHIBITION, whose first stages were planned by Cole, amid some controversy, under the Society's aegis. The Society, which became Royal in 1908, organized in 1935 the exhibition of British Art in Industry at Burlington House, and in its aftermath instituted a new title, Designer for Industry of the Royal Society of Arts (R.D.I.), in order to raise the status of the industrial designer. Among the first creation were VOYSEY, GILL, Keith MURRAY and McKnight KAUFFER, and later R.D.I.s have included most of the MODERN British design establishment, such as RUSSELL (1940), Susie COOPER (1940) and Ernest RACE (1953).

Soldani Benzi, Massimiliano (1656–1740) Born in Montevarchi, the son of an army officer of German descent, Soldani moved to Florence in 1674 with an introduction to the painter Baldassare Franceschini, and began to study sculpture. From 1678 to 1682 he studied at the Florentine Academy in Rome: he subsequently visited Paris, where he met LE BRUN. On his return to Florence, Soldani worked at first for the mint, designing many coins and medals. However, around 1690 he was also active as a designer of church metalwork, crucifixes, lamps, reliquaries and monstrances, including one for Leghorn Cathedral (1692). In about 1700 he began to design schemes of interior decoration. Soldani was extremely prolific as a sculptor, with princely patrons all over Europe. He was convinced of his descent from the noble family of Benzi, and added their name to his own. In about 1750 the Doccia porcelain factory copied two extraordinary bronze VASES by Soldani on marine themes, comparable to FUMIANI's vase designs, as well as many of his bronze groups.

Solis, Virgil (1514–62) The birthplace of Solis is not known but his career was spent in Nuremberg, where he married for the first time in 1539, and died, having had at least sixteen children by two wives. He seems to have been influenced by HIRSCHVOGEL and to have been closely linked with FLÖTNER. The Solis workshop, which was active from about 1540 to 1572, was uniquely prolific in woodcuts and engravings, thanks to the employment of numerous assistants. Already in 1548, when he executed illustrations for the influential Walter Rivius's *Vitruvius Teutsch*, Solis was well-known. As a designer Solis attempted to satisfy an insatiable demand in Nuremberg for modern designs. The introduction of his reprint of Léonard THIRY's evocations of Roman ruins, *Fragmenta Structurae Veteris* (Orleans, 1550), published by J. A. DuCERCEAU, makes it clear that Solis was more interested in modernity than quality. Accordingly he borrowed extensively from fashionable designers; one of the thirty designs, for instance, was used to fill a woodcut door design influenced by Flötner, which Solis published in about 1555, and he also used designs by DuCerceau and Cornelis FLORIS, and the views of Roman ruins published by Hieronymus Cock in Antwerp in 1551. Engraved designs published by Solis included biblical and historical subjects and figures, many in ornamental frames and niches, a suite of playing-cards, with apes, peacocks, parrots and lions as suits, many small friezes of hunting, animals and birds, and 124 designs for goldsmiths' work. The latter include double cups which combine RENAISSANCE motifs with GOTHIC lobed ornament, and a chalice of Gothic form. Other designs, for instance a ewer whose body is formed as a spiralled snail and another with lizards and a tortoise crawling over its surface and a handle formed as a snake, are exaggeratedly MANNERIST in style. Some designs are inscribed with their materials – coconut and nautilus shells, or their construction – some cups could be disassembled to form clocks, salts and candlesticks. One plate combined designs for four cups, two *tazze* and a candlestick. Solis also published forty-seven plates of jewellery, pendants, crosses and brooches, some, of about 1540, in an early Renaissance manner, others, of about 1560, in a complex mannerist style. 114 plates of MORESQUES by Solis include at least six suites and many designs for the decoration of swords and daggers; a Solis moresque frieze was copied in a later edition of Quentel's *Ein New Kunstlich Modelbuch* (1564). Solis also published numerous designs for engraving on cups and dishes, and a suite of the planets in triumphal cars which was used on a South German cabinet of 1560 and later on wall-paintings at Stodmarsh Court in Kent. Very few of Solis's engravings are dated: an exception, *Etlicher gutter Conterfetischer Laubwerck* (1553; ten plates), contains tight black foliate ornament with putti and medallion heads. AMMAN took over Solis's role as a supplier of designs, but there seems to have been no strong link between the two. In 1862 a reprint of designs for goldsmiths' work by Solis was published in London.

Solon, Léon Victor (1872–1957) Son of Marc Louis Emanuel SOLON, Léon Victor Solon worked as a ceramic designer for Mintons of Stoke-on-Trent from 1900 to 1909. He then went to the United States, where he was responsible for the decoration of the Philadelphia Museum of Fine Arts. His *Polychromy, Architectural and Structural* (New York, 1924) is a document of the interest in this subject in the 1920s, with caustic comments on HITTORFF and CHEVREUL.

Solon, Marc Louis Emanuel (1835–1913) Born in Montauban, Solon was employed from 1857 by the Sèvres porcelain factory, where he specialized in the *pâte-sur-pâte* technique of decoration, which he developed to an extraordinary degree of subtlety and virtuosity. In 1866 Solon published *Inventions Décoratives*, fifty plates of GROTESQUE designs for metalwork, ceramics and ornament based on 16th-

century Fontainebleau prototypes, but full of invention and a sinister elegance rare in the 19th century and in Solon's own ceramic works, although these sometimes possess a certain delicate eroticism. Solon also designed metalwork shown by P.-H. Froment Meurice (1837–1913) at the PARIS 1867 EXHIBITION. In 1870, after the Franco-Prussian war, Solon fled to England, where he was employed by Mintons of Stoke-on-Trent up to 1904. From the 1890s Solon wrote extensively on the history of ceramics.

Sorg, Jörg Sorg was born in Augsburg in about 1525, the son of a painter of the same name and a grandson of the celebrated armourer Kolman Helmschmied, and worked in Augsburg as a painter and etcher on armour, working for several armourers. A surviving pattern-book of armour by Sorg records designs from 1548 to 1563, and includes armours sent to Spain, Austria and Bohemia. In 1566 Sorg designed armour for the Emperor Maximilian II. In his later years he worked for the great Augsburg armourer Anton Peffenhauser (1525–1603); he died in 1603. Sorg's designs seem to have influenced Jacob Halder, the designer of the Jacope Album executed at Greenwich in about 1595. Sorg's son-in-law, Hans Stromair, etched armour for Maximilian II in 1571 and designed a partisan for the Emperor RUDOLF II in 1577.

Sottsass, Ettore Born in Innsbruck in 1917, the son of an architect, Sottsass himself graduated as an architect from the Turin Polytechnic in 1939. After serving in the army he started to practise architecture in Milan in 1946. Sottsass also designed furniture and ceramics and in 1958 became design consultant to Olivetti Electronics division. He has also designed for Driade, Zanotta and Artemide. In 1961 Sottsass visited India and developed an interest in Eastern philosophy. In 1972 he showed portable and adaptable plastic shelters at the NEW YORK MUSEUM OF MODERN ART Exhibition, Italy: The New Domestic Landscape. By this date, while maintaining his conventionally and competently MODERN work for Olivetti, Sottsass was evolving an iconoclastic and colourful new style, much influenced by 1950s popular design and often buttressed by overripe and highfalutin commentaries. Such work was done through Sottsass's Studio Alchymia and in 1981 he opened a shop in Milan, Memphis, to show his own furniture and lighting together with designs by Michael Graves, Terry Jones, Hans Hollein, Shiro Kuramata and other like-minded Post-Modernists.

Spicre, Pierre A painter active in Dijon, Spicre died in 1478. In 1474 he designed a suite of tapestries on the Life of the Virgin for Notre Dame at Beaune, and in 1475 a suite on the History of St Bernard for the same church.

Spooner, Charles Sydney (1862–1938) Spooner was trained as an architect under Sir Arthur Blomfield (1829–99). He was a member of the ART-WORKERS' GUILD from 1887 and took part in ARTS & CRAFTS EXHIBITIONS. Spooner's speciality was the design of furniture, ecclesiastical and secular; in 1892 he read a paper, 'Design Illustrative of Furniture'. In about 1905 Spooner and the architect Arthur Penty (1875–1937) set up a short-lived furniture-making firm, Elmdon & Co., in Hammersmith. Spooner taught furniture at the Central School of Arts & Crafts. His own designs, as illustrated in a lecture on 'House and Church Furniture' in Weir SCHULTZ's *The Arts Connected with Building* (1909), are typically Arts & Crafts, ranging from neat variations on modest 18th-century forms to GIMSONESQUE inlay and GOTHIC. Spooner, who also designed stained glass, retired in 1936.

Sprimont, Nicholas Sprimont, the son of a Liège goldsmith, was recorded as marrying in London in 1742. However, it is probable that he arrived in London earlier, in the late 1730s; a small group of sculpturally ROCOCO silver of about 1740, marked by the goldsmith Paul Crespin, seems to have been designed and made by Sprimont. Sprimont entered his own mark at Goldsmiths' Hall in 1743. In 1744 he was god-father to Sophie, daughter of the sculptor Louis François Roubiliac. Roubiliac lectured on sculpture at the ST MARTIN'S LANE ACADEMY in 1745, and it is likely that Sprimont was in close contact with this seed-bed of English rococo. His own silver designs, which employed vigorous NATURALISTIC ornament alongside rococo scrolls, may have exercised some influence in London, as is suggested by a Matthias LOCK spoon design identical to one executed by Sprimont in 1742. Sprimont remained a goldsmith until 1748 but from about 1745 his main preoccupation was the Chelsea porcelain factory, for which Roubiliac modelled for a short period and which converted several of Sprimont's silver designs into porcelain. In 1749 Sprimont took over the factory from its first manager, Charles Gouyn. In 1750 he was running a 'nursery of thirty lads . . . bred to designing and painting', and he began about that date to employ Joseph Willems, a Flemish teacher of drawing and modelling, as a designer. In 1762 Sprimont gave up the day-to-day running of the factory because of ill health and retired to Richmond. The business was sold to William Duesbury of Derby in 1769 and Sprimont died in 1771, when his collection of paintings was sold at Christies. According to his widow Sprimont had possessed 'superior skill and taste in the arts of drawing and modelling'.

Stabler, Harold (1872–1945) Born at Levens in Westmorland, the son of a schoolmaster, Stabler was trained as a wood-carver and metalworker at the Keswick School of Industrial Art founded in 1884 by Canon Rawnsley under the influence of RUSKIN. After a spell under R. Llewellyn Rathbone (1864–1939) in the metalworking department of Liverpool School of Art, Stabler moved to London. Designs by Stabler were illustrated in the 'ART-WORKERS' QUARTERLY'. He showed metalwork at ARTS & CRAFTS EX-HIBITIONS but after the 1912 Exhibition grew dissatisfied with the Arts & Crafts approach and became a founder of the DESIGN AND INDUSTRIES ASSOCIATION. From 1912 to 1926 Stabler taught at the Royal College of Art (see SCHOOL OF DESIGN). As a designer of goldsmiths' work he received many official commissions, including a cup presented to the City of Paris in 1937 by the Goldsmiths' Company. His silver evolved from a typical Arts & Crafts manner to a geometricized 18th-century style. He also designed glass for Chance Brothers of Birmingham and posters and tiles for the London Underground. The latter were made by the Poole pottery, Carter, Stabler & Adams Ltd, in which he had become a partner in 1921 and for which his wife Phoebe also designed. In the 1930s Stabler acted as a design consultant to Firth Vickers, the Sheffield stainless-steel manufacturers. His Cumberland stainless-steel tea set, designed in 1938, was still being produced in 1950 by J. & J. Wiggin Ltd, for whom Welch was later to design. In 1936 Stabler was appointed by the Royal SOCIETY OF ARTS one of the first Designers for Industry.

Stafford, John Apprenticed to a provincial upholsterer, Stafford became a leading upholsterer in Bath, where he had premises in Milsom Street up to at least 1830. His *A Series of Designs for Interior Decorations Comprehending Draperies and Elegancies for the Drawing-Room* (1814; eighteen coloured plates) comprises charming designs for window curtains and pelmets, one, commemorating the 'memorable epoch of 1814', in homage to Wellington. The work was published in London by James Barron 'Upholsterers' Brass Founder' and dedicated 'To Thomas HOPE, Esq., whose Pure Taste and Classical Erudition have ... directed his countrymen, by better paths, to the Distant Dome of Attic Elegance'. In a copious preface Stafford claimed to have executed most of the designs 'within the period of the last two years' and, alluding to the superiority of French taste, bemoaned the lack of design education in England. Stafford's designs were reprinted on a smaller scale in ACKERMANN'S *Repository* from 1819 to 1820.

Stalker, John With George Parker, Stalker published *A Treatise of Japanning and Varnishing* (Oxford, 1688); two further editions appeared in the same year, one with Parker's name first, the other with Stalker's name alone. Dedicated to the Countess of Darby, the book includes a lengthy technical text on 'Japaning ... Guilding ... Burnishing', etc., written in a high-flown style. The preface claims that 'The glory of one Country, Japan alone, has exceeded in beauty and magnificence all the pride of the Vatican at this time, and the Pantheon heretofore'. The *Treatise* contains twenty-four plates with 'Above an Hundred distinct patterns for JAPAN-work, in Imitation of the INDIANS, for Tables, Stands, Frames, Cabinets, Boxes &c.'. They are in a fanciful Japanese style with foliage, landscapes, buildings, birds, figures, animals, 'Pagod Worshipps', and 'An Embassy'.

Stam, Mart Born Martinus Adrianus Stam in Purmerend in 1899, Stam studied drawing in Amsterdam from 1917 to 1919, and worked as an architectural draughtsman in Rotterdam until 1922. He then moved to Berlin, where he met Poelzig, Taut and El LISSITZKY. In 1923 he worked on an exhibition at the BAUHAUS with Oud, Dudok and others. Until 1925 he was in Switzerland, and from 1925 to 1928 published articles on design, furniture, architecture and advertising, the latter with El Lissitzky, in the Constructivist journal *ABC*. Having in 1925 returned to Amsterdam via Paris, in 1926 Stam had made the first cantilevered tubular-metal chair, constructed of gas pipes. Also in 1926 he was invited by MIES VAN DER ROHE to design three houses at the DEUTSCHE WERKBUND'S STUTTGART 1927 EXHIBITION. They were furnished with a developed version of his chair and with a tubular armchair. Stam's chairs were included in SCHNECK's 1928 Der Stuhl Exhibition in Stuttgart. In 1927 Stam published an attack on *M-Kunst*, the monumental art of the past, and was, with BERLAGE and RIETVELD, one of the Dutch founders of the CONGRÈS INTERNATIONAUX D'ARCHITECTURE MODERNE. Stam designed other chairs in 1931 and 1932 while working under Ernst May as a town planner in Russia. Having returned to Amsterdam in 1934 he published articles on furniture and chairs in *Opbouw* (1937 and 1938). From 1948 to 1952 he taught in Dresden and East Berlin. He then returned to Amsterdam, but in 1966 retired to seclusion in Switzerland. That MODERN archetype, the cantilever chair, could have no more fitting creator than Stam, socialist, idealistic, intolerant and uncompromising.

Standage, Alfred Standage compiled *Practical Illustrations of Upholstery Work* (London, 1865; forty plates). It comprises curtains, portières and beds in the MODERN, GOTHIC, Elizabethan, Greek and Louis XVI styles, including a curtain designed for Windsor Castle, and ends with eight coloured plates of furniture in the 1860s synthetic geometric style.

Steinle, Matthias Born in about 1644, probably in the Salzburg area, where his father was active as a cabinet-maker and constructed many altars, Steinle worked as a sculptor in Leubus from 1676 to 1680 and from at least 1682 in Breslau. There he published four suites of ornament of six plates each. A suite of friezes (1684) is in a vigorous and dynamic ACANTHUS style influenced by DELLA BELLA. It was reissued in Nuremberg. A suite of cartouches, reissued in Nuremberg in 1686, also uses the acanthus style, in some cases applied to elongated and elegant forms. A suite of floral swags with putti is notably sculptural, but a suite of VASES carries sculptural ornament to scrolly and contorted excess. From 1688 Steinle worked in Vienna, where he held a post as a carver to the imperial court. He also taught architecture and engineering at the Academy founded by Leopold I in Vienna in 1692. Prodigiously fertile and versatile, Steinle was in 1704 described as '*viro in omni arte experto*'. He designed for goldsmiths, smiths, plasterers, embroiderers and cabinet-makers, especially those involved in church furnishing. Among his more notable designs are the great monstrance for Stift Klosterneuberg made from 1710 to 1715 by the imperial goldsmith, Johann Känischbauer, and the monstrance for Stift Herzogenburg made in 1722.

Stella, Guido Maria Balsamo (1882–1941) Born in Turin, Stella was trained as a painter but turned to designing posters and book-plates in 1904. In 1905 he moved to Munich, where he studied under Albert Welti, a Swiss pupil of Böcklin. His later book-plates were strongly influenced by Beardsley, STUCK and the Secession style; in 1914 'DEKORATIVE KUNST' devoted an article to his work. After this Stella visited the Orrefors glass factory in Sweden, and was strongly impressed by the designs of HALD and GATE. Stella was also Italian commissioner at the Stockholm 1920 Exhibition. After the First World War he devoted himself to glass design and engraving, at first in Florence and from 1925 in Venice, in collaboration with the Bohemian glass engraver, Franz Pelzel. From 1928 he designed for the SALIR glassworks of Murano. Stella's glass designs were basically NEO-CLASSICAL, but are often treated with an ART DÉCO verve and lightness and incorporate many modern motifs, for instance aeroplanes and 'Ragtime'. 'DOMUS' praised his work in 1929. From 1929 to 1933 Stella taught design at the Università di Arti Decorative at Monza.

Stella, Jacques (1596–1657) Born in Lyon, the son of a painter by whom he was taught, Stella moved to Florence in 1619 and there worked for the Grand Duke Cosimo II de' Medici. From 1623 Stella was in Rome, where he became friendly with the painter Nicolas Poussin (1594–1665), who arrived in 1624. Stella was active as a painter and also worked as an engraver for the Jesuits. Back in Paris in 1635 Stella was patronized by Cardinal Richelieu (1585–1642), and in 1644 was appointed Premier Peintre du Roi. *Divers Ornements d'Architecture* (Paris, 1658; sixty-six plates) was published after Stella's drawings by his niece, Claudine Bouzonnet Stella; it comprises mouldings, rosettes and ACANTHUS ornament and was dedi-

cated to Antoine Ratabon, Surintendant des Manufactures de France. *Livre de Vases* (1667; fifty plates) presents VASES, incense-burners, lamps and so on, handsome designs, some in a pure antique manner, others RENAISSANCE and others BAROQUE. They later inspired vases made at Meissen and by Wedgwood. In 1657, fifty plates of putti engaged in games were published after Stella's drawings.

Stent, Peter Stent was active as a publisher at the White Horse in Giltspur Street from 1643 to 1667, when he was succeeded by John OVERTON. Stent published many books of prints with such titles as *A booke of Flowers Fruicts Beastes Birds and Flies*, which were presumably of use to embroiderers. Some were designed by John Dunstall and by Wenceslas Hollar. Stent also published Francis CLEIN's *The Seven Liberall Arts*. Robert Walton was a rival.

Stevens, Alfred (1817–75) Born at Blandford Forum, Dorset, the son of a house painter, Stevens spent nine years in Italy from 1833 to 1842, including periods attached to the Academy in Florence, and in the studio of the Danish sculptor, Thorwaldsen (1770–1844), in Rome. From 1844 he lived in London and from 1845 to 1847 was employed as Assistant Master in the government SCHOOL OF DESIGN, Somerset House, to teach 'drawing and painting, ornament, geometrical drawing and modelling'. Stevens, before and after his resignation from the School, was involved in a series of painted decorative schemes directed by Leonard W. Collmann, of the firm of Collmann & Davis. A scheme for bronze doors for the Geological Museum, executed in 1848, anticipated Stevens's move in 1850 to Sheffield to become chief designer to the ironfounders Henry E. Hoole & Co. Earlier he had designed candlesticks for

William Potts of Birmingham. Although Stevens returned to London in late 1851 he continued to design for Hoole until about 1857. His grates, stoves and fenders, acclaimed at the LONDON 1851 EXHIBITION, at the PARIS 1855 EXHIBITION and at the LONDON 1862 EXHIBITION, were a great success. Hoole also produced his design for a table for the VICTORIA & ALBERT MUSEUM. Stevens designed hunting knives in 1851 for George Wostenholm & Son of Sheffield, two chimneypieces executed by the Coalbrookdale Iron Company in about 1856, and a silver table-centre and tray made by Joseph Bradbury in 1856. But Stevens's last designs for a manufacturer were for vases and plates for Minton & Co., done in about 1861 in preparation for the London 1862 Exhibition, for which he also designed a Certificate of Honourable Mention. Among his executed and unexecuted schemes of decoration that for Dorchester House, begun in 1855 but never completed, was the grandest to come to fruition. For it, and for his own house, he designed furniture and panelling as well as painted and sculptural decoration. Stevens was the most distinguished practitioner of the Victorian RENAISSANCE Revival manner, but his achievements, whether as sculptor, painter or designer, sadly failed to match his promise or opportunities. His greatest influence was through his pupils and followers including Godfrey SYKES, James Gamble and Reuben Townroe.

Stickley, Gustav (1857–1946) Born in Osceola, Wisconsin, the son of a poor farmer, Stickley trained as a stonemason from 1869. From about 1875 he worked in a chair factory in Gardner, Massachusetts, belonging to his uncle S. C. Brandt; he became its foreman in 1879. In 1883 Stickley established a furniture store in Binghampton, New York, and in 1886 began to manufacture Colonial style

chairs. In 1891 he moved his company to Syracuse. In about 1898 Stickley visited Europe where he met VOYSEY and saw BING's shop. In 1900 Stickley showed some simple Arts & Craft style furniture at Grand Rapids. This was rapidly plagiarized and at the Buffalo 1901 Pan-American exhibition Stickley showed similar furniture under his Craftsman trade name. In 1902 he turned some stables in Eastwood into the Craftsman Building; by 1903 it contained a library, lecture hall, metalwork and furniture workshops, and the offices of his magazine the 'CRAFTSMAN' (1901–16). Stickley's workshops were briefly organized on a guild basis, influenced by RUSKIN and William MORRIS, under the title The United Crafts. Stickley designed himself and also used designs by Harvey ELLIS. Burgeoning success bred a more commercial attitude and expansion into house building, farming and gardens. From 1913 the twelve-storey Craftsman Building in New York was the flagship of Stickley's empire, a piquant contrast to ASHBEE's. Stickley went bankrupt in 1915. He much resented Elbert HUBBARD's successful incursion into his field. After bankruptcy Stickley briefly designed in the Chinese CHIPPENDALE and other historic styles, but he died in obscurity.

Stier, Gustav (1807–80) Born in Berlin, Stier worked under SCHINKEL from 1828 to 1837, and from 1839 to 1842 taught design at BEUTH's Preussisches Gewerbeinstitut, contributing to his *Vorbilder*, and later at the Bauakademie. Stier supplied designs to the Berlin porcelain factory, as well as designing ironwork, including the railings round Schinkel's grave, silver, for the factory of W. F. Ehrenburg, and furniture. His designs of the 1840s incorporated late GOTHIC, NATURALISTIC, BAROQUE and ROCOCO motifs as well as rich classical ornament. Stier's *Vor-*

legeblätter für Maurer und Zimmerleute (1841) comprised thirty-seven neat plates of architectural ornament in a manner derived from Schinkel. In 1842 he designed the elaborately Schinkelesque bronze frame for a portrait on porcelain of Friedrich Wilhelm IV of Prussia, planned by Beuth, which the King presented in 1844 to Christian Bunsen (1791–1860), then Prussian Ambassador in London.

Stile Industria (1954–63) Published in Milan as an offshoot of 'DOMUS', this magazine, edited by Alberto Rosselli, acted as a forum for the best Italian industrial design of the 1950s.

Stimmer, Tobias (1539–84) Born in Schaffhausen, the son of a German schoolmaster who also worked as a glass painter, Stimmer was mainly active as a designer of stained glass in a manner strongly influenced by Jörg BREU. Both his narrative scenes and his scrollwork frames were animated by a vigour exceptional among his contemporaries. He designed woodcuts from about 1564 but was most prolific in this field after 1570 when he moved to Strasbourg, where he had a close friendship with the publisher Bernhard JOBIN. RUBENS was later an admirer of Stimmer's woodcuts. Stimmer was an accomplished mathematician and designed the case of the celebrated astronomical clock built at Strasbourg from 1571 to 1574. In about 1578 he executed decorative paintings in Baden for Margrave Philipp II. He became a citizen of Strasbourg in 1582. Stimmer also designed silver and was a poet and anti-Catholic propagandist. He enjoyed a high contemporary reputation.

Stockholm 1930 Exhibition In 1917 a successful exhibition was organized in Stockholm by the Swedish Society of Arts & Crafts (Slöjdföreningen): it included a simple living-room by the architect Erik Gunnar ASPLUND (1885–1940). The Stockholm 1930 Exhibition was organized by the director of the Society, Dr Gregor Paulsson, with Asplund as architect. Asplund's buildings were dashingly MODERN and the exhibition led to the general acceptance of FUNCTIONALISM (Funkis) in Sweden. Other designers involved were Sigurd Lewerentz (poster, wallpaper, paper manufacturers' pavilion), Erik Chambert (furniture) and Sven Markelius (interiors).

Stockmann, Johann Adam Probably born in Riedenburg in Bavaria, Stockmann married in Augsburg in 1720 and was active there as an engraver until 1783. He designed several suites of ROCOCO ornament published by HERTEL. They included fantastic ruins, landscapes and scrolly rococo allegories of the seasons and the times of day. One of his architectural models served as an inspiration for a tin-glazed earthenware sconce made in Brunswick in about 1765.

Stöer, Lorenz In 1555 Stöer, who in 1557 gave up his Nuremberg citizenship to move to Augsburg, was granted a licence to publish his *Geometria et Perspectiva*, but the first edition known is that published in Augsburg in 1567 by the engraver Hans Rogel I. It was reprinted in Augsburg in 1617. In 1557 Stöer was living in Nuremberg and in 1592–3 travelled there as a valuer but he seems to have lived in Augsburg for most of his career. He was still alive in 1621. *Geometria et Perspectiva* consists of eleven superb woodcut designs for marquetry in a style which combines the PERSPECTIVE virtuosity of HIRSCHVOGEL and Wenzel JAMNITZER with the theme of the Roman ruin developed by Léonard THIRY and others. A few drawings are the only other works by Stöer recorded, but his influence is apparent in the marquetry of many late-16th-century South German cabinets.

Stone, Reynolds (1909–79) From an upper-middle-class Dorset family, Stone became in 1930 an apprentice in printing at the Cambridge University Press, where he was influenced by MORISON and the 'FLEURON'. He was briefly taught wood engraving by Eric GILL and began to practise in 1932. His numerous engraved designs included lettering, devices, typographic ornaments and book labels. He also designed a typeface, Minerva (1955), for Linotype.

Storck, Josef von (1830–1902) Born in Vienna, Storck was trained as an architect there under Eduard von Null and August von Siccardsburg. From 1868 to 1899 Storck was Director of the design school attached to the VIENNA MUSEUM OF APPLIED ARTS, a post which involved close collaboration with the leading Viennese manufacturers. Storck's own designs included glass for Lobmeyr, metalwork for August Kleeburg and Dziedzinsky & Hanusch, two elaborate cabinets made in the Museum by the cabinet-maker Franz Michel and others (1871–81), silver by Lustig, textiles, bronzes and enamels. He also designed the interior decoration of the Vienna Opera, and of the imperial pavilion at the VIENNA 1873 EXHIBITION. He practised a rich but controlled RENAISSANCE Revival style and a synthetic classical style of similar character. His influence on Austrian design was pervasive, notably at the VIENNA 1873 EXHIBITION and the MUNICH 1876 EXHIBITION. In 1873 Storck published a book of photographs of glass designed by him and made by Lobmeyr, which had been commissioned by the Emperor in 1869 and was shown at the Vienna 1873 Exhibition; it was in the MANNERIST style of about 1600 and

had delicate gold, silver and silver-gilt mounts by the jeweller H. Ratzendorfer. His *Einfache Möbel in Charakter der Renaissance* (1875) contained designs for twelve pieces of Renaissance-style furniture, with full-scale details. Storck also published many books of models for use in design schools and from 1877 to 1897 edited 'BLÄTTER FÜR KUNSTGEWERBE', which included many of his designs. His *Die Pflanze in der Kunst* (1900) comprised large plates of mainly historical examples of plant ornament.

Stothard, Thomas (1755–1834) Born in London, the son of a publican, Stothard was from about 1770 an apprentice silk designer in Spitalfields, but spent his spare time illustrating Homer and Spenser. In 1777 he entered the Royal Academy Schools to train as a painter. Stothard illustrated Ossian and Hervey's *Naval History* in 1779 and thenceforward had a prodigious output of illustrations, *vignettes* and other ornaments, shop-cards, fashion plates and so on. An illustration of Rosinia (1791) served as the model for a Derby porcelain figure by J. J. Spängler. Stothard became a member of the Royal Academy in 1794. He did decorative paintings at Burghley in 1799 to 1803 and at Hafod in 1812; he also designed stained glass for Hafod. In about 1804 he advised the poet Samuel Rogers (1763–1855) on the decoration of his house and designed for him a cabinet for antiquities, decorating it with paintings. In 1821 Stothard won a competition for the design of a silver shield to be presented by the merchants and bankers of the City of London to the Duke of Wellington; it was made by Benjamin Smith for Green, Ward & Green in about 1822. Like his friend FLAXMAN, Stothard designed for the goldsmiths Rundell & Bridge, including salvers, knife handles, decanter labels, etc.; E. H. BAILY worked up many of these. C. J. RICHARDSON illustrated

Stothard silver designs in 1851. Stothard also designed decorations for Buckingham Palace in about 1829. His son, C. A. Stothard (1786–1821), prematurely killed in a fall, was a notable antiquarian draughtsman, whose *Monumental Effigies* (1819) was an important source-book of GOTHIC.

Strada, Jacopo da (1507–88) Born in Mantua, possibly of Flemish origin, Strada was trained as a goldsmith, and probably worked for Giulio ROMANO. From about 1544 he worked for Johann Jakob Fugger (1516–75), buying coins and antique statues in Rome and Venice on his behalf up to 1556; many were later acquired by Duke Albrecht V of Bavaria. In 1546, after Giulio Romano's death, Strada acquired many designs from his son, and applied to settle in Nuremberg. Permission was granted and Strada became a Nuremberg citizen in 1549, working there as a goldsmith. In 1552 he was given leave to go to Lyon to publish a work on coins, *Epitome Thesauri antiquitatum* (1553), illustrated with woodcuts of examples in his own collection. In 1556 he was granted an imperial privilege to publish a numismatic textbook and a universal dictionary. At this period Strada compiled a work on ancient coins with some 9,000 drawings for Fugger. Also in 1556 Strada was recommended to Archduke Ferdinand of Tyrol by Wenzel JAMNITZER, whose assistant he had become, as a suitable designer for an elaborate table fountain, Jamnitzer himself being occupied with work for the Emperor. As a result Strada went to Prague to show designs to the Archduke, but in the event ZÜNDT took over the project. Strada was then employed to advise on the redesign of the unfinished tomb of the Emperor Maximilian I in Innsbruck. He became court antiquary to the Emperor Maximilian II in 1564 and moved to Prague in 1565. In 1566, how-

ever, Strada was seconded by the Emperor to advise Duke Albrecht V of Bavaria, and not only collected coins and antiquities on his behalf in Italy in 1567, including Andrea Loredan's collection in Venice, but also from 1569 to 1571 helped to design his Antiquarium or gallery of antiques, later embellished by SUSTRIS and CANDID. In 1568 Strada had his portrait painted by Titian and until his retirement in 1579 he was active in Vienna as antiquary and pundit. In 1573 he planned a massive and comprehensive work on ancient inscriptions and a dictionary of eleven languages, and in 1577 a topography of Italy. Strada's transmission of Giulio Romano's MANNERIST style of metalwork design to Germany proved very influential, on HORNICK and many others, and copies and adaptations proliferated, some masquerading as Roman VASES. Strada was also important as a water engineer, a book of his inventions (fifty plates) being published posthumously in Frankfurt (1617–18). His son, Ottavio Strada (1550–1612), served the Emperor RUDOLF II from 1581 and followed his father as court antiquary. He compiled dissertations on symbols of rank in Rome and on the genealogy of the Hapsburgs, and also recycled his father's Giulio Romano repertoire of design as his own work, compiling in 1597 a volume of eighty-two designs for salts, vases, candelabra, etc., which display the full mannerist panoply of ornament and precious materials.

Straet, Jan van der (1523–1605) Born in Bruges of impoverished aristocratic stock, Straet was taught to paint first by his father, who died in 1535, and then by Maximilian Frans. He subsequently moved to Antwerp, where he studied under Pieter Aertsen (1508–75) and became a member of the Guild in 1545. After working for a while with Corneille de la Haye in Lyon, he travelled via

Venice to Florence, arriving by 1550. Having established contact with VASARI, he assisted him in the Vatican up to 1553. Back in Florence, Straet was active as a tapestry designer from at least 1557, but up to 1566 he seems to have been engaged in working up designs by Vasari. In 1567 Straet began to design a great series of twenty-four Hunts for the Villa Medici at Poggio a Cajano, completed in 1576; these were commemorated in prints by Philippe Galle entitled *Venationes* (1578), dedicated to Cosimo de' Medici. From 1569 to 1576 Straet designed a series on the achievements of the Medici, also engraved by Galle, as *Mediceae familiae rerum feliciter gestarum* (1583). Among his assistants were Friedrich SUSTRIS and Peter CANDID. Straet was also active as a decorative designer, designing a room for Eleonora da Toledo in the Palazzo Vecchio in 1561 to 1652, and collaborating on the catafalque of MICHELANGELO in 1564, and on triumphal arches for the marriage of Francesco de' Medici in 1565 and the entry of Christine of Lorraine in 1589.

Strapwork Ornament comprised of bands, straps or ribbons is not uncommon. Late-Gothic ornament, including that by the Master of the BANDEROLES, often used banderoles – ribbon-like scrolls. The MORESQUE ornament which was introduced to Venice from Turkey around 1500 and thence spread over Europe used interlacing bands. Flat bands were used to frame and articulate early GROTESQUE ornament, for instance in prints by Nicoletto Rosex da MODENA. At Fontainebleau in the mid-1530s ROSSO used similar ornament combined with grotesques to frame his murals in the Galerie François I, but with a crucial difference; it scrolled in three dimensions. This strapwork, as it is known, probably owes much to Venetian scrolled frames, although the

base of Hercules and Cacus (1533) by the Florentine sculptor Baccio Bandinelli (1493–1560) incorporates leathery strapwork terminals. However, Rosso seems to have been the first to develop strapwork, combined with grotesque, into a new system of ornament. Rosso's strapwork was massy and ponderous. At Antwerp from about 1540 Cornelis FLORIS and BOS introduced a new fantasy and flexibility to strapwork, and the Flemish strapwork grotesque spread rapidly over Northern Europe, notably through the prints of Hans VREDEMAN DE VRIES. When in around 1600 a more curvilinear stretched grotesque style became popular strapwork tended to lose its identity and was thenceforward absorbed as an ingredient of the grotesque. Strapwork surfaced again in the prints of BERAIN, but in a tamed minor role, compared to its hectic apogee in the work of designers such as WECHTER and ZAN.

Street, George Edmund (1824–81) Born at Woodford in Essex, the son of a solicitor, Street intended at first to enter the Church, but instead took articles with the architect Owen Carter (1806–59) of Winchester from 1841 to 1844, after which he moved to the London office of George Gilbert Scott and W. B. Moffatt (1812–87), whose partnership ended in 1845. In 1848 Street left Scott to set up office in Wantage. Friendship with Benjamin Webb, the Secretary of the ECCLESIOLOGICAL SOCIETY, and with Samuel Wilberforce, Bishop of Oxford, helped his career. In 1850 he was made diocesan architect of Oxford, and many similar appointments followed. Street moved to London in 1856, by which date his enormous practice as a builder and restorer of churches, schools and parsonages was well under way. His most important secular work was the Law Courts, of which he served as sole architect from 1868 until his death. Street frequently travelled abroad, publishing *Brick and Marble Architecture in North Italy* in 1855 and *Some Account of Gothic Architecture in Spain* in 1865. He was a completely committed and deeply religious protagonist of GOTHIC, agreeing with RUSKIN, whom he admired, on its inevitable rightness. His involvement with every detail of his buildings – he was a prodigiously fast and accurate draughtsman and never delegated design – led to a strong interest in all aspects of their decoration. A number of designs by Street are in the second series of *Instrumenta Ecclesiastica* (1856), the design guide issued by the Ecclesiological Society, of whose church plate scheme he was appointed superintendent in 1857 (he was succeeded by BURGES in 1864). At the LONDON 1851 EXHIBITION Newton, Jones & Willis (later Jones & Willis) of Birmingham showed ecclesiastical embroidery to Street's designs. Street designed many vestments and altar frontals for his churches to be executed by this firm or by the London Ecclesiastical Embroidery Society of which his sister had been a founder member in 1854. Street also designed stained glass on occasion, for example windows at Cuddesdon (by Hardman, 1852) and Deddington (about 1865), both in Oxfordshire, and in St Thomas, Oxford (by Clayton & Bell, 1860). His designs for church plate commenced with a pastoral staff made by Skidmore of Coventry in 1854. John Keith of London's prize-winning exhibit at the LONDON 1862 EXHIBITION included, alongside plate designed by William BUTTERFIELD and others, a chalice made to a Street design in 1859 for the Bishop of Brechin. Street also designed plate made by John Hardman & Co., and by Barkentin & Krall. Brass lecterns and candlesticks, wrought-iron hinges and ornament, gasoliers and screens, and monumental brasses, including that in Westminster Abbey to his master Sir George Gilbert Scott (1880), flowed from his pen. For the Rev. John Baron of Upton Scudamore he designed a series of model organcases, published in 1852, which constitute one of the earliest programmes of Reformed Gothic woodwork. Pews and choir-stalls and font-covers were naturally grist to his mill, but Street also designed highly inventive secular furniture, round tables on honest Puginian lines at Cuddesdon (1854) and a monumental bookcase by Holland & Sons in 1865 (Street's second wife (1876) was a daughter of the firm). He also designed tiles, much marble work in pulpits and reredoses, and even the bookbinding for his posthumous *Christ Church Cathedral, Dublin* (1882). One of his last churches, Holmbury St Mary, Surrey (1879), was built at his own expense, and in it almost everything was designed or given by Street. His prodigious energy and industry sometimes produced coarse or mechanical results, but his high and unaffected seriousness is never in doubt. The language is always Reformed Gothic, and at the top of his form Street achieved a classic balance between refinement and strength unequalled by other practitioners of the style. His assistants and pupils included Philip WEBB, William MORRIS, Richard Norman SHAW and J. D. SEDDING, the elite of the next generation.

Strozzi, Bernardo (1581–1644) Born in Genoa, Strozzi trained as a painter in about 1595 under the Sienese Pietro Sorri. In 1597 he was ordained a Capuchin but in 1608 he left the convent to devote more time to painting. In about 1630 he moved to Venice, where he died. A sketch design by Strozzi for a magnificent silver basin with embossed decorations survives; it probably dates from about 1620 and is influenced by the battle prints of TEMPESTA. It was executed, with modifications. The presence of well-delineated silver ewers in paintings by Strozzi suggests that he may have designed more widely in this medium.

Stuart, James 'Athenian' (1713–88) Born in London, the son of a Scottish mariner who died when Stuart was a boy, leaving him to support the family, Stuart at first worked for Lewis Goupy, the fan painter, who had accompanied Lord Burlington on his grand tour of 1714 to 1715, and may not only have encouraged Stuart in his studies of mathematics, geometry, anatomy, drawing and painting but also instilled in him an interest in classical antiquity. Stuart taught himself Latin and Greek and in 1742 set out on foot for Rome, where he probably survived as a guide to English visitors. In 1748, with the painter Gavin Hamilton and the architects Matthew Brettingham and Nicholas Revett, Stuart visited Naples, and also in 1748 Stuart and Revett issued 'Proposals for publishing an Accurate Description of the Antiquities of Athens'. The necessary trip to Athens was financed by a group of English dilettanti in Rome, and the two set out in 1750, although they were long delayed in Venice, where the British Resident, Sir James Gray, procured their election to the Society of D I L E T T A N T I, and only reached Athens in March 1751. They finally returned to England in 1755, and the first volume of *The Antiquities of Athens* was published in 1762, dedicated to the King, who was given a presentation copy in a binding designed by Stuart, who had designed a throne for Queen Charlotte in 1761. Although Revett had done the substantive work by executing the measured drawings and Stuart had merely contributed the topographical views, Stuart bought Revett's interest before the appearance of the first volume. The second volume appeared only in 1789

(dated 1787), being published by Stuart's widow; the third appeared in 1795, and the fourth, made up by the publisher Josiah Taylor out of miscellaneous papers and drawings, was issued in 1816. There were several later editions. After his return to England in 1755 Stuart established himself as a leading N E O - C L A S S I C A L pundit; he was elected a Fellow of the Royal Society, and of the Society of Antiquaries, and at Hagley in 1758 erected the earliest revived Greek Doric building in Europe. In 1757 he had begun to prepare designs for the decoration and furniture of Kedleston in a pioneering neo-classical style. Only fragments of these were executed, Stuart being supplanted by Robert A D A M in about 1760. But at Spencer House, the London palace designed by John V A R D Y for 1st Earl Spencer from 1756 to 1765, Stuart's designs for the decoration and furniture of certain rooms were executed from 1758 onwards and constitute the earliest neo-classical ensemble in England. Like Stuart, Lord Spencer was a member of the Society of Dilettanti; its secretary and treasurer, Colonel George Gray, was both Spencer's artistic adviser and brother to the Sir James Gray who had procured Stuart's election. At Spencer House, Stuart used details borrowed from his *Antiquities of Athens*, notably the capital surmounting the Choragic Monument of Lysicrates (The Lanthorn of Demosthenes), but also fluting, paterae, griffins, guilloche and anthemia, all motifs later to become part of the neo-classical stock-in-trade. The Painted Room was not only decorated with an elaborate painted scheme which integrated Greek and Roman motifs in a R A P H A E L E S Q U E framework, but also contained carved and gilt seat furniture, incorporating winged lions, and ormolu tripod perfume burners on pedestals. The tripods were identical to those Stuart had designed for Kedleston, a design also repeated at Wentworth Woodhouse in about 1760 for the Marquess of Rockingham, another Dilettante. A tripod 'from an original design of Mr Stuart's' was shown at the Free Society of Artists in 1761 by Diederich Nicolaus Anderson (died 1767), a craftsman who also executed designs for ormolu by Adam and CHAMBERS. The Kedleston design was repeated in the 1770s by Matthew Boulton, who in 1769 had been commissioned by Stuart to make the great tripod to surmount his copy of the Choragic Monument of Lysicrates at Shugborough. The bowl of this tripod was made by Josiah Wedgwood in 1771, and Wedgwood later used its design in black basaltes lamps. Stuart's patron at Shugborough was Thomas Anson (1695–1773), whose brother Lord Anson (1697–1760) had in 1758 fixed Stuart's appointment as surveyor of Greenwich Hospital, a post worth £200 a year; both Ansons were Dilettanti. Bolstered by this sinecure and of an indolent disposition, Stuart built little after the mid-1760s. He designed some monuments executed by Thomas Scheemakers (1740–1810), including that of Wedgwood's partner, Thomas Bentley (1731–80), a few medals, and frontispieces to two books by James Harris (1709–80). Although Stuart's character limited his output, and he was slandered by his contemporary rivals – Chambers opposed his Greek taste, and Adam described his work at Spencer House as 'Pityfullissimo' – his influence was wide; Wedgwood and Boulton both deferred to his authority in matters of design and he had a wide acquantance among the leading patrons. For Boulton he designed the silver Admiralty tureen in 1781. He continued long after his return from Greece to produce watercolours of Athens, some being illustrated in Allessandro Bisani's *A picturesque tour . . .* (1793), and after his death *The Antiquities of Athens*, which had given him his nickname 'Athenian', continued to serve as a basic neo-classical textbook; Thomas HOPE, for instance, cites it in the bibliography of his *Household Furniture* (1807).

Stuck, Franz von (1863–1928) Born in Tettenweis in Bavaria, the son of a miller, Stuck studied the applied arts in Munich and worked as an illustrator, drawing for *Fliegende Blätter*, the German humorous magazine, and producing suites of EMBLEMS (1883) and *vignettes* (1886–7) before establishing his reputation as a painter in 1889. Stuck was a founder member of the Munich Secession in 1892 and designed its poster in 1893. He also designed the title of 'PAN' (1895) and worked on 'JUGEND'. In 1897 to 1898 Stuck designed his own palatial house in Munich, the Villa Stuck (studio block added 1913). It was in a classical Roman style inspired by buildings in the paintings of Arnold Böcklin (1827–1901) and close in feeling to works by Wagner, Josef HOFFMANN and BEHRENS. The interior was richly polychrome, with marbles, mosaics, parquetry and lamps all designed by Stuck, who had always been responsible for his own frames. His luxurious classical furniture, executed by the Munich cabinetmaker Hiessmannseder, won a gold medal at the PARIS 1900 EXHIBITION. The house was publicized in a special issue of 'KUNST UND HANDWERK' (1899), whose title was designed by Stuck, and in 'INNEN-DEKORATION' (1909). On his ennoblement in 1905 Stuck chose a centaur for his arms: on his death he was laid out in a toga. His pupils included ALBERS, Klee and Kandinsky.

Studio, The (1893–present) Financed by the Bradford businessman Charles Holme (1848–1923), who in 1879 had been involved with Christopher DRESSER in a venture to import Japanese goods, contributed an article on 'Artistic Gardens in Japan' in 1893, and lived in William MORRIS's Red House, the *Studio*'s first editor was C. Lewis Hind, who was rapidly replaced by Gleeson White (1851–98). From the account of Aubrey Beardsley by Joseph Pennell in its first issue, the *Studio* concentrated on the most advanced artists and designers. Early contributors included VOYSEY, BAILLIE SCOTT and Aymer Vallance, and MACKINTOSH was treated at length in 1897. A stress on the applied arts and design and the involvement of readers through competitions helped towards an international success, an American edition being published from 1897. The *Studio*'s international influence was reflected in praise by MUTHESIUS in *Das Englische Haus* and an attack by SEDER in 'KUNST-GEWERBE IN ELSASS-LOTHRINGEN'. From 1898 to 1939 Special Numbers were issued, including *Modern British Domestic Architecture and Decoration* (1901), *The Art Revival in Austria* (1906) and *Posters and their Designers* (1924). The *Studio Yearbook of Decorative Art* (1907–present), since 1974 *Decorative Art and Modern Interiors*, after various changes of title, continues to provide an international survey of interior design. The *Studio* itself pursued an outmoded Arts & Crafts line under Geoffrey Holme, son of Charles, until 1928, when an article by Frederick Etchells on LE CORBUSIER and another by J. J. P. Oud on 'Architecture and the Future' heralded a switch to MODERN. From the 1960s as *Studio International* the magazine became straightforwardly *avant-garde* and erratic.

Stüler, Friedrich August (1800–65) Born in Mühlhausen in Thuringia, Stüler came to Berlin in 1818 and studied architecture at the Bauakademie. In 1824, with Eduard Knoblauch (1801–65)

he helped to found the Berlin society of architects. In 1827 Stüler began to work for SCHINKEL and started to rise as an official architect; he was friendly with Friedrich Wilhelm IV, and was appointed royal architect in 1842. In 1841 Stüler was appointed to plan the great new museum complex in Berlin, and designed the decoration of the collection of plaster casts, completed in 1852, and including wall-paintings by Wilhelm von Kaulbach (1805–74). From 1835 to 1840, with the architect J. H. Strack (1805–80), Stüler published a series of designs for furniture. He also advised the Berlin porcelain factory on design. Stüler not only worked in the classical style but also used RENAISSANCE and GOTHIC models.

Stuttgart 1927 Exhibition In spring 1926 the city of Stuttgart decided to give the DEUTSCHE WERKBUND control over the planning and design of a model suburb, the Weissenhofsiedlung, to be accessible during an exhibition in 1927 on the theme of housing and then to revert to the city. MIES VAN DER ROHE was put in charge of the project and brought together an international team of MODERN architects, including J. J. P. Oud, Mart STAM, LE CORBUSIER, Josef Frank, Peter BEHRENS, Hans Poelzig, Walter GROPIUS and SCHNECK. The houses they built were uncompromisingly Modern, proclaiming themselves functional objects, as Stam called the house in *Bau und Wohnung* (1927). Objects shown included lights by Marianne BRANDT, Poul Henningsen of Copenhagen and Adolf Meyer, metal chairs by Mies and Stam, and a moulded-plywood chair by Bodo and Heinz Rasch. However, as Werner Graeff observed in *Innenräume* (Stuttgart, 1928), most architects furnished their houses with a few industrially produced objects such as Thonet bentwood chairs. Also in *Innenräume* Stam advocated the minimal dwelling, Breuer argued for metal furniture and Schneck pronounced that 'Der Luxusgegenstand, der typisiert wird, heisst Kitsch' ('Mass-produced luxury objects are Kitsch'). Schneck's chair exhibition held at Stuttgart in 1928 followed the 1927 Exhibition in style and ideology.

Süe, Louis (1875–1968) Born in Bordeaux, the son of a doctor, Süe moved to Paris in 1895 and trained as a painter. From 1905 he was also active as an architect and in 1910 he visited Austria at the request of Paul POIRET to study contemporary Austrian design. In 1912 Süe set up an interior decorating business, the Atelier Français, inspired by Poiret's Atelier Martine. Süe designed furniture, textiles and ceramics, and in 1914 was commissioned by the PARIS UNION CENTRALE DES ARTS DÉCORATIFS to design their stand at the Lyon exhibition, a project cut short by the outbreak of war. In 1919, in partnership with André MARE he founded the Compagnie des Arts Français, which was written up in 'ART ET DÉCORATION' (1920). Its products, aimed at the luxury market, were in a synthetic style in which architecture and furniture used a plump but elegant adaptation of transitional NEO-CLASSI-CAL forms of the 1760s, often gently fluted, which was seen in the 1920s as a distillation of the Louis Philippe style of the 1830s and 1840s, while the flat pattern on textiles and wallpaper was often in a Fauve manner, with occasional use of cubist motifs. However, Süe, and the Compagnie, were explicitly opposed to the MODERN style. *Architectures* (1921; thirty-seven plates) was the de luxe manifesto of the Compagnie: most of the designs were engraved by Jacques Villon. The Compagnie, although significantly known as Süe & Mare, was conceived as a collaborative venture, and did in fact use the talents of many

craftsmen and designers, including Paul Véra, Charles Defresne and Gustave Jaulmes. At the PARIS 1925 EXHI-BITION the Compagnie won acclaim through its own pavilion, entitled grandiloquently the Musée de l'Art Contemporain, through the Salle des Fêtes in the Grand Palais, and through part of the Ambassade Française. Süe himself also designed for other manufacturers at the exhibition, including silver for Christofle. Also in 1925 Süe & Mare designed a Paris shop for Parfums d'Orsay, and in 1926 to 1927 they decorated Süe's Saint-Cloud villa for the actress Jane Renouardt, including a commode with marquetry of marine life designed by Mathurin Meheut (1882–1958). The culmination of the Compagnie's success was the 1928 Salon de Conversation on the liner *Île-de-France*. In 1928 the designer Jacques Adnet took over the direction of the Compagnie. When the Compagnie passed from his control Süe continued to be active as architect and designer. At the PARIS 1937 EXHIBITION he designed much of the interior decoration of the pavilion of the Société des Art-istes-Décorateurs, of which he became President in 1929. During the war he taught in Istanbul but after 1945 he returned to practise in France, designing Jean Patou's Paris shop in 1948, and advocating a return to classicism up to his retirement in 1953.

Sullivan, Louis Henry (1856–1924) Born in Boston, the son of an Irish dancing master, Sullivan spent a year in 1872 studying architecture at the Massachusetts Institute of Technology. In 1873 he went via New York to Philadelphia, where he worked briefly in FUR-NESS's office. He then returned to Chicago before in 1874 travelling to Paris, where he studied briefly at the École des Beaux-Arts. He was back in Chicago in 1875. In 1881 he entered into an architectural partnership with Dankmar Adler (1844–1900), dissolved in 1895. In the Chicago Auditorium Building (1886–90), the Getty Tomb (1890) and other contemporary buildings, Sullivan used a rich system of foliate ornament based partly on English Reformed GOTHIC prototypes. From 1888 Frank Lloyd WRIGHT worked for Sullivan; Wright retained a life-long reverence for his master. Sullivan was disgusted by the design of the CHICAGO 1893 WORLD COLUMBIAN EXPOSITION, apart from the Japanese pavilion. His Guaranty Building in Buffalo (1894–5), a massive four-square palazzo skyscraper, is incrusted with organic ornament, its lifts with pierced metal screens, its staircases decorated with stencilling, and his National Farmers' Bank, Owatonna, Minnesota (1907–8), has horizontal and rectilinear desks, comparable to Frank Lloyd Wright's furniture, and elaborate foliate ornament on the tellers' wickets. Sullivan's search for an organic style of ornament, influenced by evolutionary ideas, remained constant from the 1870s, in architectural ornament, in designs for hairpins and combs (1894–5) and for title-pages, and in the plates he designed in 1922 to 1923 for *A System of Architectural Ornament According with a Philosophy of Man's Powers* (1924). Sullivan expressed his ideas in *Kindergarten Chats* (1901–2), in the 'CRAFTSMAN' (1906) and in his *Autobiography* (1922–3). His statement that 'form follows function' (1895) reflects earlier thinking on design by A. W. N. PUGIN and others; it was later used as a slogan by MODERN designers whose aims were very different to those of Sullivan.

Sumner, George Heywood Maunoir (1853–1940) Born in Hampshire of a distinguished clerical family, Heywood Sumner studied law after Eton and Oxford, sharing lodgings with W. A. S. BENSON, whose support of the machine

he shared and whose sister he married in 1883. Sumner exhibited paintings and etchings at the Royal Academy from 1880 to 1883 and in the latter year contributed twelve etchings to a new edition of J. R. Wise's *The New Forest*, which Walter CRANE had illustrated in 1863. In 1882 Sumner was associated with MACKMURDO'S newly founded Century Guild and in 1884 he joined the ART-WORKERS' GUILD, whose Master he became in 1894. He was also in 1886 one of the leading activists in the splinter group from the Art-Workers' Guild who organized the ARTS & CRAFTS EXHIBITION in 1888, and in 1891 was one of the founders of the Fitzroy Picture Society, which aimed to supply good poster-like pictures to the poor, together with Selwyn IMAGE, Louis Davis, Christopher WHALL and C. M. Gere. Sumner specialized in sgraffito decoration and from 1887 to 1897 decorated a number of churches in this technique, as well as a cabinet, The Charm of Orpheus (1889), whose carcase was designed by W. A. S. Benson. Sumner published an article on this technique in the 'ART JOURNAL' ERN designers whose aims were very different to those of Sullivan.

Alexander Morton & Co., posters for his brother-in-law, Frank Benson, at the Globe Theatre, and stained glass. His wallpaper designs were praised by MUTHESIUS and VAN DE VELDE. Sumner retired early to the New Forest, where he designed his own house. His topographical *Book of Gorley* (1910) is an interesting specimen of Arts & Crafts typography and illustration. He also wrote on *Ancient Earthworks*.

Sustris, Friedrich Born in Italy in about 1540, the son of the painter Lambert Sustris, Friedrich Sustris was taught to paint by his father. From 1560 he was in Rome and from 1563 to 1567 in Florence, where he worked under VASARI on the decorations of the Ponte Vecchio. In 1564 he became a member of Vasari's Accademia del Disegno and worked on MICHELANGELO's funeral. From 1565 Sustris assisted on the design of tapestries for the Florentine manufactory. In 1568 he was summoned to Augsburg to work for Hans Fugger of the banking family. From Augsburg, Sustris moved in 1573 to the service of Crown Prince Wilhelm of Bavaria in Landshut, where he coordinated a redecoration of Burg Trausnitz. In 1579 he moved to Munich, where he was appointed in 1586 Kunstintendant to Wilhelm V, with powers as absolute director of the team of artists working at the Munich court, including CANDID and GERHARD. He designed decorative paintings, including the GROTESQUES in the Grottenhof of the Residenz, interior decoration, plasterwork, furniture, goldsmith's work and decorations for ceremonies. The Reiche Kapelle, the chapel of the Residenz, contains rich decorations designed by Sustris, including silver and engraved glass. Sustris was active as an architect and also designed title-pages, for instance that for *Trophaea Bavarica* (1597), and a suite of twenty-four plates of Augsburg saints published in 1601. After his death in 1599 Sustris's post as Kunstintendant was taken over by his son-in-law, Hans KRUMPER.

Sütterlin, Ludwig (1865–1917) Born in Lahr in Baden, Sütterlin was trained as a painter. He designed posters including a bold usage of a hammer for the Berlin 1896 Exhibition, as well as leather, textiles and glass for Fritz Heckert of Petersdorf. He also taught new approaches to handwriting and typography in Berlin.

Swan, Abraham A carpenter and joiner who in 1757 claimed thirty years' activity in architecture and in the same year designed the front staircase of Blair Castle, Swan published five architectural pattern-books, *The British Architect* (1745), *A Collection of Designs in Architecture* (1757), *One Hundred and Fifty New Designs for Chimney Pieces* (1758), *Designs in Carpentry* (1759) and *The Carpenter's Complete Instructor* (1768). They contain numerous details of ornament. The most influential was *The British Architect*, whose 1775 Philadelphia edition was the first architectural pattern-book published in America; another edition appeared in Boston in 1794. It displays frilly ROCOCO embellishments to basic Palladian forms. Some rococo brackets are surprisingly advanced for England in 1745. Among its owners was the Oxford-born American architect William Buckland (1734–74), who was trained, like Swan, as a carpenter and joiner.

Swanenburgh, Isaac Claesz van Born in about 1538, Swanenburgh worked in Leiden as a painter, and from 1596 took a vigorous part in local government there. He died in 1614. Swanenburgh was active as a designer for textiles and stained glass, and also, in 1594 to 1597, designed ceremonial staves for Leiden University. These were made by the goldsmith Jan Jansz van Griecken, and remade to the same design by Johannes Fransz de Meerschalek in about 1657.

Sykes, Godfrey (1824–66) Born in Malton, North Yorkshire, Sykes was first apprenticed to an engraver, James Bell, in Sheffield. In 1843 he entered the Sheffield School of Art where he began to teach in 1857 after a starred career as a student. Sykes was strongly influenced by Alfred STEVENS, who had come to work in Sheffield in 1850. For a period Sykes worked under Stevens at Hoole's for no pay. A tobacco jar designed by Sykes at this period, shown at the Dublin 1853 Exhibition, is an accomplished essay in Stevens's RENAISSANCE

Revival manner. Sykes also designed decorative schemes in Sheffield, including a frieze for the Mechanics' Institute (1854) and a ceiling for the Telegraphic News Room (1856). In 1859 Sykes moved to London to work on the Horticultural Society's new buildings and subsequently on the decoration of the new South Kensington Museum, now the VICTORIA & ALBERT MUSEUM, under the architect Captain Fowke, who became a close friend. The work employed a variety of media – terracotta, mosaic, bronze, maiolica, stained glass, paint and iron. Designers working under Sykes on this great scheme included Lockwood Kipling, Reuben Townroe (1833–1911), James Gamble (1835–1911) and Hugh Stannus (1840–1908). While he was in London Sykes also designed a tomb for the painter William Mulready (1786–1863) and the cover of Thackeray's *Cornhill Magazine* (1860). In 1861 to 1862 he travelled in Italy. Fowke called Sykes 'master and inventor of English cinque-cento decoration', a phrase which well expresses the Italianate character of his vigorous Renaissance manner inspired by Stevens. An alphabet for South Kensington (1864), inhabited by industrious boys, is among his happiest inventions.

Sylvius, Balthasar Born Balthasar Geertsen in Hertogenbosch, Sylvius was in Antwerp by 1543. He was admitted to the Guild of St Luke as an engraver. He worked on silver, as well as engraving prints after painters such as Frans Floris, brother of Cornelis FLORIS. It was a trade which brought him prosperity in the 1560s but after the fall of Antwerp in 1567 trade declined and Sylvius went to Innsbruck whence, on the death of his wife in 1570, he returned to Antwerp, where he died in 1580. His *Variarum protractionum quas vulgo Maurusias vocant . . . libellus* (1554; twenty-four plates of MORESQUE borders, panels and roundels derived from PELLEGRINO and BOS) was one of the most influential pattern-books of this genre of ornament. Two further books of moresque ornament by Sylvius are known, the fragmentary *Liber marusiarum duplicium . . .* (five plates) and *Une Livre contenant passement de Moresques* (twelve plates). Sylvius also issued *Un livre de grosserie & des flascons et boites de poivre & boites du sel De Couppes & tasses et grotisque* (Antwerp, 1568; twenty plates); it comprises highly vigorous GROTESQUE designs for VASES, cups, etc., for goldsmiths, embellished with STRAPWORK and masks and set in rusticated niches.

Symony, Peter Born in Vallorbe in Switzerland, Symony became a citizen of Strasbourg in 1603 and was active there as a goldsmith from 1604. His *Tabulae Gemmiferae XXIV* (Strasbourg, 1621; twenty-four plates) comprise designs for large and elaborate pendants in the scrolled foliate style known as COSSE DE POIS, combined with stretched GROTESQUES. In the corners of his plates are details for jewels and for enamelling, the latter notably *outré* and including the designer's monogram. Some plates were engraved by Isaac BRUNN, others by Pierre NOLIN. Their publisher, Jacob von der Heyden, also reissued TOUTIN's designs.

Syrlin, Jörg Born in Ulm in about 1455, the son of the great carver who executed the choir-stalls at Ulm Cathedral from 1469 to 1474, Syrlin was active as a carver from 1475 to 1521. He died in poverty after an unruly life. He published an engraving of an elaborate GOTHIC font, with a ground-plan.

T

Tagliente, Giovanni Antonio Tagliente published textbooks on writing (1524), reading (1524), arithmetic (1525) and letter-writing (about 1530). His *Essempio di recammi* (Venice, 1527; thirty-one plates) was the earliest Italian pattern-book for embroidery. Some designs were borrowed from German prototypes by SCHÖNSPERGER and Quentel, but most were innovatory designs for MORESQUES, called by Tagliente '*groppi moreschi et arabeschi*' ('moresque and arabesque knots'), of a type which had earlier interested Leonardo da Vinci and DÜRER. This was the first appearance of this type of ornament in a pattern-book, anticipating PELLEGRINO (1530), and it is significant that this should have happened in Venice, which had close links with the Islamic world. Several varying editions of the *Essempio* were published, and RENNER, Matio PAGANO and VAVASSORE all derived designs from Tagliente.

Talbert, Bruce J. (1838–81) Born in Dundee, Talbert was trained as a wood-carver under a Mr Millar. He then entered the office of a local architect, Charles Edwards, and in 1856 moved to Glasgow to the offices of W. N. Tait and Campbell Douglas, where his fellow pupils included J. J. Stevenson (1832–1908) and James Sellars (1846–88). In 1860 Talbert won a medal for architectural design and in 1862 another, from the Edinburgh Architectural Association, for drawing. Also in 1862 he began to design furniture for Doveston, Bird & Hull of Manchester. Shortly afterwards, probably in about 1864, he moved to Francis Skidmore's Art Manufactures Company in Coventry, founded in 1861, and while there did the detailed drawings for the gates of the Albert Memorial from Sir Gilbert Scott's designs. He also won a competition for a new title heading for the 'BUILDING NEWS'. In the late 1860s Talbert is said to have briefly set up business in his native Dundee, and to have published from there his *Gothic Forms Applied to Furniture, Metal Work and Decoration for Domestic Purposes* (1868, though dated 1867 on the title-page). However, his more permanent residence from about 1866 was in London. *Gothic Forms* was dedicated by permission to G. E. STREET, incorporated the RUSKINIAN motto 'Let us labour with love' in its title-page, and advocated the Reformed GOTHIC combination of honesty and massiveness both in the introduction and in its thirty plates. Some of the furniture illustrated had been shown by Holland & Sons, the first London firm to employ Talbert, at the PARIS 1867 EXHIBITION. Talbert also designed for Gillows, including the Pet sideboard shown at the LONDON 1873 EXHIBITION, for Marsh, Jones & Cribb of Leeds, who showed a Talbert sideboard in the PARIS 1878 EXHIBITION, and for Jackson & Graham, whose Juno cabinet, designed by Talbert, was a prizewinner at that exhibition, and was sold to the Viceroy of Egypt. Talbert showed drawings at the Royal Academy from 1870 to 1876 and in the latter year his *Examples of Ancient*

& *Modern Furniture, Metal Work, Tapestries, Decorations* &c., again dedicated to Street, was published by Batsford's, comprising twenty-one plates and conceived as a sequel to *Gothic Forms*. Its style is vaguely Jacobean with a stress on elaborately moulded panels, turned balusters and low-relief carving, as opposed to the Reformed Gothic geometric inlay, stump columns and chamfering of the earlier work. Talbert also designed ecclesiastical metalwork for Cox & Son, including a contribution to their prizewinning SOCIETY OF ARTS entry of 1870, as well as wallpapers for Jeffrey & Co., textiles for Cowlishaw, Nichol & Co. and for Barbone & Miller, carpets for Messrs Brinton, cast iron for the Coalbrookdale Company, and stained glass. Talbert spent his last years living in Euston Square, as an extremely active commercial designer, many of his designs being published posthumously in the 'CABINET MAKER AND ART FURNITURE'. A Talbert design was published with approbation in DRESSER's *Principles of Decorative Design* (1873) and Moyr SMITH named him as a major reformer in *Ornamental Interiors* (1887). However, it is probable that Talbert is best understood not as an original creator but as a brilliant commercial interpreter of the Reformed Gothic style forged by Street and others in the 1850s and of the Art style of which GODWIN and COLLCUTT were the pioneers in about 1870.

Talman, John (1677–1726) John Talman was the son of William Talman (1650–1719), architect and collector. He spent some twenty years travelling in Europe, in Holland and Germany in 1698, in Italy in 1702, again in Italy from 1709 to about 1716, having travelled outwards with William KENT, and back in Italy in 1719. In about 1699 Talman provided designs for a BAROQUE Trianon to be built at Hampton Court,

including elaborate marble pavements; one of his father's designs for this Trianon included a canopied bed and other furniture. In 1708 John Talman designed a pavement for St Paul's. During his 1709 trip to Italy, Talman hoped to obtain models for the proposed rebuilding of Whitehall Palace for Queen Anne, to replace the complex burnt down in 1698. In 1711 Talman gave an elaborate St Luke's Feast in Rome, of which Inigo JONES was a patron along with Palladio, RAPHAEL, Vitruvius and others. It was probably for this that he designed elaborate baroque silver, sideboards, lights, VASES and interior decoration, showing the influence of FOGGINI and his pupil Agostino Cornacchini. In 1717 Talman was first director of the Society of Antiquaries: his print of a lamp (1717) was adopted as the Society's device in 1718. In Italy, Talman employed artists to record works of art, collected prints and drawings, and was an art dealer. He certainly helped to propagate a taste for the Italian baroque style in England. In about 1724 he possessed 200 volumes of drawings including vases, utensils, jewels, regalia etc. They were sold in 1727.

Tarver, Edward John (1841–91) The son of the French master at Eton, Tarver was educated there and in 1858 articled to the architect Benjamin Ferrey (1810–80). He began to practise independently from 1863, at first an ardent Goth, but working in the Queen Anne style from 1870. Tarver designed much furniture, including GOTHIC picture frames illustrated in Charles EASTLAKE's *Hints* (1868) and an Art sideboard for Morant, Boyd & Blandford shown at the LONDON 1872 EXHIBITION. Tarver was a friend and assistant of BURGES, helping on *Architectural Drawings* (1870). In 1874, with H. W. Lonsdale, he published *Illustrations of Mediaeval Costume*, much influenced by Burges. Tarver was an activist in the Architectural Association.

Tatham, Charles Heathcote (1772–1842) Born in London, the son of an impoverished gentleman farmer, Tatham received his early artistic training, for which he was ever grateful, from John LINNELL, a relation. In 1788 he entered the office of S. P. Cockerell (1753–1827), where he was treated as a menial. In 1789 Tatham moved to the office of Henry HOLLAND, where he worked on the detailing of Carlton House and Woburn Abbey. In 1794 Holland sent Tatham to Rome to act as a researcher and draughtsman, and to collect antique fragments on his behalf. The fragments bought by Tatham in Rome for Holland were acquired by SOANE in 1821; some had been in PIRANESI's collection. In Rome, Tatham commissioned bronzes (1795) from Giuseppe Boschi, and was also in contact with the bronze casters Righetti, Valadier and Zoffoli, and with the porcelain manufactory of Volpato. He also became friendly with the Italian architect ASPRUCCI and the Spanish architect Velasquez. The antique fragments sent back from Rome by Tatham influenced Holland's work at Southill from 1796. Tatham had not prepared his drawings of Roman antiquities with a view to publication, but after returning to England he decided to publish with the immediate aim of supplying models for the cabinet-makers and other craftsmen working under Holland at Carlton House and elsewhere. *Etchings of Ancient Ornamental Architecture drawn from the Originals in Rome and other parts of Italy during the years 1794, 1795 and 1796* (1799; 102 plates, many dated 1800) stated in its introduction, which guardedly praised Piranesi, 'the works of the Ancients are a MAP TO THE STUDY OF NATURE'; the subscribers included Soane, James WYATT, YENN, HOPE, BOILEAU, Peter NICHOLSON and Velasquez. The *Etchings* comprised drawings of Roman furniture and ornament, including the Barberini candelabrum, already illustrated in Piranesi's *Vasi . . .* (1778); they were reprinted in 1803, 1810, 1826 and 1843 and an edition appeared in Weimar in 1805. *Etchings representing Fragments of Grecian and Roman architectural ornaments* (1806; twenty-four plates) illustrated more antique fragments and furniture. Tatham's *Designs for Ornamental Plate* (1806), dedicated to Lady Stafford, advocates 'Massiveness' as 'the principal characteristic of good plate', as opposed to the light and insignificant forms of the ADAM style. The designs include plate for Lord Carlisle, the Wrexham race cup (1801) and branch lights for Lord Spencer (1801), made by William Pitts, and for Earl Camden (1803). While working at Woburn in the early 1790s, Tatham had been in contact with John Linnell, a relative who, on his death in 1796, left his drawings to Tatham's brother, Thomas. In 1802 Thomas entered into a partnership to form the cabinet-making firm of Marsh & Tatham. Linnell's drawings later passed to Tatham himself, but despite his close links with the cabinet trade Tatham has proved difficult to identify as a furniture designer. In about 1800 he designed a massive Egyptian desk for Castle Howard, for which he also designed ormolu chandeliers (1802) as well as the whole decoration of the gallery, which he published in 1811. Litigious and quarrelsome, Tatham was reduced to poverty in his later years, having to sell his house and collection in 1834. PAPWORTH's *Architectural Dictionary* (1853) stated: 'To him, perhaps more than any other person, may be attributed the rise of the Anglo-Greek style which still prevails.' Thomas Hope, however, avoided any recognition of Tatham's achievement. It is possible that he was irked by Tatham's primacy.

Taute, Christian In 1749 Taute published *A Book of Ornaments useful for Jewellery* (eight plates), with designs for étuis, crosses, brooches, buckles, seals, snuff-boxes, a cane handle, a sword-hilt etc., composed of fleshy scrolled leaves and flowers in a style which looks back to the 17th century. He was presumably a jeweller in London.

Taylor, Ernest Archibald (1874–1951) Born in Greenock, Taylor was probably trained at the Glasgow School of Art in the late 1890s. He became a friend of MACKINTOSH, and in the 'STUDIO' in 1933 wrote an appreciation of Mackintosh as 'a neglected genius'. Taylor designed a drawing-room for the exhibit of the Glasgow cabinet-making firm of Wylie & Lochhead at the 1901 Glasgow International Exhibition. He also showed furniture and stained glass at the TURIN 1902 EXHIBITION, and was among the Glasgow designers praised by MUTHESIUS in his book on the English house. His style is a muted, delicate and accomplished version of the Mackintosh manner. In 1908 Taylor, who was mainly active as a painter, married Jessie Marion KING.

Taylor, Isaac (1730–1807) Born in Worcester, the son of a brass-founder, Taylor trained as a silversmith in London from 1752 and later worked as an engraver, publisher and designer of book illustrations and ornaments. In 1759 he engraved plates for the 1762 edition of CHIPPENDALE's *Director* and in 1765 he published MANWARING's *The Cabinet and Chair-Maker's Real Friend and Companion*. In the latter year he was elected to the SOCIETY OF ARTS, of which he became secretary in 1774, and at whose 1775 exhibition he showed an engraving of a sacrifice after STUART. In 1774 Taylor published a suite of coach designs and in 1775 a suite of panels of ADAM style ornament (six plates), with swags, VASES, sphinxes and relief medallions, a little ARTISAN in their complexity. He later had his son, Josiah, as partner; they published HEPPLEWHITE and many other works on architecture and design. His eldest son, another Isaac Taylor (1759–1829), was also active as illustrator and publisher; in 1796 he published a book of GOTHIC ornaments from Lavenham Church (forty plates).

Taylor, John Identifiable with a cabinet-maker and upholsterer who worked for the firm of Oakley and later had his own business at 19 Denmark Street, Soho, from about 1822 onwards. Taylor contributed several plates to ACKERMANN's *Repository* in 1821 to 1824. He also published three books of designs. *The Upholsterer's and Cabinet Maker's Pocket Assistant*, published by Josiah Taylor's Architectural Library, has 100 coloured plates in two parts, fifty of upholstery and fifty of cabinet work; it represents commercial Grecian furniture of about 1825, handsome, gaudy and sometimes barbarous. *Original and Novel Designs for Decorative Household Furniture* (about 1833) has seventy-two coloured plates, mainly of upholstery, in the same style, but with a few coarse GOTHIC designs. His *General Book of Reference for Chairs, Sofas, Couches, Easy Chairs &c.* contained sixty plates.

Teague, Walter Dorwin (1883–1960) Born in Decatur, Indiana, the son of a Methodist minister, Teague moved to New York in 1903 to become an artist, attending night school at the Art Students League and working for a while in an advertising agency. In 1911 he opened his own office, specializing in typographical designs for books and advertisements. In the mid-1920s, having diversified into packaging and piano cases, Teague set up as an industrial designer; his first major client, in 1928, was Eastman Kodak. His designs have included the 1930 Marmon car, the 1933 plastic Baby Brownie camera, the 1952 Scripto pen, Pullman coaches on the New Haven Railroad and Texaco service stations. For the New York 1939 World's Fair he designed the Ford exhibition, including chairs of aluminium and lucite (an early equivalent for perspex). In 1944 with DREYFUSS and LOEWY, Teague founded the American Society of Industrial Designers, of which he was first president. His book, *Design This Day* (1940), envisaged in its prologue 'the fundamental redesign of our world' and buttressed an exposition of the MODERN FUNCTIONALIST view of design with analyses of the proportions of the Parthenon. The Teague office grew large and promoted the bland American corporate style, most notably in its designs from 1946 for Boeing, coordinated by Teague's successor, Frank de Giudice.

Tempesta, Antonio (1555–1630) Born in Florence, Tempesta was a pupil of Jan van der STRAET and worked for VASARI on the decoration of the Palazzo Vecchio. On an early trip to Rome he worked for Pope Gregory XIII (1502–85). He later settled permanently in Rome, although he visited his native Florence in 1611. As a painter Tempesta assisted in the decorations of the Palazzo Farnese in Caprarola, and the Villa d'Este in Tivoli. His main activity however was as an engraver and he issued some 1,500 prints, mainly of battles and hunting scenes. These were widely circulated and often copied, for instance by Matthias Merian (1593–1650). They were frequently used to decorate earthenware by the potters of Castelli and of Moustiers, among others. A silver-mounted Antwerp cabinet from

Mentmore uses Tempesta subjects and in the Hunting Room at Wilton Edward PIERCE borrowed from *Venationes Ferarum, Avium, Piscium* (1602) and other works. The bold GROTESQUE ornaments framing the titles of Tempesta's illustrations to *Gerusalemme Liberata* (twenty plates) demonstrate his gifts as a designer of ornament, also apparent in his *Esemplare del Disegno* (1609; ten plates), panels of grotesque ornament dedicated to Prince Colonna.

Templier, Raymond (1891–1968) Born in Paris, Templier studied from 1909 to 1912 at the École Nationale Supérieure des Arts Décoratifs, and then entered the family jewellery business, founded in 1849. At the PARIS 1925 EXHIBITION he showed smart geometric ART DÉCO designs. In 1930 he was a founder member of the Union des Artistes Modernes. He also executed jewellery designed by MIKLOS. From 1929 to 1965 Marcel Percheron was his collaborator; Percheron then succeeded him. Templier also showed at the PARIS 1937 EXHIBITION.

Tesi, Mauro Antonio (1730–66) Born at Montalbano near Modena, Tesi was taught by the painter of ornament, Carlo Morettini, but he was largely an autodidact. In Bologna, where he was active as a designer of interiors and funerals, Tesi was friendly with BIANCONI, and with Count Francesco Algarotti (1712–64), the popularizer of science and NEO-CLASSICISM. Tesi's tomb for Algarotti in the Campo Santo at Pisa was completed by Bianconi, who designed Tesi's own tomb. In 1787 the amateur Count Massimiliano Gini engraved a *Raccolta di Disegni Originali* (forty-one plates), after drawings by Tesi. Designs by Tesi for friezes, consoles and church plate are included in PANFILI's *Frammenti di Ornati* (Bologna, 1783).

Tessier, Louis Born in about 1719, Tessier was employed as a flower painter at the Gobelins tapestry factory from 1749 to 1779. He died in 1781. Tessier often worked with Maurice JACQUES, and was mainly a designer of tapestry borders and chair covers, although in 1757 he designed a Savonnerie carpet. He published five suites of floral compositions for ornament, one of which was dedicated to the great naturalist Buffon (1707–88).

Tessin, Nicodemus (1654–1728) Born in Nyköping, the son of the Swedish architect Nicodemus Tessin (1615–81), Tessin studied architecture under his father and from 1670 to 1672 mathematics at Uppsala University. In 1673 he travelled to Italy, via Germany and Austria. Tessin was mainly in Rome until 1677. He studied the collection of Queen Christina of Sweden (1626–89) and the works of BERNINI, Carlo FONTANA and other BAROQUE painters, architects and designers. His many Roman drawings include sketches of a coach for the King of Spain and a mirror for Queen Christina, both designed by Bernini. On returning from Rome, Tessin travelled to England and then to France, where he remained until 1680 and developed a life-long admiration for LE BRUN. Back in Sweden, Tessin kept in contact with developments in Paris through the Swedish Ambassador there, Daniel Cronström (1655–1719). Tessin was appointed court architect in Stockholm in 1681 but in 1687 to 1688 travelled back to Rome via Copenhagen, Hamburg, Holland, Antwerp, Brussels and Paris. In Paris he was in close contact with BERAIN, '*fort mon ami*', and met Noel COYPEL and Le Brun. Tessin later ordered designs for a coach, a warship and tapestry borders from Berain and in 1697 was responsible for bringing Berain's pupil Jacques Demeux to Sweden. Tessin's principal architectural works were Drottningholm, where he succeeded his father, and the Royal Palace in Stockholm. In 1705 and 1714 he submitted to Louis XIV designs for rebuilding the Louvre. Tessin described his own work in Stockholm Palace as in the same taste as Versailles, but his interiors also used Italian models. He designed many court ceremonies, funerals, tombs, etc., metalwork, such as silver candelabra made for Stockholm Palace Chapel by Petter Henning in 1693, and furniture, including a baroque throne for Augustus II of Poland (1670–1733). Tessin was ennobled in 1714. By then his taste, never advanced, was very old-fashioned by Parisian standards. His son, Carl Gustaf Tessin (1695–1770), important as diplomat and statesman, was a notable collector of drawings, influenced by Pierre-Jean Mariette, whom he met in 1728; in 1728 he reported from Paris on the latest developments in design, advice to be used in Stockholm Palace.

Tetrode, Wilhelm Danielsz van Probably born in Delft, Tetrode was active as an architect and sculptor in Florence, Rome (1562), Delft (1568) and Cologne (1575). He also seems to have worked in London. Considering his excellent and international reputation as a sculptor among his contemporaries, he is an obscure figure. In 1587 a splendid design by Tetrode was published; it is for a dish, with Neptune in the centre and a border of marine creatures.

Textile Kunst und Industrie (1908–14) Edited from Dresden by Oskar Haebler this lavishly illustrated monthly included work by BEHRENS, ECKMANN, VAN DE VELDE, VOYSEY and MUCHA.

Theed, William (1764–1817) Born in London, the son of a wig-maker, Theed studied as a painter at the Royal Academy Schools from 1786. From about 1791 he spent some four years in Rome and emerged a sculptor. In 1799 Theed began to work as a designer for Messrs Wedgwood. He left them in 1804 for the goldsmiths Rundell, Bridge & Rundell, for whom he designed until his death.

Thierriat, Augustin (1789–1870) Thierriat was brought up in poverty in the aftermath of the 1793 Lyon siege. He studied painting under Alexis GROGNARD, and then at the Lyon École des Beaux-Arts. After a spell restoring medieval objects for the collector, painter and wallpaper designer Pierre Henri Révoil (1776–1842), Thierriat was in 1809 appointed professor of painting at the Lyon École des Beaux-Arts, where in 1823 he succeeded BERJON as professor of floral design. Thierriat was active as a textile designer but his main influence was as a teacher. He retired in 1854 and from 1850 to 1870 was curator of the Lyon Museum. His pupils, among them many designers and heads of design studios, included BERAUD, REIGNIER, SAINT-JEAN and CHABAL-DUSSURGEY.

Thiersch, Friedrich von (1852–1921) Born in Marburg, Thiersch was educated at the Stuttgart Polytechnic, where he became deeply imbued with SEMPER's ideas. Architectural training in Frankfurt was followed by foreign travels, during which he earned money as an illustrator. His first major commission was the decoration of the Frankfurt Opera (1879–80). He won the Reichstag competition in 1882, but his first executed monument was the Munich Palace of Justice (1887–97). He became a professor in Munich in 1880, succeeding NEUREUTHER in 1882, and taught on the Italian RENAISSANCE for forty years, his pupils including Walter GROPIUS and Ernst May. Thiersch also organized the Bavarian applied arts section at the PARIS 1900 EXHIBITION

and the German section at the TURIN 1902 EXHIBITION. He designed every decorative element of his many buildings, moving from Semper's Italian Renaissance to German Renaissance and BAROQUE, both styles encouraged by the MUNICH 1876 EXHIBITION. In 1900 he even designed a BIEDERMEIER revival interior for the Villa Hösslin. Thiersch is indeed a perfect specimen of the virtuosity and versatility of the great German establishment architect-designers of the post-Semper, pre-Secession epoque.

Thiry, Léonard A Fleming, Thiry is first recorded in 1536 working as a painter under ROSSO on the Galerie François I at Fontainebleau; he received relatively high payments and was later praised as a colourist by VASARI. From 1537 Thiry worked under PRIMATICCIO. In 1550 J. A. DUCERCEAU published in Orleans a suite of imaginary views of Roman ruins, *Fragmenta Structurae Veteris*, by Thiry, who had died in Antwerp. They were reprinted by Virgil SOLIS, who used one on a woodcut design for a doorway, probably in about 1555, and were again reissued in Nuremberg in 1565. In 1563 BOYVIN engraved *La Livre de la Conqueste de la Toison d'Or* (twenty-six plates after designs by Thiry). Dedicated to Charles IX, the book comprises narrative scenes of the Golden Fleece within Fontainebleau-style STRAPWORK GROTESQUE borders; the publisher, Jean de Mauregard, described them as '*patrons de tapisseries*', but no corresponding tapestries have survived, although the designs were often copied on Limoges enamels. Other prints by Boyvin may also have been designed by Thiry, who may have been an important promulgator of Rosso's designs. Thiry also designed stained glass.

Thomas, William A London architect

of Welsh origin with a smallish output, Thomas exhibited at the Royal Academy from 1780. His *Original Designs in Architecture* (1783) shows projects, mainly unexecuted, very much in the style of Robert ADAM, who was a subscriber. It includes Adamesque designs for pier-glasses, a girandole, a sideboard, ceilings, chimneypieces and iron railings. Thomas died in 1800.

Thomson, Peter Thomson designed the vast majority of the plates in *The Cabinet-Maker's Assistant* (Glasgow, 1853), an ambitious pattern-book which contained a comprehensive technical text as well as 101 plates of furniture designs. Their style is in the main a competent synthesis of Elizabethan, RENAISSANCE and ROCOCO elements, one ingredient sometimes predominating, most frequently the Elizabethan. Many designs incorporate NATURALISTIC ornament, which is most apparent in the few plates designed by A. H. Warren and in others by Carl Hambuch. Hambuch seems to have specialized in the Renaissance style, and to have designed objects shown at the LONDON 1851 EXHIBITION. Thomson also published *The Cabinet Maker's Sketch Book* (Glasgow), which contains designs also in *The Cabinet Maker's Assistant*.

Thonet, Michael (1796–1871) Born in Boppard-am-Rhein, Thonet established a furniture workshop there in 1819. From about 1830 he experimented with laminated wood, a frequent preoccupation of entrepreneurial craftsmen at this period. He showed chairs made by this method at the Koblenz 1841 and Mainz 1842 Exhibitions, and their success led to a move to Vienna under the patronage of Prince Metternich. In Vienna, Thonet was granted a patent for his new process in 1842 and worked with the cabinetmaker Carl Leistler on the furnishing of the Palais Liechtenstein. In 1849, backed

by Prinz Liechtenstein and his English architect, P. H. Desvignes (1804–83), Thonet set up his own factory, which he handed over to his five sons in 1853. Massive mechanization and expansion followed. Thonet's bentwood chairs were a major technical breakthrough, but their design, composed of more or less elaborate curves, should be seen not only as a response to the dictates of the manufacturing process, but also as an expression of the ROCOCO revival style which was dominant in Vienna in the 1840s. This is particularly evident in Thonet's elaborate contributions to the LONDON 1851 EXHIBITION, where he won a bronze medal. In the early 20th century Josef HOFFMANN and other advanced Viennese architects designed for Thonet, and LE CORBUSIER adopted the simpler Thonet chairs as appropriate MODERN furnishings. They have thenceforward been indelibly identified as 'CLASSICS of modern design'.

Thorn Prikker, Jan (1868–1932) Born in The Hague, Thorn Prikker, the son of a decorative painter, studied painting at the academy there from 1883 to 1887. From about 1890 he painted in an advanced Symbolist style and in about 1895, influenced by his friend VAN DE VELDE, he abandoned painting in favour of the decorative arts. He became one of the leaders of the Dutch revival in design in the 1890s, designing bookbindings, posters, batik, embroidery, tapestry, glass and pottery. From 1898 he designed furniture for Johan Th. Uiterwijk & Co. and in 1901 he executed sgraffito wall decorations for Dr Leuring in Scheveningen. From 1904 to 1910 Thorn Prikker taught at the school of applied arts in Krefeld, and he subsequently taught in Hagen (1910–19) and Essen (1913–18), Munich (1920–23), Düsseldorf (1923–6) and Cologne (1926–32). In 1910 he designed stained glass, commissioned by Karl Ernst

Osthaus, for Hagen railway station. Thorn Prikker was subsequently best known for his religious stained glass and mosaics. Evie HONE was among his admirers. Thorn Prikker's later stained glass was often abstract.

Thünckel, Johannes (1642–83) Born in Schnabelwaid, Thünckel trained as a goldsmith in Augsburg, and later worked in Creussen, where he died, having achieved some fame. He published a suite of six plates of scrolling floral and ACANTHUS ornament enlivened with butterflies and insects (1661, later edition 1664).

Thuraine *Plusieurs Models des plus nouvelles manières qui sont en usage en l'Art d'Arquebuzerie* (sixteen plates) contains designs for the decoration of guns by Thuraine and his partner Le Hollandois, who were gunsmiths to Louis XIV. It was published in several editions, one dated 1660. The ornament is mainly composed of scrolling ACANTHUS with GROTESQUE masks, figures and monsters. The first three plates show gunsmiths' workshops and cartouches with the names of many leading Parisian gunsmiths. *Plusieurs Models* was engraved by C. Jacquinet who also engraved MARCOU's contemporary pattern-book and probably collaborated on design. Some of the plates were later reprinted in Langlois's *Architecture à la Mode*. Nothing is known of Thuraine, but his partner, Le Hollandois, had a son who became Arquebusier Ordinaire du Roi in 1723 and had a lodging in the Louvre from 1724; his real name was Adrien Reynier.

Tibesar Tibesar designed a *Cahier d'Arabesques* (six plates), panels of NEO-CLASSICAL ornament, in a series published by Mondhare in about 1780 which included similar designs by MICHEL, FAY and PRIEUR.

Tidsskrift for Kunstindustri (1885–1915) Published in Copenhagen this well-illustrated journal was the leading Danish magazine of applied art and design. Its predecessors go back to 1838. In 1900 the title changed to *Tidsskrift for Industri* and the stress became industrial.

Tielt, Guillaume du A member of a Ypres family of painters and engravers, in about 1610 Tielt published a design for a monstrance, and some knife handles with figures of the arts and sciences and black GROTESQUE ornament, in the manner of DELAUNE or BRY.

Tiffany, Louis Comfort (1848–1933) The son of Charles Louis Tiffany (1812–1902), the founder of a prominent New York firm of silversmiths and jewellers, Louis Comfort Tiffany visited Europe in 1865 and then studied painting under George Inness (1825–94) in New Jersey. In 1868 to 1869 he painted in Paris under Léon Bailly. He then travelled to Spain and North Africa with Samuel Colman. Back in New York from 1870 Tiffany painted and in 1877, with John LA FARGE, founded the Society of American Artists. In the late 1870s, under the influence of Edward C. MOORE, Tiffany developed an interest in the decorative arts. In 1878 he was associated with Candace WHEELER's amateur Society of Decorative Arts and in 1879 founded a professional interior decorating firm, Louis C. Tiffany & Associated Artists. This venture was very successful, notable works including the Veterans' Room of the Seventh Regiment Armory (1879), Samuel L. Clemens' (Mark Twain's) house (1880–81) and several rooms in the White House (1882–3), all in an elaborate Art style. The art critic Clarence Cook wrote a promotional booklet, *What Shall We Do with Our Walls?* (1881). At this period Tiffany designed wallpapers with wild clematis and cobwebs for Warren, Fuller & Co. of New York. From the late 1870s Tiffany also took an interest in stained glass, using opalescent glass in 1878 and patenting lustre glass in 1881. In 1885 he founded the Tiffany Glass Company. He visited the PARIS 1889 EXHIBITION, where he met BING, who had supplied oriental goods to the Tiffany firm from the 1870s. As a result Bing became Tiffany's exclusive European distributor. A window by Tiffany, the Four Seasons, was shown in Paris in 1892 and his exhibit at the CHICAGO 1893 WORLD COLUMBIAN EXPOSITION was highly successful. In 1895 Bing showed Tiffany stained-glass windows designed by Pierre BONNARD, Vuillard, Toulouse-Lautrec and others. Tiffany's Favrile glass, iridescent, elegant and colourful, was shown at Bing's Art Nouveau in 1895; it had been patented in 1894. Thenceforward Tiffany glass was a successful and well-publicized ART NOUVEAU product; Bing wrote on Tiffany glass in the first issue of 'KUNST UND KUNSTHANDWERK' (1898) and Tiffany won a Grand Prix at both the PARIS 1900 EXHIBITION and the TURIN 1902 EXHIBITION. Tiffany also designed jewellery and produced mosaics, lighting, ceramics and textiles. He became artistic director of the family firm on his father's death in 1902. Tiffany entertained lavishly in New York up to the First World War and in 1918 set up a foundation to establish his luxurious country house, Laurelton, as a retreat for artists.

Tijou, Jean Tijou was employed to execute ornamental ironwork at Hampton Court Palace from 1689 to 1699. He also supplied ironwork to Chatsworth from 1688, and worked at St Paul's Cathedral from 1695 to 1707. He seems to have left England in 1712. His *A New Book of Drawings* (London, 1693; twenty plates) was engraved by

Blaize Gentot, who also engraved a silver table-top for the Duke of Devonshire, and had an allegorical title-page by Tijou's son-in-law, the painter Louis Laguerre (1663–1721). *A New Book* depicts the designs for Tijou's ironwork at Hampton Court, Chatsworth, Trinity College, Cambridge, Wimpole Hall and elsewhere. It was reissued by FORDRIN in Paris in 1723 without acknowledgement, and in 1740 Batty LANGLEY borrowed plates of ironwork for his *Treasury of Designs* from Tijou. Tijou's style derived from Jean I BERAIN and is closely related to the ornament of Daniel MAROT, his contemporary and superior. His influence is visible in gates supplied by Robert Bakewell to Cholmondeley Castle in 1722.

Toft, Charles Born in about 1831, Toft was educated at the School of Design in Stoke-on-Trent. In the 1860s he designed metalwork for Elkingtons and taught at the Birmingham School of Art. From at least 1872 Toft designed ceramics for Mintons. He was particularly involved in their revival of 16th-century French 'Henri II' ware, whose imitation was a preoccupation of several mid-19th-century ceramicists. He later opened his own factory in Stoke-on-Trent. Toft died in 1909.

Torelli, Giacomo (1604–78) Born in Fano, Torelli moved to Venice in about 1640 to work as an architect in the Arsenal but by 1641 had established himself as a theatrical designer. In 1645 he went to Paris to work for Louis XIV. He was described by La Fontaine (1621–95) as '*magicien expert et faiseur de miracles*'. In about 1660 Torelli designed three BAROQUE state carriages for Cardinal Mazarin (1602–61). In 1661, beset by rivals, he returned to Fano, but at his death he was planning to go back to France.

Toro, Jean Bernard Honoré
(1672–1731) Born in Toulon, the son of
a carver, Pierre Turreau, who worked in
the naval arsenal there, Toro was a
pupil of the sculptor Pierre Puget
(1620–94). He was in Avignon in 1706
and from at least 1713 to 1716 in Aix.
Toro then spent a year in Paris arranging
the publication of his works under the
auspices of Charles-Nicolas Lepas-
Dubuisson, Architecte du Roy. In 1717
Toro returned to Toulon, where he was
employed as chief carver at the Arsenal
from 1719, an arrogant and difficult
employee with ambitions to design as
well as carve, described in 1728 as 'capri-
cieux et fantasque'. In 1719 he submitted
an unexecuted design for the high altar
of the cathedral of Saint-Sauveur in Aix.
Toro's published designs comprise some
twenty-five suites of six plates each,
including tables, VASES, cartouches,
trophies and a wide range of ornament.
His style is a lighter version of the
BAROQUE GROTESQUE of Jean I
BERAIN, handled with a vehement but
controlled energy which infuses the conventions with new life and looks forward
to the ROCOCO style, especially in an
occasional use of asymmetry. Dragons
snarl, masks ogle and grimace, and
satyrs and putti contort themselves
unconscionably, all supported on a scaffolding of STRAPWORK and scrolls. Typical suites are *Trophées* (six plates),
Cartouches (six plates), *Desseins Arabesques à Plusieurs Usages* (six plates),
Nouveau Livre de Vases (six plates) and
Livre de Tables de diverses formes (six
plates). Toro's works were reissued by
the publisher Gautrot in Paris, and
Masks and Other Ornaments (London,
1745; nine plates), published by F. Noble
in St Martin's Court and aimed at coach
painters, watch engravers, chasers, carvers, etc., was but one of the works
available in England, where LOCK,
Thomas JOHNSON (2) and LINNELL,
etc., freely borrowed motifs from Toro.

Torregiani, Alfonso (1682–1764) Born
at Budrio, Torregiani was a pupil of the
Bolognese architect Giuseppe Antonio
Torri (1655–1713), and was himself
extremely prolific as an architect from
1704 to 1762. His designs included
scrolled wrought-iron well-heads and
large altar candlesticks for the church of
San Procolo (1752), in a manner similar
to that of GIARDINI.

Toulouze, Guillaume Toulouze, who
described himself as a master embroiderer of Montpelier, published two pattern-books for embroidery, *Livre de
bouquets de fleurs et oiseaux* (1655; thirty-
seven plates) and *Livre de Fleurs,
Feuilles et Oyzeaus* (1656; twenty-seven
plates). The latter, dedicated to the
painter Sébastien Bourdon (1616–71),
a native of Montpelier, contains birds
and botanically accurate flowers and
leaves.

Toutin, Jean (1578–1644) Toutin was
born in Châteaudun, the son of a goldsmith from Blois. He himself was in
Paris from about 1632. Toutin was a
virtuoso enameller and published two
suites of seven plates each, with black
designs for enamelling, in Châteaudun in
1618 and 1619. They were soon reprinted
together in Strasbourg by Jacob von der
Heyden. Toutin's designs are delightful.
The backs of pendants or miniatures are
presented hanging above figures or landscapes, or shaped as a beetle's back, a
shield held by a warrior, a leaf or even
a block of wood sawn by two sawyers.
Their manner varies between the
stretched GROTESQUE, and the scrolled
foliate style known as COSSE-DE-
POIS.

Tozzi, Pietro Paolo Tozzi published the
first lace pattern-book to be engraved
rather than woodcut, *Libro Novissimo
de recchami* (Padua, before 1596; thirteen plates). It contained relatively

simple designs some of which were later copied by Giacomo FRANCO. Tozzi also issued a writing handbook embellished with lace designs, *Ghirlanda di sei vaghi fiori* (Padua, 1604; fifty plates).

Trevelyon, Thomas Probably a writing master by profession, Trevelyon seems to have been active in London. He executed a manuscript *Miscellany*, dated 1608, with at least 327 pages, including a calendar, a gazetteer, epitomes of the Old Testament and British history, and some eighty pages of ornamental motifs and patterns, probably intended for use by embroiderers. A second Trevelyon manuscript, of at least 1,034 pages, is dated 1616. It repeats much of the first but includes a section, 'The green Dragone. For Joyners and Gardeners . . . Knotes, and Buildyngs, and Morysies, and Termes . . .', which includes the royal arms, flowers, architectural ornament, STRAPWORK, knots, alphabets and designs for inlay influenced by Hans VREDEMAN DE VRIES. Trevelyon's works are rare documents of English taste in ornament around 1600. Among the few similar compendia are the *Book of Divers Devices* (1593–1622) by Thomas Fella, a draper and scrivener of Halesworth, and *Pennarum Nitor* (dated 1608 and 1610) by Joseph Lawson.

Troy, Jean François de (1679–1752) Born in Paris, the son of a painter under whom he studied, Troy travelled in 1699 to Italy, where he stayed in Florence, Pisa and Rome before returning to Paris in 1706. Troy became a member of the Academy in 1708 and was from 1738 Director of the French Academy in Rome. In 1736 he was commissioned to design the History of Esther (seven pieces) for the Gobelins tapestry factory. The suite, completed in 1742, proved very popular, woven from the beginning to 1768 with borders by Pierre Josse Perrot and from 1772 to 1794 with bor-ders by Maurice JACQUES. Troy was subsequently commissioned to design the History of Jason (seven pieces), completed 1748.

Tschichold, Jan (1902–74) Born in Leipzig, the son of a sign painter, Tschichold was trained as a teacher of drawing. The Leipzig 1914 Exhibition of book production and graphic design and the printing magazine *Zwiebelfisch* aroused his interest in typography and calligraphy. His calligraphic studies were influenced by Edward Johnston (1872–1944) and Rudolf von Larisch (1856–1934). From 1919 to 1920 Tschichold studied typography at the Leipzig Academy under Professor Hermann Delitsch (1869–1937), whose assistant he became in 1921. Tschichold's mentors also included Walter Tiemann (1876–1951), Hugo Steiner-Prag (1880–1945) and Carl Ernst Poeschel (1874–1944) of the printers Poeschel & Trepte. He was influenced by Paul Renner's *Typographie als Kunst* (1922) and by Rudolf Koch (1876–1934) of Offenbach. Tschichold visited the first BAUHAUS Exhibition in 1923 and in 1924 designed a poster for Philobiblon in Warsaw which displayed the direct influence of MOHOLY-NAGY and El LISSITZKY. In 1925 he published his own MODERN typographic manifesto in the journal *Typographische Mitteilungen*. Tschichold established himself as a designer in Berlin in 1926 but in the same year moved to Munich to teach under Paul Renner (1878–1956). In Munich he designed many innovative posters for the Phoebus-Palast cinema from 1927 to 1928. His *Die neue Typographie* (1928) supplied a codified textbook of the new typography as practised at the Bauhaus and by Tschichold himself. In 1933 he went into exile in Basel, where he published a major work on typographic design, *Typographische Gestaltung* (1935). In 1935, thanks to a recommendation from McKnight KAUFFER, an exhibition of Tschichold's work was held in London under the aegis of the publishers Lund Humphries. In 1937 he was commissioned to design the *Penrose Annual* of 1938 (he also designed that of 1970). By 1935, without abandoning his Modern manner, he was also practising a more conventional symmetrical typography, and he was attacked as a renegade for so doing by the architect Max Bill. More books on calligraphy followed, including *Meisterbuch der Schrift* (1952). In 1945 Tschichold was employed as a designer by Penguin Books. He lived in London from 1946 to 1949, designing over 500 titles. Back in Basel he continued to be extremely active, his work including publicity material from 1955 to 1967 for the pharmaceutical firm of Hoffmann-Laroche. In 1971 he published a book on El Lissitzky, on whom he had first written in 1931. By his death Tschichold was loaded with international honours.

Tuffet, François (1809–54) Born in Mâcon, Tuffet studied at the Lyon École des Beaux-Arts, where he was taught by THIERRIAT in 1824. He served as professor of applied design at the École from 1840 to 1854, and published *Album du Dessinateur* (Lyon, 1849) and *Flore du Dessinateur*.

Tura, Cosimo Born shortly before 1430 in Ferrara, Tura worked as a painter and designer for the court there from at least 1451, becoming official court painter in the early 1460s. Tura designed tapestries in 1457, 1467, 1473, 1474 and 1479. He also designed decorations for the visit to Ferrara of Galeazzo Maria Sforza (1444–76) in 1459, a rich silver service for the marriage of Duke Ercole I and Eleanora of Aragon in 1471, and another

in 1484 to 1485 for Lodovico Il Moro. Tura was superseded as court painter in 1486 and died in poverty in 1495.

Turin 1902 Exhibition In 1899 the architects of the Circolo degli Artisti of Turin decided to organize an exhibition of design. This project developed into the 1902 Esposizione Internazionale d'Arte Decorativa Moderna, a display of ART NOUVEAU comparable to the PARIS 1900 EXHIBITION. The main buildings, by Raimondo d'Aronco (1857–1932), were flamboyant in the extreme. Designers represented included HORTA from Belgium, Walter CRANE from England, MACKINTOSH and the MACNAIRS from Scotland, BEHRENS, PANKOK and OLBRICH from Germany, BERLAGE from Holland, and QUARTI, BUGATTI and BASILE from Italy. MEIER-GRAEFE's La Maison Moderne showed furniture by VAN DE VELDE, and BING's Art Nouveau an ensemble by GAILLARD. The magazine *Arte Decorativa Moderna*, founded in 1902, was a product of the exhibition.

Tvar (1949–70) Published in Prague, this well-illustrated journal covered all aspects of Czech design.

Typographica (1949–67) Edited by Herbert Spencer, this varied and interesting London journal was rich in illustrations of all aspects of typography.

Typography (1936–9) A quarterly, edited by Robert Harling and published by James Shand's Shenval Press, *Typography* was a high-quality journal dealing with all aspects of graphic design with a brilliant variety of illustrations. A later successor was 'ALPHABET AND IMAGE'.

U

Udine, Giovanni da Born at Udine as Giovanni Nanni or Recamador, the son of a tailor, Giovanni da Udine arrived in Rome in about 1513 with an introduction from Baldassare Castiglione (1478–1529). Up to 1516 he worked in the studio of the painter PERUZZI. He then entered RAPHAEL's studio, where a Flemish colleague taught him fruit and flower painting. Udine made a detailed study of the Roman GROTESQUES in the Domus Aurea and the Roman plasterwork in the Colosseum. His name is scratched in the Domus Aurea near that of Nicoletto da MODENA and it was he who showed Raphael its Roman decorations and helped to revive them in the Stufetta, or bathroom, of Cardinal Bibbiena, commissioned from Raphael in 1516. From about 1517 to 1519 Udine was employed by Raphael on the Loggie and Loggetta in the Vatican, where he revitalized the Roman grotesque, enlivening his archaeology with lively representations of a wide range of animal and marine life. Udine was the great early master of the revived grotesque in paint and plaster; in 1537 SERLIO described his work in the Loggie as superior to the work of the Romans. He also designed tapestry borders for Raphael. In 1520 Udine designed for Pope Leo X a suite of twenty tapestries for the Sala di Costantino in the Vatican with playing putti, to be woven in Flanders. From 1520 he was in the service of Cardinal Giulio de' Medici, later Pope Clement VII, in the Villa Madama in Rome, where he collaborated with Giulio ROMANO, and the Palazzo Medici in Florence, and in 1523 he worked with Perino del VAGA in the Vatican. In 1524, after visiting Udine and Venice in 1522, Udine designed a suite of grotesque mythological tapestries for Pope Clement VII. In 1526 he was asked by MICHELANGELO to assist in the decoration of the Biblioteca Laurenziana in Florence, where he painted glass with grotesque ornament in 1532 to 1533, after a spell in Udine following the Sack of Rome in 1527 and a return to Rome in 1531. From 1534 Udine was permanently based in Udine, although in 1539 he worked with SALVIATI in the Palazzo Grimani in Venice and in 1550 he visited Rome again, where VASARI obtained him a sinecure as Keeper of the Seal, previously held by Guglielmo della PORTA. In 1552 he was appointed official architect of Udine, but he died back in Rome in 1561. In 1789 Carlo Lasinio (1759–1838) published plates of grotesques attributed to Udine, a tribute to their renewed popularity in the NEO-CLASSICAL period.

Ulm, Hochschule für Gestaltung The Hochschule für Gestaltung (High School for Design) in Ulm was founded as a private institution in 1950 by Inge Aicher-Scholl in memory of her brother and sister, Hans and Sophie Scholl, who had been executed by the Nazi regime. Teaching began in 1953 in provisional buildings but the formal opening of the Hochschule was in 1955, when it moved into new buildings designed by Max Bill. The Hochschule was formed in four divisions, product design, architecture, visual communication and information. Max Bill, director of the Hochschule up to 1956, was a product of the BAUHAUS. His successor, Tomás Maldonado, was strongly influenced by the Hannes Meyer regime at the Bauhaus. The Ulm tradition in product design was industrial, serious, thorough and purist. Teachers included Hans Gugelot and Herbert Lindinger, but the most famous product of the Hochschule was Dieter RAMS. The Hochschule closed in 1968.

Ulrich, Heinrich Ulrich was active as an engraver in Nuremberg from about 1595. He died there in 1621 after spending the years 1615 to 1619 in Vienna. His works include copies after DÜRER and the BEHAM brothers, allegories, historical subjects and a writing manual (1605). In 1602 he published a suite of designs for box-lids (twelve plates), oval with scrolled STRAPWORK GROTESQUES incorporating cheerful putti, jesters, warriors and animals.

Ungewitter, Georg Gottlob (1820–64) Born at Wanfried in Hessen, Ungewitter studied architecture at the Kassel Polytechnic and subsequently in Munich (1837). He practised in Hamburg from the fire of 1842 to 1848 and then in Leipzig. In 1851 he was appointed to teach at the school of applied arts at Kassel, where he trained a generation of GOTHIC specialists. His first book, on Gothic designs for decoration in brick and stone (Leipzig, 1849), was followed by another on Gothic timberwork (1849). From 1850 he became friendly with August Reichensperger (1808–95), the leading German ideologue of the Gothic revival; Ungewitter was later in contact with VIOLLET-LE-DUC, and kept abreast of developments in England through the 'BUILDER' and other publications. His book of Gothic furniture designs, *Entwürfe zu Gothischen Möbel* (Leipzig, 1851), contains forty-eight accurate and powerful drawings, some based on Gothic prototypes, others wholly original, with a strong stress on construction; an English translation appeared in 1858. Of Ungewitter's other books on Gothic design the most notable was his *Gothisches Musterbuch* (Leipzig, 1856–61), a collaboration with Vincenz Statz (1819–98), which contained 216 plates and an introduction and text by Reichensperger. It ranged from metalwork to alphabets and stained glass, all drawn from medieval specimens. Ungewitter had an extensive practice as a church restorer and builder. His Gothicism was ideological and emotional as well as formal; an outspoken opponent of SEMPER'S RENAISSANCE revival style, he was both a Catholic and a conservative.

Unit One In 1933 Paul NASH announced in a letter to *The Times* the formation of Unit One, a group of MODERN artists which included John ARMSTRONG, Wells COATES and the architect Colin Lucas. Its headquarters were the Mayor Gallery, whose premises were designed by O'RORKE, and a Unit One exhibition was held there in April 1934. Also in 1934 appeared an anthology of the group's work edited by Herbert Read, chief apologist for the group, whose *Art and Industry* (1934) was designed by Herbert BAYER. Unit One broke up in 1935 as a result of tensions between the abstractionists and surrealists among its members.

Unselt, Johann A cabinet-maker in Augsburg in 1681, Unselt published about six suites of ornament there, including *Neues Zierrathen Büchlein* (1690) and *Neues Zierathen Buch* (1695–6). They comprise coach ornaments, doors, frames, brackets, friezes, a bed and a sleigh in a vigorous ACANTHUS style comparable to the works of ECHTER and INDAU and based on the

Roman acanthus style of SCHOR, FERRI and PASSARINI.

Unteutsch, Friedrich Born in Berlin, the son of a master-gunner, Unteutsch travelled for nine years before settling in Frankfurt in 1628. He became a master cabinet-maker in 1631, and from 1632 onwards executed many official commissions, being appointed official town cabinet-maker in 1635. His *Neues Zieratenbuch* was published by Paulus Fürst at Frankfurt in about 1645. Its two parts include nearly eighty plates of vigorous AURICULAR designs for furniture, church woodwork and ornament.

Ursoni, Filippo Ursoni describes himself as a painter of Mantua on the title of his only known work, a book of designs for arms and armour in the VICTORIA & ALBERT MUSEUM dated 1554.

Lelio ORSI, whose name was given as Urso on his tomb and who also served the Gonzagas, may have been a relation of Ursoni's. His book of designs comprises harnesses for horses, horsemen in masquerade costume, including Roman, Turkish and Muscovite, armour, including helmets comparable to designs by Mantegna and POLIDORO DA CARAVAGGIO, stirrups and saddles and pageant helmets, some of which bear the insignias of the Emperor Charles V and Henri II of France, sword-hilts, and innumerable bits for horses, reminiscent of Grisone's pioneering book on the subject (Naples, 1550). Ursoni's armour designs are MANNERIST in style, influenced by Giulio ROMANO and comparable to those of WOEIRIOT, with masks, snakes, ACANTHUS and intertwined figures.

V

Vaga, Perino del (1501–46) Born Pietro Buonaccorsi in Florence, Vaga was trained as a painter under Andrea de' Ceri and Ridolfo del Ghirlandaio. He then became assistant to a painter named Vaga, whose name he adopted, and with whom he went to Rome in about 1517, when he worked on the triumphal arch to celebrate the entry of Pope Leo X to Florence. In Rome, Vaga was an assiduous student of the works of MICHELANGELO and RAPHAEL, and of the antique, especially GRO-TESQUE decorations. He also became friendly with Giulio ROMANO and Giovanni Francesco Penni, and worked with them on the grotesque decorations of the Vatican Loggie under Giovanni da UDINE. After the Sack of Rome in 1527 Vaga moved to Genoa and Pisa, where he worked for Andrea Doria. His works included ornaments for galleys and tapestries, for example a suite with the Story of Dido. Among Vaga's assistants in Genoa were Guglielmo della PORTA and Luzio Luzzi, called Romano. In 1537 Vaga moved back to Rome with Luzzi, as court painter to Pope Paul III. His painted decorations in the Palazzo Massimo display the influence of ROSSO's work at Fontainebleau. Vaga was a gifted and prolific designer of goldsmiths' work in an elegant MANNERIST style, although many of the surviving drawings for metalwork in his manner may be by Luzzi. The Farnese casket (1547–61) includes crystal plaques by Giovanni Benardi designed by Vaga to supplement those after Michelangelo.

Valadier, Giuseppe (1762–1839) Born in Rome, the son of the goldsmith Luigi Valadier (1726–85) who designed sanctuary lamps for Wardour Castle in 1775, Valadier was destined to inherit his father's workshop but, having displayed a precocious talent for architecture, received papal support for architectural studies at the Accademia di San Luca. In 1775 he won a prize in the Concorso Clementino and in 1781 travelled via Modena, Florence and Milan to Marseilles. He was subsequently active as a church architect in Spoleto and elsewhere, and was planning to go to Paris when his father's death by suicide in 1785 caused him to return to Rome. He then took over the workshop, which in 1789 to 1790 produced a monumental granite table made for Pope Pius VI (1717–99) supported on figures of Hercules by the sculptor Vincenzo Pacetti (1746–1820). Valadier became a master goldsmith in 1791, but continued his activity as an architect and town planner, working for the French regime in Rome from 1809 to 1814. In 1817 he sold the Valadier workshop to his brother-in-law Giuseppe Spagna. Valadier was until his death the most prominent NEO-CLASSICAL architect in Rome. He published superb archaeological drawings of ancient Roman monuments in 1810 and his *Opere di Architettura e di Ornamento* (1833) includes a silver reliquary for the relics of the Holy Cradle in Santa Maria Maggiore. In 1779 Valadier had designed neo-classical table ornaments and he later designed many state ceremonies and funerals, several in collaboration with the architect Giuseppe Camporese (1763–1822). Valadier's last ceremonial design was a canonization in 1839.

Vallée, G. Vallée was a smith in Paris who worked at Versailles in the early 1680s. *Divers Livres de Serrurerie et d'Ornement* (forty-eight plates) comprises handsome late-BAROQUE designs for ironwork, which were still being followed in houses in Liège in the 1730s.

Van de Velde, Henri (1863–1957) Born in Antwerp, the son of a chemist, Van de Velde showed musical talent at an early age. From 1881 to 1884 he studied painting at the Antwerp Academy, and then from 1884 to 1885 under Carolus Duran in Paris. In 1886 he joined the Antwerp art society Als ik Kan, and helped to found the L'Art Indépendant society. In 1886 he was elected a member of the advanced post-impressionist group Les Vingt. At this stage Van de Velde was in contact with Seurat and Signac; in about 1890 he was influenced by Van Gogh. In 1892 Van de Velde gave up painting for design. He was much influenced by English wallpapers, and by the writings of RUSKIN and William MORRIS, to which he was introduced by the painter and potter Willy Finch (1854–1930). In 1892 he showed an embroidery design, La Veillée des Anges, influenced by Gauguin, at the Salon of Les Vingt, and designed titles to *Dominikal* and *Salutations*, poems by his friend Max Elskamp, and designed ornaments for Elskamp's advanced periodical *Van Nu en Straks*, published from 1893. He also designed several bookbindings. In 1894 Van de Velde published *Déblaiement de l'art*, a plea for the unity of art, and taught on 'Arts d'Industrie et d'Ornementation' at Brussels University; at this stage he seems to have welcomed the possibilities of machine production, a position he was later to modify. In 1895 his first house, Bloemenwerf, in Uccle, was built. MEIER-GRAEFE and BING visited Bloemenwerf and as a result Van de Velde designed four rooms for the latter's new gallery, L'Art Nouveau, incorporating friezes by Georges Lemmen (1865–1916) and pottery by Finch. A room from Bloemenwerf was shown at the Brussels 1896 Salon de la Libre Esthétique. In 1897 Van de Velde's furniture was much admired at the Dresden Exhibition. He travelled there and to Berlin; he contributed an article on modern furniture to 'PAN'. Van de Velde also helped to design the Tervuren 1897 Colonial Exhibition, and in 1898 showed at the Hague Arts and Crafts Exhibition. He founded his own decorating firm and factory near Brussels and decorated the office of Meier-Graefe's Maison Moderne in Paris, including an imposing curved desk. Also in 1898 Van de Velde began to design publicity material for the food firm of Tropon in Mulheim. The first number of Meier-Graefe's 'ART DÉCORATIF' (1898) was devoted to Van de Velde's work; Van de Velde himself designed the title-page. In 1899 he designed furniture for the firm of Löffler and decorated the shops of the Habana Company in Berlin. Van de Velde moved his own office to Berlin in 1900. The decoration of the Folkwang Museum in Hagen (1900–1912) represented the culmination of Van de Velde's early curvilinear ART NOUVEAU style. His *Die Renaissance in modernen Kunstgewerbe* (Berlin, 1901) described the recent revival of the decorative arts. In Berlin Van de Velde was a prolific designer in every field, including silver and cutlery, Meissen and Bückau porcelain, jewellery and textiles. He designed decorations for Nietzsche's *Ecce Homo* (1908) and *Also Sprach Zarathustra* (1908). He became a close friend of the printing maecenas Count

Harry Kessler, for whom he designed the French edition (1915) of *Amo* (1909). In 1902 Van de Velde was appointed an artistic adviser in Weimar, and in 1904 professor of the new school of applied arts there, whose building he designed; it was officially opened in 1908. In 1907 he was a founder member of the DEUTSCHE WERKBUND. In 1914 his disagreement with MUTHESIUS about the Werkbund's basic principles came out into the open at the COLOGNE DEUTSCHE WERKBUND EXHIBITION; Muthesius's stress on standardization and the machine seemed to Van de Velde too restrictive a discipline for the individual creative designer. Van de Velde resigned his post in Weimar in the same year, suggesting OBRIST, ENDELL and Walter GROPIUS as potential successors. Gropius was appointed and the BAUHAUS resulted. In 1917 Van de Velde moved to Switzerland where he was mainly active as a writer and lecturer. In 1920 he went to Holland, succeeding BERLAGE as architect to Müller & Co., the firm owned by the Kröller-Müller family, for whom he designed the Kröller-Müller Museum, first conceived in 1923 and erected from 1937 to 1954. In 1926 he created the Institut Supérieur des Arts Décoratifs in Brussels, on the model of his earlier school in Weimar, and from 1926 to 1936 he was Professor of Architecture at the University of Ghent. Van de Velde continued to take an academic interest in ornament, publishing a paper on its classification in 1935. But his own works and his own teachings of around 1930 reflect a MODERN approach to design, displayed in the cool and geometrical use of new materials in his interiors for the steamer *Prince Baudouin* (1933–4). In 1947 Van de Velde moved to Switzerland, where he published his memoirs (1956), in which he emphasized his own role in the creation of the Modern style. He had strong misgivings about the Zürich 1952 Art Nouveau Exhibition, which he feared would draw attention to his youthful aberrations. Throughout his career Van de Velde was a prolific writer on design and ornament and was perhaps most important in this propagandist role. His early writings stressed the importance of line in ornament, and his early graphic designs are often completely abstract. Van de Velde's early metalwork also displays remarkable freedom and invention. However, much of his furniture is awkward or stolid, and his later designs are often dull, albeit theoretically sound.

Vardy, John From 1736 Vardy was Clerk of the Works at Greenwich and he continued in various posts in the Office of Works until 1763. He died in 1765. Vardy had a life-long admiration for William KENT, who had been appointed Deputy Surveyor of the Office of Works in 1735, and Vardy's *Some Designs of Mr Inigo Jones and Mr William Kent* (1744) reflects this discipleship. In 1751 he designed a building for the Society of DILETTANTI and in 1754 another for the British Museum. Neither was executed, but Vardy's links with collectors and patrons in the gestative period of NEO-CLASSICISM led to the commission to design Spencer House for the 1st Earl Spencer, under the supervision of Colonel George Gray of the Society of Dilettanti. Vardy's furniture designs for Spencer House use a Kentian vocabulary with notable refinement, incorporating sculptural supports and palm ornament which look back via Kent to Roman BAROQUE and to Inigo JONES and John WEBB respectively. These designs prefigure the explicit neo-classicism of James STUART, who took over from Vardy at Spencer House in 1759, while a table designed by Vardy for Hackwood Park in 1761 anticipates PIRANESI in form if not in detail.

Vardy's brother Thomas was a carver and it is probable that Vardy's designs may have influenced not only his brother but also the carver-designer John LINNELL.

Vasari, Giorgio (1511–74) Born in Arezzo, Vasari studied under a glass painter there before moving to Florence in 1524. He was back in Arezzo in 1527 but was in Florence again in 1529, studying goldsmiths' work as well as painting. In 1530 he collaborated on the design of triumphal arches to commemorate the coronation of the Emperor Charles V. At the end of 1531 Vasari moved to Rome, where he established a close friendship with SALVIATI and studied the works of MICHELANGELO, RAPHAEL, PERUZZI and POLIDORO. In 1532 he was back again in Florence, where in 1536 he worked on decorations for the entry of Charles V. From 1538 Vasari was mainly in Rome but also travelled to Arezzo, Urbino, Bologna, Florence, Lucca and Naples. He began to work as an architect at this period and also prepared the first edition of his *Vite de' più eccellenti Architetti, Pittori, et Scultori Italiani* (1550, second edition, 1568). In 1554 Vasari settled in Florence and worked as painter, architect and artistic impresario for Duke Cosimo I de' Medici at the Palazzo Vecchio and elsewhere. Vasari's designs for Cosimo included a cameo, tapestries on the Life of Man (from 1560), on which he was assisted by STRAET, map cupboards in the Palazzo Vecchio (1565) and a table supported by two sphinxes (1574) carved by Dionigi Nigetti and influenced by J. A. DUCERCEAU, intended for Cosimo's bedroom. Vasari also designed decorations, for example for the marriage of Giovanna d'Austria to Francesco de' Medici (1565). In 1572 he wrote that Francesco would keep him up to three o'clock in the morning to draw VASES. Vasari also designed many church fittings, including the choir stalls of Arezzo Cathedral (1554) executed by Giuliano di Baccio d'Agnolo, a wooden tabernacle for the cathedral of Sante Croce in Florence (1566), the altar in the Cappella Buonarroti in Santa Croce (1566), and the carved organ case of the church of the Cavalier di Santo Stefano, Pisa (1569–71). From 1571 Vasari spent much of his time in Rome, but he died in Florence. Vasari's hero was Michelangelo, the '*capo, padre et maestro di tutti*' of the FLORENCE ACCADEMIA DEL DISEGNO, whose funeral in 1564 he helped to organize. By translating Michelangelo's stress on the paramount importance of drawing (*disegno*) into an academic doctrine, Vasari provided an important basis for the teaching of design. His own example as an impresario of design at the Florentine court was also to have a far-reaching influence.

Vases The vase and its close relations the ewer and the urn were, from the RENAISSANCE onwards, a constant theme of designers. In 1531 the French humanist and diplomat Lazare de Baïf published a book on ancient vases: a summary of it appeared in 1536. The most influential early vase designs were those by POLIDORO DA CARAVAGGIO. Thereafter MANNERIST designers, for instance VICO, HORNICK and BUONTALENTI, BAROQUE designers, such as STELLA, Jean LE PAUTRE and STEINLE, and NEO-CLASSICAL designers, such as SALY, VIEN and BEAUVAIS, all designed vases. Piranesi's *Vasi, Candelabri, Cippi, Sarcofagi* (1778) provided pseudo-classical models for imitation, and the illustrations of HAMILTON's collections, published in 1766 to 1767 and 1791 to 1795, comprised, in effect, an archaeological pattern-book. GOTHIC vases by PETIT, NATURALISTIC vases by ZIEGLER, Renaissance Revival vases by M. L. E. SOLON, exemplify the continuing use of such forms for the pure display of design and ornament during the 19th century.

Vauquer, Jacques (1621–86) Vauquer was born and worked in Blois, where his brother, Robert (1625–70), was active as an enameller. Vauquer engraved flowers by the painter Jean-Baptiste MONNOYER (1636–99) but also engraved floral and other ornaments of his own design. His works comprise over 100 plates and include flowers in VASES, studies of individual flowers, flowers as cartouches and swags, dials, backs and borders for watches to be decorated in enamel with floral ornament, religious subjects, and putti, banderoles, trophies, interlaces, medallion heads and leaves. Other plates show panels of scrolling floral ornament interspersed with putti and birds. Typical suites are *Livre de Vase propre pour Peintres, Brodeurs et Dessinateurs* (seven plates), *Livre de Fleurs* (ten plates) and *Livre de fleurs propres pour Orfèvres et Graveurs* (eight plates). Many of Vauquer's plates were copied in Augsburg, and he seems to have been an influential practitioner of the floral BAROQUE style. His engravings were later copied on Strasbourg faience of about 1750.

Vavassore, Giovanni-Andrea Active in Venice from about 1510, Vavassore was responsible for two of the earliest Italian pattern-books for embroiderers. His first, *Corona di racammi* (Venice, about 1530; twenty-six plates), was aimed at painters and goldsmiths as well as embroiderers. Some of its designs were derived from TAGLIENTE and PAGANO. His ornament was part geometric, part MORESQUE, with some lively animals, and some curious GOTHIC foliate borders, derived from late-15th-century printers' decorations. His similar *Esemplario di Lavori* (Venice, 1530; twenty-six plates) was current for a generation, being reprinted eight times by

1552. Vavassore's last book, *Ornamento delle belle et virtuoso donne* (Venice, after 1567; thirty-two plates), was a compilation of designs from FORESTO, from Vavassore's own *Corona*, and from PELLICIOLO, whose works Vavassore had published. Among the many books which copied from Vavassore was Jean Ruelle's *Patrons pour brodeurs* (Paris, 1554).

Vecellio, Cesare Born in about 1521, Vecellio was a relation of Titian, by whom he was taught to paint and whom he accompanied to Augsburg in 1548. Vecellio published an important book on dress, *De gli habiti antichi et moderni* (Venice, 1590), and the most ambitious early lace pattern-book, *Corona delle nobili et virtuose donne*, which appeared in Venice in five parts from 1591 to 1596 with a total of 124 plates. It went through a grand total of some sixty editions up to 1625, and included a wide range of designs and techniques depicted in VINCIOLO's white on black manner. Subjects include figures, animals, musical instruments, as well as geometrical ornament. The *Corona* was widely copied and influential. Vecellio died in 1606.

Vechte, Antoine (1799–1868) Born near Avallon, Vechte was trained as a bronze caster and chaser in Paris, subsequently working for a clock-maker. In about 1835 he was influenced by Jean-Jacques FEUCHÈRE and began to execute embossed silver in the RENAISSANCE style, at which he soon attained remarkable virtuosity, producing many pieces later sold as authentic. His Amazon Shield entered the Prussian Royal Collection in 1843. Vechte executed modern designs for the leading Parisian goldsmiths Fauconnier, FROMENT-MEURICE and Wagner. After the 1848 revolution he accepted an offer to work for Hunt & Roskell in London and designed and executed many remarkable exhibition pieces, including the Titan Vase shown at the LONDON 1851 EXHIBITION and the National Medallion (1856), electrotyped as a prize for schools of art. In 1861 Vechte left England, never having learnt English, and retired to France. MOREL-LADEUIL was a pupil. A. W. N. PUGIN predictably despised Vechte's pagan Renaissance style, but his 1851 designs attracted the admiration of Prince ALBERT and many others.

Vellert, Dierick Jacobz Probably born in Amsterdam in about 1480 and trained as a glazier, Vellert became a master in the St Luke's Guild in Antwerp in 1511. He was both painter and engraver, publishing twenty prints from 1522 to 1544, but his main activity was as a stained-glass designer and painter, strongly influenced by Bernart van ORLEY and, later on, by Pieter COECK, whom he himself had influenced. In about 1515 Vellert designed a window for Antwerp Cathedral, which was burnt in 1533 and replaced, ironically, by a window designed by Pieter Coeck. A window designed by Vellert in 1517 displayed the influence of prints after Mantegna, and in 1521 he met another major influence, DÜRER. From about 1510 to 1544 Vellert was responsible for the design of many of the great windows at King's College, Cambridge, some of which he probably painted himself. These reveal borrowings from Israhel van MECKENEM, Lucas van LEYDEN, Marcantonio Raimondi and others. Vellert was still alive in 1547.

Veneziano, Agostino Born Agostino dei Musi in Venice, Veneziano was active as an engraver there from 1509, under the influence of Giulio Campagnola, Jacopo de Barbari and Albrecht DÜRER. In 1516 he moved to Florence and thence to Rome, where he became a pupil of Marcantonio Raimondi, executing numerous prints after RAPHAEL, MICHELANGELO and Giulio ROMANO. Veneziano also designed a number of vertical panels of GROTESQUE ornament incorporating ACANTHUS, putti, sea-horses, sphinxes, griffins, etc., similar to but more powerful than those of Nicoletto da MODENA. Many are based on a central candelabrum but a plate of 1521 contains grotesque ornament similar to those by Giovanni da UDINE in Raphael's Loggie. Veneziano also published *Sic Romae Antiqui sculptores ex aere et marmore faciebant* (1530–31), twelve plates of antique VASES and ewers, simple and classical compared to VICO's 1543 suite of the same title. As late as 1583 to 1584 an English silver ewer used one of Veneziano's designs. In 1528 and 1536 he published classical capitals and bases, and in 1536 *Sic Romae in impluvio ex marmore sculp* (1536), twelve plates of classical terms. However Veneziano's main importance was as one of the principal popularizers of grotesque ornament. Among the many he influenced were Lucas van LEYDEN and J. A. DuCERCEAU.

Venturoli, Alfonso (1749–1821) Born in Medicina, Venturoli studied under the decorative painter Petronio Vancelli (1734–1800), and then as an architect at the Accademia Clementina, whose principal he later became. He had a prolific architectural output from 1775 to 1820, spanning the styles from late BAROQUE to mature NEO-CLASSICISM. ROCOCO chancel doors, candlesticks of baroque form with neo-classical details, and neo-classical ironwork and monstrances are among his designs.

Vermeyen, Jan Cornelisz Born in about 1500 in Beverwijck near Haarlem, Vermeyen was trained as a painter and by about 1525 had entered the service of

Margaret of Austria at Mecheln. In 1530 he travelled to Augsburg and Innsbruck to paint Hapsburg portraits and in 1535 he accompanied Charles V on his expedition to Tunis. In 1546 Vermeyen signed a contract to design tapestries for Marie of Hungary, a suite on Vertumnus and Pomona, and another on the capture of Tunis. The tapestries, woven by Wilhelm Pannemaker, were delivered in 1554. Vermeyen died in Brussels in 1559.

Verneuil, Maurice Pillard (1869–1942) Born in Saint-Quentin, Verneuil was a pupil of GRASSET. He did several drawings for Grasset's *La Plante et ses Applications Ornementales* (1897) and Grasset introduced his *L'Animal dans la Décoration* (1898). Verneuil later published several ART NOUVEAU pattern-books of ornament, mainly based on plants and animals. In *Combinaisons ornementales* (1901) he collaborated with Georges Auriol and Alphonse MUCHA. Verneuil himself designed posters, metalwork, porcelain and wallpaper. From 1897 he wrote for 'ART ET DÉCORATION'; he was later mainly active as an art critic. In 1929 Verneuil edited a selection of foreign textiles shown at the PARIS 1925 EXHIBITION.

Ver Sacrum (1898–1903) Influenced by 'PAN' and edited successively by Wilhelm Schölermann, Alfred Roller and a committee including Gustav Klimt, *Ver Sacrum* was the organ of the Vienna-based association of Austrian artists known as the Sezession, and propagated their mainly rectilinear version of ART NOUVEAU. Josef HOFFMANN, Koloman MOSER, Ernst Stöhr, Alfred Roller and Joseph Maria OLBRICH were among the designers illustrated (even the advertisements included wallpapers designed by ECKMANN and Leistikow).

V.G. A German engraver the Master V.G. produced a few plates of ornament in the style of ALDEGREVER. They include a panel with a putto playing bagpipes surrounded by fleshy leaves and a frieze with the triumph of Bacchus dated 1534.

Vianen, Adam van Born in Utrecht in about 1565, the son of a goldsmith, Vianen remained there until his death, becoming a master goldsmith in 1593. Although his younger brother Paul van VIANEN was probably the pioneer of the mature AURICULAR style, Adam van Vianen shared in its development and after Paul's death carried auricular design to an imaginative extreme. A *tazza* of 1607 is the earliest piece of silver by Adam van Vianen to display auricular ornament, although this is confined to restrained cartouches. A complete command of the style is displayed in a ewer and basin presented in 1614 to the goldsmiths of Amsterdam in memory of his brother Paul. Adam's contemporary fame is attested by an extravagant eulogy in a 1620 poem by Balthasar Gerbier, and his silver objects, treated as works of art rather than function, are often shown in painted still-lives. He was also active as an engraver. Adam van Vianen died in 1627. His designs were disseminated long after his death by *Modelles Artificiels de divers Vaisseaux d'argent* (1650; forty-eight plates), published by his son Christiaen. It included magnificent designs for VASES, ewers, dishes and ornament in a highly developed auricular style. Christiaen, born in 1598, took over his father's mark and worked in the same style for Charles I of England from about 1630 to 1641.

Vianen, Paul van (1570–1613) The son of a Utrecht goldsmith, and the younger brother of Adam van VIANEN, Paul van Vianen worked for the court in Munich from 1596, becoming a master there in 1599. He then moved to Salzburg, where he worked from 1602 to 1603 for Archbishop Wolf Dietrich von Raitenau, who stood godfather to his son. In 1603 Vianen moved to Prague, where he was appointed goldsmith to Emperor RUDOLF II. His main output was embossed silver reliefs of great virtuosity but he was also active as a painter. Paul van Vianen may have been the first to develop the mature AURICULAR style, which is visible in one of his last works, a ewer made in Prague in 1613, with a fully auricular foot and handle. He visited Utrecht in 1610, thus maintaining contact with his elder brother, Adam, who carried the auricular style to more extreme lengths. Vianen supplied designs to other makers and his reputation long outlived him.

Vico, Enea Born in Parma in about 1523, Vico was trained as an engraver by the Roman engraver and publisher Tommaso Barlacchi, for whom he designed a suite of GROTESQUES, *Picturae quas grottesches vulgo vocant* (1541; twenty-two plates). These are very close to the Roman wall-paintings which they imitate, with a delicate combination of fantastic motifs linked by an insubstantial scaffolding of architecture. They were copied by J. A. DU CERCEAU in 1550. In 1542 Vico published three grotesque designs for candlesticks, one incorporating a fleshy stretched mask which looks forward to the AURICULAR style, and in 1543 *Sic Romae antiqui sculptores ex aere et marmore faciebant*, twenty-four plates of grotesque ewers which incorporate dogs, snakes and even stretched female heads, and were very influential on goldsmiths all over Europe. Vico was next summoned to Florence by Cosimo I de' Medici and executed some engravings there after MICHELANGELO. In 1546 he was resident in Venice. In 1553 Vico published a suite of military trophies (reprinted 1585 and 1602; sixteen plates), which

parade his archaeological learning by depicting a wide range of Roman arms and utensils; some were later copied by René BOYVIN. *Imagini... degli Imperatori* (1554; twelve plates) presented images of the Caesars based on antique coins, a theme to which Vico returned in 1562, after having depicted the Caesars' wives in *Imagini delle donne auguste* (sixty-three plates). These publications all reflect Vico's numismatic expertise, which led to his attachment to the court of Alfonso II in Ferrara as a numismatic adviser from 1563. Vico died there in 1567. The numismatic portraits published by Vico could also be used as a source for medallion head ornament, and his *Donne auguste* were surrounded by bold scrolled STRAPWORK frames in the Fontainebleau manner, which are excellent documents of Venetian 16th-century taste in ornament.

Victoria & Albert Museum, London On 6 September 1852 a Museum of Manufactures was opened in Marlborough House, under the aegis of the newly established Department of Practical Art. The prime movers in its foundation were Prince ALBERT and Henry COLE. The Museum included some objects accumulated for teaching purposes by the London SCHOOL OF DESIGN, others bought from the LONDON 1851 EXHIBITION with the aid of a £5,000 Treasury grant, and a number of loans. The purposes of the Museum, which changed its title to the Art Museum and then to the Museum of Ornamental Art, were 'the improvement of public taste in Design' and 'the application of fine art to objects of utility'. In 1857 the Museum moved to its present site in South Kensington, purchased with the profits of the 1851 Exhibition: it was then housed in an iron and glass building nicknamed the 'Brompton Boilers', moved after 1867 to Bethnal Green where it still stands. By 1862 the South

Kensington complex included the Museum of Ornamental Art and Art Library, British Paintings, Sculpture and Engravings, Architectural Examples, Appliances for Scholastic Education, and Reproductions by means of Photography and Casting. The Museum soon began to collect works of art for their intrinsic interest and quality, many of its most distinguished early acquisitions being due to the initiatives of J. C. ROBINSON. In 1860 a Select Committee of the House of Commons recommended that a more permanent museum building should be erected to the designs of Captain Francis Fowke (1823–65), who was assisted by Godfrey SYKES. After Sykes's death James Gamble, Reuben Townroe and F. W. Moody continued to design ornament for the Museum in a RENAISSANCE style. In the 1860s Owen JONES designed the decorations of the Indian and Oriental Galleries, the William MORRIS firm decorated the Green Dining Room, and Sir Edward Poynter (1836–1919) designed the Grill Room using an advanced combination of blue-and-white tiles and Anglo-Japanese ironwork. In 1864 the VIENNA MUSEUM OF APPLIED ARTS was founded in imitation of the South Kensington Museum and in 1863 the PARIS UNION CENTRALE DES ARTS DÉCORATIFS was set up to counter the threat to trade caused in part by the Museum's influence. After the erection of the Library in 1882 building work ceased until in 1899 Queen Victoria laid the foundation stone for new buildings designed by Sir Aston Webb (1849–1930), which were completed in 1909; in 1899 Queen Victoria directed that the Museum be called the Victoria & Albert Museum. In 1909 its scientific collections were formed into the separate 'Science Museum'. By 1908 purchases of specimens of contemporary design, originally an important element of the Museum's acquisitions,

had ebbed to such an extent that this role was for a while abandoned. However such events as the 1946 Britain Can Make It Exhibition and the present policy to collect 20th-century and contemporary objects are proof that the Museum's original purpose is neither forgotten nor neglected. The Victoria & Albert Museum comprises the world's most comprehensive collection of the arts of design.

Vien, Joseph-Marie (1716–1809) Born in Montpelier, Vien was a pupil of the architect and painter Jacques Giral there, and later he studied painting in Paris under Charles-Joseph Natoire (1700–1777). In 1744 Vien won the Prix de Rome. In Rome he met Mengs and witnessed the excitement caused by the discoveries at Herculaneum. Vien etched the *Mascarade Turque* (1748; thirty plates), the record of a carnival masquerade organized by the French Academy; it includes early NEO-CLASSICAL VASES possibly designed by Vien himself. Back in Paris from 1750 Vien was a protégé of CAYLUS and experimented with encaustic painting. In 1753 he designed neo-classical decorative panels. He became a member of the Academy in 1754, Director of the Academy in Rome from 1776 to 1781, and Director of the Academy and Premier Peintre du Roy in 1789. Vien was appointed to the Senate by Napoleon in 1799 and created a Comte de l'Empire in 1808. DAVID was among his pupils. In 1758 Vien designed the Rape of Proserpina for the Gobelins tapestry suite, Amours des Dieux, commissioned by MARIGNY, to which Van Loo, François BOUCHER and PIERRE also contributed. From the early 1760s Vien's paintings incorporated neo-classical furniture, notably *Une Prêtresse* (1763), engraved as *La Vertueuse Athénienne* (1765), which inspired and gave its name to a revived tripod produced by J. H.

Eberts from about 1773. In 1760 Vien published a *Suite de Vases* (twelve plates), engraved by his wife, of vases in a severe and advanced neo-classical style. In 1765, along with HALLÉ, LAGRENÉE and Boucher, Vien was commissioned by Mme Geoffrin (1699–1777) to execute a decorative painting for Stanislas Augustus Poniatowski, King of Poland (1732–98).

Vienna 1873 Exhibition The Vienna 1873 Exhibition was planned from 1871: there were about 39,500 exhibitors. It was remarkable for a strong showing of English design, including Coalbrookdale iron gates by TALBERT, Howell & James, clocks by Lewis F. DAY, Battam, Heywood & Hanks, furniture and carpets by DRESSER, Worcester Japanese-style porcelain by R. W. Binns, and Minton porcelain by Stacey Marks and by M. L. E. SOLON. Wedgwood showed the FLAXMAN chessmen and Elkingtons showed the Helicon vase and Milton shield by MOREL-LADEUIL, who also designed a ewer for Lemaire of Paris. The most notable French exhibits were pottery with Turkish enamelled decoration designed by PARVILLÉ and Christofle's enamels and furniture designs by REIBER and Rossigneux. The leading Austrian designers included STORCK, HANSEN and Valentin Teirich and the dominant Austrian style, encouraged by EITELBERGER and the VIENNA MUSEUM OF APPLIED ARTS, was a free RENAISSANCE.

Vienna Museum of Applied Arts At the LONDON 1862 EXHIBITION the Austrian Prime Minister, Archduke Rainer, requested Rudolf EITELBERGER, a member of the Austrian committee for the exhibition, to report on the art industry and the applied arts in Austria. He was also directed to consider the possible foundation of a museum to educate designers, industrialists, crafts-

men and the public; the scheme was directly founded on the success of the South Kensington Museum, now the VICTORIA & ALBERT MUSEUM, in London. Eitelberger rapidly reported in favour. A go-ahead was given in 1863 and in 1864 the Kaiserliches Königliches Österreichisches Museum für Kunst und Industrie (Imperial Royal Austrian Museum for Art and Industry) was founded with Eitelberger as its first Director; the neighbouring school of applied arts was founded in 1867. New buildings for both institutions were designed by Heinrich von Ferstel from 1868. Both Museum and School were deeply involved in the VIENNA 1873 EXHIBITION, the MUNICH 1876 EXHIBITION and the PARIS 1878 EXHIBITION; objects designed under the Museum aegis tended to favour a refined synthetic RENAISSANCE style. From 1877 a tax on titles of imperial appointment was devoted to the execution of objects for the Museum, the first cabinet designed by Professor Oskar Beyer. The magazine 'BLÄTTER FÜR KUNSTGEWERBE' illustrated many objects designed in the Museum. The Director from 1897 to 1909, Arthur von Scala (1845–1909), gave the Museum a new impetus, employing Josef HOFFMANN and Koloman MOSER as teachers, and promoting advanced design as founder-editor of 'KUNST UND KUNSTHANDWERK'.

Villard d'Honnecourt Born at Honnecourt near Cambrai, Villard was trained as a master mason in Picardy, working with Pierre de Corbie on the abbey at Vaucelles in about 1216. He later visited the cathedrals of Rheims, Chartres, Laon, Lausanne, Meaux and Saint-Quentin. Villard probably worked on the cathedral of Cambrai. He executed a sketch-book, probably in the late 1220s and early 1230s, to record useful models of all aspects of building with a commentary for his pupils; Villard must have been a recognized master by this date. The sketch-book was also conceived as a treatise on building, perhaps as a preparation for Villard's journey to Hungary, where he worked at the Cistercian abbey of Pilis in about 1233: the sketchbook contains designs for tile pavements similar to some excavated there. Although only thirty-three of the original sixty or so leaves are preserved, they include choir-stalls, an architectural clock-case, an elaborate eagle lectern with figures of evangelists and censing angels, supported by dragons, an eagle for a lectern with a movable head, a copper hand-warmer, and a trick cup surmounted by a castle and an eagle. The sketch-book also contained many drawings of architecture and ornament and is the most important surviving document by a GOTHIC designer. It was reprinted by LASSUS in Paris in 1858 and, in translation, by Robert Willis in London in 1859. BURGES was deeply influenced by Villard.

Vinciolo, Federigo de Born in Venice, Vinciolo may have been brought to France by Catherine de' Medici (1519–89). He was responsible for two highly influential pattern-books for embroidery and lace, the first to show designs for reticella lace, and the first to use white on black for all their plates, a formula later followed by VECELLIO. Both books were published in Paris by Jean Le Clerc, who stressed the Italian origin of the designs, and both had title-pages attributed to Jehan COUSIN the Younger, whose *Livre de pourtraicture* (1595) was also published by Le Clerc. Vinciolo's first book, *Les singuliers et nouveaux pourtraicts* (1587; seventy-six plates), was reprinted thirteen times up to 1612, and copied in France, Germany, Italy and, by POYNTZ, in England. Its designs were mainly geometrical but also included figures and flowers. Vinciolo's

second book, *Les secondes œuvres et subtiles inventions de lingerie* (1594; sixty plates), was similar in character and also often reprinted. In 1623 a collected edition of both Vinciolo's books was published by Jean Le Clerc's widow, with some additional designs probably not by Vinciolo.

Vinsac, Claude Dominique Born in Toulouse in 1749, the son of a goldsmith, Vinsac was active as an engraver in Paris. As well as portraits he designed a series of twelve suites of designs for goldsmiths' work, each of four plates. They are very able exercises in the NEO-CLASSICAL manner associated with the goldsmith Robert Joseph Auguste (1723–1805), and probably date from about 1780. Together with standard neo-classical, NATURALISTIC and Egyptian elements, Vinsac makes lively use of less usual motifs such as tortoises.

Viollet-le-Duc, Eugène (1814–79) Viollet-le-Duc was born in Paris, the son of a cultivated civil servant who rose to become Keeper of Louis Philippe's royal residences, with an apartment in the Tuileries, and the nephew of the painter and scholar Étienne Delécluze, who sent Viollet to an anti-clerical Republican school in Fontenay. In 1825 Viollet was taken by Delécluze to visit the collector Du Sommerard at the Hôtel de Cluny. In 1830 he joined his uncle on the barricades in Paris and in 1831 they travelled in France. Viollet refused to study architecture at the École des Beaux-Arts, and occupied himself designing ornaments and teaching drawing. From 1833 he regularly showed drawings at the Salon. He also designed clock-cases, VASES, lights etc. for a bronze-maker named Wittoz. Further travels in France followed and Viollet became a convert to GOTHIC. In 1836 he travelled to Italy, including Rome, where he was encouraged by

INGRES, then Director of the French Academy there. In 1838 Viollet began his official architectural career as an *auditeur* to the Conseil des Bâtiments Civils. In 1840 he designed stained glass for the royal chapel at Dreux made at Sèvres, and was stained-glass designer for Amboise in 1842. In 1840 Viollet was appointed to report on the abbey of Vézelay by Prosper Mérimée (1803–70), secretary of the Commission des Monuments Historiques instituted in 1837. Vézelay, only completed in 1859, was Viollet's first great restoration. Mérimée later became a close friend; Viollet designed his book-plate and dedicated to Mérimée his first book (1854), on medieval military architecture. From 1840 Viollet's career was dominated by the restoration of Gothic buildings, including the Hôtel de Cluny (from 1842), Notre Dame de Paris, with LASSUS (from 1842), the ramparts of Carcassonne (from 1851) and the Château de Pierrefonds for Napoleon III, including decorations and furniture (from 1858). In 1849 Viollet was appointed to a commission to improve the national manufactories of Sèvres, Gobelins and Beauvais, of which he strongly disapproved. In 1855 he was commissioned by the Compagnie de Chemins de Fer d'Orléans to design the furniture and decoration of a complete train for Napoleon III; he also designed decorations for Napoleon's marriage in 1853 and for the baptism of the Prince Imperial in 1856. In 1863 Viollet was appointed professor of the history of art at the École des Beaux-Arts, but he resigned in 1864 having been barracked at lectures. From 1874 he was engaged on the restoration of the Château d'Eu for the Comte de Paris, designing furniture and wall decorations. As a designer Viollet-le-Duc was disappointingly dry and timid. His polychromatic decorations for Notre Dame, published by Oradou in 1870, are incoherent for all their careful

elaboration, his metalwork is unimaginative, his furniture, whether Gothic for Pierrefonds or Roquetaillade (from 1866, designed in detail by Edmond Duthoit) or 17th-century for Eu, is lacking in vigour. None the less BURGES, a far superior designer, stated that 'we all cribbed from Viollet-le-Duc'. The key lies in Viollet's writings. His *Dictionnaire raisonnée de l'Architecture* (ten volumes, 1858–68) provided an indispensable analysis of Gothic architecture and the *Dictionnaire du Mobilier Français* (six volumes, 1858–75) is still the best guide to the Gothic decorative arts. The two volumes of his *Entretiens sur l'Architecture* (1863–72) encapsulated his rationalist architectural creed with interesting ideas on iron construction, which influenced GUIMARD and others, and from 1873 he published a series of *Histoires*, popular primers to the building of houses, fortresses and so on, and including the *Histoire d'un dessinateur* (1879), in which Viollet insisted on the vital importance of drawing as self-education. Anti-academic, disestablishmentarian, republican and romantic, Viollet's rationalism seemed to some of his contemporaries, for instance Reichensperger, to have neutered his creativity; as theorist or archaeologist he was admirable, but his Gothic lacked life. Viollet's influence on such disparate designers as GAUDÍ, Frank Lloyd WRIGHT and GRASSET, a pupil, was none the less incalculable and he is rightly regarded as, in his theoretical role, a pioneer of the MODERN style.

Vogtherr, Heinrich I (1490–1556) Born in Dillingen, the son of a doctor, Vogtherr was called 'Henricus Satrapitanus'. He spent 1522 to 1525 in Wimpfen, and then moved to Strasbourg, where he became a citizen in 1526 and was active as a publisher from 1536. In 1544 to 1546 he was in Zürich, and at some time in the 1540s in Augsburg. In 1550 he was appointed oculist and painter to Charles V, and summoned to Vienna, where he died. His *Kunstbüchlein* (Strasbourg, 1537, later editions 1538, 1539, 1540 and later, including Antwerp, 1572) was aimed at the whole range of craftsmen, and, with depictions of capitals, bases, balusters, shields, helmets, arms, columns and decorative motifs, presented a summary anthology of RENAIS-SANCE ornament.

Voisin, François Voisin published a suite of NEO-CLASSICAL lights, *Nouveau Cahier de Flambeaux* (six plates), which he claimed to have executed for Louis XVI, and a suite of neo-classical VASES, *Nouveau Cahier de Vases* (five plates). He also contributed a suite of four plates to the *Cahiers d'Arabesques* engraved by Guyot in about 1785, of which LAVALLÉE-POUSSIN designed the lion's share.

Vouet, Simon (1590–1649) Born in Paris, the son of a painter, Simon Vouet travelled in 1611 to Constantinople, thence to Venice and finally to Rome, where he arrived in 1612. In Rome, Vouet received a pension from the French crown and established himself as a successful painter patronized by, among others, the antiquarian Cassiano del Pozzo. In 1627 he was recalled to France as Premier Peintre du Roi, with a lodging in the Louvre. He executed decorative painting for Marie de' Medici at the Luxembourg Palace, for Louis XIII, and for his sister Henrietta Maria. *Livre de diverse Grotesques peintes dans le Cabinet des Bains de la Reine regente au Palais Royal* (Paris, 1647, later copied in Antwerp; fifteen plates) depicts bold GROTESQUE decorations by Vouet in the style of the CARRACCI painted in 1645 at the Palais Royal for Anne d'Autriche. Vouet was a very important tapestry designer, designing many suites, including Rinaldo and Armida (twelve

pieces), Scenes from the Old Testament (eight pieces), Scenes from the Odyssey (eight pieces) and the Loves of the Gods (twenty-three pieces). The Old Testament and Odyssey tapestries were derived from paintings by Vouet in the Hôtel de Bullion of 1634 to 1635; a set of the Old Testament was in the collection of Cardinal Richelieu in 1636. Vouet's 1643 portrait of Louis XIII, Anne d'Autriche and the royal children was reproduced by Pierre Dupont in Savonnerie technique. Although eclipsed in fame by Poussin, who visited France in 1640 to 1642, and apparently at odds with the artistic establishment towards the end of his life – he did not join the new Academy in 1648 – Vouet's influence on ornament in France was considerable; LE BRUN was his pupil, and through him the Roman BAROQUE style introduced to France by Vouet became the official style of Louis XIV's court.

Vovert, Jean Vovert, presumably a French jeweller, published two suites of six plates each (1598 and 1602), with small black scrolled and foliate designs for the use of jewellers, including pendants and enlivened by birds and other small motifs.

Voysey, Charles Francis Annesley (1857–1941) Born near Hull, Voysey was the eldest son of the Rev. Charles Voysey, an unorthodox clergyman who in 1871 was expelled from the Church of England for denying the doctrine of everlasting hell. The family then moved to London and in 1874 Voysey was articled to the architect J. P. SEDDON. In 1879 he worked briefly for Saxon Snell, and then in 1880 joined the office of George Devey, a friend of his father, who had a highly successful country house practice. In about 1882 Voysey set up as an independent architect but jobs were slow to come. His friendship with A. H. MACKMURDO led to commissions to design wallpapers for Jeffrey & Co. from 1883 onwards. In 1884 Voysey joined the newly founded ART-WORKERS' GUILD, and in 1888 showed wallpapers and printed fabrics at the first exhibition of the ARTS & CRAFTS EXHIBITION SOCIETY. Also in 1888 Voysey built his first house and thenceforth until about 1914 his architectural practice, which ended in 1920, was productive if not prolific. Flat pattern design continued, however, to be a major part of Voysey's work. From 1893 onwards he designed wallpapers under contract for Essex & Co., and from 1895 textiles for Alexander Morton & Co. He also produced designs for carpets and tiles. In this field Voysey was a commercial property: even in the 1920s Essex & Co. advertised 'many papers by C. F. A. Voysey, the Genius of Pattern', and he was still active as a pattern designer in the early 1930s long after the end of his architectural activity. Voysey attempted furniture design in the mid-1880s, but only from about 1895 did he develop a full set of furniture designs, first showing furniture at the Arts & Crafts Exhibition in 1893. His ideal was to design every item in a house, and he devised a basic range of chairs, tables, beds etc. which could be varied in detail or elaboration. For their execution he used a few craftsmen firms, notably F. C. Neilsen. Voysey's metalwork mainly comprises hinges, keys and door furniture manufactured by, among others, Thomas Elsley & Co., but he also designed cutlery, table-ware and lighting. Voysey saw himself as an heir of the tradition of GOTHIC design initiated by A. W. N. PUGIN, and although Gothic details are usually absent the direct influence of Pugin is visible in the bold heraldry of Voysey's flat pattern designs, in the cutout ornament of hinges and in the oaken directness of furniture. Voysey aimed at a cheerful simplicity, combining light-

ness and repose, and once he had formed his style – in about 1890 – it changed little except in nuances. His work enjoyed a great international reputation and influence, fostered by articles in the first volume of the 'STUDIO' (1893), whose cover he designed, in 'ART MODERNE' (1894), by Henri VAN DE VELDE, and in the first volume of 'DEKORATIVE KUNST' (1897). But Voysey despised the continental ART NOUVEAU style which he had so strongly influenced, and was equally opposed to the break with tradition expressed in the International MODERN style. In his last years he quizzically witnessed a renewed interest in his work and a series of honours – Master of the Art-Workers' Guild in 1924, one of the first Royal Designers for Industry in 1936, and the R.I.B.A. Royal Gold Medal in 1940.

Vredeman de Vries, Hans Born in 1526 in Leeuwarden, the capital of Friesland, Hans Vredeman worked under a glass painter there for five years before moving successively to Kampen, Mecheln and Kollum. In Kollum he worked for a cabinet-maker who introduced him to the edition of SERLIO (1539 onwards) by Pieter COECK (1502–50), which made such an impression on Vredeman that he is said to have copied it out night and day. After returning to Mecheln, Vredeman settled in Antwerp in about 1561. However, he had already worked there in 1549 on the elaborate STRAP-WORK triumphal arches erected for the entry of Charles V and Philip II, which were probably supervised by Pieter Coeck and are recorded in Cornille Graphaeus's *Le Triumphe d'Anvers* (1550). In 1555 and 1557 two suites of strapwork cartouches by Vredeman entitled *Multarum Variarum Protactionum*... were published in Antwerp by Gerhard de Jode. These were followed in about 1560 by *Scenographiae sive*

Perspectivae, architectural views published by Hieronymus Cock, and by a suite of twenty oval designs for inlay depicting fantastic architecture derived from Serlio, from J. A. DuCerceau's *Vues d'Optiques* (Orleans, 1551), and from the views of reconstructed Rome of 1551 by Hieronymus Cock, who was again Vredeman's publisher. Cock issued a second architectural suite by Vredeman in 1562, which displays the influence of J. A. DuCerceau's *Livre d'Architecture* (1559); DuCerceau himself reprinted the Vredeman suite and his *Leçons de Perspective Positive* (Paris, 1576) were influenced by it. The oval designs and 1562 suite were combined in a 1601 Theodore Galle reprint as *Variae Architecturae Formae*. In the early 1560s Vredeman published two further suites of cartouches combining disciplined strapwork with GROTESQUE ornament in the manner of Cornelis FLORIS, and a series of terminal figures entitled *Caryatidum* . . . In 1563 followed a series of imaginary tombs, *Pictores, Statuarii, Architecti* . . . (twenty-eight plates), and twelve plates of VASES engraved by Hieronymus Cock. However, Vredeman's most influential works of the 1560s were *Dorica Ionica* and *Corinthia Composita* (both 1565 and reprinted 1578, 1581 and later), in which Vredeman played ornamental variations on the themes of the classical ORDERS with strapwork and grotesques. His *Grottesco* series of about 1566 derives a lighter form of ornament from the 1550 versions by DuCerceau of the *Grottesches* engraved by Enea VICO in 1541. A suite of twelve heads of Caesars published by Gerhard de Jode at about the same date derives from Étienne DELAUNE's grotesque scenes on a black ground. This productive period in Vredeman's career coincided with Antwerp's greatest moment of prosperity. It was cruelly interrupted in 1567 by the fall of the city to the Duke of Alva and the consequent

Spanish Fury. However Vredeman remained in Antwerp, publishing a series of fountains entitled *Artis Perspectivae* . . . in 1568 and designing grotesque and strapwork borders for a suite of calligraphic specimens by Clemens Perret in 1569. In 1570 he designed triumphal arches for Anne of Austria's entry to Antwerp on her way to Spain to marry Philip II, but in the same year he fled Alva's inquisition to Aachen and thence to Luttich. None the less Vredeman continued to publish, *Panoplia* (1572), a series of ornamental trophies, being followed by part of a suite of heads of gods taken from antique coins (1573), selected by the great geographer Abraham Ortel (1527–98), and by a second series of fountains (1573). In 1575 he was back in Antwerp, directing the new fortifications. *Theatrum vitae humanae* (1577), which matched the ages of man to the classical orders, a suite on the Tuscan order (1578), *Architectura oder Bauung der Antiquen* (1581), and a set of garden designs *Hortorum Viridariorumque* . . . (1583), all pursued the theme of the orders, even the latter, which was reprinted in 1615 by Johann Bussemacher in Cologne, having the motto 'Dorica Ionica Corinthia'. In 1582 Vredeman designed the decorations for the entry of the Duke of Anjou into Antwerp, and in 1585 performed the same service after the city's second fall for the conquering general, Alessandro Farnese (1546–92). In 1586 he finally fled the city accompanied by his pupil, the painter Hendrick van Steenwyck the Elder. From Frankfurt, Vredeman went to Wolfenbüttel, where, under the patronage of Duke Julius, he was active as gardener, architect, painter and designer. It was probably at Wolfenbüttel that he published *Differents Pourtraicts de Menuiserie*, which, with a title and sixteen plates, is the earliest furniture pattern-book. After the death of Duke Julius in 1589 Vredeman's con-

tract was not renewed by his son, Heinrich Julius, and he moved to Hamburg
and thence in 1592 to Danzig, with an
appointment as civic architect. He was
not successful and, after a second stay in
Hamburg in 1595, he moved to Prague
in 1596, where he worked for the
Emperor RUDOLF II as both painter
and designer, until about 1598, after
which he went again to Hamburg. In
1601 Vredeman attended his son Paul's
wedding in Amsterdam and in 1604 his
Perspectiva was published at the Hague,
where he seems to have died in the same
year, having failed to secure a profes-
sorship at Leiden. In the preface to his
final work, *Perspectiva*, Vredeman
claimed that he had written nine books
on the subject. PERSPECTIVE was perceived in the 16th century as an almost
magical science, of which Vredeman
proclaimed himself and was recognized
an adept, not only in his prints but also
in his paintings, which helped to create
a whole new genre of elaborate architectural views, mainly interiors. Knowledge of the classical orders made a
similarly deep impression on his contemporaries, and in a series of variations on
their themes Vredeman helped to transform the Roman language of architecture into a free and elaborate ornamental *lingua franca* which answered the
taste of North European designers. The
ornaments he used were not original:
Vredeman was no genius and adopted
elements ready synthesized by Cornelis
Floris. But the propaganda effect of his
mass of publications, often reprinted,
was incalculable, both in interpretations
and imitations, often garbled, and in
direct borrowings, as for instance in the
work of Robert Smithson and John
Thorpe.

Vredeman de Vries, Paul Born in
Antwerp in 1567, the son of Hans
VREDEMAN DE VRIES, Paul Vredeman
was mainly active as a painter of archi-

tectural interiors, developing and refin-
ing a genre invented by his father. In
1597 he executed some celebrated PER-
SPECTIVE and architectural decorations
in Prague for the Emperor RUDOLF II.
In 1601 he married in Amsterdam, of
which he became a citizen in 1604.
Architectura (1607) was a posthumous
collaboration between Hans and Paul
including a fascinating early GOTHIC
Revival interior. But Paul's main work as
a designer was *Verscheyden Schryn-
werck* (Amsterdam, 1630), published in
two parts of nineteen plates each. This
was a furniture pattern-book similar to
Hans Vredeman's *Differents Pourtraicts
de Menuiserie* of about 1588, whose
themes it develops, providing an invaluable record of Northern MANNERIST
taste in furniture design in the early 17th
century.

Vries, Adriaen de (1545–1626) Born in
The Hague, Vries studied under Giovanni Bologna in Florence from about
1581 and was active as a sculptor. He
moved to Prague before 1593. In about
1601 Vries designed bases incorporating
Jupiter and Ganymede, and a woman
with a lion, for Florentine marble tables
belonging to the Emperor RUDOLF II.

Vulcop, Henri de From 1454 to 1455
Vulcop was court painter to Marie
d'Anjou, Queen of France, for whom he
illuminated a book of hours: from 1463
to 1465 he worked for her son Charles,
Duc de Berry, younger brother of Louis
XI. Vulcop was settled in Bourges in
1463 and died between 1470 and 1479.
His brother Conrad de Vulcop was
court painter to Charles VII from 1446
to 1459. Henri de Vulcop almost certainly designed a suite of eleven tapestries on the War of Troy woven at
Tournai from the mid or late 1460s. Sets
later belonged to Charles VIII of
France, Charles the Bold of Búrgundy,
Henry VII of England, Mathias Corvi-

nus, King of Hungary, Federigo da Mon-
tefeltre, who ordered a set from Jean
Grenier of Tournai in 1476, probably to
decorate the audience room in the Ducal
Palace in Urbino, and Ferdinand I of
Naples. The design of a suite of tapestries on the Destruction of Jerusalem is
also attributed to Vulcop.

W

W ⚲ The Master W ⚲ was probably a Flemish goldsmith, perhaps from Bruges. He seems to have worked for Charles the Bold from the late 1460s, and he may have accompanied him on campaign in 1473 or 1475. His surviving engravings, influenced by E. S., SCHONGAUER and Rogier van der Weyden, amount to eighty-one plates and include sacred subjects, military scenes and ships. He was also the most productive engraver of ornament of his period. His designs include a crozier, sixty-eight centimetres high, a cup, a censer, four monstrances (one later adapted, with Renaissance additions, in Jacob MÜLLER's *Ornatus Ecclesiasticus*, 1591), two circular motifs for goldsmiths with GOTHIC tracery, four Gothic frames for carved altarpieces, a fountain, probably intended as a silver table ornament, four Gothic canopies, three Gothic roses, and eight Gothic leaves.

Wachsmuth, Jeremias (1711–71) Born in Augsburg, Wachsmuth was a pupil of Johann Georg BERGMÜLLER (1688–1762) at the Augsburg Academy. He designed a total of fifty-two plates in suites of four for the publisher J. G. HERTEL, and 120 plates for M. ENGELBRECHT. A further suite was published by the heirs of Jeremias Wolff. Wachsmuth's designs are all in the ROCOCO style and comprise altars, monuments, cartouches, pulpits, ornaments, doors, plasterwork, VASES, sword-hilts and an alphabet. However, his most distinctive inventions are figures, sometimes allegorical, for instance the seasons, but more often WATTEAUESQUE, balanced on or in extraordinary rococo structures, part architecture, part ornament, frilly, flame-like or of a stretched almost AURICULAR quality. Of his more functional designs Wachsmuth's pulpits are perhaps the most exhilarating.

Wagenfeld, Wilhelm Born in Bremen in 1900, Wagenfeld was trained there as a goldsmith. In 1919 he attended the Drawing Academy at Hanau, and in 1923 he entered the BAUHAUS at Weimar, where his studies concentrated on metalwork and he was taught by Laszlo MOHOLY-NAGY. His early lamps and tea services of 1923 to 1924, some in collaboration with J. K. Jucker, use the clean geometric language of the MODERN style, like contemporary designs by Marianne BRANDT. From 1926 to 1930 the firm of Walter & Wagner of Schleiz produced a number of similar designs by Wagenfeld with others by Richard Winkelmayer for the Bauhaus. From 1926 Wagenfeld taught at the Bauhaus, and from 1931 in Berlin. He had been working with glass from about 1927 and in 1930 began to design for the Jenaer Glaswerke. From 1935 he designed glass for the Vereinigte Lausitze Glaswerke, whose trade-mark he designed in 1936 and whose publicity he worked out in every detail; for example, glasses specially decorated by the painter Crodel were to be used as 'entrance tickets' to museums, and every effort was to be made that VLG glasses were used in the official buildings of the Reich. Wagenfeld also designed porcelain for the Fürstenberg and Rosenthal factories in 1934 and 1938 respectively. Wagenfeld promoted his approach to design in articles in 'Die FORM' and other magazines from 1928 on, and his work for Jena, Lausitz and Fürstenberg won prizes at the PARIS 1937 EXHIBITION. From 1947 Wagenfeld taught design in Berlin, at first under Hans Scharoun. In 1950 he settled in Stuttgart, establishing a studio there in 1954. From 1950 he designed for the Württembergische Metallwarenfabrik at Geislingen. His post-war designs also include Rosenthal porcelain from 1953, lights for Lindner of Bamberg from 1955 and plastic utensils for Lufthansa from 1955 to 1958. In 1955 he resigned from the DEUTSCHE WERKBUND, which he had joined in 1925, on the basis that it was ineradicably bourgeois, ineffective and traditionalist. Wagenfeld's own status as a lionized Bauhaus pioneer has since been confirmed by a series of honours and exhibitions. Always stressing the moral, political and social responsibility of the designer, he has concentrated on the design of relatively cheap mass-produced objects, and placed an overriding importance on his intimate involvement with industry. His style, constant to the Modern ideal of self-effacement, purity and simplicity, has had a wide and continuing influence. For instance a glass tea service designed by Ilse Decho and produced at Jena in 1967 is a mannered version of a Wagenfeld design of the early 1930s. Occasionally Wagenfeld used historical prototypes, as in glass vases of 1937 of classical form. Faced with design problems which involve display, luxury or the expression of spiritual values, as flower vases, candelabra and chalices, his solutions can seem limp. His forte is the unobtrusive functional object, although he occasionally cuts a

dash, as with his zig-zag Pelikan ink bottle of 1938.

Wägmann, Hans Heinrich Born in Zürich in 1557, the son of a tradesman, Wägmann became a member of a guild there in 1580. In 1582 he married and settled in Lucerne, where he died in about 1626, after a prolific activity as painter and cartographer. Wägmann was also the leading designer of stained glass in the area.

Wagner, Carl (1799–1841) Trained as a jeweller in Berlin, Wagner was inspired by BEUTH, the director of the Preussisches Gewerbeinstitut, to revive the 16th-century technique of niello ornament. For lack of patronage he left Berlin for Paris in 1830, where he founded a jewellery firm, Mention & Wagner, to specialize in niello work. He later added repoussé silver to his repertoire. VECHTE was among his employees. At the PARIS 1834 EXHIBITION Wagner won a gold medal; he later made a triumphal showing at the PARIS 1839 EXHIBITION. Wagner was a principal pioneer in France of RENAISSANCE and Moorish styles. His early death was due to a hunting accident. *Les Ornemanistes du XIXme Siècle* (Paris, 1851) contained designs by Wagner for ornaments and metalwork in a NATURALISTIC GROTESQUE style. Wagner also designed wallpaper.

Wagner, Johann Peter Alexander (1730–1809) Born in Obertheres, Wagner was trained as a sculptor in Vienna. In 1756 he settled in Würzburg and entered the workshop of the sculptor Johann Wolfgang van der Auvera, who carved elaborate ROCOCO furniture for the Würzburg Residenz. Auvera died in 1756 and in 1764 Wagner married his widow. He was also appointed court sculptor. From about 1759 he designed rococo furniture for the Residenz; he also designed church fittings and was very prolific as a sculptor. From 1776 to 1782 Wagner designed very competent furniture for the Residenz in the German NEO-CLASSICAL manner.

Wailly, Charles de (1730–98) Born in Paris, Wailly studied architecture under J.-F. BLONDEL, Servandoni and LE GEAY. In 1752 he won the Grand Prix d'Architecture and spent from 1754 to 1756 in Rome. There he became friendly with CHAMBERS, whose Chinese designs (1757) seem later to have influenced some of Wailly's VASES. Wailly was a member of the Académie d'Architecture from 1767 and the Académie de Peinture from 1771. In 1772 he was appointed architect to the Palace of Fontainebleau. He revisited Rome in 1777. In 1785 Wailly was summoned to Kassel to work for Landgraf Friedrich II von Hessen. In 1790 he was offered the presidency of the St Petersburg Academy of Architecture by the Empress Catherine II (1729–96). Wailly's greatest architectural work was the Théâtre de l'Odéon (1779–82), on which he collaborated with J. M. Peyre (1730–85), but his works ranged from Genoa to Antwerp and included houses in Paris for himself and his friend, the sculptor Augustin Pajou (1730–1809). In 1760 he published a suite of vases and tables (ten plates); it was republished in about 1841. As with LA RUE, Wailly's line is tremulous and delicate, but his imaginative forms are either of the toughest early NEO-CLASSICAL variety or derive from late-17th-century prototypes by BOULLE; his tables even seem to envisage metal construction. At the 1761 Salon he showed a table, a vase and a column in the Greek style, the latter with gilt-bronze mounts by the goldsmith R. J. Auguste (1723–1805). In 1789 Wailly designed an extraordinary theatrical pulpit for Saint-Sulpice in Paris, a neo-classical variation on the theme of BERNINI's Cathedra Petri in St Peter's, Rome.

Waller, Pickford (1850–1930) Waller was a designer in the family firm of interior decorators, which worked mainly on the great estates which had been developed in Pimlico and Belgravia by Thomas Cubitt (1788–1855). He moved on the fringes of the aesthetic movement, and knew and admired Whistler and Conder (he owned Whistler's preliminary designs (1876–7) for the Thompson blue-and-white porcelain catalogue (1878)). Waller designed not only interiors in a range of fashionable styles, but also book covers, including Mercy Grogan's *How Women May Earn a Living* (1880), Ernest Dowson's *Decorations* (1899) and W. H. Davies's *Raptures* (1918), and many book-plates.

Wallis, George (1811–91) Born in Wolverhampton, Wallis trained as a painter. From the late 1830s he was involved in design education and in 1841 won a government exhibition to the SCHOOL OF DESIGN at Somerset House. He was appointed headmaster of the Spitalfields School of Design in 1843, and headmaster of the Manchester School in 1844, when he published *The Principles of Art as Applied to Design*. In 1846 Wallis resigned, in opposition to changes ordered from Somerset House, and set up his own 'Academy of Industrial and Fine Art'. He had in 1845 organized the first English exhibition of 'art-manufactures' at the Manchester Royal Institution. Wallis wrote on it in the *Art Union* (1846) and was later a frequent contributor to the 'ART JOURNAL'. In 1846 Wallis designed a delicately NATURALISTIC ticket for a concert to raise money for Shakespeare's birthplace. He was a deputy commissioner for the LONDON 1851 EXHIBITION and superintendent of the textile division; he was also involved in the PARIS EXHIBITIONS of

1855 and 1867 and the LONDON 1862 EXHIBITION. From 1851 to 1858 Wallis was a reforming headmaster of the Birmingham School of Art. His *The Industry of the United States* (1854) was the product of a visit to America in 1853. In 1858 Wallis was appointed by COLE senior keeper of the South Kensington art collections, remaining there until shortly before his death.

Walpole, Horace (1717–97) Born in Arlington Street, London, the son of the Prime Minister Sir Robert Walpole (1676–1745), Walpole was educated at Eton and Cambridge and travelled to France and Italy in 1739 on his Grand Tour. In 1743 he completed *Aedes Walpolianae* (1747), a description of the paintings in his father's house, and, he later claimed, designed a Palladian-style cabinet mounted with ivory carvings. In 1747 Walpole leased a small house at Twickenham, which he bought in 1749, christened Strawberry Hill, and had by his death transformed into the most influential GOTHIC house of his day. Walpole wrote a *Description of... Strawberry Hill* (1774, enlarged edition 1784). In 1748 he had a Palladian chimneypiece after KENT in his breakfast-room. In about 1750 Walpole and his friends John Chute (1701–76) and Richard BENTLEY formed a Committee on Taste to Gothicize and extend Strawberry Hill. Gothic details were borrowed from Worcester Cathedral (Staircase wallpaper, 1753), Westminster Abbey (Little Parlour chimneypiece and Library chimneypiece, 1754, and Gallery vault, 1758), Old St Paul's Cathedral (Library bookcases, 1754), Rouen Cathedral (Holbein Chamber screen, 1758), Canterbury Cathedral (Holbein Chamber chimneypiece and Gallery niches, 1758), St Alban's Abbey (Gallery doors, 1759) and Ely Cathedral (Gate piers, 1769). Walpole himself, although no draughtsman, took the closest interest in the design of furniture and interiors at Strawberry Hill. Other designers involved included Chute and Bentley, James Essex (1722–84), Robert ADAM and John CARTER. Johann Heinrich MÜNTZ (1727–98), in residence at Strawberry Hill from 1755 to 1759, was used by Walpole more as an artist than a designer. Walpole's rich and varied collection was an important influence on designers; an ebony chair from Strawberry Hill was engraved by Henry SHAW in 1834, and Bentley even designed chairs for Strawberry Hill based on a piece of 16th-century stained glass there.

Walton, George (1867–1933) Born in Glasgow, the son of an unsuccessful painter, Walton had an elder brother, E. A. Walton, who was also a painter, one of the 'Glasgow Boys', and a strong admirer of Whistler, whose decorative work was to have an influence on Walton himself. Having taken evening classes at the Glasgow School of Art, Walton in 1888 abandoned his position as a bank clerk and opened a business as 'George Walton & Co., Ecclesiastical and House Decorators', after having been commissioned to decorate a new smoking-room for one of Miss Cranston's Glasgow tea-rooms. He first showed at an ARTS & CRAFTS EXHIBITION in 1890, and seems soon to have fallen under the spell of VOYSEY, the strongest influence on his work and later a close friend. In 1896 to 1897 Walton was responsible for the design of Miss Cranston's Buchanan Street tea-rooms, for which he executed some elegant ladder-back chairs. The wall decoration was in the hands of Charles Rennie MACKINTOSH and there was a close interrelationship between the two designers at this point, continued in their collaboration on Miss Cranston's Argyle Street tea-rooms in 1897 to 1898, where Walton was responsible for décor and Mackintosh for furniture. However, as Gleeson White insisted in the 1897 'STUDIO', there was a strong distinction between the Mackintosh group and Walton. Also in 1897 Walton moved to London, although he retained his Glasgow showroom and workshop. In 1898 success was reflected in the opening of a branch shop in York, and in his commission to furnish Kodak showrooms in London, Glasgow, Brussels, Milan and Vienna, a commission which ended in 1901 and was illustrated, with an article by MUTHESIUS, in 'DEKORATIVE KUNST' (1903). In the late 1890s Walton designed for Clutha Glass and textiles for Mortons. In 1901 the special number of the *Studio* included Walton furniture, his stand at the Glasgow Exhibition was a model of understated elegance, and he turned to architecture, building The Leys, Elstree. In 1902 he participated in the Budapest Exhibition, and in 1910 in the Arts & Crafts Exhibition. Up to about 1910 Walton was busy, but later he failed to secure a post fitting his talents. From 1916 to 1921 he worked as an architect and designer for the Liquor Control Board, designing public houses in the Carlisle area. From 1926 to 1931 he designed textiles for Morton Sundour, finding it difficult to adapt to new fashions. Otherwise there were only odd architectural and stained-glass commissions. Walton was a quiet and sensitive man, and his designs are characterized by delicacy and refinement.

Wanderer, Friedrich Wilhelm (1840–1910) Educated at the Nuremberg school of applied arts, Wanderer began to teach there in 1863. Indefatigable, versatile and prolific, Wanderer was active as painter, designer, restorer and pundit. He specialized in the German late-GOTHIC and RENAISSANCE styles. In 1881 Wanderer's decoration of DÜRER's house in Nuremberg in the style of the early 16th century replaced that created by HEIDELOFF in 1826.

Stained glass was one of Wanderer's fortes and his cartoon for a window in St Lorenz, Nuremberg, won a gold medal at the Munich 1879 Exhibition. He was also responsible for innumerable diplomas, addresses and book illustrations as well as being an accomplished calligrapher.

Waring, John Burley (1823–75) Born in Lyme Regis, Waring studied from 1836 at the Bristol branch of the University of London and was then taught watercolour drawing by Samuel Jackson. In 1840 he was apprenticed to the London architect H. E. Kendall (1805–85). From 1842 Waring studied at the Royal Academy and in 1843 won a medal from the SOCIETY OF ARTS for the design of architectural ornaments. After travelling in Italy from 1843 to 1844, he worked as an architectural draughtsman. In 1847 he went to Spain with MACQUOID, a fellow pupil of Kendall, and did drawings published as *Architectural Art in Italy and Spain* (1850). In 1854 he collaborated with M. D. WYATT on guide-books to the architectural courts in the Crystal Palace at Sydenham, and in about 1856 he supplied texts on Byzantine and Elizabethan ornament for Owen JONES's *Grammar of Ornament*. Waring was involved in the Manchester 1857 Exhibition and the LONDON 1862 EXHIBITION. Some humorous poems inspired by the former he dedicated to 'The Immortal Buskin' (RUSKIN). *Art Treasures of the United Kingdom* (1857) and *Masterpieces of Industrial Art & Sculpture at the International Exhibition 1862* (1863) provided chromolithographic records of both. Waring's *Illustrations of Architecture and Ornament* (1865) included plant ornament alongside details sketched on the continent. In about 1867 Waring designed furniture for Messrs Trollope.

Waterhouse, Alfred (1830–1905) Born

at Aigburth near Liverpool, of a Quaker family, Waterhouse became a pupil of the architect Richard Lane of Manchester in 1848. He was early influenced by A. W. N. PUGIN and RUSKIN. On finishing his articles in 1853, Waterhouse travelled widely in Europe, reaching Constantinople. He set up practice in Manchester in 1854. His first great success was in the Manchester Assize Courts competition of 1859. He established a London office in 1864. The Natural History Museum in London (1873–81) and the Manchester Town Hall (1868–77) were his greatest public buildings. His greatest private commission was the rebuilding of Eaton Hall for the Duke of Westminster (1870–82). Waterhouse had a large output up to his retirement in 1901. In 1863 Waterhouse was sent to London to inspect Pugin's furniture for the Palace of Westminster as a preparation for designing furniture for the Manchester Courts, which indeed displayed strong Pugin influence. In London, Waterhouse became friendly with Norman SHAW, who designed a cradle for his son Julian in 1867. At Blackmoor (1869–73), a country house for the Earl of Selborne, Waterhouse designed accomplished furniture in a style similar to TALBERT's, supplied by James Capel of London; a corner cupboard surmounted by a peacock demonstrates a move away from the sterner and heavier forms of GOTHIC, while ebonized lattice-back chairs betray Near Eastern influence. Japanese 'pies', turned spindles and floral carving are combined on a sofa made by Doveston, Bird & Hull for Manchester Town Hall.

Watteau, Antoine (1684–1721) Born in Valenciennes, Watteau was trained by the local painters Gérin and Métayer and moved in 1702 to Paris, where from 1703 he was a pupil and assistant of GILLOT. From 1707 to 1709 Watteau worked as an assistant to Claude III AUDRAN. In 1709 he won second prize in the Prix de Rome competition and in 1717 he became a member of the Academy. Although mainly active as a painter, Watteau also designed fan leaves, a harpsichord lid similar to one by Gillot and numerous panels of ornament. Many of these were engraved from Watteau's drawings in the 1730s and these engravings reinforced Watteau's direct influence on early ROCOCO designers. Watteau's GROTESQUE panels tend to be composed of delicate and feathery figures and NATURALISTIC elements with little stress on any structural framework, and thus anticipate rococo developments. Chinese figures painted by Watteau at the Château de la Muette in about 1709 were engraved by the young François BOUCHER as *Figures Chinoises et Tartares* (twelve plates) and helped to promote the taste for Chinese subjects. OPPENORD, like Watteau a protégé of the great collector Pierre Crozat, owned at least two paintings by Watteau and the engraved *Figures de différents caractères*. Engravings after Watteau were widely used, for example by Augsburg designers and publishers such as ENGELBRECHT, MERZ and WACHSMUTH, by BICKHAM and on Worcester porcelain and English enamels. *The Ornamental Designs of Watteau Painter to Louis XIV* (Edinburgh, 1839) reinforced Watteau's reputation at the height of the rococo revival.

Weale, John (1791–1862) Weale set up as a publisher at 59 High Holborn in about 1820. From at least 1831 he published many reprints of ROCOCO ornament with titles such as *Chippendale's One Hundred and Thirty Three Designs* (1834) or *Chippendale's Ornaments and Interior Decorations in the Old French Style* – both misleading titles as the designs in the former work are from JOHNSON's 1758 book and those in the latter by LOCK. Other designers reprinted by Weale were CHIPPENDALE himself, PETHER and COPLAND. Weale's reprints were criticized in the *Architectural Magazine* (1834), but as late as 1858 he published a collection of *Old English and French Ornaments*. Later Weale published a reprint of Thomas KING's *Cabinet Maker's Sketch Book, Monograms* (1852) and many coloured illustrations of medieval stained glass, some in a short-lived de luxe periodical, *Quarterly Papers on Architecture* (1843–5).

Webb, John (1611–72) Born in London of a Somerset family, Webb became in 1628 a pupil of Inigo JONES, whose niece he married. His independent works seem to begin in 1638, but Webb continued in royal service under Jones until 1643, when Edward Carter was appointed Surveyor of the King's Works. From 1648 Webb designed interiors for the fire-damaged Wilton House, in 1654 a mirror with a broken pediment for The Vyne, and in 1655 panelling for Chevening. In 1661 to 1662 Webb enlarged the Queen's House at Greenwich. His 1666 design for the King's bedchamber at Greenwich included a bed alcove with palm-tree ornament derived from H. Prado and F. Villalpando's *In Ezechielem explicationes* (1604), a reconstruction of Solomon's temple; the design was published by VARDY and influenced the state bedroom furniture designed for Kedleston Hall by James Gravenor. From 1663 Webb designed settings for the revived court masques, including *The Tragedy of Mustapha* (1666). In 1669, deprived of official preferment, Webb retired to Butleigh Court, Somerset, an estate he had bought in 1653.

Webb, Philip (1831–1915) Born in Oxford, the son of a doctor, Webb was apprenticed to the Reading architect John Billing in 1849. After a brief period in Wolverhampton he entered STREET's office in Oxford in 1854. He came under the influence of RUSKIN at this stage, buying his *Stones of Venice* in 1855, and in 1856 met his life-long friend and hero, William MORRIS, who had also entered Street's office. Through Morris, Webb met BURNE-JONES and Charles Faulkner. Webb and Morris moved to London with Street's office in 1856. In 1858 Webb travelled to France with Morris and Faulkner and set up his own architectural practice. He designed a massive GOTHIC wardrobe, which was painted by Burne-Jones, as a wedding present to Morris, and from 1858 designed the Red House at Bexley Heath for Morris, including furniture. In 1859 Webb was elected to the Hogarth Club. He was at this period already working as a furniture designer, executing a large group of designs for Major Gillum in 1860. His style was massive, Gothic and oaken, strongly influenced by Street. In April 1861 Webb became a member of the newly founded Morris, Marshall, Faulkner & Co., and in 1862 ROSSETTI described Morris and Webb as 'our most active men of business as regards the actual conduct of the firm'. In 1861 Webb designed a group of furniture shown by the firm at the LONDON 1862 EXHIBITION, including the St George cabinet, painted by Morris. He was the firm's specialist in animals and birds, for instance the birds in Morris's Trellis wallpaper (1862). Webb designed the basic format of the firm's stained glass until the reconstitution of the firm as Morris & Co. in 1875; he also designed lettering, heraldry and canopy-work for stained glass, and silver, jewellery and embroidery. For his own use Webb designed a cast-iron bed and glass made by James Powell & Sons of Whitefriars. In 1866 to 1867 he designed the Green Dining Room at the VICTORIA & ALBERT MUSEUM and rooms redecorated at St James's Palace by the firm. In

1867, protesting, he was appointed consulting manager at £80 a year, and worked closely with Warington Taylor (1835–70), the firm's business manager, whose tomb he designed. Webb designed gesso decoration around 1880, much of which was executed by Kate FAULKNER, and iron grates made by Longden & Co. of Oxford Street. In 1882 EDIS illustrated a small neat *buffet* designed by Webb for Morris & Co. Many of Webb's houses included furniture, for instance a sideboard and sidetable in the dining-room at Rounton Grange (1872–5). His architectural practice was restricted but regular, including the country houses Clouds (1881–6) and Standon (1891). In 1896 he designed Morris's tomb. At this period he was friendly with LETHABY and GIMSON and acted as a guru to Arts & Crafts designers; MUTHESIUS praised his work. He retired in 1900, JACK, who had been his assistant, taking over his practice. In 1902 Webb designed a silver mace for Birmingham University. Norman SHAW described Webb as 'A very able man indeed, but with a strong liking for the ugly'.

Webb, Stephen (1849–1933) Webb moved to London at the age of sixteen and worked as a sculptor. From about 1885 to the winding-up of the firm in 1897 Webb designed for the cabinet-makers, Collinson & Lock. He contributed the essays 'Furniture', 'Of Carving' and 'Woods and Other Materials' to *Arts & Crafts Essays* (1893), and showed at ARTS & CRAFTS EXHIBITIONS from 1888 to 1906. He was a member of the ART-WORKERS' GUILD. Webb's speciality was the design of intarsia, which he executed in ivory and for which he published designs in the 'ART-WORKERS' QUARTERLY' (1902). In 1899 he wrote a paper on 'Intarsia', read in his absence owing to illness to the SOCIETY OF ARTS; some specimens

of his work were exhibited and attracted criticism and a defence by Lewis F. DAY. Webb also designed wallpaper friezes for Jeffrey & Co. in about 1894, and in 1910 plaster ornament for a fireplace designed by Walter CAVE. Webb later taught sculpture at the Royal College of Art (see SCHOOL OF DESIGN).

Wechter, Georg Born in Nuremberg in about 1526, Wechter died there in 1586. In 1573 Wechter was commissioned by Wenzel JAMNITZER to design the definitive masterpiece model for Nuremberg goldsmiths, an elaborately lobed piece of a type known as a columbine cup. This was among the designs Wechter engraved in his *30 Stuck zum Verzachnen Fur Die Goldschmid* (Nuremberg, 1579), thirty plates of cups, double cups, tankards, a pilgrim bottle and details of such objects. They are covered in bold STRAPWORK with masks and fruit, in a style very close to that of ZAN. One cup has a tree-trunk base in the early 16th-century style. On the title of *30 Stuck* Wechter calls himself a painter. His son, another Georg Wechter, also a painter and engraver, moved to Bamberg, where he published *Neuw Grottesken Buch allerley Frantzosischen Poesslein* (1619; thirty-one plates), a suite of GROTESQUE heads and masks.

Wegner, Hans Born in 1914, Wegner was trained as a cabinet-maker and at the Copenhagen School of Arts and Crafts, where he was later a lecturer from 1946 to 1953. Wegner set up his own office at Gentofte in 1943. He has designed furniture, silver, lamps and wallpapers, acting as a design consultant to several firms. In 1946 Wegner collaborated with MOGENSEN in designing a flat for the Copenhagen cabinet-makers' exhibition. Wegner's Chinese chair (1944), made by Fritz Hansen, Allerod, uses a well-known Chinese type as its model. His Chair 24 (1950) by Carl Hansen & Sons is also a version of a Chinese chair. A subtly curved teak, oak and cane chair of 1950 is Wegner's most influential design, the epitome of Danish 'good taste'. In 1970 he designed the spare and elegant steel and leather armchair 812 for Johannes Hansen of Copenhagen, who have produced many of his designs.

Weiner, Franz In the VIENNA MUSEUM FOR APPLIED ARTS are three volumes entitled *Practische Zimmer Mahlerei* which contain over seventy designs for the decoration of rooms by Franz Weiner. They probably date from about 1820 and admirably illustrate the BIEDERMEIER style in interior decoration, predominantly classical schemes in bright clear colours, but also including simulated landscapes and draperies.

Welch, Robert Born in Hereford in 1929, Welch was trained as a silversmith at Birmingham School of Art under Ralph Baxendale and Cyril Shiner, and then from 1952 to 1955 at the Royal College of Art (see SCHOOL OF DESIGN), where he met other silversmiths, including Gerald Benney and David MELLOR. In 1953 he visited Sweden and in 1954 Norway, where he worked under the silversmith Theodor Olsen of Bergen. Welch's Royal College thesis was on Stainless Steel Tableware, and illustrated designs by Folke Arstrom, Erik Herlow and Sigurd PERSSON, as well as three by Harold STABLER. In 1955 Welch was appointed design consultant to J. & J. Wiggin, who made Old Hall stainless-steel wares, and also set up in Chipping Campden in the former workshop of ASHBEE's Guild of Handicraft, by a coincidence of which Welch only later became aware. Welch designed a stainless-steel toast rack for Old Hall in 1955 and in 1957 collaborated with David Mellor on the Campden

range of cutlery, produced at the suggestion of the Council of Industrial Design to compete with Scandinavian models. In 1958 Welch designed stainless-steel tableware for the new liner *Oriana*. From 1959 he has had a wider activity as an industrial designer, his works including sanitary fittings for British Rail (1961–3) and a kettle for Carl Prinz of Solingen (1968). From 1962 he has designed and produced a number of cast-iron objects such as candlesticks and peppermills; he has also designed Stourbridge glass (1968) and pottery made in Devon (1970). After a tour of Scandinavia in 1966, when his work was described in 'MOBILIA', Welch effected a close association with Skjalm Peterson in Copenhagen. Throughout his designing career Welch has continued to practise as a silversmith, executing many prestige commissions for the Goldsmiths' Company and other establishment patrons. His style has progressed from slender Scandinavian elegance in the 1950s towards bold rounded forms, sometimes reminiscent of early industrial artefacts.

Welter, Michael (1808–92) Born in Cologne, Welter was trained as a painter in Paris. His main activity was as a decorative and stage painter, working in styles ranging from medieval to Moorish. From about 1860 he worked on the interior decoration and furniture of the Wartburg, a key monument of the GOTHIC Revival in Germany, which was visited by LUDWIG II of Bavaria in 1867 and served as one of the inspirations for Ludwig's Schloss Neuschwanstein. In 1871 to 1872 Welter was employed to design furniture in the Byzantine style for Neuschwanstein, but none was executed. Elsewhere he designed stained glass, textiles, parquetry and cast-iron ornaments, the latter for the factory of Graf von Stolberg-Wernigerode at Ilsenburg.

Wendingen (1918–31) This *avant-garde* Dutch magazine of architecture and design was published by the Amsterdam architects' fellowship 'Architectura et Amicitia'. The chief editor, H. Th. Wijdeveld, was also responsible for its brilliantly innovatory typography and design, in a highly rectilinear style reminiscent of 'DE STIJL'. Among the more important issues were one devoted to Eileen GRAY (1924), one devoted to Frank Lloyd WRIGHT (1925) and one devoted to interior design with an introduction by W. M. Dudok (1927).

Wennerberg, Gunnar (1863–1914) Born in Skara, Wennerberg studied painting in Uppsala, and then from 1886 under Bonnat and Gervex in Paris. He worked at the Sèvres factory, where he designed porcelain, and he also designed glass and textiles. In 1895 Wennerberg joined the Gustavsberg ceramic factory, for whom he designed influentially simple forms and floral decorations. In 1909 he returned to Paris, where he died.

Werk, Das (1914–present) This official Swiss architectural magazine contains a full coverage of design, especially in its earlier issues.

Wernle, Michael Wernle published *Livre de taille d'espargne* (1650; six plates of black scrolled floral ornament for goldsmiths), *Livre des ouvrages d'orfevrerie* (six plates of jewelled pendants), *Les Pendant. d'Oreille* (Paris; seven plates of bow-formed earrings covered in jewels), and a suite of twelve plates of ornament published in Nuremberg by Paulus Fürst.

Westlake, Nathaniel Hubert John (1833–1921) Westlake, born in Hampshire, was trained as a painter at Somerset House and later at J. M. Leigh's Life School. In 1858 he published *The Litany*,

'sketched from a Psalter executed in England about 1320'. This attracted the attention of BURGES, who recommended Westlake to his friend F. P. Barraud (1824–1900), partner and designer in the stained-glass firm of Lavers & Barraud, founded in 1858. In 1859 Westlake painted Burges's Sun Cabinet. Westlake designed stained glass for churches by Burges, William BUTTERFIELD and WHITE among others, and also collaborated with BENTLEY on stained-glass design from 1863 to 1883. Westlake's early stained glass was densely coloured and strongly leaded but he later adopted a more pictorial approach. He became a partner in Lavers & Barraud in 1868. He was also a historian of his subject, publishing *A History of Design in Painted Glass* (1881–94).

Whall, Christopher Whitworth (1849–1924) Born in Northamptonshire, the son of a clergyman, Whall trained as a painter at the Royal Academy Schools. He met MACKMURDO in 1874 but only after conversion to Catholicism in Lucca in 1878 did he come in 1880 to design his first stained glass, for St Ethelreda's, Ely Place. In 1888 Whall showed stained-glass designs at the first ARTS & CRAFTS EXHIBITION and at the Liverpool Art Congress. SEDDING'S admiration led him to commission Whall to design glass for Holy Trinity, Sloane Street, in 1889. Also in 1889 Whall joined the ART-WORKERS' GUILD and contributed to the Century Guild *Hobby Horse*; Selwyn IMAGE became a life-long friend. In 1894 Whall visited France and studied medieval glass. From 1896 he taught on stained glass at the Central School of Arts & Crafts, and from 1898 at the Royal College of Art (see SCHOOL OF DESIGN). In 1899 he helped to write the Art-Workers' Guild masque, 'Beauty's Awakening'. His *Stained Glass Work* (London, 1905) was one of the

Artistic Crafts series, edited by LETHABY. Whall was Master of the Art-Workers' Guild in 1912, and participated in the Ghent 1913, Paris 1914 and Royal Academy 1916 Exhibitions. In 1922 he formed the firm of Whall & Whall Ltd with his daughter and collaborator Veronica Whall (1887–1970), later a talented stained-glass designer in her own right. Whall had a close relationship with architects, particularly Henry WILSON, LETHABY and E. S. Prior (1852–1932), whose invention of Early English slab glass in 1889 was a major stimulus to Arts & Crafts stained-glass designers. Whall's own designs evinced deep historical and technical knowledge, with a brilliant use of white glass and plain geometric quarries, of which he published a pattern-book in 1900. His style evolved from early Pre-Raphaelitism towards an almost expressionist manner. In his later years 'Daddy' Whall became a father figure to his apprentices and to other designers, and exercised a wide influence in England, Ireland and America.

Wheeler, Candace (1827–1923) Candace Wheeler, born of a puritan family in Delhi in upstate New York, married Thomas Wheeler in 1855; they lived in Brooklyn and moved in an artistic set. Candace Wheeler was an amateur painter until 1876, when after seeing the Royal School of Art Needlework's exhibit at the PHILADELPHIA EXHIBITION she determined to create a similar institution in America. The Society of Decorative Art was thus founded in 1877 and thirty sister societies soon sprang up. To raise the standard of design she co-opted her friends TIFFANY and the artist Samuel Colman to join a committee which vetted and supplied designs. Candace Wheeler subsequently became a member of Louis C. Tiffany and Associated Artists, an interior decorating firm which began

operating in 1879, and herself designed embroideries, textiles and wallpapers, winning Warren, Fuller and Co.'s 1881 wallpaper design competition. Her designs were mainly floral with strong Japanese influence. Associated Artists flourished, being invited to redecorate the White House in 1882, and from 1883 to 1907 Wheeler ran the firm as her own. In 1893, although semi-retired, she was appointed director of the Women's Building at the CHICAGO WORLD COLUMBIAN EXPOSITION, for which she designed furniture and textiles. Her daughter, Dora Wheeler Keith, was a close collaborator and won fourth prize in the 1881 wallpaper competition. Candace Wheeler's books include *The Development of Embroidery in America* (1894), *How to Make Rugs* (1900) and *Principles of Home Decoration* (1903).

Whitaker, Henry Whitaker's *Designs of Cabinet Upholstery Furniture in the Most Modern Style* (1825) contains fifty plates mainly dated 1826 or 1827, with rich and handsome late-Grecian-style designs for furniture reminiscent of M. A. NICHOLSON's manner, and a few richly vegetal early ROCOCO revival designs. A few Grecian designs by Whitaker are included in *Practical Carpentry* (1826), whose lengthy technical text on cabinet work recognizes HOPE as the great reformer in furniture design. These plates were later included in Tredgold's *New and Improved Practical Builder* (1848–50). Plates of antique VASES and marbles by Whitaker (1827) are included in a book on Felix Hall (1833). In 1838 Whitaker showed a view of Sefton church at the Royal Academy, a church which BRIDGENS had delineated in 1822. Whitaker's *Practical Cabinet Maker and Upholsterer's Treasury of Designs* (1847; 111 plates) attacks French designs in its preface, a subject to which Whitaker later returned in the 'BUILDER' (1850), but does include designs in the Louis XIV, as well as the Grecian, Italian, Elizabethan, RENAISSANCE and GOTHIC styles. They are mainly for furniture, and Whitaker's clients include the Conservative Club, Osborne House, Crewe Hall, the Dukes of Devonshire (Chatsworth) and Sutherland (Trentham), and the Marquis of Exeter; Hollands and Bantings are mentioned as executant firms. The *Treasury* also includes designs for ironwork, silver, textiles and china, some by Copeland & Garrett. Whitaker's last book, *Materials for a New Style of Ornamentation* (1849; fifty plates), displays considerable botanical knowledge in plates of ornament which employ a somewhat limp formal NATURALISM.

White, William (1825–1900) The son of a clergyman, White trained as an architect under D. G. Squirhill of Leamington, and then worked in the office of Sir George Gilbert Scott (1811–78) in London before setting up practice in Truro in 1847. In 1857 he became a member of the Mediaeval Club; he was also active in the ECCLESIOLOGICAL SOCIETY. For the Rectory at St Columb Major (1850), White designed some GOTHIC hall chairs with octagonal inlaid backs. White's Gothic furniture for Bishopscourt (1860–64) is equally vigorous, and for its chapel he designed an altar frontal and toughly geometric iron candlesticks decorated with glass cabochons. His woodwork and furniture at Humewood (1867–70) was notched, moulded and chamfered idiosyncratically. White also designed tiles and devised a wasteless lavatory and a springless lock, among other curious inventions.

Wichmann, Joachim Wichmann was active as an engraver in Hamburg from 1674 to 1703. His *Ein Newes Büchlein von allerhandt Goldschmiedereij* (1674; six plates) contains crosses, pendants, seals, frames and a large dragon-fly brooch, heavily set with stones, with some scrolled ACANTHUS and floral ornament. Wichmann may also have worked in Amsterdam.

Wiedel, Jean Wiedel worked in Venice. He designed two suites of ornament published by Joseph Fridrich Leopold in Augsburg in 1718 and 1719. They comprise indented and very scrolly and seaweed-like ACANTHUS ornament applied to swags, consoles, cartouches, frames, a VASE handle and a chair with acanthus embroidery on seat and back, and some small STRAPWORK borders.

Wiener Werkstätte In 1897 a group of Viennese artists and designers, under the general leadership of the painter Gustav Klimt (1862–1918), made a well-publicized exit from the Künstlerhaus, an established artists' association and established themselves as the defiantly independent Secession, whose first group of honorary members included GRASSET, BURNE-JONES and Walter CRANE. From 1898 the magazine 'VER SACRUM' promulgated Secessionist ideas, including the unity of the arts and in the same year the Secession building, designed by OLBRICH, was erected. The 1898 Secession Exhibition included a *Ver Sacrum* room designed by Hoffmann. In 1899 the Vienna Museum of Applied Arts, directed from 1897 by Arthur von Scala, began to employ Secessionist designers as teachers, including Josef HOFFMANN and Koloman MOSER. The 1900 Secession Exhibition concentrated on the decorative arts and included designs by MACKINTOSH and ASHBEE. Mackintosh had a strong formal influence on Hoffmann and Moser but it was the example of Ashbee's Guild of Handicraft, which they later visited, which led to their foundation of a Viennese equivalent. The opportunity came when Moser suggested the idea of workshops on the Ashbee model to a rich young banker, Fritz Wärndorfer, who had visited England. The Wiener Werkstätte, Produktiv-Gemeinschaft von Kunsthandwerkern in Wien (Viennese Workshops, Production Cooperative of Art Workmen in Vienna), was founded in June 1903, with Wärndorfer as commercial director and Moser and Hoffmann in artistic charge. By 1905 the Wiener Werkstätte were employing over 100 workers and in the same year a Wiener Werkstätte brochure stated that all its products, including metalwork, jewellery, leatherwork, and furniture, were designed by Hoffmann and Moser. When Klimt, Wagner, Hoffmann, Moser and others left the Secession in 1905 the Wiener Werkstätte became the Viennese centre of progressive design, celebrated in the periodical 'DEUTSCHE KUNST UND DEKORATION' and in the 1906 'STUDIO' Special Summer Number. CZESCHKA designed for the Werkstätte from 1904 and other designers involved in 1908 were Otto Prutscher (1880–1949), Michael Powolny (1871–1954) and Berthold Löffler (1874–1960); the latter two had founded the ceramic factory Wiener Keramik in 1905. Fritz Zeymer (1886–1940) and Moriz Jung (1885–1915) supplied graphic designs, as did Oskar Kokoschka. In 1907, after a quarrel with Wärndorfer, Moser left the Wiener Werkstätte, but the severely rectilinear style he and Hoffmann had forged dominated its products until about 1915. However, Eduard Josef Wimmer (1882–1961), who began to design for the Wiener Werkstätte in 1908, and Dagobert PECHE, who was involved from 1915, introduced a new frivolous, eclectic and curvilinear style, which was predictably condemned by LOOS, who had earlier regarded Hoffmann and Moser as panderers to fashion. Even Hoffmann's late designs were tainted by the new curves, especially his metalwork. Peche inspired many lesser designers who worked for the Wiener

Werkstätte in the 1920s, mainly women, including Vally Wieselthier (1895–1945). The Wiener Werkstätte enjoyed a brief final flourish after celebrating its twenty-fifth anniversary in 1928 but in 1932 the business was dissolved as a result of financial difficulties.

Wieringen, Cornelis Claesz van Born in about 1580 and first recorded in 1597, Wieringen was a marine painter. In 1631 he became dean of the Haarlem Guild of St Luke. He died in 1633. In 1629 Wieringen designed a colossal tapestry depicting the Capture of Damiate for the Town Hall in Haarlem.

Wight, Peter Bonnett (1838–1925) Born in New York, Wight studied architecture from 1856 under Thomas R. Jackson (1826–1901). In 1862 he opened his own New York office and designed the National Academy of Design in the Reformed GOTHIC style, also the vehicle for Wight's Mercantile Library (1867) and a house in Louisville, Kentucky (1869). At this period Wight designed accomplished Reformed Gothic furniture and ornament. In 1871 he moved to Chicago where he was very active in the rebuilding after the fire, and worked on the CHICAGO 1893 WORLD COLUMBIAN EXPOSITION.

Wilborn, Nicolaus Wilborn became a citizen of Nuremberg in 1533. He published a number of prints from 1531 to 1537, some copied from ALDEGREVER, Jacopo de' Barbari and DÜRER. They include designs for dagger sheaths (1534 and 1536), a scrolling foliate frieze with a medallion head (1534), a GOTHIC alphabet surrounded by fleshy leaves and putti, a grotesque N with masks, a winged warrior etc., and a small and coarse suite of the seven planets in triumphal cars, comparable to Virgil SOLIS's later suite.

Will, Johann Martin (1727–1805) Will was active as an engraver and publisher in Augsburg. He issued 150 suites of four plates each with designs copied from NEO-CLASSICAL French designers, who included J.-F. BOUCHER, LALONDE and DELAFOSSE. Will also published a number of original neoclassical designs of ARTISAN quality.

Wille, Rudolf Born in Hildesheim in 1873 Wille was trained as an engineer. He was self-taught as a designer and worked in collaboration with his wife, Fia Körting (1868–1920), whom he married in 1900. They designed ART NOUVEAU glass for Graf Schaffgotsch's Josephinenhütte in the first decade of the century and from 1910 to 1915 had their own business designing lighting, carpets, glass and ironwork. After his wife's death Wille concentrated on glass and ironwork.

Willement, Thomas (1786–1871) Willement was active as a stained-glass designer from 1812 to 1865, executing over 1,000 commissions. He was heraldic artist to George IV and artist in stained glass to Queen Victoria. Willement designed mural decorations at Temple church, London (1842), praised by Henry COLE, who was introduced by Willement to Herbert Minton, and at Wilton church (1845). He also designed Elizabethan-style wallpapers, woodwork, etc., at Charlecote from 1828 to 1838, and encaustic tiles for St John & Barr of Worcester in 1844. He collaborated with A. W. N. PUGIN at Alton in 1841, but they quarrelled. Willement was friendly with Henry SHAW, subscribing to his *Tile Pavements* (1858), and many other antiquaries.

Willms, Albert Willms was active as an ornamental sculptor and silver designer in Paris, working with DIÉTERLE, KLAGMANN and others, before emigrating to London in 1848. In London, Willms designed works shown by the goldsmith Jean Valentin Morel (1794–1860) at the LONDON 1851 EXHIBITION. He moved back to Paris in 1852 and worked for Christofle, FROMENT-MEURICE and the bronze manufacturer Victor Paillard: Willms received a medal at the PARIS 1855 EXHIBITION for his designs for Paillard. In 1859 he was recruited as head of their design studio by Elkingtons, the Birmingham silversmiths and electrotype manufacturers; at the same time they brought over MOREL-LADEUIL. Willms designed objects shown by Elkingtons at the LONDON 1862 EXHIBITION and the PARIS EXHIBITIONS of 1867 and 1878. In 1897 he designed a mace for the City of Birmingham. Willms's pamphlet *Industrial Art* (1890) stressed the French contribution to English design and scorned the 'affectation of mediaeval . . . methods' at ARTS & CRAFTS EXHIBITIONS.

Willson, Alexander Willson described himself as 'Architect and Professor of Ornament' on the title of his *The Antique and Modern Embellisher* (1766; fifty plates). Published by SAYER, the *Embellisher* was said to be absolutely necessary to 'Architects . . . Upholsterers . . . Cabinet, and Chairmakers . . . Japanners . . . Goldsmiths . . . Stove Grate-makers' and so on. It included mouldings, frets, paterae, sphinxes, etc., and some interesting borders for 'Japanners China painters &c.', in the ROCOCO, 'Persian' and 'Moresque' styles.

Wilson, Henry (1864–1934) Wilson, the son of a clergyman, was trained at the Kidderminster School of Art, and then articled to a Maidenhead architect. He then passed through the offices of John Oldrid Scott (1841–1913) and John Belcher (1841–1913), before joining

J. D. SEDDING as chief assistant; he met GIMSON and Powell in Sedding's office. Wilson took over the practice on Sedding's death in 1891. From 1890 Wilson took a particular interest in the design and manufacture of metalwork, which he taught under LETHABY and George Frampton at the Central School of Arts & Crafts from 1896 and then from 1901 under Lethaby at the Royal College of Art (see SCHOOL OF DESIGN). He joined the ART-WORKERS' GUILD in 1902 and was its Master in 1917. He showed at the ARTS & CRAFTS EXHIBITION from 1889. Wilson's metalwork designs use an original combination of Byzantine and late-GOTHIC forms. His *Silverwork and Jewellery* (1903) was one of the Artistic Crafts series edited by Lethaby; its second edition included sections on Japanese and Indian techniques. Wilson also designed furniture for Charles Trask & Co., fireplaces for Longden & Co., a wallpaper, The Tree (1896), for Jeffrey & Co., and, in 1905, the bronze doors of the cathedral of St John the Divine, New York. In 1896 he was the first editor of the 'ARCHITECTURAL REVIEW'. In 1916 he was responsible for organizing the anachronistic Burlington House Arts & Crafts Exhibition and in 1917 he projected a Cotswold village with 200 craftsmen. Wilson went into exile in France in 1922.

Wilson, Robert Wilson designed ornaments for sword blades and guns around the 1770s, preserved in an album of 376 pages in the VICTORIA & ALBERT MUSEUM. He is possibly to be identified with a gun and pistol maker of the same name recorded in Birmingham in 1767. Some of his designs are in a very backward-looking STRAPWORK style, others are competent ROCOCO exercises. One bears the motto 'WILKES & LIBERTY'.

Winter, Anthony de Born in Utrecht, Winter was active as an engraver and publisher in Amsterdam from at least 1682, when he married. In 1690 he issued a book of cyphers. His *Nieux Goud Smits Lofwerck* (1696; twelve plates) was followed by a *Nouveau Livre d'Ornements et d'Ouvrages d'Orfèvrerie les plus en usage*. These contained floral or ACANTHUS ornament in the manner of Paul Androuet DUCERCEAU, with birds, masks and putti, for the use of goldsmiths.

Wirkkala, Tapio Born in Hanko in Finland in 1915, Wirkkala was trained as a sculptor at the Helsinki Institute for Arts and Crafts from 1933 to 1936. He later, from 1951 to 1954, served as its artistic director. In 1947, after practising as a sculptor and graphic artist, Wirkkala won a competition for glass design organized by the Karhula-Iittala glass company and in the same year a competition to design bank-notes for the Bank of Finland. Thenceforward Wirkkala has designed glass for Karhula-Iittala, working on a freelance basis like SARPANEVA, as well as cutlery, ceramics and lighting. His designs, often based on wooden models, tend to combine bold sculptural curves with simple outlines. In 1955 Wirkkala worked with Raymond LOEWY and since 1955 he has designed for the Rosenthal porcelain factory; he has also designed silver for Christofle. By organizing an exhibition of Finnish design in Zürich in 1951 and designing and organizing the Finnish entry to the MILAN 1954 TRIENNALE, he helped to establish the high international reputation of Finnish design.

Woeiriot, Pierre (1532–96) A member of a Lorraine family of goldsmiths and engravers, Woeiriot published engravings of portraits and classical history under the patronage of Duke Charles III of Lorraine. His *Pinax Iconicus*

Antiquorum (Lyon, 1556) incorporated a self-portrait. In 1555 and 1556 Woeiriot published a number of suites of pendants, swords and daggers. His *Livre d'Aneaux d'Orfèvrerie* (Lyon, 1561; forty plates) was dedicated to the writer Barthélemy Aneau, who died in Lyon in 1561. It comprises rings in a MANNERIST GROTESQUE style derived from Fontainebleau which Woeiriot used in all his works. His sword-hilts incorporate highly suggestive entwinements of elongated nudes.

Woensam, Anton The son of a painter who moved from Worms to Cologne in 1513, Woensam was active as a painter and produced an immense number of woodcuts. He was probably responsible for designs in four early pattern-books for embroidery published in Cologne by Peter Quentel. The first, *Eyn new Kunstlich Boich* (1527; twenty-four plates), was in part a copy of SCHÖNSPERGER'S 1524 book, but also included GOTHIC foliate friezes by Woensam. It was also published in 1527 with a French title and a little later by Willem Vorsterman of Antwerp, with an English title, *A neawe treatys as concernynge the excellency of the nedle worcke*. It thus became the earliest such pattern-book to be aimed at the English market. The second Quentel book, *Eyn newe Kunstlich Moetdelboech* (1529; twenty-four plates), was another combination of Schönsperger and Woensam; it was for the use of carvers as well as embroiderers. The third, *Ein new Kunstlich Modelbuch* (1541; fifty-two plates), repeated some designs from the first two with extra plates borrowed from RENNER'S designs for Egenolff and PAGANO's for Zoppino. The last Quentel/Woensam collaboration, *Eyn new Künstich Mödelbuech* (1544; twenty-seven plates), was again a compilation from their earlier books, with extra designs by Woensam, part NATURAL-ISTIC, part RENAISSANCE, and very like much Elizabethan embroidery.

Wölfer, Marius Wölfer taught at the art school in Gotha. From 1826 he published a series of modest pattern-books for architects, carpenters, metalworkers and gardeners. His *Modell- und Musterbuch für Bau- und Möbel-Tischler* (Quedlinburg and Leipzig, 1829) went through several editions up to 1836. It is the most characteristic BIEDERMEIER pattern-book for furniture, with a wide range of designs of every type of household furniture, even including spittoons. Most of the designs are simple and classical, others have GOTHIC details. There is even a doorway 'in the new Bavarian style' which reflects the influence of KLENZE'S RENAISSANCE Revival Residenz in Munich, begun in 1826, and some sofas 'in the latest style' which display rich late-Empire ornament.

Wolfers, Philippe (1858–1929) Born in Brussels, the son of the goldsmith Louis Wolfers (1820–92), Wolfers finished his studies at the Académie Royale in 1875. He then worked for his father, designing silver from 1880, at first mainly in a ROCOCO revival style, then using Japanese motifs from 1882, and working in a NATURALISTIC manner from about 1884. His jewellery and silver became increasingly ART NOUVEAU in character in the 1890s. He was one of the artists invited to work on ivory from the Congo in 1893 and showed ivory carvings in Antwerp in 1894 and in Brussels in 1895. His Art Nouveau jewellery, using a rich variety of materials and often endowed with symbolist titles, enjoyed great success at the Brussels 1897 Exhibition. Wolfers showed at the Munich Secession in 1898 and 1899 and his jewellery was illustrated in the 'STUDIO' winter number of 1901. HANKAR designed furniture for Wolfers' villa at La Hulpe in 1899, and in 1909 Wolfers employed HORTA to design his firm's offices in Brussels. He showed an electric lamp at the TURIN 1902 EXHIBITION and jewellery at Venice in 1907, but was mainly active as a chryselephantine sculptor from 1904. In 1925 however Wolfers designed an ensemble, Gioconda, including glass, ceramics, furniture and carpet, for the Belgian pavilion at the PARIS 1925 EXHIBITION. His son, Marcel Wolfers, born in 1886, was also active as a designer of silver and as a sculptor.

Wolpe, Berthold Born in 1905 at Offenbach near Frankfurt, Wolpe was first trained as a metalworker. He developed an interest in calligraphy and typography, which he studied from 1924 to 1928 at the Offenbach school of applied arts as a pupil of Rudolf Koch (1876–1934), a life-long influence. From 1929 to 1933 Wolpe taught at the Offenbach school. In the late 1920s he was active as designer of tapestry and metalwork as well as typographer. In 1932 he designed the Hyperion typeface, issued by the Bauer foundry. His *Schriftvorlagen* (1934) contained a series of scripts. In 1933 Wolpe was forbidden to teach by the Nazi regime, and in 1935 he came to England. On a visit to England in 1932 Wolpe had met Stanley MORISON who invited him to design a typeface for the Monotype Corporation. The result was the Albertus typeface (capitals 1935, lower case 1937, bold and light versions 1940). In 1935 Wolpe designed Tempest titling for the Fanfare Press and in 1937 the Pegasus italic face, first cut in 1938. Wolpe worked for the Fanfare Press for four years, publishing *A Book of Fanfare Ornaments* (1939), and then moved to Faber & Faber, for whom he designed at least 1,500 book-jackets. Wolpe is an accomplished and prolific scholar of calligraphy and typography and an omnivorous collector. He has taught at the Camberwell School of Art, the Royal College of Art and elsewhere. He was made a Royal Designer for Industry in 1959 and his innumerable ephemera include the menu for their twenty-fifth anniversary dinner in 1962. Wolpe has also designed posters and the masthead used by *The Times* from 1966 to 1970. His work is distinguished by boldness, humour and a strong sense of history.

Wood, Edgar (1860–1935) Born in Middleton, the son of a cotton-mill owner, Wood was apprenticed to the architects Mills & Murgatroyd of Manchester. In 1885 he set up on his own in Middleton. He opened an office in Oldham in 1889, and by 1893 had moved to Manchester. In 1887 Wood sketched ornaments from ROSSETTI picture frames. He took part in the Manchester 1895 Arts & Crafts Exhibition and became a founder member of the Northern Art Workers' Guild in 1896. Wood showed furniture, metalwork, tiles and architectural designs at their 1898 and 1903 exhibitions. His 1895 communion table for Lindley Methodist church and furniture illustrated in the 'STUDIO' (1898) display foliate ornament of an ART NOUVEAU character applied to sturdy Arts & Crafts forms. His 1903 Christian Scientist church in Manchester seems to reflect BAILLIE SCOTT's influence. From 1904 he was in partnership with James SELLERS, who designed most of the firm's furniture. From 1908 Wood developed a striking rectilinear manner in architecture and ornament. His work was praised by MUTHESIUS and illustrated by 'DOCUMENTS D'ARCHITECTURE MODERNE' and other magazines. After the First World War, Wood settled in Italy and painted.

Wood, Henry Active as a 'Decorative Artist and Draughtsman' at 24 Percy Street, Tottenham Court Road, London, in the 1840s, Wood published *A Series of Designs of Furniture and Decoration* (twenty-four coloured plates with large, elaborate but unarchaeological designs for furniture in the 'Louis XIV, François I, Elizabethan & Gothic' styles), *A Useful and Modern Work on Cheval and Pole Screens, Ottomans, Chairs and Settees for mounting Berlin Needlework* (eighteen coloured plates redolent of mid-Victorian taste) and *A Useful and Modern Work on Chairs* (twelve plates).

Wornum, Ralph Nicholson (1812–77) Born at Thornton, North Durham, the son of the piano manufacturer Robert Wornum (1780–1852), Ralph Wornum studied at London University in 1832 and then trained as a painter. Wornum was honourably mentioned in the Westminster Hall cartoon competition of 1840. In 1846 he began to write in the *Art Union* and in 1848 was appointed lecturer on art to the government schools of design. In 1851 Wornum won the 'ART JOURNAL' prize for his essay on 'The Exhibition of 1851 as a lesson in taste'. He was in 1852 appointed librarian and keeper of casts to the School of Design at Marlborough House, but after 1854, when he was made keeper of the National Gallery, Wornum was mainly active in the fine arts. He was a friend of RUSKIN. Wornum's *Analysis of Ornament* (1856) was based on lectures given in schools of design from 1848 to 1850 and long served as the basic textbook on its subject, going into an eighth edition in 1893.

Wright, Frank Lloyd (1867–1956) After two years at the Engineering School of Wisconsin University and a brief period in the office of the Chicago architect J. L. Silsbee, Wright spent the five years from 1888 to 1893 as draughtsman with Louis SULLIVAN, who became a lifelong influence, Wright's polemical biography of Sullivan, *Genius and the Mobocracy*, appearing in 1949. Wright began as an architect in 1889 with his own house in Oak Park, Illinois. He soon developed an organic approach, with structure, interior and exterior openly expressing their interrelationship, and every detail individually designed or chosen to fit, furniture often being built in or used to de-limit interior space. A penchant for rectilinearity and, often, horizontality, together with sophisticated simplicity, were early apparent. Wright was brought up with 19th-century textbooks, for example VIOLLET-LE-DUC and Owen JONES, whose *Grammar of Ornament* he owned. A taste for the conventionalized floral ornament advocated by Jones was reinforced by Sullivan's more organic designs, themselves influenced by the Reformed Gothic ornament of Sullivan's master, Frank FURNESS. Some of Wright's earliest ornament, for example in the William Winslow House (1894), is richly vegetal in the same tradition, but for the Auvergne Press edition of Keats's *Eve of St Agnes* (1896) and their *The House Beautiful* (1897) Wright evolved apparently abstract graphic ornaments, which are in fact formalized and repeated images of organic forms, a method underlined by Wright's inclusion in *The House Beautiful* of twelve photographs taken by himself of wild flowers and weeds, reflecting the influence of COLONNA's *Essay on Broom-Corn* (1887). Radical geometry is apparent in Wright's decorative glass for the Luxfer Prison Company (1894–9) and in stained glass of 1895 for his own house, directly based on H. Carot's *Kunstverglasungen* (Berlin, 1886). Wright's early architectural career was extremely successful; he had designed over fifty houses by 1900. The chairs designed for his Oak Park house in 1895 were tall with spindle backs, one of the earliest of an international type around 1900. Later Oak Park chairs (about 1903) used a single sloping board in the back, and in the Robie House (1908) slats replaced spindles. In 1897 Wright was a founding member of the Chicago Arts & Crafts Society founded at Hull House, set up in 1889 by Jane Addams, the social reformer, on the model of London's Toynbee Hall. He had a deep admiration for RUSKIN and William MORRIS but in a lecture at Hull House in 1901 on the 'Art and Craft of the Machine' he proclaimed the machine the 'normal tool of civilization'. Wright's own liking for dark stained oak, and later unstained oak, and for repoussé copper echoed Arts & Crafts taste, but Wright saw little common ground between his own carefully calculated effects and the 'plain as a barn door' simplicities of Gustav STICKLEY and the Roycrofters. His interest in Japan, sparked off by the Japanese Pavilion at the CHICAGO 1893 WORLD COLUMBIAN EXPOSITION, reflects his sophistication. It led to exhibitions of Japanese prints in 1906, 1908 and 1917, and a book in the latter year. But such refinement did not stand in the way of publicity and continued success: *House Beautiful* (1897) and the *Ladies' Home Journal* (1903) described his own house and in 1901 the latter featured his imaginary 'Home in a Prairie Town'. Up to his departure for Europe in 1909 Wright had a strong influence on his mid-West contemporaries, the so-called 'Prairie School'. For the Dana House, Springfield, Illinois (1903), for an extravagant patroness of the arts, Wright designed elaborate stained glass, lights and murals based on formalized flowers. His Larkin Company Administration Building, Buffalo, New York (1904), had pioneering rectilinear metal office chairs (1906) and in the Darwin D. Martin House, Buffalo (1906), his influence extended beyond the design of every item and its arrangement to the choice of his client's Japanese prints and ceramics. In the Avery Coonley House, Riverside, Illinois (1908), Wright's writ ran from the abstract tulip tiles on its

façade to table napkins and dresses for Mrs Coonley. While Wright was in Berlin, Wasmuth published two volumes of his *Ausgeführte Bauten und Entwürfe* (1910 and 1911), the second with a preface by C. R. ASHBEE, who had met Wright in Chicago in 1900. Wright was already familiar with the published work of MACKINTOSH, VAN DE VELDE, BERLAGE, LOOS and Wagner, and had admired OLBRICH's interiors at the 1904 Louisiana Purchase Exhibition, and on his return from Europe he was encouraged by his international reputation, enhanced by the 1925 Wright issue of 'WENDINGEN', to further originality. His stained glass for the Avery Coonley Playhouse (1912), a progressive school, is a cheerful quasi-abstract arrangement of squares and circles in strong colours, which seems to anticipate Mondrian, and the exploded and exaggerated planes of his library table for the Little House, Wayzata, Minnesota (1911), prefigure RIETVELD. For Midway Gardens, Chicago (1914), an entertainment complex, the Imperial Hotel, Tokyo (1915–22), and the Hollyhock House, Los Angeles (1920), Wright created totally integrated designs in which consistency extended to ceramics decorated with squares, hexagonal silver, and chairs with rectilinear hollyhock backs, the latter made under the supervision of Rudolf M. Schindler. Wright's twelve cover designs for *Liberty* magazine in 1926 to 1927 and his sixteen glass designs for the Leerdam Glass Company (1930) were unexecuted, but for one vase. His *Autobiography* (1932) thus appeared at a time when his career was in the doldrums of the Depression, but its graphic design displayed great vigour, also apparent in the brochures for the Taliesin Fellowship he founded in 1932. A revival was initiated by the house Fallingwater, Bear Run, Pennsylvania (1936), and the S. C. Johnson Administration Building, Racine, Wisconsin (1936–9); Wright designed furniture for both, high-quality walnut veneer at Fallingwater, painted aluminium and steel for the Johnson building. Furniture for his middle-class Usonian houses (1937 onwards) used slab-like forms of plywood. Built-in furniture and tall-back chairs (John Rayward House, 1956–8) reflect the continuity from his earliest designs, and even at the end an Arts & Crafts atmosphere survives. In 1955 Wright attempted to enter a wider market with his Taliesin Line furniture for the Heritage Henredon Company of North Carolina and textiles and wallpapers for F. Schumacher & Co. of New York. Despite promotion in *House Beautiful* reception was luke-warm; Wright's designs were too ambiguous, neither MODERN nor historicist, to appeal to the middle-class buyers at whom they were aimed. As a designer Wright was sometimes simplistic, particularly in his use of geometry, and sometimes impractical – his chairs often tipped over – but his single-mindedness and continuity reflected an organic vision of design which created no school but whose potency has remained undimmed.

Wuest, Johann Leonhard Wuest designed two suites of engraved or etched ornament for metal-workers, *Geaezt od' Geschnittene Gallanteries* (1715; six plates) and *Schneid und Etz Büchlein* (six plates), both published by Jeremias Wolff in Augsburg, where Wuest died in 1735. They comprise cups, VASES, boxes, bottles, sword-hilts, etc., all covered with a dense carpet of tightly scrolled MORESQUE ornament, varied with putti, birds and masks. This works well on smaller more geometrical objects such as boxes, but is less successful on Wuest's ungainly BAROQUE vases. The title of *Gallanteries* is a nice conceit, an arcade whose columns are covered in ornament, and which encloses a scatter of ornamented boxes.

Wyatt, Benjamin Dean (1775–1852) Born in London, the eldest son of James WYATT, Benjamin Dean Wyatt began to practise as an architect in London after uncompleted studies at Oxford, a spell working for the East India Company in Calcutta from 1797 to 1802, and employment as secretary to Sir Arthur Wellesley in Dublin from 1807 to 1809. In 1815 to 1816 Wyatt designed a NEO-CLASSICAL palace for the Duke of Wellington, never executed. Wyatt's importance for the history of design lies in his interiors for Crockford's Clubhouse (1827), Belvoir Castle (about 1825 to 1830), Londonderry House (1828), York, later Stafford House (1826–33), Apsley House (1828–30) and 6 Carlton House Terrace (1831), London, all in the Louis Quatorze style. The first interior in this style, a rich synthesis of French BAROQUE and ROCOCO motifs, was the Elizabethan Saloon at Belvoir (1824), designed by Wyatt's younger brother Matthew Cotes Wyatt (1777–1862) to incorporate genuine French rococo panelling. Benjamin Dean Wyatt's Louis Quatorze – all white and gold – was a style for the rich and powerful, intended to re-create the splendours of the *ancien régime*. It was the origin of the rococo revival, which rapidly became the most *lumpen* of *bourgeois* styles.

Wyatt, James (1746–1813) The sixth son of the architect Benjamin Wyatt of Weeford (1709–72), James Wyatt studied architecture in Venice under Antonio Visentini from about 1762 and in about 1764 moved to Rome. Back in England from about 1768 Wyatt made his reputation with the NEO-CLASSICAL London Pantheon (1769–72) and thenceforward had a brilliant and prolific architectural career, both public and private, ecclesiastical and secular, albeit bedevilled by administrative carelessness and lack of prolonged application which became notorious and would have been disastrous but for Wyatt's personal charm and conspicuous facility in design. His neo-classical stylistic vocabulary was the same as ADAM's but he avoided the filigree of Adam's later works, substituting a delicate, chaste and sometimes empty elegance. Wyatt became Adam's direct rival. He designed many interiors and much furniture, for example at Heveningham (1786–99), an organ case for Burton-on-Trent church (1770), unexecuted mirrors and table for Burton Constable (1776) and cases made by Roach in about 1783 for a set of James Tassie's gems sent to Catherine the Great, whose ambassador in London attempted to lure Wyatt to Russia. Wyatt also designed neo-classical silver and ormolu for Matthew Boulton (1728–1809), as well as Coade stone ornaments, clocks and ironwork. However, Wyatt's favourite style was GOTHIC; his most celebrated Gothic work was BECKFORD's Fonthill (1796–1812), but his cathedral restorations at Salisbury (1787–92) and elsewhere earned him the epithet 'the Destroyer' and the lasting contempt of A. W. N. PUGIN. Wyatt's Lee Priory (about 1785 to 1790) incorporated neat Gothic bookcases and he later carried out a Gothic remodelling of George III's apartments at Windsor (1800–13). Wyatt achieved a brief but disastrous Presidency of the Royal Academy in 1805.

Wyatt, Sir Matthew Digby (1820–77) Born at Rowde, the son of a magistrate who belonged to the great Wyatt architectural dynasty, Wyatt trained as an architect under his brother Thomas Henry Wyatt (1807–80), from 1836. By 1844 he had saved enough money to travel and set off to France, Italy, Sicily and Germany, returning in 1846. At the

suggestion of the terracotta manufacturer John Blashfield, Wyatt had done drawings of medieval mosaics published as *The Geometrical Mosaics of the Middle Ages* (1848) with fine chromolithographic plates. Through Blashfield, Wyatt met Herbert Minton (1793–1858), whom he advised on encaustic tiles for Osborne House. From 1850 Wyatt designed tiles for Maw & Co., including a fireplace shown at the LONDON 1862 EXHIBITION; many Wyatt designs for Maw are included in *Specimens of Geometrical Mosaics* (1857). In 1849 Wyatt reported for COLE's 'JOURNAL OF DESIGN' on the PARIS 1849 EXHIBITION. Wyatt's report helped to pave the way for the LONDON 1851 EXHIBITION, on whose Royal Commission Wyatt served as Special Commissioner and Secretary from 1850. He was superintending architect of the Crystal Palace and was thus in close contact with Owen JONES, to whose *Grammar of Ornament* Wyatt contributed remarks on RENAISSANCE and Italian ornament. Wyatt's *The Industrial Arts of the Nineteenth Century* (two volumes, 1851–3) comprised chromolithographic plates of objects shown at the 1851 Exhibition; fourteen of the descriptive articles were written by William BURGES, who also assisted on Wyatt's *Metalwork and its Artistic Design* (1852; fifty chromolithographic plates of early metalwork). Wyatt was responsible for the Pompeian, Byzantine, English GOTHIC and Italian Renaissance Courts in the Crystal Palace, when removed to Sydenham; Owen Jones was his collaborator there. In 1852 to 1854 Wyatt designed decorative ironwork for Brunel's Paddington Station in an innovative part geometric part NATURALISTIC style, and in 1865 an Islamic tiled billiard room at 12 Kensington Palace Gardens. He also designed carpets for Templeton, wallpapers for Messrs Woollam, and for Hurrell, James & Co., and cast-iron public conveniences. Wyatt's book design includes a fine cover for his *Notices of Sculpture in Ivory* (1855). He wrote an essay in W. R. Tymms's *The Art of Illuminating* (1860; 100 plates). Wyatt's Italian Renaissance courtyard for the India Office (1868), decorated with Minton maiolica designed by Wyatt, is perhaps the finest expression of the High Victorian Renaissance style, the style favoured by the official design establishment of which Wyatt himself was a key member.

Y

Yellow Book, The (1894–7) Published by Elkin Mathews and John Lane, the literary editor of *The Yellow Book* was Henry Harland (1861–1905), while its art editor was Aubrey Beardsley – until his dismissal in 1895, in response to a mistaken popular view that he was a close friend of Oscar Wilde. Beardsley had designed posters, covers and illustrations for *The Yellow Book*, which also included work by Walter CRANE and other advanced designers.

Yenn, John (1750–1821) The son of a London barber and wig-maker, Yenn became in 1764 a pupil of Sir William CHAMBERS, for whom he worked until he began to practise as an architect on his own account in the late 1770s. Chambers secured him a series of architectural sinecures, culminating in the Surveyorship of Greenwich Hospital (1788). Yenn was active in the Royal Academy, succeeding Chambers as Treasurer in 1796. He was a virtuoso draughtsman and drawings by Yenn for furniture survive at the VICTORIA & ALBERT MUSEUM and elsewhere, including Blenheim where he designed pierglasses and a tripod for the Temple of Health (1789). His style displayed a dense but refined combination of NEO-CLASSICAL motifs.

Ysenbeck, Hylko Bentes Probably born in about 1752 Ysenbeck was, with Isaak Uittenbogaert (1771–1831), one of the most famous designers of the Hoorn wallpaper factory, for which Hendrik ROSENBERGH had earlier worked. Ysenbeck was also manager of the factory and was succeeded on his death in 1822 by Arie Bakker; the factory closed in 1826.

Z

Zan, Bernhart A goldsmith in Nuremberg, Zan published two suites of designs for cups, tankards, beakers, details of feet and bowls for such vessels, and motifs of ornament to be applied to them. The first, *12 Stick* (1580; twelve plates), is the earliest dated example of engraving in the dotted manner, in which lines are made up of a series of small dots. The second, with forty plates, was published in 1581, and reissued by the goldsmith and publisher Stefan HERMAN in Ansbach in 1584 as *Allerley Gebuntznierte Fisirungen*. Zan's ornament consists almost entirely of fluently handled STRAPWORK, embellished with fruit, heads and GROTESQUE masks. The forms of his vessels are typical of his date, although two cups have tree-trunk stems in the early 16th-century manner, a motif already revived by WECHTER, whose style is very close to that of Zan.

Zanuso, Marco Born in Milan in 1916, Zanuso graduated as an architect there in 1939. After the Second World War he was active as both architect and industrial designer. From 1947 to 1949 he was chief editor of 'CASABELLA'. From 1956 he collaborated with Richard Sapper. He has designed much furniture, his armchairs Famiglia Antropus (1949), Milord (1956) and Baronet (1964) reflecting the move from attenuated elegance in the 1950s towards the more stocky shapes of the 1960s. His televisions, the subtly curved Brion Vega (1962), the smoothly rounded Doney transistor (1964) and the Black (1969),

a black perspex box, reflect a similar evolution. Zanuso has also designed kitchen units, sewing machines and many buildings, and has received many honours.

Zech, Daniel In 1615 Zech published a suite of twenty-four plates of borders and motifs for engraving on silver, in the dotted manner; they incorporate putti, fruit, birds and GROTESQUE masks. Zech is known to have been active as a goldsmith in Augsburg from at least 1623 to his death in 1657.

Zetterwall, Helgo Nikolaus (1831–1907) Born in Linköping, Zetterwall studied architecture at the Stockholm Academy of Art from 1853 to 1860. He then became the most prolific Swedish architect of the later 19th century, restoring many GOTHIC churches in a manner influenced by VIOLLET-LE-DUC. He was director of public works and in 1887 wrote its influential handbook on church restoration. Zetterwall was a prolific designer of church furnishings including those for All Saints, Lund (1877–91).

Zhurwesten, Augustinus In 1602 Zhurwesten published a competent suite of black stretched GROTESQUE designs for enamel, with an elaborate cartouche on the title-page, which states that they were, remarkably, designed and engraved in Rome. Zhurwesten is probably identical with Augustin Zervost, active as a goldsmith in Augsburg from about 1616 to 1665.

Zick, Januarius (1730–97) Born in Munich, the son of a painter, mathematician and mechanic, Zick studied painting in Paris in 1757 and thereafter in Rome under Mengs. In about 1760 he became court painter to the Electoral Court in Trier and settled in Ehrenbreitstein in 1762. His main activity was as a decorative painter, but he was also an architect and designed church furniture for the abbey of Wiblingen near Ulm (1778) and for St Caster in Coblenz (1783). From about 1773 Zick designed marquetry for David Roentgen (1743–1807), including the two great marquetry panels of the Continence of Scipio and the Rape of the Sabines, made for Charles Alexandre of Lorraine's palace in Brussels in 1779 and now in Vienna. For some marquetry designs Zick borrowed CHINOISERIES from PILLEMENT. Zick may also have designed furniture for Roentgen.

Ziegler, Jules-Claude (1804–56) Born in Langres, Ziegler was a pupil of the painters François Joseph Heim (1787–1865) and INGRES, and began to show paintings at the Paris Salon in 1831. In 1838, influenced in his choice of site by the 16th-century potter Bernard Palissy, Ziegler set up a pottery at Voisinlieu near Beauvais, where he made stoneware with relief ornament. From 1838 to 1842 Ziegler designed for the Sèvres porcelain factory. In 1850 Ziegler published *Études Céramiques*, a comprehensive theoretical treatise on the ceramic art which demonstrated his familiarity with Owen JONES's *Alhambra* and with the colour theories of CHEVREUL. It was accompanied by an album of fourteen brilliant lithographic plates, two coloured, with designs for ceramics in the Moorish, NATURALISTIC, Egyptian and other styles. In 1854 Ziegler was appointed director of the École des Beaux-Arts in Dijon.

Zuccarelli, Francesco (1702–88) Born in Pitigliano, Tuscany, Zuccarelli was a pupil of the landscape painter Paolo Anesi and the history painter Pietro Nelli (1672–1740). He settled in Venice in about 1730 but moved to London in 1752 as a result of his contacts with the great collector Consul Joseph Smith (1682–1770). He remained in London until 1771 but for a return to Venice from 1762 to 1765. He was a founder member of the Royal Academy in 1768, and was elected President of the Venetian Academy in 1772. Soon after this he retired to Florence where he died. In about 1757 Zuccarelli designed suites of tapestries, The Pilgrimage to Mecca, and Landscapes with Ruins, woven by Paul Saunders of Soho for Lord Egremont's house in Piccadilly, the latter using details from Robert Wood's *The Ruins of Palmyra* (1753). In 1758 he designed a tapestry, Asia, to supplement a suite of three continents brought by Lord Leicester from France. English enamels were on occasion decorated with landscapes from prints after Zuccarelli.

Zuccaro, Taddeo (1529–1566) Born near Urbino, Zuccaro went to Rome in about 1543 to study painting. In 1548 he decorated the Palazzo Mattei. He was thenceforward a prolific decorative painter in Rome, and also designed stucco and interior decoration. In 1551 Zuccaro went to Urbino to decorate the choir of the cathedral. In 1553 he was back in Rome, where in 1559 he executed decorations for the funeral of the Emperor Charles V. In 1560 he was summoned to Urbino to paint the portrait of the Duke's daughter Virginia on the occasion of her marriage to Federico Borromeo. He was then commissioned to design a maiolica service with scenes from the life of Julius Caesar, which was executed at Castel Durante by 1562.

The scenes are surrounded by lively GROTESQUE borders.

Zündt, Mathias Zündt was active as carver, goldsmith and engraver. He was a journeyman of Wenzel JAMNITZER from 1551 to 1553. In 1556 he was made a citizen of Nuremberg but in 1559 he was working in Prague for Archduke Ferdinand under Jamnitzer's auspices. Zündt engraved many portraits, maps, allegories and book-plates in Nuremberg, and in 1567 the illustrations to LENCKER'S *Perspectiva Literaria.* He died in Nuremberg in 1572. In 1551 Zündt published *Ein new Kunstbuch*, also known as *Novum Opus Craterogra-phicum* (31 plates), a series of designs for silver cups, beakers and lights, many decorated with a dense carpet of STRAP-WORK GROTESQUE ornament, others more thematically treated, such as a marine cup with sea-horses as its stem and Neptune on its cover. In 1553 he published a suite of twelve plates of jewels of cartouche form. Coarse but energetic, they consist of tightly scrolled strapwork grotesques peopled by grimacing masks, fruit and putti. Zündt also issued ornaments for dagger sheaths. His designs reflect the Jamnitzer workshop manner of the early 1550s, and thence that of Nuremberg as a whole.

MORE ABOUT PENGUINS, PELICANS AND PUFFINS

For further information about books available from Penguins please write to Dept EP, Penguin Books Ltd, Harmondsworth, Middlesex UB7 0DA.

In the U.S.A.: For a complete list of books available from Penguins in the United States write to Dept DG, Penguin Books, 299 Murray Hill Parkway, East Rutherford, New Jersey 07073.

In Canada: For a complete list of books available from Penguins in Canada write to Penguin Books Canada Ltd, 2801 John Street, Markham, Ontario L3R 1B4.

In Australia: For a complete list of books available from Penguins in Australia write to the Marketing Department, Penguin Books Australia Ltd, P.O. Box 257, Ringwood, Victoria 3134.

In New Zealand: For a complete list of books available from Penguins in New Zealand write to the Marketing Department, Penguin Books (N.Z.) Ltd, P.O. Box 4019, Auckland 10.

In India: For a complete list of books available from Penguins in India write to Penguin Overseas Ltd, 706 Eros Apartments, 56 Nehru Place, New Delhi 110019.

TEXTE INTÉGRAL

L'AVARE

MOLIÈRE

ÉTUDE DE L'ŒUVRE PAR
LUC BOUVIER

COLLECTION
PARCOURS D'UNE ŒUVRE

SOUS LA DIRECTION DE MICHEL LAURIN

Beauchemin
CHENELIÈRE ÉDUCATION

L'Avare
Texte intégral

Édition présentée, annotée et commentée
par Luc Bouvier

Collection « Parcours d'une œuvre »

Sous la direction de Michel Laurin

© 2000, Groupe Beauchemin, Éditeur Ltée

Édition : Sophie Gagnon
Coordination : Johanne O'Grady
Correction d'épreuves : Maryse Quesnel
Conception graphique : Josée Bégin
Infographie : Transcontinental Transmédia
Impression : Imprimeries Transcontinental

Tableau de la couverture :
L'Avare.
Œuvres complètes de Molière,
Paris (Laplace, Sanchez et Cie) /
akg-images.
Œuvre de **Maurice Sand,**
écrivain et peintre
français (1823-1889).

**Catalogage avant publication
de Bibliothèque et Archives nationales du Québec
et Bibliothèque et Archives Canada**

Molière, 1622-1673

   L'avare

   (Collection Parcours d'une œuvre)
   « Texte intégral ».

   Comprend des réf. bibliogr.
   Pour les étudiants du niveau collégial.

   ISBN 978-2-7616-5118-9

   1. Molière, 1622-1673. Avare. 2. Molière, 1622-1673 – Critique et
interprétation. I. Bouvier, Luc. II. Titre. III. Collection.

PQ1827.A2B68 2007   842'.4   C2007-941039-1

Beauchemin

CHENELIÈRE ÉDUCATION

7001, boul. Saint-Laurent
Montréal (Québec)
Canada H2S 3E3
Téléphone : 514 273-1066
Télécopieur : 514 276-0324
info@cheneliere.ca

ISBN 978-2-7616-5118-9

Dépôt légal : 2e trimestre 2007
Bibliothèque et Archives nationales du Québec
Bibliothèque et Archives Canada

Imprimé au Canada

1 2 3 4 5 ITG 11 10 09 08 07

Nous reconnaissons l'aide financière du gouvernement du Canada
par l'entremise du Programme d'aide au développement de l'industrie de l'édition (PADIÉ) pour nos activités d'édition.

Gouvernement du Québec – Programme de crédit d'impôt pour
l'édition de livres – Gestion SODEC.

DANGER

LE
PHOTOCOPILLAGE
TUE LE LIVRE

REMERCIEMENTS

L'auteur remercie Pascale Prud'homme pour sa collaboration et le Collège de l'Outaouais qui l'a libéré d'un cours à la session d'automne 1999.

TABLE DES MATIÈRES

ANNEXES

181

MOLIÈRE

INTRODUCTION

« [D]E L'AVARICE ET DES AVARICIEUX »
(*L'Avare*, ACTE I, SCÈNE 3, ligne 228.)

LE thème « de l'avarice et des avaricieux » est très présent dans la littérature universelle : l'ont traité, tantôt sur le mode comique, tantôt sur un ton dramatique, l'auteur latin Plaute avec Euclion dans *La Marmite* (195 av. J.-C.), Shakespeare avec l'usurier Shylock dans *Le Marchand de Venise* (1596), Honoré de Balzac et le père Grandet dans *Eugénie Grandet* (1833), Charles Dickens et l'avare Scrooge dans la nouvelle « Un chant de Noël » (1843), et combien d'autres encore. Le thème est de toutes les époques et de toutes les sociétés. Pourtant, *L'Avare* de Molière, jouée pour la première fois le 9 septembre 1668, au Palais-Royal, ne plaît guère au public parisien de l'époque. Après neuf représentations, l'auteur la retire.

Le succès relatif de *L'Avare* s'explique d'une part par la forme de la pièce et d'autre part par son propos. À l'époque de Molière, une grande comédie en cinq actes ne pouvait être en prose. Les spectateurs l'ont donc boudée. Quant au propos, l'avarice, il n'a pas enlevé systématiquement les rires, d'autant que tout n'est pas comique dans la pièce. Harpagon et son vice corrompent tout sentiment, toute morale. Le sérieux et le grave s'y mélangent, ce qui a désarçonné le public d'alors. À mesure qu'on se rapproche du XXᵉ siècle, le succès de la pièce se confirme. Le spectateur actuel ne s'attache plus à l'obligation d'écrire en vers, et le mélange des genres — comique et drame — s'est imposé comme une nécessité.

L'actualité de la pièce tient à son sujet, car chaque société est imprégnée d'un personnage d'avare notoire. Ainsi, Séraphin Poudrier[1], l'avare du roman *Un homme et son péché*, a fortement marqué la société québécoise. L'auteur, Claude-Henri Grignon, y présente un avare chez qui l'or suscite une véritable jouissance charnelle :

---

1. Personnage qui sera transposé à la radio puis à la télévision dans *Les Belles Histoires des pays d'en haut*.

SÉRAPHIN POUDRIER
DESSIN DE MICHÈLE GOUDRO SELON LES INDICATIONS
FOURNIES PAR CLAUDE-HENRI GRIGNON.

« Un escalier, à gauche, conduisait à l'étage supérieur où un corridor étroit longeait deux grandes chambres séparées par une mince cloison. La première de ces chambres avait toujours servi de magasin au vieux garçon qui, pendant vingt ans, y avait entassé, pêle-mêle, des horloges, des montres, des harnais [...] et quoi encore, toutes choses, vieilles ou neuves, laissées en gage. C'est encore dans cette chambre que se trouvaient les trois sacs d'avoine [...]. Dans un des sacs, l'usurier cachait une grande bourse de cuir ne renfermant jamais moins de cinq cents à mille dollars en billets de banque, en pièces d'argent, d'or ou de cuivre. [...] Alors il le regardait avec amour, puis marmonnait de vagues paroles. Une curiosité immense, suivie d'une sensation inexprimable, s'emparait de lui, coulait dans tout son être ainsi qu'une poussée de sang neuf et rapide. C'était trop de félicité : Séraphin ne pouvait plus se retenir. Il plongeait sa main osseuse et froide dans le sac. Avec lenteur, avec douceur, il tâtait, il palpait, il fouillait parmi les grains d'avoine, et lorsqu'il sentait enfin — ô suprêmes attouchements ! — la bourse de cuir ou simplement les cordons, sa jouissance atteignait à un paroxysme que ne connut jamais la luxure la plus parfaite, et son cœur battait, fondait, défaillait.

Plusieurs fois par jour, il se vautrait dans cette volupté. [...] seul dans cette pièce obscure, séparé du monde, Poudrier se retrouvait réellement soi-même, alors que sa passion dominante le précipitait dans des accès de rage ou de douceur infinie.

Les trois sacs d'avoine représentaient pour Séraphin le seul Dieu en trois personnes[1]. »

Séraphin, l'avare québécois, et Harpagon, son équivalent français, ont tous deux la même passion : l'or.

---

1. Claude-Henri Grignon, *Un homme et son péché*, Éditions internationales Alain Stanké, coll. $\frac{10}{10}$, Montréal, 1977, p. 20-22.

Salle du Palais-Royal, à Paris, où eut lieu
la première représentation de L'Avare, le 9 septembre 1668.

L'AVARE,

COMEDIE.

Par I. B. P. MOLIERE.

A PARIS,

Chez I E A N R I B O V, au Palais , vis-à-vis
la Porte de l'Eglise de la Sainte Chapelle,
à l'Image S. Louis.

M. DC. LXIX.

AVEC PRIVILEGE DV ROY.

PAGE DE TITRE DE L'ÉDITION DE 1669.

LES PERSONNAGES

HARPAGON[1], *père de Cléante et d'Élise, et amoureux de Mariane.*

CLÉANTE, *fils d'Harpagon, amant*[2] *de Mariane.*

ÉLISE, *fille d'Harpagon, amante de Valère.*

VALÈRE, *fils d'Anselme, et amant d'Élise.*

MARIANE, *amante de Cléante, et aimée d'Harpagon.*

ANSELME, *père de Valère et de Mariane.*

FROSINE, *femme d'intrigue.*

MAÎTRE SIMON, *courtier*[3].

MAÎTRE[4] Jacques, *cuisinier et cocher d'Harpagon.*

LA FLÈCHE, *valet de Cléante.*

DAME CLAUDE, *servante d'Harpagon.*

BRINDAVOINE, LA MERLUCHE, *laquais d'Harpagon.*

LE COMMISSAIRE ET SON CLERC.

LA SCÈNE EST À PARIS.

« La scène est une salle, et, sur le derrière, un jardin. Il faut deux chiquenilles[5] [ACTE III, SC. 1], des lunettes [ACTE III, SC. 5], un balai [ACTE III, SC. 1], une batte [ACTE III, SC. 1 et 2], une cassette[6] [ACTE IV, SC. 6], une table, une chaise, une écritoire, du papier, une robe [ACTE V, SC. 2], deux flambeaux sur la table au ve acte » (*Mémoire* de Mahelot).

N. B. : Le texte est conforme à l'édition de 1669. Seules les didascalies des éditions de 1682 et 1734 ont été ajoutées pour en faciliter la compréhension.
Les cinq extraits de l'œuvre qui font l'objet d'une analyse approfondie sont indiqués par une trame superposée au texte. Les mots suivis d'un astérisque sont définis dans le glossaire de l'œuvre, à la page 188.

1. *Harpagon* signifie « rapace » en grec et « grappin » en latin. Son costume lors de la création : « un manteau, chausse et pourpoint de satin noir, garni de dentelle ronde [unie] de soie noire, chapeau, perruque, souliers » (Inventaire après décès de Molière, 1673).
2. Amant, amante : personne qui aime et est aimée.
3. Courtier : intermédiaire entre le prêteur et l'emprunteur.
4. Le titre de maître lui est attribué parce qu'il est maître d'hôtel.
5. Chiquenilles [ou siquenilles] : vêtements protégeant la livrée des valets.
6. Cassette : petit coffre.

ACTE I

SCÈNE 1 : Valère, Élise

Valère : Hé quoi ? charmante Élise, vous devenez mélancolique, après les obligeantes assurances que vous avez eu la bonté de me donner de votre foi[1] ? Je vous vois soupirer, hélas ! au milieu de ma joie ! Est-ce du regret, dites-moi, de m'avoir fait heureux, et vous repentez-vous
5 de cet engagement[2] où[3] mes feux[4] ont pu vous contraindre ?

Élise : Non, Valère, je ne puis pas me repentir de tout ce que je fais pour vous. Je m'y sens entraîner par une trop douce puissance, et je n'ai pas même la force de souhaiter que les choses ne fussent pas. Mais, à vous dire vrai, le succès[5] me donne de l'inquiétude ; et je crains
10 fort de vous aimer un peu plus que je ne devrais.

Valère : Hé ! que pouvez-vous craindre, Élise, dans les bontés que vous avez pour moi ?

Élise : Hélas ! cent choses à la fois : l'emportement d'un père, les reproches d'une famille, les censures du monde[6] ; mais plus que tout,
15 Valère, le changement de votre cœur, et cette froideur criminelle dont ceux de votre sexe payent le plus souvent les témoignages trop ardents d'une innocente amour[7].

Valère : Ah ! ne me faites pas ce tort, de juger de moi par les autres. Soupçonnez-moi de tout, Élise, plutôt que de manquer à ce que je
20 vous dois : je vous aime trop pour cela, et mon amour pour vous durera autant que ma vie.

---

1. Foi : promesse de fidélité en amour.
2. La promesse de mariage que Valère et Élise ont mutuellement signée la veille (ACTE V, SCÈNE 3).
3. Où : auquel.
4. Mes feux : mon amour (langage précieux).
5. Succès : résultat (heureux ou malheureux).
6. Censures du monde : condamnations de la société.
7. Au XVIIᵉ siècle, amour est indifféremment masculin ou féminin.

ÉLISE : Ah ! Valère, chacun tient les mêmes discours. Tous les hommes sont semblables par les paroles ; et ce n'est que les actions qui les découvrent différents.

25 **VALÈRE** : Puisque les seules actions font connaître ce que nous sommes, attendez donc au moins à juger de mon cœur par elles[1], et ne me cherchez point des crimes dans les injustes craintes d'une fâcheuse prévoyance[2]. Ne m'assassinez[3] point, je vous prie, par les sensibles coups d'un soupçon outrageux, et donnez-moi le temps de vous

30 convaincre, par mille et mille preuves, de l'honnêteté de mes feux.

ÉLISE : Hélas ! qu'avec facilité on se laisse persuader par les personnes que l'on aime ! Oui, Valère, je tiens votre cœur incapable de m'abuser. Je crois que vous m'aimez d'un véritable amour, et que vous me serez fidèle ; je n'en veux point du tout douter, et je retranche mon chagrin

35 aux appréhensions du blâme qu'on pourra me donner[4].

VALÈRE : Mais pourquoi cette inquiétude ?

ÉLISE : Je n'aurais rien à craindre, si tout le monde vous voyait des yeux dont[5] je vous vois, et je trouve en votre personne de quoi avoir raison aux choses[6] que je fais pour vous. Mon cœur, pour sa défense,

40 a tout votre mérite, appuyé du secours d'une reconnaissance où le Ciel m'engage envers vous. Je me représente à toute heure ce péril étonnant[7] qui commença de nous offrir aux regards l'un de l'autre ; cette générosité surprenante qui vous fit risquer votre vie, pour dérober la mienne à la fureur des ondes[8] ; ces soins pleins de tendresse que

45 vous me fîtes éclater[9] après m'avoir tirée de l'eau, et les hommages assidus de cet ardent amour que ni le temps ni les difficultés n'ont

---

1. À juger de mon cœur par elles : pour juger mes sentiments par mes actions.
2. Dans les injustes craintes d'une fâcheuse prévoyance : à cause de votre trop grande prudence.
3. M'assassinez : m'accablez (langage précieux).
4. Je retranche mon chagrin aux appréhensions du blâme qu'on pourra me donner : je limite mon inquiétude aux reproches qu'on pourra me faire.
5. Dont : avec lesquels.
6. Avoir raison aux choses : justifier les choses.
7. Étonnant : effrayant.
8. Fureur des ondes : tempête.
9. Me fîtes éclater : m'avez prodigués.

rebuté, et qui, vous faisant négliger et parents et patrie[1], arrête vos pas en ces lieux, y tient en ma faveur votre fortune[2] déguisée, et vous a réduit, pour me voir, à vous revêtir de l'emploi de domestique[3] de
50 mon père. Tout cela fait chez moi sans doute un merveilleux effet ; et c'en est assez à mes yeux pour me justifier l'engagement où* j'ai pu consentir ; mais ce n'est pas assez peut-être pour le justifier aux autres, et je ne suis pas sûre qu'on entre dans mes sentiments[4].

ÉLISE : De tout ce que vous avez dit, ce n'est que par mon seul
55 amour que je prétends auprès de vous mériter quelque chose ; et quant aux scrupules que vous avez, votre père lui-même ne prend que trop de soin de vous justifier à tout le monde[5] ; et l'excès de son avarice, et la manière austère dont il vit avec ses enfants pourraient autoriser des choses plus étranges. Pardonnez-moi, charmante Élise,
60 si j'en parle ainsi devant vous. Vous savez que sur ce chapitre on n'en peut pas dire de bien. Mais enfin, si je puis, comme je l'espère, retrouver mes parents, nous n'aurons pas beaucoup de peine à nous le rendre favorable. J'en attends des nouvelles avec impatience, et j'en irai chercher moi-même, si elles tardent à venir.

65 **ÉLISE** : Ah ! Valère, ne bougez[6] d'ici, je vous prie ; et songez seulement à vous bien mettre dans l'esprit de mon père.

VALÈRE : Vous voyez comme[7] je m'y prends, et les adroites complaisances qu'il m'a fallu mettre en usage pour m'introduire à son service ; sous quel masque de sympathie et de rapports de sentiments[8] je me
70 déguise pour lui plaire, et quel personnage je joue tous les jours avec lui, afin d'acquérir sa tendresse. J'y fais des progrès admirables ; et

---

1. La patrie de Valère est Naples (ACTE V, SCÈNE 5).
2. Fortune : condition sociale.
3. Au XVIIe siècle, domestique désigne toute personne employée du maître de maison, quels que soient sa fonction ou son statut social.
4. Entre dans mes sentiments : partage mon opinion.
5. À tout le monde : aux yeux de tous.
6. Au XVIIe siècle, la deuxième partie de la négation (*pas*) est souvent omise avec un verbe à l'impératif.
7. Comme : comment.
8. Rapports de sentiments : synonyme de sympathie.

j'éprouve[1] que pour gagner les hommes, il n'est point de meilleure voie que de se parer à leurs yeux de leurs inclinations[2], que de donner dans leurs maximes[3], encenser[4] leurs défauts, et applaudir à ce qu'ils
75 font. On n'a que faire d'avoir peur de trop charger[5] la complaisance ; et la manière dont on les joue a beau être visible, les plus fins toujours sont de grandes dupes du côté de la flatterie ; et il n'y a rien de si impertinent[6] et de si ridicule qu'on ne fasse avaler lorsqu'on l'assaisonne en louange. La sincérité souffre un peu au métier que je fais ;
80 mais quand on a besoin des hommes, il faut bien s'ajuster à eux ; et puisqu'on ne saurait les gagner que par là, ce n'est pas la faute de ceux qui flattent, mais de ceux qui veulent être flattés.

Élise : Mais que ne tâchez-vous aussi à gagner l'appui de mon frère, en cas que la servante[7] s'avisât de révéler notre secret ?

85 Valère : On ne peut pas ménager l'un et l'autre ; et l'esprit du père et celui du fils sont des choses si opposées, qu'il est difficile d'accommoder ces deux confidences ensemble[8]. Mais vous, de votre part, agissez auprès de votre frère, et servez-vous de l'amitié[9] qui est entre vous deux pour le jeter dans nos intérêts. Il vient, je me retire. Prenez ce
90 temps pour lui parler ; et ne lui découvrez de notre affaire que ce que vous jugerez à propos.

Élise : Je ne sais si j'aurai la force de lui faire cette confidence.

---

1. J'éprouve : je constate.
2. Inclinations : goûts.
3. Donner dans leurs maximes : les approuver.
4. Encenser : flatter.
5. Charger : exagérer.
6. Impertinent : déplacé.
7. Il s'agit de dame Claude, la servante. Lors de la promesse mutuelle entre les deux amoureux, elle a servi de témoin, en conformité avec le droit ecclésiastique.
8. Accommoder ces deux confidences ensemble : obtenir à la fois la confiance du père et celle du fils.
9. Amitié : affection.

SCÈNE 2 : Cléante, Élise

Cléante : Je suis bien aise de vous trouver seule, ma sœur ; et je brûlais de vous parler, pour m'ouvrir à vous d'un secret.

95 **Élise :** Me voilà prête à vous ouïr[1], mon frère. Qu'avez-vous à me dire ?

Cléante : Bien des choses, ma sœur, enveloppées dans un mot : j'aime.

Élise : Vous aimez ?

Cléante : Oui, j'aime. Mais avant que d'aller plus loin, je sais que je dépends d'un père, et que le nom de fils me soumet à ses volontés ;
100 que nous ne devons point engager notre foi* sans le consentement de ceux dont nous tenons le jour ; que le Ciel les a faits les maîtres de nos vœux[2], et qu'il nous est enjoint[3] de n'en disposer que par leur conduite[4], que n'étant prévenus d'aucune folle ardeur[5], ils sont en état de se tromper bien moins que nous, et de voir beaucoup mieux
105 ce qui nous est propre[6] ; qu'il en faut plutôt croire les lumières de leur prudence[7] que l'aveuglement de notre passion ; et que l'emportement de la jeunesse nous entraîne le plus souvent dans des précipices fâcheux. Je vous dis tout cela, ma sœur, afin que vous ne vous donniez pas la peine de me le dire ; car enfin mon amour ne veut rien écouter,
110 et je vous prie de ne me point faire de remontrances.

Élise : Vous êtes-vous engagé, mon frère, avec celle que vous aimez ?

Cléante : Non, mais j'y suis résolu ; et je vous conjure encore une fois de ne me point apporter de raisons pour m'en dissuader.

Élise : Suis-je, mon frère, une si étrange personne ?

---

1. Ouïr : écouter, entendre.
2. Vœux : désirs amoureux.
3. Enjoint : ordonné.
4. Que par leur conduite : qu'avec leur permission.
5. Que n'étant prévenus d'aucune folle ardeur : qu'étant à l'abri des passions.
6. Est propre : convient.
7. Prudence : prévoyance, sagesse.

115 **Cléante** : Non, ma sœur ; mais vous n'aimez pas : vous ignorez la douce violence qu'un tendre amour fait sur nos cœurs, et j'appréhende votre sagesse.

Élise : Hélas ! mon frère, ne parlons point de ma sagesse. Il n'est personne qui n'en manque, du moins une fois en sa vie ! et si je vous 120 ouvre mon cœur, peut-être serai-je à vos yeux bien moins sage que vous.

Cléante : Ah ! plût au Ciel que votre âme, comme la mienne…

Élise : Finissons auparavant votre affaire, et me dites[1] qui est celle que vous aimez.

Cléante : Une jeune personne qui loge depuis peu en ces quartiers, 125 et qui semble être faite pour donner de l'amour à tous ceux qui la voient. La nature, ma sœur, n'a rien formé de plus aimable[2] ; et je me sentis transporté dès le moment que[3] je la vis. Elle se nomme Mariane, et vit sous la conduite d'une bonne femme[4] de mère, qui est presque toujours malade, et pour qui cette aimable fille a des senti-130 ments d'amitié* qui ne sont pas imaginables. Elle la sert, la plaint, et la console avec une tendresse qui vous toucherait l'âme. Elle se prend[5] d'un air le plus charmant du monde aux choses qu'elle fait, et l'on voit briller mille grâces en toutes ses actions : une douceur pleine d'attraits, une bonté tout engageante, une honnêteté[6] adorable, 135 une… Ah ! ma sœur, je voudrais que vous l'eussiez vue.

Élise : J'en vois beaucoup, mon frère, dans les choses que vous me dites ; et pour comprendre ce qu'elle est, il me suffit que vous l'aimez.

Cléante : J'ai découvert sous main[7] qu'elles ne sont pas fort accommodées[8], et que leur discrète conduite[9] a de la peine à étendre à tous

---

1. Me dites : dites-moi. Au XVIIe siècle, le pronom personnel se place devant le verbe à l'impératif.
2. Aimable : digne d'être aimé.
3. Que : où.
4. Bonne femme : femme âgée (sans nuance péjorative).
5. Se prend : s'applique.
6. Honnêteté : bonne éducation.
7. Sous main : secrètement.
8. Accommodées : riches.
9. Discrète conduite : modeste train de vie.

140 leurs besoins le bien qu'elles peuvent avoir. Figurez-vous, ma sœur,
quelle joie ce peut être que de relever la fortune d'une personne que
l'on aime ; que de donner adroitement quelques petits secours aux
modestes nécessités d'une vertueuse famille ; et concevez quel déplaisir[1] ce m'est de voir que, par l'avarice d'un père, je sois dans l'impuis-
145 sance de goûter cette joie, et de faire éclater à cette belle aucun
témoignage de mon amour.

ÉLISE : Oui, je conçois assez, mon frère, quel doit être votre chagrin.

CLÉANTE : Ah ! ma sœur, il est plus grand qu'on ne peut croire. Car
enfin peut-on rien voir de plus cruel que cette rigoureuse épargne
150 qu'on exerce sur nous, que cette sécheresse[2] étrange où l'on nous fait
languir ? Et que nous servira d'avoir du bien, s'il ne nous vient que
dans le temps que nous ne serons plus dans le bel âge d'en jouir, et si
pour m'entretenir même, il faut que maintenant je m'engage[3] de tous
côtés, si je suis réduit avec vous à chercher tous les jours le secours des
155 marchands, pour avoir moyen de porter des habits raisonnables[4] ?
Enfin j'ai voulu vous parler, pour m'aider à sonder mon père sur les
sentiments où je suis ; et si je l'y trouve contraire, j'ai résolu d'aller en
d'autres lieux, avec cette aimable personne, jouir de la fortune[5] que
le Ciel voudra nous offrir. Je fais chercher partout pour ce dessein de
160 l'argent à emprunter ; et si vos affaires, ma sœur, sont semblables aux
miennes, et qu'il faille que notre père s'oppose à nos désirs, nous le
quitterons là tous deux et nous affranchirons de cette tyrannie où
nous tient depuis si longtemps son avarice insupportable.

ÉLISE : Il est bien vrai que, tous les jours, il nous donne de plus en plus
165 sujet de regretter la mort de notre mère, et que…

CLÉANTE : J'entends sa voix. Éloignons-nous un peu, pour nous achever notre confidence ; et nous joindrons après nos forces pour venir
attaquer la dureté de son humeur.

---

1. Déplaisir : tourment.
2. Sécheresse : manque d'argent.
3. Engage : endette.
4. Raisonnables : convenables.
5. Fortune : destinée.

SCÈNE 3 : HARPAGON, LA FLÈCHE

HARPAGON : Hors d'ici tout à l'heure[1], et qu'on ne réplique pas.
170 Allons, que l'on détale de chez moi, maître juré filou[2], vrai gibier
de potence.

LA FLÈCHE, *à part :* Je n'ai jamais rien vu de si méchant que ce maudit
vieillard et je pense, sauf correction[3], qu'il a le diable au corps.

HARPAGON : Tu murmures entre tes dents.

175 **LA FLÈCHE :** Pourquoi me chassez-vous ?

HARPAGON : C'est bien à toi, pendard, à me demander des raisons ;
sors vite, que[4] je ne t'assomme.

LA FLÈCHE : Qu'est-ce que je vous ai fait ?

HARPAGON : Tu m'as fait que je veux que tu sortes.

180 **LA FLÈCHE :** Mon maître, votre fils, m'a donné ordre de l'attendre.

HARPAGON : Va-t'en l'attendre dans la rue, et ne sois point dans ma
maison planté tout droit comme un piquet, à observer ce qui se passe,
et faire ton profit de tout. Je ne veux point avoir sans cesse devant moi
un espion de mes affaires, un traître, dont les yeux maudits assiègent[5]
185 toutes mes actions, dévorent ce que je possède, et furètent de tous
côtés pour voir s'il n'y a rien à voler.

LA FLÈCHE : Comment diantre[6] voulez-vous qu'on fasse pour vous
voler ? Êtes-vous un homme volable, quand vous renfermez toutes
choses, et faites sentinelle jour et nuit ?

---

1. Tout à l'heure : tout de suite.
2. Maître juré filou : voleur professionnel. Au XVIIe siècle, les niveaux hiérarchiques
   d'une profession étaient apprenti, compagnon, maître et maître juré.
3. Sauf correction : sauf erreur (formule qui vise à atténuer les propos).
4. Que : avant que.
5. Assiègent : surveillent.
6. Diantre : diable.

190 **Harpagon**: Je veux renfermer ce que bon me semble, et faire sentinelle comme il me plaît. Ne voilà pas de mes mouchards[1], qui prennent garde à ce qu'on fait? (*À part.*) Je tremble qu'il n'ait soupçonné
quelque chose de mon argent. (*Haut.*) Ne serais-tu point homme à
aller faire courir le bruit que j'ai chez moi de l'argent caché?

195 **La Flèche**: Vous avez de l'argent caché?

Harpagon: Non, coquin[2], je ne dis pas cela. (*À part.*) J'enrage. (*Haut.*)
Je demande si malicieusement[3] tu n'irais point faire courir le bruit
que j'en ai.

La Flèche: Hé! que nous importe que vous en ayez ou que vous n'en
200 ayez pas, si c'est pour nous la même chose?

Harpagon: Tu fais le raisonneur. Je te baillerai[4] de ce raisonnement-
ci par les oreilles. (*Il lève la main pour lui donner un soufflet[5].*) Sors d'ici,
encore une fois.

La Flèche: Hé bien! je sors.

205 **Harpagon**: Attends. Ne m'emportes-tu rien?

La Flèche: Que vous emporterais-je?

Harpagon: Viens çà[6], que je voie. Montre-moi tes mains.

La Flèche: Les voilà.

Harpagon: Les autres.

210 **La Flèche**: Les autres?

Harpagon: Oui.

La Flèche: Les voilà.

---

1. Mouchards: délateurs, espions.
2. Coquin: au XVIIᵉ siècle, terme injurieux.
3. Malicieusement: méchamment.
4. Baillerai: donnerai.
5. Soufflet: gifle.
6. Çà: ici.

© Henri Paul.

HARPAGON (Jean Gascon) : Les autres.

LA FLÈCHE (Robert Gadouas) : Les autres ?

HARPAGON : Oui.

LA FLÈCHE : Les voilà.

ACTE I, SCÈNE 3, lignes 209 à 212.

THÉÂTRE DU NOUVEAU MONDE, 1951.
MISE EN SCÈNE DE JEAN GASCON.

HARPAGON, *montrant les hauts-de-chausses de La Flèche*: N'as-tu rien mis ici dedans?

215 **LA FLÈCHE**: Voyez vous-même.

HARPAGON. *Il tâte le bas de ses chausses*: Ces grands hauts-de-chausses[1] sont propres à devenir les receleurs[2] des choses qu'on dérobe; et je voudrais qu'on en eût fait pendre quelqu'un[3].

LA FLÈCHE, *à part*: Ah! qu'un homme comme cela mériterait bien ce 220 qu'il craint! et que j'aurais de joie à le voler!

HARPAGON: Euh?

LA FLÈCHE: Quoi?

HARPAGON: Qu'est-ce que tu parles de voler?

LA FLÈCHE: Je dis que vous fouillez bien partout, pour voir si je vous 225 ai volé.

HARPAGON: C'est ce que je veux faire.

Il fouille dans les poches de La Flèche.

LA FLÈCHE, *à part*: La peste soit de l'avarice et des avaricieux!

HARPAGON: Comment? que dis-tu?

230 **LA FLÈCHE**: Ce que je dis?

HARPAGON: Oui: qu'est-ce que tu dis d'avarice et d'avaricieux?

LA FLÈCHE: Je dis que la peste soit de l'avarice et des avaricieux.

HARPAGON: De qui veux-tu parler?

LA FLÈCHE: Des avaricieux.

235 **HARPAGON**: Et qui sont-ils ces avaricieux?

---

1. Chausses: culottes pour homme; hauts-de-chausses: culottes pour homme s'arrêtant aux genoux et bouffantes, à l'époque de Molière.
2. Receleurs: personnes qui cachent des objets volés.
3. Molière joue sur l'ambiguïté: «pendre un de ces hauts-de-chausses» ou «pendre un de ces receleurs».

© Henri Paul.

LA FLÈCHE (Robert Gadouas) : Voyez vous-même.

HARPAGON (Jean Gascon). *Il tâte le bas de ses chausses* : Ces grands hauts-de-chausses sont propres à devenir les receleurs des choses qu'on dérobe […]

ACTE I, SCÈNE 3, lignes 215 à 217.

THÉÂTRE DU NOUVEAU MONDE, 1951.
MISE EN SCÈNE DE JEAN GASCON.

LA FLÈCHE : Des vilains[1] et des ladres[2].

HARPAGON : Mais qui est-ce que tu entends par là ?

LA FLÈCHE : De quoi vous mettez-vous en peine ?

HARPAGON : Je me mets en peine de ce qu'il faut.

240 **LA FLÈCHE** : Est-ce que vous croyez que je veux parler de vous ?

HARPAGON : Je crois ce que je crois ; mais je veux que tu me dises à qui tu parles quand tu dis cela.

LA FLÈCHE : Je parle… je parle à mon bonnet[3].

HARPAGON : Et moi, je pourrais bien parler à ta barrette[4].

245 **LA FLÈCHE** : M'empêcherez-vous de maudire les avaricieux ?

HARPAGON : Non ; mais je t'empêcherai de jaser, et d'être insolent. Tais-toi.

LA FLÈCHE : Je ne nomme personne.

HARPAGON : Je te rosserai[5], si tu parles.

250 **LA FLÈCHE** : Qui se sent morveux, qu'il se mouche[6].

HARPAGON : Te tairas-tu ?

LA FLÈCHE : Oui, malgré moi.

HARPAGON : Ha ! ha !

LA FLÈCHE, *lui montrant une des poches de son justaucorps[7]* : Tenez, voilà
255 encore une poche ; êtes-vous satisfait ?

HARPAGON : Allons, rends-le-moi sans te fouiller[8].

---

1. Vilains : avares.
2. Ladres : avares.
3. Je parle à mon bonnet : je me parle.
4. Barrette : bonnet porté par les laquais. L'expression parler à la barrette de quelqu'un signifie faire tomber son chapeau sous les coups.
5. Rosserai : battrai.
6. Qui se sent morveux, qu'il se mouche : que celui qui se sent visé le prenne pour lui.
7. Justaucorps : veste ajustée (juste au corps) qui descendait jusqu'aux genoux en s'évasant.
8. Sans te fouiller : sans que je te fouille.

La Flèche : Quoi ?

Harpagon : Ce que tu m'as pris.

La Flèche : Je ne vous ai rien pris du tout.

260 **Harpagon** : Assurément ?

La Flèche : Assurément.

Harpagon : Adieux, va-t'en à tous les diables.

La Flèche, *à part* : Me voilà fort bien congédié.

Harpagon : Je te le mets sur ta conscience, au moins[1]. (*Seul.*) Voilà un
265 pendard de valet qui m'incommode fort, et je ne me plais point à voir
ce chien de boiteux-là[2].

SCÈNE 4 : Élise, Cléante, Harpagon

Harpagon : Certes ce n'est pas une petite peine que de garder chez
soi une grande somme d'argent ; et bienheureux qui a tout son fait[3]
bien placé, et ne conserve seulement que ce qu'il faut pour sa dépense.
270 On n'est pas peu embarrassé à inventer dans toute une maison une
cache fidèle[4] ; car pour moi, les coffres-forts me sont suspects, et je ne
veux jamais m'y fier : je les tiens justement une franche amorce à
voleurs, et c'est toujours la première chose que l'on va attaquer.
(*Harpagon se croyant seul.*) Cependant je ne sais si j'aurai bien fait
275 d'avoir enterré dans mon jardin dix mille écus[5] qu'on me rendit hier.
Dix mille écus en or chez soi est une somme assez…

---

1. Au moins : évidemment.
2. Allusion au fait que Louis Béjart, qui jouait le rôle de La Flèche lors de la création de la pièce, boitait.
3. Son fait : son argent, sa fortune.
4. Inventer […] une cache fidèle : trouver […] une cachette sûre.
5. Ancienne monnaie française, l'écu d'or valait 10 livres ou francs. Ainsi, 10 000 écus (environ 91 500 € ou 140 000 $) est une somme considérable.

Ici le frère et la sœur paraissent s'entretenant bas.

Ô Ciel! je me serai trahi moi-même: la chaleur[1] m'aura emporté, et je crois que j'ai parlé haut en raisonnant tout seul. (*À Cléante et à Élise.*)
280 Qu'est-ce?

CLÉANTE: Rien, mon père.

HARPAGON: Y a-t-il longtemps que vous êtes là?

ÉLISE: Nous ne venons que d'arriver.

HARPAGON: Vous avez entendu…

285 CLÉANTE: Quoi, mon père?

HARPAGON: Là…

ÉLISE: Quoi?

HARPAGON: Ce que je viens de dire.

CLÉANTE: Non.

290 HARPAGON: Si fait, si fait.

ÉLISE: Pardonnez-moi.

HARPAGON: Je vois bien que vous en avez ouï* quelques mots. C'est que je m'entretenais en moi-même de la peine qu'il y a aujourd'hui à trouver de l'argent, et je disais qu'il est bienheureux qui peut avoir dix
295 mille écus chez soi.

CLÉANTE: Nous feignions[2] à vous aborder, de peur de vous interrompre.

HARPAGON: Je suis bien aise de vous dire cela, afin que vous n'alliez pas prendre les choses de travers et vous imaginer que je dise que c'est moi qui ai dix mille écus.

300 CLÉANTE: Nous n'entrons point dans vos affaires.

HARPAGON: Plût à Dieu que je les eusse, dix mille écus!

---

1. Chaleur: passion.
2. Feignions: hésitions.

CLÉANTE : Je ne crois pas…

HARPAGON : Ce serait une bonne affaire pour moi.

ÉLISE : Ce sont des choses…

305 **HARPAGON** : J'en aurais bon besoin.

CLÉANTE : Je pense que…

HARPAGON : Cela m'accommoderait fort[1].

ÉLISE : Vous êtes…

HARPAGON : Et je ne me plaindrais pas, comme je fais, que le temps 310 est misérable.

CLÉANTE : Mon Dieu ! mon père, vous n'avez pas lieu de vous plaindre, et l'on sait que vous avez assez de bien.

HARPAGON : Comment ? j'ai assez de bien ! Ceux qui le disent en ont menti. Il n'y a rien de plus faux ; et ce sont des coquins* qui font 315 courir tous ces bruits-là.

ÉLISE : Ne vous mettez point en colère.

HARPAGON : Cela est étrange, que mes propres enfants me trahissent et deviennent mes ennemis !

CLÉANTE : Est-ce être votre ennemi que de dire que vous avez du bien !

320 **HARPAGON** : Oui, de pareils discours et les dépenses que vous faites seront cause qu'un de ces jours on me viendra chez moi couper la gorge[2], dans la pensée que je suis tout cousu de pistoles[3].

CLÉANTE : Quelle grande dépense est-ce que je fais ?

HARPAGON : Quelle ? Est-il rien de plus scandaleux que ce somptueux 325 équipage[4] que vous promenez par la ville ? Je querellais hier votre

---

1. M'accommoderait fort : m'arrangerait bien.
2. Allusion à l'assassinat de deux avares notoires, Jacques Tardieu et sa femme, le 24 août 1665. L'affaire fit grand bruit.
3. La pistole est une ancienne monnaie espagnole. L'expression viendrait de ce que les avares avaient la réputation de coudre des pièces dans la doublure de leurs vêtements.
4. Équipage : habillement.

sœur ; mais c'est encore pis. Voilà qui crie vengeance au Ciel ; et à vous prendre depuis les pieds jusqu'à la tête, il y aurait là de quoi faire une bonne constitution[1]. Je vous l'ai dit vingt fois, mon fils, toutes vos manières me déplaisent fort : vous donnez furieusement dans le
330 marquis[2] ; et pour aller ainsi vêtu, il faut bien que vous me dérobiez.

CLÉANTE : Hé ! comment vous dérober ?

HARPAGON : Que sais-je ? Où pouvez-vous donc prendre de quoi entretenir l'état[3] que vous portez ?

CLÉANTE : Moi, mon père ? C'est que je joue[4] ; et comme je suis fort
335 heureux, je mets sur moi tout l'argent que je gagne.

HARPAGON : C'est fort mal fait. Si vous êtes heureux au jeu, vous en devriez profiter, et mettre à honnête intérêt l'argent que vous gagnez afin de le trouver un jour. Je voudrais bien savoir, sans parler du reste, à quoi servent tous ces rubans dont vous voilà lardé[5] depuis les pieds
340 jusqu'à la tête, et si une demi-douzaine d'aiguillettes[6] ne suffit pas pour attacher un haut-de-chausses*? Il est bien nécessaire d'employer de l'argent à des perruques, lorsque l'on peut porter des cheveux de son cru, qui ne coûtent rien. Je vais gager qu'en perruques et rubans, il y a du moins vingt pistoles ; et vingt pistoles rapportent par année dix-
345 huit livres six sols huit deniers[7], à ne les placer qu'au denier douze[8].

CLÉANTE : Vous avez raison.

HARPAGON : Laissons cela, et parlons d'autre affaire. (*Apercevant Cléante et Élise qui se font des signes.*) Euh ? (*Bas, à part.*) Je crois qu'ils se font signe l'un à l'autre de me voler ma bourse. (*Haut.*) Que veulent
350 dire ces gestes-là ?

---

1. Constitution : placement d'argent.
2. Donnez furieusement dans le marquis : menez avec excès le train de vie des nobles.
3. État : habillement.
4. À cette époque à Paris, le jeu était très à la mode.
5. Lardé : couvert.
6. Aiguillettes : lacets (voir la photo, p. 95) qui permettent d'attacher le haut-de-chausses (culotte) au pourpoint (veste). La mode commandait de les remplacer par des rubans.
7. La pistole vaut 11 livres ou francs ; une livre, 20 sols ; un sol, 12 deniers. Ainsi, 220 livres ou francs valent environ 670 € ou 1 000 $.
8. Un intérêt d'un denier douze équivaut à 8,3 % (1/12). Le taux légal était de 5 %.

ÉLISE: Nous marchandons[1], mon frère et moi, à qui parlera le premier ; et nous avons tous deux quelque chose à vous dire.

HARPAGON: Et moi, j'ai quelque chose aussi à vous dire à tous deux.

CLÉANTE: C'est de mariage, mon père, que nous désirons vous parler.

355 HARPAGON: Et c'est de mariage aussi que je veux vous entretenir.

ÉLISE: Ah ! mon père !

HARPAGON: Pourquoi ce cri ? Est-ce le mot, ma fille, ou la chose, qui vous fait peur ?

CLÉANTE: Le mariage peut nous faire peur à tous deux, de la façon
360 que vous pouvez l'entendre[2] ; et nous craignons que nos sentiments ne soient pas d'accord avec votre choix.

HARPAGON: Un peu de patience. Ne vous alarmez point. Je sais ce qu'il faut à tous deux ; et vous n'aurez ni l'un ni l'autre aucun lieu de vous plaindre de tout ce que je prétends faire. Et pour commencer par
365 un bout : (à Cléante) avez-vous vu, dites-moi, une jeune personne appelée Mariane, qui ne loge pas loin d'ici ?

CLÉANTE: Oui, mon père.

HARPAGON, à Élise: Et vous ?

ÉLISE: J'en ai ouï* parler.

370 HARPAGON: Comment, mon fils, trouvez-vous cette fille ?

CLÉANTE: Une fort charmante personne.

HARPAGON: Sa physionomie ?

CLÉANTE: Tout honnête, et pleine d'esprit.

HARPAGON: Son air et sa manière ?

375 CLÉANTE: Admirables, sans doute[3].

---

1. Marchandons : hésitons.

2. Entendre : envisager.

3. Sans doute : sans aucun doute.

HARPAGON : Ne croyez-vous pas qu'une fille comme cela mériterait assez que l'on songeât à elle ?

CLÉANTE : Oui, mon père.

HARPAGON : Que ce serait un parti souhaitable ?

380 **CLÉANTE** : Très souhaitable.

HARPAGON : Qu'elle a toute la mine de faire un bon ménage ?

CLÉANTE : Sans doute.

HARPAGON : Et qu'un mari aurait satisfaction avec elle ?

CLÉANTE : Assurément.

385 **HARPAGON** : Il y a une petite difficulté : c'est que j'ai peur qu'il n'y ait pas avec elle tout le bien qu'on pourrait prétendre.

CLÉANTE : Ah ! mon père, le bien n'est pas considérable[1], lorsqu'il est question d'épouser une honnête personne.

HARPAGON : Pardonnez-moi, pardonnez-moi. Mais ce qu'il y a à dire,
390 c'est que si l'on n'y trouve pas tout le bien qu'on souhaite, on peut tâcher de regagner cela sur autre chose.

CLÉANTE : Cela s'entend[2].

HARPAGON : Enfin je suis bien aise de vous voir dans mes sentiments ; car son maintien honnête et sa douceur m'ont gagné l'âme, et je suis
395 résolu de l'épouser, pourvu que j'y trouve quelque bien.

CLÉANTE : Euh ?

HARPAGON : Comment ?

CLÉANTE : Vous êtes résolu, dites-vous… ?

HARPAGON : D'épouser Mariane.

400 **CLÉANTE** : Qui, vous ? vous ?

---

1. Considérable : important.
2. S'entend : va de soi.

Harpagon : Oui, moi, moi, moi. Que veut dire cela ?

Cléante : Il m'a pris tout à coup un éblouissement, et je me retire d'ici.

Harpagon : Cela ne sera rien. Allez vite boire dans la cuisine un grand verre d'eau claire. Voilà de mes damoiseaux flouets[1], qui n'ont
405 non[2] plus de vigueur que des poules. C'est là, ma fille, ce que j'ai résolu pour moi. Quant à ton frère, je lui destine une certaine veuve dont ce matin on m'est venu parler ; et pour toi, je te donne au seigneur[3] Anselme.

Élise : Au seigneur Anselme ?

410 **Harpagon** : Oui, un homme mûr, prudent et sage, qui n'a pas plus de cinquante ans, et dont on vante les grands biens.

Élise. *Elle fait une révérence* : Je ne veux point me marier, mon père, s'il vous plaît.

Harpagon. *Il contrefait la révérence* : Et moi, ma petite fille ma mie, je
415 veux que vous vous mariiez, s'il vous plaît.

Élise, *faisant encore la révérence* : Je vous demande pardon, mon père.

Harpagon, *contrefaisant Élise* : Je vous demande pardon, ma fille.

Élise : Je suis très humble servante au seigneur Anselme ; mais (*faisant encore la révérence*), avec votre permission, je ne l'épouserai point.

420 **Harpagon** : Je suis votre très humble valet ; mais (*contrefaisant Élise*), avec votre permission, vous l'épouserez dès ce soir.

Élise : Dès ce soir ?

Harpagon : Dès ce soir.

Élise, *faisant encore la révérence* : Cela ne sera pas, mon père.

425 **Harpagon**, *contrefaisant encore Élise* : Cela sera, ma fille.

Élise : Non.

---

1. Damoiseaux flouets : jeunes gens élégants et fragiles.

2. Non : pas.

3. Seigneur : monsieur (sans référence à la noblesse).

HARPAGON : Si.

ÉLISE : Non, vous dis-je.

HARPAGON : Si, vous dis-je.

430 ÉLISE : C'est une chose où vous ne me réduirez point.

HARPAGON : C'est une chose où je te réduirai.

ÉLISE : Je me tuerai plutôt que d'épouser un tel mari.

HARPAGON : Tu ne te tueras point, et tu l'épouseras. Mais voyez quelle audace ! A-t-on jamais vu une fille parler de la sorte à son père ?

435 ÉLISE : Mais a-t-on jamais vu un père marier sa fille de la sorte ?

HARPAGON : C'est un parti où il n'y a rien à redire ; et je gage que tout le monde approuvera mon choix.

ÉLISE : Et moi, je gage qu'il ne saurait être approuvé d'aucune personne raisonnable.

440 HARPAGON, *apercevant Valère de loin* : Voilà Valère : veux-tu qu'entre nous deux nous le fassions juge de cette affaire ?

ÉLISE : J'y consens.

HARPAGON : Te rendras-tu à son jugement ?

ÉLISE : Oui, j'en passerai par ce qu'il dira.

445 HARPAGON : Voilà qui est fait.

SCÈNE 5 : VALÈRE, HARPAGON, ÉLISE

HARPAGON : Ici, Valère. Nous t'avons élu pour nous dire qui a raison, de ma fille ou de moi.

VALÈRE : C'est vous, Monsieur, sans contredit.

Harpagon : Sais-tu bien de quoi nous parlons ?

450 **Valère** : Non, mais vous ne sauriez avoir tort, et vous êtes toute raison.

Harpagon : Je veux ce soir lui donner pour époux un homme aussi riche que sage ; et la coquine* me dit au nez qu'elle se moque de le prendre[1]. Que dis-tu de cela ?

Valère : Ce que j'en dis ?

455 **Harpagon** : Oui.

Valère : Eh, eh.

Harpagon : Quoi ?

Valère : Je dis que dans le fond je suis de votre sentiment ; et vous ne pouvez pas que vous n'ayez raison[2]. Mais aussi n'a-t-elle pas tort tout 460 à fait, et…

Harpagon : Comment ? le seigneur* Anselme est un parti considérable, c'est un gentilhomme qui est noble[3], doux, posé, sage, et fort accommodé*, et auquel il ne reste aucun enfant de son premier mariage. Saurait-elle mieux rencontrer ?

465 **Valère** : Cela est vrai. Mais elle pourrait vous dire que c'est un peu précipiter les choses, et qu'il faudrait au moins quelque temps pour voir si son inclination* pourra s'accommoder avec…

Harpagon : C'est une occasion qu'il faut prendre vite aux cheveux. Je trouve ici un avantage qu'ailleurs je ne trouverais pas, et il s'engage à 470 la prendre sans dot[4].

Valère : Sans dot ?

Harpagon : Oui.

---

1. Se moque de le prendre : n'a pas l'intention de l'épouser.
2. Que vous n'ayez raison : avoir tort.
3. Un gentilhomme est toujours noble. Trait de satire contre ceux qui usurpaient des titres de noblesse.
4. Dot : somme d'argent que fournissaient traditionnellement les parents de la future mariée.

Valère : Ah! je ne dis plus rien. Voyez-vous? voilà une raison tout à fait convaincante; il se faut rendre à cela.

475 **Harpagon** : C'est pour moi une épargne considérable.

Valère : Assurément, cela ne reçoit point[1] de contradiction. Il est vrai que votre fille vous peut représenter[2] que le mariage est une plus grande affaire qu'on ne peut croire; qu'il y va d'être heureux ou malheureux toute sa vie; et qu'un engagement qui doit durer jusqu'à
480 la mort[3] ne se doit jamais faire qu'avec de grandes précautions.

Harpagon : Sans dot.

Valère : Vous avez raison : voilà qui décide tout, cela s'entend*. Il y a des gens qui pourraient vous dire qu'en de telles occasions l'inclination d'une fille est une chose sans doute* où l'on doit avoir de
485 l'égard[4]; et que cette grande inégalité d'âge, d'humeur et de sentiments, rend un mariage sujet à des accidents très fâcheux.

Harpagon : Sans dot.

Valère : Ah! il n'y a pas de réplique à cela : on le sait bien; qui diantre* peut aller là contre? Ce n'est pas qu'il n'y ait quantité de pères qui
490 aimeraient mieux ménager la satisfaction de leurs filles que l'argent qu'ils pourraient donner[5]; qui ne les voudraient point sacrifier à l'intérêt, et chercheraient plus que toute autre chose à mettre dans un mariage cette douce conformité qui sans cesse y maintient l'honneur, la tranquillité et la joie, et que…

495 **Harpagon** : Sans dot.

Valère : Il est vrai : cela ferme la bouche à tout, *sans dot*. Le moyen de résister à une raison comme celle-là?

---

1. Ne reçoit point : n'admet pas.
2. Vous peut représenter : peut vous objecter.
3. Le divorce était interdit : l'Église permettait une «séparation de corps» et l'État, une «séparation de biens».
4. Où l'on doit avoir de l'égard : que l'on doit prendre en considération.
5. Aimeraient mieux ménager la satisfaction de leurs filles que l'argent qu'ils pourraient donner : préféreraient le bonheur de leurs filles à l'argent économisé.

HARPAGON (Luc Durand) : Sans dot.

VALÈRE (Gabriel Sabourin) : Vous avez raison :
voilà qui décide tout, cela s'entend.

ÉLISE (Annick Bergeron).

ACTE I, SCÈNE 5, lignes 481 et 482.

THÉÂTRE PROFUSION INC., 1995.
MISE EN SCÈNE DE LUC DURAND.

HARPAGON. *Il regarde vers le jardin* : Ouais ! il me semble que j'entends un chien qui aboie. N'est-ce point qu'on en voudrait à mon argent ? 500 (*À Valère.*) Ne bougez, je reviens tout à l'heure*. (*Il sort.*)

ÉLISE : Vous moquez-vous, Valère, de lui parler comme vous faites ?

VALÈRE : C'est pour ne point l'aigrir, et pour en venir mieux à bout. Heurter de front ses sentiments est le moyen de tout gâter ; et il y a de certains esprits qu'il ne faut prendre qu'en biaisant[1], des tempéra- 505 ments ennemis de toute résistance, des naturels rétifs[2], que la vérité fait cabrer, qui toujours se roidissent contre le droit chemin de la raison, et qu'on ne mène qu'en tournant[3] où l'on veut les conduire. Faites semblant de consentir à ce qu'il veut, vous en viendrez mieux à vos fins, et…

510 **ÉLISE** : Mais ce mariage, Valère ?

VALÈRE : On cherchera des biais[4] pour le rompre.

ÉLISE : Mais quelle invention trouver, s'il se doit conclure ce soir ?

VALÈRE : Il faut demander un délai, et feindre quelque maladie.

ÉLISE : Mais on découvrira la feinte, si l'on appelle des médecins.

515 **VALÈRE** : Vous moquez-vous ? Y connaissent-ils quelque chose ? Allez, allez, vous pourrez avec eux avoir quel mal il vous plaira[5], ils vous trouveront des raisons pour vous dire d'où cela vient.

HARPAGON, *à part, dans le fond du théâtre* : Ce n'est rien, Dieu merci.

VALÈRE, *sans voir Harpagon* : Enfin notre dernier recours, c'est que la 520 fuite nous peut mettre à couvert de tout ; et si votre amour, belle Élise, est capable d'une fermeté… (*Il aperçoit Harpagon.*) Oui, il faut qu'une fille obéisse à son père. Il ne faut point qu'elle regarde comme* un mari est fait, et lorsque la grande raison de *sans dot** s'y rencontre, elle doit être prête à prendre tout ce qu'on lui donne.

---

1. Biaisant : rusant.
2. Naturels rétifs : caractères difficiles à convaincre (terme d'équitation).
3. Qu'en tournant : que par des voies détournées (terme d'équitation).
4. Biais : moyens détournés.
5. Quel mal il vous plaira : la maladie de votre choix.

525 **HARPAGON** : Bon. Voilà bien parlé, cela.

VALÈRE : Monsieur, je vous demande pardon si je m'emporte un peu et prends la hardiesse de lui parler comme je fais.

HARPAGON : Comment ? j'en suis ravi, et je veux que tu prennes sur elle un pouvoir absolu. (*À Élise.*) Oui, tu as beau fuir. Je lui donne 530 l'autorité que le Ciel me donne sur toi, et j'entends que tu fasses tout ce qu'il te dira.

VALÈRE, *à Élise* : Après cela, résistez à mes remontrances. Monsieur, je vais la suivre, pour lui continuer les leçons que je lui faisais.

HARPAGON : Oui, tu m'obligeras. Certes…

535 **VALÈRE** : Il est bon de lui tenir un peu la bride haute[1].

HARPAGON : Cela est vrai. Il faut…

VALÈRE : Ne vous mettez pas en peine. Je crois que j'en viendrai à bout.

HARPAGON : Fais, fais. Je m'en vais faire un petit tour[2] en ville, et reviens tout à l'heure*.

540 **VALÈRE**, *adressant la parole à Élise, en s'en allant du côté par où elle est sortie* : Oui, l'argent est plus précieux que toutes les choses du monde, et vous devez rendre grâces au Ciel de l'honnête homme de père qu'il vous a donné. Il sait ce que c'est que de vivre. Lorsqu'on s'offre de prendre une fille sans dot*, on ne doit point regarder plus avant. Tout est 545 renfermé là-dedans, et *sans dot* tient lieu de beauté, de jeunesse, de naissance, d'honneur, de sagesse et de probité.

HARPAGON, *seul* : Ah ! le brave garçon ! Voilà parlé comme un oracle[3]. Heureux qui peut avoir un domestique de la sorte !

---

1. Lui tenir un peu la bride haute : ne pas lui laisser trop de liberté (terme d'équitation).
2. Tour : visite.
3. Oracle : personne considérée infaillible.

ACTE II

SCÈNE 1 : Cléante, La Flèche

Cléante : Ah ! traître que tu es, où t'es-tu donc allé fourrer ? Ne t'avais-
550 je pas donné ordre…

La Flèche : Oui, Monsieur, et je m'étais rendu ici pour vous attendre de pied ferme ; mais Monsieur votre père, le plus malgracieux des hommes, m'a chassé dehors malgré moi, et j'ai couru risque d'être battu.

555 **Cléante** : Comment va notre affaire ? Les choses pressent plus que jamais ; et depuis que je ne t'ai vu, j'ai découvert que mon père est mon rival.

La Flèche : Votre père amoureux ?

Cléante : Oui ; et j'ai eu toutes les peines du monde à lui cacher le
560 trouble où cette nouvelle m'a mis.

La Flèche : Lui se mêler d'aimer ! De quoi diable s'avise- t-il ? Se moque-t-il du monde ? Et l'amour a-t-il été fait pour des gens bâtis comme lui ?

Cléante : Il a fallu, pour mes péchés[1], que cette passion lui soit venue
565 en tête.

La Flèche : Mais par quelle raison lui faire un mystère de votre amour ?

Cléante : Pour lui donner moins de soupçon, et me conserver au besoin des ouvertures[2] plus aisées pour détourner ce mariage. Quelle réponse t'a-t-on faite ?

---

1. Pour mes péchés : en punition de mes fautes, pour mon malheur.
2. Ouvertures : moyens d'action.

570 **LA FLÈCHE**: Ma foi! Monsieur, ceux qui empruntent sont bien malheureux; et il faut essuyer[1] d'étranges choses lorsqu'on en est réduit à passer, comme vous, par les mains des fesse-mathieux[2].

CLÉANTE: L'affaire ne se fera point?

LA FLÈCHE: Pardonnez-moi. Notre maître Simon, le courtier*
575 qu'on nous a donné, homme agissant et plein de zèle, dit qu'il a fait rage[3] pour vous; et il assure que votre seule physionomie lui a gagné le cœur.

CLÉANTE: J'aurai les quinze mille francs que je demande?

LA FLÈCHE: Oui; mais à quelques petites conditions, qu'il faudra que
580 vous acceptiez, si vous avez dessein que les choses se fassent.

CLÉANTE: T'a-t-il fait parler à celui qui doit prêter l'argent?

LA FLÈCHE: Ah! vraiment, cela ne va pas de la sorte. Il apporte encore plus de soin à se cacher que vous, et ce sont des mystères bien plus grands que vous ne pensez. On ne veut point du tout dire son nom,
585 et l'on doit aujourd'hui l'aboucher[4] avec vous, dans une maison empruntée, pour être instruit, par votre bouche, de votre bien et de votre famille; et je ne doute point que le seul nom de votre père ne rende les choses faciles.

CLÉANTE: Et principalement notre mère étant morte, dont on ne peut
590 m'ôter le bien[5].

LA FLÈCHE: Voici quelques articles qu'il a dictés lui-même à notre entremetteur[6], pour vous être montrés, avant que de rien faire[7]:

Supposé que le prêteur voie toutes ses sûretés[8], et que l'emprunteur soit majeur, et d'une famille où le bien soit ample, solide, assuré, clair, et net

---

1. Essuyer: endurer.
2. Fesse-mathieux: usuriers (qui prêtent à un taux supérieur au taux légal).
3. A fait rage: s'est donné beaucoup de mal.
4. Aboucher: mettre en contact.
5. Les enfants héritaient des biens de leur mère, et leur père ne faisait que les gérer en attendant leur majorité.
6. Entremetteur: intermédiaire, ici le courtier.
7. Avant que de rien faire: avant de faire quoi que ce soit.
8. Voie toutes ses sûretés: ait toutes les garanties de remboursement.

595 *de tout embarras*[1], *on fera une bonne et exacte obligation*[2] *par-devant*
     un notaire, le plus honnête homme qu'il se pourra, et qui, pour cet effet,
     sera choisi par le prêteur, auquel il importe le plus que l'acte soit
     dûment dressé.

CLÉANTE : Il n'y a rien à dire à cela.

600 LA FLÈCHE : *Le prêteur, pour ne charger sa conscience d'aucun scrupule,*
     prétend ne donner son argent qu'au denier dix-huit[3].

CLÉANTE : Au denier dix-huit ? Parbleu ! voilà qui est honnête. Il n'y a
pas lieu de se plaindre.

LA FLÈCHE : Cela est vrai.

605 *Mais comme ledit prêteur n'a pas chez lui la somme dont il est question,*
     et que pour faire plaisir à l'emprunteur, il est contraint lui-même de
     l'emprunter d'un autre, sur le pied du denier cinq[4], *il conviendra que*
     ledit premier emprunteur paye cet intérêt, sans préjudice du reste[5],
     attendu que ce n'est que pour l'obliger[6] *que ledit prêteur s'engage à*
610 *cet emprunt.*

CLÉANTE : Comment diable ! quel Juif, quel Arabe[7] est-ce là ? C'est plus
qu'au denier quatre[8].

LA FLÈCHE : Il est vrai ; c'est ce que j'ai dit. Vous avez à voir[9] là-dessus.

CLÉANTE : Que veux-tu que je voie ? J'ai besoin d'argent ; et il faut
615 bien que je consente à tout.

LA FLÈCHE : C'est la réponse que j'ai faite.

CLÉANTE : Il y a encore quelque chose ?

---

1. Embarras : dette.
2. Obligation : reconnaissance de dette.
3. Taux d'intérêt de 5,5 % (1/18), légèrement supérieur au taux légal de 5 %.
4. Taux d'intérêt de 20 % (1/5).
5. L'emprunteur assume donc les deux taux (20 % + 5,5 %).
6. L'obliger : lui rendre service.
7. Quel Juif, quel Arabe : insulte. À l'époque, les non-chrétiens étaient considérés comme
   des barbares.
8. Taux d'intérêt de 25 % (1/4).
9. Voir : réfléchir.

CLÉANTE (Gabriel Gascon) : Que veut dire cela ?

LA FLÈCHE (Robert Gadouas) : Écoutez le mémoire.

ACTE II, SCÈNE 1, lignes 624 et 625.

THÉÂTRE DU NOUVEAU MONDE, 1951.
MISE EN SCÈNE DE JEAN GASCON.

La Flèche : Ce n'est plus qu'un petit article.

Des quinze mille francs qu'on demande, le prêteur ne pourra compter en
620 *argent que douze mille livres, et pour les mille écus[1] restants, il faudra*
que l'emprunteur prenne les hardes, nippes[2], et bijoux dont s'ensuit le
mémoire[3], et que ledit prêteur a mis, de bonne foi, au plus modique prix
qu'il lui a été possible.

Cléante : Que veut dire cela ?

625 La Flèche : Écoutez le mémoire.

Premièrement, un lit de quatre pieds[4], à bandes de points de Hongrie[5],
appliquées fort proprement[6] sur un drap de couleur d'olive, avec six
chaises et la courtepointe[7] de même ; le tout bien conditionné[8], et doublé
d'un petit taffetas[9] changeant rouge et bleu.
630 *Plus, un pavillon à queue[10], d'une bonne serge[11] d'Aumale rose-sèche,*
avec le mollet[12] et les franges de soie.

Cléante : Que veut-il que je fasse de cela ?

La Flèche : Attendez.

Plus, une tenture de tapisserie des amours de Gombaut et de Macée[13].
635 *Plus, une grande table de bois de noyer, à douze colonnes ou piliers*
tournés, qui se tire par les deux bouts, et garnie par le dessous de ses
six escabelles[14].

---

1. L'écu d'argent valait 3 livres ou francs. Selon le contrat, 3 000 francs ou livres sur les 15 000 (qui valent approximativement 45 750 € ou 70 000 $) sont prêtés sous forme de biens.
2. Hardes, nippes : vêtements, mais aussi meubles (sans nuance péjorative).
3. Mémoire : liste.
4. Environ 1,3 m. Il s'agit d'un lit d'enfant.
5. Bandes de points de Hongrie : lisières de broderie.
6. Proprement : élégamment.
7. Courtepointe : couvre-lit piqué.
8. Bien conditionné : en bon état.
9. Taffetas : étoffe de soie.
10. Pavillon à queue : baldaquin d'un lit, en forme de tente ronde et suspendu au plafond, en usage pour les lits de valet.
11. Serge : tissu de laine.
12. Mollet : bande de quelques millimètres qui borde les tissus d'ameublement, ici le pavillon à queue.
13. Gombaut, Macée : personnages d'un roman pastoral à la mode vers 1600.
14. Escabelles : tabourets de bois. Les pieds de table tournés et les escabelles ne sont plus à la mode en 1668.

CLÉANTE: Qu'ai-je affaire, morbleu…?

LA FLÈCHE: Donnez-vous[1] patience.

640 *Plus, trois gros mousquets[2] tout garnis de nacre de perles, avec les trois fourchettes[3] assortissantes.*

Plus, un fourneau de brique, avec deux cornues[4], et trois récipients, fort utiles à ceux qui sont curieux de distiller.

CLÉANTE: J'enrage.

645 **LA FLÈCHE**: Doucement.

Plus, un luth de Bologne, garni de toutes ses cordes, ou peu s'en faut.

Plus, un trou-madame[5], et un damier, avec un jeu de l'oie renouvelé des Grecs[6], fort propres à passer le temps lorsque l'on n'a que faire.

Plus, une peau de lézard, de trois pieds et demi[7], remplie de foin, curio-
650 *sité agréable pour pendre au plancher[8] d'une chambre.*

Le tout, ci-dessus mentionné, valant loyalement plus de quatre mille cinq cents livres, et rabaissé à la valeur de mille écus*, par la discrétion[9] du prêteur.

CLÉANTE: Que la peste l'étouffe avec sa discrétion, le traître, le bour-
655 reau qu'il est! A-t-on jamais parlé d'une usure[10] semblable? Et n'est-il pas content du furieux[11] intérêt qu'il exige, sans vouloir encore m'obliger à prendre, pour trois mille livres, les vieux rogatons[12] qu'il ramasse? Je n'aurai pas deux cents écus de tout cela; et cependant il

---

1. Donnez-vous: prenez.
2. Mousquets: armes à feu assez lourdes, passées de mode en 1668.
3. Fourchettes: fourches plantées en terre qui permettaient de supporter le mousquet au moment de tirer.
4. Cornues: récipients de verre à col allongé et recourbé.
5. Trou-madame: sorte d'ancêtre du billard électronique.
6. Jeu de l'oie renouvelé des Grecs: jeu qui se joue avec des dés et une planche.
7. Environ 1,05 m.
8. Plancher [de l'étage supérieur]: plafond.
9. Discrétion: modération.
10. Usure: prêt à un taux supérieur au taux légal.
11. Furieux: terrible.
12. Rogatons: objets sans valeur.

faut bien me résoudre à consentir à ce qu'il veut, car il est en état de me
660 faire tout accepter, et il me tient, le scélérat, le poignard sur la gorge.

LA FLÈCHE : Je vous vois, Monsieur, ne vous en déplaise, dans le grand
chemin justement que tenait Panurge[1] pour se ruiner, prenant argent
d'avance, achetant cher, vendant à bon marché, et mangeant son blé
en herbe[2].

665 CLÉANTE : Que veux-tu que j'y fasse ? Voilà où les jeunes gens sont
réduits par la maudite avarice des pères ; et on s'étonne après cela que
les fils souhaitent qu'ils meurent.

LA FLÈCHE : Il faut avouer que le vôtre animerait contre sa vilanie[3] le
plus posé homme du monde. Je n'ai pas, Dieu merci, les inclinations*
670 fort patibulaires[4] ; et parmi mes confrères que je vois se mêler de
beaucoup de petits commerces, je sais tirer adroitement mon épingle
du jeu, et me démêler prudemment de toutes les galanteries[5] qui
sentent tant soit peu l'échelle[6] ; mais, à vous dire vrai, il me donnerait,
par ses procédés, des tentations de le voler ; et je croirais, en le volant,
675 faire une action méritoire.

CLÉANTE : Donne-moi un peu ce mémoire*, que je le voie encore.

SCÈNE 2 : MAÎTRE SIMON, HARPAGON, CLÉANTE, LA FLÈCHE *dans le fond du théâtre.*

MAÎTRE SIMON : Oui, Monsieur, c'est un jeune homme qui a besoin
d'argent. Ses affaires le pressent d'en trouver, et il en passera par tout
ce que vous en prescrirez.

---

1. Panurge : personnage de *Pantagruel* (1532), roman de François Rabelais.
2. Mangeant son blé en herbe : dépensant son revenu avant même de l'obtenir.
3. Vilanie : avarice.
4. Les inclinations fort patibulaires : envie d'être pendu.
5. Galanteries : ici, ruses malhonnêtes (ironie).
6. L'échelle, sous-entendu « de la potence ».

680 **HARPAGON** : Mais croyez-vous, maître Simon, qu'il n'y ait rien à péricliter[1] ? et savez-vous le nom, les biens et la famille de celui pour qui vous parlez ?

MAÎTRE SIMON : Non, je ne puis pas bien vous en instruire à fond, et ce n'est que par aventure[2] que l'on m'a adressé à lui ; mais vous serez
685 de toutes choses éclairci par lui-même ; et son homme m'a assuré que vous serez content, quand vous le connaîtrez. Tout ce que je saurais vous dire, c'est que sa famille est fort riche, qu'il n'a plus de mère déjà, et qu'il s'obligera[3], si vous voulez, que son père mourra avant qu'il soit huit mois.

690 **HARPAGON** : C'est quelque chose que cela. La charité, maître Simon, nous oblige à faire plaisir aux personnes, lorsque nous le pouvons.

MAÎTRE SIMON : Cela s'entend*.

LA FLÈCHE, *bas, à Cléante, reconnaissant maître Simon* : Que veut dire ceci ? Notre maître Simon qui parle à votre père.

695 **CLÉANTE**, *bas, à La Flèche* : Lui aurait-on appris qui je suis ? et serais-tu pour nous trahir ?

MAÎTRE SIMON, *à La Flèche* : Ah ! ah ! vous êtes bien pressés ! Qui vous a dit que c'était céans[4] ? (*À Harpagon.*) Ce n'est pas moi, Monsieur, au moins*, qui leur ai découvert votre nom et votre logis ; mais, à mon
700 avis, il n'y a pas grand mal à cela. Ce sont des personnes discrètes, et vous pouvez ici vous expliquer ensemble.

HARPAGON : Comment ?

MAÎTRE SIMON, *montrant Cléante* : Monsieur est la personne qui veut vous emprunter les quinze mille livres dont je vous ai parlé.

705 **HARPAGON** : Comment, pendard ? c'est toi qui t'abandonnes à ces coupables extrémités ?

---

1. Péricliter : craindre.
2. Aventure : hasard.
3. S'obligera : s'engagera légalement.
4. Céans : dans la maison, ici.

CLÉANTE : Comment, mon père ? c'est vous qui vous portez à ces honteuses actions ?

Maître Simon s'enfuit et La Flèche va se cacher.

710 HARPAGON : C'est toi qui te veux ruiner par des emprunts si condamnables ?

CLÉANTE : C'est vous qui cherchez à vous enrichir par des usures* si criminelles ?

HARPAGON : Oses-tu bien, après cela, paraître devant moi !

715 CLÉANTE : Osez-vous bien, après cela, vous présenter aux yeux du monde ?

HARPAGON : N'as-tu point de honte, dis-moi, d'en venir à ces débauches-là ? de te précipiter dans des dépenses effroyables ? et de faire une honteuse dissipation du bien que tes parents t'ont amassé avec tant 720 de sueurs ?

CLÉANTE : Ne rougissez-vous point de déshonorer votre condition[1] par les commerces que vous faites ? de sacrifier gloire[2] et réputation au désir insatiable d'entasser écu* sur écu, et de renchérir, en fait d'intérêts, sur les plus infâmes subtilités qu'aient jamais inventées les plus 725 célèbres usuriers ?

HARPAGON : Ôte-toi de mes yeux, coquin* ! ôte-toi de mes yeux !

CLÉANTE : Qui est plus criminel, à votre avis, ou celui qui achète un argent dont il a besoin, ou bien celui qui vole un argent dont il n'a que faire ?

730 HARPAGON : Retire-toi, te dis-je, et ne m'échauffe pas les oreilles. (*Seul.*) Je ne suis pas fâché de cette aventure ; et ce m'est un avis de tenir l'œil, plus que jamais, sur toutes ses actions.

---

1. Condition : classe sociale.
2. Gloire : honneur.

SCÈNE 3 : Frosine, Harpagon

FROSINE : Monsieur…

HARPAGON : Attendez un moment ; je vais revenir vous parler.
735 (*À part.*) Il est à propos que je fasse un petit tour* à mon argent.

SCÈNE 4 : La Flèche, Frosine

LA FLÈCHE, *sans voir Frosine* : L'aventure est tout à fait drôle. Il faut bien qu'il ait quelque part un ample magasin de hardes* ; car nous n'avons rien reconnu au mémoire* que nous avons.

FROSINE : Hé ! c'est toi, mon pauvre La Flèche ? D'où vient cette
740 rencontre ?

LA FLÈCHE : Ah ! ah ! c'est toi, Frosine. Que viens-tu faire ici ?

FROSINE : Ce que je fais partout ailleurs : m'entremettre d'affaires[1], me rendre serviable aux gens, et profiter du mieux qu'il m'est possible des petits talents que je puis avoir. Tu sais que dans ce monde il faut
745 vivre d'adresse, et qu'aux personnes comme moi le Ciel n'a donné d'autres rentes que l'intrigue et que l'industrie[2].

LA FLÈCHE : As-tu quelque négoce[3] avec le patron du logis ?

FROSINE : Oui, je traite pour lui quelque petite affaire, dont j'espère une récompense.

750 LA FLÈCHE : De lui ? Ah, ma foi ! tu seras bien fine si tu en tires quelque chose ; et je te donne avis que l'argent céans* est fort cher.

---

1. M'entremettre d'affaires : servir d'intermédiaire.
2. Industrie : ruse, habileté.
3. Négoce : affaire.

FROSINE: Il y a de certains services qui touchent merveilleusement[1].

LA FLÈCHE: Je suis votre valet[2], et tu ne connais pas encore le seigneur* Harpagon. Le seigneur Harpagon est de tous les humains
755 l'humain le moins humain, le mortel de tous les mortels le plus dur et le plus serré. Il n'est point de service qui pousse sa reconnaissance jusqu'à lui faire ouvrir les mains. De la louange, de l'estime, de la bienveillance en paroles et de l'amitié tant qu'il vous plaira; mais de l'argent, point d'affaires. Il n'est rien de plus sec et de plus aride que
760 ses bonnes grâces et ses caresses[3]; et *donner* est un mot pour qui il a tant d'aversion[4], qu'il ne dit jamais: *Je vous donne*, mais: *Je vous prête le bonjour*.

FROSINE: Mon Dieu! je sais l'art de traire[5] les hommes, j'ai le secret de m'ouvrir leur tendresse, de chatouiller leurs cœurs, de trouver les
765 endroits par où ils sont sensibles.

LA FLÈCHE: Bagatelles[6] ici. Je te défie d'attendrir, du côté de l'argent, l'homme dont il est question. Il est turc[7] là-dessus, mais d'une turquerie à désespérer tout le monde; et l'on pourrait crever, qu'il n'en branlerait[8] pas. En un mot, il aime l'argent, plus que réputation,
770 qu'honneur et que vertu; et la vue d'un demandeur lui donne des convulsions. C'est le frapper par son endroit mortel, c'est lui percer le cœur, c'est lui arracher les entrailles; et si... Mais il revient; je me retire.

---

1. Touchent merveilleusement: rapportent beaucoup d'argent.
2. Je suis votre valet: pardonnez-moi (formule de politesse).
3. Caresses: politesses.
4. Aversion: dégoût.
5. Traire: soutirer de l'argent.
6. Bagatelles: paroles en l'air.
7. Turc: insensible comme les Turcs, qui avaient la réputation d'être cruels.
8. Branlerait: bougerait.

© Robert Etchevery.

Frosine (Sophie Clément) : Il y a de certains services qui touchent merveilleusement.

La Flèche (Robert Gadouas) : Je suis votre valet, et tu ne connais pas encore le seigneur Harpagon. Le seigneur Harpagon est de tous les humains l'humain le moins humain, le mortel de tous les mortels le plus dur et le plus serré.

Acte II, scène 4, lignes 752 à 756.

Théâtre du Nouveau Monde, 1985.
Mise en scène d'Olivier Reichenbach.

SCÈNE 5 : Harpagon, Frosine

Harpagon, *bas, à part* : Tout va comme il faut. (*Haut.*) Hé bien ! qu'est-
775 ce, Frosine ?

Frosine : Ah ! mon Dieu ! que vous vous portez bien ! et que vous avez
là un vrai visage de santé !

Harpagon : Qui, moi ?

Frosine : Jamais je ne vous vis un teint si frais et si gaillard [1].

780 **Harpagon** : Tout de bon ?

Frosine : Comment ? vous n'avez de votre vie été si jeune que vous
êtes ; et je vois des gens de vingt-cinq ans qui sont plus vieux que vous.

Harpagon : Cependant, Frosine, j'en ai soixante bien comptés.

Frosine : Hé bien ! qu'est-ce que cela, soixante ans ? Voilà bien de
785 quoi [2] ! C'est la fleur de l'âge cela, et vous entrez maintenant dans la
belle saison de l'homme.

Harpagon : Il est vrai ; mais vingt années de moins pourtant ne me
feraient point de mal, que je crois.

Frosine : Vous moquez-vous ? Vous n'avez pas besoin de cela, et vous
790 êtes d'une pâte à vivre jusques à cent ans.

Harpagon : Tu le crois !

Frosine : Assurément. Vous en avez toutes les marques. Tenez-vous un
peu. Oh ! que voilà bien là, entre vos deux yeux, un signe de longue vie !

Harpagon : Tu te connais à cela ?

795 **Frosine** : Sans doute*. Montrez-moi votre main. Ah ! mon Dieu !
quelle ligne de vie !

Harpagon : Comment ?

---

1. Gaillard : en santé.
2. Voilà bien de quoi ! : il n'y a pas de quoi s'inquiéter ! Au XVIIᵉ siècle, on était vieux à 40 ans.

FROSINE : Ne voyez-vous pas jusqu'où va cette ligne-là ?

HARPAGON : Hé bien ! qu'est-ce que cela veut dire ?

800 FROSINE : Par ma foi ! je disais cent ans ; mais vous passerez les six-vingts[1].

HARPAGON : Est-il possible ?

FROSINE : Il faudra vous assommer, vous dis-je ; et vous mettrez en terre et vos enfants, et les enfants de vos enfants.

805 HARPAGON : Tant mieux. Comment va notre affaire ?

FROSINE : Faut-il le demander ? et me voit-on mêler de rien dont je ne vienne à bout ? J'ai surtout pour les mariages un talent merveilleux ; il n'est point de partis au monde que je ne trouve en peu de temps le moyen d'accoupler ; et je crois, si je me l'étais mis en tête, que je
810 marierais le Grand Turc avec la République de Venise[2]. Il n'y avait pas sans doute* de si grandes difficultés à cette affaire-ci. Comme j'ai commerce chez elles[3], je les ai à fond l'une et l'autre entretenues de vous, et j'ai dit à la mère le dessein que vous aviez conçu pour Mariane, à la voir passer dans la rue, et prendre l'air à sa fenêtre.

815 HARPAGON : Qui a fait réponse…

FROSINE : Elle a reçu la proposition avec joie ; et quand je lui ai témoigné que vous souhaitiez fort que sa fille assistât ce soir au contrat de mariage qui se doit faire de la vôtre, elle y a consenti sans peine, et me l'a confiée pour cela.

820 HARPAGON : C'est que je suis obligé, Frosine, de donner à souper au seigneur* Anselme ; et je serais bien aise qu'elle soit du régal[4].

FROSINE : Vous avez raison. Elle doit après dîner rendre visite à votre fille, d'où elle fait son compte[5] d'aller faire un tour* à la foire, pour venir ensuite au souper.

---

1. Six-vingts : 120 ans (6 x 20).
2. La République de Venise et la Turquie étaient ennemies depuis des siècles.
3. J'ai commerce chez elles : je suis en relation avec elles.
4. Régal : festin.
5. D'où elle fait son compte : avec laquelle elle a l'intention.

825   **HARPAGON** : Hé bien ! elles iront ensemble dans mon carrosse, que je leur prêterai.

FROSINE : Voilà justement son affaire.

HARPAGON : Mais, Frosine, as-tu entretenu la mère touchant le bien qu'elle peut donner à sa fille ? Lui as-tu dit qu'il fallait qu'elle s'aidât
830 un peu, qu'elle fît quelque effort, qu'elle se saignât pour une occasion comme celle-ci ? Car encore n'épouse-t-on point une fille, sans qu'elle apporte quelque chose.

FROSINE : Comment ? c'est une fille qui vous apportera douze mille livres[1] de rente.

835 **HARPAGON** : Douze mille livres de rente !

FROSINE : Oui. Premièrement, elle est nourrie et élevée dans une grande épargne de bouche[2] ; c'est une fille accoutumée à vivre de salade, de lait, de fromage et de pommes, et à laquelle par conséquent il ne faudra ni table bien servie, ni consommés exquis, ni orges
840 mondés[3] perpétuels, ni les autres délicatesses qu'il faudrait pour une autre femme ; et cela ne va pas à si peu de chose, qu'il ne monte bien, tous les ans, à trois mille francs pour le moins. Outre cela, elle n'est curieuse[4] que d'une propreté[5] fort simple, et n'aime point les superbes habits, ni les riches bijoux, ni les meubles somptueux, où donnent ses
845 pareilles avec tant de chaleur* ; et cet article-là vaut plus de quatre mille livres par an. De plus, elle a une aversion* horrible pour le jeu, ce qui n'est pas commun aux femmes d'aujourd'hui ; et j'en sais une de nos quartiers qui a perdu, à trente-et-quarante[6], vingt mille francs cette année. Mais n'en prenons rien que le quart. Cinq mille francs au
850 jeu par an, et quatre mille francs en habits et bijoux, cela fait neuf mille livres ; et mille écus* que nous mettons pour la nourriture, ne voilà-t-il pas par année vos douze mille francs bien comptés ?

---

1. Approximativement 36 600 € ou 55 000 $.
2. Épargne de bouche : économie de nourriture.
3. Orges mondés : boisson à base de grains d'orge dépouillés de leur enveloppe et qui avait la propriété de conserver le teint frais.
4. Curieuse : soucieuse.
5. Propreté : élégance.
6. Trente-et-quarante : jeu de cartes, style black jack.

© Robert Laliberté.

HARPAGON (Luc Durand) : J'ai peur qu'un homme de mon âge ne soit pas de son goût ; et que cela ne vienne à produire chez moi certains petits désordres qui ne m'accommoderaient pas.

FROSINE (Michèle Bernard) : Ah ! que vous la connaissez mal !

ACTE II, SCÈNE 5, lignes 868 à 871.

THÉÂTRE PROFUSION INC., 1995.
MISE EN SCÈNE DE LUC DURAND.

Harpagon : Oui, cela n'est pas mal ; mais ce compte-là n'est rien de réel.

855 **Frosine** : Pardonnez-moi. N'est-ce pas quelque chose de réel, que de vous apporter en mariage une grande sobriété, l'héritage d'un grand amour de simplicité de parure, et l'acquisition d'un grand fonds de haine pour le jeu ?

Harpagon : C'est une raillerie, que de vouloir me constituer son
860 dot* de toutes les dépenses qu'elle ne fera point. Je n'irai pas donner quittance[1] de ce que je ne reçois pas ; et il faut bien que je touche quelque chose.

Frosine : Mon Dieu ! vous toucherez assez ; et elles m'ont parlé d'un certain pays où elles ont du bien dont vous serez le maître.

865 **Harpagon** : Il faudra voir[2] cela. Mais, Frosine, il y a encore une chose qui m'inquiète. La fille est jeune, comme tu vois ; et les jeunes gens d'ordinaire n'aiment que leurs semblables, ne cherchent que leur compagnie. J'ai peur qu'un homme de mon âge ne soit pas de son goût ; et que cela ne vienne à produire chez moi certains petits désor-
870 dres qui ne m'accommoderaient pas[3].

Frosine : Ah ! que vous la connaissez mal ! C'est encore une particularité que j'avais à vous dire. Elle a une aversion* épouvantable pour tous les jeunes gens, et n'a de l'amour que pour les vieillards.

Harpagon : Elle ?

875 **Frosine** : Oui, elle. Je voudrais que vous l'eussiez entendue parler là-dessus. Elle ne peut souffrir du tout la vue d'un jeune homme ; mais elle n'est point plus ravie, dit-elle, que lorsqu'elle peut voir un beau vieillard avec une barbe majestueuse. Les plus vieux sont pour elle les plus charmants, et je vous avertis de n'aller pas vous faire plus jeune
880 que vous êtes. Elle veut tout au moins qu'on soit sexagénaire ; et il n'y a pas quatre mois encore, qu'étant prête d'être mariée, elle rompit

---

1. Donner quittance : tenir quitte.
2. « *Voir* signifie aussi connaître charnellement une femme » (Furetière).
3. Ne m'accommoderaient pas : ne me conviendraient pas.

HARPAGON (Luc Durand) : En effet, si j'avais été femme, je n'aurais point aimé les jeunes hommes.

ACTE II, SCÈNE 5, lignes 896 et 897.

THÉÂTRE PROFUSION INC., 1995.
MISE EN SCÈNE DE LUC DURAND.

tout net le mariage, sur ce que son amant fit voir qu'il n'avait que cinquante-six ans, et qu'il ne prit point de lunettes[1] pour signer le contrat.

885 HARPAGON : Sur cela seulement ?

FROSINE : Oui. Elle dit que ce n'est pas contentement pour elle que cinquante-six ans ; et surtout, elle est pour les nez qui portent des lunettes.

HARPAGON : Certes, tu me dis là une chose toute nouvelle.

890 FROSINE : Cela va plus loin qu'on ne vous peut dire. On lui voit dans sa chambre quelques tableaux et quelques estampes ; mais que pensez-vous que ce soit ? Des Adonis ? des Céphales ? des Pâris ? et des Apollons[2] ? Non : de beaux portraits de Saturne, du roi Priam, du vieux Nestor, et du bon père Anchise[3] sur les épaules de son fils.

895 HARPAGON : Cela est admirable ! Voilà ce que je n'aurais jamais pensé ; et je suis bien aise d'apprendre qu'elle est de cette humeur. En effet, si j'avais été femme, je n'aurais point aimé les jeunes hommes.

FROSINE : Je le crois bien. Voilà de belles drogues[4] que des jeunes gens, pour les aimer ! Ce sont de beaux morveux, de beaux godelureaux[5],
900 pour donner envie de leur peau ; et je voudrais bien savoir quel ragoût il y a à eux[6].

HARPAGON : Pour moi, je n'y en comprends point ; et je ne sais pas comment il y a des femmes qui les aiment tant.

FROSINE : Il faut être folle fieffée[7]. Trouver la jeunesse aimable* ! est-
905 ce avoir le sens commun ? Sont-ce des hommes que de jeunes blondins[8] ? et peut-on s'attacher à ces animaux-là ?

---

1. Au XVIIe siècle, porter des lunettes est un signe évident de vieillesse.
2. Adonis, Céphales, Pâris, Apollons : dieux et héros jeunes et beaux.
3. Saturne, Priam, Nestor, Anchise : dieux et héros sages et âgés.
4. Drogues : remèdes (péjoratif).
5. Godelureaux : jeunes hommes élégants et prétentieux.
6. Quel ragoût il y a à eux : ce qui les rend séduisants.
7. Folle fieffée : complètement folle.
8. Blondins : qui portent une perruque blonde (couleur à la mode).

HARPAGON : C'est ce que je dis tous les jours : avec leur ton de poule laitée [1], et leurs trois petits brins de barbe relevés en barbe de chat [2], leurs perruques d'étoupes [3], leurs hauts-de-chausses* tout tombants, 910 et leurs estomacs débraillés [4].

FROSINE : Eh ! cela est bien bâti, auprès d'une personne comme vous. Voilà un homme cela. Il y a là de quoi satisfaire à la vue ; et c'est ainsi qu'il faut être fait, et vêtu, pour donner de l'amour.

HARPAGON : Tu me trouves bien ?

915 **FROSINE** : Comment ? vous êtes à ravir, et votre figure est à peindre. Tournez-vous un peu, s'il vous plaît. Il ne se peut pas mieux. Que je vous voie marcher. Voilà un corps taillé, libre, et dégagé comme il faut, et qui ne marque aucune incommodité.

HARPAGON : Je n'en ai pas de grandes, Dieu merci. Il n'y a que ma 920 fluxion [5], qui me prend de temps en temps.

FROSINE : Cela n'est rien. Votre fluxion ne vous sied point mal, et vous avez grâce à tousser.

HARPAGON : Dis-moi un peu : Mariane ne m'a-t-elle point encore vu ? N'a-t-elle point pris garde à moi en passant ?

925 **FROSINE** : Non ; mais nous nous sommes fort entretenues de vous. Je lui ai fait un portrait de votre personne ; et je n'ai pas manqué de lui vanter votre mérite, et l'avantage que ce lui serait d'avoir un mari comme vous.

HARPAGON : Tu as bien fait, et je t'en remercie.

930 **FROSINE** : J'aurais, Monsieur, une petite prière à vous faire. (*Il prend un air sévère.*) J'ai un procès que je suis sur le point de perdre, faute

---

1. Ton de poule laitée : voix efféminée.
2. Barbe de chat : moustache.
3. D'étoupes : de couleur jaune pâle.
4. Les jeunes élégants déboutonnaient leurs vestes et faisaient bouffer leurs chemises sur leurs poitrines (« estomacs »).
5. Fluxion : toux. Molière a attribué au personnage sa propre toux.

d'un peu d'argent ; et vous pourriez facilement me procurer le gain de ce procès, si vous aviez quelque bonté pour moi. Vous ne sauriez croire le plaisir qu'elle aura de vous voir. (*Il reprend un air gai.*) Ah ! que
935 vous lui plairez ! et que votre fraise à l'antique[1] fera sur son esprit un effet admirable ! Mais surtout elle sera charmée de votre haut-de-chausses, attaché au pourpoint[2] avec des aiguillettes*, c'est pour la rendre folle de vous ; et un amant aiguilletté[3] sera pour elle un ragoût merveilleux.

940 **HARPAGON** : Certes, tu me ravis de me dire cela.

FROSINE : En vérité, Monsieur, ce procès m'est d'une conséquence[4] tout à fait grande. (*Il reprend son visage sévère.*) Je suis ruinée, si je le perds ; et quelque petite assistance me rétablirait mes affaires. Je voudrais que vous eussiez vu le ravissement où elle était à m'entendre
945 parler de vous. (*Il reprend un air gai.*) La joie éclatait dans ses yeux, au récit de vos qualités ; et je l'ai mise enfin dans une impatience extrême de voir ce mariage entièrement conclu.

HARPAGON : Tu m'as fait grand plaisir, Frosine ; et je t'en ai, je te l'avoue, toutes les obligations du monde.

950 **FROSINE** : Je vous prie, Monsieur, de me donner le petit secours que je vous demande. (*Il reprend son air sérieux.*) Cela me remettra sur pied, et je vous en serai éternellement obligée.

HARPAGON : Adieu. Je vais achever mes dépêches[5].

FROSINE : Je vous assure, Monsieur, que vous ne sauriez jamais me
955 soulager dans un plus grand besoin.

HARPAGON : Je mettrai ordre que mon carrosse soit tout prêt pour vous mener à la foire.

---

1. Fraise à l'antique : sorte de collet à la mode vers 1600 (voir la photo, p. 95).
2. Pourpoint : veste pour homme.
3. Jeu de mots probable avec l'expression nouer l'aiguillette : maléfice réputé empêcher la consommation du mariage.
4. Conséquence : importance.
5. Dépêches : lettres d'affaires express.

FROSINE : Je ne vous importunerais pas, si je ne m'y voyais forcée par la nécessité.

960 **HARPAGON** : Et j'aurai soin qu'on soupe de bonne heure, pour ne vous point faire malades.

FROSINE : Ne me refusez pas la grâce dont je vous sollicite. Vous ne sauriez croire, Monsieur, le plaisir que…

HARPAGON : Je m'en vais. Voilà qu'on m'appelle. Jusqu'à tantôt.

965 **FROSINE**, *seule* : Que la fièvre te serre[1], chien de vilain* à tous les diables ! Le ladre* a été ferme à toutes mes attaques ; mais il ne me faut pas pourtant quitter la négociation ; et j'ai l'autre côté[2], en tout cas, d'où je suis assurée de tirer bonne récompense.

---

1. Te serre : t'étouffe.
2. L'autre côté : celui de la mère de Mariane.

ACTE III

SCÈNE 1 : HARPAGON, CLÉANTE, ÉLISE, VALÈRE, DAME CLAUDE, MAÎTRE[1] JACQUES, BRINDAVOINE, LA MERLUCHE

HARPAGON : Allons, venez çà* tous, que je vous distribue mes
970 ordres pour tantôt et règle à chacun son emploi. Approchez, dame
Claude. Commençons par vous. (*Elle tient un balai.*) Bon, vous voilà
les armes à la main. Je vous commets au soin[2] de nettoyer partout ;
et surtout prenez garde de ne point frotter les meubles trop fort, de
peur de les user. Outre cela, je vous constitue, pendant le souper, au
975 gouvernement des bouteilles[3] ; et s'il s'en écarte quelqu'une et qu'il
se casse quelque chose, je m'en prendrai à vous, et le rabattrai sur
vos gages[4].

MAÎTRE JACQUES, *à part* : Châtiment politique[5].

HARPAGON, *à dame Claude* : Allez. Vous, Brindavoine, et vous, La
980 Merluche, je vous établis dans la charge de rincer les verres, et de
donner à boire[6], mais seulement lorsque l'on aura soif, et non pas
selon la coutume de certains impertinents* de laquais, qui viennent
provoquer les gens, et les faire aviser de boire[7] lorsqu'on n'y songe
pas. Attendez qu'on vous en demande plus d'une fois, et vous ressou-
985 venez de porter toujours beaucoup d'eau.

MAÎTRE JACQUES, *à part* : Oui, le vin pur monte à la tête.

---

1. Le titre de maître lui est attribué parce qu'il est maître d'hôtel.
2. Commets au soin : confie la tâche.
3. Constitue […] au gouvernement des bouteilles : charge […] du service des boissons.
4. Rabattrai sur vos gages : déduirai de vos gages.
5. Politique : intéressé, puisque Harpagon économisera sur les gages.
6. Au XVIIᵉ siècle, les verres n'étaient pas sur la table. Un valet les apportait,
   remplis, sur demande.
7. Faire aviser de boire : pousser à boire.

La Merluche : Quitterons-nous nos siquenilles[1], Monsieur ?

Harpagon : Oui, quand vous verrez venir les personnes ; et gardez bien de gâter vos habits.

990 **Brindavoine** : Vous savez bien, Monsieur, qu'un des devants de mon pourpoint* est couvert d'une grande tache de l'huile de la lampe.

La Merluche : Et moi, Monsieur, que j'ai mon haut-de-chausses* tout troué par-derrière, et qu'on me voit, révérence parler[2]…

Harpagon, *à La Merluche* : Paix. Rangez cela adroitement du côté de la
995 muraille, et présentez toujours le devant au monde. (*Harpagon met son chapeau au-devant de son pourpoint, pour montrer à Brindavoine comment il doit faire pour cacher la tache d'huile.*) Et vous, tenez toujours votre chapeau ainsi, lorsque vous servirez. (*S'adressant à Élise.*) Pour vous, ma fille, vous aurez l'œil sur ce que l'on desservira, et prendrez garde qu'il ne
1000 s'en fasse aucun dégât[3]. Cela sied bien aux filles. Mais cependant préparez-vous à bien recevoir ma maîtresse[4], qui vous doit venir visiter et vous mener avec elle à la foire. Entendez-vous ce que je vous dis ?

Élise : Oui, mon père.

Harpagon : Et vous, mon fils le damoiseau[5], à qui j'ai la bonté de
1005 pardonner l'histoire de tantôt, ne vous allez pas aviser non plus de lui faire mauvais visage.

Cléante : Moi, mon père, mauvais visage ? Et par quelle raison ?

Harpagon : Mon Dieu ! nous savons le train[6] des enfants dont les pères se remarient, et de quel œil ils ont coutume de regarder ce qu'on
1010 appelle belle-mère. Mais si vous souhaitez que je perde le souvenir de votre dernière fredaine[7], je vous recommande surtout de régaler d'un

---

1. Siquenilles : vêtements protégeant la livrée des valets.
2. Révérence parler : si j'ose dire.
3. Dégât : gaspillage.
4. Ma maîtresse : la femme que j'aime.
5. Damoiseau : jeune homme élégant (ironique).
6. Train : façon d'agir.
7. Fredaine : écart de conduite.

bon visage[1] cette personne-là, et de lui faire enfin tout le meilleur accueil qu'il vous sera possible.

CLÉANTE : À vous dire le vrai, mon père, je ne puis pas vous promettre
1015 d'être bien aise qu'elle devienne ma belle-mère : je mentirais, si je vous le disais ; mais pour ce qui est de la bien recevoir, et de lui faire bon visage, je vous promets de vous obéir ponctuellement sur ce chapitre.

HARPAGON : Prenez-y garde au moins.

1020 CLÉANTE : Vous verrez que vous n'aurez pas sujet de vous en plaindre.

HARPAGON : Vous ferez sagement. Valère, aide-moi à ceci. Ho çà*, maître Jacques, approchez-vous, je vous ai gardé pour le dernier.

MAÎTRE JACQUES : Est-ce à votre cocher, Monsieur, ou bien à votre cuisinier, que vous voulez parler ? car je suis l'un et l'autre.

1025 HARPAGON : C'est à tous les deux.

MAÎTRE JACQUES : Mais à qui des deux le premier ?

HARPAGON : Au cuisinier.

MAÎTRE JACQUES : Attendez donc, s'il vous plaît.

Il ôte sa casaque[2] de cocher, et paraît vêtu en cuisinier.

1030 HARPAGON : Quelle diantre* de cérémonie est-ce là ?

MAÎTRE JACQUES : Vous n'avez qu'à parler.

HARPAGON : Je me suis engagé, maître Jacques, à donner ce soir à souper.

MAÎTRE JACQUES, *à part* : Grande merveille !

1035 HARPAGON : Dis-moi un peu, nous feras-tu bonne chère[3] ?

---

1. Régaler d'un bon visage : bien accueillir.
2. Casaque : livrée.
3. Bonne chère : bon repas.

Maître Jacques : Oui, si vous me donnez bien de l'argent.

Harpagon : Que diable, toujours de l'argent ! Il semble qu'ils n'aient autre chose à dire : « De l'argent, de l'argent, de l'argent. » Ah ! ils n'ont que ce mot à la bouche : « De l'argent. » Toujours parler d'argent.
1040 Voilà leur épée de chevet [1], de l'argent.

Valère : Je n'ai jamais vu de réponse plus impertinente* que celle-là. Voilà une belle merveille que de faire bonne chère* avec bien de l'argent : c'est une chose la plus aisée du monde, et il n'y a si pauvre esprit qui n'en fît bien autant ; mais pour agir en habile homme, il faut parler de
1045 faire bonne chère avec peu d'argent.

Maître Jacques : Bonne chère avec peu d'argent !

Valère : Oui.

Maître Jacques, *à Valère* : Par ma foi, Monsieur l'intendant, vous nous obligerez de nous faire voir ce secret, et de prendre mon office
1050 de cuisinier : aussi bien vous mêlez-vous céans* d'être le factoton [2].

Harpagon : Taisez-vous. Qu'est-ce qu'il nous faudra ?

Maître Jacques : Voilà Monsieur votre intendant, qui vous fera bonne chère pour peu d'argent.

Harpagon : Haye ! je veux que tu me répondes.

1055 **Maître Jacques** : Combien serez-vous de gens à table ?

Harpagon : Nous serons huit ou dix ; mais il ne faut prendre que huit ; quand il y a à manger pour huit, il y en a bien pour dix.

Valère : Cela s'entend*.

---

1. Épée de chevet : éternel argument. L'expression vient de ce que même la nuit, le gentilhomme gardait son épée sous la main.
2. Factoton : factotum, homme à tout faire.

Maître Jacques : Hé bien ! il faudra quatre grands potages [1], et cinq
1060   assiettes [2]. Potages [3]… Entrées [4]…

Harpagon : Que diable ! voilà pour traiter toute une ville entière.

Maître Jacques : Rôt [5]…

Harpagon, *en lui mettant la main sur la bouche* : Ah ! traître, tu manges
tout mon bien.

1065   **Maître Jacques** : Entremets [6]…

Harpagon, *mettant encore la main sur la bouche de maître Jacques* : Encore ?

Valère, *à maître Jacques* : Est-ce que vous avez envie de faire crever tout
le monde ? et Monsieur a-t-il invité des gens pour les assassiner à force
de mangeaille ? Allez-vous-en lire un peu les préceptes de la santé, et
1070   demander aux médecins s'il y a rien de plus préjudiciable à l'homme
que de manger avec excès.

Harpagon : Il a raison.

Valère : Apprenez, maître Jacques, vous et vos pareils, que c'est un
coupe-gorge qu'une table remplie de trop de viandes [7] ; que pour se
1075   bien montrer ami de ceux que l'on invite, il faut que la frugalité règne
dans les repas qu'on donne ; et que, suivant le dire d'un ancien, *il faut
manger pour vivre, et non pas vivre pour manger.*

---

1. Potages : volailles et légumes en pot-au-feu.
2. Assiettes : ragoûts ou entrées servis entre les plats.
3. Suit une énumération de plats qui pouvait changer selon la représentation. L'une, celle de
   l'édition de 1682, nous est parvenue : « Potages : bisque, potage de perdrix aux choux verts,
   potage de santé, potage de canards aux navets ».
4. « Entrées : fricassée de poulets, tourte de pigeonneaux, ris de veau, boudin blanc
   et morilles » (1682).
5. « Rôt [rôti] dans un grandissime bassin, en pyramide : une grande longe de veau de rivière,
   trois faisans, trois poulardes grasses, douze pigeons de volière, douze poulets de grain,
   six lapereaux de garenne, douze perdreaux, deux douzaines de cailles, trois douzaines
   d'ortolans… » (1682).
6. Entremets : ragoûts servis entre le rôti et les fruits.
7. Viandes : nourriture en général.

© Michel Boulianne.

Maître Jacques (Jacques-Henri Gagnon) : Entremets…

Harpagon (Roland Lepage), *mettant encore la main sur la bouche de maître Jacques* : Encore ?

ACTE III, SCÈNE 1, lignes 1065 et 1066.

THÉÂTRE DU TRIDENT, 1989.
MISE EN SCÈNE DE JEAN-PIERRE RONFARD.

HARPAGON: Ah! que cela est bien dit! Approche, que je t'embrasse pour ce mot. Voilà la plus belle sentence que j'aie entendue de ma vie.
1080 *Il faut vivre pour manger, et non pas manger pour vi...* Non, ce n'est pas cela. Comment est-ce que tu dis?

VALÈRE: Qu'*il faut manger pour vivre, et non pas vivre pour manger.*

HARPAGON: Oui. (*À maître Jacques.*) Entends-tu? (*À Valère.*) Qui est le grand homme[1] qui a dit cela?

1085 **VALÈRE**: Je ne me souviens pas maintenant de son nom.

HARPAGON: Souviens-toi de m'écrire ces mots: je les veux faire graver en lettres d'or sur la cheminée de ma salle.

VALÈRE: Je n'y manquerai pas. Et pour votre souper, vous n'avez qu'à me laisser faire: je réglerai tout cela comme il faut.

1090 **HARPAGON**: Fais donc.

MAÎTRE JACQUES: Tant mieux: j'en aurai moins de peine.

HARPAGON, *à Valère*: Il faudra de ces choses dont on ne mange guère, et qui rassasient d'abord[2]: quelque bon haricot[3] bien gras, avec quelque pâté en pot[4] bien garni de marrons.

1095 **VALÈRE**: Reposez-vous sur moi.

HARPAGON: Maintenant, maître Jacques, il faut nettoyer mon carrosse.

MAÎTRE JACQUES: Attendez. Ceci s'adresse au cocher. (*Il remet sa casaque.*) Vous dites...

HARPAGON: Qu'il faut nettoyer mon carrosse, et tenir mes chevaux
1100 tous prêts pour conduire à la foire...

MAÎTRE JACQUES: Vos chevaux, Monsieur? Ma foi, ils ne sont point du tout en état de marcher. Je ne vous dirai point qu'ils sont sur la

---

1. Cicéron (106-43 av. J.-C.), auteur latin.
2. D'abord: tout de suite.
3. Haricot: ragoût de mouton.
4. Pâté en pot: ragoût de bœuf.

litière, les pauvres bêtes n'en ont point, et ce serait fort mal parler ; mais vous leur faites observer des jeûnes si austères, que ce ne sont
1105 plus rien que des idées ou des fantômes, des façons[1] de chevaux.

Harpagon : Les voilà bien malades : ils ne font rien.

Maître Jacques : Et pour ne faire rien, Monsieur, est-ce qu'il ne faut rien manger ? Il leur vaudrait bien mieux, les pauvres animaux, de travailler beaucoup, de manger de même. Cela me fend le cœur, de les
1110 voir ainsi exténués ; car enfin j'ai une tendresse pour mes chevaux, qu'il me semble que c'est moi-même quand je les vois pâtir ; je m'ôte tous les jours pour eux les choses de la bouche ; et c'est être, Monsieur, d'un naturel trop dur, que de n'avoir nulle pitié de son prochain.

Harpagon : Le travail ne sera pas grand, d'aller jusqu'à la foire.

1115 **Maître Jacques** : Non, Monsieur, je n'ai pas le courage de les mener, et je ferais conscience[2] de leur donner des coups de fouet, en l'état où ils sont. Comment voudriez-vous qu'ils traînassent un carrosse, qu'ils[3] ne peuvent pas se traîner eux-mêmes ?

Valère : Monsieur, j'obligerai le voisin le Picard à se charger de les
1120 conduire ; aussi bien nous fera-t-il ici besoin[4] pour apprêter le souper.

Maître Jacques : Soit, j'aime mieux encore qu'ils meurent sous la main d'un autre que sous la mienne.

Valère : Maître Jacques fait bien le raisonnable[5].

Maître Jacques : Monsieur l'intendant fait bien le nécessaire[6].

1125 **Harpagon** : Paix !

Maître Jacques : Monsieur, je ne saurais souffrir les flatteurs ; et je vois que ce qu'il en fait, que ses contrôles perpétuels sur le pain et le

---

1. Façons : apparences.
2. Je ferais conscience : j'aurais mauvaise conscience.
3. Qu'ils : alors qu'ils.
4. Nous fera-t-il ici besoin : puisque nous en aurons besoin ici.
5. Le raisonnable : celui qui discute.
6. Le nécessaire : celui qui se rend indispensable.

vin, le bois, le sel, et la chandelle, ne sont rien que pour vous gratter [1]
et vous faire sa cour. J'enrage de cela, et je suis fâché tous les jours
1130 d'entendre ce qu'on dit de vous ; car enfin je me sens pour vous de la
tendresse, en dépit que j'en aie [2] ; et après mes chevaux, vous êtes la
personne que j'aime le plus.

HARPAGON : Pourrais-je savoir de vous, maître Jacques, ce que l'on dit
de moi ?

1135 MAÎTRE JACQUES : Oui, Monsieur, si j'étais assuré que cela ne vous
fâchât point.

HARPAGON : Non, en aucune façon.

MAÎTRE JACQUES : Pardonnez-moi, je sais fort bien que je vous
mettrais en colère.

1140 HARPAGON : Point du tout, au contraire, c'est me faire plaisir, et je suis
bien aise d'apprendre comme* on parle de moi.

MAÎTRE JACQUES : Monsieur, puisque vous le voulez, je vous dirai
franchement qu'on se moque partout de vous ; qu'on nous jette de
tous côtés cent brocards [3] à votre sujet ; et que l'on n'est point plus ravi
1145 que de vous tenir au cul et aux chausses [4], et de faire sans cesse des
contes de votre lésine [5]. L'un dit que vous faites imprimer des almanachs [6] particuliers, où vous faites doubler les quatre-temps et les
vigiles [7], afin de profiter des jeûnes où vous obligez votre monde.
L'autre, que vous avez toujours une querelle toute prête à faire à vos
1150 valets dans le temps des étrennes [8], ou de leur sortie d'avec vous [9], pour
vous trouver une raison de ne leur donner rien. Celui-là conte qu'une

---

1. Gratter : flatter.
2. En dépit que j'en aie : malgré moi.
3. Brocards : railleries, moqueries.
4. Vous tenir au cul et aux chausses : s'acharner après vous.
5. Lésine : avarice.
6. Almanachs : calendriers.
7. Jours de jeûne prescrits par l'Église : trois jours au début de chaque saison
   (« les quatre-temps ») et les veilles de grandes fêtes (« les vigiles »).
8. Étrennes : cadeaux offerts à l'occasion du premier jour de l'année.
9. De leur sortie d'avec vous : au moment où ils quittent votre service.

fois vous fîtes assigner[1] le chat d'un de vos voisins, pour vous avoir
mangé un reste d'un gigot de mouton. Celui-ci, que l'on vous surprit
une nuit, en venant dérober vous-même l'avoine de vos chevaux ; et
1155 que votre cocher, qui était celui d'avant moi, vous donna dans l'obscurité je ne sais combien de coups de bâton, dont vous ne voulûtes
rien dire. Enfin voulez-vous que je vous dise ? On ne saurait aller nulle
part où l'on ne vous entende accommoder de toutes pièces[2] ; vous
êtes la fable et la risée de tout le monde ; et jamais on ne parle de vous,
1160 que sous les noms d'avare, de ladre*, de vilain* et de fesse-mathieu*.

Harpagon, *en le battant* : Vous êtes un sot, un maraud[3], un coquin*,
et un impudent[4].

Maître Jacques : Hé bien ! ne l'avais-je pas deviné ? Vous ne m'avez
pas voulu croire : je vous l'avais bien dit que je vous fâcherais de vous
1165 dire la vérité.

Harpagon : Apprenez à parler.

SCÈNE 2 : Maître Jacques, Valère

Valère, *riant* : À ce que je puis voir, maître Jacques, on paye mal
votre franchise.

Maître Jacques : Morbleu ! Monsieur le nouveau venu, qui faites
1170 l'homme d'importance, ce n'est pas votre affaire. Riez de vos coups de
bâton quand on vous en donnera, et ne venez point rire des miens.

Valère : Ah ! Monsieur maître Jacques, ne vous fâchez pas, je vous prie.

---

1. Assigner : comparaître en justice.
2. Accommoder de toutes pièces : ridiculiser de toutes les façons.
3. Maraud : vaurien.
4. Impudent : effronté.

Maître Jacques, *bas, à part* : Il file doux. Je veux faire le brave et s'il est assez sot pour me craindre, le frotter[1] quelque peu. (*Haut.*) Savez-
1175 vous bien, Monsieur le rieur, que je ne ris pas, moi ? et que si vous m'échauffez la tête, je vous ferai rire d'une autre sorte ?

Maître Jacques pousse Valère jusques au bout du théâtre, en le menaçant.

Valère : Eh ! doucement.

Maître Jacques : Comment, doucement ? Il ne me plaît pas, moi.

1180 **Valère** : De grâce.

Maître Jacques : Vous êtes un impertinent[2].

Valère : Monsieur maître Jacques…

Maître Jacques : Il n'y a point de Monsieur maître Jacques pour un double[3]. Si je prends un bâton, je vous rosserai* d'importance.

1185 **Valère** : Comment, un bâton ?

Valère le fait reculer autant qu'il l'a fait.

Maître Jacques : Eh ! je ne parle pas de cela.

Valère : Savez-vous bien, Monsieur le fat[4], que je suis homme à vous rosser moi-même ?

1190 **Maître Jacques** : Je n'en doute pas.

Valère : Que vous n'êtes, pour tout potage[5], qu'un faquin[6] de cuisinier ?

Maître Jacques : Je le sais bien.

Valère : Et que vous ne me connaissez pas encore.

---

1. Frotter : battre.
2. Impertinent : personne qui se conduit de façon déplacée.
3. Un double : quelqu'un de peu de valeur. L'expression vient du fait que le double, ancienne monnaie, ne valait que deux deniers, donc presque rien.
4. Fat : sot.
5. Pour tout potage : en tout et pour tout.
6. Faquin : bon à rien.

1195 **Maître Jacques** : Pardonnez-moi.

Valère : Vous me rosserez, dites-vous ?

Maître Jacques : Je le disais en raillant.

Valère : Et moi, je ne prends point de goût à votre raillerie. (*Il lui donne des coups de bâton.*) Apprenez que vous êtes un mauvais railleur.

1200 **Maître Jacques**, *seul* : Peste soit la sincérité ! c'est un mauvais métier. Désormais j'y renonce, et je ne veux plus dire vrai. Passe encore pour mon maître ; il a quelque droit de me battre[1] ; mais pour ce Monsieur l'intendant, je m'en vengerai si je puis.

SCÈNE 3 : Frosine, Mariane, maître Jacques

Frosine : Savez-vous, maître Jacques, si votre maître est au logis ?

1205 **Maître Jacques** : Oui vraiment il y est, je ne le sais que trop.

Frosine : Dites-lui, je vous prie, que nous sommes ici.

SCÈNE 4 : Mariane, Frosine

Mariane : Ah ! que je suis, Frosine, dans un étrange état ! et s'il faut dire ce que je sens, que j'appréhende cette vue !

Frosine : Mais pourquoi, et quelle est votre inquiétude ?

---

1. Au XVIIe siècle, battre les domestiques était dans les mœurs.

1210 MARIANE : Hélas ! me le demandez-vous ? et ne vous figurez-vous
point les alarmes[1] d'une personne toute prête à voir le supplice où
l'on veut l'attacher ?

FROSINE : Je vois bien que, pour mourir agréablement, Harpagon n'est
pas le supplice que vous voudriez embrasser ; et je connais à votre mine
1215 que le jeune blondin* dont vous m'avez parlé vous revient un peu
dans l'esprit.

MARIANE : Oui, c'est une chose, Frosine, dont je ne veux pas me
défendre ; et les visites respectueuses qu'il a rendues chez nous ont
fait, je vous l'avoue, quelque effet dans mon âme.

1220 FROSINE : Mais avez-vous su quel[2] il est ?

MARIANE : Non, je ne sais point quel il est ; mais je sais qu'il est fait
d'un air à se faire aimer[3] ; que si l'on pouvait mettre les choses à mon
choix, je le prendrais plutôt qu'un autre ; et qu'il ne contribue pas
peu à me faire trouver un tourment effroyable dans l'époux qu'on
1225 veut me donner.

FROSINE : Mon Dieu ! tous ces blondins sont agréables, et débitent
fort bien leur fait[4] ; mais la plupart sont gueux[5] comme des rats ; et il
vaut mieux pour vous de prendre un vieux mari qui vous donne
beaucoup de bien. Je vous avoue que les sens ne trouvent pas si bien
1230 leur compte du côté que je dis, et qu'il y a quelques petits dégoûts à
essuyer* avec un tel époux ; mais cela n'est pas pour durer, et sa mort,
croyez-moi, vous mettra bientôt en état d'en prendre un plus aimable*,
qui réparera toutes choses.

MARIANE : Mon Dieu ! Frosine, c'est une étrange affaire, lorsque, pour
1235 être heureuse, il faut souhaiter ou attendre le trépas[6] de quelqu'un, et
la mort ne suit pas tous les projets que nous faisons.

---

1. Alarmes : craintes.
2. Quel : qui.
3. Fait d'un air à se faire aimer : séduisant.
4. Débitent fort bien leur fait : sont de beaux parleurs.
5. Gueux : pauvres.
6. Trépas : décès.

FROSINE: Vous moquez-vous ? Vous ne l'épousez qu'aux conditions de vous laisser veuve bientôt ; et ce doit être là un des articles du contrat. Il serait bien impertinent* de ne pas mourir dans trois mois. Le voici en propre personne.

MARIANE: Ah ! Frosine, quelle figure !

SCÈNE 5 : HARPAGON, FROSINE, MARIANE

HARPAGON, *à Mariane*: Ne vous offensez pas, ma belle, si je viens à vous avec des lunettes. Je sais que vos appas[1] frappent assez les yeux, sont assez visibles d'eux-mêmes, et qu'il n'est pas besoin de lunettes pour les apercevoir ; mais enfin c'est avec des lunettes qu'on observe les astres ; et je maintiens et garantis que vous êtes un astre, mais un astre le plus bel astre qui soit dans le pays des astres. Frosine, elle ne répond mot, et ne témoigne, ce me semble, aucune joie de me voir.

FROSINE: C'est qu'elle est encore toute surprise ; et puis les filles ont toujours honte à témoigner d'abord* ce qu'elles ont dans l'âme.

HARPAGON, *à Frosine*: Tu as raison. (*À Mariane.*) Voilà, belle mignonne[2], ma fille qui vient vous saluer.

SCÈNE 6 : ÉLISE, HARPAGON, MARIANE, FROSINE

MARIANE: Je m'acquitte bien tard, Madame, d'une telle visite.

ÉLISE: Vous avez fait, Madame, ce que je devais faire, et c'était à moi de vous prévenir[3].

---

1. Appas : charmes physiques, familièrement la poitrine.
2. Les galanteries d'Harpagon sont vieillottes même en 1668.
3. Prévenir : devancer.

HARPAGON : Vous voyez qu'elle est grande ; mais mauvaise herbe croît toujours.

MARIANE, *bas, à Frosine* : Oh ! l'homme déplaisant !

1260 HARPAGON, *bas, à Frosine* : Que dit la belle ?

FROSINE : Qu'elle vous trouve admirable.

HARPAGON[1] : C'est trop d'honneur que vous me faites, adorable mignonne.

MARIANE, *à part* : Quel animal !

1265 HARPAGON : Je vous suis trop obligé de ces sentiments.

MARIANE, *à part* : Je n'y puis plus tenir.

HARPAGON : Voici mon fils aussi qui vous vient faire la révérence[2].

MARIANE, *à part, à Frosine* : Ah ! Frosine, quelle rencontre ! C'est justement celui dont je t'ai parlé.

1270 FROSINE, *à Mariane* : L'aventure est merveilleuse[3].

HARPAGON : Je vois que vous vous étonnez de me voir de si grands enfants, mais je serai bientôt défait et de l'un et de l'autre.

SCÈNE 7 : CLÉANTE, HARPAGON, ÉLISE, MARIANE, FROSINE

CLÉANTE, *à Mariane* : Madame, à vous dire le vrai, c'est ici une aventure où* sans doute* je ne m'attendais pas ; et mon père ne m'a pas 1275 peu surpris lorsqu'il m'a dit tantôt le dessein qu'il avait formé.

---

1. Traditionnellement, les révérences d'Harpagon qu'il destine à Mariane sont bloquées par Frosine qui s'interpose entre les deux.
2. Faire la révérence : dire bonjour.
3. Merveilleuse : extraordinaire.

Mariane : Je puis dire la même chose. C'est une rencontre imprévue qui m'a surprise autant que vous ; et je n'étais point préparée à une pareille aventure.

Cléante : Il est vrai que mon père, Madame, ne peut pas faire un plus
1280 beau choix, et que ce m'est une sensible[1] joie que l'honneur de vous voir ; mais avec tout cela, je ne vous assurerai point que je me réjouis du dessein où vous pourriez être[2] de devenir ma belle-mère. Le compliment, je vous l'avoue, est trop difficile pour moi ; et c'est un titre, s'il vous plaît, que je ne vous souhaite point. Ce discours paraî-
1285 tra brutal aux yeux de quelques-uns ; mais je suis assuré que vous serez personne à le prendre comme il faudra ; que c'est un mariage, Madame, où vous vous imaginez bien que je dois avoir de la répu-gnance ; que vous n'ignorez pas, sachant ce que je suis, comme il choque[3] mes intérêts ; et que vous voulez bien enfin que je vous dise,
1290 avec la permission de mon père, que si les choses dépendaient de moi, cet hymen[4] ne se ferait point.

Harpagon : Voilà un compliment bien impertinent* : quelle belle confession à lui faire !

Mariane : Et moi, pour vous répondre, j'ai à vous dire que les choses
1295 sont fort égales[5] ; et que si vous auriez[6] de la répugnance à me voir votre belle-mère, je n'en aurais pas moins sans doute* à vous voir mon beau-fils. Ne croyez pas, je vous prie, que ce soit moi qui cherche à vous donner cette inquiétude. Je serais fort fâchée de vous causer du déplaisir* ; et si je ne m'y vois forcée par une puissance absolue, je
1300 vous donne ma parole que je ne consentirai point au mariage qui vous chagrine.

---

1. Sensible : grande.
2. Dessein où vous pourriez être : projet que vous pourriez avoir.
3. Comme il choque : combien il heurte.
4. Hymen : mariage.
5. Les choses sont fort égales : je pense comme vous.
6. Auriez : aviez.

Harpagon: Elle a raison ; à sot compliment il faut une réponse de même. Je vous demande pardon, ma belle, de l'impertinence de mon fils. C'est un jeune sot, qui ne sait pas encore la conséquence des paroles
1305 qu'il dit.

Mariane: Je vous promets que ce qu'il m'a dit ne m'a point du tout offensée ; au contraire, il m'a fait plaisir de m'expliquer ainsi ses véritables sentiments. J'aime de lui un aveu de la sorte ; et, s'il avait parlé d'autre façon, je l'en estimerais bien moins.

1310 **Harpagon**: C'est beaucoup de bonté à vous de vouloir ainsi excuser ses fautes. Le temps le rendra plus sage, et vous verrez qu'il changera de sentiments.

Cléante: Non, mon père, je ne suis point capable d'en changer, et je prie instamment Madame de le croire.

1315 **Harpagon**: Mais voyez quelle extravagance ! il continue encore plus fort.

Cléante: Voulez-vous que je trahisse mon cœur ?

Harpagon: Encore ? Avez-vous envie de changer de discours ?

Cléante: Hé bien ! puisque vous voulez que je parle d'autre façon,
1320 souffrez[1], Madame, que je me mette ici à la place de mon père, et que je vous avoue que je n'ai rien vu dans le monde de si charmant que vous ; que je ne conçois rien d'égal au bonheur de vous plaire, et que le titre de votre époux est une gloire, une félicité que je préférerais aux destinées des plus grands princes de la terre. Oui, Madame, le
1325 bonheur de vous posséder est à mes regards la plus belle de toutes les fortunes* ; c'est où j'attache[2] toute mon ambition ; il n'y a rien que je ne sois capable de faire pour une conquête si précieuse, et les obstacles les plus puissants…

---

1. Souffrez : permettez.
2. C'est où j'attache : c'est là que je mets.

HARPAGON : Doucement, mon fils, s'il vous plaît.

1330 **CLÉANTE** : C'est un compliment que je fais pour vous à Madame.

HARPAGON : Mon Dieu! j'ai une langue pour m'expliquer moi-même, et je n'ai pas besoin d'un procureur[1] comme vous. Allons, donnez des sièges.

FROSINE : Non; il vaut mieux que de ce pas nous allions à la foire, afin 1335 d'en revenir plus tôt, et d'avoir tout le temps ensuite de vous entretenir.

HARPAGON, *à Brindavoine* : Qu'on mette donc les chevaux au carrosse. (*À Mariane.*) Je vous prie de m'excuser, ma belle, si je n'ai pas songé à vous donner un peu de collation avant que de partir.

CLÉANTE : J'y ai pourvu, mon père, et j'ai fait apporter ici quelques 1340 bassins[2] d'oranges de la Chine, de citrons doux et de confitures[3], que j'ai envoyé quérir[4] de votre part.

HARPAGON, *bas, à Valère* : Valère!

VALÈRE, *à Harpagon* : Il a perdu le sens.

CLÉANTE : Est-ce que vous trouvez, mon père, que ce ne soit pas 1345 assez? Madame aura la bonté d'excuser cela, s'il lui plaît.

MARIANE : C'est une chose qui n'était pas nécessaire.

CLÉANTE : Avez-vous jamais vu, Madame, un diamant plus vif que celui que vous voyez que mon père a au doigt?

MARIANE : Il est vrai qu'il brille beaucoup.

1350 **CLÉANTE**. *Il l'ôte du doigt de son père et le donne à Mariane* : Il faut que vous le voyiez de près.

MARIANE : Il est fort beau sans doute*, et jette quantité de feux.

---

1. Procureur : personne qui agit pour une autre.
2. Bassins : coupes.
3. Au XVIIe siècle, oranges, citrons et confitures étaient des produits de luxe.
4. Quérir : chercher.

CLÉANTE. *Il se met au-devant de Mariane, qui le veut rendre*: Nenni[1], Madame: il est en de trop belles mains. C'est un présent que mon
1355 père vous a fait.

HARPAGON: Moi?

CLÉANTE: N'est-il pas vrai, mon père, que vous voulez que Madame le garde pour l'amour de vous?

HARPAGON, *à part, à son fils*: Comment?

1360 **CLÉANTE**: Belle demande! (*À Mariane.*) Il me fait signe de vous le faire accepter.

MARIANE: Je ne veux point…

CLÉANTE, *à Mariane*: Vous moquez-vous? Il n'a garde de le reprendre.

HARPAGON, *à part*: J'enrage!

1365 **MARIANE**: Ce serait…

CLÉANTE, *en empêchant toujours Mariane de rendre la bague*: Non, vous dis-je, c'est l'offenser.

MARIANE: De grâce…

CLÉANTE: Point du tout.

1370 **HARPAGON**, *à part*: Peste soit…

CLÉANTE: Le voilà qui se scandalise de votre refus.

HARPAGON, *bas, à son fils*: Ah! traître!

CLÉANTE: Vous voyez qu'il se désespère.

HARPAGON, *bas, à son fils, en le menaçant*: Bourreau que tu es!

1375 **CLÉANTE**: Mon père, ce n'est pas ma faute. Je fais ce que je puis pour l'obliger à la garder; mais elle est obstinée.

---

1. Nenni: non.

HARPAGON, *bas, à son fils, avec emportement*: Pendard!

CLÉANTE: Vous êtes cause, Madame, que mon père me querelle.

HARPAGON, *bas, à son fils, avec les mêmes grimaces*: Le coquin* !

1380 **CLÉANTE**, *à Mariane*: Vous le ferez tomber malade. De grâce, Madame, ne résistez point davantage.

FROSINE, *à Mariane*: Mon Dieu! que de façons! Gardez la bague, puisque Monsieur le veut.

MARIANE, *à Harpagon*: Pour ne vous point mettre en colère, je la garde
1385 maintenant ; et je prendrai un autre temps [1] pour vous la rendre.

SCÈNE 8 : HARPAGON, MARIANE, FROSINE, CLÉANTE, BRINDAVOINE, ÉLISE

BRINDAVOINE: Monsieur, il y a là un homme qui veut vous parler.

HARPAGON: Dis-lui que je suis empêché, et qu'il revienne une autre fois.

BRINDAVOINE: Il dit qu'il vous apporte de l'argent.

1390 **HARPAGON**, *à Mariane*: Je vous demande pardon. Je reviens tout à l'heure*.

---

1. Prendrai un autre temps : choisirai un autre moment.

SCÈNE 9 : Harpagon, Mariane, Cléante, Élise, Frosine, La Merluche

La Merluche. *Il vient en courant, et fait tomber Harpagon* : Monsieur…

Harpagon : Ah ! je suis mort.

Cléante : Qu'est-ce, mon père ? vous êtes-vous fait mal ?

1395 **Harpagon** : Le traître assurément a reçu de l'argent de mes débiteurs, pour me faire rompre le cou.

Valère : Cela ne sera rien.

La Merluche : Monsieur, je vous demande pardon, je croyais bien faire d'accourir vite.

1400 **Harpagon** : Que viens-tu faire ici, bourreau ?

La Merluche : Vous dire que vos deux chevaux sont déferrés.

Harpagon : Qu'on les mène promptement chez le maréchal.

Cléante : En attendant qu'ils soient ferrés, je vais faire pour vous, mon père, les honneurs de votre logis, et conduire Madame dans le 1405 jardin, où je ferai porter la collation.

Harpagon : Valère, aie un peu l'œil à tout cela ; et prends soin, je te prie, de m'en sauver le plus que tu pourras, pour le renvoyer au marchand.

Valère : C'est assez[1].

1410 **Harpagon,** *seul* : Ô fils impertinent*, as-tu envie de me ruiner ?

---

1. Formule ambiguë. Valère s'adresse-t-il à Cléante pour lui dire que cela suffit, ou à Harpagon pour lui signifier qu'il a compris ce qu'il veut ?

ACTE IV

SCÈNE 1 : Cléante, Mariane, Élise, Frosine

Cléante : Rentrons ici, nous serons beaucoup mieux. Il n'y a plus autour de nous personne de suspect, et nous pouvons parler librement.

Élise : Oui, Madame, mon frère m'a fait confidence de la passion qu'il a pour vous. Je sais les chagrins et les déplaisirs* que sont capables de
1415 causer de pareilles traverses[1] ; et c'est, je vous assure, avec une tendresse extrême que je m'intéresse à votre aventure.

Mariane : C'est une douce consolation que de voir dans ses intérêts une personne comme vous ; et je vous conjure, Madame, de me garder toujours cette généreuse amitié, si capable de m'adoucir les cruautés
1420 de la fortune*.

Frosine : Vous êtes, par ma foi, de malheureuses gens l'un et l'autre, de ne m'avoir point, avant tout ceci, avertie de votre affaire. Je vous aurais sans doute* détourné[2] cette inquiétude, et n'aurais point amené les choses où l'on voit qu'elles sont.

1425 **Cléante :** Que veux-tu ? C'est ma mauvaise destinée qui l'a voulu ainsi. Mais, belle Mariane, quelles résolutions sont les vôtres ?

Mariane : Hélas ! suis-je en pouvoir de faire des résolutions ? Et dans la dépendance où je me vois, puis-je former que[3] des souhaits ?

Cléante : Point d'autre appui pour moi dans votre cœur que de
1430 simples souhaits ? point de pitié officieuse[4] ? point de secourable bonté ? point d'affection agissante ?

---

1. Traverses : obstacles, difficultés.
2. Détourné : évité, épargné.
3. Que : autre chose que.
4. Officieuse : serviable.

MARIANE: Que saurais-je vous dire? Mettez-vous en[1] ma place, et voyez ce que je puis faire. Avisez, ordonnez vous-même: je m'en remets à vous, et je vous crois trop raisonnable pour vouloir exiger de 1435 moi que ce qui peut m'être permis par l'honneur et la bienséance.

CLÉANTE: Hélas! où me réduisez-vous, que de me renvoyer[2] à ce que voudront me permettre les fâcheux sentiments d'un rigoureux honneur et d'une scrupuleuse bienséance.

MARIANE: Mais que voulez-vous que je fasse? Quand je pourrais[3] 1440 passer sur quantité d'égards où notre sexe est obligé, j'ai de la considération pour ma mère. Elle m'a toujours élevée avec une tendresse extrême, et je ne saurais me résoudre à lui donner du déplaisir. Faites, agissez auprès d'elle, employez tous vos soins à gagner son esprit: vous pouvez faire et dire tout ce que vous voudrez, je vous en donne 1445 la licence[4], et s'il ne tient qu'à me déclarer en votre faveur, je veux bien consentir à lui faire un aveu moi-même de tout ce que je sens pour vous.

CLÉANTE: Frosine, ma pauvre Frosine, voudrais-tu nous servir?

FROSINE: Par ma foi! faut-il demander? je le voudrais de tout mon 1450 cœur. Vous savez que de mon naturel je suis assez humaine; le Ciel ne m'a point fait l'âme de bronze, et je n'ai que trop de tendresse à rendre de petits services, quand je vois des gens qui s'entr'aiment en tout bien et en tout honneur. Que pourrions-nous faire à ceci?

CLÉANTE: Songe un peu, je te prie.

1455 **MARIANE**: Ouvre-nous des lumières[5].

ÉLISE: Trouve quelque invention pour rompre ce que tu as fait.

FROSINE: Ceci est assez difficile. (*À Mariane.*) Pour votre mère, elle n'est pas tout à fait déraisonnable, et peut-être pourrait-on la gagner,

---

1. En: à.
2. Que de me renvoyer: en me renvoyant.
3. Quand je pourrais: même si je pouvais.
4. Licence: permission.
5. Ouvre-nous des lumières: donne-nous des idées.

et la résoudre à transporter au fils le don qu'elle veut faire au père.
1460 (*À Cléante.*) Mais le mal que j'y trouve, c'est que votre père est votre père.

CLÉANTE : Cela s'entend*.

FROSINE : Je veux dire qu'il conservera du dépit, si l'on montre qu'on le refuse ; et qu'il ne sera point d'humeur ensuite à donner son consentement à votre mariage. Il faudrait, pour bien faire, que le refus
1465 vînt de lui-même, et tâcher par quelque moyen de le dégoûter de votre personne.

CLÉANTE : Tu as raison.

FROSINE : Oui, j'ai raison, je le sais bien. C'est là ce qu'il faudrait ; mais le diantre* est d'en pouvoir trouver les moyens. Attendez : si nous
1470 avions quelque femme un peu sur l'âge[1], qui fût de mon talent, et jouât assez bien pour contrefaire une dame de qualité, par le moyen d'un train fait à la hâte[2], et d'un bizarre nom de marquise, ou de vicomtesse, que nous supposerions de la basse Bretagne, j'aurais assez d'adresse pour faire accroire à votre père que ce serait une personne
1475 riche, outre ses maisons, de cent mille écus[3] en argent comptant ; qu'elle serait éperdument amoureuse de lui, et souhaiterait de se voir sa femme, jusqu'à lui donner tout son bien par contrat de mariage[4] ; et je ne doute point qu'il ne prêtât l'oreille à la proposition ; car enfin il vous aime fort, je le sais ; mais il aime un peu plus l'argent ; et
1480 quand, ébloui de ce leurre[5], il aurait une fois consenti à ce qui vous touche, il importerait peu ensuite qu'il se désabusât, en venant à vouloir voir clair aux effets[6] de notre marquise.

CLÉANTE : Tout cela est fort bien pensé.

---

1. Un peu sur l'âge : d'un certain âge.
2. Un train fait à la hâte : une suite de serviteurs constituée rapidement.
3. Approximativement 915 000 € ou 1 400 000 $.
4. Aucun notaire sérieux n'aurait accepté une telle clause, puisque traditionnellement chaque époux gardait son bien propre.
5. Leurre : piège.
6. Qu'il se désabusât, en venant à vouloir voir clair aux effets : qu'il fût détrompé, quand il voudra toucher la fortune.

Frosine : Laissez-moi faire. Je viens de me ressouvenir d'une de mes
1485 amies, qui sera notre fait[1].

Cléante : Sois assurée, Frosine, de ma reconnaissance, si tu viens à
bout de la chose. Mais, charmante Mariane, commençons, je vous
prie, par gagner votre mère ; c'est toujours beaucoup faire que de
rompre ce mariage. Faites-y de votre part, je vous en conjure, tous les
1490 efforts qu'il vous sera possible ; servez-vous de tout le pouvoir que
vous donne sur elle cette amitié* qu'elle a pour vous ; déployez sans
réserve les grâces éloquentes, les charmes tout-puissants que le Ciel a
placés dans vos yeux et dans votre bouche ; et n'oubliez rien, s'il vous
plaît, de ces tendres paroles, de ces douces prières, et de ces caresses
1495 touchantes à qui je suis persuadé qu'on ne saurait rien refuser.

Mariane : J'y ferai tout ce que je puis, et n'oublierai aucune chose.

SCÈNE 2 : Harpagon, Cléante, Mariane,
Élise, Frosine

Harpagon, *à part, sans être aperçu* : Ouais ! mon fils baise la main de sa
prétendue[2] belle-mère, et sa prétendue belle-mère ne s'en défend pas
fort. Y aurait-il quelque mystère là-dessous ?

1500 **Élise** : Voilà mon père.

Harpagon : Le carrosse est tout prêt. Vous pouvez partir quand il
vous plaira.

Cléante : Puisque vous n'y allez pas, mon père, je m'en vais
les conduire.

1505 **Harpagon** : Non, demeurez. Elles iront bien toutes seules ; et j'ai
besoin de vous.

---

1. Sera notre fait : fera l'affaire.
2. Prétendue : future. Au XVIIe siècle, la bienséance ne permettait pas de baiser la main
de sa future belle-mère.

SCÈNE 3 : Harpagon, Cléante

Harpagon : Ô çà, intérêt de belle-mère à part[1], que te semble à toi de cette personne ?

Cléante : Ce qui m'en semble ?

1510 **Harpagon :** Oui, de son air, de sa taille, de sa beauté, de son esprit ?

Cléante : La, la.

Harpagon : Mais encore ?

Cléante : À vous en parler franchement, je ne l'ai pas trouvée ici ce que je l'avais crue. Son air est de franche coquette ; sa taille est assez
1515 gauche, sa beauté très médiocre, et son esprit des plus communs. Ne croyez pas que ce soit, mon père, pour vous en dégoûter ; car belle-mère pour belle-mère, j'aime autant celle-là qu'une autre.

Harpagon : Tu lui disais tantôt pourtant…

Cléante : Je lui ai dit quelques douceurs en votre nom, mais c'était
1520 pour vous plaire.

Harpagon : Si bien donc que tu n'aurais pas d'inclination* pour elle ?

Cléante : Moi ? point du tout.

Harpagon : J'en suis fâché ; car cela rompt une pensée qui m'était venue dans l'esprit. J'ai fait, en la voyant ici, réflexion sur mon âge ; et
1525 j'ai songé qu'on pourra trouver à redire de me voir marier à une si jeune personne. Cette considération m'en faisait quitter le dessein ; et comme je l'ai fait demander, et que je suis pour elle engagé de parole, je te l'aurais donnée, sans l'aversion* que tu témoignes.

Cléante : À moi ?

1530 **Harpagon :** À toi.

Cléante : En mariage ?

---

1. Intérêt de belle-mère à part : si tu oublies qu'elle est ta future belle-mère.

Harpagon: En mariage.

Cléante: Écoutez: il est vrai qu'elle n'est pas fort à mon goût; mais pour vous faire plaisir, mon père, je me résoudrai à l'épouser, si
1535 vous voulez.

Harpagon: Moi? Je suis plus raisonnable que tu ne penses: je ne veux point forcer ton inclination.

Cléante: Pardonnez-moi, je me ferai cet effort pour l'amour de vous.

Harpagon: Non, non; un mariage ne saurait être heureux où l'incli-
1540 nation n'est pas.

Cléante: C'est une chose, mon père, qui peut-être viendra ensuite; et l'on dit que l'amour est souvent un fruit du mariage.

Harpagon: Non: du côté de l'homme, on ne doit point risquer l'affaire, et ce sont des suites fâcheuses, où je n'ai garde de me commettre[1].
1545 Si tu avais senti quelque inclination pour elle, à la bonne heure: je te l'aurais fait épouser, au lieu de moi; mais cela n'étant pas, je suivrai mon premier dessein, et je l'épouserai moi-même.

Cléante: Hé bien! mon père, puisque les choses sont ainsi, il faut vous découvrir mon cœur, il faut vous révéler notre secret. La vérité
1550 est que je l'aime, depuis un jour que je la vis dans une promenade; que mon dessein était tantôt de vous la demander pour femme; et que rien ne m'a retenu que la déclaration de vos sentiments, et la crainte de vous déplaire.

Harpagon: Lui avez-vous rendu visite?

1555 **Cléante**: Oui, mon père.

Harpagon: Beaucoup de fois?

Cléante: Assez, pour le temps qu'il y a[2].

Harpagon: Vous a-t-on bien reçu?

---

1. Me commettre: m'aventurer.
2. Pour le temps qu'il y a: pour le peu de temps qu'il y a entre notre première rencontre et maintenant.

Cléante : Fort bien, mais sans savoir qui j'étais ; et c'est ce qui a fait
1560 tantôt la surprise de Mariane.

Harpagon : Lui avez-vous déclaré votre passion, et le dessein où vous
étiez de l'épouser ?

Cléante : Sans doute* ; et même j'en avais fait à sa mère quelque
peu d'ouverture[1].

1565 **Harpagon** : A-t-elle écouté, pour sa fille, votre proposition ?

Cléante : Oui, fort civilement.

Harpagon : Et la fille correspond-elle[2] fort à votre amour ?

Cléante : Si j'en dois croire les apparences, je me persuade, mon
père, qu'elle a quelque bonté pour moi.

1570 **Harpagon**, *bas, à part* : Je suis bien aise d'avoir appris un tel secret ; et
voilà justement ce que je demandais. (*Haut.*) Oh sus[3] ! mon fils, savez-
vous qu'il y a ? c'est qu'il faut songer, s'il vous plaît, à vous défaire
de votre amour ; à cesser toutes vos poursuites auprès d'une personne
que je prétends pour moi[4] ; et à vous marier dans peu avec celle qu'on
1575 vous destine.

Cléante : Oui, mon père, c'est ainsi que vous me jouez ! Hé bien !
puisque les choses en sont venues là, je vous déclare, moi, que je ne
quitterai point la passion que j'ai pour Mariane, qu'il n'y a point d'extré-
mité où je ne m'abandonne pour vous disputer sa conquête, et que si
1580 vous avez pour vous le consentement d'une mère, j'aurai d'autres
secours peut-être qui combattront pour moi.

Harpagon : Comment, pendard ? tu as l'audace d'aller sur mes
brisées[5] ?

Cléante : C'est vous qui allez sur les miennes ; et je suis le premier
1585 en date.

---

1. Fait à sa mère quelque peu d'ouverture : parlé un peu à sa mère.
2. Correspond-elle : répond-elle.
3. Sus : allons.
4. Je prétends pour moi : j'ai l'intention d'épouser.
5. Aller sur mes brisées : entrer en concurrence avec moi (terme de chasse).

Harpagon : Ne suis-je pas ton père ? et ne me dois-tu pas respect !

Cléante : Ce ne sont point ici des choses où les enfants soient obligés de déférer[1] aux pères ; et l'amour ne connaît personne.

Harpagon : Je te ferai bien me connaître, avec de bons coups de bâton.

1590 **Cléante** : Toutes vos menaces ne feront rien.

Harpagon : Tu renonceras à Mariane.

Cléante : Point du tout.

Harpagon : Donnez-moi un bâton tout à l'heure*.

SCÈNE 4 : Maître Jacques, Harpagon, Cléante

Maître Jacques : Eh, eh, eh, Messieurs, qu'est-ce ci[2] ? à quoi 1595 songez-vous ?

Cléante : Je me moque de cela.

Maître Jacques, *à Cléante* : Ah ! Monsieur, doucement.

Harpagon : Me parler avec cette impudence[3] !

Maître Jacques, *à Harpagon* : Ah ! Monsieur, de grâce.

1600 **Cléante** : Je n'en démordrai point.

Maître Jacques, *à Cléante* : Hé quoi ? à votre père ?

Harpagon : Laisse-moi faire.

Maître Jacques, *à Harpagon* : Hé quoi ? à votre fils ? Encore passe pour moi.

---

1. Déférer : obéir.
2. Qu'est-ce ci ? : que se passe-t-il ici ?
3. Impudence : effronterie.

1605 **HARPAGON**: Je te veux faire toi-même, maître Jacques, juge de cette affaire, pour montrer comme j'ai raison.

MAÎTRE JACQUES: J'y consens. (*À Cléante.*) Éloignez-vous un peu.

HARPAGON: J'aime une fille, que je veux épouser ; et le pendard a l'insolence de l'aimer avec moi, et d'y prétendre malgré mes ordres.

1610 **MAÎTRE JACQUES**: Ah ! il a tort.

HARPAGON: N'est-ce pas une chose épouvantable, qu'un fils qui veut entrer en concurrence avec son père ? et ne doit-il pas, par respect, s'abstenir de toucher à mes inclinations[1] ?

MAÎTRE JACQUES: Vous avez raison. Laissez-moi lui parler, et 1615 demeurez là.

Il vient trouver Cléante à l'autre bout du théâtre.

CLÉANTE, *à maître Jacques, qui s'approche de lui*: Hé bien ! oui, puisqu'il veut te choisir pour juge, je n'y recule point ; il ne m'importe qui ce soit[2] ; et je veux bien aussi me rapporter à toi, maître Jacques, de 1620 notre différend.

MAÎTRE JACQUES: C'est beaucoup d'honneur que vous me faites.

CLÉANTE: Je suis épris d'une jeune personne qui répond à mes vœux*, et reçoit tendrement les offres de ma foi* ; et mon père s'avise de venir troubler notre amour par la demande qu'il en fait faire.

1625 **MAÎTRE JACQUES**: Il a tort assurément.

CLÉANTE: N'a-t-il point de honte, à son âge, de songer à se marier ? lui sied-il bien d'être encore amoureux ? et ne devrait-il pas laisser cette occupation aux jeunes gens ?

MAÎTRE JACQUES: Vous avez raison, il se moque. Laissez-moi lui dire 1630 deux mots. (*Il revient à Harpagon.*) Hé bien ! votre fils n'est pas si étrange que vous le dites, et il se met à la raison. Il dit qu'il sait le respect qu'il vous doit, qu'il ne s'est emporté que dans la première

---

1. Mes inclinations : celle que j'aime.
2. Il ne m'importe qui ce soit : la personne choisie m'importe peu.

chaleur[1], et qu'il ne fera point refus de se soumettre à ce qu'il vous plaira, pourvu que vous vouliez le traiter mieux que vous ne faites, et
1635 lui donner quelque personne en mariage dont il ait lieu d'être content.

HARPAGON : Ah ! dis-lui, maître Jacques, que moyennant cela, il pourra espérer toutes choses de moi ; et que, hors Mariane, je lui laisse la liberté de choisir celle qu'il voudra.

MAÎTRE JACQUES : Laissez-moi faire. (*Il va au fils*). Hé bien ! votre père
1640 n'est pas si déraisonnable que vous le faites ; et il m'a témoigné que ce sont vos emportements qui l'ont mis en colère ; qu'il n'en veut seulement qu'à votre manière d'agir, et qu'il sera fort disposé à vous accorder ce que vous souhaitez, pourvu que vous vouliez vous y prendre par la douceur, et lui rendre les déférences, les respects, et les soumis-
1645 sions qu'un fils doit à son père.

CLÉANTE : Ah ! maître Jacques, tu lui peux assurer que, s'il m'accorde Mariane, il me verra toujours le plus soumis de tous les hommes ; et que jamais je ne ferai aucune chose que par ses volontés.

MAÎTRE JACQUES, *à Harpagon* : Cela est fait. Il consent à ce que
1650 vous dites.

HARPAGON : Voilà qui va le mieux du monde.

MAÎTRE JACQUES, *à Cléante* : Tout est conclu. Il est content de vos promesses.

CLÉANTE : Le Ciel en soit loué !

1655 MAÎTRE JACQUES : Messieurs, vous n'avez qu'à parler ensemble : vous voilà d'accord maintenant ; et vous alliez vous quereller, faute de vous entendre.

CLÉANTE : Mon pauvre maître Jacques, je te serai obligé toute ma vie.

MAÎTRE JACQUES : Il n'y a pas de quoi, Monsieur.

1660 HARPAGON : Tu m'as fait plaisir, maître Jacques, et cela mérite une récompense. Va, je m'en souviendrai, je t'assure.

---

1. Chaleur : mouvement de colère.

Il tire son mouchoir de sa poche[1], ce qui fait croire à maître Jacques qu'il va lui donner quelque chose.

Maître Jacques : Je vous baise les mains[2].

SCÈNE 5 : Cléante, Harpagon

1665 **Cléante** : Je vous demande pardon, mon père, de l'emportement que j'ai fait paraître.

Harpagon : Cela n'est rien.

Cléante : Je vous assure que j'en ai tous les regrets du monde.

Harpagon : Et moi, j'ai toutes les joies du monde de te voir 1670 raisonnable.

Cléante : Quelle bonté à vous d'oublier si vite ma faute !

Harpagon : On oublie aisément les fautes des enfants, lorsqu'ils rentrent dans leur devoir.

Cléante : Quoi ? ne garder aucun ressentiment de toutes mes 1675 extravagances ?

Harpagon : C'est une chose où* tu m'obliges par la soumission et le respect où tu te ranges.

Cléante : Je vous promets, mon père, que, jusques au tombeau, je conserverai dans mon cœur le souvenir de vos bontés.

1680 **Harpagon** : Et moi, je te promets qu'il n'y aura aucune chose que de moi tu n'obtiennes.

Cléante : Ah ! mon père, je ne vous demande plus rien ; et c'est m'avoir assez donné que de me donner Mariane.

---

1. Traditionnellement, le mouchoir qu'utilise Harpagon est **minuscule**.
2. Je vous baise les mains : formule de remerciement (ironique ici).

HARPAGON: Comment?

1685 **CLÉANTE**: Je dis, mon père, que je suis trop content de vous, et que je trouve toutes choses dans la bonté que vous avez de m'accorder Mariane.

HARPAGON: Qui est-ce qui parle de t'accorder Mariane?

CLÉANTE: Vous, mon père.

1690 **HARPAGON**: Moi!

CLÉANTE: Sans doute*.

HARPAGON: Comment? C'est toi qui as promis d'y renoncer.

CLÉANTE: Moi, y renoncer?

HARPAGON: Oui.

1695 **CLÉANTE**: Point du tout.

HARPAGON: Tu ne t'es pas départi d'y prétendre[1]?

CLÉANTE: Au contraire, j'y suis porté plus que jamais.

HARPAGON: Quoi? pendard, derechef[2]?

CLÉANTE: Rien ne me peut changer.

1700 **HARPAGON**: Laisse-moi faire, traître.

CLÉANTE: Faites tout ce qu'il vous plaira.

HARPAGON: Je te défends de me jamais voir.

CLÉANTE: À la bonne heure.

HARPAGON: Je t'abandonne.

1705 **CLÉANTE**: Abandonnez.

HARPAGON: Je te renonce[3] pour mon fils.

---

1. Ne t'es pas départi d'y prétendre: n'as pas renoncé à elle.
2. Derechef: encore, de nouveau.
3. Renonce: renie.

Cléante : Soit.

Harpagon : Je te déshérite.

Cléante : Tout ce que vous voudrez.

1710 **Harpagon** : Et je te donne ma malédiction.

Cléante : Je n'ai que faire de vos dons.

SCÈNE 6 : La Flèche, Cléante

La Flèche, *sortant du jardin, avec une cassette** : Ah ! Monsieur, que je vous trouve à propos ! suivez-moi vite.

Cléante : Qu'y a-t-il ?

1715 **La Flèche** : Suivez-moi, vous dis-je : nous sommes bien[1].

Cléante : Comment ?

La Flèche : Voici votre affaire.

Cléante : Quoi ?

La Flèche : J'ai guigné[2] ceci tout le jour.

1720 **Cléante** : Qu'est-ce que c'est ?

La Flèche : Le trésor de votre père, que j'ai attrapé.

Cléante : Comment as-tu fait ?

La Flèche : Vous saurez tout. Sauvons-nous, je l'entends crier.

---

1. Nous sommes bien : tout va bien pour nous.
2. Guigné : surveillé.

SCÈNE 7 : Harpagon

Il crie au voleur dès le jardin, et vient sans chapeau. Au voleur! au voleur! à
1725 l'assassin! au meurtrier! Justice, juste Ciel! je suis perdu, je suis assassiné, on m'a coupé la gorge, on m'a dérobé mon argent. Qui peut-ce
être? Qu'est-il devenu? Où est-il? Où se cache-t-il? Que ferai-je pour
le trouver? Où courir? Où ne pas courir? N'est-il point là? N'est-il
point ici? Qui est-ce? Arrête. Rends-moi mon argent, coquin*… (*Il se
1730 prend lui-même le bras.*) Ah! c'est moi. Mon esprit est troublé, et j'ignore
où je suis, qui je suis, et ce que je fais. Hélas! mon pauvre argent, mon
pauvre argent, mon cher ami! on m'a privé de toi; et puisque tu m'es
enlevé, j'ai perdu mon support, ma consolation, ma joie; tout est fini
pour moi, et je n'ai plus que faire au monde: sans toi, il m'est impos-
1735 sible de vivre. C'en est fait, je n'en puis plus; je me meurs, je suis mort,
je suis enterré. N'y a-t-il personne qui veuille me ressusciter, en me
rendant mon cher argent, ou en m'apprenant qui l'a pris? Euh? que
dites-vous? Ce n'est personne. Il faut, qui que ce soit qui ait fait le
coup, qu'avec beaucoup de soin on ait épié l'heure; et l'on a choisi
1740 justement le temps que je parlais à mon traître de fils. Sortons. Je veux
aller quérir* la justice, et faire donner la question[1] à toute la maison :
à servantes, à valets, à fils, à fille, et à moi aussi. Que de gens assem-
blés[2]! Je ne jette mes regards sur personne qui ne me donne des soup-
çons, et tout me semble mon voleur. Eh! de quoi est-ce qu'on parle
1745 là? De celui qui m'a dérobé? Quel bruit fait-on là-haut? Est-ce mon
voleur qui y est? De grâce, si l'on sait des nouvelles de mon voleur, je
supplie que l'on m'en dise. N'est-il point caché là parmi vous? Ils me
regardent tous, et se mettent à rire. Vous verrez qu'ils ont part sans
doute* au vol que l'on m'a fait. Allons vite, des commissaires[3], des
1750 archers[4], des prévôts[5], des juges, des gênes[6], des potences et des bour-
reaux. Je veux faire pendre tout le monde; et si je ne retrouve mon
argent, je me pendrai moi-même après.

---

1. Faire donner la question : soumettre à la torture pour obtenir des aveux.
2. Les spectateurs.
3. Commissaires : officiers de police chargés de l'enquête.
4. Archers : policiers chargés des arrestations.
5. Prévôts : chefs de police.
6. Gênes : instruments de torture.

© Henri Paul.

Cléante (Gabriel Gascon) : Qu'est-ce que c'est ?

La Flèche (Robert Gadouas) : Le trésor de votre père, que j'ai attrapé.

Acte iv, scène 6, lignes 1720 et 1721.

Théâtre du Nouveau Monde, 1951.
Mise en scène de Jean Gascon.

HARPAGON (Luc Durand) : Au voleur ! au voleur ! à l'assassin ! au meurtrier ! Justice, juste Ciel !

ACTE IV, SCÈNE 7, lignes 1724 et 1725.

THÉÂTRE DU NOUVEAU MONDE, 1985.
MISE EN SCÈNE D'OLIVIER REICHENBACH.

128　　L'AVARE,

ACTE V.

SCENE PREMIERE.

HARPAGON, LE COMMISSAIRE, SON CLERC.

LE COMMISSAIRE.

Aissez-moy faire. Ie sçay mon mestier, Dieu mercy. Ce n'est pas d'aujourd'huy que ie me mesle de découurir des vols; & ie voudrois auoir autant de sacs de mille francs, que i'ay fait pendre de personnes.

HARPAGON.

Tous les Magistrats sont interessez à prendre cette affaire en main; & si l'on ne me fait retrouuer mon argent, ie demanderay justice de la Iustice.

LE COMMISSAIRE.

Il faut faire toutes les poursuites requises. Vous dites qu'il y auoit dans cette Cassette?

HARPAGON.

Dix mille écus bien contez.

LE COMMISSAIRE.

Dix mille écus!

REPRODUCTION DE LA PAGE 128
DE L'ÉDITION ORIGINALE DE 1669.

ACTE V

SCÈNE 1 : HARPAGON, LE COMMISSAIRE, SON CLERC

LE COMMISSAIRE : Laissez-moi faire, je sais mon métier, Dieu merci. Ce n'est pas d'aujourd'hui que je me mêle de découvrir des vols ; et
1755 je voudrais avoir autant de sacs de mille francs que j'ai fait pendre de personnes.

HARPAGON : Tous les magistrats sont intéressés à prendre cette affaire en main ; et si l'on ne me fait retrouver mon argent, je demanderai justice de la justice.

1760 LE COMMISSAIRE : Il faut faire toutes les poursuites requises. Vous dites qu'il y avait dans cette cassette*… ?

HARPAGON : Dix mille écus* bien comptés.

LE COMMISSAIRE : Dix mille écus !

HARPAGON : Dix mille écus. *(En pleurant.)*

1765 LE COMMISSAIRE : Le vol est considérable.

HARPAGON : Il n'y a point de supplice assez grand pour l'énormité de ce crime ; et s'il demeure impuni, les choses les plus sacrées ne sont plus en sûreté.

LE COMMISSAIRE : En quelles espèces était cette somme ?

1770 HARPAGON : En bons louis d'or[1] et pistoles bien trébuchantes[2].

LE COMMISSAIRE : Qui soupçonnez-vous de ce vol ?

---

1. Le louis d'or (monnaie française) et la pistole (monnaie d'or espagnole) avaient la même valeur, soit 11 livres ou francs.
2. Trébuchantes : dont le poids d'or fait pencher la balance, appelée trébuchet, puisqu'on leur donnait un léger supplément de poids en prévision de l'usure par frottement.

Harpagon : Tout le monde ; et je veux que vous arrêtiez prisonniers la ville et les faubourgs.

Le Commissaire : Il faut, si vous m'en croyez, n'effaroucher personne,
1775 et tâcher doucement d'attraper quelques preuves, afin de procéder après par la rigueur au recouvrement des deniers qui vous ont été pris.

SCÈNE 2 : Maître Jacques, Harpagon, le Commissaire, son Clerc

Maître Jacques, *au bout du théâtre, en se retournant du côté dont il sort* : Je m'en vais revenir. Qu'on me l'égorge tout à l'heure* ; qu'on me lui fasse griller les pieds, qu'on me le mette dans l'eau bouillante, et qu'on
1780 me le pende au plancher*.

Harpagon, *à maître Jacques* : Qui ? celui qui m'a dérobé ?

Maître Jacques : Je parle d'un cochon de lait que votre intendant me vient d'envoyer, et je veux vous l'accommoder à ma fantaisie.

Harpagon : Il n'est pas question de cela ; et voilà Monsieur, à qui il
1785 faut parler d'autre chose.

Le Commissaire, *à maître Jacques* : Ne vous épouvantez point. Je suis homme à ne vous point scandaliser[1], et les choses iront dans la douceur.

Maître Jacques : Monsieur est de votre souper ?

Le Commissaire : Il faut ici, mon cher ami, ne rien cacher à votre
1790 maître.

Maître Jacques : Ma foi ! Monsieur, je montrerai tout ce que je sais faire, et je vous traiterai du mieux qu'il me sera possible.

Harpagon : Ce n'est pas là l'affaire.

---

1. Scandaliser : causer du tort.

MAÎTRE JACQUES : Si je ne vous fais pas aussi bonne chère* que je
1795 voudrais, c'est la faute de Monsieur notre intendant, qui m'a rogné les
ailes avec les ciseaux de son économie.

HARPAGON : Traître, il s'agit d'autre chose que de souper ; et je veux
que tu me dises des nouvelles de l'argent qu'on m'a pris.

MAÎTRE JACQUES : On vous a pris de l'argent ?

1800 **HARPAGON** : Oui, coquin* ; et je m'en vais te pendre, si tu ne me
le rends.

LE COMMISSAIRE, *à Harpagon* : Mon Dieu ! ne le maltraitez point. Je
vois à sa mine qu'il est honnête homme, et que sans se faire mettre en
prison, il vous découvrira ce que vous voulez savoir. Oui, mon ami, si
1805 vous nous confessez la chose, il ne vous sera fait aucun mal, et vous
serez récompensé comme il faut par votre maître. On lui a pris
aujourd'hui son argent, et il n'est pas que vous ne sachiez[1] quelques
nouvelles de cette affaire.

MAÎTRE JACQUES, *à part* : Voici justement ce qu'il me faut pour me
1810 venger de notre intendant : depuis qu'il est entré céans*, il est le favori,
on n'écoute que ses conseils, et j'ai aussi sur le cœur les coups de
bâton de tantôt.

HARPAGON : Qu'as-tu à ruminer ?

LE COMMISSAIRE, *à Harpagon* : Laissez-le faire : il se prépare à vous
1815 contenter, et je vous ai bien dit qu'il était honnête homme.

MAÎTRE JACQUES : Monsieur, si vous voulez que je vous dise les
choses, je crois que c'est Monsieur votre cher intendant qui a fait
le coup.

HARPAGON : Valère ?

1820 **MAÎTRE JACQUES** : Oui.

HARPAGON : Lui, qui me paraît si fidèle ?

---

1. Il n'est pas que vous sachiez : il n'est pas possible que vous ne sachiez pas.

© Henri Paul.

HARPAGON (Jean Gascon) : Et cette cassette, comment est-elle faite ? Je verrai bien si c'est la mienne.

MAÎTRE JACQUES (Guy Hoffman) : Comment elle est faite ?

LE COMMISSAIRE (Georges Groulx).

ACTE V, SCÈNE 2, lignes 1836 à 1838.

THÉÂTRE DU NOUVEAU MONDE, 1951.
MISE EN SCÈNE DE JEAN GASCON.

Maître Jacques : Lui-même. Je crois que c'est lui qui vous a dérobé.

Harpagon : Et sur quoi le crois-tu ?

Maître Jacques : Sur quoi ?

1825 **Harpagon** : Oui.

Maître Jacques : Je le crois… sur ce que je le crois.

Le Commissaire : Mais il est nécessaire de dire les indices que vous avez.

Harpagon : L'as-tu vu rôder autour du lieu où j'avais mis mon argent ?

1830 **Maître Jacques** : Oui, vraiment. Où était-il votre argent ?

Harpagon : Dans le jardin.

Maître Jacques : Justement : je l'ai vu rôder dans le jardin. Et dans quoi est-ce que cet argent était ?

Harpagon : Dans une cassette*.

1835 **Maître Jacques** : Voilà l'affaire : je lui ai vu une cassette.

Harpagon : Et cette cassette, comment est-elle faite ? Je verrai bien si c'est la mienne.

Maître Jacques : Comment elle est faite ?

Harpagon : Oui.

1840 **Maître Jacques** : Elle est faite… elle est faite comme une cassette.

Le Commissaire : Cela s'entend*. Mais dépeignez-la un peu, pour voir.

Maître Jacques : C'est une grande cassette.

Harpagon : Celle qu'on m'a volée est petite.

Maître Jacques : Eh ! oui, elle est petite, si on le veut prendre par là ;
1845 mais je l'appelle grande pour ce qu'elle contient.

Le Commissaire : Et de quelle couleur est-elle ?

Maître Jacques : De quelle couleur ?

Le Commissaire : Oui.

Maître Jacques : Elle est de couleur… là, d'une certaine couleur…
1850 Ne sauriez-vous m'aider à dire ?

Harpagon : Euh ?

Maître Jacques : N'est-elle pas rouge ?

Harpagon : Non, grise.

Maître Jacques : Eh ! oui, gris-rouge : c'est ce que je voulais dire.

1855 **Harpagon** : Il n'y a point de doute : c'est elle assurément. Écrivez,
Monsieur, écrivez sa déposition. Ciel ! à qui désormais se fier ? Il ne
faut plus jurer de rien ; et je crois après cela que je suis homme à me
voler moi-même.

Maître Jacques, *à Harpagon* : Monsieur, le voici qui revient. Ne lui
1860 allez pas dire au moins que c'est moi qui vous ai découvert cela.

SCÈNE 3 : Valère, Harpagon, le Commissaire, son Clerc, maître Jacques

Harpagon : Approche : viens confesser l'action la plus noire, l'atten-
tat le plus horrible qui jamais ait été commis.

Valère : Que voulez-vous, Monsieur ?

Harpagon : Comment, traître, tu ne rougis pas de ton crime ?

1865 **Valère** : De quel crime voulez-vous donc parler ?

Harpagon : De quel crime je veux parler, infâme ! comme si tu ne
savais pas ce que je veux dire. C'est en vain que tu prétendrais de le
déguiser[1] : l'affaire est découverte, et l'on vient de m'apprendre tout.

---

1. Prétendrais de le déguiser : chercherais à le cacher.

Comment abuser ainsi de ma bonté, et s'introduire exprès chez moi
1870 pour me trahir? pour me jouer un tour de cette nature?

Valère : Monsieur, puisqu'on vous a découvert tout, je ne veux point
chercher de détours et vous nier la chose.

Maître Jacques, *à part* : Oh! oh! aurais-je deviné sans y penser?

Valère : C'était mon dessein de vous en parler, et je voulais attendre
1875 pour cela des conjonctures favorables ; mais puisqu'il est ainsi, je vous
conjure de ne vous point fâcher, et de vouloir entendre mes raisons.

Harpagon : Et quelles belles raisons peux-tu me donner, voleur
infâme?

Valère : Ah! Monsieur, je n'ai pas mérité ces noms. Il est vrai que
1880 j'ai commis une offense envers vous ; mais, après tout, ma faute
est pardonnable.

Harpagon : Comment, pardonnable? Un guet-apens? un assassinat
de la sorte?

Valère : De grâce, ne vous mettez point en colère. Quand vous m'aurez
1885 ouï*, vous verrez que le mal n'est pas si grand que vous le faites.

Harpagon : Le mal n'est pas si grand que je le fais. Quoi? mon sang,
mes entrailles, pendard?

Valère : Votre sang, Monsieur, n'est pas tombé dans de mauvaises
mains. Je suis d'une condition* à ne lui point faire de tort, et il n'y a
1890 rien en tout ceci que je ne puisse bien réparer.

Harpagon : C'est bien mon intention, et que tu me restitues ce que
tu m'as ravi.

Valère : Votre honneur, Monsieur, sera pleinement satisfait.

Harpagon : Il n'est pas question d'honneur là-dedans. Mais, dis-moi,
1895 qui t'a porté à cette action?

Valère : Hélas! me le demandez-vous?

Harpagon : Oui, vraiment, je te le demande.

Valère : Un dieu qui porte les excuses de tout ce qu'il fait faire : l'Amour.

1900 **Harpagon** : L'Amour ?

Valère : Oui.

Harpagon : Bel amour, bel amour, ma foi ! l'amour de mes louis d'or.

Valère : Non, Monsieur, ce ne sont point vos richesses qui m'ont tenté ; ce n'est pas cela qui m'a ébloui, et je proteste de ne prétendre 1905 rien à tous vos biens[1], pourvu que vous me laissiez celui que j'ai.

Harpagon : Non ferai[2], de par tous les diables ! je ne te le laisserai pas. Mais voyez quelle insolence de vouloir retenir le vol qu'il m'a fait !

Valère : Appelez-vous cela un vol ?

Harpagon : Si je l'appelle un vol ? Un trésor comme celui-là !

1910 **Valère** : C'est un trésor, il est vrai, et le plus précieux que vous ayez sans doute* ; mais ce ne sera pas le perdre que de me le laisser. Je vous le demande à genoux, ce trésor plein de charmes ; et pour bien faire, il faut que vous me l'accordiez.

Harpagon : Je n'en ferai rien. Qu'est-ce à dire cela ?

1915 **Valère** : Nous nous sommes promis une foi* mutuelle, et avons fait serment de nous point abandonner.

Harpagon : Le serment est admirable, et la promesse plaisante !

Valère : Oui, nous nous sommes engagés d'être l'un à l'autre à jamais.

Harpagon : Je vous en empêcherai bien, je vous assure.

1920 **Valère** : Rien que la mort ne nous peut séparer.

Harpagon : C'est être bien endiablé après mon argent.

Valère : Je vous ai déjà dit, Monsieur, que ce n'était point l'intérêt qui m'avait poussé à faire ce que j'ai fait. Mon cœur n'a point agi

---

1. Je proteste de ne prétendre rien à tous vos biens : j'affirme que je n'en veux pas à votre argent.
2. Non ferai : je n'en ferai rien.

par les ressorts que vous pensez, et un motif plus noble m'a inspiré
1925 cette résolution.

HARPAGON : Vous verrez que c'est par charité chrétienne qu'il veut
avoir mon bien ; mais j'y donnerai bon ordre ; et la justice, pendard
effronté, me va faire raison[1] de tout.

VALÈRE : Vous en userez comme vous voudrez, et me voilà prêt à souf-
1930 frir toutes les violences qu'il vous plaira ; mais je vous prie de croire,
au moins, que, s'il y a du mal, ce n'est que moi qu'il en faut accuser, et
que votre fille en tout ceci n'est aucunement coupable.

HARPAGON : Je le crois bien, vraiment ; il serait fort étrange que ma
fille eût trempé dans ce crime. Mais je veux ravoir mon affaire, et que
1935 tu me confesses en quel endroit tu me l'as enlevée.

VALÈRE : Moi ? je ne l'ai point enlevée, et elle est encore chez vous.

HARPAGON, *bas, à part* : Ô ma chère cassette* ! (*Haut.*) Elle n'est point
sortie de ma maison ?

VALÈRE : Non, Monsieur.

1940 **HARPAGON** : Hé ! dis-moi donc un peu : tu n'y as point touché ?

VALÈRE : Moi, y toucher ? Ah ! vous lui faites tort, aussi bien qu'à moi ;
et c'est d'une ardeur toute pure et respectueuse que j'ai brûlé pour elle.

HARPAGON, *à part* : Brûlé pour ma cassette !

VALÈRE : J'aimerais mieux mourir que de lui avoir fait paraître aucune
1945 pensée offensante : elle est trop sage et trop honnête pour cela.

HARPAGON, *à part* : Ma cassette trop honnête !

VALÈRE : Tous mes désirs se sont bornés à jouir de sa vue ; et rien de
criminel n'a profané[2] la passion que ses beaux yeux m'ont inspirée.

HARPAGON, *à part* : Les beaux yeux de ma cassette ! Il parle d'elle
1950 comme un amant d'une maîtresse.

---

1. Me va faire raison : va me venger.
2. Profané : avili, dégradé.

Valère : Dame Claude, Monsieur, sait la vérité de cette aventure, et elle vous peut rendre témoignage…

Harpagon : Quoi ? ma servante est complice de l'affaire ?

Valère : Oui, Monsieur, elle a été témoin de notre engagement ; et
1955 c'est après avoir connu l'honnêteté de ma flamme[1], qu'elle m'a aidé à persuader votre fille de me donner sa foi*, et recevoir la mienne.

Harpagon : Eh ? (*À part.*) Est-ce que la peur de la justice le fait extravaguer[2] ? (*À Valère.*) Que nous brouilles-tu ici de ma fille[3] ?

Valère : Je dis, Monsieur, que j'ai eu toutes les peines du monde à
1960 faire consentir sa pudeur à ce que voulait mon amour.

Harpagon : La pudeur de qui ?

Valère : De votre fille ; et c'est seulement depuis hier qu'elle a pu se résoudre à nous signer mutuellement une promesse de mariage.

Harpagon : Ma fille t'a signé une promesse de mariage !

1965 **Valère :** Oui, Monsieur, comme de ma part je lui en ai signé une.

Harpagon : Ô Ciel ! autre disgrâce[4] !

Maître Jacques, *au Commissaire* : Écrivez, Monsieur, écrivez.

Harpagon : Rengrégement[5] de mal ! surcroît de désespoir ! Allons, Monsieur, faites le dû de votre charge[6], et dressez-lui-moi son procès,
1970 comme larron[7], et comme suborneur[8].

Valère : Ce sont des noms qui ne me sont point dus ; et quand on saura qui je suis…

---

1. Flamme : amour (langage précieux).
2. Extravaguer : divaguer.
3. Que nous brouilles-tu ici de ma fille ? : pourquoi nous embrouilles-tu en parlant de ma fille ?
4. Disgrâce : malheur.
5. Rengrégement : augmentation.
6. Le dû de votre charge : votre travail.
7. Larron : voleur.
8. Suborneur : séducteur.

SCÈNE 4 : Élise, Mariane, Frosine, Harpagon, Valère, maître Jacques, le Commissaire, son Clerc

Harpagon : Ah ! fille scélérate ! fille indigne d'un père comme moi ! c'est ainsi que tu pratiques les leçons que je t'ai données ? Tu te laisses
1975 prendre d'amour pour un voleur infâme, et tu lui engages ta foi sans mon consentement ? Mais vous serez trompés[1] l'un et l'autre. (*À Élise.*) Quatre bonnes murailles[2] me répondront de ta conduite ; (*à Valère*) et une bonne potence me fera raison de ton audace.

Valère : Ce ne sera point votre passion[3] qui jugera l'affaire ; et l'on
1980 m'écoutera, au moins, avant que de me condamner.

Harpagon : Je me suis abusé de dire[4] une potence, et tu seras roué tout vif[5].

Élise, *à genoux devant son père* : Ah ! mon père, prenez des sentiments un peu plus humains, je vous prie, et n'allez point pousser les choses
1985 dans les dernières violences du pouvoir paternel. Ne vous laissez point entraîner aux premiers mouvements de votre passion, et donnez-vous le temps de considérer ce que vous voulez faire. Prenez la peine de mieux voir celui dont vous vous offensez[6] : il est tout autre que vos yeux ne le jugent ; et vous trouverez moins étrange que je me sois
1990 donnée à lui, lorsque vous saurez que sans lui vous ne m'auriez plus il y a longtemps. Oui, mon père, c'est celui qui me sauva de ce grand péril que vous savez que je courus dans l'eau, et à qui vous devez la vie de cette même fille dont…

Harpagon : Tout cela n'est rien ; et il valait bien mieux pour moi qu'il
1995 te laissât noyer que de faire ce qu'il a fait.

---

1. Trompés : déçus.
2. Harpagon songe à faire enfermer sa fille dans un couvent. La loi lui en donne le droit.
3. Passion : colère.
4. Abusé de dire : trompé en disant.
5. Roué tout vif : condamné au supplice de la roue, sur laquelle on laissait mourir le condamné à qui l'on avait brisé les membres.
6. Dont vous vous offensez : qui, selon vous, vous offense.

ÉLISE: Mon père, je vous conjure, par l'amour paternel, de me…

HARPAGON: Non, non, je ne veux rien entendre ; et il faut que la justice fasse son devoir.

MAÎTRE JACQUES, *à part* : Tu me payeras mes coups de bâton.

2000 **FROSINE**, *à part* : Voici un étrange embarras[1].

SCÈNE 5 : ANSELME, HARPAGON, ÉLISE, MARIANE, FROSINE, VALÈRE, MAÎTRE JACQUES, LE COMMISSAIRE, SON CLERC

ANSELME: Qu'est-ce, seigneur* Harpagon ? je vous vois tout ému.

HARPAGON: Ah ! seigneur Anselme, vous me voyez le plus infortuné de tous les hommes ; et voici bien du trouble et du désordre au contrat que vous venez faire ! On m'assassine dans le bien, on m'assassine dans
2005 l'honneur[2] ; et voilà un traître, un scélérat, qui a violé tous les droits les plus saints, qui s'est coulé[3] chez moi sous le titre de domestique, pour me dérober mon argent et pour me suborner[4] ma fille.

VALÈRE: Qui songe à votre argent, dont vous me faites un galimatias[5] ?

HARPAGON: Oui, ils se sont donné l'un et l'autre une promesse de
2010 mariage. Cet affront vous regarde, seigneur Anselme, et c'est vous qui devez vous rendre partie contre lui[6], et faire toutes les poursuites de la justice, pour vous venger de son insolence.

---

1. Embarras : imbroglio, situation compliquée et confuse.
2. On m'assassine dans le bien, on m'assassine dans l'honneur : on vole mon argent, on déshonore ma fille.
3. Coulé : insinué adroitement.
4. Suborner : séduire.
5. Galimatias : discours embrouillé.
6. Vous rendre partie contre lui : l'attaquer en justice. Les frais seraient donc à la charge d'Anselme.

ANSELME : Ce n'est pas mon dessein de me faire épouser par force, et de rien prétendre à un cœur[1] qui se serait donné ; mais pour vos inté-
2015 rêts, je suis prêt à les embrasser ainsi que les miens propres.

HARPAGON : Voilà Monsieur qui est un honnête commissaire, qui n'oubliera rien, à ce qu'il m'a dit, de la fonction de son office. (*Au Commissaire, montrant Valère.*) Chargez-le[2] comme il faut, Monsieur, et rendez les choses bien criminelles.

2020 **VALÈRE** : Je ne vois pas quel crime on me peut faire de la passion que j'ai pour votre fille ; et le supplice où* vous croyez que je puisse être condamné pour notre engagement, lorsqu'on saura ce que je suis…

HARPAGON : Je me moque de tous ces contes ; et le monde aujourd'hui n'est plein que de ces larrons de noblesse[3], que de ces imposteurs, qui
2025 tirent avantage de leur obscurité, et s'habillent insolemment du premier nom illustre qu'ils s'avisent de prendre.

VALÈRE : Sachez que j'ai le cœur trop bon[4] pour me parer de quelque chose qui ne soit point à moi, et que tout Naples peut rendre témoignage de ma naissance.

2030 **ANSELME** : Tout beau[5] ! prenez garde à ce que vous allez dire. Vous risquez ici plus que vous ne pensez ; et vous parlez devant un homme à qui tout Naples est connu, et qui peut aisément voir clair dans l'histoire que vous ferez.

VALÈRE, *en mettant fièrement son chapeau*[6] : Je ne suis point homme à
2035 rien craindre, et si Naples vous est connu, vous savez qui était Dom Thomas d'Alburcy.

ANSELME : Sans doute*, je le sais ; et peu de gens l'ont connu mieux que moi.

---

1. De rien prétendre à un cœur : d'exiger quelque chose d'une personne.
2. Chargez-le : accusez-le.
3. Larrons de noblesse : faux nobles. Ils étaient nombreux.
4. Bon : noble.
5. Tout beau ! : attention !
6. Un gentilhomme garde son chapeau devant un autre gentilhomme.

L'acteur Grandmesnil (1758-1832) dans le rôle d'Harpagon.
À noter la chandelle dans la poche d'Harpagon et,
en arrière-plan, maître Jacques tenant un chandelier.

(Voir la note 2, à la page 111.)

HARPAGON : Je ne me soucie ni de Dom Thomas ni de Dom Martin[1].

2040 (*Harpagon, voyant deux chandelles allumées, en souffle une[2].*)

ANSELME : De grâce, laissez-le parler, nous verrons ce qu'il en veut dire.

VALÈRE : Je veux dire que c'est lui qui m'a donné le jour.

ANSELME : Lui ?

VALÈRE : Oui.

2045 **ANSELME** : Allez ; vous vous moquez. Cherchez quelque autre histoire, qui vous puisse mieux réussir, et ne prétendez pas vous sauver sous cette imposture.

VALÈRE : Songez à mieux parler. Ce n'est point une imposture ; et je n'avance rien qu'il ne me soit aisé de justifier.

2050 **ANSELME** : Quoi ? vous osez vous dire fils de Dom Thomas d'Alburcy ?

VALÈRE : Oui, je l'ose ; et je suis prêt de[3] soutenir cette vérité contre qui que ce soit.

ANSELME : L'audace est merveilleuse. Apprenez, pour vous confondre, qu'il y a seize ans pour le moins que l'homme dont vous nous
2055 parlez périt sur mer avec ses enfants et sa femme, en voulant dérober

---

1. Harpagon feint de croire qu'on parle de moines bénédictins qui eux aussi font précéder leur nom de dom.
2. À cette didascalie de 1682 est rattaché un jeu de scène qui remonte peut-être à l'époque de Molière et que décrit, fin du XVIIIᵉ siècle, l'acteur Grandmesnil (1758-1832) : « Les comédiens ont imaginé le jeu de la bougie pour égayer une scène que le public n'écoute jamais sans quelque impatience. Voici comment ce jeu s'exécute : Harpagon éteint une de ces deux bougies placées sur la table du notaire. À peine a-t-il tourné le dos que maître Jacques la rallume. Harpagon, la voyant brûler de nouveau, s'en empare, l'éteint et la garde dans sa main. Mais pendant qu'il écoute, les deux bras croisés, la conversation d'Anselme et de Valère, maître Jacques passe derrière lui et rallume la bougie. Un instant après, Harpagon décroise les bras, voit la bougie brûler, la souffle et la met dans la poche droite de son haut-de-chausses où maître Jacques ne manque pas de la rallumer une quatrième fois. Enfin la main d'Harpagon rencontre la flamme de la bougie… » (G. Couton, *Molière. Œuvres complètes*, t. II, p. 1396-1397).
3. Prêt de : prêt à.

leur vie[1] aux cruelles persécutions qui ont accompagné les désordres de Naples[2], et qui en firent exiler plusieurs nobles familles.

Valère : Oui ; mais apprenez, pour vous confondre, vous, que son fils, âgé de sept ans, avec un domestique, fut sauvé de ce naufrage par un
2060 vaisseau espagnol, et que ce fils sauvé est celui qui vous parle ; apprenez que le capitaine de ce vaisseau, touché de ma fortune*, prit amitié* pour moi ; qu'il me fit élever comme son propre fils, et que les armes furent mon emploi dès que je m'en trouvai capable ; que j'ai su depuis peu que mon père n'était point mort, comme je l'avais
2065 toujours cru ; que passant ici pour l'aller chercher, une aventure, par le Ciel concertée[3], me fit voir la charmante Élise ; que cette vue me rendit esclave de ses beautés ; et que la violence de mon amour, et les sévérités de son père, me firent prendre la résolution de m'introduire dans son logis, et d'envoyer un autre à la quête de mes parents.

2070 **Anselme** : Mais quels témoignages encore, autres que vos paroles, nous peuvent assurer que ce ne soit point une fable que vous ayez bâtie sur une vérité ?

Valère : Le capitaine espagnol ; un cachet de rubis qui était à mon père ; un bracelet d'agate que ma mère m'avait mis au bras ; le vieux
2075 Pedro, ce domestique qui se sauva avec moi du naufrage.

Mariane : Hélas ! à vos paroles je puis ici répondre, moi, que vous n'imposez point[4] ; et tout ce que vous dites me fait connaître clairement que vous êtes mon frère.

Valère : Vous ma sœur ?

2080 **Mariane** : Oui. Mon cœur s'est ému dès le moment que* vous avez ouvert la bouche ; et notre mère, que vous allez ravir, m'a mille fois entretenue des disgrâces* de notre famille. Le Ciel ne nous fit point aussi[5] périr dans ce triste naufrage ; mais il ne nous sauva la vie que

---

1. Dérober leur vie : échapper.
2. Allusion à la révolte de Masaniello (juillet 1647-avril 1648) contre la domination espagnole, pendant laquelle plusieurs familles nobles napolitaines furent persécutées et s'exilèrent.
3. Concertée : préparée.
4. N'imposez point : ne mentez pas.
5. Aussi : nous non plus.

par la perte de notre liberté ; et ce furent des corsaires qui nous
2085 recueillirent, ma mère et moi, sur un débris de notre vaisseau. Après
dix ans d'esclavage, une heureuse fortune nous rendit notre liberté, et
nous retournâmes dans Naples, où nous trouvâmes tout notre bien
vendu, sans y pouvoir trouver des nouvelles de notre père. Nous
passâmes à Gênes, où ma mère alla ramasser quelques malheureux
2090 restes d'une succession qu'on avait déchirée[1] ; et de là, fuyant la barbare
injustice de ses parents, elle vint en ces lieux, où elle n'a presque vécu
que d'une vie languissante.

ANSELME : Ô Ciel ! quels sont les traits de ta puissance ! et que tu
fais bien voir qu'il n'appartient qu'à toi de faire des miracles !
2095 Embrassez-moi, mes enfants, et mêlez tous deux vos transports[2] à
ceux de votre père.

VALÈRE : Vous êtes notre père ?

MARIANE : C'est vous que ma mère a tant pleuré ?

ANSELME : Oui, ma fille, oui, mon fils, je suis Dom Thomas d'Alburcy,
2100 que le Ciel garantit des ondes[3] avec tout l'argent qu'il portait, et qui
vous ayant tous crus morts durant plus de seize ans, se préparait, après
de longs voyages, à chercher dans l'hymen* d'une douce et sage
personne la consolation de quelque nouvelle famille. Le peu de sûreté[4]
que j'ai vu pour ma vie à retourner à Naples m'a fait y renoncer pour
2105 toujours ; et ayant su trouver moyen d'y faire vendre ce que j'avais, je
me suis habitué[5] ici, où, sous le nom d'Anselme, j'ai voulu m'éloigner[6] les chagrins de cet autre nom qui m'a causé tant de traverses*.

HARPAGON, à Anselme : C'est là votre fils ?

ANSELME : Oui.

---

1. Déchirée : pillée et dispersée.
2. Transports : élans de joie.
3. Garantit des ondes : sauva du naufrage.
4. Sûreté : sécurité.
5. Habitué : installé.
6. M'éloigner : éloigner de moi.

2110 **Harpagon** : Je vous prends à partie[1], pour me payer dix mille écus*
qu'il m'a volés.

Anselme : Lui, vous avoir volé ?

Harpagon : Lui-même.

Valère : Qui vous dit cela ?

2115 **Harpagon** : Maître Jacques.

Valère, *à maître Jacques* : C'est toi qui le dis ?

Maître Jacques : Vous voyez que je ne dis rien.

Harpagon : Oui, voilà Monsieur le Commissaire qui a reçu sa
déposition.

2120 **Valère** : Pouvez-vous me croire capable d'une action si lâche ?

Harpagon : Capable ou non capable, je veux ravoir mon argent.

SCÈNE 6 : Cléante, Valère, Mariane, Élise, Frosine, Harpagon, Anselme, maître Jacques, La Flèche, le Commissaire, son Clerc

Cléante : Ne vous tourmentez point, mon père, et n'accusez
personne. J'ai découvert des nouvelles de votre affaire, et je viens ici
pour vous dire que, si vous voulez vous résoudre à me laisser épouser
2125 Mariane, votre argent vous sera rendu.

Harpagon : Où est-il ?

Cléante : Ne vous en mettez point en peine : il est en lieu dont je
réponds, et tout ne dépend que de moi. C'est à vous de me dire à quoi

---

1. Prends à partie : intente un procès.

vous vous déterminez; et vous pouvez choisir, ou de me donner
2130 Mariane, ou de perdre votre cassette*.

HARPAGON: N'en a-t-on rien ôté?

CLÉANTE: Rien du tout. Voyez si c'est votre dessein de souscrire à ce
mariage, et de joindre votre consentement à celui de sa mère, qui lui
laisse la liberté de faire un choix entre nous deux.

2135 **MARIANE**, *à Cléante*: Mais vous ne savez pas que ce n'est pas assez que
ce consentement, et que le Ciel, (*montrant Valère*) avec un frère que
vous voyez, vient de me rendre (*montrant Anselme*) un père dont vous
avez à m'obtenir.

ANSELME: Le Ciel, mes enfants, ne me redonne point à vous pour être
2140 contraire à vos vœux*. Seigneur* Harpagon, vous jugez bien que le
choix d'une jeune personne tombera sur le fils plutôt que sur le père.
Allons, ne vous faites point dire ce qu'il n'est pas nécessaire d'entendre,
et consentez ainsi que moi à ce double hyménée[1].

HARPAGON: Il faut, pour me donner conseil, que je voie ma cassette.

2145 **CLÉANTE**: Vous la verrez saine[2] et entière.

HARPAGON: Je n'ai point d'argent à donner en mariage à mes enfants.

ANSELME: Hé bien! j'en ai pour eux; que cela ne vous inquiète point.

HARPAGON: Vous obligerez-vous à faire tous les frais de ces deux
mariages?

2150 **ANSELME**: Oui, je m'y oblige; êtes-vous satisfait?

HARPAGON: Oui, pourvu que pour les noces vous me fassiez faire
un habit.

ANSELME: D'accord. Allons jouir de l'allégresse que cet heureux jour
nous présente.

---

1. Hyménée: mariage.
2. Saine: intacte.

J.B. Pocquelin de Molière
Musée des Beaux-Arts, Orléans.

2155   **LE COMMISSAIRE** : Holà ! Messieurs, holà ! tout doucement, s'il vous plaît : qui me payera mes écritures[1] ?

HARPAGON : Nous n'avons que faire de vos écritures.

LE COMMISSAIRE : Oui ! mais je ne prétends pas, moi, les avoir faites pour rien.

2160   **HARPAGON**, *montrant maître Jacques* : Pour votre paiement, voilà un homme que je vous donne à pendre.

MAÎTRE JACQUES : Hélas ! comment faut-il donc faire ? On me donne des coups de bâton pour dire vrai[2], et on me veut pendre pour mentir.

ANSELME : Seigneur* Harpagon, il faut lui pardonner cette imposture.

2165   **HARPAGON** : Vous payerez donc le Commissaire ?

ANSELME : Soit. Allons vite faire part de notre joie à votre mère.

HARPAGON : Et moi, voir ma chère cassette*.

J. B. P. Molière

---

1.   Écritures : dépositions d'Harpagon, de maître Jacques et de Valère que le commissaire a consignées par écrit.
2.   Pour dire vrai : parce que je dis la vérité.

GRAVURE DE J. SAUVÉ D'APRÈS P. BRISSART
POUR L'ÉDITION DE 1682.
LE COSTUME DE CLÉANTE (À GAUCHE) CONTRASTE AVEC LA
TENUE SIMPLE ET VIEILLOTTE D'HARPAGON (AU CENTRE).

PRÉSENTATION
DE L'ŒUVRE

GRAVURE DE I. SYLVESTRE, QUI ILLUSTRE « LES PLAISIRS DE L'ISLE
ENCHANTÉE » (1664), DIVERTISSEMENTS ROYAUX QUE LOUIS XIV
AVAIT DEMANDÉ À MOLIÈRE D'ANIMER.

MOLIÈRE, SON ÉPOQUE ET SON ŒUVRE
La France en 1668

LA POLITIQUE

En 1668, année de la création de *L'Avare*, Louis XIV (1638-1715) est roi depuis 1654, mais il règne effectivement sur la France depuis seulement sept ans, soit depuis la mort de Mazarin, son ministre. Le souvenir de La Fronde (1648-1652), période durant laquelle les Grands se sont révoltés contre le pouvoir royal et qui a obligé l'enfant qu'il était alors à fuir Paris, l'a marqué. Devenu roi, il consolide la monarchie absolue et surveille étroitement les nobles. Il les occupe grâce aux fastes de la vie de cour. Il leur offre des divertissements dont Molière est l'un des principaux artisans de 1664 à sa mort, en 1673. Louis XIV fait aussi depuis sept ans bâtir Versailles, où il s'installera en 1672 et qui deviendra le symbole de la puissance française au XVIIe siècle.

LA SOCIÉTÉ

En 1668, la société française est très hiérarchisée. Au sommet, le roi règne, détenteur de toute autorité. Immédiatement sous lui, les nobles, dont il s'entoure mais dont il se méfie, détiennent de par leur naissance le monopole des hautes fonctions militaires et ecclésiastiques. Puis vient la bourgeoisie, nouvelle classe sociale à laquelle le roi confie la gestion des affaires de l'État. Colbert (1619-1683), son ministre, en est le prototype. Sous sa gouverne, l'économie française est en pleine expansion. Harpagon fait partie de cette classe émergente que la noblesse méprise.

« L'avarice bourgeoise, en ce temps-là, s'oppose comme un reproche à la prodigalité des aristocrates. Les nobles méprisent les bourgeois, qui sentent la boutique et le comptoir. Les bourgeois se vengent en ruinant les nobles et en les regardant galoper à leur ruine. Harpagon est le représentant forcené de la classe qui amasse, à laquelle Louis XIV donne le pouvoir. En crispant ses doigts sur sa cassette, il essaie de retenir cette puissance que la jeunesse et l'amour lui arrachent[1] . »

En bas de la pyramide sociale se trouve 95 % de la population, à la merci des classes supérieures.

LES IDÉOLOGIES

En 1668, deux partis idéologiques s'affrontent : les libertins et les dévots. Les premiers revendiquent la liberté de pensée, tandis que les seconds souhaitent que tous se conforment aux normes religieuses. Les libertins s'inspirent du vent de liberté qui a soufflé sur la société pendant la Renaissance.

La réforme protestante du XVIe siècle a entraîné une contre-réforme catholique. Dans le but de renouveler le catholicisme, saint Vincent de Paul (1581-1660) se fait l'apôtre de la charité chrétienne auprès des plus démunis, tandis que saint François de Sales (1567-1622) tente de promouvoir la dévotion chez les nobles et les bourgeois. De ce renouveau catholique naît le parti dévot, dont la société secrète, la Compagnie du Saint-Sacrement, lutte pour étendre la mainmise religieuse sur l'ensemble de la société.

Bien que le catholicisme soit la religion de la France, face à un roi jeune qui veut s'amuser, les libertins ont une certaine liberté. Mais à mesure que le roi vieillira, la rigueur catholique représentée par le parti dévot deviendra plus forte.

LA LITTÉRATURE

En 1668, la littérature se plie aux règles du classicisme : imitation des Anciens, les Latins et les Grecs ; primauté de la raison, le « je » est haïssable ; respect des règles, comme la règle des trois unités au théâtre. L'œuvre littéraire doit plaire et instruire tout en se pliant aux critères de vraisemblance — il faut peindre d'après nature — et de bien-séance — il faut respecter la morale. L'écrivain classique n'est guère

---

1. Paul Guth, *Histoire de la littérature française, des origines épiques au siècle des Lumières*, Paris, Fayard, 1967.

contestataire; au contraire, il veut être reconnu par le pouvoir, par le roi, être pensionné et nommé à l'Académie française qu'a fondée Richelieu en 1635.

LE THÉÂTRE

En 1668, à Paris, quatre troupes principales se partagent trois salles. La troupe royale de l'Hôtel de Bourgogne reçoit du roi une pension de 12 000 livres. Spécialisée dans la tragédie, elle prône une diction déclamatoire dont Molière se moque, privilégiant chez ses comédiens une diction plus naturelle. La troupe du roi au Marais n'est pas subventionnée; elle privilégie les pièces à grand déploiement. La troupe du roi au Palais-Royal, dont Molière est le directeur, le metteur en scène et l'auteur attitré, tire sa renommée de la comédie. Molière reçoit 6 000 livres du roi. Il partage sa salle avec la troupe des Italiens, dirigée par Tiberio Fiorelli (1608-1694), et qui défend, en italien, les couleurs de la commedia dell'arte. La troupe de Molière joue les jours « ordinaires », soit les mardi, vendredi et dimanche, tandis que la troupe de Fiorelli occupe les jours « extraordinaires », soit les lundi, mercredi, jeudi et samedi. La troupe de Scaramouche, pseudonyme de Fiorelli, reçoit 16 000 livres du roi.

Des affiches placardées aux carrefours ou encore un comédien qui se fait crieur public, avant le début de la pièce, annoncent les prochains spectacles. Les représentations ont lieu dans l'après-midi, avant la noirceur, pour garantir la sécurité des spectateurs. La salle rectangulaire du Palais-Royal contient 1 500 spectateurs, la plupart debout. Des loges et des galeries accueillent surtout des femmes. Sur la scène, en plus des comédiens, les nobles ont droit à une place assise. L'assistance est bruyante, et les bagarres ne sont pas rares. Quant à l'intransigeance de l'Église envers les comédiens, elle a diminué, d'autant que le roi les reçoit, les pensionne et les apprécie.

Molière

MOLIÈRE CHOISIT LE MÉTIER DE COMÉDIEN

À la première de *L'Avare*, le 9 septembre 1668, Molière, de son vrai nom Jean-Baptiste Poquelin, est célèbre. Il a 46 ans. Il est né en janvier 1622, dans une famille aisée. Son père, Jean Poquelin, tapissier de profession, a acheté en 1631 une charge de tapissier et valet de chambre ordinaire du roi[1]. Après des études chez les jésuites (1636-1640), au collège de Clermont (aujourd'hui lycée Louis-le-Grand), le futur Molière entreprend des études en droit. À la fonction sûre de tapissier du roi que pourrait lui léguer son père, il préfère les aléas du métier de comédien, bien que la profession soit encore mal vue à l'époque. En juin 1643, il fonde, avec Madeleine Béjart, l'Illustre-Théâtre qui veut concurrencer les troupes établies de l'époque, l'Hôtel de Bourgogne et le Marais. Mais la troupe connaît des difficultés financières. Emprisonné quelques jours pour dettes, Molière quitte Paris en 1645, pour la province.

MOLIÈRE PART EN TOURNÉE

Commence alors une tournée de treize années à travers la province française pendant lesquelles Molière apprendra non seulement le métier de comédien, mais aussi celui de metteur en scène, de directeur de troupe et d'auteur. De simple comédien dans la troupe de Dufresne protégée par le duc d'Épernon en 1646, il redevient directeur d'une troupe protégée par le prince de Conti en 1650. De cette époque datent ses premières comédies, dont *L'Étourdi* (1655) et *Le Dépit amoureux* (1656).

MOLIÈRE REVIENT À PARIS

En octobre 1658, la troupe est de retour à Paris, sous la protection de Monsieur, frère du roi. Molière joue devant Louis XIV sa comédie *Le Docteur amoureux* et la tragédie *Nicomède*, de Corneille. Il obtient

---

1. Il a la charge, avec d'autres tapissiers, de la confection et de l'entretien du mobilier
   et des accessoires de la maison du roi.

du roi, à cette occasion, le Petit-Bourbon, salle que la troupe de Molière partage avec les comédiens italiens. Un an plus tard, en 1659, il connaît un premier succès avec sa pièce *Les Précieuses ridicules*, succès confirmé en 1662 avec *L'École des femmes*.

MOLIÈRE LUTTE CONTRE LE PARTI DÉVOT

Parce que Molière s'en est pris, dans sa pièce *Tartuffe* (1664), à l'hypocrisie religieuse, Molière est en butte aux attaques du parti dévot. Malgré la protection du roi qui le pensionne depuis 1662 et qui a fait de sa troupe la troupe du roi en 1665, sa pièce *Dom Juan* est interdite, et *Tartuffe* ne peut être montée qu'en février 1669. Pour arriver à ses fins, le parti dévot non seulement taxe Molière d'irréligion et de libertinage, mais colporte les pires calomnies sur son compte, laissant entre autres sous-entendre qu'Armande Béjart, que Molière a épousée en 1662, n'est pas la sœur de sa complice de toujours, Madeleine Béjart, mais sa fille, et que le père ne serait nul autre que Molière lui-même. Sur Armande Béjart, sa femme, de vingt ans plus jeune que lui, on laisse entendre qu'elle a de multiples amants.

MOLIÈRE DEVIENT CÉLÈBRE

Malgré ces luttes, et aussi à cause d'elles, Molière devient célèbre. À la cour, il est responsable des divertissements royaux et, à la ville, chaque nouvelle pièce est impatiemment attendue. Ses succès sont nombreux, dont *Le Misanthrope* (1666), *Tartuffe* (1669), *Le Bourgeois gentilhomme* (1670), *Les Femmes savantes* (1672), *Le Malade imaginaire* (1673).

Le 17 février 1673, durant la quatrième représentation du *Malade imaginaire*, Molière est pris d'un violent malaise. Ramené chez lui, il meurt. Parce qu'il n'a pas renié sa vie de comédien devant un prêtre, aucun n'ayant voulu l'assister, il n'a, selon les règles ecclésiastiques de l'époque, pas le droit d'être inhumé en terre chrétienne. Après l'intervention du roi auprès de l'archevêque de Paris, Molière est finalement enterré sans grande cérémonie le 21 février 1673 à 21 heures dans le cimetière Saint-Joseph.

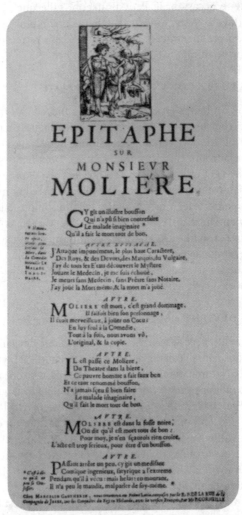

LA MORT DE MOLIÈRE, LE 17 FÉVRIER 1673,
SUSCITE PLUSIEURS RÉACTIONS QUI PRENNENT LA FORME
D'ÉPITAPHES, À LA MODE AU XVIIᵉ SIÈCLE.

L'Avare

Depuis 1664, date à laquelle le roi lui a demandé d'animer «Les plaisirs de l'Isle enchantée, ou les festes et divertissements du Roy» (voir la photo, p. 120), Molière mène une double carrière : plaire à Louis XIV et à sa cour et attirer un public nombreux dans son théâtre, c'est-à-dire depuis 1660 au Palais-Royal. L'année 1668 est chargée pour lui. En janvier, il présente *Amphitryon*, au Palais-Royal. Pour souligner la paix d'Aix-la-Chapelle, il compose *Georges Dandin*, pièce qui est présentée dans le parc de Versailles au «divertissement royal» du 18 juillet. Sa pièce *Tartuffe*, qu'il souhaite monter, est toujours interdite. Il compose donc *L'Avare*. Jouée pour la première fois le 9 septembre 1668, elle n'a guère de succès. Aux dires de Racine, en querelle avec Molière, seul Boileau aurait ri : «Je vous vis dernière-ment à *L'Avare*, et vous riiez tout seul sur le théâtre.» Ce à quoi Boileau, grand ami de Molière, réplique : «Je vous estime trop pour croire que vous n'y ayez pas ri, du moins intérieurement.» Après neuf représentations, Molière retire la pièce. Il la remet à l'affiche en décembre, mais accompagnée d'une farce, *Le Fin Lourdaud*, aujourd'hui disparue.

Plusieurs raisons peuvent expliquer cet échec. Le fait que la pièce soit écrite en prose en serait la première cause. Dans l'esprit du temps, une comédie en cinq actes commande des vers. Bien que Robinet affirme que «nonobstant les goûts divers, / Cette prose est si théâtrale / Qu'en douceur les vers elle égale[1] », elle ne semble pas avoir emporté l'adhé-sion des contemporains. «Comment, disait M. le Duc de X; Molière est-il fou et nous prend-il pour des benêts, de nous faire essuyer cinq actes de prose? A-t-on jamais vu plus d'extravagance? Le moyen d'être diverti par de la prose![2] » De plus, le ton parfois lourd de la pièce, qui montre l'avarice détruisant tout sentiment, toute moralité, était loin de ce à quoi les spectateurs de l'époque s'attendaient en matière de comédie. Le succès de *Tartuffe*, pièce à scandale très attendue, qui prendra l'affiche le 5 février 1669, sonne le glas de *L'Avare*.

---

1. Robinet, *Lettres en vers*, 15 septembre 1668.
2. Grimarest, *Vie de Molière*, 1705.

Ironiquement, le passage du temps va faire de cette mal-aimée du XVIIe siècle, une des pièces de Molière les plus jouées au XXe. Ce succès moderne de *L'Avare* s'explique du fait que sa prose est devenue un atout et que le mélange des genres, du comique et du drame, s'est imposé comme une nécessité. Enfin, l'universalité du sujet lui permet de rester d'actualité.

Les sources

SOURCE 1 : *LA MARMITE [AULULARIA]* DE PLAUTE

Pour écrire *L'Avare*, Molière s'inspire de la comédie latine *La Marmite* de Plaute (v. 195 av. J.-C). La découverte d'une marmite pleine d'or transforme la vie d'Euclion. De peur de se faire voler, il ne cesse de la changer de cachette, jusqu'à ce que l'esclave Strobile la lui vole afin de permettre le mariage du jeune Lyconide avec la fille d'Euclion. Le personnage d'Harpagon, l'histoire de la cassette et la liaison amoureuse entre Élise et Valère sont inspirés de *La Marmite*. Molière a aussi repris certaines scènes ou parties de scènes : l'inspection des mains de La Flèche par Harpagon (ACTE I, SCÈNE 3), la répétition du « sans dot » (ACTE I, SCÈNE 5), l'idée de la collation offerte à Mariane (ACTE III, SCÈNE 7), le monologue désespéré de l'avare dépouillé (ACTE IV, SCÈNE 7), les aveux de Valère sous forme de quiproquo (ACTE V, SCÈNE 3).

Voici le monologue d'Euclion après le vol de sa marmite.

EXTRAIT DE *LA MARMITE*
ACTE IV, SCÈNE 9 [*L'Avare*, ACTE IV, SCÈNE 7]

EUCLION [HARPAGON]
Je suis perdu, je suis assassiné, je suis mort ! où dois-je courir ? où dois-je ne point courir ? Tenez, tenez celui qui m'a volé. Mais qui est-il ? Je ne sais, je ne vois rien, je marche comme un aveugle, et certes je ne saurais dire où je vais, ni où je suis, ni qui je suis. Je vous prie tous tant que vous êtes de me secourir, et de me montrer celui qui me l'a dérobée. Je vous en supplie, je vous en conjure. Ils se cachent sous des habits modestes, sous la blancheur de la craie et se tiennent assis comme des personnes sérieuses. Pour toi, que dis-tu ? Se peut-on fier

à toi ? Car il me semble à voir ton visage que tu es homme de bien. Qu'y a-t-il ? Pourquoi riez-vous ? Je connais tout le monde. Je sais qu'il y a ici beaucoup de voleurs. Quoi, n'y a-t-il personne de tous ceux-là qui l'a prise ? Tu me fais mourir ! Dis donc qui l'a prise ? Ne le sais-tu point ? Ha, je suis ruiné : je suis le plus malheureux de tous les hommes ; je suis au désespoir, et je ne sais où je vais, ni comme je suis fait ; tant cette journée m'apporte de tristesse, de deuil et de maux[1].

Source 2 : *La Belle Plaideuse* de Boisrobert (1655)

Molière n'hésite pas à emprunter également à certaines comédies de son temps. Par exemple, il s'inspire de *La Belle Plaideuse* de Boisrobert pour la scène de l'usure. Un prêteur y oblige un emprunteur à remplacer par des marchandises 12 000 francs sur les 15 000 empruntés.

Extrait de *La Belle Plaideuse*

Acte IV, scène 2 [*L'Avare*, acte II, scène 1]

Ergaste [Cléante]
Où donc est le surplus ?

Filipin [La Flèche]
Je ne sais si je puis vous le conter sans rire :
Il dit que du Cap-Vert il lui vient un navire,
Et fournit le surplus de la somme en guenons
Et fort beaux perroquets, en douze gros canons,
Moitié fer, moitié fonte, et qu'on vend à la livre…

Il tire aussi de *La Belle Plaideuse* l'idée d'un père prêteur ayant son fils comme client.

Acte II, scène 8 [*L'Avare*, acte II, scène 2]

Barquet [maître Simon]
Il sort de mon étude, parlez-lui.

Ergaste [Cléante]
Quoi ! c'est là celui qui fait le prêt ?

Barquet [maître Simon]
Oui, Monsieur.

---

1. Traduction de l'abbé de Marolles (1658), celle-là même que Molière a utilisée.

AMIDOR [HARPAGON]

Quoi ! c'est là ce payeur d'intérêt ?
Quoi ! c'est donc toi, méchant filou, traîne-potence ?
C'est en vain que ton œil évite ma présence :
Je t'ai vu.

ERGASTE [CLÉANTE]

Qui doit être enfin le plus honteux,
Mon père, et qui paraît le plus sot de nous deux ?

SOURCE 3 : LES AVARES DE SON TEMPS

Molière s'est aussi inspiré des avares de son temps. Les plus célèbres sont les époux Tardieu. Tallemant des Réaux (1619-1692) trace
le portrait suivant de madame dont certains traits se retrouvent
chez Harpagon :

« […] il n'y a rien de plus ridicule que de la voir avec une robe
de velours pelé [usé], faite comme on les portait il y a vingt ans,
un collet de même âge, des rubans couleur de feu repassé, et de
vieilles mouches toutes effilochées, jouer du luth et, qui pis est,
aller chez la Reine. Elle n'a point d'enfants ; cependant sa mère,
son mari et elle n'ont pour tous valets qu'un cocher : le carrosse
est si méchant [délabré] et les chevaux aussi qu'ils ne peuvent
aller ; la mère donne l'avoine elle-même ; ils ne mangent pas leur
saoul. Elles vont elles-mêmes à la porte. Une fois que quelqu'un
leur était allé faire visite, elles le prièrent de leur prêter son
laquais, pour mener les chevaux à la rivière, car le cocher avait
pris congé. Pour récompense, elles ont été, un temps à ne vivre
toutes deux que du lait d'une chèvre. Le mari dit qu'il est fâché de
cette mesquinerie : Dieu le sait. Pour lui il dîne toujours au caba-
ret, aux dépens de ceux qui ont affaire de lui, et le soir il ne prend
que deux œufs. Il n'y a guère de gens à Paris plus riches qu'eux. Il
a mérité d'être pendu deux ou trois mille fois : il n'y a pas un plus
grand voleur au monde[1]. »

---

1. Tallemant des Réaux, *Historiettes*, tome I, Paris, Gallimard, coll. Bibliothèque de La Pléiade,
1960, p. 657-658.

**Les éléments constitutifs :
action, temps, lieu, personnages et thèmes**

L'INTRIGUE, L'ACTION

Parmi les règles propres au théâtre classique, l'unité d'action est celle avec laquelle Molière prend le plus de libertés. Il n'y a pas une intrigue dans *L'Avare*, mais plutôt quatre qui s'entremêlent : l'amour entre Élise et Valère, l'amour entre Mariane et Cléante, le mariage projeté entre Mariane et Harpagon et le vol de la cassette d'Harpagon.

> « L'unité d'action, pièce cardinale de la doctrine classique, est traitée par Molière avec une désinvolture préclassique. Bien des scènes de ses pièces sont inutiles à l'intrigue, mais toutes servent à peindre la personnalité du héros. Il y a unité d'intérêt plutôt qu'unité d'action proprement dite. Ainsi *L'Avare*, avec ses quatre intrigues peu unifiées, satisfait mal les théoriciens, mais montre admirablement, dans des domaines distincts, les ravages de l'avarice. Tout converge vers l'intérêt pour le caractère d'Harpagon ; c'est pourquoi l'on appelle parfois la pièce une comédie de caractère[1]. »

Comme l'illustre le tableau sur la structure de l'action, les différentes intrigues peuvent se fondre, surtout lorsque l'opposition entre le père et le fils se fait jour, mais l'ensemble reste assez échevelé, d'autant que Molière, entre faire rire et respecter l'unité d'action, n'hésite pas et privilégie le comique. L'unité de la pièce n'est donc pas dans l'action à proprement parler, mais bien plutôt dans le personnage d'Harpagon.

---

1. Colette et Jacques Scherer, « Le métier d'auteur dramatique », *Le Théâtre en France*, tome I, 1988.

Frontispice de C. Jaulnay, *L'Enfer burlesque*, 1668.
En représailles à *Tartuffe* et à *Dom Juan*, *L'Enfer burlesque*
peint un Molière décharné, enfariné, farceur
grotesquement vêtu entouré d'autres bouffons.

STRUCTURE DE L'ACTION

Acte	Scène	Action	Élise/Valère	Mariane/Cléante	Mariane/Harpagon	Cassette
I	1	Élise et Valère se confirment leur amour.	•			
I	2	Cléante avoue à Élise son amour pour Mariane.		•		
I	3	Harpagon fouille La Flèche.				•
I	4	Harpagon dévoile ses intentions.	•	•	•	
I	5	Valère arbitre le différend Harpagon/Élise.	•			•
II	1	La Flèche présente le contrat à Cléante.		•		
II	2	Prêteur et emprunteur se reconnaissent.		•		
II	3	Frosine arrive.			•	
II	4	La Flèche défie Frosine d'obtenir de l'argent d'Harpagon.			•	
II	5	Frosine flatte Harpagon.			•	
III	1	Harpagon planifie le repas pour la signature du contrat de mariage.			•	
III	2	Valère et maître Jacques s'affrontent.				•
III	3	Frosine et Mariane arrivent.		•	•	
III	4	Mariane avoue ses craintes à Frosine.		•	•	
III	5	Harpagon complimente Mariane.		•	•	
III	6	Harpagon complimente toujours Mariane.		•	•	
III	7	Cléante avoue implicitement son amour à Mariane.		•	•	
III	8	Harpagon est demandé.		•	•	
III	9	Cléante offre la collation à Mariane.		•	•	
IV	1	L'opposition à Harpagon s'organise.		•	•	
IV	2	Harpagon retient son fils.		•	•	
IV	3	Harpagon joue son fils.		•	•	
IV	4	Maître Jacques réconcilie le père et le fils.		•	•	
IV	5	Harpagon et Cléante se brouillent de nouveau.		•	•	
IV	6	La Flèche vole la cassette d'Harpagon.				•
IV	7	Harpagon se désespère.				•
V	1	Le Commissaire commence son enquête.				•
V	2	Maître Jacques accuse Valère.				•
V	3	Valère avoue à Harpagon son amour pour Élise.	•			
V	4	Élise implore son père.	•			
V	5	Mariane, Valère et Anselme se reconnaissent parents.	•	•	•	•
V	6	Cléante fait chanter son père.	•	•	•	•

LE TEMPS, LE LIEU

Pour le temps et le lieu, Molière est plus classique. Il respecte l'unité de temps qui demande que le temps de l'action se rapproche du temps de représentation et qu'il ne dépasse pas une journée. La pièce commence quelque part en après-midi puisque, à la SCÈNE 4 de l'ACTE I, Harpagon affirme que son fils épousera « une certaine veuve dont ce matin on [lui] est venu parler » (l. 406-407). Quant à Élise, elle doit épouser Anselme « dès ce soir » (ACTE I, SCÈNE 4, l. 421) et un souper[1] soulignera l'événement (ACTE III, SCÈNE 1). L'arrivée de Mariane et de Frosine, venues prendre une collation avant d'aller à la foire et de revenir pour le repas, a donc lieu logiquement vers 16 h 30, 17 h (ACTE III, SCÈNE 3). La Flèche vole la cassette à la fin de l'après-midi, vers 18 h. Il affirme en effet qu'il a surveillé la cassette « tout le jour » (ACTE IV, SCÈNE 6, l. 1719). Le retour de la foire d'Élise, de Mariane et de Frosine (ACTE V, SCÈNE 4) et l'arrivée d'Anselme (ACTE V, SCÈNE 5) ont lieu vers 19 h, 19 h 30, puisque le souper est prévu pour 20 h. Le temps de l'action s'étend donc sur quelques heures. En ce qui a trait au temps de la représentation, à l'époque de Molière, il était approximativement de deux heures et demie. Chaque acte, il y en a cinq, durait en effet au maximum trente-cinq minutes, soit la durée des bougies qui éclairaient la scène et qui étaient remplacées entre les actes. Puisque dans L'Avare, les deux temps, celui de l'action et celui de la représentation, se rapprochent, Molière y respecte donc l'unité de temps.

Quant à l'unité de lieu, qui demande que le lieu de l'action soit unique, Molière s'y conforme. Il situe toute l'action dans une pièce d'une maison bourgeoise à Paris. Ainsi, dans L'Avare, la satire de la justice, des femmes, des faux nobles, le portrait de l'avarice sont d'autant plus féroces que, pour les spectateurs parisiens de l'époque, tout cela se passe chez eux, dans leur bonne ville de Paris.

---

1. À l'époque de Molière, souper était encore utilisé pour désigner le repas du soir, vers 20 heures. Cette acception est toujours en usage au Québec, bien que le repas du soir soit plus tôt, vers 18 heures. En France, depuis approximativement 1830, dîner a remplacé souper qui désigne maintenant le repas ou la collation prise après le spectacle ou à une heure avancée de la nuit.

LES PERSONNAGES

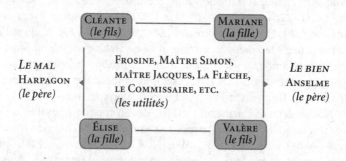

CLÉANTE *(le fils)* ———— MARIANE *(la fille)*

LE MAL HARPAGON *(le père)* ◄ FROSINE, MAÎTRE SIMON, maître JACQUES, LA FLÈCHE, le COMMISSAIRE, ETC. *(les utilités)* ► LE BIEN ANSELME *(le père)*

ÉLISE *(la fille)* ———— VALÈRE *(le fils)*

Les pères : Harpagon et Anselme

Harpagon, dont le nom signifie « rapace » en grec et « grappin » en latin, ne vit qu'en fonction de son vice. Avare au dernier degré, il ne donne rien, garde tout pour lui et fait le malheur de ses enfants, Élise et Cléante. Il veut marier son fils à « une certaine veuve » (ACTE I, SCÈNE 4, l. 406), nécessairement fort riche, et sa fille au seigneur Anselme, parce que ce dernier est « fort accommodé [riche] » et qu'il accepte de l'épouser « sans dot » (ACTE I, SCÈNE 5, l. 462-470). L'amour que sa fille a pour Valère et celui que son fils éprouve pour Mariane ne touchent pas sa fibre paternelle qui ne vibre que lorsque l'argent est en jeu. De plus, son désir de posséder, que l'âge exacerbe, l'a décidé à prendre femme. Grâce à sa richesse, il obtient la main de Mariane malgré ses 60 ans bien sonnés. Même si son fils aime la jeune fille, il se la réserve, du droit du père, du droit du plus riche.

Anselme, le père de Mariane et de Valère, est tout l'opposé. Autant Harpagon s'accroche à garder Mariane, autant Anselme rejette le mariage projeté, dès qu'il apprend qu'Élise ne l'aime pas. Il accepte que ses enfants se marient selon leurs vœux. À l'inverse d'Harpagon, il est de son temps et se conduit en conformité avec sa condition sociale. À la fin de la pièce sa générosité — il accepte même de payer le costume de l'avare — fait ressortir la ladrerie d'Harpagon.

Tout chez Harpagon faisait rire le spectateur à l'époque de Molière. Son habillement, tout de noir, est passé de mode comme le souligne particulièrement la « fraise à l'antique » (voir la photo, p. 95) à la mode cinquante ans auparavant. Son langage est parsemé de termes vieillis en 1668, tels « cache » (ACTE I, SCÈNE 4, l. 271), « damoiseau » (ACTE III, SCÈNE 1, l. 1004), « Rengrégement » (ACTE V, SCÈNE 3, l. 1968). Quand il fait sa cour à Mariane, son discours aussi est archaïque et se rapproche du langage amoureux à la mode avant 1600. Son « belle mignonne » (ACTE III, SCÈNE 5, l. 1252), par exemple, rappelle des poètes comme Joachim du Bellay (1522-1560) ou Pierre de Ronsard (1524-1585).

Non seulement Harpagon n'est pas de son époque, mais il ne tient pas son rang. Il utilise des termes à saveur populaire comme « baillerai » (ACTE I, SCÈNE 3, l. 201), « Ouais ! » (ACTE I, SCÈNE 5, l. 498). Son habillement n'a pas la richesse que son statut social commande. Ainsi, l'avare refuse de remplacer par des rubans, comme l'exigeait la mode, les aiguillettes qui permettent d'attacher la culotte (haut-de-chausses) à la veste (pourpoint). Son train de maison aussi laisse à désirer. Il ne possède que cinq domestiques, ce qui est bien peu, à l'époque, pour la maison d'un riche bourgeois. De plus, pour raisons d'économie, maître Jacques cumule les fonctions de cocher et de cuisinier, et Élise est chaperonnée par une simple servante, dame Claude, plutôt que par une suivante. Harpagon lésine aussi sur la nourriture. Le luxueux repas que souhaite préparer maître Jacques n'est pas anormal chez un riche bourgeois parisien en 1668. Que l'avare préfère un repas plus commun, fort nourrissant, et surtout plus économique, est une autre preuve de sa ladrerie.

Liés à son avarice, deux autres sentiments habitent Harpagon. D'une part, sa suspicion maladive lui fait voir des voleurs partout. Il cherche la troisième main de La Flèche, le fouille (ACTE I, SCÈNE 3), s'imagine même que ses enfants songent à le voler (ACTE I, SCÈNE 4, l. 348-349). Il va régulièrement voir si son argent est toujours bien là. Cela explique qu'il découvre le vol à peine accompli. D'autre part, son égoïsme est insondable. De ses enfants, il sera « bientôt défait et de l'un et de l'autre » (ACTE III, SCÈNE 6, l. 1272), affirme-t-il à Mariane. Il réplique à Élise, qui souligne que Valère lui a sauvé la vie : « Tout cela n'est rien ; et il valait mieux pour moi qu'il te laissât noyer que de faire ce qu'il a fait » (ACTE V, SCÈNE 4, l. 1994-1995). Son égoïsme explique sa naïveté quand il s'agit d'un domaine où l'argent n'entre pas en jeu.

Ainsi, Frosine peut soutenir qu'il est « à ravir » et que sa « figure est à peindre » (ACTE II, SCÈNE 5, l. 915), il gobe tout.

Les jeunes premiers : Valère et Cléante

Valère et Cléante, les jeunes premiers, diffèrent l'un de l'autre. Valère est noble, conscient de sa supériorité de classe. Même s'il doit cacher son identité, il s'insurge lorsque maître Jacques parle de lui donner des coups de bâton (ACTE III, SCÈNE 2). À la fin de la pièce, il revendique bien haut son statut social. Sa noblesse transparaît aussi dans ses actions. Il ne craint pas de risquer pour être près d'Élise. Il agit. Il tente d'amadouer le père, sans grand succès faut-il le préciser.

Cléante est fils de bourgeois. Il n'a pas conservé les principes de la première génération de bourgeois, selon lesquels l'argent est un capital à faire fructifier. Au contraire, pour lui, l'argent doit être dépensé, tout spécialement lorsqu'on est jeune. Il joue allègrement et dépense tous ses gains. À l'inverse de son père, il suit la mode. Ainsi, il a sur lui pour 220 livres de perruques et de rubans, soit 670 € ou 1 000 $ (ACTE I, SCÈNE 4). Sa prodigalité s'oppose à l'avarice du père. Il n'a pas l'esprit entreprenant de Valère. Incapable de trouver une solution, il demande l'aide de Frosine et reproche à Mariane de ne rien faire (ACTE IV, SCÈNE 1). Finalement, La Flèche lui offre une solution toute trouvée, mais combien peu morale, faire chanter son père (ACTE V, SCÈNE 6).

Les jeunes premières : Élise et Mariane

Les jeunes premières, Élise, la fille d'Harpagon, et Mariane, qui se révélera la fille d'Anselme, sont elles aussi différentes. La première, derrière une image de fragilité caractéristique des jeunes premières de Molière, est plutôt forte. Elle a signé une promesse de mariage avec Valère sans le consentement de son père et accepte que son amoureux se cache chez elle (ACTE I, SCÈNE 1). Elle tient tête à son père quand ce dernier lui annonce qu'il a décidé de la marier au seigneur Anselme (ACTE I, SCÈNE 4) et, finalement, tente de lui faire entendre raison (ACTE V, SCÈNE 4). Elle paraît d'autant plus forte aux yeux des spectateurs que son frère, Cléante, est faible. Quant à Mariane, si elle a accepté d'épouser Harpagon, c'est pour sortir de la misère, pour sauver sa mère. Son amour pour Cléante la place dans un dilemme, que seule la découverte providentielle de son père derrière l'identité d'Anselme viendra régler.

Les utilités : Frosine, La Flèche, maître Jacques, le Commissaire

Frosine, La Flèche, maître Jacques et le Commissaire servent de faire-valoir aux autres personnages, tout spécialement à Harpagon. Frosine fait ressortir la naïveté d'Harpagon (ACTE II, SCÈNE 5) ; La Flèche, sa suspicion maladive (ACTE I, SCÈNE 3) ; maître Jacques, sa pingrerie domestique (ACTE III, SCÈNE 1).

LES THÈMES

L'argent

Au XVIIe siècle, le système monétaire est assez complexe. L'écu d'argent vaut 3 livres ou 3 francs ; l'écu d'or, 10 livres ou 10 francs ; la pistole et le louis d'or, 11 livres ou 11 francs ; la livre ou le franc valent 20 sols ou sous ; et un sol, 12 deniers. Les pièces en or sont dites trébuchantes lorsqu'elles font pencher la balance, appelée trébuchet. On leur donnait en effet un léger supplément de poids en prévision de l'usure par frottement. À l'époque, les espèces en or sont devenues rares d'où, chez Harpagon, un attrait supplémentaire pour sa cassette. Les sommes en jeu dans *L'Avare* sont considérables. Les 10 000 écus de la cassette représentent 91 500 € ou 140 000 $, et les 15 000 francs ou livres que veut emprunter Cléante valent approximativement 45 750 € ou 70 000 $. À titre de comparaison, précisons que Molière recevait du roi une pension annuelle de 1 500 livres, qu'un domestique faisait annuellement 100 livres et une servante, 20 livres.

Au XVIIe siècle, l'intérêt sur un prêt se calcule en deniers : au denier 5, par exemple, signifie 1 denier d'intérêt par 5 deniers prêtés. En 1665, Louis XIV promulgue une loi qui n'autorise que des prêts au denier 20, soit à un taux de 5 %. Harpagon pratique donc l'usure, puisqu'il prête à des taux supérieurs, très supérieurs même, à ceux autorisés. Cette pratique est doublement interdite, et par l'Église et par l'État. Pour ce dernier, elle entre en conflit avec le mercantilisme, défendu par Colbert. Ministre des Finances en poste depuis 1665, celui-ci favorise le commerce, la circulation des produits et des capitaux. Le profit engendré par l'usure n'entraîne guère d'activité économique et est perçu comme contre productif.

« En ce temps qui manque de numéraire, l'économiste sage, en accord avec Bossuet, dénonce le mauvais riche. Nuit à la prospérité celui qui dépense mal, et plus encore celui qui ne dépense pas. L'avare est un fléau social. Il renâcle devant les placements utiles que le règne suggère : grandes compagnies de commerce, manufactures privilégiées, ateliers à vaste équipement et abondante main-d'œuvre, commerce de gros auquel la noblesse peut s'adonner sans déroger. En thésaurisant, gardant jalousement sa cassette, il refuse d'animer le marché intérieur. L'Avare est une des pièces de Molière les plus conformes aux vœux économiques et sociaux du temps[1]. »

Dans L'Avare, pour obtenir de l'argent, tous les moyens sont bons, sauf travailler : Harpagon pratique l'usure ; Cléante joue ou emprunte, misant sur la mort prochaine de son père ; Mariane accepte d'épouser un vieillard de 60 ans ; La Flèche dérobe la cassette d'Harpagon. Aucune de ces façons de gagner de l'argent n'est très morale. Molière illustre ainsi le fléau que représente l'avarice qui pervertit tout ce qu'Harpagon touche. Tout son monde, enfants et domestiques, vit dans des conditions difficiles. L'affection du père envers ses enfants se transforme en désir de se débarrasser d'eux le plus rapidement possible, tandis que le fils rêve de la mort de son père.

L'amour

Dans L'Avare, l'amour et l'argent, ces importants ressorts dramatiques, sont intimement liés. Les amours de jeunes gens contrariés par l'autorité des pères est un thème coutumier dans l'œuvre de Molière. À chaque fois, comme c'est le cas ici, le choix des amoureux triomphe du désir des parents. En amour, Molière privilégie la liberté de choix.

Le mariage est avant tout une question monétaire, le désir des enfants y semble bien secondaire. Pour être bonne à marier, une jeune fille doit être financièrement à l'aise. La dot, cette somme d'argent que

---

1. M. Bouvier-Ajam, « Le décor historique, économique et social », Europe, nov.- déc., 1972.

GRAVURE DE CHASSELAT.
DANS *L'AVARE*, TOUS LES MOYENS SONT BONS POUR OBTENIR
DE L'ARGENT, MÊME LE VOL. LA FLÈCHE DÉROBE LA CASSETTE
ET HARPAGON SE DÉSESPÈRE.

fournissent traditionnellement les parents de la future mariée, permet de mesurer le statut social du mari. La supposée dot de Mariane de 12 000 livres (ACTE II, SCÈNE 5), soit 36 600 € ou 55 000 $, est celle à laquelle s'attend un bourgeois. Quant à la supposée marquise ou vicomtesse de Basse-Bretagne, elle apporterait en mariage à Harpagon 100 000 écus (ACTE IV, SCÈNE 1), l'équivalent de 915 000 € ou de 1 400 000 $. Seul un duc pouvait s'attendre à une telle dot de la part de sa future épouse. De plus, aucun notaire sérieux n'aurait accepté une clause qui aurait laissé la somme au mari, ici Harpagon. L'usage voulait en effet que chaque époux garde son bien propre. Le fait montre jusqu'à quel point Frosine compte sur la naïveté d'Harpagon, laquelle est sans fond.

Pour les filles, le mariage est parfois une bouée de sauvetage, comme ce l'est pour Mariane. Au XVIIᵉ siècle, en effet, la meilleure solution pour une jeune fille seule et sans argent est le mariage qui lui permet d'assurer sa subsistance et son existence légale.

À l'époque, le père a tous les droits sur son enfant ; il peut le faire emprisonner sur simple désobéissance. Parce qu'Élise a signé une promesse de mariage sans son consentement, Harpagon veut l'enfermer dans un couvent (ACTE V, SCÈNE 4). Il déshérite Cléante et le maudit parce que ce dernier refuse de lui laisser la place auprès de Mariane (ACTE IV, SCÈNE 5). Les parents ont en effet toute autorité sur le mariage de leurs enfants. Ils décident de leur avenir en dehors de ces derniers, comme l'a fait Harpagon avec les siens. Leur consentement au mariage est obligatoire, jusqu'à l'âge de 30 ans pour les garçons et de 25 pour les filles. À défaut de quoi, ils peuvent le faire casser par un procès. Les enfants ne peuvent donc se marier en cachette. Élise, ayant contracté une promesse de mariage avec Valère, s'inquiète à cause de la valeur légale importante de cet engagement, car un bris de contrat peut donner lieu à des poursuites. Lors de la signature de cette promesse de mariage, la présence de dame Claude, la servante, s'explique par l'obligation qui est faite en droit ecclésiastique d'avoir un témoin. L'amour ne se conçoit pas en dehors des liens du mariage, lequel ne se termine qu'avec la mort de l'un des conjoints, puisque le divorce est interdit. À la rigueur, l'Église permet une « séparation de corps » et l'État, une « séparation de biens ».

Le masque et le théâtre dans le théâtre

La plupart des personnages de la pièce jouent un rôle, se composent un personnage, et font de *L'Avare* du théâtre dans du théâtre. Dès le départ, Valère marque le pas. D'une part, il cache sa véritable identité et joue à l'intendant auprès d'Harpagon afin d'être près d'Élise, celle qu'il aime. D'autre part, pour se faire bien voir du père, il use et abuse de la flatterie. Il porte un « masque de sympathie », se « déguise pour lui plaire », « joue tous les jours avec lui afin d'acquérir sa tendresse » (ACTE I, SCÈNE 1, l. 70-71). Mais le jeu n'est pas sans risque. Par exemple, lorsque Harpagon lui demande d'arbitrer le différend qu'il a avec sa fille, puisqu'il ne peut enlever son masque, il tergiverse, atténue même ses propres objections (ACTE I, SCÈNE 5).

Élise et Cléante aussi portent un masque. Devant leur père, ni Élise ni Cléante n'osent dévoiler l'amour qu'ils portent à Valère pour l'une et à Mariane pour l'autre. Cléante va encore plus loin. Lors de la rencontre avec Mariane, en présence de son père, il joue le rôle de ce dernier : il déclare son amour à Mariane, fait le compliment, offre la collation et le présent (ACTE III, SCÈNE 7).

Quant à maître Jacques, Frosine et La Flèche, tous trois portent un masque. Maître Jacques feint d'être courageux face à Valère (ACTE III, SCÈNE 2) et l'accuse faussement du vol de la cassette (ACTE V, SCÈNE 2). Mais il n'a pas l'art de la fourberie, sa naïveté est trop grande, et chaque fois qu'il feint, la situation se retourne contre lui. La première fois, il reçoit de Valère des coups de bâton (ACTE III, SCÈNE 2), tandis qu'à la seconde, Harpagon le donne à pendre en paiement des écritures du Commissaire (ACTE V, SCÈNE 6). En réalité, même sans masque, la naïveté de maître Jacques fait de lui une victime. Ainsi, il ne récolte que coups de bâton pour avoir dit la vérité à Harpagon (ACTE III, SCÈNE 1). À l'inverse, Frosine, la « femme d'intrigue », excelle dans l'art de « traire les hommes » (ACTE II, SCÈNE 4, l. 763), grâce au masque de la flatterie. Harpagon s'y laisse prendre tant que l'argent n'entre pas en ligne de compte (ACTE II, SCÈNE 5). Lorsqu'elle change de camp, Frosine imagine le scénario de la marquise ou vicomtesse de Basse-Bretagne. Ce scénario digne du théâtre n'aura pas lieu, mais le thème du masque y est bien présent. Quant à La Flèche, il feint la naïveté avec Harpagon (ACTE I, SCÈNE 3) et joue de l'ironie avec

Cléante (ACTE II, SCÈNE 1), cachant dans les deux cas sa véritable opinion sur ses maîtres. Quand il délaisse son masque, il trace à Frosine un portrait décapant d'Harpagon (ACTE II, SCÈNE 4).

Seul Harpagon ne porte pas systématiquement un masque. La raison en est simple : c'est par sa faute que les autres en ont un. Il s'en sert lorsqu'il veut justement que les autres enlèvent le leur. Ainsi, il se fait paternaliste quand il souhaite que maître Jacques lui dise ce que les autres racontent sur lui (ACTE III, SCÈNE 1). Mais dès qu'il le sait, il jette le masque et bat son valet. Il récidive avec son fils. Il feint le bon sens et lui offre d'épouser Mariane (ACTE IV, SCÈNE 3). Mais dès que Cléante jette le masque, il retire le sien, et le conflit entre le père et le fils atteint son paroxysme. Le comique naît de ce qu'au moins un personnage porte un masque. Dès que les deux personnages en présence le retirent, la pièce touche au romanesque, comme c'est le cas dans les deux premières scènes, ou au drame, lorsque Harpagon, le père, et Cléante, le fils, s'affrontent. La pièce se termine quand chaque personnage accepte de se dépouiller de son masque, retrouve sa véritable identité. Seul Harpagon perdure fidèle à lui-même, éternel comme son vice.

PROCÉDÉS DE FABRICATION DU COMIQUE[1]

> « C'est une étrange entreprise que celle de faire rire les honnêtes gens. »
> Molière, *La Critique de l'École des femmes*, SCÈNE 6.

Le comique demande un certain terreau pour naître. D'abord, seul l'humain fait rire. Dans *L'Avare*, ce sont les personnages, leur comportement, ce qui leur arrive qui font rire. Si un objet, par exemple la « fraise à l'antique », fait rire, c'est parce qu'un être humain la porte[2]. Ensuite, seule l'insensibilité permet que le rire éclate. Le spectateur rit d'Harpagon en autant que sa sensibilité ne s'attache pas aux conséquences dramatiques que l'avarice a sur l'entourage de l'avare. En fait, le comique s'adresse à l'intelligence seule[3]. Finalement, le rire éclate en société. Dans ce sens, une comédie est d'autant plus drôle que des spectateurs se rassemblent pour la voir. En somme, le rire naît « quand des hommes réunis en groupe dirige[…]nt toute leur attention sur un d'entre eux, faisant taire leur sensibilité et exerçant leur seule intelligence ».

Deux caractéristiques se retrouvent dans les comiques de forme, de geste, de situation, de mot et de caractère : une raideur et un automatisme, qui contrastent avec la vivacité et la diversité normales de la vie.

Le comique de forme

Selon Bergson, devient « comique toute difformité qu'une personne bien conformée arrive[…] à contrefaire ». Toute raideur physique qui rompt avec la mobilité du corps humain est donc potentiellement drôle.

---

1. Dans le texte de cette section, toutes les citations sont tirées du *Rire, essai de définition* d'Henri Bergson (Paris, Presses universitaires de France, coll. Bibliothèque de philosophie contemporaine, 1972, 157 p.).
2. Si le singe fait rire, c'est qu'il imite l'être humain ou que l'être humain l'imite.
3. Voilà pourquoi personne n'ose rire au salon funéraire de peur de passer pour sans-cœur.

LE CORPS ET LE VISAGE

Peuvent donc faire rire un La Flèche, ce «boiteux-là» (ACTE I, SCÈNE 3, l. 266), qui traîne la jambe, un maître Jacques aux joues et au ventre excessivement rebondis ou un Harpagon grimaçant et au dos voûté. Le travail du metteur en scène consiste à bien choisir la difformité physique du personnage pour qu'il soit le plus risible possible.

LES COSTUMES

Le costume aussi fait partie du comique de forme, puisqu'il est une raideur appliquée sur la fluidité corporelle de l'être humain. Les costumes qui emprisonnent le corps et rendent les personnages plus ou moins difformes font rire. L'être humain donne alors l'impression d'être une chose plus ou moins informe. Le costumier doit donc bien choisir le costume pour rendre les personnages le plus ridicules possible. Les vêtements démodés d'Harpagon et les lunettes qu'il utilise pour mieux voir les «appas» de Mariane (ACTE III, SCÈNE 5, l. 1243) relèvent du comique de forme.

LA VOIX

Une voix traînante ou nasillarde équivaut à une grimace dans l'enveloppe sonore de la voix. La plupart des metteurs en scène donnent à Harpagon une voix particulière dont la «grimace» sonore fait rire le spectateur.

Le comique de geste

«Les attitudes, gestes et mouvements du corps humain sont risibles dans l'exacte mesure où ce corps nous fait penser à une simple mécanique». Les personnages font rire lorsque leurs gestes ne sont plus le reflet de leurs sentiments intérieurs, mais tout simplement une habitude mécanique, un tic. Ainsi, tout au cours de la pièce, la toux répétitive d'Harpagon, parce que devenue mécanique, fait rire. Les révérences à répétition que s'adressent Harpagon et Élise (ACTE I, SCÈNE 4, l. 412-425) relèvent d'un pur automatisme et, à ce titre, elles font rire.

Le comique de situation

Quel que soit le procédé utilisé, à la base, une situation est comique quand elle donne à la fois « l'illusion de la vie et la sensation nette d'un agencement mécanique ».

LE DIABLE À RESSORT (LA BOÎTE À SURPRISE)

L'enfant qui actionne le mécanisme d'une boîte à surprise éclate de rire chaque fois que le diable en surgit brutalement. Il referme la boîte et recommence. Lorsqu'elle reproduit le même mécanisme, une situation est comique.

- Lorsque le diable à ressort est physique, il met aux prises deux personnages, l'un repoussant l'autre, comme dans la scène où maître Jacques repousse systématiquement Valère, alors le diable (ACTE III, SCÈNE 2, l. 1177).
- Lorsque le diable à ressort est psychologique, un sentiment et un discours qui le repousse s'opposent. Par exemple, l'avarice d'Harpagon, le diable, est repoussée par l'énumération que fait maître Jacques des plats qu'il compte servir au repas qui doit marquer la signature du contrat de mariage entre Élise et Anselme (ACTE III, SCÈNE 1, l. 1059-1066). Le mouvement de va-et-vient ainsi créé fait naître le rire.
- Un mot répété est souvent la marque d'un diable à ressort psychologique. Lorsque Harpagon demande à Valère d'arbitrer le différend qui l'oppose à Élise, l'avarice d'Harpagon, le diable, est systématiquement repoussée par l'argumentation de Valère. La répétition du « sans dot » (ACTE I, SCÈNE 5, l. 470, 471, 481, 487, 495, 496) en accentue le rythme.

LE PANTIN À FICELLE (LA MARIONNETTE)

Harpagon qui manipule son fils Cléante afin de lui soutirer l'aveu de son amour pour Mariane (ACTE IV, SCÈNE 3, l. 1507-1569), c'est l'enfant qui joue avec une marionnette. Pour le spectateur, le manipulé fait rire parce qu'il abdique inconsciemment sa liberté. Il fait preuve d'une raideur mécanique devant la vivacité du manipulateur.

Quand Frosine planifie la ruse qui doit détourner Harpagon de Mariane (ACTE IV, SCÈNE 1, l. 1468-1482), le spectateur anticipe la fourberie, la manipulation, et rit.

L'EFFET BOULE DE NEIGE

Il y a effet boule de neige lorsqu'une conséquence est inattendue. Quand Harpagon, le mystérieux prêteur, découvre que Cléante se révèle être le mystérieux emprunteur (ACTE II, SCÈNE 2), le comique naît de l'imprévu de la découverte.

LA RÉPÉTITION

La répétition est une « combinaison de circonstances, qui revient telle quelle à plusieurs reprises ». La SCÈNE 4 de l'ACTE IV, alors que maître Jacques joue le rôle du médiateur, tire son comique de la répétition d'une série de circonstances.

	HARPAGON et MAÎTRE JACQUES	CLÉANTE et MAÎTRE JACQUES
La justification	l. 1608-1615	l. 1617-1630 (jusqu'à « mots »)
La réponse	l. 1630-1639 (jusqu'à « faire »)	l. 1639-1648
L'accord	l. 1649-1651	l. 1652-1654
Le remerciement	l. 1660-1664	l. 1658-1659

L'INVERSION

- Quand « la situation se retourne et que les rôles sont intervertis », le comique naît. C'est le principe de l'arroseur arrosé. La SCÈNE 2 de l'ACTE III fait rire, entre autres, parce que les personnages changent de rôles. Dans un premier temps, maître Jacques joue au courageux et Valère feint d'avoir peur (l. 1167-1184). Puis, dans un second temps, la situation s'inverse et maître Jacques recule devant la colère de Valère (l. 1185-1199). Ici, les deux temps de l'inversion sont présents.

- Parfois, seul le deuxième l'est, le premier étant inutile parce qu'implicite. C'est le principe du monde renversé : l'enfant qui semonce ses parents, le prisonnier qui condamne un juge, un voleur qui se fait dévaliser, etc. Ainsi, quand La Flèche, le valet, sermonne Cléante, son maître (ACTE II, SCÈNE 1, l. 661-664), il y a comique par inversion. Le commentaire est d'autant plus drôle que cette inversion est double du fait que l'allusion à Panurge devrait venir du maître, normalement instruit, plutôt que du valet, normalement peu instruit.

L'INTERFÉRENCE

« Une situation est comique quand elle renvoie en même temps à deux séries d'événements absolument indépendantes, et qu'elle peut s'interpréter à la fois dans deux sens tout différents ».

- Quand une situation est interprétée différemment par deux personnages, il y a quiproquo. Ainsi, à la SCÈNE 2 de l'ACTE V, maître Jacques dit : « Qu'on me l'égorge tout à l'heure [tout de suite] ; qu'on me lui fasse griller les pieds » (l. 1778-1779). Harpagon pense qu'il s'agit possiblement de son voleur alors que maître Jacques parle d'un cochon de lait qu'il prépare pour le souper. L'erreur dans le décodage de la situation crée le quiproquo.

- Quand une situation peut être interprétée de deux façons différentes par le spectateur, il y a interférence. Ainsi, à l'époque de Molière, le spectateur interprétait de deux façons les SCÈNES 5 et 6 de l'ACTE III. Dans le contexte de la pièce (énoncé), le vieillard amoureux d'une jeune fille renvoie aux personnages d'Harpagon et de Mariane. Dans le contexte de l'écriture de la pièce (énonciation), ce barbon qui veut épouser une fille beaucoup plus jeune que lui, c'est Molière et sa femme, Armande Béjart, de vingt ans plus jeune et à qui la rumeur attribuait de nombreux amants. Puisqu'ils jouaient respectivement les rôles d'Harpagon et de Mariane, la double interprétation rendait la scène d'autant plus comique.

Le comique de mot

Le comique de mot procède de la même logique que le comique de situation.

L'INVERSION

* L'inversion consiste à retourner une phrase tout en lui gardant un sens. Ainsi, Cléante réplique en inversant systématiquement les remarques d'Harpagon.

> HARPAGON : Comment, pendard ? c'est toi qui t'abandonnes à ces coupables extrémités ?
>
> CLÉANTE : Comment, mon père ? c'est vous qui vous portez à ces honteuses actions ?
>
> HARPAGON : C'est toi qui te veux ruiner par des emprunts si condamnables ?
>
> CLÉANTE : C'est vous qui cherchez à vous enrichir par des usures si criminelles ?
>
> HARPAGON : Oses-tu bien, après cela, paraître devant moi !
>
> CLÉANTE : Osez-vous bien, après cela, vous présenter aux yeux du monde ?
>
> (ACTE II, SCÈNE 2, l. 705-716).

* Quand Harpagon reprend la maxime de Cicéron sous la forme « *Il faut vivre pour manger, et non pas manger pour vi...* », il inverse les termes et lui garde un sens (ACTE III, SCÈNE 1, l. 1080).

L'AMBIGUÏTÉ

L'ambiguïté consiste à utiliser un mot, un syntagme, une phrase qui renvoie à deux systèmes d'idées.

* Cette ambiguïté vient parfois d'une formulation syntaxiquement et volontairement peu claire. Ainsi, maître Simon affirme à propos de Cléante : « il s'obligera, si vous voulez, que son père mourra avant qu'il soit huit mois » (ACTE II, SCÈNE 2, l. 688-689). La formulation est maladroite. Cléante ne s'engage pas vraiment à ce que son

père meure dans les huit mois, mais à rembourser dans les huit mois puisque son père devrait mourir. La réplique fait rire à cause de l'ambiguïté qu'elle soulève.

- Souvent, l'ambiguïté survient parce que la phrase joue sur la polysémie, c'est-à-dire sur le fait qu'un même mot peut avoir plus d'un sens. Quand Harpagon « donne [s]a malédiction » à son fils, celui-ci lui réplique qu'il n'a « que faire de [ses] dons » (ACTE IV, SCÈNE 5, l. 1710-1711). Alors qu'Harpagon utilise le verbe *donne* dans un sens figuré (« je te donne ma malédiction » = « je te maudis »), Cléante feint de l'entendre dans le sens propre et lui répond qu'il ne veut pas de « dons », de présents.

- Parfois, l'ambiguïté naît de ce que le mot renvoie tout simplement à deux choses. Quand, par exemple, Harpagon parle de son « trésor » (ACTE V, SCÈNE 3, l. 1909), l'ambiguïté vient de ce que le terme renvoie à sa cassette pour Harpagon et à Élise pour Valère.

LA TRANSPOSITION

Le procédé consiste à transposer une idée dans un ton autre que le ton normal. Les possibilités sont innombrables, ce qui explique que le procédé est largement utilisé.

- La transposition sur la valeur consiste à valoriser quelque chose qui l'est peu, ou l'inverse. Ainsi, Valère valorise ses capacités de flatteur (ACTE I, SCÈNE 1, l. 67-82) au détriment du flatté. Pour ce faire, il utilise, entre autres, le champ lexical du théâtre : « masque », « déguise », « joue ». Moralement douteux, flatter devient un art.

- La parodie est une imitation moqueuse ou burlesque du ton, des paroles et des idées de quelqu'un. Quand Harpagon, aux SCÈNES 5 et 6 de l'ACTE III, joue à l'amoureux auprès de Mariane, il imite, bien involontairement, l'amoureux transi. Le « un astre, mais un astre le plus bel astre qui soit dans le pays des astres » (l. 1246-1247), les lunettes, son âge, son habillement, tout le rend ridicule dans ce rôle de jeune premier.

- L'ironie consiste à dire le contraire de ce que l'on pense. Quand maître Jacques remercie Harpagon, qui ne lui a rien donné, par la formule « Je vous baise les mains » (ACTE IV, SCÈNE 4, l. 1664), il ne le pense évidemment pas vraiment. À la SCÈNE 2 de l'ACTE II, Harpagon affirme à propos de l'argent qu'il va prêter : « C'est quelque chose que cela. La charité, maître Simon, nous oblige à faire plaisir aux personnes, lorsque nous le pouvons » (l. 690-691). Il va de soi qu'Harpagon n'a aucunement l'intention d'être « charitable ».

- L'humour consiste à traiter d'un sujet sérieux sur un ton léger. Ainsi, Frosine parle du mariage sur un ton pour le moins léger lorsqu'elle affirme à Mariane qui craint d'épouser un vieil homme : « Vous ne l'épousez qu'aux conditions de vous laisser veuve bientôt ; et ce doit être là un des articles du contrat. Il serait bien impertinent de ne pas mourir dans trois mois » (ACTE III, SCÈNE 4, l. 1237-1239).

- La satire consiste à critiquer les vices et les ridicules des individus et des sociétés. Dans son commentaire sur les médecins (ACTE I, SCÈNE 5, l. 515-517), Molière, par l'intermédiaire de Valère, critique le peu de valeur de la médecine de son temps. L'ensemble de la pièce est en fait une satire « de l'avarice et des avaricieux » (ACTE I, SCÈNE 3, l. 228).

- L'utilisation d'un langage technique à une fin autre que celle pour laquelle il a été établi constitue une autre forme de transposition. Ainsi, quand Harpagon traite La Flèche de « maître juré filou » (ACTE I, SCÈNE 3, l. 170), il utilise dans un contexte différent un terme, *maître juré*, qui appartient au langage des professions. Au XVIIe siècle, le maître juré représentait le plus haut niveau hiérarchique qu'un individu pouvait atteindre dans sa profession. Ici, voler devient une profession comme les autres.

Le comique de caractère

Puisque *L'Avare* tire son unité d'Harpagon, le « ladre », le « vilain », le « fesse-mathieu », le comique de caractère y est omniprésent. Ce comique demande trois conditions : un défaut (ou une vertu) poussé à l'extrême, l'insensibilité du personnage et l'insensibilité du spectateur.

© Robert Laliberté.

HARPAGON FOUILLE LA FLÈCHE, LE VALET, PARCE QU'IL SOUPÇONNE TOUJOURS QUE QUELQU'UN VEUT LE VOLER.

LA FLÈCHE (Jean-Marie Moncelet) : Je dis que vous fouillez bien partout, pour voir si je vous ai volé.

HARPAGON (Luc Durand) : C'est ce que je veux faire.
Il fouille dans les poches de La Flèche.

ACTE I, SCÈNE 3, lignes 224 à 227.

THÉÂTRE PROFUSION INC., 1995.
MISE EN SCÈNE DE LUC DURAND.

Un défaut (ou une vertu)

Le personnage est dominé par son vice. Dans *L'Avare*, l'avarice est poussée à l'extrême et régit entièrement Harpagon. Sa pingrerie lui fait chercher tous les moyens possibles et imaginables pour économiser sur son train de vie, comme l'illustre avec drôlerie la scène des préparatifs du repas devant marquer la signature du contrat de mariage entre Élise et Anselme (ACTE III, SCÈNE 1). Il donne sa fille à Anselme parce que celui-ci l'accepte sans dot (ACTE I, SCÈNE 5), il fouille La Flèche, le valet, parce qu'il soupçonne toujours que quelqu'un veut le voler (ACTE I, SCÈNE 3), etc. Toutes ses actions sont fonction de sa ladrerie.

L'insensibilité et l'automatisme du personnage

Le personnage est insensible en ce sens qu'il ne réagit qu'en fonction de son défaut, à un point tel qu'il en devient prévisible. Ainsi, Harpagon aurait dû réagir en fonction de la situation et, après que maître Jacques l'eut raccommodé avec son fils, le dédommager généreusement. Mais non, l'avarice est toujours plus forte, et tout ce qu'il tire de sa poche, c'est un mouchoir. Il est insensible aux autres, à lui-même, à tout ce qui l'entoure. Tout son comportement devient automatique, prévisible pour le spectateur qui sait qu'Harpagon réagira uniquement en fonction de son vice.

L'insensibilité du spectateur

Pour qu'un défaut fasse rire, il ne faut pas qu'il entre en conflit ouvert avec un autre sentiment. Ainsi, *L'Avare* frôle le drame quand Harpagon se retrouve face à son fils, le premier dans le rôle de l'usurier, le second dans le rôle de l'emprunteur. Ici deux sentiments entrent en conflit, l'amour de l'argent et l'amour paternel. À cause de cet état conflictuel, nous quittons presque la comédie. Si le spectateur s'attarde sur l'absence d'amour paternel chez Harpagon, il ne trouvera pas la scène drôle. Pour désamorcer le drame naissant, Molière s'arrange pour qu'après l'entrevue, Harpagon n'y fasse que

RELATION
DE LA FESTE
DE VERSAILLES.

Du dix-huit Iuillet mil six cens soixante-huit.

E Roy ayant accordé la Paix
aux instances de ses Alliez &
aux vœux de toute l'Europe,
& donné des marques d'vne
moderation & d'vne bonté sans
exemple, mesme dans le plus
fort de ses conquestes, ne pensoit plus qu'à
s'appliquer aux affaires de son Royaume, lors
que pour reparer en quelque sorte ce que la
Cour avoit perdu dans le Carnaval pendant

A ij

À L'OCCASION DU « DIVERTISSEMENT ROYAL »
DU 18 JUILLET 1668, MOLIÈRE PRÉSENTE
GEORGES DANDIN DANS LE PARC DE VERSAILLES.

très discrètement allusion : « Mais si vous voulez que je perde le sou-venir de votre dernière fredaine » (ACTE III, SCÈNE 1, l. 1010-1111). Il isole ainsi l'amour qu'éprouve Harpagon pour son argent de l'amour paternel.

Qu'il soit de forme, de geste, de situation, de mot ou de caractère, le comique reste du « mécanique plaqué sur du vivant ». Le rire naît quand une grimace, un geste, une situation, un mot ou un trait de caractère vient limiter la mobilité, la flexibilité, la vivacité du corps humain, de l'esprit humain, de la vie tout simplement.

JUGEMENTS CRITIQUES DE L'ŒUVRE

L'Avare est une de ses pièces [de Molière] où il y a le plus d'intentions et d'effets comiques. [...] Le seul défaut de la pièce est de finir par un roman postiche. [...] Mais, à cette faute près, quoi de mieux conçu que *L'Avare*.

La Harpe, *Lycée ou Cours de littérature ancienne et moderne*, 1799.

Entre toutes les pièces de Molière, *L'Avare*, dans lequel le vice détruit toute la piété qui unit le père et le fils, a une grandeur extraordinaire et est à un haut degré tragique.

Gœthe, *Conversations avec Eckermann*, 1825.

Molière, dans *L'Avare*, n'a pas entendu le moins du monde nous donner Cléante pour un fils vertueux que nous devons approuver aux dépens de son père ; il a voulu seulement opposer l'avarice à la prodigalité, parce que ce sont les deux vices qui, contrastant le plus l'un avec l'autre, peuvent, par cela même, se choquer et se punir le plus efficacement.

Saint-Marc Girardin, *Cours de littérature dramatique,* tome I, 1843.

La peinture de l'avarice se ramène à une suite de numéros de répertoire. Molière ne raisonne pas d'après un caractère, mais d'après des scènes à faire.

P. Brisson, *Molière, sa vie dans ses œuvres*, Gallimard, 1942.

Harpagon s'imagine entouré d'ennemis. Molière a poussé ce trait chez lui jusqu'aux limites de la folie : tout ce qu'il voit, dit-il lui-même, lui semble son voleur. Harpagon joint ainsi l'extrême stylisation de la caricature à la vérité psychologique la plus directe.

P. Bénichou, *Les Morales du Grand Siècle*, Gallimard, 1948.

Ce vieillard [Harpagon], physiquement épuisé, moralement traqué, est un bouffon. Bouffon devant Mariane, bouffon dans ses pauvres colères, bouffon dans sa naïveté lorsqu'il boit les flatteries de Frosine. Ce tyran est seulement ridicule. Il est au plus haut point comique, et dès lors, il devient impossible de prétendre que *L'Avare* doit son caractère de comédie aux seuls lazzis[1] qui viennent se superposer à l'intrigue de fond.

Antoine Adam, *Histoire de la littérature française au XVIIe siècle*,
tome III, Domat, 1952.

L'Avare, écrit hâtivement, sans que Molière ait eu même le temps de le versifier, est précisément instructif par le contraste de sa profondeur psychologique avec sa négligence de métier ; l'étude du vieillard avare et amoureux est de Molière homme de génie ; les plaisanteries faciles, les lazzis sans portée, l'exposition lourde et laborieuse et la langueur du dénouement appartiennent au directeur pressé, que talonne le besoin d'attirer le public et de faire vivre sa troupe.

Félix Gaiffe, *Le Rire et la scène française*, Slatkine Reprints, 1970.

---

1. Intermèdes muets et mimés de la commedia dell'arte qui servaient à briser la monotonie des dialogues.

GRAVURE DE CARS D'APRÈS F. BOUCHER
POUR L'ÉDITION DE 1734.

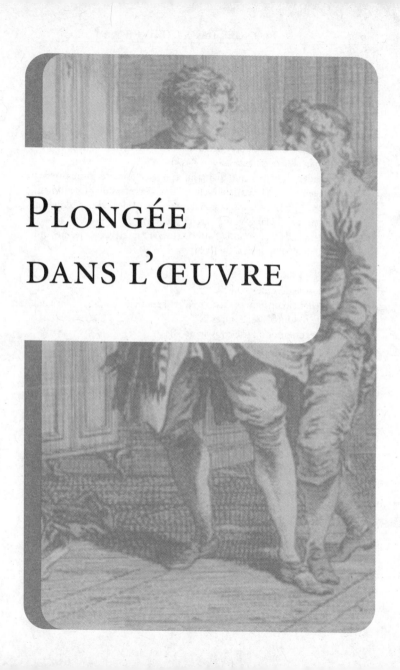

PLONGÉE
DANS L'ŒUVRE

QUESTIONS SUR L'ŒUVRE[1]

ACTE I

ACTE I, SCÈNES 1 ET 2

Compréhension

1. Quels passages des deux premières scènes permettent de comprendre pourquoi la pièce s'intitule *L'Avare* ?
2. En vogue dans les salons mondains au XVIIe siècle, la préciosité privilégie un langage recherché, particulièrement dans l'expression du sentiment amoureux. À partir de la discussion entre Élise et Valère, dégagez quelques caractéristiques du langage amoureux précieux.
3. Dans la tirade de Valère sur la flatterie (l. 67-82), relevez les termes qui renvoient au champ lexical du théâtre.

Action et personnages

1. Où l'action se déroule-t-elle ?
2. Dans quelles circonstances Élise et Valère se sont-ils connus ? Mariane et Cléante se sont-ils rencontrés ?
3. En quoi les craintes d'Élise consistent-elles ?
4. En quoi la tirade de Valère sur la flatterie (l. 67-82) est-elle utile ?
5. Que nous apprend la première tirade que Cléante adresse à sa sœur (l. 98-110) ? À quoi sert-elle sur le plan de l'action ?
6. Comment les trois personnages apparaissent-ils ?
7. Pourquoi pouvons-nous dire qu'il s'agit bien de scènes d'exposition ?
8. En quoi le suspense à la fin des deux scènes consiste-t-il ?

Comique

1. Pourquoi, durant ces deux scènes, Molière insère-t-il si peu d'éléments comiques ?
2. Expliquez le jeu de mots dans la réplique d'Élise « J'en vois beaucoup » (l. 136). Précisez le procédé comique utilisé.
3. À quel procédé du comique de mot la tirade de Valère sur la flatterie (l. 67-82) renvoie-t-elle ?

---

1. Pour toute notion reliée au théâtre (action, dénouement, comédie d'intrigue, scène de reconnaissance, ressort dramatique, théâtre dans le théâtre, règle des trois unités, etc.), référez-vous au « Lexique du théâtre » (p. 186-187).

   Pour toute notion sur le comique, référez-vous à la section « Procédés de fabrication du comique » (p. 144-155).

ACTE I, SCÈNE 3

Compréhension

1. Divisez la scène en deux parties.
2. Quels champs lexicaux Harpagon privilégie-t-il?

Action et personnages

1. Sur le plan de l'action, quelle est l'utilité de la scène? S'agit-il d'une scène d'exposition?
2. « [M]algré l'exemple de Plaute [...], je soutiens, contre Molière, qu'un avare qui n'est point fou ne va jamais jusqu'à vouloir regarder dans la troisième main de l'homme qu'il soupçonne de l'avoir volé » (Fénelon, *Lettre sur les occupations de l'Académie française*, 1716). Sur quel critère du classicisme Fénelon se base-t-il pour juger ainsi cette scène?
3. Dites quel ressort dramatique fait agir chacun des personnages.
4. Qu'est-ce qui chez La Flèche irrite Harpagon?
5. Montrez l'importance des apartés de La Flèche.

Comique

1. Sur quel procédé comique la scène est-elle construite?
2. En examinant attentivement le comportement de La Flèche avec Harpagon, dites quel procédé du comique de situation ressort tout particulièrement.
3. Dans cette scène, quel trait de caractère, lié à l'avarice, se détache particulièrement? Donnez-en deux exemples.
4. À l'aide des didascalies, expliquez en quoi pourrait consister le comique de geste dans cette scène.
5. Expliquez les comiques de mot suivants et dites à quel procédé comique respectif ils renvoient:
   a) « maître juré filou » (l. 170);
   b) « qu'on en eût fait pendre quelqu'un » (l. 218);
   c) « je pourrais bien parler à ta barrette » (l. 244).
6. De quel procédé du comique de mot le dialogue sur l'avarice et les avaricieux (l. 228-242) relève-t-il? Expliquez-en le fonctionnement.

ACTE I, SCÈNE 4, VOIR « EXTRAIT 1 » (P. 172-173)

ACTE I, SCÈNE 5

Compréhension

1. Divisez la scène en trois parties et titrez-les. Quel événement entraîne cette division? Est-il vraisemblable?
2. À l'aide du champ lexical utilisé par chacun, montrez qu'Harpagon et Valère ont des perceptions du mariage fort différentes.

Action et personnages

1. Quel ressort dramatique interne fait agir Harpagon?
2. Décrivez le comportement de Valère. Montrez que le masque qu'il porte le gêne.
3. Par quels arguments Valère tente-t-il de convaincre Harpagon de reconsidérer le mariage projeté entre Élise et Anselme?
4. Relevez les particularités syntaxiques utilisées par Valère pour atténuer, devant Harpagon, ses propres objections au mariage d'Élise avec Anselme.

Comique

1. Décrivez le procédé du comique de situation qui structure la première partie de la scène. Quelle caractéristique stylistique en accentue le rythme?
2. Toujours dans la première partie de la scène, à quel niveau l'inversion se situe-t-elle?
3. Au début de la scène, quel autre procédé du comique de situation Molière utilise-t-il?
4. Expliquez l'effet comique dans l'expression « c'est un gentilhomme qui est noble » (l. 462). Précisez le procédé comique utilisé.
5. Dans la discussion entre Valère et Élise en l'absence d'Harpagon, sur quoi la satire porte-t-elle?
6. Dans la dernière partie de la scène, quel procédé du comique de situation est privilégié?
7. Toujours dans cette dernière partie, de quel procédé du comique de mot les répliques de Valère relèvent-elles? Donnez-en deux exemples.

ACTE II

ACTE II, SCÈNE 1

Compréhension

1. Quel titre donneriez-vous à cette scène?

2. Faites l'inventaire des «hardes» et «nippes» que Cléante doit accepter comme l'équivalent d'une partie du prêt. Pour chacune d'elles, précisez, s'il existe, l'élément qui laisse supposer son peu de valeur. Aidez-vous des notes en bas de page.

3. Déterminez le taux d'intérêt réel que pratique l'usurier. N'oubliez pas de considérer que Cléante «n'aura[…] pas deux cents écus de tout cela» (l. 658), c'est-à-dire des «hardes» et des «nippes» fournies par le prêteur. Ce taux représente combien de fois le taux légal?

Action et personnages

1. Sur le plan de l'action, à quoi les premières répliques servent-elles (l. 549-569)?
2. Pourquoi Cléante veut-il emprunter de l'argent (voir ACTE I, SCÈNE 2)?
3. Comment Cléante apparaît-il dans cette scène?
4. Qu'est-ce qui permet au spectateur de s'imaginer que le prêteur est Harpagon?
5. À quoi le portrait que La Flèche trace de lui-même (l. 668-675) sert-il?
6. Molière, pour cette scène, s'inspire de *La Belle Plaideuse*, de Boisrobert (p. 129-130). Montrez que les changements apportés par Molière visent à se conformer au critère de vraisemblance du classicisme.

Comique

1. Quel procédé du comique de situation est à la base de la scène?
2. Expliquez et situez avec précision le diable à ressort du comique de situation.
3. Le mystère quant à l'identité du prêteur qui, lui-même, ne connaît pas celle de l'emprunteur, renvoie à quel procédé comique?
4. Pourquoi le commentaire de La Flèche sur la situation de Cléante (l. 661-664) fait-il sourire? Quel procédé comique est utilisé?
5. À quel procédé comique le texte du mémoire renvoie-t-il? Justifiez votre réponse.
6. La plupart des répliques de La Flèche lorsqu'il commente le mémoire relèvent du même procédé du comique de mot. Lequel? Donnez-en trois exemples précis.

ACTE II, SCÈNE 2

Compréhension

1. Quel métier Harpagon pratique-t-il? Quel rôle maître Simon y joue-t-il?
2. À l'aide des didascalies qui précisent à qui chacun s'adresse, retracez la structure de la scène.

Action et personnages

1. En quoi le coup de théâtre consiste-t-il?
2. De quoi Harpagon accuse-t-il son fils? De quoi Cléante accuse-t-il son père? Les deux hommes se ressemblent-ils?
3. Expliquez en quoi cette scène fait avancer l'action.
4. Comment le thème du masque apparaît-il dans cette scène?

Comique

1. À quel procédé comique le coup de théâtre renvoie-t-il?
2. Quelle réplique d'Harpagon est particulièrement ironique?
3. Sur quel procédé comique la querelle entre Harpagon et Cléante (l. 705-732) est-elle bâtie? Donnez-en trois exemples précis.
4. Pourquoi la formulation suivante de maître Simon est-elle comique: « il s'obligera, si vous voulez, que son père mourra avant qu'il soit huit mois » (l. 688-689)? Précisez le procédé comique utilisé.
5. De quel comique la dernière réplique qu'Harpagon s'adresse à lui-même relève-t-elle?
6. En vous aidant de la théorie sur le comique de caractère, expliquez pourquoi cette scène frôle le drame.

ACTE II, SCÈNES 3 ET 4

Compréhension

1. Que nous apprend la première réplique de La Flèche (l. 736-738)?

Action et personnages

1. À quoi la SCÈNE 3 sert-elle? Quel ressort dramatique fait agir Harpagon?
2. À quoi la SCÈNE 4 sert-elle?
3. Quel nouveau suspense la SCÈNE 4 suscite-t-elle?

Comique

1. Retracez et expliquez les trois jeux de mots qui font appel à l'ambiguïté dans la SCÈNE 4.
2. À quel niveau le comique de caractère se situe-t-il?

ACTE II, SCÈNE 5, VOIR « EXTRAIT 2 » (P. 173-174)

ACTE III

ACTE III, SCÈNE 1, VOIR « EXTRAIT 3 » (P. 174-176)

ACTE III, SCÈNE 2
Compréhension
1. Divisez cette scène en deux parties et titrez-les.
2. À quel sport vous font penser les mouvements des personnages?

Action et personnages
1. Quel ressort dramatique interne fait agir chacun des personnages?
2. Montrez que, pendant une partie de la scène, chaque personnage joue un rôle, porte un masque.
3. Sur le plan de l'action, à quoi l'aparté final de maître Jacques sert-il?

Comique
1. Sur quel procédé du comique de situation la scène est-elle construite? Décrivez-le.
2. Retracez les deux diables à ressort physiques et décrivez-les. Aidez-vous des didascalies.
3. Expliquez en quoi la réplique suivante de Valère est comique: « Que vous n'êtes pour tout potage, qu'un faquin de cuisinier? » (l. 1191-1192). À quel procédé comique renvoie-t-elle?
4. Pourquoi les coups de bâton que reçoit finalement maître Jacques font-ils rire?

ACTE III, SCÈNES 3, 4, 5 ET 6
Compréhension
1. Pourquoi Harpagon se présente-t-il avec des lunettes à la SCÈNE 5?

Action et personnages
1. À quoi chacune des scènes sert-elle (assurer la transition, faire avancer l'action, approfondir un caractère)?
2. Quel ressort dramatique externe justifie l'arrivée de Frosine et de Mariane?
3. Comment Mariane apparaît-elle?
4. En quoi Frosine et Mariane s'opposent-elles sur leur conception du mariage?
5. Montrez qu'Harpagon porte un masque dans les SCÈNES 5 et 6.

Comique

1. Expliquez les jeux de mots suivants et précisez le procédé comique utilisé :

   a) « mourir agréablement » (l. 1213) ;

   b) « Harpagon n'est pas le supplice que vous voudriez embrasser » (l. 1213-1214) ;

   c) « Je sais que vos appas frappent assez les yeux, sont assez visibles d'eux-mêmes, et qu'il n'est pas besoin de lunettes pour les apercevoir » (l. 1243-1245) ;

   d) « mais enfin c'est avec des lunettes qu'on observe les astres » (l. 1245-1246) ;

   e) « elle est encore toute surprise » (l. 1250).

2. À la SCÈNE 4, de quel procédé du comique de mot les commentaires de Frosine sur le mariage relèvent-ils ?

3. Expliquez comment fonctionnent les interférences du comique de situation dans la SCÈNE 6.

4. Expliquez le procédé du comique de situation qu'implique le jeu de scène décrit à la note 2, p. 73.

5. À quel procédé comique la surprise de Mariane à la vue de Cléante (l. 1268-1269) renvoie-t-elle ?

6. De quel comique relève la réflexion d'Harpagon : « je serai bientôt défait et de l'un et de l'autre » (l. 1272) ?

7. Dans les SCÈNES 5 et 6, en quoi le comique de forme consiste-t-il ?

8. À quel niveau se situe la parodie dans les SCÈNES 5 et 6 ?

9. En vous rappelant que, lors de la création de la pièce en 1668, Molière jouait le rôle d'Harpagon et sa femme, Armande Béjart, celui de Mariane, expliquez pourquoi les SCÈNES 5 et 6 sont un clin d'œil aux spectateurs du temps (voir « Molière lutte contre le parti dévot », p. 125). Précisez le procédé comique employé.

ACTE III, SCÈNE 7, VOIR « EXTRAIT 4 » (P. 176-177)

ACTE III, SCÈNES 8 ET 9

Action et personnages

1. Sur le plan de l'action, expliquez à quoi servent les deux scènes.

Comique

1. D'où le comique vient-il à la SCÈNE 8 ? Précisez le procédé du comique de situation utilisé et montrez qu'il s'appuie sur un comique de mot.

2. Pourquoi Harpagon fait-il rire dans les deux répliques suivantes : « Ah ! je suis mort » (l. 1393) et « Que viens-tu faire ici, bourreau ? » (l. 1400) ? Précisez le procédé comique utilisé.

3. Le comique de caractère ressort particulièrement dans trois répliques de la SCÈNE 9. Retracez-les avec précision et dites quels défauts y sont respectivement poussés à l'extrême.

4. À quel procédé du comique de situation renvoie La Merluche faisant tomber Harpagon ?

5. Pour susciter le rire, sur quel ton Cléante doit-il dire sa réplique « vous êtes-vous fait mal ? » (l. 1394) ?

6. De quel procédé comique relève le fait que Cléante assure son père qu'il fera « les honneurs de [son] logis » (l. 1404) pendant qu'on ferrera les chevaux ?

ACTE IV

ACTE IV, SCÈNE 1

Compréhension

1. Quel moyen Frosine imagine-t-elle pour tirer les jeunes amoureux du pétrin ? Sur quels traits de caractère d'Harpagon mise-t-elle ? Justifiez votre réponse en vous aidant des notes en bas de page.

Action et personnages

1. Cette scène fait-elle progresser l'action ? Justifiez votre réponse.

2. Comment Mariane apparaît-elle ici ?

3. Que reproche Cléante à Mariane ? Quels traits de Cléante ces reproches font-ils ressortir ?

4. Pour quelles raisons Frosine change-t-elle de camp ?

5. Sous quelle forme le thème du masque apparaît-il ?

Comique

1. De quel procédé du comique de situation le tour imaginé par Frosine relève-t-il ?

2. Pourquoi, dans cette scène, Molière insère-t-il si peu d'éléments comiques ?

ACTE IV, SCÈNES 2 ET 3

Compréhension

1. En examinant attentivement le pronom personnel qu'utilise Harpagon pour parler à son fils, dégagez la structure de la SCÈNE 3.

Action et personnages

1. Sur le plan de l'action, à quoi la SCÈNE 2 sert-elle?
2. Retracez les étapes de la manœuvre qu'utilise Harpagon, dans la SCÈNE 3, pour obtenir les aveux de son fils.
3. Quel ressort dramatique interne fait agir le fils? le père?
4. Comparez la réaction de Cléante lorsque Harpagon lui parle de Mariane durant cette scène avec celle de la SCÈNE 4 de l'ACTE I.
5. Montrez que, dans la SCÈNE 3, et le père et le fils portent un masque.

Comique

1. Quel comique de situation structure la première partie de la SCÈNE 3? Expliquez-le.
2. Montrez que l'appréciation que Cléante fait de Mariane au début de la SCÈNE 3 relève de l'inversion du comique de situation.
3. À l'aide de la théorie sur le comique de caractère, expliquez pourquoi la fin de la SCÈNE 3 frôle le drame.
4. Pourquoi, à la SCÈNE 3, porter un masque est-il essentiel au comique?

ACTE IV, SCÈNES 4 ET 5

Compréhension

1. Harpagon laisse-t-il toute liberté à maître Jacques dans son arbitrage?
2. Divisez la SCÈNE 5 en deux parties et titrez-les.

Action et personnages

1. Quel ressort dramatique externe entraîne le changement de situation à la SCÈNE 4?
2. La crise entre le père et le fils atteint ici son paroxysme. Retracez-en les principales étapes depuis le début de la pièce.
3. «C'est un grand vice d'être avare et de prêter à usure; mais n'en est-ce pas un plus grand encore à un fils de voler son père, de lui manquer de respect, de lui faire mille insultants reproches, et quand ce père irrité lui donne sa malédiction, de répondre, d'un air goguenard, qu'il n'a que faire de ses dons? Si la plaisanterie est excellente, en est-elle moins

punissable ? et la pièce où l'on fait aimer le fils insolent qui l'a faite, en est-elle moins une école de mauvaises mœurs ? » (Jean-Jacques Rousseau, *Lettre à d'Alembert sur les spectacles*, 1758). Sur quel critère du classicisme ce jugement de Jean-Jacques Rousseau repose-t-il ?

Comique

1. Expliquez le double diable à ressort au début de la SCÈNE 4 (l. 1594-1604) et montrez qu'il s'appuie sur des caractéristiques stylistiques.
2. Sur quel procédé du comique de situation l'essentiel de la SCÈNE 4 est-il bâti ? Montrez-en les différentes étapes et décrivez les caractéristiques stylistiques qui le renforcent.
3. Le fait que ce soit maître Jacques qui serve de médiateur entre le père et le fils relève de quel procédé comique ?
4. Quand Harpagon tire son mouchoir de sa poche, quel comique ressort, surtout si vous prenez en considération la note 1, p. 90 ?
5. À quel procédé comique renvoie la réplique finale de maître Jacques à la SCÈNE 4 : « Je vous baise les mains » (l. 1664) ?
6. Au début de la SCÈNE 5 (l. 1665-1683), quel procédé comique Molière utilise-t-il ?
7. À quel procédé comique la dernière réplique de la SCÈNE 5 renvoie-t-elle ? Expliquez-le.
8. Pourquoi la dernière partie de la SCÈNE 5 est-elle moins comique (voir « Le comique de caractère », p. 151-155) ?

ACTE IV, SCÈNE 7, VOIR « EXTRAIT 5 » (P. 177-178)

ACTE V

ACTE V, SCÈNES 1 ET 2

Compréhension

1. Décrivez le portrait de la justice que laisse transparaître, dans ces deux scènes, le comportement du Commissaire.
2. Montrez que, dans la SCÈNE 1, Harpagon ne se contrôle plus.

Action et personnages

1. Quel ressort dramatique fait agir maître Jacques ?
2. Qui porte un masque dans la SCÈNE 2 ?
3. Sur quoi le suspense repose-t-il à la fin de la SCÈNE 2 ?

Comique

1. Qu'y a-t-il de comique dans la réaction d'Harpagon à la SCÈNE 1 ? Donnez-en des exemples. À quel procédé du comique de mot cela renvoie-t-il ? En quoi pourrait consister le comique de geste dans cette scène ?

2. De quel procédé comique le portrait de la justice que laisse transparaître le comportement du Commissaire relève-t-il ?

3. Au début de la SCÈNE 2, Molière utilise par deux fois le même procédé comique. Quel est-il ? Délimitez avec précision chacun des deux moments comiques et expliquez-les.

4. Expliquez en quoi consiste le renversement de situation dans la SCÈNE 2.

5. Pourquoi l'accusation de Valère par maître Jacques est-elle comique ? Précisez le procédé comique utilisé.

6. Pourquoi l'interrogatoire de maître Jacques par Harpagon est-il comique ? Quel procédé comique est ici en cause ?

7. Quel défaut de maître Jacques ressort particulièrement dans sa dernière réplique de la SCÈNE 2 (l. 1859-1860) ? À quel type de comique renvoie-t-elle ?

ACTE V, SCÈNES 3 ET 4

Compréhension

1. Relevez les termes utilisés par Harpagon pour désigner le vol de sa cassette.

2. Qu'est-ce que la SCÈNE 4 nous apprend au sujet des relations parents-enfants ?

Action et personnages

1. Quelle est l'utilité de la SCÈNE 3 sur le plan de l'action ?

2. Quel ressort dramatique interne fait agir Harpagon ? Valère ?

3. Montrez que, dans la SCÈNE 3, Valère jette en partie le masque et qu'il se comporte différemment avec Harpagon.

4. En quoi cette scène nourrit-elle le suspense ?

5. À quoi servent les répliques avec lesquelles Valère tente de faire savoir qu'il n'est pas celui qu'on pense ?

6. À la SCÈNE 4, par quels arguments Élise tente-t-elle d'infléchir son père ?

7. Le critère de bienséance est-il respecté dans ces deux scènes ? Justifiez votre réponse.

Comique

1. Sur quel procédé du comique de situation la SCÈNE 3 est-elle construite ? Décrivez-le. Quel mot le déclenche ? À quoi les apartés servent-ils ? Relevez trois mots qui nourrissent le procédé et dites de quel procédé du comique de mot ceux-ci relèvent.

2. En quoi le comique de geste dans la SCÈNE 3 pourrait-il consister ?

3. Pourquoi la remarque d'Harpagon « tu n'y as point touché ? » (l. 1940) fait-elle rire ? Précisez le procédé comique utilisé.

4. Expliquez en quoi la réaction d'Harpagon en début de la SCÈNE 4 relève de la parodie.

5. Dans quelle réplique de la SCÈNE 4 l'égoïsme d'Harpagon est-il poussé à l'extrême ? Quel type de comique est ici en jeu ?

6. À quel procédé du comique de situation l'aveu de Valère renvoie-t-il ?

ACTE V, SCÈNES 5 ET 6

Compréhension

1. Pourquoi Valère met-il son chapeau à la SCÈNE 5 (l. 2034) ?

2. En vous aidant de la donnée historique que recèle la SCÈNE 5, déterminez vers quelles années se passe la pièce. Déduisez-en l'âge de Valère.

Action et personnages

1. Quel ressort dramatique externe justifie l'arrivée d'Anselme ?

2. Relevez les coups de théâtre dans les deux scènes.

3. Expliquez en quoi ces deux scènes sont des scènes de dénouement.

4. Soulignez les éléments qui relèvent du merveilleux dans la SCÈNE 5. Quel critère du classicisme Molière ne respecte-t-il pas ?

5. Comparez les deux pères.

6. Quel est le dilemme d'Harpagon dans la SCÈNE 6 ?

Comique

1. Quels éléments sociaux Molière satirise-t-il ?

2. À quel procédé comique le jeu de scène dit « de la chandelle » renvoie-t-il (voir la ligne 2040 et la note 2, p. 111) ? Décrivez-le.

3. Dans la SCÈNE 6, quelles répliques d'Harpagon relèvent du comique de caractère ?

4. Expliquez en quoi le dénouement, malgré son côté merveilleux, peut faire sourire les spectateurs. Précisez les procédés du comique de situation et du comique de mot en jeu.

p. 24-31

EXTRAIT 1

ACTE I, SCÈNE 4

Compréhension

1. Retracez la structure en trois parties de la scène. Pour chacune, précisez le thème.

2. Pourquoi Harpagon a-t-il caché son argent dans le jardin ? Qu'est-ce que cela laisse supposer de ses activités ?

3. Qu'apprend-on sur le mariage et les jeunes filles dans cette scène ?

Action et personnages

1. Relevez les deux répliques qui montrent que Molière tient compte de l'unité de temps.

2. En quoi le coup de théâtre consiste-t-il ?

3. Expliquez l'importance de la scène sur le plan de l'action, des conflits.

4. Comment Élise et Cléante réagissent-ils à la décision de leur père ? Qu'est-ce que cela nous apprend quant à leur caractère respectif ?

5. Étudiez les ressorts dramatiques qui font agir Harpagon dans chacune des parties de la scène.

6. Pour quelle raison Harpagon veut-il épouser Mariane ? L'aime-t-il ?

7. En quoi le suspense à la fin de la scène consiste-t-il ?

Comique

1. Dans la première partie de la scène, décrivez le diable à ressort.

2. Pourquoi, au début de la scène, après l'arrivée de ses enfants, Harpagon est-il risible ? Quel procédé comique est ici mis de l'avant ?

3. Pourquoi la discussion entre Harpagon et son fils (l. 365-401) à propos de Mariane fait-elle rire ? À quel procédé comique Molière fait-il appel ?

4. Sur quels éléments la satire porte-t-elle dans cette scène ?

5. Quel élément du comique de forme ressort particulièrement lors de la discussion entre Harpagon et Cléante sur les dépenses de ce dernier (l. 324-345) ? Justifiez votre réponse.

6. À quel procédé comique renvoie la réplique d'Harpagon : « Est-ce le mot, ma fille, ou la chose, qui vous fait peur ? » (l. 357-358) ?

7. Précisez les moments dans cette scène où le comique de caractère ressort particulièrement. Dites quel défaut est ici poussé à l'extrême.

8. Dans la dernière partie de la scène, sur quel procédé comique la discussion entre Élise et son père est-elle bâtie ? Donnez-en quatre exemples précis.

9. Toujours dans la dernière partie de la scène, expliquez, à l'aide des didascalies, en quoi consiste le comique de geste.

Sujet d'analyse littéraire

1. Après avoir situé cette scène, montrez que Molière y engage résolument l'action, tout en réussissant à faire amplement rire le spectateur.

---

p. 49-58   **EXTRAIT 2**

ACTE II, SCÈNE 5

Compréhension

1. Précisez qui est exactement chacun des dieux ou héros auxquels Frosine fait allusion.
2. Dans le contexte de la scène, qu'est-ce qu'une femme d'intrigue ?
3. Qu'est-ce que la scène nous apprend sur la vie au féminin au XVIIe siècle ?
4. Le critère de bienséance est-il toujours observé dans cette scène ? Justifiez votre réponse.

Action et personnages

1. Dans son métier de femme d'intrigue, quelle technique Frosine privilégie-t-elle ?
2. Retracez les différentes tentatives de Frosine pour convaincre Harpagon. Pour chacune, précisez si elle réussit. Quelle conclusion pouvez-vous en tirer ?
3. Qui porte un masque dans cette scène ? Pourquoi ?

Comique

1. Quel procédé comique est à la base de la scène ?
2. En début de scène, quand Frosine complimente Harpagon sur sa santé (l. 776-805), quel est le procédé du comique de situation utilisé ? Expliquez-le.
3. Pourquoi le « Tant mieux » (l. 805) d'Harpagon est-il comique ? Précisez le procédé comique utilisé.
4. À quel procédé comique renvoie la tirade de Frosine sur la rente de 12 000 livres (l. 836-852) ?
5. Expliquez les jeux de mots suivants : « vous toucherez assez » (l. 863) et « Il faudra voir cela » (l. 865). Quel est le procédé comique utilisé ?

6. Précisez les moments où le comique de forme ressort particulièrement (voir entre autres la photo, p. 52).

7. En dehors des indications fournies par les didascalies, en quoi le comique de geste pourrait-il consister dans cette scène ?

8. Quand Frosine est-elle particulièrement ironique ? Précisez dans quelles répliques.

9. Montrez que cette scène est à la fois une satire de la jeunesse et de la vieillesse.

10. Quel procédé du comique de situation est utilisé lorsque Frosine tente d'arracher de l'argent à Harpagon ? Décrivez-le. En quoi le comique de geste consiste-t-il ici ?

11. Pourquoi la remarque de Frosine « un amant aiguilletté sera pour elle un ragoût merveilleux » (l. 938-939), fait-elle sourire ? Précisez le procédé comique utilisé.

12. Par rapport à la scène précédente, à quel procédé comique renvoie l'échec de Frosine en ce qui a trait à la somme d'argent qu'elle souhaite obtenir d'Harpagon ?

13. Quels défauts d'Harpagon sont poussés à l'extrême ? Pour chacun d'eux, précisez le moment comique où il ressort particulièrement.

14. En vous rappelant que, lors de la création de la pièce en 1668, Molière jouait le rôle d'Harpagon et sa femme, Armande Béjart, celui de Mariane, expliquez pourquoi cette scène, tout spécialement quand l'avare fait part de ses craintes de « certains petits désordres » (l. 869-870), est un clin d'œil aux spectateurs du temps (voir « Molière lutte contre le parti dévot », p. 125). Précisez le procédé comique employé.

Sujet d'analyse littéraire

1. Montrez que Molière, dans cette scène, obéit aux deux finalités du classicisme : plaire, faire rire puisqu'il s'agit d'une comédie, mais aussi instruire.

p. 59-68   **EXTRAIT 3**

ACTE III, SCÈNE 1

Compréhension

1. Quel titre donneriez-vous à cette scène ?

2. En partant des différents interlocuteurs d'Harpagon, retracez la structure de la scène.

3. Qu'est-ce que cette scène nous apprend sur la vie quotidienne d'une famille bourgeoise au XVIIe siècle ?

Action et personnages

1. Quel ressort dramatique externe justifie cette scène ?
2. À quoi cette scène sert-elle ?
3. Quels traits de caractère dominent chez maître Jacques ?
4. Comparez le comportement de Valère à celui de maître Jacques. Lequel porte un masque ? Pourquoi ?
5. Comment Harpagon se comporte-t-il envers ses domestiques ? ses enfants ?
6. Montrez que cette scène ressemble à une répétition générale au théâtre et qu'à ce titre, elle est du théâtre dans du théâtre (décors, costumes, rôles, etc.).

Comique

1. Le comique de caractère est omniprésent dans cette scène. Quel défaut y est poussé à l'extrême ? Relevez dix traits qui le font particulièrement ressortir.
2. À l'aide du champ lexical utilisé par Harpagon lorsqu'il distribue ses ordres en préparation du souper de mariage, précisez le procédé comique utilisé.
3. Relevez deux répliques de maître Jacques particulièrement ironiques.
4. Harpagon transforme deux maximes. Lesquelles ? À quel procédé comique chacune de ces transformations fait-elle appel ?
5. Situez avec précision le quiproquo et expliquez-le.
6. Expliquez le procédé comique qui structure l'énumération des plats par maître Jacques (l. 1059-1066). Pour ce faire, aidez-vous des didascalies et des notes en bas de page.
7. Expliquez le jeu de mots : « tu manges tout mon bien » (l. 1063-1064). Quel est le procédé comique employé ?
8. De quelle transposition du comique de mot les deux répliques de Valère qui font l'éloge de la frugalité (l. 1067-1071 et l. 1073-1077) relèvent-elles ? Quel champ lexical utilisé par Valère rend la transposition plus probante ?
9. À l'aide de la définition de « coupe-gorge » (l. 1074), montrez qu'il y a ambiguïté.
10. À quel procédé comique renvoie le discours de maître Jacques sur les chevaux (l. 1101-1105, l. 1107-1113 et l. 1115-1118) ?
11. Retracez les deux inversions du comique de mot dans cet extrait.

12. Relevez deux moments où la naïveté de maître Jacques ressort particulièrement et qui relèvent du comique de caractère.

13. Quand Harpagon cherche à convaincre maître Jacques de le mettre au courant de ce qu'on dit de lui, quel procédé comique retrouvons-nous?

14. À quel procédé du comique de situation la fin de cette scène fait-elle appel?

15. De quels types de comique les coups de bâton à la fin de la scène relèvent-ils?

Sujet d'analyse littéraire

1. Évaluez cette scène sur les plans de l'action, du portrait social et du comique.

---

p. 73-78   **EXTRAIT 4**

ACTE III, SCÈNE 7

Compréhension

1. Divisez la scène en deux parties et titrez-les.
2. À partir du comportement de Cléante envers Mariane, déterminez les grandes étapes du code amoureux en usage au temps de Molière.
3. Relevez les caractéristiques stylistiques de la déclaration d'amour de Cléante.
4. Pourquoi la décision de Mariane en ce qui a trait à la bague satisfait-elle et le fils et le père?

Action et personnages

1. Sur le plan de l'action, cette scène est-elle importante? Justifiez votre réponse.
2. Expliquez l'importance des deux premières répliques (l. 1273-1278).
3. Pour chacun des personnages importants de cette scène, précisez quel ressort dramatique interne le fait agir.
4. Expliquez le comportement de Mariane.
5. Comment Cléante apparaît-il par rapport à son comportement antérieur?
6. Quels personnages se cachent derrière un masque dans cette scène?

Comique

1. Quel procédé comique unifie l'ensemble de la scène?

2. Trouvez deux répliques ironiques que Cléante adresse directement à son père.

3. À quel procédé comique la tirade de Cléante (l. 1279-1291) et celle de Mariane (l. 1294-1301) renvoient-elles? Pour chaque tirade, expliquez le procédé avec précision.

4. Situez exactement le double diable à ressort et décrivez-le.

5. Où le comique de geste est-il clairement précisé et en quoi consiste-t-il?

6. Pourquoi Harpagon dépouillé de sa bague fait-il rire? Précisez le procédé comique utilisé.

7. Relevez les moments où le comique de caractère ressort particulièrement.

Sujet d'analyse littéraire

1. Analysez cette scène: la structure et l'importance, les personnages et les ressorts dramatiques, le comique.

| p. 93 | **EXTRAIT 5** |

ACTE IV, SCÈNE 7

Compréhension

1. Divisez le monologue en deux parties et titrez-les.

2. Quand le spectateur a-t-il été mis au courant qu'Harpagon avait caché une cassette contenant 10 000 écus?

3. Quels champs lexicaux sont privilégiés dans le monologue d'Harpagon?

4. Relevez les termes qui personnifient l'argent.

5. Dans le monologue d'Harpagon, par quelles caractéristiques stylistiques les sentiments de l'avare ressortent-ils?

Action et personnages

1. Cherchez, dans la SCÈNE 6, l'indice de temps qui permet de situer temporellement le monologue. Molière respecte-t-il ici l'unité de temps?

2. Expliquez l'importance du vol sur le plan de l'action.

3. Quels ressorts dramatiques interne et externe expliquent cette scène?

4. Quels éléments permettent d'affirmer que la douleur d'Harpagon est si intense qu'il frôle la folie?

5. Montrez que le comportement d'Harpagon change au cours de son monologue.

Comique

1. Dans le monologue d'Harpagon, en quoi le comique de mot consiste-t-il? Précisez le procédé utilisé et les caractéristiques stylistiques qui le renforcent.

2. Expliquez en quoi pourrait consister le comique de geste dans cette scène.

3. À quel procédé comique renvoie le moment où Harpagon s'attrape lui-même?

4. De quel procédé comique l'implication du public relève-t-elle?

5. Pourquoi le fait qu'Harpagon ait été volé fait-il rire? Précisez le procédé comique utilisé.

Sujet d'analyse littéraire

1. Analysez le monologue d'Harpagon. Faites-en ressortir la structure, les caractéristiques stylistiques et lexicales, l'importance sur le plan de l'action, le comique. Comparez-le au monologue d'Euclion dans *La Marmite* de Plaute.

EXTRAIT DE *LA MARMITE*

ACTE IV, SCÈNE 9 [*L'Avare*, ACTE IV, SCÈNE 7]

EUCLION [HARPAGON]

Je suis perdu, je suis assassiné, je suis mort! où dois-je courir? où dois-je ne point courir? Tenez, tenez celui qui m'a volé. Mais qui est-il? Je ne sais, je ne vois rien, je marche comme un aveugle, et certes je ne saurais dire où je vais, ni où je suis, ni qui je suis. Je vous prie tous tant que vous êtes de me secourir, et de me montrer celui qui me l'a dérobée. Je vous en supplie, je vous en conjure. Ils se cachent sous des habits modestes, sous la blancheur de la craie et se tiennent assis comme des personnes sérieuses. Pour toi, que dis-tu? Se peut-on fier à toi? Car il me semble à voir ton visage que tu es homme de bien. Qu'y a-t-il? Pourquoi riez-vous? Je connais tout le monde. Je sais qu'il y a ici beaucoup de voleurs. Quoi, n'y a-t-il personne de tous ceux-là qui l'a prise? Tu me fais mourir! Dis donc qui l'a prise? Ne le sais-tu point? Ha, je suis ruiné: je suis le plus malheureux de tous les hommes; je suis au désespoir, et je ne sais où je vais, ni comme je suis fait; tant cette journée m'apporte de tristesse, de deuil et de maux.

QUESTIONS DE SYNTHÈSE

1. Analysez *L'Avare* de Molière : action, lieu, temps, personnages, thèmes.
2. Faites un tableau des différents procédés comiques utilisés dans *L'Avare* et illustrez-les.
3. Molière défendait la devise *Castignare mores ridendo*, soit « Châtier les mœurs en riant ». Cela s'applique-t-il à *L'Avare* ?
4. Illustrez l'importance du thème du masque dans *L'Avare*.
5. Que nous apprend *L'Avare* sur la bourgeoisie française du XVIIe siècle ?
6. En quoi la pièce *L'Avare* est-elle une comédie d'intrigue, de mœurs et de caractère ?
7. Quelle scène vous semble la plus drôle ? Justifiez votre choix.

MOLIÈRE À 35 ANS.

ANNEXES

TABLEAU CHRONOLOGIQUE

	1617	1622	1632	1633	1635	1636	1637	1638	1642	1643
ÉVÉNEMENTS CULTURELS					Fondation de l'Académie française.	Pierre Corneille, *Le Cid*.	René Descartes, *Discours de la méthode*.			
ÉVÉNEMENTS HISTORIQUES	Début du règne de Louis XIII.		Samuel de Champlain, *Voyages de la Nouvelle-France*, relation de ses voyages de 1603 à 1629.	Abjuration de Galilée devant le tribunal de l'Inquisition : « Et pourtant, elle se meut ! »				Naissance de Louis XIV.	Fondation de Ville-Marie (Montréal).	Mort de Louis XIII ; régence d'Anne d'Autriche ; Mazarin, ministre.
VIE ET ŒUVRE DE MOLIÈRE		Naissance de Jean-Baptiste Poquelin.	Mort de Marie Cressé, sa mère.							Fondation de l'Illustre-Théâtre avec Madeleine Béjart.

	1644	1645	1648	1652	1654	1655	1656	1657	1658	1659	1660	1661
	Premier séjour en France de Tiberio Fiorelli, dit « Scaramouche ».					Boisrobert, *La Belle Plaideuse*.		Tallemant des Réaux commence à écrire ses *Historiettes*.	Traduction de *La Marmite [Aulularia]* de Plaute par l'abbé de Marolles.			
			Début de la Fronde, révolte des Grands contre la royauté.	Fin de la Fronde.	Début du règne de Louis XIV.					Mariage de Louis XIV et de Marie-Thérèse, infante d'Espagne.		Mort de Mazarin ; Louis XIV gouverne seul. Début de la construction de Versailles.
	Jean-Baptiste Poquelin utilise pour la première fois son pseudonyme « Molière ».	Faillite de l'Illustre-Théâtre. Début de la tournée partout en France.				*L'Étourdi*.	*Le Dépit amoureux*.		Retour de Molière à Paris, salle du Petit-Bourbon.	*Les Précieuses ridicules*.	*Sganarelle*.	*Les Fâcheux*, *L'École des maris*. Installation au Palais-Royal.
	1644	1645	1648	1652	1654	1655	1656	1657	1658	1659	1660	1661

TABLEAU CHRONOLOGIQUE

Année	Événements culturels	Événements historiques	Vie et œuvre de Molière
1662			Mariage avec Armande Béjart. *L'École des femmes.*
1663			*L'Impromptu de Versailles.*
1664			*Tartuffe.*
1665			*Dom Juan.*
1666			*Le Misanthrope*, *Le Médecin malgré lui.*
1667	Jean Racine, *Andromaque.*		
1668	Jean de La Fontaine, *Les Fables.*		*Amphitryon*, *George Dandin*, *L'Avare.*
1669			*Tartuffe* est autorisé. *Monsieur de Pourceaugnac.*
1670	Blaise Pascal, *Pensées.*		*Le Bourgeois gentilhomme.*
1671	Début de la correspondance entre Mme de Sévigné et sa fille.		*Psyché*, *Les Fourberies de Scapin*, *La Comtesse d'Escarbagnas.*
1672		Installation de Louis XIV à Versailles.	*Les Femmes savantes*, Mort de Madeleine Béjart.
1673		Fin des *Relations des Jésuites* commencées en 1632.	*Le Malade imaginaire.* Mort de Molière après la quatrième représentation (17 février).

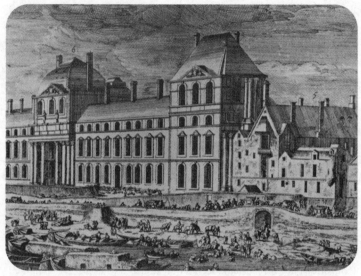

Le Petit-Bourbon (à droite) où Molière joua de 1658 à 1660.
Les représentations y avaient lieu dans l'après-midi, avant
la noirceur, pour garantir la sécurité des spectateurs.

LEXIQUE DU THÉÂTRE

Acte : partie d'une pièce qui se subdivise en scènes. À l'époque de Molière, l'acte dure trente-cinq minutes au maximum, soit la durée des bougies qui éclairent la scène et qui sont remplacées entre les actes.

Action : ce qui se passe sur la scène, ce qu'y font les différents personnages.

Aparté : convention théâtrale selon laquelle certaines paroles d'un personnage ne sont comprises que des spectateurs.

Bienséance : critère selon lequel l'écrivain doit respecter les bonnes mœurs, la morale.

Caractère (comédie de) : comédie qui peint un travers individuel.

Commedia dell'arte (comédie de l'art) : farce à l'italienne.

Conflit : affrontement entre deux personnages ou groupes de personnages.

Coup de théâtre : événement inattendu qui entraîne un rebondissement de l'action, de l'intrigue.

Dénouement : une ou plusieurs scènes, à la fin de la pièce, où les conflits se résolvent, où se dénouent les fils de l'intrigue, de l'action.

Dialogue : ensemble des répliques que s'échangent deux ou plusieurs personnages.

Didascalie : indication relative à la mise en scène et au jeu des acteurs, fournie par l'auteur (ex. : « *Il tire son mouchoir de sa poche* [...] », l. 1662). Ces indications donnent de précieuses informations pour comprendre certains comiques. À noter que la plupart des didascalies de *L'Avare* ont été ajoutées aux éditions publiées après la mort de Molière (1682, 1734).

Exposition : une ou plusieurs scènes qui, au début de la pièce, renseignent le spectateur sur l'objet de l'action, les principaux personnages, le temps et le lieu.

Farce : genre littéraire où les comiques de forme, de geste, de situation ou de mot se retrouvent sous la forme de gags, de coups de bâton, de procédés bouffons, de grosses plaisanteries, de renversements de situation, de péripéties rocambolesques, autres, et dont les personnages-types (le père avare, le valet rusé, etc.) sont facilement reconnaissables par le spectateur.

Intrigue : ensemble des événements qui forment une pièce de théâtre.

Intrigue (comédie d') : comédie qui accumule les situations nouvelles, les coups de théâtre, les quiproquos, les déguisements, les scènes de théâtre dans le théâtre.

Mœurs (comédie de) : comédie qui porte sur le comportement d'un groupe, d'une classe sociale, d'une époque.

Monologue : réplique d'un personnage qui, seul, pense à haute voix.

Reconnaissance (scène de) : scène par laquelle l'identité réelle d'un personnage est dévoilée.

Réplique : réponse d'un personnage à un autre personnage.

Ressort dramatique : élément qui fait avancer l'action. Il est externe s'il s'agit d'un fait, d'un événement, et interne s'il s'agit d'un trait de caractère, d'un sentiment, d'un point de vue d'un personnage.

Scène : partie d'un acte. Dans le théâtre classique, l'entrée ou la sortie d'un personnage entraînent un changement de scène.

Suspense : moment qui éveille chez le spectateur une attente, qui le tient en haleine.

Théâtre dans le théâtre : technique par laquelle une pièce se joue à l'intérieur d'une autre pièce.

Tirade : longue réplique d'un personnage.

Transition (scène de) : courte scène qui fait le lien entre deux autres scènes plus importantes.

Unités (règle des trois) : règle du théâtre classique qui demande que l'action soit unique (action), qu'elle ne dure qu'une journée (temps) et qu'elle se déroule en un seul endroit (lieu).

> Qu'en un lieu, qu'en un jour, un seul fait accompli
> Tienne jusqu'à la fin le théâtre rempli.
> Boileau, *L'Art poétique*, v. 45-46.

Vraisemblance : critère selon lequel l'écrivain doit peindre d'après nature.

GLOSSAIRE DE L'ŒUVRE

Accommodé: riche.

Aiguillette: lacet qui permet d'attacher le haut-de-chausses (culotte) au pourpoint (veste). La mode commandait de la remplacer par un ruban.

Aimable: digne d'être aimé.

Amitié: affection.

Au moins: évidemment.

Aversion: dégoût.

Blondin: qui porte une perruque blonde.

Bonne chère: bon repas.

Çà: ici.

Cassette: petit coffre.

Céans: dans la maison, ici.

Chaleur: passion.

Comme: comment.

Condition: classe sociale.

Coquin, coquine: au XVIIe siècle, terme injurieux.

Courtier: intermédiaire entre le prêteur et l'emprunteur.

D'abord: tout de suite.

Déplaisir: tourment.

Diantre: diable.

Disgrâce: malheur.

Dot: somme d'argent que fournissent traditionnellement les parents de la future mariée. Au XVIIe siècle, le mot est indifféremment masculin ou féminin.

Écu: l'écu d'argent valait 3 livres ou francs; l'écu d'or valait 10 livres ou francs.

Entend (s'): va de soi.

Essuyer: endurer.

Fesse-mathieu: usurier (qui prête à un taux supérieur au taux légal).

Foi: promesse de fidélité en amour.

Fortune: destinée.

Hardes: vêtements (sans nuance péjorative).

Haut-de-chausses: culotte pour homme, s'arrêtant aux genoux et bouffante, à l'époque de Molière.

Hymen: mariage.

Impertinent: déplacé; personne qui se conduit de façon déplacée.

Inclination: goût.

Ladre: avare.

Mémoire: liste.

Où : auquel, à laquelle.
Ouïr : écouter, entendre.
Plancher [de l'étage supérieur] : plafond.
Pourpoint : veste pour homme.
Que : où ; avant que ; autre chose que.
Quérir : chercher.
Rosser : battre.
Sans doute : sans aucun doute.
Seigneur : monsieur (sans référence à la noblesse).
Tour : visite.
Tout à l'heure : tout de suite.
Traverse : obstacle, difficulté.
Usure : prêt à un taux supérieur au taux légal.
Vilain : avare.
Vœux : désirs amoureux.

BIBLIOGRAPHIE

BERGSON, Henri. *Le Rire, essai de définition*, Paris, Presses universitaires de France, coll. Bibliothèque de philosophie contemporaine, 1972.

BRAY, René. *Molière, homme de théâtre*, Paris, Mercure de France, 1992.

CANOVA, Marie-Claude. *La Comédie*, Paris, Hachette, coll. Contours littéraires, 1993.

CONESA, Gabriel. *La Comédie de l'âge classique 1630-1715*, Paris, Seuil, coll. Écrivains de toujours, 1995.

DUCHÊNE, Roger. *Molière*, Paris, Librairie Arthème Fayard, 1998.

Molière. Œuvres complètes, édition par Georges Couton, Paris, Gallimard, coll. Bibliothèque de la Pléiade, 2 vol., 1983.

Molière, une vie pour le théâtre, Paris, Éditions Ilias, 1997 (cédérom).

FILMOGRAPHIE

L'Avare, mise en scène de Jean Girault, 1979, avec Louis de Funès dans le rôle d'Harpagon.

Molière, film réalisé par Ariane Mnouchkine, 1978.

ŒUVRES PARUES

FLOWERS
FOR
THE JUDGE

FLOWERS
FOR
THE JUDGE

Margery Allingham

Carroll & Graf Publishers, Inc.
New York

NOTE:

In criminal trials it is not customary for witnesses to remain in court during that part of the hearing which precedes their own testimony, but in Rex v. Wedgwood in 1931 in point of fact they did.

FLOWERS
FOR
THE JUDGE

BARNABAS LIMITED

JACOBY BARNABAS

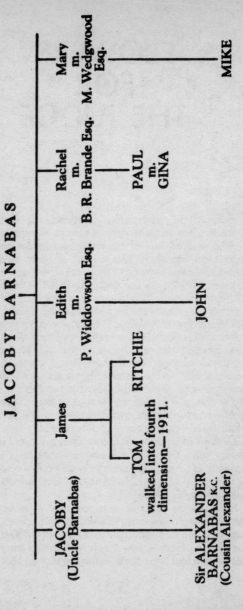

JACOBY (Uncle Barnabas)

Sir ALEXANDER BARNABAS K.C. (Cousin Alexander)

James

TOM walked into fourth dimension—1911.

RITCHIE

Edith m. P. Widdowson Esq.

JOHN

Rachel m. B. R. Brande Esq.

PAUL m. GINA

Mary m. M. Wedgwood Esq.

MIKE

1

Damp Dynamite

The story of the little man, sometimes a stockbroker, sometimes a tea merchant, but always something in the City, who walked out of his suburban house one sunny morning and vanished like a puff of grey smoke in a cloudless sky, can be recalled by nearly everyone who lived in Greater London in the first years of the century.

The details vary. Sometimes it was the inquisitive lady at Number Ten who saw him go by, and the invalid propped up in the window of Number Twelve who did not; while the letter which he was about to post was found lying pathetically upon the pavement between the two houses. Sometimes the road was bounded by two high walls, with a milkman at one end and the unfortunate gentleman's wife on her door-step at the other. In this version the wife was kissed at the garden gate and waved at from halfway down the oddly bordered road, yet the milkman saw neither hide nor hair of his patron then or afterwards.

All the stories have their own circumstantial evidence. Only the main fact and an uncomfortable impression are common to all. A man did disappear and there were reasons for supposing that he did so in no ordinary fashion. Also, of course, he never returned.

Most people know of someone who lived in the next street to the hero or victim of the tale, but the ancient firm of Barnabas and Company, publishers since 1810 at the Sign of the Golden Quiver, never referred to the story because the little man had been their junior partner on that morning

1

in May, nineteen hundred and eleven, when he bade a polite "Good morning" to his housekeeper at his front door in the Streatham Crescent, turned out into a broad suburban road and never passed the tobacconist on the corner, but vanished as neatly and unobtrusively as a raindrop in a pool.

At the time there was a certain excitement in the grand Queen Anne house in the cul-de-sac at the Holborn end of Jockey's Fields which bore the sign of the Golden Quiver, but, when it was discovered that the ledgers were still truthful and that Mr. John Widdowson, the other partner, was quite prepared to carry on while his cousin remained disintegrated or in the fourth dimension, the natural conservatism of the firm reasserted itself and the whole disturbing affair was decently forgotten.

However, although a wonder may degenerate into a funny thing after the proverbial nine days and may well become nothing but an uneasy memory after twenty years, the odd disappearance of Tom Barnabas in nineteen eleven created a sort of precedent in the firm, so that in the curious paradoxical way in which the mind works no one thought very much of it when in nineteen thirty-one Paul R. Brande, one of the directors, did not show up for a couple of days.

Gina Brande sat on the couch before the fire in her big sitting room in the top flat on the Sunday evening after Paul went. "Shop tea" was in progress. This function was part of the Barnabas tradition. On Sunday evenings all through the winter it was the custom of the cousins and Miss Curley to meet together to take tea and hold an inquest on the Sunday papers. Sometimes outsiders were present; perhaps a privileged author or visiting American or, on rare occasions, old Caldecott, that patriarch of agents who had known the Old Man.

When Paul had brought Gina back from New York and the firm had recovered from the shock of having a woman and a foreigner on the door-step, she had taken over the responsibility of providing the fire and the meal for the gatherings from John's aged housekeeper and the meetings had moved up from the flat below. It was typical of the two principal directors of the firm that they should have

2

snapped up the lease of the house next door to the office, converted its unsuitability into three flats at considerable expense, and had settled down to live in the Holborn backwater, each convinced that they should or could desire no more.

John Widdowson, managing director, senior cousin, and son of the Old Man's eldest sister, took the centre flat as befitted his position, although in size it would have better suited Paul and Gina, who were quartered above.

The ground floor and basement had been more or less wished upon Mike Wedgwood, the youngest cousin and junior director. Barnabas, Limited did things like that in the holy conviction that through minor discomforts their dignity and prestige were upheld.

The tea party was almost at an end, and as yet no one had referred to Paul. The general feeling seemed to be that the gathering was very peaceful without his crimson-faced didacticism.

Gina had folded herself on the big white sofa with its deeply buttoned back and exaggerated curves. As usual, she looked odd and lovely and unexpected amid that sober gathering.

When Pavlov, the décor man, spoke of her as "the young Bernhardt," he did her a little less than justice. Her small-boned figure, tiny hands and feet, and long modern neck would have disappeared into nothingness in the corsets and furbelows of the 'eighties. Her head was modern, too, with its wide mouth, slanting grey eyes and the small straight nose whose severity was belied by the new coxcomb coiffure which Lallé had created for her and which brought her dark chestnut hair forward into a curl faintly and charmingly reminiscent of the "bang" of the last century.

She was wearing one of her own dresses. The firm, or rather John Widdowson in the person of the firm, had not countenanced his cousin's wife continuing her career in England, and she now only designed for herself, and sometimes for Pavlov, in a strictly dignified and semi-amateur way.

The narrow gown, in a heavy dark green and black silk, accentuated her foreignness and her chic, which was so extraordinarily individual. At the moment she looked a little weary. John's weekly diatribe against the firm of Cheshunt, who flooded the book market with third-, fourth- and fifth-rate novels and advertised the figure of their mighty output with bland self-satisfaction, had seemed even a little longer and heavier than usual.

Curley sat in the corner by the fire. Her plump hands were folded on her knee and her very pale blue eyes were quiet and contemplative behind her spectacles.

Miss Florence Curley was easily the least distinguished-looking person in the room. Her iron-grey hair was not even tidy and her black velvet dress was of that variety of ill-cut, over-decorated and disgracefully expensive garments which are made in millions for the undiscerning. Her shoes were smart but looked uncomfortable, and she wore three rings which had obviously been her mother's. But Curley was the firm. Even John, glancing at her from time to time, hoped devoutly that she would outlast him.

Long ago she had been the Old Man's secretary, in the days when a lady typist was still a daring innovation, and, with the tradition of female service and unswerving loyalty to the dominant male still unshattered behind her, she had wedded herself to the firm of Barnabas, Limited as to a lover.

Thirty years later she loved the business as a son and a master. She knew more about its affairs than a roomful of ledgers, and understood its difficulties and cherished its triumphs with the insight of a first nurse.

In the office she was accepted as a benevolent and omniscient intelligence which was one of the firm's more important assets. Outside the firm she was feared, respected and faintly resented. Yet she looked a rather stupid, plain old woman sitting there by the fire.

It was very warm in the room, and John rose to his feet.

"I shall go back to it, I think, Gina," he said. "Tooth's new one is an odd sort of jumble, but I want to finish it. I'm having him up tomorrow."

John always spoke of "having authors up" when he meant that he had invited them to an interview. It was a traditional phrase of the Old Man's.

Miss Curley stirred. "Mr. Tooth is a very self-opinionated young man, Mr. Widdowson," she ventured, and added, with apparent irrelevance: "I saw him lunching with Phillips of Denver's last week. They were at school together, I think."

John, who followed her line of thought, turned round. "It's not as good as his first book," he said defensively.

"Oh, no. It's not," Miss Curley agreed. "Second books never are, are they? Still, I think he's got something in him. I shouldn't like to see him leave us. I don't like Denver's."

"Quite," said John, dry to the point of curtness. "I'll finish it," he added. "It may be just possible."

He moved over to the door, an impressive, interesting-looking person with his tall, slender figure, little dried-up yellow face and close-cropped white hair.

On the threshold he paused and looked back.

"Where is Paul? Do you know, Gina? Haven't seen him since Thursday. Off to Paris again, I suppose."

There was a moment's awkward pause, during which Curley smiled involuntarily. Paul, with his hustle methods, his bombast and his energy, while infuriating his cousin contrived to amuse her. John's remark was his first direct reference to the Tourlette biography affair, and everyone in the room recalled Paul's excited, unconvincing voice rising above the din at the September cocktail party:

"I tell you, my dear fellow, I was so thrilled, so absolutely annihilated, that I just rushed off down to Croydon and got a 'plane—didn't even remember to snatch a bag or tell Gina here—simply fled over there and bought it."

The fact that the Tourlette biography had proved of about the same interest to the British and American publics as the average first book of free verse, and that Barnabas, Limited had dropped a matter of five hundred pounds on the transaction, lent point to the comment.

Gina stirred. All her movements were very slow, and she turned her head with graceful deliberation before speaking.

"I don't know where he is. He hasn't been home since Thursday."

The quiet voice with the unexpected New England

accent betrayed no embarrassment or resentment at either the question or the fact.

"Oh, I see." John also did not seem surprised. "If he comes in tonight you might tell him to drop in and see me. I shall be reading all the evening. I've had a most extraordinary letter from Mrs. Carter. I wish Paul would learn not to enthuse to authors. It goes to their heads and then they get spiteful if a book doesn't sell."

His voice died on a plaintive note and the door closed softly behind him.

Ritchie began to laugh, a dry little cackle of which nobody took the least notice. He was out of the circle, leaning back in a chair in the shadows, a quiet, slightly melancholy or, if one felt sentimental, pathetic figure.

Ritchie Barnabas, brother of the transported Tom, was the only cousin who had received no share of the business under the Old Man's will. He had been younger in nineteen hundred and eight, of course, but not so young as Mike, who had been a baby, nor so young as Paul, who was still at school, nor even so very much younger than John himself. His own explanation of this mystery was never sought, but a clause in the will which charged the beneficiary cousins to "look after" Richard Barnabas threw some light on the Old Man's opinion of this nephew.

It was characteristic of the firm, and perhaps of publishing generally, that they fulfilled this charge by supplying Ritchie with a small room at the top of the building, a reasonable salary and the title of "The Reader." He shared the work with some twenty or thirty clergymen, maiden ladies and indigent schoolmasters scattered all over the country, but his was the official post and he lived in a world of battered manuscripts on which he made long and scholarly reports.

Like some thin and dusty ghost he was often seen on the stairs of the office, in the hall, or tramping home with long flapping strides through the network of gusty streets between the sacred cul-de-sac and his lodgings in Red Lion Square.

No one considered him and yet everyone liked him in the half-tolerant, half-condescending way with which one regards someone else's inoffensive pet.

6

Every year he was granted three weeks' holiday, and on these occasions he was never missed. Only the increasing height of the piles of manuscript in his dusty room bore witness to the genuineness of his absence.

There was a vague notion among the junior members of the staff that he spent these holidays reading in his lodgings, but no one was interested enough to find out. The cousins simply said and thought "Where's Ritchie? Oh, on holiday, of course . . ." and dismissed him for the more important matter that was always on hand.

There had been from time to time sentimental young women, although these were not encouraged in the firm, who saw in Ritchie a romantic and mysterious figure with some secret inner life too delicate or possibly too poetic for general expression, but always in time they gave up their investigations. Ritchie, they discovered, had the emotional outlook of a child and the mind of a schoolboy. He was also not even particularly unhappy.

Now, when he had finished laughing, he rose and walked over to Gina.

"I shall go too, now, my dear," he said, smiling down at her with the mildest of blue eyes.

There was a minute pause, and he added charmingly: "A delicious tea."

Gina's grey eyes narrowed as she smiled back at him.

"Sweet person, Ritchie," she said, and gave him her hand.

He took it for a moment, and then, after nodding to Curley, grinned broadly at Mike, whom he had always liked, and wandered off to find the door.

The three who were left smiled after he went out, but in a most kindly way. The warm silence remained unbroken for some time. Outside the first waves of the fog were creeping down from the park, but as yet its chill dirtiness had not penetrated into the gracious room.

Miss Curley sat in her corner, placid and apparently lost in thought. Those who knew her were used to Curley "staring through them" and her habit was a time-honoured joke in the office. She found it very useful. Her faded blue eyes were difficult to see behind the gold-rimmed spectacles, and it was, therefore, never easy to be sure whether they were focused upon one or not.

At the moment she was looking at Mike with steady inquisitiveness.

Michael Wedgwood was the son of the Old Man's youngest and favorite sister. His place in the firm had been assured to him since his childhood. He had been barely seven years old at the time of his uncle's death.

As she watched him Miss Curley reflected that his early training might easily have spoilt him altogether. A little boy brought up in cold blood to be a fitting member of any old-established publishing firm, let alone Barnabas, Limited, might have turned out to be a prig or a crank or worse. But there had been mitigating circumstances. The firm had suffered during the war and the Old Man's fortune had been very much divided, so that although the young Michael had been to the right schools he had never had quite enough money, and, in Miss Curley's opinion, there was a sobering quality in poverty greatly to be prized.

Mike had missed the war by a few months and had been actually in training at school when the Armistice was signed. Looking at him, sprawled out in the deep armchair opposite her, Curley wondered if he had not always just missed the big things. Until now she had seen him as an unscathed, untried sort of person. He was twenty-eight or nine, she supposed; kindly polite, good-looking, dependable and quiet; but, although she had understood his popularity, hitherto he had always seemed to her to be a slightly unsatisfactory being. It was as though all the vital part of him had been allowed to atrophy while his charm, his ease and his intelligence had occupied his full stage.

Curley's faded eyes did not blink. He was certainly good-looking. In his full manhood he had more of the Old Man's size and dignity than any of the cousins. The Barnabas features were there, too, the bright, sharp dark eyes, the strong characterful nose and the thin sensitive mouth. Curley's heart warmed towards him.

Now that the suspicions she had entertained for the past few weeks had virtually become a certainty, he had gained tremendously in interest for her, and, curiously, had also gone up considerably in her estimation.

She stole a glance at Gina, resting superb and quiet upon the highbacked couch.

"She doesn't know for certain yet." Curley's thoughts ran placidly on. "He's been careful not to say anything. He wouldn't, of course. People don't nowadays. The passions frighten them. They go on fighting them as though they were indecent. So they are, of course. So are lots of things. But the Old Man—" her lips curled in a faint reminiscing smile, "—he'd have got her. It wouldn't have been nice, his cousin in the firm, but he'd have got her. That was where he was different from these nephews."

Curley's old mouth pouted contemptuously as she considered them: John with his irascibility, his pomposity and his moments of sheer obstinacy; Paul lathering and shouting and making an exhibition of himself; and now the dark horse Mike, who had never really wanted anything before. Would any of them go out bald-headed for their desires, sweeping away obstacles and striding over impossible barriers to attainment, to get clean away with it in the end as the Old Man had done time and time again? Curley did not think so.

Mike was leaning back, his head partly in the shadow, so that only sometimes when the fire flickered was his face visible. Curley felt that he was very careful of his expression on these occasions.

Gina did not glance in his direction, but she was aware of him. Curley knew that by the studied calm, by the odd suggestion of tension which anybody but her, one of the most unemotional of woman, must have found unbearable.

They were "in love," then. A ridiculous but illuminating phrase, Miss Curley reflected, suggesting "an uncomfortable state." It was a very awkward thing to have happened to either of those self-possessed, intelligent young people. Mike had been woken up under his skin, Miss Curley saw with satisfaction. The fever was upon him all right. It showed painfully through his ease and politeness, turning him from a slightly austere personality into something infinitely more appealing and helpless, and at the same time somehow shameful.

Of the girl Curley was not so sure. Her poise was extraordinary. The older woman speculated upon her possible attitude towards her husband. Of course she could hardly entertain much affection for him. There might possibly be somewhere in the world a woman thick-skinned enough to be able to ignore the series of small exposures which was Paul's life, but not Gina. His fake enthusiasms and windy lies, which were always being found out, his unconvincing braggartry—surely no physical passion could counteract the blast of these upon a sensitive intelligence.

Besides, what consideration did Paul give Gina? His mind was fully occupied in the hopeless and, in the circumstances, ridiculous task of putting himself over big. Where did she think he was now, for instance? Rushing off on some wild-goose chase, throwing his importance at the head of some dazzled scribbler, to return on the morrow drunk with enthusiasm for his own cleverness, only to be sobered and left sulky by the common sense of his elder cousin.

No. If Gina had ever loved him, a possibility which Curley was inclined to doubt, she could not possibly do so now.

Her reflections and speculations were cut short by an intrusion into the warm paper-strewn sanctuary. At a glance from Gina, Mike had leapt to answer the flat buzzing of the door-bell. There was the murmur of polite greetings in the hall and he returned with the newcomer.

Curley knew of Mr. Albert Campion by repute alone and was therefore quite unprepared and a little shocked when he came wandering in behind Mike. His slender, drooping figure, pale ingenuous face and sleek yellow hair were rendered all the more indefinite by the immense and unusually solid horn-rimmed spectacles he chose to affect.

"Party over?" he enquired regretfully, casting an eye over the dismantled tea-table and scattered chairs. "What a pity!"

He shook hands with Curley and Gina, and sat down, crossing his long thin legs.

"No tea? No party? It must be business then," he chattered on, smiling affably. "Cheap, clean and trustworthy, fifteen months in last place and a conviction at the end of it. Detective work of all kinds undertaken at short notice."

10

He paused abruptly. Curley's eyes were upon him in frozen disapproval.

Mr. Campion had the grace to look abashed. Gina came to his rescue.

"You haven't met Mr. Campion before, have you, Curley? He gets some people down, but most of us grow used to him in time."

"It's an affliction," said the pale young man, with engaging embarrassment. "A form of nervousness. Think of it as a glass eye and it won't bother you any more."

Curley was only partly disarmed. The world in which she lived was besprinkled with consciously funny young men, most of them ill-mannered nincompoops. The difference between the newcomer and the average specimen dawned upon her slowly. In every case the flow of nonsense was in the nature of a protective covering, she knew, but here it was the reality which was different. Mr. Campion had more than poverty of intelligence to hide.

Meanwhile he was still talking.

"As an American, Gina, you have a thrill coming to you. We are on the eve of a real old London particular, with flares in the streets, bus-conductors on foot leading their drivers over the pavements into plateglass windows, and blind beggars guiding city magnates across the roads for a small fee. It's pretty bad in the Drury Lane vicinity now. I'm wallowing in old-world romance already."

Mike shrugged his shoulders and his dark eyes twinkled lazily.

"I hope you enjoy it," he said. "As a motorist, its romance leaves me cold. You'll hate it, Gina. It has the same effect upon the skin and clothes as a train journey from Paris to the south in midsummer."

"I see. Just another little British trick to entertain the foreigner."

The girl spoke absently, and for the first time Mr. Campion saw that the constraint in the atmosphere was not due to Miss Curley's presence alone.

"Well, ladies and gentlemen," he said cheerfully, "the Professor is here. The *ballon* she is about to mount. Bring out your misfortunes. Lost anything, Gina?"

There was a moment's awkward silence, and whereas

11

Miss Curley's astute mind took in the whole situation, Mr. Campion, who was not in possession of the facts, perceived that he had made a gaffe. Mike glanced at Gina imploringly. Miss Curley leant forward.

"If you three want to talk business, my dear, I'll get my things."

Gina hesitated, and a faintly deeper colour spread over her face. It was the first trace of embarrassment to destroy her poise, and was all the more expressive because of its restraint.

"It's not exactly that, Curley," she said. "I don't know—you might be able to help us in a way—and yet——"

She broke off deliberately. Miss Curley leant back in her chair.

"I'll stay," she said firmly. "It's about Paul, isn't it? He'll turn up, my dear. He always does. All the cousins like to disappear now and again. It's quite a tradition in the family."

She had broken the ice completely, and there was a hint of relief in Mike's laugh.

"A sort of affectation," he murmured. "Good old Curley! You see through us all, don't you?"

Miss Curley eyed him. "I *see*," she said dryly.

"Wait a minute for Mastermind to catch up," said Mr. Campion protestingly. "What's happened to Paul?"

Gina turned slowly toward him, two bright spots of colour in her face.

"I suppose it's just foolishness," she said, "but I asked Mike to get you to come over for a sort of unofficial talk. Paul hasn't been around since last Thursday, and after all, he does live here—and—and——"

"Quite," said Campion, hurrying to the rescue. "I see your point perfectly. Whereas it's one thing to call in the police, it's quite another to pretend you haven't noticed your husband's absence for three days."

"Exactly." She looked at him gratefully and went on talking, the hint of pride in her soft lazy voice making it extraordinarily appealing. "I suppose some wives would have gone haywire by this time, but with me—I mean with us—it's different. We—well, we're post-war people, Albert. Paul leads his own life, and so do I, in a way."

She paused wretchedly, only to hurry on again, forcing herself at her fences.

"What I'm trying to say is, there's nothing really unusual in Paul going off for a day or two like this without thinking to tell me, but I've never known him to stay away quite so long without my hearing even indirectly of him, and this morning I felt I ought to—well—just mention it to somebody. You do understand it, don't you?"

"Ye-es," said Mr. Campion a little dubiously.

The heavy white lids closed over the girl's eyes for a moment.

"It's not unheard of," she said, half defiantly. "Lots of people do the same sort of thing in our crowd. He may be anywhere. He may turn up tonight or tomorrow or next week, and I shall feel a fool for making such a fuss."

"Let me get this straight." Mr. Campion's precise voice was as friendly as any in the world. "I take it the dear fellow may easily have gone to a cocktail do, drifted on to an all-night binge with some of the gang, and finished up with a hangover at a week-end house-party."

"Yes," said the girl eagerly, anxious, it seemed, to convince herself. "Or he may have rushed over to Paris about this exhibition scheme he's so keen on. But even so, I don't see why he should have taken so long about it."

Mr. Campion pricked up his ears. "Is that the rare manuscript exhibition at Bumpus's in February?" he enquired.

Mike rose to give Gina a light. "Yes. Paul's putting his weight into it. It's going to be a stupendous affair. Practically the whole of the Leigh Collection will be on view."

"But not *The Gallivant*, I suppose?" murmured the visitor, venturing Miss Curley's disapproving stare.

"No, I'm afraid not." Mike seemed genuinely regretful. "Paul put up the suggestion, I believe, but John vetoed it promptly. The firm of Barnabas is hanging on to its past."

The Gallivant, that precious manuscript of Congreve's unpublished play, set down by his own hand and never printed even in his unsqueamish age, had come into the possession of the firm of Barnabas very early in its dignified career. There had been something vaguely unsavoury in the story of its acquisition, some unpleasant business of the gift of a few pounds to a starving antiquary, but that was ancient history and half forgotten.

The present grievance, shared by scholars and collectors alike, was the fact that, through a certain Puritan streak in Jacoby Barnabas, the late Old Man himself, the manuscript was never permitted to be copied or even read. John respected his uncles's wishes, and it remained therefore one of the firm's assets only.

"Too bad," said Mr. Campion aloud, and forgot *The Gallivant* as he returned to the main subject. "No line on Paul anywhere at all, then?" he said slowly. "You don't know where he went on Thursday night, for instance?"

Gina shook her head. "No. As a matter of fact, I expected him home that evening. We—er—we had some things to discuss, and I arranged a quiet meal here for seven-thirty. When he didn't show up by nine o'clock I got peevish and went out."

"Yes, yes, of course." Campion was studying her face. "When you say you went out—you didn't go to look for him?"

"Oh, no, of course not." Her cheeks were flaming. "I phoned down to Mike and we went off to the Academy to see the revival of 'Caligari.'"

Something made Mr. Campion glance at his friend. He caught the man with the visor up and a warning light flashed through his brain.

Mr. Campion was old-fashioned enough to take the marriage contract seriously, but he was also sufficiently sophisticated to know that the nicest people fall in love indiscriminately and that while under the influence of that pre-eminently selfish lunacy they may make the most outrageous demands upon their friends with no other excuse than their painful need.

It suddenly occurred to him that what Gina probably needed most was a reliable and discreet enquiry agent capable of handling divorce, and was on the point of telling her so in the friendliest of fashions when he was saved from the blunder by a remark from Miss Curley.

"Where do you *think* he is, Gina?" she said baldly. "Running round the lovely Mrs. Bell?"

Once again Gina flushed, but she laughed as she spoke:

"No, Curley, I know he's not. As a matter of fact, I phoned this morning and asked her if he was down there.

Oh, no, if it was only something like that it would be simply my own affair, wouldn't it? I mean it would be quite unpardonable of me to discuss it like this. No, I can't think where he is. That's why I'm telling someone. I mean, I'm all right. I can amuse myself. I can come down on Mike to take me around."

She smiled shyly at the other man.

"Of course," he said abruptly. "You know that. At any time."

"Oh, my hat!" reflected Mr. Campion, just as Miss Curley had done. "A genuine passion. She hasn't even been told."

His interest in the affair promptly revived.

"I say," he began diffidently. "I don't want to be inquisitive, but I must ask this. Any row between you and Paul?"

"No." Her slanting grey eyes met his squarely. "None at all, at the moment. That's another thing that made me wonder. I saw him for a moment in the office on Thursday afternoon. He'd been lunching with Caldecott and he said then that he'd come here for dinner and we'd talk. No one seems to have seen him after four. He wasn't in his room when Miss Netley took some letters for him to sign just before five. I know that because she phoned me on Friday morning to ask if she should do them herself, as they ought to go off. John phoned to ask where he was, too. He was offended with Paul for being 'so damned offhand,' as he called it."

She paused, a little breathless, and sat up on the couch, the glowing end of a cigarette between her fingers as she glanced round for an ashtray.

Mike rose and came towards her, his cupped hand held out.

"I'll take it—and chuck it in the fire," he said hastily.

She drew back in surprise. "Not like that. It'll burn you," she protested.

He did not speak, but nodded to her, his whole body expressing urgency and unconscious supplication. It was a ridiculous incident, so trivial yet curiously disquieting.

Bewildered and half amused, the girl dropped the burning fragment into the hand and Campion glanced away involuntarily so that he might not see the man's satisfaction at the pain as he carried the stub over to the fire.

The return of John Widdowson a moment later restored the trend of general thought. Gina's faithful charwoman, who had returned to do the tea things, had met him on the staircase and admitted him with her key. He nodded to Campion and glanced across at Curley.

"That book of clippings on *The Shadow Line* Fellowes sent us, Miss Curley; do you know where it is? It was a rather ornate little red thing, if I remember. What did we do with it? Send it back?"

Miss Curley considered. Somewhere neatly pigeon-holed in her mind was the information. It was this gift for relatively unimportant detail which had made her so valuable in her youth, and now in her age her skill was a fetish.

"It's on a shelf with a lot of other miscellany on the right of the doorway in the strong room," she said at last, not without a certain pride.

Mike, who caught Mr. Campion's expression of polite astonishment, hastened to explain.

"The strong room is a bit of an anachronism these days," he said. "It's a sort of fortified basement in the cellar at Twenty-three and dates from the days when authors insisted on being paid cash down in gold. We haven't much use for it now, so it's used as a junk cupboard for odds and ends we don't want to lose—addresses and that sort of thing. It's a very fine affair. Tin-lined walls in the best Victorian style."

"All very interesting," said John dryly. "Would you like to run round there and get that folder?"

Mike hesitated. The older man's tone had been unnecessarily peremptory and he was in the mood to resent it.

"I'll get it for you, Mr. Widdowson. I know just where it is." Curley was already on her feet.

"Rubbish, Curley. I'll get it. The key's in your desk as usual, isn't it? All right. I shan't be a moment."

Mike strode out of the room and John sat down in the chair he had vacated.

"Fog's getting very thick," he remarked, leaning forward to jab unceremoniously at the fire.

At sixty-three, John, the eldest of the cousins, was as forceful a personality as he ever had been. Campion, leaning back in the shadows, had opportunity to consider him. A spoilt child of his profession, he decided. A little tyrant nurtured in his uncle's carefully prepared nursery. Still, he had met his battles and had fought and won them. Not a weak face, by any means.

Conversation became desultory. Curley never expanded in John's presence, and Gina was lost in her own unhappy thoughts. Mr. Campion did his best to keep the ball rolling, but without great success, since his peculiar line in small talk was hardly appreciated by the elder man. Long silences were bound to occur, and in the last of these they heard Mike's quick steps in the passage outside.

Just for a moment a wave of apprehension touched them all. It was swiftly gone, but the sight of the young man with the red and gilt folder in his hand was somehow reassuring.

Campion might have fancied that he was unduly jumpy had it not been for John, who, after peering at his cousin inquisitively, enquired abruptly:

"What's the matter? Seen a ghost?"

They all glanced at the newcomer. His dark face was a little paler than usual and he was certainly breathless. However, he seemed genuinely surprised.

"I'm all right. A bit out of training, that's all. Fog's getting very thick outside."

John grunted, and, taking his folder, trotted out again. Campion took up the main conversation where it had left off and spoke reassuring words.

After a while Miss Curley left, and presently Mr. Campion followed, leaving Gina and Mike by the fire. Campion had reflected upon the peculiarities of other people's lives and had dismissed Gina and her truant husband from his mind by the time he turned in just after midnight, so that it came with all the more of a shock to him when Miss Curley dragged him from his bed at ten o'clock the following morning with a startling story.

"Miss Marchant, one of the typists, found him, Mr. Campion." Her voice was unnaturally businesslike over the phone, and he had a vision of her, hard, cool and practical in

17

the midst of chaos. "I sent her down to get an address file as soon as I got here, about half an hour ago. The door was locked. I gave her the key from my desk. She screamed from the basement and we all rushed down to see Mr. Paul lying there. Can you come over?"

Mr. Campion put a question and she answered it testily, as though irritated by his obtuseness.

"Yes, the strong room. Mike got the folder from it last night. Yes, the same room. Oh, and Mr. Campion—" she lowered her voice—"the doctor's here. He seems to think the poor man's been dead for some *days*."

Again Campion put a query, and this time Miss Curley's reply did not sound irritable. Her tone was awful, rather.

"Right in the middle of the room, sprawled out. No one could have opened that door without seeing him."

2
Funeral Arrangements Later

There are moments which stand out in clear detail in the recollection of an hour of horror. They are seldom dramatic, and those who are haunted by them are sometimes puzzled to discover why just they and none other should have been singled out by the brain for this especial clarity.

Neither Mike Wedgwood nor Miss Curley ever forgot the instant when the doctor looked up from his knees and said half apologetically:

"I'm afraid we shall have to move him after all. I can't possibly see here."

It may have been that the bounds of their capacity for shock had been reached and that his words coincided with the moment immediately before the first degree of merciful callousness descended upon them and they were able to begin again from a new level. But at any rate, the scene was photographed indelibly upon their minds.

The extraordinarily untidy room stood out in every detail. They saw with new eyes its lining of dusty junk-packed shelves, only broken at the far end where an old-fashioned green and black safe replaced the cooking range which had once been there. They saw the heavy table which took up nearly the whole of the centre of the room, heaped high with books and files and vast untidy brown-paper parcels.

They were even aware of the space beneath it; that, too, fully occupied by flimsy wooden boxes whose paper contents would have overflowed had it not been for the books piled carelessly on top.

The fog, which enveloped the city and now crept into every corner, hung about the air like smoke, giving the single swinging bulb a dusty halo. The body lay upon its back, the head in the shadow of the table ledge and the sagging legs and torso sprawled out towards the doorway where they stood.

The doctor rose stiffly to his feet and faced them. He was a short man, grizzled and of a good age, but still spruce, and his little eyes were shrewd beneath his fierce brows. In contrast with his sombrely smart clothes his bare forearms, muscular and very hairy, looked slightly indecent.

"Where can we take him?" he enquired.

Miss Curley, who took it for granted that the question was addressed to her, considered rapidly. Space at Twenty-three was restricted. In the basement, besides the present room, there were only the packers' hall at the end of the passage, the stock room, or the little washroom next door, none of them suitable resting-places for a corpse. Upstairs the amenities were even less inviting, since the business of the day had begun and the staff was already hysterical.

She glanced at the table.

"If we move those things on to the floor and spread a sheet on the table you'll be right under the light, Doctor," she said. "I'll get a better bulb."

The little medical man looked at her curiously. He knew Paul had been a director, and although he did not expect office employees to have quite the same attitude towards a dead man as a family might have adopted, he was surprised to find an absence of the general tendency of laymen to get the body to the most comfortable place possible at the earliest moment. Aloud he said he thought Miss Curley's a most sensible suggestion.

Mike stepped into the room, avoiding the piteous thing upon the floor, and began to shift the dusty papers to the ground on the opposite side.

The place was dry from the furnace on the other side of the passage, with occasional icy draughts from the door into the yard. Mike worked like a man in a nightmare, his tall thin figure and deep-lined sensitive face looking curiously boyish and despairing.

The doctor bent down once again, and as he worked he grunted to himself at intervals and made little breathing sounds.

Miss Curley returned with a new electric light bulb and a pair of sheets borrowed from Mike's own flat next door. Her face was grim and she moved with a suppressed energy which made the doctor look at her sharply, but Curley was all right as long as she kept going.

It was she who superintended the changing of the bulb, a feat which Mike performed with unwonted clumsiness, and she who spread one sheet over the table and stood ready with the other, waiting for the doctor to move.

The two men glanced at each other. Mike was younger and considerably stronger, but he was very pale and there was sweat upon his forehead.

Doctor Roe spoke briskly. His calm was very comforting. Thirty-five years of general practice had built up an impersonal yet friendly shell which quite concealed the rather inquisitive, ordinary little man inside.

"I'll take the shoulders, Mr. Wedgwood," he said. "If you would grip the feet, now. That's right—just above the ankles. Are you ready? Now then . . ."

Mike looked down at the square-toed brown shoes. They were familiar. They were Paul's. This dreadful helpless thing lying on the dusty floor was Paul himself. Only the physical effort of lifting steadied him. Deliberately he forced his eyes out of focus so that he should not see his cousin's face. Miss Curley's expression was quite enough.

"That's right," said the doctor. "Ah!"

And afterwards, when he looked up and saw them:

"Perhaps you'd care to wait for me outside? This—ah—isn't a very pleasant business."

In the stone corridor outside the door Mike gripped the iron banisters of the staircase which ran up beside him and hung there for a moment, his crisp shorn head pressed against the stone.

"God, Curley, this is awful," he said at last. "Where the hell is John?"

"He's coming." Miss Curley's voice was sharp. "I sent round word to him as soon as I'd phoned the doctor. The woman said he'd been up half the night reading and wasn't dressed yet, but that he'd come over right away. It's a terrible thing. I haven't sent anyone to tell Gina yet."

"Gina? Of course—I say, Curley, I'll do that. Later—not now. She might come down and see him . . ."

He broke off.

Miss Curley's sympathy for him returned and the softer emotion crowning the fear nearly undid her. She took off her spectacles and dabbed at her eyes petulantly.

Mike was silent, his brows drawn down so that his eyes seemed deep sunken and darker even than usual.

At the top of the staircase on the floor above somebody paused and a greyer shadow thickened against the wall over their heads.

"Miss Curley! Oh, Miss Curley."

A girl's voice, tremulous with its owner's effort to appear unconcerned, floated down to them.

"Mr. Tooth is here."

"Put him in the waiting room, Miss James. Put every visitor in the waiting room."

Mike spoke before Miss Curley could open her mouth and footsteps above pattered away.

The doctor came out in what seemed an extraordinarily short space of time. They pounced on him, besieging him with questions, and as he washed his hands in the little toilet next to the strong room he talked to them over his shoulder.

"He's been dead about three days, I should say. Very difficult to be more accurate once the period of rigor mortis has passed. But I put three days as the minimum. How odd he should not have been found before."

21

For the first time Miss Curley noticed that his eyes were sharp and curious under his fiery brows, and unconsciously she spoke defensively.

"This room is very seldom used, Doctor. It's virtually a safe, you know. It's really extremely lucky that we found him this morning."

"But he must have been missed," the doctor persisted. "Surely his wife . . . ?"

"Mr. Brande was a man of very uncertain habits." Miss Curley had not meant to interrupt with such chilling asperity, and Mike attempted to come to the rescue with clumsy friendliness.

"We had begun to wonder where he was. We were only talking of it last night. No one thought of looking in there, naturally."

He stopped abruptly and as clearly as though he had proclaimed it aloud it became obvious that a startling recollection had occurred to him. He grew suddenly crimson and stared at Curley, who did not meet his eyes. The doctor regarded them both with interest.

"I see," he said hastily. "I see. And now, Mr. Wedgwood, is there any heating apparatus down here at all?"

Mike looked bewildered. "How do you mean? Do you want a fire? There's the main coke furnace under the staircase here if——"

"That's what I'm asking you," interrupted the doctor shortly. "Let's have a look at it."

Together they inspected the central-heating system and the stove built into the tiny cellar-like cupboard under the staircase.

The doctor asked a great many questions and measured the distance between the cellar and the strong-room door with ridiculously exaggerated strides.

To Curley, who was only bearing up under the shock with great difficulty, the performance seemed absurd.

"But how did it happen, Doctor?" she demanded impatiently. "How did he die? That flush on his face—it's very unusual, isn't it? How did it happen?"

"That, madam," said the little man, eyeing her with a pomposity which was oddly disquieting, "I am attempting to decide."

On the whole, it was very fortunate that John should have arrived at that particular moment. He came running down the stairs, his head held slightly on one side and his excellently cut clothes looking out of place in the draughty dinginess of the basement.

He brushed past Mike and Miss Curley and shook hands perfunctorily with the doctor.

"Where is he?" he demanded.

Although no one who actually saw him during those first five minutes could possibly have doubted that John was genuinely shaken by his cousin's death, a catalogue of his words and actions would have been misleading. He moved towards the door of the strong room with little, jerky, birdlike steps, paused for a moment on the threshold and peered in at the sheeted figure on the table.

He made no attempt to enter but stepped back sharply after a second's contemplation, beating his long ivory hands softly together, cymbal fashion.

"Terrible," he said shortly. "Terrible. We must get him out of here. We must get him home."

Mike recognized that tone of quiet authority. When John spoke like that his commands were automatically carried out. The younger man turned to him.

"Gina doesn't know yet," he said. "Let me warn her, at least. Give me five minutes."

"All right. But he can't stay here, poor fellow."

Both cousins had completely forgotten the doctor, and his diffident demur came as a surprise to them.

"Mr. Widdowson," he ventured, "I hardly know whether I can advise——"

"My dear sir—" John turned upon him with raised brows, "—he can't stay here in the office, in the strong room. Can you give me any valid reason why he should not be moved?"

The doctor hesitated. He had no story ready, no actual ground on which to stand. It was a situation in which the stronger personality was bound to triumph. Mike mounted the staircase.

"Give me five minutes to tell her," he said over his shoulder.

As for Miss Curley, she hurried up to her office and phoned Mr. Campion.

Gina was pottering in the big living room, clad in a severe man-tailored pyjama suit, when the woman admitted her visitor. She looked up from the hearth rug, where she was sorting her morning's correspondence, when he entered, and his vision of her, kneeling there in the warm navy blue suit, was the only lovely thing in all that day. He remembered afterwards that her red mules made little blobs of color on the white rug and her face turned to his was radiant with sudden pleasure.

"Mike, my pet! How nice to see you. Too early for some coffee? I'm just going to have some."

Conscious that the charwoman was hovering behind him, he hesitated. All the old insufferable phrases crowded into his mind: "Gina, my dear, you must prepare yourself for a shock." Or, "I have bad news, I'm afraid." Or, "Gina, something terrible has happened."

Now that the moment had come they stuck in his throat and he was only conscious of her sitting there smiling at him, sane and lovely and adorable by a fire.

"He would like some, Mrs. Austin, please." Gina smiled at the woman and waved her hand to the sofa. "Sit down, animal, and don't stand there goggling at me. What's the matter? Can't we go to the Athertons this afternoon after all? Good heavens, it doesn't matter. Don't look like that."

Mike sat down heavily and raised his eyes to hers.

"Paul's dead," he said.

She had been in the act of placing a couple of envelopes in the flames when he spoke, and now her arrested movement, the shoulder half turned, the head bent, was more expressive than any sound she could have uttered. He dropped down on the rug beside her and put a hand on the small woollen back.

"Gina, I didn't mean to say it like that. Oh, my God, I am a fool!"

She turned to him at once. Her face was very pale, her eyes wide and dark.

"Tell me," she said quietly. "How did it happen? A car smash?"

"No." He paused. She was so close to him.

Presently he heard himself talking in a guarded unnatural way which he was unable to correct.

"He's been at Twenty-three the whole time. They've only just found him. They're going to bring him up here. You—you had to be told, you see."

"But of course I had to be told." Her deep soft voice had sharp edges. "Mike, what's happened? Was it suicide?"

"I—we—we don't know."

"But why should he? Why? Oh, Mike, why should he? We hadn't even quarrelled. He had no reason, surely. Surely, Mike?"

"Hold on, old dear." The man was gripping her shoulder tightly and she leant back into the crook of his arm.

Mrs. Austin set the coffee tray down on the table behind the sofa with a clatter and stood looking over it at them with the shrewd glance of a mendicant pigeon. Things *were* happening! She had been thinking they must get a move on for some time now, but if a man ignored his wife, well, he was asking for trouble; that was her opinion.

Gina became aware of her. She moved quietly to her feet.

"My husband is dead, Mrs. Austin," she said. "They don't know how it happened."

The full arc of Mrs. Austin's knitted bosom swelled. Her long face with its festoon of chins grew blank and she emitted a long thin sound midway between a scream and a whistle.

"No!" said Mrs. Austin. "Here," she added hastily, clattering with the coffee-jugs, "you drink this, dear. You'll need it."

Gina sat in the big white chair, and sipped the coffee obediently, while the other woman stood before her and watched her face. Mike glanced at the woman wonderingly. Hitherto Mrs. Austin had been a mechanism to open doors in his life. Now she had miraculously become a personality. It was as though a shadow had taken substance.

"Will they be bringing him up here, dear?" she demanded, and behind her ill-contrived sorrow Mike detected an awful secret glee.

Gina looked at Mike. He was still poised awkwardly, half kneeling on the rug at her feet.

"They are coming now, aren't they?" she said.

He got up stiffly. "Yes—yes, they are. But look here. Gina, there's no need for you to do anything, unless you want to, of course. I mean——"

He broke off helplessly, the situation beyond him.

"Oh," said Mrs. Austin, her little green-grey eyes fixed on him with dreadful understanding, "I think I take your meaning, sir. Oh, well, there's no need for the poor lady to see her husband for a bit. I'll do all the necessary."

She crossed over to the girl and laid a kindly crimson hand on her shoulder.

"Don't you worry, dear. Don't you worry at all."

Mike felt himself gaping at her with fascinated horror. There was a ghastliness about this practical side of death which overtopped the sum of frightfulness which had confronted him in that short morning. Mrs. Austin was kind; sympathy and friendliness oozed from her every pore; and yet she was enjoying the tragedy with all the shameful delight of the under-entertained.

He glanced at Gina. She was thinking, her face white, her eyes dark and blank.

He found himself feeling that she ought to cry and yet being relieved that she did not. He knew it would never occur to her to adopt any conventional attitude. The sudden loss of Paul could hardly be a great emotional tragedy, but it was naturally a tremendous shock.

He was looking at her, trying to divine her thoughts, when Mrs. Austin touched his sleeve.

"I'd like a few words with you outside, sir, please," she said, and before the elaborate solemnity which scarcely veiled the exuberant curiosity which consumed her he was helpless. He followed her meekly.

The fog was not yet at its worst, but the streets were as dark as at midnight and the waves of bitter, soot-laden air softened and blurred the edges of familiar objects until London was like an old brown lithograph chalked by a man with no eye for detail.

In the basement at Twenty-three John had taken

charge of the proceedings, the doctor hovering ineffectually at his side. One of the smaller packing tables had been taken off its trestles and upon it the sheeted body of Paul Brande now lay. Under John's supervision the whole affair was being managed very decently.

Old Dobson, the chief packer, a bull-necked individual with arms like the forelegs of a cart horse and a red rim round his head where a cap had sat, took the head of the improvised stretcher, while the foot was supported by a Mr. Peter Rigget from the Accounts Department. Mr. Rigget had somehow appeared upon the staircase at the critical moment and, much to his delight, had been invited to assist. He was a squat, insignificant-looking young man, long in the body and short in the leg, with a solidarity which would become fleshy in a few years. It was his misfortune that he looked like the popular conception of the less attractive black-coated worker, even to the pink sensitive nose and the very shiny gold pince-nez. In a rather futile effort to combat this disadvantage he wore his very black hair *en brosse*, and, to his eternal credit, spent much of his spare time in the Regent Street Polytechnic Gymnasium hardening his muscles.

With a certain amount of assistance from the doctor, therefore, he was quite able to manage the task for which he had angled.

Mr. Rigget had been waiting to get into the heart of the excitement downstairs ever since his sensitive perceptions had got wind of it less than three minutes after the discovery of the body, for it was a tragic fact that, in spite of his struggles against his destiny, Mr. Rigget remained what he had been born and reared to be, an inquisitive, timid, dishonorable person with a passion for self-aggrandizement which was almost a mania.

"Not through the street." John made the statement sound like an edict. "We shall have to go the back way, through the garden and into the basement at Twenty-one. We can't have a crowd in the front of the office. Are you ready?"

Not for the first time during the past ten minutes the doctor shot a curious glance at the elegant, elderly head of the firm. John Widdowson's complete preoccupation with his own particular aspect of the tragedy, and his utter disregard for any sort of pretence at conventional grief, was something unique in his experience.

He found it all the more puzzling because he did not know the man well and did not realize that it was the outcome of lifelong habit and was nothing to do with the unusual circumstances.

The procession moved off out into the yard through the narrow door between the strong room and the furnace cellar. Once in the fog the picture became macabre. The massive Dobson was blurred and transfigured into a shadow of heroic size, while Peter Rigget, bending forward under the weight, became foreshortened and spread out into something dwarfish and deformed.

The white burden between them widened and narrowed at every new angle which its path dictated, and the folds of the sheet hung limply in the cold still air.

They went down the stone way between the garage and the loading shed and turned sharply to the right, negotiating a little-used gate in the wall with difficulty.

Their progress through the other house was even more awkward, and both John and the doctor were forced to lend every assistance as they struggled and panted up the seven flights of stairs.

Mrs. Austin admitted them with red-eyed reverence as long as the door was open and whispering efficiency as soon as it was shut. She and the doctor understood each other instantly, and for the first time that morning the professional man received the mixture of awe and clumsy but well-meant assistance to which his long professional life had accustomed him.

"Mrs. Brande's quite laid out, poor thing," Mrs. Austin announced in a stage whisper, adding with ambiguous sentimentality, "Mr. Wedgwood's with her, comforting her as only he can. I've told him not to let her come out for a minute or two."

John looked at the woman as though he wondered what rather than who she was, and followed Dobson and Peter Rigget into the spare room, where nearly all the best linen had been set out by Mrs. Austin because a doctor was coming.

Dobson left at once, glad to go, but Peter Rigget lingered until bidden sharply by his employer to return to work.

Meanwhile, Mrs. Austin turned back the sheet.

John went out of the room. He felt he could not possibly be of any assistance, and he found the situation disagreeable.

Mike had only escaped from Mrs. Austin when the knock at the door heralded bigger game. He and Gina had barely spoken when John came in. He stood eyeing their questioning faces absently for a moment, his mind clearly upon other things, but as he sat down he addressed the girl.

"We brought him up, Gina, because he couldn't possible stay down there."

"But of course not. Of *course* not," she said, her deep voice rising a little. "What's the matter with you all? Of course they must bring him to his home. I'll go to him."

Mike stood in her path and she looked up at him.

"You're not protecting me, you're frightening me," she said, and swung round to John. "Where did it happen, John? Where has he been all this time?"

"In the strong room." He still spoke impersonally, his mind preoccupied.

"In the strong room?" The girl repeated the words as though she doubted her senses. "But I thought that place was kept locked; locked from the outside and the key in Curley's desk."

John blinked at her. "It's all very terrible, I admit, my dear, but there are so many things to think of besides details."

Gina sat down suddenly. The change in her face was extraordinary. She looked haggard, blue-shadowed and years older.

"Mike," she said unsteadily, "you were down there last night."

"In the strong room? Were you really, Mr. Wedgwood? You must excuse me, but this is very curious indeed, isn't it?"

Little Doctor Roe stepped forward from the doorway, where he had been hesitating for the past few moments.

"Doctor, this is Mrs. Brande." John's voice was gently reproving.

The little man was pulled up short. He looked uncomfortable.

"Er—quite, quite; I see. Er—may I say how extremely sorry I am, madam? I am afraid you must have had a very great shock." Doctor Roe's best professional manner was to the fore as he pressed Gina's hand, but he returned to Mike immediately.

"You went down to the strong room last night?" he repeated.

"Yes, Doctor, I did." Mike's tone sounded over-friendly in his eagerness to explain. "Yes, I did. I went down for a folder for my cousin. I took the key out of the desk where it is always kept, unlocked the door, found the book, relocked the place and put the key back and hurried up here. I was only in there for a second but I—I didn't see anything."

There was a long pause. The doctor's eyes had become like John's, veiled and introspective.

"Well," he said after what seemed an interminable silence, "there will be certain formalities, you understand." He coughed.

"Formalities?" John looked up. "I don't quite understand. What was the cause of death, Doctor?"

The professional man hesitated. "I shouldn't like to commit myself just now," he murmured at last. "My opinion will be tested by post-mortem before the inquest."

"Inquest?" John stiffened. "Really? Surely that's not necessary in a case like this?"

The authoritative tone somehow saved the question from sounding absurd.

The little doctor stood like a Trojan on the one piece of ground he knew to be firm.

"Mr. Widdowson," he said, "I did not attend your cousin before his death. I am not at all sure how he died and I am afraid I must refuse to grant a certificate."

"And what exactly does that mean?" John's tone was, if anything, slightly contemptuous.

The doctor looked profoundly uncomfortable.

"The case will automatically come under the cognizance of the Coroner as an uncertified death," he said slowly. "I—er I am afraid I can do nothing more."

He still hovered, his eyes beneath their heavy brows interested and bright.

Gina pulled herself together with an effort.

"Doctor," she said, "I think I will go to my husband. Will you come with me, please?"

She moved quickly out of the room, the little man at her heels.

Mike strode restlessly up and down. The cousins were not communicative as a family and a crisis did not loosen their tongues. John remained silent for some considerable time. Finally he said:

"Inquest, eh? How extremely like Paul—flamboyant to the end."

Mike stared at him, but he went on in a perfectly normal tone:

"Ring down to Miss Curley, will you? Tell her to come up here herself and bring a notebook."

Mike hesitated, opened his mouth to speak, but thought better of it and went out obediently. He had just finished phoning in the little booth at the far end of the hall when the doctor and Gina came out of the spare room. He hung back to wait for her.

The little man was all kindliness.

"Leave it all to me, Mrs. Brande," he said, holding her hand. "I quite understand. The shock has been very great. Don't worry. Leave it all to me."

It passed through Mike's mind that Gina was like that. There was something essentially feminine about her, something that inspired a spirit of protection in the most unlikely breasts. However, there was nothing shrinking about her as she came hurrying down the corridor towards him.

"Oh, Mike, what *has* happened?" she demanded. "What are you and John doing? What are you hiding?"

"Hiding? My dear girl——" Mike was aghast. "You must forgive old John," he went on hastily. "He's much more knocked up than he shows, and after all, the firm does mean such a lot to him that he can't help thinking of it even at a time like this."

The girl placed her hand on his arm and looked up into his eyes.

"Mike," she said, "I do believe you actually mean all

31

this rubbish. My dear, don't you see, the doctor won't give a certificate. He's not satisfied. How could he be in the circumstances? How could you be? How could I be? I've asked him to report to the Coroner. He was obviously going to anyway. Oh, Mike, are you listening to me? Do you understand?"

"I only know that this ghastly thing has happened to you, of all people," he said. "Look here, Gina, don't get alarmed. We'll fix it somehow so that you don't have go to the damned inquest."

The girl passed her hand over her forehead.

"Oh—oh, dear God!" she whispered, and crumpled at his feet.

Mike carried her into her bedroom.

It was over three quarters of an hour later when Mr. Rigget came creeping up the stairs. John held up his hand warningly as Mrs. Austin showed the excited young man into the room. It was one of John's peculiarities that he regarded himself as the undisputed owner of any room in the two buildings, and the fact that he was now using his bereaved cousin-in-law's studio as an office did not strike him as being in any way unfitting or extraordinary.

". . . suddenly at his place of business, Miss Curley," he was saying. "Funeral arrangements later. That's for the *Times, Morning Post* and *Telegraph*. The other paragraph Mr. Pelham can send out to the places he best thinks fit. Mr. Rigget, what do you want?"

The final phrase was uttered in such a complete change of tone that Miss Curley stared violently. But Peter Rigget was not quelled. For one of the few times in his life he was the bearer of important news.

"Mr. Widdowson," he burst out, "there are two men at the office asking for you. I slipped out through the garden and came up the back way to warn you."

"To warn me?" John eyed the young man with a nice admixture of distaste and astonishment. "What are you talking about? What two men?"

"Well, sir," said Mr. Rigget flatly, cheated of his drama, "one of them's a Coroner's Officer and the other is a plain-clothes man. They only send the plain-clothes man, sir, when it's—serious."

3
Design for an Accident

Mr. Campion sat in the waiting room at the Sign of the Golden Quiver and reflected philosophically that it is often the fate of experts to be called in and left in a corner. The young woman who had admitted him had been very firm: he was to wait.

As he sat in the shadow of the mahogany mantelpiece and sniffed the leather and tobacco-scented air he regarded the room with interest. There are publishers whose waiting rooms are like those on draughty provincial railway stations: others that resemble corners of better-class bookshops, with the wares tastefully displayed; and still others that stun by their sombre magnificence and give the odd impression that somebody very old and very rich is dying upstairs: but the waiting room at Twenty-three expressed the personality of Barnabas, Limited and was solid and comfortable and rather nice, like the dining room of a well-fed mid-Victorian household.

Mr. Campion caught himself glancing at the polished side tables and supposing the silver had gone to be cleaned. Apart from a few early editions in a locked glass and wire-fronted cupboard there was not a book in the place.

A portrait of Jacoby Barnabas, the uncle of the present directors, hung over the mantelpiece in a grand baroque frame. Head and shoulders were life size, and it was evident from a certain overpainting in the work that the artist had striven with some difficulty for a likeness.

It showed a strong, heavily boned man of sixty odd with the beard and curling white hair of a Victorian philanthropist, but the light eyes set deeply in the fine square head were imperious and very cold and the small mouth was pursed and narrow amid the beautiful fleecy whiteness of the beard. A grim old boy, thought Mr. Campion, and turned his attention to the other visitor, who stood stiffly on the other side of a centre table which ought to have had a silver epergne upon it.

He was a fat young man with a red face, who looked less as though he had a secret sorrow than a grievance which was not going to be a secret very long. He regarded Mr. Campion with what appeared to be suppressed hatred, but as soon as the other ventured to remark inanely that it was a nice foggy day he burst out into the spasmodic but more than eager conversation of one who has been in solitary confinement.

Mr. Campion, who thought privately that all young persons who voluntarily shut themselves up half their lives alone, scribbling down lies in the pathetic hope of entertaining or instructing their fellows, must necessarily be the victims of some sort of phobia, was duly sympathetic. Moreover, his curiosity concerning the business downstairs was fast becoming unbearable and he was glad to have something to crowd it out of his mind.

The fat young man flung himself down in a chair.

"I'm waiting to see Mr. Widdowson," he said abruptly. "I usually see Brande, but today I've got to go to the Headmaster. They're all infernally casual, aren't they? I've been here half an hour."

In view of all the circumstances Mr. Campion did not know quite what to say, but his silence did not worry the other man, if indeed he noticed it at all.

"I expect Brande will be down in a moment," he went on explosively. "Do you know him? A nice chap. Very enthusiastic. Gets all het up about things. He's made a lot of difference to this place since he left the army. He was in the States for a bit, you know, and then came back and started putting a bit of pep into this mausoleum."

He paused again but only for breath. Since neither of them even so much as knew the other's name Mr. Campion found him quite extraordinarily indiscreet, but he recognized the symptoms and understood that people who are forced to spend long periods alone can rarely chat noncommittally. The fat young man's tongue was running away with him again.

"Brande married an American, you know," he said accusingly. "Extraordinarily pretty girl, I believe. It seems a pity they don't . . ." He broke off hastily and rose to his feet again, glaring at Campion this time as if he had discovered him trying to surprise him into a confidence.

Mr. Campion looked comfortingly blank and as the other retired to a corner, crimson with rage and confusion, he rose himself and, wandering across to the heavily curtained windows, peered through them into the fog.

"I wonder where Brande is," said the plaintive voice behind him after a pause.

Mr. Campion stiffened and controlled the insane impulse to say, "There goes his body, anyway. Looks a fishy little procession, doesn't it?" and turned back into the room just as the door opened and a girl came in.

She was neither particularly good to look at nor possessed of an arresting personality, but she caught Mr. Campion's interest at once. She was small and very dark and affected the coiffure of a medieval page and a small straight blue serge dress with a white collar and cuffs. The effect aimed at was a twelve-year-old schoolgirl but the result was ruined by the maturity of her face, hands and neck. She smiled at the fat young man.

"Oh, Mr. Tooth," she said, "I'm so sorry you've been kept waiting. I'm afraid Mr. Widdowson won't be here today. He's been called away. Would you mind very much if we wrote you?"

Mr. Tooth grew red and then pale with indignation and Mr. Campion was inclined to sympathize with him.

"I'll go in and see Mr. Brande, then," said Mr. Tooth with dignity. "He's not engaged, is he?"

"Oh, no, he's not engaged, but I'm afraid you can't see him." There was a quality in the girl's voice which was hard to define. She was enjoying the situation, certainly, but she was not bursting to come out with the news. Rather, she was being unduly secretive about it. Mr. Campion was interested. Why should the staff of Barnabas, Limited have decided to try to keep Paul's death a secret? The death of a man is a hopeless thing to hide from his friends; after all, it is no little peccadillo or temporary embarrassment from which he may be expected to recover and afterwards prefer not to have discussed.

"Miss Netley, is there anything wrong?" Mr. Tooth had caught the savour of unrest in the air and Campion watched the girl. She did not look in the least confused.

"Well, he won't be here today," she said, not so much evasively as tantalizingly. "I'm so sorry."

A great desire to get to the heart of the trouble downstairs passed over Mr. Campion and unobtrusively he moved to the door. Mr. Tooth he dismissed from his mind. Their interests, he felt, did not meet. But there was something very curious about Miss Netley, something about her personality which was peculiar. He made a mental note of her name.

The wide entrance hall at Twenty-three was of a very simple plan and Mr. Campion had no trouble in locating the basement stairs. He sauntered through the gloomy shadows and stepped slowly down the first flight. He did not move furtively and at the first sound of his shoes upon the stone there was a warning cough from below and three men in packers' aprons slid out of a doorway below him and made for their own domain. The first two walked with their faces averted and the third glanced sharply but ineffectually at the young man's grey figure in the fog.

"Door not even locked, and plenty of visitors. The police will be pleased," murmured Mr. Campion as he wandered on towards the scene of the trouble which had been so neatly pointed out to him.

In the entrance to the strong room he paused. The retreating packers had not thought to switch off the light and the whole scene lay before him, inviting him to examine it. It was not difficult to see where the body had lain, especially as he had Miss Curley's telephoned description of its discovery firmly fixed in his mind.

The bare table puzzled him at first but it did not take a very acute mind to reconstruct roughly what had happened after the body had been found.

As Mr. Campion glanced at the heterogeneous collection of books and papers which Mike had heaped upon the floor his sympathy for any police detective who might come after him grew more intense. Since so much damage had already been done he had no hesitation in entering the room. One more set of footprints in the dust, he decided, could do little harm.

The construction of the place interested him immensely. It was clear that it had at one time been part of the kitchens of the house and its subsequent alterations had done something to enhance the dungeon-like qualities of the domestic offices of the eighteenth century.

The walls appeared to be lined first with some sort of metal and then with asbestos, while the window which had been immediately on the right of the doorway had been bricked up and covered by the shelves which ran all round the walls.

Mr. Campion sniffed the air. It was still stuffy, in spite of the open door, yet, as it seemed impossible that a room of its size could have been left entirely without ventilation, he took the opportunity of examining the outside wall.

Yet fog had penetrated even here and he could not understand it at first until his search was rewarded by the discovery of a tiny iron grating let into the wall directly beneath one of the lower shelves, where a brick had been displaced. The two centre bars of the grating had been broken, leaving a ragged hole some two inches in diameter.

At this hole Mr. Campion looked very thoughtfully. By squatting down on his heels he found that he could peer through the broken ventilator into some half-lit chamber beyond, which he erroneously decided was the loading shed.

He spent some time considering the shelf below the ventilator and restrained with difficulty his impulse to touch the papers thereon.

When at last he straightened his back and continued round the room his face was much graver than usual and narrow vertical lines had appeared between his eyebrows.

At the far end of the room, between the safe and the table, the chaos was indescribable, but, looking at it, Campion was inclined to think that it was the outcome of years of untidiness rather than the result of one frenzied five minutes indulged in by any hasty or excitable person.

It passed through his mind that the term "businesslike" rarely applied to business people. There are degrees of muddle to be found in the offices of old established firms which transcend anything ever achieved in a schoolboy's locker.

The strong room at Twenty-three seemed to have become simply one of those useful places where nothing is ever cleaned up, so that anything deposited therein may reasonably expect to remain in safety until it is again needed.

All the same, it occurred to him as he looked round that the amount of odds and ends which three generations of Barnabas directors had considered worth keeping was distressing when viewed in the bulk.

The safe, he decided, could well be the centrepiece in any museum which an enterprising burglars' guild might establish for the edification of junior members. It was massive enough in all conscience and looked as if it had been built to withstand shell-fire, but it opened with a key, a large key if the size of the highly decorated hole could be taken as a guide.

He was still looking at it when hasty footsteps pattered down the passage and the door leading out into the yard banged. Feeling a little guilty but not really deterred, Mr. Campion continued his tour.

Lying on a dusty parcel of manuscript on the shelf nearest the table he came upon an anachronism. It was a bowler hat, nearly new and only very slightly dusty. Turning it over gingerly he saw the initials "P.R.B." inside, and on the door below was a neatly rolled umbrella.

Mr. Campion's frown deepened. The problem as he saw it had certainly a great technical interest, apart from its personal side. A man, dressed for the street, found dead in his own strong room, the door locked on the outside, four days after he disappeared, presented a situation provoking thought.

Campion took another look at the ventilator and wished he might see the body.

A few minutes later he was examining the door of the room and had just decided that at no time had the lock been forced or picked when the pattering feet returned, this time from the courtyard. There was a rush of bitter air as the door swung open and next moment somebody paused and looked in at him.

Mr. Rigget and Mr. Campion exchanged glances.

For some seconds Mr. Rigget hesitated, torn between a desire to see what was going on upstairs and an inclination to investigate Mr. Campion's unexpected presence. He took stock of the stranger carefully, his eyes round and excited behind his glittering pince-nez.

He decided almost immediately that Mr. Campion was not a detective. Mr. Rigget's knowledge of detectives was small and his opinion bigoted. A thrilling alternative occurred to him and he came forward ingratiatingly.

"Could *I* help, I wonder?" he suggested, lending the offer a tinge of the underhand. "I shouldn't want my name mentioned at first, of course, but if there's anything you want to know . . . ?"

He broke off promisingly, adding a moment later as Campion's expression did not change:

"You're a journalist, of course?"

"There's no 'of course' about it," said Mr. Campion. "What's on the other side of this wall?"

"A—a garage," said Rigget, startled into speech.

Mr. Campion's eyebrows seemed in danger of disappearing.

"How many cars?"

"Only one. Mr. Wedgwood keeps his Fiat there. Why?"

Mr. Campion ignored the question. Instead he snapped out another.

"Who are you?"

Neither his tone nor manner fitted in with Mr. Rigget's idea of the jolly, hard-boiled journalist he had seen so often on the films. He grew crimson.

"I have a position here," he said stiffly.

"Fine," said Mr. Campion heartily. "Toddle along and keep it up."

"You are a journalist, aren't you?" said Mr. Rigget, now considerably alarmed.

"Certainly not." Campion looked astonished by the suggestion.

"But you're not a detective. It wasn't you who came in with the Coroner's Officer just now."

"Ah! He's here at last, is he?" said the pale young man with interest. "Splendid! Good morning."

"Shall I tell him you're waiting?" Mr. Rigget's slender pink nose quivered as he caught a glimpse of this exciting chance to visit, if only for a moment, the heart of the enquiry.

"No," said Mr. Campion. "It wouldn't be true." And, brushing past his would-be informant, he moved quietly out of the room and mounted the stairs.

Mr. Rigget stood irresolute. Some instinct told him that it would not be wise to follow immediately. Moreover, the sense of mingled shame and apprehension, inevitable aftermath of a too hastily seized conclusion, was upon him. The scene of the trouble, on the other hand, was not a healthy spot in which to linger with the police in the house. In default of any other retreat Mr. Rigget shut himself in the washroom.

Mr. Campion hurried up the stairs. His face was unusually blank and there was a strained expression in his pale eyes. He had made a discovery, or at least he had unearthed a possibility which, if it should prove to be substantiated by other facts, was going to lead to serious trouble.

At the top of the stairs he hesitated. His next step presented difficulties. He was not at all sure of his own place in the proceedings. Miss Curley had invited him to the house presumably on her own initiative; therefore he was not working with the police but in the interests of his friends. In view of everything Mr. Campion was inclined to wonder what their interests would prove to be.

However, his curiosity overrode his caution and he considered the best means of getting the information he needed.

He was still hesitating in the fog-laden hall, wondering if he should take the bull by the horns and go up to Gina's flat, when he caught sight of a shadowy figure drifting down the stairs from the floor above. Ritchie, of course; Mr. Campion had forgotten him. He stepped forward, his hand outstretched.

"Mr. Barnabas," he began, "I don't know if you remember me——"

The tall looser built man paused abruptly and a pair of astonishingly mild blue eyes peered into Campion's own.

"Yes," he said. "I do. You're a friend of Mike's, aren't you? Albert Campion. You're the man we want. You've heard, of course?"

Campion nodded. The sense of shock and regret which he had missed in the office was here very apparent. Ritchie looked haggard and the bony hand he thrust into Campion's own shook.

"They've only just told me," he said. "One of the secretaries came up to my room. I was reading. I didn't dream . . . Mike went down there last night, you know."

He paused and passed his hand through his tufty grey hair.

"Twenty years ago . . ." he added unexpectedly. "But it was May then . . . none of this awful fog about."

Mr. Campion blinked. He remembered now the other's habit of flitting from subject to subject, linked only by some erratic thought process at which one could only guess. However, he had no time to study Ritchie Barnabas's eccentricities at the moment. There was something very important that he had to find out at once.

"Look here," he said impulsively, "I'm at a great disadvantage. I really haven't any business here at all, but I do want a few words with someone who has seen the body. Do you think—I mean, could you possibly . . . ?"

Ritchie hesitated. "I'll see what I can do," he said at last, adding abruptly, his eyes fixed anxiously upon Campion's like a dog who is attempting to talk: "The body . . . that was the terrible part of it then. . . . Nothing . . . not a sign. Poor young Paul!" And afterwards, in an entirely different tone: "A mild day it was, inclined to be misty. But no fog like this."

He turned away and had gone halfway up the stairs again when he paused and finally returned.

"Go upstairs to my room," he said. "It's right at the top of the house. Forgive me for not thinking of it before."

He went off again, only to turn at the landing to look back.

"I'll meet you there," he said. "Come up now."

Mr. Campion found his way to Ritchie's office with

some difficulty. It lay at the very top of the house and was approached by a small staircase set behind the panelling of a larger room. Campion discovered it only by accident, having caught a glimpse of the swinging door as he put his head into the last room on what had at first appeared to be the top floor.

The office itself was a fitting place for its owner. It was very small and was built round an old-fashioned brick chimney, to which it seemed to cling for support. Apart from two dilapidated chairs huddled close to the minute fireplace, the whole place was a mass of manuscripts. They jostled and sat upon each other in tall unsteady piles rising up to meet the sloping ceiling.

A little window through which the fog now looked like a saffron blanket held up to the light filled one alcove, and, save for this and the glow from the fire, the place was in darkness.

Campion found the switch and a dusty reading lamp on the mantelpiece shot into prominence.

He sat down to wait. After the chill downstairs the room felt warm and musty, the air spiced with the smell of paper. It was a very personal place, he decided; like an old coat slipped off for a moment regretfully.

He had barely time to let its unexpected charm take hold of him when Ritchie returned. He came scrambling up the staircase like some overgrown spider, his long thin arms and legs barking themselves recklessly on the wooden walls.

"She's coming," he said. "Won't be a moment. Had to powder her face. Too bad . . . a child, Campion . . . only eighteen. Very pretty . . . typist or something. Good family . . . been crying . . . making statement."

He sat down.

Mr. Campion, who had deduced that he was not talking about Miss Curley, had an inspiration.

"You've got hold of the girl who found him?"

Ritchie nodded. "Terrible experience! Glad to get away from them all. Nice girl."

He brought a packet of cigarettes out of his pocket and lit one thoughtfully. He had replaced the package when, with a word of apology, he produced it again and forced a rather battered cigarette upon Campion.

"You knew Paul well?" he said. "Poor fellow! Poor fellow! You didn't? Oh, I see. . . . Well, it's a shock for everybody. It must be. . . . Dead three days, they say. Can't have been. Mike was there last night. Doctors don't know, do they?"

Mr. Campion was slowly getting used to this somewhat extraordinary method of conversation. He had experienced this jerky chatter before, but in Ritchie's case the man had a disconcerting way of fixing one with his gentle blue eyes with an earnestness which was somehow pathetic. It was evident that he wanted to be understood, but found speech very difficult.

In spite of his preoccupation with the pressing matter on hand, Campion noticed that the elder man used long sweeping gestures, completely meaningless in themselves, and he began to understand why the intolerant Jacoby Barnabas of the portrait in the waiting room had found this particular nephew so unsatisfactory.

Although he was still obviously very shaken, Ritchie seemed more at ease now that he was back in his own little room. He glanced about it, caught Mr. Campion's eye and smiled shyly.

"Been here twenty years, reading," he said.

Campion was taken off his guard.

"No remission for good conduct?" he said involuntarily.

Ritchie looked away, and for the first time the younger man was aware of something not quite frank about him.

"Get away sometimes," he said. "Week or two now and again. Why not . . . ? Must live."

His tone was so nearly angry that Campion almost apologized. He had the uncomfortable impression that the man was hiding something.

He put the idea from him as absurd, but the impression remained.

Ritchie was puffing furiously at his cigarette, his long thin fingers with their enormous knuckles gripping the little flattened tube clumsily.

"Strong personality," he said, his blue eyes once again fixed on Campion's face. "Moved very quickly . . . did foolish things. But to be found dead . . . terrible! Have you ever been in love?"

"Eh?" said Mr. Campion, completely taken aback.

"Don't understand it," said Ritchie with a wave of a long bony arm. "Never did. Paul didn't love Gina. Extraordinary. Mike's a good boy."

Campion was sorting out the possible relations between these disjointed ramblings when there was a movement on the stairs below and Ritchie got up.

"Miss Marchant," he said.

He disappeared for a moment, to return almost at once with a very pretty girl. She had been crying, and was still near tears. As he caught sight of her Mr. Campion was inclined to agree with Ritchie's sympathetic outburst. It certainly did seem a shame that this little yellow-haired girl with the big frightened eyes and demure, intelligent face should have been subjected to what must have been a very unpleasant experience.

Ritchie was already performing the introductions. He was less jerky and more at his ease when speaking to the girl, and there was a gentleness about him which was very attractive.

"Sit down," he said, taking her by the hand and leading her into the room. "This is Mr. Campion, a very clever man, not a policeman."

He peered down into her face and evidently thought he saw tears there, for he pressed a large white pocket-handkerchief into her hand without any explanation.

"Now," he said, squatting down between them on the dusty boards, "tell him."

Campion leant forward. "I'm awfully sorry to trouble you, Miss Marchant," he said. "It must be most unpleasant for you to go all through this again. But you would be doing me and Mr. Barnabas a very great service if you'd answer one or two questions. I won't keep you long."

The girl made a rather pathetic attempt at a smile.

"I don't mind," she said. "I'm glad to get away from them all. What do you want to know?"

Mr. Campion approached his point gingerly. It was not going to be easy.

"When you went down to the strong room this morning," he began, "did Miss Curley give you the key or did you take it out of her desk?"

"I—I took it. It was hanging on a little hook screwed into the underside of the flap at the back. It always hangs there."

"I see. And you just took it and went straight down-stairs?"

"Yes. But I've told all this to the Coroner's Officer." Her voice was rising, and Mr. Campion stretched out a soothing hand.

"I know," he said. "And it's really very kind of you to tell it to me again. When you unlocked the door and went in, what did you do?"

The girl took a deep breath.

"I switched on the light," she said. "Then I'm afraid I screamed."

"Oh, I see. . . ." Mr. Campion was very grave. "You saw him at once?"

"Oh, yes. He was just inside the door. My foot nearly touched his foot. When I turned on the light I was looking straight down at him."

Ritchie nodded at her, and with a wave of a flail-like arm encouraged her to use the handkerchief he had just lent her. There was something so extremely comic in the gesture that just for an instant laughter crept out behind the tears in the round eyes.

Mr. Campion proceeded cautiously.

"Look here," he said very gently, "this is going to help a lot. Try not to think of the man you found as someone you've seen in the office, someone you've worked for; think of him just as a thing, a rather ugly sight you've been called upon to look at. What struck you most about him when you first saw him?"

Miss Marchant pulled herself together. Mr. Campion had been speaking to her as though she were a child, and she was a modern young woman of eighteen.

"His colour," she said.

Mr. Campion permitted himself a long intake of breath.

"He was pink," said the girl. "I didn't think he was dead, you see. I thought he'd fallen down in a fit—apoplexy or something. I went up to him and bent down, and then I

45

saw he was dead. He was bright, bright pink, and his lips were swollen."

"And was he lying quite naturally?" said Mr. Campion, anxious to lead her away once the vital fact had been ascertained.

Miss Marchant hesitated. "I think so. He was on his back and stretched out, his hands at his sides. It wasn't—nice."

"Terrible!" said Ritchie earnestly. "Terrible! Poor girl! Poor Paul! All frightful . . ."

He hurled his cigarette stub into the fire and searched frantically for another, hoisting his gaunt body from side to side as he fought with his pockets.

Miss Marchant glanced at Mr. Campion.

"That's all," she said. "I ran out and told Miss Curley and the others after that."

"Naturally." Campion's tone was soothing and friendly. "Where was the hat?"

"The hat?" She looked at him dubiously for a moment, her brows wrinkled. "Oh, his bowler hat . . . of course. Why, it was there on the ground, just near him."

"Near his head or near his hand?" Mr. Campion persisted.

"Near his shoulder, I think . . . his left shoulder." She was screwing up her eyes in an effort of recollection.

"How was it lying?"

Miss Marchant considered. "Flat on its brim," she said at last. "I remember now. It was. I caught sight of the round black mound out of the corner of my eye and I wondered what it was at first. His umbrella was there too, lying beyond it, where it must have fallen when he fell."

She shuddered involuntarily as the picture returned to her, and looked younger than ever.

"On the left?" laboured Mr. Campion. "On *your* left?"

"No, *his* left. I told you. The side furthest from the table."

"I see," said Mr. Campion, and his face became blank. "I see."

Ritchie shepherded Miss Marchant to the floor below. When he came back his mild blue eyes rested upon Campion eagerly.

"Clearer?" he enquired, and added abruptly: "Sounds like gas, doesn't it?"

Mr. Campion regarded the other man thoughtfully. It had been slowly dawning upon him for some time now that Ritchie's disjointed phrases and meaningless gestures were disabilities behind which a mind resided. However, this last shrewdness was unexpected.

"Yes," he said slowly. "It does. Carbon monoxide, in fact. Of course one can't possibly tell for certain without taking a blood test but Miss Marchant's description does indicate it. Besides, it fits in damnably with one or two things I noticed downstairs."

Ritchie heaved a sigh of relief. "Garage next door to the strong room," he remarked. "Fumes must have percolated somehow. Accident. Poor Paul. . . ."

Mr. Campion said nothing.

Ritchie clambered into the chair Miss Marchant had vacated and sat poring over the fire, his immense bony hands held out to the tiny blaze.

"Carbon monoxide," he said. "How much of it will kill?"

Mr. Campion, who had been reflecting upon the problem for some time, gave a considered opinion.

"I'm not sure of the exact proportion," he said, "but it's something very small . . . just over four per cent in the atmosphere in some cases, I believe. The trouble with the stuff is that it's so insidious. You don't realize you're going under until you've gone, if you see what I mean. The exhaust of a car is pretty nearly the pure stuff."

Ritchie nodded sagaciously. "Dangerous," he said. "No ventilation down there with the door shut."

". . . And locked." The words were on the tip of Mr. Campion's tongue, but he did not utter them.

Ritchie continued. "Shouldn't have been there," he said. "Paul always poking about out of hours. Silly fellow . . . sorry he's dead."

The last remark was not put in as an afterthought. Every line of Ritchie's gaunt body indicated his regret, and his tone was as expressive as the most elaborate speech.

"I didn't know him well," said Campion. "I met him at most four or five times."

Ritchie shook his head. "Difficult chap," he remarked. "Great egoist. Too dominant. But good fellow. Impulsive. Not in love with Gina. Dreadful accident."

Mr. Campion's mind wandered to the little grating under the shelf in the strong room, and presently, when he and the other man went down the stairs together, it was still in his thoughts.

Ritchie was frankly overcome by the horror of the accident. The locked door and the time of death were both points that he had evidently shelved as minor details, while the significance of the position of the hat and umbrella had escaped him entirely.

As they crossed the hall, two policemen in plain clothes came up from the basement. Campion recognized one of them as Detective-Sergeant Pillow of the special branch. The man glanced up as he passed, and nodded, satisfaction in his little black eyes.

As Campion caught sight of the curious burden he carried, his heart missed a beat. Carefully wrapped round the middle with a dark handkerchief, its ends looped into drooping bows and its protected centre clasped in the Sergeant's stubby hand, was a length of rubber tubing such as is sometimes used for the improvisation of a shower-bath. Sergeant Pillow carried it as though it were his dearest possession.

4

Relations

To Gordon Roe, Esq., Surgeon.

London.
To wit.
Sir,

By virtue of this my Order as one of His Majesty's Coroners for the County of London you are hereby required to be and appear before me and the jury on Tuesday the ninth of February at eleven o'clock in the forenoon at the Court in the Parish of St. Joan's, Holborn, and then and there to give evidence on His Majesty's behalf touching the death of Paul Redfern Brande and to make or assist in making a post-mortem examination of the viscera of the Head, Chest and Abdomen of the body of the said Paul Redfern Brande without an analysis and report thereon at the said inquest. And herein fail not at your peril.

Dated the second day of February, 1931.

P. J. Salley,
Coroner.

Doctor Roe patted his pocket absently as he entered the hall of Gina's flat on the Friday following the discovery of Paul Brande's body and the Coroner's summons crackled responsively. The little doctor was following the anxious Mrs. Austin down the passage to the studio with a certain amount of curiosity.

"I really think you ought to have a look at her, Doctor." The charwoman spoke in a hushed voice and without looking round as she ploughed over the thick carpet in her soft shoes. "Not a mite of sleep she hasn't had. You can see it in her face. I said to her I said, 'You have the doctor, dear. After all, he can't make you worse nor what you are at present.' And she said to me, 'I think I will, Mrs. Austin.' 'Lie down,' I said, but she wouldn't, and there she is sitting in front of the fire like a lily."

Her speech lasted until they reached the door, but just before she entered she laid a plump, damp hand upon his own and looked up at him, a gleam of conspiratorial excitement in her eyes.

"Have they found out anything yet?"

Doctor Roe coughed. "I really don't know, Mrs. Austin," he said pleasantly. "I'm not a policeman, you know. Now where is our patient?"

Mrs. Austin raised her eyebrows, and, with many

49

ostentatious precautions against noise, tiptoed heavily into the room.

"Here's the doctor, dear," she said in a sepulchral whisper which might well have given her employer a heart attack had their entry been really quiet.

Gina was sitting in one of the big white armchairs in a tailored black wrapper which contrasted with the pallor of her face and the brilliance of her eyes and hair. She made a pathetic attempt at a smile.

"I'm glad to see you, Doctor," she said. "Won't you sit down? That'll do, Mrs. Austin."

That good lady left the room, making it plain that she did so against her better judgment. Doctor Roe remained upon his feet. His professional personality inclined to heartiness and was seen at its best astride a hearth rug.

"Well, now, Mrs. Brande," he said, "what's the trouble? Not sleeping, eh? Well, of course, that's not to be wondered at, but you can help yourself much better than anyone else can, you know. You need courage, young lady, great courage. Any other symptoms? Eating well?"

Gina leant forward, her small white hands clasped together, her elbows resting on her knees.

"Doctor," she said, "what's happened about my husband?"

The little medical man stiffened, and something that was half alarm, half resentment, flickered in his eyes.

"I came here to discuss your health, Mrs. Brande," he said warningly.

"Oh, Doctor . . ."—the soft New England accent slurred the words—". . . I don't mean to offend you. I don't understand professional etiquette and that sort of thing, but can't you see that the thing that's making me ill is not knowing what's going to happen—what is happening. What are the police doing? Why was the inquest on Tuesday adjourned for seven days? What do they expect to learn from the post-mortem?"

"My dear lady . . ." Doctor Roe's voice conveyed that his sense of decorum was outraged . . . "I'm a medical practitioner. I'm not a detective. You sent for me to ask advice about your health, and I'm prepared to give it to you. I can see you want sleep and I can prescribe something that will see to that. But I don't know anything about your other trouble, and if I did I couldn't discuss it. It would be most improper."

"But even if you're a doctor, you're human." The girl's voice was quivering. "Don't you see you're the only person who knows what the police are thinking? Just imagine my position. . . . my husband disappeared ten days ago. Four days later he was found dead. Without any warning, without any explanation, the police arrived. My husband's body was taken away. I was summoned to appear at an inquest the next day. It lasted five minutes at the outside. My cousin-in-law gave evidence of identification, and the Coroner adjourned for seven days. I've been subpoenaed for the second part of the inquest, and of course I shall go. Yet when I went out yesterday I was followed."

She paused, and the nervous tension behind her eyes was vivid and painful.

"If only they said *something*!" she said. "If only they told me! It's being kept in the dark that's getting on my nerves. Why are they watching me? Why should they think that I might run away? What's happening?"

Doctor Roe was not entirely impervious to the appeal of a very pretty woman, but there is perhaps no professional man who must protect himself more carefully than the physician.

"I'm very sorry for you," he said quite genuinely, "but I can't tell you anything about the police. They have their own methods and go about their affairs in their own mysterious way."

He frowned and looked slightly uncomfortable. Doubtless the recollection of his unpleasant morning's work with the police surgeon in the mortuary had returned to him. But he pocketed his sympathy. Some things were safe, others were not. He attempted to be consoling and at the same time noncommittal.

"I shouldn't worry," he said. "You have yourself to think of now, you know, and we mustn't have your health letting you down. Let me have your wrist, please."

He felt her pulse and compared it with his watch.

"A little excited," he announced, "but not seriously. I'll send you round something to make you sleep. You'll feel very much better in the morning. This period of suspense is very trying, I know, but you must try and pull yourself together. You've had a very great shock—a very great shock indeed—and your grief has naturally worn you down?"

The inquisitive soul which lurked behind the physician in Doctor Gordon Roe prompted the faint question contained in the last remark, and the girl responded to it without thinking.

"It's not grief," she said. "Not real grief. I'm sorry for Paul, but I was not in love with him."

Doctor Roe started. Even his most mischievous and unworthy hopes had not included a statement quite so damaging. He was both shocked and frightened by it.

"Come, come, you don't mean that, Mrs. Brande," he said peremptorily. "You're overwrought."

The girl looked at him in surprise for a moment and then her nerves seemed suddenly to fail her altogether.

"How horrible you all are!" she said explosively. "If I'd said that before my husband died you wouldn't have thought anything of it—no one would—and yet it's just as true now as it was then. Now I've only got to say that I didn't love my husband and you look at me as though you thought I'd murdered him."

Doctor Roe was panic-stricken.

"I—I must protest. Really!" he murmured into his collar, and made for the door, from which he summoned Mrs. Austin. "Get your mistress to bed," he ordered so sharply that she wondered whether he had divined that she had listened outside the door, and, having done what he considered was his duty, made his escape.

Meanwhile in a small flat over the police station in Bottle Street, Piccadilly, Mr. Campion was sitting at his desk attempting to write letters and at the same time to take a comparatively intelligent share in a conversation which he was holding with someone in the room next door.

"It's goin' to be a nasty case," a thick, inexpressibly melancholy voice announced bitterly. "Anyone can see that with 'alf an eye. You keep out of it. You don't want to get notorious. The way your name's been gettin' about lately you're a positive publicity 'ound."

"I resent that," said Mr. Campion, writing "hound"

irrelevantly in the midst of a note to his bank manager and crossing it out again. "These people are my friends, you know."

"All the more reason you want to keep away," said the voice, adopting this time a flavour of worldly wisdom. "Friends'll ask you to do things what strangers would never dare. It's a sex crime, I suppose you know that?"

"What?" said Mr. Campion. He had removed his spectacles, which somewhat obscured his vision when writing, but now he replaced them and laid down his pen.

"Sex crime," said the voice from within. "You've bin pretty lucky so far keepin' out of that sort of degradation, but you won't look so pretty trailin' about with the mud of the cheap Press all over you. I couldn't associate meself with you after that, for one thing. You'll lose all your old friends."

"Lugg," said Mr. Campion sternly. "Come in here."

There was a rumble in the other room as though a minor earthquake had disturbed it, and, preceded by the sound of deep breathing, Magersfontein Lugg surged into the room.

His girth was increasing with the years and with it his melancholy. He had also achieved a certain sartorial elegance without losing his unconventionality in that direction. At the moment he was clad in what appeared to be the hind legs of a black elephant, a spotless but collarless boiled shirt and a black velvet jacket.

His employer surveyed him coldly. "The *vie de bohême*, I see," he observed. "How are the tiny hands?"

Mr. Lugg shook his head ponderously. "Turn it aside with a light word if you like," he said mournfully, "but here we are, all respectable, nice, good class and the first nasty eruption that breaks out you're in it up to the neck."

"Where did you get that coat?"

"'Ad it made for me," said Mr. Lugg, with intent to snub. "It's a gentleman's 'ouse coat and very smart. All the wear just now. I bought it because I see in the paper that a certain important relative of yours is not too well, and if anything 'appened to 'im and you were suddenly called to take your place in the world I should like to be prepared."

"Yes, well, of course, you're revolting," said Mr.

Campion, getting up. "Ten years ago you climbed up the side of a three-story house with the agility of a monkey, let yourself through a skylight, opened a safe and got away as clean as a whistle and now look at you. You couldn't steal a bag of sweets from a two-year-old in a pram."

"I shouldn't want to, I hope," said Mr. Lugg, with dignity. "Besides," he added, lowering his puffy white lids over his little black eyes and achieving a superbly virtuous expression, "them things all belong to the past. It's the future we've got to think of, and that's why I do 'ope you'll steer clear of anything with a nasty flavour. It looked very bad in the evening newspapers and not at all the sort of thing you want to get our names mixed up with."

"You've gone soft, Lugg," said Campion, with regret. "I haven't given you enough work lately. I don't think there's much in this case for you, either."

"I'm glad to 'ear it." Mr. Lugg was positive. "When they was all talking about it at the club, discussin' the details, I said to myself, 'I do 'ope I keep out of this. It isn't as though we're on the side of the police.'"

Mr. Campion perched himself on the edge of the desk and wrapped the folds of his thin and rather dilapidated silk dressing-gown around his bony form.

"When you say 'the club,' do you mean that pub in Wardour Street?" he enquired.

A wooden expression crept into Mr. Lugg's face.

"No. I don't go there any more. I took exception to some of the members. Very low type of person, they were. If you want to know, I go to a very quiet, respectable little place in a mews up Mayfair way. There are several nice people there in me own line of business."

"Gentlemen's gentlemen, I suppose?" said Mr. Campion sarcastically.

"Exactly," agreed Mr. Lugg belligerently. "And why not? A nice superior class of people I meet and I hear all the gossip."

"I'm disgusted with you." Campion sounded genuine. "You make me sick. I've a good mind to sack you."

"You try," said Mr. Lugg, with a return of his old fire. "I'd like to know where you'd be—as helpless as a babe unborn. I've trained you not to be able to do without me.

You drop the case and we won't say anything more about it. Nothin' could be fairer than that.

"After all," he went on persuasively as he noticed no sign of capitulation in Mr. Campion's expression, "once sex rears its ugly 'ead it's time to steer clear. You know that as well as I do."

Mr. Campion's mystified expression deepened.

"You're not trying to be funny?" he suggested.

"Do I ever try to be funny?" said Mr. Lugg, with justifiable reproach. "It's not a funny subjec'."

Campion stirred. "Where did you get this—this sex idea?" he said. "I thought the papers were very reticent. They must be, of course, the law of libel being what it is."

"Readin' between the lines," said Mr. Lugg darkly. "Libel or no libel, if you reads the newspapers properly it's always clear what's 'appened. It's not what they say: it's the way they say it."

Campion frowned. "There's a lot of truth in that, unfortunately," he observed. "After your little mug between the lines, what do you deduce?"

"The wife did it, of course. They published 'er photograph. Did you see it? Nice-lookin' little bit—just the type."

Mr. Campion shuddered. "Lugg, you've done it this time," he said. "Get out."

Before the vigour of the command Mr. Lugg was abashed.

"No offence, Cock," he said hastily. "I don't know anything about the inside story. I'm only tellin' you how it appears to the man in the street. That's what you want to know, isn't it?"

Campion was silent for a moment, a slightly less vacuous expression than usual upon his pale, inoffensive face.

"I know these people, Lugg," he said at last. "They're all right, I tell you. Charming, straightforward, decent people. Mrs. Brande is one of the most delightful women I've ever met, and yet you see, apart from the tragedy of losing her husband, her portrait appears in the newspapers and the opinion in the Mayfair pubs is that she did him in."

Mr. Lugg was rebuked, but it was not his temperament to admit the fact.

"The tragedy of losin' 'er 'usband?" he said contemptuously. "That's good, that is! Hadn't the fellow been missin' since the Thursday and found dead in the office next door on the Monday? That's not my idea of a nice lovin' wife. Lets 'er old man be missin' three or four days and doesn't say a word."

"She sent for me," said Mr. Campion.

"Ho, she did, did she?" Lugg was interested. "That makes all the difference. Still, it didn't come out in the Press, did it? So how was I to know, or anybody else? Who do you think done it?"

Mr. Campion passed his hand over his fair hair and his eyes clouded.

"I don't know, Lugg," he said. "I don't know at all. I'm on the inside, you see, and yet you and your pals at the club have fixed the guilt already."

"Ah," said Mr. Lugg, "and I shouldn't be at all surprised if we wasn't right. Outsiders see most of the game, you know. You mark my words," he went on, gathering confidence, "before we know where we are up'll crop some nice young fellow she's 'ad her eye on. There'll be the motive and—there you are!"

Mr. Campion's reply was silenced by the trilling of the front-door bell. Lugg pressed his tongue against the back of his front teeth and emitted a clucking sound expressing both annoyance and resignation.

"What a time for anyone to come visitin'," he said.

Moving across the room, he opened the bottom drawer of a bureau and took therefrom, to Mr. Campion's horror, a remarkable contraption consisting of a stiff collar with a black bow tie attached. With perfect solemnity and a certain amount of pride, Mr. Lugg fastened this monstrosity round his neck by means of a button at the back, and moved ponderously out of the room, leaving his employer momentarily speechless.

Mike came into the room unannounced. The last two or three days had made a great difference in his appearance. His shorn black curls seemed to have receded a little and the skin over his forehead looked taut and lined. The old sleepy expression was still lurking in his eyes, but there was anxiety there also.

"I had to come round," he said abruptly. "I want to see you." He paused and glanced hesitantly at the sepulchral figure behind him, and Campion took the hint.

"That's all right, Lugg, please," he said.

The old ex-burglar raised his eyebrows. "I shall be in the kitchenette, sir, if you should require me," he said in so affected a voice that Campion gaped.

Mike was in no condition to notice extraneous details, however. As soon as he was alone he threw himself down in one of the deep chairs by the fire and sighed.

"This is damned awful, Campion," he said. "Losing old Paul's bad enough, but you can't imagine what it's been like this week. We haven't been able to call ourselves our own. Gina seems to be going to pieces altogether. Is there any way of finding out what the police have in their minds? I know you'll do your best for us. Have you found out anything?"

Mr. Campion, who was employed with a cocktail-shaker at the cabinet on the other side of the room, spoke over his shoulder.

"I went down to Scotland Yard," he said, "but Stanislaus Oates is on leave, and Tanner and Pillow, the men in charge of your business, were quite polite, but they weren't giving anything away. However, I shouldn't worry. Old Salley, the Coroner, is a good scout; a fierce old boy, rather abrupt, but hasn't held the office all this time without learning a thing or two. Have the police been round much since the postponement?"

"Round much . . . !" Mike groaned. "They're living in the office. We've all made statements till we're black in the face. Gina had a beastly experience, too. I persuaded her to go out a bit—sitting indoors brooding was doing her no good. She had a luncheon date with the Adelaide Chappel woman—the soprano. They went down to Boulestin's, and afterwards Madame Chappel had to go to Cook's, of all places. She always books through them, apparently, and she was off to Belgrade to sing in a concert there. Gina had nothing better to do, and went with her. She got the impression she was being followed, and actually saw a detective enquiring about her from a clerk. Since then there's been a man outside the flat. It's damnable, Campion, absolutely damnable! Why shouldn't she turn up at the inquest? Why shouldn't any of us? What have the police got up their sleeves?"

Mr. Campion handed his guest a cocktail before he spoke.

"What about all these statements you've been making?" he said. "I suppose they've been questioning you on your original essay dictated to the Coroner's Officer?"

"Have they not!" Mike spoke explosively. "I've gone over all that a dozen times, and so has Gina, to say nothing of poor old Curley and the poor little beast who found the body. They come to see us every day. This morning they were on a new track."

He drank the cocktail without tasting it and his eyes were fixed anxiously on Campion.

"They ask questions the whole time," he said, "but they never tell you anything. Today it was all the Thursday night stuff. Can you remember what you did last Thursday night—not yesterday, but the week before?"

Campion pricked up his ears. "Thursday night?" he said. "Did they ask everybody?"

"Oh, rather! I asked Pillow—a funny little chap, Campion, a sort of good-class head gardener, the last person on earth to be a detective—if they'd fixed the time of death, but he wouldn't say anything. Simply smiled surreptitiously."

Mr. Campion sat down on the edge of the opposite chair.

"Did he ask you about any special time on Thursday?"

"Yes. Between eight and nine o'clock. You've never heard such a tedious business. The whole office went through it. Poor Curley was nearly off her head. John couldn't remember where he was and she had to hunt up engagement books and phone through to inquisitive friends and business acquaintances. Finally it transpired that he was at the dinner given by the Quill Club to Lutzow, the psychologist. The secretary remembered him arriving at ten to eight and he didn't get back till eleven or twelve. Curley herself appears to have been in a Tube train on the Morden line. I was out until ten to nine. Gina was alone in the flat waiting for Paul. All simple ordinary activities, but difficult to remember when you're asked suddenly. Frankly, what's worrying me is that as far as I can see there's an ordinary explanation for the poor chap's death. The carbon monoxide must have soaked into the room and gassed him. The explanation of the locked door I suggested to Pillow was something like this: I think he went down there, let himself in, and left the key in the lock. The door swung to, and someone else, one of the employees, saw the key in the lock, turned it and took it upstairs and put it back in its place. Now they're probably too frightened to admit it."

Mr. Campion considered. "What did Sergeant Pillow say to that?"

Mike shrugged his shoulders. "Oh, you know what these policemen are! They're so darned clever. He said he'd look into it, and went on questioning me."

"How's your cousin taking it?" Mr. Campion put the question mildly.

"Who? John?" Mike permitted himself a faint smile. "He's quite fantastic. Simply doesn't realize that anything's up. Treats the police as though they were literary agents he'd never heard of, and spends his spare time thinking out little obscure paragraphs to send to the newspapers explaining why the funeral has been delayed. John's only thinking about Barnabas, Limited. He's believed so long that its reputation is sacred that he doesn't recognize a scandal when it comes along. He's had all the staff in crêpe bands, if you please, and has made arrangements for a very quiet and respectable funeral at Golders Green on the day after the inquest."

Campion replenished the empty glass.

"Mrs. Brande doesn't mind all these details taken off her hands, of course," he ventured.

"Gina? Oh, no." Mike spoke bitterly. "I think Gina always realized that Paul belonged to the firm more than to her. He—well, he neglected her in an impossible fashion, you know."

He lowered his eyes as he spoke and busied himself lighting a cigarette.

Mr. Campion did not speak, and after a pause the other man went on.

"Paul wasn't a subtle soul at all," he said, "and he had

the disconcerting habit of working himself into a fever to get hold of beautiful things and then forgetting all about them. It was the same with everything. He didn't appreciate the things he had."

Mr. Campion heaved a piece of coal into the centre of the blaze.

"As much as you might have done?" he suggested softly.

Rather to his surprise, Mike's dark eyes met his own squarely.

"That's the trouble," the younger man said quietly.

"How far has it gone?" enquired Mr. Campion.

"Not at all, thank God." Mike spoke fervently. "She's not particularly interested in me. I've just been about and we've naturally gone around together, but that's all. You don't understand Gina, Campion. No one does. I hope to heaven we can keep her out of this."

Mr. Campion was silent. For a moment he was aware of forces and counter-forces beneath the surface of the quiet lives surrounding Barnabas, Limited. There were revelations to come, he knew, some of them hideous, some of them piteous and others fantastic in their unexpectedness. He also knew that the man in front of him did not dream that once the searchlight of police and Press was turned on them there could be nothing hidden, nothing protected, and that beneath the glare little intimate things would stand out in unnatural prominence.

Aloud he said: "You ought to have married years ago, Mike."

The other man stirred. "I'm damned glad I didn't. Things are complicated enough as they are. Forget it and shut up about it. I don't know why I come to you, blethering about my secret affairs when there's open trouble to discuss. Hullo, who's this?"

His last remark was occasioned by the sound of a woman's voice in the hall. They had not heard her ring, and when Lugg showed the black-clad figure into the room a moment later they were taken by surprise.

"Gina! What are you doing here?" Mike rose to his feet and went towards her. All trace of his nerviness of a moment before had vanished. He had himself well in hand, Mr. Campion noticed approvingly.

Gina stared at him without a word of greeting and turned abruptly to Campion.

"You didn't mind me coming, did you?" she said hastily. "I'm going mad sitting up alone in the flat, wondering what the police are thinking. I even sent for the doctor, but he wouldn't tell me anything. Albert, what are they going to *do* on Tuesday?"

"Talk and talk and talk for hours, and write it all down by hand in the copybook," said Mike easily. "Look, here, suppose you come and sit down in this expensive-looking chair and let Campion give you a White Lady."

She turned to him and her wide grey eyes searched his face anxiously. He met her scrutiny smiling.

"Things are going to be all right," he said. "There's nothing to worry about. You look very fine. Did you design all that white collaretting? What d'you call it—a jabot or a bertha?"

"Mike, I can't bear it," she said, turning away from him. "Albert, tell me, what's happened?"

She sat down in the chair as she spoke and her pale face was raised to Campion's appealingly.

"He doesn't know any more than we do, Gina, but he says the Coroner is a wise old boy who isn't likely to make mistakes."

Mike spoke soothingly and pulled another chair forward and sat down in it between them. The girl seized at the straw of comfort.

"Still, people do make mistakes, don't they?" she said slowly. "To the police things look different, worse then they are. I could see that when I was interviewed by Inspector Tanner last night. I told him something, and I could see as he wrote it down that he thought—well, that he thought about it in a different way from the one in which it happened."

"Tell us about it." Campion handed her a glass as he made the suggestion.

She hesitated, and some of the colour returned to her face.

"It doesn't seem so important now," she said. "I'm behaving very badly, I'm afraid."

"Let's have it."

"Well—" Gina cleared her throat, "—I didn't know you were going to be here, Mike. It's something you don't know about, and you'll probably be surprised or shocked, but there was my side to it, and it wasn't all my fault."

She hesitated again, and the two men watched her as she sat there, so small and fragile in her sophisticated clothes.

"The Inspector was asking me about Thursday night. I told him Paul and I were going to discuss something over a meal and that I waited in for Paul until nine o'clock, when I phoned Mike and asked him to take me out."

She paused and her eyes met Campion's gravely.

"The Inspector asked me what Paul and I were going to talk about, and I told him. When he heard, he seemed to think it important. It was only an impression I got, of course, and yet . . ."

"What were you going to discuss with your husband?"

Campion saw the danger signal before he heard her confirming words.

"A divorce. I'd been trying to get Paul to give me one for some time," she said.

"A divorce?" Mike's whisper seemed to fill the room. She turned slowly round to him.

"Don't," she said. "Don't! No reproaches—not now. I'm just telling you what I told the Inspector."

A tremor passed over the younger man's face and it occurred to Campion that she did not realize her injustice.

"The Inspector was very interested," Gina went on. "He asked me if we'd spoken of it before, and I told him we had, lots of times, and that Paul wouldn't hear of it. But on the Wednesday I went to see a solicitor and that brought matters to a head. I knew where I stood. I knew I was tied to Paul if he—he—wouldn't desert me or beat me, so I begged him to have an evening at home so we could discuss it."

"You told the Inspector all this?" Mike's voice was very quiet.

"He got it out of me," she said helplessly. "Does it matter, Albert, does it matter? Will it make any difference?"

Mr. Campion rose to his feet. His face was very grave.

"I don't think so," he said at last, hoping his voice carried conviction. "You weren't quite alone in the flat when you were waiting for Paul, were you? I mean your woman was there to serve dinner?"

"Oh, yes, of course." Gina spoke carelessly. "Mrs. Austin was there until eight o'clock."

"Eight o'clock?" Mr. Campion's brows were rising.

She nodded. "I couldn't keep the woman all night," she said. "When Paul was a whole hour late for our conference and the dinner was spoiled, I told her I didn't care when he came in and I sent her off."

"Oh dear!" said Mr. Campion, and, after a little pause, again, "Oh, dear!"

5

Inquisition

It is perhaps not extraordinary that the mixture of anxiety, irritation and excitement typical of the backstage of amateur theatricals is nearly always reproduced at the moment when a family sets off for a public performance, be it wedding, funeral, or as in this case, inquest.

John had arrived, already dressed for the ordeal, at Gina's flat no later than half past eight in the morning of Tuesday, the 17th. By a quarter of nine he had phoned Mike three times and had upbraided the startled Mrs. Austin because Curley had not yet appeared.

Gina very wisely kept to her own room and left him to rampage up and down the studio.

When Curley came, pink and breathless with the exertion of climbing the stairs, he pounced upon her with a grunt of relief.

"We've got to be there in less than an hour," he said. "We don't want to be late. Let me see, there's Scruby to come yet. Hang the fellow! I told him to be punctual. You told him, Miss Curley, over the telephone. We were all to meet here at nine o'clock. I thought I'd made that quite plain."

Miss Curley, who was making frantic and futile efforts to tuck her wispy grey curls under the tight headband of her fashionable but unbecoming tricorne, was apologetic.

"He has a long way to come, Mr. Widdowson. He lives out at Hampstead, you know. Don't you remember, I told you he said we weren't to wait for him, but he'd meet us at the court."

John sank down in a chair, placing his speckless bowler on a table within arm's reach.

"Well, I suppose as a lawyer he knows well enough it doesn't do to be late for court proceedings," he said. "But I should have liked him to have been here. Miss Curley, go and ring down to Mike. Tell him we're all waiting. No one seems to realize the publicity involved in an affair of this sort, and not at all the right sort of publicity for a firm of our standing. I was fond of Paul, as you know, Miss Curley, but this final piece of sensationalism makes it very difficult for one to respect his memory as one would have liked."

"Oh, well, he won't do it again," said Miss Curley absently, and then, realizing the impropriety and inanity of the remark grew crimson with confusion.

To her relief John did not appear to have heard. He was entirely absorbed with his own angle on the tragedy.

"It's holding up everything. There's three quarters of the Spring list to come out and the Autumn one not half made up," he observed. "Still, we must put all that behind us now. We've all got to be calm and courageous. We must see this thing through with dignity and then we must bury our grief and get on with the work."

He seemed to be much more at ease after he had delivered this little homily and Miss Curley suspected that he had been saving it for a larger audience which had not materialized. She glanced at him curiously. He was getting older than she had thought, she decided, and wondered why it was that the cares of a firm aged a man so much more unattractively than the cares of a family. There was a great deal that was positively inhuman about John.

"Mr. Wellington rang up yesterday," she said, drawing

on her short black suéde gloves bought for the occasion,
"and he asked me in confidence whether I thought you'd
mind if he made an attempt to get into the public part of the
court today. He wanted to make it very clear that he was not
going after copy, but simply as an old friend of yours and
Mr. Paul's."

The mention of the distinguished author's name
seemed to cheer John immensely.

"Oh, not at all, not at all. I hope you told him not at
all," he said. "Like to feel we had friends there. It did go
through my mind that we might ask one or two people, but
it didn't seem our prerogative, so to speak."

Miss Curley looked at him sharply, but there was no
shadow of a smile upon his deeply lined, yellow little face.

"I wore a band," he said. "I think we all ought to wear
bands, don't you? Mourning's out of fashion I know,
nowadays, but it looked well, I thought. I told Mike about
it."

Miss Curley was growing calmer. There was something
extraordinarily soothing about John's attitude towards the
terrifying business. At night, when she went home and she
had a little leisure to think of the facts, she found herself
growing frightened of the disaster which had overtaken
them, but back in John's presence the habit of a lifetime
reasserted itself and she found herself adopting his attitude
against her better judgment.

When the Dresden clock on Gina's mantelpiece
chimed the quarter John could bear it no longer.

"We must go," he said. "It may take us several minutes
to find a cab at this hour of the morning. We don't want to
be late. Getting about in London is very difficult."

Miss Curley hesitated. "It couldn't possibly take us
more than ten minutes on foot, Mr. Widdowson," she said.
"The court's only just round the corner. And, anyway,
there's a cab rank at the end of Bedford Row."

"All the same, I wish you'd ask Mrs. Brande to come in
here at once." John was fidgeting. "As for Mike, I don't
know what the boy's up to. With so many Press people
about we can't afford to make a bad impression."

When Miss Curley was out of the room he rose to his
feet and walked over to the long mirror on the far side of the

room and stood there for a moment, surveying himself critically. No one who saw him could have dreamed for a moment that he regarded himself as anything but the Head of the Firm. His poise and stance proclaimed it. He was faultlessly dressed in a dark suit and overcoat, upon which the crêpe band was only just visible. His short grey hair was clipped to a point at which it would seem that its growth was discouraged and his perfect hat completed the picture.

He looked, as he hoped, a distinguished public man, shaken, but not bowed, by private grief.

He turned away from the mirror as Gina and Miss Curley entered. It did not occur to him for a moment to apologize for having commandeered her room for the family meeting place. Instead he regarded her critically and on the whole with approval.

Her black clothes suited her. They were smart yet very severe. The only touch of softness was the crisp white ruff at her throat, and to this he took exception.

"I don't know that I should wear that, Gina," he said. "It's very nice, my dear, very becoming, but I don't know whether it's quite the thing for an occasion of this sort. Let me see how you look with it off."

The girl stared at him. Her face was drawn and colourless and her eyes had receded until there were dark hollows where they should have been. She looked ill and on the verge of collapse.

She plucked at the ruff obediently, but the touch of its crispness against her fingers seemed to steady her. She stared at him coldly.

"Don't be absurd, John. I'm not going to appear on the stage. Leave me alone—for God's sake, leave me alone!"

The man was obstinate, but like others of his generation he had a horror of nerves in women.

"Just as you like, my dear," he said coldly. "Just as you like. But I do think you'd look better without it."

"What the hell does it matter what she wears?"

Mike spoke from the doorway, where he had just appeared.

John fixed his younger cousin with a disapproving stare.

"There's no need to lose your temper," he said stiffly. "I'm only trying to think what would be wisest and most dignified for us all to do. We share a common misfortune and we are going to share a common ordeal."

Mike swallowed his temper. "That's all right, John," he said. "But you might remember that Paul was Gina's husband."

"Paul was my cousin and my partner," said John, with dignity.

There was a pause and Miss Curley seized it.

"I think we should all go down now, Mr. Widdowson," she ventured. "It'll take us two or three minutes to get down to Bedford Row."

Mrs. Austin put her head round the door, and they stared at it not without justification, since it was adorned by all the rakish splendour of Mrs. Austin's "Best that had once belonged to a titled lady."

"I think I'll slip along now, M'm, if you don't mind," she said. "I don't want to be late."

Gina turned to her eagerly. "Mrs. Austin, I'll come with you. We'll go together."

She moved unsteadily across the room and the charwoman put an arm round her.

"That's right, duck," she said. "You come along with me. You've lost your 'usband and there's nobody else but me in *this* room that knows what that means."

And with this Parthian shot she swept the girl out into the passage.

"Gina's gone mad. . . . Stop her, Mike. Who is that woman? Where are they going?"

John was halfway out of the door before Mike detained him.

"They're going to the inquest," he said wearily. "We're all going to the inquest. Hundreds of people are going to be there—it's not just our show. And for God's sake come along."

Miss Curley touched his arm. "I think Mrs. Brande should come with us," she said.

The boy looked at her curiously. "Oh, let her go," he said. "She's escaped from this family, Curley. Let her go with her friends."

In the end they all straggled down Bedford Row together, Gina and Mrs. Austin stumbling along in front and John, in high dudgeon, stalking between them and Mike and Curley, who brought up the rear. They arrived at the court with fifteen minutes to spare.

There were still remnants of the last week's fog hanging about the city and the court seemed to have trapped more than its fair share. To Gina at least the whole place seemed to be filled with a thick brown mist, through which the faces of people she knew and did not know loomed out towards her and peered at her questioningly, only to disappear again in the general maelstrom.

She avoided Mike and clung to Mrs. Austin, whose grim determination to assert herself and whose contempt for the police and all their works made her a very comforting pillar on which to lean.

Mike and Curley remained side by side. The old woman's shrewd eyes took in every detail. She saw the Press benches were crowded and had the presence of mind to nod to the immaculately dressed Mr. Wellington, who was doing his best to look sympathetic at a distance of twenty feet.

John had buttonholed old Scruby, the firm's solicitor, and was talking to him rather than listening to what he had to say, as was his custom.

Scruby was a little skeleton of a man with sparse white hair that had yellow lights in it. At the moment he was peering at his client with protuberant pale blue eyes. As his practice largely consisted of libel and copyright he felt somewhat out of his element in the present situation and was doing his best not to say so. Mike, catching sight of the two of them, experienced a sense of sudden irritation well-nigh unbearable.

Scruby evidently had an inkling of the seriousness of the situation, but it was quite beyond him to impress his fears upon John, whose principal concern seemed to be the probable newspaper reports.

A pale young man with horn-rimmed spectacles, accompanied by an enormous person in a long black overcoat, sidled into the back of the court. Mr. Lugg and Mr. Campion were not on speaking terms that morning. No open rupture had occurred, but each, it seemed, thought it better not to intrude himself upon the other's private thoughts.

The inquest began in an unorthodox way. Mr. Salley addressed the jury. His voice, like his appearance, which was small and fierce, was unexpected. It was deep and very quiet, with a quality of naturalness which took Gina by surprise. He was like the best type of country doctor, she decided; blunt and straightforward and obviously completely without fancies of any sort.

His first words to the jury provoked furious activity at the Press table. He leant over his desk and his sharp eyes ranged over the seven embarrassed-looking citizens.

"Before you hear the evidence in this case," he said, "perhaps it would be as well if I defined your duty to you. I do this because possibly some of you may be under a misapprehension concerning this important matter, due to recent misleading criticisms of Coroners and Coroners' juries which have appeared in the Press.

"In the laws of England your duties are specifically laid down. There can be no question about them. They are clear and rigid.

"First of all let me repeat the oath which you took before me on this day one week ago. I must ask you to listen carefully and judge for yourselves what is the meaning of these very plain words."

He paused and they blinked at him owlishly. Taking a card from his desk he peered at it through his spectacles.

"This is your oath," he said, "listen to it—understand it. 'I swear by Almighty God that I will diligently enquire and a true presentment make of all such matters and things as are here given me in charge on behalf of our Sovereign Lord the King touching the death of Paul Redfern Brande, now lying dead, and will, without fear or favour, affection, or ill-will, a true verdict give according to the evidence and the best of my skill and knowledge.'

"There," he said, throwing down the card. "You have each of you repeated these words and I now ask you to consider to what you stand pledged. When the evidence has been set before you the law will demand of you that you answer several questions, and I think it will be as well if I told you now what those questions will be.

"Firstly, you will be required to state who the deceased was. Then how and where he died and afterwards how he came by his death."

He paused and regarded them steadily.

"This will constitute the first part of your verdict. But afterwards, and it is this point to which I want to call your attention because there has been much mischievous and misleading rubbish talked and written about it, you may possibly be called upon to answer another question. There is set down in Halsbury's *Laws of England,* a book whose authority cannot be questioned, the following incontrovertible decree. It is there stated that if the jury find that the deceased came by his death by murder or manslaughter those persons whom they find to have been guilty of such an offence, or of being accessories before the fact of murder, must be pointed out. It is the jury's responsibility, and they are in duty bound, if they know the persons guilty, to say their names."

Everybody in court save the seven people to whom these sober words were addressed seemed to be more than startled by them. The jury merely looked uncomfortable and cold. In the back of the court Mr. Lugg nudged Mr. Campion.

The Coroner had not quite finished.

"I wish to make it clear that this duty of yours does not apply in any particular or special way to the case you are about to hear today. It is your general duty. It is the duty of all Coroners' juries and I have called attention to it because I have found so much misapprehension on the subject, not only among the public, but even among members of the legal profession.

"Now we will hear the first witness."

6
By These Witnesses

Gina shrank back in her seat and waited for a merciful unreality to settle over the proceedings. In the past embarrassing or even harassing situations had always had for her this mitigating quality. Today, however, it was absent.

Instead the reverse seemed to have taken place. Faces seemed clearer, their less pleasing qualities emphasized, while each spoken word appeared to be charged with underlying menace.

The Coroner and the jury took on a Hogarthian quality, and those witnesses whom she knew resembled brilliantly cruel caricatures of themselves.

She tried to disassociate herself from it all, and to look upon the enquiry as though it were a play, but it was not possible even when she forced her eyes out of focus and persuaded her ears to hear only meaningless unrelated sounds.

Presently she found herself listening intently to Miss Marchant giving evidence about the discovery of the body. The Coroner was taking her gently through her written statement, but his tone became peremptory at the point where the actual appearance of the corpse was mentioned, warning her that any display of nerves which she might have contemplated would not be received sympathetically.

The fair-haired girl stepped down, relieved and a little nettled, the colour in her demure face heightened and her blue eyes embarrassed. The jury looked studiously disinterested.

The two doctors followed, one after the other. Consequential little Doctor Roe bustled forward, giving everyone in the court the impression that he wished to appear in a great hurry. Gina stirred uneasily. Was this awful clarity to be the peculiarity of the whole enquiry? In other circumstances Doctor Roe's hurry might have passed as genuine, but here in court it seemed monstrously overdone, his self-importance and his vanity painfully obvious.

The repetition of his statement already made to the police went slowly on, the Coroner interpolating an occasional question and writing down the replies with unhurried calm.

Gina tried to fix her mind on the evidence, but the mannerisms of the man, his love of the Latin cherished by his profession, his unction and gratification at his own importance obtruded themselves and all but eclipsed his information.

The Coroner kept him only a very short time, and the police doctor, a wholly unexpected person called Ferdie, appeared upon the stand.

Doctor Ferdie was a Scot from Dundee, and thirty years of work in London had not robbed him of his accent. He was a vast, untidy old person draped in elephant-grey clothes which managed to convey that there was something extraordinary about their cut without being actually peculiar in any definable particular. His face was seamed and rucked like the bark of an oak and from out its mass of indentations two very bright and knowing blue eyes peered at the world.

He cocked an eye at the Coroner with the confiding air of a trusted expert confronting an old client and the whole court became alive.

Preliminaries, the names and addresses of witnesses who had attested to Doctor Ferdie that the body of Paul Redfern Brande was the body of Paul Redfern Brande and not any spare corpse which might have been lying around at the time; the little matter of the warrant for examination and the address of the mortuary were all disposed of with perfunctory speed, and the doctor passed on to the external appearances of the body indicative of the time of death.

"The body was that of a well-nourished pairson," he remarked, his bright inquisitive eyes fixed upon the Coroner. "Not sae lean an' not sae stout. Just ordinary, ye see. There was no death stiffening, or, as ma colleague

Doctor Roe here would put it, rigor mortis. I examined the body carefully, and in my opeenion death had taken place within three to five days."

He paused and added confidentially:

"There were certain signs, ye see."

The Coroner nodded comprehendingly and turned to his personal notes.

"The man was last seen alive on Thursday afternoon, January the twenty-eighth; that is to say, somewhere between ninety-four and ninety-five hours before you saw him," he began at last. "In your opinion would the condition of the body be consistent with the suggestion that his death took place within an hour or so of his disappearance?"

Doctor Ferdie considered, and Gina found her heart beating suffocatingly fast.

"Ah, it might," he said at last. "It might indeed. But I couldn't commit myself, ye see. There were definite signs of the beginning of decomposition and in ordinary condeetions these do not appear until after the third day. But I wouldn't go further than that."

"Quite." The Coroner seemed satisfied, and after he had written for some moments he looked up again. "In regard to these ordinary conditions, you have said that the deceased was a well-nourished person of normal weight."

"Ah, he was," Doctor Ferdie agreed. "A healthy normal pairson."

"I see. Did you examine the room where the body was found?"

"I did."

"Was there anything about it which might have hastened or retarded the natural decomposition of the body?"

"No. It was a cool dry room, very badly ventilated, but otherwise nothing extraordinary."

"I see." The Coroner glanced at the jury, who made a visible effort to appear more intelligent. "Would the coolness hurry the termination of the period of death stiffening?"

The doctor cocked an eye again and spoke to the jury rather than to the Coroner.

"No, ye see, it would rather tend to prolong it."

"Death might easily have taken place between eighty-eight and eight-four hours before you saw him, then?"

"Ah, it might." The Scotsman hesitated. "I'd say it was very probable."

"Thank you, Doctor." The Coroner wrote again. "Now, as to the cause of death . . ."

Doctor Ferdie cleared his throat and launched into a careful and extremely delicate description of the colour of the face and chest, followed by a technical account of the autopsy which he and Doctor Roe had performed.

Gina's head began to swim. The brutality of the facts related in the soothing Scotch voice produced in her a sense of outrage.

She turned her head and caught a glimpse of Mrs. Austin. The woman was watching her with kindly but almost hungry eyes.

"Feel faint, duck?" she whispered hopefully.

Gina shook her head and passed her tongue over her dry lips. Mrs. Austin seemed disappointed.

Doctor Ferdie was still talking.

"It's lairgely a question of the colour of the bluid, ye see. I applied Haldane's test, and in my opeenion there was between forty and fifty per cent of carbon monoxide in the bluid. I took a test-tube containing a one per cent solution of the bluid to be examined. Then in a second tube I put a solution of normal bluid of like strength. Then I took a third tube an' . . ."

On and on it went, the details explained with endless patience to the seven self-conscious individuals whose acute embarrassment had given place to a sort of settled discomfort.

By the time Doctor Ferdie left the stand there could have been no reasonable doubt in anybody's mind that Paul Redfern Brande had died from carbon monoxide poisoning, and no very great question but that he had done so within eight hours of his last appearance in the office.

The doctor lolloped back to his seat and the Coroner's Officer, a plump uniformed person with a sternly avuncular manner, produced the next witness.

At the back of the court Mr. Campion sat up as Miss Netley walked hesitantly forward. Her schoolgirl affectation was enhanced today and she looked little more than fourteen in her severe blue jacket and sailor hat.

She gave her evidence in a very low voice, but her timidity did not quite ring true, and even Mr. Lugg's sympathetic expression faded into one of doubt as her plaintive answers reached him.

The Coroner was very gentle with her, and she smiled at him confidingly as he helped her through her very simple tale. It transpired that she had been Paul's secretary and that so far as anybody knew she had been the last person to see him alive.

"You say Mr. Brande went out of the office at about half past three of the afternoon of Thursday, the twenty-eighth of last month, and that was the last time you saw him alive? Is that so?"

"Yes, sir."

"And you say here"—the Coroner went on, tapping the statement upon his desk—"that when Mr. Brande went out he seemed to be excited. Suppose you tell the jury what you meant by that?"

Miss Netley blushed painfully.

"I don't know, sir," she stammered at last. "He just seemed to be excited."

Some of the Coroner's tenderness vanished.

"Was he pleased or worried? Alarmed? Anxious about something?"

"No, sir. He was just—excited."

Mr. Campion pricked up his ears. There it was again, that same indefinable thing he had noticed about the girl before. She wanted to be tantalizing and did not mind appearing a fool in order to achieve that end.

"How did you know he was excited?" the Coroner suggested.

Miss Netley considered.

"He moved as though he was," she said at last.

Mr. Lugg nudged his employer and made an expressive depreciatory gesture with his thumb, an indication which in the days of his vulgarity would have been accomplished by the succinct expression "Out her!"

The Coroner breathed deeply through his nose.

"You just knew by the way he moved that he was excited?"

"Yes, sir."

The Coroner returned to facts.

"How did you know it was half past three when Mr. Brande went out?"

"Because," said Miss Netley, "the afternoon post comes at five-and-twenty minutes past three."

"And the post had just come when Mr. Brande went out?"

"Yes, sir." Her expectancy was as evident as if she had expressed it in words.

The Coroner looked up.

"Did anything come by the post for Mr. Brande?"

"Yes, sir. One letter."

"Did you see it?"

"I saw it was addressed to him and I handed it to him," she said. "It was marked 'Personal.'"

The court began to sit up and even the police looked interested.

"After Mr. Brande had read the letter, did he decide to go out?"

"Yes, sir."

"Did he tell you where he was going?"

"No."

"Did he say when he was coming back?"

"No."

"Did he say anything at all?"

"No, sir."

The Coroner sighed.

"You are here to give us all the help you can, Miss Netley," he said sternly. "To return to this excitement you noticed in Mr. Brande; had it anything to do with the letter?"

The girl considered.

"It may have had," she said. "I noticed it after he had read the letter. He got up hurriedly, put on his hat and coat and went out."

"What did he do with the letter?"

"He put it in the fire, sir."

"And that's all you know about this business?"

"Yes, sir."

The Coroner glanced at the written page in front of him.

"All you can tell us, then, is that a letter came for your employer at five-and-twenty minutes past three on the twenty-eighth, that it was marked 'Personal,' and that after he had read it he thrust it in the fire, put on his hat and coat and went out and was never seen again alive as far as you know?"

"Yes, sir."

"You've taken a great deal of time to tell us that, Miss Netley. You're not hiding anything, are you?"

"Hiding anything, sir?" The big dark eyes grew round and shocked. The small mouth trembled. The years dropped away from the girl until she looked a child. "Of course not, sir."

"All right. You may sit down."

Miss Netley returned to her seat with all eyes upon her and Mr. Campion wondered. She was not quite the ordinary notoriety-seeker, and once again he made a mental note of her name.

The next witness was Detective-Inspector Tanner. He was tall, thick-set, and the possessor of a figure predestined to wear a uniform. His face was expressionless, but forbidding in structure, while his light blue eyes looked shrewd and obstinately honest. He gave his evidence in a flat careful voice, obviously different from the one in which he usually spoke. He made his statement with the awful conviction of the slightly inhuman, while the Coroner nodded to him from time to time and wrote it all down.

In the beginning it was the same story told from yet another angle. Gina glanced restlessly round the court and was startled to catch Mike's eyes resting upon her. He looked away abruptly, but she had seen and turned back to the witness, her body suddenly cold.

Mrs. Austin leant against her.

"Bear up, dear," she murmured.

The Inspector was making a great point of the fact that the body had been moved by the doctor after its discovery. Doctor Roe was recalled and stated amid much self-conscious protestation that the step had been necessary, or so he had been assured by Miss Curley and Mr. Michael Wedgwood.

Having successfully shifted the blame from his own shoulders to theirs, he bustled back to his seat and the Inspector was recalled.

As soon as he reappeared a tremor of interest passed through the whole court. The Press men scribbled vigorously and Mr. Lugg leaned forward to catch a glimpse of the Barnabas party seated in front of him.

"After I and my colleague, Sergeant Pillow, had taken statements from the witnesses present on the premises at Number Twenty-three, Horsecollar Yard, I made a detailed search of the said premises."

The flat voice droned out the words like a child reciting.

"In the room where the deceased was discovered I noticed a small ventilator beneath one of the shelves which surround the room. The ventilator is situated three feet from the ground and five and a half feet from the ceiling. This ventilator is not easily observed by anyone entering the room because it is hidden by the projection of the shelf beneath which it is situated. I and my colleague removed the ventilator from its position and took it to headquarters as evidence."

There was a sensation as the ragged piece of iron was produced and solemnly handed round to the jury.

"I observed," Inspector Tanner continued, "that two of the centre bars of the ventilator had been recently broken. The sharp metal edges were bright and there were signs indicative of force having been used upon them. I also noticed a quantity of soot of a certain nature sprayed over the papers and débris on the lower shelf beneath the ventilator. My colleague and I then examined the lock of the door of the room and found that it had not been tampered with in any way. We then traced the outside wall of the building and discovered that the ventilator gave into a garage used by the directors of the firm. In the garage was a twenty-horse-power Fiat car, number PQ 348206, which we subsequently discovered belonged to Mr. Michael Wedgwood, junior partner in the firm of Barnabas, Limited and first cousin to the deceased.

"Continuing our search, we entered the building next door, known as Twenty-one, Horsecollar Yard, where the residences of Mr. Michael Wedgwood, Mr. John Barnabas and the deceased are situated. Among some miscellany in the passageway outside the heating plant of these premises we found a length of rubber pipe, eight feet three inches in length and one and a half inches in diameter. As far as we could ascertain it had once formed part of a shower-bath apparatus, but did not appear to have been used for this purpose for some considerable time. One end of the pipe had been hacked off recently and the other end, which was fitted with a nozzle designed to fit over a water tap, had been considerably stretched and mutilated.

"The pipe was black with soot on the inside and the nozzle end showed signs of burning."

He paused again and the length of tubing was passed round.

The inference was obvious and the Inspector proceeded to show how the cut end of the tube had passed through the ventilator and was able to point out the indention some six inches from the end where it had been held by the ends of the broken bars.

Gina closed her eyes. It seemed to her for a moment that everyone was staring not at the exhibit but at herself. She dared not look at Mike. At her side Mrs. Austin was breathing heavily, her eyes snapping with excitement.

The Coroner took the Inspector over his statement very carefully.

"In your opinion, Inspector, this pipe was passed through the ventilator recently?" he suggested.

The Inspector stated that in his opinion there was no possible doubt whatever about the matter; he went on to say that the other end of the pipe had been tested in connection with the end of the exhaust pipe on the Fiat and finished up by producing that part of the car.

The jury stared at these three component parts and on their faces there appeared a gleam of something that could only be called satisfaction.

The Inspector stepped down and for a moment the court was full of whispers. Old Mr. Scruby was talking to John with an animation and authority quite foreign to his nature. Two or three reporters slipped out of their places and Mr. Lugg turned to Campion triumphantly.

"What did I tell you?" he murmured. "Here it comes."

Mr. Salley restored order and the next witness was thrust forward. He was a small square person with a large head, respectable clothes and innocent baby-blue eyes. It transpired that his name was Henry Cecil Pastern and that he had an expert knowledge of central-heating plants.

He made his statement with machine-gun rapidity.

"On the evening of the twenty-ninth of last month, at the invitation of Detective-Inspector Tanner, I made a detailed investigation of the boiler situated in the basement of the premises known as Twenty-three, Horsecollar Yard. It is a type of stove well known to me and when I examined it I found no defect of any kind whatsoever. Nor did I find evidences of any repairs having been made to it at any time. The stove is a comparatively new stove, not more than eighteen months installed. I do not see how any water gas or carbon monoxide gas could have escaped from it into the basement at any time."

Careful and scrupulously fair questioning by the Coroner made it clear to the jury and the court that Mr. Pastern knew perfectly well what he was saying and that even if his words had a slightly official flavour they did in fact represent his true and honest opinion.

It was during the interval after this evidence that Gina caught sight of Ritchie leaning forward in his seat, a bewildered expression upon his face. The sight of him almost made her laugh. He was so hopelessly out of place. So were they all, John, Curley and certainly poor Mr. Scruby. She found herself wishing desperately that it would end. It was a nightmare which had gone on too long.

The midday adjournment came unexpectedly. Miss Curley came bustling over, consternation on her plain plump face and her tricorne thrust unbecomingly to the back of her head.

"I've got to go with Mr. John and Mr. Scruby. They want to talk," she said breathlessly. "Will you be all right, my dear?"

"No one shall touch an 'air of 'er 'ead while I'm beside 'er," said Mrs. Austin valiantly but unnecessarily.

Gina was amazed at herself. One part of her mind was half irritated, half amused by the banality of the woman.

But there was another which was timidly grateful for her support.

As she came out of the court clinging to Mrs. Austin's arm she caught a glimpse of Ritchie mooching along, his hands in his pockets, his chin thrust out, and his lean, rangy figure looking unexpectedly distinguished. He did not see her but wandered over to Mr. Campion, who was standing in the lobby with a funereal individual whose face was only vaguely familiar to her.

The two women came out into bright sunlight completely unaware of the extraordinary picture they presented. Gina, with her hair sleeked beneath her Schiaparelli hat and her severe black suit clinging to her exquisitely fashionable figure, made a contrast with Mrs. Austin's exuberant Sunday Best which was positively arresting.

For a moment they stood hesitating, startled by the staring group on the pavement and the battery of cameras thrust mercilessly into their faces.

Glancing round her wildly, Gina suddenly saw Mike.

He was standing on the fringe of the crowd, his face turned towards her. As their eyes met he made an involuntary step forward, but immediately afterwards, as though a sudden recollection had occurred to him, he turned away and made off down the road at an exaggerated pace.

Somebody in the crowd laughed hysterically and Mrs. Austin gripped her firmly by the arm.

"If you ask my opinion," she said firmly, "what you want is a small port."

7
The Lying Straws

The woman came forward to the stand self-consciously,
constraining her natural gait into little mincing steps and
holding her large hands, exaggerated by impossibly ornate
gloves, in an affected position neither comfortable nor
becoming.

John Widdowson turned to Mr. Scruby.

"Who's this?" he demanded with the startled expression of an author at rehearsal finding an unexpected
character in his play. "I've never seen her before."

"Ssh," said Mr. Scruby apprehensively as the Coroner's
glance shot towards them.

John gobbled in silence and the witness took her place.

She was a large woman, asthmatic and unhealthy-
looking, with a white face, a pursed mouth, and gold pince-
nez looped to her ear with a small chain. She wore a cheap
black fur coat much too small for her and had filled up its
deficiency in front with a heavily frilled blouse. She gave
her evidence in tones of staggering refinement.

For a moment she was so absorbed by her unusual
prominence and a delicacy either real or assumed that she
did not hear the Coroner when he asked her name, but was
at length prevailed upon to inform the court that she was
Mrs. Rosemary Ethel Tripper, that she lived in the
basement flat at Number Twenty-five, Horsecollar Yard,
and that her occupation was assistant caretaker with her
husband of the two blocks of offices, Numbers Twenty-five
and Twenty-seven. She also took the oath.

Once again the sense of outrage crept over Gina. She
realized that the police were under no compulsion to
broadcast their affairs, but when those affairs were so very
intimately her own it seemed unnecessarily cruel to have
kept her so much in the dark.

At the Coroner's request Mrs. Tripper cast her mind back both to her statement and the evening of the twenty-eighth.

"I had been to the pictures with a lady friend," said Mrs. Tripper with the air of one recounting an interesting social experience. "I parted with her at the end of the street—at about five minutes to seven o'clock, I should say it was—and then I entered my flat and went straight into the kitchenette, where I made myself a cup of tea.

"Going into the bedroom to change my shoes, a habit I have had from a girl, I suddenly said to myself, 'Why, there's that car started up!'"

She paused triumphantly and the Coroner coughed.

"Perhaps you'll explain to us, Mrs. Tripper," he said, "what exactly you meant by that?"

Mrs. Tripper was taken off her balance.

"I was referring to the car in the garage at Number Twenty-three," she said sharply, her refined accent temporarily deserting her. "Although we can't hear the car in the daytime, of course, because of the traffic, any time after six o'clock the Crescent is so quiet you could hear a pin drop and of course you can hear the car then, because the walls are so thin—I often say it's a disgrace."

"The Crescent?" said the Coroner enquiringly.

The faint colour flowed into Mrs. Tripper's pale face.

"Well then, the Yard," she said defiantly. "Horsecollar Yard. It's really a crescent."

"I see," said the Coroner and bowed his head over his papers. "What time was it exactly, Mrs. Tripper, when you thought you heard the car start up?"

"I heard it start up at ten minutes past seven," said Mrs. Tripper. "I left my friend at five minutes to. Five minutes to walk up the street, five minutes to make myself a cup of tea, and five minutes to go into the bedroom."

"Five minutes to go into the bedroom?" enquired the Coroner in some astonishment.

Once again Mrs. Tripper was put off her stride.

"Well, let's say five past seven I heard the car," she temporized.

"Are you sure you heard the car start up soon after you came in?" said the Coroner with some asperity.

"Yes, I did. I heard it as plain as anything when I was in the bedroom after I'd had my cup of tea."

"I see. And how long did you stay in the house?"

"Till about half past seven," said Mrs. Tripper promptly. "And the car was running all the time. It was running when I went out. I noticed it because I said to myself, 'It's bad enough to hear that engine being turned on and off, without having it running in your ear the whole time,' and I meant to speak to the janitor at Twenty-three about it."

"You say about half past seven, Mrs. Tripper—" the Coroner was very gentle. "Could you be more exact?"

"Well, I *think* it was half past seven. Anyway I left the house and went down to wherever I was going, and when I got there it was ten minutes to eight—because I saw the clock."

"Where was this?"

Once again Mrs. Tripper flushed.

"It was a shop in Red Lion Street—a fried-fish shop, if you must know. It was very foggy and I hadn't been able to get about to do my ordinary shopping, and I knew my husband would like something hot for his supper and so I thought I might as well try some of their more expensive pieces. Some of these places are very high class, and the Red Lion shop is very nice indeed."

"Quite, quite," said the Coroner, rather taken aback by the vehemence of her confession. "You went straight to the fried-fish shop when you left your house and you arrived there at ten minutes to eight?"

"Yes, I did."

It was evident that Mrs. Tripper was torn between the desire to acquire kudos by admitting to a knowledge of interesting facts and irritation at having to disclose the more humble activities of her private life.

"And when I returned," she went on triumphantly, "the car was still running. I heard it turned off at ten minutes to nine or thereabouts."

The Coroner leant forward across the desk.

"I feel these times are important, Mrs. Tripper," he said. "I wonder would it be possible for you to cast your mind back and think of any concrete fact by which you can fix them? For instance, are you quite sure that it was not half past eight, or even a quarter past nine, when you heard the car turned off?"

Mrs. Tripper's narrow black eyes behind her gold pince-nez snapped.

"I've told you there was a clock," she said. "Haven't I? I stood talking in the shop a little while and suddenly I looked up and saw it was a quarter to nine. 'Oh, dear!' I said. 'My husband comes in for his supper at nine,'—he goes down to the club on Thursdays—'and I must get home,' I said. I remember saying it. I hurried off and I got home at ten minutes to, as far as I can judge."

The Coroner returned to his notes.

"I see that it took you twenty minutes to get from your home to the fried-fish shop, Mrs. Tripper, and only five minutes to get back . . ."

Mrs. Tripper's mouth set obstinately.

"That's all I can tell you," she said. "I hurried back and as far as I can judge it was ten minutes to, because my husband came in just as I'd got everything on the table, and he's always punctual. I came in at the door, I listened, and I heard the car still running. Then just as I was saying something to myself about it, off it went."

As she stepped down off the stand a sigh passed round the court and the jury whispered together.

Gina felt that she was crouching in her seat. She dared not think ahead. In her heart she felt there was nothing to be gained by thinking. There was a slow inexorable quality about this enquiry. Nothing could deter it. It was simple, brutal and unescapable.

She was still dithering when she heard her own name called, but for the first time, as she walked to the stand, she felt the longed-for sensation of remoteness. A wall of apathy seemed to have descended between her and the nightmare around her. Faces became vague and indistinct, voices heard from afar off.

She gave her name, her address and the fact that she was Paul's wife with a calm detachment which passed for extreme self-possession. Her voice was soft and carefully modulated and she held herself rigidly.

She repeated the oath calmly, unconsciously imitating the lack of expression of the Coroner's Officer.

The Coroner became a nonentity, a questioning machine, gentle and not at all unpleasant. He took her quietly through her statement. She remembered making it, remembered signing it, but only in an impersonal far-off way as though it had not been of very great interest.

"I last saw my husband at two o'clock on the afternoon that he disappeared. It was only for a few minutes. I went into his office and caught him, as he had returned early from lunch. We had a short conversation. Then I went back to my flat. I never saw him again alive."

She was completely unaware of the impression she was creating.

The average British crowd is quick to admire beauty, especially in distress, but there is a curious streak in the temperament which makes it distrust the quality of smartness, especially when it is allied, however remotely, to something questionable or suspicious.

The fact that she was a foreigner told in her favour naturally—foreigners may be forgiven for having chic—but her calm weighed heavily against her. Widows should weep and emotional display is not only expected but demanded of them.

The questioning continued.

"You say in your statement, Mrs. Brande, that you expected your husband to come home to dinner at half past seven and that you waited for him until nine, at which time you rang up your husband's cousin, Mr. Michael Wedgwood, who took you to see a film. Were you not worried when your husband did not appear for dinner?"

She repeated the word. "Worried? No. I don't think so. I was annoyed."

It occurred to her that she might explain that Paul was always late for appointments with her, that his neglect of her, his indifference to her feelings, had rendered her completely impervious to the sensation of alarm where he was concerned, but she did not want to explain. It seemed so unnecessary to go into details to all these stupid gaping people, who could never be expected to understand. She held her tongue.

The Coroner went on.

"You say that when you went to see your husband in his

office that afternoon you had something very particular to ask him. What was it?"

"I wanted to impress upon him that he must dine with me that evening, because I wanted to talk to him."

It appeared to occur to the Coroner that she was making no effort to help herself and he bent forward.

"Mrs. Brande," he said, "how long have you been married?"

"Four years."

"Would you say your marriage has been a happy one?"

"No," she said, more vehemently than she intended. "No, I don't think it was."

There was excitement in the court and John would have risen had not Mr. Scruby held him down. The Coroner pursed up his lips.

"Perhaps you'd like to amplify that, Mrs. Brande," he said. "This is a court of enquiry, you know, and we want to arrive at the truth. Did you quarrel with your husband?"

"No," she said. "We were indifferent to one another."

As soon as she had spoken she was sorry. The publicity of the whole business struck her again, but not forcibly enough to make her angry. She was past anger.

The Coroner sighed and his manner became a little less friendly.

"Mrs. Brande," he said, "you made this statement voluntarily to the Inspector and the Coroner's Officer, I understand?"

"Of course," she said stiffly. "I had nothing to hide."

"She's a cool one." The court's comment was almost audible.

"Of course not," the Coroner agreed. "You say in your statement that you were particularly anxious to confer with your husband on the evening of the twenty-eighth because you wanted to persuade him to help you to get a divorce?"

"Yes," she said.

"You do not wish to add anything to that statement now?"

"No, I don't think so."

The Coroner looked at her under his eyebrows. He had seen many frightened women and to him her reaction was not incomprehensible, but his duty was to enquire and she was not helpful.

"Why were you so anxious to talk to him about it at that particular time, Mrs. Brande?"

"It is all in the statement," she said wearily. "I told Inspector Tanner that I had visited a solicitor and found out exactly how I was placed. I realized that I could not get a divorce from my husband unless he assisted me."

There was an audible murmur in the court and little Mr. Scruby bounded to his feet. The Coroner acceded to his request that he might be allowed to question the witness and Gina became aware of the little man staring at her anxiously across the crowded room.

"Had you had any violent quarrels with your husband upon this subject, Mrs. Brande?"

"No, of course not," she said in some surprise. "It was only that we saw really very little of each other and I wanted Paul to consider my point of view."

Mr. Scruby sat down, not at all sure that he had been of any real assistance. The Coroner returned to the statement.

"You say you had ordered dinner in your flat for half past seven. Were you alone?"

"No. I had my charwoman, Mrs. Austin, with me."

"I see. And you waited for your husband until nine o'clock?"

"Yes, until almost nine."

"Was your charwoman with you then?"

"No. I let her go about eight o'clock. I saw no point in keeping her after that."

"You were pretty sure your husband would not come then?"

"I thought it extremely unlikely."

"Yet you waited for him yourself?"

"Yes. I hoped, you see."

The jury stirred. This was more like it.

"And at nine o'clock, or nearly nine o'clock—eight fifty-five, to be exact—you rang up Mr. Michael Wedgwood in the flat below and suggested that you go out together? The rest of the evening you spent in a picture palace?"

"Yes. That is true."

There was a long pause while the Coroner wrote.

"Now," he said at last, "were you in the habit of ringing up Mr. Wedgwood and suggesting that he should take you out?"

She hesitated. Something odd about the question warned her to be careful, but there was no time for adroit manoeuvring, even had she been capable of it.

"Yes," she said. "I was. We have been about a good deal together."

Mr. Campion felt the hair on his scalp rising and Mr. Lugg granted him a single reproachful glance.

"You were very great friends?"

"Yes. We are."

"Are you lovers, Mrs. Brande?"

She stared at him, hardly believing that she had heard the words. She was so completely taken aback that for a moment she was silent and during that instant of stupefaction her anger and indignation were transmuted into helplessness. The old apathy reclaimed her.

"No," she said evenly.

"You are not shocked by the suggestion?"

She opened her mouth to protest violently but thought better of it.

"It is too utterly ridiculous," she said and the proud quiet words were momentarily convincing.

A few unimportant questions followed and she was allowed to step down. She walked to her seat with the eyes of the whole court upon her, but it was not until she saw Mrs. Austin's sympathetic but horribly knowing face raised to hers that she realized quite what had happened.

Panic seized her. What had she said? What were they all driving at? The blood drained out of her face and Mrs. Austin caught her arm.

"Put your head between your knees," she whispered. "Shall I get you out?"

Gina had sufficient strength to shake her head and to turn her eyes resolutely towards the desk. She knew that John was staring at her angrily and in imagination she could see the startled little face of Mr. Scruby by his side.

Mike was the next witness.

The jury were wide awake now and their interest was not assumed. They had completely forgotten their own prominence and were absorbed by the story being unfolded so lucidly before them.

Gina did not take her eyes from Mike's face during the whole of his evidence. She felt she was seeing him for the first time. He was extraordinarily handsome, with the tall, lank Barnabas figure and the crisp curls shorn tightly to his head.

To those who knew him he betrayed his nervousness. He spoke with a drawl not natural with him and the ease of his stance was assumed.

His written statement was necessarily brief. He admitted helping the doctor to move the body on to the table and afterwards up to the flat, and gave a brief account of his cousin's position and activities in the firm.

The Coroner questioned him about the strong room. Evidence that had been given by other witnesses concerning its use was confirmed by him and he repeated that the car in the garage belonged to him.

"The yard gates are kept locked," he said, "but not the garage itself. I never considered there was any need for that."

The Coroner returned to the question of the strong room.

"I see in your statement, Mr. Wedgwood," he said, "that you admit to having visited the strong room on the night of the thirty-first, three days after your cousin's disappearance and on the evening before the discovery of his body."

The excitement at this point was intense and the Coroner had to enforce silence.

Mike's lank form seemed to be leaning back upon the air and his drawl became more pronounced.

"That is so," he said.

"Will you describe exactly what you did upon that occasion? It is all written down, I know, but I should like to hear it from you again."

Mike complied. He described how he had left the flat on Sunday night, had gone into the darkened office, taken the key from its usual place, opened the strong room and taken the folder which John had needed from its shelf, and had come away, locking the door behind him.

The Coroner seemed puzzled and he took the young man through the story again and again. Finally Mike's evidence was interrupted while Miss Curley and Miss Marchant were called to describe the exact place in which the body was found.

When the Coroner returned to Mike again his tone was peremptory.

"Can you offer any explanation why you did not see the body of your cousin on Sunday night?" he said.

"I'm sorry, I can't. It wasn't there. Or, if it was, I didn't see it."

Mike's exasperation was not unmixed with defiance. The Coroner dismissed the matter for the time being and went back to the Thursday night.

"Mr. Wedgwood," he said, "will you tell us what you did from three o'clock in the afternoon of Thursday the twenty-eighth until you answered the telephone at nine o'clock and went out to a picture palace with Mrs. Brande?"

Mike stiffened slightly and when he spoke his tone was defensive.

"I worked in my office all the afternoon," he said slowly. "My secretary was there the whole time. I left about half past five, intending to go to a cocktail party, and because it was slightly foggy and I was early I decided to walk. The house I intended to visit was in Manchester Square, but before I reached it I changed my mind and decided that I would go on walking."

He paused. The Coroner was looking at him and the seven pairs of eyes from the jury benches watched him narrowly.

"Yes?" said the Coroner.

"Well, I went on walking," said Mike lamely. "I had various things on my mind and I wanted to think them out. I went on walking until about half past eight. Then I got on a bus and came home."

The Coroner's pen traced idle designs on the blotting paper in front of him.

"Half past five till half past eight," he said. "That's three hours. It's a long time to walk on a foggy winter night, Mr. Wedgwood. Can you tell us where you went, exactly?"

"Yes. I went down to the far end of Westbourne Grove.

I walked down Holborn, Oxford Street, Edgware Road, Praed Street, and Bishop's Road. Then I turned back and I went up one of those long terraces to the Park, I cut through from Lancaster Gate to Hyde Park Corner and came up Piccadilly. I went up Shaftesbury Avenue, Charing Cross Road and I took a bus at St. Giles's Circus. It's a long way and I was not walking fast."

"Did you stop anywhere? Speak to anyone?"

"No. I don't think so."

"Well, can you tell us, Mr. Wedgwood, why you went to Westbourne Grove? Had you any purpose in going there?"

A faint smile passed over the man's expressive face.

"Yes, I had, vaguely. I meant to visit a shop there. There's a little secondhand jeweller's and curio shop about halfway down the right-hand side. I don't know the name of it. When I got there it was shut. It was Thursday anyway—I'd forgotten that."

The Coroner was inclined to be impatient.

"You must see that this is a very unsatisfactory story," he said testily. "You say you walked nearly four miles to visit a shop and found it shut. Had you any particular purpose in going to that shop?"

"No, not really. I mean, nothing urgent." Mike seemed unduly embarrassed. "I thought I might find something of interest there, I have done so before."

"Some piece of jewellery?"

"Well, yes."

"I see." The Coroner paused significantly. "Well, then, when you found the shop was shut you walked back for no other reason than that you wished to walk?"

"That is so."

"And it was cold and slightly foggy—not a pleasant night for walking?"

"No, it wasn't. But I didn't really mind about that. I had things on my mind and wanted to work them out."

"Those things, I see, Mr. Wedgwood, were private affairs which have no bearing on this case?"

"They were business matters," said Mike briefly and unconvincingly.

"When you returned home to Horsecollar Yard what did you do?"

"I went down through my own flat, out of the back door, through the gate in the wall to the garage behind the office, and started my car."

The court gasped.

"Why did you do that?"

"The fog had cleared a little and I thought it would probably be quite bright in the country. I thought I would go out somewhere by myself for a run round."

"You were tired of walking?" observed the Coroner dryly.

"Yes, I was."

"According to your evidence, Mr. Wedgwood, you had nothing to eat all this time . . ."

"No. I wasn't hungry. I just wanted to be by myself."

"And so you started up the car?"

"Yes. I always do that. I let her run for a little while, five or ten minutes at the outside, before I take her out into the traffic in the cold weather. I find she runs much more easily."

"And then?"

"Then I remembered that the key of the yard gates was in my coat in the flat. I went up to get it. While I was there Mrs. Brande rang up and explained that Paul had not returned and I suggested that we should go out somewhere. As it was too late for a theatre we went to a film. Before I went up to fetch Mrs. Brande I returned to the garage and switched off my car engine. I estimate it had been running seven minutes."

"I see." The Coroner cleared his throat. "Now there are just one or two questions I want to ask you concerning this statement. When Mrs. Brande told you that her husband had not returned and that he was two hours late for an appointment, weren't you alarmed? Didn't you wonder what had happened to him?"

"No. Paul was like that. He was a most erratic person. Neither Gina—I mean Mrs. Brande—nor we at the office ever knew when he was going to turn up."

The Coroner wrote.

"But on the Sunday, Mr. Wedgwood, when you were having tea—with others—at Mrs. Brande's flat, didn't you wonder then what had happened to your cousin?"

"I did. I thought he had stayed away rather a long time, but I wasn't worried. As I say, my cousin was unreliable."

"Well, then, one other point. You say you were getting your car out, intending to crawl through the fog until you got to the open country, because you wanted to be by yourself. And yet as soon as Mrs. Brande phoned you you suggested you should take her out to see a film? How do you explain that?"

Mike shrugged. "I don't explain it," he said. "I'm just telling you what happened."

"Mr. Wedgwood, is there a love affair between you and Mrs. Brande?"

"Certainly not."

"You have never at any time treated her in any way other than as your cousin's wife?"

"Never."

"You realize you are on oath?"

"I do."

"Very well. Will you stand down, please."

Much to everybody's astonishment, including her own, the next witness was Mrs. Austin.

She swept forward, a fine belligerent figure, skirts and streamers flying, and after climbing into position turned and surveyed the court, Coroner and police with self-possessed hostility.

She gave her name as Mrs. Dorothy Austin; her age (which was unasked) as forty-two; and an address in Somers Town.

"I've been visiting my lady, Mrs. Brande, for nearly four years now," she explained, "and if anybody knows her I do."

The Coroner looked up and smiled.

"We will stick to your statement as much as possible, Mrs. Austin," he murmured. "You say here that you were in the habit of arriving at Mrs. Brande's flat at eight o'clock every morning, that you stayed until twelve and returned again to cook and wash up after the evening meal if necessary."

Mrs. Austin concurred.

"I don't see anything wrong in that," she said.

"No, no, of course not. Now, during your visits to the flat you have had an opportunity of studying your employer and her husband. Would you say their married life was a happy one?"

"No, I wouldn't," said Mrs. Austin vehemently. "If my husband had treated me as Mr. Brande treated my lady I'd have left him long ago. It was only her sweet nature that made her put up with him as long as she did."

From the back of the court Gina looked at the woman imploringly, but there was no way of stopping that well-meaning tongue or forcing a little enlightenment into that short-sighted mind. Mrs. Austin imagined herself a counsel for the defence and already saw her name large in the newspaper as the champion of the downtrodden wife.

Pleasant, sturdy Sergeant Pillow looked down his nose. When he had taken her statement it had seemed to him almost a pity that she should have been so very much "in the mood," but after all the truth was the truth and the more easily it came out the better for everyone.

The Coroner had hardly any need to speak at all. Mrs. Austin not only remembered her statement but was quite willing to amplify it.

"They never came to blows—I will say that for them," she said, "but I often think it's a pity they didn't. The way he neglected her! Half the time he wasn't there at all and the other half he didn't notice she was there. No one could blame her if she went out a bit with Mr. Mike. A lady's got to have someone to take her about. She can't sit up like a sparrow on a housetop, not going anywhere. It's more than human nature can stand."

The Coroner interrupted the flow.

"Mrs. Austin," he said, "you say that you rarely stayed at the flat later than nine o'clock in the evening and never arrived there before eight o'clock in the morning. You are therefore not in a position to say whether, in the absence of Mr. Brande, Mr. Wedgwood ever stayed in the flat at night?"

"Well, of all the minds!" she began indignantly, but was silenced by the Coroner.

"You must answer me 'Yes' or 'No.' Did you ever know for a certainty that in the absence of Mr. Brande Mr. Wedgwood had stayed in the Brandes' flat overnight?"

"No," said Mrs. Austin, choked by the constraint put upon her. "But if he had I wouldn't have blamed him—or her, and that's the truth."

"That'll do," said the Coroner. "Now you were in the room, I understand, when Mr. Wedgwood came to tell Mrs. Brande that her husband was dead. I want you to describe that scene a little more fully than it is set down here. You admitted Mr. Wedgwood to the flat at about ten o'clock on Monday morning, the first of February. Do you remember that?"

"As clearly as the night my husband died," said Mrs. Austin a little unnecessarily.

"Very well. Now before Mr. Wedgwood arrived you saw your mistress?"

"Of course I did. I'd been running in and out of her room all the morning."

"At that time Mr. Brande had been missing for three days and four nights. Did Mrs. Brande seem worried?"

Mrs. Austin considered.

"Not exactly worried. I think she was relieved to be without him. One of us passed the remark that it was strange he hadn't come in."

"It did not occur to you that any harm might have befallen him?"

A ray of recollection flickered over Mrs. Austin's broad face.

"Now I come to think of it, I did say when I brought in her morning tea, 'I see the master's not back. I wonder if he's been runned over.'"

"Ah. And what did Mrs. Brande say to that?"

"Oh, she turned over on her side and said, 'No such luck,' or something like that."

Anyone of a more sensitive nature than the worthy Mrs. Austin must have noticed the tremendous sensation she was providing. The Coroner picked her up.

"When you say things like this, you must realize what they mean," he said severely. "Did Mrs. Brande use the actual words 'No such luck' in reply to your suggestion that her husband had been run over and killed?"

Mrs. Austin looked abashed.

96

"I think her actual words were, 'No, there's no escape that way.' I took it to mean 'No such luck.'"

"You're sure of these words, Mrs. Austin? Are you— yes or no?"

"Yes, I am. 'No, there's no escape that way'—that's what she said."

"And after that no mention of Mr. Brande was made?"

"No."

"You say you remember Mr. Wedgwood coming to the flat at ten o'clock that morning very distinctly. Will you describe it, please?"

"There was a ring at the bell," said Mrs. Austin dramatically. "I was just going to make some coffee, but I popped off my apron and opened the door. There stood Mr. Mike, white as a sheet, his hands twitching, his eyes starting out of his head. I knew at once something was up."

"Not unnaturally." The Coroner opened his mouth to say the words, but thought better of them. Instead he wrote down "Seemed greatly agitated" and put a further question.

"I see that you took Mr. Wedgwood into the room where your mistress was kneeling by the fire in pyjamas. Do you remember what she said?"

"Yes. She said, 'Mike, my pet, I'm glad to see you,' and asked him if he'd have some coffee. Her face lit up—she looked quite different."

"Then you went out of the room?"

"Yes, to make the coffee."

"And when you came back, what did you see then?"

"They were clinging together," said Mrs. Austin, with sentimental relish. "Clinging together on the hearth rug like a couple of children. Of course, when they heard me they sprung apart—as was only natural, me being an older person—and my lady said, 'My husband's dead, Mrs. Austin.' 'No!' I said. 'Yes,' she said. I give her some coffee quick. Then we all had some coffee and Mr. Wedgwood told us that they was bringing the body up. I made him come out and give me all the details so I should know what to get ready. As soon as he could he slipped back to her."

"Then you can't tell us any more about the conversation which took place between them after the death had been discovered," said the Coroner firmly. "Can you tell us what effect the news had upon your mistress? Did she seem surprised?"

"Surprised? She was horrified! I never saw such a change in anyone in all my life. One moment she was a bright laughing girl, not a care in the world except Mr. Brande's neglect and mental cruelty to her, and the next she was a drawn haggard woman, as you might say."

"Yes, but was she surprised?"

"She was thunderstruck, if you ask me," said Mrs. Austin.

Mr. Scruby, who jumped up some little time before and had only just succeeded in catching the Coroner's eye, begged to be allowed to put a question.

"When you say your mistress was in pyjamas, Mrs. Austin," he said, "do you mean her night clothes?"

The woman stared at him. "No, I don't," she said. "It's a new fashion. Little serge romper suits. Ladies wear them in the morning about the house. Very nice and respectable, they are, something after the style of a naval uniform."

"Thank you." Mr. Scruby sat down amid a titter of laughter and Mrs. Austin's appearance in the limelight came to an end.

She went back to her seat bursting with pride.

"I showed 'em," she said, sitting down beside Gina. "They didn't get much change out of me—nosy parkers!"

Gina said nothing.

The last witness was so well known to the whole of the Barnabas group that they stared at him in astonishment in this new setting. He was a little wizened person, very spruce and smart, but so nervous that he was almost incoherent. He gave his name as William Robert Dyke and explained that he was the janitor in charge of Twenty-one and Twenty-three, Horsecollar Yard, and had been in the employment of Messrs. Barnabas, Limited for twenty years.

He identified the piece of rubber tubing reluctantly as part of an old shower-bath attachment which he had saved some years before when it had been thrown out of Mike's flat during a spring-cleaning. Thinking that it might come in useful at some time or other, he had hung it over a large nail on the wall of the cupboard next to the furnace at Number Twenty-one, where a great deal of other odds and ends were stored. The cupboard had no door and its contents were easily visible to anyone and everyone who passed in and out of the building by the basement garden exit.

On the morning of Friday, the twenty-ninth, the day after the deceased had disappeared, he had noticed it lying upon the floor beside the other rubbish and had picked it up. He thought it looked a little dirty, but had not examined it carefully, simply replacing it upon its nail and forgetting it until the Coroner's Officer questioned him about it on the following Monday morning.

And there, with astonishing abruptness, the larger part of the enquiry came to an end.

Gina sat quite still. She did not want to look about her. Miss Curley tried to catch her eye, to give her a timidly reassuring nod, but the younger woman did not stir nor did she ever raise her eyes from her white-gloved hands folded tightly in her lap.

John and Mr. Scruby were conversing animatedly in whispers while Mr. Campion leant back in his seat, his arms folded and an even more vacuous expression than usual upon his face.

Outside the later editions of the evening papers were being unfolded at windy street corners by excited youths. Home news was scarce and the "Strong-Room Mystery Inquest" was a godsend.

Much had been made of the morning's disclosures and a photograph of Gina and Mrs. Austin leaving the court appeared on the front page of each paper.

Inside the courtroom the sense of drama was growing. It had been by no means a tedious inquisition and now there was breathlessness in the air as the Coroner began to sum up. From beginning to end he was scrupulously fair. His deep, matter-of-fact voice lent no hint of theatricality to his oration, but rather brought a salutary commonplaceness into the business, reminding his hearers that they were enquiring into the death of a man of no less or more importance than themselves.

He dissected the evidence of the various witnesses, but was careful to make no comment.

"Let me quote to you from a very old and respected book," he said at last, leaning across his desk and addressing the jury intimately. "I refer to Burke's *Justice*. There these words are set down for our instruction. I will read them to you.

> "*It is peculiarly the province of the jury to investigate and determine the facts of the case. They are neither to expect nor should they be bound by any specific or direct opinion of the Coroner upon the whole of the case, except so far as regards the verdict, which in point of law they ought to find as dependent and contingent upon their conclusions in point of fact. The verdict should be compounded of the facts as detailed to the jury by the witnesses and of the law as stated to them by the court.'*"

He looked up from his book.

"I have told you the law. You know what you must do and what questions you must answer. You may now consider your verdict."

The jury retired and were gone only fifteen minutes. When they returned the foreman was perspiring and the faces of the others were studiously blank. On ascertaining that they were agreed Mr. Salley put the first question, his pen poised.

"Who do you find the deceased was?"

The foreman, his voice squeaky and breathless with discomfort, spoke hurriedly.

"We find, sir, that he was Paul Redfern Brande, of Twenty-one, Horsecollar Yard, of this parish."

"How do you find that the deceased met his death?"

"Sir, we find that he met his death by poisoning from carbon monoxide gas."

"Where do you find that he died?"

"In the strong room in the basement at his place of business at Twenty-three, Horsecollar Yard, of this parish, on the twenty-eighth day of January in this year."

The Coroner wrote rapidly.

"Do you find how he came by his death?"

"Yes, sir. We find that he was murdered wilfully and with malice aforethought."

There was a long pause and the court was unnaturally silent. The reporters waited like greyhounds in the traps and Inspector Tanner sat up, his ears pricked.

The quiet voice of the Coroner continued.

"That is the first part of the verdict. We now come to the final question, about which you already know. You have declared that the deceased was murdered. If you know who is guilty of this terrible offence it is your duty to say his name. From the evidence which you have heard, do you find anyone so guilty? Remember, you must speak from the certainty in your hearts and not from any suspicion, but if you have that certainty it is your bounden duty to speak. Do you find anyone guilty of the murder of Paul Redfern Brande?"

"Yes, sir, we do." The foreman's voice squeaked ridiculously as his nervousness robbed him of his breath.

"Then will you say his or her name?"

The foreman gulped.

"We find that Michael Wedgwood did wilfully murder his cousin Paul Redfern Brande."

Gina's head fell forward and she sank against the woman at her side.

John struggled to his feet, his dignity forgotten in his astounded horror.

The Coroner went on evenly.

"Do you find anyone guilty of being accessory before the fact of murder?"

"No, sir." The foreman mopped his dripping forehead. "We find no one guilty of being accessory before or after the fact."

8
Presumed Innocent

Since the arrest which he had just made was not technically legal until the Coroner had finished with the jury's formalities and had signed the warrant, Inspector Tanner was content to wait patiently in a corner of the anteroom while John and Mr. Scruby monopolized his prisoner.

Mike stood looking at the two elderly men with unseeing eyes. He was pale and the lines of his face had deepened, leaving the skin taut and his skull oddly apparent, but his body had not lost its ease or his manner its natural lazy calm.

The sudden catastrophe seemed to have burnt up over him like the flare of a new gas mantle, leaving him visibly the same but stricken with a new vulnerability.

As though conscious of this he held himself mentally apart from the others, whose thoughts and words were still protected.

John was frankly hysterical. Little pinkish pouches had appeared in the loose flesh beneath his jaw and his eyes were flickering.

"We must keep our heads," he was saying, his long bony fingers gripping Mr. Scruby's arm with painful pressure. "We must keep our heads. It's a monstrous mistake—we know that. The Coroner has exceeded his powers and in due course he will be reprimanded and removed, but meanwhile the publicity involved is terrible. No compensation can make up for it."

"Mr. Widdowson, Mr. Widdowson." Mr. Scruby's timid voice was imploring. "This is not the time. We must talk later when we can see what is best to be done. Now we have only a few moments and I want to assure Mr. Wedgwood that we shall leave no stone unturned to defend him at his trial. You will receive a visit from someone at my office to discuss the defence," he hurried on, speaking directly to Mike. "Rest assured that we shall do everything in our power."

Mike was vaguely aware of an anxious, sympathetic face raised to his and he nodded to it gratefully.

John gaped at them both. The pouches in his neck quivered and his lips moved helplessly.

"But it was an accident. Obviously an accident. I *know* it was an accident."

"Doubtless," said Mr. Scruby dryly, and added with unexpected briskness: "It now remains for us to prove it. I do not know at this juncture, of course, what line the defence will take. That is for Counsel to decide."

John sat down suddenly on the bench which ran round the dirty pale green walls. He looked very old.

Mr. Scruby eyed him thoughtfully for a moment and returned to Mike.

"I need hardly advise you not to discuss your—ah—your situation with anyone at all until I or someone from my office can see you," he murmured. "Keep as cheerful as you can and——"

He broke off abruptly and swung round. The Inspector was interviewing someone at the door. After a considerable amount of whispering he stepped back to admit Mr. Campion, and behind him Gina and Miss Curley.

The Inspector was sympathetic.

"They'll clear off in a little while," he said confidentially to Campion. "You told your man to take the car round to the back of Chequers Street, did you? That's right. You'll be able to get the ladies away quite comfortably in a minute or two. It's the newspaper photographers, not the crowd, today. The crowd won't come until the trial."

His voice flattened and died as he became aware that they were all listening to him. He returned to his corner and presently, as Sergeant Pillow came to relieve him, went down to the courtroom for the warrant.

Mr. Scruby had stepped aside as the newcomers entered and now, his mild eyes unexpectedly shrewd, he watched the meeting between Gina and Mike. No woman, however lovely, is really improved in appearance by any of

the tragic emotions, but to some a certain interestingness is
lent by crisis. Now that the worst had come Gina had
achieved a cold poise and an almost porcelain hardness in
her face which gave her features a new decision. She looked
at Mike and their eyes met steadily.

Mr. Campion and Miss Curley were firing remarks at
John, practically speaking, at random, and Mr. Scruby was
the only frank observer of the meeting.

For a moment Gina's lips moved, hovered over words,
rejecting them unspoken. Finally she said the one thing
which her brain had refused to consider ever since the
discovery of the body. The words were jerked out of her,
her voice unnatural.

"It's happened then," she said.

For an instant the man's self-possession wavered and
the nakedness of his heart was exposed. The expression
rushed back into his eyes and incredulity mingled with the
other emotion there. He recovered immediately, however,
and for the first time since the verdict a smile appeared
upon his wide mouth.

"The vanity of the woman!" he said, and turned away.

The damage was done. The colour poured into the
girl's face, her poise was destroyed and she stood awkwardly, suddenly looking very young and gawky.

There was a moment of acute discomfort and then the
door opened once more, and Sergeant Pillow rose to admit
a telegraph boy with an envelope for John.

The old man tore it open with hands that trembled
uncontrollably and, because it was his habit to do so at the
office, read the message aloud.

> *"Astounded have not been informed. Incal-*
> *culable harm may result incomprehensible ne-*
> *glect. Do nothing till arrive. Barnabas."*

John looked up, genuine astonishment in his eyes.

"God bless my soul! Cousin Alexander," he said. "I
never thought——No, no answer, boy. Miss Curley, give
him sixpence."

Mr. Scruby came forward dubiously.

"Alexander Barnabas, the counsel?" he enquired, and

there was no telling whether there was reverence or sheer apprehension in his tone.

John blinked at him. "Yes, my cousin. My uncle's only son. Took silk a good few years ago now. Great man in criminal cases, I believe. Great reputation——"

"Oh, yes," said Mr. Scruby gently, "I know him," and there was a little silence.

It was broken by the return of Inspector Tanner.

"You can get the ladies away comfortably now, sir," he said meaningly, and Mr. Campion, who saw that there was nothing to be gained by waiting, turned to Gina enquiringly.

She went with him willingly, almost eagerly, and Miss Curley followed after leaving a whispered message with the Sergeant for John, who had begun to talk to Mr. Scruby again, and a friendly handclasp with Mike.

In the doorway Gina hesitated without looking back, and the man under arrest, glancing up, caught a last glimpse of her small black figure, her head bent and the soft arc of her chestnut hair showing under her black hat.

At one of the back doors of the court Mr. Lugg sat proud and disapproving in the shining glory which was Mr. Campion's new Lagonda. He sprang out with an agility astonishing in one of his bulk and bundled the two women somewhat unceremoniously into the back.

"Now let's sheer off before we're seen," he said in a husky undertone to his employer.

Mr. Campion, who had the same idea but for less selfish reasons, slid in behind the wheel and the great car moved away.

When they were held up in a traffic jam in Holborn he glanced over his shoulder.

"I'm going to take you back to my flat for half an hour or so, Gina, if you don't mind," he said. "These Press photographers are tenacious beggars, and you don't want to run into a battery of them waiting on your door-step."

The girl did not answer, but Miss Curley's voice, brisk and practical, came from the darkness of the hood.

"I'm so glad you thought of it, Mr. Campion," she said. "It had been on my mind. Of course, I hadn't liked to suggest it." And in a lower voice they heard her add: "Keep your head well down, my dear. You'll feel better."

"I'm all right," said Gina, and her voice sounded unutterably weary.

The person who did not approve of the suggestion was Mr. Lugg. Mr. Campion caught a glimpse of his face reflected in the windscreen and smiled in spite of himself.

It was a dark, wet night and they were caught in the home-going rush, so that it took them some considerable time to reach Bottle Street.

There the lights were subdued and shed little puddles of radiance on the streaming pavements. Campion took Gina's arm and steered her towards the brightly lit entrance beside the police station. Miss Curley followed him and Lugg put the car away.

As Campion and the two women came up the staircase to the small hall on the second landing which contained Campion's front door, a woman rose from the chair which was the only furniture in the minute passageway and stepped forward.

Her appearance was vaguely familiar to Campion, and he had the impression that he had seen her somewhere recently. She was not a usual type and he was struck by something indefinable about her which he could only describe to himself as passive rather than active grief. She was middle-aged and, although smartly dressed, had none of Gina's essential style. It occurred to him that she belonged to the category known to his father's generation as "handsome women." She came forward timidly.

"I don't know if you're Mr. Campion," she said, "but if you are, could I speak to you for a minute?"

Her voice came as a surprise. Without being actually vulgar or uneducated, its refinement was not quite genuine.

Mr. Campion took out his key.

"Why, yes, of course. In just one moment," he said, and unlocked the door.

Miss Curley took Gina inside and as the light from the inner hall fell upon the girl's face Campion heard a smothered exclamation from his unknown visitor. He turned round to find her looking after Gina, an embarrassed and defeated expression in her eyes.

"That's Mrs. Brande, isn't it?" she said. "I didn't recognize her at first, in this light. I'm sorry I bothered you, Mr. Campion. Good evening."

She was halfway across the passage to the stairs before she had finished speaking, and Mr. Campion was puzzled.

"Won't you leave your name?" he said rather idiotically.

"No, no, it doesn't matter. I made a mistake. It doesn't matter in the least."

Her voice came back to him as she clattered down the staircase in her high-heeled black patent shoes. Looking over the banisters he saw her fox fur flopping up and down on her plumpish shoulders as she hurried.

Slightly bewildered, he went into the flat and put a question.

Gina looked up from the depths of his big armchair.

"Yes, I saw her," she said wearily, "but I didn't know her. I've never seen her before in my life. What did she want?"

"Goodness knows," said Mr. Campion.

9

The Daring Young Man

On any other occasion and in any other circumstances the spectacle of Mr. Lugg in his latest rôle, serving afternoon tea to one of the principals in a *cause célèbre*, might easily have delighted Mr. Campion; but as it happened, such is the perversity of fortune, he found it irritating.

The change which had occurred to Gina in the anteroom of the court still persisted. The agitation and ill-suppressed terror of the last few days had now given place to a weary, broken weakness a thousand times more pathetic.

Miss Curley, on the other hand, had reacted by becoming an intensified edition of her normal self. Campion suspected her of being extra busy and efficient so that she might not have time to think. All the same, it was a difficult gathering and John's arrival was a relief.

He came in, scowled at Lugg, sat down in the chair which Campion had vacated on rising to welcome him, and announced querulously that he would like a cup of tea.

Lugg served him ungraciously, the expression in his little black eyes intimating clearly that he did not like his manners and was quite prepared to subject him to a course of instruction if the opportunity arose.

Having averted this danger by banishing Lugg, Campion glanced enquiringly at his new visitor.

Mr. Widdowson was fast recovering from his hysteria of earlier in the afternoon. The pink pouches had disappeared from his gills and his eyes were cold and steady.

"I've been talking to Scruby," he began peremptorily, his thin, academic voice raised a little above its normal tone, "and he agrees with me, of course, that the police are making a fantastic mistake. Apparently the Coroner is strictly within his rights, although Scruby feels he may come in for considerable censure. However, that's not the point. What we have to think about now is the best way of clearing up the ghastly business satisfactorily."

Mr. Campion eyed the man and wondered if it could be possible that even now he had not realized the full gravity of the position.

John leant back in his chair.

"I think Scruby feels that the police used the inquest to avoid shouldering full responsibility for the arrest," he announced. "He didn't say so in as many words, of course, but that's what I understood."

Gina had shrunk back into her chair and he appeared to notice her for the first time.

"We shall need you, Gina," he observed, pointing a long bony finger at her. "Scruby wanted me to impress it upon you that you're likely to be a very important witness."

She did not speak, and he evidently did not expect her to, for he returned to Campion.

"Scruby feels with me that an independent investigation on behalf of the family is absolutely necessary," he said slowly. "Time, you see, is going to be short."

Mr. Campion, who had drawn up a small, hard chair, now sat upon it and blinked at his client, his pale eyes vague behind his horn-rimmed spectacles.

"I'm sure Mr. Campion will do all he can to help Mike," put in Miss Curley so hastily that he smiled at her.

"Of course he will. Of course." John brushed aside the interruption irritably. "Now. Campion, we all know Paul's death was an accident. What I ask you to do is to prove it to the satisfaction of the most unintelligent member of the police and Press."

Mr. Campion rose. Wandering across the room, he took up a position of vantage, his hands in his pockets and his body supported by the edge of the desk.

"I say, I do hope you won't mind my saying it," he began gently, "but you're making a most unfortunate mistake, you know."

John stared at him. The quiet authority in the casual voice was unexpected.

Mr. Campion continued diffidently.

"I don't want to alarm you all, but frankly, you know, I've a tremendous respect for the police. They're about as good at their jobs as people ever get. Their occasional mistakes are the exceptions which prove the rule. They aren't trying anything out, or shelving any responsibility, or anything like that. I'm afraid it's much more devastating. You see, they feel they've got an open-and-shut case and so they're dealing with it in the quickest and most efficient manner possible. It's rather revolting when you see it from our present angle, I know, but there you are. . . ."

Mr. Widdowson appeared to be temporarily silenced, and it was Gina who spoke, her voice husky.

"Albert, you don't think Mike killed Paul, do you?"

"No, old dear," said Mr. Campion, "but somebody did. Don't let's lose sight of that."

There was a long pause. Miss Curley moistened her lips with the tip of her tongue, a regular movement more nervous than feverish.

"Moreover, someone murdered him very neatly indeed." Campion sounded apologetic when he spoke again. "And in spite of that the method has been detected already. That's another point I don't think we should miss. Our astute friends Tanner and Pillow aren't so very inefficient.

They've dogged that much out all right, although they didn't get on the scene until the body had been moved and the most appalling mess made of the strong room. They're not fools and they're not dishonest. They don't want to arrest an innocent man, believe me. That's every policeman's nightmare. But on the other hand, they do want to do their job decently. Someone has murdered Paul and they're employed to catch him and stop him doing it to anybody else."

John sat up slowly and turned the full force of his famous disapproving eye upon Campion.

"You seem to be a very outspoken young man," he observed.

Mr. Campion appeared to be embarrassed.

"It's a very outspoken business," he said. "Do you still want me to have a look round?"

"Albert, you must." Gina had risen. The pallor of her face was accentuated, and her mouth quivered uncontrollably. "I do see the danger. I've seen it all the time. It's been haunting me ever since that dreadful Monday morning. You must find out that Mike couldn't have locked the strongroom door and put the key away. You must find out why he didn't say he'd seen Paul when he went down there on Sunday—because he must have been there—and you must. find out what he was really doing before I phoned him on Thursday night."

Her voice ceased abruptly and she stood holding out her hand to him, an involuntary gesture oddly appealing. He looked at her gravely.

"I'll do all I can," he promised.

John rose. "I know it was an accident," he said, and there was conviction in his tone. "If you want to oblige me, Campion, you'll prove it. Get to the bottom of the mystery and you'll find I'm right. Now, Gina, you're to come back with me. I want you in the house when Cousin Alexander arrives."

The girl rose obediently. A lifetime of authority had endowed John with a gift for it.

"An accident," he repeated firmly as he shook hands with Campion in the hall, adding naïvely: "Terrible publicity. Good night."

Gina clutched Campion's hand; her lips were trembling.

"Let me know what's happening, won't you—please," she whispered.

John was halfway to the staircase and she glanced over her shoulder at him, dropping her voice to a whisper.

"Albert, will they open his letters there?"

Campion met her eyes.

"I shouldn't write if I were you," he said earnestly.

"I see." Her voice died away and the dullness returned to her eyes. "Good-bye, and thank you."

Campion watched her until she disappeared and then went slowly back into the sitting room. He had forgotten Miss Curley, and now the sight of her sitting quietly in an armchair, her hat slipping back until it looked like a three-cornered halo and her near-sighted eyes thoughtful behind her pince-nez, startled him. He smiled at her guiltily.

"I thought I had better stay to tell you that I'll give you all the help I can," she said. "Mr. Widdowson is really terribly grateful to you for taking up the case, but of course he's worried just now. The shock has been tremendous, for one thing. But I thought I'd like to tell you that if you care to examine any room in the office or get access to any papers I'll see that you can do it without interference."

"I shall hold you to that," he said gratefully, and added impulsively: "I'm not really the sensitive soul you seem to think."

She sighed. "Well, as long as you're not . . ." she said. "Mr. Widdowson does give offence quite unconsciously at times. It's being in the office so long, I suppose."

And then, to his consternation, her voice broke and she began to cry.

"I'm all right—I'm all right," she said, waving him away with one hand and dabbing at her eyes with the other. "I don't know what made me so stupid. It's the suddenness of it all, I suppose, although I've woken up in terror of something very like it every night this week. Mr. Campion, why didn't they arrest her as an accomplice?"

Before this mixture of muddled thought and penetration Mr. Campion found himself a trifle bewildered, but he answered the direct question.

"Gina came out very well on the stand," he said cautiously. "Besides, there's no direct evidence of an affair—no letters or anything. The charwoman was pretty damaging, but it was fairly obvious she'd go to pieces in cross-examination."

"But there's no direct evidence against Mike," Miss Curley protested. "It's all circumstantial."

He nodded gloomily. "I know. But there's a devil of a lot of it. I rather fancy that Salley has been stewing up for a row with his critics for some time and is spoiling for a showdown. You see," he went on gently, "the police evidently believe not only that they're right, but that they're obviously right."

Miss Curley's moist eyes darkened reflectively.

"I've known Mike ever since he was a child," she said, "and I don't think——"

She paused and he regarded her quizzically.

"Are you sure?"

The old woman looked up at him.

"Men in love are not quite normal," she said. "I've seen it over and over again. But I don't—I can't think Mike would *kill* Paul. And, anyway," she added triumphantly, "if he had he wouldn't have done it like that."

Campion brightened. "That's what I'm banking on," he said.

Lugg put his head round the door.

"Bloke outside," he remarked, and then, catching sight of Miss Curley, started visibly. "I thought you had gorn, madam," he remarked when he had recovered his composure, and straightening up announced with remarkable change of personality: "A gentleman is waiting in the hall, sir. Would you see 'im?"

"Of course," said Campion, slightly ashamed of his old friend. "Do drop that accent, it's getting on my nerves."

A spiteful expression appeared in Mr. Lugg's small black eyes and he surpassed himself.

"Very blinking good, sir," he said, and stalked out.

Ritchie came in, stooping unconsciously to avoid the lintel.

"Gina gone?" he enquired. "Oh, hello, Miss Curley. Thought I'd come and see you, Campion. Been down to the

112

place with some of Mike's things—pyjamas, toothbrush, comb, and so on. Still got to live, wash, eat, poor chap. It's a mistake, Campion."

He dropped into a chair as he spoke and his pale blue eyes regarded the younger man with that questioning, inarticulate expression which Campion had seen there before.

"Got to find out who did it," said Ritchie. "Must."

Miss Curley rose and held out her hand.

"Don't forget," she repeated, "if there's anything you want to see in the office, come to me."

Campion showed her out and on the steps she looked up at him.

"You're a good boy to help us," she said suddenly, and patted his arm.

Campion went back to Ritchie, who had drawn up to the fire and was gloating over it like some huge but benevolent spider trying to get warm.

"Cousin Alexander," he remarked, without turning round. "Eloquent—dramatic."

Campion took his mind off the immediate problem for a moment to consider Alexander Barnabas, K.C. The grand old man had been comparatively quiet for a month or so, he reflected. He could not remember seeing his name about since the Shadows trials in the summer. In view of the circumstances, he regretted that he had never seen the barrister in the flesh, although photographs of that magnificent head were familiar enough and the very mention of his name brought recollections of dramatic cross-examinations and sensational speeches.

Sir Alexander's history was stormy. Although he was Jacoby Barnabas's only son, he had avoided publishing and taken to law, with his father's full consent and approval, and had made his name as a junior in the great days of Marshall Hall before the bar had followed stage into a quieter and less rhetorical style. After taking silk his practice had grown and he had been greatly sought after as a leader, until the unfortunate quarrel with the Judge in the Leahbourne case had done his reputation irreparable damage.

However, although it was still felt that his temper was not to be trusted, his triumphal return in the Dallas trial had restored him to popular, if not academic, favour, and he was now considered a fine showy counsel for the defence in sensational criminal trials and was often briefed by solicitors whose clients were backed by a newspaper.

Campion thought he understood Mr. Scruby's apprehension. A remark from Ritchie recalled his attention.

"Thought of something. Ought to mention it."

The man had turned in his chair and was looking up anxiously.

"Hose pipe—car exhaust—locked room—all that, not original," he blurted out at last. "Plagiarism. All in a book."

"In a book?" enquired Mr. Campion, a trifle mystified.

A vigorous nodding affirmed the question.

"Book called *Died on a Saturday*. Most of it in there. Read it myself. Recognized it in court."

"Who published it?"

Ritchie's face lengthened. "Us. Ten—twelve months ago. Not much of a sale."

Mr. Campion was looking at him anxiously.

"Who read this book besides you?—in the office, I mean?"

Ritchie's tremendous bony shoulders hunched in a shrug.

"Anyone. Handled by Mike's department."

"Are you saying that Mike brought out a book describing the method of murder which was used to kill Paul less than a year ago?" Campion demanded, aghast.

Ritchie's wretchedness increased.

"Fifteen months perhaps," he suggested.

Mr. Campion passed his hand over his sleek yellow hair and whistled.

Ritchie was silent for some moments, his awkward figure twisted over the arm of his chair.

"Somebody did it," he said at last. "Evidence showed that."

Campion looked down at him.

"What's your private opinion?" he enquired unexpectedly. "You were much closer to it all than I was. Who did it?"

Ritchie shook his ponderous head.

114

"Anyone," he murmured, and added with a sigh and a flail-like gesture: "No one."

Mr. Campion pursued his private thoughts.

"That Miss Netley, tell me about her."

Ritchie wrinkled his nose and achieved a masterpiece of pantomimic disapproval.

"Affected girl," he said. "Silly. Sly. Superior. Little snob. Stupid clothes."

"Anything else?"

The other man hesitated.

"Don't know much. Only seen her about. Fond of the ballet. Has a Post Office Savings Book. Arch," he added in triumph. "That's it—she's arch. Don't like her."

He rose to go shame-facedly, evidently feeling that he had not been very helpful in the cause, for he shook hands earnestly and, his blue eyes peering beseechingly into Campion's own, made a long and for him coherent speech.

"Do what you can, Campion, Mike's a good fellow—decent fellow. Never hurt a soul. Kind fellow—kind. Pleasant, friendly to me. Couldn't possibly get anything out of it. If we don't find out who killed affected ass Paul they'll hang Mike—kill him. Stop it, there's a dear chap."

After he had gone Mr. Campion sat at his desk and scribbled idly on the blotting-paper. He had no illusions concerning the task in front of him. Events had moved more swiftly than he had contemplated and the need for urgency was great.

Suddenly the thought which had been playing round the edges of his conscious mind so irritatingly for some time past came out into the open. He reached for the telephone directory and got on to Miss Curley just as she had entered her home in Hammersmith.

She heard his question with surprise.

"Mr. *Tom* Barnabas?" she echoed. "The one who—who disappeared?"

"That's the man." Campion's voice sounded eager. "What sort of person was he? What was he like?"

Miss Curley cast her mind back twenty years.

"A nice man," she said at last. "Good-looking, inclined to be reserved, but very odd. Why?"

"Odd?" Campion seized upon the word. "In what way?"

Miss Curley laughed, but when she spoke her words had a flavour of the macabre.

"He could walk upstairs on his hands," she said.

10
Twenty Years After

It was wet and bitterly cold, with sludge on the pavement and dark grey blankets in the sky, when Mr. Campion walked thoughtfully down Nemetia Crescent, Streatham, and tried to imagine it as it had been on a May morning twenty years before.

To his relief, there was no sign of any recent building operations, and, although the neighborhood had gone down a little, he suspected, there was no evidence of any structural alteration.

It was a melancholy little enclosure, a half hoop of flat-fronted houses looking out across a strip of wet tarmac at a bank of dilapidated shrubs.

He found the house out of which Tom Barnabas had walked on May the eighth, nineteen hundred and eleven, and stood in the rain looking at it. Dingy lace curtains covered the windows and a fly-blown black card in the transom over the unexpectedly nice door announced in silver letters that there were apartments within.

Mr. Campion passed on and turned the corner at the end of the Crescent. To his relief he saw that the deserted road in front of him tallied exactly with the description Miss Curley had given. A wall over six feet high and completely blank ran down the whole length of the road on the side nearest the Crescent, while on the other a row of little villas recessed from the road by overgrown gardens straggled down to the trams and the main street.

Campion paused and let his imagination dwell upon the facts of the story as he knew them.

It had been about nine o'clock in the morning. Mr. Barnabas had come striding from his house in the Crescent, had turned the corner, and was apparently marching on to the little tobacconist's at the end of the street, where it was his custom to stop and pick up a copy of the *Times* and the *Standard*, when unfortunately he stepped into the fourth dimension or was the victim of spontaneous combustion or some sort of accident to an atom.

The tobacconist's was still there. A row of newspaper boards decorated the far end of the wall, in spite of the rain. Mr. Campion wandered on, pausing now and again in spite of the weather and reflecting upon the few facts he had been able to glean that morning from the files of a newspaper.

For May 8th, 1911, the prophets had predicted fair to fine weather, warm temperature and slight mist. There had been an air smash in the Paris to Madrid race on the day before, when Monsieur Train had crashed at Issy, killing himself and seriously injuring Monsieur Monis, Premier of France, who had been present to see him start. The Court was just out of mourning for Edward VII, the Imperial Conference was opening the following day, and Freeman (J.) had been bowled by Hobbs for twenty-one in the presence of Their Royal Highnesses the Prince of Wales and Prince George.

The information was not very helpful. The world, in fact, seemed to have been going on in much the same way as ever. And since it is always easier to believe in a miracle which happened twenty years ago than in one of yesterday morning, Mr. Campion felt his suspicions aroused.

He looked at the wall. There was no way of telling what was on the other side. It might have hidden a pool, a back garden, or fairyland itself.

He walked on to the newspaper and tobacconist's shop. As he entered it his spirits rose. This stuffy little room with its doorway narrowed to the verge of the impassable by ancient paper-racks filled with brightly coloured periodicals, its acrid smell of newsprint, its two counters, one piled high with papers and the other decorated with every known brand of tobacco grouped round an immense pair of shining scales, could not have altered for forty or fifty, much less twenty, years.

He stood hesitating on the square foot or so of floor space for some moments before he realized that he was not alone in this sanctuary of smoke and light literature.

Over the paper department there was a species of canopy composed of yet more periodicals clipped into wire frames, and in the narrow opening between this and the counter he caught sight of two very bright eyes peering at him from out a pepper-and-salt wilderness of hair and whisker.

"Paper or a nice box of cigarettes, sir?" said a voice at once friendly and a trifle pert.

Mr. Campion bought both and had the satisfaction of seeing the remainder of the man as he came running out of his lurking place to attend to the tobacconist's side of his business.

He was very small, spry and compact, and his feet, which were tiny, were thrust into old sheep-skin slippers which flapped as he walked.

"Haven't seen you about here before, sir?" he enquired. "Moved into the district?"

"Not yet," said Mr. Campion cautiously.

"No offence meant and none taken, I hope," said the old man, running all the words together until they formed a single apologetic sound. "Only I saw you wandering up and down the road just now and it came into my head that you might be looking for lodgings. This part isn't what it used to be, but I could put you on to several nice respectable women who'd look after you very well. Perhaps you'd like a widow, now?" he finished, his little bright eyes watching Campion with the inquisitive yet impersonal interest of a sparrow.

"Not at present," said Mr. Campion, who had a literal mind. "As a matter of fact, I came down here on a sort of sentimental errand. A friend of mine disappeared, or is supposed to have disappeared, walking along this street."

Tremendous interest appeared at once on the small face.

"I believe you're referring to my phenomenon," he

said. "I always call it mine, although it wasn't really. I just happened to be there. Now that *was* a funny thing, if you like."

"Do you remember it?"

"Remember it? Wasn't I in this very shop?" The little man seemed hurt. "Wasn't it me who gave interviews to all the newspapers?—or would have done, only they didn't believe me. It was hushed up really. Did you know that? In my opinion, sir," he went on, eyeing Mr. Campion with portentous solemnity, "that was the most important thing that ever happened to me in all my life. And, luck being what it is—" he spread out his hands and hunched his shoulders in a gesture of resignation, "—I turned me back on it."

"Infuriating," murmured Mr. Campion sympathetically.

"It was," said his informant and, returning to his position behind the paper counter, leant across it and took a deep breath. "I didn't always talk about this," he began. "My name's Higgleton, by the way."

"How d'you do?" said Campion pleasantly.

"Pleased to meet *you*, sir," complied Mr. Higgleton, with grace, and plunged into his story. "It was on a Monday—no, a Tuesday morning, I think it was. Or it may have been a Thursday—I can't really remember—but I can see it as plain as daylight. I didn't talk about it much at the time because—well, you know what people are. Once you start seeing things that other people know can't have happened, you're apt to get the reputation of being a bit queer."

"Fanciful," suggested Mr. Campion.

"Exactly. But I remember that Wednesday morning as though it was yesterday. Only it was May then, not February like it is now. It was a beautiful clear morning, bright sunlight—we didn't have summertime then, so there was no hanky-panky—just a bright clear summer's day. This place is very pretty in the summer, though you might not think so. When there's leaves on those trees over there you can't see the houses. There were more trees in those days. It was when the children kept getting run over that they had one or two of 'em down. The children couldn't see the road from the gardens because of the trees and they used to run out and—there you are, as the saying is."

"I suppose that's why no one saw Mr. Barnabas from the houses?" said Mr. Campion.

"Barnabas!" said Mr. Higgleton, pouncing on the name. "That's it! That's it! Couldn't remember it for a moment, although it was on the tip of me tongue. That's why I was hedging about. Oh, I knew him as well as I know—you, I was going to say. Used to come in here every day for his papers. He was an ornament to the neighbourhood. I don't know what his business was; it was something in the City. But he used to turn out to it as though he was going to a——" Mr. Higgleton paused and searched in his mind for a simile.

"Ball?" suggested Mr. Campion idiotically.

His new friend glanced at him reproachfully.

"Well, not exactly a ball, but a wedding. City gentlemen used to dress more tastefully then than they do now. You probably wouldn't remember it very well, but they did. Silk hats and tail coats and fancy trousers were all the go, and a nice pair of yellow gloves to top everything off."

"And was Mr. Barnabas dressed like that when he disappeared?" said Mr. Campion.

"He was. A very well-dressed man indeed was Mr. Barnabas. I can see him now—in me mind's eye, of course—silk hat, nicely brushed, gold-topped cane and spats. A big handsome man he was, too, and very nicely spoken."

"How did it happen?" The question escaped Mr. Campion involuntarily.

"In the twinkling of a hand—like that!" said Mr. Higgleton, and snapped his fingers.

He had an odd trick of pausing after he had made an announcement and surveying his listener with a wide-eyed expression, as though inviting him to join in a wonder.

Mr. Campion, who had liked him from the start, began to feel a positive affection for him.

"I'll show you how it happened," said Mr. Higgleton, and, running out from behind the counter, he planted himself on the door-step. "Now here am I—see," he said over his shoulder, "standing on the corner of the street. It's nine o'clock in the morning, but I'm not so busy as all that, and I'm just standing here taking a deep breath of the ozone."

He gulped a lungful of rain-soaked, soot-laden air, and glanced at Campion for approval.

"Well, I see Mr. Barnabas turn the corner of the street down there."

He waved his hand in the direction of Nemetia Crescent.

"Now I *know* it is him—there's no doubt about that. (My eyes are better than what they are now, it being twenty years ago.) And I watch him coming up the street for a bit. There he is, striding along in the sunlight swinging his cane, looking as calm and happy as you please.

"Well, when he's about fifty yards away I say to myself, 'I'd better get his papers.' So I turn back into me shop like this," he trotted back to the counter and picked up a couple of newspapers which he thrust under Campion's nose. "There they are—see? Then I hurry back to the door and—" he stopped, and peered up and down the street, ventured out into the rain, and finally returned, bewilderment expressed in every line of his features, "—not a sign of him," he said. "Street empty all ways. You could knock me down with a wave of the hand, as the saying has it.

"'Well,' I said, 'he's vanished!' And he had, too."

Again the look of wonder.

"Of course you'll say," he continued after a silence which Mr. Campion had not liked to break, "that he must have snapped into a trot and run past the shop. But he couldn't have done. I wasn't in here above five seconds. Besides, the constable who was standing on the corner saw him go. One minute he was there and one minute he wasn't. In the middle of the pavement about fifteen yards from this shop, just along by the wall there, he disappeared and was never seen by mortal eye again."

"Top hat, gold-headed cane and all?" said Mr. Campion.

"Yellow gloves *and* spats," said Mr. Higgleton. "Clean as kiss yer hand."

"I'd like to have met the policeman." Mr. Campion sounded wistful.

"So you should have. I'd have taken you round myself if he hadn't retired and gone to live in the country. Somewhere Norfolk way he is. But he drops in here now and again when he comes to town. He was here as little as two years ago. Next time I see him I'll tell him you're interested and perhaps he'll let you have his side of the story. His name's on tip of me tongue, but I've forgotten it."

Mr. Higgleton thought for a while but to no purpose.

Mr. Campion expressed his thanks and made an attempt to leave, but he was not to get away so easily.

"I don't like to pretend I know what happened because I don't," said his new friend, skilfully edging between him and the exit. "But then funny things do happen. There was a man in that house over there—you can see it if you stand on the step—who ran off with every servant-girl his wife had in the course of twelve years. Every single one of them!"

This time the expression of wonder was a little overdone.

"She fetched him back one week and off he'd go with the new girl the next."

"What happened in the end?" said Mr. Campion, interested in spite of himself.

"Cut his throat on a golf-course in Scotland," said Mr. Higgleton. "And then there was the woman with the snakes."

"Really?" murmured Mr. Campion, moving adroitly to the right and gaining six inches in his progress to the door.

"She used to live in this house at the back of mine, on the other side," said Mr. Higgleton frantically. "Her garden used to run down behind mine and finish up alongside this wall. Of course, she left before the war, but at one time her place was *alive* with 'em. She used to breed 'em and train 'em. Some of them were very clever, I believe, but I never liked them."

He sighed. Mr. Campion was going to get away; he could see it.

"If ever that police sergeant should drop it, sir, perhaps you'd like me to give him your name?" he ventured, breathless with defeat.

"That's very kind of you." Campion drew a card from his wallet and Mr. Higgleton took it and placed it with great care behind a jar of tobacco on the shelf at the back of the shop. "Any time you want to know anything about this district," he said wistfully, "you'll come to me, won't you?"

Mr. Campion felt a cad.

"I certainly shall," he said. "Thank you very much."

"It's been a pleasure, sir," said Mr. Higgleton truthfully, and Campion went down to the High Street to find a cab, convinced in spite of his stern belief in the material that something very odd indeed had happened to Tom Barnabas twenty years before.

When he arrived back at Bottle Street he was still absorbed by the past and the urgent message from the present head of the firm of Barnabas and Company, Limited, demanding his immediate attendance at Twenty-three, Horsecollar Yard, brought him back to the problem of the moment with uncomfortable conviction that he had spent an unprofitable morning.

He arrived at the office at a little after two o'clock and was shown at once into John's big room on the ground floor, where a conference was in progress. Before he entered the room, while he was still in the hall, the sonorous voice from within warned him what to expect, and he did not come upon Cousin Alexander altogether unprepared.

The first thing he saw upon entering the room was the back of John's head and the arc of his forehead. He was leaning back in his chair, which had been turned away from the door, and appeared to be entranced or even stupefied by the spectacle confronting him.

On the hearth rug Sir Alexander Barnabas stood in one of his more famous attitudes, and Campion had the full benefit of his commanding presence. He was a big man, tall and heavy, with a magnificent physique and a great head surmounted by a mass of iron-grey curls parted sleekly down the middle and brushed up at the sides so that, whether by accident or design, one was almost deceived into thinking that his barrister's wig was a fixture.

His face was handsome in an orthodox way and its clean-shaven mobility had a trick of emphasizing the slightest inflection in its owner's voice with appropriate expression.

At the moment he was radiating authority. One long

graceful hand was upraised to drive home some point while the other rested behind his broad, dark-coated back.

"There is no question of that," he was saying. "Ab-so-lute-ly no question." And Mr. Campion was quite convinced that, whatever the subject of conversation might be, there could indeed be absolutely no question about it.

At Campion's entrance John pulled himself out of the stupor into which he had fallen and performed the introduction.

Mr. Campion was aware of a personage condescending to do a great honour. Two immense fingers rested in his hand for a second, and then he was dismissed to the realm of unimportant things and Cousin Alexander's melodious voice took up the thread of his discourse once again.

"We must have an acquittal," he said. "Complete and unconditional acquittal with no stain left upon the boy's character. I shall work for that and I shall achieve it."

Mr. Campion sat down on the edge of a chair in the far corner of the room and listened politely. Miracles seemed to be the order of the day.

"But you must understand, John," the Counsel continued firmly. "The case against Mike is very strong. Circumstantial evidence can be very deadly indeed. At the moment Michael is in a position of the gravest danger."

Mr. Campion pulled himself together with a jerk. The effect of so powerful a personality at close range was disconcerting. When Sir Alexander spoke of gravity one automatically thought of international crises and in his mouth the word "danger" had the shrill insistence of a fire alarm.

John attempted to speak, but was answered before a word had left his mouth.

"I have seen the boy," said Cousin Alexander, "and I am convinced of his innocence. Innocence," he repeated and stared at Campion, who found himself feeling like a rabbit caught in the glare of a headlight. "Innocent." Sir Alexander again dropped his voice to a whisper. "I heard his statement. Only an innocent man would have dared to make such a damaging confession. Why did he admit he had no alibi? Because he was telling the truth. Because he was innocent."

His glance swept round the room.

"Can't you see what happened?" he went on passionately. "Are you blind? Or does the very nakedness of truth offend your modesty? Imagine it . . ."

His voice had become persuasive, his excitement passing as rapidly as it had arisen.

"Think of the story he told the police. Think of the damaging history of that fatal night, related as simply as a child might have told it, a child not only innocent, but so guileless as to believe that not for a moment would its innocence be called into question."

Mr. Campion settled back in his chair and reflected how much more bearable drama was when it had a little art to help it along. On the witness-stand Mike had presented a depressing tale, but in Sir Alexander's hands his story became an exhilarating experience if not in particularly good taste. Meanwhile the great man was off again filling the room with melodious but overpowering sound.

"The Coroner demanded to know where Mike was between the hours of five and nine in the evening, hours which have since proved to be critical in the history of this terrible case. What did the boy do? Did he invent a history of little alibis to be broken down one by one by a pitiless police enquiry? Or did he tell the truth? 'I walked,' he said. 'I walked alone through the London streets, amid thousands of my fellow men, not one of whom will come forward to bear me witness. I was unknown to them—a stranger. I was alone.'"

"Yes, but what was he doing?" said John irritably, the paralyzing quality of Cousin Alexander's peroration having apparently passed over his head. "What purpose could he possibly have had in wandering about like that?"

Just for a moment the great man seemed to have been taken off his balance. He was evidently not used to interruptions, for his eye wavered and when he spoke again there was a reproving quality in the beautiful voice which had very little to do with art.

"If you will have patience," he said, "I will tell you. Mike is a young man and he committed a crime which, although reprehensible, is one of those misfortunes which overtake young men in spite of themselves. He fell in love with another man's wife. But he did not tell her so. He stood by and saw her neglected and tyrannized over by a man who did not realize her worth. From beginning to end their association was innocent. It does not follow that because of this restraint his passion was any the less real. An evening came when he knew the woman he loved was going to have a long interview with the man to whom she was bound by every legal and moral tie which our civilization has devised. Imagine him——"

The sonorous voice took on a hushed quality that Mr. Campion, who felt he was listening to the truth in dramatized form, found a little shocking.

"Imagine him sitting at his desk early in the evening of that cold January day. He was due to attend some literary function where a great deal of rubbish, some of it witty, some of it not, would be bandied from mouth to mouth, while in the very house in which he lived, in the very room two floors above that in which he slept, the woman whose being was the very core of his existence was talking to the man against whom she was completely defenceless, the man to whom the law gave every conceivable right in her, the man from whom she could not escape and from whom he dared not protect her.

"Do you see him there?" he went on, fixing Campion with a steely blue eye strangely reminiscent of the portrait in the waiting room. And then, in an even quieter voice: "I do. He cannot work, he does not want to go to the witty gathering whose chatter cannot save him from himself, nor can he go to his own home because he knows that in the room upstairs *she* is talking to his rival, her husband.

"What more natural for him, then——" the voice became musical as its rich tones played over the euphonious words, "——than to feel he must get away? Even his car is denied him: the fog is too thick. So he walks. He takes refuge in the time-honoured escape which men of every age and every generation have used to soothe their troubled spirits.

"He walks through London, through the crowds, thinking of her, trying to reason with himself, no doubt: trying to wrest himself from the cloying embraces of the pitiless emotion which consumes him."

John attempted to rise to his feet at this juncture, but was subdued by the famous eye.

"The little shop in Bayswater," said Cousin Alexander. "A secondhand jewellery store. A little place of curios, sentimental trifles scarcely of any value. He went there to buy her something, so engrossed in his thoughts that he forgot the day, forgot that it was a Thursday afternoon, upon which the keeper of the shop took his holiday and closed the shutters over the little trinkets, bidding lovers and their ladies wait until the morrow."

He paused, evidently feeling that he was navigating a dangerous stretch, and his keen eyes appraised their discomfort.

"He turned back. He walked on through the wet, cold streets. He did not notice they were wet, he did not notice they were cold; he was thinking of her, he was thinking of the woman. When he reached his home he had still come no nearer his goal, he had still not thrashed out his problem. It remained as large, as terrifying, as piteous, as wearying as ever before. He still felt the need of escape."

The great voice quivered and boomed, and at such close quarters was well-nigh pulverizing.

"What did he do? He saw the night was clearer. He thought of his car. He thought of the cool roads, the open fields, little remote villages—freedom, solitude. He went round to the garage and because it was his habit, because he wanted complete obedience from his car, he switched on the engine, intending to let it run for a while so that the cylinders should be warm, the oil moving smoothly and evenly.

"And at that time he was completely unaware that his car had been, or was going to be, used by some enemy to destroy the very man to whom the woman he loved was tied. Unfortunately for him he did not take the car straight out of the garage. Instead he remembered the key of the yard gate and went to his lonely little flat to fetch it.

"Imagine the thoughts which must have come into his mind as he entered that room and realized that she was above him, closeted, so he thought, remember, with the husband who neglected and had no respect for her.

"Then, just as he was about to take the key, what happened? The telephone bell rang and he heard her voice. He went down, turned off the car, and these two young

127

people went out together. Is that the sort of man who would have gone to see a moving picture if he knew that down in the strong room beneath the office, in the very house next to the one in which he was going to sleep that night, a man lay suffocated to death? Of course not! It is not feasible."

He allowed the last word to die away and then quite surprisingly dropped his artificial manner and became a different sort of person altogether.

"That's the truth, you know," he said. "That's what happened."

John pulled a crisp white handkerchief out of his pocket and wiped his forehead.

"I think you're right about Mike," he said. "You convinced me."

A smile, pleased and schoolboyish, appeared upon Cousin Alexander's handsome face.

"It's effective, isn't it?" he said, including Campion in the question. "Awfully effective, and true. But we can't possibly use it."

Mr. Campion said nothing. A purely academic consideration concerning the importance of technique in all phases of modern life had sprung unbidden to his mind.

"Not use it?" said John in exasperation.

"Oh, no, we couldn't use it." Sir Alexander was quite definite. "Not in this case, not in London. It's not suitable. We simply must not admit any love at all. In law love is suspicious. Bendex—he's going to be one junior and is devilling for me at the moment—points out that that is absolutely without question, and I see that he's right. I was only telling you privately why I know Mike's innocent. We'll think of something else. But that's the truth of that point, I'm sure of it. Who is that?"

The final remark was made with a trace of his old manner and both John and Mr. Campion turned towards the door, through which faint sounds, as of a slight scuffle, reached them.

"Come in," said John peremptorily and, the handle turning abruptly, the door burst open and Mr. Rigget was precipitated into the room.

It was evident at once that something more than the business of the Accounts Department had occasioned his sudden appearance. He was neat, as usual, but considerably more pink and clearly a little above himself. He was also breathless.

At the sight of the K.C. he wavered and for a moment it seemed as though his determination would desert him, but a glimpse of John's stony face seemed to pull him together.

"I thought it my duty to come to you at once, sir," he said in a squeaky rush, his eyes snapping behind his pince-nez and his phraseology oddly stilted. "I reached the decision to tell something of which I had become cognizant to the police only this morning and now that I have done so I thought it would be only fair to tell you as well."

He stood for a moment wavering. John was looking at him as though he were some particularly unpleasant species of life, repellent but not dangerous.

Cousin Alexander, on the other hand, was staring over his head, no doubt considering Truth from yet another angle. Mr. Campion alone remained politely interested.

From pink Mr. Rigget became crimson and a dappling of sweat appeared upon his forehead.

"I've just told Sergeant Pillow about the quarrel I heard," he said sulkily. "It was on the Wednesday morning before the Thursday on which Mr. Paul was killed. The door between Mr. Paul's rooms and the File Copy Office was ajar and I didn't like to shut it."

Cousin Alexander bent his gaze upon the wretched man for the first time.

"Eavesdropping?" he enquired blandly.

"I happened to hear certain words," said Mr. Rigget indignantly. "And," he added, a suggestion of a snarl appearing for a fleeting instant across his mouth with the surprisingly white teeth, "I thought it was my duty to repeat them to the police."

"Get out!" said John, suddenly losing his temper. "Get out! Get straight out of the Office."

"Wait a minute." Cousin Alexander's voice had become pleasant again. "Let's hear what this gentleman has to say. You've come here to help us, haven't you? That's extremely kind of you. My cousin appreciates it. What did you hear when the door was ajar? First of all, who was speaking? You were sure of the voices, were you?"

"Yes, I was," said Mr. Rigget, considerably taken aback by this mercurial change in the magnificent-looking old gentleman in front of him. "Besides, I'd seen Mr. Paul and Mr. Mike when I went through the room first."

"Mr. Paul and Mr. Michael . . ." said Cousin Alexander soothingly. "And what were the words you heard?"

"Well, they'd stopped talking when I went in first," said Mr. Rigget truculently, "and then I suppose they thought the door was shut so they went on with their quarrel."

"Or conversation," murmured Sir Alexander pleasantly. "And then what?"

Mr. Rigget swung round on John. There was intense satisfaction upon his ignoble face.

"Mr. Paul said, 'You mind your own damned business, Mike. She's mine and I'll manage my own life in my own way.'"

There was complete silence in the room after he had spoken and he had the satisfaction of knowing that he had achieved a sensation.

"And did you hear anything else?" Cousin Alexander's voice was cloying.

"Yes," said Mr. Rigget, blushing to the roots of his black hair. "He said, 'Make love to her if you want—God knows I'm not stopping you.'"

"And then?"

"I didn't hear any more," said Mr. Rigget. "I came out then. But I could see what Mr. Mike was thinking."

"That's not evidence," said Cousin Alexander.

11

Fuse Cap

After a tedious magisterial hearing Michael Wedgwood was committed for trial and on the afternoon before the day on which he was to appear at the Old Bailey Mr. Campion, with Ritchie at his side, steered the Lagonda through the traffic in New Oxford Street. It was one of those warm blowy days when every street corner is a flower garden presided over by a stalwart London nymph still clad in the wools and tippets of winter and the air is redolent with an exciting mixture of tar, exhaust and face powder.

However, neither of the men in the big car was in the mood to appreciate the eternal hopefulness of spring. Ritchie was talking, curbing his gestures with considerable difficulty because of the confined space.

"Want you to see her," he said. "Don't like her like this. It's getting her down, Campion. She's fond of him, you know. Loves him and probably feels responsible. Women always take responsibility. It's a form of vanity. Can't help it. Natural with them."

His anxiety seemed to have loosened his tongue and the fact that he now considered Campion an old friend made him more coherent.

"Bound to get him off, don't you think?" he added, cocking a wistful eye at the young man beside him. "Terrible experience anyway. All terrible," he went on, waving a tremendous arm between Mr. Campion's eyes and the windscreen. "All this. All these people. They're all in prison. All miserable. All slaves. All got to work when they don't want to, eat when they don't want to, sleep when they don't want to. Can't drink until someone says they may. Can't hide their faces, got to hide their bodies. No freedom anywhere. I hate it. Frightens me. Knew a man once who chucked it. I couldn't."

"It's a feeling one does get sometimes," Mr. Campion conceded.

"I always feel like it," said Ritchie and hesitated on the brink of some further confidence but thought better of it and was silent.

They found Gina sitting by the open window in the big studio and Campion, who had not seen her for some weeks, was shocked by the change in her. She was harder, more sophisticated, older. Nervous exhaustion had been replaced by general deterioration. She looked less chic, less graceful, less charming.

Her greeting was artificial and it was not until he had been sitting on the big white sofa for some minutes that she suddenly turned to him with something of her old genuineness.

"It was good of you to come," she said. "I'm not going to cry or do anything silly and I shall be perfectly composed in the witness-box. It's not hearing from him," she added, her defences suddenly collapsing. "No mental contact at all. He's just gone. He might be dead."

The natural embarrassment which the confidence might have engendered was swept away by the relief which Campion felt at seeing that her artificiality went no deeper. This was only a warning then of the damage which might be done to her and had not the awful finality of the accomplished fact.

"You—you haven't found out what really happened? I know you haven't. You'd have told me, of course. But haven't you got just an inkling—haven't you got a clue? When I asked John he said something about a new witness. Can't you tell me about that? Or is it all a secret, like everything else?"

The mixture of bitterness and pleading in her deep voice was disturbing. Mr. Campion wished in his heart that he had better news for her.

"The new witness may be useful," he said. "His name's Widgeon. I had an awful job getting hold of him. He didn't want to talk but when he realized how much depended on it he shelved his private considerations like a sportsman and came out with all he knew. He's employed by the Tolleshunt Press people. They've got a small office on the second floor of Number Twenty-one. Apparently he got tight at lunch on the Thursday and it took him all the afternoon to sober up, so that he came to himself about five with a splitting headache and all the afternoon's work on his hands. So he stayed and did it and was still hard at it between six and nine, when Mrs. Tripper was making herself cups of tea and coming home from pictures and trotting along to the fried-fish shop."

He paused and smiled at her encouragingly.

"His story is that he heard the car start up soon after six—he can't say how soon—and that the engine was running continuously until eight or thereabouts, and that he didn't hear it again until ten to nine, when it ran for only a short time."

"But that lets Mike out! That bears out Mike's story!"

For the first time during the interview a faint tinge of colour appeared in her pale cheeks and she seemed to take new life.

Campion looked uncomfortable.

"It bears out his story," he said, "but it doesn't let him out. He can't establish his alibi between six and the time you phoned him, remember."

"I see," she said. She sank back again, her slender body in the sleek, man-tailored gown lifeless and pathetic.

"It'll help," said Campion, anxious to be reassuring. "Apart from fixing in the jury's mind that the whole thing probably happened on the Thursday, it refutes the evidence of the Tripper woman, or muddles it at any rate."

"And you've discovered nothing else?"

"Nothing of value," he confessed. "There's been so little to go upon. Usually in these things you can get your teeth in somewhere and worry the whole thing out, but in this business there hasn't been a gripping place. I had great hopes of Miss Netley, but either she can't talk and simply tried to look as though she could out of vanity, or else there's no earthly reason why she should and she doesn't want to."

"Netley," said Ritchie and, getting to his feet, walked out of the room.

His exit was so abrupt that they both looked after him. Gina's eyes were wet when she returned to Campion.

"He's been so kind," she said. "I used to think he was inhuman, a sort of creature; not a lunatic, you know, but, well, just not quite a right thing; but since—since Paul died he's been the only person who's behaved normally, to me at any rate. He's genuinely sorry for me and terrified for Mike. The others, John and even dear old Curley and Mrs. Austin and the doctor and all the other normal people who I always thought were ordinary and real, and who I expected to have ordinary human reactions, have their own points of view so strongly that they have no room for mine or Mike's. D'you know, John's *only* thinking about the publicity and the firm, and Curley follows him. Mrs. Austin's thinking about her personal appearance. It's as though she was going on the stage . . ."

Mr. Campion looked sympathetic.

"They're in it, you see, old dear," he said. "It's touched their lives."

She nodded gloomily. "It's the first time I've ever seen anything terrible close to," she said. "I haven't shown up very well to myself."

There was a silence which Mr. Campion did not like to break and presently she spoke again.

"John brought that man he calls Cousin Alexander up here. I got hysterical and they sent a doctor to me. I didn't mean to but he just wasn't human as far as I was concerned. He was like an author planning a book or a play. They talked about hostile witnesses and witness for the defence not as though they were people but as though they were stray ideas, little pieces of construction."

"Sir Alexander is convinced that he'll get an acquittal," said Campion.

"I know." Her voice became strident. "Insufficient evidence! And what good'll that be? I talked all this out with Ritchie and he was as appalled as I was when he realized it. Don't you see an acquittal will only save Mike's life? The great damage is done."

She leant forward, her intelligent face turned to him and her eyes very steady.

"Don't you see," she said, speaking carefully, as though he were a child, "if they acquit him without finding the man who did the murder everyone will always believe Mike did it, and if ever he is seen speaking to me that'll prove it from their point of view."

"I suppose what other people think matters?" said Mr. Campion weakly.

"Of course it matters," she said angrily. "It becomes the truth. What everybody thinks *is* the truth."

Mr. Campion was silent, knowing from experience that a discourse on ethics is rarely comforting to anyone in genuine distress.

"Somebody must have done it," she said. "Who was it? I've gone over it again and again so often that I sometimes think I shall go mad and imagine I did it myself. It was someone clever enough to think of arranging an accident, someone who had no idea how clever the police are. Albert, it wasn't Mike, was it?"

"No," said Mr. Campion quietly but with complete conviction. "It wasn't Mike."

She laughed unsteadily.

"When you're alone thinking, you believe anything."

Her voice died on the last word and she turned round. The door clattered open and Ritchie returned. Because of his excitement he was clumsier than ever and he lurched across the room dangerously.

"Any good?" he enquired, dropping something into Mr. Campion's lap.

Mr. Campion turned over the battered cardboard-backed book in some astonishment.

"Post Office Savings Bank?" he said. "Whose is it?"

"Girl Netley's." Ritchie seemed tremendously pleased with himself. "Might be interesting. Never know. Often thought it funny she brought it to the office. Keep bank books at home, not lying about."

"Where did you get it from?" Mr. Campion turned over the pages carefully.

"Out of her bag," said Ritchie without hesitation or attempt at mitigation. "Can't be conventional at a time like this."

Mr. Campion made no comment. Something in the book had attracted his attention and he sat for some considerable time turning over the pages and comparing entries.

135

"Thrifty kid," he said at last. "She saves ten bob a week regularly, every Saturday. There it is. It goes back nearly a year. Handed in at the same office just down the road here in Holborn. There were several sums paid in at Christmas—that's presents, I suppose—and she took out three pounds then too. I'm afraid it doesn't tell us much about her, unless—Hello! What's this?"

Gina rose to look over his shoulder while Ritchie leant back in his chair, his long hands dropping over the arms and his eyes mild and inquisitive, like a dog who has brought a parcel and is content to see his master open it.

Mr. Campion ran a finger down a paying-in column and traced certain entries across the page to the circular stamp which showed at which office the deposits had been made.

"These can't all be birthdays," he said. "They're funny amounts, too; so irregular. A pound on October the twenty-second last year, paid in at St. James's of all places. Ten shillings in the middle of the first week in November at the same place. Then there's just the ordinary ten shillings until December the first, when she paid two pounds in at the St. Martin's Lane office. Then nothing odd until January, and then there's quite a lot. Three pounds on the tenth, another three pounds on the thirteenth, two pounds on the seventeenth, then three again on the twentieth and—I say—five pounds on the twenty-ninth. That was the day after Paul disappeared. I wonder . . ."

He turned over the pages and his frown deepened.

"And there's nothing since. That's odd in a way."

"Source of blackmail dead," suggested Ritchie crudely.

Mr. Campion did not scout the suggestion openly.

"It's not very much for blackmail," he murmured. "Eighteen pounds odd all told. It's the paying-in places that strike me as being odd. They're all over the shop. Only the first two alike. Of course, we're catching at straws now, you know. This doesn't prove anything. It may mean absolutely nothing. Still, it's worth looking up."

He closed the book and slipped it into his pocket.

"I think I'll go across and have a word with her."

"Say I took it if you have to," said Ritchie recklessly.

"God forbid." Mr. Campion spoke piously and left them.

In spite of the fact that he had become a familiar figure at Twenty-three during the last few months, custom insisted that he should be shown into the waiting room and there left to kick his heels until the person whom he sought should be discovered and delivered to him.

He was standing with his back to the door, surveying the portrait of Jacoby Barnabas afresh, when Miss Netley came in. She went to meet him, a smile upon her lips and the same smug secretiveness in her eyes which he had noticed at their first meeting.

"Here again, Mr. Campion?" she said pleasantly but with the faintest suggestion of amusement in her tone. "I thought perhaps you'd brought us a manuscript!"

Mr. Campion's smile was wholly charming.

"That's what I call intuition," he said. "Look at this."

He had the satisfaction of seeing her complaisance vanish as she caught sight of the little brown book in his hand. Her round eyes lost their ingenuous expression and her colour vanished.

"It's mine," she said. "Where did you get it? Thank you for returning it."

"Ah, but I'm not returning it," murmured Mr. Campion and she gaped at him.

"I've never heard such impudence in all my life," she burst out finally. "How dare you! Where *did* you get it anyway?"

"Took it," said Mr. Campion and put the book back in his pocket.

Miss Netley trembled. "It's outrageous!" she said unsteadily. "It's illegal, it's—it's stealing!"

"Of course it is," he agreed. "Let's go and tell Inspector Tanner all about it, shall we? He's a policemen."

She drew back from him, her lips sulky, her eyes narrowed and frightened.

"What do you want to know? I can't tell you anything."

Mr. Campion sighed with relief. They taught them to be quick-witted in offices, he reflected.

"I thought we might have a chat," he said.

"I've told the police everything—absolutely everything."

"About the murder? Yes, of course you have," he said,

wondering how long they were going to be left alone in peace in the waiting room. "Let's talk about yourself."

Her suspicion increased.

"I don't understand."

Mr. Campion leant on the large table which filled the centre of the room. His expression was vague to the point of idiocy and his eyes looked guileless behind his spectacles.

"I hate to sound inquisitive and my question may sound a little in bad taste," he began, "but however much one's upset by a death one has to face facts, hasn't one? I do hope you won't think it impertinent of me to ask if your finanical position has been very much upset by Mr. Paul Brande's death? It is frightfully inquisitive, I know, but I would be really obliged if you'd tell me."

She looked relieved and he saw at once that he was on a wrong tack.

"Well, I haven't lost my job, if that's what you mean," she said. "What other difference could it make?"

"None, of course. If you're staying on that's all right." Mr. Campion covered his tracks but her interest had been aroused.

"Just exactly what are you getting at?" she demanded.

He took the bank book out of his pocket, looked at it thoughtfully, and replaced it again.

"You told the police exactly what happened when Mr. Paul Brande got a letter by the afternoon post on the Thursday that he disappeared. You haven't remembered anything else since, have you?"

"I've told it all, every single word, over and over again."

There was an edge to her voice which warned him to be careful. He smiled at her brightly.

"You've got awfully strong nerves, haven't you?" he said. "Let's go into his old office and—just go through it. Please don't think I'm being a nuisance, but I would like to know just exactly what happened. It'll fix the picture in my mind, you see."

Miss Netley looked at him witheringly but the retort which rose to her lips did not come and without a word she led him up to the first floor and into the big comfortable room, a little too preciously furnished for an office, in which Paul had worked.

Mr. Campion sat down at the desk after placing his hat and stick carefully on a side table.

"Now," he said, "where were you when the letter came?"

Still sullen, and looking her contempt, Miss Netley seated herself at the typewriter in the corner.

"Now," said Mr. Campion, "I suppose the boy brought the letter in, gave it to you and you handed it to Mr. Brande?"

She bowed her head. It was evident that she did not trust herself to speak. Mr. Campion tore open an imaginary envelope, exhibiting much pantomimic skill.

"Now," he demanded briskly, "what do I do now?"

"Mr. Paul got up," said Miss Netley, indicating that she was not going to play, "scrunched up the paper and envelope and threw them into the fireplace."

"Like that?" said Mr. Campion, hurling an imaginary ball from him violently.

"No," she said unwillingly. "Just casually."

"And it burned?" he enquired, his eyes resting on her quizzically.

"It did."

"All of it? Every scrap of it?"

"Every tiny bit."

"You looked to see?"

She met his eyes defiantly. "After he had gone, yes, I did."

"We're getting on," said Mr. Campion cheerfully. "Now I get up, don't I? And I seem excited? What happens? Do I get red and seem a little flustered? Do I take up my hat and stick and make for the door without a word or a glance in your direction? Or do I say something?"

The girl hesitated. She seemed to be considering her course of action.

"No," she said at last, grudgingly. "Mr. Paul asked me if a parcel had come."

"Oh, did he? What did he say? Can you remember his actual words?"

"He said"—she still spoke unwillingly—"'Has that parcel come from Fortnum and Mason's yet?'"

"Fortnum and Mason's? And what did you say?"

139

"I said, 'No, Mr. Brande, I don't think it has.' And he said, 'Oh, well, it doesn't matter,' and went out without it. And now I hope you're satisfied."

"Well, it's a crumb," said Mr. Campion. "It's a crumb. Ten bob here, a pound there. Two pounds and five pounds—it all tells up, doesn't it?"

He stopped abruptly. If he had meant to terrify her he could not have been more successful. She was staring at him, her eyes wide and her lips open.

"What do you know?" she asked huskily.

"Much more than you'd think." Mr. Campion spoke cryptically and he hoped convincingly. "Let's get back to Mr. Paul. You said the parcel hadn't come and then what happened?"

"I told you. He said it didn't matter. 'It does not matter,' he said. 'I will go without it.' Then he went out and shut the door and I never saw him again."

"Splendid!" said Mr. Campion. "You're not a good witness, you know, but it makes a lot of difference when you try. Now what happened to the parcel? Did it ever come?"

"Yes. It came about an hour after he left. I put it in that cupboard over there."

"Is it still there?"

"I don't know. I haven't looked."

"Then shall we look now?" he suggested.

She got up, sauntered across the room and jerked open the cupboard.

"Yes," she said. "There it is."

"Bring it here," said Mr. Campion. "I wouldn't have you for a secretary as a gift."

Miss Netley reddened and opened her mouth to speak. A single unprintable epithet left her lips and then, as he looked completely shocked, she strode over to her typewriter and burst into tears.

Campion examined the parcel. There seemed to be nothing in any way extraordinary about it and he loosened the string. Inside was a square box, tastefully ornamented and containing two pounds of crystallized Cape gooseberries.

He sat looking at them in their green and pink sugar jackets, his head slightly on one side and his eyes puzzled.

"Who was the lady?" he enquired at last.

Miss Netley wiped her eyes.

"I don't know."

"Of course you do. Ten bob—two pounds—"

She laughed. "You're wrong. I knew you were wrong."
Her watery-eyed triumph was vindictive.

"Well, I know now," said Mr. Campion mercilessly.
"Come on, I want the address."

"I don't know it."

He had the uncomfortable impression that she was
telling the truth.

"Look here, young woman," he said severely, "an
accident of nature has given you a certain amount of
intelligence. Believe me when I tell you that now is the
time to use it. Think! Pull your scattered little wits
together. Get it into your head that now is the time to talk."

This sudden ferocity from the hitherto mild young man
had the desired effect.

"There was a telephone number he used to ring up
sometimes," she admitted. "He used to send me out of the
room and then just as I was going I would hear him give the
number."

"Well, then, out with it, for the love of Mike," said Mr.
Campion, using the expression unconsciously.

"Maida Vale 58423. Now I can't tell you any more. I
can't—can't! I don't know any more!"

"Maida Vale 58423," said Mr. Campion, scribbling the
number on the blotter in front of him. "All right. You clear
off now and get your face washed."

"What about my book? You can't keep my book."

"I should trust me with it for a day or two," said Mr.
Campion. "I might put something in it. You never know."

A stifled scream escaped the girl. He had a vision of
her, white and trembling, and then the door banged behind
her. Enlightenment dawned in Mr. Campion's pale eyes.

"So that's how he did it," he said and pulled the
telephone towards him.

He heard the bell ringing in the far-off room for some
time before a voice answered him.

"Yes? Maida Vale 58423. Who is it, please?"

Mr. Campion was puzzled. It was a woman's voice and

it was familiar, but he could not place it. Completely in the dark, he proceeded cautiously.

"I say, I'm afraid you'll think it frightfully odd of me ringing up like this," he began. "I wonder if it would be too much to ask you if I could come along and see you? It really is important and I wouldn't take up more than ten minutes of your time."

"Do you know the address?" whispered the voice. "It's Thirty-two, Dorothy Studios, Denbigh Road, Kilburn. You open the garden gate and come down the steps."

"Splendid. I'll be right along," he said, completely startled. "My name's Campion, by the way."

"Yes, I know. I've been expecting you. My name's Teddie Dell."

Mr. Campion hung up the receiver slowly.

He was very conscious of the fact that he had never heard either the name or the address in his life before.

12

Somebody Died

Mr. Campion saw the studio as soon as he pushed open the gate in the blank wall behind the huge margarine-coloured block of flats and came out on to the iron staircase high above the untidy strip of sunken garden.

It sat opposite him in the grass, trying to look like a country cottage and succeeding in suggesting a garden suburb. Its four tall windows faced south and the back of the flats and had diamond panes. The skylight had been leaded over.

There was a trimness about the whole building and a preponderance of bright colours which conveyed a personality childish or at least uneducated. The paint was green, the curtains blue, the window sills and step red-ochred, while a ridiculous little green dog kennel stood beside the door. It looked extraordinarily clean and new in the dinginess of Kilburn and no more in bad taste than a painted Noah's Ark, which it resembled.

It was six o'clock and not yet dusk, although the sun had gone in. The flats and the studio appeared to be deserted and there was a quiet evening melancholy upon the scene.

Mr. Campion went slowly down the iron staircase and, picking his way over the grass, tapped with the brass knocker which bore a relief of Worcester cathedral and had come from Birmingham via Bruges.

An excited yapping from within answered him, followed by a woman's voice admonishing the dog. Then the door opened.

"Come in," said Teddie Dell.

Enlightenment came to Mr. Campion as he recognized the woman who had been waiting for him outside the Bottle Street flat when he had come home from the inquest with Gina and Curley. She looked bigger and older in her indoor clothes. Her fairish hair was dressed close to her head and was cut in a thin unfashionably curled fringe, while her smooth capable body was sturdy and unsuitably dressed in a very smooth blue skirt and a very frilly blouse.

There was a suggestion of strength about her face also, with its square jawbone and thick cream skin, its good teeth and wide-set blue-grey eyes.

"I'm glad you came," she said. "I've been wondering if I ought to ring you. Come in and sit down and have a cigarette."

The over-carefulness of her pronunciation struck him again, but her self-possession was unconscious and superb.

The dog was frantic with delight at his arrival and danced round him noisily in spite of his mistress's rebuke. He was a small smooth-haired yellow mongrel, spry and wiry on thin legs. Campion put out a hand and he offered a paw instantly. Campion took it and laughed.

"George, don't be a fool. Lie down! He's absurd, isn't he?"

The woman was laughing as she spoke and Campion glanced up to see that her eyes were swimming. She turned away to the mantelshelf and brought back cigarettes and matches, waiting on her visitor with the complete lack of self-consciousness of a nurse or a teashop waitress.

He found himself fumbling for a case to offer her at the moment when she held a lighted match to his cigarette.

The room in which they stood reflected the outside of the building. The floor was covered with imitation red and grey tiles and shone like a ship's deck. The dark oak furniture was ordinary and unpretentious. There was a divan under the windows and a comfortable chesterfield, flanked by two chintz-covered easy chairs by the fire.

Teddie Dell drew up the largest and most comfortable chair.

"Sit down," she said, indicating it, and he obeyed her.

Mr. Campion, the most unassuming of men, did not imagine for a moment that her solicitude for his comfort, her tacit acceptance of the fact that his ease was all-important, was due in any way to his personal charm. Teddie Dell, he realized, was behaving as she always had and always would behave, since she belonged to that most ill-used sisterhood, some of them wives, some of them mothers, and all of them lovers, who really believe that there is in the mere quality of manhood something magnificent and worthy to be served.

"You were pointed out to me at the inquest and I heard you were interested in the case," she said, seating herself opposite him and holding one hand up to the fire to shield her face from the blaze. "I didn't want to go to the police for obvious reasons. He wouldn't have liked it and she's only a kid, isn't she, and mixed up with nice people who don't understand this sort of thing. So I went round to your place. When I saw her come up with you I thought I'd better slip off. She's never heard of me, you see."

Mr. Campion nodded. He was wondering irrelevantly what Teddie Dell thought she meant by "nice people."

"It's been on my mind," she continued. "He came here when he left the office on the Thursday and the police don't know that. I wanted to ask someone about it and find out if it was any good telling. He kept me a secret from his family for fourteen years and I didn't see any point in it all coming out now if it wouldn't help."

"Fourteen years?" said Mr. Campion involuntarily.

Her eyes rested upon him for a moment.

"We met in the war, in France," she said. "I've had this place since '23."

Her glance left his face and travelled round the yellow walls and there was an indefinable expression in her eyes.

"I never thought he'd marry," she went on abruptly. "But he was right: it didn't make any difference. That's why I was sorry for the kid. That's no marriage for a girl. I suppose she got hold of the young cousin and egged him on and teased him till he went out of his mind—although I don't know why they think he did it. My dear old boy had a lot of other enemies—ooh, he had a temper——!"

She broke off. Her eyes were a blank and her mouth very hard.

Mr. Campion looked at the dog, who lay upon the hearth rug, his nose between his paws and his ears cocked. Gradually he became aware of other things: a small silver golf trophy on the dresser and a pair of slippers, grey with age and long discarded, stuffed behind the coal-box, which was also a fireside seat.

"Was Mr. Brande here very long on the Thursday?"

He put the question diffidently but the woman gave him her whole attention at once.

"No, he couldn't stay. That often happened. He was such a busy man. I suppose they'll miss him at the office. He held the business together, didn't he?"

She spoke wistfully and for a moment Mr. Campion was able to take the impulsive, excitable, slightly ridiculous Paul at the dead man's own valuation. The woman was still speaking.

"We were going to have a bit of dinner and then he was going to read. We didn't go out much together since he got so well known. I didn't ask him to take me; I'm not a fool. But he came in just about four and said he couldn't stay, so I made him a cup of tea and he went. I wondered why he didn't ring up on the Sunday, but on the Monday I saw the papers."

Her voice wavered on the last word but she controlled it magnificently, out of deference, Mr. Campion felt, to the presence of a stranger.

"Do you know where he went when he left here?" he enquired.

"I know where he said he was going and there was no point in him lying. Besides, he never did to me. We knew each other too well. He said, 'I'm so sorry I can't stay, Ted. I've got to go down to fetch a key from Camden Town of all places, and then I've got to dash back and slip into the British Museum.' I asked him if there was any chance of him dropping in later but he said, 'No luck, I'm going to be busy tonight. I'll ring you Sunday.'"

Her voice ceased and she moved her position slightly so that her face was in the shadow. Mr. Campion felt he dared intrude no more.

"It's been very kind of you," he began awkwardly. "I'll let you know, of course, if I think you ought to come forward, but it's quite possible that it won't be at all necessary—if you don't want to."

She got up, raising herself wearily as if her bones were unusually heavy.

"Why should I?" she said. "It's not as if he were ill. He's dead."

The dog rose and yawned and stretched himself, only to lie down again, his nose between his forepaws. The room was growing dark and the firelight flickered over the bright floor and was reflected in some little bits of brass on the dresser. There was comfort in the place and an utterly unbearable sense of waiting. Mr. Campion hurried.

Teddie Dell escorted him to the door.

"I'll keep in touch with you," he promised and paused. Paul had not died penniless and Campion had a strong sense of justice. "Forgive me if I am saying the wrong thing," he ventured, "but are you all right for cash?"

She smiled and there were so many varying emotions in her expression that he only understood that she appreciated his thoughtfulness.

"Better let her have it," she said. "There isn't much. He spent like a lunatic. It would be charity too. I haven't any rights."

She was silent for a moment and he had a very vivid impression of her, square and sturdy in her little painted home, the dog peering round her skirts.

"We loved each other," she said and her voice was as proud and forlorn as high tragedy itself.

Mr. Campion came away.

13

A Craftsman of Camden Town

"Would it be possible, Lugg," enquired Mr. Campion delicately, "for you to forget for a moment this respectability to which you are not accustomed and delve into the past?"

Mr. Lugg, who was taking off his collar because it was only his employer whom he had admitted, kept his back turned to the speaker and his attention fixed upon the drawer into which he was tucking this badge of refinement. The white roll of fat at the back of his neck looked smug and obstinate. Mr. Lugg had not heard.

"I suppose if I asked you to come off it," Mr. Campion began sarcastically.

Mr. Lugg swung round, his small black eyes unconvincingly innocent.

"I shouldn't understand what you meant," he said placidly, and returned to the drawer. "Some of the fellows down at the Mews wear butterfly collars and some wear straight," he observed over his shoulder. "I 'aven't made up me mind for good yet. Butterflies let yer neck through, but they're apt to look untidy."

Mr. Campion made no response to this implied question. Instead he put another.

"Lugg," he said, "if a man who had something to hide went to Camden Town to get a key, who would he go to?"

Surprise took Mr. Lugg unawares.

"Lumme," he said, "old Wardie Samson! He's not still at it, is 'e? Must be well over a 'undred. I remember 'im in my dad's day."

This family reminiscence was cut short by what was no

147

doubt a recollection of the rigid society of the hostelry in the "Mews."

"A very low person," said the new Mr. Lugg. "Dishonest, reely."

"Do you know him?"

Lugg wriggled uncomfortably.

"I visited 'im as a lad with my father," he said at last, "but I shouldn't think 'e was the party to which you was referrin'."

"Well, take off that awful coat and get in the car, which is downstairs," said Mr. Campion. "We're going to see him."

"Not me." Mr. Lugg was defiant. "I'll give you 'is address if you like, but I'm not coming with you. It's more than me reputation's worth. You never know 'ow a thing like this might tell two or three years hence when your relation 'as gorn the way all good relations should go and you and me are established in our rightful place. What sort of a position should I be in if one of the 'ousemaids, or per'aps another gentleman who'd come up in the world, should say, 'Surely I saw you in Camden Town, Mr. Lugg?' What sort of position should I be in then?"

"Even if I become a Duke," said Mr. Campion brutally, "the chances of you becoming a respectable person are remote—or at any rate, I shouldn't count on it. Come on. Hurry."

Before the authority in the tone Mr. Lugg's defiance turned to pathos.

"What's the good of me tryin' to better meself if you keep draggin' me down?" he said. "I've put the old life be'ind me. I've forgot it, see?"

"Well, this is where you do a spot of remembering," insisted Mr. Campion heartlessly. "And don't spoil everything by trying to impress your old pal with your new vulgarity, you fat oaf."

Mr. Lugg bridled. "That's a bit too thick, that is," he said. "You're destroying my ambition, that's about what you're doing. Mucking up me perishin' soul, see? All right, I'll come with you."

They drove for some time in silence, but as the wealthier parts of the city were left behind and they slid into the noisy poverty of the Hampstead Road some of Mr. Lugg's gloom deserted him.

"It's like old times, isn't it?" he observed.

Campion accepted the olive branch.

"We've got a delicate job ahead," he said. "I suppose your friend Wardie would give away a client if he was dead?"

"Wardie doesn't *give* anything." Lugg spoke reminiscently. "Doesn't know the meanin' of the word 'tick' either. Still, we can but try 'im. I 'aven't seen 'im for ten years, remember."

"When you were a lad," said Mr. Campion unkindly.

"When I was one of the lads," said Mr. Lugg, whose spirits were soaring. "'E was a clever old bloke, Wardie," he continued. "Give 'im an impression one day and in a little while 'e'd drop you a line and down you'd go to find a better key than the original. 'E did name plates, too—not for the same people. Only one thing aginst 'im, 'e was slow. Lumme, 'ow slow that man was! So busy making snide 'e never 'ad time for honest work. Used to make lovely 'alf-crowns. Made 'em out of the tops of soda-water siphons. That metal's just the right weight, y'know."

Mr. Campion showed polite interest. "Was he pinched?"

"Wardie? No. He was too careful. 'E never passed 'em. Wouldn't let any of 'is relations 'andle 'em either. Used to sell 'em—so much a gross—to one of these lads in the Ditch. 'E's a handy man, if you take me. I'm surprised at 'im still working, especially for outsiders. It's round 'ere, guv'nor. Better leave the car at a garridge. It's no good parkin' it. We don't want to turn up to Wardie's lookin' like bloomin' millionaires. Might give 'im ideas."

They left the car and continued on foot. For one who professed to have left this particular world behind him Mr. Lugg found his way among the maze of small streets with remarkable precision.

"'Ere we are," he said at last. "Now, look casual but not 'alf-witted. I don't want 'im to think I've turned up with a Killarney."

Mr. Campion, who in the course of a long association had come to realize that living up to Mr. Lugg was an impossibility, remained much as usual and they paused in the narrow, dusty little road littered with paper bags and kitchen refuse while Lugg went through an elaborate pantomime of noticing a small shop some few doors down on the opposite side.

"Why, there's Mr. Samson's joint!" he said, with theatrical astonishment. "I wonder if 'e's still alive? I'd better go and look 'im up. Just the same! The ole place 'asn't changed since I was a boy."

At first sight the Samson emporium was not impressive. It consisted of a very narrow door and a small window. Both were incredibly dirty and, while one revealed an even dingier interior, the other displayed a collection of old-iron ranging from nails to the back of bedsteads, a notice which announced that shoe leather could be purchased within, and a quantity of cheap new razor blades. There was also, Mr. Campion noticed, a hank of bass, two large bales of twine and a skein of very thick elastic labelled "For Catapults." This last was crossed out very lightly and "Model Aëroplanes" substituted in wavering pencil.

With the nonchalance of a loiterer observing a policeman, Mr. Lugg lounged into the shop, beckoning Mr. Campion to follow him with a jerk of his shoulder.

It took them some moments to accustom their eyes to the darkness. The atmosphere, which was composed of a nice blend of rust, leather and Irish stew, took a bit of assimilating also, and Campion felt his feet sink into a sand of dust and iron filings.

There was a movement in the shop, followed by a snuffling, and presently a bright young man with a white face, dusty yellow hair and an enquiring manner sauntered towards them. Mr. Lugg showed surprise.

"Business changed 'ands?" he asked suspiciously. "I come reely to enquire after an old friend, Mr. Samson."

The young man eyed Mr. Lugg from the toes of his boots to the top of his hat.

"One of the old brigade, aren't yer?" he said cheekily, his narrow blue eyes astute and appraising.

Mr. Lugg was momentarily taken off his balance.

"'Ere, what're you gettin' at?" he said, taking a

menacing step forward. "When I want any lip from two penn'orth of string-bag I'll ask for it."

In spite of a certain flabbiness induced by high life, Mr. Lugg was still a formidable opponent, and he was not alone. The young man retreated.

"Gran'dad's in the back," he said. "If you'll tell me your name I'll go and see if he remembers you."

"Gran'dad?" said Mr. Lugg, a repulsively sentimental smile appearing on his great white face. "Don't tell me you're little Alfie? Not little Alfie what I danced up an' down on my knee?"

"Charlie," said the young man, without enthusiasm.

"Charlie! That was it. Rosie's boy—little Rosie. 'Ow's your mother, son?"

"'Aven't seen 'er since she went off with a rozzer," said the young man, with that complete carelessness which is more chilling than any rebuke. "I'll go and tell Gran'dad. What's yer name?"

"Just tell 'im Maggers is 'ere," said Lugg, who was beginning to enjoy himself for the first time, Mr. Campion felt, for years.

"Shall I come with you?"

"No. You stay 'ere," said Charlie, with the first show of animation he had yet exhibited and disappeared into the darkness.

Mr. Lugg chuckled in a fatherly fashion.

"I remember 'im being born," he said, with inexplicable pride. "'Ear what 'e called me?—'Old Brigade!' That's 'cos 'e knows I'm after a key. 'Is pals use oxy-acetylene. Nasty dangerous stuff. When that come on the market I knew my time was over."

"'E'll see yer. Come on."

Charlie did not emerge from the shadows to make this announcement and they groped forward in the direction of his voice. After passing through a living room, into which the iron filings had percolated in the course of years, and which was apparently the fountainhead of the Irish stew, they came quite unexpectedly into the bright light of day. Their way led across a minute yard, dirty to a degree unknown by most users of the word, and into a small shed festooned with old bicycle tyres.

Seated at a bench was a large blank-faced old man, bald as an egg and clad in a very loose shirt and surprisingly tight trousers whose original colour could only be surmised. The round face was at once mild and cunning and possessed the serenity of a Buddha.

"Wardie!" said Mr. Lugg, enraptured, adding a little inopportunely: "I thought you was dead."

The old man smiled enigmatically as he held out a hand, and it occurred to Mr. Campion that he was deaf.

"Afternoon, gentlemen," he said, and his voice had a husky, secretive quality.

Lugg deserted Campion. He went round the back of the bench and seated himself beside the old man.

"I'm Maggers, Wardie," he said, thrusting a mighty arm round the other man's shoulders. "You remember me. I'm the fellow what was sweet on yer second daughter—the one what died. I'm coming back to yer, aren't I?"

"Lugg," said the old man suddenly. "Young Lugg."

They shook hands again solemnly and with great sentiment.

"Can you 'ear me?" said Mr. Lugg, rumbling into one of the great ears.

"Course," said the old man. "'Eard you all the time. Didn't know oo you were. Oo's yer friend?"

"Young fellow I go round with," said Mr. Lugg shamelessly. "You know me, Wardie: I wouldn't tell you wrong. Me and my pal we want a bit of 'elp from you."

He cocked an eye at his employer.

"You tell 'im, Bert."

Mr. Campion explained his business as well as he could.

"It's about a key," he said. "Lugg and I wondered if you could tell us anything about a key which a man picked up down here in Camden Town on Thursday, the twenty-eighth of January last. It's a long time ago, I know, but I thought you might remember. He was a well-dressed fellow, forty-fiveish, dark, and spoke well."

Wardie Samson shook his large round head.

"I don't know anything about keys," he said. "We don't sell 'em."

Lugg burst into a roar of unnatural laughter.

"You're takin' Bert for a 'tec!" he said. "That's a good one, that is! Old Bert a split! That'll be one to tell the boys!"

Wardie's inflamed and rheumy eyes shifted nervously. "Can't tell yer about a key," he said. "Don't know."

Mr. Campion took a chance.

"It's private information I want," he said. "I'm willing to pay for it and I'll give you any assurance you like that you will never be questioned about it again. I am a detective, if you like, but I'm not a police detective. I'm not interested in your business, and all I want is a description, or, better still, a mould, of a key which the man I am interested in had made in this district. That's all I want. After I walk out of this shop you can swear blindly you've never seen me before. Lugg won't act as a witness."

The old man, who had been watching Campion carefully throughout this recital, seemed impressed.

"What date did you say, guv'nor? The twenty-eighth of January? Seems to me I read an interestin' bit in the paper about a gentleman who got his on that day. It wouldn't be him you was interested in, would it?"

"That's the ticket," said Mr. Lugg heartily. "Now you're bein' sensible. We're just blokes oo've come to an old pal for a bit of 'elp. As for that chap, 'e can't buy anything off you again, can 'e? 'E's in 'is box."

Mr. Samson seemed to have decided that his visitors were on the level, but he retained his caution of voice and expression, which seemed to be habitual.

"I sent 'im a letter telling 'im it was ready and 'e come down right away. Said 'e'd destroyed the letter for 'is own sake."

He cocked an eye at Campion, who nodded reassuringly.

"He had. We come to you by chance. Have you destroyed the impression?"

The old man nodded and seemed to debate within himself for a moment or so. Then, with a glance at Lugg that was almost affectionate, he opened a small drawer in the bench in front of him and, after rummaging in it for some time, produced a large, old-fashioned key. He threw it down in front of Campion.

"Always make two for luck," he said, and the faintest

suggestion of a smile flickered for an instant round his mouth.

Another search in the drawer produced a dirty envelope. "Paul R. Brande," he spelt out awkwardly. "Twenty-three, Horsecollar Yard, Holborn, W.C.1."

Mr. Campion took the key and Lugg waved him out of the shed.

"Me and Wardie will fix this little matter up between us," he said magnificently.

Mr. Campion waited in the filth of the yard for some considerable time, and Lugg finally appeared.

"Three pound ten," he said. "I know it's a lot, but you 'ave to pay for these things."

Mr. Campion parted with the money and presently, with the key safely stowed in his pocket, he once more approached the garage where the car was parked. As they settled down and Campion turned the Lagonda out into Hampstead Road Lugg nudged him.

"'Ere's thirty-five shillings that belongs to you," he said. "I did a split with Wardie. It's the worst of these dishonest people. They always expect you to live down to 'em."

14
The Damned

Even if Mr. Lugg was as hurt as he looked when his employer dropped him at the corner of Regent Street, at least he refrained from referring to himself as a "worn-out glove," an unsuitable simile of which he was very fond, having, so he said, read it somewhere and thought it "the ticket."

Campion went on alone to Horsecollar Yard. He had no desire to discuss his afternoon's work with Gina, and was wondering how he could get into Number Twenty-three without disturbing her, John, or an inquisitive policeman when he observed a familiar figure striding out of the cul-de-sac.

Ritchie Barnabas possessed a striking appearance at all times, but, seen at a reasonable distance in the lamp-lit dusk of a spring evening, he presented a spectacle of fantasy. He lolloped along at a great pace, each knee giving a little as it took his weight, and his great arms flapping about him like the wings of an intoxicated crow.

He pulled up with a jerk which almost overbalanced him as the Lagonda slid to a standstill at his side and thrust an anxious face into Campion's own.

"The key of the office?" he repeated after the younger man had made the request. "Certainly. Let you in myself. All the cousins and Miss Curley have keys. John's out, anyway. Gone to see Alexander."

All the time he was speaking he watched Campion's face with the eager but diffident curiosity of a child. The other man found himself apologizing.

"If I had anything definite I'd tell you," he said, "but at the moment I've only got an idea, supported by two or three dubious facts."

Ritchie nodded humbly and his blue eyes blinked trustingly at his friend. He opened the front door of Twenty-three and hesitated.

"Wait for you?" he enquired hopefully.

"I shouldn't." Unconsciously Mr. Campion spoke in that firm but regretful tone with which one tries to persuade a strange and friendly dog not to accompany one home.

"All right," Ritchie agreed sadly. "Lock up behind you. Good night."

He strode off, to return at once.

"Only live in Red Lion Square, you know address," he murmured. "There if wanted. Any hour."

He went off again, successfully this time, and Mr. Campion set about his investigations, blessing the idiosyncrasy of the firm of Barnabas which made them elect to have their offices cleaned out in the early morning instead of at night.

It was practically dark indoors, and the big untidy

rooms looked unfamiliar in the gloom; nor were they particularly silent. The ticking of clocks, the stir of papers in a draught and the vibrations of the nearby Underground railway combined to make the place sound alive.

Anxious not to advertise himself, Campion did not turn on the lights, but relied upon his torch. He went up to Miss Curley's room, a neatly kept glass-and-panelling cubicle built round one window in the typists' office. The strong-room key hung upon its hook on the inside of the old-fashioned desk. As soon as he handled it one of Mr. Campion's minor theories collapsed gently, to be replaced by a sense of misgiving and a wholly unwarrantable suspicion of the innate honesty of Wardie Samson.

He compared the two keys as they lay side by side on the desk in the gleam of his torch. Apart from the fact that they were both of the ordinary or old-fashioned type and were both over four inches long, it would have been difficult to find two such instruments more dissimilar. The key of the strong-room door was long and slender with three wards, but the key which Wardie Samson had made for luck was squat and heavy and had that curious unsatis-factory appearance which is peculiar to old-fashioned patent devices which have never been really successful.

Mr. Campion turned it over thoughtfully and an idea occurred to him. Placing both keys in his pocket, he went slowly downstairs. It was growing darker and the well of the front hall, which had no windows to admit the gleam from the street lamps, was completely black.

Because it is natural to keep quiet in the dark, Mr. Campion trod gently. At the top of the stone staircase leading down into the basement he paused to listen. His quick ears had detected something that was not one of the ordinary night noises and his interest quickened. It did not come again, however, and he went on.

On the landing, where the stair turned to face the basement wall, he paused abruptly, extinguishing his torch. Below him, at the end of the passage, a thin angle of light gleamed in the darkness. The strong-room door was ajar and there was a light within, a fact which might not have been so very astonishing even out of office hours had he not carried the only official key in his pocket.

Campion advanced cautiously, feeling his way down the shallow worn stone steps. His foot had just touched the concrete floor of the passage when the angle vanished as the light in the room went out.

He stood motionless, listening. The silence was uncanny and he hesitated to use the torch until he knew more of the situation. An unarmed man with a torch is an admirable target.

He was some half-dozen yards from the door and the basement was less disturbed by vibrations and draught-disturbed papers than the rest of the building, yet he could hear nothing. There was not a breath, not a rustle, not even the almost undetectable whisper of a well-oiled hinge. It was a paralyzed silence, not altogether natural.

Mr. Campion did not consider himself a nervous man, but neither was he sufficiently thick-skinned to let the piquancy of the situation pass by him. Someone, presumably with a guilty conscience and possibly with a gun, was aware of his presence and was waiting for him.

Campion stood quite still, holding his breath lest any sound should reveal his exact position.

The silence continued.

It came to an end at last, and in so unnerving a fashion that all his preparation was wasted. At the moment when he had decided that he must breathe deeply or burst, a yell so loud that its nature or even its origin was indeterminate sounded within a few feet of his ear and practically at the same time something apparently demoniacal struck him in the chest, knocking the torch out of his hand and most of the breath from his body.

There is to most of us a secret savage satisfaction in receiving a blow that one knows that one can repay with interest. As Campion staggered back against the wall beside the staircase his left came in contact with something that was hard enough to be a man's head. He heard a grunt and deep breathing and, as the knee came up to catch him in the stomach, he threw his arms round it, hurling his weight forward so that he went down on top of his unknown adversary.

During the next few seconds he had little time for speculation, but he became aware that he was fighting something human, since it was clothed, and of an iron hardness and ferocity which suggested a hank of steel rope temporarily possessed by a fiend.

Campion had some experience of catch-as-catch-can fighting. During his adventurous life he had enjoyed scraps in most stratas of society, so that he was aware that the Queensberry rules have many variations, but that evening in the pitch-dark basement he received an education.

The unseen creature bit, clawed, sobbed and pummelled, interspersing this unconventionality with occasional scientific blows. Campion was temporarily outclassed and was only relieved that his enemy had no weapon.

He was lying upon his face with a teetering, kicking thing trying to force him through the concrete floor when his groping hand caught an iron banister and he dragged himself up and let out with his right, the full weight of his body behind the blow.

It dawned upon him then, as he felt the wet chin go back under his fist, that he was fighting with a man in terror. The sobbing ceased and something thudded satisfactorily at his feet. Campion shook himself and waited, but there was no further sound from the floor. He moved unsteadily down the passage and, after a considerable delay, discovered the switch.

The first thing he saw as his surroundings leapt into view was a reflection of his own face in the mirror which hung just inside the open door of the little washroom. It was not a reassuring spectacle.

He did not stop to examine the damage, but swung round just in time to see a tousled object creeping furtively towards the stairs.

Mr. Campion leapt upon it, caught it by the remnants of what had once been a collar, and jerked back its head.

Shivering, whimpering, his face covered with blood and tears, cowered a star witness for the Crown, Mr. Peter Rigget.

Campion gaped at him and let him go. He dropped to the floor, crawled into a sitting position on the bottom step of the staircase, and wept. Never an irritable man, Mr. Campion felt himself excused in the exhibition of a little impatience. He pulled out his handkerchief and wiped some of the blood off his face.

"What in the name of all that's holy do you think you've been doing?" he enquired.

Mr. Rigget continued to blubber. Presently he stopped and his head fell forward on his chest. Campion bent over him, his eyebrows raised. But Mr. Rigget had not fainted. He was asleep.

Campion was not surprised. He had seen the same thing happen before when great physical exertion had been allied to the emotional upheaval. Since it is a natural phenomenon, only occurring to young people in exceptional health, Mr. Campion felt unreasonably angry with Mr. Rigget.

He left him where he was and retired to the washroom, where, with the door open, he could keep an eye upon the heavily breathing figure at the foot of the stairs.

A wrenched shoulder, a cut over the left eye, and four weals left by four fingernails travelling from his right temple to the top of his collar seemed to be his principal injuries. His clothes were in ribbons. There was a piece missing from the sleeve of his jacket which could only have been bitten away, and there was blood all over him.

He cleaned himself up as best he could and felt better after his head had been under the cold tap for a minute or two.

He let Mr. Rigget sleep for half an hour, and woke him by pouring a jug of cold water over his head. The puffed eyes opened sleepily and closed again.

Campion raised the stocky little body which was in such surprisingly good condition, and dragged it into the washroom, where he repeated his treatment until Mr. Rigget showed signs of returning life and intelligence.

"All right?" Campion enquired when once again the blue eyes looked out clearly from beneath their battered lids.

Mr. Rigget said nothing. He turned his back on Mr. Campion and began to wash his hands.

"I think we'd better have a chat, don't you, having been properly introduced?"

Still Mr. Rigget was silent. His hands seemed to require a lot of attention.

"What were you doing down here? You'll have to explain to somebody, you know. You'd better tell me."

Mr. Rigget was trembling violently, but no sound left his lips and he went on washing his hands.

Campion leant forward, turned off the tap and threw him a towel.

"Come on," he said, taking the other man by the arm. "We'll go into the strong room."

Mr. Rigget remained perfectly still. He was staring straight in front of him, his face pink where it was not discoloured and his eyes narrowed to pin-points.

Mr. Campion choked down his growing irritation.

"Since that face of yours is going to create a scandal in the witness-box, anyway, we may as well have the whole truth," he said. "And by the way, next time you go leaping on people in the dark don't lose your head, or you'll find yourself landed with a corpse which has been the victim of a murderous attack. Keeping yourself fit is all very well, but you don't want to turn yourself into a dangerous machine every time you get the wind up."

Mr. Rigget's trembling increased and suddenly, with an effect which was completely unnerving, he began to pray aloud. Mr. Campion took him by the shoulders and shook him.

"Pull yourself together!" he said firmly. "Don't try to mesmerize yourself. You need your brain at the moment. Use it."

Mr. Rigget relaxed cautiously.

"Where are you going to take me?" he demanded.

"Nowhere," said Campion. "We're going to stay here."

Mr. Rigget shuddered and glanced at the strong room.

"Not in there. I'll tell you. I'll tell you everything. I'm not really as bad as I look—at least I am, only I can't help it. Oh, God, I'm so tired!"

Mr. Campion sighed.

"My car's outside," he said. "I'll take you back to the flat."

Peter Rigget seemed agreeable to this suggestion, and they had started down the passage when he remembered the strong-room door and went back to it. To Mr. Campion's intense interest he thrust his hand into his tattered pocket, drew out a slender three-ward key identical with the one which Campion himself had borrowed from Miss Curley's desk, locked the door and returned.

"I'm tired," he said again.

He dropped to sleep in the back of the car, and Campion had to wake him again when they arrived at Bottle Street. Lugg, curious and openly appalled at his employer's condition, went down obligingly to put the car away and Campion and his captive were alone.

In the bright light of Mr. Campion's comfortable room Peter Rigget made a pathetic and embarrassing spectacle. His pince-nez were gone, and his normally red thin sensitive nose was no longer thin, and his puffy red wrists stuck out some three inches from his torn shirt-cuffs.

Mr. Campion, who knew a great deal about exhaustion, gave him some food, which he ate eagerly, swallowing great hunks of bread and lump sugar as though he realized instinctively how great was his need of them.

Gradually his unnatural lassitude disappeared, leaving him weary, but otherwise normal. Mr. Campion sat opposite him.

"Still feel like talking?" he enquired pleasantly.

Mr. Rigget looked at the ground. He was young, Campion decided, younger than he had thought; twenty-five or six at the most.

"I'm not a nice chap," he said. "I can't help it. I fight against it, but my instincts are all wrong. I keep letting myself down."

A dreadful sincerity in the statement robbed it of its humour and made it merely embarrassing. Mr. Rigget appeared to be speaking the simple truth from the depths of a resigned rather than a contrite heart.

"I've been educated," he went on, "but it hasn't altered me. I'm a cad. I'm dirty."

"Let's get back to the strong room, shall we?" suggested Mr. Campion gently. "You've got a key, I see."

Mr. Rigget shuddered. "I had it made. It was so easy. They ought not to put temptation in your way like that. I know I'm rotten, but I was tempted. Fancy leaving the key

there where anybody could get it! I took it home with me
for a week-end in the summer and had another one made.
Nobody noticed. Nobody asked any questions. Even the
man at the shop believed me when I said it was the key of
my own front door. I live with my people. They're very
respectable. This is going to break them. They've educated
me and made me a better class than they are, and now I've
disgraced them."

He spoke sullenly and with a sort of masochistic
satisfaction.

"Been using the key pretty regularly?" Mr. Campion
enquired.

The young man stirred. "Fairly often. Whenever I
could stay behind. There wasn't much in there. I didn't do
anything. I didn't take anything. I only turned things over.
They didn't keep anything valuable there. It's a sort of junk
room."

"What was the idea?" Mr. Campion sounded merely
curious, even friendly.

"I'm nasty," said Mr. Rigget, raising very blue eyes
bright with tears to his inquisitor's face. "I just wanted to
see if there was anything interesting there—something that
might be useful. You don't understand me. I'm not ordinary.
I'm not decent. I haven't got any instincts against prying
into other people's affairs. Most firms are dirty, and I wanted
to find out anything I could."

Mr. Campion had an inspiration.

"Like little evasions of income tax?" he suggested.

A secretive, rather repulsive smile appeared on Mr.
Rigget's swollen lips.

"Yes," he said. "That's the sort of thing. Only I couldn't
find any books or anything. They didn't keep 'em there. I
suppose they're in the safe. Or more probably the important ones'd be at the bank," he added gloomily. "You're
shocked, aren't you?" He looked at Campion resentfully.
"You ought to be if you've got the right instincts. But I'm
not. I used to try to be, but I'm not. I'm dirty and mean and
low and underhand, and all the things they educate you not
to be."

It was all very distressing. Mr. Rigget's excellent accent
and obvious misery made him well-nigh unbearable.

"Did you ever get the safe open?" Mr. Campion found himself trying to put the question so casually that it would not sound offensive.

"Oh, no, I didn't touch the safe! That's criminal. I haven't done anything criminal."

Mr. Rigget uttered the word as though it were blasphemous.

"I've had the key in my hand, I admit that, but I've never used it." He writhed in his chair. "I've got a key of the safe, I may as well admit that, but I've never used it. I swear I've never used it! I daren't do anything criminal. I want to, but I'm afraid to. That's the sort of chap I am. I ought never to be in. the sort of job I'm in. I'm only educated. I haven't got any instincts."

Mr. Campion realized that he was confronted by a serious modern sociological problem, but he decided that it was far too large to tackle, especially at the moment. He concentrated on the keys. Producing the instrument which Wardie Samson had made "for luck," he handed it to the man whom he was trying not to think of as his victim.

"That's it! Where did you get it? It was in my collar drawer, locked up at home. Mother didn't know it was there, nor did Father, nor did anyone. Oh, God, you've been to them! They know about me. I'll never dare to go home now. I never want to see them again." Peter Rigget trembled on the verge of hysterics.

"This is my key," said Mr. Campion firmly. "It's nothing to do with your key. Pull yourself together."

Mr. Rigget wiped the tears angrily from his eyes and squared his powerful shoulders.

"I give way," he said unexpectedly. "That's weak. That shows I'm all wrong. I've been hiding myself up ever since I was a kid, but it's coming out now. You can't alter your instincts. You are what you are born to be, whatever you learn. If I'd been brave I'd have told what I knew on the Friday night, but I didn't want anybody to know I'd been down there. I was glad," he added, his voice rising. "I was *glad* it had happened, and I knew about it. I was *glad* there was going to be trouble. It made me feel excited and important."

It occurred to Mr. Campion that what Mr. Rigget really

needed was some sort of reverse process of psychoanalysis. To know the truth about oneself, if it were both unpleasant and incurable, must be a variety of hell, he decided. He became quite sorry for him, but there was obviously much to be learnt.

"When you say the Friday night, was that the evening after Mr. Brande disappeared?"

Mr. Rigget nodded. "I got a fright when I saw him. Afterwards I was pleased. I knew he was there, you see. I knew he was there all the week-end."

Mr. Campion sat up, but Mr. Rigget was too engrossed in his own unfortunate reactions to life to notice any added interest in his hearer.

"I stayed behind on Friday. It's easier on Fridays. People go home earlier and don't notice you're hanging about. I shut myself in the washroom with the light out until they'd all gone—I did that tonight, and then I let myself out and unlocked the strong-room door with my own key and went in. I didn't see the body at first. It wasn't by the door where they found it. It was lying crumpled up in a corner beside the safe, hidden from the door by a lot of boxes and things under the table."

He hesitated.

"That's where I got my key of the safe," he explained at last. "It was in the lock and the safe door was open. I thought the key might be useful, so I shut the door and turned it. I was frightened, of course, but I was excited, too. I never liked Mr. Paul."

Mr. Campion sat enthralled. He did not like to break the thread of the story, but at the same time the man's attitude towards his important discovery was incomprehensible.

"You were terrified, I suppose?" he ventured.

"No," said Mr. Rigget. "I wasn't frightened because he was dead—I made sure he *was* dead. I'd have been more frightened if he'd been alive."

He caught Mr. Campion's expression and attempted to excuse himself.

"It wasn't anything to do with me, I hadn't killed him. I didn't think he had been killed then. I thought he'd just fallen down in a fit. I was frightened they'd catch me by the

164

safe and think I'd opened it. I ought not to have taken the key of the safe. That's criminal, really. But I didn't use it. I never used it. I didn't bring it tonight because I thought I might use it and I wanted to put the temptation behind me. I took the other key, too," he went on, averting his eyes. "It was in the lock when I pushed mine in and it fell out on the floor on the inside. I picked it up and when I went out I put it back in Miss Curley's desk after I'd locked the door."

"Why on earth did you do that?" Campion demanded in astonishment.

Mr. Rigget was silent for some seconds and the sulkiness on his face increased in intensity.

"Well, I thought I ought to leave the door locked in case someone had tried it earlier in the day and had looked for the key and found it wasn't there. Then I thought they'd have to get him out some time, and I thought they'd probably smash the lock. Then my own key that I'd had made wouldn't fit any more. I'm mean!" he burst out passionately. "I do things like that. I'm always thinking of myself and how to save myself trouble—little petty things like that."

Mr. Campion's face was very severe.

"Look here," he demanded, "do you realize that Mike Wedgwood has been arrested and is going to be tried for his life largely on the evidence that Brande was found dead in a room locked on the outside? Now, according to your story, the dead man was in a room locked on the inside. You must see the difference."

Mr. Rigget shrugged his shoulders. "It wasn't anything to do with me, as far as I saw. I've told you, I'm selfish, I'm narrow, I'm mean."

Mr. Campion ignored the last part of his remark.

"You say when you found the body on the Friday night it was lying in a corner so that no one entering the door could see it immediately?"

"I didn't see it until I went over to the safe."

"But, good heavens!" exploded Mr. Campion. "Don't you see, you're corroborating Wedgwood's story? Didn't you follow the inquest?"

Mr. Rigget leant back in his chair. He looked exhausted.

"It wasn't any affair of mine," he said stubbornly.

"Had you got a grudge against Wedgwood?"

"No." Mr. Rigget's sullenness increased. "I didn't have much to do with him. *I tell you*," he said, his voice breaking, "you think I'm a beastly filthy little twip, don't you? Well, *I am!* That's what I keep telling you. I am and I can't help it. I know I'm being an unspeakable cad not to own up to what I did, to get him off. I know I am: that makes it worse."

"Why did you go back there tonight?"

Mr. Rigget's wretchedness would have been distressing on any less momentous occasion.

"I shall get the sack when the trial's over," he muttered. "You were there that day when I went to Mr. Widdowson and Sir Alexander and told them about the quarrel I'd overheard. They daren't sack me now, but as soon as the trial's over they will—unless I can get something on them first. That's why I was hunting for something that I could use."

"Yes, well," said Mr. Campion, with disgust, "I don't think much of an education which taught you that tampering with a safe was criminal but didn't mention blackmail."

"Oh, it wouldn't be blackmail," murmured Mr. Rigget. "It would only be something I could just mention. All this is going to come out now, isn't it?"

"Some of it'll have to."

"How d'you know I shan't kill myself?" Mr. Rigget spoke cunningly.

Mr. Campion looked at him. "You poor little beast, you might," he murmured. "That's why I'm going to take you over to Scruby immediately."

Mr. Rigget shrank back in his chair.

"I'm a witness for the Crown. You can't tamper with me. You can't persuade me to say anything I don't want to. I've been talking to you as I've never talked to anybody else, but I'm not going to do it in court."

Mr. Campion got up heavily.

"I shouldn't worry so much about coming clean," he said. "Ever heard of Nemesis? Come on."

15
Night Shift

Those who live in that ghostly part of London which is the most crowded square mile by day and the most deserted by night insist that at three o'clock in the morning it is as peaceful as a country churchyard, and that there the black rats dance a leisurely saraband down the centres of the glossy streets.

Mr. Campion's hurrying footsteps made sharp echoes on the pavements as he strode through the unsavoury alley which is Red Lion Passage and came out into the shabby comfort of the square.

Most of the flat houses had been converted into offices long ago. Standing back from the road, they turned blank eyes to the street lamps and only a single brightly lit third-floor window twinkled at him mellowly through the budding plane trees in the dusty centre garden.

He made for it and was rewarded. Ritchie was evidently a man of his word and was sitting up. Having no desire to wake the whole house, Mr. Campion paused on the edge of the pavement and pitched a halfpenny expertly into the centre of the lighted pane.

Immediately a somewhat fantastic silhouette appeared at the sash, waved reassuringly and vanished.

Campion wandered up to the door, and it opened before him with so little delay that he experienced a slight shock of astonishment.

"Slide down the banisters?" he enquired facetiously.

Ritchie did not answer, and Campion, who could not see his face, received the disquieting impression that he was disconcerted. It was a ridiculous incident and passed at once. Ritchie's great hand caught his arm and forced him up the dark staircase of the house which had seen much better days.

"People asleep," his host confided in a whisper which was like a roar of the wind in a turret. "Only kind to be quiet."

It was a long way up, but the older man moved at a great rate and Mr. Campion came thankfully and a trifle breathlessly into the bed-sitting-room which was Ritchie's home.

It was a huge apartment with a very high ceiling, some two feet below which a shelf had been constructed round all four sides of the room. This ledge was the most striking feature of the place, and first caught a visitor's attention, since it evidently contained practically all Mr. Richard Barnabas's worldly possessions. Books, clothes and manuscripts were there stacked together neatly, albeit a trifle dustily, and were, of course, extraordinarily inaccessible.

What furniture the room contained was huddled together along the darkest wall, as though space were restricted. The wash-stand stood at the end of the iron bedstead, rubbing elbows uncomfortably with a minute dressing-table.

The rest of the room was virtually bare, the floor covered with several layers of dusty under-felting. A small gas fire burned in the grate and a single folding armchair was drawn up before it.

"Sit down. Rather stand—sit all day."

A sweeping but completely meaningless gesture of one arm accompanied the hospitality, and Mr. Campion, who was beginning to understand his friend, obeyed meekly.

He was about to drop into the chair when he caught sight of something among the corduroy cushions and retrieved it in some astonishment. It was a spangled black tulle frill which immediately suggested to Mr. Campion a sentimental relic of a lady in tights dancing upon a *fin de siècle* stage.

If he showed surprise it was nothing to the effect the discovery had upon Ritchie. For a moment he stood gaping, utter consternation on his face, and then, whipping the furbelow out of Campion's hand, he thrust it for want of a better hiding place under the pillow on the iron bedstead.

"Never ask," he commanded, bright spots of colour appearing in his thin cheeks and his blue eyes unexpectedly belligerent. "Never ask."

Mr. Campion, who was tired and had by no means recovered from his encounter with the athletic Mr. Rigget, began to wonder if he himself were not a trifle light-headed. However, Ritchie was still regarding him truculently and he hastened to reassure him.

"Of course not," he said, with dignity.

There was a pause, during which Ritchie seated himself upon the floor, tucking his long awkward legs beneath him with extraordinary dexterity. His excitement evaporated and his eyes became mild and friendly, albeit a trifle worried.

Mr. Campion blinked. The vision of a youthful Ritchie and a lady in spangled tights provided a bizarre note in the sober business of the evening and he reflected what an odd, attractive, simple soul his host was. Ritchie glanced at Campion.

"Been fighting?" he observed.

Campion gave him a rough outline of his evening's adventure.

"I roused poor old Scruby and left Rigget with him," he finished at last. "It means a flutter among the legal gents tomorrow, I'm afraid, but that can't very well be helped. The important thing is that the little rat's story contains two pieces of new evidence: one that Paul was murdered, the key being on the inside of the strong-room door, and the other that the body was moved after rigor mortis had passed and probably Mike went down to the strong room on Sunday night."

He paused and Ritchie regarded him owlishly from the ground. Campion continued.

"I rather thought that something like that last had happened when I first heard about the hat. A man doesn't set his hat upon the floor and then lie down carefully beside it to die. But there was no proof, you see. Everything had been so mucked about by the time the police arrived that they were hampered on all sides."

Ritchie nodded his comprehension.

"New evidence important?" he enquired. "Vital? Mean release?"

"Oh, no, I'm afraid not." Mr. Campion succumbed to the impulse to explain things gently to Ritchie. "It'll weaken the case, of course, but Mike must stand his trial. You see, to do everybody justice, Mike is the obvious person to have killed Paul. He had opportunity, he admits going to the garage and starting the car, the shower tube had belonged to him, he had bought and read a book describing the method of murder in detail, and in the police opinion he had a motive."

"Gina?"

Mr. Campion bowed his battered head.

"The degrees of familiarity between the sexes in ordinary social life differ from clique to clique and class to class more than anything else," he pointed out. "It's practically the only subject on which the authorities are consistently muddled. I'm afraid police circles are inclined to be prurient-minded and lawyers worse."

"Understandable," said Ritchie unexpectedly. "Always having unfortunate experiences."

Mr. Campion continued his dissertation.

"That's the positive legal case, roughly. But then there's all the negative evidence, which only counts in the back of people's minds. Someone killed Paul, someone killed him intentionally and ingeniously. That someone apparently killed him between six in the evening, when the office went home, and nine in the same evening, when Mike turned off his engine and both Mrs. Tripper and my new friend Widgeon noticed the noise had ceased. That someone had access to either Twenty-three or Twenty-one, because it was only through either of these houses that the car could be reached. That someone either knew that Paul would be in the strong room at that particular time or inveigled him into the place. That someone knew of the hose pipe and therefore also knew the back entrance at Twenty-one. The only people who could have known and done all these things are Mike, you, Gina, John, Curley and the janitor—or possibly Paul himself, although it seems an idiotic way to commit suicide. And, anyway, in that case who moved the body?"

"Might be others," said Ritchie dubiously. "If Rigget stayed behind why not others? Girl Netley. Rigget himself. Anyone in the office?"

"Well, let's hope so," said Mr. Campion cheerfully. "Otherwise Mike and Gina are very unfortunately placed. Everyone else has an alibi."

He leant back in his chair and removed his spectacles as Ritchie's eyes watched his face.

"Miss Curley left the office on the Thursday evening at half past five and went to Peter Robinson's to have her hair shampooed. She left there at six and hurried on to the cocktail party which Mike should have attended in Manchester Square. At seven-thirty she left and went on to dinner at Rule's with Miss Betcherley of Blenheim's literary agency, and at eight-fifty she caught a Tube train to Hammersmith."

He paused and smiled.

"Then there's you. You left the office early and came back here, where you collected your landlord——"

"Landlady's husband," corrected Ritchie in the interests of strict accuracy.

"——And went to the circus at Olympia," continued Mr. Campion imperturbably, "where you stayed until ten-thirty. John left his office at five and went to his club, where he was recognized and where he had a business interview. He returned to his flat and dressed for the evening with his usual deliberation and attention to detail. His housekeeper waited upon him the whole time. At seven-forty he went off in a taxi to the Dorchester for the Quill Club dinner, at which he spent the evening. The janitor left the office at six sharp and went off with some pals to the Holborn Empire. In fact, everyone behaved normally except Mike, who went walking, an exercise he hardly ever takes."

His voice died away and he regarded Ritchie steadily.

"Do you realize," he demanded suddenly, "that whoever killed Paul must have stood by and let that car pump gas into the strong room for at least an hour, probably an hour and a half? It wouldn't take long to put Paul under, of course, but the murderer must have gone on with the treatment for some considerable time to make sure of death. That's why these alibis are so very convincing."

Ritchie was silent. He sat upon his feet, rocking gently before the fire, his eyes hidden.

"No motives," he murmured almost, it seemed to Mr. Campion, regretfully. "No motives either."

"All the same," Campion put in hastily, "it's not a strong case against Mike, and all that row the Coroner came in for will prejudice both Judge and Jury in his favour. He's almost certain to get off."

Ritchie shook his head gloomily.

"Not good enough. Stigma all his life. In love—can't marry. Poor fellow!"

He was quiet for a full minute, his huge bony hands twitching in little indeterminate gestures. Suddenly he sat up and Campion was surprised by the purpose and vigour in his tone.

"Got to prove who did it. Only way. Where now?"

Mr. Campion glanced at his watch. It was a quarter past four.

"I came to get your key to Twenty-three again," he said. "I'm going to burgle the safe. Like to come?"

"Yes," he said simply, and Campion grinned at him, despite his weariness.

They accomplished their short eerie walk without mishap and let themselves in through the big Queen Anne door at Twenty-three during that darkest moment of the night when the street lamps suddenly go out half an hour before the dawn.

"Can see in the dark," Ritchie remarked unexpectedly as he piloted Campion across the pitch-black hall to the top of the basement stairs. "Not like day, of course, but fairly well. Ten steps down to the landing and then twelve."

They reached the strong-room door and Campion unlocked it with Mr. Rigget's cherished key. There was something ghostly about the chaotic little apartment, and Mr. Campion found his mind, which was not used to such fancies, dwelling upon the crumpled body which had lain for so many hours among the dusty boxes by the safe and on the murderer who must have returned and dragged the helpless thing out to the clear space by the door at a time when the ravages of death were beginning to show.

There was no sign of Mr. Rigget's activities. His little inquisitions had been performed with the greatest discretion. Campion turned his attention to the safe and was glad that Lugg was not with him to express an opinion on a firm which entrusted anything of value to such an antiquated contraption. Ritchie divined his thoughts.

"Cupboard really," he observed apologetically. "Safe cupboard. Valuables at the bank."

Mr. Campion inserted the squat key which Mr. Samson had made for luck and mastered within a minute or two the simple arrangement of turns and half turns which shot back extremely heavy bolts. The door, which must have weighed a quarter of a ton at the lowest estimation, swung back, and Mr. Campion and Ritchie peered into the steel recess within.

At first sight the contents were not enlightening. Two or three half-calf ledgers, two small notebooks containing addresses, and a file of letters were neatly arranged upon the lower shelf. And that was all, save for a package neatly wrapped in green baize and tied with pink tape.

Mr. Campion took it out carefully and unpacked it on the table which Mike had cleared to receive Paul's body. Inside the baize wrapping was a well-made blue leather case designed to look like a book and very beautifully gilded. Examination proved that it had no lock, but pulled out in two pieces like a card-case and contained a slender manuscript.

"Gallivant," Ritchie remarked, looking over Campion's shoulder. "Never examined it. Uncle Jacoby Barnabas very strict. Thought it indecent. Would have destroyed it but for the value. John carries on tradition. Probably dull."

Campion turned back the thin octavo sheets, which were unbound save for the faded ribbon tied about the centre of the bundle. The brown ink made a spidery but decipherable pattern on the soft rag paper. He read a line or two.

> *"Gagewell: 'O Sir, since Lady Frippet hath a bee in her bonnet, you must allow if the bee's not a queen the bonnet is at least à la mode.'"*

"Clean bit," said Ritchie, with that complete simplicity which was the mainspring of his personality. "Nothing to help us there. Valuable, of course. Wrote it himself, in his own hand. Insured. Stands at twenty thousand pounds in the balance-sheet."

Mr. Campion raised his eyebrow.

"Along with the office freehold and the printing plant at Gravesend?" he suggested.

"That's right," the older man agreed. "Best place for it. Never liked the classics. Put it away."

Campion was some little time repacking the treasure, and Ritchie wandered over to the safe.

"Nothing else," he observed, without turning round. "What are we looking for?"

"Whatever it was that made Paul go to the trouble of getting a key to the safe made for him," Campion explained as he tied the pink tape round the green baize once more and stowed it away in the safe. "There's only one official key to this elegant invention, I suppose. Who keeps it?"

"Head of the firm," said Ritchie. "Another tradition. Explains why there's nothing much kept in it."

"I see. That means that John had the original key?"

Ritchie considered.

"Probably Curley," he said at last. "One or the other. Only a fetish."

Mr. Campion took off his spectacles and perched himself on the edge of the table.

"It seems very careless to keep *The Gallivant* there," he began. "I should have thought the insurance johnnies might have objected to a thing like that."

Ritchie's eyes clouded.

"Ought to go back to the bank," he agreed. "Fact is, this dreadful business—death, murder, trial, and so on— has probably put the whole thing out of their minds. Very likely they haven't been down here since. Can't blame them."

"Oh, it's usually kept at the bank, is it?" said Campion, pricking up his ears. "When was it put in here? Do you know?"

Ritchie's discomfort increased.

"Before Christmas. Silly business. Curley annoyed. Couldn't really blame her."

Mr. Campion was patient. Ritchie's cryptogrammic

replies were tantalizing, and he was thankful for everybody's sake that the well-meaning, inarticulate soul had not been subpœnaed for the morrow's trial.

After a certain amount of persuasion Ritchie amplified his story.

"Nothing in it," he said wretchedly. "Paul made an ass of himself over *The Gallivant*. Wanted to lend it to rare-manuscript exhibition. Up against tradition at once. Grand old firm's vulgar classic. Wouldn't do. Old-fashioned. Stupid. But John and Curley had last word. Paul not content—silly fellow. Tried to get it from bank manager. Being partner, succeeded. Curley saw messenger who brought it. Went to John. John furious, backed her up. *Gallivant* put in safe."

Mr. Campion was bewildered. It seemed incredible that such a little domestic quarrel in the firm could have any connection with the grave issues at stake. He was silent for some moments, considering. John, he knew, had a fanatical pride in the honour of the firm; Miss Curley might easily have hidden depths of prudery; and Paul certainly seemed to have made a nuisance of himself all round. But compared with the scandal which had burst about their ears the public burning of *The Gallivant* by the police—an eventuality, after all, unlikely, since authors dead over a hundred years are permitted great license on the principle, no doubt, that their work has had time to air—would have been negligible, unless——? An idea occurred to him and he looked up, a startled expression in his pale eyes.

"Look here, I'll have to wander off now, Ritchie," he said. "I've been rather late for the bus all along, but I believe I'm catching up with it now. I shan't be down at the Old Bailey at the beginning this morning, but I'll come along later. Keep an eye on Gina, but don't tell her anything."

"No," said Ritchie, with the obedience of a child, and Campion, looking at him affectionately, wondered how much of the mystery about him he saw and what, if anything, he thought of it.

It was half past six on a cold spring morning, with drizzle in the air, when they parted, and Mr. Campion went home to bathe and shave, since it was too early to begin his day's business. He also took the opportunity to submit himself to a patching process, of which Mr. Lugg was a past master. The spectacle of that mournful figure, clad solely in a pair of trousers, standing upon a bath mat at seven-thirty in the morning, a minute pair of surgical scissors in one enormous hand and an even smaller strip of sticking-plaster in the other, was one of those experiences that Mr. Campion frankly enjoyed.

He was sorry that they were not on conversational terms. Mr. Lugg was the victim of a two-way complex. His newer self revolted at the unpleasant publicity with which he saw his employer's name surrounded as the trial progressed, while his elder spirit was deeply hurt that Campion should have enjoyed a scrap in which he had not been permitted to take part.

"There you are," he said at last, stepping back from his handiwork. "Now I've wasted my time on you making you look like a gent again, go and smear yourself with society filth. Roll in it like a dawg—but don't ask me to clean yer. Mud sticks closer than them patches I've put on your dial."

"Mud of the soul?" enquired Mr. Campion affably.

"You know what I mean," said Lugg warningly. "And if we 'ad that charwoman I've ben thinking of I'd drive 'ome me contemp' in the way I was brought up to, even if I 'ave learnt spittin's not quite the thing."

Mr. Campion dressed in silence. At nine o'clock he was waiting outside the door of a little office on the third floor of a building in St. Martin's Lane.

Ex-Detective-Inspector Beth found him there when he came heavily up the stairs to open the little private enquiry office he had established on his retirement.

"Can't get my assistant to turn up before half past, Mr. Campion," he explained as he unlocked the door. "My word, if I had him in the Force for half an hour!"

He paused, enquiry on his round good-natured face.

"Surely *we* can't do anything for you, can we? Well, well, I thought they even took in your laundry work down at the Yard these days."

"Working a little light humour into the act, I see," said his visitor approvingly. "'Divorce with a laugh' and 'Blackmail made fun'? It's not a bad idea. However, unfortunately, there's nothing very amusing about the small commission I am about to entrust to you at the moment. It is merely odd."

He took a limp brown bank book from his pocket and, opening it, entered into some careful instructions. The ex-inspector was puzzled.

"If it was a case of impersonation—someone taking it out—I could understand it," he said. "But who cares who pays money in?"

"I do," said Mr. Campion, who was very tired. "I'm a very proud young fellow, and I like to know where my money's coming from."

Beth turned the book over.

"Since when have you been called Dora Phyllis Netley?" he enquired suspiciously.

Campion leant forward confidentially.

"You must let a man have his secrets," he murmured. "Get on to it and let me have a report tonight."

"Tonight? What do you think we are?" protested his host.

"Private and enterprising. I read it on the door," said Mr. Campion, and hurried away.

It was just after ten when he reached the British Museum, and he paused for a moment at the foot of the great soot-stained granite flight of steps to feel in his breast pocket. His weariness was making him absent-minded, and just for a moment he could not remember if on changing his clothes he had slipped into his pocket a wallet containing a page of *The Gallivant* which he had stolen so shamelessly from beneath Ritchie's very nose. It was here, however, and he went on thankfully.

Time at the Museum is given the treatment it deserves from the custodians of the treasure of historic man, and Mr. Campion's godfather, Professor Bunney, did not arrive until late, so that the morning was considerably advanced when the tall pale young man in the horn-rimmed spectacles at last came out between the granite columns.

Mr. Campion walked slowly, accustoming himself to an idea. His godfather had been most helpful and he now knew without a possibility of doubt that the manuscript of *The Gallivant* in the blue leather box, which was insured for twenty thousand pounds and appeared in the balance-sheet of the famous firm of Barnabas, Limited as representing that sum, was certainly not, however genuine its contents might be, penned by the hand of Wm. Congreve, Dec. 1729, nor was the paper on which it was written manufactured one year earlier than 1863.

16
The Fourth Chair

One of the unexpected things about the Central Criminal Court at the Old Bailey is that it is perfectly new. The carving above the Judge's chair, where the great sword hangs, is not an old carving, and the light oak of the contraption so like a Punch and Judy show, which is the witness-box, is not worn by the nervous hands of a thousand testators but retains some of the varnished brightness of the cabinet-maker's shop.

This newness might perhaps destroy some of the court's undeniable impressiveness were it not for one significant difference between this particular new room and others of the time.

Here ancient things have been replaced not by copies vulgarly disguised to appear old, nor yet by new things different in design and purpose from the old out of deference to the changing manners and customs which have altered the surface of life during the past five hundred years, but by new things replacing those worn out in a room where customs and manners do not change and where the business conducted is not concerned with the surface but with that deeply set, unchangeable streak embedded in the rock of civilization which is crime.

Miss Curley sat beside Gina in the block of seats at the back of the court which is reserved for witnesses and, looking about her, wondered if Mike had been properly fed in Pentonville.

The two women were wedged in a corner some three rows from the front. Gina, at Cousin Alexander's hinted instigation, had succeeded in making herself look almost dowdy. Certainly she appeared very young and very tragic, the high collar of her black coat shadowing her pale, distinctive face.

Immediately before them in the well of the court was the enormous dock, looking as large as and not at all unlike a very superior sheep pen in a country market.

Three chairs, the one in the middle a little in front of the others and directly facing the judicial desk, stood lonely and inadequate in the midst of the expanse.

Beyond was Counsels' table, already littered with papers and glasses of water, with the jury and witness-boxes and the Press table on its left and the solicitors' table and the bank of expert witnesses on its right.

Farther away still were the clerks' desks, directly beneath the dais and facing into the well.

Last of all was the Bench itself.

The seven chairs on the dais were equidistant and all very much alike, since the Lord Mayor and Aldermen of London are entitled to sit. They each had high leather backs emblazoned with the city arms and managed to look impressive even when unoccupied.

The fourth chair fascinated Miss Curley. It stood between the carved columns, the state sword, hilt downward, immediately above it, while before it, at the wide desk, a little clerk was arranging sheaves of paper.

The court was full of people. The witness benches were crammed and the public gallery over the solicitors' table seemed in danger of bursting and jettisoning its load into the dock. Press and solicitors' tables were full and junior counsel and the clerks were clustering round their own headquarters. Everyone was talking. Men in gowns hurried to and fro with papers, their shoes squeaking noisily on the wood. Now and again a late arrival was thrust into a seat in the witness benches by a fatherly official clad in what appeared to be some sort of police uniform augmented by a beadle's gown.

The jury, ten men and two women, looked on at the preparations like an absurdly small audience at an amateur theatrical show which had got completely out of hand and swamped the auditorium. They looked apprehensive and painfully uncomfortable and the foreman, an elderly man with pince-nez and a bald head, mopped his face repeatedly although the morning was inclined to be cold.

John sat at the solicitors' table oddly in the picture, his round head held slightly on one side and his long thin neck sticking stiffly out of his elegant grey collar.

Ritchie was behind Gina and his expression of frightened disgust as he noticed each new evidence of human bondage was pathetic or comic according to the onlooker's fancy. He showed no signs of fatigue, but his gentle eyes were anxious and his enormous bony hands fidgeted on his knees.

Among the legal broiling circulating round the court with a familiarity which proclaimed it their own fishpond there was a certain amount of pleasurable anticipation. A *cause célèbre* at the Old Bailey is bound to have its moments. The Lord Chief Justice, Lord Lumley, affectionately called "Lor Lumme" by his admirers in the best legal, police and criminal circles, still preserved sufficient humanity in his omnipotence to lose his temper on occasions and there was a persistent rumour, utterly unfounded, that he cherished a personal antipathy towards Sir Alexander Barnabas.

Then, in accordance with the custom at poisoning trials at the Old Bailey, the Attorney-General himself, Sir Montague Brooch, was appearing for the Crown and was leading Sir Andrew Phelps, with Jerome Fyshe and Eric Battersby as juniors.

There were rumors of last-minute trouble with important witnesses and altogether the prospects looked good.

Gina sat trembling.

"I'm going to see him—I'm going to see him—I'm going to see him—I'm going to see him——"

The words made a singsong pattern completely without meaning in her brain, neither conveying nor expressing any thought at all, but providing a deadening chatter which prevented her from thinking.

Miss Curley sat forward, straining her eyes to see Counsels' table. Something was happening and she could see flickers of amusement appearing on dark faces beneath blue-white periwigs.

A clerk entered, laden with an assortment of paraphernalia which he proceeded to arrange. First a dark cushion was placed carefully on a chair, then a portfolio laid reverently on the table and round it a little ring of oddments carefully set out. Miss Curley discerned a pile of exquisite cambric handkerchiefs, a bottle of smelling salts, another of sal volatile, a box of throat pastilles and a glass of water.

There was a long pause. The clerk stepped back and gazed expectantly at the doorway behind him. His interest was not unnaturally echoed by those about him and finally, when everyone in the court was aware that somebody of importance was about to enter, a little door swung open, there was a rustle of an old silk gown, a glimpse of a grey-blue wig, and then, looking like a middle-aged Apollo in fancy dress, Cousin Alexander swept up to the table and sat down.

Miss Curley waited for the Attorney-General and, disappointed, had allowed her eyes to wander back to Cousin Alexander and away again before she suddenly caught sight of him at the same table and wondered if he had been there all the time.

The big hand of the court clock reached the half hour and there was a sudden silence, followed by a mighty rustle as everybody rose. The door on the right of the dais opened and an old gentleman in red appeared.

The squad of wigs bowed, looking slightly comic as black, brown and even pink heads appeared for an instant beneath the queues as necks were bent.

The Judge returned the bow as he settled himself, not in the fourth chair beneath the sword but in the one beside it, and the untidy little clerk rearranged his papers. The position brought him nearer the jury and the witness-box and farther from Counsel, and the change was probably pure pernicketiness and the desire to break the symmetry of the design.

The Lord Chief Justice, Lord Lumley, was a large old

man with the drooping jowls and bald bony eyesockets of a
bloodhound. His upper lip was shaven but he affected a
square of close-clipped white hair about as big as a piece of
confetti in the centre of his lower one, which gave him a
slightly sporting appearance. He was over seventy and
forced from time to time to use eyeglasses, which he wore
on a wide black ribbon.

As he sat in his high leather chair his scarlet robe fell
sleekly with deep wine-coloured shadows over his heavy
form, and his square wig, which was brown and inclined to
look as though it were made of the bristles usually fashioned
into carpet brooms, overshadowed his face.

In his hand he held a formal bouquet, the nosegay
dating from the time when the air of the courtroom was not
so hygienic as modern cleanliness has made it and a handful
of flowers and herbs was at least some barrier between a
fastidious gentleman and the plague.

After a pause, he seemed to remember it suddenly, for
he leant forward and placed it carefully in the tumbler of
water on his desk, where it stood for the remainder of the
day looking like a motif from a Tudor tapestry or a chapter
end for *Alice in Wonderland*.

Meanwhile there was a whispering hush over the
room, and presently, from somewhere below the court, the
sound of a door banging heralded the arrival of the prisoner.

Gina was unfamiliar with the geography of the place
and Mike's sudden appearance from the well staircase in the
bottom right-hand corner of the dock almost unnerved her.
He came up slowly between two warders, whose care of
him was that of hospital attendants. They were both square,
short-legged men, considerably his senior, and they patted
him and murmured what must have been encouraging
words as he towered above them in the vast and shining
sheep pen below the dome.

Miss Curley caught her breath. She had not seen him
since his arrest and was unprepared for the change in him.
He did not look particularly ill. His features were finer and
his pallor made his eyes look darker, but his crisp shorn
head was grey and, as he stood facing the Judge with his
back directly to her, she saw the wide bones of his shoulders
hunched under his coat.

She stole a glance at Gina. The girl was crying; angry, indignant tears hovering on the fringe of her lashes, and Miss Curley, who was liable to unexpected flashes of feminine intuition, realized that, whatever her other thoughts and emotions might be, Gina wept because his hair was grey.

She looked away abruptly. An entirely new personality had taken charge of the proceedings. The Clerk, who until now had been just another dark-faced, grey-wigged person sitting at a desk directly beneath the Judge's dais, had risen to his feet and revealed himself to be an unexpectedly distinguished man with a deep, cultured voice and a casual manner which robbed his words of their formality without over-emphasizing their meaning.

"Michael Wedgwood, you are charged for that you, on the twenty-eighth day of January, nineteen thirty-one, at London, murdered Paul Redfern Brande. You are also charged on a Coroner's inquisition with murder. How say you, Michael Wedgwood? Are you guilty or not guilty?"

As the last word left his lips he sat down again with a great rustle of papers and there was a pause until one of the wardens nudged his prisoner gently.

"Not guilty."

Mike's voice was unexpectedly loud and infused a note of tension into the friendly, businesslike atmosphere of the court. He remained upon his feet while the Clerk turned his attention to the business of swearing in the jury, and Lord Justice Lumley raised that part of his face where his left eyebrow should have been and remarked affably:

"You may sit down. The only time you have to stand in this court is when you are receiving sentence or when I address you."

He had a pleasant rumbling voice with a slight squeak in it at commas, which did nothing to detract from the magnificent oddity of his appearance or his unshakable dignity which clothed him as surely as his robe.

The jury being sworn, a proceeding conducted with the neatness and efficiency of a first-class acrobatic turn, the Clerk addressed them as they sat wriggling before him, twelve busy citizens with troubles enough of their own.

He sat down at last and bent over his desk and, while

Miss Curley trembled, the Attorney-General rose to open the case for the prosecution.

Montague Brooch was a little crow of a man. His silk gown enveloped him and his wig gave his face an even sharper, beakier appearance than it possessed without it. In repose he was inclined to look insignificant, and few would remark him, if even for his ugliness, but the moment he opened his mouth he became a personality that was as unforgettable as it was utterly charming.

"May it please Your Lordship, Members of the Jury——"

The voice was virile yet confiding, attractive, deferential and pleasing in the extreme.

"—the charge against the prisoner, as you have heard, is murder. I must, I am afraid, open to you with a story of considerable detail, and, while it is not without its difficulties, it must, I think, show a very serious case indeed against the prisoner."

For the first time since the arrival of Cousin Alexander upon the scene Miss Curley felt genuinely afraid. Until now she had accepted John's valuation of the famous man without question and had allayed all her qualms for Mike's eventual safety by a recollection of that handsome, sanguine figure with the face of a hero and the confidence of a Harley Street specialist. But here was a real adversary. Cousin Alexander's charm was definable and all the more vulnerable because of it, but the personality of Montague Brooch was not capable of analysis and had a disconcerting habit of confusing itself with clear and reasoned argument, so that it was his thought and not the man one most remembered.

Miss Curley glanced at John now and saw him sitting forward in his chair, his head held on one side and his cold eyes fixed unwaveringly upon the little crow with the sweet voice who spoke so convincingly, and at the same time somehow so regretfully, of the crime. There was no way of telling his thought but Miss Curley fancied that he was disconcerted.

Behind her Ritchie was breathing heavily and down in the other witness benches she caught a glimpse of Mrs. Austin's broad back and untidy hair.

". . . Now what happens on the Sunday night? On
January the thirty-first you will hear that quite fortuitous-
ly, and when in the company of friends, the accused is
asked to go down to the room where, it is the Crown's case,
he knew the body lay. . . ."

To Gina the Attorney-General was just a voice repeat-
ing facts she already knew and had heard proved over and
over again until their significance was lost upon her.

To her the one reality was Mike himself, sitting
directly in front of her. She could see his grey head and the
short hairs at the nape of his neck and her throat contracted
until the pain of it alone seemed sufficient to suffocate her.

There was not complete silence in the court while the
speech went on. To Miss Curley's surprise there seemed to
be no rule against whispering, and clerks, with great
armfuls of papers and noisy shoes, tiptoed about.

Cousin Alexander, looking tremendously important
and more handsome than any man over fifty has any right to
be in his immaculate wig and bands, was rustling his
papers, conferring with his juniors and polishing his glasses
with a great flourish of the topmost handkerchief.

". . . Let me take the next stage. Doctor Ferdie
arrives. He agrees with Doctor Roe as to the cause of death
and together these two men make a very careful autopsy. . . ."

The delightful voice played over the unpleasant words,
giving them just sufficient emphasis. Miss Curley found
herself listening with detached interest. At the inquest the
central figure had been the dead man but here Mike had
taken his place and the story was told afresh from a new
angle.

It occurred to Miss Curley, who had known Paul and
had been amused by him, that he was easily the least
important person in the whole story and that his personality
alone did not emerge in the dreadful résumé of the manner
of his dying. She could not see the public gallery and even if
she had been able she would not have recognized Teddie
Dell.

". . . Inspector Tanner visited the strong room,
where you have heard the body lay, and, after making a

careful survey of the room and its environs, discovered a most ingenious device, of which he will tell you. . . ."

Miss Curley, having located Doctors Ferdie and Roe in the benches behind the solicitors' table, was looking about for Inspector Tanner in the seats behind her when a large elderly man at her side turned round and, seeing her placid friendly face, whispered huskily:

"Makes you think, don't he? I remember him in a stuff gown."

Miss Curley gave the remark the conventional smile it needed and wondered who he was. There were a great many people in the benches whom she had never seen before and next time the stranger confided his admiration of Counsel to her with a muttered, "What a way with him!" she ventured to whisper back.

"Are you a witness?"

"No. Come in to watch."

He did not volunteer any information concerning the method by which he had obtained a seat and Miss Curley eyed his pleasant face, whose only striking feature was enormous eyebrows, covertly and reflected that it was difficult to generalize and that he was not at all the type she would have suspected of morbid curiosity.

Meanwhile, Sir Montague had spoken for the best part of an hour and his gentle voice was apologizing to Judge and Jury.

". . . I have little more to say now. You will hear in detail every part of the tragic and abominable story I have outlined to you. But there are a few points which I should like to put into your minds at this stage. It is usual to look for a motive in any crime and, although in this case you will not find a motive which you, or I, I hope, would think adequate, I think you will see that it is more than possible that the accused had a motive sufficient for him. I must admit to you that the Crown has no direct evidence of immoral relations between the murdered man's wife and the accused. It may be that when you see Mrs. Brande you will decide that she is not the sort of woman whose principles are those which would permit her to stoop to that sort of irregularity, but you will hear on her own submission that she was a neglected wife, and the accused has admitted in

his statement, which I have read to you, that he was in the habit of spending much of his time with her and that in fact at the very moment when, as I shall prove to you, her husband was lying dead in a basement room in the house next door, he took her to a cinema, bringing her back afterwards to the flat which she shared with her husband and returning immediately, I have no doubt, to his own home in the same building.

"You will also hear from Mrs. Austin, the honest woman who attended to Mrs. Brande's household work, of the scene which she witnessed when the accused came to break the news of Paul Brande's death to Mrs. Brande.

"Mrs. Austin came into the room to find them on the hearth rug, 'clinging together,' as she so graphically puts it. You may feel that this is not evidence of immoral relations and I would reiterate that the Crown does not allege immoral relations, but it does insist that there was deep friendship between the accused and Mrs. Brande, dating over a period of some years and increasing in intensity as Mrs. Brande's husband increased in his neglect.

"At what point, if any, a deep affection cherished by a young and virile man for a beautiful and virtuous woman some years his junior may grow into an overwhelming passion, in the grip of which his moral fibre is broken down utterly, it is for you to consider. The Crown is not dealing with conjecture. The Crown merely contends that a deep affection was entertained by the accused for Mrs. Brande.

"Mrs. Brande will tell you that she had visited a solicitor some days before her husband's death and had learned from him that there was no way open to her to obtain a divorce save through her husband's cruelty or through his co-operation. She will also tell you that the accused knew nothing of this, and indeed that he had no idea that any such project had entered her head. You must believe what you see to be the truth. If you believe that a deep friendship existed between these two you may think that it is improbable, even impossible, that any woman should keep such an important matter from such an intimate friend who saw her every day. If there was nothing but friendship between them, why should she hide it? If

there was more, might it not have been even at the accused's suggestion that she approached the solicitor?

"However, you will hear that Mr. Brande would not consider a divorce and that it was to discuss this very matter, and to make his strong views known to his wife, that he had arranged to meet her on the very evening that he met his death, an appointment which he never kept. . . ."

Miss Curley stirred in her seat. Gina was rigid, her cheeks pallid and her lips compressed. A woman in the gallery craned her neck to catch a glimpse of her.

Gradually the speech came to an end. The Attorney-General's voice had never lost its gentle and impartial reasonableness and now it became even more soothing, even more deferential, than before.

"It has been necessary to address you at this length because you must know exactly what the facts are in this story, the burden of which the Crown will attempt to prove. If you feel, as I feel you must, that the evidence leads you to the conclusion beyond all reasonable doubt that this man, in order to marry his cousin's wife, did kill his cousin on the night of January the twenty-eighth in this year, you will have no hesitation in doing your duty.

"If, however, you find there is insufficient direct evidence to make you so sure, and that you have a reasonable doubt, then again you will have no hesitation in doing your duty.

"The case is a difficult one. All the Crown will do is to set out the facts on which you must rely. This is not a case in which you will be concerned with any possible verdicts such as manslaughter. A murder has been done and it is for you to decide if it was committed by the accused. If it was, if the Crown proves to you, as I believe it will, that this man did what he is charged with doing, then it is a crime utterly foul and unpardonable. His cousin had done him no wrong. At worst he had neglected his own wife. And yet, if you so find it, he sent him slowly and insidiously to his death with a callousness which no rigour of the law can equal.

"If you think it is fairly proved against this man that he so murdered his cousin, then it will be your duty to send him to his account."

He paused, bowed to the Judge, and sat down.

And then, while the court was still tingling, a police

photographer bobbed up in the Punch and Judy witness-box, and began to testify as to photographs taken in connection with the crime.

A surveyor had taken his place and was painfully describing the survey of the ground floors and garden of Twenty-three and Twenty-one which he had made, and had produced plans and had sworn to them, when Miss Curley's neighbour turned to her.

"Shan't come back. Nothing more of interest today. Fireworks tomorrow," he confided in a warm whisper. "They'll adjourn in a minute."

"Adjourn?" murmured Miss Curley, who already saw Mike on the scaffold. "What for?"

Her neighbour gaped at her as at a lunatic.

"Lunch, of course," he said.

17

Mr. Campion's Case for the Defence

Ritchie was standing in the huge multi-coloured marble hall at the Old Bailey, which had the smell of a public library and was full of people who talked together with that peculiar excited anxiety almost always reserved for other people's troubles, when Mr. Campion found him and led him to one side.

He was obviously shaken by the experience of the morning and it was some time before Campion, who was tired, could be sure that he was getting his full attention.

"There won't be anything more of interest today," Campion repeated slowly and with emphasis. "I want you to come away with me now and give me a hand. It's important."

"Leave the court?" said Ritchie, his gentle eyes blinking at his friend.

"Yes, if you would." Mr. Campion was very patient. "I've seen Sir Alexander and Miss Curley will look after Gina. Are you coming?"

The sweet air, or it may have been the sweet freedom, of Newgate Street, revived Ritchie's powers of speech. He strode along to the car park talking with what was for him lucidity and volubility.

"Awful, Campion!" he shouted. "Ghastly! Jolly things like fancy dress, boxes for seats, coloured robes and policemen all made horrible and frightening. Like a serious harlequinade. Mike's grey. Hair's grey. Two men in delightful clothes arguing for his life. Like a game . . . rules . . . places to stand. Felt ill. Sick. Wanted to spew. Frightened, Campion."

The young man in the horn-rimmed spectacles was silent. The project he had in hand was a delicate one and he required co-operation. It seemed to him best in the circumstances to allow Ritchie's startled wits to reassort themselves without assistance.

As they climbed into the car and waited to slip out into the slothful stream of traffic Ritchie sighed and shook himself.

"Like a dream," he said. "Absurd, like a dream. They'll hang him, Campion. That fellow with the voice is cleverer than Cousin Alexander. That's what counts."

By the time they reached Ludgate Hill he was better and his companion, recognizing in him a worried edition of his normal self, thought it safe to broach the subject in hand.

"You get on very well with Mrs. Peel, don't you?" he enquired.

"John's housekeeper? Known her for years. Nice old body. Why?"

"She doesn't like me," explained Campion regretfully. "She didn't like to trust me in the flat. Afraid I was going to pinch the ormolu clock with the china figures. That's why I had to come and get hold of you."

He paused and concentrated on his driving, wondering how far Ritchie's perception would lead him and with what results.

The elder man did not seem to perceive at all. He

acquiesced quietly as they drove on in silence. It was warm and sunny when they arrived at the cul-de-sac and Twenty-one seemed to be deserted. Twenty-three was not closed but there was little sign of activity and the Morris sign of the Golden Quiver swung disconsolately in the light breeze.

"Mrs. Peel," remarked Mr. Campion as he sprang out of the car and came round to help Ritchie with the door, whose simple mechanism had defeated him, "thinks I am (A) a thief and (B) the police. You are coming with me to dispel both these delusions. Do you think you can do it?"

"Dear good intelligent woman." Ritchie observed, apparently in answer to the question. "Kind. Always liked her."

She stood in the dark entrance hall of John's flat when they presented themselves at the door a few minutes later and surveyed them with belligerent beady eyes, like some large elderly beetle surprised in its tree-trunk home.

She had a harsh unpleasing voice and when she said, "Back again?" Mr. Campion could not help feeling some of the shame which she intended to stir in him.

Ritchie stood looking at her helplessly for a moment and then, either by accident or design, achieved a master-stroke.

"No lunch. Peely . . . cocoa . . . bread and butter . . . anything," he murmured. "Campion and me, tired, hungry, want to sit down."

Mrs. Peel led the way into the dining room, grumbling as she went. Her brown serge dress hitched at the back, revealing untidy ankles, but her sparse hair was groomed and dressed to a neatness which suggested that each separate strand knew its duty in emergency and was determined to make up for its scarcity of companions.

As they sat waiting for food at the heavy mahogany table in the dark book-lined room with the thick curtains and half-drawn venetian blinds, Mr. Barnabas made a very curious remark.

"Pity about the food, Campion. Know how you feel. Old shibboleth, though. Couldn't be helped."

Mr. Campion's eyebrows rose and he shot his friend a single penetrating glance which completely destroyed for an instant the habitual vacuity of his expression, but Ritchie said no more and presently rose from his chair and opened a window, which Mrs. Peel promptly closed as soon as she returned with bread, butter, Gorgonzola and two cups of weak unpalatable cocoa.

"That two grown men with money in their pockets can't look after their creature comforts in a town of this size is extraordinary," she remarked angrily but as she looked only at Ritchie as she spoke Mr. Campion realized with relief that he was accepted, if ignored.

He even ate the horrible meal, Mrs. Peel waiting upon him as if he had been a six-year-old, buttering his bread and cutting him small chunks of odoriferous cheese.

"Been to the trial," Ritchie mumbled into his cocoa cup.

Mrs. Peel made an indignant sound like a French railway engine.

"That murder! I never heard such utter nonsense in all my born days. It was an accident. Mr. John told me so himself."

"Were you here on the night it happened?" Mr. Campion ventured.

The woman turned round and looked at him.

"Well, of all the questions!" she exclaimed. "Of course I was. What are you trying to insinuate? That I was turning on the gas in the office? No. I was in this flat the whole time. At four o'clock I began to lay out Mr. John's clothes and when he came in at five-thirty I went to my room and sat with the door open, so that I could hear when he called me."

"And did he call you?"

Mr. Campion's face expressed polite interest.

"Of course he did," she said impatiently. "If Mr. John could dress by himself I should think he was ill. He called me to turn on the bath and when it was ready I told him so and went back to my room."

Campion was silent for some time and his eyes were thoughtful. He was forming the next question carefully when she answered it unbidden.

"The murder wasn't the only accident that happened that night," she observed in the tone of one mentioning a genuine trouble in the midst of a discussion on imaginary ills. "When I knocked on Mr. John's bedroom door to tell him the bath was ready he didn't hear me and all the time I thought he was having his bath he was in here. He sat down for a moment and must have dozed off. Anyway, he didn't hear me and at a quarter to seven I hear him come out of the bathroom in a fine rage. He had been to see if the bath was ready and had found it lukewarm, I had to hot it up for him. In the end he didn't go into that bath until seven o'clock and of course he wouldn't hurry himself—never would, not if the house was afire. And finally he went off to his dinner at a quarter to eight, dressed nicely but not shaved. He hadn't, I know, because I looked at his brush and it was dry. That shows you how accidents happen."

"Yes," agreed Mr. Campion with a solemnity quite out of keeping with the circumstances. "Yes, that's exactly what it does do."

"Well, then," said Mrs. Peel and began to clear away with a great clatter.

Mr. Campion rose to his feet.

"Where is the bathroom?" he enquired.

The woman stared at him, her brows raised into acute angles on her wrinkled forehead and a flush spreading upward over her face.

"I never did!" she said at last. "Really! Oh, all right . . . the second door across the passage. There is a clean towel there."

A few minutes later when Ritchie entered the old-fashioned bathroom with the big copper geyser and the enormous antiquated bath he found Mr. Campion leaning out of the window. The younger man drew in his head and straightened his back. Ritchie took his place.

A fire escape sprawled its ungainly way up the back of the elegant old house and one green-painted iron landing stage abutted on to the wall less than two feet below the sill over which he leant. He looked at it for a moment and then stepped back and he and Mr. Campion eyed each other. Ritchie was first to speak.

"Talk," he said urgently. "Downstairs."

Mrs. Peel made it clear that she was glad to see the end of them, if indeed, as she very much doubted, it was the end. She also mentioned that something for nothing was a very common quarry in her experience, but that since Mr. Ritchie was a relation she did not see that she was entitled to begrudge the cocoa. She also wished them a very good afternoon.

Ritchie led Campion downstairs to the ground floor and let himself into Mike's domain.

"Mike gave it to me," he explained, observing Campion's eyes on the latchkey. "Had to fetch him some clothes when they took him to that place. He won't mind us here. Good fellow, Mike. Grey hair, poor chap."

He waved his friend toward a dusty armchair in the sitting room which they both knew well and perched himself opposite on the edge of the table, where he sat with his long arms swinging and his shaggy head held up alertly.

"Know now?" he asked anxiously and for the last time the younger man surprised the dog-like, enquiring expression in his face. "Clear?"

"Yes, I think so," said Mr. Campion and sighed.

"*Gallivant* only a copy?"

Although he put the words as a question Ritchie seemed to have very little doubt as to the answer and Campion wondered afresh at his extraordinary mixture of shrewdness and simplicity. Aloud he said:

"They think the stuff itself may be genuine, but it's not the original manuscript. It's probably a copy made sometime in the last half of the last century."

"Uncle Jacoby," observed Ritchie blandly. "All prudish Victorians secretly dirty. Probably had it made for private reading. Like him, rather. Funny old man. What happened to Paul?"

Mr. Campion leaned back in his chair. He looked very tired but his eyes were bright and intelligent.

"Paul was too energetic," he said slowly, and added apologetically, "You'll have to forgive me if I take my time, but I've learnt the story the wrong way round."

"Tell it that way. Begin at the end."

"I don't know the end," said Mr. Campion. "That's the trouble."

Ritchie sat silent and expectant and presently Campion went on.

"Paul made himself a nuisance in the firm for four years, ever since he returned from America," he said. "In that time he seems to have got on the nerves of most people in publishing generally. Then he was bitten by the idea of exhibiting *The Gallivant* and, of course, there were excellent reasons why the manuscript should not be shown in a place where interfering people might ask awkward questions about the age of the paper and the quality of the ink, not to mention the authenticity of the handwriting. So he was stopped, but, being an enquiring and obstinate beggar, it dawned upon him that there was probably something fishy about the precious manuscript and he decided to examine it. He got the bank to give it up, but again he was stopped from looking at it and the manuscript was put in the safe. Whether that was done with malice aforethought I don't know, but I rather think so, for the safe key was left in his way long enough for him to take an impression of it and from that time on a pretty close watch was kept on Paul's activities and the watcher was paid small sums for her trouble."

He paused and Ritchie nodded comprehendingly.

"The day came," continued Mr. Campion, "when the watcher reported that a letter had arrived which had made Paul dash off in excitement. It was a letter from Wardie Samson, for which he and his observers had waited. It was a signal for action.

"This is what happened to Paul. He came back to Twenty-three just after six o'clock, when he knew the place would be closed, let himself in and went up to Curley's desk, where he got the key of the strong room. He then went down to the basement. His new key fitted the safe, but the arrangement of turns and half turns got him bothered because he was nervous and in a high state of excitement. He had just got the safe door open when he was disturbed by footsteps in the yard outside. I imagine that a characteristic cough warned him, quite intentionally, that the newcomer was the one particular person he did not wish to find him there and I think he behaved quite normally and in the way the murderer foresaw he would behave, and not like that hysterical maniac Peter Rigget, who lost his head and went berserk."

Ritchie looked interested but so completely in the da[r]
that Campion wondered if he could possibly be followi[ng]
this complicated reconstruction.

"Paul locked himself in and turned out the light[s,]
Campion continued. "He knew, or thought he knew, that h[e]
had the only key of the strong room, so that he was sa[fe]
from the intruder, and as long as no chink of light showe[d]
anywhere there was no reason at all why anyone shoul[d]
suspect the place was occupied.

"In the dark he crept away from the door and waite[d]
for the other man to go. But the newcomer remained. H[e]
went into the garage and started the car and Paul, not su[re]
if the back door was standing open, dared not slip out, eve[n]
if he wanted to. Personally I think he decided to wait unt[il]
the other man had gone. Probably he imagined that Mik[e]
was with him. Anyway, whatever he thought, it did n[ot]
occur to him that carbon monoxide fumes were pouring int[o]
the unventilated room through the rubber pipe pushe[d]
through the grating in the opposite wall.

"He noticed the smell of exhaust gas, of course, bu[t]
since he could hear the car and probably guessed there wa[s]
an air brick leading into the garage somewhere he though[t]
nothing of it.

"Within five minutes he was drowsy and sat down, [I]
think by the safe. Five minutes later he was unconscious[,]
and after the best part of an hour, when the murdere[r]
returned and switched off the engine, he was dead."

"Murderer returned?"

Mr. Campion looked up.

"Yes," he said. "In the interim he went back to hi[s]
home by the way he had come, found his bath was cold[,]
blew up his housekeeper, had the bath heated again an[d]
bathed. When he had finished he put on his underclothe[s]
and trousers, probably, under a dressing-gown, and wen[t]
out once more through the bathroom window, down the fir[e]
escape, through the door in the garden wall, switched o[ff]
the car, threw the rubber tubing in at the basement door a[nd]
he returned, then finished his dressing and went out t[o]
dinner, unfortunately not having had time to shave.

"I'm open to bet that he wore gloves not because o[f]

fingerprints, but so that he should not dirty or burn his hands."

There was a long silence. Ritchie was rocking himself slowly backwards and forwards.

"Not dozing in dining room, watching street for Paul to go into Twenty-three," he said at last. "Wouldn't have been seen on fire escape from street at other end of yard. Foggy all that week. Risky, Campion."

"Risky!" Mr. Campion caught his breath. "It was so risky that no one who did not imagine himself a species of god about the place would have thought of it, much less attempted it. Mike might have come home earlier, although, of course, he was supposed to be at the cocktail party. But anyone might have gone into the garage to see why the car was running. Hang it! Even a policeman might have enquired. . . . Besides, Paul might not have stayed there. He might have come out at the very beginning and asked him what the hell he thought he was up to."

"Wouldn't have mattered," Ritchie observed. "He'd have won. He'd have told Paul to mind his own business and go away. Paul would have gone. Strong personality . . . strict, you know . . . authoritative."

Mr. Campion remained thoughtful.

"On Sunday he must have been getting restive when he sent Mike down to the strong room," he said quietly. "He sent him to get a folder, expecting him to find the door locked and the key missing and so start the excitement which would lead to the finding of the body. It would have been a weak move if Mike had found Paul. As it turned out, of course, it complicated the issue tremendously. Mike didn't see the corpse and came back as though nothing had happened. That must have jolted our man considerably. So afterwards, probably late at night, he went down there himself, dragged the body into a prominent position, and, after placing the hat by its side, left it for Miss Marchant to find in the morning. He couldn't very well leave the door locked on the inside, so he put the key back in Miss Curley's desk.

"It's a mad sort of crime, so mad that it came off. It was the man's mental make-up which made it possible. All murderers are a little crazy. The people who get away with incredible things are those who never look round the subject, but just go straight ahead and make for their objective with blinkers on. It's like the drunk who walks across the parapet. He only knows he wants to get to a window next door, sees a straight path and takes it, oblivious to the ten-story drop on either side of him."

"John . . ." Ritchie. "Obvious really."

"Obvious?" enquired Mr. Campion, his professional pride stirring in its latent bed.

"From the beginning," said Ritchie placidly. "John said he knew it was an accident. John's not a fool. Got a logical mind. Reasonable, except where personal infallibility is concerned. If he knew it was an accident he must have arranged it himself: everyone else thought it was a murder. Queer chap . . . law of his own. Terrible for Mike."

"Not too good for Paul," murmured Mr. Campion dryly. "But that's not the question at the moment. The trouble is I can't prove this story. It depends too much on your friend Mrs. Peel, and even if she could be persuaded to tell the same yarn in the witness-box what should we have then? A case against John just about as strong as the one they've already got against Mike. The police wouldn't consider it. Why should they?"

Ritchie sat silent for a long time. Finally he looked at the younger man, his mild blue eyes dark and pained.

"Terrible for Mike," he repeated. "Caught, imprisoned, killed."

"No," said Campion hastily. "He'll be acquitted. I'm sure of it. If I wasn't I'd be at the Yard now doing anything I could, making a fool of myself probably. I'm banking on an acquittal. Anyway, there'll be the appeal. That's not the point. Unfortunately in an imperfect world acquittal does not mean that a man is proved innocent to the satisfaction of the people with whom he has got to live."

"What shall we do?"

Ritchie invited a command and Mr. Campion made up his mind. He rose and walked over to Mike's desk.

"I think we'll leave a note," he said.

Taking an envelope from a pigeon-hole, he addressed it to John, adding briefly: "With Mr. Campion's compliments."

Inside he placed the folded page from the copy of *The Gallivant* and the key of the safe which he had received from Mr. Rigget. Together he and Ritchie carried the missive up stairs and left it with Mrs. Peel.

18
In Reply to Your Letter

Their visit to John's flat and subsequent conversation had taken much longer than either Ritchie or Mr. Campion had dreamed, and when they met Gina and Miss Curley on the door-step of Twenty-one they were astounded to learn that the court had adjourned for the day.

Miss Curley was grimly capable, keeping her head with a conscious effort. Gina was silent and, had it not been for a glazed expression in her eyes, might have appeared sullen. Her chestnut hair warmed the whiteness of her skin and her mouth was resolute.

"She must eat," said Miss Curley in an undertone to Ritchie. "You come up with me and talk to her until I find something."

Gina looked at Campion.

"They're making a strong case," she whispered. "Even John's beginning to see it now. He stayed behind to speak to Cousin Alexander. It all fits in so horribly the way they put it."

"Wait till you hear the defence," said Campion, with forced cheerfulness. "The prosecution is always convincing till you hear the defence. Don't worry."

She looked at him as though he had said something absurd, smiled mechanically and passed on up the stairs, Miss Curley following her. Ritchie turned to Campion.

"Better go," he said. "Poor girl!"

There was a pause in which he seemed to be struggling for words. Campion thought he had never seen such intensity of feeling in a face before.

"To escape," said Ritchie suddenly. "Escape, Campion. Escape all . . . this."

A great wave of a flail-like arm included, as far as his hearer could judge, the civilized world and all that lay within it.

Mr. Campion made no direct reply. Apart from the fact that no one could ever be quite sure what Ritchie was talking about, there seemed to be no comment upon such passionate feeling which would not be an impertinence.

"Good-bye," he said. "See you to-morrow."

"To-morrow," said Ritchie, and in his mouth the word had the bitterness of eternity.

Mr. Campion went home. Age, he reflected, was beginning to tell on him, and, since he was a person not given to self-consideration, it came to him with all the force of a major discovery that nearly thirty-five and nearly twenty-five are two very different kettles of fish where nervous stamina and the ability to do without sleep are concerned.

He was so depressed by the thought that he decided to go to bed immediately upon arriving at Bottle Street, and would have done so had it not been for the visitor who awaited him.

Ex-Inspector Beth rose from his chair in the sitting room and grinned as his host came in.

"Didn't expect to see me here, did you?" he said. "And with the goods."

"No," said Campion truthfully. "I did not."

"He's bin 'ere for an hour talking about 'imself, until you'd think 'e was still a flattie," observed Mr. Lugg, who had wandered in from the next room, collarless and in his house coat.

"Oh, I have, have I? Well, no one would think you were still a cat burglar," countered the ex-inspector spitefully.

"No, I've bettered meself," said Lugg, with ineffable complacency. "I'm a house gentleman now."

"What's the report?" cut in Mr. Campion, who was not in the mood for cross-talk. "Anything definite?"

The visitor became businesslike immediately.

"Pretty good, Mr. Campion, pretty good. As far as I

can ascertain, nearly all the amounts paid into the bank book since December last, and not handed in at the Holborn post office, were paid in by an elderly gentleman. Is that what you expected?"

"Only 'nearly all'?" enquired Campion, with interest.

"All those I could ascertain," said the Inspector firmly and with reproach. "There are five instances in which the assistant remembered, because he or she thought it queer; two doubtfuls; and one plain rude and unhelpful."

"Any description of the man?"

"Fair." The ex-inspector consulted his notes. "Tall, thin, sixty-ish, well-dressed, yellow face—that's some person's word alone—quiet, stranger to each office. Any good?"

"Good enough," said Mr. Campion. "Good enough for my own information. No good as evidence."

"I don't see why not." The inspector was hurt. "Some of them remember him clearly. The idea of him doing it tickled 'em. You know what these youngsters are nowadays."

"Oh, it's not your end. That's fine." Campion spoke soothingly. "It's the information received. That's the part of the story I couldn't pin down."

Ex-Inspector Beth's large face assumed a puzzled expression. He had never been a man who liked to see good work wasted, and now mentioned the fact in passing.

"For information received, was it?" he continued. "That makes it darker still to me. I can't see at all what you're driving at, Mr. Campion. The amounts were so small. If there was any hanky-panky you'd imagine they'd have been paid in cash."

Campion sat down. He felt the ex-inspector was entitled to an explanation, but had never felt less like making one in his life.

"Beth," he demanded, "have you ever met a woman who conveyed interested information without actually saying it?"

"Hinting?" enquired the inspector dubiously.

"No, not exactly." Campion hesitated, looking for the word. "A woman who gossiped to the point," he said at last. "She knows, and you know, that she's telling you something, and yet for reasons of discipline or dignity or discretion neither of you ever admits to the other that you are interested or she is informing. See what I mean?"

"Exactly."

Beth nodded sagaciously and Mr. Campion, finding it easier than he had expected, went on.

"Now suppose you want to reward such a woman. You want to encourage her and yet you don't want to commit yourself by giving her money in her hand. You can't trust her not to come out into the open with a direct question if you leave a pound note on her typewriter."

"Yes?"

"Well, suppose she sees your difficulty and one day you find her Post Office Savings Bank Book lying in your room. It may have been a mistake; it may not. What is to prevent you paying a pound or two in at an unfamiliar post office? If she likes to query it you know nothing about it. If she accepts the cash and it encourages her, well, you're on the same footing as you were before. You've never come off your pedestal. You've never descended to a familiar word. You've done it and yet you haven't done it."

"And if an old ex-policeman goes round asking questions?" murmured the practical Inspector Beth.

"Ah," agreed Mr. Campion, "but I don't think you're the sort of man who would imagine that possible. You're a conceited beggar. You think your dignity gives you a special pass to ignore enquiring policemen and all their works. It's your own personal dignity in relation to the woman who is your employee which counts with you. That's the sort of man you are."

"Oh, am I?" said the ex-inspector. "Well, in that case, Mr. Campion, you can take it from me that I might do abso-bally-lutely anything. What a tale! If you'll pardon a professional question, how did you get on to it?"

"She's that sort of woman," said Mr. Campion, and Beth was satisfied.

It was half an hour later before Campion got rid of him. Lugg was in lordly mood and in the vein for a bout with an old sparring partner, while the ex-inspector evidently had time to waste. Eventually, however, he departed and Campion was thinking affectionately of his bed when the telephone summoned him to his feet again.

"Hello, is that you, Campion?" The dry precise voice sent a thrill through him. "John Widdowson here. I got your note."

"Oh, yes?" Campion heard his own voice studiously noncommittal.

"You made a most natural mistake." The tone was conciliatory, but by no means ingratiating. "You've discovered the manuscript in the safe is a copy, of course. I don't think anyone knew that except myself. I congratulate you. It was made for my uncle many years ago and for reasons of extra-special safety I put it in the place of the real play, so that if there should be any attempt at theft I should be doubly protected. You follow me?"

"Perfectly." Campion's inflection was unmistakable.

"Good. Well, what I want to say is this. I feel that since you have made the discovery and it has evidently led you to a mistaken conclusion, I naturally very much want you to see the real manuscript, so that any—ah—unfortunate surmises you may have made can be contradicted. That's quite reasonable, isn't it?"

Mr. Campion's tired brain considered the concrete evidence he had gathered against the man at the other end of the wire and found it nil. He had no doubt that John Widdowson could have murdered his cousin, and in his heart he believed he had done so, but he realized that if the real *Gallivant* was still in the firm's possession the motive he had so carefully reconstructed was gone, and if there was no motive the strongest part of the case fell to the ground.

John was still speaking.

"I want you to see that manuscript and I want you to see it at once, so that you can concentrate on finding the truth. Mike's life is in danger. We've got to move quickly before those imbeciles decide to hang him. I'm in conference with Sir Alexander now. He's hopeful, I may tell you, but he realizes that it's going to be a hard fight. We're grateful for Rigget, Campion, but it's not enough."

There were urgency and anxiety in the voice not unmixed with a hint of reproof, and Mr. Campion found himself shaken by that rarest of the emotions, honest astonishment.

John went on.

"I'm a little irritated, naturally. Although I do see exactly how the misapprehension arose. You are a friend of poor Mike's, but you don't know me. We will say no more about that. I admit that were I unable to produce the genuine manuscript my own position might very well be open to question. I see that now, although it certainly gave me a shock when you pointed it out. I want you to see the real manuscript, Campion."

"I should like to." Campion sounded annoyed, in spite of himself.

"You must. You must see it at once. I want all your energies concentrated on Mike's trouble. Will you give me your promise that you'll settle this point tonight?"

Mr. Campion's weariness had given place to bewildered resignation.

"Yes, of course. I want to see it."

"You'll be able to recognize it, you think?"

"I think so."

"Splendid. It's not in a very inaccessible spot, thank God, but one of the safest I know, one where I keep things when I want them protected from the inquisitiveness of my own family. Do you know our Paul Jones premises?"

"No," said Campion, who felt like a child waiting to see what would happen next.

"They're in the phone book, of course." John was clearly trying to keep civil in the face of crass idiocy, and finding it difficult. "Eighty-seven, Parrot Street, Pimlico. It's a large building. Take a cab. Any driver will know it. I can't come with you myself, unfortunately, because I shall be closeted with Sir Alexander into the small hours. But I want you to go at once. You can't do anything useful while you're still on a wild-goose chase. You see that?"

Mr. Campion found himself thinking, quite unpardonably, that he had never been treated as a blundering employee before and that the experience was refreshing, stimulating and probably good for the soul. Aloud he said:

"All right. I'll go."

"You'd be behaving like a young ass if you didn't," said the voice, with some asperity. "I'll telephone to the caretaker to admit you on your card. He won't know where the manuscript is, of course. You'll have to find that yourself from what I tell you now. It's very simple. The last room on the fourth floor, that is to say, at the top of the building, is the directors' office. The room number is forty-five. If you forget it the caretaker will show you. In the room is a carved desk—oak or ebony, I forget which—and in the left-hand top drawer you will find the key of the cupboard. Open it, and the manuscript is in a newspaper parcel on the second shelf with two or three others. My uncle always kept it like that. His contention was that no one would look for it there or recognize it if they found it, and when he gave over he passed the tip on to me. Lock up after you, of course."

"Yes," said Mr. Campion meekly.

"I shall expect you to phone me later in the evening to tell me you're satisfied, and, perhaps—" the cold authoritative voice betrayed a hint of condescending amusement, "—to apologize. I'll phone the caretaker immediately. Oh, wait a moment; Sir Alexander may want to speak to you."

There was a considerable pause while, presumably, Cousin Alexander was fetched from another room, and then the magnificent voice rumbled over the wire.

"That you, Campion? I'm sorry, but I must have John here some time yet. Terribly sorry, my dear fellow, but anxious times, you know—anxious times. Good night."

Before Mr. Campion could reply he had gone and John had taken his place again.

"Go along and satisfy your mind, my boy," he said. "You'll know where you are then. As soon as you clear the line I'll ring Jenkinson. He'll be waiting for you. Good-bye."

Mr. Campion hung up the receiver and walked slowly back across the room. Standing by the window, looking down into the lamplit street, he tried to sort out thought from instinct and wished he were not so incredibly tired. That afternoon he had been sure of John's guilt. Even now, when he considered his painfully forged chain of half-facts, he could not believe that it was composed entirely of unrelated coincidences; and yet, if John were innocent, could he possibly have made any more reasonable move than the present one? On the other hand, if he were guilty, what could he hope to gain by the production of yet another faked manuscript, or even no manuscript at all?

There was one other alternative, and Campion considered it in cold blood. In the course of an adventurous career he had received many invitations which had subsequently proved to be not at all as innocent as they at first appeared, and the common or garden trap was not by any means unknown to him. And yet, in cold blood, the absurdity of such a suggestion in the present case was inclined to overwhelm every other aspect.

While he was still wavering there returned to his mind a maxim often expounded by old Sergeant McBain, late of H Division: "If you think it's a frame, go and see. Frames is evidence."

Mr. Campion put on his coat and had reached the front door when another thought occurred to him, and rather shamefacedly he returned to his desk and, taking a little Webley from its drawer, slid it into his pocket.

Leaning back in a taxi cab nearly fifteen minute later he surveyed Parrot Street, Pimlico, with interest. It was a long dingy road lined with solid slabs of Georgian housing, intersected by occasional side streets or great yawning gaps where demolition and rebuilding were in progress. Office staffs had long ago displaced the comfortable families for whom the houses were built, and at eight o'clock in the evening Parrot Street was a gloomy and deserted thoroughfare.

Number Eighty-seven was a dishevelled building. Its windows were dirty and uncurtained and here and there patches of plaster had chipped away, showing the brick beneath. One of its immediate neighbours had been taken down and huge wooden joists supporting the structure along one side did not add to its distinction. Altogether it was not a likely sister for the elegant Twenty-three, Horsecollar Yard.

The explanation, of course, was the old one. Like hairdressing and hotel-keeping, publishing is forced to be class-conscious, and just as front-rank restaurateurs are sometimes known to have smaller, cheaper establishments tucked away in the back streets, where, under less dignified names, money is made and odds and ends used up without waste, so sometimes distinguished publishing houses have humbler sisters where less rare but equally filling mental dishes are prepared and distributed.

Messrs. Paul Jones, Ltd. published children's picture-books, light love stories of the cheaper sort, translations, and a vast quantity of reprints, and were kept alive by the possession of some twenty or thirty copyrights of the great Fairgreen Fields' earlier works, which they republished at three and six, half a crown, one and three, one shilling, ninepence, sixpence, and fourpence simultaneously and over a period of years, without ever, apparently, overlapping or saturating any of that fine "blood" writer's many markets.

The firm was owned by Messrs. Barnabas, without being in any way affiliated to them socially, and was run by a separate staff.

The taximan pulled up outside the dilapidated doorway and Mr. Campion got out. The dirty transom showed a faint light in the entrance hall, and as soon as he knocked the door was opened by a woman as untidy and disheartened as the house itself.

"Me husband's hurt his foot," she said before he had time to open his mouth, "and I said for him not to move himself now he was got comfortable. I knew you wouldn't mind."

She looked up at him with a confiding leer which showed gappy teeth in pale gums.

A wail from the lighted doorway at the far end of the passage indicated that she was not in attendance upon her husband alone.

"I'm coming!" she shouted in a voice surprisingly raucous after her husky conversation tone. "See to 'im, Dad, do!"

Mr. Campion gave her his card, and she took it under the bulb to read.

"That's right," she said, with idiotic but ingratiating surprise. "Campion. That was the name Mr. Widdowson said. Shall I keep this, sir? D'you know where to go? It's Room Forty-five, right at the top of the 'ouse."

She glanced abjectly at the dusty wooden staircase and back again.

"I can turn on the 'all lights from 'ere," she added, and rubbed her hands on the back of her skirt.

Mr. Campion looked down at her.

"How long ago did your husband hurt his foot?" he enquired unexpectedly.

"Week last Monday. One of the van boys let a box down on 'im—clumsy young monkey! Mr. Widdowson said surely it was well by now. I didn't 'alf tell 'im off over the phone. 'Well,' I said, ''he's not an idol, Mr. Widdowson.'"

She spoke without heat or humour, and her tired face turned towards the stairs again. In the back room the baby roared.

"I'll come up with you if you like," she said.

Suddenly Campion laughed.

"Don't bother. Is the door locked?"

"Oh, no, sir. We're always here, you see. There's only this entrance and the one at the back which we use. Nobody could get in. You'll go up, then?"

"I will. I'll see you when I come down."

"Thank you, sir." He saw her quick hopeful smile and she wiped her hands again. "I'll just turn on the lights."

The beautiful staircase, which had been a Georgian housewife's pride and responsibility and was now a danger trap to van boys and caretakers, was flooded with dusty light as Campion set foot upon it.

The premises at Eighty-seven were even less attractive inside than out. The two lower floors were used as a warehouse and stretched out behind over what once had been a garden in vast ramifications of the book-producer's trade. The very air was thick with dust and the sweet, acrid smell of ink.

Campion went up slowly, his hand on the Webley. In spite of his conviction that the idea of attack was absurd, he took no risks. His senses were alert and he walked with quiet springy steps.

He was not disturbed. The rows of greasy doors on each landing were silent and no creaking board, either behind or above him, answered the tread of his own feet.

It was a long way up. He climbed steadily on, pausing only once to look down the well to the hall, small and far away below.

The fourth floor was a little cleaner than the rest of the house. One or two of the doors had been freshly painted, throwing the shabbiness of the walls into painful prominence, and there was a strip of floor-covering of sorts down the centre of the passage.

Outside room number forty-five he paused and stood for a moment, listening. The silence was everywhere. Very gently he tried the handle. It turned easily and the door swung open, revealing an apartment only faintly lit by the light from the street lamps below.

With his left hand, his gun in his right, he shone his torch round the room. It was unoccupied and appeared to be in normal order.

A glance at the light fixtures assured him that there was nothing untoward in that direction, and he turned over the switch.

It was a big room, comfortably furnished with that particular brand of red Turkey carpet which is to the City office what the bowler hat is to the City clerk, a bookcase, a few chairs and the desk of which John had spoken. The walls were covered with show-cards, book jackets and galleys of advertisements.

Mr. Campion looked for the cupboard door and saw two, one beside the desk, the other behind it. They were both used as notice boards, the wooden panelling being particularly suitable for the reception of drawing-pins. The miscellany hanging there told him little more than the date, several publication fixtures for books of which he had never heard, and the details of the train service to Chelmsford.

He did not hurry. In the back of his mind something was warning him of impending danger. Looking about him, the instinct seemed ridiculous, and he remembered that he was tired and probably jumpy.

He went over to the desk unwillingly and pulled open the first drawer on the left-hand side. It contained at first sight nothing more remarkable than a tin of biscuits and a pair of gloves, but after removing these cautiously he saw a key with a piece of string through the ring lying half under the paper with which the drawer was lined.

He took it out and looked at it suspiciously, but it was quite ordinary and of no particular interest in itself.

Feeling foolish but still puzzled, he carried it over to the door behind the desk.

It fitted the lock, but he did not get the door open until he realized with a wave of self-dislike that it opened outwards and was not even locked. He thrust it open and stepped back, taking out his torch once more.

The cupboard proved to be a cloak-room containing an incredibly dirty wash-basin and a row of clothes-hooks, upon one of which a dilapidated umbrella hung dejectedly.

He came out and went over to the other door. Once again he fitted the key in the lock, the old sense of danger assailed him, and he swung round to face the landing, but all was silent and dirty and ordinary as before.

Then, from far below, he heard a little angry sound, thin, high and furious. Mrs. Jenkinson's baby was protesting violently at some parental indignity. It was too much. Mr Campion cursed himself for his hysteria, his cowardice and his approaching age. He turned the bolt over and pulled the handle.

The jamb did not move and he remembered it probably opened outwards. He tried it gently, but it was stuck and he drew himself back to throw his shoulder against it.

That miraculous sense which is either second sight or the lightning calculation of the subconscious mind, which nothing escapes, arrested him, and, changing his mind on the instant, he pulled his gun and kicked the door open, police fashion.

For a moment it still stuck and then shattered open sickeningly and he stood overbalancing, shuddering horror fighting with the realization of a certainty.

There was nothing there at all; only the wide sky threadbare with stars and fringed with a million chimney-pots, and, far, far below him in the cool darkness, the jagged stone foundations of the house that had been next door.

19
Under the Sword

Miss Curley cleared her throat, pushed her hat a little further on to the back of her head, and wondered rather helplessly if the truth could be any more apparent after five days' talk, when it seemed to be so hopelessly hidden after one and a half.

At her side Gina sat immobile. All through the day she had preserved the same aloof expression. Her eyes were no longer dazed, but had assumed instead a settled coldness. Miss Curley was anxious about her.

In the luncheon recess she had taken the girl to a city restaurant and had made her eat, but she had done so without interest and had not talked.

Even John's absence, the non-appearance of Ritchie, and the unaccountable desertion of Mr. Campion had passed her by as unworthy of comment and only once, when Mike had been brought back into the dock, had she shown by a single quickening glance the least sign of interest in the proceedings.

Miss Curley's other neighbour, on the contrary, was evidently not only following, but enjoying, the case. He had reappeared at the morning session as eager as a child at a play, and Miss Curley, a patient, tolerant woman, had gradually become used to his muttered commentary.

The afternoon was very warm for the time of the year, and the sun shone on the dome, making the court comfortable and bright. Lord Lumley leant back in his high leather chair, his scarlet robe catching the sunlight and the colour flickering on the lenses of his eyeglasses. Before him the eternal bustle of the court continued.

Cousin Alexander sat in his place, his silk gown shining

and his eyes eloquent, ready at any moment to leap up an
pounce upon a witness.

The first three sessions of the enquiry had establishe
much of the Crown case and the Attorney-General ha
reason to be pleased with the way events were shaping. Th
jury now fully understood the mechanics of the crime. The
had examined the hose pipe, seen the photographs of th
strong room and garage, and had heard the medica
evidence.

They had also heard Mrs. Austin do her well-meaning
damnedest, and Mrs. Tripper had repeated her story of th
running car engine.

At the moment the red-headed and vivacious Robert
Jeeves, author of *Died on a Saturday*, was giving he
evidence, struggling between the desire to escape al
responsibility and a certain shy pride in having invented a
murder which would work.

She had, she said, no idea whether Mr. Michael
Wedgwood had read her book or not. It did happen some
times that a publisher did not read every book he spon
sored.

Was that not usually only in the case of well-estab
lished authors? Fyshe put the question innocently.

Miss Jeeves reluctantly supposed it would be, and
Counsel begged leave to enquire if Miss Jeeves considered
that she had been a well-established author at the time o
the publication of *Died on a Saturday*.

Miss Jeeves confessed with not unnatural irritation
that she had no idea.

Fyshe asked humbly if it were true that in view of the
complicated mechanics of the device described and the
faithfulness with which they had been executed in real life
Miss Jeeves had felt it her duty to call the attention of the
police to her book.

Miss Jeeves, holding strong views on the subject o
coincidence, was fairly embarked upon a dissertation upon
them when she was gently and courteously stopped by the
Judge.

Cousin Alexander did not cross-examine.

Miss Curley stirred and smiled nervously in reply to
her unknown neighbour's wink and nod of appreciation. She
looked round the court again. Until now she had believed

that court proceedings were tedious beyond all bearing and that the greatest ordeal participators had to face was one by ennui, but so far the effect of cumulative drama had never faltered and always just in front of her there had been that strong wide back of the young man she knew, who might be going to die.

Others might find the technicalities of doctors and central-heating experts dull, but to Miss Curley every word was of vital importance, every point reached her, and every time the jury whispered together her heart contracted painfully.

Miss Jeeves having returned to her seat, there was a rustle at Counsels' table. Fyshe sat down and the Attorney-General rose to examine as Peter Rigget stepped into the box.

His slightly dilapidated appearance was not enhanced by the green reading light which, shining down upon his papers, was reflected up into his face. He looked puffy because of Mr. Campion, unhealthy because of the light, and thoroughly vindictive, which was his own affair.

Miss Curley, who knew nothing about his secret self-deploration, had no sympathy for him at all.

"Strong case," whispered the man at her side. "Now they're coming to it . . ."

Miss Curley wondered if it was her imagination or that a new excitement was, in fact, growing in the big bright room. The Lord Chief Justice looked as placid as before, but there was certainly a rustle among the clerks and the jury leant forward to see the witness better.

It was evident at once that Mr. Rigget was aware of his importance. He even permitted himself a sickly nervous smile, which was rendered frankly horrific by the green light reflected in his glasses.

Cousin Alexander noticed the little man's self-satisfaction with grim approval.

Miss Curley glanced at Gina. The girl was very still; her eyes fixed upon the silent figure in the dock. It occurred to the older woman that she was praying.

The Attorney-General began gently in his softest, most ingratiating tone, and Mr. Rigget made his opening statement happily.

"I am an accountant employed by Messrs. Barnabas. I have known the accused and the deceased for about two years, ever since I came to work in the office. On January the twenty-seventh I went into the deceased's room at the office and on into the book-file room, which leads off it. When I entered the room the two men were talking. They ceased when they saw me, but when I went into the little office they continued their conversation."

"Was the door open or shut?"

"Open."

"Could you hear what was said?"

"Clearly."

"Can you repeat what you overheard, word for word?"

"I can."

"Is it not extraordinary that you should remember a chance conversation so clearly?"

"No, because it was an extraordinary conversation."

"Will you repeat it?"

Mr. Rigget considered and began in a slightly affected voice.

"Mr. Paul, the deceased, said: 'You mind your own damned business, Mike. She's mine. I'll manage my own life in my own way.' And then after a pause he said: 'Make love to her if you want to. God knows I'm not stopping you.'"

"Did you hear any more?"

"No. I came out then and they stopped talking."

"Did you see both men?"

"Of course."

"How close to them were you?"

"I passed quite close to Mr.—to the accused, within two feet."

"Did you notice anything about him?"

"He was very white. His hands were clenched. He looked as if he could—he looked very angry."

"Had you ever seen him like that before?"

"I had never seen him like that before."

Miss Curley's neighbour nudged her.

"They'll get him," he whispered jubilantly, and then, as she turned to him, coughed apologetically into his handkerchief and reddened round the ears.

Cousin Alexander rose majestically and scattered a sheaf of papers to the floor with the sleeve of his gown. While Mr. Rigget's attention was still distracted by the incident he put his first question.

"Some time before you entered the employment of Messrs. Barnabas, Limited, you were employed by Messrs. Fitch and Sons, paper merchants, were you not?"

Mr. Rigget started violently.

"Yes."

"Is it true that after you left them you gave evidence for the prosecution in an action brought against that firm by the Inland Revenue Department and were rewarded by that Department for information received?"

The Attorney-General sprang up and protested violently, and for the first time real heat was infused into the chill argument which had taken place between the two Counsels. Lord Lumley blinked at Cousin Alexander.

"I confess I don't see the purpose of such a question, Sir Alexander," he rumbled mildly.

Cousin Alexander bowed.

"I will not press it, My Lord," he said virtuously, and Mr. Rigget was sufficiently ill-advised to smile.

"Are you an accountant?"

"I am."

"Have you very little to do with the book publishing side of Messrs. Barnabas' business?"

"I suppose I have." Mr. Rigget spoke grudgingly.

"Is it true you do not know even the titles of all the books they publish?"

"No, not all," said Mr. Rigget nervously.

"Is it true that you did not know, for instance, that in January Messrs. Barnabas acquired the rights of an autobiography entitled *My Own Life*, by Lady Emily Trumpington?"

"No—o."

"Did you or did you not?"

Cousin Alexander's chill eyes suddenly reminded Mr. Rigget of the portrait in the waiting room.

"I may have heard of it."

"Did it occur to you then or does it occur to you now that what you really overheard the deceased say on the

215

occasion when you were 'overhearing' in the next office was: 'You mind your own damned business, Mike. She's mine. I'll manage *My Own Life* in my own way,' meaning, of course, the author, Lady Trumpington, is my client and I will manage her book—that is to say, I will publish her book—in my own way.'

"No," said Mr. Rigget, turning a dull brown in the green light. "No. I thought he was talking about his wife."

"You thought . . . !" began Cousin Alexander, apparently temporarily overwhelmed by the iniquity of fools, but recovering himself with pretty dignity. "What made you think that he was talking about his wife?"

"Well," said Mr. Rigget uncomfortably, "there had been a bit of talk in the office about Mrs. Brande and the accused carrying on, and I naturally thought—"

His voice trailed away.

"A bit of talk." Cousin Alexander's tone rose melodiously. "A bit of talk in the office. Tittle-tattle among the employees. A's wife has been seen with B, and so when A and B talk heatedly it must be about Mrs. A. Is that how you reasoned, Mr. Rigget?"

"I—I may have done."

Lord Lumley leant forward.

"When you heard the words 'my own life,' did they sound like the title of a book? Were they said with equal emphasis on each word, or on one or two words only?"

The quiet affable question brought the whole tricksy business back to earth again, out of the realms of cleverness into the quiet line of enquiry the results of which should determine if Mike was to hang by the neck until he was dead.

Mr. Rigget dithered while the court held its breath.

"I can't remember," he said at last, and the ready tears which were such a constant source of embarrassment to him crept into his eyes.

Cousin Alexander let the admission sink in before he tackled the next stage of his enquiry.

"You have told us that you cannot remember the inflection on the words 'my own life,'" he said quietly. "Are you sure that you remember the words 'make love to her if you want to, God knows I'm not stopping you'? You are sure you heard them?"

"I am sure."

"Did the accused say anything at all while you were in the inner office?"

"Nothing."

"Are you saying that you heard him say nothing?"

"I heard nothing."

"Might he have whispered?"

"No. I should have heard him if he had."

"Were you listening carefully?"

"I was."

"Were you remembering everything you heard?"

"Everything."

"And yet you are not sure if the deceased was talking about his own life or the title of a book."

"That's your suggestion," sneered Mr. Rigget.

"Yes, it is," said Cousin Alexander, with lightning heat. "And it is also my suggestion that in order to convince yourself that you had heard Mr. Brande talking about his wife, you imagined the second part of the statement."

"No."

Cousin Alexander took a deep breath.

"Consider those two remarks, first side by side and then concurrently. Do you think they could have been made by the same man, the same man in the same mood and on the same point? Are they not directly contradictory? 'I'll manage my own married life in my own way; make love to my wife if you want to.' Taken together, do they not sound absurd?"

"I heard it," said Mr. Rigget obstinately.

"I suggest," said Cousin Alexander, "that you thought you heard it."

"No, I heard it."

"Is it possible, Mr. Rigget, that you may have been mistaken in what you heard?"

There was a blessed quality of moral absolution in the word "mistaken," and Mr. Rigget fell for it.

"Perhaps," he said, and Cousin Alexander sighed.

"Do you like the accused?—or rather, is it true that you bear no grudge against him?"

"I hardly know him."

"Yet you knew the intimate affairs of his life. You knew he had been 'carrying on' with Mrs. Brande."

"I had heard it."

"Do you think now that you may have been mistaken?"

"I had heard it."

"May it have been untrue?"

"It may."

Cousin Alexander began to enjoy himself. His elation, which had been slowly growing ever since Mr. Rigget had entered the box, was shared by all those whose personal feelings were not harrowed by the case. Throughout the last part of the cross-examination people had been coming into the room. Barristers from other courts slipped in unobtrusively and the undercurrent of whispers which broke out in every pause became a natural part of the proceedings.

Miss Curley was stirred by the excitement of it all, in spite of herself. She could not help reacting to the general animation which had arisen so suddenly. It frightened her. She felt that it was at moments like these when mistakes were made, but she could feel the exhilaration and her neighbour was quite frankly beside himself with delight.

There was so much movement going on all round the room that she did not notice that the Attorney-General had left the court. It was Gina who called her attention to the fact.

"Where's Sir Montague Brooch gone?" she whispered. "A note was brought in to him and he hurried out. Did you see? Where's Albert Campion? They'll need him, won't they? Something's happening."

Miss Curley realized with a shock of self-reproach that the different atmosphere in the court had not registered upon the girl. Gina was concerned only with the truth and the man in the dock. Cousin Alexander's dexterities had passed her by.

"I don't notice anything," she whispered back, and before she had time to consider the suggestion Cousin Alexander began again.

"We will leave for a moment the question of what you do and do not remember, Mr. Rigget," he said graciously, "what you are sure you heard and what you cannot remember if you heard, and go on to something which happened so short a while ago that I am sure you will have no difficulty in calling it to mind. I put it to you that you visited the strong room where the deceased was found after office hours on the ninth of this month on the eve of this trial. Did you or did you not?"

Mr. Rigget's glance turned nervously towards the prosecution and he saw for the first time that Sir Montague Brooch was not present. Sir Alexander was still waiting.

"Did you or did you not?"

"I may have done."

"Come, come, Mr. Rigget, that's no answer to a perfectly straightforward question. It is now Thursday. Did you on Tuesday night go down to the strong room of the office where you are employed after office hours?"

Again Mr. Rigget looked round helplessly, and this time even Miss Curley was aware that something untoward was afoot. Cousin Alexander's junior tugged his gown and slipped a note into his hand, and at the same time the Clerk, who had been in conference for some minutes with Fyshe, rose and whispered to the Judge.

Mr. Rigget, finding himself temporarily forgotten, said "Yes" sulkily, and the whole court waited.

"'Ullo? 'Ullo?" murmured Miss Curley's unknown neighbour expressively, and at the same time Gina caught the older woman's hand.

"I told you something had happened. What is it? More evidence against Mike? I can't bear it, Curley, I can't bear it!"

"Hush, dear, hush," said Miss Curley, patting the hand she held and moistening her lips with the tip of her tongue.

Cousin Alexander bustled out of court and his junior rose to take his place. The Clerk still stood whispering and Lord Lumley, looking more like a very old and very wise bloodhound than ever, sat forward, his head on one side. Now and again he nodded gravely and sometimes put a muttered question, which was answered by more whispered volubility from the Clerk.

The junior for the defence repeated Cousin Alexander's last question and received the same sulky reply from Mr.

Rigget, but its importance was lost. The jury were whispering heatedly, and only the little group in the dock sat stolidly silent, waiting.

"While you were there, what did you do?"

"I looked for things."

"Were you on the firm's business?"

"Yes."

"Did anyone from the office know you were there?"

"They may have done."

Mr. Rigget's eyes were snapping. He saw his opportunity and was taking it. The junior had no terrors for him, and he saw his chance to deny the truth of the statement he had made in Mr. Scruby's office. He supposed he could get that respected firm of solicitors and the odious Mr. Campion into the devil of a row if he played his cards carefully.

Looking up, he saw Mike's eyes resting upon him, and he turned away hastily from that pale unhappy face.

"Will you tell the court what was the nature of the business on which you were engaged in the strong room at that unlikely hour?"

The fact that the court was certainly not listening to anything Mr. Rigget might have to tell unnerved the young barrister and the question lacked authority.

"I was looking up some royalty accounts for our department," said Mr. Rigget mendaciously, and remembered suddenly that perjury is a crime.

"Had you any authority to do that?"

"No, but I like to do my job thoroughly."

The whispered conversation at the bench had ceased, and now Sir Andrew Phelps was talking to the Clerk.

The cross-examination went on its desultory way.

"While you were there were you disturbed?"

"Yes, I was. I was set upon and nearly killed."

"Did you not attack the man who discovered you there?"

"No, he attacked me."

"You must be more explicit. Did your assailant come straight into the room and hit you?"

The quiet voice from the bench at his side startled Mr. Rigget out of his wits. Under cover of the mysterious upheaval which seemed to have distracted the entire court, he had been happily chirruping on. Now it was as though God had stretched out a great finger and pinned an impudent sparrow to the gate. He gasped.

"No. I went out to see who it was, and he hit me then."

Counsel continued.

"Did you turn on the light?"

"No, I ran out into the passage in the dark."

Mr. Rigget's face grew rigid after he had spoken. His eyes blinked piteously and he trembled, waiting for the next question.

It was a very long time in coming, and at last he looked up in sheer desperation, only to see the Attorney-General and Cousin Alexander back at the table again. Both men seemed slightly excited. There was a flush on Sir Montague Brooch's thin dark cheekbones and Cousin Alexander was forcing a smile, which was clearly not genuine. There was a pause. The Attorney-General looked at the Judge, and when His Lordship nodded to him imperceptibly he rose.

"My Lord—" the beautiful voice was a little thin, "—in view of certain circumstances which have arisen, and of which I understand Your Lordship is already aware, it is the intention of the prosecution to call no further evidence."

Before the words were finally out of his mouth, Cousin Alexander was on his feet beside him. Even in that moment of bewilderment it flashed through Miss Curley's mind that his agility was extraordinary for his age and weight. An usher signalled Mr. Rigget out of the box, and was too startled to notice whether he obeyed.

"My Lord," said Cousin Alexander, "in view of my learned friend's decision, it is my duty to demand a verdict from the jury."

Mr. Rigget was still in the box, forgotten and too terrified to move.

The Lord Chief Justice cleared his throat and tapped gently with his eyeglasses upon the vivid sleeve of his robe.

"Yes, Sir Alexander," he said in a quiet unemotional voice which temporarily robbed, for Miss Curley at least, his words of their momentous meaning. "I think that is a very proper request."

He turned to the jury, where they sat gaping at him like a double row of somebody's stupid relations, and addressed them simply.

"Members of the Jury, as you have just heard, certain circumstances have arisen which have caused the prosecution to decide to call no further evidence in this case. That means the Crown does not press the charge against the accused. Therefore it is my duty to direct you to find the prisoner not guilty and to acquit him of the charges which have been brought against him. Do you understand?"

There was a mutter in the jury-box, too confused and hasty to be dignified by the word "consultation," and the foreman stumbled to his feet with a nervous nod.

"We have—I mean we do, My Lord, Not guilty, My Lord."

As the jury writhed and murmured, overcome with delight and relief, the Judge addressed the prisoner. Mike rose stiffly to his feet. He looked young, broken, and inexpressibly alone in the great bare dock. The Judge's voice was very kind.

"Michael Wedgwood, you have been found not guilty of the charges brought against you. You may go."

The young man stood quite still. The whispering around him turned into a roar, and Cousin Alexander hurried over to him.

" 'S'truth," said the man next to Miss Curley, as they rose while the Judge made his stately exit, his flowers in his hand, "what's happened now?"

Gina clutched Curley's arm.

"I want to get out!" she said wildly. "I want to get out!"

Miss Curley put her arm round Gina's shoulders and they were swept by an excited throng to the doorway. Mike was surrounded, she saw, and it occurred to her that it would be better if the two young people did not leave the court together.

What's happened? Why? What's happened? The question overtopped all the other crowding thoughts racing through her bewildered mind. Mike free—no need for Gina to give evidence—what's happened?—where are they all?—what's happened?

Over her shoulder she had her last glimpse of the court, the empty bench, the sword, the coats-of-arms, the excited throng, wigs, bands and silk gowns shining in the sunlight under the dome, and the witness-box with Mr. Rigget still inside it, peeping out like a bewildered green parrot in a cage.

What's happened?

They came out into Newgate Street, running almost, with the weight of the crowd behind them. The sun shone in their eyes and the hubbub of the traffic surged about them.

What's happened? With the return from the slightly *Alice in Wonderland* atmosphere of the court to the sturdy matter-of-factness of a London afternoon the question became urgent.

"What's happened?" The words themselves were on her lips when Gina stopped abruptly on the pavement. "Look!" she said huskily.

An old man in a ragged raincoat, who wore three out-of-date hospital flags in his cap, was leaning against a brilliant pillar-box, an apron of newspaper bills round his waist.

WEDGWOOD TRIAL
MAN DEAD

Miss Curley's eyes let her down. She took the paper the old man proffered her and fumbled with it blindly.

"What's happened?"

Gina's voice sounded very harsh and far away.

Miss Curley was aware of a red, unshaven Cockney face and two very bright sparrow eyes looking at her with kindly curiosity.

"There it is, lady, right on the first page. It happened this morning, but trust the perlice to keep it dark until they knoo what was what. 'John Widdowson, cousin of the man on trial, found dead.' Look, Ma, *there.*"

Miss Curley did not speak. She was staring through the paper and her shoulders shook a little.

"Found dead in 'is bath, killed the same way as the

other bloke was, with carbon monoxide gas. 'Ousekeeper found 'im."

The paper-seller supplied the details out of pure kindness of heart.

"Suicide," said Gina, and drew a long breath.

"Very likely," agreed the old man, politely noncommittal. "But it looks to me as if the perlice thought it was murder. What price the case for the prosecution now? Get you a taxi, lady?"

20
The Fourth Dimension

It was nearly dark in the hallway at Twenty-one when Mike came home. He was alone. Because of John's death there was a man on the outside door and reporters, friends and sightseers were temporarily kept at bay.

He came slowly down the passage, feeling for his second key. His lean figure did not droop, but some of the dignity of his ordeal still clung to him, and he looked unapproachable, like a man in great grief.

As he paused to open the door a shadow detached itself from the darkness of the first half-landing and came slowly down to meet him. It was Gina.

She looked smaller and thinner then he remembered her, and her old quiet self-assurance had gone, leaving her pretty and young but not a commanding personality.

"Hallo, Mike," she said.

He paused and looked at her awkwardly, wishing she had not come.

"Hallo, Gina."

There was a painful silence and she stood on the bottom step, hesitating.

"I'm glad you're free."

"Thank you."

There was another gap, and he felt weary and very glad he could not see her face.

"It's terrible about John." Her voice had a quiver in it, and, because he could not bear any more emotion and because he felt sick and so flat that the Day of Judgment might have come and he been overlooked, he snubbed her.

"Quite terrible," he said over his shoulder, and he bent to unlock the door.

He did not step inside instantly, but turned back apologetically. She was in the passage and the light from the door caught her face.

"I'm tired, old girl," he said awkwardly. "Hopelessly tired." He went in and shut the door. The girl went quietly upstairs.

On the threshold of his sitting room Mike stopped abruptly. Mr. Campion was sitting there alone.

"Have a drink?" he suggested, raising a glass.

Without a word the newcomer helped himself from a decanter and siphon on the elbow-table and accepted a cigarette. He did not speak until he was seated and had half finished his glass. Then he looked at his friend and a hint of the old lazy humour returned to his eyes.

"What a mess," he said.

Mr. Campion stretched himself.

"The best possible thing in a way," he murmured depreciatingly.

"We couldn't have brought him to trial, poor chap, even if we'd felt like it."

"Alexander's been telling me." Mike shook his grey-black head. "I was in a bedroom at his club, hiding from newspapermen, while he was talking to you. Poor old chap! He seems quite cut up. I think he'd been looking forward to his speech in my defence. I was sorry I missed you, but I've heard all about *The Gallivant* and the fire escape and—"

"—the ever-open door," murmured Mr. Campion. "But I forgot, you don't know about that. John was a difficult chap. This was the best way."

"It was suicide, wasn't it?" Mike put the question anxiously. "Cousin Alexander struck me as being a trifle

reticent on that point. What happened exactly? How did h
die?"

Mr. Campion sipped his whiskey.

"At nine o'clock this morning," he said, "John turne
on the bath in his flat, locking the door probably out of forc
of habit, although he was alone in the apartment. Mrs. Pee
had been called out, so he had to light the geyser himsel
The window wouldn't open—stuck or something—and h
was shut in with that awful old brass death-trap, one of th
first geysers ever produced, I should think. Water takes o
the stink of carbon monoxide, you know, and very little o
the beastly stuff can do you in. Anyway, when Mrs. Pee
returned at about eleven o'clock she found the door stil
locked and, getting no reply to her knock, she got th
janitor up and they forced the door open. John was in th
bath, his head under the water. He had passed out with th
gas and slipped under. Actually he was drowned."

Mike sat up and passed his hand wearily over hi
forehead.

"It sounds like an accident to me," he said. "How di
I—I mean, how did it affect me?"

Mr. Campion blinked at him.

"Mrs. Peel had the presence of mind not to raise
general alarm. She phoned Tanner and he came herein
round to find that the vent-pipe on the geyser had bee
bunged up with a towel. You can reach it quite easily from
the fire escape. From one or two other things Tanner bega
to suspect he'd made a mistake. Very soon he was quite sur
he had. I had a little yarn to tell him which had a bearing o
the case, and finally he did the necessary. The police don'
want to convict the innocent, you know! That's the on
thing they say their prayers about."

"What an extraordinary way to commit suicide," sai
Mike. "I suppose John thought it was self-explanatory, sinc
he left no note."

Mr. Campion nodded absently. There were one or tw
points which he had no intention of mentioning at th
moment. One of them was that the bathroom window ha
been wedged from the outside and another that th
telegram which had summoned Mrs. Peel to her marrie

daughter's untelephoneable house in East Putney had not been sent by the lady whose name appeared as its signature.

Mike leaned back and closed his eyes.

"It's true, Campion," he said. "The awful thing is that it's not a nightmare. It's happened."

"Let's clear off," said Campion unexpectedly. "Let's go abroad. Miss Curley is cut up now, but she'll get over it and running the office will—er—take her mind off things. Besides, you've got some good men. A personal telephone call to each author will keep the business sweeter than anything; that's one thing, authors do understand the desire for solitude."

A flicker of interest appeared in Mike's eyes.

"It wouldn't be bad."

"I'll hold you to it," said Campion. "Going to stay here alone now?"

"No. Jimmy Bengers was in court. He came up to me after the trial and suggested he should come round this evening. Know him?"

"The golfer?"

"That's him. He'll be here any minute now. Good chap, Jimmy. Understands how to shut up. I've know him all my life. Ritchie will roll in too, I expect. I suppose someone's told the poor old beggar about everything?"

"I suppose so," said Mr. Campion vaguely. "I say, I think I'll go now. I've got one or two things to look into. I'll phone you in the morning."

He left Mike in the armchair and had the satisfaction of passing Mr. James Bengers in the outside hall. That large young man had a straw-covered bottle in one hand, a hamper in the other and a hastily caught-up toothbrush peeping shyly from his breast pocket.

Mr. Campion nodded to the man on duty and pushed his way through the crowd on the pavement. Afterwards he went down to Scotland Yard and stayed there for some time, talking to Superintendent Stanislaus Oates, an old friend who had much that was interesting to tell him.

It was just after ten when he returned at last to Bottle Street, and was met by Lugg in the hall of the flat. Lugg was wearing his collar, a certain portent of strange company, and Campion's heart sank. Lugg was indignant.

"Bloomin' ex-rozzer," he murmured in an all-too audible undertone. "Old Beth's bad enough for one wee and all right in 'is way, but this chap's never bin more than *sergeant*. Can't get rid of 'im. You 'ave a try."

Had Miss Curley been with Mr. Campion as he entered the sitting room she would have recognized the visitor immediately. Mr. Campion saw a large, oldish ex policeman, with a round red face and very bushy eyebrows who rose as he appeared and grinned at him in a fashion both shy and friendly.

"Mr. Campion, I presume?" he said. "I'm Mr. Living stone, late of the Met-ro-politan Police. You'll have to excuse me calling on you so late in the evening, but I'm off on the six-forty back to Norwich to-morrow."

The mention of the Norfolk town brought a great light to Mr. Campion, and to Lugg's disgust he shook the newcomer's hand warmly.

"This is an Act of God," he said. "You're the man I want to see. Higgleton sent you, I suppose?"

"Yes." Mr. Livingstone sat down again and accepted the drink Campion offered him. "Old Charlie Higgleton and me are what you'd call friends, although we don't see much of each other now I've retired. On the quiet, I came up for the trial," he added confidentially. "I like to keep in touch with old times, as it were, and when I see a certain firm was implicated, in which I was interested because of a funny thing which happened in the past, I said to my wife, 'I'll have to go and see that.' And so I came."

"Did you get in?"

Mr. Livingtone drooped a heavy eyelid.

"There's ways and means," he said darkly, "naming no names, of course. But we—er—we—" He hesitated.

"Old blues?" suggested Mr. Campion affably.

Mr. Livingstone beamed.

"Exactly. We police, we stick together and remember old pals. The end come a a real shock to me this afternoon. I thought the youngster was for it."

He looked at Campion enquiringly, but his host did not

rise to the implied question, and after a pause he continued.

"Well, when I went back to Charlie's, where I'm staying, and was talking about it and about old times, he remembered you and found your card. I recollected seeing your name in connection with the case, so I hopped on a bus and here I am."

Mr. Campion purred over him.

"You're providential," he said. "Tell me, did Mr. Higgleton tell you about our conversation in the spring?"

Mr. Livingstone looked pointedly at Lugg, and when that excellent person had been persuaded to leave them he smiled self-consciously at Campion.

"It's not a tale to put about," he murmured apologetically, "but since you was interested I thought I'd like you to hear my side of it. We're referrin' to a certain party who disappeared about twenty years ago, aren't we?"

"That's right," said Campion. "Tom Barnabas was walking down the road from Nemetia Crescent, Streatham, when he vanished."

"And was never seen of more," added Ex-Sergeant Livingstone in a voice so sepulchral that Campion jumped. "Well, since you're interested I may tell you it's true. It was a sunny May morning with a touch of mist in the air and that shimmery look on the pavements and the trees. Mr. Barnabas was walking along the road on the side nearest the wall. Charlie Higgleton saw 'im and went in to get his paper for 'im, and I was standing on the corner on the opposite side of the road. I saw 'im coming and I recognized 'im. I didn't watch 'im closely, of course—why should I? I didn't know 'e was going to walk into the fourth dimension."

"Of course not," agreed Mr. Campion reasonably.

"It's a high wall," said his visitor. "You've seen it, so you know. As high as the top of 'is silk hat. I mention it because him being against it, as it were, he stood out very clear, if you take me."

Mr. Campion nodded comprehendingly and Livingstone went on earnestly.

"When he was about a hundred yards away from me on the opposite side of the road, and there wasn't another soul in sight, I looked away from him and glanced into Charlie's shop. But I could still see Mr. Barnabas, although it was only out of the tail of me eye and I wasn't really lookin' at him. You follow me?"

"Perfectly."

"Well, 'e vanished," said Mr. Livingstone, staring at Campion with boot-button eyes.

Mr. Campion was suitably impressed.

"Look here," he said, "let's get this right. When you looked once he was there, and when you looked a second time he wasn't."

"No, that was the funny thing," said Mr. Livingstone. "I saw 'im out of the corner of me eye the whole time. I saw 'im go."

"Did you, by Jove? Which way?"

"He went . . . up," said Mr. Livingstone.

There was a slightly uncanny silence and Mr. Campion rose.

"Higher than the wall?" he enquired at last.

"I think he did. I remember him melting into the foliage above the wall and then 'e was gone. It happened like *that*."

He struck one palm noiselessly against the other, an oddly expressive gesture.

"Of course I didn't report it quite like that at the station," Mr. Campion's visitor continued in a different tone. "We wasn't used to miracles twenty years ago, and if I'd gone to the Inspector and said I'd seen a big heavy bloke in a top hat, tail coat, white spats and gold-headed cane disappear into thin air in front of me very eyes I'd have been sent to the doctor and never heard the end of it all me born days. So I took the wise course, and you'll see in my reports that I saw 'im coming along and I looked away, and after that I didn't notice 'im any more. I thought he must have gone into the shop. It was Charlie Higgleton who stuck to the miracle story, although it was me who saw it. That was a funny road altogether. On the other side of the wall was a garden full of snakes. A woman used to breed 'em. London's a rum place. I miss it sometimes up there in Norwich. London's got the fascination of a girl you never quite get to know."

He made the final remark regretfully and without affectation.

Mr. Campion was silent for some time. Finally he looked up.

"Do you like miracles?" he enquired.

"Like 'em?"

"Do you mind them explained?"

"Oh, I see what you mean." Mr. Livingstone had the honesty to hesitate, and his host liked him for it. "Yes," he said at last. "Yes, I'd like to know what really happened. He wasn't never seen again, you know."

Mr. Campion went to the cupboard in the bureau and, after rummaging for some time in its depths with his back towards his visitor, he suddenly swung round, his left arm outstretched.

"Look," he commanded.

Mr. Livingstone's eyes bulged and he sprang to his feet with an exclamation. A particularly murderous-looking knife was sticking through Campion's forearm with about three inches of crimson blade projecting from the side opposite the hilt.

Mr. Campion was apologetic.

"Sorry to startle you," he said. "I thought you'd probably seen these things. They sell 'em at the toyshops. It's a sort of bracelet, see?"

He took the contraption off his arm and revealed its secret, which was no more mysterious than a half circle of steel wire connecting the hilt with a three-inch length of painted blade.

Ex-Sergeant Livingstone took a child-like delight in the trick.

"You startled me!" he said, chuckling. "I thought, 'Lumme! 'E's barmy,' before I see you laugh."

"Yes, well, there you are. There's the explanation of your miracle." Mr. Campion sounded a little regretful.

His visitor was still puzzled.

"Do you mean it was a trick wall, sir?" he ventured dubiously. "I dare say you know best, sir, but I knew that road pretty well and I'd have known at once if there was anything funny about the wall."

231

"Oh, no, not a trick wall," said Mr. Campion. "A trick man."

"A trick man, sir?"

"Yes, look here. Suppose if instead of a stolid city gentleman advancing on middle age you'd seen a great strong fellow in shorts and a singlet striding down the road towards you; and if you had read a poster which told you that Mr. Tom Barnabas, the vaulting champion of the world, was going to perform; and if, while you were looking at him, he suddenly swung up an enormous right arm, and caught the top of the wall, which was six foot ten high, and pulled himself over it as swiftly and neatly as a dog swallows a chunk of fish, would you still have thought it a miracle? No. You'd have thought what a first-class performance it was."

Mr. Livingstone took some moments to digest this revelation.

"Was Mr. Barnabas a champion vaulter, sir?" he said. "I never heard that."

"No," said Campion. "He wasn't. That's why it was such a good trick. I don't even know if there were such things; but he could walk upstairs on his hands and I imagine that he had one or two other accomplishments of a like nature. He also had a sense of theatre and I suspect a touch of humour."

"But the snakes . . ." protested Mr. Livingstone, impressed in spite of himself. "The garden on the other side of that wall was full of snakes."

Mr. Campion eyed the ex-sergeant.

"I think he was probably very fond of snakes," he said. "And I think he knew those particular creatures very well."

"Well!" said Mr. Livingstone, and was silent.

He sat quiet for some little time and finally glanced up wistfully.

"You've got it," he said. "I remember now after all these years I caught a glimpse of him turnin' in the air and I thought he was going up in a sort of spiral. But when I got me head round he was gone. Still," he added, taking leave of his miracle with reluctance, "what about his belongings, if he disappeared on purpose? He left everything, you know. Money in the bank as well."

"I think," said Mr. Campion, with deliberation, "that he only took one piece of luggage into the fourth dimension, and he sent that in advance."

It was clear that he did not mean to dilate further upon the subject, and Mr. Livingstone did not press him. The explanation of his miracle had saddened him and he was subdued.

Gradually, however, his thoughts drifted from the past to the present and he sat up.

"I'll be going," he said. "It's late. Thank you very much for your information, sir. It's explained a lot to me. I'm glad you told me, I am really. I wonder if you could tell me one other thing? In the present case the Crown stopped that trial because the police believed there'd been another murder done in exactly the same way as the first, and probably by the same man. Now are they going to hunt out the murderer, or are they going to let the papers think it was a case of suicide done in remorse and leave things alone?"

Campion looked at him, heavy-eyed.

"My dear chap, I don't know," he said, and his voice was sharp with anxiety. "I only wish I did."

After his visitor had gone he flung himself down in his chair and stared morosely at the carpet, a strange heaviness in his heart. For what he had not told Mike, and what the police were so far attempting to hide from the Press, was the indisputable fact that at eight o'clock that morning Mr. Ritchie Barnabas had paid his bill at his lodgings, divided his personal effects impartially between his landlady and his landlady's husband, and had gone out ostensibly to take his annual holiday and had vanished as utterly and unobtrusively as his brother had done twenty years before.

21
The Spangled Frill

It was September, and the hot airs of the long summer were beginning to be dispersed by the light breezes which precede the mistral, when Mr. Campion and Mike stood upon the long concrete platform of the railway station at Avignon and waited for the Paris train.

It was just dusk and inside the walls of the city the plane trees were making high tents against the sky, while down in the *place* the rival cafés jostled each other off the cobbles, the different colours of their painted chairs alone proclaiming their irregular boundaries.

Both men looked well and exceedingly pleased with themselves. Mike especially was frankly jubilant, as every now and again he glanced at his wrist-watch.

"I still think we ought to have gone on to Paris," he said. "I can't see why you're so insistent about staying here. Of course, I am very grateful to you. I shouldn't have sent that wire by myself. I hope it'll be all right though: this isn't exactly a pleasure city."

"It's a lovely town," said Mr. Campion, with dignity. "The French Colchester. When you compare the two you see the essential differences between the French and English temperaments. We've had a nice vulgar holiday all over the show, and this is journey's end, and very nice, too."

Mike grunted, and after a pause glanced at his friend sharply.

"I don't want to butt in," he said diffidently, "but have you had any idea in your mind while we've been gadding about?"

"Idea?" echoed Mr. Campion, a trifle hurt.

"Well, purpose. All this trip, ever since May, you've

been jittering around the Continent like an agitated tourist. We've avoided the cities, but I should think we've visited every second-size town in Italy, Dalmatia and France, stayed about ten minutes and rushed off again. Now at last you've settled down in Avignon of all places. Found anything?"

Mr. Campion was silent. He did not appear to have heard. Mike hesitated.

"Don't think I'm not grateful," he went on seriously. "I am. I've got everything in perspective now and my own troubles don't quite fill up the landscape any more. I had a line from Curley. Everything seems to have blown over. It seems extraordinary when you think back, but people soon forget. The latest rumpus in our world is the autobiography row. The author's hiding in a nursing home terrified of all the angry females who haven't been put in the book."

He laughed shortly, and Campion, eyeing him, decided that his cure was practically complete.

"Train's due," he said.

"Is it?" Mike swung round and gazed up the track and Mr. Campion felt himself forgotten.

The engine came roaring in, and instantly the dozens of recumbent blue figures who had hitherto lain moribund sprang to vociferous life and, amid all the excitement of the arrival of the winners in a motor rally, the daily mid-evening train drew in.

The door of the Pullman burst open and Campion heard Mike's "Gina" above the parrot-house hubbub all round him.

She stepped out, radiant and coolly excited, and Campion, who had a proper respect for any woman who could end a twelve-hour summer journey in a Paris-Sud train looking as though she had stepped out of a bandbox rather than an ash-pit, admired her elegance.

She did not see him at first. Mike absorbed her complete attention.

"I got your wire," she was saying as Campion drifted up to them.

Mike held her at arms' length, his eyes eloquent, although his words were hardly inspired.

"And you came?"

"I came," she said quietly, and he caught his breath as she linked her arm through his.

Mr. Campion shook hands hastily and said he was going to the circus. They watched him stride off, a long, thin, inoffensive figure, personable, but by no means arresting.

"We owe him a lot, that one," the girl remarked quietly.

"Too much," said Mike fervently. "I daren't think of it. Look here, sweetheart, you've got to hurry. The chef of the hotel is waiting for you. He tells me he is a man of perception. I'm afraid he may come and cry over us."

She laughed and they stepped out of the station together and climbed into the crazy old *voiture* which was to carry them into the walled city.

Mr. Campion crossed the bridge over the wide, lazy Rhone, reflecting idiotically that the new bridge was better than the old Pont d'Avignon of the nursery rhyme because there was enough of it to reach to the other side.

It was a magnificent dusky evening, the air soft and tainted by the wine-presses and jubilant with the excitement of autumn, which is so much more comfortable than the excitement of spring.

In the fields on the other bank of the river, on the road to Villeneuve, the *cirque* was already established. It was not a grand affair, designed to attract the *tourisme*, but a little noisy jollification for the natives now that the visitors had gone and left a few spare centimes behind them.

There was one big tent, five or six side-shows mainly of the freak variety, and a cluster of painted living wagons. Electric light bulbs strung on yards of dangerous cable sprawled everywhere and the Provençal *en toute famille* laughed and joked about the frankly comic sides of ordinary life which seem to be so very offensive if one is not amused.

The show in the big tent would not begin for half an hour, and Campion, having seen the spider lady and the tallest Ethiopian in the world, found himself outside the largest of the living wagons. This was a slightly baroque affair, decorated with the Queen of Sheba on one side and a view of Naples on the other, and glittered with brass rails and several varieties of scroll-work. A man sat upon the steps reading a newspaper by the light of a festoon of coloured bulbs draped over the wagon.

He was a large man, still tough at sixty and very fine to look at, in spite of a pink shirt, stiff collar, tight black trousers and Texan sombrero. There were two diamond rings on his fingers and his shoes were English hand-sewn.

He looked up at Campion, who saw his face and rejoiced.

"M'sieu'?" he enquired.

Campion presented him with his card. The stranger took it between an enormous finger and thumb and sat looking at it thoughtfully for some time. Campion bent forward.

"I came to tell you," he said quietly in French, "that John Widdowson killed his cousin Paul Brande, and afterwards, when he was discovered, was found dead in his bath. The general opinion in England now is that he committed suicide."

"And the police? What do they think?"

"The police," explained Mr. Campion, "preserve an open mind. There is one whom they would interview if they found him, but I do not think they are looking for him. As long as he does not reappear . . ." He shrugged his shoulders expressively.

The man rose to his feet and held out his hand.

"How d'you do?" he said in English. "Let me introduce you to Madame."

He went slowly up the steps and bent his head to enter the caravan. He was extremely tall, a giant of a man, with the long supple muscles of an acrobat. Campion caught a few of the murmured words within.

"*Un ami vrai . . . absolument. C'est lui . . . le jeune gen lui-même. Ne vous enquietez pas.*"

There was a rustle and Madame appeared. She was large, dark and gracious, wearing a trifle too much jewellery for camping, perhaps, but she gave Mr. Campion her hand and flashed her black eyes at him and he liked her, snakes, diamonds and all.

They entertained him on the steps. It was a warm night, and it occurred to Campion that she might just possibly keep her more favourite pets in the caravan.

"How did you find us, my friend?"

It was Madame who enquired, and Mr. Campion, feeling he could do no less, explained.

"I went through the old mailing lists, and when I found that M. Robert, proprietor of Robert's *Cirque*, one time c/o the World's Fair, received copies of Spring and Autumn catalogues in company with several thousand householders, I thought he might be worth looking up. It has taken me three months."

The man who called himself Pierre Robert smiled, and reminded Campion of his brother.

"Rubbish!" he said. "It has taken you twenty years. Remember," he continued, speaking English carefully as though he were not used to the tongue, "you are a friend of his. We feel you are his friend."

"But of course," agreed Madame, "the young man is a friend. I knew it as soon as I saw him. "You see," she added, beaming upon Campion, "for so many years now he has spent his holidays with us. Now it is all holiday."

"He is free—that's the main thing," her husband remarked. "Been imprisoned, as I was, all his life. Now the fellow's free—free as air."

Mr. Campion hesitated. There was something he very much wanted to ask, and was wondering how to put it.

"It seems—er—unexpected," he ventured at last. "I mean, after *publishing* . . ."

His host turned to his wife.

"The portrait," he commanded, and while she scrambled into the wagon he launched into a brief and formal history.

"My father was an impulsive man, but very much under his brother Jacoby's influence. He fell in love with a beautiful woman, carried her off and married her. She gave up everything for him, but Jacoby still considered it a mésalliance, and after her two sons were born she died of a broken heart. They kept her mewed up in the country, where she was looked down upon and misunderstood."

His visitor had just time to nod his comprehension when Madame returned with a faded cabinet photograph, which she placed reverently in his hands.

Mr. Campion's startled eyes rested upon one of the most supremely comic figures of his life. A corseted lady in tights and a bustle had been caught in the act of gripping a broken column as though for support. He had a fleeting impression of gentle eyes, a coronet of flowers and a fine piece of gilt script announcing *"La Palone, the Queen of the Wires."*

His host took the photograph away.

"My mother," he said, with a dignity which was as unassailable as Lord Lumley's own. "That's the explanation. My grandfather was a tumbler."

It was altogether a most delightful gathering. Madame brought glasses and a bottle of Royal Provence, that wine of Paradise which the tourist ices and derides because it does not taste like champagne. They drank it in the dusk and Mr. Campion no longer felt anxious.

As he rose to leave he turned to his new friends.

"Mr. Barnabas," he enquired unexpectedly, "what did you do with *The Gallivant*?"

"Sold it to a collector," said Tom Barnabas promptly. "Fellow was a crook. Believe he cheated me. Anyway, I got enough to buy the show, which was all that mattered."

A grin passed over his face and Campion saw him as he must have been in the days when Miss Curley had admired him.

"I didn't steal it, you know," he continued. "I wanted to sell out my share in the business when Uncle Jacoby died, but old John wouldn't hear of it. So to save trouble I took the firm's most mobile asset and went off, leaving John with my share in exchange. It was quite fair."

"Taking his fortune, he leapt into space?" murmured Mr. Campion under his breath.

Tom Barnabas sighed.

"What a leap that was!" he said. "I couldn't do it now."

Madame laid a plump hand on his shoulder.

"Do you want to?" she demanded. "Of course not."

Tom Barnabas looked at Campion and laughed.

" 'Voir, M'sieu. Au 'voir."

Mr. Campion wandered off into the fair. The big tent was crowded. An appreciative audience was applauding a lady who was hanging by her teeth from a trapeze, while her son and daughter swung lightheartedly from her ankles.

The turn finished with much bowing and kissing of hands and, while a resplendent attendant wound up their trapeze, a wild exuberant cry sounded from the artists' entrance and a flying figure came whooping into the ring.

He was attired as only French clowns are dressed, in a monstrous caricature of everyday clothes. An enormous black sleeping-suit, on which a white shirt and waistcoat front had been crudely painted, enveloped his gaunt form. Grease-paint half an inch thich obliterated his features and gave him a wide, pathetic smile.

A little white head covering, which Campion saw with a shock was a regulation barrister's wig, decorated his skull and round his neck was a tulle frill spangled with gold.

From the moment he appeared he was a success. His flail-like gestures were here understood. Here his mute appeal was answered, his wide smile echoed. The children shouted his name: "Moulin-Mou! Moulin-Mou! Moulin-Mou!"

He bowed to them gravely and lolloped to the side of the ring purposefully. There he took a basin from an unexpected cupboard in the skirting. He broke eggs in it and added sawdust from the track. His face, now miraculously anxious in spite of his painted smile, appealed to them to sympathize with him in his insuperable difficulties.

To his foredoomed concoction he added all sorts of unlikely ingredients, his dubiety growing and his eyes wild and apprehensive. He stirred, he looked, he smelled. He offered the basin to a little white dog, who lay down and covered its nose with its fore-feet. He wept. He went on stirring.

Then just at the moment when defeat and disgrace seemed inevitable he started. He smiled. He beamed at the breathless company and finally, amid howls of delight, produced triumphantly half a dozen very stale buns and threw five of them to the delirious audience. The sixth he held in his hand for an instant, looking about him with bright child-like eagerness.

Campion was aware of two very gentle blue eyes, infinitely appealing, infinitely friendly, and so far away that they peered at him from another world.

The sixth bun dropped into his lap.

He rose to his feet and waved and some of his neighbours rose with him. Moulin-Mou threw up his arms and bellowed. Campion saw him, rigid for an instant, his great flail-like arms outstretched, his face hidden forever behind the most impenetrable disguise in the world.

The next moment he had gone and a young lady on a horse had taken his place.

Mr. Campion went back over the Pont Neuf, the bun in his hand. He was still carrying it when Mike and Gina met him on the steps of the hotel.

"Horrible," said Mike, staring at the unattractive object with suspicion. "Who gave you that?"

Mr. Campion looked at them solemnly.

"The King's Executioner," he said so gravely that they did not question him.

ABOUT THE AUTHOR

MARGERY ALLINGHAM, who was born in London in 1904, came
from a long line of writers. "I was brought up from babyhood in
an atmosphere of ink and paper," she claimed. One ancestor
wrote early nineteenth century melodramas, another wrote
popular boys' school stories, and her grandfather was the
proprietor of a religious newspaper. But it was her father, the
author of serials for the popular weeklies, who gave her her
earliest training as a writer. She began studying the craft at the
age of seven and had published her first novel by the age of
sixteen while still at boarding school. In 1927 she married Philip
Youngman Carter, and the following year she produced the first
of her Albert Campion detective stories, *The Crime at Black
Dudley*. She and her husband lived a life "typical of the English
countryside" she reported, with "horses, dogs, our garden and
village activities" taking up leisure time. One wonders how
much leisure time Margery Allingham, the author of more than
thirty-three mystery novels in addition to short stories, serials
and book reviews, managed to have.

FINE MYSTERY AND SUSPENSE
TITLES FROM CARROLL & GRAF

❏ Allingham, Margery/THE ALLINGHAM CASE-BOOK	$3.95
❏ Allingham, Margery/MR. CAMPION'S FARTHING	$3.95
❏ Allingham, Margery/MR. CAMPION'S QUARRY	$4.50
❏ Allingham, Margery/MYSTERY MILE	$3.95
❏ Allingham, Margery/NO LOVE LOST	$3.95
❏ Allingham, Margery/POLICE AT THE FUNERAL	$3.95
❏ Allingham, Margery/THE WHITE COTTAGE MYSTERY	$3.50
❏ Ambler, Eric/BACKGROUND TO DANGER	$3.95
❏ Ambler, Eric/A COFFIN FOR DIMITRIOS	$3.95
❏ Ambler, Eric/EPITAPH FOR A SPY	$3.95
❏ Ambler, Eric/JOURNEY INTO FEAR	$3.95
❏ Ambler, Eric/STATE OF SIEGE	$3.95
❏ Ball, John/IN HEAT OF THE NIGHT	$3.95
❏ Ball, John/THE KIWI TARGET	$3.95
❏ Bentley, E.L./TRENT'S LAST CASE	$4.95
❏ Bentley, E.C./TRENT'S OWN CASE	$3.95
❏ Blake, Nicholas/A TANGLED WEB	$3.50
❏ Block, Lawrence/AFTER THE FIRST DEATH	$4.50
❏ Block, Lawrence/THE GIRL WITH THE LONG GREEN HEART	$3.95
❏ Block, Lawrence/MONA	$3.95
❏ Block, Lawrence/THE TRIUMPH OF EVIL	$3.95
❏ Brand, Christianna/DEATH IN HIGH HEELS	$3.95
❏ Brand, Christianna/FOG OF DOUBT	$4.95
❏ Brown, Fredric/THE LENIENT BEAST	$3.50
❏ Brown Fredric/THE SCREAMING MIMI	$3.50
❏ Buchan, John/JOHN MACNAB	$3.95
❏ Buchan, John/WITCH WOOD	$3.95
❏ Burnett, W.R./LITTLE CAESAR	$3.50
❏ Butler, Gerald/KISS THE BLOOD OFF MY HANDS	$3.95
❏ Carr, John Dickson/BRIDE OF NEWGATE	$4.95

☐ Wallace, Edgar/THE FOUR JUST MEN $2.9
☐ Waugh, Hillary/A DEATH IN A TOWN $3.9
☐ Waugh, Hillary/SLEEP LONG, MY LOVE $3.9
☐ Web, Martha G./DARLING COREY'S DEAD $3.9
☐ Westlake, Donald E./THE MERCENARIES $3.9
☐ Willeford, Charles/THE WOMAN CHASER $3.9

Available from fine bookstores everywhere or use this coupon for ordering.

- -

Carroll & Graf Publishers, Inc., 260 Fifth Avenue, N.Y., N.Y. 10001

Please send me the books I have checked above. I am enclosing $_____
(please add $1.75 per title to cover postage and handling.) Send check
or money order—no cash or C.O.D.'s please. N.Y. residents please add
8¼% sales tax.

Mr/Mrs/Ms _____

Address _____

City_____ State/Zip_____

Please allow four to six weeks for delivery.

- -